CRITICISM: THE MAJOR TEXTS

ENLARGED EDITION

CRITICISM:
THE MAJOR TEXTS

ENLARGED EDITION

Edited by Walter Jackson Bate

LOWELL PROFESSOR OF THE HUMANITIES, HARVARD UNIVERSITY

HARCOURT BRACE JOVANOVICH, PUBLISHERS
San Diego   New York   Chicago   Austin
London   Sydney   Toronto

ISBN: 0-15-516148-2

Library of Congress Catalog Card Number: 70-136968

Printed in the United States of America

TABLE OF CONTENTS

II. The Development of Modern Criticism: Romanticism and After

PREFACE

THIS REVISION includes corrections of details as well as a careful reconsideration and updating of the bibliographies. But the principal problem was how to use most effectively an additional hundred pages allowed for further selections from twentieth-century criticism.

The need to concentrate on major critics has become more urgent since the 1950's, when the first edition of this book appeared. We become intimidated before the sheer bulk of critical writing; and our only alternative to confusion, paralysis, or what Johnson called "the superiority of inattention" is to seek out the essential ways of looking at literature, to try to see them as clearly as we can, and, if possible, to sift them. Repeatedly we find that when this is done, the student is less intimidated and learns, if nothing else, what to reduce to size. He shares the experience Justice Oliver Wendell Holmes described of his first years as a jurist. When he faced a new situation or a new case, he was often frightened or bewildered. When he walked courageously to the thing, however, and placed his hands upon it, the lion's skin fell off, and he saw that it was "only the same old donkey" underneath. By reverting to primary texts and central issues in criticism, we have found time and again that we can avoid an immense waste of anxiety and confusion. We need not be doctrinaire and push our own prejudices or stock responses; we need only allow major statements to be presented clearly and fairly.

In this edition, as in the first edition, I have aimed, within the available space, to represent as fully as possible the great literary critics from Aristotle to the present day, and then to supplement the selections with more abundant interpretation and commentary than are usually found. Where this book departs from existing anthologies, it does so, in the editor's opinion, in the following ways: It stresses some critics, particularly Hazlitt, whom other available collections have largely neglected. It represents some of the main critics since the Renaissance,

especially Johnson, Coleridge, Arnold, and Eliot, much more copiously. There is no attempt to offer small excerpts, of a paragraph or a page or two, from a wide variety of writers. Instead, the editor has frankly reacted against the "snippet" kind of anthology. Certainly the most common temptation an anthologist faces is to try to please everyone by including a brief selection from every possible writer—to try, in Johnson's description of the "modest man," to "please principally by not offending." But this negative procedure, of course, ends by pleasing no one. By yielding to it, all anthologies become much the same, repeating each other (like the common run of motion pictures) for fear of violating a taste and canon they themselves have arbitrarily created. Furthermore, such brief excerpts by themselves are of negligible value, and, if they do remain in the mind of the student for a while, they remain only as titles. Major writers are thus reduced to almost the same level as minor ones, each limping with a title apiece into the egalitarian kingdom of the college anthology.

Moreover, this volume tries, where possible, to offer complete selections. If separate chapters of books are counted (such as the two chapters from Coleridge's *Biographia Literaria*, or "Doctrine in Poetry" from I. A. Richards's *Practical Criticism*), then forty-nine of the ninety-three selections are complete units. The editor believes that this number compares very favorably with that in other anthologies which also aspire to cover the entire range of the history of criticism. Furthermore, many of the remaining selections are virtually complete units. The most notable example of the latter is the critical portion of Johnson's *Life of Pope*, which is printed entire, although it is not, strictly speaking, a complete selection.

A final distinctive feature of this volume may be found in the amount and character of the commentary. Biographical and bibliographical information has been condensed and confined to notes. It was felt that whatever space was available for introductions should be used for a more valuable purpose, and that at least an attempt should be made toward remedying a surprising but very real lack—the lack of a brief but comprehensive introduction for English-speaking readers to the history of criticism as a whole. For this reason, and also because of the well-known lack of any general history of the subject at all since Saintsbury's *History of Criticism* of seventy years ago, the commentary in the present volume tries to provide—in necessarily brief space, of course—an introductory history of criticism which exploits problems, issues, and points of view that have risen since the time of Saintsbury.

In turning to the entire subject afresh, my intention in the commentary has been to approach literary criticism, first, through a concentrated focusing on major critics. Second, I have aimed to approach the subject through discussing the rise and development of historical trends in criticism, suggesting their interrelation with each other and with the general intellectual background, and indicating the range and significance of the key terms used. Third, it has not seemed the smallest part of my editorial function to note, over and beyond their historical development, the general premises and implications that underlie or emerge from the various ways of approaching art, and the extent to which these intertwine with other values. All three of these aims find expression in the introductions to individual critics, but the longer general introductions to the Classical Tradition and to the period since the later eighteenth century, treated under the heading, "The Development of Modern Criticism: Romanticism and After," were designed as a supplement to embody more fully the second and third aims. In the case of the classical tradition, the task was more simple and clear-cut. But for the period since the later eighteenth century, which is characterized by no one dominant premise but rather by a bewildering variety of tendencies, it has seemed almost impossible to be comprehensive in a brief space without letting the discussion degenerate into a mere listing of names and titles, provided in the desperate hope that one is not neglecting this trend or that one. Still, the editor has wished to abstain from this temptation, and has tried to synthesize modern developments in criticism in the light of general intellectual and moral values, aims, and presuppositions, and to unify them into some four or five basic categories, all of which interlace with each other. Though the attempt seems naïve, the editor felt it was necessary because of the absence of any other available survey of the subject as a whole, in three pages or in three volumes.

To determine the relative importance of various critics is probably an even more arbitrary act than to make similar decisions for other kinds of writers. For the history of criticism is a recent field, and those present-day works that deal with it are concerned with specific aspects, especially with the criticism of particular periods in individual countries. Accordingly, both students and, to some extent, teachers have been forced to depend, for any over-all picture of the history of criticism, on anthologies themselves. The present editor has deliberately tried—so far as he is capable—to reconsider the whole subject freshly, and to bring to bear as wide a perspective as possible in determining what critics to emphasize.

Re-evaluation of the importance of various critics has not induced the editor to omit commonly known critical monuments or critics of acknowledged supremacy. Instead he was induced to include more. Thus, for reasons that have nothing to do with readability, historical importance, or intrinsic value, Johnson, as compared with Dryden, has been lightly represented in critical anthologies. Yet during the past half century English-speaking writers and scholars have increasingly turned back to Johnson not only as the broadest exponent of the neoclassic tradition but also as a critic who has particular affinities with present-day interests—with the contemporary desire to rediscover basic classical aims, and with the contemporary interest in problems of form and in incisive intellectuality of language and poetic structure. Or again, among romantic critics, Coleridge, as a rule, is heavily stressed, while Hazlitt is virtually neglected. One possible explanation is that no informed selection from Hazlitt's criticism has been made that would immediately indicate his critical range and penetration. Only the casual essays frequently reprinted throughout the nineteenth and early twentieth centuries, before the history of criticism was seriously pursued, are readily available and well known to anthologists. Yet Hazlitt's prolific writing not only supplies the most representative English criticism of the romantic movement; it also brings into focus and directly discusses poetic values that have persisted throughout the century after his death. But doing justice to Johnson and to Hazlitt has not, I believe, meant any slighting of such figures as Dryden and Coleridge, either in selections or in commentary. Finally, in the specific introductions to the critics most emphasized, the editor, in each case, has tried to indicate the criteria that justify the stress given the particular writer.

Another governing consideration has been the practical fact that this volume is intended for English-speaking readers and students—for readers whose interest in literature has, rightly and inevitably, led them primarily to the literature of their own language. The editor has naturally wished to avoid provinciality; and Continental critics, at least since the later eighteenth century, are represented and discussed in this collection. Yet, if there was a choice between two very similar works, one English and one Continental, and if other considerations were more or less equal, the English work was given preference. For example, there is little reason, in a general volume of this size, for printing both Boileau's *Art Poétique* and Pope's *Essay on Criticism:* they are equally valuable monuments of the Horatian verse-essay of their period, and each is about as original (or unoriginal) as the other. To print Boileau rather than Pope, however, would reflect either an affected xenophilia or a distorted sense of the importance of a few years' priority. Pope is more relevant in every way to the interests and knowledge of the readers that the editor has in mind.

For other reasons, moreover, the critics from whom the largest amount of material is drawn tend to be English. To read criticism with any understanding, needless to say, demands some knowledge of what is being criticized. Sainte-Beuve's discussion of Chateaubriand is a model of critical intelligence; but it means comparatively little to the student who has never read Chateaubriand. Familiarity of subject, then, has been an important consideration. And this has operated in favor of English critics in other ways besides their general familiarity as literary figures. For Continental criticism, at its best, tends to deal with specific works or authors. The best English criticism, however, when it deals with a particular writer, is often concerned simply with Shakespeare; or else it focuses on general types of literature—in a speculative, imaginative, and suggestive way rather than with detailed analysis of a variety of works; or else on the psychology of the imagination, on the relation of art to the common moral problems of life; or—if the critic is himself a practicing writer in other forms—on his experience with his own craft.

In keeping with this decision to utilize English criticism wherever it is appropriate and fruitful has been the concern with readability generally. Where possible, critical works that require no specialized knowledge have been selected. Moreover, the editor has used modernized spelling for such works as Sidney's *Apology for Poetry* and Daniel's *Defence of Rhyme*, which are only too often left in their Elizabethan spelling, with the burden thus shifted from the editor to the student. Similarly, in making his own translations of several selections, the editor has viewed readability, without any sacrifice of accuracy, as the quality most desired. Again, the notes, it is hoped, have been added only where they will be really helpful. As in the case of Coleridge's essays on the philosophy of art, where they seemed particularly necessary, they generally tend to be explanatory, or else they cite significant parallels. Routine annotation, particularly the identifying of quotations, has been dispensed with, however, in the case of Hazlitt, who quotes brief remarks and fragmentary phrases so constantly from memory that, to have identified them all, would have been simply to waste valuable space.

A final consideration throughout has been the desire never to lose sight of the most basic problem of all—the problem of the end of art and of literature in particular. If the student can vividly see the end of art as a heightened awareness of reality, however variously reality may be conceived, then he is less likely to feel that the special technical aspects of art with which criticism must deal—the conventions, forms, and techniques indigenous to the art—

are hopelessly arbitrary, like the chance rules of a game, each ultimately as valuable as the other. Instead, these formal elements may come to be sensed for what they really are. They may be viewed, that is, as *means* to a desired and valuable end, and may therefore be seriously discussed and even evaluated. Accordingly, the commentary in this book has often analyzed the different approaches of literature in the light of the various general ends they assume. And in the selections the attempt has been made to catch the critic in the process either of stating or of working toward a conception of this end as he sees it, and of justifying or evolving his more strictly technical standards or criteria as means to that end. Where the critic himself has explicitly stated a central or ultimate ideal, this statement, where possible, has also been included even though it may not, at first glance, appear to be "criticism" in a strict and confined sense of the term. An example would be the first chapter of Arnold's *Culture and Anarchy*, "Sweetness and Light," most of which is here included. This is not specifically a critical essay, yet it states or at least sketches the central concern of all Arnold's writing: a guiding conception of "culture" or human fulfillment that clarifies his actual criticism and makes it more vitally pertinent to general and basic human aims.

Moreover, though the chief concern of this book has been *criticism* rather than *esthetics*, or the philosophy of art, the line between the two is arbitrary. To adhere closely to such a line— especially in the case of practicing literary critics who have worked toward a more abstract concern with the theory of art—would be to confine the intellectual range and dignity of critical thinking. Accordingly, as in the cases of Lessing, Schiller, or Coleridge, writing openly concerned with the theory of art has unhesitatingly been included. Especially for Coleridge a deliberate effort has been made to offer and interpret material of this sort. For one of the paradoxes in the study of literary criticism is that Coleridge, at least in England and America, is always referred to as a suggestive and penetrating philosophical critic, and yet the works that show this side of him do not always appear to have been read and understood by the people who thus exalt him. It is stated abstractly that Coleridge

was a critic of profound, if fragmentary, insights, and that his main importance lies in his excursions into the murkier aspects of the theory of art and in his attempt to rest his theory of art on a metaphysical basis. Yet selections from Coleridge's criticism are usually just the chapters from the *Biographia Literaria* on Wordsworth's theory and use of poetic language. The present editor has felt that this volume should depart from precedent and show the reader a little of the dark side of the moon:—that, in moderate doses, it should really illustrate and attempt to elucidate the side of Coleridge most generally extolled and really most neglected. Hence what seem to the editor to be the most central statements of Coleridge's ideas—the three brief essays "On the Principles of Genial Criticism" and the fragmentary "On Poesy or Art"—are included entire; and both the relatively heavy annotation to these works and the introduction try to make this essential side of Coleridge more familiar and less forbidding.

The great justification of criticism at any time is that it can help to bring into focus and emphasize the function of the arts and of the humanities themselves. The humanities, by definition, do not seek to offer analysis without synthesis, description without evaluation, or abstractions without feeling. This, indeed, is the most obvious distinction between them and the physical and social sciences. And the activity that *subserves* the humanities—critical theory— fulfills its purpose only if it is as fully aware as possible of the aim and character of what it subserves. Criticism of the humanities, that is, must itself be humanistic; and to be humanistic is to be aware of basic human values, to prize them as something more than idle abstractions to talk about, and to evaluate things in the light of the ends that these values characterize. Especially for the beginning student of literature today, faced with a rapidly growing diversity of literary works and qualities, and too often introduced to them only through a hasty and meaningless survey of names, titles, and other routine external data, the main value of studying criticism is that it may arouse in him the desire to think through what he is reading in literature generally, and sharpen in him the ability to do so. Its first and most important fruit is to make him realize that evaluation—seeing things for what they are, seeing them in their importance—is not a matter of caprice, custom, or affectation, but that it can emerge from intelligently conceived premises and aims. Such a realization is salutary in the highest degree. It is the greatest encouragement one can have to go ahead and think further. Criticism can thus bring into activity the noblest of human qualities: namely, the quality of sincerity, the desire to discern the truth, to see some point in what one is doing or thinking, and to keep penetrating until the answer is found.

Our approach to criticism through major texts of a general or theoretical character is faced with special complications when we come to critical writing in the middle third of the twentieth century. To begin with, there is the general embarrassment felt by the political, economic, and cultural historian or anthologist of almost any kind of writing as soon as he comes to the contemporary, for the past cannot help him here in sifting things into perspective. As a result, his choice is either to infuriate most of his readers by presenting an inevitably subjective and exclusive selection, or more mildly to irritate everyone (including himself) by presenting a little of as much as possible. With the timidities that experience creates in most of us by middle age, the latter is the alternative usually preferred.

But aside from this general embarrassment, we confront two more special problems in criticism itself:

(1) Of the finest critical writing since the Second World War, especially in the English-speaking world, by far the largest portion concentrates on particular writers. Eclectic, refusing doctrinaire single-mindedness, this writing employs a variety of critical approaches in combination. But one of the premises of this anthology, from the start, is that we should concentrate on general theory or on general approach to literature, with the recognition that a course in the history of critical theory could not, by definition, hope also to be a course in the history of literature itself, where particular works (dictated by the selections in the anthology rather than chosen by the teacher) are read simultaneously. Exceptions could be made for

discussions of particular authors only when the discussions were frankly essayistic, fundamental in importance, and concerned with writers, knowledge of whom could either be taken for granted or was not necessary. As Johnson said about poetic imitations: "An imitation of Spenser is nothing to a reader, however acute, by whom Spenser has never been perused." And the same is true for much, if not all, detailed, particularized criticism. Ideally, a course on the history of critical thought would parallel a three- or four-year course in literature itself. But, as every teacher of critical theory knows, we must learn (as Coleridge kept telling himself, without much effect) to "do one thing at a time."

(2) Of the most important general discussions of literature and the arts during the last fifty years, some are by writers who could hardly be called "critics" in the more specialized sense. For example, teachers have asked for selections from writers primarily associated with drama, poetry, or the novel—such writers as Wilde, Yeats, Woolf, and Mann. In another category are more philosophical writers like Santayana, Dewey, Whitehead, and Ortega y Gasset. Their works, at once central and readable, have provided a capital on which the criticism of the last fifty years has drawn heavily. If we devoted the necessarily limited additional space to merely three such writers, what space would be left for the more specifically "belletristic" authors?

The cumulative advice of teachers who use this anthology was to cut the Gordian knot by adding, with substantial selections, one more primarily theoretical critic, and then providing a capacious supplement of a dozen or so other centrally important critical essays, including some by novelists and poets; some by critics primarily valued for their discussions of particular authors and movements, but who stand aside here and speak more generally; and some by writers concerned with subjects broader than literature itself. The hope also was not to confine ourselves to the English-speaking world, even though the anthology is designed for English-speaking students. I sympathized with the hope of teachers that this revision would include a substantial selection from Northrop Frye, with a fairly detailed introduction. Certainly, in the English-speaking world, Frye's importance since 1957 (the date of his *Anatomy of Criticism*) is unique. But how best to use the remaining pages? The founders of what, after the 1930's, was called the New Criticism—Eliot, Richards, and Hulme—were already fairly represented in the original edition, and the major premises were there. Later, more refined examples of the New Criticism concentrated, by definition, not only on particular writers but on particular texts. Meanwhile, a decision had to be reached as to what could be presented from continental Europe, which had less interest in these things. Freud and psychoanalysis, Existentialism, and the new sociological interest in art, of which Ortega y Gasset was the pioneer, had to be considered, as did the recent humanistic attempt to meet all these new concepts and interests, and to take them for granted, and still retain its bearings.

In our supplement, "Further Modern Developments," we added (at the request of many teachers) the central portions of Wilde's "Decay of Lying," which presents, in distillation, one of the premises of modern formalism; Yeats's manifesto and discussion of the new symbolism; Virginia Woolf on the modern novel; a section from Picasso's manifesto; and Santayana's clairvoyant essay on "Penitent Art," which no thoughtful student of the arts can forget and which now seems more timely than ever. Ortega y Gasset's "The Dehumanization of Art," at once the most lucid and, on the continent, most influential statement of the distinction between modernism and the nineteenth century, was from the start a favorite work of English and American critics, although it was perhaps less widely known to general students of literature in the English-speaking world. With the revival, in the later 1960's, of interest in the social significance of literature, this clear-headed and seminal discussion of the arts by one of the great sociologists of our century has again deservedly leaped into general prominence. By far the most thoughtful consideration by any major author of our century of the relation of Freud and psychoanalysis to literature in general is that by Thomas Mann. For a more theoretical statement by one of the major New Critics, following Eliot and Richards, we turn to a central essay by R. P. Blackmur; and for statements by Anglo-American poets since the Second World War, we turn to W. H. Auden and Wallace Stevens. For the post-war movement of Existentialism, we turn naturally to Sartre himself. Two classic essays, Harry Levin's "Literature as an Institution" and Douglas Bush's "Literary History and Literary Criticism," allow us to excerpt a moment of profound reflection from two of the principal contemporary humanistic minds, who are at once historical and analytic in their approach, but whose primary works are devoted to particular authors and particular periods. The order of the essays in the supplement is by date of composition, not by date of the author's birth.

In making this revision, I wish to thank all those mentioned in the first preface, particularly Professors Harry Levin, René Wellek, Douglas Bush, David Perkins, and the late Professor Werner Jaeger; to express my gratitude to the scores of teachers who have since talked with me about an enlarged edition; and to add special thanks to Professor John Paul Russo, who has helped me in every part of the revision.

W.J.B.

Cambridge, Massachusetts
1970

I. THE CLASSICAL TRADITION

INTRODUCTION

LIKE OTHER comprehensive terms, the word "classical" can be approached or used in many ways. Since it is an appealing word, it is often applied abstractly to certain qualities of art or thought that a particular critic believes desirable. But the word is most concretely and perhaps most profitably used when it is applied, as a historical term, to the principles and values that characterized the art and thought of ancient Greece, and also to the later attitudes and developments in Western culture that were most obviously and directly influenced by these principles and values. In the conception of art and especially literature that arose in Greece and has persisted throughout the classical tradition, the various aspects are compactly interwoven with each other. Perhaps the most convenient starting point—and one that immediately begins to involve all the other attitudes—is the basic classical premise that art is an *imitation of nature*.

I

To say that art is an *imitation of nature* at once implies the existence of something outside the artist's own mind which he is trying to imitate. This external reality is the primary concern; the classical attitude has always meant a comparative lack of interest, therefore, in the artist himself—in the psychological character of his imagination, for example, and especially in his own subjective feelings. In judging an *imitation* of something, the first and last consideration is the success with which the imitation is able to duplicate what is most essential and important in its original model. Hence art should seek to be *objective*. To the classical writer, it would have been meaningless to hold up, as an end in itself, what the romantics later called "originality." For one can be "original" in any number of ways. For example, to react counter to the truth in every respect is, after all, a form of "originality." On the other hand, if "original" is equated with "unusual" or "rare," nothing is more "original" than really to react in accordance with the truth. The term, in fact, is meaningless as an *ideal for which to strive*. The end is awareness or insight; and whether the awareness is "original" is not even secondary but irrelevant.

It is important to note why such romantic catchwords as "originality," "imagination," and "creative" are absent in classical criticism. For it is sometimes assumed that classical thought is *opposed* to the qualities such words suggest. It is not. It is concerned with another aim: to *know*, and to employ art in order to duplicate and transmit that knowledge. In the pursuit of this aim, "originality" may or may not be present. According to classical standards the "imagination" is of value to the degree that it helps give substance to the insight and make it concrete. As for being "creative"—the Greek word for poet, after all, is "maker," and to fashion an imitation is to make or create—everything depends on the value and truth of what is being created: on whether the artist, in Aristotle's words, is "creative *according to a true idea*." In short, if art is regarded as imitation, its ideal or purpose can never be to communicate the artist's own feelings, however well informed his feelings may be, or however much they may be directed to an objective reality outside himself. Such feelings will necessarily enter into the work of art, of course. The artist could not very well create or even be alive without reactions. But to admit this is different from urging that his *aim*, his ideal, should be to express those reactions or feelings. Rather, the aim is to descry the total character, meaning, and form of his model, and to imitate it with truth and vitality. He can achieve this aim only by using his reactions and, in fact, every form of awareness he has, as fully and vividly as possible.

Moreover, if art is said to imitate nature, then the character of art is governed by one's conception of what it imitates. The classical theory of art, therefore, is firmly based upon the far more important conception of what constitutes nature itself. In this sense, the foundation of the classical tradition is its confidence in a rationally ordered and harmonious universe, working according to fixed laws, principles, and forms. The universe is not a meaningless hurly-burly of atoms; least of all is it something the qualities and characteristics of which are made up in our own minds. Rather, the universe is regarded as a meaningful process, in which all the parts are interrelated with the living whole; and because of their confidence in such an ordered universe and their eager desire to pierce through to increasingly more basic and general principles, the Greeks succeeded in creating philosophy as we know it—systematic philosophical thinking, in place of the isolated maxims and observations of earlier civilizations. According to this philosophy universal forms and principles constitute the essential character of nature. Plato held the extreme conviction that these forms are the sole genuine reality; while Aristotle after him maintained the modified view that the universal forms must work through the material and the concrete in order to fulfill themselves, i.e., they must have *something to form* in order to become *forming* agents, although the concrete itself is nothing except as it is being formed. But in the views of both Plato and Aristotle, as well as in Greek thought generally, the focal point of interest is the permanent rules that govern and pervade all events.

Art, as an *imitation of what is essential in nature,* is therefore concerned with *persisting, objective forms.* Thus the classical theory of art as imitation by no means implies what we now call *realism,* and the realistic concentration on concrete detail for its own sake. For, to begin with, the very subject matter on which the theory focuses is that which is permanent and ordered rather than isolated and particular. Hence Aristotle says that poetry is "more philosophical" than history. For history relates circumstances as they occurred in time, one after another. Only as it tries to be philosophical does history concentrate on the causal interconnection of things, leaving out details that are irrelevant to the general pattern or meaning. Now poetry, like philosophy, looks at once for the general form: it is selective, and omits all particular events or characteristics that do not emphasize or lead directly

to the general order it is trying to disclose. This is what Aristotle means when he says that poetry is concerned with the *"ideal,"* or *"what ought to be."* The "ideal," in most classical writing, does not refer to what we ordinarily mean when we say something is "idealized," that is, something we have made up in our own minds, or the way we might want things to be in our private wish-fulfillment dreams. It refers to the *way things would be if the form, the principle, that is operating through them were carried out to its logical fulfillment, its final completion.* Hence the dramatist, in taking a historical subject for a play, may omit some details and compress others in order to emphasize solely the interconnection of incidents that leads to the logical end. Again, in his portrayal of character, he should concentrate on the *type* rather than on particular and personal mannerisms: he must show the character as it "ought to be," that is, he must show how a particular type of character would act and feel when subjected to a certain series of incidents. Similarly, classical sculpture does not seek to accentuate individual features and expression; rather, it seeks to subdue them and to present in their place the total capacity of the human figure, endowed with a proportion and a finality that could have emerged only from a complete and unobstructed development.

Poetry, says Aristotle, rests upon two instincts in man—the instinct for *imitation,* and the instinct for *harmony.* And in addition to taking general truths and persisting forms as its model, as its subject matter, art also subdues and recasts the imitation it is making into a new harmony—a harmonious treatment, this time, of the materials through which a given medium of art works—of line and color in painting, of sounds in music, of words in poetry. Art, that is, attempts to duplicate nature, within the particular medium into which it is transposing its subject. The classical term "imitation" is thus to be viewed in a flexible, imaginative way. It is especially important to cut off any associations of the term with photographic copying. In the middle and late eighteenth century, the meaning of the word "imitation" became narrower, and it was then set up in opposition to words like "creativity" and "originality." Because this more restricted definition implied literal copying, it seemed strange, for example, to call music an "imitative" art—to call any art "imitative," for that matter, except painting and sculpture. But the original Greek use of the term was more liberal and far-reaching, and was quite applicable to music. Thus, in Aristotle's suggestive discussion of music in his *Politics* (and it is characteristically Greek that, in an analysis of statecraft, the educational value of music should have a prominent place), music is viewed as an even more valuable and essential form of "imitation" than painting. For music can "imitate" the "moral habits" and "states of feeling" that take place in the human mind or soul. The soul is an "activity"; so is music. Feeling, moral persuasions, habits of reacting, all take place in *time*; they have *duration*. Music, unlike painting, also has duration. Sounds following one another, the use of melody and rhythm, make up a pattern or form that exists through the passage of time. Music can thus "imitate" directly the ebb and flow of feeling, states of mind, "moral *habits*," and different varieties of "character"; it can especially imitate more highly ordered feelings, attitudes, or traits of character than we ordinarily have, and then infiltrate them directly into *our* feelings, at once deepening the intensity of our feeling and molding and channeling it by a harmonious and ordered form. Painting, however, is confined to figures and colors. It must work through them, and try to use them *symbolically* if it is going to suggest anything beyond the mere spatial shape and color. For "figures and colors are not imitations; they are only [symbols or] signs of moral habits—indications which the body gives of states of feeling."

The points to be stressed in attempting to understand the classical conception of "imitation" are (1) that "imitation" should generally be construed in a more liberal sense than we now use it; (2) that "imitation" is less a detailed copying than an attempt to offer an active *counterpart* of its model; (3) that insofar as it can, "imitation" takes as its model the essential and persisting forms of nature; and (4) that in translating its subject or object of imitation into a new form or medium—words, sounds, or shapes—art employs forms appropriate to the particular materials it is using, and by doing so it presents a *living* imitation or counterpart. Through a harmonious design bent toward a logical end and a finished totality, art thus offers an active rival or duplication of the ordered process of nature itself. This view explains the general classical concern with *form* in the arts: with completeness of outline and with subduing the part to the whole—or rather with treating the part only as it contributes to or emerges into a rounded finality of structure. General examples would be the classical emphasis on plot rather than character in the drama, on the total figure rather than individual features in sculpture, and on line rather than color in painting. In every case, form is stressed, not because it gives us a change from our daily lives, not because it shows inventive or technical cleverness on the part of the artist, but because it is believed to be the transmuting or duplicating of what is *real* (i.e., what pervades and controls nature itself), and because we are the better for knowing what is true with as vivid and full a realization as we can. Accordingly, the classical qualities of decorum and balance—of rhythm, symmetry, and integration of parts—are not pursued as ends in themselves (classicism is not deliberate and self-conscious *formalism*). They evolve as by-products of the attempt to imitate or duplicate an ordered nature or reality—of the attempt to offer a heightened and harmonious presentation of truth.

II

Thus art, according to the classical tradition, might most generally be described as *an attempt on the part of man to complete or fulfill nature*. In Aristotle's distinction between the "useful" and the "fine" arts, both are grounded upon this common aim, and differ only in their way of carrying it out. The "useful" arts—ranging from handicrafts through architecture to some professions, like medicine, which we would now call sciences—all *co-operate* with nature, so to speak. They spin and weave cloth, mold clay, quarry marble, rear buildings, make medicines to assist the body, and in other ways attempt to complete or carry out nature's uses, designs, and potentialities to the end of satisfying man's practical needs. The "fine" arts also use and co-operate with the processes of nature; but they do so by trying to duplicate them. They complete nature, that is, by offering a purified and *completed imitation*—an imitation that rivals but still concurs with nature by duplicating and not differing from its original. And just as the "useful" arts complete nature in order to minister to human practical needs, the "fine" arts complete nature through imitation in order to enlarge, nourish, and develop human awareness and insight.

The classical view emphasizes, then, that art is formative in the most valuable sense by assisting man to fulfill *his* own end. For man's end is to *complete himself:* to carry out, to the fullest extent, what is best and most distinctive in him. And what is best in him, as an aware creature, is the capacity to realize what is without, to profit and grow by means of this knowledge, and to react and desire in accordance with the awareness that has informed him. Freedom and self-fulfillment arise, in Samuel Johnson's noble phrase, only as the mind can "repose on the stability of truth." This, the greatest of Greek premises, is the end; this is the crucial and all-important goal. And all of man's pursuits are to be *evaluated* according to the degree that they further and promote this end. It is on this firm and enduring base that the great classical justification of the arts is built. For by taking permanent truths and persisting forms as its model, art attempts to discover and duplicate objective reality. But it not only seeks to capture and imitate reality. It seeks to *convey* what it has caught and portrayed—to familiarize and bring home its insight, and thus to *complete* human awareness by extending and converting that awareness into emotion—into felt persuasions and active response. It is here that poetry, for example, transmits a more reaching effect than even philosophy. For philosophy, as Sir Philip Sidney later said in his great Renaissance restatement of classical attitudes, deals only with general and abstract notions; and these strike home only if one has already concretely and vividly experienced what these ideas are built upon. In this sense, the philosopher, with his definitions and abstract categories, "teacheth them that are already taught"; and "happy is that man who may understand him, and more happy that can *apply* what he doth understand." To take an elementary example: A man (says Sidney) who had never seen an animal like a rhinoceros or an elephant, or never seen an imposing palace, might hear a detailed description of them, and might be able afterwards to repeat the description, word for word; and yet he might have no valid idea of what they were really like, and know them less than he might if he were given even a single image or picture of them. And so with more complex matters. There is no substitute for the actual *experience* of a thing as it exists concretely. Poetry, on the other hand—though it is focussed on the universal, persisting forms, on the interconnection and completed potentiality of things—reveals the form *in the concrete.* It exhibits the concrete—sounds, visual images, human characters and events—in the process of *taking on* or *disclosing* universal form and value. To this extent, as Aristotle points out in his *Nichomachean Ethics,* the imitative arts are again like nature in needing both form and matter. As in nature itself, the forms of art are dynamic, emerging, working through concrete material; they are not abstractions. In other words, poetry does not *describe or define,* as philosophy does. It *exhibits or portrays by imitating.* It couples, as Sidney said, "the general notion with the particular example," and thus gives to the mind a concrete *experience,* an actual "*image* of that whereof the Philosopher bestoweth but a wordish description"—a description that can never "strike, pierce, nor *possess* the sight of the soul" to the degree that a living experience can.

Hence the confidence of the Greeks in the immense power of art—which they called *psychagogia* (a *leading* or *persuading* of the soul)—as a molding or formative agent in developing human feelings and motivations. Thus the artist's function—despite the lack of interest in his own personality and self-expression—was given, for the first time, an unparalleled importance and dignity. For with the vision of human perfection before them, the Greeks raised the whole concept of education far above the routine acquirement of simple memory, mechanical skills, and vocational apprenticeship. In an imperishable example to the human race, their desire to *educate*—their wish to mold and shape human character, as they conceived it, and thus to complete human potentiality in the light of the highest standard of excellence or nobility—became the most distinctive and all-important of Greek ideals. That ideal serves as the inspiring and massive theme of the great interpretation of Greece for the modern era, Werner Jaeger's *Paideia*. Indeed, "virtue," as Aristotle said in the *Politics*, "consists in *rejoicing and loving and hating aright;* and there is clearly nothing which we are so much concerned to acquire and to cultivate as the *power* of forming right judgments, and of taking delight in good dispositions and noble actions." One should dwell on the active implication of the verbs here—"*rejoicing* and *loving* and *hating* aright," and the "power of *forming* right judgments, and of taking delight" in what is really worthy of the delight. Virtue, in the Greek sense, does not consist in being able to repeat a list of platitudes. It is not even the self-enforced abidance by literal precepts, though perhaps this is better than nothing. Rather, virtue is the *active desiring and moving toward* the good or valuable: it is *reacting* and *feeling* in the light of what is true—of what is known to be essential, basic, and therefore valuable. The end, in short, is the assimilation of truth, and the automatic desiring and acting in accordance with it. "The heart," as Coleridge later said, "should have *fed* upon the *truth,* as insects on a leaf, until it is tinged with its food, and shows the color . . . in every minutest fibre." By gradually enlarging and unconsciously shaping man as a desiring, reacting, and living organism, and by calling forth his ability to convert insight or awareness into feeling, art is capable of developing his capacity to react vitally and sympathetically to the truth. It thus assumes dignity and genuine value as a nourisher, enlarger, and shaper of the mind and heart, offering insight through a true representation and at the same time stimulating and arousing a dynamic and feeling response.

The flexible but relatively clear-cut premises of classical criticism are best exemplified in the work of Aristotle, particularly his *Poetics* and, to a lesser extent, his *Rhetoric*. The influence of Plato on the history of criticism arises more from his general metaphysics and theory of knowledge than from his scattered remarks on art and literature. He raises, to be sure, certain questions, particularly two: the general problem of what "imitation" is; and the enormous problem of the moral and therefore social effects of

art. The very fact that a man of Plato's general intellectual eminence and imaginative literary power should have taken an adverse stand against the arts was challenging.

Aristotle's re-examination of the aim and function of poetry was, indeed, partly an attempt to answer Plato's position. The great merit of this re-examination is that Aristotle did not deduce a theory of art from an abstract theory of esthetics. Rather, he observed art directly in order to see what it is, what it can do, and how it affects man. In other words, he drew on the actual concrete experience of the Greeks with art. He may be said, in fact, to sum up the character and aim of Greek literature, and his writings serve as the critical basis of the classical tradition. By considering the psychological effect of art, if only briefly, Aristotle prepared the way for later speculation on the subject—speculation that led to greater interest in the imaginative and emotional elements of art, as in Philostratus and later Plotinus, and that culminated in the direct emphasis on imaginative power and emotional transport in the famous work, attributed to Longinus, *On the Sublime*.

But the general tendency of ancient criticism after Aristotle was to analyze the technical problems of writing in more detail, to classify devices—the ancient treatises on rhetoric, including much of Longinus, are examples—and, in so far as general aims and purposes were concerned, to codify many of Aristotle's precepts and extend them in a less flexible way. The *Art of Poetry*, by the Roman Horace, though it differs in its casual, familiar manner, also looked back to Greece; and Horace did not hesitate to present as *rules* many of the observations and suggestions of his Greek predecessors. Ancient criticism in the later years thus set something of the pattern that was—after comparative indifference to literary speculation during the Middle Ages—to characterize the great restatement of classical values and aims throughout the European Renaissance. It is significant that in the large movement throughout the Renaissance, which we now call *neoclassicism* and which extends down to the middle eighteenth century, the indirect influence of Aristotle was paralleled by the strong, direct influence of Horace's *Art of Poetry*.

III

The most notable example of Renaissance neo-classicism is Sir Philip Sidney's great and moving credo, the *Apology for Poetry*. Some local and special problems also occupied European criticism from the close of the Middle Ages throughout the Renaissance. The attempt to justify the use of modern languages instead of Latin was one such problem. Dante's *De Vulgari Eloquentia* (about 1304) was the first and most significant of these justifications which continued down through the notable defence of the French vernacular by Joachim du Bellay (1549). They are significant more as historical signposts than as active influences. The very fact that the *Divine Comedy*, for example, was written in Italian instead of Latin was an immeasurably more important influence in encouraging the use of the vernacular than was Dante's brief discussion of the matter. Another special problem is exemplified by Samuel Daniel's *Defence of Rhyme*.

In its broadest aspect, however, the critical writing of the Renaissance may be described as a self-conscious reassertion of classical aims and values, less flexible, much more thoroughly systematized, and buttressed now by a deliberate appeal to tradition. Its approach may be described, in short, as *neoclassicism* or a "new classicism." The effect of neoclassic theory on the actual art and literature of western Europe was only gradual. There was, in fact, a marked split between the rather rigid critical or theoretical approach to art in the Renaissance and much of the greatest art and literature of the same epoch. It is one of the ironies of cultural history that, as neoclassic theory began at last to affect art and literature during the declining years of the European Renaissance in the seventeenth century, and afterwards in the early eighteenth century, neoclassic criticism should have become increasingly more liberal, more inclusive, and more psychologically penetrating and sophisticated. In its final form in mid-eighteenth-century England, it attained a largeness of outlook and a humane applicability that can be called genuinely classical.

Of the new elements that enter into the neoclassic reformulation of classical values, at least three may be briefly noted: the influence of religion; the deliberate emphasis on tradition and past examples; the influence of philosophical rationalism. The moral fervor of the Christian church sharpened and made more specific the traditional classical principle that art is formative and therefore moral. It was a common belief that the "great Design of Arts," as one critic said, "is to restore the Decays that happened to human nature by the Fall [of Man], by restoring Order." Classical thought had never placed its trust in emotion or any other aspect of man's nonrational nature except to the degree that the emotions and the will of man are informed, shaped, and directed by rational insight. Christian thinking was not only suspicious of man's emotional and imaginative nature, but more often than not sought rigorously to suppress it. The effect of this attitude on critical thought was extensive, particularly on the moral aspects of the general conception of *decorum*, or propriety. For Christian moral criteria were at once more specific and literal, and at the same time more eagerly and zealously applied.

A second element that lent an authoritarian quality to neoclassic theory, and tended to restrict some of its premises, was the deliberate use of classical authority as a model. To imitate the *Iliad*, as an eighteenth-century critic said, is not to imitate Homer; for Homer did not himself sit down to imitate another *Iliad*. In a similar way, one might suggest that to transcribe and codify Aristotle's *Poetics* is not following the tentative and experimental practice of Aristotle, who would have done no such thing. The gain in having classical models was enormous; it is hardly possible that European literature or art could have developed very far without them. The point to be stressed is simply that neoclassic critical theory now added a strong and studied emphasis on tradition, and on the use of past works as specific models or guides.

A third element that helped to codify neoclassic theory into a coherent framework was the pervasive influence of rationalistic philosophy, with its optimistic confidence in the ability of reason, method, and system to reach final and conclusive answers. For the most extreme period of European rationalism is to be found, not in Greece, nor during the period when medieval Scholastic philosophy flourished, but in the late Renaissance, reaching its peak in the flowering of mathematics in the seventeenth century and in the great rationalistic systems of Descartes, Spinoza, and Leibniz. The result was to encourage the belief that the "law of nature" is made up of rational and unalterable regulations; and mathematics in particular stood out as a prototype of what reason could discover if only it used the right "method." The temptation, at times, was to regard the "rules" of art as part also of the infallible machinery of the universal order—as existing, to quote an early eighteenth-century critic, among the "Laws of Nature, which always acts with Uniformity, and gives them a perpetuate Existence." And another critic, impressed as were so many by the success of the great mathematician, Sir Isaac Newton, hopefully felt that the rules for dramatic poetry were now standing on "the same footing with our noble system of Newtonian philosophy." Such sentiments were fairly general by the end of the seventeenth century; and though they were just as often opposed, especially in England, they indicate the extent to which the pervasive trust in method and regulation affected neoclassic theory and helped to enhance its authority.

An academic respect for rules had already become pronounced by the close of the sixteenth century, particularly in Italy. Marco Girolamo Vida's *Art of Poetry* (1527), patterned after Horace's, had reapplied the more self-conscious conception of decorum that Horace himself expressed. By studying examples from ancient literature, other critics had attempted to construct a series of specific regulations. The most famous was the doctrine of the three "unities." Aristotle had spoken of the importance of a "unity of action" in the drama. He also mentioned that, in Greek dramatic tragedy, the time during which the action took place was usually not more than a day. In the Renaissance, however, an Italian critic, Giraldi Cinthio, attempted to make a rule of this "unity of time," and it was quickly taken over by other critics. His fellow countryman, Ludovico Castelvetro, shortly afterwards added the "unity of place" as a third rule. The justification was that, if the scene of the play changed from one place to another, it would cease to seem real; for we, as the audience, could not be expected to believe that the same stage which we have been watching all the time could be first one place and then another. Castelvetro even

felt that the unities of time and place were more important than the one unity—that of action—on which Aristotle had insisted. In his great *Preface to Shakespeare,* almost two centuries later, Samuel Johnson undercut the argument for the unities of time and place with telling common sense. But, until then, the three unities retained a strong hold on the imagination of European critics. An example of their influence on practicing writers, especially in France, is the extent to which a great dramatist like Corneille felt compelled to defend and apologize for any slight modification he made of them.

Other refinements in decorum continued to be made. The most notable is the rise of the conception of "poetic justice," according to which the good should be rewarded and the bad punished. A formidable defender of "poetic justice" in the seventeenth century was Thomas Rymer, who also went so far as to maintain that a character should not be permitted to kill another in a play unless their ranks were appropriate to the "laws of the duel." It is characteristic that Rymer felt that even learning and liberal study were not necessary in order to arrive at proper critical rules. "Common sense alone suffices," for the rules are self-evident, and as "convincing and clear as any demonstration of Mathematics."

With critical regulation now becoming so fixed and self-confident, it was perhaps inevitable that even the great works of classical antiquity should have been weighed in the balance and found wanting. And that is precisely what happened, as the seventeenth century wore on, in the famous critical war between the Ancients and the Moderns. For the Moderns were not objecting that the Ancients had created rules that were too confining. They were objecting that the Ancients did not observe the rules as carefully and correctly as they should have done. Critics who took a more liberal and elastic view thus found themselves defending the classical tradition. Accordingly, Swift, in burlesquing this whole quarrel between the Ancients and the Moderns in his *Battle of the Books,* uses the bee as the symbol for the Ancients, and portrays the Moderns as a spider. For the bee lives upon what is *outside* it, in a 'universal plunder upon nature," and brings home honey and wax, thus furnishing man with "the two noblest of things, which are sweetness and light." The complicated rules and regulations of the Moderns, on the other hand, are not acquired from a direct turning to nature. They are made up or invented by the Moderns, who mistake the means for the end, are interested in system and complication for their own sake, wish to reduce everything to mathematical method, and are filled with short-sighted pride in their achievements. The spider that represents them, therefore, is "a domestic animal, furnished with a native stock," jealous of his originality, spinning regulations in the form of complicated cobwebs out of his own entrails, and absorbed and fascinated by the complexities and schemes he has constructed in his own corner.

I V

By the close of the seventeenth century, neoclassic theory attained its most complete form. At least four general characteristics may here be noted, though each is usually interrelated with others in the writings of particular critics: (1) There is the extreme neoclassic regulation, with its trust in system and method, its emphasis on "correctness" in structure and style, its feeling of superiority to the ancients, and its belief that its rules are grounded on the "law of nature." This extreme form of neoclassic rationalism is found mainly in France. (2) Almost in direct reaction to extreme neoclassic rationalism, is a strong tendency toward an emotional conception of taste—a tendency to rest it upon feeling. Critics who swung over to this extreme often used the phrase *je ne sais quoi* ("I do not know what") to apply to the subjective sentiment in which they put their faith. This individualism resulting from antipathy to the rules became much stronger in England than on the Continent, for the English have always been unusually individualistic in their writing, disregarding "schools" or "movements." Moreover, unlike France, England already possessed a large body of remarkable literature—that of the Elizabethan period and of the early seventeenth century—written without much direct influence from neoclassic theory. (3) British philosophy has always been individualistic, empirical, introspective, and interested in psychology. And at the close of the seventeenth century, influenced by philosophers like Thomas Hobbes and especially John Locke, English critics began to be interested in the imagination and the way it works. This interest in the *psychology of art* was to develop rapidly during the eighteenth century, and to have a widespread influence on the romantic movement. But during the first half of the eighteenth century, its main effect was to make at least some English critics more sophisticated: more aware, that is, of psychological factors, more open-minded, and more skeptical of the authority of hard-and-fast rules. (4) There was also a general concern with the neoclassic ideals of "good sense," "refinement," and "correctness," particularly in the use of language. But it did not base itself upon a rigid and exclusive rationalism. The combination of urbanity, grace, and unsystematic good sense, which characterized Horace as a critic, served as a guide and model. It is characteristic, indeed, that the most representative examples of these values and attitudes should have been the two famous verse-essays, written in the manner of Horace's *Art of Poetry*: Boileau's *Art Poétique* (1674) and Pope's *Essay on Criticism* (1711).

The great critical writing from the later seventeenth century through the following hundred years avoids the exclusive confidence in rules and method, but it includes something of the other three aspects listed above. It includes, for example, the ideals of "correctness," "refinement," and "good sense." On the other hand, it not only makes allowance for individual reactions and emotional appeal; it takes them for granted as necessary and even desirable, though it does not dwell on them as ends to be pursued for their own sake. Again, it appropriates to itself and profits from the empirical spirit and the descriptive psychology that continued to develop in England after John Locke. It was therefore further encouraged to distrust facile generalization and premature systematizing. Neoclassic theory, then, during its concluding century, attained its broadest and most flexible form. And it is characteristic that its chief spokesmen, in this concluding, liberal stage, should have been English: Dryden, Johnson, and, to a lesser extent, Sir Joshua Reynolds. Explanations for this are easily available: one is the traditional individualism of the English, and their refusal to follow authority blindly. "It ought to be the first endeavour of a writer," said Johnson, "to *distinguish nature from custom;* or that which is established because it is right, from that which is right only because it is established." Other elements include the English distrust of system-mongering and of excessive methodology, their interest in psychology and especially the imagination, their trust in experience, and the successful example of their own literary achievement with all its rich diversity and individuality. Some of these qualities have often, of course, encouraged the English to be anticritical and even crotchety and whimsical. But when joined with analytic power, they have led to a rare common sense and a pliable open-mindedness. A further element has been the traditional English concern with moral values. This concern has all too often shown itself in a restricted, preachy conception of what is morally desirable, and a disregard of significant technical problems of art. But when combined with imaginative range and sympathetic flexibility, it has resulted in a healthful grasp of the essential: an ability to distinguish between ends and means, and to evaluate means as they lead to fundamental ends. Indeed, nothing is more genuinely classical than the continual desire to make such a distinction, and the ability to do so with experimental openness, imaginative pliability, and yet sincerity of purpose. In one sense, neoclassicism may be said to have argued itself out of existence. As it became broader in its applicability, that is, it overturned many of its own rules, attitudes, and preconceptions; and it rejected them on *classical* grounds. Johnson, in particular, offers many such instances. One example is his pushing beyond certain fixed and artificial neoclassic "types" of character in the drama—types based originally on the classical interest in the general form and outline—by appealing to more basic but less simplified types of human character, and by invoking a broader and more classical conception of "general nature."

Neoclassic theory thus ended with a breadth of outlook that is in some ways reminiscent of the large openness and sincere grasp of essentials that characterized the start of the classical tradition in ancient Greece. It has been pointed out that, in the controversy between the Ancients and the Moderns during the preceding century, when neoclassic "methodolatry" had reached its apex, critics who espoused the liberal position were those who defended the Ancients. The ex-

ample is revealing. For to return to the basic classical premises, and to the ideals that surrounded their origin, has always had a liberating and salutary effect on the human spirit. It has helped—as Sir Joshua Reynolds said of Johnson—to "clear the mind of a great deal of rubbish." It has helped to free the mind from confusing the means with the end, and from the passive, unthinking acceptance of custom and habit as the desirable or even necessary norm. At the same time, it has assisted in bringing the mind back to the desire to discover fundamental aims and aspirations, to assimilate these aims, and to weigh, evaluate, and prize the means to the degree that they further the end. Above all, to return to the source and fountainhead of the classical legacy in ancient Greece is to witness—as an actual, historical example—just how such premises and values concretely helped to lead a small body of people into a creative flowering, without parallel in its rapidity and extent. It is to witness how such aims and ideals guided the sudden growth of diverse achievements which have served as the capital from which the Western world has frequently drawn, which have stayed occidental civilization through difficult times, and which, in brilliant creative epochs, especially the European Renaissance, have always furnished for reinvestment the ready and impelling nucleus.

BIBLIOGRAPHICAL NOTE

By far the most comprehensive and penetrating discussion of the origin, premises, and ideals of the classical tradition generally, on which the classical conception of the aim and value of art is based, is Werner Jaeger's *Paideia: the Ideals of Greek Culture* (trans. Gilbert Highet, 3 vols., 1939-1944). For classical criticism specifically, see especially J. W. H. Atkins, *Literary Criticism in Antiquity* (2 vols., Cambridge, 1934); S. H. Butcher, *Aristotle's Theory of Poetry and The Fine Arts* (1895; rev. 1911) and the essays on "Greek Literary Criticism" in *Harvard Lectures on Greek Subjects* (1904), reprinted as *Harvard Lectures on the Originality of Greece* (1920). Other works, including collections as well as commentaries, include: (1) Classical antiquity: Leo Aylen, *Greek Tragedy and the Modern World* (1964); M. W. Bundy, *Theory of Imagination in Classical and Medieval Thought* (Urbana, 1927); J. F. D'Alton, *Roman Literary Criticism* (1931); J. D. Denniston (ed.), *Greek Literary*

Criticism (1924) ; A. W. Gomme, *The Greek Attitude to Poetry and History* (Berkeley, 1954) ; G. M. A. Grube, *The Greek and Roman Critics* (1965) ; Rosemary Harriott, *Poetry and Criticism Before Plato* (1965) ; J. Jones, *On Aristotle and Greek Tragedy* (1962) ; H. D. F. Kitto, *Form and Meaning in Drama* (1959) and *Poesis: Structure and Thought* (Berkeley, 1966) ; Marsh H. McCall, Jr., *Ancient Rhetorical Theories of Simile and Comparison* (Cambridge, Mass., 1962) ; P. E. More, *The Greek Tradition* (5 Vols., Princeton, 1917-1927) ; W. R. Roberts, *Greek Rhetoric and Literary Criticism* (1928) ; E. E. Sikes, *The Greek View of Poetry* (1931). (2) Renaissance to the later eighteenth century: A. Bosker, *Literary Criticism in the Age of Johnson* (The Hague, 1930) ; Donald Clark, *Rhetoric and Poetry in the Renaissance* (1922) ; A. F. B. Clark, *Boileau and the French Classical Critics in England* (Paris, 1925) ; A. H. Gilbert, *Literary Criticism, Plato to Dryden* (1940), valuable for English translations of Renaissance Italian critics; Baxter Hathaway, *The Age of Criticism: the Late Renaissance in Italy* (Ithaca, 1962) ; S. H. Monk, *The Sublime . . . Critical Theories in XVIII Century England* (1935) ; Douglas Radclif-Umstead, *The Birth of Modern Comedy in Renaissance Italy* (Chicago, 1969) ; J. E. Spingarn, *Literary Criticism in the Renaissance* (1899) ; E. J. Sweeting, *Early Tudor Criticism* (Oxford, 1940) ; Bernard Weinberg, *A History of Literary Criticism in the Renaissance* (2 vols., Chicago, 1962) ; and the five collections, G. W. Chapman (ed.), *Literary Criticism in England, 1660-1800* (1966) ; W. H. Durham (ed.), *Critical Essays of the Eighteenth Century, 1700-1725* (New Haven, 1915) ; O. B. Hardison (ed.), *English Literary Criticism: the Renaissance* (1963) ; G. G. Smith (ed.), *Elizabethan Critical Essays* (2 vols., Oxford, 1904) ; J. E. Spingarn (ed.), *Critical Essays of the Seventeenth Century* (3 vols., Oxford, 1908-09). (3) General works include: C. S. Baldwin, *Ancient Rhetoric and Poetic* (1924), *Medieval Rhetoric and Poetic* (1928), and *Renaissance Literary Theory and Practice* (1939) ; W. J. Bate, *From Classic to Romantic* (Cambridge, Mass., 1946), Chs. I-III; Bernard Bosanquet, *A History of Aesthetic*, 2d ed. (1940) ; Ronald Crane (ed.), *Critics and Criticism: Ancient and Modern* (Chicago, 1952) ; Philip Damon (ed.), *Literary Criticism and Historical Understanding* (1967) ; K. Gilbert and H. Kuhn, *A History of Aesthetics* (1939) ; George Saintsbury, *History of Criticism* (3 vols., 1900-04) ; W. K. Wimsatt and Cleanth Brooks, *Literary Criticism: a Short History* (1957) ; and, for discussion of a subject of central importance, John D. Boyd, S.J., *The Function of Mimesis and Its Decline* (Cambridge, Mass., 1968). Here, and in the following bibliographical notes, place of publication is listed only if it is not London or New York.

1. Classical Antiquity

ARISTOTLE   (384 B.C.-322 B.C.)

ARISTOTLE's *Poetics* is not only the most important critical work of classical antiquity. It is also perhaps the most influential work in the entire history of criticism. The unique value of the *Poetics* may be expressed in at least three ways, not to mention others. (1) It marks the beginning of literary criticism. The beginning of critical analysis and the discovery of principles by which analysis can proceed are obviously larger and more essential steps than any one later elaboration or development of these principles. (2) Throughout some periods, particularly the Renaissance and the early eighteenth century, the *Poetics* served as a starting point and sometimes a guide for literary criticism. Even those critics whose works have appeared since the decline of neoclassicism, have revealed their awareness of it as a document which is very much to be reckoned with. (3) The *Poetics* is the best key to the temper and aims of Greek art generally. Aristotle, as we have said, did not try to deduce a theory of literature from an abstract theory of esthetics. He looked at literature directly, almost as a naturalist would regard it. He scrutinized it as a province of knowledge with a concrete body of material of its own; and this body of material was Greek literature itself. He not only described the technical characteristics of Greek literature, drawing from it general aims and principles. In answering Plato's suspicions about the moral effect of art, he also stressed, as we have indicated earlier, the healthful and formative effect of art on the mind; and, in doing so, he was quite in accord with the general Greek confidence in the power of art as *psychagogia, the leading out of the soul,* and as a molder and developer of human character. More than any other critical statement of antiquity, the *Poetics* offers, however briefly and incompletely, the ap-

ARISTOTLE. One of the greatest figures in the history of human thought, Aristotle was born in Stagira, Macedonia, the son of a court physician. While still a youth, he became a student of Plato at Athens. After teaching in Asia Minor and studying in Lesbos, he was asked by King Philip of Macedon to serve as tutor to the young Alexander (342-336 B.C.). Afterwards, Aristotle returned to Athens, where he founded the famous Peripatetic School and lectured on subjects covering widely diverse fields, including physics, zoology, politics, ethics, metaphysics, logic, rhetoric, and poetry.

English translations include: *Works* (ed. W. D. Ross. 11 vols., 1908-24); and, of the *Poetics*, those in S. H. Butcher, *Aristotle's Theory of Poetry and Fine Art* (1895; 4th ed., 1923), and in

proach to literature of one of the most gifted peoples in history—a people, indeed, which virtually created the premises and values of Western civilization. It thus has more than the ordinary importance of a critical work that mirrors a particular, local background. Many of the issues it raises have a perennial importance—an importance that results from the range and penetration of Aristotle's own mind, and also from the remarkable success and fertile creativity of the Greek approach to art upon which the *Poetics* rests.

2

In so far as it is an answer to Plato, Aristotle's *Poetics* justifies poetry on two grounds: the truth and validity, first of all, of poetry as an *imitation of nature*—or as a form of knowledge—and, secondly, the morally desirable effect of this awareness upon the human mind. Both of these justifications Plato had seriously questioned. Whereas Plato regarded ultimate reality as consisting of pure "Ideas," divorced from the concrete, material world, Aristotle conceived of reality or nature as a *process of becoming or developing:* a process in which form manifests itself through concrete material, and in which the concrete *takes on form and meaning,* working in accordance with persisting, ordered principles. Now art, as Aristotle said in the *Physics,* has this characteristic in common with nature. For art, too, employs materials—concrete images, human actions, and sounds—and it deals with these materials as form or meaning emerges or dawns through them.

Poetry, then, although it imitates concrete nature, as Plato charged, does not imitate *just* the concrete. In fact, its focal point of interest—the process of which it is trying to offer a duplicate or counterpart—is *form shaping, guiding, and developing the concrete* into a unified meaning and completeness. The word "form" here should be interpreted broadly, and not as a synonym for mere "technique" in art. It applies to the *direction* which something would take if it were permitted to carry itself out to its final culmination. It thus applies to what is distinctive, significant, or true about that person, object, or event, if *accidental* elements are not allowed to intervene or obstruct its fulfillment. Thus, classical sculpture concerns itself not with individual features, expressions, or isolated acts, but with the total capacity of the figure carried out to the fulfillment which it would attain if it were permitted to do so. Or again, in a drama, the plot does not include every

Ingram Bywater, *Aristotle on the Art of Poetry* (Oxford, 1909). Lane Cooper's translations of the *Poetics* (1913) and the *Rhetoric* (1932) offer examples from modern literature in place of the original Greek examples. See also D. W. Lucas's edition with an introduction, commentary, and notes (Oxford, 1968). English commentaries include, besides W. D. Ross's general *Aristotle* (2d ed., 1930), the critical analyses accompanying Butcher's and Bywater's translations; Lane Cooper, *The Poetics of Aristotle: Its Meaning and Influence* (Boston, 1923); Gerald F. Else, *Aristotle's Poetics: the Argument* (Cambridge, Mass., 1957); Leon Golden and O. B. Hardison, Jr., *Aristotle's Poetics* (Englewood Cliffs, 1968); Humphrey House, *Aristotle's Poetics* (Chester Springs, Pa., 1956); Richard McKeon, "Literary Criticism and the Concept of Imitation in Antiquity," *Modern Philology,* XXXIV (1936), 1-35; Elder Olson (ed.), *Aristotle's Poetics and English Literature: a Collection of Critical Essays* (Chicago, 1965).

incident that might happen to us in ordinary life. For any number of casual incidents occur that are irrelevant to certain other events that interlock with each other and lead to a conclusion; and it is this chain of events interlocked through cause and effect upon which the dramatist concentrates, the form and meaning of which he is attempting to disclose. Hence Aristotle's remark that poetry can be "a more philosophical and higher thing than history: for poetry tends to express the *universal,* history the *particular.*" That is, history concentrates on specific details as they happened, regardless of the ultimate form (the "universal") that things would take if they were allowed to carry themselves out to their logical conclusion. The dramatist, however, is selective: he omits the irrelevant, and draws out the potential form or pattern of an event as a complete unit. The word "form," then, may here be applied to the direction in which something is capable of reaching its complete fulfillment, and in such way as to reveal its distinctive nature.

3

The term "form" also applies to the *value* of that object or event—to its full meaning and character, and hence to its worth and importance. Accordingly, the object or event must have, said Aristotle, "a certain magnitude," if the development of it is to have a significance worth the disclosing. This ordered carrying out of an object to an unobstructed and completed fulfillment is also what is meant by the classical conception of the "ideal" or what "ought to be": not something subjectively "idealized," not something as it "ought to be" in the way that one might, for any private feeling, wish it to be, but rather the way things *would* be, to use Aristotle's own phrase, "according to the law of probability or necessity," if they were to fulfill their total end and complete their potential form. Aristotle applied this principle not only to *what* poetry should seek to disclose or "imitate," but also to the *way* (the *harmonia*) in which this imitation is made and presented as a unified thing in itself. For this reason his emphasis was on plot rather than particular characters; indeed, for Aristotle, the plot was the "soul" or proper form of the drama. The drama imitates *actions;* otherwise it is not a drama, but something else. In imitating actions, therefore, the drama should appropriately be an *activity* itself; and this activity is the plot; hence Aristotle's emphasis on unity of interconnection and on a rounded completeness in this activity that comprises the plot. The plot must contain *within itself* the conditions that lead to its culmination rather than rely on mere chance or some external *deus ex machina* who suddenly resolves all the difficulties artificially. And if tragedy occupied most of Aristotle's attention, it is because, more than any other genre or type, it can best fulfill the general aim of poetry: to present a heightened and harmonious imitation of nature, and, in particular, those aspects of nature that touch most closely upon human life. Because it is itself an activity, and because of its necessary brevity, tragedy can offer a more packed, vivid, and closely unified imitation of events than narrative verse offers.

There must, in short, be *probability*. For "probability," as Aristotle used the term, does not mean a narrow, realistic verisimilitude, nor does it mean "ordinary"; great events and remarkable persons, such as tragedy deals with, may both be rare. "Probability" applies to the inner coherence and structure, the ordered interconnection and working out of a plot. As opposed to mere chance—however "possible" that chance may be—"probability" implies that the culmination of what happens arises naturally and inevitably, by causal interrelation, out of what precedes it. The plot, in other words, must possess what Aristotle called a "unity of action." It must have "a beginning, middle, and end." Nothing in our experience, of course, is really a beginning or an end: related events or causes always exist before any one point, and further results always follow. What is meant is simply a beginning that does not need preceding action on the stage in order to explain it; a development (or "middle"); and an end that generally concludes this development so that more action is not needed to complete the total sequence. Except for a descriptive remark about the amount of time covered in most Greek tragedies, Aristotle did not insist on the other two unities—those of "time" and "place"—which Renaissance critics were to formulate into rules.

Aristotle's emphasis on probability of dramatic structure, and on the ordered self-sufficiency of the plot, also led him to suggest another desirable principle: that the main character of tragedy should have a "tragic flaw." To allow the character to be simply the victim of unpredictable and undeserved calamities would violate the complete, self-contained unity of action. But there are also psychological justifications for selecting, as the central character, a man of some stature "brought from prosperity to adversity" as a result "of some great error or frailty." For if the character is superhumanly good, it is difficult to identify oneself with him sympathetically; he appears almost an abstraction. Moreover, if the calamity that befalls a virtuous man is completely undeserved, our sense of shock may be so violent that it prevents or obstructs other emotional reactions: the emotional and imaginative elevation, for example, that comes in witnessing the working out of a pattern of events to their culmination, and seeing the total significance emerge into universal applicability. On the other hand, the character should have standing and capacity; he must certainly be above average, whether in rank, mind, or capacity to feel. For, unless the character is *too* far removed above us, admiration stimulates sympathetic identification; we all like to regard ourselves as at least somewhat better than we are, and are more likely to surrender our identification to someone we consider worthy of it. Moreover, the tragic fall is much greater to the degree that the character has more "multiplicity of consciousness," in Samuel Johnson's phrase, and to the degree that he himself is aware, therefore, of what is happening. Again, the tragic character must have a place from which to fall. And the loftier his position is, the more disastrous the fall. Needless to say, "the downfall of the utter villain," as Aristotle stated, is not tragic; it "would, doubtless, satisfy the moral sense, but it would inspire neither pity nor fear; for pity is aroused by unmerited misfortune, fear by the misfortune of a man like ourselves." The "tragic flaw," it should be added, is not stated to be *necessary* for a tragedy. It is regarded as desirable in an ideal or "perfect tragedy . . . arranged not on the simple but complex plan": a tragedy in which the calamity does not simply descend from above, but emerges as a closely interconnected series of incidents which arise from various sources including qualities in the character himself.

4

Aristotle's belief in the formative and morally desirable effect of art is implicit in many of his writings. This attitude is quite in accord with Greek thought generally; and it was Plato who took a novel and atypical position by voicing the misgivings he did. One must not, therefore, expect to find a real *defense* of art in Aristotle. He would doubtless have regarded a detailed defense as unnecessary. He did state, however, more or less in answer to Plato, that tragedy produces a healthful effect on the human character through what he called a *katharsis*, "through pity and fear effecting a proper purgation of these emotions." A successful tragedy, then, exploits and appeals at the start to two basic emotions. One is "fear"—the painful sense, as Aristotle elsewhere describes it, "of impending evil which is destructive. . . ." Tragedy, in other words, deals with the element of evil, with what we least want and most fear to face, with what is destructive to human life and values; it is this concern that makes the theme of the play *tragic*. In addition, tragedy exploits our sense of "pity": it draws out our ability to sympathize with others, so that, in our identification with the tragic character, we ourselves feel something of the impact and extent of the evil befalling him. But tragedy does more than simply *arouse* sympathetic identification and a vivid sense of tragic evil or destructiveness. It offers a *katharsis*, a "proper purgation" of "pity and terror."

It is plain that the subject of *katharsis* had an important place in Aristotle's conception of poetry. For he used the term in discussing music in the *Politics*, and mentioned that a fuller account was to be found in the *Poetics*. The reference may well have been to an entire chapter now missing. The term has consequently caused as much discussion as any in the history of criticism. However one may interpret it, at least a few general implications may be borne in mind. To begin with, the *katharsis* that tragedy offers is not merely an outlet or escape for emotion. It is not simply that men **go** about full of pent-up emotions, and that the sight of a dramatic tragedy every once in a while serves as a safety valve, so to speak, by which they let off steam. More than this, tragedy first of all deliberately *excites* in the spectator the emotions of pity and fear which are then to undergo the "proper purgation." The tragic *katharsis* operates by a process which first excites and then tranquillizes emotion; and it does the first in order to accomplish the second. It is, in short, a *controlling* and *directing* of emotion. Whereas Plato, in the *Republic,* had adversely criticized poetry because it "feeds and waters the passions instead of starving them," Aristotle—both psychologically more sophisticated and also more typically Greek—took for granted that it is undesirable to "starve" the emotions; and assumed feeling—though he believed it should be directed and controlled by intelligence —to be a necessary aspect of human life.

Katharsis, as Aristotle employed the term, may be described as the use, control, and *purification* of emotion. In the medical language of the school of Hippocrates, as S. H. Butcher points out, the Greek word "strictly denotes the removal of a painful or disturbing element . . . and hence the purifying of what remains." Something desirable, in other words, happens to emotion when it is aroused and managed by poetic tragedy: the personally disturbing and morbid is purged or shed off, and the emotion, after undergoing this "purgation," has been purified and lifted, as it were, to a harmonious serenity.

Now from what we know of the direction of Aristotle's thought as a whole, and from what we know of his conception of the mind in particular, we can generalize even further. The morbid element purged from the emotion is the subjective, the purely personal and egoistic element. The emotion is caught up, as it were, by sympathetic identification with the tragic character and the tragic situation. It is extended *outward,* that is, away from self-centered absorption. This enlarging of the soul through sympathy, this lifting of one above the egocentric, is itself desirable and operates to the advantage of one's psychological and moral health: it joins emotion to awareness, directing it outward to what is being conceived. But in addition to this, there is a further effect on the emotion of the observer. Tragic drama not only arouses our sympathetic identification through presenting an "imitation" of human actions; but, by appealing to our instinct for *harmonia* as well as for *mimesis* (imitation), it also presents an ordered and proportioned regularity of structure, interrelated through "the law of probability and necessity." And to the degree that the tragedy has been successful in offering, in its own completed and harmonious form, a truthful duplication of the forms of events significant in human life, it rises into universality. The meaning of what has occurred—its inevitability, the various respects in which it is applicable to human life and destiny—is caught with a full and vivid awareness. Moreover, it is reduced to a clarity of outline, and transmuted—purified and heightened—into a harmonious form created through the medium of poetic language. Accordingly, the emotion of the spectator, after being drawn out and identified with the "imitation" before him, is then carried along and made a part of the harmonious development and working out of the particular drama. And the intellectual realization of what has happened, emerging through the ordered structure and body of the drama, is therefore also emerging through the spectator's *own* feelings; in so emerging, the intellectual realization lifts our feelings to a state of harmonized serenity and tranquillity. It has "purged" them of the subjective and self-centered. It has enlarged and extended them through sympathy. Above all, it has joined feeling to insight, conditioning our habitual emotion to that awareness of the essential import of human actions which poetry, through "imitation," is capable of offering. For beneath the theory of *katharsis* lies the general Greek premise that art, in presenting a heightened and harmonious "imitation" of reality, is formative; that, in enlarging, exercising, and refining one's feelings, and in leading them outward, art possesses a unique power to form the "total man," in whom emotion has been reconciled to intelligence and harmoniously integrated with it.

Poetics

I PROPOSE to treat of Poetry in itself and of its various kinds, noting the essential quality of each; to inquire into the structure of the plot as requisite to a good poem; into the number and nature of the parts of which a poem is composed; and similarly into whatever else falls within the same inquiry. Following, then, the order of nature, let us begin with the principles which come first.

2. Epic poetry and Tragedy, Comedy also and Dithyrambic poetry, and the music of the flute and of the lyre in most of their forms, are all in their general conception modes of imitation. 3. They differ, however, from one another in three respects,—the medium, the objects, the manner or mode of imitation, being in each case distinct.

4. For as there are persons who, by conscious

art or mere habit, imitate and represent various objects through the medium of colour and form, or again by the voice; so in the arts above mentioned, taken as a whole, the imitation is produced by rhythm, language, or "harmony," either singly or combined.

Thus in the music of the flute and of the lyre, "harmony" and rhythm alone are employed; also in other arts, such as that of the shepherd's pipe, which are essentially similar to these. 5. In dancing, rhythm alone is used without "harmony"; for even dancing imitates character, emotion, and action, by rhythmical movement.

6. There is another art which imitates by means of language alone, and that either in prose or verse—which verse, again, may either combine different metres or consist of but one kind—but this has hitherto been without a name. 7. For there is no common term we could apply to the mimes of Sophron and Xenarchus and the Socratic dialogues on the one hand; and, on the other, to poetic imitations in iambic, elegiac, or any similar metre. People do, indeed,

Poetics. Translated by S. H. Butcher (1895; rev. 1911). In his translation Butcher puts into brackets phrases and entire passages—the whole of Chapter **XX** and the last paragraph of Chapter **XXXI**—which have been sometimes regarded as insertions by scribes or copyists, or which have been otherwise disputed.

add the word "maker" or "poet" to the name of the metre, and speak of elegiac poets, or epic (that is, hexameter) poets, as if it were not the imitation that makes the poet, but the verse that entitles them all indiscriminately to the name. 8. Even when a treatise on medicine or natural science is brought out in verse, the name of poet is by custom given to the author; and yet Homer and Empedocles have nothing in common but the metre, so that it would be right to call the one poet, the other physicist rather than poet.[1] 9. On the same principle, even if a writer in his poetic imitation were to combine all metres, as Chaeremon did in his Centaur, which is a medley composed of metres of all kinds, we should bring him too under the general term poet. So much then for these distinctions.

10. There are, again, some arts which employ all the means above mentioned,—namely, rhythm, tune and metre. Such are Dithyrambic and Nomic poetry,[2] and also Tragedy and Comedy; but between them the difference is, that in the first two cases these means are all employed in combination, in the latter, now one means is employed, now another.

Such, then, are the differences of the arts with respect to the medium of imitation.

II

Since the objects of imitation are men in action, and these men must be either of a higher or a lower type (for moral character mainly answers to these divisions, goodness and badness being the distinguishing marks of moral differences), it follows that we must represent men either as better than in real life, or as worse, or as they are.[3] It is the same in painting. Polygnotus depicted men as nobler than they are, Pauson as less noble, Dionysius drew them true to life.

2. Now it is evident that each of the modes of imitation above mentioned will exhibit these differences, and become a distinct kind in imitating objects that are thus distinct. 3. Such diversities may be found even in dancing, flute-playing, and lyre-playing. So again in language, whether prose or verse unaccompanied by music. Homer, for example, makes men better than they are; Cleophon as they are; Hegemon the Thasian, the inventor of parodies, and Nicochares, the author of the Deiliad, worse than they are. 4. The same thing holds good of Dithyrambs and Nomes; here too one may portray different types, as Timotheus and Philoxenus differed in representing their Cyclopes. The same distinction marks off Tragedy from Comedy; for Comedy aims at representing men as worse, Tragedy as better than in actual life.

III

There is still a third difference—the manner in which each of these objects may be imitated. For the medium being the same, and the objects the same, the poet may imitate by narration—in which case he can either take another personality as Homer does, or speak in his own person, unchanged—or he may present all his characters as living and moving before us.

2. These, then, as we said at the beginning, are the three differences which distinguish artistic imitation—the medium, the objects and the manner. So that from one point of view, Sophocles is an imitator of the same kind as Homer—for both imitate higher types of character; from another point of view, of the same kind as Aristophanes—for both imitate persons acting and doing. 3. Hence, some say, the name of "drama" is given to such poems, as representing action.[4] For the same reason the Dorians claim the invention both of Tragedy and Comedy. The claim to Comedy is put forward by the Megarians,—not only by those of Greece proper, who allege that it originated under their democracy, but also by the Megarians of Sicily, for the poet Epicharmus, who is much earlier than Chionides

---

[1] Compare Sidney, *An Apology for Poetry,* p. 87.

[2] Dithyrambic poetry consisted of lyrics written in an impassioned manner (formerly choric hymns in honor of Dionysus, and sung to the accompaniment of a flute). Nomes were poems written for music, solemn and staid in character, and sung to the movements of the Chorus.

[3] Implied here is the classical conviction that value (moral worth) is inseparable from any event or action: that to show anything really essential in life is—if it is portrayed truly and *inclusively*—to show its potential *value* for one thing or another, or, in other words, its worth or moral significance (using the word "moral" in its broadest sense). Compare Arnold's statements that poetry really dealing with "life" necessarily deals with "moral" ideas—with evaluation ("Wordsworth," p. 477).

[4] The Greek word for "drama" comes from the verb (*dran*) meaning to *act* or *do*.

and Magnes, belonged to that country. Tragedy too is claimed by certain Dorians of the Peloponnese. In each case they appeal to the evidence of language. Villages, they say, are by them called κῶμαι, by the Athenians δῆμοι: and they assume that Comedians were so named not from κωμάζειν, "to revel," but because they wandered from village to village (κατὰ κώμας), being excluded contemptuously from the city. They add also that the Dorian word for "doing" is δρᾶν, and the Athenian, πράττειν.

4. This may suffice as to the number and nature of the various modes of imitation.

I V

Poetry in general seems to have sprung from two causes, each of them lying deep in our nature.[5] 2. First, the instinct of imitation is implanted in man from childhood, one difference between him and other animals being that he is the most imitative of living creatures; and through imitation he learns his earliest lessons; and no less universal is the pleasure felt in things imitated. 3. We have evidence of this in the facts of experience. Objects which in themselves we view with pain, we delight to contemplate when reproduced with minute fidelity: such as the forms of the most ignoble animals and of dead bodies. 4. The cause of this again is, that to learn gives the liveliest pleasure, not only to philosophers but to men in general; whose capacity, however, of learning is more limited. 5. Thus the reason why men enjoy seeing a likeness is, that in contemplating it they find themselves learning or inferring, and saying perhaps, "Ah, that is he." For if you happen not to have seen the original, the pleasure will be due not to the imitation as such, but to the execution, the colouring, or some such other cause.

6. Imitation, then, is one instinct of our nature. Next, there is the instinct for "harmony" and rhythm, metres being manifestly sections of rhythm. Persons, therefore, starting with this natural gift developed by degrees their special

aptitudes, till their rude improvisations gave birth to Poetry.

7. Poetry now diverged in two directions, according to the individual character of the writers. The graver spirits imitated noble actions, and the actions of good men. The more trivial sort imitated the actions of meaner persons, at first composing satires, as the former did hymns to the gods and the praises of famous men. 8. A poem of the satirical kind cannot indeed be put down to any author earlier than Homer; though many such writers probably were. But from Homer onward, instances can be cited,—his own *Margites*, for example, and other similar compositions. The appropriate metre was also here introduced; hence the measure is still called the iambic or lampooning measure, being that in which people lampooned one another. 9. Thus the older poets were distinguished as writers of heroic or of lampooning verse.

As, in the serious style, Homer is pre-eminent among poets, for he alone combined dramatic form with excellence of imitation, so he too first laid down the main lines of Comedy, by dramatising the ludicrous instead of writing personal satire. His *Margites*[6] bears the same relation to Comedy that the Iliad and Odyssey do to Tragedy. 10. But when Tragedy and Comedy came to light, the two classes of poets still followed their natural bent: the lampooners became writers of Comedy, and the Epic poets were succeeded by Tragedians, since the drama was a larger and higher form of art.

11. Whether Tragedy has as yet perfected its proper types or not; and whether it is to be judged in itself, or in relation also to the audience,—this raises another question. 12. Be that as it may, Tragedy—as also Comedy—was at first mere improvisation. The one originated with the leaders of the Dithyramb, the other with those of the phallic songs, which are still in use in many of our cities. Tragedy advanced by slow degrees; each new element that showed itself was in turn developed. Having passed through many changes, it found its natural form, and there it stopped.

13. Aeschylus first introduced a second actor; he diminished the importance of the Chorus, and assigned the leading part to the dialogue. Soph-

---

[5] This is one of the key passages in the *Poetics*. For it is widely assumed that Aristotle—because he treats poetry as imitation so extensively—rests poetry upon the instinct for imitation alone. But the emphasis here is clearly upon poetry as a completed and *harmonized* imitation of nature.

[6] A comic poem no longer regarded as Homer's.

ocles raised the number of actors to three, and added scene-painting. 14. Moreover, it was not till late that the short plot was discarded for one of greater compass, and the grotesque diction of the earlier satyric form for the stately manner of Tragedy. The iambic measure then replaced the trochaic tetrameter, which was originally employed when the poetry was of the satyric order, and had greater affinities with dancing. Once dialogue had come in, Nature herself discovered the appropriate measure. For the iambic is, of all measures, the most colloquial: we see it in the fact that conversational speech runs into iambic form more frequently than into any other kind of verse; rarely into hexameters, and only when we drop the colloquial intonation. 15. The additions to the number of "episodes" or acts, and the other improvements of which tradition tells, must be taken as already described; for to discuss them in detail would, doubtless, be a large undertaking.

V

Comedy is, as we have said, an imitation of characters of a lower type—not, however, in the full sense of the word bad, the Ludicrous being merely a subdivision of the ugly.[7] It consists in some defect or ugliness which is not painful or destructive. To take an obvious example, the comic mask is ugly and distorted, but does not imply pain.

2. The successive changes through which Tragedy passed, and the authors of these changes, are well known, whereas Comedy has had no history, because it was not at first treated seriously. It was late before the Archon granted a comic chorus to a poet; the performers were till then voluntary. Comedy had already taken definite shape when comic poets, distinctively so called, are heard of. 3. Who introduced masks, or prologues, or increased the number of actors—these and other similar details remain unknown. As for the plot, it came originally from Sicily; but

of Athenian writers Crates was the first who, abandoning the "iambic" or lampooning form, generalised his themes and plots.

4. Epic poetry agrees with Tragedy in so far as it is an imitation in verse of characters of a higher type. They differ, in that Epic poetry admits but one kind of metre, and is narrative in form. They differ, again, in their length: for Tragedy endeavours, as far as possible, to confine itself to a single revolution of the sun, or but slightly to exceed this limit; whereas the Epic action has no limits of time.[8] This, then, is a second point of difference; though at first the same freedom was admitted in Tragedy as in Epic poetry.

5. Of their constituent parts some are common to both, some peculiar to Tragedy. Whoever, therefore, knows what is good or bad Tragedy, knows also about Epic poetry: for all the elements of an Epic poem are found in Tragedy, but the elements of a Tragedy are not all found in the Epic poem.[9]

VI

Of the poetry which imitates in hexameter verse, and of Comedy, we will speak hereafter. Let us now discuss Tragedy, resuming its formal definition, as resulting from what has been already said.

2. Tragedy then, is an imitation of an action that is serious, complete, and of a certain magnitude; in language embellished with each kind of artistic ornament, the several kinds being found in separate parts of the play; in the form of action, not of narrative; through pity and fear effecting the proper purgation of these emotions.[10] 3. By "language embellished," I mean language into which rhythm, "harmony," and song enter. By "the several kinds in separate parts," I mean, that some parts are rendered through the medium of verse alone, others again with the aid of song.

---

[7] Greek thought conceived of beauty as consisting of the *harmonious integration* of parts into a whole—the proper or appropriate adaptation of all aspects or means to an end (an appropriate form or value). The laughable, resting on incongruity, or lack of integration, is thus a species of the ugly.

[8] Here is the only mention in Aristotle of what Renaissance neoclassicism later made into a rule, the "unity of time." Aristotle, of course, is not advancing it as a "rule" but as a description of common Greek practice.

[9] Tragedy is thus a more complex, concentrated, and challenging form than the epic. See Ch. XXVI.

[10] This is the famous theory of *katharsis*. See p. 17. The word "proper" here should be given weight.

4. Now as tragic imitation implies persons acting, it necessarily follows, in the first place, that Spectacular equipment will be a part of Tragedy. Next, Song and Diction, for these are the medium of imitation. By "Diction" I mean the mere metrical arrangement of the words: as for "Song," it is a term whose sense every one understands.

5. Again, Tragedy is the imitation of an action; and an action implies personal agents, who necessarily possess certain distinctive qualities both of character and thought; for it is by these that we qualify actions themselves, and these—thought and character—are the two natural causes from which actions spring, and on actions again all success or failure depends. 6. Hence, the Plot is the imitation of the action:—for by plot I here mean the arrangement of the incidents. By Character I mean that in virtue of which we ascribe certain qualities to the agents. Thought is required wherever a statement is proved, or, it may be, a general truth enunciated. 7. Every Tragedy, therefore, must have six parts, which parts determine its quality—namely, Plot, Character, Diction, Thought, Spectacle, Song.[11] Two of the parts constitute the medium of imitation, one the manner, and three the objects of imitation. And these complete the list. 8. These elements have been employed, we may say, by the poets to a man; in fact, every play contains Spectacular elements as well as Character, Plot, Diction, Song, and Thought.

9. But most important of all is the structure of the incidents. For Tragedy is an imitation, not of men, but of an action and of life, and life consists in action, and its end is a mode of action, not a quality. 10. Now character determines men's qualities, but it is by their actions that they are happy or the reverse. Dramatic action, therefore, is not with a view to the representation of character: character comes in as subsidiary to the actions. Hence the incidents and the plot are the end of a tragedy; and the end is the chief thing of all. 11. Again, without action there cannot be a tragedy;[12] there may

be without character. The tragedies of most of our modern poets fail in the rendering of character; and of poets in general this is often true. It is the same in painting; and here lies the difference between Zeuxis and Polygnotus. Polygnotus delineates character well: the style of Zeuxis is devoid of ethical quality. 12. Again, if you string together a set of speeches expressive of character, and well finished in point of diction and thought, you will not produce the essential tragic effect nearly so well as with a play which, however deficient in these respects, yet has a plot and artistically constructed incidents. 13. Besides which, the most powerful elements of emotional interest in Tragedy—Peripeteia or Reversal of Intention, and Recognition scenes—are parts of the plot. 14. A further proof is, that novices in the art attain to finish of diction and precision of portraiture before they can construct the plot. It is the same with almost all the early poets.

The Plot, then, is the first principle, and, as it were, the soul of a tragedy: Character holds the second place. 15. A similar fact is seen in painting. The most beautiful colours, laid on confusedly, will not give as much pleasure as the chalk outline of a portrait. Thus Tragedy is the imitation of an action, and of the agents, mainly with a view to the action.

16. Third in order is Thought,—that is, the faculty of saying what is possible and pertinent in given circumstances. In the case of oratory, this is the function of the political art and of the art of rhetoric: and so indeed the older poets make their characters speak the language of civic life; the poets of our time, the language of the rhetoricians.

17. Character is that which reveals moral purpose, showing what kind of things a man chooses or avoids. Speeches, therefore, which do not make this manifest, or in which the speaker does not choose or avoid anything whatever, are not expressive of character. Thought, on the other hand, is found where something is proved to be or not to be, or a general maxim is enunciated.

18. Fourth among the elements enumerated comes Diction; by which I mean, as has been

[11] The order is significant. Nothing more strikingly illustrates its importance than to contrast the order in which Aristotle ranks these aspects of the drama with the exactly opposite order found in the average motion picture.

[12] One may note here the characteristic Greek tendency to define something in terms, first of all, of its most nearly basic single attribute; in the case of the drama, for example, there is above all else an *activity* going on. See note 4, p. 20.

already said, the expression of the meaning in words; and its essence is the same both in verse and prose.

19. Of the remaining elements Song holds the chief place among the embellishments.

The Spectacle has, indeed, an emotional attraction of its own, but, of all the parts, it is the least artistic, and connected least with the art of poetry. For the power of Tragedy, we may be sure, is felt even apart from representation and actors. Besides, the production of spectacular effects depends more on the art of the stage machinist than on that of the poet.

VII

These principles being established, let us now discuss the proper structure of the Plot, since this is the first and most important part of Tragedy.

2. Now, according to our definition, Tragedy is an imitation of an action that is complete, and whole, and of a certain magnitude; for there may be a whole that is wanting in magnitude. 3. A whole is that which has a beginning, a middle, and an end. A beginning is that which does not itself follow anything by causal necessity, but after which something naturally is or comes to be. An end, on the contrary, is that which itself naturally follows some other thing, either by necessity, or as a rule, but has nothing following it. A middle is that which follows something as some other thing follows it. A well constructed plot, therefore, must neither begin nor end at haphazard, but conform to these principles.

4. Again, a beautiful object, whether it be a picture of a living organism or any whole composed of parts, must not only have an orderly arrangement of parts, but must also be of a certain magnitude; for beauty depends on magnitude and order.[13] Hence an exceedingly small picture cannot be beautiful; for the view of it is confused, the object being seen in an almost imperceptible moment of time. Nor, again, can one

[13] The attitude here should be contrasted with extreme formalism (such as modern abstractionism). Though there must be a harmonizing of parts (order), there must be something of significance being harmonized. Aristotle, who has been emphasizing *harmonia* in the preceding paragraph, is now stressing the other of the two "instincts" upon which poetry rests—that of *mimesis* or "imitation."

of vast size be beautiful; for as the eye cannot take it all in at once, the unity and sense of the whole is lost for the spectator; as for instance if there were a picture a thousand miles long. 5. As, therefore, in the case of animate bodies and pictures a certain magnitude is necessary, and a magnitude which may be easily embraced in one view; so in the plot, a certain length is necessary, and a length which can be easily embraced by the memory. 6. The limit of length in relation to dramatic competition and sensuous presentment, is no part of artistic theory. For had it been the rule for a hundred tragedies to compete together, the performance would have been regulated by the water-clock—as indeed we are told was formerly done. 7. But the limit as fixed by the nature of the drama itself is this:— the greater the length, the more beautiful will the piece be by reason of its size, provided that the whole be perspicuous. And to define the matter roughly, we may say that the proper magnitude is comprised within such limits, that the sequence of events, according to the law of probability or necessity, will admit of a change from bad fortune to good, or from good fortune to bad.

VIII

Unity of plot does not, as some persons think, consist in the unity of the hero.[14] For infinitely various are the incidents in one man's life, which cannot be reduced to unity; and so, too, there are many actions of one man out of which we cannot make one action. 2. Hence the error, as it appears, of all poets who have composed a Heracleid, a Theseid, or other poems of the kind. They imagine that as Heracles was one man, the story of Heracles must also be a unity. 3. But Homer, as in all else he is of surpassing merit, here too—whether from art or natural genius— seems to have happily discerned the truth. In composing the Odyssey he did not include all the adventures of Odysseus—such as his wound on Parnassus, or his feigned madness at the mustering of the host—incidents between which there was no necessary or probable connexion: but he made the Odyssey, and likewise the Iliad, to centre round an action that in our sense of the

[14] The unity cannot, in other words, be biographical: it must be found not in character but in a given action.

word is one. 4. As therefore, in the other imitative arts, the imitation is one when the object imitated is one, so the plot, being an imitation of an action, must imitate one action and that a whole, the structural union of the parts being such that, if any one of them is displaced or removed, the whole will be disjointed and disturbed. For a thing whose presence or absence makes no visible difference, is not an organic part of the whole.

IX

It is, moreover, evident from what has been said, that it is not the function of the poet to relate what has happened, but what may happen —what is possible according to the law of probability or necessity. 2. The poet and the historian differ not by writing in verse or in prose. The work of Herodotus might be put into verse, and it would still be a species of history, with metre no less than without it. The true difference is that one relates what has happened, the other what may happen. 3. Poetry, therefore, is a more philosophical and a higher thing than history: for poetry tends to express the universal, history the particular. 4. By the universal I mean how a person of a certain type will on occasion speak or act, according to the law of probability or necessity; and it is this universality at which poetry aims in the names she attaches to the personages. The particular is—for example—what Alcibiades did or suffered. 5. In Comedy this is already apparent: for here the poet first constructs the plot on the lines of probability, and then inserts characteristic names;—unlike the lampooners who write about particular individuals. 6. But tragedians still keep to real names, the reason being that what is possible is credible: what has not happened we do not at once feel sure to be possible: but what has happened is manifestly possible: otherwise it would not have happened. 7. Still there are some tragedies in which there are only one or two well known names, the rest being fictitious. In others, none are well known,—as in Agathon's Antheus, where incidents and names alike are fictitious, and yet they give none the less pleasure. 8. We must not, therefore, at all costs keep to the received legends, which are the usual subjects of Tragedy. Indeed, it would be

absurd to attempt it; for even subjects that are known are known only to a few, and yet give pleasure to all. 9. It clearly follows that the poet or "maker" should be the maker of plots rather than of verses; since he is a poet because he imitates, and what he imitates are actions.[15] And even if he chances to take an historical subject, he is none the less a poet; for there is no reason why some events that have actually happened should not conform to the law of the probable and possible, and in virtue of that quality in them he is their poet or maker.

10. Of all plots and actions the epeisodic are the worst. I call a plot "epeisodic" in which the episodes or acts succeed one another without probable or necessary sequence. Bad poets compose such pieces by their own fault, good poets, to please the players; for, as they write show pieces for competition, they stretch the plot beyond its capacity, and are often forced to break the natural continuity.

11. But again, Tragedy is an imitation not only of a complete action, but of events terrible and pitiful. Such an effect is best produced when the events come on us by surprise; and the effect is heightened when, at the same time, they follow as cause and effect. 12. The tragic wonder will then be greater than if they happened of themselves or by accident; for even coincidences are most striking when they have an air of design. We may instance the statue of Mitys at Argos, which fell upon his murderer while he was a spectator at a festival, and killed him. Such events seem not to be due to mere chance. Plots, therefore, constructed on these principles are necessarily the best.

X

Plots are either Simple or Complex, for the actions in real life, of which the plots are an imitation, obviously show a similar distinction. 2. An action which is one and continuous in the sense above defined, I call Simple, when the change of fortune takes place without Reversal of Intention and without Recognition.

A Complex action is one in which the change is accompanied by such Reversal, or by Recog-

[15] Compare Arnold's adverse criticism of his own play, *Empedocles on Etna*, on these grounds, p. 446.

nition, or by both. 3. These last should arise from the internal structure of the plot, so that what follows should be the necessary or probable result of the preceding action. It makes all the difference whether any given event is a case of *propter hoc* or *post hoc*.

XI

Reversal of Intention is a change by which the action veers round to its opposite, subject always to our rule of probability or necessity. Thus in the Oedipus, the messenger comes to cheer Oedipus and free him from his alarms about his mother, but by revealing who he is, he produces the opposite effect. Again in the Lynceus, Lynceus is being led away to his death, and Danaus goes with him, meaning to slay him; but the outcome of the action is, that Danaus is killed and Lynceus saved.

2. Recognition, as the name indicates, is a change from ignorance to knowledge, producing love or hate between the persons destined by the poet for good or bad fortune. The best form of recognition is coincident with a Reversal of Intention, as in the Oedipus. 3. There are indeed other forms. Even inanimate things of the most trivial kind may sometimes be objects of recognition. Again, we may recognise or discover whether a person has done a thing or not. But the recognition which is most intimately connected with the plot and action is, as we have said, the recognition of persons. 4. This recognition, combined with Reversal, will produce either pity or fear; and actions producing these effects are those which, by our definition, Tragedy represents. Moreover, it is upon such situations that the issues of good or bad fortune will depend. 5. Recognition, then, being between persons, it may happen that one person only is recognised by the other—when the latter is already known—or it may be necessary that the recognition should be on both sides. Thus Iphigenia is revealed to Orestes by the sending of the letter; but another act of recognition is required to make Orestes known to Iphigenia.

6. Two parts, then, of the Plot—Reversal of Intention and Recognition—turn upon surprises. A third part is the Tragic Incident. The Tragic Incident is a destructive or painful action, such as death on the stage, bodily agony, wounds, and the like.

XII

[The parts of Tragedy which must be treated as elements of the whole, have been already mentioned. We now come to the quantitative parts—the separate parts into which Tragedy is divided—namely, Prologue, Episode, Exodos, Choric song; this last being divided into Parodos and Stasimon. These are common to all plays: peculiar to some are the songs of actors from the stage and the Commoi.

2. The Prologos is that entire part of a tragedy which precedes the Parodos of the Chorus. The Episode is that entire part of a tragedy which is between complete choric songs. The Exodos is that entire part of a tragedy which has no choric song after it. Of the Choric part the Parodos is the first undivided utterance of the Chorus: the Stasimon is a Choric ode without anapaests or trochaic tetrameters: the Commos is a joint lamentation of Chorus and actors. 3. The parts of Tragedy which must be treated as elements of the whole have been already mentioned. The quantitative parts—the separate parts into which it is divided—are here enumerated.]

XIII

As the sequel to what has already been said, we must proceed to consider what the poet should aim at, and what he should avoid, in constructing his plots; and by what means the specific effect of Tragedy will be produced.

2. A perfect tragedy should, as we have seen, be arranged not on the simple but on the complex plan. It should, moreover, imitate actions which excite pity and fear, this being the distinctive mark of tragic imitation. It follows plainly, in the first place, that the change of fortune presented must not be the spectacle of a virtuous man brought from prosperity to adversity: for this moves neither pity nor fear; it merely shocks us. Nor, again, that of a bad man passing from adversity to prosperity: for nothing can be more alien to the spirit of Tragedy; it possesses no single tragic quality; it neither satisfies the moral sense, nor calls forth pity or

fear. Nor, again, should the downfall of the utter villain be exhibited. A plot of this kind would, doubtless, satisfy the moral sense, but it would inspire neither pity nor fear; for pity is aroused by unmerited misfortune, fear by the misfortune of a man like ourselves. Such an event, therefore, will be neither pitiful nor terrible. 3. There remains, then, the character between these two extremes,—that of a man who is not eminently good and just, yet whose misfortune is brought about not by vice or depravity, but by some error or frailty. He must be one who is highly renowned and prosperous,—a personage like Oedipus, Thyestes, or other illustrious men of such families.

4. A well constructed plot should, therefore, be single in its issue, rather than double as some maintain. The change of fortune should be not from bad to good, but, reversely, from good to bad. It should come about as the result not of vice, but of some great error or frailty, in a character either such as we have described, or better rather than worse. 5. The practice of the stage bears out our view. At first the poets recounted any legend that came in their way. Now, the best tragedies are founded on the story of a few houses,—on the fortunes of Alcmaeon, Oedipus, Orestes, Meleager, Thyestes, Telephus, and those others who have done or suffered something terrible. A tragedy, then, to be perfect according to the rules of art should be of this construction. 6. Hence they are in error who censure Euripides just because he follows this principle in his plays, many of which end unhappily. It is, as we have said, the right ending. The best proof is that on the stage and in dramatic competition, such plays, if well worked out, are the most tragic in effect; and Euripides, faulty though he may be in the general management of his subject, yet is felt to be the most tragic of the poets.

7. In the second rank comes the kind of tragedy which some place first. Like the Odyssey, it has a double thread of plot, and also an opposite catastrophe for the good and for the bad. It is accounted the best because of the weakness of the spectators; for the poet is guided in what he writes by the wishes of his audience. 8. The pleasure, however, thence derived is not the true tragic pleasure. It is proper rather to Comedy, where those who, in the piece, are the deadliest

enemies—like Orestes and Aegisthus—quit the stage as friends at the close, and no one slays or is slain.

XIV

Fear and pity may be aroused by spectacular means; but they may also result from the inner structure of the piece, which is the better way, and indicates a superior poet. For the plot ought to be so constructed that, even without the aid of the eye, he who hears the tale told will thrill with horror and melt to pity at what takes place. This is the impression we should receive from hearing the story of the Oedipus. 2. But to produce this effect by the mere spectacle is a less artistic method, and dependent on extraneous aids. Those who employ spectacular means to create a sense not of the terrible but only of the monstrous, are strangers to the purpose of Tragedy; for we must not demand of Tragedy any and every kind of pleasure, but only that which is proper to it. 3. And since the pleasure which the poet should afford is that which comes from pity and fear through imitation, it is evident that this quality must be impressed upon the incidents.

Let us then determine what are the circumstances which strike us as terrible or pitiful.

4. Actions capable of this effect must happen between persons who are either friends or enemies or indifferent to one another. If an enemy kills an enemy, there is nothing to excite pity either in the act or the intention,—except so far as the suffering in itself is pitiful. So again with indifferent persons. But when the tragic incident occurs between those who are near or dear to one another—if, for example, a brother kills, or intends to kill, a brother, a son his father, a mother her son, a son his mother, or any other deed of the kind is done—these are the situations to be looked for by the poet. 5. He may not indeed destroy the framework of the received legends—the fact, for instance, that Clytemnestra was slain by Orestes and Eriphyle by Alcmaeon—but he ought to show invention of his own, and skilfully handle the traditional material. Let us explain more clearly what is meant by skilful handling.

6. The action may be done consciously and with knowledge of the persons, in the manner of the older poets. It is thus too that Euripides

makes Medea slay her children. Or, again, the deed of horror may be done, but done in ignorance, and the tie of kinship or friendship be discovered afterwards. The Oedipus of Sophocles is an example. Here, indeed, the incident is outside the drama proper; but cases occur where it falls within the action of the play: one may cite the Alcmaeon of Astydamas, or Telegonus in the Wounded Odysseus. 7. Again, there is a third case,—<to be about to act with knowledge of the persons and then not to act. The fourth case is> when some one is about to do an irreparable deed through ignorance, and makes the discovery before it is done. These are the only possible ways. For the deed must either be done or not done,—and that wittingly or unwittingly. But of all these ways, to be about to act knowing the persons, and then not to act, is the worst. It is shocking without being tragic, for no disaster follows. It is, therefore, never, or very rarely, found in poetry. One instance, however, is in the Antigone, where Haemon threatens to kill Creon. 8. The next and better way is that the deed should be perpetrated. Still better, that it should be perpetrated in ignorance, and the discovery made afterwards. There is then nothing to shock us, while the discovery produces a startling effect. 9. The last case is the best, as when in the Cresphontes Merope is about to slay her son, but, recognising who he is, spares his life. So in the Iphigenia, the sister recognises the brother just in time. Again in the Helle, the son recognises the mother when on the point of giving her up. This, then, is why a few families only, as has been already observed, furnish the subjects of tragedy. It was not art, but happy chance, that led poets to look for such situations and so impress the tragic quality upon their plots. They are compelled, therefore, to have recourse to those houses whose history contains moving incidents like these.

Enough has now been said concerning the structure of the incidents, and the proper constitution of the plot.

X V

In respect of Character there are four things to be aimed at. First, and most important, it must be good. Now any speech or action that manifests moral purpose of any kind will be ex-

pressive of character: the character will be good if the purpose is good. This rule is relative to each class. Even a woman may be good, and also a slave; though the woman may be said to be an inferior being, and the slave quite worthless. 2. The second thing to aim at is propriety There is a type of manly valour; but valour in a woman, or unscrupulous cleverness, is inappropriate. 3. Thirdly, character must be true to life: for this is a distinct thing from goodness and propriety, as here described. 4. The fourth point is consistency: for though the subject of the imitation, who suggested the type, be inconsistent, still he must be consistently inconsistent. 5. As an example of motiveless degradation of character, we have Menelaus in the Orestes: of character indecorous and inappropriate, the lament of Odysseus in the Scylla, and the speech of Melanippe: of inconsistency, the Iphigenia at Aulis,—for Iphigenia the suppliant in no way resembles her later self.

6. As in the structure of the plot, so too in the portraiture of character, the poet should always aim either at the necessary or the probable. Thus a person of a given character should speak or act in a given way, by the rule either of necessity or of probability; just as this event should follow that by necessary or probable sequence. 7. It is therefore evident that the unravelling of the plot, no less than the complication, must arise out of the plot itself,[16] it must not be brought about by the *Deus ex Machina*—as in the Medea, or in the Return of the Greeks in the Iliad. The *Deus ex Machina* should be employed only for events external to the drama,—for antecedent or subsequent events, which lie beyond the range of human knowledge, and which require to be reported or foretold; for to the gods we ascribe the power of seeing all things. Within the action there must be nothing irrational. If the irrational cannot be excluded, it should be outside the scope of the tragedy. Such is the irrational element in the Oedipus of Sophocles.

8. Again, since Tragedy is an imitation of per-

---

[16] As a *completed* action, or imitation of an action, showing what "ought to be" (that is, what *would* happen, given certain circumstances and developments), the plot must necessarily work out as an interlocked and self-contained activity or process, with its own form or culmination emerging organically from its own details or materials.

sons who are above the common level, the example of good portrait-painters should be followed. They, while reproducing the distinctive form of the original, make a likeness which is true to life and yet more beautiful. So too the poet, in representing men who are irascible or indolent, or have other defects of character, should preserve the type and yet ennoble it.[17] In this way Achilles is portrayed by Agathon and Homer.

9. These then are rules the poet should observe. Nor should he neglect those appeals to the senses, which, though not among the essentials, are the concomitants of poetry; for here too there is much room for error. But of this enough has been said in the published treatises.

XVI

What Recognition is has been already explained. We will now enumerate its kinds.

First, the least artistic form, which, from poverty of wit, is most commonly employed—recognition by signs. 2. Of these some are congenital,—such as "the spear which the earth-born race bear on their bodies," or the stars introduced by Carcinus in his Thyestes. Others are acquired after birth; and of these some are bodily marks, as scars; some external tokens, as necklaces, or the little ark in the Tyro by which the discovery is effected. 3. Even these admit of more or less skilful treatment. Thus in the recognition of Odysseus by his scar, the discovery is made in one way by the nurse, in another by the herdsmen. The use of tokens for the express purpose of proof—and, indeed, any formal proof with or without tokens—is a less artistic mode of recognition. A better kind is that which comes about by a turn of incident, as in the Bath Scene in the Odyssey.

4. Next come the recognitions invented at will by the poet, and on that account wanting in art. For example, Orestes in the Iphigenia reveals the fact that he is Orestes. She, indeed, makes herself known by the letter; but he, by speaking himself, and saying what the poet, not what the plot requires. This, therefore, is nearly allied to the fault above mentioned:—for Orestes might as well have brought tokens with him. Another similar instance is the "voice of the shuttle"[18] in the Tereus of Sophocles.

5. The third kind depends on memory when the sight of some object awakens a feeling: as in the Cyprians of Dicaeogenes, where the hero breaks into tears on seeing the picture; or again in the "Lay of Alcinous," where Odysseus, hearing the minstrel play the lyre, recalls the past and weeps; and hence the recognition.

6. The fourth kind is by process of reasoning. Thus in the Choëphori:—"Some one resembling me has come: no one resembles me but Orestes: therefore Orestes has come." Such too is the discovery made by Iphigenia in the play of Polyidus the Sophist. It was a natural reflexion for Orestes to make, "So I too must die at the altar like my sister." So, again, in the Tydeus of Theodectes, the father says, "I came to find my son, and I lose my own life." So too in the Phineidae: the women, on seeing the place, inferred their fate:—"Here we are doomed to die, for here we were cast forth." 7. Again, there is a composite kind of recognition involving false inference on the part of one of the characters, as in the Odysseus Disguised as a Messenger. A said $<$that no one else was able to bend the bow; . . . hence B (the disguised Odysseus) imagined that A would$>$ recognise the bow which, in fact, he had not seen; and to bring about a recognition by this means—the expectation that A would recognise the bow—is false inference.

8. But, of all recognitions, the best is that which arises from the incidents themselves, where the startling discovery is made by natural means. Such is that in the Oedipus of Sophocles, and in the Iphigenia; for it was natural that Iphigenia should wish to dispatch a letter. These recognitions alone dispense with the artificial aid of tokens or amulets. Next come the recognitions by process of reasoning.

XVII

In constructing the plot and working it out with the proper diction, the poet should place

---

[17] To "preserve the type" is necessary for the sake of truthful portrayal. To "ennoble" the type—to present it in the form of an individual above the average—is necessary if there is to be any admiration and any sense of distance in the fall of the tragic character.

[18] In this play Philomela, who was raped and then had her tongue cut out to prevent her telling about it, wove with her shuttle a web which revealed the story.

the scene, as far as possible, before his eyes. In this way, seeing everything with the utmost vividness, as if he were a spectator of the action, he will discover what is in keeping with it, and be most unlikely to overlook inconsistencies. The need of such a rule is shown by the fault found in Carcinus. Amphiaraus was on his way from the temple. This fact escaped the observation of one who did not see the situation. On the stage, however, the piece failed, the audience being offended at the oversight.

2. Again, the poet should work out his play, to the best of his power, with appropriate gestures; for those who feel emotion are most convincing through natural sympathy with the characters they represent; and one who is agitated storms, one who is angry rages, with the most life-like reality. Hence poetry implies either a happy gift of nature or a strain of madness. In the one case a man can take the mould of any character; in the other, he is lifted out of his proper self.[19]

3. As for the story, whether the poet takes it ready made or constructs it for himself, he should first sketch its general outline, and then fill in the episodes and amplify in detail. The general plan may be illustrated by the Iphigenia. A young girl is sacrificed; she disappears mysteriously from the eyes of those who sacrificed her; she is transported to another country, where the custom is to offer up all strangers to the goddess. To this ministry she is appointed. Some time later her own brother chances to arrive. The fact that the oracle for some reason ordered him to go there, is outside the general plan of the play. The purpose, again, of his coming is outside the action proper. However, he comes, he is seized, and, when on the point of being sacrificed, reveals who he is. The mode of recognition may be either that of Euripides or of Polyidus, in whose play he exclaims very natu-

rally:—"So it was not my sister only, but I too, who was doomed to be sacrificed"; and by that remark he is saved.

4. After this, the names being once given, it remains to fill in the episodes. We must see that they are relevant to the action. In the case of Orestes, for example, there is the madness which led to his capture, and his deliverance by means of the purificatory rite. 5. In the drama, the episodes are short, but it is these that give extension to Epic poetry. Thus the story of the Odyssey can be stated briefly. A certain man is absent from home for many years; he is jealously watched by Poseidon, and left desolate. Meanwhile his home is in a wretched plight—suitors are wasting his substance and plotting against his son. At length, tempest-tost, he himself arrives; he makes certain persons acquainted with him; he attacks the suitors with his own hand, and is himself preserved while he destroys them. This is the essence of the plot; the rest is episode.

XVIII

Every tragedy falls into two parts,—Complication and Unravelling or *Dénouement*. Incidents extraneous to the action are frequently combined with a portion of the action proper, to form the Complication; the rest is the Unravelling. By the Complication I mean all that extends from the beginning of the action to the part which marks the turning-point to good or bad fortune. The Unravelling is that which extends from the beginning of the change to the end. Thus, in the Lynceus of Theodectes, the Complication consists of the incidents presupposed in the drama, the seizure of the child, and then again * * <The Unravelling> extends from the accusation of murder to the end.

2. There are four kinds of Tragedy, the Complex, depending entirely on Reversal and Recognition; the Pathetic (where the motive is passion),—such as the tragedies on Ajax and Ixion; the Ethical (where the motives are ethical),—such as the Phthiotides and the Peleus. The fourth kind is the Simple. <We here exclude the purely spectacular element>, exemplified by the Phorcides, the Prometheus, and scenes laid in Hades. 3. The poet should endeavour, if possible, to combine all poetic merits; or failing

[19] Aristotle's emphasis on the value of sympathetic identification with characters should be compared with the romantic theory of sympathetic imagination, particularly in Hazlitt. See p. 284. Aristotle here is stressing the extent to which the poet is lifted beyond his ordinary self. The poet can transcend his ordinary state in two ways: in emotional enthusiasm, akin to "madness"; or in an intense but objective awareness of the characters of others through sympathetic identification. There are indications that Aristotle prefers the latter. See especially, XXIV, 7.

that, the greatest number and those the most important; the more so, in face of the cavilling criticism of the day. For whereas there have hitherto been good poets, each in his own branch, the critics now expect one man to surpass all others in their several lines of excellence.

In speaking of a tragedy as the same or different, the best test to take is the plot. Identity exists where the Complication and Unravelling are the same. Many poets tie the knot well, but unravel it ill. Both arts, however, should always be mastered.

4. Again, the poet should remember what has been often said, and not make a Tragedy into an Epic structure. By an Epic structure I mean one with a multiplicity of plots: as if, for instance, you were to make a tragedy out of the entire story of the Iliad. In the Epic poem, owing to its length, each part assumes its proper magnitude. In the drama the result is far from answering to the poet's expectation. 5. The proof is that the poets who have dramatised the whole story of the Fall of Troy, instead of selecting portions, like Euripides; or who have taken the whole tale of Niobe, and not a part of her story, like Aeschylus, either fail utterly or meet with poor success on the stage. Even Agathon has been known to fail from this one defect. In his Reversals of Intention, however, he shows a marvellous skill in the effort to hit the popular taste,—to produce a tragic effect that satisfies the moral sense. 6. This effect is produced when the clever rogue, like Sisyphus, is outwitted, or the brave villain defeated. Such an event is probable in Agathon's sense of the word: "it is probable," he says, "that many things should happen contrary to probability."

7. The Chorus too should be regarded as one of the actors; it should be an integral part of the whole, and share in the action, in the manner not of Euripides but of Sophocles. As for the later poets, their choral songs pertain as little to the subject of the piece as to that of any other tragedy. They are, therefore, sung as mere interludes,—a practice first begun by Agathon. Yet what difference is there between introducing such choral interludes, and transferring a speech, or even a whole act, from one play to another?

XIX

It remains to speak of Diction and Thought, the other parts of Tragedy having been already discussed. Concerning Thought, we may assume what is said in the Rhetoric, to which inquiry the subject more strictly belongs. 2. Under Thought is included every effect which has to be produced by speech, the subdivisions being,—proof and refutation; the excitation of the feelings, such as pity, fear, anger, and the like; the suggestion of importance or its opposite. 3. Now, it is evident that the dramatic incidents must be treated from the same points of view as the dramatic speeches, when the object is to evoke the sense of pity, fear, importance, or probability. The only difference is, that the incidents should speak for themselves without verbal exposition; while the effects aimed at in speech should be produced by the speaker, and as a result of the speech. For what were the business of a speaker, if the Thought were revealed quite apart from what he says?

4. Next, as regards Diction. One branch of the inquiry treats of the Modes of Expression. But this province of knowledge belongs to the art of Delivery, and to the masters of that science. It includes, for instance,—what is a command, a prayer, a narrative, a threat, a question, an answer, and so forth. 5. To know or not to know these things involves no serious censure upon the poet's art. For who can admit the fault imputed to Homer by Protagoras,—that in the words, "Sing, goddess, of the wrath," he gives a command under the idea that he utters a prayer? For to tell some one to do a thing or not to do it is, he says, a command. We may, therefore, pass this over as an inquiry that belongs to another art, not to poetry.

XX [20]

[Language in general includes the following parts:—Letter, Syllable, Connecting word, Noun, Verb, Inflexion or Case, Sentence or Phrase.

[20] This and the following chapter, which are less essential for the student than the others, afford one illustration of Aristotle's approach in the *Poetics*; in this first treatment of poetry as a province of knowledge suitable for analytic investigation, the investigation would naturally include language as the material through which poetic imitation works.

2. A Letter is an indivisible sound, yet not every such sound, but only one which can form part of a group of sounds. For even brutes utter indivisible sounds, none of which I call a letter. 3. The sound I mean may be either a vowel, a semi-vowel, or a mute. A vowel is that which without impact of tongue or lip has an audible sound. A semi-vowel, that which with such impact has an audible sound, as S and R. A mute, that which with such impact has by itself no sound, but joined to a vowel sound becomes audible, as G and D. 4. These are distinguished according to the form assumed by the mouth, and the place where they are produced; according as they are aspirated or smooth, long or short; as they are acute, grave, or of an intermediate tone; which inquiry belongs in detail to a treatise on metre.

5. A Syllable is a non-significant sound, composed of a mute and a vowel: for GR without A is a syllable, as also with A,—GRA. But the investigation of these differences belongs also to metrical science.

6. A Connecting word is a non-significant sound, which neither causes nor hinders the union of many sounds into one significant sound; it may be placed at either end or in the middle of a sentence. Or, a non-significant sound, which out of several sounds, each of them significant, is capable of forming one significant sound,— as ἀμφί, περί, and the like. 7. Or, a non-significant sound, which marks the beginning, end, or division of a sentence; such, however, that it cannot correctly stand by itself at the beginning of a sentence,—as μέν, ἤτοι, δέ.

8. A Noun is a composite significant sound, not marking time, of which no part is in itself significant: for in double or compound words we do not employ the separate parts as if each were in itself significant. Thus in Theodorus, "god-given," the δῶρον or "gift" is not in itself significant.

9. A Verb is a composite significant sound, marking time, in which, as in the noun, no part is in itself significant. For "man," or "white" does not express the idea of "when"; but "he walks," or "he has walked" does connote time, present or past.

10. Inflexion belongs both to the noun and verb, and expresses either the relation "of," "to," or the like; or that of number, whether one or many, as "man" or "men"; or the modes or tones in actual delivery, e.g. a question or a command. "Did he go?" and "go" are verbal inflexions of this kind.

11. A Sentence or Phrase is a composite significant sound, some at least of whose parts are in themselves significant; for not every such group of words consists of verbs and nouns—"the definition of man," for example—but it may dispense even with the verb. Still it will always have some significant part, as "in walking," or "Cleon son of Cleon." A sentence or phrase may form a unity in two ways,—either as signifying one thing, or as consisting of several parts linked together. Thus the Iliad is one by the linking together of parts, the definition of man by the unity of the thing signified.]

XXI

Words are of two kinds, simple and double. By simple I mean those composed of non-significant elements, such as γῆ. By double or compound, those composed either of a significant and non-significant element (though within the whole word no element is significant), or of elements that are both significant. A word may likewise be triple, quadruple, or multiple in form, like so many Massilian expressions, e.g. "Hermo-caico-xanthus <who prayed to Father Zeus.>"

2. Every word is either current, or strange, or metaphorical, or ornamental, or newly-coined, or lengthened, or contracted, or altered.

3. By a current or proper word I mean one which is in general use among a people; by a strange word, one which is in use in another country. Plainly, therefore, the same word may be at once strange and current, but not in relation to the same people. The word σίγυνον, "lance," is to the Cyprians a current term but to us a strange one.

4. Metaphor is the application of an alien name by transference either from genus to species, or from species to genus, or from species to species, or by analogy, that is, proportion. 5. Thus from genus to species, as: "There lies my ship"; for lying at anchor is a species of lying. From species to genus, as: "Verily ten thousand noble deeds hath Odysseus wrought"; for ten thousand is a species of large number, and is here used for a large number generally. From species to spe-

cies, as: "With blade of bronze drew away the life," and "Cleft the water with the vessel of unyielding bronze." Here ἀρύσαι, "to draw away," is used for ταμεῖν, "to cleave," and ταμεῖν again for ἀρύσαι,—each being a species of taking away. 6. Analogy or proportion is when the second term is to the first as the fourth to the third. We may then use the fourth for the second, or the second for the fourth. Sometimes too we qualify the metaphor by adding the term to which the proper word is relative. Thus the cup is to Dionysus as the shield to Ares. The cup may, therefore, be called "the shield of Dionysus," and the shield, "the cup of Ares." Or, again, as old age is to life, so is evening to day. Evening may therefore be called "the old age of the day," and old age, "the evening of life," or, in the phrases of Empedocles, "life's setting sun." 7. For some of the terms of the proportion there is at times no word in existence; still the metaphor may be used. For instance, to scatter seed is called sowing: but the action of the sun in scattering his rays is nameless. Still this process bears to the sun the same relation as sowing to the seed. Hence the expression of the poet "sowing the god-created light." 8. There is another way in which this kind of metaphor may be employed. We may apply an alien term, and then deny of that term one of its proper attributes; as if we were to call the shield, not "the cup of Ares," but "the wineless cup."

<An ornamental word . . .>

9. A newly-coined word is one which has never been even in local use, but is adopted by the poet himself. Some such words there appear to be: as ἐρνύγες, "sprouters," for κέρατα, "horns," and ἀρητήρ, "supplicator," for ἱερεύς, "priest."

10. A word is lengthened when its own vowel is exchanged for a longer one, or when a syllable is inserted. A word is contracted when some part of it is removed. Instances of lengthening are,—πόληος for πόλεως, and Πηληιάδεω for Πηλείδου: of contraction,—κρῖ, δῶ and ὄψ as in μία γίνεται ἀμφοτέρων ὄψ.

11. An altered word is one in which part of the ordinary form is left unchanged, and part is re-cast; as in δεξιτερὸν κατὰ μαζόν, δεξιτερόν is for δεξιόν.

12. [Nouns in themselves are either masculine, feminine, or neuter. Masculine are such as end in ν, ρ, ς, or in some letter compounded with ς,—these being two, ψ and ξ. Feminine, such as end in vowels that are always long, namely η and ω and—of vowels that admit of lengthening—those in α. Thus the number of letters in which nouns masculine and feminine end is the same; for ψ and ξ are equivalent to endings in ς. No noun ends in a mute or vowel short by nature. Three only end in ι,—μέλι, κόμμι, πέπερι: five end in υ. Neuter nouns end in these two latter vowels; also in ν and ς.]

XXII

The perfection of style is to be clear without being mean. The clearest style is that which uses only current or proper words; at the same time it is mean:—witness the poetry of Cleophon and of Sthenelus. That diction, on the other hand, is lofty and raised above the commonplace which employs unusual words. By unusual, I mean strange (or rare) words, metaphorical, lengthened,—anything, in short, that differs from the normal idiom. 2. Yet a style wholly composed of such words is either a riddle or a jargon; a riddle, if it consists of metaphors; a jargon, if it consists of strange (or rare) words. For the essence of a riddle is to express true facts under impossible combinations. Now this cannot be done by any arrangement of ordinary words, but by the use of metaphor it can. Such is the riddle:—"A man I saw who on another man had glued the bronze by aid of fire," and others of the same kind. A diction that is made up of strange (or rare) terms is a jargon. 3. A certain infusion, therefore, of these elements is necessary to style; for the strange (or rare) word, the metaphorical, the ornamental, and the other kinds above mentioned, will raise it above the commonplace and mean, while the use of proper words will make it perspicuous. 4. But nothing contributes more to produce a clearness of diction that is remote from commonness than the lengthening, contraction, and alteration of words. For by deviating in exceptional cases from the normal idiom, the language will gain distinction; while, at the same time, the partial conformity with usage will give perspicuity. 5. The critics, therefore, are in error who censure these licenses of speech, and hold the author up to ridicule. Thus Eucleides, the elder, declared that it would be an easy matter to be a poet if you might lengthen syllables at will. He caricatured the practice in the very form of his diction, as in the verse:

Ἐπιχάρην εἶδον Μαραθῶνάδε βαδίζοντα,

or,

οὔκ ἄν γ' ἐράμενος τὸν ἐκείνου ἐλλέβορον.

6. To employ such license at all obtrusively is, no doubt, grotesque; but in any mode of poetic diction there must be moderation. Even metaphors, strange (or rare) words, or any similar forms of speech, would produce the like effect if used without propriety, and with the express purpose of being ludicrous. 7. How great a difference is made by the appropriate use of lengthening, may be seen in Epic poetry by the insertion of ordinary forms in the verse. So, again, if we take a strange (or rare) word, a metaphor, or any similar mode of expression, and replace it by the current or proper term, the truth of our observation will be manifest. For example Aeschylus and Euripides each composed the same iambic line. But the alteration of a single word by Euripides, who employed the rarer term instead of the ordinary one, makes one verse appear beautiful and the other trivial. Aeschylus in his Philoctetes says:

φαγέδαινα <δ'> ἥ μου σάρκας ἐσθίει ποδός.[21] Euripides substitutes θοινᾶται "feasts on" for ἐσθίει "feeds on." Again, in the line,

νῦν δέ μ' ἐὼν ὀλίγος τε καὶ οὐτιδανὸς καὶ ἀεικής,[22]

the difference will be felt if we substitute the common words,

νῦν δέ μ' ἐὼν μικρός τε καὶ ἀσθενικὸς καὶ ἀειδής.[23]

Or, if for the line,

δίφρον ἀεικέλιον καταθεὶς ὀλίγην τε τράπεζαν,[24]

we read,

δίφρον μοχθηρὸν καταθεὶς μικράν τε τράπεζαν.[25]

Or, for ἠιόνες βοόωσιν, ἠιόνες κράζουσιν.[26]

8. Again, Ariphrades ridiculed the tragedians for using phrases which no one would employ in ordinary speech: for example, δωμάτων ἄπο instead of ἀπὸ δωμάτων, σέθεν, ἐγὼ δέ νιν, Ἀχιλλέως πέρι instead of περὶ Ἀχιλλέως, and the like. It is precisely because such phrases are not part of the current idiom that they give distinction to the style. This, however, he failed to see.

9. It is a great matter to observe propriety in these several modes of expression—compound words, strange (or rare) words, and so forth. But the greatest thing by far is to have a command of metaphor. This alone cannot be imparted by another; it is the mark of genius,—for to make good metaphors implies an eye for resemblances.

10. Of the various kinds of words, the compound are best adapted to dithyrambs, rare words to heroic poetry, metaphors to iambic. In heroic poetry, indeed, all these varieties are serviceable. But in iambic verse, which reproduces, as far as may be, familiar speech, the most appropriate words are those which are found even in prose. These are,—the current or proper, the metaphorical, the ornamental.

Concerning Tragedy and imitation by means of action this may suffice.

XXIII

As to that poetic imitation which is narrative in form and employs a single metre, the plot manifestly ought, as in a tragedy, to be constructed on dramatic principles. It should have for its subject a single action, whole and complete, with a beginning, a middle, and an end. It will thus resemble a single and coherent picture of a living being, and produce the pleasure proper to it. It will differ in structure from historical compositions, which of necessity present not a single action, but a single period, and all that happened within that period to one person or to many, little connected together as the events may be. 2. For as the sea-fight at Salamis and the battle with the Carthaginians in Sicily

[21] "The ulcer feeds on the flesh of my foot."
[22] "Now being small, powerless, of no standing."
[23] "Now being little, spindly, and ugly."
[24] "He set a simple stool and a meager table."
[25] "He set a little stool and a piddling little table."
[26] "Shores roar, shores scream."

took place at the same time, but did not tend to any one result, so in the sequence of events, one thing sometimes follows another, and yet no single result is thereby produced. Such is the practice, we may say, of most poets. 3. Here again, then, as has been already observed, the transcendent excellence of Homer is manifest. He never attempts to make the whole war of Troy the subject of his poem, though that war had a beginning and an end. It would have been too vast a theme, and not easily embraced in a single view. If, again, he had kept it within moderate limits, it must have been over-complicated by the variety of the incidents. As it is, he detaches a single portion, and admits as episodes many events from the general story of the war—such as the Catalogue of the ships and others—thus diversifying the poem. All other poets take a single hero, a single period, or an action single indeed, but with a multiplicity of parts. Thus did the author of the Cypria and of the Little Iliad. 4. For this reason the Iliad and the Odyssey each furnish the subject of one tragedy, or, at most, of two; while the Cypria supplies materials for many, and the Little Iliad for eight—the Award of the Arms, the Philoctetes, the Neoptolemus, the Eurypylus, the Mendicant Odysseus, the Laconian Women, the Fall of Ilium, the Departure of the Fleet.

XXIV

Again, Epic poetry must have as many kinds as Tragedy: it must be simple, or complex, or "ethical," or "pathetic." The parts also, with the exception of song and scenery, are the same; for it requires Reversals of Intention, Recognitions, and Tragic Incidents. 2. Moreover, the thoughts and the diction must be artistic. In all these respects Homer is our earliest and sufficient model. Indeed each of his poems has a twofold character. The Iliad is at once simple and "pathetic," and the Odyssey complex (for Recognition scenes run through it), and at the same time "ethical." Moreover, in diction and thought he is supreme.

3. Epic poetry differs from Tragedy in the scale on which it is constructed, and in its metre. As regards scale or length, we have already laid down an adequate limit:—the beginning and the end must be capable of being brought within a single view. This condition will be satisfied by poems on a smaller scale than the old epics, and answering in length to the group of tragedies presented at a single sitting.

4. Epic poetry has, however, a great—a special—capacity for enlarging its dimensions, and we can see the reason. In Tragedy we cannot imitate several lines of actions carried on at one and the same time; we must confine ourselves to the action on the stage and the part taken by the players. But in Epic poetry, owing to the narrative form, many events simultaneously transacted can be presented; and these, if relevant to the subject, add mass and dignity to the poem. The Epic has here an advantage, and one that conduces to grandeur of effect, to diverting the mind of the hearer, and relieving the story with varying episodes. For sameness of incident soon produces satiety, and makes tragedies fail on the stage.

5. As for the metre, the heroic measure has proved its fitness by the test of experience. If a narrative poem in any other metre or in many metres were now composed, it would be found incongruous. For of all measures the heroic is the stateliest and the most massive; and hence it most readily admits rare words and metaphors, which is another point in which the narrative form of imitation stands alone. On the other hand, the iambic and the trochaic tetrameter are stirring measures, the latter being akin to dancing, the former expressive of action. 6. Still more absurd would it be to mix together different metres, as was done by Chaeremon. Hence no one has ever composed a poem on a great scale in any other than heroic verse. Nature herself, as we have said, teaches the choice of the proper measure.

7. Homer, admirable in all respects, has the special merit of being the only poet who rightly appreciates the part he should take himself. The poet should speak as little as possible in his own person, for it is not this that makes him an imitator.[27] Other poets appear themselves upon the scene throughout, and imitate but little and rarely. Homer, after a few prefatory words, at once brings in a man, or woman, or other personage; none of them wanting in characteristic qualities, but each with a character of his own.

[27] Sympathetic identification with the object is thus necessary for successful imitation. See note 19, p. 30.

8. The element of the wonderful is admitted in Tragedy. The irrational, on which the wonderful depends for its chief effects, has wider scope in Epic poetry, because there the person acting is not seen. Thus, the pursuit of Hector would be ludicrous if placed upon the stage—the Greeks standing still and not joining in the pursuit, and Achilles waving them back. But in the Epic poem the absurdity passes unnoticed. Now the wonderful is pleasing: as may be inferred from the fact that, in telling a story, every one adds something startling of his own, knowing that his hearers like it. 9. It is Homer who has chiefly taught other poets the art of telling lies skilfully. The secret of it lies in a fallacy. For, assuming that if one thing is or becomes, a second is or becomes, men imagine that, if the second is, the first likewise is or becomes. But this is a false inference. Hence, where the first thing is untrue, it is quite unnecessary, provided the second be true, to add that the first is or has become. For the mind, knowing the second to be true, falsely infers the truth of the first. There is an example of this in the Bath Scene of the Odyssey.

10. Accordingly, the poet should prefer probable impossibilities to improbable possibilities.[28] The tragic plot must not be composed of irrational parts. Everything irrational should, if possible, be excluded; or, at all events, it should lie outside the action of the play (as, in the Oedipus, the hero's ignorance as to the manner of Laius' death); not within the drama,—as in the Electra, the messenger's account of the Pythian games; or, as in the Mysians, the man who comes from Tegea to Mysia without speaking. The plea that otherwise the plot would have been ruined, is ridiculous; such a plot should not in the first instance be constructed. But once the irrational has been introduced and an air of likelihood imparted to it, we must accept it in spite of the absurdity. Take even the irrational incidents in the Odyssey, where Odysseus is left upon the shore of Ithaca. How intolerable even these might have been would be apparent if an inferior poet

---

[28] Another key statement of the *Poetics*. A "probable impossibility" would be such a monster as Caliban in the *Tempest:* though he is impossible, his actions are consistent, and would be appropriate to such a monster if he did exist. An "improbable possibility" would be a freak accident in the plot, or, in the form of character, an ordinary and very possible human being who acted in an improbable way.

were to treat the subject. As it is, the absurdity is veiled by the poetic charm with which the poet invests it.

11. The diction should be elaborated in the pauses of the action, where there is no expression of character or thought. For, conversely, character and thought are merely obscured by a diction that is over brilliant.

XXV

With respect to critical difficulties and their solutions, the number and nature of the sources from which they may be drawn may be thus exhibited.

The poet being an imitator, like a painter or any other artist, must of necessity imitate one of three objects,—things as they were or are, things as they are said or thought to be, or things as they ought to be. 2. The vehicle of expression is language,—either current terms or, it may be, rare words or metaphors. There are also many modifications of language, which we concede to the poets. 3. Add to this, that the standard of correctness is not the same in poetry and politics, any more than in poetry and any other art. Within the art of poetry itself there are two kinds of faults,—those which touch its essence, and those which are accidental. 4. If a poet has chosen to imitate something, <but has imitated it incorrectly> through want of capacity, the error is inherent in the poetry. But if the failure is due to a wrong choice—if he has represented a horse as throwing out both his off legs at once, or introduced technical inaccuracies in medicine, for example, or in any other art—the error is not essential to the poetry. These are the points of view from which we should consider and answer the objections raised by the critics.

5. First as to matters which concern the poet's own art. If he describes the impossible, he is guilty of an error; but the error may be justified, if the end of the art be thereby attained (the end being that already mentioned),—if, that is, the effect of this or any other part of the poem is thus rendered more striking. A case in point is the pursuit of Hector. If, however, the end might have been as well, or better, attained without violating the special rules of the poetic art, the error is not justified: for every kind of error should, if possible, be avoided.

Again, does the error touch the essentials of the poetic art, or some accident of it? For example,—not to know that a hind has no horns is a less serious matter than to paint it inartistically.

6. Further, if it be objected that the description is not true to fact, the poet may perhaps reply,—"But the objects are as they ought to be": just as Sophocles said that he drew men as they ought to be; Euripides, as they are. 7. In this way the objection may be met. If, however, the representation be of neither kind, the poet may answer,—"This is how men say the thing is." This applies to tales about the gods. It may well be that these stories are not higher than fact nor yet true to fact: they are, very possibly, what Xenophanes says of them. But anyhow, "this is what is said." Again a description may be no better than the fact: "still, it was the fact"; as in the passage about the arms: "Upright upon their butt-ends stood the spears." This was the custom then, as it now is among the Illyrians.

8. Again, in examining whether what has been said or done by some one is poetically right or not, we must not look merely to the particular act or saying, and ask whether it is poetically good or bad. We must also consider by whom it is said or done, to whom, when, in whose interest, or for what end; whether, for instance, it be to secure a greater good, or avert a greater evil.

9. Other difficulties may be resolved by due regard to the usage of language. We may note a rare word, as in οὐρῆας μὲν πρῶτον, where the poet perhaps employs οὐρῆας not in the sense of mules, but of sentinels. So, again, of Dolon: "ill-favoured indeed he was to look upon." It is not meant that his body was ill-shaped, but that his face was ugly; for the Cretans use the word εὐειδές, "well-favoured," to denote a fair face. Again, ζωρότερον δὲ κέραιε, "mix the drink livelier," does not mean "mix it stronger" as for hard drinkers, but "mix it quicker."

10. Sometimes an expression is metaphorical, as "Now all gods and men were sleeping through the night,"—while at the same time the poet says: "Often indeed as he turned his gaze to the Trojan plain, he marvelled at the sound of flutes and pipes." "All" is here used metaphorically for "many," all being a species of many. So in the verse,—"alone she hath no part . . . ," οἴη,

"alone," is metaphorical; for the best known may be called the only one.

11. Again, the solution may depend upon accent or breathing. Thus Hippias of Thasos solved the difficulties in the line,—δίδομεν (διδόμεν) δέ οἱ, and τὸ μὲν οὗ (οὐ) καταπύθεται ὄμβρῳ.[29]

12. Or again, the question may be solved by punctuation, as in Empedocles,—"Of a sudden things became mortal that before had learnt to be immortal, and things unmixed before mixed."

13. Or again, by ambiguity of construction,—as in παρῴχηκεν δὲ πλέω νύξ,[30] where the word πλέω is ambiguous.

14. Or by the usage of language. Thus any mixed drink is called οἶνος, "wine." Hence Ganymede is said "to pour the wine to Zeus," though the gods do not drink wine. So too workers in iron are called χαλκέας, or workers in bronze. This, however, may also be taken as a metaphor.

15. Again, when a word seems to involve some inconsistency of meaning, we should consider how many senses it may bear in the particular passage. 16. For example: "there was stayed the spear of bronze"—we should ask in how many ways we may take "being checked there." The true mode of interpretation is the precise opposite of what Glaucon mentions. Critics, he says, jump at certain groundless conclusions; they pass adverse judgment and then proceed to reason on it; and, assuming that the poet has said whatever they happen to think, find fault if a thing is inconsistent with their own fancy. The question about Icarius has been treated in this fashion. The critics imagine he was a Lacedaemonian. They think it strange, therefore, that Telemachus should not have met him when he went to Lacedaemon. But the Cephallenian story may perhaps be the true one. They allege that Odysseus took a wife from among themselves, and that her father was Icadius not Icarius. It is merely a mistake, then, that gives plausibility to the objection.

17. In general, the impossible must be justified by reference to artistic requirements, or to the higher reality, or to received opinion. With re-

[29] He explained "We grant he will receive what he prayed for" as "Allow him to receive . . ."; and "It is not rotted by rain" as "A part of it is rotted . . ."

[30] "The greater part," in Greek, is ambiguous in the statement, "The greater part of the night had passed."

spect to the requirements of art, a probable impossibility is to be preferred to a thing improbable and yet possible. Again, it may be impossible that there should be men such as Zeuxis painted. "Yes," we say, "but the impossible is the higher thing; for the ideal type must surpass the reality." To justify the irrational, we appeal to what is commonly said to be. In addition to which, we urge that the irrational sometimes does not violate reason; just as "it is probable that a thing may happen contrary to probability."

18. Things that sound contradictory should be examined by the same rules as in dialectical refutation—whether the same thing is meant, in the same relation, and in the same sense. We should therefore solve the question by reference to what the poet says himself, or to what is tacitly assumed by a person of intelligence.

19. The element of the irrational, and, similarly, depravity of character, are justly censured when there is no inner necessity for introducing them. Such is the irrational element in the Aegeus of Euripides, and the badness of Menelaus in the Orestes.

20. Thus, there are five sources from which critical objections are drawn. Things are censured either as impossible, or irrational, or morally hurtful, or contradictory, or contrary to artistic correctness. The answers should be sought under the twelve heads above mentioned.

XXVI

The question may be raised whether the Epic or Tragic mode of imitation is the higher. If the more refined art is the higher, and the more refined in every case is that which appeals to the better sort of audience, the art which imitates anything and everything is manifestly most unrefined. The audience is supposed to be too dull to comprehend unless something of their own is thrown in by the performers, who therefore indulge in restless movements. Bad flute-players twist and twirl, if they have to represent "the quoit-throw," or hustle the coryphaeus when they perform the "Scylla." 2. Tragedy, it is said, has this same defect. We may compare the opinion that the older actors entertained of their successors. Mynniscus used to call Callippides "ape" on account of the extravagance of his action,

and the same view was held of Pindarus. Tragic art, then, as a whole, stands to Epic in the same relation as the younger to the elder actors. So we are told that Epic poetry is addressed to a cultivated audience, who do not need gesture; Tragedy, to an inferior public. 3. Being then unrefined, it is evidently the lower of the two.

Now, in the first place, this censure attaches not to the poetic but to the histrionic art: for gesticulation may be equally overdone in epic recitation, as by Sosistratus, or in lyrical competition, as by Mnasitheus the Opuntian. Next, all action is not to be condemned—any more than all dancing—but only that of bad performers. Such was the fault found in Callippides, as also in others of our own day, who are censured for representing degraded women. Again, Tragedy like Epic poetry produces its effect even without action; it reveals its power by mere reading. If, then, in all other respects it is superior, this fault, we say, is not inherent in it.

4. And superior it is, because it has all the epic elements—it may even use the epic metre—with the music and scenic effects as important accessories; and these produce the most vivid of pleasures. Further, it has vividness of impression in reading as well as in representation. 5. Moreover, the art attains its end within narrower limits; for the concentrated effect is more pleasurable than one which is spread over a long time and so diluted. What, for example, would be the effect of the Oedipus of Sophocles, if it were cast into a form as long as the Iliad? 6. Once more, the Epic imitation has less unity; as is shown by this, that any Epic poem will furnish subjects for several tragedies. Thus if the story adopted by the poet has a strict unity, it must either be concisely told and appear truncated; or, if it conform to the Epic canon of length, it must seem weak and watery. <Such lengths implies some loss of unity,> if, I mean, the poem is constructed out of several actions, like the Iliad and the Odyssey, which have many such parts, each with a certain magnitude of its own. Yet these poems are as perfect as possible in structure; each is, in the highest degree attainable, an imitation of a single action.

7. If, then, Tragedy is superior to Epic poetry in all these respects, and, moreover, fulfils its specific function better as an art—for each art

ought to produce, not any chance pleasure, but the pleasure proper to it, as already stated—it plainly follows that Tragedy is the higher art, as attaining its end more perfectly.[31]

8. Thus much may suffice concerning Tragic

and Epic poetry in general; their several kinds and parts, with the number of each and their differences; the causes that make a poem good or bad; the objections of the critics and the answers to these objections.

---

[31] Tragedy, in short, is a more concentrated, unified, and vivid form of imitation than narrative verse. It is also itself, by definition, an *activity* in a more direct and thoroughgoing way than is a narrative poem. Accordingly, in imitating or portraying human actions, it

offers a closer counterpart than mere narrative can present—just as music can imitate human feeling more vitally than can the visual arts, since feeling is an activity taking place in time, and so is music (see p. 5).

PLATO   (427 B.C.-347 B.C.)

I F THE great name of Plato is closely connected with the history of literary criticism, it is principally through the influence of his philosophy as a whole upon literary theorists and critics, especially beginning with the Renaissance. To attempt to suggest in a few sentences the central thesis of any great thinker is even more inadequate in the case of Plato than it usually is. For his philosophy is less an actual *system* of thought than it is a series of experimental and tentative probings, in which argument and poetic suggestion interplay, and from which the salient outlines emerge only gradually. Still, some understanding of what Plato conceived to be reality is obviously necessary if one is to begin to sense the meaning of his general influence on the theory of art, and also of his own specific remarks on art and literature.

To begin with, Plato's philosophy may be described as a search for *certainty*—a search for a reality that never changes but is absolute, perfect, and fixed. It is, in part, a reaction against the popular skepticism of the Greek Sophists, who spread the doctrine that everything is *relative*—that all knowledge, judgment, or evaluation of any sort depends upon the particular person's individual reactions. In answer, Plato turned back to the

PLATO. Born of an aristocratic family, Plato early became a friend and disciple of Socrates; and his later attitude toward poetry was then symbolically foreshadowed, according to legend, by his burning the poems he had written before turning to the study of philosophy. After traveling widely, he founded a school (the Academy) in the grove called Academus at Athens, taught philosophy, and there wrote the works associated with his name.

Of the translations of his writings, the most famous is that of Benjamin Jowett (5 vols., Oxford, 1871; 1875; 1892). Relevant commentary will be found in works dealing with ancient criticism listed under "The Classical Tradition" (see pp. 11-12), particularly J. W. H. Atkins, "The Attack on Poetry: Plato," in *Literary Criticism in Antiquity* (Cambridge, 1934), I, Ch. III, and Werner Jaeger, *Paideia* (tr. Gilbert Highet, Oxford, 1939-44), II, especially pp. 208-30, 358-70. See also Eric Havelock, *Preface to Plato* (Cambridge, Mass., 1963); R. C. Lodge, *Plato's Theory of Art* (1953); P. Vicaire, *Platon: Critique Littéraire* (Paris, 1960).

general Greek confidence—still common in Greek thought despite the popularity of the Sophists as teachers—that there is a meaning, an order, or purpose in things, and that the mind, if it is alert enough, can discern this significance. But Plato carried out this point of view in a much more thoroughgoing way than did those before him. The persisting order of the universe and the "forms" through which it works were for him the sole reality. The fluctuating and uncertain world of matter, of concrete circumstances, Plato viewed variously. At times he regarded it as a mere "shadow" of reality —a shadow that we feel is there only because our own minds are not sufficiently awake and attuned to what *is* real. It is, in short, a world of mere "appearance" rather than reality. On other occasions, he viewed the material world as a chaos of imperfect elements, all struggling vainly to fulfill themselves according to the absolute forms or "ideas" that constitute ultimate reality. At all events, the world of matter is at most an imperfect "copy" of a final and absolute reality. Through reason, man is potentially capable of conceiving the "ideas" and thus attaining certainty. Man's other capacities—sense, imagination, emotion—are of value only if they subserve reason. Otherwise they are actually hindrances. For they tend by themselves to focus upon the world of matter, the unstable world of mere appearance, of flux, of sensations, and of emotional "opinion."

The introductions throughout this volume stress some of the occasions on which the Platonic philosophy has touched critical theory or even become an important element in it. But it should be remembered that, whatever else he was, Plato was not himself a literary "critic" or theorist in the specific sense that Aristotle was. He did, to be sure, discuss general problems and aspects of art. The passages in the *Gorgias* and *Phaedrus* dealing with rhetoric afford one example. A second would be the lyrical and half-ironical praise of poetic inspiration in the *Ion:* the poet is said to be divinely inspired, not wholly responsible for what he utters, and to be in a state akin to enthusiastic "madness." This theme has been often repeated at various times since Plato's day, but it is hardly a subject for serious literary criticism. Third, and more important, there is Plato's famous questioning of the worth of poetry both as an educative, and therefore moral, agent, and also as a means of insight into truth.

It is largely because of Plato's misgivings about the social and intellectual value of poetry, particularly as his opinions are expressed in Book X of the *Republic*, that the history of criticism is sometimes said to have begun specifically with him. For Aristotle's *Poetics*, it is argued, is essentially an answer to Plato, and cannot be understood apart from the circumstances that prompted it. Yet it is worth remembering that the *Poetics* is one of a series of several works by Aristotle, each investigating a particular field of knowledge; and as such, it would probably have been written whether Plato had questioned the value of poetry or not. Moreover, it would probably have been written in the same spirit. For it rests upon widespread Greek principles, although it also elaborates them. Chief among these principles is the belief in the unique value of poetry as a formative developer of the human mind and emotions. Aristotle, particularly so far as any justification of poetry was concerned, did not have to look very far for an "answer" to Plato. The answer already existed and had existed in the Greek art and the commonly accepted Greek values of his own day and earlier. For the arts, especially poetry, were the very basis of Greek education.

Indeed, Plato, who took for granted the immense power of poetry over the human mind, would not have attacked poetry as he did had it not been given so central a place in Greek education. Accordingly, as Werner Jaeger says, "We cannot understand Plato's criticisms of poetry unless we remember that the Greeks thought it was the epitome of all knowledge and culture"; and Plato, far from wishing to banish poetry from human life, was protesting against the belief that poetry rather than philosophy should have the highest rank among human pursuits and that it is the ideal "teacher of mankind." To begin with, Plato maintained that poetry, as a fictional creation, does not offer "reality" but unreal "imitations." It not only offers mere imitations, but its imitations are confined to copying only the concrete world. Ultimate truth, however, is absolute: it transcends the changing flux of material things, which themselves are only shadows and imitations of the fixed principles, forms, and "ideas" that comprise the final reality. Philosophy, not poetry, is directed to ultimate truth. Moreover, while philosophy exercises and appeals to reason, poetry and the arts openly address the feelings. "Poetry," according to Plato, "feeds and waters the passions instead of starving them." Plato's attitude thus illuminates, by contrast, the contribution of Aristotle to the theory of art and literature. Aristotle admitted that art is very much concerned with the concrete world about us—the world of "Becoming" as distinct from Plato's world of ideal, absolute "Being." But, in the first place, this activity, this process of "becoming" *is* reality, as Aristotle conceived it. Moreover, art is not confined to the mere material side of this activity of nature, but can draw out and emphasize the general form emerging through it. Instead of being a copy of a copy, as Plato thought, art is, according to Aristotle, a duplicating of the living process of nature, completing and accentuating its potential form. As for the emotional appeal of art, that is all to its credit. The soul, said Aristotle, is an "activity"; and the capacity to feel should be educated, developed, and extended, not suppressed or starved.

Although it is superficial, then, to regard Plato as the beginning or source of the classical theory of art as "imitation," since the concept of "imitation" was already basic in Greek moral and esthetic thought, it is true that he sharpened and emphasized this concept. At times, he even gave a moving expression to it. In Book III of the *Republic,* for example, where the education of the guardians of the ideal state is being traced, Plato puts into the mouth of Socrates a persuasive presentation of the educational value of music. Rhythm and harmony, says Socrates, are able to imitate desirable moral qualities of character, such as temperance, measure, and serenity, just as they can also imitate the reverse of these qualities. Such rhythms and harmonies, in turn, can have a permanent and molding effect on the soul—on the character and habitual feelings—of the hearer, inducing it to assimilate grace, proportion, and regulated harmony into itself. Plato, in such an instance as this, follows the general Greek tendency to connect the conception of art as "imitation" with the formative shaping and development of human character. But it should be repeated and emphasized that his more specific contribution to the idea of "imitation" is to narrow the range of what imitative art can do. It remained for later Platonists, especially Plotinus, to justify art by pleading that, at its best, it can approximately "imitate" those very "ideas" that for Plato were the final reality. In Plato's own theory of art, the tendency is to conceive art as essentially an imitation of objects or aspects of the *material* world, and as being therefore of limited moral and educational value. This very restricting of the range of "imitation," on the other hand, served to focus attention even more strongly upon the imitative character of art, supplying a provocative stimulus for later theorists to try to interpret the concept of imitation in a more liberal way.

Besides concentrating attention more strongly on the theory of art as "imitation," Plato also gave a further prominence, not, as is sometimes thought, to the importance of the social influence of art—that importance was taken for granted by the Greeks—but to the philosophical questioning about the *desirability* of that influence. And this question Plato illuminated in so thoroughgoing a way that it has remained ever since an imposing challenge to apologists for the arts. In this particular respect, as in so many others, the situation illustrates the justice of Alfred North Whitehead's remark that the history of European philosophy is "a series of footnotes to Plato." Even so, the real significance of Plato for the history of criticism lies mainly in the effect of his philosophy as a whole rather than in his specific remarks on art and literature.

From Ion

SOCRATES: I perceive, Ion; and I will proceed to explain to you what I imagine to be the reason of this. The gift which you possess of speaking excellently about Homer is not an art, but, as I was just saying, an inspiration; there is a divinity moving you, like that contained in the stone which Euripides calls a magnet, but which is commonly known as the stone of Heraclea. This stone not only attracts iron rings, but also imparts to them a similar power of attracting other rings; and sometimes

Ion. Translated by Benjamin Jowett.

you may see a number of pieces of iron and rings suspended from one another so as to form quite a long chain: and all of them derive their power of suspension from the original stone. In like manner the Muse first of all inspires men herself; and from these inspired persons a chain of other persons is suspended, who take the inspiration. For all good poets, epic as well as lyric, compose their beautiful poems not by art, but because they are inspired and possessed. And as the Corybantian revellers when they dance are not in their right mind, so the lyric poets are not in their right mind when they are composing their beautiful strains: but when falling under the power of music and metre they are inspired and possessed; like Bacchic maidens who draw milk and honey from the rivers when they are under the influence of Dionysus but not when they are in their right mind. And the soul of the lyric poet does the same, as they themselves say; for they tell us that they bring songs from honeyed fountains, culling them out of the gardens and dells of the Muses; they, like the bees, winging their way from flower to flower. And this is true. For the poet is a light and winged and holy thing, and there is no invention in him until he has been inspired and is out of his senses, and the mind is no longer in him: when he has not attained to this state, he is powerless and is unable to utter his oracles. Many are the noble words in which poets speak concerning the actions of men; but like yourself when speaking about Homer, they do not speak of them by any rules of art: they are simply inspired to utter that to which the Muse impels them, and that only; and when inspired, one of them will make dithyrambs, another hymns of praise, another choral strains, another epic or iambic verses—and he who is good at one is not good at any other kind of verse: for not by art does the poet sing, but by power divine. . . .

From Book X of The Republic

OF THE many excellences which I perceive in the order of our State, there is none which upon reflection pleases me better than the rule about poetry.[1]

To what do you refer?

To the rejection of imitative poetry, which certainly ought not to be received; as I see far more clearly now that the parts of the soul have been distinguished.

What do you mean?

Speaking in confidence, for I should not like to have my words repeated to the tragedians and the rest of the imitative tribe—but I do not mind saying to you, that all poetical imitations are ruinous to the understanding of the hearers, and that the knowledge of their true nature is the only antidote to them.

Explain the purport of your remark.

Well, I will tell you, although I have always from my earliest youth had an awe and love of Homer, which even now makes the words falter on my lips, for he is the great captain and teacher of the whole of that charming tragic company; but a man is not to be reverenced more than the truth, and therefore I will speak out.

Very good, he said.

Listen to me then, or rather, answer me.

Put your question.

Can you tell me what imitation is? for I really do not know.

A likely thing, then, that I should know.

Why not? for the duller eye may often see a thing sooner than the keener.

Very true, he said; but in your presence, even if I had any faint notion, I could not muster courage to utter it. Will you enquire yourself?

Well then, shall we begin the enquiry in our usual manner: Whenever a number of individuals have a common name, we assume them to have also a corresponding idea or form:—do you understand me?

I do.

Let us take any common instance; there are beds and tables in the world—plenty of them, are there not?

Yes.

[1] Socrates is speaking to Glaucon.

But there are only two ideas or forms of them —one the idea of a bed, the other of a table.

True.

And the maker of either of them makes a bed or he makes a table for our use, in accordance with the idea—that is our way of speaking in this and similar instances—but no artificer makes the ideas themselves: how could he?

Impossible.

And there is another artist,—I should like to know what you would say of him.

Who is he?

One who is the maker of all the works of all other workmen.

What an extraordinary man!

Wait a little, and there will be more reason for your saying so. For this is he who is able to make not only vessels of every kind, but plants and animals, himself and all other things—the earth and heaven, and the things which are in heaven or under the earth; he makes the gods also.

He must be a wizard and no mistake.

Oh! you are incredulous, are you? Do you mean that there is no such maker or creator, or that in one sense there might be a maker of all these things but in another not? Do you see that there is a way in which you could make them all yourself?

What way?

An easy way enough; or rather, there are many ways in which the feat might be quickly and easily accomplished, none quicker than that of turning a mirror round and round—you would soon enough make the sun and the heavens, and the earth and yourself, and other animals and plants, and all the other things of which we were just now speaking, in the mirror.

Yes, he said; but they would be appearances only.

Very good, I said, you are coming to the point now. And the painter too is, as I conceive, just such another—a creator of appearances, is he not?

Of course.

But then I suppose you will say that what he creates is untrue. And yet there is a sense in which the painter also creates a bed?

Yes, he said, but not a real bed.

And what of the maker of the bed? were you not saying that he too makes, not the idea which, according to our view, is the essence of the bed, but only a particular bed?

Yes, I did.

Then if he does not make that which exists he cannot make true existence, but only some semblance of existence; and if any one were to say that the work of the maker of the bed, or of any other workman, has real existence, he could hardly be supposed to be speaking the truth.

At any rate, he replied, philosophers would say that he was not speaking the truth.

No wonder, then, that his work too is an indistinct expression of truth.

No wonder.

Suppose now that by the light of the examples just offered we enquire who this imitator is?

If you please.

Well, then, here are three beds: one existing in nature, which is made by God, as I think that we may say—for no one else can be the maker?

No.

There is another which is the work of the carpenter?

Yes.

And the work of the painter is a third?

Yes.

Beds, then, are of three kinds, and there are three artists who superintend them: God, the maker of the bed, and the painter?

Yes, there are three of them.

God, whether from choice or from necessity, made one bed in nature and one only; two or more such ideal beds neither ever have been nor ever will be made by God.

Why is that?

Because even if He had made but two, a third would still appear behind them which both of them would have for their idea, and that would be the ideal bed and not the two others.

Very true, he said.

God knew this, and He desired to be the real maker of a real bed, not a particular maker of a particular bed, and therefore He created a bed which is essentially and by nature one only.

So we believe.

Shall we, then, speak of Him as the natural author or maker of the bed?

Yes, he replied; inasmuch as by the natural process of creation He is the author of this and of all other things.

And what shall we say of the carpenter—is not he also the maker of the bed?

Yes.

But would you call the painter a creator and maker?

Certainly not.

Yet if he is not the maker, what is he in relation to the bed?

I think, he said, that we may fairly designate him as the imitator of that which the others make.

Good, I said; then you call him who is third in the descent from nature an imitator?

Certainly, he said.

And the tragic poet is an imitator, and therefore, like all other imitators, he is thrice removed from the king and from the truth?

That appears to be so.

Then about the imitator we are agreed. And what about the painter?—I would like to know whether he may be thought to imitate that which originally exists in nature, or only the creations of artists?

The latter.

As they are or as they appear? you have still to determine this.

What do you mean?

I mean, that you may look at a bed from different points of view, obliquely or directly or from any other point of view, and the bed will appear different, but there is no difference in reality. And the same of all things.

Yes, he said, the difference is only apparent.

Now let me ask you another question: Which is the art of painting designed to be—an imitation of things as they are, or as they appear—of appearance or of reality?

Of appearance.

Then the imitator, I said, is a long way off the truth, and can do all things because he lightly touches on a small part of them, and that part an image. For example: A painter will paint a cobbler, carpenter, or any other artist, though he knows nothing of their arts; and, if he is a good artist, he may deceive children or simple persons, when he shows them his picture of a carpenter from a distance, and they will fancy that they are looking at a real carpenter.

Certainly.

And whenever any one informs us that he has found a man who knows all the arts, and all things else that anybody knows, and every single thing with a higher degree of accuracy than any other man—whoever tells us this, I think that we can only imagine him to be a simple creature who is likely to have been deceived by some wizard or actor whom he met, and whom he thought all-knowing, because he himself was unable to analyse the nature of knowledge and ignorance and imitation.

Most true.

And so, when we hear persons saying that the tragedians, and Homer, who is at their head, know all the arts and all things human, virtue as well as vice, and divine things too, for that the good poet cannot compose well unless he knows his subject, and that he who has not this knowledge can never be a poet, we ought to consider whether here also there may not be a similar illusion. Perhaps they may have come across imitators and been deceived by them; they may not have remembered when they saw their works that these were but imitations thrice removed from the truth, and could easily be made without any knowledge of the truth, because they are appearances only and not realities? Or, after all, they may be in the right, and poets do really know the things about which they seem to the many to speak so well?

The question, he said, should by all means be considered.

Now do you suppose that if a person were able to make the original as well as the image, he would seriously devote himself to the image-making branch? Would he allow imitation to be the ruling principle of his life, as if he had nothing higher in him?

I should say not.

The real artist, who knew what he was imitating, would be interested in realities and not in imitations; and would desire to leave as memorials of himself works many and fair; and, instead of being the author of encomiums, he would prefer to be the theme of them.

Yes, he said, that would be to him a source of much greater honour and profit.

Then, I said, we must put a question to Homer; not about medicine, or any of the arts to which his poems only incidentally refer: we are not going to ask him, or any other poet, whether he has cured patients like Asclepius, or left behind him a school of medicine such as the

Asclepiads were, or whether he only talks about medicine and other arts at second-hand; but we have a right to know respecting military tactics, politics, education, which are the chiefest and noblest subjects of his poems, and we may fairly ask him about them. 'Friend Homer,' then we say to him, 'if you are only in the second remove from truth in what you say of virtue, and not in the third—not an image maker or imitator—and if you are able to discern what pursuits make men better or worse in private or public life, tell us what State was ever better governed by your help? The good order of Lacedaemon is due to Lycurgus, and many other cities great and small have been similarly benefited by others; but who says that you have been a good legislator to them and have done them any good? Italy and Sicily boast of Charondas, and there is Solon who is renowned among us; but what city has anything to say about you?' Is there any city which he might name?

I think not, said Glaucon; not even the Homerids themselves pretend that he was a legislator.

Well, but is there any war on record which was carried on successfully by him, or aided by his counsels, when he was alive?

There is not.

Or is there any invention of his, applicable to the arts or to human life, such as Thales the Milesian or Anacharsis the Scythian, and other ingenious men have conceived, which is attributed to him?

There is absolutely nothing of the kind. . . .

Thus far we are pretty well agreed that the imitator has no knowledge worth mentioning of what he imitates. Imitation is only a kind of play or sport, and the tragic poets, whether they write in Iambic or in Heroic verse, are imitators in the highest degree?

Very true.

And now tell me, I conjure you, has not imitation been shown by us to be concerned with that which is thrice removed from the truth?

Certainly.

And what is the faculty in man to which imitation is addressed?

What do you mean?

I will explain: The body which is large when seen near, appears small when seen at a distance?

True.

And the same objects appear straight when looked at out of the water, and crooked when in the water; and the concave becomes convex, owing to the illusion about colours to which the sight is liable. Thus every sort of confusion is revealed within us; and this is that weakness of the human mind on which the art of conjuring and of deceiving by light and shadow and other ingenious devices imposes, having an effect upon us like magic.

True.

And the arts of measuring and numbering and weighing come to the rescue of the human understanding—there is the beauty of them—and the apparent greater or less, or more or heavier, no longer have the mastery over us, but give way before calculation and measure and weight?

Most true.

And this, surely, must be the work of the calculating and rational principle in the soul?

To be sure.

And when this principle measures and certifies that some things are equal, or that some are greater or less than others, there occurs an apparent contradiction?

True.

But were we not saying that such a contradiction is impossible—the same faculty cannot have contrary opinions at the same time about the same thing?

Very true.

Then that part of the soul which has an opinion contrary to measure is not the same with that which has an opinion in accordance with measure?

True.

And the better part of the soul is likely to be that which trusts to measure and calculation?

Certainly.

And that which is opposed to them is one of the inferior principles of the soul?

No doubt.

This was the conclusion at which I was seeking to arrive when I said that painting or drawing, and imitation in general, when doing their own proper work, are far removed from truth, and the companions and friends and associates of a principle within us which is equally removed from reason, and that they have no true or healthy aim. . . .

But when a man is drawn in two opposite directions, to and from the same object, this, as we affirm, necessarily implies two distinct principles in him?

Certainly.

One of them is ready to follow the guidance of the law?

How do you mean?

The law would say that to be patient under suffering is best, and that we should not give way to impatience, as there is no knowing whether such things are good or evil; and nothing is gained by impatience; also, because no human thing is of serious importance, and grief stands in the way of that which at the moment is most required.

What is most required? he asked.

That we should take counsel about what has happened, and when the dice have been thrown order our affairs in the way which reason deems best; not, like children who have had a fall, keeping hold of the part struck and wasting time in setting up a howl, but always accustoming the soul forthwith to apply a remedy, raising up that which is sickly and fallen, banishing the cry of sorrow by the healing art.

Yes, he said, that is the true way of meeting the attacks of fortune.

Yes, I said; and the higher principle is ready to follow this suggestion of reason?

Clearly.

And the other principle, which inclines us to recollection of our troubles and to lamentation, and can never have enough of them, we may call irrational, useless, and cowardly?

Indeed, we may.

And does not the latter—I mean the rebellious principle—furnish a great variety of materials for imitation? Whereas the wise and calm temperament, being always nearly equable, is not easy to imitate or to appreciate when imitated, especially at a public festival when a promiscuous crowd is assembled in a theatre. For the feeling represented is one to which they are strangers.

Certainly.

Then the imitative poet who aims at being popular is not by nature made, nor is his art intended, to please or to affect the rational principle in the soul; but he will prefer the passionate and fitful temper, which is easily imitated?

Clearly.

And now we may fairly take him and place him by the side of the painter, for he is like him in two ways: first, inasmuch as his creations have an inferior degree of truth—in this, I say, he is like him; and he is also like him in being concerned with an inferior part of the soul; and therefore we shall be right in refusing to admit him into a well-ordered State, because he awakens and nourishes and strengthens the feelings and impairs the reason. As in a city when the evil are permitted to have authority and the good are put out of the way, so in the soul of man, as we maintain, the imitative poet implants an evil constitution, for he indulges the irrational nature which has no discernment of greater and less, but thinks the same thing at one time great and at another small—he is a manufacturer of images and is very far removed from the truth.

Exactly.

But we have not yet brought forward the heaviest count in our accusation:—the power which poetry has of harming even the good (and there are very few who are not harmed), is surely an awful thing?

Yes, certainly, if the effect is what you say.

Hear and judge: The best of us, as I conceive, when we listen to a passage of Homer, or one of the tragedians, in which he represents some pitiful hero who is drawling out his sorrows in a long oration, or weeping, and smiting his breast —the best of us, you know, delight in giving way to sympathy, and are in raptures at the excellence of the poet who stirs our feelings most.

Yes, of course I know.

But when any sorrow of our own happens to us, then you may observe that we pride ourselves on the opposite quality—we would fain be quiet and patient; this is the manly part, and the other which delighted us in the recitation is now deemed to be the part of a woman.

Very true, he said.

Now can we be right in praising and admiring another who is doing that which any one of us would abominate and be ashamed of in his own person?

No, he said, that is certainly not reasonable.

Nay, I said, quite reasonable from one point of view.

What point of view?

If you consider, I said, that when in misfortune we feel a natural hunger and desire to relieve our sorrow by weeping and lamentation, and that this feeling which is kept under control in our own calamities is satisfied and delighted by the poets;—the better nature in each of us, not having been sufficiently trained by reason or habit, allows the sympathetic element to break loose because the sorrow is another's; and the spectator fancies that there can be no disgrace to himself in praising and pitying any one who comes telling him what a good man he is, and making a fuss about his troubles; he thinks that the pleasure is a gain, and why should he be supercilious and lose this and the poem too? Few persons ever reflect, as I should imagine, that from the evil of other men something of evil is communicated to themselves. And so the feeling of sorrow which has gathered strength at the sight of the misfortunes of others is with difficulty repressed in our own.

How very true!

And does not the same hold also of the ridiculous? There are jests which you would be ashamed to make yourself, and yet on the comic stage, or indeed in private, when you hear them, you are greatly amused by them, and are not at all disgusted at their unseemliness;—the case of pity is repeated;—there is a principle in human nature which is disposed to raise a laugh, and this which you once restrained by reason, because you were afraid of being thought a buffoon, is now let out again; and having stimulated the risible faculty at the theatre, you are betrayed unconsciously to yourself into playing the comic poet at home.

Quite true, he said.

And the same may be said of lust and anger and all the other affections, of desire and pain and pleasure, which are held to be inseparable from every action—in all of them poetry feeds and waters the passions instead of drying them up; she lets them rule, although they ought to be controlled, if mankind are ever to increase in happiness and virtue.

I cannot deny it.

Therefore, Glaucon, I said, whenever you meet with any of the eulogists of Homer declaring that he has been the educator of Hellas, and that he is profitable for education and for the ordering of human things, and that you should take

him up again and again and get to know him and regulate your whole life according to him, we may love and honour those who say these things—they are excellent people, as far as their lights extend; and we are ready to acknowledge that Homer is the greatest of poets and first of tragedy writers; but we must remain firm in our conviction that hymns to the gods and praises of famous men are the only poetry which ought to be admitted into our State. For if you go beyond this and allow the honeyed muse to enter, either in epic or lyric verse, not law and the reason of mankind, which by common consent have ever been deemed best, but pleasure and pain will be the rulers in our State.

That is most true, he said.

And now since we have reverted to the subject of poetry, let this our defence serve to show the reasonableness of our former judgment in sending away out of our State an art having the tendencies which we have described; for reason constrained us. But that she may not impute to us any harshness or want of politeness, let us tell her that there is an ancient quarrel between philosophy and poetry; of which there are many proofs, such as the saying of 'the yelping hound howling at her lord,' or of one 'mighty in the vain talk of fools,' and 'the mob of sages circumventing Zeus,' and the 'subtle thinkers who are beggars after all'; and there are innumerable other signs of ancient enmity between them. Notwithstanding this, let us assure our sweet friend and the sister arts of imitation, that if she will only prove her title to exist in a well-ordered State we shall be delighted to receive her—we are very conscious of her charms; but we may not on that account betray the truth. I dare say, Glaucon, that you are as much charmed by her as I am, especially when she appears in Homer?

Yes, indeed, I am greatly charmed.

Shall I propose, then, that she be allowed to return from exile, but upon this condition only—that she make a defence of herself in lyrical or some other metre?

Certainly.

And we may further grant to those of her defenders who are lovers of poetry and yet not poets the permission to speak in prose on her behalf: let them show not only that she is pleasant but also useful to States and to human life, and we will listen in a kindly spirit; for if this can be proved we shall surely be the gainers— I mean, if there is a use in poetry as well as a delight?

Certainly, he said, we shall be the gainers.

If her defence fails, then, my dear friend, like other persons who are enamoured of something, but put a restraint upon themselves when they think their desires are opposed to their interests, so too must we after the manner of lovers give her up, though not without a struggle. We too are inspired by that love of poetry which the education of noble States has implanted in us, and therefore we would have her appear at her best and truest; but so long as she is unable to make good her defence, this argument of ours shall be a charm to us, which we will repeat to ourselves while we listen to her strains; that we may not fall away into the childish love of her which captivates the many. At all events we are well aware that poetry being such as we have described is not to be regarded seriously as attaining to the truth; and he who listens to her, fearing for the safety of the city which is within him, should be on his guard against her seductions and make our words his law. . . .

HORACE (65 B.C.-8 B.C.)

To MODERN students of critical theory, Horace's *Art of Poetry* is more interesting for its important historical influence than for its intrinsic value as criticism. Though it is a plea to take poetry seriously, it does not confront, as does Aristotle's *Poetics,* the most central problems and the highest uses of poetry. It couches its argument in terms that would appeal to the sophisticated Roman of the time. For besides dwelling on the importance of clarity of outline, and a clear-cut sense of technique, it stresses the general intellectual qualities of prudence, good sense, and an amiable if aloof fastidiousness of taste. Moreover, the poem tries to heighten interest in these qualities by suggesting their social desirability. For example, it appeals to the Roman of wealth and leisure to distinguish himself, in what he patronizes, from the attitudes and tastes of those in the theater audience who eat roasted peas and chestnuts. It would not be true to say that the *Art*

HORACE. Q. Horatius Flaccus, the son of an energetic and ambitious freedman, was carefully educated at Rome, and then sent to Athens to study philosophy. He fought in Brutus's army at Philippi, returned to Rome to find his father's estate confiscated, took a position as a clerk, and began writing verse. Virgil and Varius brought him to the attention of the noted patron, Maecenas, who rescued him from poverty and presented him with the famous Sabine Farm; where, except for visits to Rome, he henceforth lived and wrote.

Texts include *Epistles* (ed. A. S. Wilkins, 1885); *Ars Poetica* (ed. A. Rostagni, 1930). Available translations are those of A. S. Cook (1892), E. H. Blakeney (1928), and H. R. Fairclough (Loeb Classical Library, 1929). Relevant commentary may be found in J. W. H. Atkins, *Literary Criticism in Antiquity* (1934), II, Ch. ii; C. O. Brink, *Horace on Poetry* (Cambridge, 1963); G. C. Fiske, *Lucilius and Horace, a Study in the Classical Theory of Imitation* (Madison, 1920); E. Fraenkel, *Horace* (Oxford, 1957); Pierre Grimal, *Essai sur l'Art Poétique d'Horace* (Paris, 1968); T. E. Maresca, "Horace" in *Pope's Horatian Poems* (Columbus, Ohio, 1966).

of Poetry advocates a discriminating taste mainly as a social accomplishment. However, the conception of taste that underlies the *Art of Poetry* is characterized more by urbanity than by depth. It lacks the larger overtones implicit in the Greek conception of art as *psychagogia,* or a developing and leading out of the soul: a conception which had included urbanity, good sense, decorum, and the other values stressed by Horace, but in which these values had been viewed only as by-products that arose in attempting to fulfill more basic ends or ideals.

The *Art of Poetry,* as Scaliger said in the sixteenth century, is "an *Art* written without art." Even if one agrees with Pope that "Horace still charms with graceful negligence,/And without method talks us into sense," it may seem surprising that a poem that insists so strongly upon ordered coherence should itself be so casual, formless, and in some places needlessly verbose. On the other hand, we should remember that the *Epistle to the Pisos* (see note 1) was intended not as an essay but as a verse-letter, purposely discursive and informal. It was not Horace but the Roman rhetorician, Quintilian, who later referred to it as the *Art of Poetry.* Moreover, though the point may have been overemphasized by recent commentators, there is a structure of sorts. For Horace, in a loose way, is following the arrangement of many Greek and Roman treatises on poetry and rhetoric, with the general divisions of (1) *poesis,* or poesy as a whole (ll. 1-45); (2) *poema,* or technical problems in the poem itself (ll. 46-294); and (3) *poeta,* or the qualification and duties of the poet (ll. 295-476). The *poesis* division is slight, to say the least. But the other two categories are clearly apparent, even though the order of the subdivisions within them is rather arbitrary. It has been suggested that Horace, at least in places, was actually copying and versifying an earlier treatise. The passage describing the "satyric" plays (ll. 220-250) would particularly suggest that he was doing this, for the plays had been long extinct. Horace could have no reason for wishing to revive them; their literary value had been unimportant. Therefore, the argument runs, he was probably turning into verse an older treatise that happened to contain a discussion of them.

Historically considered, the *Art of Poetry* is significant less in its building upon or synthesizing from the past than in its anticipation of the Renaissance restatement of classical aims and values. For the general temper of the *Art of Poetry,* and the comparative limitations of its outlook, already illustrate critical theory in a more self-conscious and retrospective state, acutely aware of tradition and of past models, and deliberately emphasizing the qualities—often only external—associated with these models. In this sense, Horace looks forward to the Italian theorists of the sixteenth century, to Sir Philip Sidney (though what is best in Sidney is not derived from Horace), to French neoclassic theory of the seventeenth century, and to the enlightened urbanity of early eighteenth-century England and France.

Indirectly, through the series of verse-essays from the *Art of Poetry* of Vida through Boileau to Pope's *Essay on Criticism*, and directly through his influence on neoclassic theory as a whole, he inspired the hope, as Edmund Waller said of the Earl of Roscommon's translation of the *Art of Poetry*, that

> Horace will our superfluous branches prune,
> Give us new rules and keep our harp in tune;
> Direct us how to back the wingèd horse,
> Favor his flight and moderate his force.

Art of Poetry

[*Unity and simplicity of form.*] If a painter should decide to join the neck of a horse to a human head, and to lay many-colored feathers upon limbs taken from here or there, so that what is a comely woman above ended as a dark, grotesque fish below, could you, my friends, if you were allowed to see it, keep from laughing? Believe me, dear Pisos,[1] a book may be like just such a picture if it portray idle imaginings shaped like the dreams of a sick man, so that neither head nor foot can be properly ascribed to any one shape. You may say, "Painters and Poets have always had an equal privilege of daring to do anything they wish." This is true; as poets, we claim this licence for ourselves, and grant it to others. But we do not carry it so far as to allow that savage animals should be united with tame, serpents with birds, lambs with tigers.

Works with solemn beginnings, which start with great promises, often have one or two purple patches tacked on, in order to catch the eye. For example, there may be a description of Diana's grove and altar, and of "the moving stream that winds through the fair fields," or the River Rhine, or a description of a rainbow. This is not the place for such things. Perhaps you can sketch a cypress tree. But what has that to do with the matter if you have been commissioned to portray a sailor struggling in despair to escape from a shipwreck? A wine-jar may be intended at the start; why, then, from the potter's wheel, does it end up as a pitcher? In short, whatever your

work may be, let it at least have simplicity and unity.

Among us poets, most—O father and sons worthy of you—are deceived by a superficial idea of the correct thing to do. I try to be brief, and only end by being obscure. Attempting to be smooth, one simply ends up lacking vigor and fire. Another, in striving for the sublime, may fall into bombast; while still another, by being too cautious and afraid of the storm, creeps along the ground. If one has a single subject, and then tries too eagerly to vary it by any means possible, one is then like a painter who puts a dolphin into a forest, or a wild boar on top of the ocean-waves. Avoiding a fault [in this case attempting to avoid monotony], one may fall into a worse one unless there be real artistic skill.

The humblest craftsman over near the Aemilian school [2] will model fingernails and imitate waving hair in bronze; but the total work will be unhappy because he does not know how to represent it as a unified whole. I should no more wish to be like him, if I desired to compose something, than to be praised for my dark hair and eyes and yet go through life with my nose turned awry. You who write, take a subject equal to your powers, and consider at length how much your shoulders can bear. Neither proper words nor lucid order will be lacking to the writer who chooses a subject within his powers. The excellence and charm of the arrangement, I believe, consists in the ability to say only what needs to be said at the time, deferring or omitting many

Art of Poetry. Translated by the editor.

[1] Horace's *Art of Poetry* is in the form of an epistle addressed to the father and two sons of the Piso family.

[2] A school for gladiators; the shops of the bronze-workers were located here.

points for the moment. The author of the long-promised poem must accept and reject as he proceeds. (Ll. 1-45.)

[*Words.*] In addition to using taste and care in arranging words, you will express yourself most effectively if you give novelty to a familiar word by means of a skilful setting. If you have to use new terms for out-of-the-way things, you then have a chance to coin words unheard of by the Cethegi, who wear loincloths [and are thus too old-fashioned to wear tunics]; and you will be allowed the licence of doing this if you do it moderately. New and lately coined words will also be accepted if they are drawn from the Greek fountain; but the spring must be tapped sparingly. Why should a Roman refuse this privilege to Virgil and Varius when it was allowed to Caecilius and Plautus? Why should I be grudged the liberty of adding a few words when Cato and Ennius have enriched our native language and brought forth new terms for things? [3] It has always been and always will be allowed to issue words bearing the stamp of the present day.

As the forest changes its leaves at the decline of the year, so, among words, the oldest die; and like all things young, the new ones grow and flourish. We, and all that belongs to us, are destined for death. And this is so whether we build a harbor, channeling the sea into the shelter of the land in order to protect our fleets from the north winds—a kingly work indeed; or whether a marsh, long a waste and passable only by boats, is drained and tilled in order to feed neighboring cities; or whether a river that formerly destroyed crops has been diverted into a better channel. All mortal things shall perish; still less shall the currency and charm of words always endure. Many words that have lapsed in use will be reborn, and many now in high repute will die, if custom wills it, within whose power

lie the judgment, rule, and standard of speech. (Ll. 46-72.)

[*Meter.*] Homer has shown in what meter [dactylic hexameter] the deeds of kings and captains and the sorrows of war may be written. Verses of unequal lengths, paired in couplets,[4] were used for elegies, and later for the sentiments felt when prayers were granted. But it is unknown and still disputed who the writer was who first used these elegiac verses. Anger armed Archilochus [5] with his own verse form, the *iambic.* Both Comedy and Tragedy have adopted this meter as best fitted for dialogue, able to drown out the noise of the audience, and suitable for action. (Ll. 73-82.)

[*Appropriateness of style.*] The Muse has granted to the lyre the task of celebrating gods and the children of gods, the champion in boxing, the victorious horse in a race, the desire of lovers, and the carefree pleasure in wine. If I am unable to understand and retain these clear-cut distinctions and poetic genres, why should I be considered a poet? Why, through false shame, should I prefer to be ignorant rather than to know? A subject for Comedy refuses to be written in verse suitable for Tragedy. In a similar way, the banquet of Thyestes could not be related in lines suitable to ordinary life and hence appropriate for Comedy. Let each style keep the place to which it belongs. Yet these are times when even Comedy elevates its style, and an angry Chremes raves with swelling voice. Also, in Tragedy, Telephus and Peleus [6] often give vent to their sorrow in the language of prose when, in poverty and exile, they discard their bombast and *sesquipedalian* words [words a foot and a half long] in order to touch the heart of the spectator with their grief. (Ll. 83-98.)

[*Dramatic characters must be convincing: the poet must identify himself with them, and also must portray them with probability and consistency, and thus maintain decorum.*] It is not enough for poems to be beautiful; they must be affecting, and must lead the heart of the hearer

---

[3] Lucius Varius Rufus (c. 74-14 B.C.), friend of Virgil and Horace, was author of the tragedy *Thyestes.* Of the earlier writers, mentioned by Horace as coining words, Caecilius Statius (died c. 168 B.C.), was a Roman comic poet; and his friend Ennius was noted as a tragic and narrative poet who tried to adapt the Latin language to the Homeric hexameter, and to refine literature and the language according to Greek example. M. Portius Cato (234-149 B.C.) or "Cato the Elder" was the first important Latin prose writer. The plays of Plautus (c. 250-184 B.C.), the Roman comic dramatist, were closely modeled after Greek originals.

[4] The "elegiac" couplet consisted of a hexameter followed by a pentameter, the shorter second line giving the couplet a melancholy and falling rhythm.

[5] A remarkable Greek satirist (seventh century B.C.), famous for his bitter and effective realism.

[6] Chremes was a comic character in Terence. Peleus was the father of Achilles, and Telephus, the son-in-law of Priam, was wounded and later cured by Achilles.

as they will. As people's faces smile on those who smile, in a similar way they sympathize with those who weep. If you wish me to weep, you must first feel grief yourself. Only then, O Telephus or Peleus, will your misfortunes affect me. If your words are not appropriate, I shall laugh or go to sleep. Sad words are appropriate to a sorrowful face, furious words are fitting to the angry, gay jests to the merry, serious words to the solemn. For Nature first forms us within to meet all the changes of fortune. She causes us to rejoice or impels us to anger, or burdens us down to the ground with a heavy grief. Afterwards, with the tongue as her interpreter, she expresses the emotions of the heart. If the words of a speaker seem inappropriate to his situation, the Romans, both the aristocracy and the populace, will simply laugh. It will make a great difference whether it is a god who is speaking or a hero, a ripe old man or a youth still in his flower, a wealthy woman or a bustling nurse, a traveling merchant or the tiller of a fertile farm, a Colchian or an Assyrian, one raised in Thebes or in Argos.

Either follow tradition or else make what you invent be consistent. If, in writing, you wish to bring in the famous Achilles, let him be restless, irascible, unyielding, and fierce. Let him refuse to allow any laws to apply to himself; let him place his trust in his sword. Let your Medea be fierce and firm, your Ino sorrowful, your Ixion faithless, your Io a wanderer, your Orestes despondent.[7] If you try something not yet attempted in the theater, and boldly create a new character, have him remain to the close the sort of person he was when he first appeared, and keep him consistent. It is hard to treat a commonly known subject in an original way. It is better to dramatize the *Iliad* into acts than to

offer a subject unknown and unsung. In publicly known matters, you will be able to achieve originality if you do not translate word for word, nor jump into a narrow imitative groove, from which both fear and the rules followed in the given work prevent your escape. (Ll. 99-135.)

[*The building up of interest.*] Nor should you begin as the Cyclic writer of old began: "I shall sing the fortune of Priam, and the noble war." What will this boaster produce worthy of this mouthing? Mountains will labor, and bring forth a mere mouse. How much more fitting for a writer not to make such an inept claim: "Muse, tell me of the man who, after Troy fell, saw the cities and manners of many people."[8] He does not intend to give you smoke after the first flash, but rather light after the smoke, so that he will set forth in time some notable and striking tales: Antiphates, Scylla, Charybdis, the Cyclops. Nor does he start the tale of Diomed's return with the story of Meleager's death, nor begin the Trojan war by telling of the twin eggs.[9] Instead, he always hastens to the climax, and plunges the listener into the middle of things as though they were already known. He leaves out what he is afraid he cannot make more illustrious with his touch, and he invents, mixing fiction with truth, in such a way that the beginning, middle, and end are all appropriate with each other. (Ll. 136-252.)

[*Types of character and other rules of decorum.*] Hear what I, and the people with me, expect. If you want an appreciative listener who waits till the close, staying until the singing attendant cries out, "Applaud!"—you must mark the characteristics of each period of life and present what is fitting to the various natures and ages. The boy who has just learned to speak and walk loves to play with his friends, flies into anger, and forgets it quickly, changing every hour. The beardless stripling, now free from his tutor, delights in horses, dogs, and in the grassy, sunlit field. He is soft as wax in being influenced by evil; he is rude to advisers, slow to provide sensibly for himself, wasteful with

---

[7] Because of her husband's desertion of her, Medea (the subject of the tragedy by Euripides) killed her children in order to make her husband suffer. Ino lost one of her children because she angered the goddess Hera. Ixion, who slew his father-in-law after inviting him to a feast, was shunned by men, rescued by Zeus, proved faithless to him, was then banished to Hades, and as punishment was tied to a perpetually revolving wheel. Io, the mistress of Zeus, was transformed into a heifer, was pursued by jealous Hera, Zeus's wife, and forced to wander. Orestes, son of Agamemnon, avenged his mother's killing of his father by slaying her and her consort.

[8] The opening of the *Odyssey*.

[9] Meleager, an uncle of Diomed, died before Diomed was born. The twin eggs were the offspring of Leda and Zeus, who assumed the form of a swan when with Leda. From one of the eggs came Helen, and thus ultimately the Trojan war.

money, high-spirited, passionate, but quick to change in his desires. With different interests, the maturer mind of the man seeks wealth and friendship. He serves ambition, and is afraid of doing whatever he might later wish undone. Many evils plague the old man, whether he seeks wealth and then like a miser abstains from using it, or because he is without spirit or courage in all his affairs, slow, greedy for a longer life, petulant, obstinate, or the sort of person who glorifies his own boyhood days and damns the present youth. Old age brings many blessings; it also takes many away. Lest the role of old age be assigned to a youth, or that of grown manhood to a child, we should always emphasize the characteristics appropriate to each age.

Events are either acted out on the stage or else they are narrated. Now the mind is much less stirred by hearing things described than it is by actually seeing them, with one's own eyes, as a spectator. On the other hand, you must not show on the stage itself the kind of thing that should have taken place behind the scenes. In fact, many things must be kept from sight for an actor to tell about later. For example, Medea should not butcher her children in plain view of the audience, nor the wicked Atreus cook human flesh in public.[10] Nor, of course, should Procne be transformed into a bird, nor Cadmus into a serpent. Whatever you try to show me openly in this way simply leaves me unbelieving and rather disgusted.

Let your play, if it is to continue to have appeal and be produced, have five acts, no more nor less. And do not have a god—a *deus ex machina*—intervene unless there is a knot worthy of having such a deliverer to untie it! Nor should there be a fourth actor trying to speak.[11] (Ll. 153-192.)

[*The Chorus.*] The Chorus ought to maintain the part and function of an actor with vigor, and not sing anything between the acts that does not advance the action or fit into the plot. It should take the side of the good, give them friendly advice, control the angry, and show affection to those who are afraid to do evil. It should praise moderation in eating, healthful justice and laws, and peace, with the gates of cities lying open. It should respect secrets, and it should implore the gods to remove good fortune from the arrogant and bring it back to the miserable. (Ll. 193-200.)

[*The use of music.*] At one time, the flute, not decked out in brass as it is now, rivaling the trumpet, but slight, simple, and with few stops, was used to set the tone and accompany the Chorus. With its sound, it filled the benches, which were not yet too crowded, and where—when people gathered—there were few enough so that they could be easily counted, and those were thrifty, virtuous, and honest. But later on, nations that were victorious in war began to widen their boundaries, and longer walls were built around their cities. On feast-days, people were able to give themselves up freely to drinking in the daytime; and then greater licence was given to music and rhythm. For what taste could one expect to find in an ignorant crowd, free from its daily toil, in the peasant mixed with the city-dweller, the low-born with the nobles? Therefore, the flute-player added movement and decoration to his earlier art. He now began to strut across the stage, trailing a robe. New sounds were added to the restrained music of the lyre. A hurried style brought with it a new sort of language; and wise, prophetic sayings were also brought forth to sound like the oracles of Delphi. (Ll. 201-219.)

[*Satyric drama.*[12]] The poet who first competed in tragic verse for the prize of a wretched goat soon began to bring on to the stage naked, rustic satyrs. Without losing dignity, he introduced coarse jests; for only by the lure and charm of novelty could he hold the sort of spec-

---

[10] Atreus, king of Mycenae, killed the two sons of his brother Thyestes, and placed their flesh before their father at a banquet. Procne, the sister of Philomela (see p. 29, note 18), was according to the Latin version of the legend, changed into a swallow. Another ancient legend tells the story of Cadmus, king of Illyria and his wife Harmonia, who were changed into serpents and carried to the Elysian fields.

[11] Compare Aristotle (*Poetics*, Ch. IV) on the number of actors.

[12] Horace supposes that the term "tragedy" (that is, "goat-song") arose because the dramas had once been written for the prize of a goat. Actually, the participants were originally dressed in goat skins; hence the origin of the word. Satyric dramas (not to be confused with *satiric*) mark a survival of this custom. Greek tragedies were performed in trilogies; and at their conclusion, as a fourth drama, was presented a *satyric* play, partly serious and partly jesting, in which the chorus consisted of satyrs clothed in goat skins.

tator who, after the Bacchic rites, was completely drunk and wild. In amusing the audience with the laughter and jests of your satyrs, however, and in passing from grave to gay, it is more fitting to do it in such a way that no god or hero whom you are bringing on the stage, and whom we have been accustomed to see in royal gold and purple, should be allowed to sink down into the low talk of dingy taverns, or, in trying to raise himself, simply clutch at clouds and emptiness. Tragedy scorns any temptation to babble light verses, as a matron who is asked to dance on festal days takes her place among the impudent satyrs with modest shame. If I were writing Satyric plays, O Pisos, I should not, for my part, wish to use only ordinary, unadorned language, I should not wish to get so far away from the language of Tragedy that no one could tell who is speaking—whether it is Davus, or bold Pythias, who cheated Simo out of a talent, or whether it is Silenus,[13] who guards and serves his divine charge.

For me, the ideal of poetic style is to mould familiar material with such skill that anyone might hope to achieve the same feat. And yet so firmly would the material be ordered and interconnected (and such is the beauty that one may draw out in that way from the familiar) that he would work and sweat in vain to rival it. Therefore, to my mind, when these rustic fauns are introduced on the stage, they should not act as though they had dwelt in the streets and the forum, languishing with adolescent love-verses, or cracking obscene and embarrassing jokes. The knights, and people of any standing or estate, do not enjoy and wish to offer a crown to everything that pleases the sort of people who buy popcorn and candy.[14] (Ll. 220-250.)

[*Rhythms and verse-forms.*] A short syllable followed by a long one is called an "iambus." This is a rapid foot. Hence the term "trimeter" was given to straight iambic lines that had as many as six beats.[15] Not long ago, however, since it is a tolerant and accommodating form of meter, it admitted the weighty spondee [two long stresses], in order to allow the line to move with more stately slowness, but still with the provision that the iambic always retain its place at least in the second and fourth feet of the line. In what some like to call the "noble" trimeters of Accius, the iambic foot rarely appears; and also in the pompous lines with which Ennius blessed the stage one sees either hasty or careless work, or else sheer ignorance of the art of poetry. Not all critics can notice faulty meter. Therefore our Roman poets have been granted an indulgence quite undeserved. Is that any excuse for me to run wild and write without restraint? Or, supposing that my faults will be noticed by everyone, should I consider myself safe just because I keep within the limits of whatever is pardoned? I may perhaps escape blame by doing that, but I shall have deserved no praise. As for yourselves, thumb through and study the Greek masterpieces by day and night. But, you will say, our forefathers admired the wit and meter of Plautus! Yes, they admired both with tolerance, not to say stupidity, if you and I are any judges of the difference between coarse and urbane language, or have any ability to detect true rhythm by the ear and the finger. (Ll. 251-274.)

[*Origin and early development of the drama.*] Thespis[16] is said to have been the man who discovered Tragedy—a type of poetry hitherto unknown—and to have carried his plays around on wagons to be sung and acted by players whose faces had been smeared with wine-lees. Later on, Aeschylus, who invented the use of the mask and the tragic robe, had his players act on a stage built of small planks, and taught them to talk in lofty words and move in a stately manner with buskined feet. Then came the Old Comedy, popular with everyone. But its free manner degenerated into an excess of violence that deserved to be restrained. It yielded to regulation, and the Chorus, with its ability to do harm now removed, simply sank into silence, to its own shame. Our own poets have left no style unattempted. Nor is it least to their credit that they have been

---

13 Not to be confused with Damon and Pythias. Davus, a male slave, and Pythias, a female, who deceived her master, Simo, are typical comic characters in Terence; whereas Silenus, the teacher of Bacchus and the merry and wise father of the satyrs, was a philosopher.

14 That is, the Roman equivalent, roasted peas and chestnuts.

15 Because it was sufficiently rapid for two feet to make one metrical unit, a six-foot iambic line would nevertheless be called a "trimeter."

16 The Greek poet (sixth century B.C.) who first introduced an actor to reply to the Chorus.

courageous enough to leave the footsteps of the Greeks and celebrate the deeds of their own nation, whether in Comedy or Tragedy. Rome would be as eminent in literature as it is in valor and arms if its poets, one and all, did not find a laborious use of the file [17] so exasperating. O descendants of Numa Pompilius, condemn a poem that time and labor have not corrected and refined tenfold, down to the very fingernail. (Ll. 275-294.)

[*The importance of urbanity and serious craftsmanship.*] Just because Democritus believes that sheer native genius is better than wretched art, and excludes sane poets from Helicon,[18] a good number do not cut their fingernails and beards. They live in solitude and stay away from the baths, since anyone can acquire the distinction and name of a poet if he never entrusts to Licinus, the barber, a head that three Anticyras [19] could not remedy! I suppose I am quite a fool, then, to go and purge myself of bile when the spring comes. Otherwise no one could write better poems! But then, the game would hardly be worth it. So what I shall try to do, therefore, is to serve as a whetstone which, though it cannot itself do any cutting, is able to sharpen steel. Though I myself write nothing worth while, I shall at least teach the duty and office of the poet, instruct him where to get his materials, show what moulds and develops him, what is fitting to him and what is not, where the good can lead him and where the wrong. (Ll. 295-308.)

[*Wisdom and intellectual insight the first requisite of the poet.*] In all good writing the source and fountain is wisdom. The Socratic writings can offer you the material; and when the subject is grasped, the words will come easily. He who has learned what he owes his nation and his friends, what love is due to a parent, brother, and guest, what is the duty of a senator or a judge, what the role of a general sent to war, will know how to give the appropriate nature to each character. I should counsel one who has learned the art of imitation to turn to life and real manners as his model, and draw from there a living language. Sometimes a play, interspersed with commonplaces and having an appropriate characterization, even though lacking in beauty, power, and art, still gives delight to the people and entertains them more than do verses without matter or mere trifling songs.

To the Greeks, who desired only glory, the Muse gave genius and greatness of style. Our Roman youth, however, learn how to divide the *as* [20] into a hundred parts. "Let the son of Albinus answer: if you take from five-twelfths an ounce, how much is left? You ought to know by now!" "A third of an *as*." "Splendid! *You'll* be able to look after *yourself*! And if you add an ounce, how much is that?" "One half an *as*." When this interest in commercial gain has stained the soul, how can we expect to have poems worthy of being preserved in cedar oil and kept in cypress cases? (Ll. 309-332.)

[*The end of poetry.*] The aim of the poet is to inform or delight, or to combine together, in what he says, both pleasure and applicability to life. In instructing, be brief in what you say in order that your readers may grasp it quickly and retain it faithfully. Superfluous words simply spill out when the mind is already full. Fiction invented in order to please should remain close to reality. Your play must not demand that the audience believe anything you take a whim to portray. You cannot have a living child snatched from the belly of Lamia [21] after she has devoured him. The elders of Rome censure poetry that lacks instruction; the young aristocrats, on the other hand, scorn austere poetry. He who combines the useful and the pleasing wins out by both instructing and delighting the reader. That is the sort of book that will make money for the publisher, cross the seas, and extend the fame of the author. (Ll. 333-347.)

[*The difference between isolated faults and habitual blundering.*] There are faults, however, that we can willingly forgive. For the string does not always give out the sound that the mind and hand wished. When you desire a flat, it often gives you a sharp. The arrow, too, does not always hit its mark. When the beauties in a poem predominate, I shall not make an issue of a few

---

[17] The metaphor is drawn from sculpture, the file being used to give a completely smooth finish.

[18] A mountain sacred to the Muses, where the fountain Hippocrene flowed.

[19] Anticyra was a town famous for producing hellebore, a drug useful in killing lice and other insects.

[20] A Roman unit of money which is divisible into twelve "ounces."

[21] A witch, in Greek nursery lore, who ate children.

blemishes that have resulted from carelessness or human frailty. How shall we sum up the matter, then? As a copyist deserves to be condemned if, after being constantly warned, he keeps on making the same mistake, and as a musician is laughed at if he always falters on the same note, in a similar way I regard the poet that blunders constantly as being like Choerilus,[22] whose two or three good lines cause surprised laughter. I am also irritated whenever the great Homer nods. But then, when a work is long, sleep inevitably creeps over it. Poetry is like painting. One work will please you more if you stand close to it; the other strikes more if you stand farther away. One shows more to advantage when seen in the shadow; another, unafraid of the sharp view of the critic, ought to be viewed in the light. One will please only once; the other, though looked at ten times, will continue to please. (Ll. 347-365.)

[*Prudent awareness of one's own limitations.*] You, elder youth of the Piso family, though your judgment has profited from your father's training and though you are sensible in your own right, take this to heart and remember it: only in certain things can mediocrity be tolerated or forgiven. A lawyer, pleading an ordinary suit, may fall short of the eloquent Messalla, and know less than Aulus Cascellius, but he is still respected. But neither gods, men, nor booksellers, tolerate a mediocre poet. At a pleasant banquet, poor music, cheap perfume, and poppy seeds mixed with Sardinian honey, are offensive; the banquet could have done very well without them. And in a similar way, a poem, born and created in order to give the soul delight, if once it falls short of the highest excellence, sinks to the lowest level. If a person cannot play a game, he refrains from trying to handle the weapons used in the Campus Martius; and if he is unfamiliar with the ball, quoit, or hoop, he remains apart lest, with perfectly good reason, the nearby crowd laugh at him. On the other hand, a person will dare to write poetry without knowing how

to do it. "Why not?" he thinks. He is a free man, well born, perhaps with a knight's income, and has a good character. But *you,* I am sure, will do or say nothing stupid; you have enough judgment and good sense not to do so. Still, if you ever do write anything, show it first to Maecius the critic, or to your father, or to me. Then put your manuscript back in the closet, and keep it for nine years. One can always destroy what one has not yet published; but a word that is published can never be canceled. (Ll. 366-389.)

[*The traditional power of poetry in influencing man.*] While men still dwelt in the woods, Orpheus, the priest and interpreter of the gods, drew them away from slaughtering each other and from foul living. Hence the legend that he tamed tigers and fierce lions. Hence also the story that Amphion, founder of Thebes, moved stones by the sound of his lyre, and led them to go wherever he wished by his supplicating magic. In olden times, this was regarded as wisdom: to mark a line between the public and private rights, the differences between sacred and secular, to prohibit promiscuous living, assign rights to the married, build towns, and engrave laws on wooden tablets. Thus honor and fame came to poets and their verses, as if they were divine. Afterwards, Homer became renowned; and Tyrtaeus [23] with his songs inspired men's hearts to perform warlike deeds. Oracles were delivered in verse, and the conduct of life was taught in them. The favor of kings was solicited in Pierian [24] strains, and festal dramas celebrated the conclusion of great labors. Therefore you do not need to feel ashamed for the Muse, skilled at the lyre, and for Apollo, the god of poetry. (Ll. 391-407.)

[*The importance to the poet of informed labor and rational restraint.*] It is asked whether a praiseworthy poem is the product of Nature or of conscious Art. For my own part, I do not see the value of study without native ability, nor of genius without training: so completely does each depend on the other and blend with it. The athlete who wishes to reach the longed-for goal has striven and borne much in boyhood, has endured heat and cold, and kept away from women

---

[22] A minor epic poet (fourth century B.C.) who accompanied Alexander the Great on his campaigns. Alexander, who said that he would rather have been the Thersites of Homer than the Achilles of Choerilus, offered him a piece of gold for every good verse he wrote, and apparently did not deplete his treasury in doing so.

[23] A Greek schoolmaster who composed war songs that were popular with the Spartans.

[24] Pieria was the birthplace of the Muses.

and wine. The flute-player at the Pythian games has learned his lessons and submitted to a teacher. Today people think it enough to say: "I fashion wonderful poems. The devil take the hindmost [as though poetry were a game]. It's not right for me to be left behind, and admit I do not know what I have never really learned."

Like a crier who collects a crowd to buy his wares, a poet, if rich in land or investments, bids his flatterers come to the call of gain. Though he can serve a costly banquet, go surety for a man who is bankrupt, or rescue someone snared in the grim suit-at-law, I should be surprised if, with all his good fortune, he can distinguish between a false and true friend. When you give someone a present, do not then ask him, when he is filled with joy because of your gift, to listen to your verses. For he will simply exclaim: "Beautiful! good! perfect!" He will change color, drop tears from his friendly eyes, leap up, and stamp the ground. Just as the hired mourners at a funeral lament and do more than those who really grieve, so the insincere admirer seems to be more moved than a true one. We are told that kings, when they wish to see whether a man is worthy of their friendship, test him by getting him drunk. In a similar way, if you write poems, do not be taken in by the spirit of the fox. If you read anything to Quintilius,[25] however, he would say "Correct this or that, please." If after trying it vainly two or three times, you said you could not do better, he would have you cut out the offending lines and take them back to the anvil. If you chose simply to defend the passage rather than improve it, he would waste no more words or effort. And you might then love yourself and your work all alone, without rivals. A good, sensible critic will censure weak lines and condemn harsh ones. He will draw a line through those that are awkward, and will cut off pretentious decorations. He will force you to clarify obscure passages; he will point out doubtful meanings, and mark what ought to be changed. He will prove to be another Aristarchus.[26] He will not say: "Why should I disagree with my friend about trifles?" For it is trifles of this sort that get the friend into trouble when he has been laughed at and unfavorably received.

As people avoid someone afflicted with the itch, with jaundice, the fits, or insanity, so sensible men stay clear of a mad poet. Children tease him and rash fools follow him. Spewing out verses, he wanders off, with his head held high, like a fowler with his eyes on the blackbirds; and if he falls into a well or ditch, he may call out, "Help, fellow citizens!"—but no one cares to help him. If anyone did wish to aid him by letting down a rope, I should say: "How do you know he didn't throw himself down on purpose, and doesn't want to be saved?" And I should tell him how the Sicilian poet, Empedocles, met his end: wishing to be thought an immortal god, he deliberately leapt into the burning crater of Aetna. You must allow poets to have the right and ability to destroy themselves. Saving a man against his will is as bad as murder. He is not doing this for the first time. And if he is pulled out now, he will not become like other people and get over this desire for a famous death. Nor is it clear why he writes verses. Perhaps he defiled the family grave, or disturbed a consecrated spot. He is mad, at any rate; and like a bear that has been strong enough to break the bars of its cage, he frightens away both the learned and the ignorant by reciting his verses. If he catches a victim, he clings to him and reads him to death, like a leech that will not leave the skin until it is filled with blood. (Ll. 408-476.)

25 A famous Homeric scholar of Alexandria (second century B.C.).

26 A Greek critic of Alexandria (c. 220-143 B.C.), supposed author of more than eight hundred commentaries, editor of the major Greek poets and tragedians, particularly Homer, and famous in antiquity as the prototype of the severely alert and demanding critic.

LONGINUS　　　　　　　　　　　　　　(First Century, A.D.)

THE TREATISE *On the Sublime* stands out as the first great example of an approach to literature that was to become especially common in critical writing after the mid-eighteenth century. It stresses the importance of emotional transport, of imaginative grandeur, and of the sympathetic reaction of the individual reader or hearer. This is not to say, of course, that Longinus is a "romantic," even if one were to apply the term "romantic" loosely. It is simply that the general tenor of the treatise is less characteristic of classical criticism as a whole than it is of criticism written since the middle of the eighteenth century.

The title is misleading. The subject is not quite what the word "sublime" has come to mean since the term became current in the eighteenth century. Instead, the subject may be better described as elevation of style, or that which lifts literary style above the ordinary and commonplace to the highest excellence. The work, moreover, is a treatise on rhetoric, though it continually crosses the border line—a border line that is thin in most classical writing—between the style of prose-rhetoric and that of poetry. After discussing instances of false sublimity (Chs. 1-6), to which he returns at the close (Chs. 41-44), Longinus cites five main sources of the sublime (Ch. 8). Two of them are the result of innate, natural capacity: "elevation of mind" or the "power of forming great conceptions" (Chs. 8-15), and "vehement and inspired passion" (discussion of which was reserved for another work). The other three sources of the sublime are largely technical, and are acquired mainly by study and habit: figurative language (Chs. 16-29), the choice of "noble diction" (Chs. 30-38), and the rhythmic and elevated arrangement of words (Chs. 39-40).

Almost half of the treatise as we have it is devoted to the subjects of fig-

LONGINUS. Both the date and the author are unknown. In the earliest extant manuscript (tenth century, A.D., first published by Robertello in 1554), the writer is said to be "Dionysius or Longinus." The work is quite unlike that of the famous rhetorician, Dionysius of Halicarnassus; and there is little chance that it was written by Cassius Longinus (d. 273 A.D.), to whom, until recently, it was often assigned. Whoever the author may have been, the treatise was probably written in the first half of the first century A.D. It mentions no writers after that time; and the work of Caecilius, *On the Sublime*, is cited in such a way as to imply that it had appeared rather recently. The manuscript, as we have it, is fragmentary; about two fifths, consisting of scattered sections, is lost. Nor does this include the loss at the end; for the work is unfinished.

Translations include those of W. Rhys Roberts (Cambridge, 1899); W. Hamilton Fyfe (Loeb Classical Library, 1927); and Benedict Einarson (1945). For commentary, see especially J. W. H. Atkins, *Literary Criticism in Antiquity* (Cambridge, 1934), II, Ch. 6; Jules Brody, *Boileau and Longinus* (Geneva, 1958); T. R. Henn, *Longinus and English Criticism* (Cambridge, 1934); S. H. Monk, *The Sublime: a Study of Critical Theories in Eighteenth-Century England* (1935); D. A. Russell's edition of *On the Sublime* (Oxford, 1964).

urative language, choice of diction, and word order. Some of the analysis and illustration in the sections dealing with these technical matters, as well as in other sections, is confusing to the modern student, who is usually unfamiliar both with the Greek language and with the complexities of ancient rhetorical classification. Indeed, the beginning student has often been deterred from a sympathetic reading of Longinus by the relative abundance and unfamiliarity of specific rhetorical analysis. Hence the omission by the present editor of portions that appear inessential to the present purpose.

Yet despite the technical nature of its material, the treatise, when compared with most ancient analyses of rhetoric, discusses the subject of language and figures of speech in a way that is far from mechanical. It is concerned less with the mere classification of rhetorical devices than with their use as a means of arousing emotional transport. Indeed, from one point of view, Longinus' *On the Sublime* is actually directed against the mechanical handbook of rhetoric, for it takes as its starting point the inadequacies of just such a handbook by the rhetorician Caecilius, and deliberately attempts to supply the deficiencies of that work. Hence the continual generalizing tendency throughout the treatise, not only in those sections of it that are openly concerned with grandeur of conception and emotional intensity, but also, now and then, throughout the more technical portions. And the style of Longinus, for the most part, is in keeping with his subject. It is easy, familiar, gracefully insinuating, and at times it rises to a genuine loftiness in which, as Pope says, Longinus'

> own example strengthens all his laws;
> And is himself that great Sublime he draws.

The closeness of Longinus to criticism since about 1750 is shown in the way his general concern with the emotional response to art governs his approach to style. We find him interested in the organic relation between feeling and expression. He is the first extant critic, for example, to emphasize strongly the importance of metaphor in appealing or giving outlet to intense emotion. Moreover, we find him anticipating Matthew Arnold's famous "touchstone" theory (Ch. 14, par. 1). For, in contrast to Aristotle's concern with the total structure of a work, Longinus, like many critics from the romantic movement to the present day, tended to concentrate somewhat more on particular examples of language and expression—on what, in the eighteenth century, were often called the "beauties" of a work. They are highlighted and discussed, moreover, with a vivid impressionism. The extent to which this approach encouraged the psychological impressionism of the later eighteenth century is illustrated by Gibbon's remark, in his *Journal* (Oct. 3, 1762):

Till now, I was acquainted only with two ways of criticizing a beautiful passage: the one, to show, by an exact anatomy of it, the distinct beauties of it, and from whence they sprung; the other, an idle exclamation, or a general encomium, which leaves nothing behind it. Longinus has shown me that there is a third. He tells me his own feelings upon reading it; and tells them with such energy that he communicates them. I almost doubt which is the most sublime, Homer's battle of the gods, or Longinus's apostrophe to Terentianus upon it.

But if the critical views of Longinus are reflected in criticism of the past two centuries, their reflection is particularly strong in the critical writing of the later eighteenth century, when a strong romantic impressionism existed side by side with a neoclassic emphasis upon experience, wide learning, and a respect for great models of the past. Thus, on the one hand, Longinus stressed the extent to which emotional intensity and imaginative power are innate and "beyond the reach of art" and of rules. On the other hand, Longinus took issue (Ch. 2, pars. 1-2) with those who feel that genius is degraded by rules, and who would turn art into mere self-expression, uninhibited and "unballasted" with knowledge. "Greatness of soul," according to Longinus, is admittedly the prime requisite for great writing. But it must be fed and developed by an enthusiastic "imitation and emulation of previous great poets and writers." We grow by taking into us and imitating what is good. By sympathetically identifying ourselves with great writers of the past, we shall find ourselves unconsciously catching and imitating their ways of thinking, feeling, and expressing. Indeed, "from the great natures of the men of old there are borne in upon the souls of those who emulate them . . . what we may describe as *effluences,* so that even those who seem little likely to be possessed are thereby inspired and succumb to the spell of the others' greatness" (Ch. 13, par. 2). Hence, the "judgment of style is the last and crowning fruit of long experience." The position is that which is later so eloquently urged by Sir Joshua Reynolds, particularly in his sixth *Discourse:* that, as distinct from mere passive copying, a prolonged contact and an active imaginative sympathy with the works of great predecessors afford the most fruitful way of developing the potential capacities of an artist. Emotional and imaginative response, in other words, should be guided and educated by qualities of works which, as eighteenth-century critics were to stress, have stood the "test of time." For "what has pleased, and continues to please," as Reynolds echoed from Longinus, "is likely to please again"; and through the "habit of contemplating and brooding" over the works of major artists, "the accumulated experience of mankind may . . . be acquired." Hence, as Longinus said,

In general, consider those examples of sublimity to be fine and genuine which please all and always. For when men of different pursuits, lives, ambitions, ages, languages, hold identical views on one and the same subject, then that verdict which results, so to speak, from a concert of discordant elements makes our faith in the object of admiration strong and unassailable. (Ch. 7, par. 4.)

The influence of Longinus on European criticism came relatively late. The treatise was virtually unknown until it was published during the Renaissance (1554). After being edited and translated into Latin and various other languages, it became widely known in the late seventeenth century, especially when Boileau's translation into French appeared (1674). From then on, the influence of Longinus began to gather force. It is, indeed, with the eighteenth century, especially in England, that his influence is most frequently and justly associated. His influence, then, was varied. But one aspect should be especially noted. More than any other ancient critic—more, perhaps, than any other critic at all from the time of Aristotle down to the middle of the eighteenth century—he served as a source of authoritative encouragement in the great shift in critical approach and values that was to culminate in European romanticism.

From On the Sublime

YOU WILL remember, my dear Postumius Terentianus, that when we examined together the treatise of Caecilius on the Sublime, we found that it fell below the dignity of the whole subject, while it failed signally to grasp the essential points, and conveyed to its readers but little of that practical help which it should be a writer's principal aim to give. In every systematic treatise two things are required. The first is a statement of the subject; the other, which although second in order ranks higher in importance, is an indication of the methods by which we may attain our end. Now Caecilius seeks to show the nature of the sublime by countless instances as though our ignorance demanded it, but the consideration of the means whereby we may succeed in raising our own capacities to a certain pitch of elevation he has, strangely enough, omitted as unnecessary. 2. However, it may be that the man ought not so much to be blamed for his shortcomings as praised for his happy thought and his enthusiasm. But since you have urged me, in my turn, to write a brief essay on the sublime for your special gratification, let us consider whether the views I have formed contain anything which will be of use to public men. You will yourself, my friend, in

accordance with your nature and with what is fitting, join me in appraising each detail with the utmost regard for truth; for he answered well who, when asked in what qualities we resemble the Gods, declared that we do so in benevolence and truth. 3. As I am writing to you, my good friend, who are well versed in literary studies, I feel almost absolved from the necessity of premising at any length that sublimity is a certain distinction and excellence in expression, and that it is from no other source than this that the greatest poets and writers have derived their eminence and gained an immortality of renown. 4. The effect of elevated language upon an audience is not persuasion but transport. At every time and in every way imposing speech, with the spell it throws over us, prevails over that which aims at persuasion and gratification. Our persuasions we can usually control, but the influences of the sublime bring power and irresistible might to bear, and reign supreme over every hearer. Similarly, we see skill in invention, and due order and arrangement of matter, emerging as the hard-won result not of one thing nor of two, but of the whole texture of the composition, whereas Sublimity flashing forth at the right moment scatters everything before it like a thunderbolt, and at once displays the power of the orator in all its plenitude. But enough; for these reflexions, and others like

On the Sublime. Translated by W. Rhys Roberts (Cambridge, 1899). Reprinted by permission of the Cambridge University Press.

them, you can, I know well, my dear Terentianus, yourself suggest from your own experience.

II

First of all, we must raise the question whether there is such a thing as an art of the sublime or lofty. Some hold that those are entirely in error who would bring such matters under the precepts of art. A lofty tone, says one, is innate, and does not come by teaching; nature is the only art that can compass it. Works of nature are, they think, made worse and altogether feebler when wizened by the rules of art. 2. But I maintain that this will be found to be otherwise if it be observed that, while nature as a rule is free and independent in matters of passion and elevation, yet is she wont not to act at random and utterly without system. Further, nature is the original and vital underlying principle in all cases, but system can define limits and fitting seasons, and can also contribute the safest rules for use and practice. Moreover, the expression of the sublime is more exposed to danger when it goes its own way without the guidance of knowledge,—when it is suffered to be unstable and unballasted,—when it is left at the mercy of mere momentum and ignorant audacity. It is true that it often needs the spur, but it is also true that it often needs the curb. 3. Demosthenes expresses the view, with regard to human life in general, that good fortune is the greatest of blessings, while good counsel, which occupies the second place, is hardly inferior in importance, since its absence contributes inevitably to the ruin of the former. This we may apply to diction, nature occupying the position of good fortune, art that of good counsel. Most important of all, we must remember that the very fact that there are some elements of expression which are in the hands of nature alone, can be learnt from no other source than art. If, I say, the critic of those who desire to learn were to turn these matters over in his mind, he would no longer, it seems to me, regard the discussion of the subject as superfluous or useless. . . .

III

Quell they the oven's far-flung splendour-glow!
Ha, let me but one hearth-abider mark—

One flame-wreath torrent-like I'll whirl on high;
I'll burn the roof, to cinders shrivel it!—
Nay, now my chant is not of noble strain.[1]

Such things are not tragic but pseudo-tragic— "flame-wreaths," and "belching to the sky," and Boreas represented as a "flute-player," and all the rest of it. They are turbid in expression and confused in imagery rather than the product of intensity, and each one of them, if examined in the light of day, sinks little by little from the terrible into the contemptible. But since even in tragedy, which is in its very nature stately and prone to bombast, tasteless tumidity is unpardonable, still less, I presume, will it harmonise with the narration of fact. 2. And this is the ground on which the phrases of Gorgias of Leontini are ridiculed when he describes Xerxes as the "Zeus of the Persians" and vultures as "living tombs." So is it with some of the expressions of Callisthenes which are not sublime but high-flown, and still more with those of Cleitarchus, for the man is frivolous and blows, as Sophocles has it,[2]

On pigmy hautboys: mouthpiece have they none.

Other examples will be found in Amphicrates and Hegesias and Matris, for often when these writers seem to themselves to be inspired they are in no true frenzy but are simply trifling. 3. Altogether, tumidity seems particularly hard to avoid. The explanation is that all who aim at elevation are so anxious to escape the reproach of being weak and dry that they are carried, as by some strange law of nature, into the opposite extreme. They put their trust in the maxim that "failure in a great attempt is at least a noble error." 4. But evil are the swellings, both in the body and in diction, which are inflated and unreal, and threaten us with the reverse of our aim; for nothing, say they, is drier than a man who has the dropsy. While tumidity desires to transcend the limits of the sublime, the defect which is termed puerility is the direct antithesis of elevation, for it is utterly low and mean and in real truth the most ignoble vice of style. What, then, is this puerility? Clearly, a pedant's thoughts, which begin in learned trifling and end in frigidity. Men slip into this kind of error because, while they aim at the uncommon and

---

[1] From the lost *Oreithyia* of Aeschylus.
[2] The play does not now exist.

elaborate and most of all at the attractive, they drift unawares into the tawdry and affected. 5. A third, and closely allied, kind of defect in matters of passion is that which Theodorus[3] used to call *parenthyrsus*. By this is meant unseasonable and empty passion, where no passion is required, or immoderate, where moderation is needed. For men are often carried away, as if by intoxication, into displays of emotion which are not caused by the nature of the subject, but are purely personal and wearisome. In consequence they seem to hearers who are in no wise affected to act in an ungainly way. And no wonder; for they are beside themselves, while their hearers are not. But the question of the passions we reserve for separate treatment.

I V

Of the second fault of which we have spoken —frigidity—Timaeus supplies many examples. Timaeus was a writer of considerable general ability, who occasionally showed that he was not incapable of elevation of style. He was learned and ingenious, but very prone to criticise the faults of others while blind to his own. Through his passion for continually starting novel notions, he often fell into the merest childishness. 2. I will set down one or two examples only of his manner, since the greater number have been already appropriated by Caecilius. In the course of a eulogy on Alexander the Great, he describes him as "the man who gained possession of the whole of Asia in fewer years than it took Isocrates to write his *Panegyric* urging war against the Persians."[4] Strange indeed is the comparison of the man of Macedon with the rhetorician. How plain it is, Timaeus, that the Lacedaemonians, thus judged, were far inferior to Isocrates in prowess, for they spent thirty years in the conquest of Messene, whereas he composed his *Panegyric* in ten. 3. Consider again the way in which he speaks of the Athenians who were captured in Sicily. "They were punished because they had acted impiously towards Hermes and mutilated his images, and the infliction of punishment was chiefly due to Hermocrates the son

of Hermon, who was descended, in the paternal line, from the outraged god." I am surprised, beloved Terentianus, that he does not write with regard to the despot Dionysius that "Dion and Heracleides deprived him of his sovereignty because he had acted impiously towards Zeus and Heracles." 4. But why speak of Timaeus when even those heroes of literature, Xenophon and Plato, though trained in the school of Socrates, nevertheless sometimes forget themselves for the sake of such paltry pleasantries? Xenophon writes in the *Polity of the Lacedaemonians:* "You would find it harder to hear their voice than that of busts of marble, harder to deflect their gaze than that of statues of bronze; you would deem them more modest than the very maidens in their eyes."[5]

It was worthy of an Amphicrates and not of a Xenophon to call the pupils of our eyes "modest maidens." Good heavens, how strange it is that the pupils of the whole company should be believed to be modest notwithstanding the common saying that the shamelessness of individuals is indicated by nothing so much as the eyes! "Thou sot, that hast the eyes of a dog," as Homer has it.[6] 5. Timaeus, however, has not left even this piece of frigidity to Xenophon, but clutches it as though it were hid treasure. At all events, after saying of Agathocles that he abducted his cousin, who had been given in marriage to another man, from the midst of the nuptial rites, he asks, "Who could have done this had he not had wantons, in place of maidens, in his eyes?" 6. Yes, and Plato (usually so divine) when he means simply *tablets* says, "They shall write and preserve *cypress memorials* in the temples."[7]

And again, "As touching walls, Megillus, I should hold with Sparta that they be suffered to lie asleep in the earth and not summoned to arise."[8] 7. The expression of Herodotus to the effect that beautiful women are "eye-smarts" is not much better.[9] This, however, may be condoned in some degree since those who use this particular phrase in his narrative are barbarians and in their cups, but not even in the mouths of such characters is it well that an author should

---

[3] A minor rhetorician (c. 30 B.C.).

[4] Timaeus was a Sicilian historian (fourth century B.C.); Caecilius a Sicilian rhetorician (first century B.C.).

[5] *De Rep. Laced.*, III, 5.

[6] *Iliad*, I, 225.

[7] Plato, *Laws*, V, 741 C.

[8] *Ibid.*, VI, 778 D.

[9] V, 18.

suffer, in the judgment of posterity, from an unseemly exhibition of triviality.

V

All these ugly and parasitical growths arise in literature from a single cause, that pursuit of novelty in the expression of ideas which may be regarded as the fashionable craze of the day. Our defects usually spring, for the most part, from the same sources as our good points. Hence, while beauties of expression and touches of sublimity, and charming elegances withal, are favourable to effective composition, yet these very things are the elements and foundation, not only of success, but also of the contrary. Something of the kind is true also of variations and hyperboles and the use of the plural number, and we shall show subsequently the dangers to which these seem severally to be exposed. It is necessary now to seek and to suggest means by which we may avoid the defects which attend the steps of the sublime.

V I

The best means would be, my friend, to gain, first of all, clear knowledge and appreciation of the true sublime. The enterprise is, however, an arduous one. For the judgment of style is the last and crowning fruit of long experience. None the less, if I must speak in the way of precept, it is not impossible perhaps to acquire discrimination in these matters by attention to some such hints as those which follow.

V I I

You must know, my dear friend, that it is with the sublime as in the common life of man. In life nothing can be considered great which it is held great to despise. For instance, riches, honours, distinctions, sovereignties, and all other things which possess in abundance the external trappings of the stage, will not seem, to a man of sense, to be supreme blessings, since the very contempt of them is reckoned good in no small degree, and in any case those who could have them, but are high-souled enough to disdain them, are more admired than those who have them. So also in the case of sublimity in poems and prose writings, we must consider whether some supposed examples have not simply the appearance of elevation with many idle accretions, so that when analysed they are found to be mere vanity—objects which a noble nature will rather despise than admire. 2. For, as if instinctively, our soul is uplifted by the true sublime; it takes a proud flight, and is filled with joy and vaunting, as though it had itself produced what it has heard.[10] 3. When, therefore, a thing is heard repeatedly by a man of intelligence, who is well versed in literature, and its effect is not to dispose the soul to high thoughts, and it does not leave in the mind more food for reflexion than the words seem to convey, but falls, if examined carefully through and through, into disesteem, it cannot rank as true sublimity because it does not survive a first hearing. For that is really great which bears a repeated examination, and which it is difficult or rather impossible to withstand, and the memory of which is strong and hard to efface. 4. In general, consider those examples of sublimity to be fine and genuine which please all and always. For when men of different pursuits, lives, ambitions, ages, languages, hold identical views on one and the same subject, then that verdict which results, so to speak, from a concert of discordant elements makes our faith in the object of admiration strong and unassailable.

V I I I

There are, it may be said, five principal sources of elevated language. Beneath these five varieties there lies, as though it were a common foundation, the gift of discourse, which is indispensable. First and most important is the power of forming great conceptions, as we have elsewhere explained in our remarks on Xenophon. Secondly, there is vehement and inspired passion. These two components of the sublime are for the most part innate. Those which remain are partly the product of art. The due formation of figures deals with two sorts of figures,

[10] The statement is unusual in classical writing, suggesting that poetry can secure a powerful appeal by arousing the subjective activity of the reader's or hearer's mind, and inducing it to create its own conception. Longinus anticipates one of the common romantic attitudes (see p. 274).

first those of thought and secondly those of expression. Next there is noble diction, which in turn comprises choice of words, and use of metaphors, and elaboration of language. The fifth cause of elevation—one which is the fitting conclusion of all that have preceded it—is dignified and elevated composition. Come now, let us consider what is involved in each of these varieties, with this one remark by way of preface, that Caecilius has omitted some of the five divisions, for example, that of passion. 2. Surely he is quite mistaken if he does so on the ground that these two, sublimity and passion, are a unity, and if it seems to him that they are by nature one and inseparable. For some passions are found which are far removed from sublimity and are of a low order, such as pity, grief and fear; and on the other hand there are many examples of the sublime which are independent of passion, such as the daring words of Homer with regard to the Aloadae, to take one out of numberless instances,

Yea, Ossa in fury they strove to upheave on Olympus on high,
With forest-clad Pelion above, that thence they might step to the sky.[11]

And so of the words which follow with still greater force:—

Ay, and the deed had they done.[12]

3. Among the orators, too, eulogies and ceremonial and occasional addresses contain on every side examples of dignity and elevation, but are for the most part void of passion. This is the reason why passionate speakers are the worst eulogists, and why, on the other hand, those who are apt in encomium are the least passionate. 4. If, on the other hand, Caecilius thought that passion never contributes at all to sublimity, and if it was for this reason that he did not deem it worthy of mention, he is altogether deluded. I would affirm with confidence that there is no tone so lofty as that of genuine passion, in its right place, when it bursts out in a wild gust of mad enthusiasm and as it were fills the speaker's words with frenzy.

[11] *Odyssey*, XI, 315, 316.
[12] *Ibid.*, XI, 317.

IX

Now the first of the conditions mentioned, namely elevation of mind, holds the foremost rank among them all. We must, therefore, in this case also, although we have to do rather with an endowment than with an acquirement, nurture our souls (as far as that is possible) to thoughts sublime, and make them always pregnant, so to say, with noble inspiration. 2. In what way, you may ask, is this to be done? Elsewhere I have written as follows: "Sublimity is the echo of a great soul." Hence also a bare idea, by itself and without a spoken word, sometimes excites admiration just because of the greatness of soul implied. Thus the silence of Ajax in the Underworld is great and more sublime than words.[13] 3. First, then, it is absolutely necessary to indicate the source of this elevation, namely, that the truly eloquent must be free from low and ignoble thoughts. For it is not possible that men with mean and servile ideas and aims prevailing throughout their lives should produce anything that is admirable and worthy of immortality. Great accents we expect to fall from the lips of those whose thoughts are deep and grave. 4. Thus it is that stately speech comes naturally to the proudest spirits. . . . 9. Similarly, the legislator of the Jews,[14] no ordinary man, having formed and expressed a worthy conception of the might of the Godhead, writes at the very beginning of his Laws, "God said,"—what? "Let there be light, and there was light; let there be land, and there was land." 10. Perhaps I shall not seem tedious, my friend, if I bring forward one passage more from Homer—this time with regard to the concerns of *men*—in order to show that he is wont himself to enter into the sublime actions of his heroes. In his poem the battle of the Greeks is suddenly veiled by mist and baffling night. Then Ajax, at his wits' end, cries:

Zeus, Father, yet save thou Achaia's sons from beneath the gloom,
And make clear day, and vouchsafe unto us with our eyes to see!
So it be but in light, destroy us! [15]

[13] *Ibid.*, XI, 543.
[14] Moses, in Gen.: 1, 3 ff.
[15] *Iliad*, XVII, 645-647.

That is the true attitude of an Ajax. He does not pray for life, for such a petition would have ill beseemed a hero. But since in the hopeless darkness he can turn his valour to no noble end, he chafes at his slackness in the fray and craves the boon of immediate light, resolved to find a death worthy of his bravery, even though Zeus should fight in the ranks against him. 11. In truth, Homer in these cases shares the full inspiration of the combat, and it is neither more nor less than true of the poet himself that

Mad rageth he as Arês the shaker of spears, or as mad flames leap
Wild-wasting from hill unto hill in the folds of a forest deep,
And the foam-froth fringeth his lips.[16]

He shows, however, in the Odyssey (and this further observation deserves attention on many grounds) that, when a great genius is declining, the special token of old age is the love of marvellous tales. . . . 15. These observations with regard to the Odyssey should be made for another reason—in order that you may know that the genius of great poets and prose-writers, as their passion declines, finds its final expression in the delineation of character. For such are the details which Homer gives, with an eye to characterisation, of life in the home of Odysseus; they form as it were a comedy of manners.

X

Let us next consider whether we can point to anything further that contributes to sublimity of style. Now, there inhere in all things by nature certain constituents which are part and parcel of their substance. It must needs be, therefore, that we shall find one source of the sublime in the systematic selection of the most important elements, and the power of forming, by their mutual combination, what may be called one body. The former process attracts the hearer by the choice of the ideas, the latter by the aggregation of those chosen. . . .

X I

An allied excellence to those already set forth is that which is termed *amplification*. This fig-

16 *Ibid.*, XV, 605-607.

ure is employed when the narrative or the course of a forensic argument admits, from section to section, of many starting-points and many pauses, and elevated expressions follow, one after the other, in an unbroken succession and in an ascending order. 2. And this may be effected either by way of the rhetorical treatment of commonplaces, or by way of intensification (whether events or arguments are to be strongly presented), or by the orderly arrangement of facts or of passions; indeed, there are innumerable kinds of amplification. Only, the orator must in every case remember that none of these methods by itself, apart from sublimity, forms a complete whole, unless indeed where pity is to be excited or an opponent to be disparaged. In all other cases of amplification, if you take away the sublime, you will remove as it were the soul from the body. For the vigour of the amplification at once loses its intensity and its substance when not resting on a firm basis of the sublime. 3. Clearness, however, demands that we should define concisely how our present precepts differ from the point under consideration a moment ago, namely the marking-out of the most striking conceptions and the unification of them; and wherein, generally, the sublime differs from amplification.

X I I

Now the definition given by the writers on rhetoric does not satisfy me. Amplification is, say they, discourse which invests the subject with grandeur. This definition, however, would surely apply in equal measure to sublimity and passion and figurative language, since they too invest the discourse with a certain degree of grandeur. The point of distinction between them seems to me to be that sublimity consists in elevation, while amplification embraces a multitude of details. Consequently, sublimity is often comprised in a single thought, while amplification is universally associated with a certain magnitude and abundance. 2. Amplification (to sum the matter up in a general way) is an aggregation of all the constituent parts and topics of a subject, lending strength to the argument by dwelling upon it, and differing herein from proof that, while the latter demonstrates the matter under investigation. . . .

With his vast riches Plato swells, like some sea,

into a greatness which expands on every side.
3. Wherefore it is, I suppose, that the orator in
his utterance shows, as one who appeals more to
the passions, all the glow of a fiery spirit. Plato,
on the other hand, firm-planted in his pride and
magnificent stateliness, cannot indeed be accused
of coldness, but he has not the same vehemence.
4. And it is in these same respects, my dear
friend Terentianus, that it seems to me (supposing always that we Greeks are allowed to
have an opinion upon the point) that Cicero
differs from Demosthenes in elevated passages.
For the latter is characterised by sublimity which
is for the most part rugged, Cicero by profu-
sion. Our orator,[17] owing to the fact that in his
vehemence,—aye, and in his speed, power and
intensity,—he can as it were consume by fire and
carry away all before him, may be compared to
a thunderbolt or flash of lightning. Cicero, on
the other hand, it seems to me, after the manner
of a wide-spread conflagration, rolls on with all-
devouring flames, having within him an ample
and abiding store of fire, distributed now at this
point now at that, and fed by an unceasing succession. . . .

XIII

To return from my digression. Although Plato
thus flows on with noiseless stream, he is none
the less elevated. You know this because you
have read the *Republic* and are familiar with
his manner. "Those," says he, "who are destitute of wisdom and goodness and are ever present at carousals and the like are carried on the
downward path, it seems, and wander thus
throughout their life. They never look upwards
to the truth, nor do they lift their heads, nor
enjoy any pure and lasting pleasure, but like
cattle they have their eyes ever cast downwards
and bent upon the ground and upon their feed-
ing-places, and they graze and grow fat and
breed, and through their insatiate desire of these
delights they kick and butt with horns and hoofs
of iron and kill one another in their greed." [18]
2. This writer shows us, if only we were willing to pay him heed, that another way (beyond
anything we have mentioned) leads to the sublime. And what, and what manner of way, may

that be? It is the imitation and emulation of previous great poets and writers. And let this, my
dear friend, be an aim to which we steadfastly
apply ourselves. For many men are carried away
by the spirit of others as if inspired, just as it is
related of the Pythian priestess when she approaches the tripod, where there is a rift in the
ground which (they say) exhales divine vapour.
By heavenly power thus communicated she is impregnated and straightway delivers oracles in
virtue of the afflatus. Similarly from the great
natures of the men of old there are borne in upon
the souls of those who emulate them (as from
sacred caves) what we may describe as *effluences*, so that even those who seem little likely
to be possessed are thereby inspired and succumb to the spell of the others' greatness. 3. Was
Herodotus alone a devoted imitator of Homer?
No, Stesichorus even before his time, and Archilochus, and above all Plato, who from the
great Homeric source drew to himself innumerable tributary streams. And perhaps we should
have found it necessary to prove this, point by
point, had not Ammonius and his followers selected and recorded the particulars. 4. This proceeding is not plagiarism; it is like taking an
impression from beautiful forms or figures or
other works of art. And it seems to me that there
would not have been so fine a bloom of perfection on Plato's philosophical doctrines, and that
he would not in many cases have found his way
to poetical subject-matter and modes of expression, unless he had with all his heart and mind
struggled with Homer for the primacy, entering
the lists like a young champion matched against
the man whom all admire, and showing perhaps
too much love of contention and breaking a
lance with him as it were, but deriving some
profit from the contest none the less. For, as
Hesiod says, "This strife is good for mortals." [19]
And in truth that struggle for the crown of
glory is noble and best deserves the victory in
which even to be worsted by one's predecessors
brings no discredit. . . .

XV

Images, moreover, contribute greatly, my
young friend, to dignity, elevation, and power

---

[17] Sc. Demosthenes.
[18] *Republic*, IX, 586A.

[19] *Works and Days*, 24.

as a pleader. In this sense some call them mental representations. In a general way the name of *image* or *imagination* is applied to every idea of the mind, in whatever form it presents itself, which gives birth to speech. But at the present day the word is predominantly used in cases where, carried away by enthusiasm and passion, you think you see what you describe, and you place it before the eyes of your hearers. 2. Further, you will be aware of the fact that an image has one purpose with the orators and another with the poets, and that the design of the poetical image is enthralment, of the rhetorical—vivid description. Both, however, seek to stir the passions and the emotions.

Mother!—'beseech thee, hark not thou on me
Yon maidens gory-eyed and snaky-haired!
Lo there!—lo there!—they are nigh—they leap on
   me!

And:

Ah! she will slay me! whither can I fly? . . .[20]

XVI

Here, however, in due order comes the place assigned to Figures; for they, if handled in the proper manner, will contribute, as I have said,[21] in no mean degree to sublimity. But since to treat thoroughly of them all at the present moment would be a great, or rather an endless task, we will now, with the object of proving our proposition, run over a few only of those which produce elevation of diction. 2. Demosthenes is bringing forward a reasoned vindication of his public policy. What was the natural way of treating the subject? It was this. "You were not wrong, you who engaged in the struggle for the freedom of Greece. You have domestic warrant for it. For the warriors of Marathon did no wrong, nor they of Salamis, nor they of Plataea." [22] When, however, as though suddenly inspired by heaven and as it were frenzied by the God of Prophecy, he utters his famous oath by the champions of Greece ("assuredly ye did no wrong; I swear it by those who at Marathon stood in the forefront of the danger"), in the

public view by this one Figure of Adjuration, which I here term *Apostrophe*, he deifies his ancestors. He brings home the thought that we ought to swear by those who have thus nobly died as we swear by Gods, and he fills the mind of the judges with the high spirit of those who there bore the brunt of the danger, and he has transformed the natural course of the argument into transcendent sublimity and passion and that secure belief which rests upon strange and prodigious oaths. He instils into the minds of his hearers the conviction—which acts as a medicine and an antidote—that they should, uplifted by these eulogies, feel no less proud of the fight against Philip than of the triumph at Marathon and Salamis. By all these means he carries his hearers clean away with him through the employment of a single figure. . . .

XIX

The words issue forth without connecting links and are poured out as it were, almost outstripping the speaker himself. "Locking their shields," says Xenophon, "they thrust fought slew fell." [23] 2. And so with the words of Eurylochus:—

We passed, as thou badst, Odysseus, midst twilight
   of oak-trees round.
There amidst of the forest-glens a beautiful palace
   we found.[24]

For the lines detached from one another, but none the less hurried along, produce the impression of an agitation which interposes obstacles and at the same time adds impetuosity. This result Homer has produced by the omission of conjunctions.

XX

A powerful effect usually attends the union of figures for a common object, when two or three mingle together as it were in partnership, and contribute a fund of strength, persuasiveness, beauty. Thus, in the speech against Meidias, examples will be found of *asyndeton*,[25] interwoven

---

[20] Euripides, *Orestes*, 255, and *Iphigenia*, 291.
[21] In Ch. VIII above.
[22] *On the Crown*, 208.

[23] *Hellenica*, IV, 3, 19.
[24] *Odyssey*, X, 251, 2.
[25] Broken sentences.

with instances of *anaphora*[26] and *diatyposis*.[27] "For the smiter can do many things (some of which the sufferer cannot even describe to another) by attitude, by look, by voice."[28] 2. Then, in order that the narrative may not, as it advances, continue in the same groove (for continuance betokens tranquillity, while passion—the transport and commotion of the soul—sets order at defiance), straightway he hurries off to other *Asyndeta* and *Repetitions*. "By attitude, by look, by voice, when he acts with insolence, when he acts like an enemy, when he smites with his fists, when he smites you like a slave." By these words the orator produces the same effect as the assailant—he strikes the mind of the judges by the swift succession of blow on blow. 3. Starting from this point again, as suddenly as a gust of wind, he makes another attack. "When smitten with blows of fists," he says, "when smitten upon the cheek. These things stir the blood, these drive men beyond themselves, when unused to insult. No one can, in describing them, convey a notion of the indignity they imply." So he maintains throughout, though with continual variation, the essential character of the *Repetitions* and *Asyndeta*. In this way, with him, order is disorderly, and on the other hand disorder contains a certain element of order. . . .

XXII

Hyperbata, or *inversions,* must be placed under the same category. They are departures in the order of expressions or ideas from the natural sequence; and they bear, it may be said, the very stamp and impress of vehement emotion. Just as those who are really moved by anger, or fear, or indignation, or jealousy, or any other emotion (for the passions are many and countless, and none can give their number), at times turn aside, and when they have taken one thing as their subject often leap to another, foisting in the midst some irrelevant matter, and then again wheel round to their original theme, and driven by their vehemence, as by a veering wind, now this way now that with rapid changes, transform their expressions, their thoughts, the

order suggested by a natural sequence, into numberless variations of every kind; so also among the best writers it is by means of *hyperbaton* that imitation approaches the effects of nature. For art is perfect when it seems to be nature, and nature hits the mark when she contains art hidden within her. We may illustrate by the words of Dionysius of Phocaea in Herodotus. "Our fortunes lie on a razor's edge, men of Ionia; for freedom or for bondage, and that the bondage of runaway slaves. Now, therefore, if you choose to submit to hardships, you will have toil for the moment, but you will be able to overcome your foes."[29] 2. Here the natural order would have been: "Men of Ionia, now is the time for you to meet hardships; for our fortunes lie on a razor's edge." But the speaker postpones the words "Men of Ionia." He starts at once with the danger of the situation, as though in such imminent peril he had no time at all to address his hearers. Moreover, he inverts the order of ideas. For instead of saying that they ought to endure hardships, which is the real object of his exhortation, he first assigns the reason because of which they ought to endure hardships, in the words "our fortunes lie on a razor's edge." The result is that what he says seems not to be premeditated but to be prompted by the necessities of the moment. . . .

XXIII

The figures which are termed *polyptota*—accumulations, and variations, and climaxes—are excellent weapons of public oratory, as you are aware, and contribute to elegance and to every form of sublimity and passion. Again, how greatly do changes of cases, tenses, persons, numbers, genders, diversify and enliven exposition. 2. Where the use of numbers is concerned, I would point out that style is not adorned only or chiefly by those words which are, as far as their forms go, in the singular but in meaning are, when examined, found to be plural: as in the lines

> A countless crowd forthright
> Far-ranged along the beaches were clamouring
> "Thunny in sight!"[30]

[26] Repetition of words.
[27] Vivid description.
[28] *Meidias,* 72.

[29] VI, 11.
[30] By an unknown writer.

The fact is more worthy of observations that in certain cases the use of the plural (for the singular) falls on the ear with still more imposing effect and impresses us by the very sense of multitude which the number conveys. . . .

XXIV

Further (to take the converse case) particulars which are combined from the plural into the singular are sometimes most elevated in appearance. "Thereafter," says Demosthenes, "all Peloponnesus was at variance." [31] "And when Phrynichus had brought out a play entitled the *Capture of Miletus*, the whole theatre burst into tears." [32] For the compression of the number from multiplicity into unity gives more fully the feeling of a single body. 2. In both cases the explanation of the elegance of expression is, I think, the same. Where the words are singular, to make them plural is the mark of unlooked-for passion; and where they are plural, the rounding of a number of things into a fine-sounding singular is surprising owing to the converse change.

XXV

If you introduce things which are past as present and now taking place, you will make your story no longer a narration but an actuality. Xenophon furnishes an illustration. "A man," says he, "has fallen under Cyrus' horse, and being trampled strikes the horse with his sword in the belly. He rears and unseats Cyrus, who falls." [33] This construction is specially characteristic of Thucydides.

XXVI

In like manner the interchange of persons produces a vivid impression, and often makes the hearer feel that he is moving in the midst of perils:—

Thou hadst said that with toil unspent, and all unwasted of limb,
They closed in the grapple of war, so fiercely they rushed to the fray; [34]

[31] *On the Crown*, 18.
[32] Herodotus, VI, 21.
[33] *Cyropaedia*, VII, 1, 37.
[34] *Iliad*, XV, 346.

and the line of Aratus:—

Never in that month launch thou forth amid lashing seas. [35]

2. So also Herodotus: "From the city of Elephantine thou shalt sail upwards, and then shalt come to a level plain; and after crossing this tract, thou shalt embark upon another vessel and sail for two days, and then shalt come to a great city whose name is Meroe." [36] Do you observe, my friend, how he leads you in imagination through the region and makes you *see* what you hear? All such cases of direct personal address place the hearer on the very scene of action. 3. So it is when you seem to be speaking, not to all and sundry, but to a single individual:—

But Tydeides—thou wouldst not have known him, for whom that hero fought. [37]

You will make your hearer more excited and more attentive, and full of active participation, if you keep him on the alert by words addressed to himself.

XXVII

There is further the case in which a writer, when relating something about a person, suddenly breaks off and converts himself into that selfsame person. This species of figure is a kind of outburst of passion:—

Then with a far-ringing shout to the Trojans Hector cried,
Bidding them rush on the ships, bidding leave the spoils blood-dyed—
And whomso I mark from the galleys aloof on the farther side,
I will surely devise his death. [38]

The poet assigns the task of narration, as is fit, to himself, but the abrupt threat he suddenly, with no note of warning, attributes to the angered chief. It would have been frigid had he inserted the words, "Hector said so and so." As it is, the swift transition of the narrative has outstripped the swift transitions of the narrator. 2. Accordingly this figure should be used by preference when a sharp crisis does not suffer the writer to tarry, but constrains him to pass at

[35] *Phaenomena*, 287.
[36] II, 29.
[37] *Iliad*, V, 85.
[38] *Ibid.*, XV, 346.

once from one person to another. An example will be found in Hecataeus: "Ceyx treated the matter gravely, and straightway bade the descendants of Heracles depart; for I am not able to succour you. In order, therefore, that ye may not perish yourselves and injure me, get you gone to some other country." . . .

XXXIX

The fifth of those elements contributing to the sublime which we mentioned, my excellent friend, at the beginning, still remains to be dealt with, namely the arrangement of the words in a certain order. In regard to this, having already in two treatises sufficiently stated such results as our inquiry could compass, we will add, for the purpose of our present undertaking, only what is absolutely essential, namely the fact that harmonious arrangement is not only a natural source of persuasion and pleasure among men but also a wonderful instrument of lofty utterance and of passion. 2. For does not the flute instil certain emotions into its hearers and as it were make them beside themselves and full of frenzy, and supplying a rhythmical movement constrain the listener to move rhythmically in accordance therewith and to conform himself to the melody, although he may be utterly ignorant of music? Yes, and the tones of the harp, although in themselves they signify nothing at all, often cast a wonderful spell, as you know, over an audience by means of the variations of sounds, by their pulsation against one another, and by their mingling in concert. 3. And yet these are mere semblances and spurious copies of persuasion, not (as I have said) genuine activities of human nature. Are we not, then, to hold that composition (being a harmony of that language which is implanted by nature in man and which appeals not to the hearing only but to the soul itself), since it calls forth manifold shapes of words, thoughts, deeds, beauty, melody, all of them born at our birth and growing with our growth, and since by means of the blending and variation of its own tones it seeks to introduce into the minds of those who are present the emotion which affects the speaker and since it always brings the audience to share in it and by the building of phrase upon phrase raises a sublime and harmonious structure: are

we not, I say, to hold that harmony by these selfsame means allures us and invariably disposes us to stateliness and dignity and elevation and every emotion which it contains within itself, gaining absolute mastery over our minds? But it is folly to dispute concerning matters which are generally admitted, since experience is proof sufficient. 4. An example of a conception which is usually thought sublime and is really admirable is that which Demosthenes associates with the decree: "This decree caused the danger which then beset the city to pass by just-as a cloud." [39] But it owes its happy sound no less to the harmony than to the thought itself. For the thought is expressed throughout in dactylic rhythms, and these are most noble and productive of sublimity; and therefore it is that they constitute the heroic, the finest metre that we know. For if you derange the words of the sentence and transpose them in whatever way you will, as for example "This decree just-as a cloud caused the danger of the time to pass by"; nay, if you cut off a single syllable only and say "caused to pass by as a cloud," you will perceive to what an extent harmony is in unison with sublimity. For the very words "just-as a cloud" begin with a long rhythm, which consists of four metrical beats; but if one syllable is cut off and we read "as a cloud," we immediately maim the sublimity by the abbreviation. Conversely, if you elongate the word and write "caused to pass by just-as-if a cloud," it means the same thing, but no longer falls with the same effect upon the ear, inasmuch as the abrupt grandeur of the passage loses its energy and tension through the lengthening of the concluding syllables.

XL

Among the chief causes of the sublime in speech, as in the structure of the human body, is the collocation of members, a single one of which if severed from another possesses in itself nothing remarkable, but all united together make a full and perfect organism. So the constituents of grandeur, when separated from one another, carry with them sublimity in distraction this way and that, but when formed into a body by association and when further encircled in a chain

[39] *On the Crown*, 188.

of harmony they become sonorous by their very rotundity; and in periods sublimity is, as it were, a contribution made by a multitude. 2. We have, however, sufficiently shown that many writers and poets who possess no natural sublimity and are perhaps even wanting in elevation have nevertheless, although employing for the most part common and popular words with no striking associations of their own, by merely joining and fitting these together, secured dignity and distinction and the appearance of freedom from meanness. Instances will be furnished by Philistus among many others, by Aristophanes in certain passages, by Euripides in most. . . .

XLII

Further, excessive concision of expression tends to lower the sublime, since grandeur is marred when the thought is brought into too narrow a compass. Let this be understood not of proper compression, but of what is absolutely petty and cut into segments. For concision curtails the sense, but brevity goes straight to the mark. It is plain that, *vice versa*, prolixities are frigid, for so is everything that resorts to unseasonable length.

XLIII

Triviality of expression is also apt to disfigure sublimity. In Herodotus, for example, the tempest is described with marvellous effect in all its details, but the passage surely contains some words below the dignity of the subject. The following may serve as an instance—"when the sea seethed." [40] The word "seethed" detracts greatly from the sublimity because it is an ill-sounding one. Further, "the wind," he says, "grew fagged," and those who clung to the spars met "an unpleasant end." [41] The expression "grew fagged" is lacking in dignity, being vulgar; and the word "unpleasant" is inappropriate to so great a disaster. 2. Similarly, when Theopompus [42] had dressed out in marvellous fashion the descent of the Persian king upon Egypt, he spoilt the whole by some petty words. "For which of the cities (he says) or which of the tribes in

[40] VII, 188.
[41] VII, 191; VIII, 13.
[42] Greek historian (c. 350 B.C.), pupil of Isocrates.

Asia did not send envoys to the Great King? Which of the products of the earth or of the achievements of art was not, in all its beauty or preciousness, brought as an offering to his presence? Consider the multitude of costly coverlets and mantles, in purple or white or embroidery; the multitude of pavilions of gold furnished with all things useful; the multitude, too, of tapestries and costly couches. Further, gold and silver plate richly wrought, and goblets and mixing-bowls, some of which you might have seen set with precious stones, and others finished with care and at great price. In addition to all this, countless myriads of Greek and barbaric weapons, and beasts of burden beyond all reckoning and victims fattened for slaughter, and many bushels of condiments, and many bags and sacks and sheets of papyrus and all other useful things, and an equal number of pieces of salted flesh from all manner of victims, so that the piles of them were so great that those who were approaching from a distance took them to be hills and eminences confronting them." 3. He runs off from the more elevated to the more lowly, whereas he should, on the contrary, have risen higher and higher. With his wonderful description of the whole outfit he mixes bags and condiments and sacks, and conveys the impression of a confectioner's shop! For just as if, in the case of those very adornments, between the golden vessels and the jewelled mixing-bowls and the silver plate and the pavilions of pure gold and the goblets, a man were to bring and set in the midst paltry bags and sacks, the proceeding would have been offensive to the eye, so do such words when introduced out of season constitute deformities and as it were blots on the diction. 4. He might have described the scene in broad outline just as he says that hills blocked their way, and with regard to the preparations generally have spoken of "waggons and camels and the multitude of beasts of burden carrying everything that ministers to the luxury and enjoyment of the table," or have used some such expression as "piles of all manner of grain and things which conduce preeminently to good cookery and comfort of body," or if he must necessarily put it in so uncompromising a way, he might have said that "all the dainties of cooks and caterers were there." 5. In lofty passages we ought not to descend to sordid and contemptible language unless constrained by some overpowering necessity, but it is fitting that we should use words worthy of the subject and imitate nature the artificer of man, for she has not placed in full view our grosser parts or the means of purging our frame, but has hidden them away as far as was possible, and as Xenophon says has put their channels in the remotest background, so as not to sully the beauty of the entire creature. 6. But enough; there is no need to enumerate, one by one, the things which produce triviality. For since we have previously indicated those qualities which render style noble and lofty, it is evident that their opposites will for the most part make it low and base.

XLIV

It remains however (as I will not hesitate to add, in recognition of your love of knowledge) to clear up, my dear Terentianus, a question which a certain philosopher has recently mooted. "I wonder," he says, "as no doubt do many others, how it happens that in our time there are men who have the gift of persuasion to the utmost extent, and are well fitted for public life, and are keen and ready, and particularly rich in all the charms of language, yet there no longer arise really lofty and transcendent natures unless quite exceptionally. So great and world-wide a dearth of high utterance attends our age." 2. "Can it be," he continued, "that we are to accept the trite explanation that democracy is the kind nursing-mother of genius, and that literary power may be said to share its rise and fall with democracy and democracy alone? For freedom, it is said, has power to feed the imaginations of the lofty-minded and to inspire hope, and where it prevails there spreads abroad the eagerness of mutual rivalry and the emulous pursuit of the foremost place. 3. Moreover, owing to the prizes which are open to all under popular government, the mental excellences of the orator are continually exercised and sharpened, and as it were rubbed bright, and shine forth (as it is natural they should) with all the freedom which inspires the doings of the state. To-day," he went on, "we seem in our boyhood to learn the lessons of a righteous servitude, being all but enswathed in its customs and observances, when our thoughts are yet young and tender, and never

tasting the fairest and most productive source of eloquence (by which," he added, "I mean freedom), so that we emerge in no other guise than that of sublime flatterers." 4. This is the reason, he maintained, why no slave ever becomes an orator, although all other faculties may belong to menials. In the slave there immediately bursts out signs of fettered liberty of speech, of the dungeon as it were, of a man habituated to buffetings. 5. "For the day of slavery," as Homer has it, "takes away half our manhood." [43] "Just as," he proceeded, "the cages (if what I hear is true) in which are kept the Pygmies, commonly called *nani*, not only hinder the growth of the creatures confined within them, but actually attenuate them through the bonds which beset their bodies, so one has aptly termed all servitude (though it be most righteous) the cage of the soul and a public prison-house." 6. I answered him thus: "It is easy, my good sir, and characteristic of human nature, to find fault with the age in which one lives. But consider whether it may not be true that it is not the world's peace that ruins great natures, but far rather this war illimitable which holds our desires in its grasp, aye, and further still those passions which occupy as with troops our present age and utterly harry and plunder it. For the love of money (a disease from which we all now suffer sorely) and the love of pleasure make us their thralls, or rather, as one may say, drown us body and soul in the depths, the love of riches being a malady which makes men petty, and the love of pleasure one which makes them most ignoble. 7. On reflexion I cannot discover how it is possible for us, if we value boundless wealth so highly, or (to speak more truly) deify it, to avoid allowing the entrance into our souls of the evils which are inseparable from it. For vast and unchecked wealth is accompanied, in close conjunction and step for step as they say, by extravagance, and as soon as the former opens the gates of cities and houses, the latter immediately enters and abides. And when time has passed the pair build nests in the lives of men, as the wise say, and quickly give themselves to the rearing of offspring, and breed ostentation, and vanity, and luxury, no spurious progeny of theirs, but only too legitimate. If these children of wealth are permitted to come to ma-

[43] *Odyssey*, XVII, 322.

turity, straightway they beget in the soul inexorable masters—insolence, and lawlessness, and shamelessness. 8. This must necessarily happen, and men will no longer lift up their eyes or have any further regard for fame, but the ruin of such lives will gradually reach its complete consummation and sublimities of soul fade and wither away and become contemptible, when men are lost in admiration of their own mortal parts and omit to exalt that which is immortal. 9. For a man who has once accepted a bribe for a judicial decision cannot be an unbiassed and upright judge of what is just and honourable (since to the man who is venal his own interests must seem honourable and just), and the same is true where the entire life of each of us is ordered by bribes, and huntings after the death of others, and the laying of ambushes for legacies, while gain from any and every source we purchase—each one of us—at the price of life itself, being the slaves of pleasure. In an age which is ravaged by plagues so sore, is it possible for us to imagine that there is still left an unbiassed and incorruptible judge of works that are great and likely to reach posterity, or is it not rather the case that all are influenced in their decisions by the passion for gain? 10. Nay, it is perhaps better for men like ourselves to be ruled than to be free, since our appetites, if let loose without restraint upon our neighbours like beasts from a cage, would set the world on fire with deeds of evil. 11. Summing up, I maintained that among the banes of the natures which our age produces must be reckoned that half-heartedness in which the life of all of us with few exceptions is passed, for we do not labour or exert ourselves except for the sake of praise and pleasure, never for those solid benefits which are a worthy object of our own efforts and the respect of others. 12. But " 'tis best to leave these riddles unresolved," [44] and to proceed to what next presents itself, namely the subject of the Passions, about which I previously undertook to write in a separate treatise. These form, as it seems to me, a material part of discourse generally and of the Sublime itself.

[44] Euripides, *Electra*, 379.

2. *The Renaissance Restatement*

SIR PHILIP SIDNEY   (1554-1586)

SIDNEY is hardly a major critic in the sense that Johnson, Hazlitt, the Schlegels, Sainte-Beuve, or Arnold, for example, are major critics. For literary criticism had not yet in his time become a genre that attracted an extensive effort from talented writers. Sidney's critical reputation, therefore, rests only upon his *Apology for Poetry*, written in the early 1580's and published after his death in 1595. Yet the *Apology* gives Sidney a unique place in English literature; he is the first of the great English poet-critics. It is difficult to find, in any other literature, a parallel to the impressive group of poets in England who have discussed their own art critically—a group that includes, in the neoclassic tradition, Ben Jonson, Dryden, and Samuel Johnson; or, among the romantics, Wordsworth, Coleridge, and Shelley; or, still later, Arnold and Eliot. The distinction and uniqueness of such an array of poet-critics go far toward disproving the belief, popularized by Matthew Arnold and encouraged by the English themselves, that English writers are not "critical." This belief, if it has any justification at all, is valid only for the period since about 1830. Even then, the justification exists only if one is thinking in terms of professional and systematic critics rather than critically informed and critically interested writers.

Moreover, apart from its special importance for English literature, the *Apology for Poetry* clearly stands out as the greatest of all Renaissance critical writings. It does so not only because of its range, its humane largeness of outlook, and its combined grace and concreteness of style, but also because of its typicality and representativeness. For, taking the Aristotelian

SIR PHILIP SIDNEY. Educated at Shrewsbury and Christ Church, Oxford, Sidney visited extensively on the Continent (1572-75), then served on various diplomatic missions, and became widely known and admired throughout the courts of Europe. Interested in American colonization, he received the dedication of Hakluyt's *Voyages*; he became well acquainted with literary circles, was appointed governor of Flushing (1584), and, while still in his early thirties, was killed fighting the Spanish (1586).

Texts include the Arber reprint (1858), and the editions of E. S. Shuckburgh (Cambridge, 1891), J. C. Collins (Oxford, 1907), and A. Feuillerat (1923). For discussion of the *Apology* and its background, see K. O. Myrick, *Sir Philip Sidney as a Literary Craftsman* (Cambridge, Mass., 1935); J. E. Spingarn, *Literary Criticism in the Renaissance* (1899); and F. M. Krouse, "Plato and Sidney's *Defence of Poesie*," *Comparative Literature*, VI (1954), 138-47. A German dissertation, by C. Quossek, relates the *Apology* to Aristotle's *Poetics* (Crefeld, 1880).

theory of poetry as its backbone, it fills out its discussion with criteria and arguments drawn from Plato—from Plato's philosophy as a whole rather than from his remarks on literature itself. Moreover, the influence of Horace, directly and also indirectly through the sixteenth-century Italian critics, is superadded to that of Plato and Aristotle. By combining these three influences, together with that of Christian religious thought, Sidney's *Apology for Poetry* offers the most rounded and comprehensive synthesis we have of the Renaissance conception of the aim and function of literature. It thus has a general and European-wide significance as an eloquent summation of the Renaissance restatement of classical values and ideals.

2

If the *Apology for Poetry* presents a larger synthesis of Renaissance ideals than do other critical works, one reason is simply the bold generality of its subject. With a few exceptions, earlier Renaissance criticism had been restricted in scope and had concentrated on technical rules. It had usually been concerned with such problems as the dramatic "unities," the use of meter, and especially with the analysis and classification of forms of speech and of rhetorical devices. Critical writing in England had been especially meager before Sidney. There had been some works on rhetoric, the most notable of which was Thomas Wilson's *Art of Rhetoric* (1553). There had also been a brief discussion of versification, George Gascoigne's *Certain Notes of Instruction Concerning the Making of Verse or Rhyme in English* (1575), later used for a handbook on meter by James VI of Scotland (1584). If the *Apology for Poetry* completely transcends such works in breadth of subject and treatment, this is partly because it does not pretend to be a "critical" analysis, and Sidney therefore felt no need to adhere strictly to the subject matter and form of critical treatises of the time. Instead, as its two different titles indicate, the work is openly a "defense" or "apology" for imaginative writing in general. Stephen Gosson's Puritan attack on poetry, *The School of Abuse* (1579) had been dedicated, without permission, to Sidney. Partly as an answer to Gosson, but even more as a reply to the general attitudes of which *The School of Abuse* was one example, Sidney's *Apology* takes the form of a persuasive and moving oration. Indeed, in the actual structure of the *Apology*, as Kenneth Myrick has pointed out, one may discover, in order, the seven different parts of the classical oration: (1) the *exordium*, or the winning of the hearer's attention to what follows; (2) the *narratio*, in which Sidney offers a historical survey of the role of poetry; (3) the *propositio*, or resolving of what has been said, with Sidney's definition of poetry, drawn primarily from Aristotle; (4) the *partitio*, or dividing up and stating of what arguments remain to be answered; (5) the *confirmatio*, or proving of the case; (6) the *repre-*

hensio, or final refutation in the form of reproof or censure of the other side; and lastly (7) the *peroratio*, or final summing up.

3

The body of Sidney's argument or defense falls under three general headings. First, by turning to history itself, he notes the extent to which poetry has been the first educator and mental nourisher of primitive peoples, leading them gradually into a more civilized state and a more sensitive receptivity to knowledge of every sort. From this, he moves to a second argument, buttressing his previous historical survey by a more philosophical discussion of the ideal aim of poetry—of what poetry at its best is able to do: namely, to present reality, and human experience with reality, in a vivid and persuasive form. Sidney's third argument, the moral value of poetry as a formative molder and enlarger of the human mind and character, is built upon the preceding two.

Like the Roman Horace, Renaissance writers were inevitably more aware of history than were the Greeks. For they had the history of Greece itself before them as an example. In urging the cultural role of poetry throughout history, Sidney thought mainly of Greece. But he also cited the example of other peoples, thus employing an approach that foreshadowed that of modern comparative anthropology. In a primitive people, said Sidney, oral poetry—chants, rituals, heroic lays, and sagas—exists before any *written* literature. Without writing, no other form of literature except poetry can be perpetuated. Precise, scientific description or philosophical analysis are not stored in the memory and easily transmitted. Indeed, the writing down of language often begins in order to record poetry. Unless there is something present to write, there is not much incentive to discover a way of writing; and about the only form of literature that primitive peoples have to write is poetry. Hence poetry is often the cause or incentive in creating a written language, thus making other studies and sciences possible. Moreover, according to Sidney, it is poetry that first opens the "untamed wits" of "stony and beastly people" by presenting a knowledge of men and their actions, and by arousing the curiosity and imagination to take note of this knowledge. For these reasons, it has served as the "first light-giver to ignorance"—as the "nurse" whose milk gradually enables a people "to feed afterwards of tougher knowledges." Hence the high esteem in which poetry was held in earlier cultures, so that other forms of learning often took their start as branches of poetry. In Greece, especially, the telling of historical incidents, political and moral philosophy, and scientific speculation were at first put into the form of verse. Nor could these have aroused attention and won entrance into men's minds at that stage had they not first "taken a great passport of Poetry."

4

In defining the aim and function of poetry after his historical survey, Sidney mainly repeated and enlarged upon Aristotle's conception of poetry as an effective form of "imitating" nature. Certain literal-minded moralists, he observed, regard poetry as a "mother of lies." Because it is *fictional,* that is, it was said to offer as real what is not real—the assumption being that whatever is not literally true is automatically false. But, to begin with, Sidney pointed out, poetic fiction is not presented as literal truth. No one who attends a play in which the scene is laid in Thebes can say that he is being "deceived" by a matter-of-fact assertion that the wooden stage before him is really Thebes. In fact, by not being tied down to actual, specific happenings, poetry is able to concentrate more on the general pattern and general meaning of things. It can thus, as Aristotle said, be "more philosophical" than the mere historical chronicling of details would be.

If poetry is "more philosophical" than history, it is more effective than philosophy because it gives concrete body to the general truth it is disclosing. The abstract precepts, the general formulations of the philosopher do not so easily strike home to the heart. One can memorize exactly and then repeat by rote the "wordish description" of a thing that one has never seen— a palace, said Sidney, or an unusual animal like an elephant or a rhinoceros —and yet never have so clear an idea of it as a single picture would give. Without concrete experience, philosophical generalizations are rarely effective. One may admit they are true but still not feel them vividly. Poetry, while it offers what is general, can also give one the concrete experience; for at its best it "coupleth the general notion with the particular example." In doing so, it insinuates knowledge more thoroughly into the heart. If, for example, certain philosophers should fly into a rage because they cannot agree on their definitions of anger, they would illustrate—however subtle and precise their analyses were—that their knowledge had not been appropriated into their feeling; and they could hardly be said to possess it, therefore.

5

Sidney's statement of the function of poetry as an effective presentation of general truth thus leads directly to his third argument: the formative, educational value of imaginative writing. Here he reverted to the basic classical conviction that the knowledge which is of greatest value, the knowledge which is most truly known and possessed, is that which has entered into one so completely that it has really enlarged one's way of feeling and thinking. In other words, the final "end of all earthly learning," said Sidney, is "virtuous action": it is the ability to feel, react, and live in accordance with the truth. Poetry ministers directly to this end by opening awareness and susceptibility, and also by "purifying" the intellect, "enriching" the memory, and "enlarging" the capacity to conceive of things imaginatively.

In making general truth familiar and understandable, poetry also acts formatively in a more direct way. For Sidney, it should be noted, went beyond Aristotle in his conception of general or ideal truth; he also included Plato's theory of perfect and absolute "ideas." Accordingly, he further justified the formative value of poetry by pointing out that, because it is not chained to literal detail, poetry is able to portray "ideal" characters— "ideal" in a stricter moral sense than Aristotle had in mind—and to render the image of the good in such a way as to persuade men to follow it. This use of the Platonic "ideas" in a specific moral way is characteristic of much Renaissance thinking, and of the extent to which the moral ideas of the Christian tradition were coalescing with classical precepts. Indeed, it is especially on this ground—its freedom to portray persuasive moral examples of human character, and to induce us to follow them—that imaginative, fictional poetry becomes more valuable than any other sort of writing. It, especially, is able to "teach and delight"—a phrase common from the Renaissance through the eighteenth century, adapted from Horace's *aut prodesse aut delectare* (poetry should "either instruct or delight"). And it fulfills this joint function by emotionally moving men "to take that goodness in hand, which without delight they would fly as from a stranger." As for the charge that poetry can also lure us away from the morally desirable, and can thus cater to idle indulgence or wildly improbable fancies, Sidney sensibly replied that any instrument or function can be misused. If any undesirable effects could ever be traced to poetry, it would be a result of man misusing poetry, not of poetry abusing man. One might as well condemn the gift of speech because it can be used for bad as well as good, and because, through communication, men are able to work more harm than otherwise. But when used for good, needless to say, the ability to communicate is more desirable than the inability to do so.

6

This stricter interpretation of the moral function of art, by Sidney and by other sixteenth-century critics as well, was to become one of the distinctive characteristics of neoclassic criticism. A particular example was Sidney's approval of what a century later was to be called "poetic justice," in which, as Sidney said, "We see virtue exalted, and vice punished." Beside the principle of "poetic justice," which was to serve as a narrow petrification of the broad classical belief in the formative aim of art, the *Apology* applied other criteria that were to become increasingly common in neoclassic criticism. The rigid distinction of genres—tragedy, comedy, pastoral, heroic, and the like—though classical in origin, is an instance, together with Sidney's dislike of the "mongrel tragi-comedy" of the English stage. Others were his concern for the three "unities," and for keeping strict decorum in presenting fixed types of character. Another, more general neoclassic characteristic is the pervasive self-conscious awareness of the authority of tradition and of the example of past models. In the neoclassic bent of the *Apology*, we may see the influence of J. C. Scaliger's *Poetice* (1561), on which Sidney directly drew. More general, if indirect, is the influence of Horace, which was to bulk larger in later neoclassic criticism. Because of these various qualities, the *Apology for Poetry* may be viewed as a lucid and graphic signpost of the direction that the neoclassic theory of literature was to take through the seventeenth to the mid-eighteenth century.

But what is best in the *Apology* transcends both Scaliger and Horace, and reaches back to the basic source and inspiration of the classical tradition. By doing so, it invigorates the Renaissance neoclassic theory of literature with the philosophical concern for basic issues and with something of the imaginative largeness of mind that had characterized classical theory at its origin. With this active and open concern behind it, Sidney's *Apology* coalesces into luminous form the various principles and ideals by which Renaissance Europe was guided in its attempt to discover a high and compelling value in humane learning and to justify to itself, on the widest possible grounds, its own vivid interest and creative brilliance in the arts. Beneath its attempt to restate for itself the basic aim of art, we can sense the eager hope that—by disclosing and adhering to such a goal—the Renaissance might even rival the challenge it found in its haunting dream of classical antiquity. This "new classicism," or "neoclassicism," is not, to be sure, the classicism of ancient Greece. But that it differs in some respects is only another sign of what is more strikingly indicated—though often in very different ways—by the originality and rich diversity of Renaissance literature, art, and philosophy. It is one more illustration that the Renaissance was not a "rebirth" of classical premises, forms, and values, but rather a new birth that came about through and by means of them.

An Apology for Poetry

WHEN the right virtuous Edward Wotton and I were at the Emperor's Court together, we gave ourselves to learn horsemanship of John Pietro Pugliano, one that with great commendation had the place of an esquire in his stable. And he, according to the fertileness of the Italian wit, did not only afford us the demonstration of his practice, but sought to enrich our minds with the contemplations therein

An Apology for Poetry. Written probably in 1583, and first published in 1595 in two slightly different versions: the *Defense of Poesie* (printed by Ponsonby) and the *Apologie for Poetrie* (printed by Olney). The latter text is used here, and the spelling has been modernized.

which he thought most precious. But with none I remember mine ears were at any time more loaden, than when (either angered with slow payment, or moved with our learner-like admiration) he exercised his speech in the praise of his faculty. He said, soldiers were the noblest estate of mankind, and horsemen the noblest of soldiers. He said they were the masters of war and ornaments of peace; speedy goers and strong abiders; triumphers both in camps and courts. Nay, to so unbelieved a point he proceeded, as that no earthly thing bred such wonder to a prince as to be a good horseman. Skill of government was but a *pedanteria* [1] in comparison. Then would he add certain praises, by telling what a peerless beast a horse was, the only serviceable courtier without flattery, the beast of most beauty, faithfulness, courage, and such more, that, if I had not been a piece of a logician before I came to him, I think he would have persuaded me to have wished myself a horse. But thus much at least with his no few words he drove into me, that self-love is better than any gilding to make that seem gorgeous wherein ourselves are parties. Wherein, if Pugliano's strong affection and weak arguments will not satisfy you, I will give you a nearer example of myself, who (I know not by what mischance) in these my not old years and idlest times having slipped into the title of a poet, am provoked to say something unto you in the defence of that my unelected vocation, which if I handle with more good will than good reasons, bear with me, since the scholar is to be pardoned that followeth the steps of his master. And yet I must say that, as I have just cause to make a pitiful defence of poor Poetry, which from almost the highest estimation of learning is fallen to be the laughing-stock of children, so have I need to bring some more available proofs, since the former is by no man barred of his deserved credit, the silly latter hath had even the names of philosophers used to the defacing of it, with great danger of civil war among the Muses.

And first, truly, to all them that professing learning inveigh against Poetry may justly be objected, that they go very near to ungratefulness, to seek to deface that which, in the noblest nations and languages that are known, hath been the first light-giver to ignorance, and first nurse, whose milk by little and little enabled them to feed afterwards of tougher knowledges. And will they now play the hedgehog that, being received into the den, drove out his host, or rather the vipers, that with their birth kill their parents? Let learned Greece in any of her manifold sciences be able to show me one book before Musaeus, Homer, and Hesiod, all three nothing else but poets. Nay, let any history be brought that can say any writers were there before them, if they were not men of the same skill, as Orpheus, Linus, and some other are named, who, having been the first of that country that made pens deliverers of their knowledge to their posterity, may justly challenge to be called their fathers in learning, for not only in time they had this priority (although in itself antiquity be venerable) but went before them, as causes to draw with their charming sweetness the wild untamed wits to an admiration of knowledge, so, as Amphion was said to move stones with his poetry to build Thebes, and Orpheus to be listened to by beasts—indeed stony and beastly people.[2] So among the Romans were Livius Andronicus, and Ennius. So in the Italian language the first that made it aspire to be a treasure-house of Science were the poets Dante, Boccaccio, and Petrarch. So in our English were Gower and Chaucer.

After whom, encouraged and delighted with their excellent fore-going, others have followed, to beautify our mother tongue, as well in the same kind as in other arts. This did so notably show itself, that the philosophers of Greece durst not a long time appear to the world but under the masks of poets. So Thales, Empedocles, and Parmenides sang their natural philosophy in verses; so did Pythagoras and Phocylides their moral counsels; so did Tyrtaeus in war matters, and Solon in matters of policy: or rather, they, being poets, did exercise their delightful vein in those points of highest knowledge, which before them lay hid to the world. For that wise Solon was directly a poet it is manifest, having written in verse the notable fable of the Atlantic Island, which was continued by Plato.

And truly, even Plato, whosoever well con-

---

[1] That is, mere pedantry, or schoolbook knowledge, in comparison.

[2] See Horace, *Art of Poetry*, ll. 391 ff., above, p. 57.

sidereth shall find that in the body of his work, though the inside and strength were Philosophy, the skin as it were and beauty depended most of Poetry: for all standeth upon dialogues, wherein he feigneth many honest burgesses of Athens to speak of such matters, that, if they had been set on the rack, they would never have confessed them, besides his poetical describing the circumstances of their meetings, as the well ordering of a banquet, the delicacy of a walk, with interlacing mere tales, as Gyges' Ring, and others, which who knoweth not to be flowers of poetry did never walk into Apollo's garden.

And even historiographers (although their lips sound of things done, and verity be written in their foreheads) have been glad to borrow both fashion and perchance weight of poets. So Herodotus entitled his history by the name of the nine Muses; and both he and all the rest that followed him either stole or usurped of Poetry their passionate describing of passions, the many particularities of battles, which no man could affirm, or, if that be denied me, long orations put in the mouths of great kings and captains, which it is certain they never pronounced. So that, truly, neither philosopher nor historiographer could at the first have entered into the gates of popular judgements, if they had not taken a great passport of Poetry, which in all nations at this day, where learning flourisheth not, is plain to be seen, in all which they have some feeling of Poetry. In Turkey, besides their law-giving divines, they have no other writers but poets. In our neighbour country Ireland, where truly learning goeth very bare, yet are their poets held in a devout reverence. Even among the most barbarous and simple Indians where no writing is, yet have they their poets, who make and sing songs, which they call *Areytos*, both of their ancestors' deeds and praises of their gods—a sufficient probability that, if ever learning come among them, it must be by having their hard dull wits softened and sharpened with the sweet delights of Poetry. For until they find a pleasure in the exercises of the mind, great promises of much knowledge will little persuade them that know not the fruits of knowledge. In Wales, the true remnant of the ancient Britons, as there are good authorities to show the long time they had poets, which they called bards, so through all the conquests of

Romans, Saxons, Danes, and Normans, some of whom did seek to ruin all memory of learning from among them, yet do their poets, even to this day, last; so as it is not more notable in soon beginning than in long continuing. But since the authors of most of our sciences were the Romans, and before them the Greeks, let us a little stand upon their authorities, but even so far as to see what names they have given unto this now scorned skill.

Among the Romans a poet was called *Vates*, which is as much as a diviner, foreseer, or prophet, as by his conjoined words *vaticinium* and *vaticinari* is manifest: so heavenly a title did that excellent people bestow upon this heart-ravishing knowledge. And so far were they carried into the admiration thereof, that they thought in the chanceable hitting upon any such verses great foretokens of their following fortunes were placed. Whereupon grew the word of *Sortes Virgilianae*, when, by sudden opening Virgil's book, they lighted upon any verse of his making: whereof the histories of the emperors' lives are full, as of Albinus, the governor of our island, who in his childhood met with this verse,

Arma amens capio nec sat rationis in armis; [3]

and in his age performed it: which, although it were a very vain and godless superstition, as also it was to think that spirits were commanded by such verses—whereupon this word charms, derived of *carmina*, cometh—so yet serveth it to show the great reverence those wits were held in. And altogether not without ground, since both the Oracles of Delphos and Sibylla's prophecies were wholly delivered in verses. For that same exquisite observing of number and measure in words, and that high flying liberty of conceit proper to the poet, did seem to have some divine force in it.

And may not I presume a little further, to show the reasonableness of this word *Vates*, and say that the holy David's Psalms are a divine poem? If I do, I shall not do it without the testimony of great learned men, both ancient and modern. But even the name Psalms will speak for me, which, being interpreted, is nothing but

[3] "I seize upon arms, while frenzied; nor is there enough reason for arms" (*Aeneid*, II, 314).

Songs; then that it is fully written in metre, as all learned Hebricians agree, although the rules be not yet fully found; lastly and principally, his handling his prophecy, which is merely poetical. For what else is the awaking his musical instruments, the often and free changing of persons, his notable *prosopopeias*,[4] when he maketh you, as it were, see God coming in His majesty, his telling of the beasts' joyfulness, and hills' leaping, but a heavenly poesy, wherein almost he showeth himself a passionate lover of that unspeakable and everlasting beauty to be seen by the eyes of the mind, only cleared by faith? But truly now having named him, I fear me I seem to profane that holy name, applying it to Poetry, which is among us thrown down to so ridiculous an estimation. But they that with quiet judgements will look a little deeper into it, shall find the end, and working of it such, as, being rightly applied, deserveth not to be scourged out of the Church of God.

But now, let us see how the Greeks named it, and how they deemed of it. The Greeks called him "a poet," which name hath, as the most excellent, gone through other languages. It cometh of this word *Poiein*, which is "to make": wherein, I know not whether by luck or wisdom, we Englishmen have met with the Greeks in calling him "a maker": which name, how high and incomparable a title it is, I had rather were known by marking the scope of other sciences than by my partial allegation.

There is no art delivered to mankind that hath not the works of Nature for his principal object, without which they could not consist, and on which they so depend, as they become actors and players, as it were, of what Nature will have set forth. So doth the astronomer look upon the stars, and, by that he seeth, setteth down what order Nature hath taken therein. So do the geometrician and arithmetician in their diverse sorts of quantities. So doth the musician in times tell you which by nature agree, which not. The natural philosopher thereon hath his name, and the moral philosopher standeth upon the natural virtues, vices, and passions of man; and "follow Nature" (saith he) "therein, and thou shalt not err." The lawyer saith what men have determined; the historian what men have done. The

grammarian speaketh only of the rules of speech; and the rhetorician and logician, considering what in Nature will soonest prove and persuade, thereon give artificial rules, which still are compassed within the circle of a question according to the proposed matter. The physician weigheth the nature of a man's body, and the nature of things helpful or hurtful unto it. And the metaphysic, though it be in the second and abstract notions, and therefore be counted supernatural, yet doth he indeed build upon the depth of Nature. Only the poet, disdaining to be tied to any such subjection, lifted up with the vigour of his own invention, doth grow in effect another nature, in making things either better than Nature bringeth forth, or, quite anew, forms such as never were in Nature, as the Heroes, Demi-gods, Cyclopes, Chimeras, Furies, and such like: so as he goeth hand in hand with Nature, not enclosed within the narrow warrant of her gifts, but freely ranging only within the zodiac of his own wit.

Nature never set forth the earth in so rich tapestry as divers poets have done—neither with pleasant rivers, fruitful trees, sweet-smelling flowers, nor whatsoever else may make the too much loved earth more lovely. Her world is brazen, the poets only deliver a golden. But let those things alone, and go to man—for whom as the other things are, so it seemeth in him her uttermost cunning is employed—and know whether she have brought forth so true a lover as Theagenes, so constant a friend as Pylades, so valiant a man as Orlando, so right a prince as Xenophon's Cyrus, so excellent a man every way as Virgil's Aeneas. Neither let this be jestingly conceived, because the works of the one be essential, the other in imitation or fiction; for any understanding knoweth the skill of the artificer standeth in that idea or foreconceit of the work, and not in the work itself. And that the poet hath that idea is manifest, by delivering them forth in such excellency as he hath imagined them. Which delivering forth also is not wholly imaginative, as we are wont to say by them that build castles in the air: but so far substantially it worketh, not only to make a Cyrus, which had been but a particular excellency, as Nature might have done, but to bestow a Cyrus upon the world, to make many

---

[4] Use of personification.

Cyruses, if they will learn aright why and how that maker made him.

Neither let it be deemed too saucy a comparison to balance the highest point of man's wit with the efficacy of Nature; but rather give right honour to the heavenly Maker of that maker, who, having made man to His own likeness, set him beyond and over all the works of that second nature: which in nothing he showeth so much as in Poetry, when with the force of a divine breath he bringeth things forth far surpassing her doings, with no small argument to the incredulous of that first accursed fall of Adam, since our erected wit maketh us know what perfection is, and yet our infected will keepeth us from reaching unto it. But these arguments will by few be understood, and by fewer granted. Thus much (I hope) will be given me, that the Greeks with some probability of reason gave him the name above all names of learning. Now let us go to a more ordinary opening of him, that the truth may be more palpable: and so I hope, though we get not so unmatched a praise as the etymology of his names will grant, yet his very description, which no man will deny, shall not justly be barred from a principal commendation.

Poesy therefore is an art of imitation, for so Aristotle[5] termeth it in his word *Mimesis*, that is to say, a representing, counterfeiting, or figuring forth—to speak metaphorically, a speaking picture; with this end, to teach and delight.[6] Of this have been three several kinds. The chief, both in antiquity and excellency, were they that did imitate the inconceivable excellencies of God. Such were David in his Psalms; Solomon in his Song of Songs, in his Ecclesiastes, and Proverbs; Moses and Deborah in their Hymns; and the writer of Job, which, beside other, the learned Emanuel Tremellius and Franciscus Junius do entitle the poetical part of the Scripture. Against these none will speak that hath the Holy Ghost in due holy reverence.

In this kind, though in a full wrong divinity, were Orpheus, Amphion, Homer in his Hymns, and many other, both Greeks and Romans, and this poesy must be used by whosoever will follow St. James's counsel in singing psalms when they are merry, and I know is used with the fruit of comfort by some, when, in sorrowful pangs of their death-bringing sins, they find the consolation of the never-leaving goodness.

The second kind is of them that deal with matters philosophical: either moral, as Tyrtaeus, Phocylides, and Cato; or natural, as Lucretius and Virgil's Georgics; or astronomical, as Manilius and Pontanus; or historical, as Lucan; which who mislike, the fault is in their judgements quite out of taste, and not in the sweet food of sweetly uttered knowledge. But because this second sort is wrapped within the fold of the proposed subject, and takes not the course of his own invention, whether they properly be poets or no let grammarians dispute; and go to the third, indeed right poets, of whom chiefly this question ariseth, betwixt whom and these second is such a kind of difference as betwixt the meaner sort of painters, who counterfeit only such faces as are set before them, and the more excellent, who, having no law but wit, bestow that in colours upon you which is fittest for the eye to see, as the constant though lamenting look of Lucretia, when she punished in herself another's fault.

Wherein he painteth not Lucretia whom he never saw, but painteth the outward beauty of such a virtue. For these third be they which most properly do imitate to teach and delight, and to imitate borrow nothing of what is, hath been, or shall be; but range, only reined with learned discretion, into the divine consideration of what may be, and should be.[7] These be they that, as the first and most noble sort may justly be termed *Vates*, so there are waited on in the excellentest languages and best understandings, with the foredescribed name of Poets; for these indeed do merely make to imitate, and imitate both to delight and teach, and delight to move men to take that goodness in hand, which without delight they would fly as from a stranger, and teach, to make them know that goodness whereunto they are moved: which being the noblest scope to which ever any learning was directed, yet want there not idle tongues to bark at them. These be subdivided into sundry more special denominations. The most notable be the Heroic, Lyric, Tragic, Comic, Satiric, Iambic,

---

[5] *Poetics*, above, p. 21.
[6] Taken from Horace, *Art of Poetry*, ll. 333, 361, above, pp. 56-57.

[7] *Poetics*, above, p. 25.

Elegiac, Pastoral, and certain others, some of these being termed according to the matter they deal with, some by the sorts of verses they liked best to write in; for indeed the greatest part of poets have apparelled their poetical inventions in that numbrous kind of writing which is called verse—indeed but apparelled, verse being but an ornament and no cause to Poetry, since there have been many most excellent poets that never versified, and now swarm many versifiers that need never answer to the name of poets. For Xenophon,[8] who did imitate so excellently as to give us *effigiem iusti imperii*, "the portraiture of a just Empire," under name of Cyrus (as Cicero saith of him), made therein an absolute heroical poem.

So did Heliodorus in his sugared invention of that picture of love in Theagenes and Chariclea;[9] and yet both these writ in prose: which I speak to show that it is not rhyming and versing that maketh a poet—no more than a long gown maketh an advocate, who though he pleaded in armour should be an advocate and no soldier. But it is that feigning notable images of virtues, vices, or what else, with that delightful teaching, which must be the right describing note to know a poet by, although indeed the Senate of Poets hath chosen verse as their fittest raiment, meaning, as in matter they passed all in all, so in manner to go beyond them—not speaking (table talk fashion or like men in a dream) words as they chanceably fall from the mouth, but peizing each syllable of each word by just proportion according to the dignity of the subject.

Now therefore it shall not be amiss first to weigh this latter sort of Poetry by his works, and then by his parts, and, if in neither of these anatomies he be condemnable, I hope we shall obtain a more favourable sentence. This purifying of wit, this enriching of memory, enabling of judgement, and enlarging of conceit, which commonly we call learning, under what name soever it come forth, or to what immediate end soever it be directed, the final end is to lead and draw us to as high a perfection as our degenerate souls, made worse by their clayey lodgings, can be capable of. This, according to the inclination of the man, bred many formed impressions. For some that thought this felicity principally to be gotten by knowledge and no knowledge to be so high and heavenly as acquaintance with the stars, gave themselves to Astronomy; others, persuading themselves to be demigods if they knew the causes of things, became natural and supernatural philosophers; some an admirable delight drew to Music; and some the certainty of demonstration to the Mathematics. But all, one and other, having this scope—to know, and by knowledge to lift up the mind from the dungeon of the body to the enjoying his own divine essence. But when by the balance of experience it was found that the astronomer looking to the stars might fall into a ditch, that the inquiring philosopher might be blind in himself, and the mathematician might draw forth a straight line with a crooked heart, then, lo, did proof, the overruler of opinions, make manifest that all these are but serving sciences, which, as they have each a private end in themselves, so yet are they all directed to the highest end of the mistress-knowledge, by the Greeks called *Architectonike*, which stands (as I think) in the knowledge of a man's self, in the ethic and politic consideration, with the end of well doing and not of well knowing only:[10]— even as the saddler's next end is to make a good saddle, but his farther end to serve a nobler faculty, which is horsemanship; so the horseman's to soldiery, and the soldier not only to have the skill, but to perform the practice of a soldier. So that, the ending end of all earthly learning being virtuous action, those skills, that most serve to bring forth that, have a most just title to be princes over all the rest. Wherein we can show the poet's nobleness, by setting him before his other competitors, among whom as principal challengers step forth the moral philosophers, whom, me thinketh, I see coming towards me with a sullen gravity, as though they could not abide vice by daylight, rudely clothed

8 Xenophon's *Education of Cyrus* (or *Cyropaedia*), which is written in prose. Sidney is following Aristotle in refusing to regard the distinction between prose and verse as a distinction between what is poetry and what is not.

9 Heliodorus' *Aethiopica*, probably written in the third century A.D.

10 Sidney is here voicing a basic classical tenet. Cf. Aristotle (*Politics*, VIII, 5): virtue, as distinct from learning abstract precepts, consists of an *active desiring* of what is known to be truly valuable, and an active moving toward it and fulfilling of it.

for to witness outwardly their contempt of outward things, with books in their hands against glory, whereto they set their names, sophistically speaking against subtlety, and angry with **any** man in whom they see the foul fault of anger. These men casting largesse as they go of definitions, divisions, and distinctions, with a scornful interrogative do soberly ask whether it be possible to find any path so ready to lead a man to virtue as that which teacheth what virtue is— and teacheth it not only by delivering forth his very being, his causes, and effects, but also by making known his enemy, Vice (which must be destroyed), and his cumbersome servant, Passion (which must be mastered), by showing the generalities that containeth it, and the specialities that are derived from it; lastly, by plain setting down, how it extendeth itself out of the limits of a man's own little world to the government of families, and maintaining of public societies.

The historian scarcely giveth leisure to the moralist to say so much, but that he, laden with old mouse-eaten records, authorizing himself (for the most part) upon other histories, whose greatest authorities are built upon the notable foundation of hearsay; having much ado to accord differing writers and to pick truth out of partiality; better acquainted with a thousand years ago than with the present age, and yet better knowing how this world goeth than how his own wit runneth: curious for antiquities and inquisitive of novelties; a wonder to young folks and a tyrant in table talk, denieth, in a great chafe, that any man for teaching of virtue, and virtuous actions, is comparable to him. "I am *Lux vitae, Temporum magistra, Vita memoriae, Nuncia vetustatis*," &c.[11]

The philosopher (saith he) "teacheth a disputative virtue, but I do an active. His virtue is excellent in the dangerless Academy of Plato, but mine showeth forth her honourable face in the battles of Marathon, Pharsalia, Poitiers, and Agincourt. He teacheth virtue by certain abstract considerations, but I only bid you follow the footing of them that have gone before you. Old-aged experience goeth beyond the fine-witted philosopher, but I give the experience of many ages. Lastly, if he make the song-book, I put the learner's hand to the lute; and if he be the guide, I am the light."

Then would he allege you innumerable examples, conferring story by story, how much the wisest senators and princes have been directed by the credit of history, as Brutus, Alphonsus of Aragon, and who not, if need be? At length the long line of their disputation maketh a point in this, that the one giveth the precept, and the other the example.

Now, whom shall we find (since the question standeth for the highest form in the School of Learning) to be Moderator? Truly, as me seemeth, the poet; and if not a Moderator, even the man that ought to carry the title from them both, and much more from all other serving sciences. Therefore compare we the poet with the historian, and with the moral philosopher; and, if he go beyond them both, no other human skill can match him. For as for the Divine, with all reverence it is ever to be excepted, not only for having his scope as far beyond any of these as eternity exceedeth a moment, but even for passing each of these in themselves.

And for the lawyer, though Jus be the daughter of Justice, and Justice the chief of virtues, yet because he seeketh to make men good rather *formidine poenae* than *virtutis amore*,[12] or, to say righter, doth not endeavour to make men good, but that their evil hurt not others, having no care, so he be a good citizen, how bad a man he be: therefore, as our wickedness maketh him necessary, and necessity maketh him honourable, so is he not in the deepest truth to stand in rank with these who all endeavour to take naughtiness away, and plant goodness even in the secretest cabinet of our souls. And these four are all that any way deal in that consideration of men's manners, which being the supreme knowledge, they that best breed it deserve the best commendation.

The philosopher therefore and the historian are they which would win the goal, the one by precept, the other by example. But both, not having both, do both halt. For the philosopher, setting down with thorny argument the bare rule, is so hard of utterance, and so misty to be conceived, that one that hath no other guide but him shall wade in him till he be old before he shall find sufficient cause to be honest. For his

---

[11] "The light of life, the master of the times, the life of memory, the messenger of antiquity" (Cicero, *De Oratore*, II, 9, 36).

[12] "By fear of punishment rather than love of virtue."

knowledge standeth so upon the abstract and general, that happy is that man who may understand him, and more happy that can apply what he doth understand.

On the other side, the historian, wanting the precept, is so tied, not to what should be but to what is, to the particular truth of things and not to the general reason of things, that his example draweth no necessary consequence, and therefore a less fruitful doctrine.

Now doth the peerless poet perform both: for whatsoever the philosopher saith should be done, he giveth a perfect picture of it in some one by whom he presupposeth it was done; so as he coupleth the general notion with the particular example. A perfect picture I say, for he yieldeth to the powers of the mind an image of that whereof the philosopher bestoweth but a wordish description: which doth neither strike, pierce, nor possess the sight of the soul so much as that other doth.

For as in outward things, to a man that had never seen an elephant or a rhinoceros, who should tell him most exquisitely all their shapes, colour, bigness, and particular marks, or of a gorgeous palace the architecture, with declaring the full beauties might well make the hearer able to repeat, as it were by rote, all he had heard, yet should never satisfy his inward conceits with being witness to itself of a true lively knowledge: but the same man, as soon as he might see those beasts well painted, or the house well in model, should straightways grow, without need of any description, to a judicial comprehending of them: so no doubt the philosopher with his learned definition—be it of virtue, vices, matters of public policy or private government—replenisheth the memory with many infallible grounds of wisdom, which, notwithstanding, lie dark before the imaginative and judging power, if they be not illuminated or figured forth by the speaking picture of Poesy.

Tully taketh much pains, and many times not without poetical helps, to make us know the force love of our country hath in us. Let us but hear old Anchises speaking in the midst of Troy's flames, or see Ulysses in the fullness of all Calypso's delights bewail his absence from barren and beggarly Ithaca. Anger, the Stoics say, was a short madness: let but Sophocles bring you Ajax on a stage, killing and whipping sheep

and oxen, thinking them the army of Greeks, with their chieftains Agamemnon and Menelaus, and tell me if you have not a more familiar insight into anger than finding in the Schoolmen his genus and difference. See whether wisdom and temperance in Ulysses and Diomedes, valour in Achilles, friendship in Nisus and Euryalus, even to an ignorant man carry not an apparent shining, and, contrarily, the remorse of conscience in Oedipus, the soon repenting pride of Agamemnon, the self-devouring cruelty in his father Atreus, the violence of ambition in the two Theban brothers, the sour-sweetness of revenge in Medea, and, to fall lower, the Terentian Gnatho and our Chaucer's Pandar so expressed that we now use their names to signify their trades; and finally, all virtues, vices, and passions so in their own natural seats laid to the view, that we seem not to hear of them, but clearly to see through them. But even in the most excellent determination of goodness, what philosopher's counsel can so readily direct a prince, as the feigned Cyrus in Xenophon; or a virtuous man in all fortunes, as Aeneas in Virgil; or a whole Commonwealth, as the way of Sir Thomas More's *Utopia?* I say the way, because where Sir Thomas More erred, it was the fault of the man and not of the poet, for that way of patterning a Commonwealth was most absolute, though he perchance hath not so absolutely performed it. For the question is, whether the feigned image of Poesy or the regular instruction of Philosophy hath the more force in teaching: wherein if the philosophers have more rightly showed themselves philosophers than the poets have attained to the high top of their profession, as in truth,

> *Mediocribus esse poetis,*
> *Non Dii, non homines, non concessere Columnae;* [13]

it is, I say again, not the fault of the art, but that by few men that art can be accomplished.

Certainly, even our Saviour Christ could as well have given the moral commonplaces of uncharitableness and humbleness as the divine narration of Dives and Lazarus; or of disobedience and mercy, as that heavenly discourse of the lost child and the gracious father; but that His

---

[13] "Mediocre poets are not endured by gods, men, or booksellers" (Horace, *Art of Poetry*, ll. 372-373).

through-searching wisdom knew the estate of Dives burning in hell, and of Lazarus being in Abraham's bosom, would more constantly (as it were) inhabit both the memory and judgement. Truly, for myself, meseems I see before my eyes the lost child's disdainful prodigality, turned to envy a swine's dinner: which by the learned Divines are thought not historical acts, but instructing parables. For conclusion, I say the Philosopher teacheth, but he teacheth obscurely, so as the learned only can understand him; that is to say, he teacheth them that are already taught. But the poet is the food for the tenderest stomachs, the poet is indeed the right popular philosopher, whereof Aesop's tales give good proof: whose pretty allegories, stealing under the formal tales of beasts, make many, more beastly than beasts, begin to hear the sound of virtue from these dumb speakers.

But now may it be alleged that, if this imagining of matters be so fit for the imagination, then must the historian needs surpass, who bringeth you images of true matters, such as indeed were done, and not such as fantastically or falsely may be suggested to have been done. Truly, Aristotle himself, in his discourse of Poesy, plainly determineth this question, saying that Poetry is *Philosophoteron* and *Spoudaioteron*, that is to say, it is more philosophical and more studiously serious than history. His reason is, because Poesy dealeth with *Katholou*, that is to say, with the universal consideration, and the history with *Kathekaston*, the particular: "now," saith he, "the universal weighs what is fit to be said or done, either in likelihood or necessity (which the Poesy considereth in his imposed names), and the particular only marks whether Alcibiades did, or suffered, this or that." [14] Thus far Aristotle: which reason of his (as all his) is most full of reason. For indeed, if the question were whether it were better to have a particular act truly or falsely set down, there is no doubt which is to be chosen, no more than whether you had rather have Vespasian's picture right as he was, or at the painter's pleasure nothing resembling. But if the question be for your own use and learning, whether it be better to have it set down as it should be, or as it was, then certainly is more doctrinable the feigned Cyrus in Xenophon than the true

[14] *Poetics*, IX, above, p. 25.

Cyrus in Justin, and the feigned Aeneas in Virgil than the right Aeneas in Dares Phrygius.

As to a lady that desired to fashion her countenance to the best grace, a painter should more benefit her to portrait a most sweet face, writing Canidia upon it, than to paint Canidia as she was, who, Horace sweareth, was foul and ill favoured.

If the poet do his part aright, he will show you in Tantalus, Atreus, and such like, nothing that is not to be shunned; in Cyrus, Aeneas, Ulysses, each thing to be followed; where the historian, bound to tell things as things were, cannot be liberal (without he will be poetical) of a perfect pattern, but, as in Alexander or Scipio himself, show doings, some to be liked, some to be misliked. And then how will you discern what to follow but by your own discretion, which you had without reading Quintus Curtius? And whereas a man may say, though in universal consideration of doctrine the poet prevaileth, yet that the history, in his saying such a thing was done, doth warrant a man more in that he shall follow.

The answer is manifest: that if he stand upon that *was*—as if he should argue, because it rained yesterday, therefore it should rain to-day —then indeed it hath some advantage to a gross conceit; but if he know an example only informs a conjectured likelihood, and so go by reason, the poet doth so far exceed him, as he is to frame his example to that which is most reasonable, be it in warlike, politic, or private matters; where the historian in his bare *was* hath many times that which we call fortune to overrule the best wisdom. Many times he must tell events whereof he can yield no cause: or, if he do, it must be poetical. For that a feigned example hath as much force to teach as a true example (for as for to move, it is clear, since the feigned may be tuned to the highest key of passion), let us take one example wherein a poet and a historian do concur.

Herodotus and Justin do both testify that Zopyrus, King Darius's faithful servant, seeing his master long resisted by the rebellious Babylonians, feigned himself in extreme disgrace of his king: for verifying of which, he caused his own nose and ears to be cut off, and so flying to the Babylonians, was received, and for his known valour so far credited, that he did find means to deliver them over to Darius. Much like matter doth Livy record of Tarquinius and his son. Xenophon excellently feigneth such another stratagem performed by Abradates in Cyrus's behalf. Now would I fain know, if occasion be presented unto you to serve your prince by such an honest dissimulation, why you do not as well learn it of Xenophon's fiction as of the other's verity—and truly so much the better, as you shall save your nose by the bargain; for Abradates did not counterfeit so far. So then the best of the historian is subject to the poet; for whatsoever action, or faction, whatsoever counsel, policy, or war stratagem the historian is bound to recite, that may the poet (if he list) with his imitation make his own, beautifying it both for further teaching, and more delighting, as it pleaseth him, having all, from Dante's heaven to his hell, under the authority of his pen. Which if I be asked what poets have done so, as I might well name some, yet say I, and say again, I speak of the art, and not of the artificer.

Now, to that which commonly is attributed to the praise of histories, in respect of the notable learning is gotten by marking the success, as though therein a man should see virtue exalted and vice punished—truly that commendation is peculiar to Poetry, and far off from History. For indeed Poetry ever setteth virtue so out in her best colours, making Fortune her well-waiting handmaid, that one must needs be enamoured of her. Well may you see Ulysses in a storm, and in other hard plights; but they are but exercises of patience and magnanimity, to make them shine the more in the near-following prosperity. And of the contrary part, if evil men come to the stage, they ever go out (as the tragedy writer answered to one that misliked the show of such persons) so manacled as they little animate folks to follow them. But the historian, being captived to the truth of a foolish world, is many times a terror from well doing, and an encouragement to unbridled wickedness.

For see we not valiant Miltiades rot in his fetters: the just Phocion and the accomplished Socrates put to death like traitors; the cruel Severus live prosperously; the excellent Severus miserably murdered; Sylla and Marius dying in their beds; Pompey and Cicero slain then when they would have thought exile a happiness?

See we not virtuous Cato driven to kill him-self, and rebel Caesar so advanced that his name yet, after 1,600 years, lasteth in the highest honour? And mark but even Caesar's own words of the forenamed Sylla (who in that only did honestly, to put down his dishonest tyranny), *Literas nescivit*,[15] as if want of learning caused him to do well. He meant it not by Poetry, which, not content with earthly plagues, deviseth new punishments in hell for tyrants, nor yet by Philosophy, which teacheth *Occidendos esse;*[16] but no doubt by skill in History, for that indeed can afford your Cypselus, Periander, Phalaris, Dionysius, and I know not how many more of the same kennel, that speed well enough in their abominable injustice or usurpation. I conclude, therefore, that he excelleth History, not only in furnishing the mind with knowledge, but in setting it forward to that which deserveth to be called and accounted good: which setting forward, and moving to well doing, indeed setteth the laurel crown upon the poet as victorious, not only of the historian, but over the philosopher, howsoever in teaching it may be questionable.

For suppose it be granted (that which I suppose with great reason may be denied) that the philosopher, in respect of his methodical proceeding, doth teach more perfectly than the poet, yet do I think that no man is so much *Philophilosophos*[17] as to compare the philosopher, in moving, with the poet.

And that moving is of a higher degree than teaching, it may by this appear, that it is well-nigh the cause and the effect of teaching. For who will be taught, if he be not moved with desire to be taught, and what so much good doth that teaching bring forth (I speak still of moral doctrine) as that it moveth one to do that which it doth teach? For, as Aristotle saith, it is not *Gnosis* but *Praxis*[18] must be the fruit. And how *Praxis* cannot be, without being moved to practise, it is no hard matter to consider.

The philosopher showeth you the way, he informeth you of the particularities, as well of the tediousness of the way, as of the pleasant lodging you shall have when your journey is ended, as of the many by-turnings that may divert you

[15] "He did not know literature."
[16] "They are to be killed."
[17] "A lover of the philosopher."
[18] Not mere abstract *knowledge*, that is, but *action.*

from your way. But this is to no man but to him that will read him, and read him with attentive studious painfulness; which constant desire whosoever hath in him, hath already passed half the hardness of the way, and therefore is beholding to the philosopher but for the other half. Nay truly, learned men have learnedly thought that where once reason hath so much overmastered passion as that the mind hath a free desire to do well, the inward light each mind hath in itself is as good as a philosopher's book; seeing in nature we know it is well to do well, and what is well and what is evil, although not in the words of art which philosophers bestow upon us. For out of natural conceit the philosophers drew it; but to be moved to do that which we know, or to be moved with desire to know, *Hoc opus, hic labor est.*[19]

Now therein of all sciences (I speak still of human, and according to the humane conceits) is our poet the monarch. For he doth not only show the way, but giveth so sweet a prospect into the way, as will entice any man to enter into it. Nay, he doth, as if your journey should lie through a fair vineyard, at the first give you a cluster of grapes, that, full of that taste, you may long to pass further. He beginneth not with obscure definitions, which must blur the margent[20] with interpretations, and load the memory with doubtfulness; but he cometh to you with words set in delightful proportion, either accompanied with, or prepared for, the well enchanting skill of music; and with a tale forsooth he cometh unto you, with a tale which holdeth children from play, and old men from the chimney corner. And, pretending no more, doth intend the winning of the mind from wickedness to virtue: even as the child is often brought to take most wholesome things by hiding them in such other as have a pleasant taste: which, if one should begin to tell them the nature of aloes or rhubarb they should receive, would sooner take their physic at their ears than at their mouth. So is it in men (most of which are childish in the best things, till they be cradled in their graves): glad they will be to hear the tales of Hercules, Achilles, Cyrus, and Aeneas; and, hear-

ing them, must needs hear the right description of wisdom, valour, and justice; which, if they had been barely, that is to say philosophically, set out, they would swear they be brought to school again.

That imitation whereof Poetry is, hath the most conveniency to Nature of all other, insomuch that, as Aristotle saith, those things which in themselves are horrible, as cruel battles, unnatural monsters, are made in poetical imitation delightful.[21] Truly, I have known men, that even with reading *Amadis de Gaule* (which God knoweth wanteth much of a perfect poesy) have found their hearts moved to the exercise of courtesy, liberality, and especially courage.

Who readeth Aeneas carrying old Anchises on his back, that wisheth not it were his fortune to perform so excellent an act? Whom do not the words of Turnus move, the tale of Turnus having planted his image in the imagination?—

> *Fugientem haec terra videbit?*
> *Usque adeone mori miserum est?*[22]

Where the philosophers, as they scorn to delight, so must they be content little to move, saving wrangling whether Virtue be the chief or the only good, whether the contemplative or the active life do excel: which Plato and Boethius well knew, and therefore made Mistress Philosophy very often borrow the masking raiment of Poesy. For even those hard-hearted evil men who think virtue a school name, and know no other good but *indulgere genio*,[23] and therefore despise the austere admonitions of the philosopher, and feel not the inward reason they stand upon, yet will be content to be delighted—which is all the good fellow poet seemeth to promise—and so steal to see the form of goodness, which seen they cannot but love ere themselves be aware, as if they took a medicine of cherries. Infinite proofs of the strange effects of this poetical invention might be alleged; only two shall serve, which are so often remembered as I think all men know them.

The one of Menenius Agrippa, who, when the whole people of Rome had resolutely divided themselves from the Senate, with apparent show

---

[19] "This is the work, this the labor" (*Aeneid*, VI, 129).

[20] Notes, at the time of Sidney, were often put in the margins of the page.

[21] *Poetics*, IV, above, p. 21.

[22] "Shall this land see [Turnus] fleeing away? Is it so wretched a thing to die as that?" (*Aeneid*, XII, 645-646).

[23] "To indulge one's nature."

of utter ruin, though he were (for that time) an excellent orator, came not among them upon trust of figurative speeches or cunning insinuations, and much less with farfetched maxims of Philosophy, which (especially if they were Platonic) they must have learned geometry before they could well have conceived; but forsooth he behaves himself like a homely and familiar poet. He telleth them a tale, that there was a time when all the parts of the body made a mutinous conspiracy against the belly, which they thought devoured the fruits of each other's labour: they concluded they would let so unprofitable a spender starve. In the end, to be short (for the tale is notorious, and as notorious that it was a tale), with punishing the belly they plagued themselves. This applied by him wrought such effect in the people, as I never read that ever words brought forth but then so sudden and so good an alteration; for upon reasonable conditions a perfect reconcilement ensued. The other is of Nathan the Prophet, who, when the holy David had so far forsaken God as to confirm adultery with murder, when he was to do the tenderest office of a friend, in laying his own shame before his eyes, sent by God to call again so chosen a servant, how doth he it but by telling of a man whose beloved lamb was ungratefully taken from his bosom?—the application most divinely true, but the discourse itself feigned. Which made David (I speak of the second and instrumental cause) as in a glass to see his own filthiness, as that heavenly Psalm of Mercy well testifieth.

By these, therefore, examples and reasons, I think it may be manifest that the Poet, with that same hand of delight, doth draw the mind more effectually than any other art doth: and so a conclusion not unfitly ensueth, that, as Virtue is the most excellent resting place for all worldly learning to make his end of, so Poetry, being the most familiar to teach it, and most princely to move towards it, in the most excellent work is the most excellent workman. But I am content not only to decipher him by his works (although works in commendation or dispraise must ever hold an high authority), but more narrowly will examine his parts: so that, as in a man, though all together may carry a presence full of majesty and beauty, perchance in some one defectious piece we may find a blemish. Now

in his parts, kinds, or species (as you list to term them), it is to be noted that some poesies have coupled together two or three kinds, as tragical and comical, whereupon is risen the tragi-comical. Some, in the like manner, have mingled prose and verse, as Sannazzaro and Boethius. Some have mingled matters heroical and pastoral. But that cometh all to one in this question, for, if severed they be good, the conjunction cannot be hurtful. Therefore, perchance forgetting some, and leaving some as needless to be remembered, it shall not be amiss in a word to cite the special kinds, to see what faults may be found in the right use of them.

Is it then the Pastoral Poem which is misliked? For perchance where the hedge is lowest they will soonest leap over. Is the poor pipe disdained, which sometime out of Melibaeus' mouth can show the misery of people under hard lords or ravening soldiers, and again, by Tityrus, what blessedness is derived to them that lie lowest from the goodness of them that sit highest? sometimes, under the pretty tales of wolves and sheep, can include the whole considerations of wrongdoing and patience; sometimes show that contention for trifles can get but a trifling victory; where perchance a man may see that even Alexander and Darius, when they strave who should be cock of this world's dunghill, the benefit they got was that the afterlivers may say,

Haec memini et victum frustra contendere Thirsin:
Ex illo Coridon, Coridon est tempore nobis.[24]

Or is it the lamenting Elegiac, which in a kind heart would move rather pity than blame, who bewails with the great philosopher Heraclitus the weakness of mankind and the wretchedness of the world; who surely is to be praised, either for compassionate accompanying just causes of lamentation, or for rightly pointing out how weak be the passions of woefulness? Is it the bitter but wholesome Iambic, which rubs the galled mind, in making shame the trumpet of villainy with bold and open crying out against naughtiness? Or the Satiric, who

Omne vafer vitium ridenti tangit amico;[25]

[24] "I recall those things, and that the conquered Thyrsis strove in vain: From that time, Corydon for us is Corydon" (Virgil, *Eclogue*, VII, 69-70).
[25] "The rogue touches every vice while causing his friend to laugh" (Persius, *Satires*, I, 116-117).

who sportingly never leaveth until he make a man laugh at folly, and, at length ashamed, to laugh at himself, which he cannot avoid, without avoiding the folly; who, while

circum praecordia ludit,[26]

giveth us to feel how many headaches a passionate life bringeth us to; how, when all is done,

Est Ulubris animus si nos non deficit aequus? [27]

No, perchance it is the Comic, whom naughty play-makers and stage-keepers have justly made odious. To the argument of abuse I will answer after. Only thus much now is to be said, that the Comedy is an imitation of the common errors of our life, which he representeth in the most ridiculous and scornful sort that may be, so as it is impossible that any beholder can be content to be such a one.

Now, as in Geometry the oblique must be known as well as the right, and in Arithmetic the odd as well as the even, so in the actions of our life who seeth not the filthiness of evil wanteth a great foil to perceive the beauty of virtue. This doth the Comedy handle so in our private and domestical matters, as with hearing it we get as it were an experience, what is to be looked for of a niggardly Demea, of a crafty Davus, of a flattering Gnatho, of a vainglorious Thraso; and not only to know what effects are to be expected, but to know who be such, by the signifying badge given them by the comedian. And little reason hath any man to say that men learn evil by seeing it so set out; since, as I said before, there is no man living but, by the force truth hath in nature, no sooner seeth these men play their parts, but wisheth them in *pistrinum;* [28] although perchance the sack of his own faults lie so behind his back that he seeth not himself dance the same measure; whereto yet nothing can more open his eyes than to find his own actions contemptibly set forth. So that the right use of Comedy will (I think) by nobody be blamed, and much less of the high and excellent Tragedy, that openeth the greatest

wounds, and showeth forth the ulcers that are covered with tissue; that maketh kings fear to be tyrants, and tyrants manifest their tyrannical humours; that, with stirring the affects of admiration and commiseration, teacheth the uncertainty of this world, and upon how weak foundations gilden roofs are builded; that maketh us know,

Qui sceptra saevus duro imperio regit,
Timet timentes, metus in auctorem redit.[29]

But how much it can move, Plutarch yieldeth a notable testimony of the abominable tyrant Alexander Pheraeus, from whose eyes a tragedy, well made and represented, drew abundance of tears, who, without all pity, had murdered infinite numbers, and some of his own blood, so as he, that was not ashamed to make matters for tragedies, yet could not resist the sweet violence of a tragedy.

And if it wrought no further good in him, it was that he, in despite of himself, withdrew himself from hearkening to that which might mollify his hardened heart. But it is not the Tragedy they do mislike; for it were too absurd to cast out so excellent a representation of whatsoever is most worthy to be learned. Is it the Lyric that most displeaseth, who with his tuned lyre, and well-accorded voice, giveth praise, the reward of virtue, to virtuous acts, who gives moral precepts, and natural problems, who sometimes raiseth up his voice to the height of the heavens, in singing the lauds of the immortal God? Certainly, I must confess my own barbarousness, I never heard the old song of Percy and Douglas that I found not my heart moved more than with a trumpet; and yet is it sung but by some blind crowder, with no rougher voice than rude style; which, being so evil apparelled in the dust and cobwebs of that uncivil age, what would it work, trimmed in the gorgeous eloquence of Pindar? In Hungary I have seen it the manner at all feasts, and other such meetings, to have songs of their ancestors' valour; which that right soldierlike nation think the chiefest kindlers of brave courage. The incomparable Lacedemonians did not only carry that kind of music ever with them to the field,

[26] "He plays around the heart-strings" (same passage).

[27] "Happiness is found in Ulabrae [an extinct or dead city] if we have a sane mind" (Horace, *Epistles,* I, 11, 30).

[28] A Roman mill to which slaves were often condemned as punishment.

[29] "The savage ruler who wields the sceptre with a hard hand fears his frightened subjects, and fear thus returns to the author of it" (Seneca, *Oedipus,* 705-706)

but even at home, as such songs were made, so were they all content to be the singers of them, when the lusty men were to tell what they did, the old men what they had done, and the young men what they would do. And where a man may say that Pindar many times praiseth highly victories of small moment, matters rather of sport than virtue; as it may be answered, it was the fault of the poet, and not of the poetry, so indeed the chief fault was in the time and custom of the Greeks, who set those toys at so high a price that Philip of Macedon reckoned a horse-race won at Olympus among his three fearful felicities. But as the inimitable Pindar often did, so is that kind most capable and most fit to awake the thoughts from the sleep of idleness, to embrace honourable enterprises.

There rests the Heroical, whose very name (I think) should daunt all backbiters; for by what conceit can a tongue be directed to speak evil of that which draweth with it no less champions than Achilles, Cyrus, Aeneas, Turnus, Tydeus, and Rinaldo? who doth not only teach and move to a truth, but teacheth and moveth to the most high and excellent truth; who maketh magnanimity and justice shine throughout all misty fearfulness and foggy desires; who, if the saying of Plato and Tully be true, that who could see Virtue would be wonderfully ravished with the love of her beauty—this man sets her out to make her more lovely in her holiday apparel, to the eye of any that will deign not to disdain until they understand. But if anything be already said in the defence of sweet Poetry, all concurreth to the maintaining the Heroical, which is not only a kind, but the best and most accomplished kind of Poetry.[30] For as the image of each action stirreth and instructeth the mind, so the lofty image of such worthies most inflameth the mind with desire to be worthy, and informs with counsel how to be worthy. Only let Aeneas be worn in the tablet of your memory, how he governeth himself in the ruin of his country, in the preserving his old father, and carrying away his religious ceremonies, in obeying the god's commandment to leave Dido, though not only all passionate kindness, but even the human consideration of virtuous gratefulness,

would have craved other of him; how in storms, how in sports, how in war, how in peace, how a fugitive, how victorious, how besieged, how besieging, how to strangers, how to allies, how to enemies, how to his own; lastly, how in his inward self, and how in his outward government, and I think, in a mind not prejudiced with a prejudicating humour, he will be found in excellency fruitful, yea, even as Horace saith,

Melius Chrysippo et Crantore.[31]

But truly I imagine it falleth out with these poet-whippers, as with some good women, who often are sick, but in faith they cannot tell where. So the name of Poetry is odious to them, but neither his cause nor effects, neither the sum that contains him nor the particularities descending from him, give any fast handle to their carping dispraise.

Since then Poetry is of all human learning the most ancient and of most fatherly antiquity, as from whence other learnings have taken their beginnings; since it is so universal that no learned nation doth despise it, nor no barbarous nation is without it; since both Roman and Greek gave divine names unto it, the one of "prophesying," the other of "making," and that indeed that name of "making" is fit for him, considering that whereas other Arts retain themselves within their subject, and receive, as it were, their being from it, the poet only bringeth his own stuff, and doth not learn a conceit out of a matter, but maketh matter for a conceit; since neither his description nor his end containeth any evil, the thing described cannot be evil; since his effects be so good as to teach goodness and to delight the learners; since therein (namely in moral doctrine, the chief of all knowledges) he doth not only far pass the historian, but, for instructing, is wellnigh comparable to the philosopher, and, for moving, leaves him behind him; since the Holy Scripture (wherein there is no uncleanness) hath whole parts in it poetical, and that even our Saviour Christ vouchsafed to use the flowers of it; since all his kinds are not only in their united forms but in their severed dissections

---

[30] One of the notable departures of Renaissance critics from Aristotle was to place the epic above tragedy as a poetic form. Cf. *Poetics*, XXVI, above, p. 38.

[31] "Better than do Chrysippus and Crantor" (*Epistles*, I, 2, 4). Horace is stating that the knowledge of the good is better learned from Homer than from the above two philosophers.

fully commendable; I think (and think I think rightly) the laurel crown appointed for triumphing captains doth worthily (of all other learnings) honour the poet's triumph. But because we have ears as well as tongues, and that the lightest reasons that may be will seem to weigh greatly, if nothing be put in the counterbalance, let us hear, and, as well as we can, ponder, what objections may be made against this art, which may be worthy either of yielding or answering.

First, truly I note not only in these *Mysomousoi*, poet-haters, but in all that kind of people who seek a praise by dispraising others, that they do prodigally spend a great many wandering words in quips and scoffs, carping and taunting at each thing, which, by stirring the spleen, may stay the brain from a thorough beholding the worthiness of the subject.

Those kind of objections, as they are full of very idle easiness, since there is nothing of so sacred a majesty but that an itching tongue may rub itself upon it, so deserve they no other answer, but, instead of laughing at the jest, to laugh at the jester. We know a playing wit can praise the discretion of an ass, the comfortableness of being in debt, and the jolly commodity of being sick of the plague. So of the contrary side, if we will turn Ovid's verse,

Ut lateat virtus proximitate mali,

that "good lie hid in nearness of the evil," Agrippa will be as merry in showing the vanity of Science as Erasmus was in commending of folly. Neither shall any man or matter escape some touch of these smiling railers. But for Erasmus and Agrippa, they had another foundation than the superficial part would promise. Marry, these other pleasant faultfinders, who will correct the verb before they understand the noun, and confute others' knowledge before they confirm their own, I would have them only remember that scoffing cometh not of wisdom; so as the best title in true English they get with their merriments is to be called good fools, for so have our grave forefathers ever termed that humorous kind of jesters. But that which giveth greatest scope to their scorning humours is rhyming and versing. It is already said (and, as I think, truly said) it is not rhyming and versing that maketh Poesy. One may be a poet without versing, and a versifier without poetry. But yet presuppose

it were inseparable (as indeed it seemeth Scaliger judgeth) truly it were an inseparable commendation.[32] For if *Oratio* next to *Ratio*, Speech next to Reason, be the greatest gift bestowed upon mortality, that cannot be praiseless which doth most polish that blessing of speech; which considers each word, not only (as a man may say) by his forcible quality, but by his best measured quantity, carrying even in themselves a harmony (without, perchance, number, measure, order, proportion be in our time grown odious). But lay aside the just praise it hath, by being the only fit speech for Music (Music, I say, the most divine striker of the senses), thus much is undoubtedly true, that if reading be foolish without remembering, memory being the only treasurer of knowledge, those words which are fittest for memory are likewise most convenient for knowledge.

Now, that verse far exceedeth prose in the knitting up of the memory, the reason is manifest,—the words (besides their delight, which hath a great affinity to memory) being so set as one word cannot be lost but the whole work fails; which accuseth itself, calleth the remembrance back to itself, and so most strongly confirmeth it. Besides, one word so, as it were, begetting another, as, be it in rhyme or measured verse, by the former a man shall have a near guess to the follower: lastly, even they that have taught the art of memory have showed nothing so apt for it as a certain room divided into many places well and thoroughly known. Now, that hath the verse in effect perfectly, every word having his natural seat, which seat must needs make the words remembered. But what needeth more in a thing so known to all men? Who is it that ever was a scholar that doth not carry away some verses of Virgil, Horace, or Cato, which in his youth he learned, and even to his old age serve him for hourly lessons? But the fitness it hath for memory is notably proved by all delivery of Arts: wherein for the most part, from Grammar to Logic, Mathematic, Physic, and the rest, the rules chiefly necessary to be borne away are compiled in verses. So that, verse being in itself sweet and orderly, and being best for memory, the only handle of knowledge, it

---

[32] See note 8, above. Scaliger states that the word "poet" is derived not from making imaginative inventions but from making verses (*Poetice*, 1, 2).

must be in jest that any man can speak against it. Now then go we to the most important imputations laid to the poor poets. For aught I can yet learn, they are these. First, that there being many other more fruitful knowledges, a man might better spend his time in them than in this. Secondly, that it is the mother of lies. Thirdly, that it is the nurse of abuse, infecting us with many pestilent desires, with a siren's sweetness drawing the mind to the serpent's tale of sinful fancy,—and herein, especially, comedies give the largest field to ear (as Chaucer saith),—how both in other nations and in ours, before poets did soften us, we were full of courage, given to martial exercises, the pillars of manlike liberty, and not lulled asleep in shady idleness with poets' pastimes. And lastly, and chiefly, they cry out with an open mouth, as if they outshot Robin Hood, that Plato banished them out of his Commonwealth.[33] Truly, this is much, if there be much truth in it. First, to the first, that a man might better spend his time is a reason indeed: but it doth (as they say) but *petere principium:* [34] for if it be, as I affirm, that no learning is so good as that which teacheth and moveth to virtue, and that none can both teach and move thereto so much as Poetry, then is the conclusion manifest that ink and paper cannot be to a more profitable purpose employed. And certainly, though a man should grant their first assumption, it should follow (methinks) very unwillingly, that good is not good because better is better. But I still and utterly deny that there is sprung out of earth a more fruitful knowledge. To the second therefore, that they should be the principal liars, I answer paradoxically, but truly, I think truly, that of all writers under the sun the poet is the least liar, and, though he would, as a poet can scarcely be a liar. The astronomer, with his cousin the geometrician, can hardly escape, when they take upon them to measure the height of the stars.

How often, think you, do the physicians lie, when they aver things good for sicknesses, which afterwards send Charon a great number of souls drowned in a potion before they come to his ferry? And no less of the rest, which take upon them to affirm. Now, for the poet, he nothing affirms, and therefore never lieth. For, as I take it, to lie is to affirm that to be true which is false; so as the other artists, and especially the historian, affirming many things, can, in the cloudy knowledge of mankind, hardly escape from many lies. But the poet (as I said before) never affirmeth. The poet never maketh any circles about your imagination, to conjure you to believe for true what he writes. He citeth not authorities of other histories, but even for his entry calleth the sweet Muses to inspire into him a good invention; in truth, not labouring to tell you what is, or is not, but what should or should not be. And therefore, though he recount things not true, yet because he telleth them not for true, he lieth not,—without we will say that Nathan lied in his speech, before alleged, to David; which as a wicked man durst scarce say, so think I none so simple would say that Aesop lied in the tales of his beasts: for who thinks that Aesop writ it for actually true were well worthy to have his name chronicled among the beasts he writeth of.

What child is there that, coming to a play, and seeing *Thebes* written in great letters upon an old door, doth believe that it is Thebes? If then a man can arrive, at that child's age, to know that the poets' persons and doings are but pictures what should be, and not stories what have been, they will never give the lie to things not affirmatively but allegorically and figuratively written. And therefore, as in History, looking for truth, they go away full fraught with falsehood, so in Poesy, looking for fiction, they shall use the narration but as an imaginative ground-plot of a profitable invention.

But hereto is replied, that the poets give names to men they write of, which argueth a conceit of an actual truth, and so, not being true, proves a falsehood. And doth the lawyer lie then, when under the names of "John a Stile" and "John a Noakes" he puts his case? But that is easily answered. Their naming of men is but to make their picture the more lively, and not to build any history; painting men, they cannot leave men nameless. We see we cannot play at chess but that we must give names to our chessmen; and yet, methinks, he were a very partial champion of truth that would say we lied for giving a piece of wood the reverend title of a bishop.

[33] See above, p. 47.
[34] "Beg the question."

The poet nameth Cyrus or Aeneas no other way than to show what men of their fames, fortunes, and estates should do.

Their third is, how much it abuseth men's wit, training it to wanton sinfulness and lustful love: for indeed that is the principal, if not the only, abuse I can hear alleged. They say the Comedies rather teach than reprehend amorous conceits. They say the Lyric is larded with passionate sonnets, the Elegiac weeps the want of his mistress, and that even to the Heroical Cupid hath ambitiously climbed. Alas, Love, I would thou couldst as well defend thyself as thou canst offend others. I would those on whom thou dost attend could either put thee away, or yield good reason why they keep thee. But grant love of beauty to be a beastly fault (although it be very hard, since only man, and no beast, hath that gift to discern beauty); grant that lovely name of Love to deserve all hateful reproaches (although even some of my masters the philosophers spent a good deal of their lamp-oil in setting forth the excellency of it); grant, I say, whatsoever they will have granted; that not only love, but lust, but vanity, but (if they list) scurrility, possesseth many leaves of the poets' books: yet think I, when this is granted, they will find their sentence may with good manners put the last words foremost, and not say that Poetry abuseth man's wit, but that man's wit abuseth Poetry.

For I will not deny but that man's wit may make Poesy, which should be *Eikastike*, which some learned have defined, "figuring forth good things," to be *Phantastike*, which doth, contrariwise, infect the fancy with unworthy objects, as the painter, that should give to the eye either some excellent perspective, or some fine picture, fit for building or fortification, or containing in it some notable example, as Abraham sacrificing his son Isaac, Judith killing Holofernes, David fighting with Goliath, may leave those, and please an ill-pleased eye with wanton shows of better hidden matters. But what, shall the abuse of a thing make the right use odious? Nay truly, though I yield that Poesy may not only be abused, but that being abused, by the reason of his sweet charming force, it can do more hurt than any other army of words, yet shall it be so far from concluding that the abuse should give reproach to the abused, that contrariwise it is a

good reason, that whatsoever, being abused, doth most harm, being rightly used (and upon the right use each thing conceiveth his title), doth most good.

Do we not see the skill of Physic (the best rampire to our often-assaulted bodies), being abused, teach poison, the most violent destroyer? Doth not knowledge of Law, whose end is to even and right all things, being abused, grow the crooked fosterer of horrible injuries? Doth not (to go to the highest) God's word abused breed heresy, and His Name abused become blasphemy? Truly, a needle cannot do much hurt, and as truly (with leave of ladies be it spoken) it cannot do much good. With a sword thou mayest kill thy father, and with a sword thou mayest defend thy prince and country. So that, as in their calling poets the fathers of lies they say nothing, so in this their argument of abuse they prove the commendation.

They allege herewith, that before poets began to be in price our nation hath set their heart's delight upon action, and not upon imagination, rather doing things worthy to be written, than writing things fit to be done. What that beforetime was, I think scarcely Sphinx can tell, since no memory is so ancient that hath the precedence of Poetry. And certain it is that, in our plainest homeliness, yet never was the Albion nation without Poetry. Marry, this argument, though it be levelled against Poetry, yet is it indeed a chain-shot against all learning, or bookishness, as they commonly term it. Of such mind were certain Goths, of whom it is written that, having in the spoil of a famous city taken a fair library, one hangman, belike, fit to execute the fruits of their wits, who had murdered a great number of bodies, would have set fire on it. "No," said another very gravely, "take heed what you do, for while they are busy about these toys, we shall with more leisure conquer their countries."

This indeed is the ordinary doctrine of ignorance, and many words sometimes I have heard spent in it: but because this reason is generally against all learning, as well as Poetry, or rather, all learning but Poetry; because it were too large a digression to handle, or at least too superfluous (since it is manifest that all government of action is to be gotten by knowledge, and knowledge best by gathering many knowledges, which is reading), I only, with Horace, to him that is of that opinion,

Iubeo stultum esse libenter; [35]

for as for Poetry itself, it is the freest from this objection. For Poetry is the companion of the camps.

I dare undertake, Orlando Furioso, or honest King Arthur, will never displease a soldier: but the quiddity of *Ens* and *Prima materia* will hardly agree with a corslet. And therefore, as I said in the beginning, even Turks and Tartars are delighted with poets. Homer, a Greek, flourished before Greece flourished. And if to a slight conjecture a conjecture may be opposed, truly it may seem, that, as by him their learned men took almost their first light of knowledge, so their active men received their first motions of courage. Only Alexander's example may serve, who by Plutarch is accounted of such virtue, that Fortune was not his guide but his footstool; whose acts speak for him, though Plutarch did not,—indeed the Phoenix of warlike princes. This Alexander left his schoolmaster, living Aristotle, behind him, but took dead Homer with him. He put the philosopher Callisthenes to death for his seeming philosophical, indeed mutinous, stubbornness, but the chief thing he ever was heard to wish for was that Homer had been alive. He well found he received more bravery of mind by the pattern of Achilles than by hearing the definition of fortitude: and therefore, if Cato misliked Fulvius for carrying Ennius with him to the field, it may be answered that, if Cato misliked it, the noble Fulvius liked it, or else he had not done it: for it was not the excellent Cato Uticensis (whose authority I would much more have reverenced), but it was the former, in truth a bitter punisher of faults, but else a man that had never well sacrificed to the Graces. He misliked and cried out upon all Greek learning, and yet, being 80 years old, began to learn it, belike fearing that Pluto understood not Latin. Indeed, the Roman laws allowed no person to be carried to the wars but he that was in the soldier's roll, and therefore, though Cato misliked his unmustered person, he misliked not his work. And if he had, Scipio Nasica, judged by common consent

the best Roman, loved him. Both the other Scipio brothers, who had by their virtues no less surnames than of Asia and Afric, so loved him that they caused his body to be buried in their sepulchre. So as Cato's authority being but against his person, and that answered with so far greater than himself, is herein of no validity. But now indeed my burden is great; now Plato's name is laid upon me, whom, I must confess, of all philosophers I have ever esteemed most worthy of reverence, and with great reason, since of all philosophers he is the most poetical. Yet if he will defile the fountain out of which his flowing streams have proceeded, let us boldly examine with what reasons he did it. First truly, a man might maliciously object that Plato, being a philosopher, was a natural enemy of poets. For indeed, after the philosophers had picked out of the sweet mysteries of Poetry the right discerning true points of knowledge, they forthwith, putting it in method, and making a school art of that which the poets did only teach by a divine delightfulness, beginning to spurn at their guides, like ungrateful prentices, were not content to set up shops for themselves, but sought by all means to discredit their masters; which by the force of delight being barred them, the less they could overthrow them, the more they hated them. For indeed, they found for Homer seven cities strove who should have him for their citizen; where many cities banished philosophers as not fit members to live among them. For only repeating certain of Euripides' verses, many Athenians had their lives saved of the Syracusians, when the Athenians themselves thought many philosophers unworthy to live.

Certain poets, as Simonides and Pindarus, had so prevailed with Hiero the First, that of a tyrant they made him a just king; where Plato could do so little with Dionysius, that he himself of a philosopher was made a slave. But who should do thus, I confess, should requite the objections made against poets with like cavillation against philosophers; as likewise one should do that should bid one read Phaedrus or Symposium in Plato, or the discourse of love in Plutarch, and see whether any poet do authorize abominable filthiness, as they do. Again, a man might ask out of what Commonwealth Plato did banish them. In sooth, thence where he himself alloweth community of women. So as belike this banish-

---

[35] "I ask him to be as much of a fool as he wishes" (*Satires*, I, 1, 63).

ment grew not for effeminate wantonness, since little should poetical sonnets be hurtful when a man might have what woman he listed. But I honour philosophical instructions, and bless the wits which bred them: so as they be not abused, which is likewise stretched to Poetry.

St. Paul himself, who yet, for the credit of poets, allegeth twice two poets, and one of them by the name of a prophet, setteth a watchword upon Philosophy,—indeed upon the abuse. So doth Plato upon the abuse, not upon Poetry. Plato found fault that the poets of his time filled the world with wrong opinions of the gods, making light tales of that unspotted essence, and therefore would not have the youth depraved with such opinions. Herein may much be said; let this suffice: the poets did not induce such opinions, but did imitate those opinions already induced. For all the Greek stories can well testify that the very religion of that time stood upon many and many-fashioned gods, not taught so by the poets, but followed according to their nature of imitation. Who list may read in Plutarch the discourses of Isis and Osiris, of the cause why oracles ceased, of the divine providence, and see whether the theology of that nation stood not upon such dreams which the poets indeed superstitiously observed, and truly (since they had not the light of Christ) did much better in it than the philosophers, who, shaking off superstition, brought in atheism. Plato therefore (whose authority I had much rather justly construe than unjustly resist) meant not in general of poets, in those words of which Julius Scaliger saith, *Qua authoritate barbari quidam atque hispidi abuti velint ad poetas e republica exigendos;* [36] but only meant to drive out those wrong opinions of the Deity (whereof now, without further law, Christianity hath taken away all the hurtful belief), perchance (as he thought) nourished by the then esteemed poets. And a man need go no further than to Plato himself to know his meaning: who, in his Dialogue called *Ion,* giveth high and rightly divine commendation to Poetry. So as Plato, banishing the abuse, not the thing, not banishing it, but giving due honour unto it, shall be our patron and not our adversary. For indeed I had much rather

[36] "The rude and barbarous would abuse such an authority in order to drive the poets out of the state" (*Poetice,* 1, 2).

(since truly I may do it) show their mistaking of Plato (under whose lion's skin they would make an ass-like braying against Poesy) than go about to overthrow his authority; whom, the wiser a man is, the more just cause he shall find to have in admiration; especially since he attributeth unto Poesy more than myself do, namely, to be a very inspiring of a divine force, far above man's wit, as in the afore-named Dialogue is apparent.

Of the other side, who would show the honours have been by the best sort of judgements granted them, a whole sea of examples would present themselves: Alexanders, Caesars, Scipios, all favourers of poets; Laelius, called the Roman Socrates, himself a poet, so as part of *Heautontimorumenos* in Terence was supposed to be made by him, and even the Greek Socrates, whom Apollo confirmed to be the only wise man, is said to have spent part of his old time in putting Aesop's fables into verses. And therefore, full evil should it become his scholar Plato to put such words in his master's mouth against poets. But what need more? Aristotle writes the Art of Poesy: and why, if it should not be written? Plutarch teacheth the use to be gathered of them, and how, if they should not be read? And who reads Plutarch's either history or philosophy, shall find he trimmeth both their garments with guards of Poesy. But I list not to defend Poesy with the help of her underling Historiography. Let it suffice that it is a fit soil for praise to dwell upon; and what dispraise may set upon it, is either easily overcome, or transformed into just commendation. So that, since the excellencies of it may be so easily and so justly confirmed, and the low-creeping objections so soon trodden down; it not being an art of lies, but oft true doctrine; not of effeminateness, but of notable stirring of courage; not of abusing man's wit, but of strengthening man's wit; not banished, but honoured by Plato; let us rather plant more laurels for to engarland our poets' heads (which honour of being laureate, as besides them only triumphant captains wear, is a sufficient authority to show the price they ought to be had in) than suffer the ill-favouring breath of such wrong-speakers once to blow upon the clear springs of Poesy.

But since I have run so long a career in this matter, methinks, before I give my pen a full stop, it shall be but a little more lost time to inquire why England (the mother of excellent minds) should be grown so hard a stepmother to poets, who certainly in wit ought to pass all other, since all only proceedeth from their wit, being indeed makers of themselves, not takers of others. How can I but exclaim,

Musa, mihi causas memora, quo numine laeso! [37]

Sweet Poesy, that hath anciently had kings, emperors, senators, great captains, such as, besides a thousand others, David, Adrian, Sophocles, Germanicus, not only to favour poets, but to be poets; and of our nearer times can present for her patrons a Robert, king of Sicily, the great King Francis of France, King James of Scotland; such cardinals as Bembus and Bibbiena: such famous preachers and teachers as Beza and Melancthon; so learned philosophers as Fracastorius and Scaliger; so great orators as Pontanus and Muretus; so piercing wits as George Buchanan; so grave counsellors as, besides many, but before all, that Hospital of France, than whom (I think) that realm never brought forth a more accomplished judgement, more firmly builded upon virtue—I say these, with numbers of others, not only to read others' poesies, but to poetize for others' reading—that Poesy, thus embraced in all other places, should only find in our time a hard welcome in England, I think the very earth lamenteth it, and therefore decketh our soil with fewer laurels than it was accustomed. For heretofore poets have in England also flourished, and, which is to be noted, even in those times when the trumpet of Mars did sound loudest. And now that an overfaint quietness should seem to strew the house for poets, they are almost in as good reputation as the mountebanks at Venice. Truly even that, as of the one side it giveth great praise to Poesy, which like Venus (but to better purpose) hath rather be troubled in the net with Mars than enjoy the homely quiet of Vulcan; so serves it for a piece of a reason why they are less grateful to idle England, which now can scarce endure the pain of a pen. Upon this necessarily followeth, that base men with servile wits undertake it, who think it enough if they can be rewarded of the printer. And so as Epaminondas is said, with the honour of his virtue, to have made an office, by his exercising it, which before was contemptible, to become highly respected, so these, no more but setting their names to it, by their own disgracefulness disgrace the most graceful Poesy. For now, as if all the Muses were got with child, to bring forth bastard poets, without any commission they do post over the banks of Helicon, till they make the readers more weary than posthorses, while, in the meantime, they,

Queis meliore luto finxit praecordia Titan, [38]

are better content to suppress the outflowing of their wit, than, by publishing them, to be accounted knights of the same order. But I that, before ever I durst aspire unto the dignity, am admitted into the company of the paper-blurrers, do find the very true cause of our wanting estimation is want of desert, taking upon us to be poets in despite of Pallas. Now, wherein we want desert were a thankworthy labour to express: but if I knew, I should have mended myself. But I, as I never desired the title, so have I neglected the means to come by it. Only, overmastered by some thoughts, I yielded an inky tribute unto them. Marry, they that delight in Poesy itself should seek to know what they do, and how they do, and, especially, look themselves in an unflattering glass of reason, if they be inclinable unto it. For Poesy must not be drawn by the ears; it must be gently led, or rather it must lead; which was partly the cause that made the ancient-learned affirm it was a divine gift, and no human skill; since all other knowledges lie ready for any that hath strength of wit; a poet no industry can make, if his own genius be not carried unto it; and therefore is it an old proverb, *Orator fit, Poeta nascitur.* [39] Yet confess I always that as the fertilest ground must be manured, so must the highest-flying wit have a Daedalus to guide him. That Daedalus, they say, both in this and in other, hath three wings to bear itself up into the air of due commendation: that is, Art, Imitation, and Exercise. But these, neither artificial rules nor imitative patterns, we much cumber ourselves withal. Exercise indeed we do, but that very fore-backwardly: for where

[37] "Tell me, O Muse, in what way was her divinity being injured?" (*Aeneid*, I, 8.)

[38] "Whose hearts Titan has fashioned of finer clay" (Juvenal, *Satires*, XIV, 35).

[39] "The orator is made, the poet is born."

we should exercise to know, we exercise as having known: and so is our brain delivered of much matter which never was begotten by knowledge. For, there being two principal parts—matter to be expressed by words and words to express the matter—in neither we use Art or Imitation rightly. Our matter is *Quodlibet* indeed, though wrongly performing Ovid's verse,

> *Quicquid conabar dicere, versus erat:* [40]

never marshalling it into an assured rank, that almost the readers cannot tell where to find themselves.

Chaucer, undoubtedly, did excellently in his *Troilus and Cressida;* of whom, truly, I know not whether to marvel more, either that he in that misty time could see so clearly, or that we in this clear age walk so stumblingly after him. Yet had he great wants, fit to be forgiven in so reverent antiquity. I account the *Mirrour of Magistrates* meetly furnished of beautiful parts, and in the Earl of Surrey's *Lyrics* many things tasting of a noble birth, and worthy of a noble mind. The *Shepheard's Calendar* hath much poetry in his Eclogues, indeed worthy the reading, if I be not deceived. That same framing of his style to an old rustic language I dare not allow, since neither Theocritus in Greek, Virgil in Latin, nor Sannazzaro in Italian did affect it. Besides these, do I not remember to have seen but few (to speak boldly) printed, that have poetical sinews in them: for proof whereof, let but most of the verses be put in prose, and then ask the meaning; and it will be found that one verse did but beget another, without ordering at the first what should be at the last; which becomes a confused mass of words, with a tingling sound of rhyme, barely accompanied with reason.

Our Tragedies and Comedies (not without cause cried out against), observing rules neither of honest civility nor of skilful Poetry, excepting *Gorboduc* (again, I say, of those that I have seen), which notwithstanding, as it is full of stately speeches and well-sounding phrases, climbing to the height of Seneca's style, and as full of notable morality, which it doth most delightfully teach, and so obtain the very end of Poesy, yet in truth it is very defectious in the circumstances,

which grieveth me, because it might not remain as an exact model of all Tragedies. For it is faulty both in place and time,[41] the two necessary companions of all corporal actions. For where the stage should always represent but one place, and the uttermost time presupposed in it should be, both by Aristotle's precept and common reason, but one day, there is both many days, and many places, inartificially imagined. But if it be so in *Gorboduc,* how much more in all the rest, where you shall have Asia of the one side, and Afric of the other, and so many other under-kingdoms, that the player, when he cometh in, must ever begin with telling where he is, or else the tale will not be conceived? Now ye shall have three ladies walk to gather flowers and then we must believe the stage to be a garden. By and by we hear news of shipwreck in the same place, and then we are to blame if we accept it not for a rock.

Upon the back of that comes out a hideous monster, with fire and smoke, and then the miserable beholders are bound to take it for a cave. While in the meantime two armies fly in, represented with four swords and bucklers, and then what hard heart will not receive it for a pitched field? Now, of time they are much more liberal, for ordinary it is that two young princes fall in love. After many traverses, she is got with child, delivered of a fair boy; he is lost, groweth a man, falls in love, and is ready to get another child; and all this in two hours' space: which, how absurd it is in sense, even sense may imagine, and Art hath taught, and all ancient examples justified, and, at this day, the ordinary players in Italy will not err in. Yet will some bring in an example of Eunuchus in Terence,[42] that containeth matter of two days, yet far short of twenty years. True it is, and so was it to be played in two days, and so fitted to the time it set forth. And though Plautus hath in one place done amiss, let us hit with him, and not miss with him. But they will say, How then shall we set forth a story, which containeth both many places and many times? And do they not know that a Trag-

---

[40] "Whatever I tried to say was verse" (*Tristia,* IV,

[41] That is, it fails to abide by the unities of time and place. See above, p. 9. Here and in succeeding passages, Sidney is closely following the neoclassic precepts of sixteenth-century Italian critics.

[42] The *Heautontimorumenos* (or *Self-Punisher*) of Terence, not the *Eunuchus.*

edy is tied to the laws of Poesy, and not of History; not bound to follow the story, but, having liberty, either to feign a quite new matter, or to frame the history to the most tragical conveniency? Again, many things may be told which cannot be showed, if they know the difference betwixt reporting and representing. As, for example, I may speak (though I am here) of Peru, and in speech digress from that to the description of Calicut; but in action I cannot represent it without Pacolet's horse. And so was the manner the ancients took, by some Nuncius [43] to recount things done in former time or other place. Lastly, if they will represent an history, they must not (as Horace saith) begin *ab ovo*,[44] but they must come to the principal point of that one action which they will represent. By example this will be best expressed. I have a story of young Polydorus, delivered for safety's sake, with great riches, by his father Priam to Polymnestor, king of Thrace, in the Trojan war time. He, after same years, hearing the overthrow of Priam, for to make the treasure his own, murdereth the child. The body of the child is taken up by Hecuba. She, the same day, findeth a slight to be revenged most cruelly of the tyrant. Where now would one of our tragedy writers begin, but with the delivery of the child? Then should he sail over into Thrace, and so spend I know not how many years, and travel numbers of places. But where doth Euripides? Even with the finding of the body, leaving the rest to be told by the spirit of Polydorus. This need no further to be enlarged; the dullest wit may conceive it. But besides these gross absurdities, how all their plays be neither right tragedies, nor right comedies, mingling kings and clowns, not because the matter so carrieth it, but thrust in clowns by head and shoulders, to play a part in majestical matters, with neither decency [45] nor discretion, so as neither the admiration and commiseration, nor the right sportfulness, is by their mongrel tragi-comedy obtained. I know Apuleius did somewhat so, but that is a thing recounted with space of time, not represented in one moment: and I know the ancients have one or two examples of tragi-comedies, as

Plautus hath *Amphitrio*. But, if we mark them well, we shall find, that they never, or very daintily, match hornpipes and funerals. So falleth it out that, having indeed no right comedy, in that comical part of our tragedy we have nothing but scurrility, unworthy of any chaste ears, or some extreme show of doltishness, indeed fit to lift up a loud laughter, and nothing else: where the whole tract of a comedy should be full of delight, as the tragedy should be still maintained in a well-raised admiration. But our comedians think there is no delight without laughter; which is very wrong, for though laughter may come with delight, yet cometh it not of delight, as though delight should be the cause of laughter; but well may one thing breed both together. Nay, rather in themselves they have, as it were, a kind of contrariety: for delight we scarcely do but in things that have a conveniency to ourselves or to the general nature: laughter almost ever cometh of things most disproportioned to ourselves and nature. Delight hath a joy in it, either permanent or present. Laughter hath only a scornful tickling.

For example, we are ravished with delight to see a fair woman, and yet are far from being moved to laughter. We laugh at deformed creatures, wherein certainly we cannot delight. We delight in good chances, we laugh at mischances; we delight to hear the happiness of our friends, or country, at which he were worthy to be laughed at that would laugh. We shall, contrarily, laugh sometimes to find a matter quite mistaken and go down the hill against the bias, in the mouth of some such men, as for the respect of them one shall be heartily sorry, yet he cannot choose but laugh; and so is rather pained than delighted with laughter. Yet deny I not but that they may go well together. For as in Alexander's picture well set out we delight without laughter, and in twenty mad antics we laugh without delight, so in Hercules, painted with his great beard and furious countenance, in woman's attire, spinning at Omphale's commandment, it breedeth both delight and laughter. For the representing of so strange a power in love procureth delight: and the scornfulness of the action stirreth laughter. But I speak to this purpose, that all the end of the comical part be not upon such scornful matters as stirreth laughter only, but, mixed with it, that delightful teaching which is

[43] Messenger.

[44] From the egg (or beginning); *Art of Poetry*, l. 147, above, p. 53.

[45] Decorum (what is suitable or fitting).

the end of Poesy. And the great fault even in that point of laughter, and forbidden plainly by Aristotle,[46] is that they stir laughter in sinful things, which are rather execrable than ridiculous; or in miserable, which are rather to be pitied than scorned. For what is it to make folks gape at a wretched beggar, or a beggarly clown; or, against the law of hospitality, to jest at strangers, because they speak not English so well as we do? What do we learn, since it is certain

Nil habet infelix paupertas durius in se,
Quam quod ridiculos homines facit? [47]

But rather a busy loving courtier, a heartless threatening Thraso, a self-wise-seeming schoolmaster, an awry-transformed traveller—these if we saw walk in stage names, which we play naturally, therein were delightful laughter, and teaching delightfulness: as in the other, the tragedies of Buchanan do justly bring forth a divine admiration. But I have lavished out too many words of this play matter. I do it because, as they are excelling parts of Poesy, so is there none so much used in England, and none can be more pitifully abused; which, like an unmannerly daughter showing a bad education, causeth her mother Poesy's honesty to be called in question. Other sorts of Poetry almost have we none, but that lyrical kind of songs and sonnets: which, Lord, if He gave us so good minds, how well it might be employed, and with how heavenly fruit, both private and public, in singing the praises of the immortal beauty, the immortal goodness of that God who giveth us hands to write and wits to conceive; of which we might well want words, but never matter; of which we could turn our eyes to nothing, but we should ever have new budding occasions. But truly many of such writings as come under the banner of unresistible love, if I were a mistress, would never persuade me they were in love; so coldly they apply fiery speeches, as men that had rather read lovers' writings, and so caught up certain swelling phrases (which hang together like a man which once told me the wind was at north-west, and by south, because he would be sure to name winds enough), than that in truth they feel those passions, which easily (as I

think) may be betrayed by that same forcibleness or *Energia* (as the Greeks call it) of the writer. But let this be a sufficient though short note, that we miss the right use of the material point of Poesy.

Now, for the outside of it, which is words, or (as I may term it) Diction, it is even well worse. So is that honey-flowing matron Eloquence apparelled, or rather disguised, in a courtesan-like painted affectation: one time with so far-fetched words, they may seem monsters, but must seem strangers, to any poor Englishman; another time, with coursing of a letter, as if they were bound to follow the method of a dictionary; another time, with figures and flowers, extremely winter-starved. But I would this fault were only peculiar to versifiers, and had not as large possession among prose-printers, and (which is to be marvelled) among many scholars, and (which is to be pitied) among some preachers. Truly I could wish, if at least I might be so bold to wish in a thing beyond the reach of my capacity, the diligent imitators of Tully and Demosthenes (most worthy to be imitated) did not so much keep Nizolian paper-books of their figures and phrases, as by attentive translation (as it were) devour them whole, and make them wholly theirs. For now they cast sugar and spice upon every dish that is served to the table, like those Indians, not content to wear earrings at the fit and natural place of the ears, but they will thrust jewels through their nose and lips, because they will be sure to be fine.

Tully, when he was to drive out Catiline, as it were with a thunderbolt of eloquence, often used that figure of repetition, *Vivit. Vivit? Imo in Senatum venit,* &c.[48] Indeed, inflamed with a well-grounded rage, he would have his words (as it were) double out of his mouth, and so do that artificially which we see men do in choler naturally. And we, having noted the grace of those words, hale them in sometime to a familiar epistle, when it were too much choler to be choleric. Now for similitudes in certain printed discourses, I think all Herberists, all stories of beasts, fowls, and fishes are rifled up, that they come in multitudes to wait upon any of our conceits; which certainly is as absurd a surfeit to the ears as is possible: for the force of a similitude

---

[46] *Poetics*, V, above, p. 22.

[47] "Unhappy poverty has nothing worse than that it makes men ridiculous" (Juvenal, *Satires*, III, 152-153).

[48] "He lives. Lives?—He even comes into the senate."

not being to prove anything to a contrary disputer, but only to explain to a willing hearer; when that is done, the rest is a most tedious prattling, rather over-swaying the memory from the purpose whereto they were applied, than any whit informing the judgment, already either satisfied, or by similitudes not to be satisfied. For my part, I do not doubt, when Antonius and Crassus, the great forefathers of Cicero in eloquence, the one (as Cicero testifieth of them) pretended not to know art, the other not to set by it, because with a plain sensibleness they might win credit of popular ears; which credit is the nearest step to persuasion; which persuasion is the chief mark of Oratory—I do not doubt (I say) that but they used these knacks very sparingly; which, who doth generally use, any man may see doth dance to his own music; and so be noted by the audience more careful to speak curiously than to speak truly.

Undoubtedly (at least to my opinion undoubtedly) I have found in divers small-learned courtiers a more sound style than in some professors of learning: of which I can guess no other cause, but that the courtier, following that which by practice he findeth fittest to nature, therein (though he know it not) doth according to Art, though not by Art: where the other, using Art to show Art, and not to hide Art (as in these cases he should do), flieth from nature, and indeed abuseth Art.

But what? Methinks I deserve to be pounded for straying from Poetry to Oratory: but both have such an affinity in this wordish consideration, that I think this digression will make my meaning receive the fuller understanding—which is not to take upon me to teach poets how they should do, but only, finding myself sick among the rest, to show some one or two spots of the common infection grown among the most part of writers: that, acknowledging ourselves somewhat awry, we may bend to the right use both of matter and manner; whereto our language giveth us great occasion, being indeed capable of any excellent exercising of it. I know some will say it is a mingled language. And why not so much the better, taking the best of both the other? Another will say it wanteth grammar. Nay truly, it hath that praise, that it wanteth grammar: for grammar it might have, but it needs it not; being so easy of itself, and so void of those cumbersome differences of cases, genders, moods, and tenses, which I think was a piece of the Tower of Babylon's curse, that a man should be put to school to learn his mother-tongue.[49] But for the uttering sweetly and properly the conceits of the mind, which is the end of speech, that hath it equally with any other tongue in the world: and is particularly happy in compositions of two or three words together, near the Greek, far beyond the Latin: which is one of the greatest beauties can be in a language.

Now, of versifying there are two sorts, the one ancient, the other modern: the ancient marked the quantity of each syllable, and according to that framed his verse; the modern observing only number (with some regard of the accent), the chief life of it standeth in that like sounding of the words, which we call rhyme. Whether of these be the most excellent, would bear many speeches. The ancient (no doubt) more fit for music, both words and tune observing quantity, and more fit lively to express divers passions, by the low and lofty sound of the well-weighed syllable. The latter likewise, with his rhyme, striketh a certain music to the ear: and, in fine, since it doth delight, though by another way, it obtains the same purpose: there being in either sweetness, and wanting in neither majesty. Truly the English, before any other vulgar language I know, is fit for both sorts: for, for the ancient, the Italian is so full of vowels that it must ever be cumbered with elisions; the Dutch so, of the other side, with consonants, that they cannot yield the sweet sliding fit for a verse; the French, in his whole language, hath not one word that hath his accent in the last syllable saving two, called *Antepenultima;* and little more hath the Spanish: and, therefore, very gracelessly may they use dactyls. The English is subject to none of these defects.

Now, for the rhyme, though we do not observe quantity, yet we observe the accent very precisely: which other languages either cannot do, or will not do so absolutely. That *caesura,* or breathing place in the midst of the verse, neither Italian nor Spanish have, the French, and we,

[49] Sidney's defense of English instead of Latin as the proper language for English writers is one of the notable Renaissance statements on behalf of the vernacular. See above, p. 8.

never almost fail of. Lastly, even the very rhyme itself the Italian cannot put in the last syllable, by the French named the "masculine rhyme," but still in the next to the last, which the French call the "female," or the next before that, which the Italians term *sdrucciola*. The example of the former is *buono : suono*, of the *sdrucciola*, *femina : semina*. The French, of the other side, hath both the male, as *bon : son*, and the female, as *plaise : taise*, but the *sdrucciola* he hath not: where the English hath all three, as *due : true*, *father : rather*, *motion : potion*, with much more which might be said, but that I find already the triflingness of this discourse is much too much enlarged. So that since the ever-praiseworthy Poesy is full of virtue-breeding delightfulness, and void of no gift that ought to be in the noble name of learning; since the blames laid against it are either false or feeble; since the cause why it is not esteemed in England is the fault of poet-apes, not poets; since, lastly, our tongue is most fit to honour Poesy, and to be honoured by Poesy; I conjure you all that have had the evil luck to read this ink-wasting toy of mine, even in the name of the Nine Muses, no more to scorn the sacred mysteries of Poesy, no more to laugh at the name of "poets," as though they were next inheritors to fools, no more to jest at the reverent title of a "rhymer"; but to believe, with Aristotle, that they were the ancient treasurers of the Grecians' Divinity; to believe, with Bembus, that they were first bringers-in of all civility; to believe, with Scaliger, that no philosopher's precepts can sooner make you an honest man than the reading of Virgil; to believe, with Clauserus, the translator of Cornutus, that it pleased the heavenly Deity, by Hesiod and Homer, under the veil of fables, to give us all knowledge, Logic, Rhetoric, Philosophy, natural and moral, and *Quid non?*;[50] to

believe, with me, that there are many mysteries contained in Poetry, which of purpose were written darkly, lest by profane wits it should be abused; to believe, with Landino, that they are so beloved of the gods that whatsoever they write proceeds of a divine fury; lastly, to believe themselves, when they tell you they will make you immortal by their verses.

Thus doing, your name shall flourish in the printers' shops; thus doing, you shall be of kin to many a poetical preface; thus doing, you shall be most fair, most rich, most wise, most all; you shall dwell upon superlatives. Thus doing, though you be *libertino patre natus*, you shall suddenly grow *Herculea proles*,

Si quid mea carmina possunt.[51]

Thus doing, your soul shall be placed with Dante's Beatrix, or Virgil's Anchises. But if (fie of such a but) you be born so near the dull-making cataract of Nilus that you cannot hear the planet-like music of Poetry, if you have so earth-creeping a mind that it cannot lift itself up to look to the sky of Poetry, or rather, by a certain rustical disdain, will become such a Mome as to be a Momus of Poetry; then, though I will not wish unto you the ass's ears of Midas, nor to be driven by a poet's verses (as Bubonax was) to hang himself, nor to be rhymed to death, as is said to be done in Ireland; yet thus much curse I must send you, in the behalf of all poets, that while you live, you live in love, and never get favour for lacking skill of a Sonnet, and, when you die, your memory die from the earth for want of an Epitaph.

---

[50] "What not?"

[51] The whole sentence may be rendered, "Thus doing, though you be the son of a former slave, you shall suddenly grow Herculean offspring, if my poems are able to do anything." The Latin phrases are, in order, from Horace, Ovid, and Virgil.

SAMUEL DANIEL   (1563-1619)

D ANIEL'S *Defence of Rhyme* (published between 1602 and 1607) illustrates one of the ways in which the Renaissance, in attempting to
rival classical antiquity, asserted its own independence. But in seeking to attain its own ends the Renaissance also did not neglect to imitate
the ancients directly, often with great profit. One of the less profitable imitations, however, was the attempt to introduce into English, after the classical
model, quantitative instead of accentual verse. A by-product of this attempt
was a tendency to disparage the nonclassical device of rhyme. By the time
of Daniel's *Defence,* quantitative verse had been an issue in England for
more than half a century. Movements to introduce a quantitative versification
in Italy had been followed in England by Thomas Watson (between 1540
and 1550), who regarded rhyme as a barbaric invention of the Middle
Ages. In 1580, letters between Spenser and Gabriel Harvey reveal that a
more deliberate attempt was being made to establish quantitative meter in
English. There were extremists as well as moderates, like Harvey himself.
Other writers included Richard Stanyhurst, who translated part of the *Aeneid*
(1582); William Webbe, in his *Discourse of English Poetry* (1586); and
especially Thomas Campion, whose *Observations on the Art of English
Poesy* (1603) was the immediate provocation of Daniel's reply.
especially Thomas Campion, whose *Observations on the Art of English
Poesy* (1602) was the immediate provocation of Daniel's reply.

In defending the use of rhyme, Daniel is stating, in effect, that the practice of classical antiquity should not be taken as the sole standard or criterion. But Daniel's thesis nonetheless rests upon a classical premise—a
confidence in the value of what has traditionally persisted and has therefore
secured, as he says, the "approbation of many ages." For Daniel cites the
use of rhyme by various peoples at different times. In doing so, he comes
closer than any other critic of his day to using a historical approach to the
study of poetry.

SAMUEL DANIEL. Daniel entered Magdalen Hall, Oxford (1581), but left without taking a degree,
visited Italy, and served as tutor to William Herbert, third Earl of Pembroke. He published his
sonnets, *Delia* (1592), some plays, and the *Civil Wars* (1595) and, as Master of the Queen's
Revels, composed masques for the court.
    Editions include the *Complete Works* (ed. A. B. Grosart, 5 vols., 1885-96), and *Poems and a
Defense of Ryme* (ed. A. C. Sprague, Cambridge, Mass., 1930). For commentary on the general
background, see J. E. Spingarn, *Literary Criticism in the Renaissance* (1899). For more specific
analysis, see Joan Rees, *Samuel Daniel: a Critical and Biographical Study* (Liverpool, 1964); and
Pierre Spriet, *Samuel Daniel, 1563-1619: Sa Vie, Son Oeuvre* (Paris, 1968).

A Defence of Rhyme

THE GENERAL custom and use of Rhyme in this kingdom, noble lord, having been so long (as if from a grant of Nature) held unquestionable, made me to imagine that it lay altogether out of the way of contradiction, and was become so natural, as we should never have had a thought to cast it off into reproach, or be made to think that it ill became our language. But now I see, when there is opposition made to all things in the world by words, we must now at length likewise fall to contend for words themselves, and make a question whether they be right or not. For we are told how that our measures go wrong, all rhyming is gross, vulgar, barbarous; which if it be so, we have lost much labour to no purpose; and, for mine own particular, I cannot but blame the fortune of the times and mine own genius, that cast me upon so wrong a course, drawn with the current of custom and an unexamined example. Having been first encouraged or framed thereunto by your most worthy and honourable mother, and receiving the first notion for the formal ordering of those compositions at Wilton—which I must ever acknowledge to have been my best school, and thereof always am to hold a feeling and grateful memory—, afterward drawn farther on by the well liking and approbation of my worthy lord, the fosterer of me and my Muse; I adventured to bestow all my whole powers therein, perceiving it agreed so well, both with the complexion of the times and mine own constitution, as I found not wherein I might better employ me. But yet now, upon the great discovery of these new measures, threatening to overthrow the whole state of Rhyme in this kingdom, I must either stand out to defend, or else be forced to forsake myself and give over all. And though irresolution and a self-distrust be the most apparent faults of my nature, and that the least check of reprehension, if it savour of reason, will as easily shake my resolution as any man's living;

yet in this case I know not how I am grown more resolved, and, before I sink, willing to examine what those powers of judgement are that must bear me down and beat me off from the station of my profession, which by the law of nature I am set to defend. And the rather for that this detractor (whose commendable rhymes, albeit now himself an enemy to Rhyme, have given heretofore to the world the best notice of his worth) is a man of fair parts and good reputation . . .

We could well have allowed of his numbers, had he not disgraced our Rhyme, which both custom and nature doth most powerfully defend: custom that is before all law, nature that is above all art. Every language hath her proper number or measure fitted to use and delight, which custom, entertaining by the allowance of the ear, doth endenize and make natural. All verse is but a frame of words confined within certain measure, differing from the ordinary speech, and introduced the better to express men's conceits, both for delight and memory. Which frame of words consisting of *rhythmus* or *metrum*, number or measure, are disposed into divers fashions, according to the humour of the composer and the set of the time. And these *rhythmi*, as Aristotle saith, are familiar amongst all nations, and *e naturali et sponte fusa compositione:* [1] and they fall as naturally already in our language as ever art can make them, being such as the ear of itself doth marshal in their proper rooms; and they of themselves will not willingly be put out of their rank, and that in such a verse as best comports with the nature of our language. And for our Rhyme (which is an excellency added to this work of measure, and a harmony far happier than any proportion antiquity could ever show us) doth add more grace, and hath more of delight than ever bare numbers, howsoever they can be forced to run in our slow language, can possibly yield. Which, whether it be derived of *rhythmus* or of romance, which were songs the Bards and Druids about rhymes used, and thereof were called

A Defence of Rhyme. Written as an answer to Thomas Campion's *Observations in the Art of English Poesie* (1602), and published about 1603 or 1604. It is addressed to William Herbert, Earl of Pembroke. The spelling has been modernized.

[1] "From natural and spontaneous composition."

Remensi, as some Italians hold, or howsoever, it is likewise number and harmony of words, consisting of an agreeing sound in the last syllables of several verses, giving both to the ear an echo of a delightful report, and to the memory a deeper impression of what is delivered therein. For as Greek and Latin verse consists of the number and quantity of syllables, so doth the English verse of measure and accent. And though it doth not strictly observe long and short syllables, yet it most religiously respects the accent; and as the short and the long make number, so the acute and grave accent yield harmony. And harmony is likewise number; so that the English verse then hath number, measure, and harmony in the best proportion of music. Which, being more certain and more resounding, works that effect of motion with as happy success as either the Greek or Latin. And so natural a melody is it, and so universal, as it seems to be generally born with all the nations of the world as an hereditary eloquence proper to all mankind. The universality argues the general power of it: for if the barbarian use it, then it shows that it sways the affection of the barbarian; if civil nations practise it, it proves that it works upon the hearts of civil nations; if all, then that it hath a power in nature on all. Georgeviez, *De Turcarum Moribus,* hath an example of the Turkish rhymes just of the measure of our verse of eleven syllables, in feminine rhyme; never begotten, I am persuaded, by any example in Europe, but born no doubt in Scythia, and brought over Caucasus and Mount Taurus. The Sclavonian and Arabian tongues acquaint a great part of Asia and Africa with it; the Moscovite, Polack, Hungarian, German, Italian, French, and Spaniard use no other harmony of words. The Irish, Briton, Scot, Dane, Saxon, English, and all the inhabiters of this island either have hither brought or here found the same in use. And such a force hath it in nature, or so made by nature, as the Latin numbers, notwithstanding their excellence, seemed not sufficient to satisfy the ear of the world thereunto accustomed, without this harmonical cadence: which made the most learned of all nations labour with exceeding travail to bring those numbers likewise unto it; which many did with that happiness as neither their purity of tongue nor their material contemplations are thereby any way disgraced, but rather deserve to be rever-

enced of all grateful posterity, with the due regard of their worth. . . .

"Ill customs are to be left." I grant it; but I see not how that can be taken for an ill custom which nature hath thus ratified, all nations received, time so long confirmed, the effects such as it performs those offices of motion for which it is employed; delighting the ear, stirring the heart, and satisfying the judgment in such sorts as I doubt whether ever single numbers will do in our climate, if they show no more work of wonder than yet we see. And if ever they prove to become anything, it must be by the approbation of many ages that must give them their strength for any operation, as before the world will feel where the pulse, life, and energy lies; which now we are sure where to have in our rhymes, whose known frame hath those due stays for the mind, those encounters of touch, as makes the motion certain, though the variety be infinite. . . .

All excellences being sold us at the hard price of labour, it follows, where we bestow most thereof we buy the best success: and Rhyme, being far more laborious than loose measures (whatsoever is objected), must needs, meeting with wit and industry, breed greater and worthier effects in our language. So that, if our labours have wrought out a manumission from bondage, and that we go at liberty, notwithstanding these ties, we are no longer the slaves of Rhyme, but we make it a most excellent instrument to serve us. Nor is this certain limit observed in sonnets any tyrannical bounding of the conceit, but rather reducing it in *girum* and a just form, neither too long for the shortest project, nor too short for the longest, being but only employed for a present passion. For the body of our imagination being as an unformed chaos without fashion, without day, if by the divine power of the spirit it be wrought into an orb of order and form, is it not more pleasing to Nature, that desires a certainty and comports not with that which is infinite, to have these closes, rather than not to know where to end, or how far to go, especially seeing our passions are often without measure? . . .

Methinks we should not so soon yield our consents captive to the authority of antiquity, unless we saw more reason; all our understandings are not to be built by the square of Greece and

Italy. We are the children of nature as well as they; we are not so placed out of the way of judgement, but that the same sun of discretion shineth upon us; we have our portion of the same virtues as well as of the same vices . . . It is not the observing of trochaics nor their iambics that will make our writings aught the wiser. All their Poesy, all their Philosophy is nothing, unless we bring the discerning light of conceit with us to apply it to use. It is not books, but only that great book of the world and the all-overspreading grace of heaven that makes men truly judicial. Nor can it be but a touch of arrogant ignorance to hold this or that nation barbarous, these or those times gross, considering how this manifold creature man, wheresoever he stand in the world, hath always some disposition of worth, entertains the order of society, affects that which is most in use, and is eminent in some one thing or other that fits his humour and the times. The Grecians held all other nations barbarous but themselves; yet Pyrrhus, when he saw the well-ordered marching of the Romans, which made them see their presumptuous error, could say it was no barbarous manner of proceeding. The Goths, Vandals, and Lombards, whose coming down like an inundation overwhelmed, as they say, all the glory of learning in Europe, have yet left us still their laws and customs as the originals of most of the provincial constitutions of Christendom, which well considered with their other courses of government may serve to clear them from this imputation of ignorance. And though the vanquished never yet spake well of the conqueror, yet even through the unsound coverings of malediction appear those monuments of truth as argue well their worth and proves them not without judgement, though without Greek and Latin.

Will not experience confute us, if we should say the state of China, which never heard of Anapaestics, Trochees, and Tribrachs, were gross, barbarous, and uncivil? And is it not a most apparent ignorance, both of the succession of learning in Europe and the general course of things, to say "that all lay pitifully deformed in those lack-learning times from the declining of the Roman Empire till the light of the Latin tongue was revived by Reuchlin, Erasmus, and More"?—when for three hundred years before them, about the coming down of Tamerlane into Europe, Francis Petrarch (who then no doubt likewise found whom to imitate) showed all the best notions of learning, in that degree of excellency both in Latin, prose and verse, and in the vulgar Italian, as all the wits of posterity have not yet much overmatched him in all kinds to this day . . .

We must not look upon the immense course of times past as men overlook spacious and wide countries from off high mountains, and are never the near to judge of the true nature of the soil or the particular site and face of those territories they see. Nor must we think, viewing the superficial figure of a region in a map, that we know straight the fashion and place as it is. Or reading an history (which is but a map of men, and doth no otherwise acquaint us with the true substance of circumstances than a superficial card doth the seaman with a coast never seen, which always proves other to the eye than the imagination forecast it), that presently we know all the world, and can distinctly judge of times, men, and manners, just as they were: when the best measure of man is to be taken by his own foot bearing ever the nearest proportion to himself, and is never so far different and unequal in his powers, that he hath all in perfection at one time, and nothing at another. The distribution of gifts are universal, and all seasons have them in some sort. We must not think but that there were Scipios, Caesars, Catos, and Pompeys born elsewhere than at Rome; the rest of the world hath ever had them in the same degree of nature, though not of state. And it is our weakness that makes us mistake or misconceive in these delineations of men the true figure of their worth. And our passion and belief is so apt to lead us beyond truth, that unless we try them by the just compass of humanity, and as they were men, we shall cast their figures in the air, when we should make their models upon earth. . . .

BEN JONSON   (1572-1637)

JONSON's judicious and critical approach to literature colors almost all of his writing. It especially reveals itself in his careful and even self-conscious craftsmanship in attempting to follow ancient models. More through his own example than through his critical writing he was to influence the future course of English neoclassicism. Still, his criticism presents his aims and standards in a compact form; and in illustrating the development of neoclassicism from Sidney to Dryden, it has historical, if not great intrinsic, importance. Jonson's main critical work, a commentary based on Horace, was lost in a fire. What we have left, aside from his Prefaces and the record of his literary conversations with the Scottish poet, William Drummond, consists of the collection of miscellaneous notes and brief essays called *Timber; or, Discoveries*, published posthumously in 1641, for which he drew heavily upon continental critics of his own time and earlier as well as on the classics.

For Jonson the end of poetry, as of any other humanistic pursuit, is the further development of man. It seeks to present a "Pattern of living well, and happily; disposing us to all Civil offices of Society." It draws upon other fields of learning for its materials. But what particularly makes it "poetry" is that it offers its knowledge in such a way as to "delight," and presents it in a completed and unified "proportion," "harmony," or "consent of parts." Besides its stress on the moral function of art, and also on "proportion"—or what Dryden later called "propriety"—Jonson's approach is shown to be neoclassic even more in what he considered most necessary for the poet himself: (1) "a goodness of natural wit," or a fertile inventive and imaginative power of mind; (2) continual "exercise" and "habit" in writing; and (3) the study and imitation of past writers. The second and third qualifications reveal an attitude strongly opposed to the romantic trust

BEN JONSON. After attending Westminster and possibly Cambridge, Jonson worked as a bricklayer's apprentice, and then volunteered for military service in the Low Countries. Returning to London, he began his brilliant career as a playwright, serving also for a while as an actor. During the next forty years he became acquainted with many of the celebrated men of his day, and as an acknowledged literary giant developed a considerable following among admiring younger writers.

The standard edition of Jonson's works is that of C. H. Herford and P. Simpson (1925 ff.). Annotated editions of the *Discoveries* are those of F. E. Schelling (1892), M. Castelain (Paris, 1906), R. S. Walker (1953), and J. D. Redwine, Jr. (1969). An edition that also includes the *Conversations with Drummond* is G. B. Harrison's (1923). Detailed commentary in English is not plentiful. The introduction and notes in J. E. Spingarn, *Critical Essays of the Seventeenth Century* (Oxford, 1908), I, and Wesley Trimpi, *Ben Jonson's Poems* (Stanford, 1962), Part I, "Discoveries," are helpful. Students who read German may consult H. Reinsch, *Ben Jonson's Poetik und seine Beziehungen zu Horaz* (1898).

in "original genius," and the writer's belief, as Jonson said, that "he can leap forth suddenly a Poet, by dreaming he hath been in *Parnassus,* or, having washt his lips (as they say) in Helicon." The emphasis on exercise and habit exemplifies Jonson's own definition of the art of poetry as a "habit," a "skill, or Craft of making." By persevering, the poetic ability will gradually learn to "lift and dilate itself, as men of low stature, raise themselves on their toes; and so oft times get even, if not eminent." But it is especially in adding his own concept of "imitation"—the ability to "convert the substance, or Riches of another *Poet,* to his own use"—that Jonson illustrates the "new classicism," a classicism no longer quite that of Aristotle and now buttressed by strong and self-conscious recognition of authority.

From Timber: or, Discoveries

[*Shakespeare*]

I REMEMBER, the Players have often mentioned it as an honour to Shakespeare, that in his writing, (whatsoever he penn'd) hee never blotted out [a] line. My answer hath beene, would he had blotted a thousand. Which they thought a malevolent speech. I had not told posterity this, but for their ignorance, who choose that circumstance to commend their friend by, wherein he most faulted. And to justifie mine owne candor, (for I lov'd the man, and doe honour his memory (on this side Idolatry) as much as any.) Hee was (indeed) honest, and of an open, and free nature: had an excellent *Phantsie;* brave notions, and gentle expressions: wherein hee flow'd with that facility, that sometime it was necessary he should be stop'd: *Sufflaminandus erat;* as *Augustus* said of *Haterius.* His wit was in his owne power; would the rule of it had beene so too. Many times hee fell into those things, could not escape laughter: As when hee said in the person of *Caesar,* one speaking to him; *Caesar thou dost me wrong.* Hee replyed: *Caesar did never wrong, but with just cause:* and such like, which were ridiculous. But hee redeemed his vices, with his vertues. There was ever more in him to be praysed, then to be pardoned.

Timber: or, Discoveries. Probably written during the years 1620-35, and posthumously published in 1641.

[*Style*] [1]

For a man to write well, there are required three Necessaries. To read the best Authors, observe the best Speakers: and much exercise of his owne style. In style to consider, what ought to be written: and after what manner: Hee must first thinke, and excogitate his matter; then choose his words, and examine the weight of either. Then take care in placing, and ranking both matter, and words, that the composition be comely; and to doe this with diligence, and often. No matter how slow the style be at first, so it be labour'd, and accurate; seeke the best, and be not glad of the forward conceipts, or first words, that offer themselves to us, but judge of what wee invent; and order what wee approve. Repeat often, what wee have formerly written; which beside, that it helpes the consequence, and makes the juncture better, it quickens the heate of imagination, that often cooles in the time of setting downe, and gives it new strength, as if it grew lustier, by the going back. As wee see in the contention of leaping, they jumpe farthest, that fetch their race largest: or, as in throwing a Dart, or Iavelin, wee force back our armes, to make our loose the stronger. Yet, if we have a faire gale of wind, I forbid not the steering out of our sayle, so the favour of the gale deceive us not. For all that wee invent doth

[1] Much of this section is borrowed, and in some places directly translated from Quintilian, and also from the Renaissance humanists, Vives and Lipsius.

please us in the conception, or birth; else we would never set it downe. But the safest is to re-turne to our Judgement, and handle over againe those things, the easinesse of which might make them justly suspected. So did the best Writers in their beginnings; they impos'd upon them-selves care, and industry. They did nothing rashly. They obtain'd first to write well, and then custome made it easie, and a habit. By little and little, their matter shew'd it selfe to 'hem more plentifully; their words answer'd, their composition followed; and all, as in a well-order'd family, presented it selfe in the place. So that the summe of all is: Ready writing makes not good writing: but good writing brings on ready writing: Yet when wee thinke wee have got the faculty, it is even then good to resist it: as to give a Horse a check sometimes with bit, which doth not so much stop his course, as stirre his mettle. Againe, whether a mans *Genius* is best able to reach thither, it should more and more contend, lift and dilate it selfe, as men of low stature, raise themselves on their toes; and so oft times get even, if not eminent. Besides, as it is fit for grown and able Writers to stand of themselves, and worke with their owne strength, to trust and endeavour by their owne faculties: so it is fit for the beginner, and learner, to study others, and the best. For the mind, and memory are more sharpely exercis'd in comprehending an other mans things, and are familiar with the best Authors, shall ever and anon find some-what of them in themselves, and in the expres-sion of their minds, even when they feele it not, be able to utter something like theirs, which hath an Authority above their owne. Nay, sometimes it is the reward of a mans study, the praise of quoting an other man fitly: And though a man be more prone, and able for one kind of writ-ing, then another, yet hee must exercise all. For as in an Instrument, so in style, there must be a Harmonie, and consent of parts.

I take this labour in teaching others, that they should not be alwayes to bee taught; and I would bring my precepts into practise. For rules are ever of lesse force, and valew, then experiments. Yet with this purpose, rather to shew the right way to those that come after, then to detect any that have slipt before by errour, and I hope it will bee more profitable. For men doe more willingly listen, and with more favour to precept, then reprehension. Among diverse opinions of an Art, and most of them contrary in themselves, it is hard to make election; and therefore, though a man cannot invent new things after so many, he may doe a welcome worke yet to helpe pos-terity to judge rightly of the old. But Arts and Precepts availe nothing, except nature be bene-ficiall, and ayding. And therefore these things are no more written to a dull disposition, then rules of husbandry to a barren Soyle. No pre-cepts will profit a Foole; no more then beauty will the blind, or musicke the deafe. As wee should take care, that our style in writing, be neither dry, nor empty; wee should looke againe it be not winding, or wanton with far-fetcht-descriptions; Either is a vice. But that is worse which proceeds out of want, then that which riots out of plenty. The remedy of fruitfulnesse is easie, but no labour will helpe the contrary; I will like, and praise some things in a young Writer; which yet if hee continue in, I cannot, but justly hate him for the same. There is a time to bee given all things for maturity; and that even your Countrey-husbandman can teach; who to a young plant will not put the proyning knife, because it seemes to feare the iron, as not able to admit the scarre. No more would I tell a greene Writer all his faults, lest I should make him grieve and faint, and at last despaire. For nothing doth more hurt, then to make him so afraid of all things, as hee can endeavour noth-ing. Therefore youth ought to be instructed be-times, and in the best things: for we hold those longest, wee take soonest. As the first sent of a Vessell lasts: and that tinct the wooll first re-ceives. Therefore a Master should temper his owne powers, and descend to the others infirm-ity. If you powre a glut of water upon a Bottle, it receives little of it; but with a Funnell, and by degrees, you shall fill many of them, and spill little of your owne; to their capacity they will all receive, and be full. And as it is fit to reade the best Authors to youth first, so let them be of the openest, and clearest. As *Livy* before *Salust*, *Sydney* before *Donne*: and beware of letting them taste *Gower*, or *Chaucer* at first, lest falling too much in love with Antiquity, and not appre-hending the weight, they grow rough and barren in, language onely. When their judgements are firme, and out of danger, let them reade both, the old and the new: but no lesse take heed, that their new flowers, and sweetnesse doe not as much corrupt, as the others drinesse, and squallor, if they choose not carefully. *Spencer*, in affecting the Ancients writ no Language: Yet I would have him read for his matter; but as *Virgil* read *Ennius*. The reading of *Homer* and *Virgil* is counsell'd by *Quintilian*, as the best way of informing youth, and confirming man. For besides that, the mind is rais'd with the height, and sublimity of such a verse, it takes spirit from the greatnesse of the matter, and is tincted with the best things.

[The Function of the Poet]

A Poet is that, which by the *Greeks* is call'd ἐξοχὴν, ὁ ποιητὴς, a Maker, or a fainer: His Art, an Art of imitation, of faining; expressing the life of man in fit measure, numbers, and harmony, according to Aristotle: From the word ποιεῖν, which signifies to make or fayne. Hence, hee is call'd a *Poet*, not hee which writeth in measure only; but that fayneth and formeth a fable, and writes things like the Truth. For, the Fable and Fiction is (as it were) the forme and Soule of any Poeticall worke, or Poeme.

[A Poem as Distinct from Poesy]

A Poeme, as I have told you is the worke of the Poet; the end, and fruit of his labour, and studye. *Poesy* is his skill, or Crafte of making: the very Fiction it selfe, the reason, or forme of the worke. And these three voices differ, as the thing done, the doing, and the doer; the thing fain'd, the faining, and the fainer: so the *Poeme*, the Poesy, and the Poet. Now, the *Poesy* is the habit, or the Art: nay, rather the Queene of Arts: which had her Originall from heaven, received thence from the 'Ebrewes, and had in prime estimation with the Greeks, transmitted to the Latines, and all Nations, that profess'd Civility. The Study of it (if wee will trust *Aristotle*) offers to mankinde a certain rule, and Patterne of living well, and happily; disposing us to all Civill offices of Society. If wee will beleive Tully, it nourisheth, and instructeth our Youth; delights our Age; adornes our prosperity; comforts our Adversity; entertaines us at home; keepes us company abroad, travailes with

us; watches; divides the times of our earnest, and sports; shares in our Country recesses, and recreations; insomuch as the wisest, and best learned have thought her the absolute Mistresse of manners; and neerest of kin to Vertue.[2] And, wheras they entitle *Philosophy* to bee a rigid, and austere *Poesie*: they have (on the contrary) stiled *Poesy*, a dulcet, and gentle *Philosophy*, which leades on, and guides us by the hand to Action, with a ravishing delight, and incredible Sweetnes.[3] But, before wee handle the kindes of *Poems*, with their speciall differences: or make court to the Art it selfe, as a Mistresse, I would leade you to the knowledge of our Poet, by a perfect Information, what he is, or should bee by nature, by exercise, by imitation, by Studie; and so bring him downe through the disciplines of Grammar, Logicke, Rhetoricke, and the Ethicks, adding somewhat, out of all, peculiar to himselfe, and worthy of your Admittance, or reception.

First, wee require in our *Poet*, or maker, (for that Title our Language affordes him, elegantly, with the *Greeke*) a goodnes of naturall wit. For, wheras all other Arts consist of Doctrine, and Precepts; the *Poet* must bee able by nature, and instinct, to powre out the Treasure of his minde; and, as *Seneca* saith, *Aliquando secundum Anacreontem insanire jucundum esse:*[4] by which hee understands, the *Poeticall Rapture*. And according to that of *Plato; Frustra Poeticas fores sui compos pulsavit:*[5] And of *Aristotle; Nullum magnum ingenium sine mixtura dementiae fuit. Nec potest grande aliquid, & supra caeteros loqui, nisi mota mens.*[6] Then it riseth higher, as by a devine Instinct, when it contemnes common, and knowne conceptions. It utters somewhat above a mortall mouth. Then it gets a loft, and flies away with his Ryder, whether, before, it was doubtfull to ascend. This the Poets under-

[2] Cicero, *Pro Archia*, 7.

[3] Compare Sidney, above, p. 92.

[4] "Sometimes, like a second Anacreon, it is delightful to rave" (*De Tranquillitate Animi*, 15).

[5] "He who is his own master beats vainly at the gates of Poetry."

[6] "There has been no great genius who has not been touched by madness, nor can you say anything great above other things unless the mind is excited." Jonson is quoting these passages from Plato's *Ion* and Aristotle's *Poetics* (xvii, 1), not directly, but from Seneca.

stood by their *Helicon, Pegasus,* or *Parnassus;* and this made *Ovid* to boast:

Est, Deus in nobis; agitante calescimus illo:
Sedibus aethereis spiritus ille venit.[7]

And *Lipsius,* to affirme; *Scio, Poetam neminem praestantem fuisse, sine parte quadam uberiore divinae aurae.*[8] And, hence it is, that the comming up of good Poets, (for I minde not *mediocres,* or *imos*) is so thinne and rare among us; Every beggerly Corporation affoords the State a *Major,* or two *Bailiffs,* yearly: but, *solus Rex, aut Poeta, non quotannis nascitur.*[9] To this perfection of Nature in our *Poet,* wee require Exercise of those parts, and frequent. If his wit will not arrive soddainly at the dignitie of the Ancients, let him not yet fall out with it, quarrell, or be over hastily Angry: offer, to turne it away from Study, in a humor; but come to it againe upon better cogitation; try an other time, with labour. If then it succeed not, cast not away the Quills, yet: nor scratch the Wainescott, beate not the poore Deske; but bring all to the forge, and file, againe; tourne it a newe. There is no Statute *Law* of the Kingdome bids you bee a Poet, against your will; or the first Quarter. If it come, in a yeare, or two, it is well. The common Rymers powre forth Verses, such as they are, (*ex tempore*) but there never come from them one Sense, worth the life of a Day. A Rymer, and a *Poet,* are two things. It is said of the incomparable *Virgil,* that he brought forth his verses like a Beare, and after form'd them with licking. *Scaliger,* the Father, writes it of him, that he made a quantitie of verses in the morning, which a fore night hee reduced to a lesse number. But, that which *Valerius Maximus* hath left recorded of *Euripides, the tragicke Poet,* his answer to *Alcestis,* an other *Poet,* is as memorable, as modest: who, when it was told to Alcestis, that *Euripides* had in three daies brought forth, but three verses, and those with some difficultie, and throwes: *Alcestis,* glorying hee could with ease have sent forth a hundred in the space; *Eurip-*

ides roundly repl'd, like enough. But, here is the difference; Thy verses will not last those three daies; mine will to all time. Which was, as to tell him; he could not write a verse. I have met many of these Rattles, that made a noyse, and buz'de. They had their humme; and, no more. Indeed, things, wrote with labour, deserve to be so read, and will last their Age. The third requisite in our *Poet,* or *Maker,* is *Imitation,* to bee able to convert the substance, or Riches of an other *Poet,* to his owne use. To make choise of one excellent man above the rest, and so to follow him, till he grow very *Hee:* or, so like him, as the Copie may be mistaken for the Principall. Not, as a Creature, that swallowes, what it takes in, crude, raw, or indigested; but, that feedes with an Appetite, and hath a Stomacke to concoct, devide, and turne all into nourishment. Not, to imitate servilely, as *Horace* saith, and catch at vices, for vertue: but, to draw forth out of the best, and choisest flowers, with the Bee, and turne all into Honey, worke it into one relish, and savour:[10] make our *Imitation* sweet: observe, how the best writers have imitated, and follow them. How *Virgil,* and *Statius* have imitated *Homer:* how *Horace, Archilochus;* how *Alcaeus,* and the other *Liricks:* and so of the rest. But, that, which wee especially require in him is an exactness of Studie, and multiplicity of reading, which maketh a full man, not alone enabling him to know the *History,* or Argument of a *Poeme,* and to report it: but so to master the matter, and Stile, as to shew, hee knowes, how to handle, place, or dispose of either, with elegancie, when need shall bee. And not thinke, hee can leape forth suddainely a Poet, by dreaming hee hath been in *Parnassus,* or, having washt his lipps (as they say) in *Helicon.* There goes more to his making, then so. For to Nature, Exercise, Imitation, and Studie, *Art* must bee added, to make all these perfect. And, though these challenge to themselves much, in the making up of our Maker, it is Art only can lead him to perfection, and leave him there in possession, as planted by her hand. . . .

---

[7] "There is, in us, a god; by his urging, we grow warm; it is from the etherial regions that the spirit comes" (*Fasti,* vii, 5).

[8] "I know that, without the divine breath, or inspiration, in abundance no poet has become illustrious."

[9] "It is only a king or a poet who is not born every year."

[10] This is a common figure in Renaissance writing. It was later applied by Swift to the great writers of classical antiquity in comparing them with the modern writers who, like the spider, spin out their works from themselves. See above, pp. 9-10.

[*The Fable or Plot of a Poem*]

To the resolving of this *Question*,[11] wee must first agree in the definition of the Fable. The Fable is call'd the *Imitation* of one intire, and perfect Action; whose parts are so joyned, and knitt together, as nothing in the structure can be chang'd; or taken away, without imparing, or troubling the whole; of which there is a proportionable magnitude in the members. As for example; if a man would build a house, he would first appoint a place to build it in, which he would define within certaine bounds: So in the Constitution of a *Poeme*, the Action is aym'd at by the *Poet*, which answers Place in a building; and that Action hath his largenesse, compasse, and proportion. But, as a Court of Kings Palace requires other dimensions then a private house: So the *Epick* askes a magnitude, from other Poëms. Since, what is Place in the one, is Action in the other, the difference is in space. So that by this definition wee conclude the fable, to be the *imitation* of one perfect, and intire Action; as one perfect, and intire place is requir'd to a building. By perfect, wee understand that, to which nothing is wanting; as Place to the building, that is rais'd, and Action to the fable, that is form'd. It is perfect, perhaps, not for a Court, or Kings Palace, which requires a greater ground; but for the structure wee would raise, so the space of the Action, may not prove large enough for the *Epick Fable*, yet bee perfect for the *Dramatick*, and whole.

Whole, wee call that, and perfect, which hath a *beginning*, a *mid'st*, and an *end*. So the place of any building may be whole, and intire, for that worke; though too little for a palace. As, to a *Tragedy* or a *Comedy*, the Action may be convenient, and perfect, that would not fit an *Epicke*

[11] The question of "the magnitude and compasse of any Fable, Epicke, or Dramaticke."

Poeme in Magnitude. So a Lion is a perfect creature in himselfe, though it bee lesse, then that of a *Buffalo*, or a *Rhinocerote*. They differ, but in *specie:* either in the kinde is absolute. Both have their parts, and either the whole. Therefore, as in every body; so in every Action, which is the subject of a just worke, there is requir'd a certaine proportionable greatnesse, neither too vast, nor too minute. For that which happens to the Eyes, when wee behold a body, the same happens to the Memorie, when wee contemplate an action. I looke upon a monstrous Giant, as *Tityus*, whose body cover'd nine Acres of Land, and mine eye stickes upon every part; the whole that consists of those parts, will never be taken in at one intire view. So in a *Fable*, if the Action be too great wee can never comprehend the whole together in our Imagination. Againe, if it be too little, there ariseth no pleasure out of the object, it affords the view no stay: It is beheld and vanisheth at once. As if wee should looke upon an Ant or Pismyre, the parts fly the sight, and the whole considered is almost nothing. The same happens in Action, which is the object of Memory, as the body is of sight. Too vast oppresseth the Eyes, and exceeds the Memory: too little scarce admits either. . . .

For the *whole*, as it consisteth of parts; so without all the parts it is not the whole; and to make it absolute, is requir'd, not only the parts, but such parts as are true. For a part of the whole was true; which if you take away, you either change the whole, or it is not the whole. For if it be such a part, as being present or absent, nothing concernes the whole, it cannot be call'd a part of the whole: and such are the *Episodes*, of which hereafter. For the present, here is one example; The single Combat of *Ajax* with *Hector*, as it is at large describ'd in *Homer* nothing belongs to this *Ajax* of *Sophocles*.

PIERRE CORNEILLE   (1606-1684)

CORNEILLE's three *Discourses,* and the *Examens* he wrote of his plays, are lucid illustrations of the extreme neoclassic theory of drama that became prevalent in seventeenth-century France. It is not that Corneille himself was an eager advocate of the rules. What is significant is that this great dramatist felt compelled to adhere to them so closely. Much of his critical writing, indeed, has a note of apology for interpreting the rules a little more liberally than perhaps he should.

French dramatic criticism was by now justifying the rules of plot structure and character-portrayal by invoking the ideals of *vraisemblance* and *le nécessaire.* The three "unities" of plot, for example, were felt to give added verisimilitude to the action. If we are asked to believe that the first scene is Paris, we cannot be expected to believe that the same stage, which we have been watching all the time, is now Rouen. Nor can we, when we are sitting for two or three hours, be expected to believe that years have passed. Necessity or probability join with verisimilitude to make the *liaison des scenes* also desirable. In character, there must be propriety—consistency with the type—and truth to life. Corneille's often melodramatic desire to portray passionate and strong-willed characters, such as we find also in the English "Heroic Plays" of the Restoration, led him to chafe against the demand for *vraisemblance.* Nor was he happy about the restrictions imposed by the unities. He had been hurt by earlier criticism of his general lack of strict regularity, and tried gently to suggest, to "theoretical critics," some of the almost impossible difficulties that arise in trying to follow the unities of time and place. It remained for Johnson, a century later, to dismiss these two unities bluntly as giving "more trouble to the poet, than pleasure to the auditor," and as "the product of superfluous and ostentatious art, by which is shown rather, what is possible, than what is necessary."

PIERRE CORNEILLE. Born at Rouen, Corneille became a lawyer, and served as a royal attorney at Rouen till 1650. After some early comedies (the first was produced in 1629), he turned to tragedy and became the founder of classical tragedy in France. Since he was never too docile to fashionable tastes, he was not very popular among influential court and literary circles, and in his later years his plays were put into the background by those of Racine.

A complete edition is that of Ch. Marty-Laveaux (12 vols., 1862-68). For general background, there are René Bray, *La Formation de la Doctrine Classique en France* (Paris, 1927), and C. H C. Wright, *French Classicism* (Cambridge, Mass., 1920). Students acquainted with French may be referred to Sainte-Beuve's essays on Corneille, to J. Lemaître, *Corneille et la Poétique d'Aristote* (1888), and to M. O. Sweetser, *Les Conceptions Dramatiques de Corneille* (Geneva, 1962). Also helpful are Herbert Fogel, *The Criticism of Cornelian Tragedy: a Study of Critical Writing from the Seventeenth to the Twentieth Century* (1967); and P. J. Yarrow, *Corneille* (1963).

Discourse on the Three Unities

I CONTEND then, and have already stated it, that the unity of action, in comedy, consists in a unity of *intrigue,* or in obstacles to the designs of the main characters; and, in tragedy, it consists in a unity of *danger,* whether the hero succumbs to it or escapes from it. I do not say that one cannot admit several intrigues and obstacles into the former, and several dangers into the latter, provided each necessarily winds into the other. For then the disappearance of the first danger does not render the action complete, since it leads into a second one; and the clearing up of one intrigue does not leave the actors idle, since it encumbers them with another intrigue. . . .

In the second place, this term "unity of action" does not mean that there should be only one action in the play. What the poet selects for his subject ought to have a beginning, a middle, and an end; and these three parts are not only so many actions coming to a center in the principal action; but each of them, moreover, can contain several parts in a similar subordination. There ought only to be a *complete* action, which leaves the mind of the spectator composed. But it can only result through several incomplete parts, which contribute to the progress of the whole, and maintain the spectator in an agreeable suspension. It is necessary that the writer contrive at the end of each act to make the action continuous.

The *liaison des scènes* [1] which unites all the particular actions of each act, the one with the other, and of which I have spoken in the *examen* to the *Suivante,* is an important ornament to a poem, and greatly helps to form a continuity of action by giving a continuity of representation. But, in the last analysis, it is only an ornament, and not a rule. The ancients have not always submitted to it, even though most of their acts are filled with two or three scenes; this makes it much easier for them than for us, who sometimes have nine or ten. . . .

Although the action of a dramatic poem ought to have unity, it must be regarded as having two elements: the knotting together, or complication, and the *dénouement,* or unravelling. "The complication," according to Aristotle, "is composed in part of what has passed outside the theater before the commencement of the action . . . the rest belongs to the *dénouement* . . ." [2] The complication depends entirely on the choice and illustrious imagination of the poet; and one cannot give for it any rules except that everything ought to be arranged according to probability or necessity . . .

In the *dénouement* I find two things to avoid —a simple change of heart in the character, and the use of the *deus ex machina.*[3] There is no great skill in finishing a poem when that which comprizes an obstacle to the designs of the principal characters, during four acts, simply ceases to exist in the fifth act, without any notable event to make it that way . . . Nor does the use of the machine show any more skill when it only serves to have a god descend in order to conclude everything when the actors no longer know how to settle matters. . . .

From the subject of the action I turn to that of the division of a play into acts, which ought each to contain a part, but not so equal that one does not reserve more for the last act than for the others, and offer less in the first than in the remaining ones. . . . Aristotle does not prescribe the number of acts. Horace limits the number to five . . .

The number of scenes in each act is not subject to any rule. But as every act ought to have a certain number of verses, which keeps its dura-

Discourse on the Three Unities. Published in 1660; translated by the editor.

[1] According to this rule of French neoclassic drama, the various scenes of a play should be connected by having present, at the start of a scene, an actor who had been on the stage at the end of the preceding scene. The hope of giving an illusion of unity by this means created obvious difficulties. Amusing attempts were made to interpret the rule more elastically without abandoning it. The French critic, D'Aubignac, for example, was willing to permit a connection by having an actor appear at the start of a scene who was "looking for" a character present in the previous one, or who had heard a noise made then.

[2] See Aristotle's *Poetics,* above, p. 30.
[3] *Ibid.,* above, p. 28.

tion equal to that of the others, one can insert more or fewer scenes according as they are shorter or longer, in order to fill out the time that every complete act ought to consume. . . .

The rule for the unity of time has its basis in the statement of Aristotle that "tragedy ought to confine the length of its action within one revolution of the sun, or try not to exceed it very much." [4] This remark gives rise to that famous dispute whether it applies to a natural day of twenty-four hours, or an artificial day of twelve . . . I, for my own part, find there are subjects so hard to enclose in so little time that I will not only accord them the entire twenty-four hours, but I will even avail myself of the license given by the philosopher to exceed them a bit, and without scruple push them up to thirty hours. . . .

Many declaim against this rule, which they call tyrannical; and they would have reason if it was founded only on the authority of Aristotle. But what ought to make it accepted is the natural reason that gives it support. A dramatic poem is an imitation, or, to put it better, a portrait of men's actions; and without doubt the portraits are more excellent to the degree that they resemble the original. The representation lasts two hours; and it would resemble the original perfectly if the action it represents did not demand any longer in the imitation itself. Thus let us not at all stop at twelve or at twenty-four hours. But let us confine the action of the poem in the least time that we can, so that the representation resembles more closely and is more perfect. . . .

So far as the unity of place is concerned, I do not find any rule about it in Aristotle or Horace. This is why some are led to believe that the rule was established only as a result of the unity of time, and accordingly to persuade themselves that one can extend it to include whatever place one can go to and return in twenty-four hours. This opinion is a bit licentious; and if one had an actor ride past, the two sides of the theater could represent Paris and Rouen. . . .

Our ancients, who have their kings speak in a public place, give this rigorous unity of place rather easily to their tragedies. Sophocles, however, has not observed it in his *Ajax*, who leaves the theater in order to find a lonely place in which to kill himself, and kills himself before

the spectators. . . . We cannot take the same liberty of drawing kings and princesses from their apartments. And as the difference and opposition of interests of those who are lodged in the same palace often permit them to make their confidences and disclose their secrets only in their own chambers, it is necessary to look for some other way of arranging for the unity of place if we wish to preserve it in all our poems. . . .

I contend, then, that one should expect this unity to be as exact as possible. But as it does not adapt itself to every sort of subject, I should very willingly admit that whatever took place in a single city would have unity of place. It is not that I wish the theater to represent the city as a whole; that would be too spacious a scene; but the stage might present merely two or three particular places enclosed within its walls. . . . In order to rectify in some fashion this changing of place, when it is inevitable, I should wish to suggest two things. The first is that one should never change the scene in the same act, but solely from one act to another, as is done in the first three acts of *Cinna*. The second suggestion is that the two places should not need to have different scenery, and that neither should be named specifically, but simply be the general place in which the two places are included, such as Paris, Rome, Lyons, Constantinople, and the like. This will help to beguile the spectator, who, not seeing anything that marks the difference in place, does not become aware of it; at least he will not note the difference in a malicious and critical spirit (of which there are a few quite capable), the majority of them attaching themselves with warmth to the action they see represented. . . .

Many of my works will be lacking if one does not wish to admit a modification [of the unity of place], of which I shall content myself in the future when I cannot satisfy the utmost rigor of the rule. . . . It is easy for theoretical critics to be severe. But if they wished to offer ten or twelve poems of this sort to the public, they perhaps would enlarge the rules still more than I have done as soon as they recognized, by experience, how much restraint there is in abiding by them exactly and how many beautiful things are thereby banished from the theater. Be that as it may, these are my opinions, or, if you wish, my heresies touching the principal points of the art. . . .

[4] *Ibid.*, above, p. 22.

JOHN MILTON   (1608-1674)

MILTON'S critical writing, aside from the two brief prefaces printed here, is found mainly in the second book of the *Reason of Church Government* (1642) and in some passages in the *Apology for Smectymnuus* (1642). His brief criticism is largely of historical value in showing the extent to which the greatest epic poet of his time assumed the common premises and ideals of Renaissance criticism. The Preface to *Paradise Lost* protests against the "modern bondage of Riming" by invoking the great example of ancient heroic verse. The technical problems touched on in the Preface to *Samson Agonistes*—plot structure, the "unities," the mixture of comic and tragic scenes, decorum in character portrayal, the use of appropriate meters—had been general concerns in neoclassic theory since the mid-sixteenth century. But Milton's discussion of the Aristotelian *katharsis,* though based on that of the Italian critic, Antonio Minturno, is a broader psychological interpretation of the moral function of art than that commonly found in the critical theory of the time.

JOHN MILTON. Educated at St. Paul's school and at Christ's College, Cambridge, Milton's conscious preparation for the vocation of poet by wide reading and study is common knowledge to the student of English literature. So, too, is his later career, when, after writing his earlier verse, and making a trip abroad (1638-39), chiefly to Italy, Milton became involved in the Puritan cause, was appointed Latin Secretary to Cromwell (1649), and, after the Restoration, published *Paradise Lost* (1667), *Paradise Regained* (1671), and *Samson Agonistes* (1671).

Texts are too numerous and available to need citation. The standard complete edition is that published by Columbia University (20 vols., 1931-40). Specific commentary on Milton's criticism is small; I. Langdon, *Milton's Theory of Poetry and Fine Art* (New Haven, 1924) may be mentioned; but general works on Renaissance critical theory are more helpful (see above, p. 12). More particular studies include F. T. Prince, *The Italian Element in Milton's Verse* (Oxford, 1954); M. E. Miller, "*Pathos* and *Katharsis* in *Samson Agonistes,*" *Journal of English Literary History*, XXXI (1964), 156-74; and Martin Mueller, "Sixteenth-Century Italian Criticism and Milton's Theory of Catharsis," *Studies in English Literature*, VI (1966), 139-50.

Preface to Paradise Lost

THE VERSE

THE MEASURE is *English* Heroic Verse without Rime, as that of *Homer* in *Greek* and of *Virgil* in *Latin*,—Rime being no necessary Adjunct or true Ornament of Poem or good Verse, in longer Works especially, but the Invention of a barbarous Age, to set off wretched matter and lame meeter—grac't indeed since by the use of some famous modern Poets, carried away by Custom, but much to their own vexation, hindrance, and constraint to express many things otherwise, and for the most part worse, than else they would have exprest them. Not without cause, therefore, some both *Italian* and *Spanish* Poets of prime note have rejected Rime both in longer and shorter Works, as have also long since our best *English* tragedies, as a thing of itself, to all judicious ears, trivial and of no true musical delight; which consists only in apt Numbers, fit quantity of Syllables, and the sense variously drawn out from one Verse into another, not in the jingling sound of like endings, a fault avoided by the learned Ancients both in Poetry and all good Oratory. This neglect then of Rime so little is to be taken for a defect, though it may seem so perhaps to vulgar Read-ers, that it rather is to be esteem'd an example set, the first in *English*, of ancient liberty recov-er'd to Heroic Poem from the troublesom and modern bondage of Riming.

Preface to Samson Agonistes

OF THAT SORT OF DRAMATIC POEM WHICH
IS CALLED TRAGEDY

TRAGEDY, as it was antiently compos'd, hath been ever held the gravest, moralest, and most profitable of all other Poems: there-fore said by *Aristotle* to be of power, by rais-ing pity and fear, or terror, to purge the mind of those and such like passions, that is, to temper and reduce them to just measure with a kind of delight, stirr'd up by reading or seeing those passions well imitated.[1] Nor is Nature wanting in her own effects to make good his assertion; for so, in Physic, things of melancholic hue and quality are us'd against melancholy, sowr against sowr, salt to remove salt humours. Hence Philoso-phers and other gravest Writers, as *Cicero, Plu-tarch*, and others, frequently cite out of *Tragic Poets*, both to adorn and illustrate their dis-course. The Apostle *Paul* himself thought it not unworthy to insert a verse of *Euripides* into the text of Holy Scripture, I Cor. 15.33; and *Paraeus*, commenting on the *Revelation*, divides the whole Book as a Tragedy, into Acts, distin-guisht each by a Chorus of Heavenly Harpings and Song between. Heretofore Men in highest dignity have labour'd not a little to be thought able to compose a Tragedy. Of that honor *Dio-nysius* the elder was no less ambitious than be-fore of his attaining to the Tyranny. *Augustus Caesar* also had begun his *Ajax*, but, unable to please his own judgment with what he had be-gun, left it unfinisht. *Seneca* the Philosopher is by some thought the Author of those Tragedies (at lest the best of them) that go under that name. *Gregory Nazianzen*, a Father of the Church, thought it not unbeseeming the sanctity of his person to write a Tragedy, which he en-titl'd *Christ suffering*. This is mention'd to vin-dicate Tragedy from the small esteem, or rather infamy, which in the account of many it under-goes at this day, with other common Interludes;

[1] See the *Poetics,* above, p. 22.

hap'ning through the Poet's error of intermix-ing Comic stuff with Tragic sadness and gravity, or introducing trivial and vulgar persons: which by all judicious hath bin counted absurd, and brought in without discretion, corruptly to grati-fie the people. And though antient Tragedy use no Prologue, yet using sometimes, in case of self defence, or explanation, that which *Martial* calls an Epistle; in behalf of this Tragedy, coming forth after the antient manner, much different from what among us passes for best, thus much before-hand may be Epistl'd: that *Chorus* is here introduc'd after the Greek manner, not antient only, but modern, and still in use among the *Italians*. In the modelling therefore of this Poem, with good reason, the Antients and *Italians* are rather follow'd, as of much more authority and fame. The measure of Verse us'd in the Chorus is of all sorts, call'd by the Greeks *Monostrophic*, or rather *Apolelymenon*, without regard had to *Strophe, Antistrophe*, or *Epode*, which were a kind of Stanzas fram'd only for the Music, then us'd with the Chorus that sung; not essential to the Poem, and therefore not material; or, being divided into Stanzas or Pauses, they may be called *Alloeostropha*. Division into Act and Scene, referring chiefly to the Stage (to which this work never was intended), is here omitted.

It suffices if the whole drama be found not pro-duc't beyond the fift Act. Of the style and uni-formitie, and that commonly call'd the Plot, whether intricate or explicit,—which is nothing indeed but such oeconomy, or disposition of the fable, as may stand best with verisimilitude and decorum,—they only will best judge who are not unacquainted with *Aeschylus, Sophocles*, and *Euripides*, the three Tragic Poets unequall'd yet by any, and the best rule to all who endeavour to write Tragedy. The circumscription of time, wherein the whole Drama begins and ends, is, according to antient rule and best example, within the space of 24 hours.

3. Neoclassic Developments and Reactions

JOHN DRYDEN   (1631-1700)

I
N THE codifying and final development of what we now call "neoclassicism," Dryden has a key position. With the possible exception of Ben
Jonson, Dryden was the first great English poet to discuss in detail and
also to embody extensively in his own writings the neoclassic ideals of "refinement," "correctness," strict unity, and simple clarity. For these reasons,
and also because Dryden wrote in so many different literary genres—didactic poetry, satire, the lyric, poetic drama, and critical prose—eighteenth-
century England looked back on him as the first great model of the "new
classicism." Nor, up to the time of Dryden, was there any one major writer
on the Continent who fulfilled neoclassic ideals in so many different forms
of literature.

Moreover, because Dryden wrote so much more critical prose—usually
in the form of prefaces—than any other important English man-of-letters
before him, the eighteenth century also looked back on him as the virtual
founder of serious English criticism. This esteem of Dryden as a critic has
deservedly continued to the present day. In the nineteenth century, indeed,
he seems to have been regarded as just about the only neoclassic critic worth
reading. For with its limited idea of neoclassicism, the nineteenth century
often assumed, in an automatic way, that any neoclassic writer must have
had a radically different taste from its own. Hence it was almost taken for
granted that the neoclassicist would see nothing to admire in writers like

JOHN DRYDEN. After attending Westminster School, Dryden was educated at Trinity College,
Cambridge (A.B. 1654), settled in London, and attempted to earn his living by writing. After
writing his early poems, he concentrated on plays, became prosperous and well known, was made
a member of the Royal Society (1662), and later succeeded Davenant as poet laureate (1668).
Partly because of the political responsibilities of his position as laureate, partly because of
theatrical and other disagreements, he increasingly devoted his energy to poetic satire, in which,
except for Pope, he has no rival. He became a Catholic on the succession of James II (1685), and
thus lost his position as laureate when the Catholic James was deposed (1688). During his later
years he was therefore forced again to support himself by constant writing.

The standard edition of Dryden's criticism is *Essays* (ed. W. P. Ker, 2 vols., Oxford, 1900).
Commentary includes Ker's admirable introduction and notes; L. I. Bredvold, *Intellectual Milieu
of John Dryden* (Ann Arbor, 1934); T. S. Eliot, *Homage to John Dryden* (1924) and *John
Dryden: the Poet, the Dramatist, the Critic* (1932); Samuel Johnson, "Dryden," *Lives of the
English Poets* (1779-81); Mark Van Doren, *The Poetry of John Dryden* (1920; rev. 1945);
A. W. Verrall, *Lectures on Dryden* (Cambridge, 1914); and F. H. Moore, *The Nobler Pleasure:
Dryden's Comedy in Theory and Practice* (Chapel Hill, 1963). Critical opinions of Dryden are
collected in dictionaries by J. M. Aden (Nashville 1963) and H. J. Jensen (Minneapolis, 1969).

Chaucer, Shakespeare, or even the great English "neoclassic" idol, Milton. But partly because Dryden already had for so long a high reputation as a critic, partly because he wrote with so simple and easy a style, and partly because his criticism had something of the personal intimacy and relaxed informality that we find in romantic and Victorian essayists, the nineteenth century occasionally read his criticism in a way that it rarely read that of other neoclassic writers. And because it found in Dryden commendatory statements about Chaucer and Shakespeare, it assumed he was a unique example of a neoclassic critic who rose above the "rule-mongering" of his own age. This belief is still occasionally found even at the present day.

On the other hand, many students in this generation are less convinced that Dryden is, apart from his historical importance, the greatest critical exponent of neoclassicism. For, to begin with, Dryden did not deal with the ultimate problems of literature. He tended, instead, to discuss specific matters, usually questions of technique and method. Though warmly debated in his own day, many of these matters are now felt to have been rather local and temporary in importance. His lengthy discussions of the question whether tragedy should or should not be written in rhyme is an example. Moreover, Dryden did not systematically develop a point, but took it up, dropped it for something else, and returned to it at his leisure. Indeed, to an age eager for an incisive and searching treatment of basic issues, Dryden's casual and personal method of writing criticism may arouse a less urgent attention than his critical importance really justifies. A final reason why Dryden's comparative standing as a neoclassic critic is being slightly revised is that the twentieth century, in enlarging its understanding of neoclassic thought, has begun once again, with renewed insight, to read the critical writing of Samuel Johnson.

Still, though Dryden was not unique as a liberal exponent of neoclassicism, his distinctive virtues as a practicing critic compel admiration. There is usually present in his critical writings a ready and flexible good sense. He was always willing to reconsider, and to change his opinions. He lacked dogma to such an extent that he often presented attitudes different from his own more effectively than did their own supporters. Finally, his vivid enjoyment of literature breathes through his writing in a way that is too often absent in literary criticism.

2

The general neoclassic principle of "decorum" or "propriety" pervades Dryden's approach to every aspect of literature, from problems of style and language to those involving character portrayal, plot structure, and the moral purpose of the writer. So far as language is concerned, his own practice especially illustrates the movement then taking place in England toward refined propriety and a clear, denotative diction. His criticism was also an important advocate for this movement. The new meaning of the key term "wit," as Dryden discussed it, is an example. For it was at this time, as Johnson says, "that wit, which had been till then used for intellection . . . took the meaning, whatever it be, which it now bears." The meaning it frequently bore after Dryden is indicated in Pope's line, "What oft was thought, but ne'er so well expressed,"—a definition which reduces wit, as Johnson believed, "from strength of thought to happiness of language." Dryden's interpretation leads to that of Pope. For wit, as he defined it in his *Apology for Heroic Poetry* (1677), and indeed elsewhere, is "propriety of thoughts and words; or, in other terms, thoughts and words elegantly adapted to the subject." Hence Dryden's emphasis, in his *Essay on the Dramatic Poetry of the Last Age* (1672), on the superior refinement of wit and language found in the drama of his own day.

But the ideal of "propriety," as Dryden said in his Preface to *Albion and Albanius* (1685), applies to far more than to language alone. Rather, it signifies "proportion": the smooth and fitting adaptation of every part of a work of art toward the unified whole. It may be defined, indeed, as the subordination of the means to the end, as the use of only those means, those parts or details that, with least interference on their own part, fulfill and blend into the central design. "Propriety" may thus be regarded as the quality that permits or encourages the integrity, the total harmony of a work of art. But for Dryden it was less a subject of explicit consideration than a governing ideal, pervasive but taken for granted.

Indeed, Dryden's approach to criticism was largely in terms of particular genres or types of literature. He was primarily concerned with the various demands peculiar to the aims and appropriate techniques of each genre. Thus, in the *Discourse Concerning the Original and Progress of Satire* (1693), he discussed what best fulfills the aim of that genre, which, as he said, "is of the nature of moral philosophy, as being instructive." Or he discussed what properties and qualities characterize the epic or "heroic poem," as in the Preface to *Annus Mirabilis* (1667) or the Dedication to his translation of the *Aeneid* (1697). Above all, Dryden's writing serves as a prototype of genres criticism when it treats of poetic drama: in the *Essay of Dramatic Poesy* and its *Defence* (1668); the essay of *Heroic Plays*, published as a Preface to the *Conquest of Granada* (1672), together with an *Essay on the Dramatic Poetry of the Last Age*; and finally in his important and unusually packed discussion of tragedy in the Preface to *Troilus and Cressida* (1679). Here especially, in his dramatic criticism, the principle of decorum or "propriety" is extensively and systematically applied, but— particularly in the *Essay of Dramatic Poesy*—with flexibility and imaginative discernment.

3

"As in perspective," said Dryden in the Preface to *Troilus and Cressida,* so in a drama "there must be a point of sight in which all the lines terminate." Hence a unified plot, he went on to say, is the very "foundation of the play." Based upon the plot, and deriving from it, are the human "manners" or "inclinations" that motivate the characters; and these should be "suitable to the age, quality, country, dignity, etc., of the character." Just as these motivations should rise necessarily and automatically out of the single design or unified "action" that comprises the plot, so the individual characters themselves are in turn derived from the sort of motivations or inclinations that the plot demands. Similarly, the attitudes and remarks fit the characters, and the diction follows appropriately from them. We thus have something like a pyramidic structure, the plot serving as the base, with the other aspects of the drama built successively on it, and with the language or expression emerging as the final layer and end-point.

This approach contrasts not only with the romantic interest in character rather than plot; it contrasts even more with what Arnold was later to point out as one of the weaknesses of nineteenth-century poetry. Attention has become so frequently devoted, said Arnold, "to detached expressions, not to the action itself," that, as in Keats's *Isabella,* we "have poems which seem to exist merely for the sake of single lines and passages; not for the sake of producing any total-impression." The various "rules" of the drama —such as the "unities," or the keeping of decorum in character portrayal by preserving the "type"—were thus regarded by Dryden as means of attaining "propriety." They are the methodical means of "imitating nature" —an ordered, harmonious nature—by presenting a closely knit and probable action, in which, as in nature itself, each part is subordinated and contributes to the central design. Hence, as Dryden quoted from the French neoclassic critic, René Rapin, "If the rules be well considered, we shall find them to be made only to reduce Nature into method, to trace her step by step . . . 'tis only by these, that probability in fiction is maintained, which is the soul of poetry. They are founded upon good sense, and sound reason . . ."

But Dryden's theory of dramatic propriety, even as he expounded it in the Preface to *Troilus and Cressida,* is not quite that of Rapin and the French neoclassicists. His conception of the drama is more capacious and complex. For Dryden was acutely mindful of more than one way of writing drama. His awareness of diverse possibilities is particularly shown in the famous *Essay of Dramatic Poesy* (1668), in which four people—each with a somewhat different point of view—discuss what qualities and techniques are most effective in poetic drama. The body of the dialogue is concerned with the relative merits of ancient and modern drama; and, in modern drama, with the comparative virtues of strict French neoclassic drama and the native English drama of the Elizabethan and Jacobean periods. Crites (Sir Robert Howard) begins by urging the superiority of ancient drama. According to him, each age has a specific genius; that of the present is in science, not poetry. The high esteem in which poetry was held by the Greeks indicates the direction of their genius. Moreover, the Greeks created the drama; we are only followers. In reply, Eugenius (Lord Buckhurst, Dryden's patron) presents arguments typical of those urged for the Moderns in the Quarrel of the Ancients and the Moderns, that vigorous exposition of rival claims to pre-eminence in learning to which Swift gave the *coup de grace* in his *Battle of the Books*. Poetry can improve by study and effort just as the sciences can, and indeed it has improved in refinement. The ancients were not "regular" enough. The Greeks did not divide their tragedies into acts in the way we do. They did not always preserve the "unities"; Aristotle, indeed, even failed to mention the "unity of place." The Ancients did not apply "poetic justice" in their plays. Eugenius even deplores the lack of romantic love in ancient tragedy—a lack that later critics, long weary of its monopoly in the modern theater, have found refreshing. Lisideius (Sir Charles Sedley) then urges the superiority of the French over the English stage, and in passing condemns English tragicomedy and Shakespeare's neglect of the "unities."

Neander (Dryden himself), though he takes a more balanced position, is generally a Modern. But he is not a Modern in the sense that Eugenius and Lisideius are. His argument becomes a defense of the vigor and wide diversity of the English drama from Shakespeare to Dryden's own day. He points out the advantages of contrast from mixing tragic with comic scenes, and the greater range and variety of character portrayal in English drama. The use of double plots, though less neat, gives a further variety of action. The language of the English drama is more effective and natural. Its closer truth to nature can arouse a more intense sympathetic identification than the declamatory set speeches of French drama. Moreover, English drama has an older and more vital tradition. Finally, though it offers a more "lively imitation of nature" through its variety of plot and character and its greater realism and imaginative power of language, it can also, in the hands of such a writer as Ben Jonson, be quite as regular in form as French drama. Jonson's *Silent Woman* is discussed as an example. The dialogue then concludes on a more restricted topic, with Dryden defending the use of rhyme in tragedy.

4

Dryden's merit as a critic lies less in his general theory than in his actual approach when a work is immediately before him. Indeed, his theoretical stand often changes, and seems readily influenced by other critics of the time. If the *Essay of Dramatic Poesy*, therefore, represents his approach to drama more fully than do his other works, this is partly because it is not a theoretical discussion of the drama in the sense that the Preface to *Troilus and Cressida* is. Instead, it is a practical treatment of the problems facing the English dramatist of the later seventeenth century—a dramatist who has before him three different, and perhaps impressively intimidating models: ancient drama, with its settled types and aims; seventeenth-century French neoclassic drama, of which Corneille was the outstanding prototype, with its strict regulation and stylized patterns of plot; and, closer at hand, the rich and varied, if somewhat chaotic, body of native English drama, stretching from the late sixteenth to the mid-seventeenth century—the generation just before Dryden. It is because Dryden was sympathetically aware of the virtues of each that his position is more complex and less easily systematized than that, for example, of Corneille, Rapin, or Thomas Rymer.

The Preface to the *Fables* (1700), written at the close of Dryden's life and published the year of his death, sums up, with ripe breadth and tolerance, a variety of opinions that had gradually matured throughout his life. The Preface to the *Fables* is particularly notable in revealing Dryden's strong admiration for the traditional qualities of English poetry—its range, its imaginative vitality, and even its interest in character portrayal. In Dryden's favorable comparison of Chaucer with Ovid, we may note a nationalistic feeling rare in neoclassic criticism, though common in the romantic criticism of a century later, and also a certain historical awareness of Chaucer's position. More important to note are the qualities of Chaucer that attract Dryden: his energetic gusto; the abundant variety of characters (to which Dryden applies the henceforth famous proverb, "Here is God's plenty"); and perhaps—though the inference may be carried too far— there is a secret fondness on Dryden's part for realistic verisimilitude in the portraying of character. In this collection of miscellaneous opinions and insights that comprises the Preface to the *Fables*, Dryden illustrates once again how impossible it is to systematize English criticism, taste, or thought in general into movements or schools. For English literature, Dryden comes nearer than anyone else to offering a synthesis of neoclassic ideals in their final form, and as they were to persist through most of the eighteenth century. But from a broader point of view—that of European criticism as a whole—he is less important as a synthesizer of neoclassic ideals, which, indeed, had already been brought into a sharp, focal application by French criticism. Rather, he is a distinguished example of how neoclassic ideals could be combined with the traditional characteristics of English literature, and thus gain a greater pertinence to the richness and wide diversity of modern literature in general.

An Essay of Dramatic Poesy

IT WAS that memorable day, in the first summer of the late war, when our navy engaged the Dutch; a day wherein the two most mighty and best appointed fleets which any age had ever seen, disputed the command of the greater half of the globe, the commerce of nations, and the riches of the universe: while these vast floating bodies, on either side, moved against each other in parallel lines, and our countrymen, under the happy conduct of his Royal Highness, went breaking, by little and little, into the line of the enemies; the noise of the cannon from both navies reached our ears about the City, so that all men being alarmed with it, and in a dreadful suspense of the event, which they knew was then deciding, every one went following the sound as his fancy led him; and leaving the town almost empty, some took towards the park, some cross the river, others down it; all seeking the noise in the depth of silence.

Among the rest, it was the fortune of Eugenius, Crites, Lisideius, and Neander,[1] to be in company together; three of them persons whom their wit and quality have made known to all the town; and whom I have chose to hide under these borrowed names, that they may not suffer by so ill a relation as I am going to make of their discourse.

Taking then a barge, which a servant of Lisideius had provided for them, they made haste to shoot the bridge, and left behind them that great fall of waters which hindered them from hearing what they desired: after which, having disengaged themselves from many vessels which rode at anchor in the Thames, and almost blocked up the passage towards Greenwich, they ordered the watermen to let fall their oars more gently; and then, every one favour-

ing his own curiosity with a strict silence, it was not long ere they perceived the air to break about them like the noise of distant thunder, or of swallows in a chimney: those little undulations of sound, though almost vanishing before they reached them, yet still seeming to retain somewhat of their first horror, which they had betwixt the fleets. After they had attentively listened till such time as the sound by little and little went from them, Eugenius, lifting up his head, and taking notice of it, was the first who congratulated to the rest that happy omen of our Nation's victory: adding, that we had but this to desire in confirmation of it, that we might hear no more of that noise, which was now leaving the English coast. When the rest had concurred in the same opinion, Crites, a person of a sharp judgment, and somewhat too delicate a taste in wit, which the world have mistaken in him for ill-nature, said, smiling to us, that if the concernment of this battle had not been so exceeding great, he could scarce have wished the victory at the price he knew he must pay for it, in being subject to the reading and hearing of so many ill verses as he was sure would be made on that subject. Adding, that no argument could scape some of those eternal rhymers, who watch a battle with more diligence than the ravens and birds of prey; and the worst of them surest to be first in upon the quarry: while the better able, either out of modesty writ not at all, or set that due value upon their poems, as to let them be often desired and long expected. "There are some of those impertinent people of whom you speak," answered Lisideius, "who to my knowledge are already so provided, either way, that they can produce not only a Panegyric upon the victory, but, if need be, a Funeral Elegy on the Duke; wherein, after they have crowned his valour with many laurels, they will at last deplore the odds under which he fell, concluding that his courage deserved a better destiny." All the company smiled at the conceipt of Lisideius; but Crites, more eager than before, began to make particular exceptions against some writers, and said, the public mag-

An Essay of Dramatic Poesy. First published in 1668. Dryden's slightly revised edition of 1684 is reprinted here; and because modernized spelling is generally used in the available reprints of Dryden's criticism, it is employed here as well.

[1] For the identification of the characters, see p. 127, above.

istrate ought to send betimes to forbid them; and that it concerned the peace and quiet of all honest people, that ill poets should be as well silenced as seditious preachers. "In my opinion," replied Eugenius, "you pursue your point too far; for as to my own particular, I am so great a lover of poesy, that I could wish them all rewarded who attempt but to do well; at least, I would not have them worse used than one of their brethren was by Sylla the Dictator:— *Quem in concione vidimus* (says Tully), *cum ei libellum malus poeta de populo subjecisset, quod epigramma in eum fecisset tantummodo alternis versibus longiusculis, statim ex iis rebus quas tunc vendebat jubere ei praemium tribui, sub ea conditione ne quid postea scriberet.*"[2] "I could wish with all my heart," replied Crites, "that many whom we know were as bountifully thanked upon the same condition,—that they would never trouble us again. For amongst others, I have a mortal apprehension of two poets, whom this victory, with the help of both her wings, will never be able to escape." "'Tis easy to guess whom you intend," said Lisideius; "and without naming them, I ask you, if one of them does not perpetually pay us with clenches upon words, and a certain clownish kind of raillery? if now and then he does not offer at a catachresis or Clevelandism, wresting and torturing a word into another meaning: in fine, if he be not one of those whom the French would call *un mauvais buffon;* one who is so much a well-willer to the satire, that he intends at least to spare no man; and though he cannot strike a blow to hurt any, yet he ought to be punished for the malice of the action, as our witches are justly hanged, because they think themselves to be such; and suffer deservedly for believing they did mischief, because they meant it." "You have described him," said Crites, "so exactly, that I am afraid to come after you with my other extremity of poetry. He is one of those who, having had some advantage of education and converse, knows better than the other what a poet should be, but puts it into practice more unluckily than any man; his style and matter are every where alike:

he is the most calm, peaceable writer you ever read: he never disquiets your passions with the least concernment, but still leaves you in as even a temper as he found you; he is a very Leveller in poetry: he creeps along with ten little words in every line,[3] and helps out his numbers with *For to,* and *Unto,* and all the pretty expletives he can find, till he drags them to the end of another line; while the sense is left tired half way behind it: he doubly starves all his verses, first for want of thought, and then of expression; his poetry neither has wit in it, nor seems to have it; like him in Martial:

Pauper videri Cinna *vult, et est pauper.*[4]

"He affects plainness, to cover his want of imagination: when he writes the serious way, the highest flight of his fancy is some miserable antithesis, or seeming contradiction; and in the comic he is still reaching at some thin conceit, the ghost of a jest, and that too flies before him, never to be caught; these swallows which we see before us on the Thames are the just resemblance of his wit: you may observe how near the water they stoop, how many proffers they make to dip, and yet how seldom they touch it; and when they do, it is but the surface: they skim over it but to catch a gnat, and then mount into the air and leave it."

"Well, gentlemen," said Eugenius, "you may speak your pleasure of these authors; but though I and some few more about the town may give you a peaceable hearing, yet assure yourselves, there are multitudes who would think you malicious and them injured: especially him whom you first described; he is the very Withers of the city: they have bought more editions of his works than would serve to lay under all their pies at the Lord Mayor's Christmas. When his famous poem first came out in the year 1660, I have seen them reading it in the midst of 'Change time; nay so vehement they were at it, that they lost their bargain by the candles' ends; but what will you say if he has been received amongst great persons? I can assure you he is, this day, the envy of one who is lord in the art of quibbling, and who does not take it well that any man should intrude so far into his prov-

---

[2] "Once, in a crowd, a bad poet offered him a volume of elegies he had written on the general. Sylla ordered that he be given a reward from the war-booty provided he never write anything afterwards" (Cicero, *Pro Archia,* 10, 25).

[3] See Pope's *Essay on Criticism,* ll. 345 ff., below, for a repetition and illustration.

[4] "Cinna wishes to appear a pauper; and he is."

ince." "All I would wish," replied Crites, "is, that they who love his writings, may still admire him, and his fellow poet: *Qui Bavium non odit, etc.,*[5] is curse sufficient." "And farther," added Lisideius, "I believe there is no man who writes well, but would think he had hard measure, if their admirers should praise anything of his: *Nam quos contemnimus, eorum quoque laudes contemnimus.*"[6] "There are so few who write well in this age," says Crites, "that methinks any praises should be welcome; they neither rise to the dignity of the last age, nor to any of the Ancients: and we may cry out of the writers of this time, with more reason than Petronius of his, *Pace vestrâ liceat dixisse, primi omnium eloquentiam perdidistis:*[7] you have debauched the true old poetry so far, that Nature, which is the soul of it, is not in any of your writings."

"If your quarrel," said Eugenius, "to those who now write, be grounded only on your reverence to antiquity, there is no man more ready to adore those great Greeks and Romans than I am: but on the other side, I cannot think so contemptibly of the age in which I live, or so dishonourably of my own country, as not to judge we equal the Ancients in most kinds of poesy, and in some surpass them; neither know I any reason why I may not be as zealous for the reputation of our age as we find the Ancients themselves were in reference to those who lived before them. For you hear your Horace saying,

Indignor quidquam reprehendi, non quia crasse
Compositum, illepidève putetur, sed quia nuper.

And after:

Si meliora dies, ut vina, poemata reddit,
Scire velim, pretim chartis quotus arroget annus?[8]

"But I see I am engaging in a wide dispute, where the arguments are not like to reach close on either side; for Poesy is of so large an ex-

tent, and so many both of the Ancients and Moderns have done well in all kinds of it, that in citing one against the other, we shall take up more time this evening than each man's occasions will allow him: therefore I would ask Crites to what part of Poesy he would confine his arguments, and whether he would defend the general cause of the Ancients against the Moderns, or oppose any age of the Moderns against this of ours?"

Crites, a little while considering upon this demand, told Eugenius, that if he pleased, he would limit their dispute to Dramatic Poesy; in which he thought it not difficult to prove, either that the Ancients were superior to the Moderns, or the last age of this of ours.

Eugenius was somewhat surprised, when he heard Crites make choice of that subject. "For aught I see," said he, "I have undertaken a harder province than I imagined; for though I never judged the plays of the Greek or Roman poets comparable to ours, yet, on the other side, those we now see acted come short of many which were written in the last age: but my comfort is, if we are overcome, it will be only by our own countrymen: and if we yield to them in this one part of poesy, we more surpass them in all the other: for in the epic or lyric way, it will be hard for them to show us one such amongst them, as we have many now living, or who lately were: they can produce nothing so courtly writ, or which expresses so much the conversation of a gentleman, as Sir John Suckling; nothing so even, sweet, and flowing as Mr. Waller; nothing so majestic, so correct, as Sir John Denham; nothing so elevated, so copious, and full of spirit as Mr. Cowley; as for the Italian, French, and Spanish plays, I can make it evident, that those who now write surpass them; and that the Drama is wholly ours."

All of them were thus far of Eugenius his opinion, that the sweetness of English verse was never understood or practised by our fathers; even Crites himself did not much oppose it; and every one was willing to acknowledge how much our poesy is improved by the happiness of some writers yet living; who first taught us to mould our thoughts into easy and significant words,— to retrench the superfluities of expression,—and to make our rhyme so properly a part of the

---

[5] "Who does not hate Bavius?"

[6] "We despise the praise of those we despise."

[7] "You were the first, if I may say so, to lose the eloquence everyone before you had."

[8] "I dislike to see something condemned not because it is clumsy and witless but only because it is new"; and "If age makes poems better, as it does wines, how many years are necessary for the process?" (*Epistles,* II, i, 76 and 34).

verse, that it should never mislead the sense, but itself be led and governed by it.

Eugenius was going to continue this discourse, when Lisideius told him that it was necessary, before they proceeded further, to take a standing measure of their controversy; for how was it possible to be decided who writ the best plays, before we know what a play should be? But, this once agreed on by both parties, each might have recourse to it, either to prove his own advantages, or to discover the failings of his adversary.

He had no sooner said this, but all desired the favour of him to give the definition of a play; and they were the more importunate, because neither Aristotle, nor Horace, nor any other, who had writ of that subject, had ever done it.

Lisideius, after some modest denials, at last confessed he had a rude notion of it; indeed, rather a description than a definition; but which served to guide him in his private thoughts, when he was to make a judgment of what others writ: that he conceived a play ought to be, *A just and lively image of human nature, representing its passions and humours, and the changes of fortune to which it is subject, for the delight and instruction of mankind.*

This definition, though Crites raised a logical objection against it—that it was only *a genere et fine,* and so not altogether perfect, was yet well received by the rest; and after they had given order to the watermen to turn their barge, and row softly, that they might take the cool of the evening in their return, Crites, being desired by the company to begin, spoke on behalf of the Ancients, in this manner:—

"If confidence presage a victory, Eugenius, in his own opinion, has already triumphed over the Ancients: nothing seems more easy to him, than to overcome those whom it is our greatest praise to have imitated well; for we do not only build upon their foundations, but by their models. Dramatic Poesy had time enough, reckoning from Thespis (who first invented it) to Aristophanes, to be born, to grow up, and to flourish in maturity. It has been observed of arts and sciences, that in one and the same century they have arrived to great perfection; and no wonder, since every age has a kind of universal genius, which inclines those that live in it to some particular studies: the work then, be-

ing pushed on by many hands, must of necessity go forward.

"Is it not evident, in these last hundred years, (when the study of philosophy has been the business of all the Virtuosi in Christendom), that almost a new nature has been revealed to us? That more errors of the school have been detected, more useful experiments in philosophy have been made, more noble secrets in optics, medicine, anatomy, astronomy, discovered, than in all those credulous and doting ages from Aristotle to us?—so true it is, that nothing spreads more fast than science, when rightly and generally cultivated.

"Add to this, the more than common emulation that was in those times of writing well; which though it be found in all ages and all persons that pretend to the same reputation, yet Poesy, being then in more esteem than now it is, had greater honours decreed to the professors of it, and consequently the rivalship was more high between them; they had judges ordained to decide their merit, and prizes to reward it; and historians have been diligent to record of Eschylus, Euripides, Sophocles, Lycophron, and the rest of them, both who they were that vanquished in these wars of the theatre, and how often they were crowned: while the Asian kings and Grecian commonwealths scarce afforded them a nobler subject than the unmanly luxuries of a debauched court, or giddy intrigues of a factious city:—*Alit aemulatio ingenia* (says Paterculus), *et nunc invidia, nunc admiratio incitationem accendit:* Emulation is the spur of wit; and sometimes envy, sometimes admiration, quickens our endeavours.

"But now, since the rewards of honour are taken away, that virtuous emulation is turned into direct malice; yet so slothful, that it contents itself to condemn and cry down others, without attempting to do better: it is a reputation too unprofitable, to take the necessary pains for it; yet, wishing they had it, that desire is incitement enough to hinder others from it. And this, in short, Eugenius, is the reason why you have now so few good poets, and so many severe judges. Certainly, to imitate the Ancients well, much labour and long study is required; which pains, I have already shown, our poets would want encouragement to take, if yet they had ability to go through the work. Those Ancients have been faithful imitators and wise observers of that Nature which is so torn and ill represented in our plays; they have handed down to us a perfect resemblance of her; which we, like ill copiers, neglecting to look on, have rendered monstrous, and disfigured. But, that you may know how much you are indebted to those your masters, and be ashamed to have so ill requited them, I must remember you, that all the rules by which we practise the Drama at this day (either such as relate to the justness and symmetry of the plot, or the episodical ornaments, such as descriptions, narrations, and other beauties, which are not essential to the play,) were delivered to us from the observations which Aristotle made, of those poets, who either lived before him, or were his contemporaries: we have added nothing of our own, except we have the confidence to say our wit is better; of which, none boast in this our age, but such as understand not theirs. Of that book which Aristotle has left us, περὶ τῆς Ποιητικῆς, Horace his Art of Poetry is an excellent comment, and, I believe, restores to us that Second Book of his concerning *Comedy*, which is wanting in him.

"Out of these two have been extracted the famous Rules, which the French call *Des Trois Unitez*, or, The Three Unities, which ought to be observed in every regular play; namely, of Time, Place, and Action.

"The Unity of Time they comprehend in twenty-four hours, the compass of a natural day, or as near as it can be contrived; and the reason of it is obvious to every one,—that the time of the feigned action, or fable of the play, should be proportioned as near as can be to the duration of that time in which it is represented: since, therefore, all plays are acted on the theatre in the space of time much within the compass of twenty-four hours, that play is to be thought the nearest imitation of nature, whose plot or action is confined within that time; and, by the same rule which concludes this general proportion of time, it follows, that all the parts of it are (as near as may be) to be equally subdivided; namely, that one act take not up the supposed time of half a day, which is out of proportion to the rest; since the other four are then to be straitened within the compass of the remaining half: for it is unnatural that one act, which being spoke or written is not longer than

the rest, should be supposed longer by the audience; it is therefore the poet's duty, to take care that no act should be imagined to exceed the time in which it is represented on the stage; and that the intervals and inequalities of time be supposed to fall out between the acts.[9]

"This rule of time, how well it has been observed by the Ancients, most of their plays will witness: you see them in their tragedies (wherein to follow this rule is certainly most difficult), from the very beginning of their plays, falling close into that part of the story which they intend for the action or principal object of it, leaving the former part to be delivered by narration: so that they set the audience, as it were, at the post where the race is to be concluded; and, saving them the tedious expectation of seeing the poet set out and ride the beginning of the course, they suffer you not to behold him, till he is in sight of the goal, and just upon you.

"For the second Unity, which is that of Place, the Ancients meant by it, that the scene ought to be continued through the play, in the same place where it was laid in the beginning: for, the stage on which it is represented being but one and the same place, it is unnatural to conceive it many,—and those far distant from one another. I will not deny but, by the variation of painted scenes, the fancy, which in these cases will contribute to its own deceit, may sometimes imagine it several places, with some appearance of probability; yet it still carries the greater likelihood of truth if those places be supposed so near each other as in the same town or city; which may all be comprehended under the larger denomination of one place; for a greater distance will bear no proportion to the shortness of time which is allotted, in the acting, to pass from one of them to another; for the observation of this, next to the Ancients, the French are to be most commended. They tie themselves so strictly to the Unity of Place that you never see in any of their plays a scene changed in the middle of an act: if the act begins in a garden, a street, or chamber, 'tis ended in the same place; and that you may know it to be the same, the stage is so supplied with persons, that it is never empty all the time: he who enters second, has business with him who was

[9] See above, p. 117.

on before; and before the second quits the stage, a third appears who has business with him. This Corneille calls *la liaison des scenes*, the continuity or joining of the scenes; and 'tis a good mark of a well-contrived play, when all the persons are known to each other, and every one of them has some affairs with all the rest.

"As for the third Unity, which is that of Action, the Ancients meant no other by it than what the logicians do by their *finis*, the end or scope of any action; that which is the first in intention, and last in execution: now the poet is to aim at one great and complete action, to the carrying on of which all things in his play, even the very obstacles, are to be subservient; and the reason of this is as evident as any of the former. For two actions, equally laboured and driven on by the writer, would destroy the unity of the poem; it would be no longer one play, but two: not but that there may be many actions in a play, as Ben Jonson has observed in his *Discoveries;* but they must be all subservient to the great one, which our language happily expresses in the name of *under-plots:* such as in Terence's *Eunuch* is the difference and reconcilement of Thais and Phaedria, which is not the chief business of the play, but promotes the marriage of Chaerea and Chremes's sister, principally intended by the poet. There ought to be but one action, says Corneille, that is, one complete action, which leaves the mind of the audience in a full repose; but this cannot be brought to pass but by many other imperfect actions, which conduce to it, and hold the audience in a delightful suspence of what will be.

"If by these rules (to omit many other drawn from the precepts and practice of the Ancients) we should judge our modern plays, 'tis probable that few of them would endure the trial: that which should be the business of a day, takes up in some of them an age; instead of one action, they are the epitomes of a man's life; and for one spot of ground, which the stage should represent, we are sometimes in more countries than the map can show us.

"But if we allow the Ancients to have contrived well, we must acknowledge them to have written better. Questionless we are deprived of a great stock of wit in the loss of Menander among the Greek poets, and of Caecilius, Afra-

nius, and Varius, among the Romans; we may guess at Menander's excellency by the plays of Terence, who translated some of his; and yet wanted so much of him, that he was called by C. Caesar the half-Menander; and may judge of Varius, by the testimonies of Horace, Martial, and Velleius Paterculus. 'Tis probable that these, could they be recovered, would decide the controversy; but so long as Aristophanes and Plautus are extant, while the tragedies of Euripides, Sophocles, and Seneca, are in our hands, I can never see one of those plays which are now written but it increases my admiration of the Ancients. And yet I must acknowledge further, that to admire them as we ought, we should understand them better than we do. Doubtless many things appear flat to us, the wit of which depended on some custom or story, which never came to our knowledge; or perhaps on some criticism in their language, which being so long dead, and only remaining in their books, 'tis not possible they should make us understand perfectly. To read Macrobius, explaining the propriety and elegancy of many words in Virgil, which I had before passed over without consideration as common things, is enough to assure me that I ought to think the same of Terence; and that in the purity of his style (which Tully so much valued that he ever carried his works about him) there is yet left in him great room for admiration, if I knew but where to place it. In the meantime I must desire you to take notice that the greatest man of the last age (Ben Jonson) was willing to give place to them in all things: he was not only a professed imitator of Horace, but a learned plagiary of all the others; you track him everywhere in their snow: if Horace, Lucan, Petronius Arbiter, Seneca, and Juvenal, had their own from him, there are few serious thoughts which are new in him: you will pardon me, therefore, if I presume he loved their fashion, when he wore their clothes. But since I have otherwise a great veneration for him, and you, Eugenius, prefer him above all other poets, I will use no farther argument to you than his example: I will produce before you Father Ben, dressed in all the ornaments and colours of the Ancients; you will need no other guide to our party, if you follow him; and whether you consider the bad plays of our age, or regard the good plays of the last, both the best and worst of the modern poets will equally instruct you to admire the Ancients."

Crites had no sooner left speaking, but Eugenius, who had waited with some impatience for it, thus began:

"I have observed in your speech, that the former part of it is convincing as to what the Moderns have profited by the rules of the Ancients; but in the latter you are careful to conceal how much they have excelled them; we own all the helps we have from them, and want neither veneration nor gratitude, while we acknowledge that, to overcome them, we must make use of the advantages we have received from them: but to these assistances we have joined our own industry; for, had we sat down with a dull imitation of them, we might then have lost somewhat of the old perfection, but never acquired any that was new. We draw not therefore after their lines, but those of Nature; and having the life before us, besides the experience of all they knew, it is no wonder if we hit some airs and features which they have missed. I deny not what you urge of arts and sciences, that they have flourished in some ages more than others; but your instance in philosophy makes for me: for if natural causes be more known now than in the time of Aristotle, because more studied, it follows that poesy and other arts may, with the same pains, arrive still nearer to perfection; and, that granted, it will rest for you to prove that they wrought more perfect images of human life than we; which seeing in your discourse you have avoided to make good, it shall now be my task to show you some part of their defects, and some few excellencies of the Moderns. And I think there is none among us can imagine I do it enviously, or with purpose to detract from them; for what interest of fame or profit can the living lose by the reputation of the dead? On the other side, it is a great truth which Velleius Paterculus affirms: *Audita visis libentius laudamus; et praesentia invidia praeterita admiratione prosequimur; et his nos obrui, illis instrui credimus:* [10] that praise or censure is certainly the most sincere, which unbribed posterity shall give us.

"Be pleased then in the first place to take notice that the Greek poesy, which Crites has affirmed to have arrived to perfection in the reign of the Old Comedy, was so far from it that the distinction of it into acts was not known to them; or if it were, it is yet so darkly delivered to us that we cannot make it out.

"All we know of it is from the singing of their Chorus; and that too is so uncertain, that in some of their plays we have reason to conjecture they sung more than five times. Aristotle indeed divides the integral parts of a play into four. First, the *Protasis*, or entrance, which gives light only to the characters of the persons, and proceeds very little into any part of the action. Secondly, the *Epitasis*, or working up of the plot; where the play grows warmer, the design or action of it is drawing on, and you see something promising that it will come to pass. Thirdly, the *Catastasis*, called by the Romans, *Status*, the height and full growth of the play: we may call it properly the counter-turn, which destroys that expectation, imbroils the action in new difficulties, and leaves you far distant from that hope in which it found you; as you may have observed in a violent stream resisted by a narrow passage,—it runs round to an eddy, and carries back the waters with more swiftness than it brought them on. Lastly, the *Catastrophe*, which the Grecians called λύσις, the French *le dénouement*, and we the discovery, or unravelling of the plot: there you see all things settling again upon their first foundations; and, the obstacles which hindered the design or action of the play once removed, it ends with that resemblance of truth and nature, that the audience are satisfied with the conduct of it. Thus this great man delivered to us the image of a play; and I must confess it is so lively, that from thence much light has been derived to the forming it more perfectly into acts and scenes: but what poet first limited to five the number of the acts, I know not; only we see it so firmly established in the time of Horace, that he gives it for a rule in comedy,— *Neu brevior quinto, neu sit productior actu.* [11] So that you see the Grecians cannot be said to have consummated this art; writing rather by entrances than by acts, and having rather a gen-

---

[10] "We praise more freely what we *hear* than what we *see;* and we regard the present with envy, the past with admiration: and we feel injured by the first [the present], instructed by the latter."

[11] "Let it be neither more nor less than five acts" (*Art of Poetry*, above, p. 54).

eral indigested notion of a play, than knowing how and where to bestow the particular graces of it.

"But since the Spaniards at this day allow but three acts, which they call *Jornadas,* to a play, and the Italians in many of theirs follow them, when I condemn the Ancients, I declare it is not altogether because they have not five acts to every play, but because they have not confined themselves to one certain number: it is building an house without a model; and when they succeeded in such undertakings, they ought to have sacrificed to Fortune, not to the Muses.

"Next, for the plot, which Aristotle called τὸ μῦθος, and often τῶν πραγμάτων σύνθεσις,[12] and from him the Romans *Fabula;* it has already been judiciously observed by a late writer, that in their tragedies it was only some tale derived from Thebes or Troy, or at least something that happened in those two ages; which was worn so threadbare by the pens of all the epic poets, and even by tradition, itself of the talkative Greeklings (as Ben Jonson calls them), that before it came upon the stage it was already known to all the audience: and the people, so soon as ever they heard the name of Oedipus, knew as well as the poet, that he had killed his father by a mistake, and committed incest with his mother, before the play; that they were now to hear of a great plague, an oracle, and the ghost of Laius: so that they sat with a yawning kind of expectation, till he was to come with his eyes pulled out, and speak a hundred or more verses in a tragic tone, in complaint of his misfortunes. But one Oedipus, Hercules, or Medea, had been tolerable: poor people, they escaped not so good cheap; they had still the *Chapon bouille*[13] set before them, till their appetites were cloyed with the same dish, and, the novelty being gone, the pleasure vanished; so that one main end of Dramatic Poesy in its definition, which was to cause delight, was of consequence destroyed.

"In their comedies, the Romans generally borrowed their plots from the Greek poets; and theirs was commonly a little girl stolen or wandered from her parents, brought back unknown to the city, there [falling into the hands of] some young fellow, who, by the help of his servant, cheats his father; and when her time comes, to cry,—*Juno Lucina fer opem,*[14]—one or other sees a little box or cabinet which was carried away with her, and so discovers her to her friends, if some god do not prevent it, by coming down in a machine, and taking the thanks of it to himself.

"By the plot you may guess much of the characters of the persons. An old father, who would willingly, before he dies, see his son well married; his debauched son, kind in his nature to his mistress, but miserably in want of money; a servant or slave, who has so much wit to strike in with him, and help to dupe his father; a braggadocio captain, a parasite, and a lady of pleasure.

"As for the poor honest maid, on whom the story is built, and who ought to be one of the principal actors in the play, she is commonly a mute in it: she has the breeding of the old Elizabeth way, which was for maids to be seen and not to be heard; and it is enough you know she is willing to be married, when the fifth act requires it.

"These are plots built after the Italian mode of houses, you see through them all at once: the characters are indeed the imitation of Nature, but so narrow, as if they had imitated only an eye or an hand, and did not dare to venture on the lines of a face, or the proportion of a body.

"But in how strait a compass soever they have bounded their plots and characters, we will pass it by, if they have regularly pursued them, and perfectly observed those three Unities of Time, Place, and Action; the knowledge of which you say is derived to us from them. But in the first place give me leave to tell you, that the Unity of Place, however it might be practised by them, was never any of their rules: we neither find it in Aristotle, Horace, or any who have written of it, till in our age the French poets first made it a precept of the stage. The Unity of Time, even Terence himself, who was the best and most regular of them, has neglected: his *Heautontimorumenos,* or Self-Punisher, takes up visibly two days, says Scaliger; the two first acts concluding the first day, the three last the day en-

---

[12] "The putting together of actions."
[13] "Sop at bread."

[14] "Juno Lucina [goddess of childbirth], give help to me."

suing; and Euripides, in tying himself to one day, has committed an absurdity never to be forgiven him; for in one of his tragedies he has made Theseus go from Athens to Thebes, which was about forty English miles, under the walls of it to give battle, and appear victorious in the next act; and yet, from the time of his departure to the return of the Nuntius, who gives the relation of his victory, Æthra and the Chorus have but thirty-six verses; which is not for every mile a verse.

"The like error is as evident in Terence his *Eunuch,* when Laches, the old man, enters by mistake into the house of Thais; where, betwixt his exit and the entrance of Pythias, who comes to give ample relation of the disorders he has raised within, Parmeno, who was left upon the stage, has not above five lines to speak. *C'est bien employer un temps si court,*[15] says the French poet, who furnished me with one of the observations: and almost all their tragedies will afford us examples of the like nature.

"It is true, they have kept the continuity, or, as you called it, *liaison des scenes,* somewhat better: two do not perpetually come in together, talk, and go out together; and other two succeed them, and do the same throughout the act, which the English call by the name of single scenes; but the reason is, because they have seldom above two or three scenes, properly so called, in every act; for it is to be accounted a new scene, not only every time the stage is empty; but every person who enters, though to others, makes it so; because he introduces a new business. Now the plots of their plays being narrow, and the persons few, one of their acts was written in a less compass than one of our well-wrought scenes; and yet they are often deficient even in this. To go no further than Terence; you find in the *Eunuch,* Antipho entering single in the midst of the third act, after Chremes and Pythias were gone off; in the same play you have likewise Dorias beginning the fourth act alone; and after she had made a relation of what was done at the Soldier's entertainment (which by the way was very inartificial, because she was presumed to speak directly to the audience, and to acquaint them with what was necessary to be known, but yet should have

been so contrived by the poet as to have been told by persons of the drama to one another, and so by them to have come to the knowledge of the people), she quits the stage, and Phaedria enters next, alone likewise: he also gives you an account of himself, and of his returning from the country, in monologue; to which unnatural way of narration Terence is subject in all his plays. In his *Adelphi,* or Brothers, Syrus and Demea enter after the scene was broken by the departure of Sostrata, Geta, and Canthara; and indeed you can scarce look unto any of his comedies, where you will not presently discover the same interruption.

"But as they have failed both in laying of their plots, and in the management, swerving from the rules of their own art by misrepresenting Nature to us, in which they have ill satisfied one intention of a play, which was delight; so in the instructive part they have erred worse: instead of punishing vice and rewarding virtue, they have often shewn a prosperous wickedness, and an unhappy piety: they have set before us a bloody image of revenge in Medea, and given her dragons to convey her safe from punishment; a Priam and Astyanax murdered, and Cassandra ravished, and the lust and murder ending in the victory of him who acted them: in short, there is no indecorum in any of our modern plays, which if I would excuse, I could not shadow with some authority from the Ancients.

"And one farther note of them let me leave you: tragedies and comedies were not writ then as they are now, promiscuously, by the same person; but he who found his genius bending to the one, never attempted the other way. This is so plain, that I need not instance to you, that Aristophanes, Plautus, Terence, never any of them writ a tragedy; Æschylus, Euripides, Sophocles, and Seneca, never meddled with comedy: the sock and buskin were not worn by the same poet. Having then so much care to excel in one kind, very little is to be pardoned them, if they miscarried in it; and this would lead me to the consideration of their wit, had not Crites given me sufficient warning not to be too bold in my judgment of it; because, the languages being dead, and many of the customs and little accidents on which it depended lost to us, we are not competent judges of it. But

---

[15] "It is well to employ a time so short."

though I grant that here and there we may miss the application of a proverb or a custom, yet a thing well said will be wit in all languages; and though it may lose something in the translation, yet to him who reads it in the original, 'tis still the same: he has an idea of its excellency, though it cannot pass from his mind into any other expression or words than those in which he finds it. When Phaedria, in the *Eunuch,* had a command from his mistress to be absent two days, and, encouraging himself to go through with it, said, *Tandem ego non illa caream, si sit opus, vel totum triduum?*—Parmeno, to mock the softness of his master, lifting up his hands and eyes, cries out, as it were in admiration, *Hui! universum triduum!* [16] the elegancy of which *universum,* though it cannot be rendered in our language, yet leaves an impression on our souls: but this happens seldom in him; in Plautus oftener, who is infinitely too bold in his metaphors and coining words, out of which many times his wit is nothing; which questionless was one reason why Horace falls upon him so severely in those verses:

Sed proavi nostri Plautinos et numeros et
Laudavere sales, nimium patienter utrumque,
Ne dicam stolidè. [17]

For Horace himself was cautious to obtrude a new word on his readers, and makes custom and common use the best measure of receiving it into our writings:

Multa renascentur quae nunc cecidere, cadentque
Quae nunc sunt in honore vocabula, si volet usus,
Quem penes arbitrium est, et jus, et norma lo-
quendi. [18]

"The not observing this rule is that which the world has blamed in our satirist, Cleveland: to express a thing hard and unnaturally, is his new way of elocution. 'Tis true, no poet but may sometimes use a catachresis: Virgil does it—

Mistaque ridenti colocasia fundet acantho—

in his eclogue of *Pollio;* and in his 7th *Aeneid:*

mirantur et undae,
Miratur nemus insuetum fulgentia longe
Scuta virum fluvio pictasque innare carinas. [19]

And Ovid once so modestly, that he asks leave to do it:

si verbo audacia detur,
Haud metuam summi dixisse Palatia caeli.

calling the court of Jupiter by the name of Augustus his palace; though in another place he is more bold, where he says,—*et longas visent Capitolia pompas.* [20] But to do this always, and never be able to write a line without it, though it may be admired by some few pedants, will not pass upon those who know that wit is best conveyed to us in the most easy language; and is most to be admired when a great thought comes dressed in words so commonly received, that it is understood by the meanest apprehensions, as the best meat is the most easily digested: but we cannot read a verse of Cleveland's without making a face at it, as if every word were a pill to swallow: he gives us many times a hard nut to break our teeth, without a kernel for our pains. So that there is this difference betwixt his Satires and doctor Donne's; that the one gives us deep thoughts in common language, though rough cadence; the other gives us common thoughts in abstruse words: 'tis true, in some places his wit is independent of his words, as in that of the rebel Scot:

Had *Cain* been *Scot,* God would have chang'd his doom;
Not forc'd him wander, but confin'd him home.

"*Si sic, omnia dixisset!* [21] This is wit in all languages: 'tis like Mercury, never to be lost or killed:—and so that other—

For beauty, like white powder, makes no noise,
And yet the silent hypocrite destroys.

---

[16] "Shall I not do without her for even three days if necessary?" and "Alas, the total of three days!" (II, i).

[17] "But our ancestors praised the meter and wit of Plautus, admiring each of them tolerantly if not stupidly" (*Art of Poetry,* ll. 270-72).

[18] "Many words now disused shall revive, and many now esteemed shall wither, if custom wills; for custom determines right usage in language" (*Ibid.,* see above, p. 52).

[19] "The bean shall flower, joined with the laughing acanthus" (*Eclogues,* IV, 20); and "Woods and the waters marvel at the shining shields and painted ships on the waves" (*Aeneid,* VIII, 91).

[20] "If verbal license is allowed, I shall not fear to call it the imperial palace"; and "The Capitol sees long processions" (*Metamorphoses,* I, 175, 561).

[21] "If only he had spoken everything thus."

You see the last line is highly metaphorical, but it is so soft and gentle, that it does not shock us as we read it.

"But, to return from whence I have digressed, to the consideration of the Ancients' writing, and their wit (of which by this time you will grant us in some measure to be fit judges). Though I see many excellent thoughts in Seneca, yet he of them who had a genius most proper for the stage, was Ovid; he had a way of writing so fit to stir up a pleasing admiration and concernment, which are the objects of a tragedy, and to show the various movements of a soul combating betwixt two different passions, that, had he lived in our age, or in his own could have writ with our advantages, no man but must have yielded to him; and therefore I am confident the *Medea* is none of his: for, though I esteem it for the gravity and sententiousness of it, which he himself concludes to be suitable to a tragedy,—*Omne genus scripti gravitate tragaedia vincit*,[22]—yet it moves not my soul enough to judge that he, who in the epic way wrote things so near the drama as the story of Myrrha, of Caunus and Biblis, and the rest, should stir up no more concernment where he most endeavoured it. The masterpiece of Seneca I hold to be that scene in the *Troades*, where Ulysses is seeking for Astyanax to kill him: there you see the tenderness of a mother so represented in Andromache, that it raises compassion to a high degree in the reader, and bears the nearest resemblance of anything in the tragedies of the ancients to the excellent scenes of passion in Shakespeare, or in Fletcher: for love-scenes, you will find few among them; their tragic poets dealt not with that soft passion, but with lust, cruelty, revenge, ambition, and those bloody actions they produced; which were more capable of raising horror than compassion in an audience: leaving love untouched, whose gentleness would have tempered them; which is the most frequent of all the passions, and which, being the private concernment of every person, is soothed by viewing its own image in a public entertainment.

"Among their comedies, we find a scene or two of tenderness, and that where you would

least expect it, in Plautus; but to speak generally, their lovers say little, when they see each other, but *anima mea, vita mea;* Ζωὴ καὶ ψυχῆ,[23] as the women in Juvenal's time used to cry out in the fury of their kindness. Any sudden gust of passion (as an ecstasy of love in an unexpected meeting) cannot better be expressed than in a word and a sigh, breaking one another. Nature is dumb on such occasions; and to make her speak would be to represent her unlike herself. But there are a thousand other concernments of lovers, as jealousies, complaints, contrivances, and the like, where not to open their minds at large to each other, were to be wanting to their own love, and to the expectation of the audience; who watch the movements of their minds, as much as the changes of their fortunes. For the imagining of the first is properly the work of a poet; the latter he borrows from the historian."

Eugenius was proceeding in that part of his discourse, when Crites interrupted him. "I see," said he, "Eugenius and I are never like to have this question decided betwixt us; for he maintains, the Moderns have acquired a new perfection in writing; I can only grant they have altered the mode of it. Homer described his heroes men of great appetites, lovers of beef broiled upon the coals, and good fellows; contrary to the practice of the French Romances, whose heroes neither eat, nor drink, nor sleep, for love. Virgil makes Æneas a bold avower of his own virtues:

Sum pius Aeneas, fama super aethera notus;[24]

which, in the civility of our poets is the character of a fanfaron or Hector: for with us the knight takes occasion to walk out, or sleep, to avoid the vanity of telling his own story, which the trusty 'squire is ever to perform for him. So in their love-scenes, of which Eugenius spoke last, the ancients were more hearty, were more talkative: they writ love as it was then the mode to make it; and I will grant thus much to Eugenius, that perhaps one of their poets had he lived in our age, *si foret hoc nostrum fato delapsus in aevum* [25] (as Horace says of Lucilius), he had altered many things; not that they were not

---

[22] "Tragedy exceeds every other kind of writing in gravity."

[23] "My soul, my life."

[24] "I am pious Aeneas, whose fame is known above the heavens" (*Aeneid*, I, 378-79).

[25] "If he had been dropped into our age by fate."

natural before, but that he might accommodate himself to the age in which he lived. Yet in the meantime, we are not to conclude anything rashly against those great men, but preserve to them the dignity of masters, and give that honour to their memories, *quos Libitina sacravit*,[26] part of which we expect may be paid to us in future times."

This moderation of Crites, as it was pleasing to all the company, so it put an end to that dispute; which Eugenius, who seemed to have the better of the argument, would urge no farther: but Lisideius, after he had acknowledged himself of Eugenius his opinion concerning the Ancients, yet told him, he had forborne, till his discourse were ended, to ask him why he preferred the English plays above those of other nations? and whether we ought not to submit our stage to the exactness of our next neighbours?

"Though," said Eugenius, "I am at all times ready to defend the honour of my country against the French, and to maintain, we are as well able to vanquish them with our pens, as our ancestors have been with their swords; yet, if you please," added he, looking upon Neander, "I will commit this cause to my friend's management; his opinion of our plays is the same with mine, and besides, there is no reason, that Crites and I, who have now left the stage, should re-enter so suddenly upon it; which is against the laws of comedy."

"If the question had been stated," replied Lisideius, "who had writ best, the French or English, forty years ago, I should have been of your opinion, and adjudged the honour to our own nation; but since that time" (said he, turning towards Neander), "we have been so long together bad Englishmen that we had not leisure to be good poets. Beaumont, Fletcher, and Jonson (who were only capable of bringing us to that degree of perfection which we have), were just then leaving the world; as if in an age of so much horror, wit, and those milder studies of humanity, had no farther business among us. But the Muses, who ever follow peace, went to plant in another country: it was then that the great Cardinal Richelieu began to take them into his protection; and that, by his encouragement, Corneille, and some other French-

men, reformed their theatre (which before was as much below ours, as it now surpasses it and the rest of Europe). But because Crites in his discourse for the Ancients has prevented me, by observing many rules of the stage which the Moderns have borrowed from them, I shall only, in short, demand of you, whether you are not convinced that of all nations the French have best observed them? In the Unity of Time you find them so scrupulous that it yet remains a dispute among their poets, whether the artificial day of twelve hours, more or less, be not meant by Aristotle, rather than the natural one of twenty-four; and consequently, whether all plays ought not to be reduced into that compass. This I can testify, that in all their dramas writ within these last twenty years and upwards, I have not observed any that have extended the time to thirty hours: in the Unity of Place they are full as scrupulous; for many of their critics limit it to that very spot of ground where the play is supposed to begin; none of them exceed the compass of the same town or city. The Unity of Action in all plays is yet more conspicuous; for they do not burden them with under-plots, as the English do: which is the reason why many scenes of our tragi-comedians carry on a design that is nothing of kin to the main plot; and that we see two distinct webs in a play, like those in ill-wrought stuffs; and two actions, that is, two plays, carried on together, to the confounding of the audience; who, before they are warm in their concernments for one part, are diverted to another; and by that means espouse the interest of neither. From hence likewise it arises that the one half of our actors are not known to the other. They keep their distances, as if they were Montagues and Capulets, and seldom begin an acquaintance till the last scene of the fifth act, when they are all to meet upon the stage. There is no theatre in the world has anything so absurd as the English tragi-comedy; 'tis a drama of our own invention, and the fashion of it is enough to proclaim it so; here a course of mirth, there another of sadness and passion, and a third of honour and a duel: thus, in two hours and a half, we run through all the fits of Bedlam. The French affords you as much variety on the same day, but they do it not so unseasonably, or *mal à propos*, as we: our poets present you the play and the farce together; and our stages still re-

---

[26] "Which Libitina has consecrated."

tain somewhat of the original civility of the Red Bull:

Atque ursum et pugiles media inter carmina poscunt.[27]

The end of tragedies or serious plays, says Aristotle, is to beget admiration, compassion, or concernment; but are not mirth and compassion things incompatible? and is it not evident that the poet must of necessity destroy the former by intermingling of the latter? that is, he must ruin the sole end and object of his tragedy, to introduce somewhat that is forced into it, and is not of the body of it. Would you not think that physician mad, who, having prescribed a purge, should immediately order you to take restringents?

"But to leave our plays, and return to theirs. I have noted one great advantage they have had in the plotting of their tragedies; that is, they are always grounded upon some known history: according to that of Horace, *Ex noto fictum carmen sequar;* [28] and in that they have so imitated the Ancients that they have surpassed them. For the Ancients, as was observed before, took for the foundation of their plays some poetical fiction, such as under that consideration could move but little concernment in the audience, because they already knew the event of it. But the French goes farther:

Atque ita mentitur, sic veris falsa remiscet
Primo ne medium, medio ne discrepet imum.[29]

He so interweaves truth with probable fiction that he puts a pleasing fallacy upon us; mends the intrigues of fate, and dispenses with the severity of history, to reward that virtue which has been rendered to us there unfortunate. Sometimes the story has left the success so doubtful that the writer is free, by the privilege of a poet, to take that which of two or more relations will best suit with his design: as for example, in the death of Cyrus, whom Justin and some others report to have perished in the Scythian war, but Xenophon affirms to have died in his bed of extreme old age. Nay more, when the event is past dispute, even then we are willing to be deceived, and the poet, if he contrives it with appearance of truth, has all the audience of his party; at least during the time his play is acting: so naturally we are kind to virtue, when our own interest is not in question, that we take it up as the general concernment of mankind. On the other side, if you consider the historical plays of Shakespeare, they are rather so many chronicles of kings, or the business many times of thirty or forty years, cramped into a representation of two hours and a half; which is not to imitate or paint Nature, but rather to draw her in miniature, to take her in little; to look upon her through the wrong end of a perspective, and receive her images not only much less, but infinitely more imperfect than the life: this, instead of making a play delightful, renders it ridiculous:—

Quodcunque ostendis mihi sic, incredulus odi.[30]

For the spirit of man cannot be satisfied but with truth, or at least verisimility; and a poem is to contain, if not τὰ ἔτυμα, yet ἐτύμοισιν ὁμοῖα,[31] as one of the Greek poets has expressed it.

"Another thing in which the French differ from us and from the Spaniards, is that they do not embarrass, or cumber themselves with too much plot; they only represent so much of a story as will constitute one whole and great action sufficient for a play; we, who undertake more, do but multiply adventures which, not being produced from one another, as effects from causes, but rarely following, constitute many actions in the drama, and consequently make it many plays.

"But by pursuing closely one argument, which is not cloyed with many turns, the French have gained more liberty for verse, in which they write; they have leisure to dwell on a subject which deserves it; and to represent the passions (which we have acknowledged to be the poet's work), without being hurried from one thing to another, as we are in the plays of Calderon, which we have seen lately upon our theatres

---

[27] "In the middle of plays they ask for a bear and boxers."

[28] "I should write a poem from a well-known story" (*Art of Poetry*, l. 240).

[29] "He so lies, and mingles the true and false, that you cannot tell the beginning, middle, or end apart" (*Ibid.*, l. 151).

[30] "Whatever you show me in that way I find unbelievable and disgusting" (*Ibid.*, l. 188).

[31] "True things," yet "things like the truth."

under the name of Spanish plots. I have taken notice but of one tragedy of ours whose plot has that uniformity and unity of design in it, which I have commended in the French; and that is *Rollo*, or rather, under the name of Rollo, the Story of Bassianus and Geta in Herodian: there indeed the plot is neither large nor intricate, but just enough to fill the minds of the audience, not to cloy them. Besides, you see it founded upon the truth of history,—only the time of the action is not reduceable to the strictness of the rules; and you see in some places a little farce mingled, which is below the dignity of the other parts, and in this all our poets are extremely peccant: even Ben Jonson himself, in *Sejanus* and *Catiline*, has given us this oleo of a play, this unnatural mixture of comedy and tragedy; which to me sounds just as ridiculously as the history of David with the merry humours of Golias. In *Sejanus* you may take notice of the scene betwixt Livia and the physician which is a pleasant satire upon the artificial helps of beauty: in *Catiline* you may see the parliament of women; the little envies of them to one another; and all that passes betwixt Curio and Fulvia: scenes admirable in their kind, but of an ill mingle with the rest.

"But I return again to the French writers, who, as I have said, do not burden themselves too much with plot, which has been reproached to them by an *ingenious person* of our nation as a fault; for, he says, they commonly make but one person considerable in a play; they dwell on him, and his concernments, while the rest of the persons are only subservient to set him off. If he intends this by it,—that there is one person in the play who is of greater dignity than the rest, he must tax, not only theirs, but those of the Ancients, and which he would be loth to do, the best of ours; for it is impossible but that one person must be more conspicuous in it than any other, and consequently the greatest share in the action must devolve on him. We see it so in the management of all affairs; even in the most equal aristocracy, the balance cannot be so justly poised but some one will be superior to the rest, either in parts, fortune, interest, or the consideration of some glorious exploit; which will reduce the greatest part of business into his hands.

"But, if he would have us to imagine, that in exalting one character the rest of them are neglected, and that all of them have not some share or other in the action of the play, I desire him to produce any of Corneille's tragedies, wherein every person, like so many servants in a well-governed family, has not some employment, and who is not necessary to the carrying on of the plot, or at least to your understanding it.

"There are indeed some protatic persons in the Ancients, whom they make use of in their plays, either to hear or give the relation: but the French avoid this with great address, making their narrations only to, or by such, who are some way interested in the main design. And now I am speaking of relations, I cannot take a fitter opportunity to add this in favour of the French, that they often use them with better judgment and more *à propos* than the English do. Not that I commend narrations in general,—but there are two sorts of them. One, of those things which are antecedent to the play, and are related to make the conduct of it more clear to us. But 'tis a fault to choose such subjects for the stage as will force us on that rock because we see they are seldom listened to by the audience and that is many times the ruin of the play; for, being once let pass without attention, the audience can never recover themselves to understand the plot: and indeed it is somewhat unreasonable that they should be put to so much trouble, as that, to comprehend what passes in their sight, they must have recourse to what was done, perhaps, ten or twenty years ago.

"But there is another sort of relations, that is, of things happening in the action of the play, and supposed to be done behind the scenes; and this is many times both convenient and beautiful; for by it the French avoid the tumult to which we are subject in England, by representing duels, battles, and the like; which renders our stage too like the theatres where they fight prizes. For what is more ridiculous than to represent an army with a drum and five men behind it; all which the hero of the other side is to drive in before him; or to see a duel fought, and one slain with two or three thrusts of the foils, which we know are so blunted that we might give a man an hour to kill another in good earnest with them.

"I have observed that in all our tragedies, the audience cannot forbear laughing when the actors are to die; it is the most comic part of the whole play. All *passions* may be lively represented on the stage, if to the well-writing of them the actor supplies a good commanded voice, and limbs that move easily, and without stiffness; but there are many *actions* which can never be imitated to a just height: dying especially is a thing which none but a Roman gladiator could naturally perform on the stage, when he did not imitate or represent, but do it; and therefore it is better to omit the representation of it.

"The words of a good writer, which describe it lively, will make a deeper impression of belief in us than all the actor can insinuate into us, when he seems to fall dead before us; as a poet in the description of a beautiful garden, or a meadow, will please our imagination more than the place itself can please our sight. When we see death represented, we are convinced it is but fiction; but when we hear it related, our eyes, the strongest witnesses, are wanting, which might have undeceived us; and we are all willing to favour the sleight, when the poet does not too grossly impose on us. They therefore who imagine these relations would make no concernment in the audience, are deceived, by confounding them with the other, which are of things antecedent to the play: those are made often in cold blood, as I may say, to the audience; but these are warmed with our concernments, which were before awakened in the play. What the philosophers say of motion, that, when it is once begun, it continues of itself, and will do so to eternity, without some stop put to it, is clearly true on this occasion: the soul being already moved with the characters and fortunes of those imaginary persons, continues going of its own accord; and we are no more weary to hear what becomes of them when they are not on the stage, than we are to listen to the news of an absent mistress. But it is objected, that if one part of the play may be related, then why not all? I answer, some parts of the action are more fit to be represented, some to be related. Corneille says judiciously that the poet is not obliged to expose to view all particular actions which conduce to the principal: he ought to select such of them to be seen, which will appear with the greatest beauty, either by the magnificence of the show, or the vehemence of passions which they produce, or some other charm

which they have in them; and let the rest arrive to the audience by narration. 'Tis a great mistake in us to believe the French present no part of the action on the stage; every alteration or crossing of a design, every new-sprung passion, and turn of it, is a part of the action, and much the noblest, except we conceive nothing to be action till the players come to blows; as if the painting of the hero's mind were not more properly the poet's work than the strength of his body. Nor does this anything contradict the opinion of Horace, where he tells us,

Segnius irritant animos demissa per aurem,
Quam quae sunt oculis subjecta fidelibus.[32]

"For he says immediately after,

> *Non tamen intus*
> *Digna geri promes in scenam; multaq; tolles*
> *Ex oculis, quae mox narret facundia praesens.*

"Among which many he recounts some:

Nec pueros coram populo Medea trucidet,
Aut in avem Procne mutetur, Cadmus in anguem,
etc.

That is, those actions which by reason of their cruelty, will cause aversion in us, or by reason of their impossibility, unbelief, ought either wholly to be avoided by a poet, or only delivered by narration. To which we may have leave to add, such as, to avoid tumult (as was before hinted), or to reduce the plot into a more reasonable compass of time, or for defect of beauty in them, are rather to be related than presented to the eye. Examples of all these kinds are frequent, not only among all the Ancients, but in the best received of our English poets. We find Ben Jonson using them in his *Magnetic Lady*, where one comes out from dinner, and relates the quarrels and disorders of it, to save the undecent appearance of them on the stage, and to abbreviate the story; and this in express imitation of Terence, who had done the same before

[32] This and the following two quotations may be translated thus: "What we hear through our ears stirs us less strongly than what we see through our eyes." "You should not bring onto the stage what should be done off it: many things should be kept out of sight and told instead with vivid readiness." "Medea should not cut up her children in front of the audience; Procne should not be changed into a bird there, nor Cadmus into a snake" (*Art of Poetry*, above, p. 54).

him in his *Eunuch,* where Pythias makes the like relation of what had happened within at the Soldier's entertainment. The relations likewise of Sejanus's death, and the prodigies before it, are remarkable; the one of which was hid from sight, to avoid the horror and tumult of the representation; the other, to shun the introducing of things impossible to be believed. In that excellent play, *The King and no King,* Fletcher goes yet farther; for the whole unravelling of the plot is done by narration in the fifth act, after the manner of the Ancients; and it moves great concernment in the audience, though it be only a relation of what was done many years before the play. I could multiply other instances, but these are sufficient to prove that there is no error in choosing a subject which requires this sort of narrations; in the ill management of them, there may.

"But I find I have been too long in this discourse, since the French have many other excellencies not common to us; as that you never see any of their plays end with a conversion, or simple change of will, which is the ordinary way which our poets use to end theirs. It shows little art in the conclusion of a dramatic poem, when they who have hindered the felicity during the four acts, desist from it in the fifth, without some powerful cause to take them off their design; and though I deny not but such reasons may be found, yet it is a path that is cautiously to be trod, and the poet is to be sure he convinces the audience that the motive is strong enough. As for example, the conversion of the Usurer in *The Scornful Lady* seems to me a little forced; for, being an Usurer, which implies a lover of money to the highest degree of covetousness,— and such the poet has represented him,—the account he gives for the sudden change is, that he has been duped by the wild young fellow; which in reason might render him more wary another time, and make him punish himself with harder fare and coarser clothes, to get up again what he had lost: but that he should look on it as a judgment, and so repent, we may expect to hear in a sermon, but I should never endure it in a play.

"I pass by this; neither will I insist on the care they take that no person after his first entrance shall ever appear, but the business which brings him upon the stage shall be evident;

which rule, if observed, must needs render all the events in the play more natural; for there you see the probability of every accident, in the cause that produced it; and that which appears chance in the play, will seem so reasonable to you, that you will there find it almost necessary: so that in the exit of the actor you have a clear account of his purpose and design in the next entrance (though, if the scene be well wrought, the event will commonly deceive you); for there is nothing so absurd, says Corneille, as for an actor to leave the stage only because he has no more to say.

"I should now speak of the beauty of their rhyme, and the just reason I have to prefer that way of writing in tragedies before ours in blank verse; but because it is partly received by us, and therefore not altogether peculiar to them, I will say no more of it in relation to their plays. For our own, I doubt not but it will exceedingly beautify them; and I can see but one reason why it should not generally obtain, that is, because our poets write so ill in it. This indeed may prove a more prevailing argument than all others which are used to destroy it, and therefore I am only troubled when great and judicious poets, and those who are acknowledged such, have writ or spoke against it: as for others, they are to be answered by that one sentence of an ancient author:—*Sed ut primo ad consequendos eos quos priores ducimus, accendimur, ita ubi aut proeteriri, aut aequari eos posse desperavimus, studium cum spe senescit: quod, scilicet, assequi non potest, sequi desinit; . . . praeteritoque eo in quo eminere non possumus, aliquid in quo nitamur, conquirimus.*" [33]

Lisideius concluded in this manner; and Neander, after a little pause, thus answered him:

"I shall grant Lisideius, without much dispute, a great part of what he has urged against us; for I acknowledge that the French contrive their plots more regularly, and observe the laws of comedy, and decorum of the stage (to speak generally), with more exactness than the English. Farther, I deny not but he has taxed us

[33] "Just as we are inspired to follow those we consider most worthy, so—when we despair of excelling or equalling them—our enthusiasm and hope diminish. For what it cannot attain, it ceases to follow. . . . When that we cannot excel is over, we look for something else for which to strive" (Velleius Paterculus, I, 17).

justly in some irregularities of ours, which he has mentioned; yet, after all, I am of opinion that neither our faults nor their virtues are considerable enough to place them above us.

"For the lively imitation of Nature being in the definition of a play, those which best fulfil that law ought to be esteemed superior to the others. 'Tis true, those beauties of the French poesy are such as will raise perfection higher where it is, but are not sufficient to give it where it is not: they are indeed the beauties of a statue, but not of a man, because not animated with the soul of Poesy, which is imitation of humour and passions: and this Lisideius himself, or any other, however biassed to their party, cannot but acknowledge, if he will either compare the humours of our comedies, or the characters of our serious plays, with theirs. He who will look upon theirs which have been written till these last ten years, or thereabouts, will find it a hard matter to pick out two or three passable humours amongst them. Corneille himself, their arch-poet, what has he produced except *The Liar,* and you know how it was cried up in France; but when it came upon the English stage, though well translated, and that part of Dorant acted to so much advantage as I am confident it never received in its own country, the most favourable to it would not put it in competition with many of Fletcher's or Ben Jonson's. In the rest of Corneille's comedies you have little humour; he tells you himself, his way is, first to show two lovers in good intelligence with each other; in the working up of the play to embroil them by some mistake, and in the latter end to clear it, and reconcile them.

"But of late years Molière, the younger Corneille, Quinault, and some others, have been imitating afar off the quick turns and graces of the English stage. They have mixed their serious plays with mirth, like our tragi-comedies, since the death of Cardinal Richelieu; which Lisideius and many others not observing, have commended that in them for a virtue which they themselves no longer practise. Most of their new plays are, like some of ours, derived from the Spanish novels. There is scarce one of them without a veil, and a trusty Diego, who drolls much after the rate of *The Adventures.* But their humours, if I may grace them with that name, are so thin-sown, that never above one of them comes up in any play. I dare take upon me to find more variety of them in some one play of Ben Jonson's than in all theirs together; as he who has seen *The Alchemist, The Silent Woman,* or *Bartholomew-Fair,* cannot but acknowledge with me.

"I grant the French have performed what was possible on the ground-work of the Spanish plays; what was pleasant before, they have made regular: but there is not above one good play to be writ on all those plots; they are too much alike to please often; which we need not the experience of our own stage to justify. As for their new way of mingling mirth with serious plot, I do not, with Lisideius, condemn the thing, though I cannot approve their manner of doing it. He tells us, we cannot so speedily recollect ourselves after a scene of great passion and concernment, as to pass to another of mirth and humour, and to enjoy it with any relish: but why should he imagine the soul of man more heavy than his senses? Does not the eye pass from an unpleasant object to a pleasant in a much shorter time than is required to this? and does not the unpleasantness of the first commend the beauty of the latter? The old rule of logic might have convinced him, that contraries, when placed near, set off each other. A continued gravity keeps the spirit too much bent; we must refresh it sometimes, as we bait in a journey that we may go on with greater ease. A scene of mirth, mixed with tragedy, has the same effect upon us which our music has betwixt the acts; which we find a relief to us from the best plots and language of the stage, if the discourses have been long. I must therefore have stronger arguments, ere I am convinced that compassion and mirth in the same subject destroy each other; and in the meantime cannot but conclude, to the honour of our nation, that we have invented, increased, and perfected a more pleasant way of writing for the stage, than was ever known to the ancients or moderns of any nation, which is tragi-comedy.

"And this leads me to wonder why Lisideius and many others should cry up the barrenness of the French plots above the variety and copiousness of the English. Their plots are single; they carry on one design, which is pushed forward by all the actors, every scene in the play contributing and moving towards it. Our plays, besides the main design, have under-plots or by-concernments, of less considerable persons and intrigues, which are carried on with the motion of the main plot: as they say the orb of the fixed stars, and those of the planets, though they have motions of their own, are whirled about by the motion of the *primum mobile,* in which they are contained. That similitude expresses much of the English stage; for if contrary motions may be found in nature to agree; if a planet can go east and west at the same time;—one way by virtue of his own motion, the other by the force of the First Mover;—it will not be difficult to imagine how the under-plot, which is only different, not contrary to the great design, may naturally be conducted along with it.

"Eugenius has already shown us, from the confession of the French poets, that the Unity of Action is sufficiently preserved, if all the imperfect actions of the play are conducing to the main design; but when those petty intrigues of a play are so ill ordered, that they have no coherence with the other, I must grant that Lisideius has reason to tax that want of due connection; for co-ordination in a play is as dangerous and unnatural as in a state. In the meantime he must acknowledge, our variety, if well ordered, will afford a greater pleasure to the audience.

"As for his other argument, that by pursuing one single theme they gain an advantage to express and work up the passions, I wish any example he could bring from them would make it good; for I confess their verses are to me the coldest I have ever read. Neither, indeed, is it possible for them, in the way they take, so to express passion, as that the effects of it should appear in the concernment of an audience, their speeches being so many declamations, which tire us with the length; so that instead of persuading us to grieve for their imaginary heroes, we are concerned for our own trouble, as we are in tedious visits of bad company; we are in pain till they are gone. When the French stage came to be reformed by Cardinal Richelieu, those long harangues were introduced to comply with the gravity of a churchman. Look upon the *Cinna* and the *Pompey;* they are not so properly to be called plays, as long discourses of reason of state; and *Polieucte* in matters of religion is as solemn as the long stops upon our organs. Since that time it is grown into a custom, and their

actors speak by the hour-glass, like our parsons; nay, they account it the the grace of their parts, and think themselves disparaged by the poet, if they may not twice or thrice in a play entertain the audience with a speech of an hundred lines. I deny not but this may suit well enough with the French; for as we, who are a more sullen people, come to be diverted at our plays, so they, who are of an airy and gay temper, come thither to make themselves more serious: and this I conceive to be one reason why comedies are more pleasing to us, and tragedies to them. But to speak generally: it cannot be denied that short speeches and replies are more apt to move the passions and beget concernment in us, than the other; for it is unnatural for any one in a gust of passion to speak long together, or for another in the same condition to suffer him, without interruption. Grief and passion are like floods raised in little brooks by a sudden rain; they are quickly up; and if the concernment be poured unexpectedly in upon us, it overflows us: but a long sober shower gives them leisure to run out as they came in, without troubling the ordinary current. As for Comedy, repartee is one of its chiefest graces; the greatest pleasure of the audience is a chase of wit, kept up on both sides, and swiftly managed. And this our forefathers, if not we, have had in Fletcher's plays, to a much higher degree of perfection than the French poets can reasonably hope to reach.

"There is another part of Lisideius his discourse, in which he rather excused our neighbours than commended them; that is, for aiming only to make one person considerable in their plays. 'Tis very true what he has urged, that one character in all plays, even without the poet's care, will have advantage of all the others; and that the design of the whole drama will chiefly depend on it. But this hinders not that there may be more shining characters in the play: many persons of a second magnitude, nay, some so very near, so almost equal to the first, that greatness may be opposed to greatness, and all the persons be made considerable, not only by their quality, but their action. 'Tis evident that the more the persons are, the greater will be the variety of the plot. If then the parts are managed so regularly, that the beauty of the whole be kept entire, and that the variety become not a perplexed and confused mass of accidents, you will find it infinitely pleasing to be led in a labyrinth of design, where you see some of your way before you, yet discern not the end till you arrive at it. And that all this is practicable, I can produce for examples many of our English plays: as *The Maid's Tragedy, The Alchemist, The Silent Woman:* I was going to have named *The Fox,* but that the unity of design seems not exactly observed in it; for there appear two actions in the play; the first naturally ending with the fourth act; the second forced from it in the fifth; which yet is the less to be condemned in him, because the disguise of Volpone, though it suited not with his character as a crafty or covetous person, agreed well enough with that of a voluptuary; and by it the poet gained the end at which he aimed, the punishment of vice, and the reward of virtue, both which that disguise produced. So that to judge equally of it, it was an excellent fifth act, but not so naturally proceeding from the former.

"But to leave this, and pass to the latter part of Lisideius his discourse, which concerns relations: I must acknowledge with him, that the French have reason to hide that part of the action which would occasion too much tumult on the stage, and to choose rather to have it made known by narration to the audience. Farther, I think it very convenient, for the reasons he has given, that all incredible actions were removed; but whether custom has so insinuated itself into our countrymen, or nature has so formed them to fierceness, I know not; but they will scarcely suffer combats and other objects of horror to be taken from them. And indeed, the indecency of tumults is all which can be objected against fighting: for why may not our imagination as well suffer itself to be deluded with the probability of it, as with any other thing in the play? For my part, I can with as great ease persuade myself that the blows are given in good earnest, as I can that they who strike them are kings or princes, or those persons which they represent. For objects of incredibility,—I would be satisfied from Lisideius, whether we have any so removed from all appearance of truth, as are those of Corneille's *Andromede;* a play which has been frequented the most of any he has writ. If the Perseus, or the son of a heathen god, the Pegasus, and the

Monster, were not capable to choke a strong belief, let him blame any representation of ours hereafter. Those indeed were objects of delight; yet the reason is the same as to the probability: for he makes it not a Ballette or masque, but a play, which is to resemble truth. But for death, that it ought not to be represented, I have, besides the arguments alleged by Lisideius, the authority of Ben Jonson, who has forborne it in his tragedies; for both the death of Sejanus and Catiline are related: though in the latter I cannot but observe one irregularity of that great poet; he has removed the scene in the same act from Rome to Catiline's army, and from thence again to Rome; and besides, has allowed a very inconsiderable time, after Catiline's speech, for the striking of the battle, and the return of Petreius, who is to relate the event of it to the senate: which I should not animadvert on him, who was otherwise a painful observer of τὸ πρέπον, or the *decorum* of the stage, if he had not used extreme severity in his judgment on the incomparable Shakespeare for the same fault.—To conclude on this subject of relations; if we are to be blamed for showing too much of the action, the French are as faulty for discovering too little of it: a mean betwixt both should be observed by every judicious writer, so as the audience may neither be left unsatisfied by not seeing what is beautiful, or shocked by beholding what is either incredible or undecent. I hope I have already proved in this discourse, that though we are not altogether so punctual as the French in observing the laws of Comedy, yet our errors are so few, and little, and those things wherein we excel them so considerable, that we ought of right to be preferred before them. But what will Lisideius say, if they themselves acknowledge they are too strictly bounded by those laws, for breaking which he has blamed the English? I will allege Corneille's words, as I find them in the end of his Discourse of the Three Unities: *Il est facile aux speculatifs d'estre severes, etc.* ' 'Tis easy for speculative persons to judge severely; but if they would produce to public view ten or twelve pieces of this nature, they would perhaps give more latitude to the rules than I have done, when by experience they had known how much we are limited and constrained by them, and how many beauties of the stage they banished from it.' To illustrate a little what he has said: By their servile observations of the Unities of Time and Place, and integrity of scenes, they have brought on themselves that dearth of plot, and narrowness of imagination, which may be observed in all their plays. How many beautiful accidents might naturally happen in two or three days, which cannot arrive with any probability in the compass of twenty-four hours? There is time to be allowed also for maturity of design, which, amongst great and prudent persons, such as are often represented in Tragedy, cannot, with any likelihood of truth, be brought to pass at so short a warning. Farther; by tying themselves strictly to the Unity of Place, and unbroken scenes, they are forced many times to omit some beauties which cannot be shown where the act began; but might, if the scene were interrupted, and the stage cleared for the persons to enter in another place; and therefore the French poets are often forced upon absurdities; for if the act begins in a chamber, all the persons in the play must have some business or other to come thither, or else they are not to be shown that act; and sometimes their characters are very unfitting to appear there: as, suppose it were the king's bed-chamber; yet the meanest man in the tragedy must come and dispatch his business there, rather than in the lobby or courtyard (which is fitter for him), for fear the stage should be cleared, and the scenes broken. Many times they fall by it in a greater inconvenience; for they keep their scenes unbroken, and yet change the place; as in one of their newest plays, where the act begins in the street. There a gentleman is to meet his friend; he sees him with his man, coming out from his father's house; they talk together, and the first goes out: the second, who is a lover, has made an appointment with his mistress; she appears at the window, and then we are to imagine the scene lies under it. This gentleman is called away, and leaves his servant with his mistress; presently her father is heard from within; the young lady is afraid the serving-man should be discovered, and thrusts him into a place of safety, which is supposed to be her closet. After this, the father enters to the daughter, and now the scene is in a house; for he is seeking from one room to another for this poor Philipin, or French Diego, who is heard from within, drolling and breaking many a miserable conceit on the subject of his sad condition. In this ridiculous manner the play goes forward, the stage being never empty all the while: so that the street, the window, the houses, and the closet, are made to walk about, and the persons to stand still. Now what, I beseech you, is more easy than to write a regular French play, or more difficult than to write an irregular English one, like those of Fletcher, or of Shakespeare?

"If they content themselves, as Corneille did, with some flat design, which, like an ill riddle, is found out ere it be half proposed, such plots we can make every way regular, as easily as they; but whenever they endeavour to rise to any quick turns and counterturns of plot, as some of them have attempted, since Corneille's plays have been less in vogue, you see they write as irregularly as we, though they cover it more speciously. Hence the reason is perspicuous why no French plays, when translated, have, or ever can succeed on the English stage. For, if you consider the plots, our own are fuller of variety; if the writing, ours are more quick and fuller of spirit; and therefore 'tis a strange mistake in those who decry the way of writing plays in verse, as if the English therein imitated the French. We have borrowed nothing from them; our plots are weaved in English looms: we endeavour therein to follow the variety and greatness of characters which are derived to us from Shakespeare and Fletcher; the copiousness and well-knitting of the intrigues we have from Jonson; and for the verse itself we have English precedents of elder date than any of Corneille's plays. Not to name our old comedies before Shakespeare, which were all writ in verse of six feet, or Alexandrines, such as the French now use,—I can show in Shakespeare many scenes of rhyme together, and the like in Ben Jonson's tragedies: in *Catiline* and *Sejanus* sometimes thirty or forty lines,—I mean besides the Chorus, or the monologues; which, by the way, showed Ben no enemy to this way of writing, especially if you read his *Sad Shepherd*, which goes sometimes on rhyme, sometimes on blank verse, like an horse who eases himself on trot and amble. You find him likewise commending Fletcher's pastoral of *The Faithful Shepherdess*, which is for the most part rhyme, though not refined to that purity to which it hath since been brought·

And these examples are enough to clear us from a servile imitation of the French.

"But to return whence I have digressed: I dare boldly affirm these two things of the English drama;—First, that we have many plays of ours as regular as any of theirs, and which, besides, have more variety of plot and characters; and secondly, that in most of the irregular plays of Shakespeare or Fletcher (for Ben Jonson's are for the most part regular), there is a more masculine fancy and greater spirit in the writing than there is in any of the French. I could produce, even in Shakespeare's and Fletcher's works, some plays which are almost exactly formed; as *The Merry Wives of Windsor*, and *The Scornful Lady:* but because (generally speaking) Shakespeare, who writ first, did not perfectly observe the laws of comedy, and Fletcher, who came nearer to perfection, yet through carelessness made many faults; I will take the pattern of a perfect play from Ben Jonson, who was a careful and learned observer of the dramatic laws, and from all his comedies I shall select *The Silent Woman;* of which I will make a short examen, according to those rules which the French observe."

As Neander was beginning to examine *The Silent Woman*, Eugenius, earnestly regarding him; "I beseech you, Neander," said he, "gratify the company, and me in particular, so far, as before you speak of the play, to give us a character of the author; and tell us frankly your opinion, whether you do not think all writers, both French and English, ought to give place to him."

"I fear," replied Neander, "that in obeying your commands I shall draw some envy on myself. Besides, in performing them, it will be first necessary to speak somewhat of Shakespeare and Fletcher, his rivals in poesy; and one of them, in my opinion, at least his equal, perhaps his superior.

"To begin, then, with Shakespeare. He was the man who of all modern, and perhaps ancient poets, had the largest and most comprehensive soul. All the images of Nature were still present to him, and he drew them, not laboriously, but luckily; when he describes anything, you more than see it, you feel it too. Those who accuse him to have wanted learning, give him the greater commendation: he was naturally learned; he needed not the spectacles of books to read Nature; he looked inwards, and found her there. I cannot say he is everywhere alike; were he so, I should do him injury to compare him with the greatest of mankind. He is many times flat, insipid; his comic wit degenerating into clenches,[34] his serious swelling into bombast. But he is always great, when some great occasion is presented to him; no man can say he ever had a fit subject for his wit, and did not then raise himself as high above the rest of poets,

Quantum lenta solent inter viburna cupressi.[35]

The consideration of this made Mr. Hales of Eaton say, that there was no subject of which any poet ever writ, but he would produce it much better done in Shakespeare; and however others are now generally preferred before him, yet the age wherein he lived, which had contemporaries with him Fletcher and Jonson, never equalled them to him in their esteem: and in the last King's court, when Ben's reputation was at highest, Sir John Suckling, and with him the greater part of the courtiers, set our Shakespeare far above him.

"Beaumont and Fletcher, of whom I am next to speak, had, with the advantage of Shakespeare's wit, which was their precedent, great natural gifts, improved by study: Beaumont especially being so accurate a judge of plays, that Ben Jonson, while he lived, submitted all his writings to his censure, and, 'tis thought, used his judgment in correcting, if not contriving, all his plots. What value he had for him, appears by the verses he writ to him; and therefore I need speak no farther of it. The first play that brought Fletcher and him in esteem was their *Philaster:* for before that, they had written two or three very unsuccessfully, as the like is reported of Ben Jonson, before he writ *Every Man in his Humour*. Their plots were generally more regular than Shakespeare's, especially those which were made before Beaumont's death; and they understood and imitated the conversation of gentlemen much better; whose wild debaucheries, and quickness of wit in repartees, no poet before them could paint as they have done.

[34] Puns.

[35] "As cypresses commonly do among pliant shrubs."

Humour, which Ben Jonson derived from particular persons, they made it not their business to describe: they represented all the passions very lively, but above all, love. I am apt to believe the English language in them arrived to its highest perfection: what words have since been taken in, are rather superfluous than ornamental. Their plays are now the most pleasant and frequent entertainments of the stage; two of theirs being acted through the year for one of Shakespeare's or Jonson's: the reason is, because there is a certain gaiety in their comedies, and pathos in their more serious plays, which suit generally with all men's humours. Shakespeare's language is likewise a little obsolete, and Ben Jonson's wit comes short of theirs.

"As for Jonson, to whose character I am now arrived, if we look upon him while he was himself (for his last plays were but his dotages), I think him the most learned and judicious writer which any theatre ever had. He was a most severe judge of himself, as well as others. One cannot say he wanted wit, but rather that he was frugal of it. In his works you find little to retrench or alter. Wit, and language, and humour also in some measure, we had before him; but something of art was wanting to the Drama till he came. He managed his strength to more advantage than any who preceded him. You seldom find him making love in any of his scenes, or endeavouring to move the passions; his genius was too sullen and saturnine to do it gracefully, especially when he knew he came after those who had performed both to such an height. Humour was his proper sphere; and in that he delighted most to represent mechanic people. He was deeply conversant in the Ancients, both Greek and Latin, and he borrowed boldly from them: there is scarce a poet or historian among the Roman authors of those times whom he has not translated in *Sejanus* and *Catiline*. But he has done his robberies so openly, that one may see he fears not to be taxed by any law. He invades authors like a monarch; and what would be theft in other poets is only victory in him. With the spoils of these writers he so represents old Rome to us, in its rites, ceremonies, and customs, that if one of their poets had written either of his tragedies, we had seen less of it than in him. If there was any fault in his language, 'twas that he weaved it too closely and laboriously, in his comedies especially: perhaps, too, he did a little too much Romanise our tongue, leaving the words which he translated almost as much Latin as he found them: wherein, though he learnedly followed their language, he did not enough comply with the idiom of ours. If I would compare him with Shakespeare, I must acknowledge him the more correct poet, but Shakespeare the greater wit. Shakespeare was the Homer, or father of our dramatic poets; Jonson was the Virgil, the pattern of elaborate writing; I admire him, but I love Shakespeare. To conclude of him; as he has given us the most correct plays, so in the precepts which he has laid down in his *Discoveries*, we have as many and profitable rules for perfecting the stage, as any wherewith the French can furnish us.

"Having thus spoken of the author, I proceed to the examination of his comedy, *The Silent Woman.*

EXAMEN OF THE SILENT WOMAN

"To begin first with the length of the action; it is so far from exceeding the compass of a natural day, that it takes not up an artificial one. 'Tis all included in the limits of three hours and a half, which is no more than is required for the presentment on the stage: a beauty perhaps not much observed; if it had, we should not have looked on the Spanish translation of *Five Hours* with so much wonder. The scene of it is laid in London; the latitude of place is almost as little as you can imagine; for it lies all within the compass of two houses, and after the first act, in one. The continuity of scenes is observed more than in any of our plays, except his own *Fox* and *Alchemist*. They are not broken above twice or thrice at most in the whole comedy; and in the two best of Corneille's plays, the *Cid* and *Cinna*, they are interrupted once. The action of the play is entirely one; the end or aim of which is the settling Morose's estate on Dauphine. The intrigue of it is the greatest and most noble of any pure unmixed comedy in any language; you see in it many persons of various characters and humours, and all delightful. As first, Morose, or an old man, to whom all noise but his own talking is offensive. Some who would be thought critics, say this humour of his is forced: but to remove that objection, we may consider him first to be naturally of a delicate hearing, as many are, to whom all sharp sounds are unpleasant; and secondly, we may attribute much of it to the peevishness of his age, or the wayward authority of an old man in his own house, where he may make himself obeyed; and to this the poet seems to allude in his name Morose. Besides this, I am assured from divers persons, that Ben Jonson was actually acquainted with such a man, one altogether as ridiculous as he is here represented. Others say, it is not enough to find one man of such an humour; it must be common to more, and the more common the more natural. To prove this, they instance in the best of comical characters, Falstaff. There are many men resembling him; old, fat, merry, cowardly, drunken, amorous, vain, and lying. But to convince these people, I need but tell them that humour is the ridiculous extravagance of conversation, wherein one man differs from all others. If then it be common, or communicated to many, how differs it from other men's? or what indeed causes it to be ridiculous so much as the singularity of it? As for Falstaff, he is not properly one humour, but a miscellany of humours or images, drawn from so many several men: that wherein he is singular is his wit, or those things he says *praeter expectatum*, unexpected by the audience; his quick evasions, when you imagine him surprised, which, as they are extremely diverting of themselves, so receive a great addition from his person; for the very sight of such an unwieldy old debauched fellow is a comedy alone. And here, having a place so proper for it, I cannot but enlarge somewhat upon this subject of humour into which I am fallen. The ancients had little of it in their comedies; for the τὸ γελοῖον [36] of the old Comedy, of which Aristophanes was chief, was not so much to imitate a man, as to make the people laugh at some odd conceit, which had commonly somewhat of unnatural or obscene in it. Thus, when you see Socrates brought upon the stage, you are not to imagine him made ridiculous by the imitation of his actions, but rather by making him perform something very unlike himself; something so childish and absurd, as by comparing it with the gravity of the true Socrates, makes a ridiculous object for the spectators. In their

new Comedy which succeeded, the poets sought indeed to express the ἦθος, [37] as in their tragedies the πάθος [38] of mankind. But this ἦθος contained only the general characters of men and manners; as old men, lovers, serving-men, courtezans, parasites, and such other persons as we see in their comedies; all which they made alike: that is, one old man or father, one lover, one courtezan, so like another, as if the first of them had begot the rest of every sort: *Ex homine hunc natum dicas.*[39] The same custom they observed likewise in their tragedies. As for the French, though they have the word *humeur* among them, yet they have small use of it in their comedies or farces; they being but ill imitations of the *ridiculum*, or that which stirred up laughter in the Old Comedy. But among the English 'tis otherwise: where by humour is meant some extravagant habit, passion, or affection, particular (as I said before) to some one person, by the oddness of which, he is immediately distinguished from the rest of men; which being lively and naturally represented, most frequently begets that malicious pleasure in the audience which is testified by laughter; as all things which are deviations from customs are ever the aptest to produce it: though by the way this laughter is only accidental, as the person represented is fantastic or bizarre; but pleasure is essential to it, as the imitation of what is natural. The description of these humours, drawn from the knowledge and observation of particular persons, was the peculiar genius and talent of Ben Jonson; to whose play I now return.

"Besides Morose, there are at least nine or ten different characters and humours in *The Silent Woman;* all which persons have several concernments of their own, yet are all used by the poet to the conducting of the main design to perfection. I shall not waste time in commending the writing of this play; but I will give you my opinion, that there is more wit and acuteness of fancy in it than in any of Ben Jonson's. Besides that he has here described the conversation of gentlemen in the persons of True-Wit, and his friends, with more gaiety, air, and freedom, than in the rest of his comedies. For the contrivance of the plot, 'tis extreme, elaborate, and yet withal

[36] The laughable.

[37] *Ethos,* or character.
[38] *Pathos,* or feeling.
[39] "You would say he was born from the other man."

easy; for the λύσις, or untying of it, 'tis so admirable, that when it is done, no one of the audience would think the poet could have missed it; and yet it was concealed so much before the last scene, that any other way would sooner have entered into your thoughts. But I dare not take upon me to commend the fabric of it, because it is altogether so full of art, that I must unravel every scene in it to commend it as I ought. And this excellent contrivance is still the more to be admired, because 'tis comedy, where the persons are only of common rank, and their business private, not elevated by passions or high concernments, as in serious plays. Here every one is a proper judge of all he sees, nothing is represented but that with which he daily converses: so that by consequence all faults lie open to discovery, and few are pardonable. 'Tis this which Horace has judiciously observed:

> *Creditur, ex medio quia res arcessit, habere*
> *Sudoris minimum; sed habet Comedia tanto*
> *Plus oneris, quanto veniae minus.*[40]

But our poet who was not ignorant of these difficulties has made use of all advantages; as he who designs a large leap takes his rise from the highest ground. One of these advantages is that which Corneille has laid down as the greatest which can arrive to any poem, and which he himself could never compass above thrice in all his plays; viz., the making choice of some signal and long-expected day, whereon the action of the play is to depend. This day was that designed by Dauphine for the settling of his uncle's estate upon him; which to compass, he contrives to marry him. That the marriage had been plotted by him long beforehand, is made evident by what he tells True-Wit in the second act, that in one moment he had destroyed what he had been raising many months.

"There is another artifice of the poet, which I cannot here omit, because by the frequent practice of it in his comedies he has left it to us almost as a rule; that is, when he has any character or humour wherein he would show a *coup de Maistre*, or his highest skill, he recommends it to your observation by a pleasant description of it before the person first appears. Thus, in *Bartholomew-Fair* he gives you the pictures of Numps and Cokes, and in this those of Daw, Lafoole, Morose, and the Collegiate Ladies; all which you hear described before you see them. So that before they come upon the stage, you have a longing expectation of them, which prepares you to receive them favourably; and when they are there, even from their first appearance you are so far acquainted with them, that nothing of their humour is lost to you.

"I will observe yet one thing further of this admirable plot; the business of it rises in every act. The second is greater than the first; the third than the second; and so forward to the fifth. There too you see, till the very last scene, new difficulties arising to obstruct the action of the play; and when the audience is brought into despair that the business can naturally be effected, then, and not before, the discovery is made. But that the poet might entertain you with more variety all this while, he reserves some new characters to show you, which he opens not till the second and third act; in the second Morose, Daw, the Barber, and Otter; in the third the Collegiate Ladies: all which he moves afterwards in by-walks, or under-plots, as diversions to the main design, lest it should grow tedious, though they are still naturally joined with it, and somewhere or other subservient to it. Thus, like a skilful chess-player, by little and little he draws out his men, and makes his pawns of use to his greater persons.

"If this comedy and some others of his were translated into French prose (which would now be no wonder to them, since Molière has lately given them plays out of verse, which have not displeased them), I believe the controversy would soon be decided betwixt the two nations, even making them the judges. But we need not call our heroes to our aid. Be it spoken to the honour of the English, our nation can never want in any age such who are able to dispute the empire of wit with any people in the universe. And though the fury of a civil war, and power for twenty years together abandoned to a barbarous race of men, enemies of all good learning, had buried the muses under the ruins of monarchy; yet, with the restoration of our happiness, we see revived poesy lifting up its head, and already shaking off the rubbish which lay so heavy on

---

[40] "Comedy is thought to demand the least work; for it draws its subjects from ordinary life. But the less indulgence it has, the more work it requires" (*Epistles,* II, i).

it. We have seen since his majesty's return, many dramatic poems which yield not to those of any foreign nation, and which deserve all laurels but the English. I will set aside flattery and envy: it cannot be denied but we have had some little blemish either in the plot or writing of all those plays which have been made within these seven years; (and perhaps there is no nation in the world so quick to discern them, or so difficult to pardon them, as ours:) yet if we can persuade ourselves to use the candour of that poet, who, though the most severe of critics, has left us this caution by which to moderate our censures—

ubi plura nitent in carmine, non ego paucis Offendar maculis;— [41]

if, in consideration of their many and great beauties, we can wink at some slight and little imperfections, if we, I say, can be thus equal to ourselves, I ask no favour from the French. And if I do not venture upon any particular judgment of our late plays, 'tis out of the consideration which an ancient writer gives me: *vivorum, ut magna admiratio, ita censura difficilis:* [42] betwixt the extremes of admiration and malice, 'tis hard to judge uprightly of the living. Only I think it may be permitted me to say, that as it is no lessening to us to yield to some plays, and those not many, of our own nation in the last age, so can it be no addition to pronounce of our present poets, that they have far surpassed all the Ancients, and the modern writers of other countries."

This was the substance of what was then spoken on that occasion; and Lisideius, I think, was going to reply, when he was prevented thus by Crites: "I am confident," said he, "that the most material things that can be said have been already urged on either side; if they have not, I must beg of Lisideius that he will defer his answer till another time: for I confess I have a joint quarrel to you both, because you have concluded, without any reason given for it, that rhyme is proper for the stage. I will not dispute how ancient it hath been among us to write this way; perhaps our ancestors knew no better till Shakespeare's time. I will grant it was not alto-

gether left by him, and that Fletcher and Ben Jonson used it frequently in their Pastorals, and sometimes in other plays. Farther,—I will not argue whether we received it originally from our own countrymen, or from the French; for that is an inquiry of as little benefit, as theirs who, in the midst of the late plague, were not so solicitous to provide against it, as to know whether we had it from the malignity of our own air, or by transportation from Holland. I have therefore only to affirm, that it is not allowable in serious plays; for comedies, I find you already concluding with me. To prove this, I might satisfy myself to tell you, how much in vain it is for you to strive against the stream of the people's inclination; the greatest part of which are prepossessed so much with those excellent plays of Shakespeare, Fletcher, and Ben Jonson, which have been written out of rhyme, that except you could bring them such as were written better in it, and those too by persons of equal reputation with them, it will be impossible for you to gain your cause with them, who will still be judges. This it is to which, in fine, all your reasons must submit. The unanimous consent of an audience is so powerful, that even Julius Caesar (as Macrobius reports of him), when he was perpetual dictator, was not able to balance it on the other side; but when Laberius, a Roman Knight, at his request contended in the *Mime* with another poet, he was forced to cry out, *Etiam favente me victus es, Laberi.* [43] But I will not on this occasion take the advantage of the greater number, but only urge such reasons against rhyme, as I find in the writings of those who have argued for the other way. First, then, I am of opinion that rhyme is unnatural in a play, because dialogue there is presented as the effect of sudden thought: for a play is the imitation of Nature; and since no man, without premeditation, speaks in rhyme, neither ought he to do it on the stage. This hinders not but the fancy may be there elevated to an higher pitch of thought than it is in ordinary discourse; for there is a probability that men of excellent and quick parts may speak noble things *extempore:* but those thoughts are never fettered with the numbers or sound of verse without study, and therefore it cannot be but unnatural to present

[41] "When many beauties shine out in a poem, I shall not be offended at small faults" (*Art of Poetry*, l. 351).

[42] "Just as admiration for the living is great, it is difficult to criticize them."

[43] "Even with me on your side, you are defeated, Laberius."

the most free way of speaking in that which is the most constrained. For this reason, says Aristotle, 'tis best to write tragedy in that kind of verse which is the least such, or which is nearest prose: and this amongst the Ancients was the Iambic, and with us is blank verse, or the measure of verse kept exactly without rhyme. These numbers therefore are fittest for a play; the others for a paper of verses, or a poem; blank verse being as much below them as rhyme is improper for the Drama. And if it be objected that neither are blank verses made *extempore*, yet, as nearest nature, they are still to be preferred.—But there are two particular exceptions, which many besides myself have had to verse; by which it will appear yet more plainly how improper it is in plays. And the first of them is grounded on that very reason for which some have commended rhyme; they say, the quickness of repartees in argumentative scenes receives an ornament from verse. Now what is more unreasonable than to imagine that a man should not only light upon the wit, but the rhyme too, upon the sudden? This nicking of him who spoke before both in sound and measure, is so great an happiness, that you must at least suppose the persons of your play to be born poets: *Arcades omnes, et cantare pares, et respondere parati:* they must have arrived to the degree of *quicquid conabar dicere;* [44]—to make verses almost whether they will or no. If they are anything below this, it will look rather like the design of two, than the answer of one: it will appear that your actors hold intelligence together; that they perform their tricks like fortune-tellers, by confederacy. The hand of art will be too visible in it, against that maxim of all professions—*Ars est celare artem;* [45] that it is the greatest perfection of art to keep itself undiscovered. Nor will it serve you to object, that however you manage it, 'tis still known to be a play; and, consequently, the dialogue of two persons understood to be the labour of one poet. For a play is still an imitation of Nature; we know we are to be deceived, and we desire to be so; but no man ever was deceived but with a probability of truth; for who will suffer a gross lie to be

fastened on him? Thus we sufficiently understand that the scenes which represent cities and countries to us are not really such, but only painted on boards and canvas; but shall that excuse the ill painture or designment of them? Nay, rather ought they not be laboured with so much the more diligence and exactness, to help the imagination? since the mind of man does naturally tend to truth; and therefore the nearer anything comes to the imitation of it, the more it pleases.

"Thus, you see, your rhyme is uncapable of expressing the greatest thoughts naturally, and the lowest it cannot with any grace: for what is more unbefitting the majesty of verse, than to call a servant, or bid a door be shut in rhyme? and yet you are often forced on this miserable necessity. But verse, you say, circumscribes a quick and luxuriant fancy, which would extend itself too far on every subject, did not the labour which is required to well-turned and polished rhyme, set bounds to it. Yet this argument, if granted, would only prove that we may write better in verse, but not more naturally. Neither is it able to evince that; for he who wants judgment to confine his fancy in blank verse, may want it as much in rhyme: and he who has it will avoid errors in both kinds. Latin verse was as great a confinement to the imagination of those poets as rhyme to ours; and yet you find Ovid saying too much on every subject. *Nescivit* (says Seneca) *quod bene cessit relinquere:* [46] of which he gives you one famous instance in his description of the deluge:

Omnia pontus erat, deerant quoque litora ponto.
Now all was sea, nor had that sea a shore.

Thus Ovid's fancy was not limited by verse, and Virgil needed not verse to have bounded his.

"In our own language we see Ben Jonson confining himself to what ought to be said, even in the liberty of blank verse; and yet Corneille, the most judicious of the French poets, is still varying the same sense an hundred ways, and dwelling eternally on the same subject, though confined by rhyme. Some other exceptions I have to verse; but since these I have named are for the most part already public, I conceive it reasonable they should first be answered."

44 "Both Arcadians, prepared to sing on equal terms and to reply" (Virgil, *Eclogues*, VII, 4) ; "whatever I tried to say [would be verse]."

45 "It is an art to conceal art."

46 "He did not know how to end when he should have done so" (*Controversies*, IX, 5).

"It concerns me less than any," said Neander (seeing he had ended), "to reply to this discourse; because when I should have proved that verse may be natural in plays, yet I should always be ready to confess, that those which I have written in this kind come short of that perfection which is required. Yet since you are pleased I should undertake this province, I will do it, though with all imaginable respect and deference, both to that person from whom you have borrowed your strongest arguments, and to whose judgment, when I have said all, I finally submit. But before I proceed to answer your objections, I must first remember you, that I exclude all Comedy from my defence; and next that I deny not but blank verse may be also used; and content myself only to assert, that in serious plays where the subject and characters are great, and the plot unmixed with mirth, which might allay or divert these concernments which are produced, rhyme is there as natural and more effectual than blank verse.

"And now having laid down this as a foundation,—to begin with Crites,—I must crave leave to tell him, that some of his arguments against rhyme reach no farther than, from the faults or defects of ill rhyme, to conclude against the use of it in general. May not I conclude against blank verse by the same reason? If the words of some poets who write in it are either ill chosen, or ill placed, which makes not only rhyme, but all kind of verse in any language unnatural, shall I, for their vicious affectation, condemn those excellent lines of Fletcher, which are written in that kind? Is there anything in rhyme more constrained than this line in blank verse? *I heaven invoke, and strong resistance make;* where you see both the clauses are placed unnaturally, that is, contrary to the common way of speaking, and that without the excuse of a rhyme to cause it: yet you would think me very ridiculous, if I should accuse the stubbornness of blank verse for this, and not rather the stiffness of the poet. Therefore, Crites, you must either prove that words, though well chosen, and duly placed, yet render not rhyme natural in itself; or that, however natural and easy the rhyme may be, yet it is not proper for a play. If you insist on the former part, I would ask you, what other conditions are required to make rhyme natural in itself, besides an election of

apt words, and a right disposition of them? For the due choice of your words expresses your sense naturally, and the due placing them adapts the rhyme to it. If you object that one verse may be made for the sake of another, though both the words and rhyme be apt, I answer, it cannot possibly so fall out; for either there is a dependence of sense betwixt the first line and the second, or there is none: if there be that connection, then in the natural position of the words the latter line must of necessity flow from the former; if there be no dependence, yet still the due ordering of words makes the last line as natural in itself as the other: so that the necessity of a rhyme never forces any but bad or lazy writers to say what they would not otherwise. 'Tis true, there is both care and art required to write in verse. A good poet never establishes the first line till he has sought out such a rhyme as may fit the sense, already prepared to heighten the second: many times the close of the sense falls into the middle of the next verse, or farther off, and he may often prevail himself of the same advantages in English which Virgil had in Latin,—he may break off in the hemistich, and begin another line. Indeed, the not observing these two last things makes plays which are writ in verse so tedious: for though, most commonly, the sense is to be confined to the couplet, yet nothing that does *perpetuo tenore fluere*, run in the same channel, can please always. 'Tis like the murmuring of a stream, which not varying in the fall, causes at first attention, at last drowsiness. Variety of cadences is the best rule; the greatest help to the actors, and refreshment to the audience.

"If then verse may be made natural in itself, how becomes it unnatural in a play? You say the stage is the representation of nature, and no man in ordinary conversation speaks in rhyme. But you foresaw when you said this, that it might be answered—neither does any man speak in blank verse, or in measure without rhyme. Therefore you concluded, that which is nearest nature is still to be preferred. But you took no notice that rhyme might be made as natural as blank verse, by the well placing of the words, etc. All the difference between them, when they are both correct, is, the sound in one, which the other wants; and if so, the sweetness of it, and all the advantage resulting from it, which are handled in the Preface to *The Rival Ladies,* will yet stand good. As for that place of Aristotle, where he says, plays should be writ in that kind of verse which is nearest prose, it makes little for you; blank verse being properly but measured prose. Now measure alone, in any modern language, does not constitute verse; those of the Ancients in Greek and Latin consisted in quantity of words, and a determinate number of feet. But when, by the inundation of the Goths and Vandals into Italy, new languages were introduced, and barbarously mingled with the Latin, of which the Italian, Spanish, French, and ours (made out of them and the Teutonic) are dialects, a new way of poesy was practised; new, I say, in those countries, for in all probability it was that of the conquerors in their own nations: at least we are able to prove, that the eastern people have used it from all antiquity. This new way consisted in measure or number of feet, and rhyme; the sweetness of rhyme, and observation of accent, supplying the place of quantity in words, which could neither exactly be observed by those Barbarians, who knew not the rules of it, neither was it suitable to their tongues, as it had been to the Greek and Latin. No man is tied in modern poesy to observe any farther rule in the feet of his verse, but that they be dissyllables; whether Spondee, Trochee, or Iambic, it matters not; only he is obliged to rhyme: neither do the Spanish, French, Italian, or Germans, acknowledge at all, or very rarely, any such kind of poesy as blank verse amongst them. Therefore, at most 'tis but a poetic prose, a *sermo pedestris;* and as such, most fit for comedies, where I acknowledge rhyme to be improper. Farther; as to that quotation of Aristotle, our couplet verses may be rendered as near prose as blank verse itself, by using those advantages I lately named,—as breaks in an hemistich, or running the sense into another line,—thereby making art and order appear as loose and free as nature: or not tying ourselves to couplets strictly, we may use the benefit of the Pindaric way practised in *The Siege of Rhodes;* where the numbers vary, and the rhyme is disposed carelessly, and far from often chiming. Neither is that other advantage of the Ancients to be despised, of changing the kind of verse when they please, with the change of the scene, or some new entrance; for they confine

not themselves always to iambics, but extend their liberty to all lyric numbers, and sometimes even to hexameter. But I need not go so far to prove that rhyme, as it succeeds to all other offices of Greek and Latin verse, so especially to this of plays, since the custom of nations at this day confirms it; the French, Italian, and Spanish tragedies are generally writ in it; and sure the universal consent of the most civilised parts of the world, ought in this, as it doth in other customs, to include the rest.

"But perhaps you may tell me, I have proposed such a way to make rhyme natural, and consequently proper to plays, as is unpracticable; and that I shall scarce find six or eight lines together in any play, where the words are so placed and chosen as is required to make it natural. I answer, no poet need constrain himself at all times to it. It is enough he makes it his general rule; for I deny not but sometimes there may be a greatness in placing the words otherwise; and sometimes they may sound better; sometimes also the variety itself is excuse enough. But if, for the most part, the words be placed as they are in the negligence of prose, it is sufficient to denominate the way practicable; for we esteem that to be such, which in the trial oftener succeeds than misses. And thus far you may find the practice made good in many plays: where you do not, remember still, that if you cannot find six natural rhymes together, it will be as hard for you to produce as many lines in blank verse, even among the greatest of our poets, against which I cannot make some reasonable exception.

"And this, Sir, calls to my remembrance the beginning of your discourse, where you told us we should never find the audience favourable to this kind of writing, till we could produce as good plays in rhyme as Ben Jonson, Fletcher, and Shakespeare had writ out of it. But it is to raise envy to the living, to compare them with the dead. They are honoured, and almost adored by us, as they deserve; neither do I know any so presumptuous of themselves as to contend with them. Yet give me leave to say thus much, without injury to their ashes; that not only we shall never equal them, but they could never equal themselves, were they to rise and write again. We acknowledge them our fathers in wit; but they have ruined their estates themselves, before they came to their children's hands. There is scarce an humour, a character, or any kind of plot, which they have not used. All comes sullied or wasted to us: and were they to entertain this age, they could not now make so plenteous treatments out of such decayed fortunes. This therefore will be a good argument to us, either not to write at all, or to attempt some other way. There is no bays to be expected in their walks: *tentanda via est, quà me quoque possum tollere humo.*[47]

"This way of writing in verse they have only left free to us; our age is arrived to a perfection in it, which they never knew; and which (if we may guess by what of theirs we have seen in verse, as *The Faithful Shepherdess,* and *Sad Shepherd*) 'tis probable they never could have reached. For the genius of every age is different; and though ours excel in this, I deny not but to imitate Nature in that perfection which they did in prose, is a greater commendation than to write in verse exactly. As for what you have added—that the people are not generally inclined to like this way,—if it were true, it would be no wonder, that betwixt the shaking off an old habit, and the introducing of a new, there should be difficulty. Do we not see them stick to Hopkins' and Sternhold's psalms, and forsake those of David, I mean Sandys his translation of them? If by the people you understand the multitude, the οἱ πολλοί, 'tis no matter what they think; they are sometimes in the right, sometimes in the wrong: their judgment is a mere lottery. *Est ubi plebs rectè putat, est ubi peccat.*[48] Horace says it of the vulgar, judging poesy. But if you mean the mixed audience of the populace and the noblesse, I dare confidently affirm that a great part of the latter sort are already favourable to verse; and that no serious plays written since the King's return have been more kindly received by them than *The Siege of Rhodes,* the *Mustapha, The Indian Queen,* and *Indian Emperor.*

"But I come now to the inference of your first argument. You said that the dialogue of plays is presented as the effect of sudden thought, but no man speaks suddenly, or *extem-*

pore, in rhyme; and you inferred from thence, that rhyme, which you acknowledge to be proper to epic poesy, cannot equally be proper to dramatic, unless we could suppose all men born so much more than poets, that verses should be made in them, not by them.

"It has been formerly urged by you, and confessed by me, that since no man spoke any kind of verse *extempore,* that which was nearest Nature was to be preferred. I answer you, therefore, by distinguishing betwixt what is nearest to the nature of Comedy, which is the imitation of common persons and ordinary speaking, and what is nearest the nature of a serious play: this last is indeed the representation of Nature, but 'tis Nature wrought up to a higher pitch. The plot, the characters, the wit, the passions, the descriptions, are all exalted above the level of common converse, as high as the imagination of the poet can carry them, with proportion to verisimility. Tragedy, we know, is wont to image to us the minds and fortunes of noble persons, and to portray these exactly; heroic rhyme is nearest Nature, as being the noblest kind of modern verse.

> *Indignatur enim privatis et prope socco*
> *Dignis carminibus narrari coena Thyestae,*

says Horace: and in another place,

> *Effutire leves indigna tragoedia versus.*[49]

Blank verse is acknowledged to be too low for a poem, nay more, for a paper of verses; but if too low for an ordinary sonnet, how much more for Tragedy, which is by Aristotle, in the dispute betwixt the epic poesy and the dramatic, for many reasons he there alleges, ranked above it?

"But setting this defence aside, your argument is almost as strong against the use of rhyme in poems as in plays; for the epic way is everywhere interlaced with dialogue, or discoursive scenes; and therefore you must either grant rhyme to be improper there, which is contrary to your assertion, or admit it into plays by the same title which you have given it to poems. For though Tragedy be justly preferred above

---

[47] "I must explore to find out a way by which I can raise myself" (Virgil, *Georgics,* III, 8-9).

[48] "Sometimes the people think rightly, sometimes not" (*Epistles,* II, 1, 63).

[49] "The banquet of Thyestes should not be told in the familiar verses appropriate to comedy"; and "It is not proper for tragedy to babble in light verse" (*Art of Poetry,* ll. 90-91, 231).

the other, yet there is a great affinity between them, as may easily be discovered in that definition of a play which Lisideius gave us. The *genus* of them is the same, a just and lively image of human nature, in its actions, passions, and traverses of fortune: so is the end—namely, for the delight and benefit of mankind. The characters and persons are still the same, viz., the greatest of both sorts; only the manner of acquainting us with those actions, passions, and fortunes, is different. Tragedy performs it *viva voce*, or by action, in dialogue; wherein it excels the Epic Poem, which does it chiefly by narration, and therefore is not so lively an image of human nature. However, the agreement betwixt them is such, that if rhyme be proper for one, it must be for the other. Verse, 'tis true, is not the effect of sudden thought; but this hinders not that sudden thought may be represented in verse, since those thoughts are such as must be higher than Nature can raise them without premeditation, especially to a continuance of them, even out of verse; and consequently you cannot imagine them to have been sudden either in the poet or in the actors. A play, as I have said, to be like Nature, is to be set above it; as statues which are placed on high are made greater than the life, that they may descend to the sight in their just proportion.

"Perhaps I have insisted too long on this objection; but the clearing of it will make my stay shorter on the rest. You tell us, Crites, that rhyme appears most unnatural in repartees, or short replies: when he who answers (it being presumed he knew not what the other would say, yet) makes up that part of the verse which was left incomplete, and supplies both the sound and measure of it. This, you say, looks rather like the confederacy of two, than the answer of one.

"This, I confess, is an objection which is in every man's mouth, who loves not rhyme: but suppose, I beseech you, the repartee were made only in blank verse, might not part of the same argument be turned against you? for the measure is as often supplied there as it is in rhyme; the latter half of the hemistich as commonly made up, or a second line subjoined as a reply to the former; which any one leaf in Jonson's plays will sufficiently clear to you. You will often find in the Greek tragedians, and in Seneca, that when a scene grows up into the warmth of repartees, which is the close fighting of it, the latter part of the trimeter is supplied by him who answers; and yet it was never observed as a fault in them by any of the ancient or modern critics. The case is the same in our verse, as it was in theirs; rhyme to us being in lieu of quantity to them. But if no latitude is to be allowed a poet, you take from him not only his licence of *quidlibet audendi*,[50] but you tie him up in a straiter compass than you would a philosopher. This is indeed *Musas colere severiores*.[51] You would have him follow Nature, but he must follow her on foot: you have dismounted him from his Pegasus. But you tell us, this supplying the last half of a verse, or adjoining a whole second to the former, looks more like the design of two, than the answer of one. Suppose we acknowledge it: how comes this confederacy to be more displeasing to you, than in a dance which is well contrived? You see there the united design of many persons to make up one figure: after they have separated themselves in many petty divisions, they rejoin one by one into a gross: the confederacy is plain amongst them, for chance could never produce anything so beautiful; and yet there is nothing in it that shocks your sight. I acknowledge the hand of art appears in repartee, as of necessity it must in all kind of verse. But there is also the quick and poignant brevity of it (which is an high imitation of Nature in those sudden gusts of passion) to mingle with it; and this, joined with the cadency and sweetness of the rhyme, leaves nothing in the soul of the hearer to desire. 'Tis an art which appears; but it appears only like the shadowings of painture, which being to cause the rounding of it, cannot be absent; but while that is considered, they are lost: so while we attend to the other beauties of the matter, the care and labour of the rhyme is carried from us, or at least drowned in its own sweetness, as bees are sometimes buried in their honey. When a poet has found the repartee, the last perfection he can add to it, is to put it into verse. However good the thought may be, however apt the words in which 'tis couched, yet he finds himself at a little unrest, while rhmye is wanting: he cannot leave it till that comes naturally, and then is at ease, and sits down contented.

[50] "Of taking any liberty he wishes."
[51] "To cultivate the more serious Muses."

"From replies, which are the most elevated thoughts of verse, you pass to those which are most mean, and which are common with the lowest of household conversation. In these, you say, the majesty of verse suffers. You instance in the calling of a servant, or commanding a door to be shut, in rhyme. This, Crites, is a good observation of yours, but no argument: for it proves no more but that such thoughts should be waived as often as may be, by the address of the poet. But suppose they are necessary in the places where he uses them, yet there is no need to put them into rhyme. He may place them in the beginning of a verse, and break it off, as unfit, when so debased, for any other use: or granting the worst,—that they require more room than the hemistich will allow, yet still there is a choice to be made of the best words, and least vulgar (provided they be apt), to express such thoughts. Many have blamed rhyme in general, for this fault, when the poet with a little care might have redressed it. But they do it with no more justice than if English Poesy should be made ridiculous for the sake of the Water Poet's rhymes. Our language is noble, full, and significant; and I know not why he who is master of it may not clothe ordinary things in it as decently as the Latin, if he use the same diligence in his choice of words: *delectus verborum origo est eloquentiae.*[52] It was the saying of Julius Caesar, one so curious in his, that none of them can be changed but for a worse. One would think, *unlock the door,* was a thing as vulgar as could be spoken; and yet Seneca could make it sound high and lofty in his Latin:

Reserate clusos regii postes laris.
Set wide the palace gates.

"But I turn from this conception, both because it happens not above twice or thrice in any play that those vulgar thoughts are used; and then too (were there no other apology to be made, yet), the necessity of them, which is alike in all kind of writing, may excuse them. For if they are little and mean in rhyme, they are of consequence such in blank verse. Besides that the great eagerness and precipitation with which they are spoken, makes us rather mind the sub-

52 "Proper choice in words is the source of eloquence."

stance than the dress; that for which they are spoken, rather than what is spoken. For they are always the effect of some hasty concernment, and something of consequence depends on them.

"Thus, Crites, I have endeavoured to answer your objections; it remains only that I should vindicate an argument for verse, which you have gone about to overthrow. It had formerly been said that the easiness of blank verse renders the poet too luxuriant, but that the labour of rhyme bounds and circumscribes an over-fruitful fancy; the sense there being commonly confined to the couplet, and the words so ordered that the rhyme naturally follows them, not they the rhyme. To this you answered, that it was no argument to the question in hand; for the dispute was not which way a man may write best, but which is most proper for the subject on which he writes.

"First, give me leave, Sir, to remember you that the Argument against which you raised this objection, was only secondary: it was built on this hypothesis,—that to write in verse was proper for serious plays. Which supposition being granted (as it was briefly made out in that discourse, by showing how verse might be made natural), it asserted, that this way of writing was an help to the poet's judgment, by putting bounds to a wild overflowing fancy. I think, therefore, it will not be hard for me to make good what it was to prove on that supposition. But you add, that were this let pass, yet he who wants judgment in the liberty of his fancy, may as well show the defect of it when he is confined to verse; for he who has judgment will avoid errors, and he who has it not, will commit them in all kinds of writing.

"This argument, as you have taken it from a most acute person, so I confess it carries much weight in it: but by using the word judgment here indefinitely, you seem to have put a fallacy upon us. I grant, he who has judgment, that is, so profound, so strong, or rather so infallible a judgment, that he needs no helps to keep it always poised and upright, will commit no faults either in rhyme or out of it. And on the other extreme, he who has a judgment so weak and crazed that no helps can correct or amend it, shall write scurvily out of rhyme, and worse in it. But the first of these judgments is nowhere to be found, and the latter is not fit to write at all. To speak therefore of judgment as it is in the best poets; they who have the greatest proportion of it, want other helps than from it, within. As for example, you would be loth to say that he who is endued with a sound judgment has no need of History, Geography, or Moral Philosophy, to write correctly. Judgment is indeed the master-workman in a play; but he requires many subordinate hands, many tools to his assistance. And verse I affirm to be one of these; 'tis a rule and line by which he keeps his building compact and even, which otherwise lawless imagination would raise either irregularly or loosely; at least, if the poet commits errors with this help, he would make greater and more without it: 'tis, in short, a slow and painful, but the surest kind of working. Ovid, whom you accuse for luxuriancy in verse, had perhaps been farther guilty of it, had he writ in prose. And for your instance of Ben Jonson, who, you say, writ exactly without the help of rhyme; you are to remember, 'tis only an aid to a luxuriant fancy, which his was not: as he did not want imagination, so none ever said he had much to spare. Neither was verse then refined so much, to be an help to that age, as it is to ours. Thus then the second thoughts being usually the best, as receiving the maturest digestion from judgment, and the last and most mature product of those thoughts being artful and laboured verse, it may well be inferred, that verse is a great help to a luxuriant fancy; and this is what that argument which you opposed was to evince."

Neander was pursuing this discourse so eagerly that Eugenius had called to him twice or thrice, ere he took notice that the barge stood still, and that they were at the foot of Somerset-stairs, where they had appointed it to land. The company were all sorry to separate so soon, though a great part of the evening was already spent; and stood a-while looking back on the water, upon which the moonbeams played, and made it appear like floating quick-silver: at last they went up through a crowd of French people, who were merrily dancing in the open air, and nothing concerned for the noise of guns which had alarmed the town that afternoon. Walking thence together to the Piazze, they parted there; Eugenius and Lisideius to some pleasant appointment they had made, and Crites and Neander to their several lodgings.

Preface to Fables, Ancient and Modern

'TIS WITH a Poet, as with a man who designs to build, and is very exact, as he supposes, in casting up the cost beforehand; but, generally speaking, he is mistaken in his account, and reckons short of the expense he first intended. He alters his mind as the work proceeds, and will have this or that convenience more, of which he had not thought when he began. So has it happened to me; I have built a house, where I intended but a lodge; yet with better success than a certain nobleman, who, beginning with a dog kennel, never lived to finish the palace he had contrived.

From translating the First of Homer's *Iliads*, (which I intended as an essay to the whole work,) I proceeded to the translation of the Twelfth Book of Ovid's *Metamorphoses*, because it contains, among other things, the causes, the beginning, and ending, of the Trojan war. Here I ought in reason to have stopped; but the speeches of Ajax and Ulysses lying next in my way, I could not balk 'em. When I had compassed them, I was so taken with the former part of the Fifteenth Book, (which is the masterpiece of the whole *Metamorphoses*,) that I enjoined myself the pleasing task of rendering it into English. And now I found, by the number of my verses, that they began to swell into a little volume; which gave me an occasion of looking backward on some beauties of my author, in his former books: There occurred to me the *Hunting of the Boar, Cinyras and Myrrha,* the good-natured story of *Baucis and Philemon,* with the rest, which I hope I have translated closely enough, and given them the same turn of verse which they had in the original; and this, I may say without vanity, is not the talent of every poet. He who has arrived the nearest

Preface to Fables, Ancient and Modern. First published in 1700. Reprinted with modernized spelling.

to it, is the ingenious and learned Sandys, the best versifier of the former age; if I may properly call it by that name, which was the former part of this concluding century. For Spenser and Fairfax both flourished in the reign of Queen Elizabeth; great masters in our language, and who saw much further into the beauties of our numbers than those who immediately followed them. Milton was the poetical son of Spenser, and Mr. Waller of Fairfax; for we have our lineal descents and clans as well as other families. Spenser more than once insinuates, that the soul of Chaucer was transfused into his body, and that he was begotten by him two hundred years after his decease. Milton has acknowledged to me, that Spenser was his original; and many besides myself have heard our famous Waller own that he derived the harmony of his numbers from the *Godfrey of Bulloign,* which was turned into English by Mr. Fairfax.

But to return: having done with Ovid for this time, it came into my mind that our old English poet, Chaucer, in many things resembled him, and that with no disadvantage on the side of the modern author, as I shall endeavour to prove when I compare them; and as I am, and always have been, studious to promote the honour of my native country, so I soon resolved to put their merits to the trial, by turning some of the *Canterbury Tales* into our language, as it is now refined; for by this means, both the poets being set in the same light, and dressed in the same English habit, story to be compared with story, a certain judgment may be made betwixt them by the reader, without obtruding my opinion on him. Or, if I seem partial to my countryman and predecessor in the laurel, the friends of antiquity are not few; and besides many of the learned, Ovid has almost all the *Beaux,* and the whole Fair Sex, his declared patrons. Perhaps I have assumed somewhat more to myself than they allow me, because I have adventured to sum up the evidence; but the readers are the jury, and their privilege remains entire, to decide according to the merits of the cause; or, if they please, to bring it to another hearing before some other court. In the mean time, to follow the thrid of my discourse (as thoughts, according to Mr. Hobbes,[1] have always some connec-

tion,) so from Chaucer I was led to think on Boccace, who was not only his contemporary, but also pursued the same studies; wrote novels in prose, and many works in verse; particularly is said to have invented the octave rhyme, or stanza of eight lines, which ever since has been maintained by the practice of all Italian writers who are, or at least assume the title of heroic poets. He and Chaucer, among other things, had this in common, that they refined their mother-tongues; but with this difference, that Dante had begun to file their language, at least in verse, before the time of Boccace, who likewise received no little help from his master Petrarch. But the reformation of their prose was wholly owing to Boccace himself, who is yet the standard of purity in the Italian tongue; tho' many of his phrases are become obsolete, as in process of time it must needs happen. Chaucer (as you have formerly been told by our learned Mr. Rymer)[2] first adorned and amplified our barren tongue from the Provençal, which was then the most polished of all the modern languages; but this subject has been copiously treated by that great critic, who deserves no little commendation from us his countrymen. For these reasons of time, and resemblance of genius, in Chaucer and Boccace, I resolved to join them in my present work; to which I have added some original papers of my own; which whether they are equal or inferior to my other poems, an author is the most improper judge, and therefore I leave them wholly to the mercy of the reader. I will hope the best, that they will not be condemned; but if they should, I have the excuse of an old gentleman, who, mounting on horseback before some ladies, when I was present, got up somewhat heavily, but desired of the fair spectators that they would count fourscore and eight before they judged him. By the mercy of God, I am already come within twenty years of his number, a cripple in my limbs, but what decays are in my mind, the reader must determine. I think myself as vigorous as ever in the faculties of my soul, excepting only my memory, which is not impaired to any great degree; and if I lose not more of it, I have no great reason to complain. What judgment I had, increases rather than di-

[1] Thomas Hobbes (1588-1679), the great English philosopher and psychologist.

[2] Thomas Rymer, perhaps the outstanding English exponent of extreme neoclassic rationalism (see above, p. 9).

minishes; and thoughts, such as they are, come crowding in so fast upon me, that my only difficulty is to choose or to reject; to run them into verse, or to give them the other harmony of prose: I have so long studied and practised both, that they are grown into a habit, and become familiar to me. In short, tho' I may lawfully plead some part of the old gentleman's excuse, yet I will reserve it till I think I have greater need, and ask no grains of allowance for the faults of this my present work, but those which are given of course to human frailty. I will not trouble my reader with the shortness of time in which I writ it, or the several intervals of sickness. They who think too well of their own performances, are apt to boast in their prefaces how little time their works have cost them, and what other business of more importance interfered; but the reader will be as apt to ask the question, why they allowed not a longer time to make their works more perfect? and why they had so despicable an opinion of their judges as to thrust their indigested stuff upon them, as if they deserved no better?

With this account of my present undertaking, I conclude the first part of this discourse: in the second part, as at a second sitting, tho' I alter not the draught, I must touch the same features over again, and change the dead-colouring of the whole. In general, I will only say, that I have written nothing which savours of immorality or profaneness; at least, I am not conscious to myself of any such intention. If there happen to be found an irreverent expression, or a thought too wanton, they are crept into my verses thro' my inadvertency: if the searchers find any in the cargo, let them be staved or forfeited, like counterbanded goods; at least, let their authors be answerable for them, as being but imported merchandise, and not of my own manufacture. On the other side, I have endeavoured to choose such fables, both ancient and modern, as contain in each of them some instructive moral; which I could prove by induction, but the way is tedious, and they leap foremost into sight, without the reader's trouble of looking after them. I wish I could affirm, with a safe conscience, that I had taken the same care in all my former writings; for it must be owned, that supposing verses are never so beautiful or pleasing, yet, if they contain anything which shocks religion or good

manners, they are at best what Horace says of good numbers without good sense, *Versus inopes rerum, nugaeque canorae*.[3] Thus far, I hope, I am right in court, without renouncing to my other right of self-defense, where I have been wrongfully accused, and my sense wire-drawn into blasphemy or bawdry, as it has often been by a religious lawyer, in a late pleading against the stage; in which he mixes truth with falsehood, and has not forgotten the old rule of calumniating strongly, that something may remain.

I resume the thrid of my discourse with the first of my translations, which was the first *Iliad* of Homer. If it shall please God to give me longer life, and moderate health, my intentions are to translate the whole *Ilias*; provided still that I meet with those encouragements from the public, which may enable me to proceed in my undertaking with some cheerfulness. And this I dare assure the world beforehand, that I have found, by trial, Homer a more pleasing task than Virgil, tho' I say not the translation will be less laborious; for the Grecian is more according to my genius than the Latin poet. In the works of the two authors we may read their manners, and natural inclinations, which are wholly different. Virgil was of a quiet, sedate temper; Homer was violent, impetuous, and full of fire.[4] The chief talent of Virgil was propriety of thoughts, and ornament of words: Homer was rapid in his thoughts, and took all the liberties, both of numbers and of expressions, which his language, and the age in which he lived, allowed him. Homer's invention was more copious, Virgil's more confined; so that if Homer had not led the way, it was not in Virgil to have begun heroic poetry; for nothing can be more evident, than that the Roman poem is but the second part of the *Ilias*; a continuation of the same story, and the persons already formed. The manners of Aeneas are those of Hector, superadded to those which

---

[3] "Verses empty of matter, trifling songs" (*Art of Poetry*, l. 322).

[4] The contrast between Homer and Virgil as a contrast between "genius" and "judgment," between "vigor," "the sublime," etc., and "refinement," "correctness," and the like is extremely common in neoclassic criticism after Dryden. Its most famous appearance is in Pope's Preface to the *Iliad*. A somewhat similar contrast between Dryden and Pope is found in Johnson's *Life of Pope*, below, pp. 228-29.

Homer gave him. The adventures of Ulysses in the *Odysseis* are imitated in the first Six Books of Virgil's *Aeneis;* and tho' the accidents are not the same, (which would have argued him of a servile copying, and total barrenness of invention,) yet the seas were the same, in which both the heroes wandered; and Dido cannot be denied to be the poetical daughter of Calypso. The six latter Books of Virgil's poem are the four-and-twenty *Iliads* contracted; a quarrel occasioned by a lady, a single combat, battles fought, and a town besieged. I say not this in derogation to Virgil, neither do I contradict anything which I have formerly said in his just praise; for his episodes are almost wholly of his own invention, and the form which he has given to the telling makes the tale his own, even tho' the original story had been the same. But this proves, however, that Homer taught Virgil to design; and if invention be the first virtue of an epic poet, then the Latin poem can only be allowed the second place. Mr. Hobbes, in the preface to his own bald translation of the *Ilias* (studying poetry as he did mathematics, when it was too late,) Mr. Hobbes, I say, begins the praise of Homer where he should have ended it. He tells us, that the first beauty of an epic poem consists in diction; that is, in the choice of words, and harmony of numbers; now the words are the colouring of the work, which, in the order of nature, is last to be considered. The design, the disposition, the manners, and the thoughts, are all before it: [5] where any of those are wanting or imperfect, so much wants or is imperfect in the imitation of human life, which is in the very definition of a poem. Words, indeed, like glaring colours, are the first beauties that arise and strike the sight; but, if the draught be false or lame, the figures ill disposed, the manners obscure or inconsistent, or the thoughts unnatural, then the finest colours are but daubing, and the piece is a beautiful monster at the best. Neither Virgil nor Homer were deficient in any of the former beauties; but in this last, which is expression, the Roman poet is at least equal to the Grecian, as I have said elsewhere: supplying the poverty of his language by his musical ear, and by his diligence.

But to return: our two great poets being so different in their tempers, one choleric and san-

guine, the other phlegmatic and melancholic; that which makes them excel in their several ways is, that each of them has followed his own natural inclination, as well in forming the design, as in the execution of it. The very heroes shew their authors: Achilles is hot, impatient, revengeful, *Impiger, iracundus, inexorabilis, acer,* &c., Aeneas patient, considerate, careful of his people, and merciful to his enemies; ever submissive to the will of Heaven—*Quo fata trahunt retrahuntque, sequamur.*[6]

I could please myself with enlarging on this subject, but am forced to defer it to a fitter time. From all I have said, I will only draw this inference, that the action of Homer, being more full of vigour than that of Virgil, according to the temper of the writer, is of consequence more pleasing to the reader. One warms you by degrees; the other sets you on fire all at once, and never intermits his heat. 'Tis the same difference which Longinus makes betwixt the effects of eloquence in Demosthenes and Tully; one persuades, the other commands. You never cool while you read Homer, even not in the Second Book (a graceful flattery to his countrymen); but he hastens from the ships, and concludes not that book till he has made you an amends by the violent playing of a new machine. From thence he hurries on his action with variety of events, and ends it in less compass than two months. This vehemence of his, I confess, is more suitable to my temper; and, therefore, I have translated his First Book with greater pleasure than any part of Virgil; but it was not a pleasure without pains. The continual agitations of the spirits must needs be a weakening of any constitution, especially in age; and many pauses are required for refreshment betwixt the heats; the *Iliad* of itself being a third part longer than all Virgil's works together.

This is what I thought needful in this place to say of Homer. I proceed to Ovid and Chaucer; considering the former only in relation to the latter. With Ovid ended the golden age of the Roman tongue; from Chaucer the purity of the English tongue began. The manners of the poets were not unlike. Both of them were well-bred, well-natured, amorous, and libertine, at least in

---

[5] Dryden is largely repeating Aristotle here (see above, p. 23)

[6] "Energetic, angry, relentless, bitter" (*Art of Poetry,* l. 121); and "Where the fates lead us, let us follow" (*Aeneid,* V, 709).

their writings; it may be, also in their lives. Their studies were the same, philosophy and philology. Both of them were knowing in astronomy; of which Ovid's books of the *Roman Feasts,* and Chaucer's *Treatise of the Astrolabe,* are sufficient witnesses. But Chaucer was likewise an astrologer, as were Virgil, Horace, Persius, and Manilius. Both writ with wonderful facility and clearness; neither were great inventors: for Ovid only copied the Grecian fables, and most of Chaucer's stories were taken from his Italian contemporaries, or their predecessors. Boccace his *Decameron* was first published, and from thence our Englishman has borrowed many of his *Canterbury Tales:* yet that of *Palamon and Arcite* was written, in all probability, by some Italian wit, in a former age, as I shall prove hereafter. The tale of Grizild was the invention of Petrarch; by him sent to Boccace; from whom it came to Chaucer. *Troilus and Cressida* was also written by a Lombard author, but much amplified by our English translator, as well as beautified; the genius of our countrymen, in general, being rather to improve an invention than to invent themselves, as is evident not only in our poetry, but in many of our manufactures. I find I have anticipated already, and taken up from Boccace before I come to him: but there is so much less behind; and I am of the temper of most kings, who love to be in debt, are all for present money, no matter how they pay it afterwards: besides, the nature of a preface is rambling, never wholly out of the way, nor in it. This I have learned from the practice of honest Montaigne, and return at my pleasure to Ovid and Chaucer, of whom I have little more to say.

Both of them built on the inventions of other men; yet since Chaucer had something of his own, as *The Wife of Bath's Tale, The Cock and the Fox,* which I have translated, and some others, I may justly give our countryman the precedence in that part; since I can remember nothing of Ovid which was wholly his. Both of them understood the manners, under which name I comprehend the passions, and, in a larger sense, the descriptions of persons, and their very habits. For an example, I see Baucis and Philemon as perfectly before me, as if some ancient painter had drawn them; and all the pilgrims in the *Canterbury Tales,* their humours, their fea-

tures, and the very dress, as distinctly as if I had supped with them at the *Tabard* in Southwark. Yet even there, too, the figures of Chaucer are much more lively, and set in a better light; which tho' I have not time to prove, yet I appeal to the reader, and am sure he will clear me from partiality. The thoughts and words remain to be considered in the comparison of the two poets, and I have saved myself one-half of that labour, by owning that Ovid lived when the Roman tongue was in its meridian; Chaucer, in the dawning of our language: therefore that part of the comparison stands not on an equal foot, any more than the diction of Ennius and Ovid, or of Chaucer and our present English. The words are given up, as a post not to be defended in our poet, because he wanted the modern art of fortifying. The thoughts remain to be considered; and they are to be measured only by their propriety; that is, as they flow more or less naturally from the persons described, on such and such occasions. The vulgar judges, which are nine parts in ten of all nations, who call conceits and jingles wit, who see Ovid full of them, and Chaucer altogether without them, will think me little less than mad for preferring the Englishman to the Roman. Yet, with their leave, I must presume to say, that the things they admire are only glittering trifles, and so far from being witty, that in a serious poem they are nauseous, because they are unnatural. Would any man, who is ready to die for love, describe his passion like Narcissus? Would he think of *inopem me copia fecit,*[7] and a dozen more of such expressions, poured on the neck of one another, and signifying all the same thing? If this were wit, was this a time to be witty, when the poor wretch was in the agony of death? This is just John Little-wit, in *Bartholomew Fair,* who had a conceit (as he tells you) left him in his misery; a miserable conceit. On these occasions the poet should endeavour to raise pity; but, instead of this, Ovid is tickling you to laugh. Virgil never made use of such machines when he was moving you to commiserate the death of Dido: he would not destroy what he was building. Chaucer makes Arcite violent in his love, and unjust in the pursuit of it; yet,

7 "Wealth has impoverished me" (*Metamorphoses,* III, 466).

when he came to die, he made him think more reasonably: he repents not of his love, for that had altered his character; but acknowledges the injustice of his proceedings, and resigns Emilia to Palamon. What would Ovid have done on this occasion? He would certainly have made Arcite witty on his deathbed. He had complained he was farther off from possession, by being so near, and a thousand such boyisms, which Chaucer rejected as below the dignity of the subject. They who think otherwise, would, by the same reason, prefer Lucan and Ovid to Homer and Virgil, and Martial to all four of them. As for the turn of words, in which Ovid particularly excels all poets, they are sometimes a fault, and sometimes a beauty, as they are used properly or improperly; but in strong passions always to be shunned, because passions are serious, and will admit no playing. The French have a high value for them; and, I confess, they are often what they call delicate, when they are introduced with judgment; but Chaucer writ with more simplicity, and follow'd Nature more closely than to use them. I have thus far, to the best of my knowledge, been an upright judge betwixt the parties in competition, not meddling with the design nor the disposition of it; because the design was not their own; and in the disposing of it they were equal. It remains that I say somewhat of Chaucer in particular.

In the first place, as he is the father of English poetry, so I hold him in the same degree of veneration as the Grecians held Homer, or the Romans Virgil. He is a perpetual fountain of good sense; learn'd in all sciences; and, therefore, speaks properly on all subjects. As he knew what to say, so he knows also when to leave off; a continence which is practiced by few writers, and scarcely by any of the ancients, excepting Virgil and Horace. One of our late great poets is sunk in his reputation, because he could never forgive any conceit which came in his way; but swept like a drag-net, great and small. There was plenty enough, but the dishes were ill sorted; whole pyramids of sweetmeats for boys and women, but little of solid meat for men. All this proceeded not from any want of knowledge, but of judgment. Neither did he want that in discerning the beauties and faults of other poets, but only indulged himself in the luxury of writing; and perhaps knew it was a fault, but hoped

the reader would not find it. For this reason, tho' he must always be thought a great poet, he is no longer esteemed a good writer; and for ten impressions, which his works have had in so many successive years, yet at present a hundred books are scarcely purchased once a twelve-month; for, as my last Lord Rochester said, tho' somewhat profanely, *Not being of God, he could not stand.*

Chaucer followed Nature everywhere, but was never so bold to go beyond her; and there is a great difference of being *poeta* and *nimis poeta*,[8] if we may believe Catullus, as much as betwixt a modest behaviour and affectation. The verse of Chaucer, I confess, is not harmonious to us; but 'tis like the eloquence of one whom Tacitus commends, it was *auribus istius temporis accommodata:* [9] they who lived with him, and some time after him, thought it musical; and it continued so, even in our judgment, if compared with the numbers of Lydgate and Gower, his contemporaries: there is the rude sweetness of a Scotch tune in it, which is natural and pleasing, tho' not perfect. 'Tis true, I cannot go so far as he who published the last edition of him; for he would make us believe the fault is in our ears, and that there were really ten syllables in a verse where we find but nine: but this opinion is not worth confuting; 'tis so gross and obvious an error, that common sense (which is a rule in everything but matters of Faith and Revelation) must convince the reader, that equality of numbers, in every verse which we call *heroic,* was either not known, or not always practiced, in Chaucer's age. It were an easy matter to produce some thousands of his verses, which are lame for want of half a foot, and sometimes a whole one, and which no pronunciation can make otherwise. We can only say, that he lived in the infancy of our poetry, and that nothing is brought to perfection at the first. We must be children before we grow men. There was an Ennius, and in process of time a Lucilius, and a Lucretius, before Virgil and Horace; even after Chaucer there was a Spenser, a Harrington, a Fairfax, before Waller and Denham were in being; and our numbers were in their nonage till these last appeared. I need say little of his parentage, life, and fortunes; they are to be found

---

8 "Too much of a poet."

9 "Accommodated to the ears of the time."

at large in all the editions of his works. He was employed abroad and favoured by Edward the Third, Richard the Second, and Henry the Fourth, and was poet, as I suppose, to all three of them. In Richard's time, I doubt, he was a little dipt in the rebellion of the Commons; and being brother-in-law to John of Ghant, it was no wonder if he followed the fortunes of that family; and was well with Henry the Fourth when he had deposed his predecessor. Neither is it to be admired, that Henry, who was a wise as well as a valiant prince, who claimed by succession, and was sensible that his title was not sound, but was rightfully in Mortimer, who had married the heir of York; it was not to be admired, I say, if that great politician should be pleased to have the greatest Wit of those times in his interests, and to be the trumpet of his praises. Augustus had given him the example, by the advice of Maecenas, who recommended Virgil and Horace to him; whose praises helped to make him popular while he was alive, and after his death have made him precious to posterity. As for the religion of our poet, he seems to have some little bias towards the opinions of Wycliffe, after John of Ghant his patron; somewhat of which appears in the tale of *Piers Plowman:* Yet I cannot blame him for inveighing so sharply against the vices of the clergy in his age: their pride, their ambition, their pomp, their avarice, their worldly interest, deserved the lashes which he gave them, both in that, and in most of his *Canterbury Tales.* Neither has his contemporary Boccace spared them: Yet both those poets lived in much esteem with good and holy men in orders; for the scandal which is given by particular priests reflects not on the sacred function. Chaucer's *Monk,* his *Canon,* and his *Friar,* took not from the character of his *Good Parson.* A satirical poet is the check of the laymen on bad priests. We are only to take care, that we involve not the innocent with the guilty in the same condemnation. The good cannot be too much honoured, nor the bad too coarsely used; for the corruption of the best becomes the worst. When a clergyman is whipped, his gown is first taken off, by which the dignity of his order is secured. If he be wrongfully accused, he has his action of slander; and 'tis at the poet's peril if he transgress the law. But they will tell us, that all kind of satire, tho' never so well deserved by particular priests, yet brings the whole order into contempt. Is then the peerage of England anything dishonoured when a peer suffers for his treason? If he be libelled or any way defamed, he has his *scandalum magnatum* [10] to punish the offender. They who use this kind of argument, seem to be conscious to themselves of somewhat which has deserved the poet's lash, and are less concerned for their public capacity than for their private; at least there is pride at the bottom of their reasoning. If the faults of men in orders are only to be judged among themselves, they are all in some sort parties; for, since they say the honour of their order is concerned in every member of it, how can we be sure that they will be impartial judges? How far I may be allowed to speak my opinion in this case, I know not; but I am sure a dispute of this nature caused mischief in abundance betwixt a King of England and an Archbishop of Canterbury; one standing up for the laws of his land, and the other for the honour (as he called it) of God's Church; which ended in the murther of the prelate, and in the whipping of his Majesty from post to pillar for his penance. The learned and ingenious Dr. Drake has saved me the labour of inquiring into the esteem and reverence which the priests have had of old; and I would rather extend than diminish any part of it: yet I must needs say, that when a priest provokes me without any occasion given him, I have no reason, unless it be the charity of a Christian, to forgive him: *prior laesit* [11] is justification sufficient in the civil law. If I answer him in his own language, self-defence, I am sure must be allowed me; and if I carry it further, even to a sharp recrimination, somewhat may be indulged to human frailty. Yet my resentment has not wrought so far, but that I have followed Chaucer, in his character of a holy man, and have enlarged on that subject with some pleasure; reserving to myself the right, if I shall think fit hereafter, to describe another sort of priests, such as are more easily to be found than the Good Parson; such as have given the last blow to Christianity in this age, by a practice so contrary to their doctrine. But this will keep cold till another time. In the mean while, I take up Chaucer where I left him.

[10] "[Law of] slander extraordinary."
[11] "He gave the first offence."

He must have been a man of a most wonderful comprehensive nature, because, as it has been truly observed of him, he has taken into the compass of his *Canterbury Tales* the various manners and humours (as we now call them) of the whole English nation, in his age. Not a single character has escaped him. All his pilgrims are severally distinguished from each other; and not only in their inclinations, but in their very physiognomies and persons. Bapista Porta could not have described their natures better, than by the marks which the poet gives them. The matter and manner of their tales, and of their telling, are so suited to their different educations, humours, and callings, that each of them would be improper in any other mouth. Even the grave and serious characters are distinguished by their several sorts of gravity: their discourses are such as belong to their age, their calling, and their breeding; such as are becoming of them, and of them only. Some of his persons are vicious, and some virtuous; some are unlearn'd, or (as Chaucer calls them) lewd, and some are learn'd. Even the ribaldry of the low characters is different: the Reeve, the Miller, and the Cook, are several men, and distinguished from each other as much as the mincing Lady-Prioress and the broad-speaking gap-toothed Wife of Bath. But enough of this; there is such a variety of game springing up before me, that I am distracted in my choice, and know not which to follow. 'Tis sufficient to say, according to the proverb, that *here is God's plenty*. We have our forefathers and great-grandames all before us, as they were in Chaucer's days: their general characters are still remaining in mankind, and even in England, tho' they are called by other names than those of Monks, and Friars, and Canons, and Lady Abbesses; and Nuns; for mankind is ever the same, and nothing lost out of Nature, tho' everything is altered. May I have leave to do myself the justice (since my enemies will do me none, and are so far from granting me to be a good poet, that they will not allow me so much as to be a Christian, or a moral man), may I have leave, I say, to inform my reader, that I have confined my choice to such tales of Chaucer as savour nothing of immodesty. If I had desired more to please than to instruct, the *Reeve*, the *Miller*, the *Shipman*, the *Merchant*, the *Sumner*, and, above all, the *Wife of Bath*, in the Prologue to her *Tale*, would have procured me as many friends and readers, as there are *beaux* and ladies of pleasure in the town. But I will no more offend against good manners: I am sensible as I ought to be of the scandal I have given by my loose writings; and make what reparation I am able, by this public acknowledgment. If anything of this nature, or of profaneness, be crept into these poems, I am so far from defending it, that I disown it. *Totum hoc indictum volo.*[12] Chaucer makes another manner of apology for his broad speaking, and Boccace makes the like; but I will follow neither of them. Our countryman, in the end of his *Characters*, before the *Canterbury Tales*, thus excuses the ribaldry, which is very gross in many of his novels—

But firste, I pray you, of your courtesy,
That ye ne arrete it not my villainy,
Though that I plainly speak in this mattere,
To tellen you her words, and eke her chere:
Ne though I speak her words properly,
For this ye knowen as well as I,
Who shall tellen a tale after a man,
He mote rehearse as nye as ever he can:
Everich word of it ben in his charge,
All speke he, never so rudely, ne large:
Or else he mote tellen his tale untrue,
Or feine things, or find words new:
He may not spare, altho he were his brother,
He mote as well say o word as another.
Crist spake himself ful broad in holy Writ,
And well I wote no villainy is it,
Eke *Plato* saith, who so can him rede,
The words mote been cousin to the dede.

Yet if a man should have enquired of Boccace or of Chaucer, what need they had of introducing such characters, where obscene words were proper in their mouths, but very undecent to be heard; I know not what answer they could have made; for that reason, such tales shall be left untold by me. You have here a specimen of Chaucer's language, which is so obsolete, that his sense is scarce to be understood; and you have likewise more than one example of his unequal numbers, which were mentioned before. Yet many of his verses consist of ten syllables, and the words not much behind our present English: as for example, these two lines, in the description of the Carpenter's young wife—

Wincing she was, as is a jolly colt,
Long as a mast, and upright as a bolt.

I have almost done with Chaucer, when I have answered some objections relating to my present work. I find some people are offended that I have turned these tales into modern English; because they think them unworthy of my pains, and look on Chaucer as a dry, old-fashioned wit, not worth reviving. I have often heard the late Earl of Leicester say, that Mr. Cowley himself was of that opinion; who, having read him over at my Lord's request, declared he had no taste of him. I dare not advance my opinion against the judgment of so great an author; but I think it fair, however, to leave the decision to the public. Mr. Cowley was too modest to set up for a dictator; and being shocked perhaps with his old style, never examined into the depth of his good sense. Chaucer, I confess, is a rough diamond, and must first be polished, ere he shines. I deny not likewise, that, living in our early days of poetry, he writes not always of a piece; but sometimes mingles trivial things with those of greater moment. Sometimes also, tho' not often, he runs riot, like Ovid, and knows not when he has said enough. But there are more great wits beside Chaucer, whose fault is their excess of conceits, and those ill sorted. An author is not to write all he can, but only all he ought. Having observed this redundancy in Chaucer, (as it is an easy matter for a man of ordinary parts to find a fault in one of greater,) I have not tied myself to a literal translation; but have often omitted what I judged unnecessary, or not of dignity enough to appear in the company of better thoughts. I have presumed further, in some places, and added somewhat of my own where I thought my author was deficient, and had not given his thoughts their true luster, for want of words in the beginning of our language. And to this I was the more emboldened, because (if I may be permitted to say it of myself) I found I had a soul congenial to his, and that I had been conversant in the same studies. Another poet, in another age, may take the same liberty with my writings; if at least they live long enough to deserve correction. It was also necessary sometimes to restore the sense of Chaucer, which was lost or mangled in the errors of the press. Let this example suffice at present: in the story of *Pala-*

mon and Arcite, where the temple of Diana is described, you find these verses, in all the editions of our author:—

There saw I *Danè* turned unto a tree,
I mean not the goddess *Diane*,
But *Venus* daughter, which that hight *Danè*.

Which, after a little consideration, I knew was to be reformed into this sense, that *Daphne*, the daughter of Peneus, was turned into a tree. I durst not make thus bold with Ovid, lest some future Milbourne should arise, and say, I varied from my author, because I understood him not.

But there are other judges, who think I ought not to have translated Chaucer into English, out of a quite contrary notion: they suppose there is a certain veneration due to his old language; and that it is little less than profanation and sacrilege to alter it. They are farther of opinion, that somewhat of his good sense will suffer in this transfusion, and much of the beauty of his thoughts will infallibly be lost, which appear with more grace in their old habit. Of this opinion was that excellent person, whom I mentioned, the late Earl of Leicester, who valued Chaucer as much as Mr. Cowley despised him. My Lord dissuaded me from this attempt, (for I was thinking of it some years before his death,) and his authority prevailed so far with me, as to defer my undertaking while he lived, in deference to him: yet my reason was not convinced with what he urged against it. If the first end of a writer be to be understood, then, as his language grows obsolete, his thoughts must grow obscure—

*Multa renascentur, quae nunc cecidere; cadentque
Quae nunc sunt in honore vocabula, si volet usus,
Quem penes arbitrium est et jus et norma loquendi.*[13]

When an ancient word, for its sound and significancy, deserves to be revived, I have that reasonable veneration for antiquity to restore it. All beyond this is superstition. Words are not like landmarks, so sacred as never to be removed; customs are changed, and even statutes are silently repealed, when the reason ceases for which they were enacted. As for the other part of the argument, that his thoughts will lose of their original beauty by the innovation of words;

[13] See *Essay of Dramatic Poesy*, above, note 18.

in the first place, not only their beauty, but their being is lost, where they are no longer understood, which is the present case. I grant that something must be lost in all transfusion, that is, in all translations; but the sense will remain, which would otherwise be lost, or at least be maimed, when it is scarce intelligible, and that but to a few. How few are there, who can read Chaucer so as to understand him perfectly? And if imperfectly, then with less profit, and no pleasure. It is not for the use of some old Saxon friends, that I have taken these pains with him: let them neglect my version, because they have no need of it. I made it for their sakes, who understand sense and poetry as well as they, when that poetry and sense is put into words which they understand. I will go farther, and dare to add, that what beauties I lose in some places, I give to others which had them not originally: but in this I may be partial to myself; let the reader judge, and I submit to his decision. Yet I think I have just occasion to complain of them, who because they understand Chaucer, would deprive the greater part of their countrymen of the same advantage, and hoard him up, as misers do their grandam gold, only to look on it themselves, and hinder others from making use of it. In sum, I seriously protest, that no man ever had, or can have, a greater veneration for Chaucer than myself. I have translated some part of his works, only that I might perpetuate his memory, or at least refresh it, amongst my countrymen. If I have altered him anywhere for the better, I must at the same time acknowledge, that I could have done nothing without him. *Facile est inventis addere* [14] is no great commendation; and I am not so vain to think I have deserved a greater. I will conclude what I have to say of him singly, with this one remark: A lady of my acquaintance, who keeps a kind of correspondence with some authors of the fair sex in France, has been informed by them, that Mademoiselle de Scudery, who is as old as Sibyl, and inspired like her by the same God of Poetry, is at this time translating Chaucer into modern French. From which I gather, that he has been formerly translated into the old Provençal; for how she should come to

[14] "It is easy to add to what has already been invented."

understand old English, I know not. But the matter of fact being true, it makes me think that there is something in it like fatality; that, after certain periods of time, the fame and memory of great Wits should be renewed, as Chaucer is both in France and England. If this be wholly chance, 'tis extraordinary; and I dare not call it more, for fear of being taxed with superstition.

Boccace comes last to be considered, who, living in the same age with Chaucer, had the same genius, and followed the same studies. Both writ novels, and each of them cultivated his mother tongue. But the greatest resemblance of our two modern authors being in their familiar style, and pleasing way of relating comical adventures, I may pass it over, because I have translated nothing from Boccace of that nature. In the serious part of poetry, the advantage is wholly on Chaucer's side; for tho' the Englishman has borrowed many tales from the Italian, yet it appears, that those of Boccace were not generally of his own making, but taken from authors of former ages, and by him only modelled; so that what there was of invention, in either of them, may be judged equal. But Chaucer has refined on Boccace, and has mended the stories, which he has borrowed, in his way of telling; tho' prose allows more liberty of thought, and the expression is more easy when unconfined by numbers. Our countryman carries weight, and yet wins the race at disadvantage. I desire not the reader should take my word; and, therefore, I will set two of their discourses, on the same subject, in the same light, for every man to judge betwixt them. I translated Chaucer first, and, amongst the rest, pitched on *The Wife of Bath's Tale*; not daring, as I have said, to adventure on her Prologue, because 'tis too licentious. There Chaucer introduces an old woman, of mean parentage, whom a youthful knight, of noble blood, was forced to marry, and consequently loathed her. The crone being in bed with him on the wedding-night, and finding his aversion, endeavours to win his affection by reason, and speaks a good word for herself, (as who could blame her?) in hope to mollify the sullen bridegroom. She takes her topics from the benefits of poverty, the advantages of old age and ugliness, the vanity of youth, and the silly pride of ancestry and titles, without inherent virtue, which is the true nobility. When

I had closed Chaucer, I returned to Ovid, and translated some more of his fables; and, by this time, had so far forgotten *The Wife of Bath's Tale,* that, when I took up Boccace, unawares I fell on the same argument, of preferring virtue to nobility of blood and titles, in the story of *Sigismonda;* which I had certainly avoided, for the resemblance of the two discourses, if my memory had not failed me. Let the reader weigh them both; and, if he thinks me partial to Chaucer, 'tis in him to right Boccace.

I prefer, in our countryman, far above all his other stories, the noble poem of *Palamon and Arcite,* which is of the epic kind, and perhaps not much inferior to the *Ilias,* or the *Aeneis.* The story is more pleasing than either of them, the manners as perfect, the diction as poetical, the learning as deep and various, and the disposition full as artful: only it includes a greater length of time, as taking up seven years at least; but Aristotle has left undecided the duration of the action; which yet is easily reduced into the compass of a year, by a narration of what preceded the return of Palamon to Athens. I had thought, for the honour of our nation, and more particularly for his, whose laurel, tho' unworthy, I have worn after him, that this story was of English growth, and Chaucer's own: but I was undeceived by Boccace; for, casually looking on the end of his seventh *Giornata,* I found Dioneo, (under which name he shadows himself,) and Fiametta, (who represents his mistress, the natural daughter of Robert, King of Naples,) of whom these words are spoken: *Dioneo e Fiametta gran pezza cantarono insieme d' Arcita, e di Palamone;*[15] by which it appears, that this story was written before the time of Boccace; but the name of its author being wholly lost, Chaucer is now become an original; and I question not but the poem has received many beauties, by passing thro' his noble hands. Besides this tale, there is another of his own invention, after the manner of the Provençals, called *The Flower and the Leaf,* with which I was so particularly pleased, both for the invention and the moral, that I cannot hinder myself from recommending it to the reader.

As a corollary to this preface, in which I have done justice to others, I owe somewhat to myself; not that I think it worth my time to enter the lists with one M——, or one B——,[16] but barely to take notice, that such men there are, who have written scurrilously against me, without any provocation. M——, who is in orders, pretends, amongst the rest, this quarrel to me, that I have fallen foul on priesthood: if I have, I am only to ask pardon of good priests, and am afraid his part of the reparation will come to little. Let him be satisfied that he shall not be able to force himself upon me for an adversary. I contemn him too much to enter into competition with him. His own translations of Virgil have answered his criticisms on mine. If, (as they say, he has declared in print), he prefers the version of Ogleby [17] to mine, the world has made him the same compliment; for 'tis agreed, on all hands, that he writes even below Ogleby. That, you will say, is not easily to be done; but what cannot M—— bring about? I am satisfied, however, that, while he and I live together, I shall not be thought the worst poet of the age. It looks as if I had desired him underhand to write so ill against me; but upon my honest word I have not bribed him to do me this service, and am wholly guiltless of his pamphlet. 'Tis true, I should be glad if I could persuade him to continue his good offices, and write such another critique on anything of mine; for I find, by experience, he has a great stroke with the reader, when he condemns any of my poems, to make the world have a better opinion of them. He has taken some pains with my poetry; but nobody will be persuaded to take the same with his. If I had taken to the Church, as he affirms, but which was never in my thoughts, I should have had more sense, if not more grace, than to have turned myself out of my benefice, by writing libels on my parishioners. But his account of my manners and my principles are of a piece with his cavils and his poetry; and so I have done with him for ever.

As for the City Bard, or Knight Physician, I hear his quarrel to me is, that I was the author of *Absalom and Achitophel,* which, he thinks, is a little hard on his fanatic patrons in London.

---

[15] "Dioneo and Fiametta sang together for a long while of Arcite and of Palamon."

[16] Luke Milbourn and Sir Richard Blackmore. See Pope's *Essay on Criticism,* below, note 15.

[17] John Ogilby, who translated not only Virgil (1649-50) but Homer (1660-65).

But I will deal the more civilly with his two poems, because nothing ill is to be spoken of the dead; and therefore peace be to the *manes* of his *Arthurs*. I will only say, that it was not for this noble Knight that I drew the plan of an epic poem on *King Arthur*, in my preface to the translation of *Juvenal*. The Guardian Angels of kingdoms were machines too ponderous for him to manage; and therefore he rejected them, as Dares did the whirl-bats of Eryx when they were thrown before him by Entellus: Yet from that preface, he plainly took his hint; for he began immediately upon the story, tho' he had the baseness not to acknowledge his benefactor, but instead of it, to traduce me in a libel.

I shall say the less of Mr. Collier, because in many things he has taxed me justly; and I have pleaded guilty to all thoughts and expressions of mine, which can be truly argued of obscenity, profaneness, of immorality, and retract them. If he be my enemy, let him triumph; if he be my friend, as I have given him no personal occasion to be otherwise, he will be glad of my repentance. It becomes me not to draw my pen in the defence of a bad cause, when I have so often drawn it for a good one. Yet it were not difficult to prove, that in many places he has perverted my meaning by his glosses, and interpreted my words into blasphemy and bawdry, of which they were not guilty. Besides that, he is too much given to horse-play in his raillery, and comes to battle like a dictator from the plow. I will not say, *the zeal of God's house has eaten him up;* but I am sure it has devoured some part of his good manners and civility. It might also be doubted, whether it were altogether zeal which prompted him to this rough manner of proceeding; perhaps, it became not one of his function to rake into the rubbish of ancient and modern plays: a divine might have employed his pains to better purpose, than in the nastiness of Plautus and Aristophanes, whose examples, as they excuse not me, so it might be possibly supposed that he read them not without some pleasure. They who have written commentaries on those poets, or on Horace, Juvenal, and Martial, have explained some vices, which, without their interpretation, had been unknown to modern times. Neither has he judged impartially betwixt the former age and us.

There is more bawdry in one play of Fletcher's, called *The Custom of the Country*, than in all ours together. Yet this has been often acted on the stage, in my remembrance. Are the times so much more reformed now, than they were five-and-twenty years ago? If they are, I congratulate the amendment of our morals. But I am not to prejudice the cause of my fellow poets, tho' I abandon my own defence: they have some of them answered for themselves; and neither they nor I can think Mr. Collier so formidable an enemy, that we should shun him. He has lost ground, at the latter end of the day, by pursuing his point too far, like the Prince of Condé, at the battle of Senneph: from immoral plays to no plays, *ab abusu ad usum, non valet consequentia.*[18] But, being a party, I am not to erect myself into a judge. As for the rest of those who have written against me, they are such scoundrels, that they deserve not the least notice to be taken of them. B—— and M—— are only distinguished from the crowd by being remembered to their infamy:—

> . . . *Demetri, teque Tigelli,*
> *Discipulorum inter jubeo plorare cathedras.*[19]

[18] "It is not a valid argument to apply the *abuse* of a thing to its proper *use.*"
[19] "I bid you, Demetrius and Tigellius, lament among the seats of your scholars."

ALEXANDER POPE (1688-1744)

IN THE *Essay on Criticism* (1711), written in 1709 when he was hardly twenty-one, Pope was trying to write a poetical essay which would hold the same important place in English that Boileau's *Art Poétique* (1674) was holding in French criticism. If it did not quite attain this position, the reason is not that Pope's essay is inferior to Boileau's. It is simply that English writers of any period, including the age of Pope, have a way of refusing to form schools and follow manifestoes. Still, Pope's *Essay on Criticism* is not only the last but perhaps the most rewarding of the important critical essays in verse modeled on Horace's *Art of Poetry*. It draws upon the previous verse-essays of Horace, Vida, and Boileau, as well as those of two minor Restoration writers, the Earls of Mulgrave and Roscommon. It also draws upon precepts from the Roman Quintilian and the French critics, Rapin and Le Bossu. Above all, its general tone is kept comparatively liberal and flexible by the influence of Dryden, and, to some extent, of Longinus. The background is broad. This may partly explain why the *Essay on Criticism* is more comprehensive in what it covers than any other of the Horatian verse-essays, including that of Boileau. It also quite equals Boileau in edge of style, and it surpasses him in compactness.

The *Essay on Criticism* is more profitably introduced by a topical summary of its themes than by an analysis of its premises. For its premises and aims are those of the entire neoclassic tradition. And the poem itself is a statement or summary of them rather than an individual argument or analysis. The essay may be described as falling into three parts, with the following subdivisions:

I. General qualities needed by the critic (1-200):
   A. Awareness of his own limitations (46-67).
   B. Knowledge of Nature in its general forms (68-87).

ALEXANDER POPE. Reared as a Catholic, Pope was privately educated, and at a precocious age began writing gifted poetry. With his early pastorals and the *Essay on Criticism*, his acquaintance with literary and social circles began to widen. Addison, for a while, and especially Swift, Gay, and Arbuthnot were among his friends. After his translation of the *Iliad* (1715-20), his fame was established. He tried his hand at philosophical verse in the *Essay on Man* (1733-34); but he is especially eminent in ranking with Dryden as one of the greatest satirists in either English or Continental poetry.

The standard text of the *Essay on Criticism* is that of the Twickenham Edition, I (ed. E. Audra and A. Williams, 1961). For the prose criticism, especially the Preface to the *Iliad*, see *Prose Works* (ed. N. Ault, Oxford, 1936), and J. Spence, *Anecdotes, Observations, and Characters of Books and Men* (ed. J. M. Osborn, Oxford, 1966). Among commentary, see the introductory material in George Sherburn, *Selections* (1929; later reprinted as the *Best of Pope*); Geoffrey Tillotson, *On the Poetry of Pope* (Oxford, 1938); Austin Warren, *Pope as Critic and Humanist* (Princeton, 1929); and William Empson, *The Structure of Complex Words* (Norfolk, Conn., 1951).

1. Nature defined (70-79).
2. Need of both wit and judgment to conceive it (80-87).
C. Imitation of the ancients, and the use of rules (88-200).
   1. Value of ancient poetry and criticism as models (88-103).
   2. Censure of slavish imitation and codified rules (104-117).
   3. Need to study the *general* aims and qualities of the ancients (118-140).
   4. Exceptions to the rules (141-168).

II. Particular laws for the critic (201-559):
[Digression on the need for humility (201-232).]
   A. Consider the work as a total unit (233-252).
   B. Seek the author's aim (253-266).
   C. Examples of false critics who mistake the part for the whole (267-383).
      1. The pedant who forgets the end and judges by rules (267-288).
      2. The critic who judges by imagery and metaphor alone (289-304).
      3. The rhetorician who judges by the pomp and color of the diction (305-336).
      4. Critics who judge by versification only (337-343).
         [Pope's digression to exemplify "representative meter" (344-383).]
   D. Need for tolerance and for aloofness from extremes of fashion and personal mood (384-559).
      1. The fashionable critic: the cults, as ends in themselves, of the foreign (398-405), the new (406-423), and the esoteric (424-451).
      2. Personal subjectivity and its pitfalls (452-559).

III. The ideal character of the critic (560-744):
   A. Qualities needed: integrity (562-565), modesty (566-571), tact (572-577), courage (578-583).
   B. Their opposites (584-630).
   C. Concluding eulogy of ancient critics as models (643-744).

The intention of this outline is simply to clarify the topics discussed by Pope. It is by no means intended to attribute an argumentative or reasoned order to the poem. For as Johnson said of Warburton's attempt to discover the order or design of the *Essay on Criticism:*

Almost every poem, consisting of precepts, is so far arbitrary and immethodical, that many of the paragraphs may change place with no apparent inconvenience; for of two and more positions, depending upon some remote or general principle, there is seldom any cogent reason why one should precede the other. But for the order in which they stand, whatever it be, a little ingenuity may easily give a reason.

An Essay on Criticism

PART I

'Tis hard to say, if greater want of skill
Appear in writing or in judging ill;
But, of the two, less dang'rous is th' offence
To tire our patience, than mislead our sense:
Some few in that, but numbers err in this,
Ten censure wrong for one who writes amiss;
A fool might once himself alone expose;
Now one in verse makes many more in prose.

'Tis with our judgments as our watches, none
Go just alike, yet each believes his own.　　10
In poets as true genius is but rare,
True taste as seldom is the critic's share;
Both must alike from heav'n derive their light,
These born to judge, as well as those to write.
Let such teach others who themselves excel,
And censure freely, who have written well.
Authors are partial to their wit, 'tis true,
But are not critics to their judgment too?

Yet, if we look more closely, we shall find
Most have the seeds of judgment in their mind.　20
Nature affords at least a glimm'ring light;
The lines, tho' touch'd but faintly are drawn right:
But as the slightest sketch, if justly trac'd,
Is by ill colouring but the more disgrac'd,
So by false learning is good sense defac'd:
Some are bewilder'd in the maze of schools,
And some made coxcombs Nature meant but fools:
In search of wit, these lose their common sense,
And then turn critics in their own defence:
Each burns alike, who can, or cannot write,　　30
Or with a rival's, or an eunuch's spite.
All fools have still an itching to deride,
And fain would be upon the laughing side.
If Maevius scribble in Apollo's spite,
There are who judge still worse than he can write.

Some have at first for wits, then poets past,
Turn'd critics next, and prov'd plain fools at last.
Some neither can for wits nor critics pass,
As heavy mules are neither horse nor ass.
Those half-learn'd witlings, num'rous in our isle,　40
As half-form'd insects on the banks of Nile;
Unfinish'd things, one knows not what to call,
Their generation's so equivocal;

An Essay on Criticism. First published in 1711.

To tell them would a hundred tongues require,
Or one vain wit's, that might a hundred tire.

But you who seek to give and merit fame,
And justly bear a Critic's noble name,
Be sure yourself and your own reach to know,
How far your genius, taste, and learning go;
Launch not beyond your depth, but be discreet, 50
And mark that point where sense and dulness meet.

Nature to all things fix'd the limits fit,
And wisely curb'd proud man's pretending wit.
As on the land while here the ocean gains,
In other parts it leaves wide sandy plains;
Thus in the soul while memory prevails,
The solid pow'r of understanding fails;
Where beams of warm imagination play,
The memory's soft figures melt away.
One science only will one genius fit;　　　　60
So vast is art, so narrow human wit:
Not only bounded to peculiar arts,
But oft' in those confin'd to single parts.
Like kings we lose the conquests gain'd before,
By vain ambition still to make them more:
Each might his sev'ral province well command,
Would all but stoop to what they understand.

First follow Nature, and your judgment frame
By her just standard, which is still the same:
Unerring Nature! still divinely bright,　　　70
One clear, unchang'd, and universal light,
Life, force, and beauty, must to all impart,
At once the source, and end, and test of art.[1]
Art from that fund each just supply provides;
Works without show, and without pomp presides:
In some fair body thus th' informing soul
With spirits feeds, with vigour fills the whole;
Each motion guides, and ev'ry nerve sustains,
Itself unseen, but in th' effects remains.
Some, to whom Heav'n in wit has been profuse, 80
Want as much more, to turn it to its use;
For wit and judgment often are at strife,
Tho' meant each other's aid, like man and wife.

[1] One of the key lines of the *Essay on Criticism.* Nature, the fundamental process of reality as it reveals persisting forms, is the object of imitation, or the "source"; the "end" of art is to duplicate and express the character of this reality; and the "test" is the success with which this is done.

'Tis more to guide, than spur the Muse's steed;
Restrain his fury, than provoke his speed:
The winged courser, like a gen'rous horse,
Shows most true mettle when you check his course.

Those Rules of old discover'd, not devis'd,
Are Nature still, but Nature methodiz'd: [2]
Nature, like liberty, is but restrain'd   90
By the same laws which first herself ordain'd.

Hear how learn'd Greece her useful rules indites,
When to repress, and when indulge our flights:
High on Parnassus' top her sons she show'd,
And pointed out those arduous paths they trod;
Held from afar, aloft, th' immortal prize,
And urg'd the rest by equal steps to rise.
Just precepts thus from great examples giv'n,
She drew from them what they deriv'd from Heav'n;
The gen'rous critic fann'd the poet's fire,   100
And taught the world with reason to admire.
Then Criticism the Muse's handmaid prov'd,
To dress her charms, and make her more belov'd:
But following wits from that intention stray'd;
Who could not win the mistress, woo'd the maid;
Against the poets their own arms they turn'd,
Sure to hate most the men from whom they learn'd.
So modern 'pothecaries, taught the art
By doctors' bills to play the doctor's part,
Bold in the practice of mistaken rules,   110
Prescribe, apply, and call their masters fools.
Some on the leaves of ancient authors prey;
Nor time nor moths e'er spoil'd so much as they:
Some dryly plain, without invention's aid,
Write dull receipts how poems may be made;
These leave the sense, their learning to display,
And those explain the meaning quite away.

You then whose judgment the right course would steer,
Know well each ancient's proper character;
His fable, subject, scope in ev'ry page;   120
Religion, country, genius of his age:
Without all these at once before your eyes,
Cavil you may, but never criticise.
Be Homer's works your study and delight,
Read them by day, and meditate by night;
Thence form your judgment, thence your maxims bring,
And trace the Muses upward to their spring.

Still with itself compar'd, his text peruse;
And let your comment be the Mantuan Muse.   129
When first young Maro [3] in his boundless mind
A work t' outlast immortal Rome design'd,
Perhaps he seem'd above the critic's law,
And but from Nature's fountain scorn'd to draw:
But when t' examine every part he came,
Nature and Homer were, he found, the same.
Convinc'd, amaz'd, he checks the bold design,
And rules as strict his labour'd work confine
As if the Stagyrite [4] o'erlook'd each line.
Learn hence for ancient rules a just esteem;
To copy Nature is to copy them.   140

Some beauties yet no precepts can declare,
For there's a happiness as well as care.[5]
Music resembles poetry; in each
Are nameless graces which no methods teach,
And which a master-hand alone can reach.
If, where the rules not far enough extend,
(Since rules were made but to promote their end)
Some lucky licence answer to the full
Th' intent propos'd, that licence is a rule.
Thus Pegasus, a nearer way to take,   150
May boldly deviate from the common track.
Great wits sometimes may gloriously offend,
And rise to faults true critics dare not mend;
From vulgar bounds with brave disorder part,
And snatch a grace beyond the reach of art,
Which, without passing thro' the judgment, gains
The heart, and all its end at once attains.
In prospects thus some objects please our eyes,
Which out of Nature's common order rise,
The shapeless rock, or hanging precipice.   160
But tho' the Ancients thus their rules invade,
(As kings dispense with laws themselves have made)
Moderns, beware! or if you must offend
Against the precept, ne'er transgress its end;
Let it be seldom, and compell'd by need;
And have, at least, their precedent to plead;
The critic else proceeds without remorse,
Seizes your fame, and puts his laws in force.
I know there are, to whose presumptuous thoughts
Those freer beauties, ev'n in them, seem faults. 170

---

[2] "If the rules be well considered, we shall find them to be made only to reduce Nature into method . . . 'tis only by these, that probability . . . is maintained, which is the soul of poetry" (Dryden, Preface to "Troilus and Cressida," *Essays* [ed. Ker, 1926], I, 213).

[3] Virgil.

[4] Aristotle, who was born in Stagira, Macedonia.

[5] An element of good fortune, or lucky chance, as well as industry or caution ("care"). Here, and in the following fifteen lines, Pope is repeating the argument of the critics who were reacting against the extreme neoclassic faith in rules (see above, p. 10).

Some figures monstrous and mis-shap'd appear,
Consider'd singly, or beheld too near,
Which, but proportion'd to their light, or place,
Due distance reconciles to form and grace.
A prudent chief not always must display
His pow'rs in equal ranks, and fair array,
But with th' occasion and the place comply,
Conceal his force, nay, seem sometimes to fly.
Those oft' are stratagems which errors seem,
Nor is it Homer nods but we that dream.   180
  Still green with bays each ancient altar stands,
Above the reach of sacrilegious hands;
Secure from flames, from envy's fiercer rage,
Destructive war, and all-involving age.
See, from each clime, the learn'd their incense
      bring;
Hear, in all tongues consenting Paeans ring!
In praise so just let ev'ry voice be join'd,
And fill the gen'ral chorus of mankind.
Hail, Bards triumphant! born in happier days;
Immortal heirs of universal praise!   190
Whose honours with increase of ages grow,
As streams roll down, enlarging as they flow;
Nations unborn your mighty names shall sound,
And worlds applaud, that must not yet be found!
O may some spark of your celestial fire,
The last, the meanest of your sons inspire,
(That on weak wings, from far, pursues your flights;
Glows while he reads, but trembles as he writes,)
To teach vain wits a science little known,
T' admire superior sense, and doubt their own!   200

PART II

  Of all the causes which conspire to blind
Man's erring judgment, and misguide the mind,
What the weak head with strongest bias rules,
Is pride, the never-failing vice of fools.
Whatever Nature has in worth deni'd,
She gives in large recruits of needful pride;
For as in bodies, thus in souls, we find
What wants in blood and spirits, swell'd with wind:
Pride, where wit fails, steps in to our defence,
And fills up all the mighty void of sense: 210
If once right reason [6] drives that cloud away,
Truth breaks upon us with resistless day.
Trust not yourself; but, your defects to know,
Make use of ev'ry friend—and ev'ry foe.

[6] The Renaissance phrase for rational insight into the
absolute forms and principles of Nature.

A little learning is a dang'rous thing;
Drink deep, or taste not the Pierian spring:
There shallow draughts intoxicate the brain,
And drinking largely sobers us again.
Fir'd at first sight with what the Muse imparts,
In fearless youth we tempt the heights of arts,   220
While from the bounded level of our mind,
Short views we take, nor see the lengths behind;
But more advanc'd, behold with strange surprise,
New distant scenes of endless science rise!
So pleas'd at first the tow'ring Alps we try,
Mount o'er the vales, and seem to tread the sky,
Th' eternal snows appear already past,
And the first clouds and mountains seem the last:
But those attain'd, we tremble to survey
The growing labours of the lengthen'd way;   230
Th' increasing prospect tires our wand'ring eyes,
Hills peep o'er hills, and Alps on Alps arise!
  A perfect judge will read each work of wit
With the same spirit that its author writ;
Survey the whole, nor seek slight faults to find
Where Nature moves, and rapture warms the mind;
Nor lose for that malignant dull delight,
The gen'rous pleasure to be charm'd with wit.
But in such lays as neither ebb nor flow,
Correctly cold, and regularly low,   240
That, shunning faults, one quiet tenour keep,
We cannot blame indeed—but we may sleep.
In wit, as nature, what affects our hearts
Is not th' exactness of peculiar parts;
'Tis not a lip, or eye, we beauty call,
But the joint force and full result of all.
Thus when we view some well-proportion'd dome,
(The world's just wonder, and ev'n thine, O Rome!)
No single parts unequally surprise,
All comes united to th' admiring eyes;   250
No monstrous height, or breadth, or length, appear;
The whole at once is bold, and regular.
  Whoever thinks a faultless piece to see,
Thinks what ne'er was, nor is, nor e'er shall be.
In ev'ry work regard the writer's end,
Since none can compass more than they intend;
And if the means be just, the conduct true,
Applause, in spite of trivial faults, is due.
As men of breeding, sometimes men of wit,
T' avoid great errors, must the less commit;   260
Neglect the rules each verbal critic lays,
For not to know some trifles is a praise.
Most critics, fond of some subservient art,
Still make the whole depend upon a part:

They talk of principles, but notions prize,
And all to one lov'd folly sacrifice.
    Once on a time, La Mancha's Knight, they say,
A certain bard encount'ring on the way,
Discours'd in terms as just, with looks as sage,
As e'er could Dennis,[7] of the Grecian stage;   270
Concluding all were desp'rate sots and fools,
Who durst depart from Aristotle's rules.
Our author, happy in a judge so nice,
Produc'd his play, and begg'd the Knight's advice;
Made him observe the subject, and the plot,
The manners, passions, unities; what not?
All which, exact to rule, were brought about,
Were but a combat in the lists left out.
"What! leave the combat out?" exclaims the Knight.
"Yes, or we must renounce the Stagyrite."   280
"Not so, by Heav'n!" (he answers in a rage)
"Knights, squires, and steeds, must enter on the
    stage."
"So vast a throng, the stage can ne'er contain."
"Then build a new, or act it in a plain."
    Thus critics of less judgment than caprice,
Curious, not knowing, not exact but nice,
Form short ideas, and offend in arts
(As most in manners) by a love to parts.
    Some to Conceit [8] alone their taste confine,
And glitt'ring thoughts struck out at ev'ry line; 290
Pleas'd with a work where nothing's just or fit;
One glaring chaos and wild heap of wit.
Poets, like painters, thus unskill'd to trace
The naked nature, and the living grace,
With golds and jewels cover ev'ry part,
And hide with ornaments their want of art.
True wit is Nature to advantage dress'd;
What oft' was thought, but ne'er so well express'd;[9]
Something, whose truth convinc'd at sight we find,
That gives us back the image of our mind.   300
As shades more sweetly recommend the light,
So modest plainness sets off sprightly wit:
For works may have more wit than does them good,
As bodies perish thro' excess of blood.
    Others for Language all their care express,
And value books, as women men, for dress:

Their praise is still,—the style is excellent;
The sense, they humbly take upon content.
Words are like leaves, and where they most abound,
Much fruit of sense beneath is rarely found.   310
False eloquence, like the prismatic glass,
Its gaudy colours spreads on ev'ry place;
The face of Nature we no more survey,
All glares alike, without distinction gay;
But true expression, like th' unchanging sun,
Clears and improves whate'er it shines upon,
It gilds all objects, but it alters none.
Expression is the dress of thought, and still
Appears more decent, as more suitable:
A vile conceit in pompous words express'd   320
Is like a clown in regal purple dress'd:
For diff'rent styles with diff'rent subjects sort,
As several garbs with country, town, and court.
Some by old words to fame have made pretence,
Ancients in praise, mere Moderns in their sense;
Such labour'd nothings, in so strange a style,
Amaze th' unlearn'd, and make the learned smile.
Unlucky, as Fungoso [10] in the play,
These sparks with aukward vanity display
What the fine gentleman wore yesterday;   330
And but so mimic ancient wits at best,
As apes our grandsires, in their doublets drest.
In words, as fashions, the same rule will hold;
Alike fantastic, if too new, or old:
Be not the first by whom the new are try'd,
Nor yet the last to lay the old aside.
    But most by Numbers [11] judge a poet's song,
And smooth or rough, with them, is right or wrong:
In the bright Muse, tho' thousand charms conspire,
Her voice is all these tuneful fools admire;   340
Who haunt Parnassus but to please their ear,
Not mend their minds; as some to church repair
Not for the doctrine, but the music there.
These equal syllables alone require,
Tho' oft' the ear the open vowels tire;
While expletives their feeble aid do join,
And ten low words oft' creep in one dull line:
While they ring round the same unvary'd chimes,
With sure returns of still expected rhymes;   349
Where'er you find "the cooling western breeze,"
In the next line, it "whispers thro' the trees:"

---

[7] John Dennis (1657-1734), a well-known English critic whom Pope frequently attacked.

[8] Figurative language. Pope is here disparaging the sort of critic who looks merely for the isolated happy image or metaphor, neglecting the whole for the part.

[9] See Johnson's discussion of this definition of wit in his *Life of Cowley*, below, p. 218.

[10] In Ben Jonson's *Every Man out of his Humour*.

[11] Versification. Pope uses this theme as an excuse to show his own skill in versification, particularly (ll. 356-373) in what the eighteenth century called "representative meter," or "suiting the sound to the sense" (see Johnson's *Life of Pope*, below, pp. 231-32).

If crystal streams "with pleasing murmurs creep,"
The reader's threaten'd (not in vain) with "sleep:"
Then, at the last and only couplet, fraught
With some unmeaning thing they call a thought,
A needless Alexandrine ends the song,
That, like a wounded snake, drags its slow length
    along.
Leave such to tune their own dull rhymes, and know
What's roundly smooth, or languishingly slow;
And praise the easy vigour of a line   360
Where Denham's strength, and Waller's sweetness
    join.
True ease in writing comes from art, not chance,
As those move easiest who have learn'd to dance.
'Tis not enough no harshness gives offence;
The sound must seem an echo to the sense.
Soft is the strain when zephyr gently blows,
And the smooth stream in smoother numbers flows;
But when loud surges lash the sounding shore,
The hoarse, rough verse should like the torrent roar:
When Ajax strives some rock's vast weight to throw,
The line too labours, and the words move slow:
Not so when swift Camilla scours the plain,   372
Flies o'er th' unbending corn, and skims along the
    main.
Hear how Timotheus' vary'd lays surprise,
And bid alternate passions fall and rise,
While at each change, the son of Libyan Jove
Now burns with glory, and then melts with love;
Now his fierce eyes with sparkling fury glow,
Now sighs steal out, and tears begin to flow: 379
Persians and Greeks like turns of Nature found,
And the world's victor stood subdu'd by sound!
The pow'r of music all our hearts allow,
And what Timotheus was, is Dryden now.
    Avoid extremes, and shun the fault of such
Who still are pleas'd too little or too much.
At ev'ry trifle scorn to take offence,
That always shews great pride, or little sense:
Those heads, as stomachs, are not sure the best,
Which nauseate all, and nothing can digest.
Yet let not each gay turn thy rapture move;   390
For fools admire, but men of sense approve:
As things seem large which we thro' mists descry,
Dulness is ever apt to magnify.
    Some foreign writers, some our own despise;
The Ancients only, or the moderns prize.
Thus wit, like faith, by each man is apply'd
To one small sect, and all are damn'd beside.
Meanly they seek the blessing to confine,
And force that sun but on a part to shine,

Which not alone the southern wit sublimes,   400
But ripens spirits in cold northern climes;
Which, from the first has shone on ages past,
Enlights the present, and shall warm the last;
Tho' each may feel increases and decays,
And see now clearer and now darker days;
Regard not then if wit be old or new,
But blame the false, and value still the true.
    Some ne'er advance a judgment of their own,
But catch the spreading notion of the town;
They reason and conclude by precedent,   410
And own stale nonsense which they ne'er invent.
Some judge of authors' names, not works, and then
Nor praise nor blame the writings, but the men.
Of all this servile herd, the worst is he
That in proud dulness joins with quality;
A constant critic at the great man's board,
To fetch and carry nonsense for my Lord.
What woful stuff this madrigal would be,
In some starv'd hackney sonnetteer, or me!
But let a lord once own the happy lines,   420
How the wit brightens! how the style refines!
Before his sacred name flies ev'ry fault,
And each exalted stanza teems with thought!
    The vulgar thus thro' imitation err,
As oft the learn'd by being singular;
So much they scorn the crowd, that if the throng
By chance go right, they purposely go wrong:
So schismatics the plain believers quit,
And are but damn'd for having too much wit.   429
Some praise at morning what they blame at night,
But always think the last opinion right.
A muse by these is like a mistress us'd,
This hour she's idoliz'd, the next abus'd;
While their weak heads, like towns unfortify'd,
'Twixt sense and nonsense daily change their side.
Ask them the cause; they're wiser still they say;
And still to-morrow's wiser than to-day.
We think our fathers fools, so wise we grow;
Our wiser sons, no doubt, will think us so.   439
Once school-divines this zealous isle o'erspread;
Who knew most Sentences,[12] was deepest read:
Faith, gospel, all, seem'd made to be disputed,
And none had sense enough to be confuted.
Scotists and Thomists,[13] now in peace remain,
Amidst their kindred cobwebs in Duck Lane.[14]

[12] *The Book of Sentences* of Peter Lombard.
[13] Followers of the two medieval philosophers, Duns
Scotus and St. Thomas Aquinas.
[14] Where old and secondhand books were sold.

If faith itself has diff'rent dresses worn,
What wonder modes in wit should take their turn?
Oft' leaving what is natural and fit,
The current folly proves the ready wit;
And authors think their reputation safe,   450
Which lives as long as fools are pleas'd to laugh.
  Some, valuing those of their own side or mind,
Still make themselves the measure of mankind:
Fondly we think we honour merit then,
When we but praise ourselves in other men.
Parties in wit attend on those of state,
And public faction doubles private hate.
Pride, malice, folly, against Dryden rose,
In various shapes of parsons, critics, beaus;   459
But sense surviv'd when merry jests were past;
For rising merit will buoy up at last.
Might he return, and bless once more our eyes,
New Blackmores and new Milbourns [15] must arise:
Nay, should great Homer lift his awful head,
Zoilus [16] again would start up from the dead.
Envy will merit, as its shade, pursue;
But like a shadow, proves the substance true:
For envy'd wit, like Sol eclips'd, makes known
Th' opposing body's grossness, not its own.   469
When first that sun too pow'rful beams displays,
It draws up vapours which obscure its rays;
But ev'n those clouds at last adorn its way,
Reflect new glories, and augment the day.
  Be thou the first true merit to befriend;
His praise is lost, who stays till all commend.
Short is the date, alas! of modern rhymes,
And 'tis but just to let them live betimes.
No longer now that golden age appears,
When patriarch wits surviv'd a thousand years;
Now length of fame (our second life) is lost,   480
And bare threescore is all ev'n that can boast;
Our sons their fathers' failing language see,
And such as Chaucer is, shall Dryden be.
So when the faithful pencil has design'd
Some bright idea of the master's mind,
Where a new world leaps out at his command,
And ready Nature waits upon his hand;
When the ripe colours soften and unite,
And sweetly melt into just shade and light;   489
When mellowing years their full perfection give,
And each bold figure just begins to live,

The treach'rous colours the fair art betray,
And all the bright creation fades away!
  Unhappy wit, like most mistaken things,
Atones not for that envy which it brings;
In youth alone its empty praise we boast,
But soon the short-liv'd vanity is lost;
Like some fair flow'r the early spring supplies,
That gaily blooms, but ev'n in blooming dies.
What is this wit, which must our cares employ? 500
The owner's wife, that other men enjoy;
Then most our trouble still when most admir'd,
And still the more we give, the more requir'd;
Whose fame with pains we guard, but lose with ease,
Sure some to vex, but never all to please;
'Tis what the vicious fear, the virtuous shun,
By fools 'tis hated, and by knaves undone!
  If wit so much from ign'rance undergo,
Ah let not learning too commence its foe!
Of old, those met rewards who could excel,   510
And such were prais'd who but endeavour'd well:
Tho' triumphs were to gen'rals only due,
Crowns were reserv'd to grace the soldiers too.
Now, they who reach Parnassus' lofty crown,
Employ their pains to spurn some others down;
And while self-love each jealous writer rules,
Contending wits become the sport of fools;
But still the worst with most regret commend,
For each ill author is as bad a friend.
To what base ends, and by what abject ways,   520
Are mortals urg'd thro' sacred lust of praise!
Ah ne'er so dire a thirst of glory boast,
Nor in the critic let the man be lost.
Good nature and good sense must ever join;
To err is human, to forgive, divine.
  But if in noble minds some dregs remain
Not yet purg'd off, of spleen and sour disdain,
Discharge that rage on more provoking crimes,
Nor fear a dearth in these flagitious times.
No pardon vile obscenity should find,   530
Tho' wit and art conspire to move your mind;
But dulness with obscenity must prove
As shameful sure as impotence in love.
In the fat age of pleasure,[17] wealth, and ease,
Sprung the rank weed, and thriv'd with large increase:
When love was all an easy monarch's care;
Seldom at council, never in a war,
Jilts rul'd the state, and statesmen farces writ;
Nay, wits had pensions, and young lords had wit;

[15] Sir Richard Blackmore and Luke Milbourn were among those who attacked Dryden's plays as immoral (see Dryden's *Preface to the Fables,* above, p. 170).
[16] An ancient critic who attacked Homer.

[17] The reign of Charles II (1660-85).

The fair sat panting at a courtier's play,   540
And not a mask went unimprov'd away;
The modest fan was lifted up no more,
And virgins smil'd at what they blush'd before.
The foll'wing licence of a foreign reign [18]
Did all the dregs of bold Socinus [19] drain;
Then unbelieving priests reform'd the nation,
And taught more pleasant methods of salvation;
Where Heaven's free subjects might their rights
     dispute,
Lest God himself should seem too absolute:
Pulpits their sacred satire learn'd to spare,   550
And Vice admir'd to find a flatt'rer there!
Encourag'd thus, Wit's Titans braved the skies,
And the press groan'd with licens'd blasphemies.
These monsters, Critics! with your darts engage,
Here point your thunder, and exhaust your rage!
Yet shun their fault, who, scandalously nice,
Will needs mistake an author into vice:
All seems infected that th' infected spy,
As all looks yellow to the jaundic'd eye.

PART III

Learn then what morals critics ought to show,
For 'tis but half a judge's task, to know.   561
'Tis not enough, taste, judgment, learning, join;
In all you speak, let truth and candour shine,
That not alone what to your sense is due
All may allow, but seek your friendship too.

Be silent always when you doubt your sense,
And speak, tho' sure, with seeming diffidence:
Some positive, persisting fops we know,
Who, if once wrong, will needs be always so;
But you with pleasure own your errors past,   570
And make each day a critique on the last.

'Tis not enough your counsel still be true;
Blunt truths more mischief than nice falsehoods do;
Men must be taught as if you taught them not,
And things unknown propos'd as things forgot.
Without good-breeding truth is disapprov'd;
That only makes superior sense belov'd.

Be niggards of advice on no pretence,
For the worst avarice is that of sense.   579
With mean complaisance ne'er betray your trust,
Nor be so civil as to prove unjust.
Fear not the anger of the wise to raise;
Those best can bear reproof, who merit praise.

[18] That of William III (1689-1702).
[19] Faustus and Laelius Socinus denied the divinity of
Christ. Pope is here speaking of Deism.

'Twere well might critics still this freedom take,
But Appius [20] reddens at each word you speak,
And stares, tremendous, with a threat'ning eye,
Like some fierce tyrant in old tapestry.
Fear most to tax an Honourable fool,
Whose right it is, uncensur'd, to be dull:
Such, without wit, are poets when they please,   590
As without learning they can take degrees.
Leave dang'rous truths to unsuccessful satires,
And flattery to fulsome dedicators,
Whom, when they praise, the world believes no
     more,
Than when they promise to give scribbling o'er.
'Tis best sometimes your censure to restrain,
And charitably let the dull be vain;
Your silence there is better than your spite,
For who can rail so long as they can write?   599
Still humming on, their drowsy course they keep,
And lash'd so long, like tops, are lash'd asleep.
False steps but help them to renew the race,
As, after stumbling, jades will mend their pace.
What crowds of these, impenitently bold,
In sounds and jingling syllables grown old,
Still run on poets in a raging vein,
Ev'n to the dregs and squeezing of the brain,
Strain out the last dull droppings of their sense,
And rhyme with all the rage of impotence.   609

Such shameless bards we have; and yet, 'tis true,
There are as mad, abandon'd critics too.
The bookful blockhead, ignorantly read,
With loads of learned lumber in his head,
With his own tongue still edifies his ears,
And always list'ning to himself appears:
All books he reads, and all he reads assails,
From Dryden's Fables down to Durfey's Tales.
With him most authors steal their works, or buy;
Garth did not write his own Dispensary.
Name a new play, and he's the poet's friend,   620
Nay, show'd his faults—but when would poets
     mend?
No place so sacred from such fops is barr'd,
Nor is Paul's church more safe than Paul's church-
     yard: [21]
Nay, fly to altars, there they'll talk you dead;
For fools rush in where angels fear to tread.
Distrustful sense with modest caution speaks,
It still looks home, and short excursions makes;
But rattling nonsense in full volleys breaks,

[20] John Dennis. See note 7, above.
[21] Several booksellers were located here.

And never shock'd, and never turn'd aside,
Bursts out, resistless, with a thund'ring tide.   630
  But where's the man, who counsel can bestow,
Still pleas'd to teach, and yet not proud to know?
Unbiass'd, or by favour, or by spite,
Not dully prepossess'd, nor blindly right;
Tho' learn'd, well-bred; and tho' well-bred, sincere;
Modestly bold, and humanly severe;
Who to a friend his faults can freely show,
And gladly praise the merit of a foe?
Bless'd with a taste exact, yet unconfin'd;
A knowledge both of books and human-kind;   640
Gen'rous converse; a soul exempt from pride;
And love to praise, with reason on his side?
  Such once were Critics; such the happy few
Athens and Rome in better ages knew.
The mighty Stagyrite first left the shore,
Spread all his sails, and durst the deeps explore;
He steer'd securely, and discover'd far,
Led by the light of the Maeonian star.
Poets, a race long unconfin'd and free,
Still fond and proud of savage liberty,   650
Receiv'd his laws, and stood convinc'd 'twas fit,
Who conquer'd Nature, should preside o'er wit.
  Horace still charms with graceful negligence,
And without method talks us into sense;
Will, like a friend, familiarly convey
The truest notions in the easiest way.
He, who supreme in judgment, as in wit,
Might boldly censure, as he boldly writ,
Yet judg'd with coolness, tho' he sung with fire;
His precepts teach but what his works inspire.
Our critics take a contrary extreme,   661
They judge with fury, but they write with phlegm:
Nor suffers Horace more in wrong translations
By wits, than critics in as wrong quotations.
  See Dionysius [22] Homer's thoughts refine,
And call new beauties forth from ev'ry line!
  Fancy and art in gay Petronius [23] please,
The scholar's learning, with the courtier's ease.
  In grave Quintilian's [24] copious work, we find
The justest rules, and clearest method join'd;   670
Thus useful arms in magazines we place,
All rang'd in order, and dispos'd with grace;

[22] Dionysius of Halicarnassus (first century B.C.), a
Greek rhetorician.
[23] Petronius Arbiter (first century A.D.), a Roman
critic and satirist.
[24] The noted Roman critic (first century A.D.), author
of *De Institutione Oratoria,* which strongly influenced
eighteenth-century theories of rhetoric and prose style.

But less to please the eye, than arm the hand,
Still fit for use, and ready at command.
  Thee, bold Longinus! all the Nine inspire,
And bless their critic with a poet's fire:
An ardent judge, who, zealous in his trust,
With warmth gives sentence, yet is always just;
Whose own example strengthens all his laws;
And is himself that great Sublime he draws.   680
  Thus long succeeding critics justly reign'd,
Licence repress'd, and useful laws ordain'd.
Learning and Rome alike in empire grew,
And arts still follow'd where her Eagles flew;
From the same foes, at last, both felt their doom,
And the same age saw Learning fall, and Rome.
With Tyranny, then Superstition join'd,
As that the body, this enslav'd the mind;
Much was believ'd, but little understood,
And to be dull was constru'd to be good;   690
A second deluge Learning thus o'er-run,
And the Monks finish'd what the Goths begun.
  At length Erasmus, that great injur'd name,
(The glory of the priesthood, and the shame!)
Stemm'd the wild torrent of a barb'rous age,
And drove those holy Vandals off the stage.
  But see! each Muse, in Leo's [25] golden days,
Starts from her trance, and trims her wither'd bays;
Rome's ancient Genius, o'er its ruins spread,   699
Shakes off the dust, and rears his rev'rend head.
Then Sculpture and her sister arts revive;
Stones leap'd to form, and rocks began to live;
With sweeter notes each rising temple rung;
A Raphael painted, and a Vida [26] sung.
Immortal Vida: on whose honour'd brow
The poet's bays and critic's ivy grow:
Cremona now shall ever boast thy name,
As next in place to Mantua, next in fame!
  But soon by impious arms from Latium chas'd,
Their ancient bounds the banish'd Muses pass'd:
Thence arts o'er all the northern world advance,
But critic learning flourish'd most in France;   712
The rules a nation, born to serve, obeys;
And Boileau still in right of Horace sways.
But we, brave Britons, foreign laws despis'd,
And kept unconquer'd, and unciviliz'd;
Fierce for the liberties of wit, and bold,
We still defy'd the Romans, as of old.
Yet some there were, among the sounder few
Of those who less presum'd, and better knew,   720

[25] Leo X (1475-1521).
[26] Italian critic, author of an *Art of Poetry* in verse
(see above, p. 9).

Who durst assert the juster ancient cause,
And here restor'd Wit's fundamental laws.
Such was the Muse, whose rules and practice tell
"Nature's chief master-piece is writing well."
Such was Roscommon,[27] not more learn'd than good,
With manners gen'rous as his noble blood;
To him the wit of Greece and Rome was known,
And ev'ry author's merit, but his own.
Such late was Walsh [28]—the Muse's judge and
    friend,
Who justly knew to blame or to commend;   730

[27] Wentworth Dillon, Earl of Roscommon, translated Horace's *Art of Poetry* (1680) and wrote an *Essay on Translated Verse* (1684).

[28] William Walsh, a minor poet who befriended the young Pope, had recently died.

To failings mild, but zealous for desert;
The clearest head, and the sincerest heart.
Thus humble praise, lamented Shade! receive;
This praise at least a grateful Muse may give:
The Muse, whose early voice you taught to sing,
Prescrib'd her heights, and prun'd her tender wing,
(Her guide now lost) no more attempts to rise,
But in low numbers short excursions tries;
Content, if hence th' unlearn'd their wants may
    view,
The learn'd reflect on what before they knew: 740
Careless of censure, nor too fond of fame;
Still pleas'd to praise, yet not afraid to blame;
Averse alike to flatter, or offend;
Not free from faults, nor yet too vain to mend.

JOSEPH ADDISON   (1672-1719)

THE ESSAYS in the *Spectator* (1711-12) are unrivaled in giving a clear, if by no means profound, picture of interests and ideas current in early eighteenth-century England. Addison's critical essays, which comprize a fair portion of the *Spectator,* quickly illustrate the taste and critical approach of the informed English society of the time. The papers on "true and false wit" (Nos. 58-63) reveal the neoclassic reaction away from ingenuity for its own sake and toward a sophisticated but simple elegance. The famous paper on the old ballad, *Chevy Chase,* shows once again how catholic and unsystematized English neoclassic taste could be. For the ballad is extolled on neoclassic grounds for its noble simplicity and universality of appeal. The eighteen papers on *Paradise Lost* (starting with No.

JOSEPH ADDISON. Educated at the Charterhouse and at Oxford, Addison acquired something of a name as a classical scholar, and traveled on the Continent (1699-1703). He became connected with the Whig party, was appointed under-secretary of state (1706), and was a member of Parliament from 1708 till his death (1719). With his friend Richard Steele, he published the *Tatler* (1709-11), which appeared three times a week, and later the daily *Spectator.*

Editions of the *Spectator* are numerous: those of G. Gregory Smith (1897-98), G. A. Aitken (1898), and D. F. Bond (5 vols., Oxford, 1965) may be mentioned. Selections of the papers on Milton have been edited by H. Morley (1889) and A. S. Cook (1892). Commentary includes E. K. Broadus, "Joseph Addison as a Literary Critic," *University Magazine* (Montreal), Feb., 1909; Clarence D. Thorpe, "Addison's Theory of Imagination," *Michigan Academy of Science, Arts, and Letters,* XXI (1935), 509-30, and "Addison and Hutcheson on the Imagination," *Journal of English Literary History,* II (1935), 215-34; and Lee A. Elioseff, *The Cultural Milieu of Addison's Literary Criticism* (Austin, 1963).

267, and continuing thenceforth on Saturdays to No. 369) illustrate the extent to which Milton's imaginative power was to operate as a strong influence on English neoclassic thought, helping to prevent it from becoming thin and academically routine.

But it is especially in the papers that he entitled *The Pleasures of the Imagination* (Nos. 411-21) that Addison reveals the open-minded interest of English neoclassicism in the *psychology* of art. These essays also point to future developments in criticism. For this English interest in psychology was eventually, during the later eighteenth century, to culminate in the focal concentration on psychological theory, especially about the imagination, that underlay romantic criticism. Addison is the first clear and popular example of the influence of British empirical psychology; and, through his writing, some Continental critics were first led to explore the possibilities of psychological criticism.

Addison began by limiting his subject to the "pleasures of the imagination" that come from *sight*—from images, or visible objects. And the pleasure in images is either *primary* (seeing the object directly) or *secondary* (calling up images through memory, and arranging them into new combinations). He then continued by declaring that this pleasurable activity of the imagination is experienced in reacting to three qualities: (1) "greatness," or sublimity, which frees the mind from restraint, and lifts it to a state of transport; (2) the "new or uncommon," in which surprise or novelty increases interest; and (3) "beauty," or the harmonious adaptation of parts to the whole. It is important to note that by approaching art psychologically—by taking the pleasurable activity of the imagination as an end in itself—Addison was led to sanction other qualities in art besides beauty: that is, the sublime, or what can arouse the most intensely felt emotion, and, secondly, the new or strange. Both qualities were to become guiding criteria in romantic criticism, and on similar grounds. Addison also anticipated later critics, especially Hazlitt, in another way. The *secondary* function of the imagination which compares ideas or images with each other is itself pleasurable. Hence the pleasure we take in *imitations* of all kinds—in comparing the original object, whatever it may be, with the imitation. This premise was later to have important results for romantic and modern criticism, for if the *activity of mind*, comparing original and imitation, is itself desirable, then what most stimulates it is desirable in art. And this activity is stimulated by *suggestion*, by not being too close and precise. The premise was to lead to the nineteenth-century emphasis on "suggestiveness" in art.

The Pleasures of the Imagination

No. 412.   Monday, June 23, 1712.

I SHALL first consider those Pleasures of the Imagination, which arise from the actual View and Survey of outward Objects: And these, I think, all proceed from the Sight of what is *Great, Uncommon,* or *Beautiful.* There may, indeed, be something so terrible or offensive, that the Horrour or Loathsomeness of an Object may over-bear the Pleasure which results from its *Greatness, Novelty* or *Beauty;* but still there will be such a Mixture of Delight in the very Disgust it gives us, as any of these three Qualifications are most conspicuous and prevailing.

By *Greatness,*[1] I do not only mean the Bulk of any single object, but the Largeness of a whole View, considered as one entire Piece. Such are the Prospects of an open Champian Country, a vast uncultivated Desart, of huge Heaps of Mountains, high Rocks and Precipices, or a wide Expanse of Waters, where we are not struck with the Novelty or Beauty of the Sight, but with that rude kind of Magnificence which appears in many of these stupendous Works of Nature. Our Imagination loves to be filled with an Object, or to grasp at any thing that is too big for its Capacity. We are flung into a pleasing Astonishment at such unbounded Views, and feel a delightful Stilness and Amazement in the Soul at the Apprehension of them. The Mind of Man naturally hates every thing that looks like a Restraint upon it, and is apt to fancy it self under a sort of Confinement, when the Sight is pent up in a narrow Compass, and shortened on every side by the Neighbourhood of Walls or Mountains. On the contrary, a spacious Horizon is an Image of Liberty, where the Eye has Room to range abroad, to expatiate at large on the Immensity of its Views, and to lose it self amidst the Variety of Objects that offer themselves to

its Observation. Such wide and undetermined Prospects are as pleasing to the Fancy, as the Speculations of Eternity or Infinitude or to the Understanding. But if there be a Beauty or Uncommonness joined with this Grandeur, as in a troubled Ocean, a Heaven adorned with Stars and Meteors, or a spacious Landskip cut out into Rivers, Woods, Rocks, and Meadows, the Pleasure still grows upon us, as it arises from more than a single Principle.

Every thing that is *new* or *uncommon* raises a Pleasure in the Imagination, because it fills the Soul with an agreeable Surprise, gratifies its Curiosity, and gives it an Idea of which it was not before possest. We are indeed so often conversant with one Sett of Objects, and tired out with so many repeated Shows of the same Things, that whatever is *new* or *uncommon* contributes a little to vary human Life, and to divert our Minds, for a while, with the Strangeness of its Appearance: It serves us for a Kind of Refreshment, and takes off from that Satiety we are apt to complain of in our usual and Ordinary Entertainments. It is this that bestows Charms on a Monster, and makes even the Imperfections of Nature please us. It is this that recommends Variety, where the Mind is every Instant called off to something new, and the Attention not suffered to dwell too long, and waste it self on any particular Object. It is this, likewise, that improves what is great or beautiful, and makes it afford the Mind a double Entertainment. Groves, Fields, and Meadows, are at any Season of the Year pleasant to look upon, but never so much as in the opening of the Spring, when they are all new and fresh, with their first Gloss upon them, and not yet too much accustomed and familar to the Eye. For this Reason there is nothing that more enlivens a Prospect than Rivers, Jetteaus, or Falls of Water, where the Scene is perpetually shifting, and entertaining the Sight every Moment with something that is new. We are quickly tired with looking upon Hills and Vallies, where every thing continues fixt and settled in the same Place and Posture, but find our Thoughts a little agi-

---

The Pleasures of the Imagination. This series in the *Spectator* includes, besides a prefatory essay on taste (No. 409), eleven papers (Nos. 411-21). One is printed here in part (No. 412), and another (No. 416) in its entirety.

[1] Addison is here speaking of what eighteenth-century critics usually called the "sublime."

tated and relieved at the Sight of such Objects as are ever in Motion, and sliding away from beneath the Eye of the Beholder.

But there is nothing that makes its way more directly to the Soul than *Beauty*, which immediately diffuses a secret Satisfaction and Complacency through the Imagination, and gives a Finishing to any thing that is Great or Uncommon. The very first Discovery of it strikes the Mind with an inward Joy, and spreads a Chearfulness and Delight through all its Faculties. There is not perhaps any real Beauty or Deformity more in one piece of Matter than another, because we might have been so made, that whatsoever now appears loathsom to us, might have shewn it self agreeable; but we find by Experience, that there are several Modifications of Matter which the Mind, without any previous Consideration, pronounces at first sight Beautiful or Deformed. Thus we see that every different Species of sensible Creatures has its different Notions of Beauty, and that each of them is most affected with the Beauties of its own Kind. . . .

As the Fancy delights in every thing that is Great, Strange, or Beautiful, and is still more pleased the more it finds of these Perfections in the same Object, so it is capable of receiving a new Satisfaction by the Assistance of another Sense. Thus any continued Sound, as the Musick of Birds, or a Fall of Water, awakens every moment the Mind of the Beholder, and makes him more attentive to the several Beauties of the Place that lye before him. Thus if there arises a Fragrancy of Smells or Perfumes, they heighten the Pleasures of the Imagination, and make even the Colours and Verdure of the Landskip appear more agreeable; for the Ideas of both Senses recommend each other, and are pleasanter together, than when they enter the Mind separately: As the different Colours of a Picture, when they are well disposed, set off one another, and receive an additional Beauty from the Advantage of their Situation.

No. 416.   Friday, June 27, 1712.

I AT first divided the Pleasures of the Imagination, into such as arise from Objects that are actually before our Eyes, or that once entered in at our Eyes, and are afterwards called up into the Mind either barely by its own Operations, or on occasion of something without us, as Statues, or Descriptions. We have already considered the first Division, and shall therefore enter on the other, which, for Distinction sake, I have called the Secondary Pleasures of the Imagination. When I say the Ideas we receive from Statues, Descriptions, or such like Occasions, are the same that were once actually in our View, it must not be understood that we had once seen the very Place, Action, or Person which are carved or described. It is sufficient, that we have seen Places, Persons, or Actions in general, which bear a Resemblance, or at least some remote Analogy with what we find represented. Since it is in the Power of the Imagination, when it is once Stocked with particular Ideas, to enlarge, compound, and vary them at her own Pleasure.

Among the different Kinds of Representation, *Statuary* is the most natural, and shews us something *likest* the Object that is represented. To make use of a common Instance, let one who is born Blind take an Image in his Hands, and trace out with his Fingers the different Furrows and Impressions of the Chissel, and he will easily conceive how the Shape of a Man, or Beast, may be represented by it; but should he draw his Hand over a *Picture*, where all is smooth and uniform, he would never be able to imagine how the several Prominencies and Depressions of a human Body could be shewn on a plain Piece of Canvas, that has in it no Unevenness or Irregularity. *Description* runs yet further from the things it represents than Painting; for a Picture bears a real Resemblance to its Original, which Letters and Syllables are wholly void of. Colours speak all Languages, but Words are understood only by such a People or Nation. For this reason, tho' Men's Necessities quickly put them on finding out Speech, Writing is probably of a later Invention than Painting; particularly we are told, that in *America* when the *Spaniards* first arrived there, Expresses were sent to the Emperor of *Mexico* in Paint, and the News of his Country delineated by the Strokes of a Pencil, which was a more natural Way than that of Writing, tho' at the same time much more imperfect, because it is impossible to draw the little connexions of Speech, or to give the Picture of a Conjunction or an Adverb. It would be yet more strange, to represent visible Objects by Sounds that have no Ideas annexed to them, and to make something like Description in *Musick*. Yet it is certain, there may be confused, imperfect Notions of this Nature raised in the Imagination by an Artificial Composition of Notes; and we find that great Masters in the Art are able, sometimes to set their Hearers in the heat and hurry of a Battel, to overcast their Minds with melancholy Scenes and Apprehensions of Deaths and Funerals, or to lull them into pleasing Dreams of Groves and Elisiums.

In all these Instances, this Secondary Pleasure of the Imagination proceeds from that Action of the Mind,[2] which compares the Ideas arising from the Original Objects, with the Ideas we receive from the Statue, Picture, Description, or Sound that represents them. It is impossible for us to give the necessary Reason, why this Operation of the Mind is attended with so much Pleasure, as I have before observed on the same Occasion; but we find a great variety of Entertainments derived from this single Principle: For it is this that not only gives us a relish of Statuary, Painting and Description, but makes us delight in all the Actions and Arts of Mimickry. It is this that makes the several kinds of Wit pleasant, which consists, as I have formerly shewn, in the Affinity of Ideas: And we may add, it is this also that raises the little Satisfaction we sometimes find in the different Sorts of false Wit; whether it consist in the Affinity of Letters, as an Anagram, Acrostick; or of Syllables, as in Doggerel Rhimes, Echos; or of Words, as in Puns, Quibbles; or of a whole Sentence or Poem, to Wings, and Altars. The *final Cause,* probably, of annexing Pleasure to this Operation of the Mind, was to quicken and encourage us in our Searches after Truth, since the distinguishing one thing from another, and the right discerning betwixt our Ideas, depends wholly upon our comparing them together, and observing the Congruity or Disagreement that appears among the several Works of Nature.

But I shall here confine my self to those Pleasures of the Imagination, which proceed from Ideas raised by *Words*, because most of the

Observations that agree with Descriptions, are equally Applicable to Painting and Statuary.

Words, when well chosen, have so great a Force in them, that a Description often gives us more lively Ideas than the Sight of Things themselves. The Reader finds a Scene drawn in Stronger Colours, and painted more to the Life in his Imagination, by the help of Words, than by an actual Survey of the Scene which they describe. In this Case the Poet seems to get the better of Nature; he takes, indeed, the Landskip after her, but gives it more vigorous Touches, heightens its Beauty, and so enlivens the whole Piece, that the Images which flow from the Objects themselves appear weak and faint, in Comparison of those that come from the Expressions. The Reason, probably, may be, because in the Survey of any Object, we have only so much of it painted on the Imagination, as comes in at the Eye; but in its Description, the Poet gives us as free a View of it as he pleases, and discovers to us several Parts, that either we did not attend to, or that lay out of our Sight when we first beheld it. As we look on any Object, our Idea of it is, perhaps, made up of two or three simple Ideas; but when the Poet represents it, he may either give us a more complex Idea of it, or only raise in us such Ideas as are most apt to affect the Imagination.

It may be here worth our while to examine, how it comes to pass that several Readers, who are all acquainted with the same Language, and know the Meaning of the Words they read, should nevertheless have a different Relish of the same Descriptions. We find one transported with a Passage, which another runs over with Coldness and Indifference, or finding the Representation extremely natural, where another can perceive nothing of Likeness and Conformity. This different Taste must proceed either from the *Perfection of Imagination* in one more than in another, or from the *different Ideas* that several Readers affix to the same Words. For, to have a true Relish, and form a right Judgment of a Description, a Man should be born with a good Imagination, and must have well weighed the Force and Energy that lye in the several Words of a Language, so as to be able to distinguish which are most significant and expressive of their proper Ideas, and what additional Strength and Beauty they are capable of receiv-

---

[2] Addison is here anticipating the romantic interest in "suggestiveness" as an important quality in art. See below, p. 274, and Hazlitt's discussion of the subject, below, p. 298.

ing from Conjunction with others. The Fancy must be warm, to retain the Print of those Images it hath received from outward Objects; and the Judgment discerning, to know what Expressions are most proper to cloath and adorn them to the best Advantage. A Man who is deficient in either of these Respects, tho' he may receive the general Notion of a Description, can never see distinctly all its particular Beauties: As a Person with a weak Sight may have the confused Prospect of a Place that lyes before him, without entering into its several Parts, or discerning the variety of its Colours in their full Glory and Perfection.

HENRY FIELDING   (1707-1754)

IF BY the term "novel" we mean simply prose fiction of some length, this literary form has a long history indeed. But if we define it with some rigor in terms of a regular structure of plot, then the novel first begins as a serious genre in mid-eighteenth-century England. Its development at this time owes more to the novels of Fielding than to those of any other writer. Moreover, the Preface to *Joseph Andrews* (1742) and the introductory chapters to the various books of *Tom Jones* are the first serious criticism of the novel that we have.

In the Preface to *Joseph Andrews* Fielding states his theory of the novel as a "comic epic poem in prose." This designation at once indicates that Fielding's main purpose was to dissociate the novel from the old prose-romance by urging that it should have a specific form and structure of its own, and thus to place it on both a higher technical and higher intellectual level. Just as the drama is generally divided into tragedy and comedy, the epic poem may be justifiably divided in a similar way. That is, one can write a long poem that bears a relation to the *Iliad* analogous, say, to that of a dramatic comedy to a tragedy; and because it possesses a less serious theme, it may, like dramatic comedy, be written in prose. Such a work, if well designed, would have all the other qualities of a comic verse-epic except meter. Its characters, its plot outline, would employ similar techniques. So the novel may more justly be classed with the epic poem, Fielding

HENRY FIELDING. After attending Eton and studying law at Leyden, Fielding lived in London, wrote for the stage, was called to the bar (1740), wrote the periodical, the *Champion* (1739-41), and in 1742 published the first of his great novels, *Joseph Andrews*. He became justice of the peace for Westminster, was actively interested in legal and philanthropic work, but continued to write prolifically until his premature death.

The standard edition of his *Works* is still that of W. E. Henley, *et al.* (16 vols., 1903), but the Wesleyan Edition is in progress, and J. C. Battestin has edited the Preface in *Joseph Andrews* (Oxford, 1967). Of the abundant commentary available, see especially E. M. Thornbury, *Henry Fielding's Theory of the Comic Prose Epic* (Madison, 1931); F. P. Van der Voorde, *Henry Fielding, Critic and Satirist* (The Hague, 1931); F. O. Bissell, *Fielding's Theory of the Novel* (Ithaca, 1933); M. Johnson, *Fielding's Art of Fiction* (Philadelphia, 1961); and Sheldon Sacks, *Fiction and the Shape of Belief* (Berkeley, 1964).

argues, than with the old prose-romance, to which its only similarity is that it is written in prose.

The Preface to *Joseph Andrews* is important for the theory of comedy as well as for the theory of the novel. Fielding argues for a "naturalistic" comedy, in the broadest sense of the word—a comedy that reveals and highlights the ridiculous in real life, as distinct from comedy of wit and of burlesque, which he implies are less basic. The richest source of the ridiculous, in human life, is pretense or "affectation." Of this there are two varieties, vanity and hypocrisy, each of which can offer incongruity through the contrast between the pretense of the character—either to himself or to others—and his true nature. By stressing, at the close, that comedy is not present in the incongruity of undeserved imperfections or misfortunes, Fielding anticipates a conception of the comic later implied by Hazlitt and expounded in our time by Henri Bergson: the view that the comic is incongruity viewed without a strong sympathetic concern, and that one's sympathetic identification must be first disengaged from the character before the incongruous events that befall him can be viewed as ridiculous.

Preface to Joseph Andrews

THE COMIC EPIC POEM IN PROSE

As it is possible the mere English reader may have a different idea of romance with the author of these little volumes; and may consequently expect a kind of entertainment, not to be found, nor which was even intended, in the following pages; it may not be improper to premise a few words concerning this kind of writing, which I do not remember to have seen hitherto attempted in our language.

The EPIC, as well as the DRAMA, is divided into tragedy and comedy. HOMER, who was the father of this species of poetry, gave us the pattern of both these, though that of the latter kind is entirely lost; which Aristotle tells us, bore the same relation to comedy which his Iliad bears to tragedy. And perhaps, that we have no more instances of it among the writers of antiquity, is owing to the loss of this great pattern, which, had it survived, would have found its imitators equally with the other poems of this great original.

And farther, as this poetry may be tragic or comic, I will not scruple to say it may be like-

Preface to *Joseph Andrews*. Published in 1742.

wise either in verse or prose: for though it wants one particular, which the critic enumerates in the constituent parts of an epic poem, namely, metre; yet, when any kind of writing contains all its other parts, such as fable, action, characters, sentiments, and diction, and is deficient in metre only, it seems, I think, reasonable to refer it to the epic; at least, as no critic hath thought proper to range it under any other head, or to assign it a particular name to itself.

Thus the Telemachus of the Archbishop of Cambray appears to me of the epic kind, as well as the Odyssey of Homer; indeed, it is much fairer and more reasonable to give it a name common with that species from which it differs only in a single instance, than to confound it with those which it resembles in no other. Such are those voluminous works, commonly called Romances, namely, Clelia, Cleopatra, Astraea, Cassandra, the Grand Cyrus, and innumerable others which contain, as I apprehend, very little instruction or entertainment.

Now, a comic romance is a comic epic poem in prose; differing from comedy, as the serious epic from tragedy: its action being more extended and comprehensive; containing a much larger circle of incidents, and introducing a greater variety of characters. It differs from the serious romance in its fable and action in this; that as in the one these are grave and solemn, so in the other they are light and ridiculous: it differs in its characters, by introducing persons of inferior rank, and consequently of inferior manners, whereas the grave romance sets the highest before us; lastly in its sentiments and diction, by preserving the ludicrous instead of the sublime. In the diction, I think, burlesque itself may be sometimes admitted; of which many instances will occur in this work, as in the description of the battles, and some other places not necessary to be pointed out to the classical reader, for whose entertainment those parodies or burlesque imitations are chiefly calculated.

But though we have sometimes admitted this in our diction, we have carefully excluded it from our sentiments and characters; for there it is never properly introduced, unless in writings of the burlesque kind, which this is not intended to be. Indeed, no two species of writing can differ more widely than the comic and the burlesque: for as the latter is ever the exhibition of what is monstrous and unnatural, and where our delight, if we examine it, arises from the surprising absurdity, as in appropriating the manners of the highest to the lowest, or *e converso*; so in the former, we should ever confine ourselves strictly to nature, from the just imitation of which will flow all the pleasure we can this way convey to a sensible reader. And perhaps, there is one reason why a comic writer should of all others be the least excused for deviating from nature, since it may not be always so easy for a serious poet to meet with the great and the admirable; but life everywhere furnishes an accurate observer with the ridiculous.

I have hinted this little, concerning burlesque; because I have often heard that name given to performances, which have been truly of the comic kind, from the author's having sometimes admitted it in his diction only; which, as it is the dress of poetry, doth like the dress of men establish characters, (the one of the whole poem, and the other of the whole man), in vulgar opinion, beyond any of their greater excellences: but surely, a certain drollery in style, where characters and sentiments are perfectly natural, no more constitutes the burlesque,

than an empty pomp and dignity of words, where everything else is mean and low, can entitle any performance to the appellation of the true sublime.

And I apprehend, my Lord Shaftesbury's opinion of mere burlesque agrees with mine, when he asserts, "There is no such thing to be found in the writings of the ancients." But perhaps I have less abhorrence than he professes for it: and that not because I have had some little success on the stage this way; but rather as it contributes more to exquisite mirth and laughter than any other; and these are probably more wholesome physic for the mind, and conduce better to purge away spleen, melancholy, and ill affections, than is generally imagined. Nay, I will appeal to common observation, whether the same companies are not found more full of good-humour and benevolence, after they have been sweetened for two or three hours with entertainments of this kind, than when soured by a tragedy or a grave lecture.

But to illustrate all this by another science, in which, perhaps, we shall see the distinction more clearly and plainly: let us examine the works of a comic history-painter, with those performances which the Italians call Caricatura, where we shall find the greatest excellence of the former to consist in the exactest copy of nature; insomuch, that a judicious eye instantly rejects anything *outré*; any liberty which the painter hath taken with the features of that *alma mater*. Whereas in the Caricatura we allow all licence. Its aim is to exhibit monsters not men; and all distortions and exaggerations whatever are within its proper province.

Now what Caricatura is in painting, Burlesque is in writing; and in the same manner the comic writer and painter correlate to each other. And here I shall observe, that as in the former the painter seems to have the advantage; so it is in the latter infinitely on the side of the writer: for the Monstrous is much easier to paint than describe, and the Ridiculous to describe than paint.

And though perhaps this latter species doth not in either science so strongly affect and agitate the muscles as the other; yet it will be owned, I believe, that a more rational and useful pleasure arises to us from it. He who should call the ingenious Hogarth a burlesque painter, would, in my opinion, do him very little honour: for sure it is much easier, much less the subject of admiration, to paint a man with a nose, or any other feature of a preposterous size, or to expose him in some absurd or monstrous attitude, than to express the affections of men on canvas. It hath been thought a vast commendation of a painter to say his figures seem to breathe; but surely it is a much greater and nobler applause, that they appear to think.

But to return. The Ridiculous only, as I have before said, falls within my province in the present work. Nor will some explanation of this word be thought impertinent by the reader, if he considers how wonderfully it hath been mistaken, even by writers who have professed it: for to what but such a mistake can we attribute the many atempts to ridicule the blackest villainies; and what is yet worse, the most dreadful calamities? What could exceed the absurdity of an author who should write the comedy of Nero, with the merry incident of ripping up his mother's belly; or what would give a greater shock to humanity than an attempt to expose the miseries of poverty and distress to ridicule? And yet, the reader will not want much learning to suggest such instances to himself.

Besides, it may seem remarkable, that Aristotle, who is so fond and free of definitions, hath not thought proper to define the Ridiculous. Indeed, where he tells us it is proper to comedy, he hath remarked that villainy is not its object: but he hath not, as I remember, positively asserted what is. Nor doth the Abbé Bellegarde, who hath written a treatise on this subject, though he shows us many species of it, once trace it to its fountain.

The only source of the true Ridiculous (as it appears to me) is affectation. But though it arises from one spring only, when we consider the infinite streams into which this one branches, we shall presently cease to admire at the copious field it affords to an observer. Now affectation proceeds from one of these two causes: vanity, or hypocrisy; for as vanity puts us on affecting false characters, in order to purchase applause; so hypocrisy sets us on an endeavour to avoid censure by concealing our vices under an appearance of their opposite virtues. And though these two causes are often confounded, (for there is some difficulty in distinguishing them),

yet, as they proceed from very different motives, so they are as clearly distinct in their operations: for indeed, the affectation which arises from vanity is nearer to truth than the other; as it hath not that violent repugnancy of nature to struggle with, which that of the hypocrite hath. It may be likewise noted, that affectation doth not imply an absolute negation of those qualities which are affected: and therefore, though, when it proceeds from hypocrisy, it be nearly allied to deceit; yet when it comes from vanity only, it partakes of the nature of ostentation: for instance, the affectation of liberality in a vain man, differs visibly from the same affectation in the avaricious; for though the vain man is not what he would appear, or hath not the virtue he affects, to the degree he would be thought to have it; yet it sits less awkwardly on him than on the avaricious man, who is the very reverse of what he would seem to be.

From the discovery of this affectation arises the Ridiculous—which always strikes the reader with surprise and pleasure; and that in a higher and stronger degree when the affectation arises from hypocrisy, than when from vanity: for, to discover any one to be the exact reverse of what he affects, is more surprising, and consequently more ridiculous, than to find him a little deficient in the quality he desires the reputation of. I might observe that our Ben Jonson, who of all men understood the Ridiculous the best, hath chiefly used the hypocritical affectation.

Now from affectation only, the misfortunes and calamities of life, or the imperfections of nature, may become the objects of ridicule. Surely he hath a very ill-framed mind, who can look on ugliness, infirmity, or poverty, as ridiculous in themselves: nor do I believe any man living who meets a dirty fellow riding through the streets in a cart, is struck with an idea of the Ridiculous from it; but if he should see the same figure descend from his coach and six, or bolt from his chair with his hat under his arm, he would then begin to laugh, and with justice. In the same manner, were we to enter a poor house and behold a wretched family shivering with cold and languishing with hunger, it would not incline us to laughter, (at least we must have very diabolical natures, if it would): but should we discover there a grate, instead of coals, adorned with flowers, empty plate or china dishes on the side-board, or any other affectation of riches and finery either on their persons or in their furniture, we might then indeed be excused for ridiculing so fantastical an appearance. Much less are natural imperfections the object of derision: but when ugliness aims at the applause of beauty, or lameness endeavours to display agility; it is then that these unfortunate circumstances, which at first moved our compassion, tend only to raise our mirth.

The poet carries this very far;

None are for being what they are in fault,
But for not being what they would be thought.

Where if the metre would suffer the word Ridiculous to close the first line, the thought would be rather more proper. Great vices are the proper objects of our detestation, smaller faults of our pity: but affectation appears to me the only true source of the Ridiculous.

But perhaps it may be objected to me, that I have against my own rules introduced vices, and of a very black kind, into this work. To which I shall answer: first, that it is very difficult to pursue a series of human actions and keep clear from them. Secondly, that the vices to be found here are rather the accidental consequences of some human frailty, or foible, than causes habitually existing in the mind. Thirdly, that they are never set forth as the objects of ridicule, but detestation. Fourthly, that they are never the principal figure at that time on the scene; and lastly, they never produce the intended evil.

Having thus distinguished Joseph Andrews from the productions of romance writers on the one hand and burlesque writers on the other, and given some few very short hints (for I intended no more) of this species of writing, which I have affirmed to be hitherto unattempted in our language; I shall leave to my good-natured reader to apply my piece to my observations, and will detain him no longer than with a word concerning the characters in this work.

And here I solemnly protest I have no intention to vilify or asperse any one; for though everything is copied from the book of nature, and scarce a character or action produced which I have not taken from my own observations and experience; yet I have used the utmost care to obscure the persons by such different circumstances, degrees, and colours, that it will be impossible to guess at them with any degree of certainty; and if it ever happens otherwise, it is only where the failure characterised is so minute, that it is a foible only which the party himself may laugh at as well as any other.

As to the character of Adams, as it is the most glaring in the whole, so I conceive it is not to be found in any book now extant. It is designed a character of perfect simplicity; and as the goodness of his heart will recommend him to the good-natured, so I hope it will excuse me to the gentlemen of his cloth; for whom, while they are worthy of their sacred order, no man can possibly have a greater respect. They will therefore excuse me, notwithstanding the low adventures in which he is engaged, that I have made him a clergyman; since no other office could have given him so many opportunities of displaying his worthy inclinations.

DAVID HUME   (1711-1776)

IN THE philosophy of Hume more than that of any other writer, the tradition of classical rationalism, which underlies the thought of antiquity, the Middle Ages, Renaissance humanism, and the great rationalistic systems of the seventeenth century, came to its conclusion. In his writings, human reason was dissected with such devastating effect that philosophy has never since quite recovered the traditional classical confidence in reason. The repercussions in the history of criticism—as in the history of literature and art in general—have been far-reaching. But they have come indirectly, through the medium of successive writers who have been influenced by Hume's metaphysics. Hume's occasional and informal essays in the field of literary criticism itself hardly begin to suggest his general intellectual significance, though they are all readable and informative, and though at least one—"Of Tragedy"—offers the most incisive brief analysis of its subject that can be found in European criticism of the eighteenth century.

The essay "Of Tragedy" illustrates the increasingly psychological approach of eighteenth-century criticism. Hume concentrated on the problem of determining why, and in what ways, tragedy pleases. The subject, of course, had been treated before. Addison, in *Spectator* No. 418, gave one of the typical answers. We make a partly unconscious comparison, according to Addison, between the object of the tragedy, who is suffering, and ourselves, and prize by contrast our own good fortune. In real life, the suffering of another would press too closely on our sympathy; but when we know that the tragedy is fiction, the sympathetic pressure is lighter, and we are able to enjoy the contrast. Where Addison's answer, which is an old one, is naïve, Hume's is far more sophisticated in regarding the pleasure in tragedy as a combination of various elements. These may be roughly summarized under four headings. There is, first, the natural desire of the mind for strong or intense impressions. This is not a sadistic pleasure in the suffering of others, nor is it a mere matter of feeling good by comparison. Rather,

DAVID HUME. Born in Edinburgh, Hume studied at La Flèche (1734-37), published his famous *Treatise of Human Nature* (1739-40), and, gradually, through other works, became known as a philosopher, particularly in France. He became keeper of the Advocate's Library at Edinburgh (1752), and, while serving as secretary to the Embassy in Paris (1763-65), became acquainted with French literary and court circles. On returning to Edinburgh, he became a prominent member of the gifted literary and philosophical group there.

Complete editions are those of 1826, 1836, and 1854. Editions of the *Essays* include those of T. H. Green and T. H. Grose (2 vols., 1874) and L. A. Selby-Bigge (1894; 1902). Commentary includes W. J. Bate, *The Burden of the Past and the English Poet* (Cambridge, Mass., 1970), Ch. III, "The Eighteenth-Century Reconsideration: Hume and the Essential Diagnosis"; T. Brunius, *David Hume on Criticism* (Stockholm, 1952); R. Cohen, "The Transformation of Passion," *Philological Quarterly*, XLI (1962), 450-64; and Jan Wilbanks, *Hume's Theory of Imagination* (The Hague, 1968).

if the impression is strong enough (and scenes of happiness or contentment on the stage are not so strongly impressive as are those of suffering and tragedy), the mind is caught up through sympathetic identification. Second, there is the awareness that the tragedy is fiction. Third, "tragedy is an imitation, and imitation is always of itself agreeable." Fourth, the mixed emotions aroused by these various elements are given direction and form by the expression of sentiments or thought, the use of imagery and meter, and the structure or design of the drama. They are channeled, in other words, and harmonized by the esthetic form of the drama. Hume's essay is a psychologically informed elaboration of Aristotle's thesis that poetry, especially dramatic tragedy, appeals simultaneously to two "instincts": the instinct for "imitation" and the instinct for *harmonia*.

Of Tragedy

IT SEEMS an unaccountable pleasure which the spectators of a well-written tragedy receive from sorrow, terror, anxiety, and other passions that are in themselves disagreeable and uneasy. The more they are touched and affected, the more are they delighted with the spectacle; and as soon as the uneasy passions cease to operate, the piece is at an end. One scene of full joy and contentment and security is the utmost that any composition of this kind can bear; and it is sure always to be the concluding one. If in the texture of the piece there be interwoven any scenes of satisfaction, they afford only faint gleams of pleasure, which are thrown in by way of variety, and in order to plunge the actors into deeper distress by means of that constrast and disappointment. The whole art of the poet is employed in rousing and supporting the compassion and indignation, the anxiety and resentment, of his audience. They are pleased in proportion as they are afflicted, and never are so happy as when they employ tears, sobs, and cries, to give vent to their sorrow, and relieve their heart, swollen with the tenderest sympathy and compassion.

The few critics who have had some tincture of philosophy have remarked this singular phenomenon, and have endeavoured to account for it.

L'Abbé Dubos,[1] in his Reflections on Poetry

Of Tragedy. First published in Hume's *Four Dissertations* (1757).

[1] Jean Baptiste Dubos, author of *Réflexions critiques sur la Poésie et sur la Peinture* (1719).

and Painting, asserts, that nothing is in general so disagreeable to the mind as the languid, listless state of indolence into which it falls upon the removal of all passion and occupation. To get rid of this painful situation, it seeks every amusement and pursuit: business, gaming, shows, executions; whatever will rouse the passions and take its attention from itself. No matter what the passion is: let it be disagreeable, afflicting, melancholy, disordered; it is still better than that insipid languor which arises from perfect tranquillity and repose.

It is impossible not to admit this account as being, at least in part, satisfactory. You may observe, when there are several tables of gaming, that all the company run to those where the deepest play is, even though they find not there the best players. The view, or, at least, imagination of high passions, arising from great loss or gain, affects the spectator by sympathy, gives him some touches of the same passions, and serves him for a momentary entertainment. It makes the time pass the easier with him, and is some relief to that oppression under which men commonly labour when left entirely to their own thoughts and meditations.

We find that common liars always magnify, in their narrations, all kinds of danger, pain, distress, sickness, deaths, murders, and cruelties, as well as joy, beauty, mirth, and magnificence. It is an absurd secret which they have for pleasing their company, fixing their attention, and attaching them to such marvellous relations by the passions and emotions which they excite.

There is, however, a difficulty in applying to the present subject, in its full extent, this solution, however ingenious and satisfactory it may appear. It is certain that the same object of distress which pleases in a tragedy, were it really set before us, would give the most unfeigned uneasiness; though it be then the most effectual cure to languor and indolence. Monsieur Fontenelle [2] seems to have been sensible of this difficulty, and accordingly attempts another solution of the phenomenon, at least makes some addition to the theory above mentioned.

"Pleasure and pain," says he, "which are two sentiments so different in themselves, differ not so much in their cause. From the instance of tickling it appears, that the movement of pleasure pushed a little too far, becomes pain, and that the movement of pain, a little moderated, becomes pleasure. Hence it proceeds, that there is such a thing as a sorrow, soft and agreeable: It is a pain weakened and diminished. The heart likes naturally to be moved and affected. Melancholy objects suit it, and even disastrous and sorrowful, provided they are softened by some circumstance. It is certain, that, on the theatre, the representation has almost the effect of reality; yet it has not altogether that effect. However we may be hurried away by the spectacle, whatever dominion the senses and imagination may usurp over the reason, there still lurks at the bottom a certain idea of falsehood in the whole of what we see. This idea, though weak and disguised, suffices to diminish the pain which we suffer from the misfortunes of those whom we love, and to reduce that affliction to such a pitch as converts it into a pleasure. We weep for the misfortune of a hero to whom we are attached. In the same instant we comfort ourselves by reflecting, that it is nothing but a fiction: And it is precisely that mixture of sentiments which composes an agreeable sorrow, and tears that delight us. But as that affliction which is caused by exterior and sensible objects is stronger than the consolation which arises from an internal reflection, they are the effects

[2] Bernard Le Bovier, sieur de Fontenelle, in *Réflexions sur la Poétique* (1691), section 36.

and symptoms of sorrow that ought to predominate in the composition."

This solution seems just and convincing; but perhaps it wants still some new addition, in order to make it answer fully the phenomenon which we here examine. All the passions, excited by eloquence, are agreeable in the highest degree, as well as those which are moved by painting and the theatre. The epilogues of Cicero are, on this account chiefly, the delight of every reader of taste; and it is difficult to read some of them without the deepest sympathy and sorrow. His merit as an orator, no doubt, depends much on his success in this particular. When he had raised tears in his judges and all his audience, they were then the most highly delighted, and expressed the greatest satisfaction with the pleader. The pathetic description of the butchery made by Verres of the Sicilian captains, is a masterpiece of this kind. But I believe none will affirm, that the being present at a melancholy scene of that nature would afford any entertainment. Neither is the sorrow here softened by fiction. For the audience were convinced of the reality of every circumstance. What is it then which in this case raises a pleasure from the bosom of uneasiness, so to speak, and a pleasure which still retains all the features and outward symptoms of distress and sorrow?

I answer: this extraordinary effect proceeds from that very eloquence with which the melancholy scene is represented. The genius required to paint objects in a lively manner, the art employed in collecting all the pathetic circumstances, the judgment displayed in disposing them; the exercise, I say, of these noble talents, together with the force of expression, and beauty of oratorial numbers, diffuse the highest satisfaction on the audience, and excite the most delightful movements. By this means, the uneasiness of the melancholy passions is not only overpowered and effaced by something stronger of an opposite kind, but the whole impulse of those passions is converted into pleasure and swells the delight which the eloquence raises in us. The same force of oratory, employed on an uninteresting subject, would not please half so much, or rather would appear altogether ridiculous; and the mind, being left in absolute calmness and indifference, would relish none of those beauties of imagination or expression, which, if joined to passion, give it such exquisite entertainment. The impulse or vehemence arising from sorrow, compassion, indignation, receives a new direction from the sentiments of beauty.[3] The latter, being the predominant emotion, seize the whole mind, and convert the former into themselves, at least tincture them so strongly as totally to alter their nature. And the soul being at the same time roused by passion and charmed by eloquence, feels on the whole a strong movement, which is altogether delightful.

The same principle takes place in tragedy; with this addition, that tragedy is an imitation, and imitation is always of itself agreeable. This circumstance serves still further to smooth the motions of passion, and convert the whole feeling into one uniform and strong enjoyment. Objects of the greatest terror and distress please in painting, and please more than the most beautiful objects that appear calm and indifferent.[4] The affection, rousing the mind, excites a large stock of spirit and vehemence; which is all transformed into pleasure by the force of the prevailing movement. It is thus the fiction of tragedy softens the passion, by an infusion of a new feeling, not merely by weakening or diminishing the sorrow. You may by degrees weaken a real sorrow, till it totally disappears; yet in none of its gradations will it ever give pleasure; except, perhaps, by accident, to a man sunk under lethargic indolence, whom it rouses from that languid state.

[3] The combination Hume is stressing is similar to Aristotle's thesis that poetry appeals to two instincts: the instinct for *mimesis* (imitation, sympathetic identification) and *harmonia*. See the introduction above, and Aristotle's *Poetics*, also above, p. 21.

[4] "Painters make no scruple of representing distress and sorrow, as well as any other passion: But they seem not to dwell so much on these melancholy affections as the poets, who, though they copy every motion of the human breast, yet pass quickly over the agreeable sentiments. A painter represents only one instant; and if that be passionate enough, it is sure to affect and delight the spectator: But nothing can furnish to the poet a variety of scenes, and incidents, and sentiments, except distress, terror, or anxiety. Complete joy and satisfaction is attended with security and leaves no further room for action" (Hume).

To confirm this theory, it will be sufficient to produce other instances, where the subordinate movement is converted into the predominant, and gives force to it, though of a different, and even sometimes though of a contrary nature.

Novelty naturally rouses the mind, and attracts our attention; and the movements which it causes are always converted into any passion belonging to the object, and join their force to it. Whether an event excites joy or sorrow, pride or shame, anger or good-will, it is sure to produce a stronger affection, when new or unusual. And though novelty of itself be agreeable, it fortifies the painful, as well as agreeable passions.

Had you any intention to move a person extremely by the narration of any event, the best method of increasing its effect would be artfully to delay informing him of it, and first excite his curiosity and impatience before you let him into the secret. This is the artifice practised by Iago in the famous scene of Shakespeare; and every spectator is sensible that Othello's jealousy acquires additional force from his preceding impatience, and that the subordinate passion is here readily transformed into the predominant one.

Difficulties increase passions of every kind; and by rousing our attention, and exciting our active powers, they produce an emotion which nourishes the prevailing affection.

Parents commonly love that child most whose sickly infirm frame of body has occasioned them the greatest pains, trouble, and anxiety, in rearing him. The agreeable sentiment of affection here acquires force from sentiments of uneasiness.

Nothing endears so much a friend as sorrow for his death. The pleasure of his company has not so powerful an influence.

Jealousy is a painful passion; yet without some share of it, the agreeable affection of love has difficulty to subsist in its full force and violence. Absence is also a great source of complaint among lovers, and gives them the greatest uneasiness: yet nothing is more favourable to their mutual passion than short intervals of that kind. And if long intervals often prove fatal, it is only because, through time, men are accustomed to them, and they cease to give uneasiness. Jealousy and absence in love compose the *dolce peccante* [5] of the Italians, which they suppose so essential to all pleasure.

There is a fine observation of the elder Pliny, which illustrates the principle here insisted on. "It is very remarkable," says he,[6] "that the last works of celebrated artists, which they left imperfect, are always the most prized, such as the *Iris* of Aristides, the *Tyndarides* of Nicomachus, the *Medea* of Timomachus, and the *Venus* of Apelles. These are valued even above their finished productions. The broken lineaments of the piece, and the half-formed idea of the painter, are carefully studied; and our very grief for that curious hand, which had been stopped by death, is an additional increase to our pleasure."

These instances (and many more might be collected) are sufficient to afford us some insight into the analogy of nature, and to show us, that the pleasure which poets, orators, and musicians give us, by exciting grief, sorrow, indignation, compassion, is not so extraordinary or paradoxical as it may at first sight appear. The force of imagination, the energy of expression, the power of numbers, the charms of imitation; all these are naturally, of themselves, delightful to the mind. And when the object presented lays hold also of some affection, the pleasure still rises upon us, by the conversion of this subordinate movement into that which is predominant. The passion, though perhaps naturally, and when excited by the simple appearance of a real object, it may be painful; yet is so smoothed, and softened, and mollified, when raised by the finer arts, that it affords the highest entertainment.

To confirm this reasoning, we may observe, that if the movements of the imagination be not predominant above those of the passion, a contrary effect follows; and the former, being now subordinate, is converted into the latter, and still further increases the pain and affliction of the sufferer.

Who could ever think of it as a good expedient for comforting an afflicted parent, to exaggerate, with all the force of elocution, the irreparable loss which he has met with by the death of a favourite child? The more power of imagination and expression you here employ, the more you increase his despair and affliction.

The shame, confusion, and terror of Verres, no doubt, rose in proportion to the noble eloquence and vehemence of Cicero: So also did his pain and uneasiness. These former passions were too strong for the pleasure arising from the beauties of elocution; and operated, though from the same principle, yet in a contrary manner, to the sympathy, compassion, and indignation of the audience.

Lord Clarendon,[7] when he approaches towards the catastrophe of the royal party, supposes that his narration must then become infinitely disagreeable; and he hurries over the king's death without giving us one circumstance of it. He considers it as too horrid a scene to be contemplated with any satisfaction, or even without the utmost pain and aversion. He himself, as well as the readers of that age, were too deeply concerned in the events, and felt a pain from subjects which an historian and a reader of another age would regard as the most pathetic and most interesting, and, by consequence, the most agreeable.

An action, represented in tragedy, may be too bloody and atrocious. It may excite such movements of horror as will not soften into pleasure; and the greatest energy of expression, bestowed on descriptions of that nature, serves only to augment our uneasiness. Such is that action represented in the *Ambitious Step-mother*,[8] where a venerable old man, raised to the height of fury and despair, rushes against a pillar, and, striking his head upon it, besmears it all over with mingled brains and gore. The English theatre abounds too much with such shocking images.

Even the common sentiments of compassion require to be softened by some agreeable affection, in order to give a thorough satisfaction to the audience. The mere suffering of plaintive virtue, under the triumphant tyranny and oppression of vice, forms a disagreeable spectacle, and is carefully avoided by all masters of the drama. In order to dismiss the audience with

---

[5] Sweet sinning.

[6] *Natural History*, XXXV, 40, 20. Hume is here stressing the importance of "suggestiveness" in art: the ability of art, increasingly prized in romantic criticism, to arouse, by suggestion, the subjective energy of the reader's or observer's own imagination, and thus encourage it to create its own conception. Cf. Addison, above, p. 186, and especially Hazlitt, below, p. 298.

[7] Author of the *History of the Rebellion* (1702-04).

[8] By Nicholas Rowe (1700).

entire satisfaction and contentment, the virtue must either convert itself into a noble courageous despair, or the vice receive its proper punishment.

Most painters appear in this light to have been very unhappy in their subjects. As they wrought much for churches and convents, they have chiefly represented such horrible subjects as crucifixions and martyrdoms, where nothing appears but tortures, wounds, executions, and passive suffering, without any action or affection. When they turned their pencil from this ghastly mythology, they had commonly recourse to Ovid, whose fictions, though passionate and agreeable, are scarcely natural or probable enough for painting.

The same inversion of that principle which is here insisted on, displays itself in common life, as in the effects of oratory and poetry. Raise so the subordinate passion that it becomes the predominant, it swallows up that affection which it before nourished and increased. Too much jealousy extinguishes love; too much difficulty renders us indifferent; too much sickness and infirmity disgusts a selfish and unkind parent.

What so disagreeable as the dismal, gloomy, disastrous stories, with which melancholy people entertain their companions? The uneasy passion being there raised alone, unaccompanied with any spirit, genius, or eloquence, conveys a pure uneasiness, and is attended with nothing that can soften it into pleasure or satisfaction.

4. *Close of the Classical Tradition:*
Humanism and Classical Realism

SAMUEL JOHNSON   (1709-1784)

I F JOHNSON's criticism rests on any one principle more than another it is on the classical conviction that the aim of art—as indeed of all humanistic pursuits—is the mental and moral enlargement of man, and that art attains this end through a moving and imaginative presentation of truth. In justifying Shakespeare's intermingling of tragic and comic scenes, Johnson stated that "there is always an appeal open from criticism to nature." Despite his acute and informed interest in the technical problems of literature, his primary concern was with its ultimate end and function, and, as a true classicist, he evaluated the means to the degree that they furthered that end. For Johnson, the knowledge to be desired is the knowledge of what principles, qualities, or values are most universal or persisting. It is the objective knowledge of what he called "*general* nature." The more universal and far-reaching the truth desired or conveyed by art, the closer art comes to fulfilling its primary aim. Moreover, "nothing can please many, and please long, but just representations of general nature." The poet, as "the interpreter of Nature," must therefore try to "divest himself of the prejudices of his age and country," and attempt to grasp and disclose general truths, "which will always be the same." With this point of view in mind, one sees that most of Johnson's adverse criticism is directed against whatever distorts "general nature" or abandons it in order to concentrate on isolated details, cater to temporary fashions, or satisfy arbitrary "rules" of art. In opposing this last tendency, Johnson overturned extreme neoclassic dogma, not on romantic, but on broadly classical grounds.

SAMUEL JOHNSON. Born at Lichfield, the son of a bookseller, Johnson attended Pembroke College, Oxford, for a while, and after trying to teach school, he went to London (1737), and worked as a hack writer, living in the direst poverty. His writing covered a wide area, ranging from poetry to reports of parliamentary debates. His periodical, the *Rambler* (1750-52) and especially his famous *Dictionary* (1755) brought him more notice. By the time he published his edition of Shakespeare (1765), Johnson was the center of the noted group that included Burke, Reynolds, Goldsmith, Garrick, and others. Because of Boswell's biography of him, Johnson's life during his remaining twenty years is perhaps better known than that of any other writer.

The critical essays in the *Rambler* are most easily consulted in any of the available editions of the complete *Works* (ed. Sir John Hawkins, 15 vols., 1787-89; and the numerous republications down to 1825), now superseded by the Yale Edition of the *Works of Samuel Johnson*, III-V (ed. W. J. Bate and A. Strauss, 1969). Standard editions for the other criticism are *Johnson on Shakespeare* (ed. A. Sherbo, 1958), and the *Lives of the Poets* (ed. G. B. Hill, Oxford, 3 vols.,

2

Of the innumerable "novels and romances that wit or idleness, vanity or indigence, have pushed into the world, there are very few of which the end cannot be conjectured from the beginning." Far from demanding more real imagination, improbable fiction requires the author to do little more, as Johnson said, than to gain a moderate "fluency of language" and then "retire to his closet, let loose his invention, and heat his mind with incredibilities." Johnson also viewed askance in the drama the growing obsession which made of romantic love the "universal agent . . . by whose power all good and evil is distributed, and every action quickened or retarded." By such false emphasis, "probability is violated" and "life is misrepresented." It is significant to Johnson that romantic love has little place in the dramas of Shakespeare, "who caught his ideas from the living world." Similarly, like the great neoclassic realist, Jonathan Swift, Johnson despised pastoral poetry: "an intelligent reader acquainted with the scenes of real life sickens at the mention of the *crook,* the *pipe,* the *sheep,* and the *kids,*" which can please only "barbarians in the dawn of literature, and children in the dawn of life." This dislike of the pastoral as a genre should be borne in mind in reading Johnson's famous remarks on Milton's *Lycidas.* Though his bias does not justify, it helps at least to explain his approach.

Truth to life, then, is the first criterion. But this does not mean for Johnson a naturalistic concentration on particular details. The excessive use of what we now call "local color," the interest in unique and individual traits of character, the portraying of transitory, local fashions and manners, in whatever level of society, will in the future give a work little more than documentary interest; though it "easily finds readers," it also "quickly loses them." The Puritans satirized in Butler's *Hudibras* have only historical importance. Homer, on the other hand, survives because his "positions are general . . . with very little dependence on local or temporary customs." In Shakespeare, who is probably without equal as a poet of "general nature," the characters are "not modified by the customs of particular places, unpractised by the rest of the world . . . or by the accidents of transient fashions or temporary opinions: they are the genuine progeny of common humanity, such as the world will always supply . . ." The aim of the poet,

1905). The selections offered in *The Critical Opinions of Samuel Johnson* (ed. J. E. Brown, Princeton, 1926) are arranged by subject and author to give immediate reference to the whole body of Johnson's criticism. Commentary on Johnson's criticism is abundant and covers many different aspects. Among general discussions are: W. J. Bate, *The Achievement of Samuel Johnson* (1955), Ch. V; Jean Hagstrum, *Samuel Johnson's Literary Criticism* (Minneapolis, 1952); and Sir Walter Raleigh, *Six Essays on Johnson* (Oxford, 1910). A fuller treatment of the general point of view presented above is W. J. Bate, *From Classic to Romantic* (1946), Ch. III. More specific discussions include: Bergen Evans, "Dr. Johnson's Theory of Biography," *Review of English Studies,* X (1934), 301-10; W. B. C. Watkins, *Johnson and English Poetry Before 1660* (Princeton, 1936); Karl Young, *Samuel Johnson on Shakespeare,* Wisconsin Univ. Studies, XVIII (1923).

in other words, is not to "number the streaks of the tulip." Hence Johnson's strictures on detailed particularity of style, by which the "grandeur of generality," he felt, was lost. One example is his attitude toward the specific metaphors and images in the more extreme "metaphysical" poets. Despite his respect for the learning and original thinking of these poets, Johnson believed that, because of their "laboured particularities," the mind of the reader "is turned more upon . . . that from which the illustration is drawn, than that to which it is applied," and that so "analytic" a style fails effectively to exhibit the wide "prospects of nature, or the scenes of life." Another example is Johnson's opposition to "pedantry" in style—the use of out-of-the-way references, or deliberate "imitations" of past writers—as in Milton's Latin idiom, or Shakespeare's more ostentatious allusions in some of the longer set speeches, or the specialized knowledge assumed for reading Pope's *Imitations of Horace*. Johnson particularly censured imitations, such as those of Spenser that were common in the eighteenth century. They may show industry and please the learned by unexpected parallels. However, they "appeal not to reason or passion," but to "accidental" memory: "An imitation of Spenser is nothing to a reader, however acute, by whom Spenser has never been perused."

3

In the eighteenth-century approach to "imitations" of authors, one may at once see the two diverse sides of neoclassicism: the more self-conscious and restricted side, based on authority and past models, that leads to the writing of "imitations"; and the broader side that rejects them by placing truth to "general nature," and the direct appeal to "reason or passion," as the first requirement of art. Johnson, more than any other neoclassic critic, either in England or the Continent, exemplifies the latter, broader side. In a general sense, he admitted that some imitation of earlier writers is unavoidable. Especially in the great works of antiquity, the approach to the general characteristics of nature has been tested by the repeated judgment of centuries. The writer, therefore, may profit from studying the principles and aims of these works. But to copy the specific and external qualities of earlier writing is to "tread a beaten walk." In this respect, "no man ever yet became great by imitation." We may again remember the maxim of Edward Young: he that imitates the *Iliad* is not imitating Homer. And in reading Young's *Conjectures on Original Composition*, Johnson was surprised to find Young "receive as novelties" what Johnson himself "thought very common thoughts."

An even greater neglect of "general nature" is the arbitrary codifying of "rules" such as we find in Thomas Rymer or in "the minute and slender criticism of Voltaire." Indeed, one of the most notable achievements of Johnson is that, by broadly applying the principle of "general nature," he repudiated, on rational and classical grounds, many of the external neo-classic rules. "It ought," he said in *Rambler,* No. 156, "to be the first endeavour of a writer to distinguish nature from custom; or that which is established because it is right, from that which is right only because it is established." Self-authorized critics, "out of various means by which the same end [the compact and truthful presenting of nature] may be attained, selected such as happened to occur to their own reflexion," and then arbitrarily tried to give them "the certainty and stability of science." Hence Johnson, in his great *Preface to Shakespeare,* justifies Shakespeare's neglect of three major neoclassic "rules" by bringing to bear a more open-minded and flexible conception of decorum, based directly on nature itself. In wishing, for example, to stress the general "type" rather than the particular individual, neoclassic theory had interpreted its belief in keeping "decorum of type" to apply to what Coleridge would call the "exterior" rather than the "interior" character of a man. Thus Dennis and Rymer, said Johnson, in reacting to Shakespeare's characters "think his Romans not sufficiently Roman; and Voltaire censures his kings as not completely royal." Shakespeare preserves the "essential character" of the type. But his types are more pervasive than the mere classes and the external and changeable "drapery" of local customs that Rymer and Voltaire have in mind; in Johnson's words, "a poet overlooks the casual distinction of country and condition, as a painter, satisfied with the figure, neglects the drapery."

Again, in answering the neoclassic charges against Shakespeare's use of both tragic and comic elements in the same play, Johnson undercuts such complaints by returning to the central classical premise: "the end of poetry is to instruct by pleasing," to enlarge our conception of nature, to infiltrate knowledge into our awareness through a process of pleasing. The "mingled drama," therefore, is easily justified both by its closeness to nature and by the obvious pleasure it has given. Finally, Johnson sweeps aside the traditional arguments for the "unities" of time and place as a means of verisimilitude in a searching and common-sense analysis of "dramatic illusion." We are often told that the drama will not seem real if the scene keeps changing, and if the time supposedly covered by the action is much longer than the two or three hours that we sit in the theater. But the spectator does not believe he is actually at Alexandria to begin with, and therefore is not surprised or incredulous at finding himself later in Rome. As for time, the imagination can as easily conceive "a lapse of years . . . as a passage of hours." No more heed of time and place need be given by the spectator of a play "than by the reader of a narrative, before whom may pass in an hour the life of a hero, or the revolutions of an empire." It is significant in this respect that what to a noted French writer should seem revolutionary and "romantic" was, to the conservative English classicist, Johnson, simply common sense. For, as W. P. Ker pointed out, Stendhal, in his *Racine et*

Shakespeare (1822), translated Johnson's remarks on the unities and appropriated them as a romantic manifesto.

4

Johnson's reassertion of classical aims is therefore broadly positive and affirmative. Hence it is not easy to account for the nineteenth-century belief that his criticism was usually negative and carping, and that he was a rigid advocate of extreme neoclassic standards of "correctness." For the only "rules" that we find Johnson occasionally stressing are the classical and in some cases neoclassic rules concerning diction, metaphor, and versification. Even these, more often than not, he applies flexibly and with common sense; and the ideal he has in mind is an intellectually active and alertly effective use of language. The *Life of Gray* contains several examples. In Gray's playful "Ode on the Death of a Favourite Cat," the cat, looking for goldfish, falls into the tub and is drowned. Johnson points out the irrelevance of the conclusion, "all that glisters" is not "gold." If, says Johnson, *"what glistered had been gold,* the cat would not have gone into the water; and, if she had, would not less have been drowned." By some nineteenth-century writers Johnson would here be dismissed as "unimaginative" and too literal. Twentieth-century critics, however, would be quick to agree that the poem is structurally weak, and that the conclusion does not organically develop from the body of the poem. In such a work as the *Life of Gray*, therefore, Johnson should not be regarded as vaguely opposing what we now call "romanticism." Rather, he anticipated such present-day critics as T. S. Eliot in feeling the poverty of "wit" and intellectual energy in the poetry of his own day and in decrying the substitution of stock devices, employed in the belief, as Johnson said, that "not to write prose is certainly to write poetry." He also doubted, as did Eliot later, the value of Milton's influence on minor poets, particularly in their blank verse. Speaking of Thomas Warton, for example, he made up a parody ending, "Wearing out life's evening gray": *"Gray evening,"* added Johnson, "is common enough; but *evening gray* he'd think fine."

Moreover, Johnson was still a critic in the original sense—a sense that includes evaluating and judging. Where some nineteenth-century English writers eulogized Shakespeare and Milton indiscriminately, and considered Johnson insensitive for not doing likewise, he did not hesitate, in evaluating the work of these poets, to point out what he believed to be its lacks or faults as well as its merits. If, for example, some of the conclusions of Shakespeare's plays seem weak or sudden, as in *Henry V* and *All's Well That Ends Well,* Johnson did not scruple to say as much, and to add, as in the case of *All's Well*, "Of all this Shakespeare could not be ignorant, but Shakespeare wanted to conclude his play." Similarly, Johnson openly noted what he considered faults of style that resulted from Shakespeare's rapid writing. But in such instances, as Sir Walter Raleigh has said, he was "not attacking Shakespeare; he is assuming his greatness, and helping to define it . . ." Again, if Johnson irritated admirers of Milton by his comments on *Lycidas* and by saying of *Paradise Lost* that no one "ever wished it longer," it should be remembered that he offers the first great critique of *Paradise Lost* and that he concludes his *Life of Milton* by stating, of this "wonderful performance," that it "is not the greatest of heroic poems, only because it is not the first"—that is, only because it had Homer before it as an original model.

Even at the present time it is too quickly assumed that, in the *Life of Cowley,* Johnson is merely presenting the classical charge against the "metaphysical" poets. In a sense he is doing that. He points out what he considers to be their weaknesses when they are judged against the highest standards of poetry. But he also suggests the basis on which they can be defended or justified. And he does this so effectively that recent exponents of the "metaphysical" style often build upon his premises, and even use his terminology as a starting point: the *"discordia concors;* a combination of dissimilar images, or discovery of occult resemblances in things apparently unlike." It should be noted that Johnson, in the *Life of Cowley*, attempted to broaden again the idea of "wit," which—as in Pope's definition, "What oft was thought, but ne'er so well expressed,"—had become "reduced," Johnson felt, "from strength of thought to happiness of language." To write in the "metaphysical" style—and this was high praise from Johnson— "it was at least necessary to read and think." The variety of "wit" that he found in the "metaphysical" poets, moreover, was one that he described as "more rigorously and philosophically considered." If Johnson presented the classical charge against the "metaphysical" poets, he also offered at least the basis for the classical defense of them. He did not, it is true, view them as ideal models. His concern was to see them, in a balanced way, for what they were, and, at a time when they were almost forgotten, to find a critical framework for them, and to discover a basis on which they could be understood and evaluated.

5

It was manifest to Johnson, that in order to grasp general reality and portray it in the form of art, the first requirement is "reason." But by "reason" he meant a far more complete activity of mind than mere deductive abstraction. He would not have agreed with the extreme neoclassic rationalists that sheer method and abstract logic are the main key to anything except the particular sciences built specifically upon them. For Johnson, who was very English in his empirical-mindedness, firmly believed in the value of concrete experience. On the other hand, he felt that every effort should be made to widen this experience by drawing upon that of others. Moreover, "to judge rightly of the present, we must oppose it to the past; for all judgment is comparative . . ." Hence the importance of studying the practical experiences of the past as shown in the history of manners, judgments, tastes, and values. Special attention should be given to those that have persisted beyond a particular age or locality, for what the majority of intelligent and discriminating people persist in valuing over different periods of time can greatly assist us toward a flexible standard for judging what will continue to appeal. It is on this basis that Johnson begins the *Preface to Shakespeare* with the statement that "to works not raised upon principles demonstrative and scientific, but appealing wholly to observation and experience, no other test can be applied than length of duration and continuance of esteem."

But, according to Johnson, this full exertion of mind, directed by reason and the intelligent use of experience, must also include emotion and the imagination. Among the primary subjects of the poet, none is more important than human nature itself and its motivating passions. The poet, needless to say, can hardly understand and portray human passion without being himself susceptible to it. Moreover, if the "end of poetry is to instruct *by pleasing*," poetry must tap human feeling in order to relate it to insight. Johnson's only qualification was that *mere* emotion, by itself, was not a trustworthy guide, and that emotion is of value only to the degree that it is fed and informed by reason and knowledge. His attitude toward the function of the imagination was similar. It is frequently said that Johnson "distrusted" the imagination, but what he distrusted was the use of the imagination as a practical, moral guide. For him the term still meant "image-making," not the entire play of mind that Coleridge, for example, meant by the word. Hence Johnson rightly took it for granted that mere unguided "image-making," left to itself, can lead to any end, including nightmares and insanity. Johnson's distrust of imagination and emotion as exclusive moral guides was increased by his fear of his own vivid imagination and strong feelings. Much of his life was devoted to a courageous struggle against what he called "that hunger of imagination which preys incessantly upon life." On the other hand, he also took it for granted that imagination is necessary in art. The more of it one has, the better, provided it be informed and "regulated" by knowledge. Since imagination and feeling tend to follow whatever is before them—an object, a remembered image, an association, a fear or hope—it is the task of reason to make sure that what they follow is not the result of mere whim, accident, or local custom and chance environment.

The aim, in short, is to cleave to the rational conception of what is true with such vigor and firmness that this conception will then arouse, lead, and channel the feelings and the imagination toward it. This broad classical conviction is as far from the narrow, anti-imaginative bias of extreme neo-classicism as it is from the loose, watery emotionalism of the extreme romantic. And the conviction gains force as Johnson applied it, because his own life may be described as an energetic effort to realize, deeply and emotionally, the truths that his reason perceived. He was not entirely successful, of course, nor did the temper or character of his own period offer much encouragement. "Lonely in his life," as T. S. Eliot has said, "Johnson seems . . . still more lonely in his intellectual and moral significance." Yet both as a critic and as a moralist, Johnson never lost sight of what is centrally important. The outstanding characteristic of his writing, therefore, is its *sanity*; and it is a sanity that is all the stronger and more genuine because it is a rational attitude to which Johnson clung, with a powerful exertion of will, in self-preservation against his own emotionally turbulent nature. In the mind and the literary achievement of Johnson, the classical tradition, at least as an unbroken continuity, finally comes to its close. But in doing so, it rises once again to a living and pervasive applicability to literature and human life.

Rasselas

CHAPTER X

IMLAC'S HISTORY CONTINUED. A DISSERTATION
UPON POETRY

WHEREVER I went, I found that poetry was considered as the highest learning, and regarded with a veneration somewhat approaching to that which man would pay to the Angelic Nature. And yet it fills me with wonder, that, in almost all countries, the most ancient poets are considered as the best: whether it be that every other kind of knowledge is an acquisition gradually attained, and poetry is a gift conferred at once; or that the first poetry of every nation surprised them as a novelty, and retained the credit by consent which it received by accident at first: or whether, as the province of poetry is to describe Nature and Passion, which are always the same, the first writers took possession of the most striking objects for description, and the most probable occurrences for fiction, and left nothing to those that followed them, but transcription of the same events, and new combinations of the same images. What-

Rasselas. Published in 1759.

ever be the reason, it is commonly observed that the early writers are in possession of nature, and their followers of art: that the first excel in strength and invention, and the latter in elegance and refinement.

"I was desirous to add my name to this illustrious fraternity. I read all the poets of Persia and Arabia, and was able to repeat by memory the volumes that are suspended in the mosque of Mecca. But I soon found that no man was ever great by imitation. My desire of excellence impelled me to transfer my attention to nature and to life. Nature was to be my subject, and men to be my auditors: I could never describe what I had not seen: I could not hope to move those with delight or terror, whose interests and opinions I did not understand.

"Being now resolved to be a poet, I saw every thing with a new purpose; my sphere of attention was suddenly magnified: no kind of knowledge was to be overlooked. I ranged mountains and deserts for images and resemblances, and pictured upon my mind every tree of the forest and flower of the valley. I observed with equal care the crags of the rock and the pinnacles of the palace. Sometimes I wandered along the mazes of the rivulet, and sometimes watched the changes of the summer clouds. To a poet nothing can be useless. Whatever is beautiful, and whatever is dreadful, must be familiar to his imagination: he must be conversant with all that is awfully vast or elegantly little. The plants of the garden, the animals of the wood, the minerals of the earth, and meteors of the sky, must all concur to store his mind with inexhaustible variety: for every idea is useful for the enforcement or decoration of moral or religious truth; and he, who knows most, will have most power of diversifying his scenes, and of gratifying his reader with remote allusions and unexpected instruction.

"All the appearances of nature I was therefore careful to study, and every country which I have surveyed has contributed something to my poetical powers."

"In so wide a survey," said the prince, "you must surely have left much unobserved. I have lived, till now, within the circuit of these mountains, and yet cannot walk abroad without the sight of something which I had never beheld before, or never heeded."

"The business of a poet," said Imlac, "is to examine, not the individual, but the species; to remark general properties and large appearances; he does not number the streaks of the tulip, or describe the different shades in the verdure of the forest. He is to exhibit in his portraits of nature such prominent and striking features, as recall the original to every mind; and must neglect the minuter discriminations, which one may have remarked, and another have neglected, for those characteristics which are alike obvious to vigilance and carelessness.

"But the knowledge of nature is only half the task of a poet; he must be acquainted likewise with all the modes of life. His character requires that he estimate the happiness and misery of every condition; observe the power of all the passions in all their combinations, and trace the changes of the human mind as they are modified by various institutions and accidental influences of climate or custom, from the sprightliness of infancy to the despondence of decrepitude. He must divest himself of the prejudices of his age or country; he must consider right and wrong in their abstracted and invariable state; he must disregard present laws and opinions, and rise to general and transcendental truths, which will always be the same: he must therefore content himself with the slow progress of his name; contemn the applause of his own time, and commit his claims to the justice of posterity. He must write as the interpreter of nature, and the legislator of mankind, and consider himself as presiding over the thoughts and manners of future generations; as a being superior to time and place.

"His labour is not yet at an end: he must know many languages and many sciences; and, that his style may be worthy of his thoughts, must, by incessant practice, familiarize to himself every delicacy of speech and grace of harmony."

From the Preface to Shakespeare

THAT praises are without reason lavished on the dead, and that the honours due only to excellence are paid to antiquity, is a complaint likely to be always continued by those, who, being able to add nothing to truth, hope for eminence from the heresies of paradox; or those, who, being forced by disappointment upon consolatory expedients, are willing to hope from posterity what the present age refuses, and flatter themselves that the regard which is yet de-

Preface to Shakespeare. First published in 1765.

nied by envy, will be at last bestowed by time.

Antiquity, like every other quality that attracts the notice of mankind, has undoubtedly votaries that reverence it, not from reason, but from prejudice. Some seem to admire indiscriminately whatever has been long preserved, without considering that time has sometimes co-operated with chance; all perhaps are more willing to honour past than present excellence; and the mind contemplates genius through the shades of age, as the eye surveys the sun through artificial opacity. The great contention of criticism is to find the faults of the moderns, and the beauties of the ancients. While an authour is yet living we estimate his powers by his worst performance, and when he is dead, we rate them by his best.

To works, however, of which the excellence is not absolute and definite, but gradual and comparative; to works not raised upon principles demonstrative and scientifick, but appealing wholly to observation and experience, no other test can be applied than length of duration and continuance of esteem. What mankind have long possessed they have often examined and compared; and if they persist to value the possession, it is because frequent comparisons have confirmed opinion in its favour. As among the works of nature no man can properly call a river deep, or a mountain high, without the knowledge of many mountains, and many rivers; so in the productions of genius, nothing can be stiled excellent till it has been compared with other works of the same kind. Demonstration immediately displays its power, and has nothing to hope or fear from the flux of years; but works tentative and experimental must be estimated by their proportion to the general and collective ability of man, as it is discovered in a long succession of endeavours. Of the first building that was raised, it might be with certainty determined that it was round or square; but whether it was spacious or lofty must have been referred to time. The Pythagorean scale of numbers was at once discovered to be perfect; but the poems of *Homer* we yet know not to transcend the common limits of human intelligence, but by remarking, that nation after nation, and century after century, has been able to do little more than transpose his incidents, new-name his characters, and paraphrase his sentiments.

The reverence due to writings that have long subsisted arises therefore not from any credulous confidence in the superior wisdom of past ages, or gloomy persuasion of the degeneracy of mankind, but is the consequence of acknowledged and indubitable positions, that what has been longest known has been most considered, and what is most considered is best understood.

The Poet, of whose works I have undertaken the revision, may now begin to assume the dignity of an ancient, and claim the privilege of established fame and prescriptive veneration.

He has long outlived his century, the term commonly fixed as the test of literary merit. Whatever advantages he might once derive from personal allusions, local customs, or temporary opinions, have for many years been lost; and every topick of merriment, or motive of sorrow, which the modes of artificial life afforded him, now only obscure the scenes which they once illuminated. The effects of favour and competition are at an end; the tradition of his friendships and his enmities has perished; his works support no opinion with arguments, nor supply any faction with invectives; they can neither indulge vanity nor gratify malignity; but are read without any other reason than the desire of pleasure, and are therefore praised only as pleasure is obtained; yet, thus unassisted by interest or passion, they have past through variations of taste and changes of manners, and, as they devolved from one generation to another, have received new honours at every transmission.

But because human judgment, though it be gradually gaining upon certainty, never becomes infallible; and approbation, though long continued, may yet be only the approbation of prejudice or fashion; it is proper to inquire, by what peculiarities of excellence *Shakespeare* has gained and kept the favour of his countrymen.

Nothing can please many, and please long, but just representations of general nature. Particular manners, can be known to few, and therefore few only can judge how nearly they are copied. The irregular combinations of fanciful invention may delight a-while, by that novelty of which the common satiety of life sends us all in quest; but the pleasures of sudden wonder are soon exhausted, and the mind can only repose on the stability of truth.

Shakespeare is above all writers, at least above all modern writers, the poet of nature; the poet that holds up to his readers a faithful mirrour of manners and of life. His characters are not modified by the customs of particular places, unpractised by the rest of the world; by the peculiarities of studies or professions, which can operate but upon small numbers; or by the accidents of transient fashions or temporary opinions: they are the genuine progeny of common humanity, such as the world will always supply, and observation will always find. His persons act and speak by the influence of those general passions and principles by which all minds are agitated, and the whole system of life is continued in motion. In the writings of other poets a character is too often an individual; in those of *Shakespeare* it is commonly a species.

It is from this wide extension of design that so much instruction is derived. It is this which fills the plays of *Shakespeare* with practical axioms and domestic wisdom. It was said of *Euripides*, that every verse was a precept; and it may be said of *Shakespeare*, that from his works may be collected a system of civil and oeconomical prudence. Yet his real power is not shewn in the splendour of particular passages, but by the progress of his fable, and the tenour of his dialogue; and he that tries to recommend him by select quotations, will succeed like the pedant in *Hierocles*, who, when he offered his house to sale, carried a brick in his pocket as a specimen.

It will not easily be imagined how much *Shakespeare* excells in accommodating his sentiments to real life, but by comparing him with other authours. It was observed of the ancient schools of declamation, that the more diligently they were frequented, the more was the student disqualified for the world, because he found nothing there which he should ever meet in any other place. The same remark may be applied to every stage but that of *Shakespeare*. The theatre, when it is under any other direction, is peopled by such characters as were never seen, conversing in a language which was never heard, upon topicks which will never rise in the commerce of mankind. But the dialogue of this authour is often so evidently determined by the incident which produces it, and is pursued with so much ease and simplicity, that it seems scarcely to claim the merit of fiction, but to have been gleaned by diligent selection out of common conversation, and common occurrences.

Upon every other stage the universal agent is love, by whose power all good and evil is distributed, and every action quickened or retarded. To bring a lover, a lady and a rival into the fable; to entangle them in contradictory obligations, perplex them with oppositions of interest, and harrass them with violence of desires inconsistent with each other; to make them meet in rapture and part in agony; to fill their mouths with hyperbolical joy and outrageous sorrow;

to distress them as nothing human ever was distressed; to deliver them as nothing human ever was delivered; is the business of a modern dramatist. For this probability is violated, life is misrepresented, and language is depraved. But love is only one of many passions; and as it has no great influence upon the sum of life, it has little operation in the dramas of a poet, who caught his ideas from the living world, and exhibited only what he saw before him. He knew, that any other passion, as it was regular or exorbitant, was a cause of happiness or calamity.

Characters thus ample and general were not easily discriminated and preserved, yet perhaps no poet ever kept his personages more distinct from each other. I will not say with *Pope*, that every speech may be assigned to the proper speaker, because many speeches there are which have nothing characteristical; but perhaps, though some may be equally adapted to every person, it will be difficult to find, any that can be properly transferred from the present possessor to another claimant. The choice is right, when there is reason for choice.

Other dramatists can only gain attention by hyperbolical or aggravated characters, by fabulous and unexampled excellence or depravity, as the writers of barbarous romances invigorated the reader by a giant and a dwarf; and he that should form his expectations of human affairs from the play, or from the tale, would be equally deceived. *Shakespeare* has no heroes; his scenes are occupied only by men, who act and speak as the reader thinks that he should himself have spoken or acted on the same occasion: Even where the agency is supernatural the dialogue is level with life. Other writers disguise the most natural passions and most frequent incidents; so that he who contemplates them in the book will not know them in the world: *Shakespeare* approximates the remote, and familiarizes the wonderful; the event which he represents will not happen, but if it were possible, its effects would probably be such as he has assigned; and it may be said, that he has not only shewn human nature as it acts in real exigencies, but as it would be found in trials, to which it cannot be exposed.

This therefore is the praise of *Shakespeare*, that his drama is the mirrour of life; that he who has mazed his imagination, in following the phantoms which other writers raise up before him, may here be cured of his delirious extasies, by reading human sentiments in human language, by scenes from which a hermit may estimate the transactions of the world, and a confessor predict the progress of the passions.

His adherence to general nature has exposed him to the censure of criticks, who form their judgments upon narrow principles. *Dennis* and *Rhymer* think his *Romans* not sufficiently *Roman*; and *Voltaire* censures his kings as not completely royal. *Dennis* is offended, that *Menenius*, a senator of *Rome*, should play the buffoon; and *Voltaire* perhaps thinks decency violated when the *Danish* Usurper is represented as a drunkard. But *Shakespeare* always makes nature predominate over accident; and if he preserves the essential character, is not very careful of distinctions superinduced and adventitious. His story requires Romans or kings, but he thinks only on men. He knew that *Rome*, like every other city, had men of all dispositions; and wanting a buffoon, he went into the senate-house for that which the senate-house would certainly have afforded him. He was inclined to shew an usurper and a murderer not only odious but despicable, he therefore added drunkenness to his other qualities, knowing that kings love wine like other men, and that wine exerts its natural power upon kings. These are the petty cavils of petty minds; a poet overlooks the casual distinction of country and condition, as a painter, satisfied with the figure, neglects the drapery.

The censure which he has incurred by mixing comick and tragick scenes, as it extends to all his works, deserves more consideration. Let the fact be first stated, and then examined.

Shakespeare's plays are not in the rigorous and critical sense either tragedies or comedies, but compositions of a distinct kind; exhibiting the real state of sublunary nature, which partakes of good and evil, joy and sorrow, mingled with endless variety of proportion and innumerable modes of combination; and expressing the course of the world, in which the loss of one is the gain of another; in which, at the same time, the reveller is hasting to his wine, and the mourner burying his friend; in which the malignity of one is sometimes defeated by the frolick of another; and many mischiefs and

many benefits are done and hindered without design.

Out of this chaos of mingled purposes and casualties the ancient poets, according to the laws which custom had prescribed, selected some the crimes of men, and some their absurdities; some the momentous vicissitudes of life, and some the lighter occurrences; some the terrours of distress, and some the gayeties of prosperity. Thus rose the two modes of imitation, known by the names of *tragedy* and *comedy*, compositions intended to promote different ends by contrary means, and considered as so little allied, that I do not recollect among the *Greeks* or *Romans* a single writer who attempted both.

Shakespeare has united the powers of exciting laughter and sorrow not only in one mind, but in one composition. Almost all his plays are divided between serious and ludicrous characters, and, in the successive evolutions of the design, sometimes produce seriousness and sorrow, and sometimes levity and laughter.

That this is a practice contrary to the rules of criticism will be readily allowed; but there is always an appeal open from criticism to nature. The end of writing is to instruct; the end of poetry is to instruct by pleasing. That the mingled drama may convey all the instruction of tragedy or comedy cannot be denied, because it includes both in its alternations of exhibition and approaches nearer than either to the appearance of life, by shewing how great machinations and slender designs may promote or obviate one another, and the high and the low cooperate in the general system by unavoidable concatenation.

It is objected, that by this change of scenes the passions are interrupted in their progression, and that the principal event, being not advanced by a due gradation of preparatory incidents, wants at last the power to move, which constitutes the perfection of dramatick poetry. This reasoning is so specious, that it is received as true even by those who in daily experience feel it to be false. The interchanges of mingled scenes seldom fail to produce the intended vicissitudes of passion. Fiction cannot move so much, but that the attention may be easily transferred; and though it must be allowed that pleasing melancholy be sometimes interrupted by unwelcome levity, yet let it be considered likewise, that melancholy is often not pleasing, and that the disturbance of one man may be the relief of another; that different auditors have different habitudes; and that, upon the whole, all pleasure consists in variety.

The players, who in their edition divided our authour's works into comedies, histories, and tragedies, seem not to have distinguished the three kinds by any very exact or definite ideas.

An action which ended happily to the principal persons, however serious or distressful through its intermediate incidents, in their opinion, constituted a comedy. This idea of a comedy continued long amongst us; and plays were written, which, by changing the catastrophe, were tragedies to-day, and comedies to-morrow.

Tragedy was not in those times a poem of more general dignity or elevation than comedy; it required only a calamitous conclusion, with which the common criticism of that age was satisfied, whatever lighter pleasure it afforded in its progress.

History was a series of actions, with no other than chronological succession, independent on each other, and without any tendency to introduce or regulate the conclusion. It is not always very nicely distinguished from tragedy. There is not much nearer approach to unity of action in the tragedy of *Antony and Cleopatra,* than in the history of *Richard the Second.* But a history might be continued through many plays; as it had no plan, it had no limits.

Through all these denominations of the drama, *Shakespeare's* mode of composition is the same; an interchange of seriousness and merriment, by which the mind is softened at one time, and exhilarated at another. But whatever be his purpose, whether to gladden or depress, or to conduct the story, without vehemence or emotion, through tracts of easy and familiar dialogue, he never fails to attain his purpose; as he commands us, we laugh or mourn, or sit silent with quiet expectation, in tranquillity without indifference.

When *Shakespeare's* plan is understood, most of the criticisms of *Rhymer* and *Voltaire* vanish away. The play of *Hamlet* is opened, without impropriety, by two sentinels; *Iago* bellows at *Brabantio's* window, without injury to the scheme of the play, though in terms which a modern audience would not easily endure; the character of *Polonius* is seasonable and useful; and the Grave-diggers themselves may be heard with applause.

Shakespeare engaged in dramatick poetry with the world open before him; the rules of the ancients were yet known to few; but publick judgment was unformed; he had no example of such fame as might force him upon imitation, nor criticks of such authority as might restrain his extravagance: He therefore indulged his natural disposition, and his disposition, as *Rhymer* has remarked, led him to comedy. In tragedy he often writes, with great appearance of toil and study, what is written at last with little felicity; but in his comick scenes, he seems to produce without labour what no labour can improve. In tragedy he is always struggling after some occasion to be comick; but in comedy he seems to repose, or to luxuriate, as in a mode of thinking congenial to his nature. In his tragick scenes there is always something wanting,[1] but his comedy often surpasses expectation or desire. His comedy pleases by the thoughts and the language, and his tragedy for the greater part by incident and action. His tragedy seems to be skill, his comedy to be instinct.

The force of his comick scenes has suffered little diminution from the changes made by a century and a half, in manners or in words. As his personages act upon principles arising from genuine passion, very little modified by particular forms, their pleasures and vexations are communicable to all times and to all places; they are natural, and therefore durable; the adventitious peculiarities of personal habits, are only superficial dies, bright and pleasing for a little while, yet soon fading to a dim tinct, without any remains of former lustre; but the discriminations of true passion are the colours of nature; they pervade the whole mass, and can only perish with the body that exhibits them. The accidental compositions of heterogeneous modes are dissolved by the chance which combined them; but the uniform simplicity of primitive qualities neither admits increase, nor suffers decay. The sand heap by one flood is scattered by another, but the rock always continues in its

---

[1] On the other hand, "every man," Johnson says later, "finds his mind more strongly seized by the tragedies of Shakespeare than of any other writer" (see below, p. 217).

place. The stream of time, which is continually washing the dissoluble fabricks of other poets, passes without injury by the adamant of *Shakespeare*.

If there be, what I believe there is, in every nation, a stile which never becomes obsolete, a certain mode of phraseology so consonant and congenial to the analogy and principles of its respective language as to remain settled and unaltered; this style is probably to be sought in the common intercourse of life, among those who speak only to be understood, without ambition of elegance. The polite are always catching modish innovations, and the learned depart from established forms of speech, in hope of finding or making better; those who wish for distinction forsake the vulgar, when the vulgar is right; but there is a conversation above grossness and below refinement, where propriety resides, and where this poet seems to have gathered his comick dialogue. He is therefore more agreeable to the ears of the present age than any other authour equally remote, and among his other excellencies deserves to be studied as one of the original masters of our language.

These observations are to be considered not as unexceptionably constant, but as containing general and predominant truth. *Shakespeare's* familiar dialogue is affirmed to be smooth and clear, yet not wholly without ruggedness or difficulty; as a country may be eminently fruitful, though it has spots unfit for cultivation: His characters are praised as natural, though their sentiments are sometimes forced, and their actions improbable; as the earth upon the whole is spherical, though its surface is varied with protuberances and cavities.

Shakespeare with his excellencies has likewise faults, and faults sufficient to obscure and overwhelm any other merit. I shall shew them in the proportion in which they appear to me, without envious malignity or superstitious veneration. No question can be more innocently discussed than a dead poet's pretensions to renown; and little regard is due to that bigotry which sets candour higher than truth.

His first defect is that to which may be imputed most of the evil in books or in men. He sacrifices virtue to convenience, and is so much more careful to please than to instruct, that he seems to write without any moral purpose. From his writings indeed a system of social duty may be selected, for he that thinks reasonably must think morally; but his precepts and axioms drop casually from him; he makes no just distribution of good or evil, nor is always careful to shew in the virtuous a disapprobation of the wicked; he carries his persons indifferently through right and wrong, and at the close dismisses them without further care, and leaves their examples to operate by chance. This fault the barbarity of his age cannot extenuate; for it is always a writer's duty to make the world better, and justice is a virtue independent on time or place.

The plots are often so loosely formed, that a very slight consideration may improve them, and so carelessly pursued, that he seems not always fully to comprehend his own design. He omits opportunities of instructing or delighting which the train of his story seems to force upon him, and apparently rejects those exhibitions which would be more affecting, for the sake of those which are more easy.

It may be observed, that in many of his plays the latter part is evidently neglected. When he found himself near the end of his work, and, in view of his reward, he shortened the labour to snatch the profit. He therefore remits his efforts where he should most vigorously exert them, and his catastrophe is improbably produced or imperfectly represented.

He had no regard to distinction of time or place, but gives to one age or nation, without scruple, the customs, institutions, and opinions of another, at the expence not only of likelihood, but of possibility. These faults *Pope* has endeavoured, with more zeal than judgment, to transfer to his imagined interpolators. We need not wonder to find *Hector* quoting *Aristotle*, when we see the loves of *Theseus* and *Hippolyta* combined with the *Gothick* mythology of fairies. *Shakespeare*, indeed, was not the only violator of chronology, for in the same age *Sidney*, who wanted not the advantages of learning, has, in his *Arcadia*, confounded the pastoral with the feudal times, the days of innocence, quiet and security, with those of turbulence, violence, and adventure.

In his comick scenes he is seldom very successful, when he engages his characters in reciprocations of smartness and contests of sarcasm; their jests are commonly gross, and their pleasantry licentious; neither his gentlemen nor his ladies have much delicacy, nor are sufficiently distinguished from his clowns by any appearance of refined manners. Whether he represented the real conversation of his time is not easy to determine; the reign of *Elizabeth* is commonly supposed to have been a time of stateliness, formality and reserve; yet perhaps the relaxations of that severity were not very elegant. There must, however, have been always some modes of gayety preferable to others, and a writer ought to chuse the best.

In tragedy his performance seems constantly to be worse, as his labour is more. The effusions of passion which exigence forces out are for the most part striking and energetick; but whenever he solicits his invention, or strains his faculties, the offspring of his throes is tumour, meanness, tediousness, and obscurity.

In narration he affects a disproportionate pomp of diction, and a wearisome train of circumlocution, and tells the incident imperfectly in many words, which might have been more plainly delivered in few. Narration in dramatick poetry is naturally tedious, as it is unanimated and inactive, and obstructs the progress of the action; it should therefore always be rapid, and enlivened by frequent interruption. *Shakespeare* found it an encumberance, and instead of lightening it by brevity, endeavoured to recommend it by dignity and splendour.

His declamations or set speeches are commonly cold and weak, for his power was the power of nature; when he endeavoured, like other tragick writers, to catch opportunities of amplification, and instead of inquiring what the occasion demanded, to show how much his stores of knowledge could supply, he seldom escapes without the pity or resentment of his reader.

It is incident to him to be now and then entangled with an unwieldy sentiment, which he cannot well express, and will not reject; he struggles with it a while, and if it continues stubborn, comprises it in words such as occur, and leaves it to be disentangled and evolved by those who have more leisure to bestow upon it.

Not that always where the language is intricate the thought is subtle, or the image always great where the line is bulky; the equality of words to things is very often neglected, and trivial sentiments and vulgar ideas disappoint the attention, to which they are recommended by sonorous epithets and swelling figures.

But the admirers of this great poet have never less reason to indulge their hopes of supreme excellence, than when he seems fully resolved to sink them in dejection, and mollify them with tender emotions by the fall of greatness, the danger of innocence, or the crosses of love. He is not long soft and pathetick without some idle conceit, or contemptible equivocation. He no sooner begins to move, than he counteracts himself; and terrour and pity, as they are rising in the mind, are checked and blasted by sudden frigidity.

A quibble is to *Shakespeare,* what luminous vapours are to the traveller; he follows it at all adventures; it is sure to lead him out of his way, and sure to engulf him in the mire. It has some malignant power over his mind, and its fascinations are irresistible. Whatever be the dignity or profundity of his disquisition, whether he be enlarging knowledge or exalting affection, whether he be amusing attention with incidents, or enchaining it in suspense, let but a quibble spring up before him, and he leaves his work unfinished. A quibble is the golden apple for which he will always turn aside from his career, or stoop from his elevation. A quibble, poor and barren as it is, gave him such delight, that he was content to purchase it, by the sacrifice of reason, propriety and truth. A quibble was to him the fatal *Cleopatra* for which he lost the world, and was content to lose it.

It will be thought strange, that, in enumerating the defects of this writer, I have not yet mentioned his neglect of the unities; his violation of those laws which have been instituted and established by the joint authority of poets and criticks.

For his other deviations from the art of writing I resign him to critical justice, without making any other demand in his favour, than that which must be indulged to all human excellence: that his virtues be rated with his failings: But, from the censure which this irregularity may bring upon him, I shall, with due reverence to that learning which I must oppose, adventure to try how I can defend him.

His histories, being neither tragedies nor comedies are not subject to any of their laws; nothing more is necessary to all the praise which they expect, than that the changes of action be so prepared as to be understood, that the incidents be various and affecting, and the characters consistent, natural, and distinct. No other unity is intended, and therefore none is to be sought.

In his other works he has well enough preserved the unity of action. He has not, indeed, an intrigue regularly perplexed and regularly unravelled: he does not endeavour to hide his design only to discover it, for this is seldom the order of real events, and *Shakespeare* is the poet of nature: But his plan has commonly what *Aristotle* requires, a beginning, a middle, and an end; one event is concatenated with another, and the conclusion follows by easy consequence. There are perhaps some incidents that might be spared, as in other poets there is much talk that only fills up time upon the stage; but the general system makes gradual advances, and the end of the play is the end of expectation.

To the unities of time and place he has shewn no regard; and perhaps a nearer view of the principles on which they stand will diminish their value, and withdraw from them the veneration which, from the time of *Corneille*, they have very generally received, by discovering that they have given more trouble to the poet, than pleasure to the auditor.

The necessity of observing the unities of time and place arises from the supposed necessity of making the drama credible. The criticks hold it impossible, that an action of months or years can be possibly believed to pass in three hours; or that the spectator can suppose himself to sit in the theatre, while ambassadors go and return between distant kings, while armies are levied and towns besieged, while an exile wanders and returns, or till he whom they saw courting his mistress, shall lament the untimely fall of his son. The mind revolts from evident falsehood, and fiction loses its force when it departs from the resemblance of reality.

From the narrow limitation of time necessarily arises the contraction of place. The spectator, who knows that he saw the first act at *Alexandria*, cannot suppose that he sees the next at *Rome*, at a distance to which not the dragons of *Medea* could, in so short a time, have transported him; he knows with certainty that he has not changed his place, and he knows that place

cannot change itself; that what was a house cannot become a plain; that what was *Thebes* can never be *Persepolis*.

Such is the triumphant language with which a critick exults over the misery of an irregular poet, and exults commonly without resistance or reply. It is time therefore to tell him by the authority of *Shakespeare*, that he assumes, as an unquestionable principle, a position, which, while his breath is forming it into words, his understanding pronounces to be false. It is false, that any representation is mistaken for reality; that any dramatick fable in its materiality was ever credible, or, for a single moment, was ever credited.

The objection arising from the impossibility of passing the first hour at *Alexandria*, and the next at *Rome*, supposes, that when the play opens, the spectator really imagines himself at *Alexandria*, and believes that his walk to the theatre has been a voyage to *Egypt*, and that he lives in the days of *Antony* and *Cleopatra*. Surely he that imagines this may imagine more. He that can take the stage at one time for the palace of the *Ptolemies*, may take it in half an hour for the promontory of *Actium*. Delusion, if delusion be admitted, has no certain limitation; if the spectator can be once persuaded, that his old acquaintance are *Alexander* and *Caesar*, that a room illuminated with candles is the plain of *Pharsalia*, or the bank of *Granicus*, he is in a state of elevation above the reach of reason, or of truth, and from the heights of empyrean poetry, may despise the circumscriptions of terrestrial nature. There is no reason why a mind thus wandering in extasy should count the clock, or why an hour should not be a century in that calenture of the brains that can make the stage a field.

The truth is, that the spectators are always in their senses, and know, from the first act to the last, that the stage is only a stage, and that the players are only players. They came to hear a certain number of lines recited with just gesture and elegant modulation. The lines relate to some action, and an action must be in some place; but the different actions that complete a story may be in places very remote from each other; and where is the absurdity of allowing that space to represent first *Athens*, and then

Sicily, which was always known to be neither *Sicily* nor *Athens,* but a modern theatre?

By supposition, as place is introduced, time may be extended; the time required by the fable elapses for the most part between the acts; for, of so much of the action as is represented, the real and poetical duration is the same. If, in the first act, preparations for war against *Mithridates* are represented to be made in *Rome,* the event of the war may, without absurdity, be represented, in the catastrophe, as happening in *Pontus;* we know that there is neither war, nor preparation for war; we know that we are neither in *Rome* nor *Pontus;* that neither *Mithridates* nor *Lucullus* are before us. The drama exhibits successive imitations of successive actions; and why may not the second imitation represent an action that happened years after the first, if it be so connected with it, that nothing but time can be supposed to intervene? Time is, of all modes of existence, most obsequious to the imagination; a lapse of years is as easily conceived as a passage of hours. In contemplation we easily contract the time of real actions, and therefore willingly permit it to be contracted when we only see their imitation.

It will be asked, how the drama moves, if it is not credited. It is credited with all the credit due to a drama. It is credited, whenever it moves, as a just picture of a real original; as representing to the auditor what he would himself feel, if he were to do or suffer what is there feigned to be suffered or to be done. The reflection that strikes the heart is not, that the evils before us are real evils, but that they are evils to which we ourselves may be exposed. If there be any fallacy, it is not that we fancy the players, but that we fancy ourselves unhappy for a moment; but we rather lament the possibility than suppose the presence of misery, as a mother weeps over her babe, when she remembers that death may take it from her. The delight of tragedy proceeds from our consciousness of fiction; if we thought murders and treasons real, they would please no more.

Imitations produce pain or pleasure, not because they are mistaken for realities, but because they bring realities to mind. When the imagination is recreated by a painted landscape, the trees are not supposed capable to give us shade, or the fountains coolness; but we consider, how we should be pleased with such fountains playing beside us, and such woods waving over us. We are agitated in reading the history of *Henry* the Fifth, yet no man takes his book for the field of *Agencourt.* A dramatick exhibition is a book recited with concomitants that encrease or diminish its effect. Familiar comedy is often more powerful in the theatre, than in the page; imperial tragedy is always less. The humour of *Petruchio* may be heightened by grimace; but what voice or what gesture can hope to add dignity or force to the soliloquy of *Cato.*

A play read, affects the mind like a play acted. It is therefore evident, that the action is not supposed to be real; and it follows, that between the acts a longer or shorter time may be allowed to pass, and that no more account of space or duration is to be taken by the auditor of a drama, than by the reader of a narrative, before whom may pass in an hour the life of a hero, or the revolutions of an empire.

Whether *Shakespeare* knew the unities, and rejected them by design, or deviated from them by happy ignorance, it is, I think, impossible to decide, and useless to enquire. We may reasonably suppose, that, when he rose to notice, he did not want the counsels and admonitions of scholars and criticks, and that he at last deliberately persisted in a practice, which he might have begun by chance. As nothing is essential to the fable, but unity of action, and as the unities of time and place arise evidently from false assumptions, and, by circumscribing the extent of the drama, lessen its variety, I cannot think it much to be lamented, that they were not known by him, or not observed: Nor, if such another poet could arise, should I very vehemently reproach him, that his first act passed at *Venice,* and his next in *Cyprus.* Such violations of rules merely positive, become the comprehensive genius of *Shakespeare,* and such censures are suitable to the minute and slender criticism of *Voltaire:*

> *Non usque adeo permiscuit imis*
> *Longus summa dies, ut non, si voce Metelli*
> *Serventur leges, malint a Caesare tolli.*[2]

[2] "A long time does not so confuse the highest with the lowest but that laws made by Metellus may wish to be abolished by Caesar."

Yet when I speak thus slightly of dramatick rules, I cannot but recollect how much wit and learning may be produced against me; before such authorities I am afraid to stand, not that I think the present question one of those that are to be decided by mere authority, but because it is to be suspected, that these precepts have not been so easily received but for better reasons than I have yet been able to find. The result of my enquiries, in which it would be ludicrous to boast of impartiality, is, that the unities of time and place are not essential to a just drama, that though they may sometimes conduce to pleasure, they are always to be sacrificed to the nobler beauties of variety and instruction; and that a play, written with nice observation of critical rules, is to be contemplated as an elaborate curiosity, as the product of superfluous and ostentatious art, by which is shewn, rather what is possible, than what is necessary.

He that, without diminution of any other excellence, shall preserve all the unities unbroken, deserves the like applause with the architect, who shall display all the orders of architecture in a citadel, without any deduction from its strength; but the principal beauty of a citadel is to exclude the enemy; and the greatest graces of a play, are to copy nature and instruct life.

Perhaps what I have here not dogmatically but deliberately written, may recall the principles of the drama to a new examination. I am almost frighted at my own temerity; and when I estimate the fame and the strength of those that maintain the contrary opinion, am ready to sink down in reverential silence; as *Aeneas* withdrew from the defence of *Troy*, when he saw *Neptune* shaking the wall, and *Juno* heading the besiegers.

Those whom my arguments cannot persuade to give their approbation to the judgment of *Shakespeare*, will easily, if they consider the condition of his life, make some allowance for his ignorance.

Every man's performances, to be rightly estimated, must be compared with the state of the age in which he lived, and with his own particular opportunities; and though to the reader a book be not worse or better for the circumstances of the authour, yet as there is always a silent reference of human works to human abilities, and as the enquiry, how far man may extend his designs, or how high he may rate his native force, is of far greater dignity than in what rank we shall place any particular performance, curiosity is always busy to discover the instruments, as well as to survey the workmanship, to know how much is to be ascribed to original powers, and how much to casual and adventitious help. The palaces of *Peru* or *Mexico* were certainly mean and incommodious habitations, if compared to the houses of *European* monarchs; yet who could forbear to view them with astonishment, who remembered that they were built without the use of iron?

The *English* nation, in the time of *Shakespeare*, was yet struggling to emerge from barbarity. The philology of *Italy* had been transplanted hither in the reign of *Henry* the Eighth; and the learned languages had been successfully cultivated by *Lilly*, *Linacer*, and *More*; by *Pole*, *Cheke*, and *Gardiner*; and afterwards by *Smith*, *Clerk*, *Haddon*, and *Ascham*. Greek was now taught to boys in the principal schools; and those who united elegance with learning, read, with great diligence, the *Italian* and *Spanish* poets. But literature was yet confined to professed scholars, or to men and women of high rank. The publick was gross and dark; and to be able to read and write, was an accomplishment still valued for its rarity.

Nations, like individuals, have their infancy. A people newly awakened to literary curiosity, being yet unacquainted with the true state of things, knows not how to judge of that which is proposed as its resemblance. Whatever is remote from common appearances is always welcome to vulgar, as to childish credulity; and of a country unenlightened by learning, the whole people is the vulgar. The study of those who then aspired to plebeian learning was laid out upon adventures, giants, dragons, and enchantments. *The Death of Arthur* was the favourite volume.

The mind, which has feasted on the luxurious wonders of fiction, has no taste of the insipidity of truth. A play which imitated only the common occurrences of the world, would, upon the admirers of *Palmerin* and *Guy* of *Warwick*, have made little impression; he that wrote for such an audience was under the necessity of looking round for strange events and fabulous transactions, and that incredibility, by which maturer knowledge is offended, was the chief recommendation of writings, to unskilful curiosity.

Our authour's plots are generally borrowed from novels, and it is reasonable to suppose, that he chose the most popular, such as were read by many, and related by more; for his audience could not have followed him through the intricacies of the drama, had they not held the thread of the story in their hands.

The stories, which we now find only in remoter authours, were in his time accessible and familiar. The fable of *As you like it,* which is supposed to be copied from *Chaucer's* Gamelyn, was a little pamphlet of those times; and old Mr. *Cibber* remembered the tale of *Hamlet* in plain *English* prose, which the cricks have now to seek in *Saxo Grammaticus.*

His *English* histories he took from *English* chronicles and *English* ballads; and as the ancient writers were made known to his countrymen by versions, they supplied him with new subjects; he dilated some of *Plutarch's* lives into plays, when they had been translated by *North.*

His plots, whether historical or fabulous, are always crouded with incidents, by which the attention of a rude people was more easily caught than by sentiment or argumentation; and such is the power of the marvellous even over those who despise it, that every man finds his mind more strongly seized by the tragedies of *Shakespeare* than of any other writer; others please us by particular speeches, but he always makes us anxious for the event, and has perhaps excelled all but *Homer* in securing the first purpose of a writer, by exciting restless and unquenchable curiosity and compelling him that reads his work to read it through.

The shows and bustle with which his plays abound have the same original. As knowledge advances, pleasure passes from the eye to the ear, but returns, as it declines, from the ear to the eye. Those to whom our authour's labours were exhibited had more skill in pomps or processions than in poetical language, and perhaps wanted some visible and discriminated events, as comments on the dialogue. He knew how he should most please; and whether his practice is more agreeable to nature, or whether his example has prejudiced the nation, we still find that on our stage something must be done as well as said, and inactive declamation is very coldly heard, however musical or elegant, passionate or sublime.

Voltaire expresses his wonder, that our authour's extravagances are endured by a nation, which has seen the tragedy of *Cato.* Let him be answered, that *Addison* speaks the language of poets, and *Shakespeare,* of men. We find in *Cato* innumerable beauties which enamour us of its authour, but we see nothing that acquaints us with human sentiments or human actions; we place it with the fairest and the noblest progeny which judgment propagates by conjunction with learning, but *Othello* is the vigorous and vivacious offspring of observation impregnated by genius. *Cato* affords a splendid exhibition of artificial and fictitious manners, and delivers just and noble sentiments, in diction easy, elevated and harmonious, but its hopes and fears communicate no vibration to the heart; the composition refers us only to the writer; we pronounce the name of *Cato,* but we think on *Addison.* . . .

From the Life of Cowley

COWLEY, like other poets who have written with narrow views, and, instead of tracing intellectual pleasures in the mind of man, paid their court to temporary prejudices, has been at one time too much praised, and too much neglected at another.

Wit, like all other things subject by their nature to the choice of man, has its changes and fashions, and at different times takes different forms. About the beginning of the seventeenth century appeared a race of writers that may be termed the *metaphysical poets,* of whom, in a criticism on the works of Cowley, it is not improper to give some account.

Life of Cowley. From *Lives of the English Poets* (1779-81). This celebrated discussion of the "metaphysical" poets, which comprises a distinct unit in the *Life of Cowley,* is not an "attack," as has occasionally been thought. It is an attempt to analyze and offer a balanced estimate of their distinctive characteristics.

The metaphysical poets were men of learning, and to show their learning was their whole endeavour; but, unluckily resolving to show it in rhyme, instead of writing poetry they only wrote verses, and very often such verses as stood the trial of the finger better than of the ear; for the modulation was so imperfect, that they were only found to be verses by counting the syllables.

If the father of criticism has rightly denominated poetry τέχνη μιμητική, *an imitative art,* these writers will, without great wrong, lose their right to the name of poets, for they cannot be said to have imitated anything; they neither copied nature nor life, neither painted the forms of matter, nor represented the operations of intellect.

Those, however, who deny them to be poets, allow them to be wits. Dryden confesses of himself and his contemporaries, that they fall below Donne in wit, but maintains that they surpass him in poetry.

If wit be well described by Pope, as being "that which has been often thought, but was never before so well expressed," they certainly never attained, nor ever sought it; for they endeavoured to be singular in their thoughts, and were careless of their diction. But Pope's account of wit is undoubtedly erroneous: he depresses it below its natural dignity, and reduces it from strength of thought to happiness of language.[1]

If by a more noble and more adequate conception that be considered as wit which is at once natural and new, that which, though not obvious, is, upon its first production, acknowledged to be just; if it be that which he that never found it wonders how he missed, to wit of this kind the metaphysical poets have seldom risen. Their thoughts are often new, but seldom natural; they are not obvious, but neither are they just; and the reader, far from wondering that he missed them, wonders more frequently by what perverseness of industry they were ever found.

But wit,[2] abstracted from its effects upon the hearer, may be more rigorously and philosophically considered as a kind of *discordia concors;* a combination of dissimilar images, or discovery of occult resemblances in things apparently unlike. Of wit, thus defined, they have more than enough. The most hetrogeneous ideas are yoked by violence together; nature and art are ransacked for illustrations, comparisons, and allusions; their learning instructs, and their subtlety surprises; but the reader commonly thinks his improvement dearly bought, and, though he sometimes admires, is seldom pleased.

From this account of their compositions it will be readily inferred that they were not successful in representing or moving the affections. As they were wholly employed on something unexpected and surprising, they had no regard to that uniformity of sentiment which enables us to conceive and to excite the pains and the pleasure of other minds: they never inquired what, on any occasion, they should have said or done, but wrote rather as beholders than partakers of human nature; as beings looking upon good and evil, impassive and at leisure; as Epicurean deities, making remarks on the actions of men, and the vicissitudes of life, without interest and without emotion. Their courtship was void of fondness, and their lamentation of sorrow. Their wish was only to say what they hoped had been never said before.

Nor was the sublime more within their reach than the pathetic; for they never attempted that comprehension and expanse of thought which at once fills the whole mind, and of which the first effect is sudden astonishment, and the second rational admiration. Sublimity is produced by aggregation, and littleness by dispersion. Great thoughts are always general, and consist in positions not limited by exceptions, and in descriptions not descending to minuteness. It is with great propriety that subtlety, which in its original import means exility of particles, is taken in its metaphorical meaning for nicety of

---

[1] The conception of wit discussed here is one generally assumed in much neoclassic writing of the late seventeenth and the eighteenth centuries. "Wit" had become increasingly connected with "taste," "judgment," and "propriety"—including propriety of language. It is characteristic of Johnson's emphasis on "strength of thought" in poetry that he should feel that such a conception of wit "depresses it below its natural dignity."

[2] It is here that Johnson advances a definition of "wit" that can include the "metaphysical" poets. In doing so, he is somewhat elaborating the old distinction between *wit written* (in the poem) and *wit writing* (the energetic activity of mind in the poet, "abstracted from its effects upon the hearer"). It is "wit" in this latter sense that Johnson finds most eminently characteristic of the "metaphysical" poets, that is, wit considered "more rigorously and philosophically," and as a psychological process or activity of mind.

distinction. Those writers who lay on the watch for novelty could have little hope of greatness; for great things cannot have escaped former observation. Their attempts were always analytic; they broke every image into fragments; and could no more represent, by their slender conceits and laboured particularities, the prospects of nature, or the scenes of life, than he who dissects a sunbeam with a prism can exhibit the wide effulgence of a summer noon.

What they wanted however of the sublime, they endeavoured to supply by hyperbole; their amplification had no limits; they left not only reason but fancy behind them; and produced combinations of confused magnificence, that not only could not be credited, but could not be imagined.

Yet great labour, directed by great abilities, is never wholly lost: if they frequently threw away their wit upon false conceits, they likewise sometimes struck out unexpected truth; if their conceits were far-fetched, they were often worth the carriage. To write on their plan, it was at least necessary to read and think. No man could be born a metaphysical poet, nor assume the dignity of a writer, by descriptions copied from descriptions, by imitations borrowed from imitations, by traditional imagery, and hereditary similes, by readiness of rhyme, and volubility of syllables.

In perusing the works of this race of authors, the mind is exercised either by recollection or inquiry; either something already learned is to be retrieved, or something new is to be examined. If their greatness seldom elevates, their acuteness often surprises; if the imagination is not always gratified, at least the powers of reflection and comparison are employed; and in the mass of materials which ingenious absurdity has thrown together, genuine wit and useful knowledge may be sometimes found buried perhaps in grossness of expression, but useful to those who know their value; and such as, when they are expanded to perspicuity, and polished to elegance, may give lustre to works which have more propriety though less copiousness of sentiment.

From the Life of Dryden

DRYDEN may be properly considered as the father of English criticism, as the writer who first taught us to determine upon principles the merit of composition. Of our former poets, the greatest dramatist wrote without rules, conducted through life and nature by a genius that rarely misled, and rarely deserted him. Of the rest, those who knew the laws of propriety had neglected to teach them.

Two *Arts of English Poetry* were written in the days of Elizabeth by Webb and Puttenham, from which something might be learned, and a few hints had been given by Jonson and Cowley; but Dryden's *Essay on Dramatic Poetry* was the first regular and valuable treatise on the art of writing.

He who, having formed his opinions in the present age of English literature, turns back to peruse this dialogue, will not perhaps find much increase of knowledge, or much novelty of in-

struction; but he is to remember that critical principles were then in the hands of a few, who had gathered them partly from the ancients, and partly from the Italians and French. The structure of dramatic poems was then not generally understood. Audiences applauded by instinct; and poets perhaps often pleased by chance.

A writer who obtains his full purpose loses himself in his own lustre. Of an opinion which is no longer doubted, the evidence ceases to be examined. Of an art universally practised, the first teacher is forgotten. Learning once made popular is no longer learning; it has the appearance of something which we have bestowed upon ourselves, as the dew appears to rise from the field which it refreshes.

To judge rightly of an author, we must transport ourselves to his time, and examine what were the wants of his contemporaries, and what were his means of supplying them. That which is easy at one time was difficult at another. Dryden at least imported his science, and gave his country what it wanted before; or, rather, he im-

Life of Dryden. From *Lives of the English Poets* (1779-81).

ported only the materials, and manufactured them by his own skill.

The *Dialogue on the Drama* was one of his first essays of criticism, written when he was yet a timorous candidate for reputation, and therefore laboured with that diligence which he might allow himself somewhat to remit, when his name gave sanction to his positions, and his awe of the public was abated, partly by custom, and partly by success. It will not be easy to find, in all the opulence of our language, a treatise so artfully variegated with successive representations of opposite probabilities, so enlivened with imagery, so brightened with illustrations. His portraits of the English dramatists are wrought with great spirit and diligence. The account of Shakespeare may stand as a perpetual model of encomiastic criticism; exact without minuteness, and lofty without exaggeration. The praise lavished by Longinus, on the attestation of the heroes of Marathon, by Demosthenes, fades away before it. In a few lines is exhibited a character, so extensive in its comprehension, and so curious in its limitations, that nothing can be added, diminished, or reformed; nor can the editors and admirers of Shakespeare, in all their emulation of reverence, boast of much more than of having diffused and paraphrased this epitome of excellence, of having changed Dryden's gold for baser metal, of lower value though of greater bulk.

In this, and in all his other essays on the same subject, the criticism of Dryden is the criticism of a poet; not a dull collection of theorems, nor a rude detection of faults, which perhaps the censor was not able to have committed; but a gay and vigorous dissertation, where delight is mingled with instruction, and where the author proves his right of judgment by his power of performance.

The different manner and effect with which critical knowledge may be conveyed, was perhaps never more clearly exemplified than in the performances of Rymer [1] and Dryden. It was said of a dispute between two mathematicians, "malim cum Scaligero errare, quam cum Clavio recte sapere"; that "it was more eligible to go wrong with one than right with the other." A tendency of the same kind every mind must feel at the perusal of Dryden's prefaces and Rymer's

[1] See above, p. 9.

discourses. With Dryden we are wandering in quest of Truth; whom we find, if we find her at all, dressed in the graces of elegance; and, if we miss her, the labour of the pursuit rewards itself; we are led only through fragrance and flowers. Rymer, without taking a nearer, takes a rougher way; every step is to be made through thorns and brambles; and Truth, if we meet her, appears repulsive by her mien, and ungraceful by her habit. Dryden's criticism has the majesty of a queen; Rymer's has the ferocity of a tyrant.

As he had studied with great diligence the art of poetry, and enlarged or rectified his notions by experience perpetually increasing, he had his mind stored with principles and observations; he poured out his knowledge with little labour; for of labour, notwithstanding the multiplicity of his productions, there is sufficient reason to suspect that he was not a lover. To write *con amore*, with fondness for the employment, with perpetual touches and retouches, with unwillingness to take leave of his own idea, and an unwearied pursuit of unattainable perfection, was, I think, no part of his character.

His criticism may be considered as general or occasional. In his general precepts, which depend upon the nature of things, and the structure of the human mind, he may doubtless be safely recommended to the confidence of the reader; but his occasional and particular positions were sometimes interested, sometimes negligent, and sometimes capricious. . . .

What he wishes to say, he says at hazard; he cited *Gorboduc*, which he had never seen; gives a false account of Chapman's versification; and discovers in the preface to his *Fables* that he translated the first book of the Iliad, without knowing what was in the second.

It will be difficult to prove that Dryden never made any great advances in literature. As having distinguished himself at Westminster under the tuition of Busby, who advanced his scholars to a height of knowledge very rarely attained in grammar-schools, he resided afterwards at Cambridge; it is not to be supposed that his skill in the ancient languages was deficient, compared with that of common students, but his scholastic acquisitions seem not proportionate to his opportunities and abilities. He could not, like Milton or Cowley, have made his name illustrious merely by his learning. He mentions but few books, and those such as lie in the beaten track of regular study; from which if ever he departs, he is in danger of losing himself in unknown regions.

In his *Dialogue on the Drama* he pronounces with great confidence that the Latin tragedy of *Medea* is not Ovid's, because it is not sufficiently interesting and pathetic. He might have determined the question upon surer evidence; for it is quoted by Quintilian as the work of Seneca; and the only line which remains of Ovid's play—for one line is left us—is not there to be found. There was therefore no need of the gravity of conjecture, or the discussion of plot or sentiment, to find what was already known upon higher authority than such discussions can ever reach.

His literature, though not always free from ostentation, will be commonly found either obvious, and made his own by the art of dressing it; or superficial, which, by what he gives, shows what he wanted; or erroneous, hastily collected, and negligently scattered.

Yet it cannot be said that his genius is ever unprovided of matter, or that his fancy languishes in penury of ideas. His works abound with knowledge, and sparkle with illustrations. There is scarcely any science or faculty that does not supply him with occasional images and lucky similitudes; every page discovers a mind very widely acquainted both with art and nature, and in full possession of great stores of intellectual wealth. Of him that knows much, it is natural to suppose that he has read with diligence; yet I rather believe that the knowledge of Dryden was gleaned from accidental intelligence and various conversation, by a quick apprehension, a judicious selection, and a happy memory, a keen appetite of knowledge, and a powerful digestion; by vigilance that permitted nothing to pass without notice, and a habit of reflection that suffered nothing useful to be lost. A mind like Dryden's, always curious, always active, to which every understanding was proud to be associated, and of which every one solicited the regard, by an ambitious display of himself, had a more pleasant, perhaps a nearer way to knowledge than by the silent progress of solitary reading. I do not

suppose that he despised books, or intentionally neglected them; but that he was carried out by the impetuosity of his genius to more vivid and speedy instructors; and that his studies were rather desultory and fortuitous than constant and systematical.

It must be confessed that he scarcely ever appears to want book-learning but when he mentions books; and to him may be transferred the praise which he gives his master Charles:

> His conversation, wit, and parts,
> His knowledge in the noblest useful arts,
>   Were such, dead authors could not give,
>   But habitudes of those that live;
> Who lighting him, did greater lights receive;
>   He drain'd from all, and all they knew,
> His apprehensions quick, his judgment true:
>   That the most learn'd with shame confess
> His knowledge more, his reading only less.

Of all this, however, if the proof be demanded, I will not undertake to give it; the atoms of probability, of which my opinion has been formed, lie scattered over all his works; and by him who thinks the question worth his notice, his works must be perused with very close attention.

Criticism, either didactic or defensive, occupies almost all his prose, except those pages which he has devoted to his patrons; but none of his prefaces were ever thought tedious. They have not the formality of a settled style, in which the first half of the sentence betrays the other. The clauses are never balanced, nor the periods modelled: every word seems to drop by chance, though it falls into its proper place. Nothing is cold or languid; the whole is airy, animated, and vigorous; what is little is gay; what is great is splendid. He may be thought to mention himself too frequently; but while he forces himself upon our esteem, we cannot refuse him to stand high in his own. Everything is excused by the play of images and the sprightliness of expression. Though all is easy, nothing is feeble; though all seems careless, there is nothing harsh; and though since his earlier works more than a century has passed, they have nothing yet uncouth or obsolete.

From the Life of Pope

THE PERSON of Pope is well known not to have been formed by the nicest model. He has, in his account of the "Little Club," compared himself to a spider, and by another is described as protuberant behind and before. He is said to have been beautiful in his infancy; but he was of a constitution originally feeble and weak; and as bodies of a tender frame are easily distorted, his deformity was probably in part the effect of his application. His stature was so low, that, to bring him to a level with common tables, it was necessary to raise his seat. But his face was not displeasing, and his eyes were animated and vivid.

By natural deformity, or accidental distortion, his vital functions were so much disordered, that his life was a "long disease." His most frequent assailant was the headache, which he used to relieve by inhaling the steam of coffee, which he very frequently required.

Most of what can be told concerning his petty peculiarities was communicated by a female domestic of the Earl of Oxford, who knew him perhaps after the middle of life. He was then so weak as to stand in perpetual need of female attendance; extremely sensible of cold, so that he wore a kind of fur doublet under a shirt of a very coarse warm linen with fine sleeves. When he rose, he was invested in bodice made of stiff canvas, being scarce able to hold himself erect till they were laced, and he then put on a flannel waistcoat. One side was contracted. His legs were so slender, that he enlarged their bulk with three pair of stockings, which were drawn on and off by the maid; for he was not able to dress or undress himself, and neither went to bed nor rose without help. His weakness made it very difficult for him to be clean.

His hair had fallen almost all away; and he used to dine sometimes with Lord Oxford, privately, in a velvet cap. His dress of ceremony was black, with a tye-wig and a little sword.

The indulgence and accommodation which his

sickness required had taught him all the unpleasing and unsocial qualities of a valetudinary man. He expected that everything should give way to his ease or humour, as a child whose parents will not hear her cry, has an unresisted dominion in the nursery.

> C'est que l'enfant toujours est homme,
> C'est que l'homme est toujours enfant.[1]

When he wanted to sleep, he "nodded in company"; and once slumbered at his own table while the Prince of Wales was talking of poetry.

The reputation which his friendship gave procured him many invitations; but he was a very troublesome inmate. He brought no servant, and had so many wants that a numerous attendance was scarcely able to supply them. Wherever he was, he left no room for another, because he exacted the attention and employed the activity of the whole family. His errands were so frequent and frivolous that the footmen in time avoided and neglected him; and the Earl of Oxford discharged some of the servants for their resolute refusal of his messages. The maids, when they had neglected their business, alleged that they had been employed by Mr. Pope. One of his constant demands was of coffee in the night, and to the woman that waited on him in his chamber he was very burthensome: but he was careful to recompense her want of sleep; and Lord Oxford's servant declared, that in a house where her business was to answer his call she would not ask for wages.

He had another fault, easily incident to those who, suffering much pain, think themselves entitled to what pleasures they can snatch. He was too indulgent to his appetite; he loved meat highly seasoned and of strong taste; and, at the intervals of the table, amused himself with biscuits and dry conserves. If he sat down to a variety of dishes, he would oppress his stomach with repletion; and though he seemed angry when a dram was offered him, did not forbear to drink it. His friends, who knew the avenues

Life of Pope. From *Lives of the English Poets.* Johnson's treatment of the general character of Pope and of his work, which follows the biography of Pope, is here printed complete.

[1] "It is true that the child is always the man, and the man is always the child."

to his heart, pampered him with presents of luxury, which he did not suffer to stand neglected. The death of great men is not always proportioned to the lustre of their lives. Hannibal, says Juvenal, did not perish by a javelin or a sword; the slaughters of Cannae were revenged by a ring. The death of Pope was imputed by some of his friends to a silver saucepan, in which it was his delight to heat potted lampreys.

That he loved too well to eat is certain; but that his sensuality shortened his life will not be hastily concluded, when it is remembered that a conformation so irregular lasted six and fifty years, notwithstanding such pertinacious diligence of study and meditation.

In all his intercourse with mankind he had great delight in artifice, and endeavoured to attain all his purposes by indirect and unsuspected methods. "He hardly drank tea without a stratagem." If, at the house of his friends, he wanted any accommodation, he was not willing to ask for it in plain terms, but would mention it remotely as something convenient; though, when it was procured, he soon made it appear for whose sake it had been recommended. Thus he teased Lord Orrery till he obtained a screen. He practised his arts on such small occasions, that Lady Bolingbroke used to say, in a French phrase, that "he played the politician about cabbages and turnips." His unjustifiable impression of *The Patriot King*, as it can be imputed to no particular motive, must have proceeded from his general habit of secrecy and cunning; he caught an opportunity of a sly trick, and pleased himself with the thought of outwitting Bolingbroke.

In familiar or convivial conversation it does not appear that he excelled. He may be said to have resembled Dryden as being not one that was distinguished by vivacity in company. It is remarkable that, so near his time, so much should be known of what he has written and so little of what he has said: traditional memory retains no sallies of raillery nor sentences of observation; nothing either pointed or solid, either wise or merry. One apophthegm only stands upon record. When an objection raised against his inscription for Shakespeare was defended by the authority of Patrick, he replied—"horresco referens"—that "he would allow the publisher of a Dictionary to know the meaning of a single word, but not of two words put together."

He was fretful and easily displeased, and allowed himself to be capriciously resentful. He would sometimes leave Lord Oxford silently, no one could tell why, and was to be courted back by more letters and messages than the footmen were willing to carry. The table was indeed infested by Lady Mary Wortley, who was the friend of Lady Oxford, and who, knowing his peevishness, could by no intreaties be restrained from contradicting him, till their disputes were sharpened to such asperity that one or the other quitted the house.

He sometimes condescended to be jocular with servants or inferiors; but by no merriment, either of others or his own, was he ever seen excited to laughter.

Of his domestic character frugality was a part eminently remarkable. Having determined not to be dependent, he determined not to be in want, and therefore wisely and magnanimously rejected all temptations to expense unsuitable to his fortune. This general care must be universally approved; but it sometimes appeared in petty artifices of parsimony, such as the practice of writing his compositions on the back of letters, as may be seen in the remaining copy of the Iliad, by which perhaps in five years five shillings were saved; or in a niggardly reception of his friends and scantiness of entertainment, as, when he had two guests in his house, he would set at supper a single pint upon the table; and, having himself taken two small glasses, would retire and say, "Gentlemen, I leave you to your wine." Yet he tells his friends that "he has a heart for all, a house for all, and, whatever they may think, a fortune for all."

He sometimes, however, made a splendid dinner, and is said to have wanted no part of the skill or elegance which such performances require. That this magnificence should be often displayed, that obstinate prudence with which he conducted his affairs would not permit; for his revenue, certain and casual, amounted only to about eight hundred pounds a year, of which however he declares himself able to assign one hundred to charity.

Of this fortune, which, as it arose from public approbation, was very honourably obtained, his imagination seems to have been too full: it would be hard to find a man, so well entitled to notice by his wit, that ever delighted so much in talking of his money. In his letters and in his poems, his garden and his grotto, his quincunx and his vines, or some hints of his opulence, are always to be found. The great topic of his ridicule is poverty; the crimes with which he reproaches his antagonists are their debts, their habitation in the Mint, and their want of a dinner. He seems to be of an opinion not very uncommon in the world, that to want money is to want everything.

Next to the pleasure of contemplating his possessions seems to be that of enumerating the men of high rank with whom he was acquainted, and whose notice he loudly proclaims not to have been obtained by any practices of meanness or servility, a boast which was never denied to be true, and to which very few poets have ever aspired. Pope never set genius to sale; he never flattered those whom he did not love, or praised those whom he did not esteem. Savage however remarked, that he began a little to relax his dignity when he wrote a distich for "his Highness's dog."

His admiration of the great seems to have increased in the advance of life. He passed over peers and statesmen to inscribe his *Iliad* to Congreve, with a magnanimity of which the praise had been complete, had his friend's virtue been equal to his wit. Why he was chosen for so great an honour it is not now possible to know; there is no trace in literary history of any particular intimacy between them. The name of Congreve appears in the letters among those of his other friends, but without any observable distinction or consequence.

To his latter works, however, he took care to annex names dignified with titles, but was not very happy in his choice; for, except Lord Bathurst, none of his noble friends were such as that a good man would wish to have his intimacy with them known to posterity: he can derive little honour from the notice of Cobham, Burlington, or Bolingbroke.

Of his social qualities, if an estimate be made from his Letters, an opinion too favourable cannot easily be formed; they exhibit a perpetual and unclouded effulgence of general benevolence and particular fondness. There is nothing but liberality, gratitude, constancy, and tenderness. It has been so long said as to be commonly believed, that the true characters of men may be found in their letters, and that he who writes to his friends lays his heart open before him. But the truth is, that such were the simple friendships of the "Golden Age," and are now the friendships only of children. Very few can boast of hearts which they dare lay open to themselves, and of which, by whatever accident exposed, they do not shun a distinct and continued view; and, certainly, what we hide from ourselves we do not show to our friends. There is, indeed, no transaction which offers stronger temptations to fallacy and sophistication than epistolary intercourse. In the eagerness of conversation the first emotions of the mind often burst out before they are considered; in the tumult of business, interest and passion have their genuine effect; but a friendly letter is a calm and deliberate performance, in the cool of leisure, in the stillness of solitude, and surely no man sits down to depreciate by design his own character.

Friendship has no tendency to secure veracity; for by whom can a man so much wish to be thought better than he is, as by him whose kindness he desires to gain or keep? Even in writing to the world there is less constraint; the author is not confronted with his reader, and takes his chance of approbation among the different dispositions of mankind; but a letter is addressed to a single mind, of which the prejudices and partialities are known, and must therefore please, if not by favouring them, by forbearing to oppose them.

To charge those favourable representations which men give of their own minds with the guilt of hypocritical falsehood, would show more severity than knowledge. The writer commonly believes himself. Almost every man's thoughts, while they are general, are right; and most hearts are pure while temptation is away. It is easy to awaken generous sentiments in privacy; to despise death when there is no danger; to glow with benovelence when there is nothing to be given. While such ideas are formed they are felt, and self-love does not suspect the gleam of virtue to be the meteor of fancy.

If the Letters of Pope are considered merely as compositions, they seem to be premeditated and artificial. It is one thing to write, because there is something which the mind wishes to discharge; and another to solicit the imagination, because ceremony or vanity requires something to be written. Pope confesses his early letters to be vitiated with *affectation and ambition:* to know whether he disentangled himself from these perverters of epistolary integrity his book and his life must be set in comparison.

One of his favourite topics is contempt of his own poetry. For this, if it had been real, he would deserve no commendation; and in this he was certainly not sincere, for his high value of himself was sufficiently observed; and of what could he be proud but of his poetry? He writes, he says, when "he has just nothing else to do"; yet Swift complains that he was never at leisure for conversation, because he "had always some poetical scheme in his head." It was punctually required that his writing-box should be set upon his bed before he rose; and Lord Oxford's domestic related, that in the dreadful winter of Forty [1740] she was called from her bed by him four times in one night to supply him with paper lest he should lose a thought.

He pretends insensibility to censure and criticism, though it was observed by all who knew him that every pamphlet disturbed his quiet, and that his extreme irritability laid him open to perpetual vexation; but he wished to despise his critics, and therefore hoped that he did despise them.

As he happened to live in two reigns when the Court paid little attention to poetry, he nursed in his mind a foolish disesteem of Kings, and proclaims that "he never sees Courts." Yet a little regard shown him by the Prince of Wales melted his obduracy; and he had not much to say when he was asked by his Royal Highness, "How he could love a Prince while he disliked Kings?"

He very frequently professes contempt of the world, and represents himself as looking on mankind, sometimes with gay indifference, as on emmets of a hillock, below his serious attention; and sometimes with gloomy indignation, as on monsters more worthy of hatred than of pity. These were dispositions apparently counterfeited. How could he despise those whom he lived by pleasing, and on whose approbation his esteem of himself was superstructed? Why should he hate those to whose favour he owed his honour and his ease? Of things that terminate in human life, the world is the proper judge; to despise its sentence, if it were possible, is not just; and if it were just, is not possible. Pope was far enough

from this unreasonable temper; he was sufficiently *a fool to Fame,* and his fault was, that he pretended to neglect it. His levity and his sullenness were only in his Letters; he passed through common life, sometimes vexed, and sometimes pleased, with the natural emotions of common men.

His scorn of the Great is repeated too often to be real; no man thinks much of that which he despises; and as falsehood is always in danger of inconsistency, he makes it his boast at another time that he lives among them.

It is evident that his own importance swells often in his mind. He is afraid of writing, lest the clerks of the Post-office should know his secrets; he has many enemies; he considers himself as surrounded by universal jealousy; "after many deaths, and many dispersions, two or three of us," says he, "may still be brought together, not to plot, but to divert ourselves, and the world too, if it pleases"; and they can live together, and "show what friends wits may be, in spite of all the fools in the world." All this while it was likely that the clerks did not know his hand; he certainly had no more enemies than a public character like his inevitably excites; and with what degree of friendship the wits might live, very few were so much fools as ever to inquire.

Some part of this pretended discontent he learned from Swift, and expresses it, I think, most frequently in his correspondence with him. Swift's resentment was unreasonable, but it was sincere; Pope's was the mere mimicry of his friend, a fictitious part which he began to play before it became him. When he was only twenty-five years old, he related that "a glut of study and retirement had thrown him on the world," and that there was danger lest "a glut of the world should throw him back upon study and retirement." To this Swift answered with great propriety, that Pope had not yet either acted or suffered enough in the world to have become weary of it. And, indeed, it must be some very powerful reason that can drive back to solitude him who has once enjoyed the pleasures of society.

In the Letters both of Swift and Pope there appears such narrowness of mind as makes them insensible of any excellence that has not some affinity with their own, and confines their esteem and approbation to so small a number, that who-ever should form his opinion of the age from their representation, would suppose them to have lived amidst ignorance and barbarity, unable to find among their contemporaries either virtue or intelligence, and persecuted by those that could not understand them.

When Pope murmurs at the world, when he professes contempt of fame, when he speaks of riches and poverty, of success and disappointment, with negligent indifference, he certainly does not express his habitual and settled sentiments, but either wilfully disguises his own character, or, what is more likely, invests himself with temporary qualities, and sallies out in the colours of the present moment. His hopes and fears, his joys and sorrows, acted strongly upon his mind; and if he differed from others, it was not by carelessness; he was irritable and resentful; his malignity to Philips, whom he had first made ridiculous, and then hated for being angry, continued too long. Of his vain desire to make Bentley contemptible, I never heard any adequate reason. He was sometimes wanton in his attacks; and, before Chandos, Lady Wortley, and Hill, was mean in his retreat.

The virtues which seem to have had most of his affection were liberality and fidelity of friendship, in which it does not appear that he was other than he describes himself. His fortune did not suffer his charity to be splendid and conspicuous; but he assisted Dodsley with a hundred pounds, that he might open a shop; and of the subscription of forty pounds a year that he raised for Savage, twenty were paid by himself. He was accused of loving money, but his love was eagerness to gain, not solicitude to keep it.

In the duties of friendship he was zealous and constant; his early maturity of mind commonly united him with men older than himself; and therefore, without attaining any considerable length of life, he saw many companions of his youth sink into the grave; but it does not appear that he lost a single friend by coldness or by injury; those who loved him once, continued their kindness. His ungrateful mention of Allen in his will was the effect of his adherence to one whom he had known much longer, and whom he naturally loved with greater fondness. His violation of the trust reposed in him by Bolingbroke could have no motive inconsistent with the warm-est affection; he either thought the action so near to indifferent that he forgot it, or so laudable that he expected his friend to approve it.

It was reported, with such confidence as almost to enforce belief, that in the papers intrusted to his executors was found a defamatory Life of Swift, which he had prepared as an instrument of vengeance, to be used if any provocation should be ever given. About this I inquired of the Earl of Marchmont, who assured me that no such piece was among his remains.

The religion in which he lived and died was that of the Church of Rome, to which in his correspondence with Racine he professes himself a sincere adherent. That he was not scrupulously pious in some part of his life, is known by many idle and indecent applications of sentences taken from the Scriptures; a mode of merriment which a good man dreads for its profaneness, and a witty man disdains for its easiness and vulgarity. But to whatever levities he has been betrayed, it does not appear that his principles were ever corrupted, or that he ever lost his belief of Revelation. The positions which he transmitted from Bolingbroke he seems not to have understood, and was pleased with an interpretation that made them orthodox.

A man of such exalted superiority, and so little moderation, would naturally have all his delinquencies observed and aggravated: those who could not deny that he was excellent, would rejoice to find that he was not perfect.

Perhaps it may be imputed to the unwillingness with which the same man is allowed to possess many advantages, that his learning has been depreciated. He certainly was, in his early life, a man of great literary curiosity; and when he wrote his *Essay on Criticism* had, for his age, a very wide acquaintance with books. When he entered into the living world, it seems to have happened to him as to many others, that he was less attentive to dead masters; he studied in the academy of Paracelsus, and made the universe his favourite volume. He gathered his notions fresh from reality, not from the copies of authors, but the originals of Nature. Yet there is no reason to believe that literature ever lost his esteem; he always professed to love reading; and Dobson, who spent some time at his house translating his *Essay on Man*, when I asked him what learning he found him to possess, answered,

"More than I expected." His frequent references to history, his allusions to various kinds of knowledge, and his images selected from art and nature, with his observations on the operations of the mind and the modes of life, show an intelligence perpetually on the wing, excursive, vigorous, and diligent, eager to pursue knowledge, and attentive to retain it.

From this curiosity arose the desire of travelling, to which he alludes in his verses to Jervas, and which, though he never found an opportunity to gratify it, did not leave him till his life declined.

Of his intellectual character, the constituent and fundamental principle was good sense, a prompt and intuitive perception of consonance and propriety. He saw immediately, of his own conceptions, what was to be chosen, and what to be rejected; and, in the works of others, what was to be shunned, and what was to be copied.

But good sense alone is a sedate and quiescent quality, which manages its possessions well, but does not increase them; it collects few materials for its own operations, and preserves safety, but never gains supremacy. Pope had likewise genius; a mind active, ambitious, and adventurous, always investigating, always aspiring; in its widest searches still longing to go forward, in its highest flights still wishing to be higher; always imagining something greater than it knows, always endeavouring more than it can do.

To assist these powers, he is said to have had great strength and exactness of memory. That which he had heard or read was not easily lost; and he had before him not only what his own meditations suggested, but what he had found in other writers, that might be accommodated to his present purpose.

These benefits of nature he improved by incessant and unwearied diligence; he had recourse to every source of intelligence, and lost no opportunity of information; he consulted the living as well as the dead; he read his compositions to his friends, and was never content with mediocrity when excellence could be attained. He considered poetry as the business of his life; and, however he might seem to lament his occupation, he followed it with constancy; to make verses was his first labour, and to mend them was his last.

From his attention to poetry he was never diverted. If conversation offered anything that could be improved, he committed it to paper; if a thought, or perhaps an expression more happy than was common, rose to his mind, he was careful to write it; an independent distich was preserved for an opportunity of insertion; and some little fragments have been found containing lines, or parts of lines, to be wrought upon at some other time.

He was one of those few whose labour is their pleasure: he was never elevated to negligence, nor wearied to impatience; he never passed a fault unamended by indifference, nor quitted it by despair. He laboured his works first to gain reputation and afterwards to keep it.

Of composition there are different methods. Some employ at once memory and invention, and, with little intermediate use of the pen, form and polish large masses by continued meditation, and write their productions only when, in their own opinion, they have completed them. It is related of Virgil, that his custom was to pour out a great number of verses in the morning, and pass the day in retrenching exuberances and correcting inaccuracies. The method of Pope, as may be collected from his translation, was to write his first thoughts in his first words, and gradually to amplify, decorate, rectify, and refine them.

With such faculties, and such dispositions, he excelled every other writer in poetical prudence; he wrote in such a manner as might expose him to few hazards. He used almost always the same fabric of verse; and, indeed, by those few essays which he made of any other, he did not enlarge his reputation. Of this uniformity the certain consequence was readiness and dexterity. By perpetual practice, language had, in his mind, a systematical arrangement; having always the same use for words, he had words so selected and combined as to be ready at his call. This increase of facility he confessed himself to have perceived in the progress of his translation.

But what was yet of more importance, his effusions were always voluntary, and his subjects chosen by himself. His independence secured him from drudging at a task, and labouring upon a barren topic: he never exchanged praise for money, nor opened a shop of condolence or congratulation. His poems, therefore. were scarce ever temporary. He suffered coronations and royal marriages to pass without a song, and derived no opportunities from recent events, nor any popularity from the accidental disposition of his readers. He was never reduced to the necessity of soliciting the sun to shine upon a birthday, of calling the Graces and Virtues to a wedding, or of saying what multitudes have said before him. When he could produce nothing new, he was at liberty to be silent.

His publications were for the same reason never hasty. He is said to have sent nothing to the press till it had lain two years under his inspection: it is at least certain that he ventured nothing without nice examination. He suffered the tumult of imagination to subside, and the novelties of invention to grow familiar. He knew that the mind is always enamoured of its own productions, and did not trust his first fondness. He consulted his friends, and listened with great willingness to criticism; and, what was of more importance, he consulted himself, and let nothing pass against his own judgment.

He professed to have learned his poetry from Dryden, whom, whenever an opportunity was presented, he praised through his whole life with unvaried liberality; and perhaps his character may receive some illustration, if he be compared with his master.

Integrity of understanding and nicety of discernment were not allotted in a less proportion to Dryden than to Pope. The rectitude of Dryden's mind was sufficiently shown by the dismission of his poetical prejudices, and the rejection of unnatural thoughts and rugged numbers. But Dryden never desired to apply all the judgment that he had. He wrote, and professed to write, merely for the people; and when he pleased others, he contented himself. He spent no time in struggles to rouse latent powers; he never attempted to make that better which was already good, nor often to mend what he must have known to be faulty. He wrote, as he tells us, with very little consideration; when occasion or necessity called upon him, he poured out what the present moment happened to supply, and, when once it had passed the press, ejected it from his mind; for when he had no pecuniary interest, he had no further solicitude.

Pope was not content to satisfy; he desired to excel, and therefore always endeavoured to do his best: he did not court the candour, but dared the judgment of his reader, and, expecting no indulgence from others, he showed none to himself. He examined lines and words with minute and punctilious observation, and retouched every part with indefatigable diligence, till he had left nothing to be forgiven.

For this reason he kept his pieces very long in his hands, while he considered and reconsidered them. The only poems which can be supposed to have been written with such regard to the times as might hasten their publication were the two satires of *Thirty-eight*; of which Dodsley told me that they were brought to him by the author, that they might be fairly copied. "Almost every line," he said, "was then written twice over; I gave him a clean transcript, which he sent some time afterwards to me for the press, with almost every line written twice over a second time."

His declaration that his care for his works ceased at their publication was not strictly true. His parental attention never abandoned them; what he found amiss in the first edition, he silently corrected in those that followed. He appears to have revised the Iliad, and freed it from some of its imperfections; and the *Essay on Criticism* received many improvements after its first appearance. It will seldom be found that he altered without adding clearness, elegance, or vigour. Pope had perhaps the judgment of Dryden; but Dryden certainly wanted the diligence of Pope.

In acquired knowledge, the superiority must be allowed to Dryden, whose education was more scholastic, and who before he became an author had been allowed more time for study, with better means of information. His mind has a larger range, and he collects his images and illustrations from a more extensive circumference of science. Dryden knew more of man in his general nature, and Pope in his local manners. The notions of Dryden were formed by comprehensive speculation, and those of Pope by minute attention. There is more dignity in the knowledge of Dryden, and more certainty in that of Pope.

Poetry was not the sole praise of either; for both excelled likewise in prose; but Pope did not borrow his prose from his predecessor. The style of Dryden is capricious and varied; that of Pope is cautious and uniform. Dryden observes the motions of his own mind; Pope constrains his mind to his own rules of composition. Dryden is sometimes vehement and rapid; Pope is always smooth, uniform, and gentle. Dryden's page is a natural field, rising into inequalities, and diversified by the varied exuberance of abundant vegetation; Pope's is a velvet lawn, shaven by the scythe, and levelled by the roller.

Of genius, that power which constitutes a poet; that quality without which judgment is cold, and knowledge is inert; that energy which collects, combines, amplifies, and animates; the superiority must, with some hesitation, be allowed to Dryden. It is not to be inferred that of this poetical vigour Pope had only a little, because Dryden had more; for every other writer since Milton must give place to Pope; and even of Dryden it must be said, that, if he has brighter paragraphs, he has not better poems. Dryden's performances were always hasty, either excited by some external occasion, or extorted by domestic necessity; he composed without consideration, and published without correction. What his mind could supply at call, or gather in one excursion, was all that he sought, and all that he gave. The dilatory caution of Pope enabled him to condense his sentiments, to multiply his images, and to accumulate all that study might produce or chance might supply. If the flights of Dryden therefore are higher, Pope continues longer on the wing. If of Dryden's fire the blaze is brighter, of Pope's the heat is more regular and constant. Dryden often surpasses expectation, and Pope never falls below it. Dryden is read with frequent astonishment, and Pope with perpetual delight.

This parallel will, I hope, when it is well considered, be found just; and if the reader should suspect me, as I suspect myself, of some partial fondness for the memory of Dryden, let him not too hastily condemn me; for meditation and inquiry may, perhaps, show him the reasonableness of my determination.

The Works of Pope are now to be distinctly examined, not so much with attention to slight faults or petty beauties, as to the general character and effect of each performance.

It seems natural for a young poet to initiate himself by pastorals, which, not professing to imitate real life, require no experience; and, exhibiting only the simple operation of unmingled passions, admit no subtle reasoning or deep inquiry. Pope's *Pastorals* are not, however, composed but with close thought; they have reference to the time of the day, the seasons of the year, and the periods of human life. The last, that which turns the attention upon age and death, was the author's favourite. To tell of disappointment and misery, to thicken the darkness of futurity, and perplex the labyrinth of uncertainty, has been always a delicious employment of the poets. His preference was probably just. I wish, however, that his fondness had not overlooked a line in which the *Zephyrs* are made *to lament in silence.*

To charge these *Pastorals* with want of invention, is to require what was never intended. The imitations are so ambitiously frequent, that the writer evidently means rather to show his literature than his wit. It is surely sufficient for an author of sixteen, not only to be able to copy the poems of antiquity with judicious selection, but to have obtained sufficient power of language and skill in metre to exhibit a series of versification which had in English poetry no precedent, nor has since had an imitation.

The design of *Windsor Forest* is evidently derived from *Cooper's Hill*, with some attention to Waller's poem on *The Park*; but Pope cannot be denied to excel his masters in variety and elegance, and the art of interchanging description, narrative, and morality. The objection made by Dennis is the want of plan, of a regular subordination of parts terminating in the principal and original design. There is this want in most descriptive poems, because as the scenes, which they must exhibit successively, are all subsisting at the same time, the order in which they are shown must by necessity be arbitrary, and more is not to be expected from the last part than from the first. The attention, therefore, which cannot be detained by suspense, must be excited by diversity, such as his poem offers to its reader.

But the desire of diversity may be too much indulged; the parts of *Windsor Forest* which deserve least praise, are those which were added to enliven the stillness of the scene, the appearance of Father Thames, and the transformation of Lodona. Addison had in his *Campaign* derided the rivers that "rise from their oozy beds" to tell stories of heroes; and it is therefore strange that Pope should adopt a fiction not only unnatural, but lately censured. The story of Lodona is told with sweetness; but a new metamorphosis is a ready and puerile expedient: nothing is easier than to tell how a flower was once a blooming virgin, or a rock an obdurate tyrant.

The *Temple of Fame* has, as Steele warmly declared, "a thousand beauties." Every part is splendid; there is great luxuriance of ornaments; the original vision of Chaucer was never denied to be much improved; the allegory is very skilfully continued, the imagery is properly selected, and learnedly displayed: yet, with all this comprehension of excellence, as its scene is laid in remote ages, and its sentiments, if the concluding paragraph be excepted, have little relation to general manners or common life, it never obtained much notice, but is turned silently over, and seldom quoted or mentioned with either praise or blame.

That the *Messiah* excels the *Pollio* is no great praise, if it be considered from what original the improvements are derived.

The *Verses on the Unfortunate Lady* have drawn much attention by the illaudable singularity of treating suicide with respect; and they must be allowed to be written in some parts with vigorous animation, and in others with gentle tenderness; nor has Pope produced any poem in which the sense predominates more over the diction. But the tale is not skilfully told; it is not easy to discover the character of either the Lady or her Guardian. History relates that she was about to disparage herself by a marriage with an inferior; Pope praises her for the dignity of ambition, and yet condemns the uncle to detestation for his pride; the ambitious love of a niece may be opposed by the interest, malice, or envy of an uncle, but never by his pride. On such an occasion a poet may be allowed to be obscure, but inconsistency never can be right.

The *Ode for St. Cecilia's Day* was undertaken at the desire of Steele: in this the author is generally confessed to have miscarried, yet he has miscarried only as compared with Dryden; for he has far outgone other competitors. Dryden's plan is better chosen; history will always take stronger hold of the attention than fable: the passions excited by Dryden are the pleasures and

pains of real life, the scene of Pope is laid in imaginary existence; Pope is read with calm acquiescence, Dryden with turbulent delight; Pope hangs upon the ear, and Dryden finds the passes of the mind.

Both the odes want the essential constituent of metrical compositions, the stated recurrence of settled numbers. It may be alleged, that Pindar is said by Horace to have written *numeris lege solutis:* but as no such lax performances have been transmitted to us, the meaning of that expression cannot be fixed; and perhaps the like return might properly be made to a modern Pindarist, as Mr. Cobb received from Bentley, who, when he found his criticisms upon a Greek Exercise, which Cobb had presented, refuted one after another by Pindar's authority, cried out at last, "Pindar was a bold fellow, but thou art an impudent one."

If Pope's ode be particularly inspected, it will be found that the first stanza consists of sounds well chosen indeed, but only sounds.

The second consists of hyperbolical commonplaces, easily to be found, and perhaps without much difficulty to be as well expressed.

In the third, however, there are numbers, images, harmony, and vigour, not unworthy the antagonist of Dryden. Had all been like this— but every part cannot be the best.

The next stanzas place and detain us in the dark and dismal regions of mythology, where neither hope nor fear, neither joy nor sorrow, can be found: the poet, however, faithfully attends us; we have all that can be performed by elegance of diction or sweetness of versification; but what can form avail without better matter?

The last stanza recurs again to commonplaces. The conclusion is too evidently modelled by that of Dryden; and it may be remarked that both end with the same fault; the comparison of each is literal on one side, and metaphorical on the other.

Poets do not always express their own thoughts: Pope, with all this labour in the praise of music, was ignorant of its principles, and insensible of its effects.

One of his greatest, though of his earliest works, is the *Essay on Criticism*, which, if he had written nothing else, would have placed him among the first critics and the first poets, as it exhibits every mode of excellence that can embellish or dignify didactic composition—selection of matter, novelty of arrangement, justness of precept, splendour of illustration, and propriety of digression. I know not whether it be pleasing to consider that he produced this piece at twenty, and never afterwards excelled it: he that delights himself with observing that such powers may be soon attained, cannot but grieve to think that life was ever after at a stand.

To mention the particular beauties of the *Essay* would be unprofitably tedious; but I cannot forbear to observe, that the comparison of a student's progress in the sciences with the journey of a traveller in the Alps, is perhaps the best that English poetry can show. A simile, to be perfect, must both illustrate and ennoble the subject; must show it to the understanding in a clearer view, and display it to the fancy with greater dignity; but either of these qualities may be sufficient to recommend it. In didactic poetry, of which the great purpose is instruction, a simile may be praised which illustrates, though it does not ennoble; in heroics that may be admitted which ennobles, though it does not illustrate. That it may be complete, it is required to exhibit, independently of its references, a pleasing image; for a simile is said to be a short episode. To this antiquity was so attentive, that circumstances were sometimes added, which, having no parallels, served only to fill the imagination, and produced what Perrault ludicrously called "comparisons with a long tail." In their similes the greatest writers have sometimes failed: the ship-race, compared with the chariot-race, is neither illustrated nor aggrandised; land and water make all the difference: when Apollo, running after Daphne, is likened to a greyhound chasing a hare, there is nothing gained; the ideas of pursuit and flight are too plain to be made plainer; and a god and the daughter of a god are not represented much to their advantage by a hare and dog. The simile of the Alps has no useless parts, yet affords a striking picture by itself; it makes the foregoing position better understood, and enables it to take faster hold on the attention; it assists the apprehension and elevates the fancy.

Let me likewise dwell a little on the celebrated paragraph in which it is directed that "the sound should seem an echo to the sense"; a precept which Pope is allowed to have observed beyond any other English poet.

This notion of representative metre, and the desire of discovering frequent adaptations of the sound to the sense, have produced, in my opinion, many wild conceits and imaginary beauties. All that can furnish this representation are the sounds of the words considered singly, and the time in which they are pronounced. Every language has some words framed to exhibit the noises which they express, as *thump, rattle, growl, hiss*. These, however, are but few; and the poet cannot make them more, nor can they be of any use but when sound is to be mentioned. The time of pronunciation was in the dactylic measures of the learned languages capable of considerable variety; but that variety could be accommodated only to motion or duration, and different degrees of motion were perhaps expressed by verses rapid or slow, without much attention of the writer, when the image had full possession of his fancy; but our language having little flexibility, our verses can differ very little in their cadence. The fancied resemblances, I fear, arise sometimes merely from the ambiguity of words; there is supposed to be some relation between a *soft* line and *soft* couch, or between *hard* syllables and *hard* fortune.

Motion, however, may be in some sort exemplified; and yet it may be suspected that in such resemblances the mind often governs the ear, and the sounds are estimated by their meaning. One of their most successful attempts has been to describe the labour of Sisyphus:

With many a weary step, and many a groan,
Up the high hill he heaves a huge round stone;
The huge round stone, resulting with a bound,
Thunders impetuous down, and smokes along the
    ground.

Who does not perceive the stone to move slowly upward, and roll violently back? But set the same numbers to another sense:

While many a merry tale, and many a song,
Cheer'd the rough road, we wish'd the rough road
    long;
The rough road then, returning in a round,
Mock'd our impatient steps, for all was fairy
    ground.

We have now surely lost much of the delay, and much of the rapidity.

But, to show how little the greatest master of numbers can fix the principles of representative harmony, it will be sufficient to remark that the poet who tells us that

When Ajax strives some rock's vast weight to throw,
The line too labours, and the words move slow;
Not so when swift Camilla scours the plain,
Flies o'er th' unbending corn, and skims along the
    main;

when he had enjoyed for about thirty years the praise of Camilla's lightness of foot, he tried another experiment upon *sound* and *time,* and produced this memorable triplet:

Waller was smooth; but Dryden taught to join ⎞
The varying verse, the full resounding line, ⎬
The long majestic march, and energy divine. ⎠

Here are the swiftness of the rapid race, and the march of slow-paced majesty, exhibited by the same poet in the same sequence of syllables, except that the exact prosodist will find the line of *swiftness* by one time longer than that of *tardiness.*

Beauties of this kind are commonly fancied; and, when real, are technical and nugatory, not to be rejected, and not to be solicited.

To the praises which have been accumulated on *The Rape of the Lock* by readers of every class, from the critic to the waiting-maid, it is difficult to make any addition. Of that which is universally allowed to be the most attractive of all ludicrous compositions, let it rather be now inquired from what sources the power of pleasing is derived.

Dr. Warburton, who excelled in critical perspicacity, has remarked that the preternatural agents are very happily adapted to the purposes of the poem. The heathen deities can no longer gain attention: we should have turned away from a contest between Venus and Diana. The employment of allegorical persons always excites conviction of its own absurdity; they may produce effects, but cannot conduct actions: when the phantom is put in motion, it dissolves: thus *Discord* may raise a mutiny; but *Discord* cannot conduct a march, nor besiege a town. Pope brought in view a new race of beings, with powers and passions proportionate to their operation. The sylphs and gnomes act at the toilet and the tea-table, what more terrific and more

powerful phantoms perform on the stormy ocean or the field of battle; they give their proper help, and do their proper mischief.

Pope is said, by an objector, not to have been the inventor of this petty nation; a charge which might with more justice have been brought against the author of the Iliad, who doubtless adopted the religious system of his country; for what is there but the names of his agents which Pope has not invented? Has he not assigned them characters and operations never heard of before? Has he not, at least, given them their first poetical existence? If this is not sufficient to denominate his work original, nothing original ever can be written.

In this work are exhibited, in a very high degree, the two most engaging powers of an author. New things are made familiar, and familiar things are made new. A race of aerial people, never heard of before, is presented to us in a manner so clear and easy, that the reader seeks for no further information, but immediately mingles with his new acquaintance, adopts their interests, and attends their pursuits, loves a sylph, and detests a gnome.

That familiar things are made new, every paragraph will prove. The subject of the poem is an event below the common incidents of common life; nothing real is introduced that is not seen so often as to be no longer regarded; yet the whole detail of a female-day is here brought before us, invested with so much art of decoration, that, though nothing is disguised, everything is striking, and we feel all the appetite of curiosity for that from which we have a thousand times turned fastidiously away.

The purpose of the poet is, as he tells us, to laugh at "the little unguarded follies of the female sex." It is therefore without justice that Dennis charges *The Rape of the Lock* with the want of a moral, and for that reason sets it below the *Lutrin,* which exposes the pride and discord of the clergy. Perhaps neither Pope nor Boileau has made the world much better than he found it; but, if they had both succeeded, it were easy to tell who would have deserved most from public gratitude. The freaks, and humours, and spleen, and vanity of women, as they embroil families in discord, and fill houses with disquiet, do more to obstruct the happiness of life in a year than the ambition of the clergy in many centuries. It has been well observed, that the misery of man proceeds not from any single crush of overwhelming evil, but from small vexations continually repeated.

It is remarked by Dennis likewise that the machinery is superfluous; that, by all the bustle of preternatural operation, the main event is neither hastened nor retarded. To this charge an efficacious answer is not easily made. The Sylphs cannot be said to help or to oppose, and it must be allowed to imply some want of art, that their power has not been sufficiently intermingled with the action. Other parts may likewise be charged with want of connection; the game at *ombre* might be spared; but if the Lady had lost her hair while she was intent upon her cards, it might have been inferred that those who are too fond of play will be in danger of neglecting more important interests. Those perhaps are faults; but what are such faults to so much excellence?

The *Epistle of Eloisa to Abelard* is one of the most happy productions of human wit; the subject is so judiciously chosen, that it would be difficult, in turning over the annals of the world, to find another which so many circumstances concur to recommend. We regularly interest ourselves most in the fortune of those who most deserve our notice. Abelard and Eloisa were conspicuous in their days for eminence of merit. The heart naturally loves truth. The adventures and misfortunes of this illustrious pair are known from undisputed history. Their fate does not leave the mind in hopeless dejection, for they both found quiet and consolation in retirement and piety. So new and so affecting is their story, that it supersedes invention, and imagination ranges at full liberty without straggling into scenes of fable.

The story, thus skilfully adopted, has been diligently improved. Pope has left nothing behind him which seems more the effect of studious perseverance and laborious revisal. Here is particularly observable the *curiosa felicitas*, a fruitful soil and careful cultivation. Here is no crudeness of sense, nor asperity of language.

The sources from which sentiments which have so much vigour and efficacy have been drawn, are shown to be the mystic writers by the learned author of the *Essay on the Life and Writings of Pope*; a book which teaches how the brow of Criticism may be smoothed, and how she may be enabled, with all her severity, to attract and to delight.

The train of my disquisition has now conducted me to that poetical wonder, the translation of the Iliad, a performance which no age or nation can pretend to equal. To the Greeks translation was almost unknown; it was totally unknown to the inhabitants of Greece. They had no recourse to the Barbarians for poetical beauties, but sought for everything in Homer, where indeed there is but little which they might not find.

The Italians have been very diligent translators, but I can hear of no version, unless perhaps Anguillara's Ovid may be excepted, which is read with eagerness. The Iliad of Salvini every reader may discover to be punctiliously exact; but it seems to be the work of a linguist skilfully pedantic, and his countrymen, the proper judges of its power to please, reject it with disgust.

Their predecessors the Romans have left some specimens of translation behind them, and that employment must have had some credit in which Tully and Germanicus engaged; but unless we suppose, what is perhaps true, that the plays of Terence were versions of Menander, nothing translated seems ever to have risen to high reputation. The French, in the meridian hour of their learning, were very laudably industrious to enrich their own language with the wisdom of the ancients; but found themselves reduced, by whatever necessity, to turn the Greek and Roman poetry into prose. Whoever could read an author could translate him. From such rivals little can be feared.

The chief help of Pope in this arduous undertaking was drawn from the versions of Dryden. Virgil had borrowed much of his imagery from Homer, and part of the debt was now paid by his translator. Pope searched the pages of Dryden for happy combinations of heroic diction; but it will not be denied that he added much to what he found. He cultivated our language with so much diligence and art that he has left in his Homer a treasure of poetical elegances to posterity. His version may be said to have tuned the English tongue; for since its appearance no writer, however deficient in other powers, has wanted melody. Such a series of lines, so elaborately corrected and so sweetly modulated, took possession of the public ear; the vulgar was enamoured of the poem, and the learned wondered at the translation.

But in the most general applause discordant voices will always be heard. It has been objected by some, who wish to be numbered among the sons of learning, that Pope's version of Homer is not Homerical; that it exhibits no resemblance of the original and characteristic manner of the father of poetry, as it wants his awful simplicity, his artless grandeur, his unaffected majesty. This cannot be totally denied; but it must be remembered that *necessitas quod cogit defendit*; that may be lawfully done which cannot be forborne. Time and place will always enforce regard. In estimating this translation, consideration must be had of the nature of our language, the form of our metre, and above all of the change which two thousand years have made in the modes of life and the habits of thought. Virgil wrote in a language of the same general fabric with that of Homer, in verses of the same measure, and in an age nearer to Homer's time by eighteen hundred years, yet he found, even then, the state of the world so much altered, and the demand for elegance so much increased, that mere nature would be endured no longer; and perhaps, in the multitude of borrowed passages, very few can be shown which he has not embellished.

There is a time when nations emerging from barbarity, and falling into regular subordination, gain leisure to grow wise, and feel the shame of ignorance and the craving pain of unsatisfied curiosity. To this hunger of the mind plain sense is grateful; that which fills the void removes uneasiness, and to be free from pain for a while is pleasure; but repletion generates fastidiousness; a saturated intellect soon becomes luxurious, and knowledge finds no willing reception till it is recommended by artificial diction. Thus it will be found, in the progress of learning, that in all nations the first writers are simple, and that every age improves in elegance. One refinement always makes way for another; and what was expedient to Virgil was necessary to Pope.

I suppose many readers of the English Iliad, when they have been touched with some unexpected beauty of the lighter kind, have tried to enjoy it in the original, where, alas! it was not to be found. Homer doubtless owes to his trans-lator many Ovidian graces not exactly suitable to his character; but to have added can be no great crime, if nothing be taken away. Elegance is surely to be desired, if it be not gained at the expense of dignity. A hero would wish to be loved as well as to be reverenced.

To a thousand cavils one answer is sufficient: the purpose of a writer is to be read, and the criticism which would destroy the power of pleasing must be blown aside. Pope wrote for his own age and his own nation; he knew that it was necessary to colour the images and point the sentiments of his author; he therefore made him graceful, but lost him some of his sublimity.

The copious notes with which the version is accompanied, and by which it is recommended to many readers, though they were undoubtedly written to swell the volumes, ought not to pass without praise: commentaries which attract the reader by the pleasure of perusal have not often appeared; the notes of others are read to clear difficulties, those of Pope to vary entertainment.

It has, however, been objected, with sufficient reason, that there is in the commentary too much of unseasonable levity and affected gaiety; that too many appeals are made to the ladies, and the ease which is so carefully preserved is sometimes the ease of a trifler. Every art has its terms, and every kind of instruction its proper style; the gravity of common critics may be tedious, but is less despicable than childish merriment.

Of the Odyssey nothing remains to be observed: the same general praise may be given to both translations, and a particular examination of either would require a large volume. The notes were written by Broome, who endeavoured, not unsuccessfuly, to imitate his master.

Of *The Dunciad* the hint is confessedly taken from Dryden's *Mac Flecknoe*; but the plan is so enlarged and diversified as justly to claim the praise of an original, and affords perhaps the best specimen that has yet appeared of personal satire ludicrously pompous.

That the design was moral, whatever the author might tell either his readers or himself, I am not convinced. The first motive was the desire of revenging the contempt with which Theobald had treated his Shakespeare, and regaining the honour which he had lost, by crushing his opponent. Theobald was not of bulk enough to fill a poem, and therefore it was necessary to find other enemies with other names, at whose expense he might divert the public.

In this design there was petulance and malignity enough; but I cannot think it very criminal. An author places himself uncalled before the tribunal of criticism, and solicits fame at the hazard of disgrace. Dullness or deformity are not culpable in themselves, but may be very justly reproached when they pretend to the honour of wit or the influence of beauty. If bad writers were to pass without reprehension, what should restrain them? *impune diem consumpserit ingens Telephus;* and upon bad writers only will censure have much effect. The satire which brought Theobald and Moore into contempt, dropped impotent from Bentley like the javelin of Priam.

All truth is valuable, and satirical criticism may be considered as useful when it rectifies error and improves judgment; he that refines the public taste is a public benefactor.

The beauties of this poem are well known; its chief fault is the grossness of its images. Pope and Swift had an unnatural delight in ideas physically impure, such as every other tongue utters with unwillingness, and of which every ear shrinks from the mention.

But even this fault, offensive as it is, may be forgiven for the excellence of other passages—such as the formation and dissolution of Moore, the account of the Traveller, the misfortune of the Florist, and the crowded thoughts and stately numbers which dignify the concluding paragraph.

The alterations which have been made in *The Dunciad*, not always for the better, require that it should be published, as in the present collection, with all its variations.

The *Essay on Man* was a work of great labour and long consideration, but certainly not the happiest of Pope's performances. The subject is perhaps not very proper for poetry, and the poet was not sufficiently master of his subject; metaphysical morality was to him a new study, he was proud of his acquisitions, and, supposing himself master of great secrets, was in haste to teach what he had not learned. Thus he tells us, in the first epistle, that from the nature of the Supreme Being may be deduced an order of beings such as mankind, because Infinite Excellence can do only what is best. He finds out that

these beings must be "somewhere," and that "all the question is whether man be in a wrong place." Surely if, according to the poet's Leibnitian reasoning, we may infer that man ought to be, only because he is, we may allow that his place is the right place because he has it. Supreme Wisdom is not less infallible in disposing than in creating. But what is meant by *somewhere* and *place*, and *wrong place*, it had been vain to ask Pope, who probably had never asked himself.

Having exalted himself into the chair of wisdom, he tells us much that every man knows, and much that he does not know himself: that we see but little, and that the order of the universe is beyond our comprehension—an opinion not very uncommon; and that there is a chain of subordinate beings "from infinite to nothing," of which himself and his readers are equally ignorant. But he gives us one comfort which, without his help, he supposes unattainable, in the position "that though we are fools, yet God is wise."

This essay affords an egregious instance of the predominance of genius, the dazzling splendour of imagery, and the seductive powers of eloquence. Never were penury of knowledge and vulgarity of sentiment so happily disguised. The reader feels his mind full, though he learns nothing; and when he meets it in its new array, no longer knows the talk of his mother and his nurse. When these wonder-working sounds sink into sense, and the doctrine of the *Essay*, disrobed of its ornaments, is left to the powers of its naked excellence, what shall we discover? That we are, in comparison with our Creator, very weak and ignorant—that we do not uphold the chain of existence—and that we could not make one another with more skill than we are made. We may learn yet more—that the arts of human life were copied from the instinctive operations of other animals—that if the world be made for man, it may be said that man was made for geese. To these profound principles of natural knowledge are added some moral instructions equally new: that self-interest, well understood, will produce social concord—that men are mutual gainers by mutual benefits— that evil is sometimes balanced by good—that human advantages are unstable and fallacious, of uncertain duration and doubtful effect—that our true honour is, not to have a great part, but to act it well—that virtue only is our own—and that happiness is always in our power.

Surely a man of no very comprehensive search may venture to say that he has heard all this before; but it was never till now recommended by such a blaze of embellishments, or such sweetness of melody. The vigorous contraction of some thoughts, the luxuriant amplification of others, the incidental illustrations, and sometimes the dignity, sometimes the softness of the verses, enchain philosophy, suspend criticism, and oppress judgment by overpowering pleasure.

This is true of many paragraphs; yet if I had undertaken to exemplify Pope's felicity of composition before a rigid critic, I should not select the *Essay on Man;* for it contains more lines unsuccessfully laboured, more harshness of diction, more thoughts imperfectly expressed, more levity without elegance, and more heaviness without strength, than will easily be found in all his other works.

The *Characters of Men and Women* are the product of diligent speculation upon human life; much labour has been bestowed upon them, and Pope very seldom laboured in vain. That his excellence may be properly estimated, I recommend a comparison of his *Characters of Women* with Boileau's Satire; it will then be seen with how much more perspicacity female nature is investigated, and female excellence selected; and he surely is no mean writer to whom Boileau shall be found inferior. The *Characters of Men,* however, are written with more, if not with deeper thought, and exhibit many passages exquisitely beautiful. The "Gem and the Flower" will not easily be equalled. In the women's part are some defects: the character of Atossa is not so neatly finished as that of Clodio; and some of the female characters may be found perhaps more frequently among men; what is said of Philomede was true of Prior.

In the Epistles to Lord Bathurst and Lord Burlington, Dr. Warburton has endeavoured to find a train of thought which was never in the writer's head, and, to support his hypothesis, has printed that first which was published last. In one, the most valuable passage is perhaps the Elegy on "Good Sense"; and the other, the "End of the Duke of Buckingham."

The *Epistle to Arbuthnot,* now arbitrarily called the *Prologue to the Satires,* is a performance consisting, as it seems, of many fragments wrought into one design, which by this union of scattered beauties contains more striking paragraphs than could probably have been brought together into an occasional work. As there is no stronger motive to exertion than self-defence, no part has more elegance, spirit, or dignity than the poet's vindication of his own character. The meanest passage is the satire upon Sporus.

Of the two poems which derived their names from the year, and which are called the *Epilogue to the Satires,* it was very justly remarked by Savage, that the second was in the whole more strongly conceived, and more equally supported, but that it had no single passages equal to the contention in the first for the dignity of Vice, and the celebration of the triumph of Corruption.

The *Imitations of Horace* seem to have been written as relaxations of his genius. This employment became his favourite by its facility; the plan was ready to his hand, and nothing was required but to accommodate as he could the sentiments of an old author to recent facts or familiar images; but what is easy is seldom excellent; such imitations cannot give pleasure to common readers; the man of learning may be sometimes surprised and delighted by an unexpected parallel; but the comparison requires knowledge of the original, which will likewise often detect strained applications. Between Roman images and English manners there will be an irreconcileable dissimilitude, and the works will be generally uncouth and party-coloured; neither original nor translated, neither ancient nor modern.

Pope had, in proportions very nicely adjusted to each other, all the qualities that constitute genius. He had *Invention,* by which new trains of events are formed, and new scenes of imagery displayed, as in *The Rape of the Lock;* and by which extrinsic and adventitious embellishments and illustrations are connected with a known subject, as in the *Essay on Criticism.* He had *Imagination,* which strongly impresses on the writer's mind, and enables him to convey to the reader, the various forms of nature, incidents of life, and energies of passion, as in his *Eloisa, Windsor*

Forest, and the *Ethic Epistles.* He had *Judgment,* which selects from life or nature what the present purpose requires, and by separating the essence of things from its concomitants, often makes the representation more powerful than the reality: and he had colours of language always before him, ready to decorate his matter with every grace of elegant expression, as when he accommodates his diction to the wonderful multiplicity of Homer's sentiments and descriptions.

Poetical expression includes sound as well as meaning. "Music," says Dryden, "is inarticulate poetry"; among the excellences of Pope, therefore, must be mentioned the melody of his metre. By perusing the works of Dryden, he discovered the most perfect fabric of English verse, and habituated himself to that only which he found the best; in consequence of which restraint, his poetry has been censured as too uniformly musical, and as glutting the ear with unvaried sweetness. I suspect this objection to be the cant of those who judge by principles rather than perception; and who would even themselves have less pleasure in his works, if he had tried to relieve attention by studied discords, or affected to break his lines and vary his pauses.

But though he was thus careful of his versification, he did not oppress his powers with superfluous rigour. He seems to have thought with Boileau, that the practice of writing might be refined till the difficulty should overbalance the advantage. The construction of his language is not always strictly grammatical; with those rhymes which prescription had conjoined he contented himself, without regard to Swift's remonstrances, though there was no striking consonance; nor was he very careful to vary his terminations, or to refuse admission, at a small distance, to the same rhymes.

To Swift's edict for the exclusion of alexandrines and triplets he paid little regard; he admitted them, but, in the opinion of Fenton, too rarely; he uses them more liberally in his translation than his poems.

He has a few double rhymes; and always, I think, unsuccessfully, except once in *The Rape of the Lock.*

Expletives he very early ejected from his verses; but he now and then admits an epithet rather commodious than important.

Each of the six first lines of the Iliad might lose two syllables with very little diminution of the meaning; and sometimes, after all his art and labour, one verse seems to be made for the sake of another. In his latter productions the diction is sometimes vitiated by French idioms, with which Bolingbroke had perhaps infected him.

I have been told that the couplet by which he declared his own ear to be most gratified was this:

Lo, where Maeotis sleeps, and hardly flows
The freezing Tanais through a waste of snows.

But the reason of this preference I cannot discover.

It is remarked by Watts, that there is scarcely a happy combination of words, or a phrase poetically elegant in the English language, which Pope has not inserted into his version of Homer. How he obtained possession of so many beauties of speech, it were desirable to know. That he gleaned from authors, obscure as well as eminent, what he thought brilliant or useful, and preserved it all in a regular collection, is not unlikely. When, in his last years, Hall's Satires were shown him, he wished that he had seen them sooner.

New sentiments and new images others may produce; but to attempt any further improvement of versification will be dangerous. Art and diligence have now done their best, and what shall be added will be the effort of tedious toil and needless curiosity.

After all this, it is surely superfluous to answer the question that has once been asked, Whether Pope was a poet? otherwise than by asking in return, If Pope be not a poet, where is poetry to be found? To circumscribe poetry by a definition will only show the narrowness of the definer, though a definition which shall exclude Pope will not easily be made. Let us look round upon the present time, and back upon the past; let us inquire to whom the voice of mankind has decreed the wreath of poetry; let their productions be examined, and their claim stated, and the pretensions of Pope will be no more disputed. Had he given the world only his version, the name of poet must have been allowed him: if the writer of the *Iliad* were to class his successors, he would assign a very high place to his translator, without requiring any other evidence of Genius.

From the Life of Gray

GRAY'S poetry is now to be considered; and I hope not to be looked on as an enemy to his name, if I confess that I contemplate it with less pleasure than his life.

His ode on *Spring* has something poetical, both in the language and the thought; but the language is too luxuriant, and the thoughts have nothing new. There has of late arisen a practice of giving to adjectives derived from substantives, the termination of participles; such as the *cultured* plain, the *daisied* bank; but I was sorry to see, in the lines of a scholar like Gray, the *honied* Spring. The morality is natural, but too stale; the conclusion is pretty.

The poem *On the Cat* was doubtless by its author considered as a trifle, but it is not a happy trifle. In the first stanza "the azure flowers *that* blow," show how resolutely a rhyme is sometimes made when it cannot easily be found. Selima, the Cat, is called a nymph, with some violence both to language and sense; but there is good use made of it when it is done; for of the two lines,

> What female heart can gold despise?
> What cat's averse to fish?

the first relates merely to the nymph, and the second only to the cat. The sixth stanza contains a melancholy truth, that "a favourite has no friend"; but the last ends in a pointed sentence of no relation to the purpose: if *what glistered* had been *gold*, the cat would not have gone into the water; and if she had, would not less have been drowned.

The *Prospect of Eton College* suggests nothing to Gray which every beholder does not equally think and feel. His supplication to Father Thames, to tell him who drives the hoop or tosses the ball, is useless and puerile. Father Thames has no better means of knowing than himself. His epithet "buxom health" is not elegant; he seems not to understand the word. Gray thought his language more poetical as it was more remote from common use: finding in Dryden "honey redolent of Spring," an expres-

Life of Gray. From *Lives of the English Poets.*

sion that reaches the utmost limits of our language, Gray drove it a little more beyond common apprehension by making "gales" to be "redolent of joy and youth."

Of the *Hymn to Adversity*, the hint was at first taken from "O Diva, gratum quae regis Antium"; but Gray has excelled his original by the variety of his sentiments, and by their moral application. Of this piece, at once poetical and rational, I will not by slight objections violate the dignity.

My process has now brought me to the *wonderful* "Wonder of Wonders," the two Sister Odes; by which, though either vulgar ignorance or common sense at first universally rejected them, many have been since persuaded to think themselves delighted. I am one of those that are willing to be pleased, and therefore would gladly find the meaning of the first stanza of the *Progress of Poetry*.

Gray seems in his rapture to confound the images of "spreading sound and running water." A "stream of music" may be allowed; but where does "music," however "smooth and strong," after having visited the "verdant vales, roll down the steep amain," so as that "rocks and nodding groves rebellow to the roar"? If this be said of music, it is nonsense; if it be said of water, it is nothing to the purpose.

The second stanza, exhibiting Mars's car and Jove's eagle, is unworthy of further notice. Criticism disdains to chase a school-boy to his commonplaces.

To the third it may likewise be objected that it is drawn from mythology, though such as may be more easily assimilated to real life. Idalia's "velvet-green" has something of cant. An epithet or metaphor drawn from nature ennobles art: an epithet or metaphor drawn from art degrades nature. Gray is too fond of words arbitrarily compounded. "Many-twinkling" was formerly censured as not analogical; we may say "many-spotted," but scarcely "many-spotting." This stanza, however, has something pleasing.

Of the second ternary of stanzas, the first

endeavours to tell something, and would have told it had it not been crossed by Hyperion: the second describes well enough the universal prevalence of poetry; but I am afraid that the conclusion will not rise from the premises. The caverns of the North and the plains of Chili are not the residences of "glory and generous shame." But that poetry and virtue go always together is an opinion so pleasing, that I can forgive him who resolves to think it true.

The third stanza sounds big with "Delphi," and "Egean," and "Ilissus," and "Meander," and "hallowed fountains," and "solemn sound"; but in all Gray's odes there is a kind of cumbrous splendour which we wish away. His position is at last false: in the time of Dante and Petrarch, from whom we derive our first school of poetry, Italy was overrun by "tyrant power" and "coward vice"; nor was our state much better when we first borrowed the Italian arts.

Of the third ternary, the first gives a mythological birth of Shakespeare. What is said of that mighty genius is true; but it is not said happily: the real effects of this poetical power are put out of sight by the pomp of machinery. Where truth is sufficient to fill the mind, fiction is worse than useless; the counterfeit debases the genuine.

His account of Milton's blindness, if we suppose it caused by study in the formation of his poem—a supposition surely allowable—is poetically true, and happily imagined. But the *car* of Dryden, with his *two coursers*, has nothing in it peculiar; it is a car in which any other rider may be placed.

The Bard appears at the first view to be, as Algarotti and others have remarked, an imitation of the prophecy of Nereus. Algarotti thinks it superior to its original, and if preference depends only on the imagery and animation of the two poems, his judgment is right. There is in *The Bard* more force, more thought, and more variety. But to copy is less than to invent, and the copy has been unhappily produced at a wrong time. The fiction of Horace was to the Romans credible; but its revival disgusts us with apparent and unconquerable falsehood. *Incredulus odi.*

To select a singular event, and swell it to a giant's bulk by fabulous appendages of spectres and predictions, has little difficulty; for he that forsakes the probable may always find the marvellous. And it has little use: we are affected only as we believe; we are improved only as we find something to be imitated or declined. I do not see that *The Bard* promotes any truth, moral or political.

His stanzas are too long, especially his epodes; the ode is finished before the ear has learned its measures, and consequently before it can receive pleasure from their consonance and recurrence.

Of the first stanza the abrupt beginning has been celebrated; but technical beauties can give praise only to the inventor. It is in the power of any man to rush abruptly upon his subject that has read the ballad of *Johnny Armstrong:*

Is there ever a man in all Scotland.

The initial resemblances, or alliterations, "ruin, ruthless, helm or hauberk," are below the grandeur of a poem that endeavours at sublimity.

In the second stanza the Bard is well described; but in the third we have the puerilities of obsolete mythology. When we are told that "Cadwallo hush'd the stormy main," and that "Modred made huge Plinlimmon bow his cloud-topp'd head," attention recoils from the repetition of a tale that, even when it was first heard, was heard with scorn.

The *weaving* of the *winding sheet* he borrowed, as he owns, from the Northern bards; but their texture, however, was very properly the work of female powers, as the act of spinning the thread of life in another mythology. Theft is always dangerous; Gray has made weavers of slaughtered bards, by a fiction outrageous and incongruous. They are then called upon to "weave the warp, and weave the woof," perhaps with no great propriety; for it is by crossing the *woof* with the *warp* that men *weave* the *web* or piece; and the first line was dearly bought by the admission of its wretched correspondent, "Give ample room and verge enough." He has, however, no other line as bad.

The third stanza of the second ternary is commended, I think, beyond its merit. The personification is indistinct. *Thirst* and *hunger* are not alike; and their features, to make the imagery perfect, should have been discriminated. We are told in the same stanza how "towers are fed." But I will no longer look for particular faults;

yet let it be observed that the ode might have been concluded with an action of better example; but suicide is always to be had without expense of thought.

These odes are marked by glittering accumulations of ungraceful ornaments; they strike, rather than please; the images are magnified by affectation; the language is laboured into harshness. The mind of the writer seems to work with unnatural violence. "Double, double, toil and trouble." He has a kind of strutting dignity, and is tall by walking on tiptoe. His art and his struggle are too visible, and there is too little appearance of ease and nature.

To say that he has no beauties, would be unjust: a man like him, of great learning and great industry, could not but produce something valuable. When he pleases least, it can only be said that a good design was ill directed.

His translations of Northern and Welsh poetry deserve praise; the imagery is preserved, perhaps often improved; but the language is unlike the language of other poets.

In the character of his Elegy I rejoice to concur with the common reader; for by the common sense of readers uncorrupted with literary prejudices, after all the refinements of subtilty and the dogmatism of learning, must be finally decided all claim to poetical honours. The *Churchyard* abounds with images which find a mirror in every mind, and with sentiments to which every bosom returns an echo. The four stanzas beginning "Yet even these bones" are to me original: I have never seen the notions in any other place; yet he that reads them here, persuades himself that he has always felt them. Had Gray written often thus, it had been vain to blame, and useless to praise him.

EDWARD YOUNG (1683-1765)

AN EAGER interest in originality, and a tendency to equate it with "genius," marked the growing romanticism of the eighteenth century. If man's emotional nature is by itself good and trustworthy, as much romantic writing was to assume, then in art the ideal course for him to follow is to express his feelings—to disregard rules, traditions, custom, and look into his heart and write. To the degree that art follows this practice, it becomes original and unique; and originality and uniqueness increasingly take on the connotation of greatness. Critical works with titles like *An Essay on Genius*, or *On Original Genius* indicate the shift in emphasis. They also illustrate the growing interest in the psychology of art.

Young's *Conjectures on Original Composition* (1759) is another instance of the concern with originality, though it is not a psychological in-

EDWARD YOUNG. After studying at Winchester and Oxford, Young entered the Church and became rector of Welwyn (1730), where he lived for the remaining thirty-five years of his life. In addition to his famous blank-verse poem, *Night Thoughts on Life, Death, and Immortality* (1742-45), he wrote some excellent satires (*The Universal Passion*) and two unimpressive plays.

Modern editions of the *Conjectures* are those of M. W. Steinke (Philadelphia, 1917), and especially E. J. Morley (Manchester, 1918). See also A. D. McKillop, "Richardson, Young, and the *Conjectures*," *Modern Philology*, XXII (1925), 391-404, and W. J. Bate, *The Burden of the Past and the English Poet* (Cambridge, Mass., 1970), Ch. II.

vestigation. It is the more characteristic because in it we have a typical English neoclassic writer actively urging the need for originality. Through "imitation"—and Young is speaking not of the "imitation of nature," but the close imitation of past writers—we actually "counteract nature. . . . She brings us into the world all Originals . . . how comes it to pass that we die Copies?" Great models of the past, if we study them too zealously, "prejudice" us in favor of their own particular virtues so that we fail to develop our own. They also "intimidate" us and inhibit our effort. In some ways, Young is romantic in equating "originality" with the organic and vital spontaneity that the romantics themselves prized. "An Original," he says, is "of a vegetable nature; it rises spontaneously from the vital root of genius; it grows, it is not made." No classical theorist, of course, ever believed that genius results from merely following rules or precepts. On the other hand, he would never have felt that any amount of spontaneous vitality was worth much unless it had been educated and developed by reason. But Young is not a romantic extremist who urges complete self-expression as the aim of literature. He really takes it for granted that one should know great predecessors. But he would add, as would Johnson or Reynolds: "Let our understanding feed on theirs . . . But let them nourish, not annihilate, our own. . . . It is by a sort of noble contagion . . . and not by any particular sordid theft, that we can be the better for those who went before us."

From Conjectures on Original Composition

IMITATIONS are of two kinds: one of nature, one of authors. The first we call originals, and confine the term imitation to the second. I shall not enter into the curious inquiry of what is, or is not, strictly speaking, original, content with what all must allow, that some compositions are more so than others; and the more they are so, I say, the better. Originals are, and ought to be, great favourites, for they are great benefactors; they extend the republic of letters, and add a new province to its dominion. Imitators only give us a sort of duplicates of what we had, possibly much better, before; increasing the mere drug of books, while all that makes them valuable, knowledge and genius, are at a stand. The pen of an original writer, like Armida's wand, out of a barren waste calls a blooming spring. Out of that blooming spring an imitator is a transplanter of laurels, which

Conjectures on Original Composition. Published in 1759.

sometimes die on removal, always languish in a foreign soil.

But suppose an imitator to be most excellent (and such there are), yet still he but nobly builds on another's foundation; his debt is, at least, equal to his glory; which, therefore, on the balance, cannot be very great. On the contrary, an original, though but indifferent (its originality being set aside), yet has something to boast; it is something to say with him in *Horace, Meo sum Pauper in aere;* and to share ambition with no less than Caesar, who declared he had rather be the first in a village than the second at Rome.

Still farther: an imitator shares his crown, if he has one, with the chosen object of his imitation; an original enjoys an undivided applause. An original may be said to be of a vegetable nature; it rises spontaneously from the vital root of genius; it grows, it is not made. Imitations are often a sort of manufacture wrought up by those mechanics, art and labour, out of pre-existent materials not their own. . . .

But why are originals so few? not because the writer's harvest is over, the great reapers of antiquity having left nothing to be gleaned after them; nor because the human mind's teeming time is past, or because it is incapable of putting forth unprecedented births; but because illustrious examples engross, prejudice, and intimidate. They engross our attention, and so prevent a due inspection of ourselves; they prejudice our judgement in favour of their abilities, and so lessen the sense of our own; and they intimidate us with the splendour of their renown, and thus under diffidence bury our strength. Nature's impossibilities, and those of diffidence lie wide asunder.

Let it not be suspected, that I would weakly insinuate anything in favour of the moderns, as compared with ancient authors; no, I am lamenting their great inferiority. But I think it is no necessary inferiority; that it is not from divine destination, but from some cause far beneath the moon: I think that human souls, through all periods, are equal; that due care and exertion would set us nearer our immortal predecessors than we are at present; and he who questions and confutes this, will show abilities not a little tending toward a proof of that equality which he denies.

After all, the first ancients had no merit in being originals: they could not be imitators. Modern writers have a choice to make; and therefore have a merit in their power. They may soar in the regions of liberty, or move in the soft fetters of easy imitation; and imitation has as many plausible reasons to urge, as pleasure had to offer to Hercules. Hercules made the choice of an hero, and so became immortal.

Yet let not assertors of classic excellence imagine, that I deny the tribute it so well deserves. He that admires not ancient authors, betrays a secret he would conceal, and tells the world that he does not understand them. Let us be as far from neglecting, as from copying, their admirable compositions: sacred be their rights, and inviolable their fame. Let our understanding feed on theirs; they afford the noblest nourishment; but let them nourish, not annihilate, our own. When we read, let our imagination kindle at their charms; when we write, let our judgement

shut them out of our thoughts; treat even Homer himself as his royal admirer was treated by the cynic; bid him stand aside, nor shade our composition from the beams of our own genius; for nothing original can rise, nothing immortal can ripen, in any other sun.

Must we then, you say, not imitate ancient authors? Imitate them by all means; but imitate aright. He that imitates the divine *Iliad* does not imitate Homer; but he who takes the same method, which Homer took, for arriving at a capacity of accomplishing a work so great. Tread in his steps to the sole fountain of immortality; drink where he drank, at the true Helicon, that is, at the breast of Nature: imitate; but imitate not the composition, but the man. For may not this paradox pass into a maxim? viz. "The less we copy the renowned ancients, we shall resemble them the more."

But possibly you may reply, that you must either imitate Homer, or depart from Nature. Not so: for suppose you was to change place, in time, with Homer; then, if you write naturally, you might as well charge Homer with an imitation of you. Can you be said to imitate Homer for writing so, as you would have written, if Homer had never been? As far as a regard to Nature, and sound sense, will permit a departure from your great predecessors; so far, ambitiously, depart from them; the farther from them in similitude, the nearer are you to them in excellence; you rise by it into an original; become a noble collateral, not an humble descendant from them. Let us build our compositions with the spirit, and in the taste, of the ancients; but not with their materials: thus will they resemble the structures of Pericles at Athens, which Plutarch commends for having had an air of antiquity as soon as they were built. All eminence, and distinction, lies out of the beaten road; excursion and deviation are necessary to find it; and the more remote your path from the highway, the more reputable; if, like poor Gulliver (of whom anon), you fall not into a ditch, in your way to glory.

What glory to come near, what glory to reach, what glory (presumptuous thought!) to surpass our predecessors! And is that then in Nature absolutely impossible? Or is it not, rather, contrary to Nature to fail in it? Nature herself sets the ladder, all wanting is our ambition to climb. For by the bounty of Nature we are as strong as our predecessors; and by the favour of time (which is but another round in Nature's scale) we stand on higher ground. As to the first, were they more than men? Or are we less? Are not our minds cast in the same mould with those before the flood? . . . It is by a sort of noble contagion, from a general familiarity with their writings, and not by any particular sordid theft, that we can be the better for those who went before us.

GOTTHOLD EPHRAIM LESSING   (1729-1781)

LESSING marks not only the beginning of serious German criticism but the beginning of the great period of German literature in general. Though Germany was later to feel that the romantic movement was distinctively its own, and probably did, in fact, carry the philosophy of romanticism farther than any other nation, the inaugurator of its critical theory, Lessing, is quite in the neoclassic tradition. His *Laokoon* (1766), though it turns into a general discussion of poetry that has romantic as well as classical affinities, is a protest against what was to become a common romantic tendency, the inclination to confuse the different arts. We may later see such a tendency illustrated in Richard Wagner's dream of a *Gesammtkunst*, in which the various arts are to be mingled together; in the later nineteenth-century eagerness to compose music that conveys a picture; in the desire to paint in such a way as to incite feelings ordinarily aroused by music; or in the use of so-called *synaesthetic* imagery in poetry —imagery that usually appeals to one sense but is also made to address another sense (as in Keats's phrases, "the *touch* of *scent*," "*fragrant* and enwreathèd *light*," or "embalmèd darkness").

Long before the romantic movement, however, there were frequent attempts to overcome the divisions between the arts. Particularly after the

GOTTHOLD EPHRAIM LESSING. Educated by his father, a clergyman, and at schools in Kamenz and Meissen, Lessing abandoned the study of theology for literature, attended the University of Wittenberg, and became known as a dramatist and poet by his middle thirties. He lived for a while in Leipzig, in close association with the theater there, and then in Berlin. He served as a military secretary (1760-65) while continuing to write, and then moved to Hamburg, where his contact with the theater led him to write the *Hamburgische Dramaturgie* (1767-68). During the last decade of his life, he was librarian to the Prince of Brunswick.

Translations of the *Laokoon* include those of E. C. Beasley (1853), Ellen Frothingham (1873), Sir Robert Phillimore (1874), A. Hamann (1892), L. E. Upcott (1895), and E. A. McCormick (Indianapolis, 1962). A translation of excerpts from the *Hamburg Dramaturgy* is in *Selected Prose Works* (tr. E. C. Beasley and H. Zimmern, and ed. by Edward Bell, Bohn Library, 1879). For commentary in English, see especially Irving Babbitt, *The New Laokoon* (1910); E. H. Gombrich, "Lessing," *Proceedings of the British Academy*, XLIII (1957), 133-56; Peter Heller, *Dialectics and Nihilism* (Amherst, 1966); F. O. Nolte, *Lessing's "Laocoön"* (1940); and John G. Robertson, *Lessing's Dramatic Theory* (Cambridge, 1939).

Renaissance, Horace's phrase, *ut pictura poesis* ("as is a painting, so is poetry"), had given a quasi-authoritative sanction to an interest in drawing parallels between the two arts. The immediate occasion of Lessing's *Laokoon* was Johann Winckelmann's discussion of the celebrated sculpture of the Laocoön group in his great work on Greek art (1755). Winckelmann defined the dominant characteristic of Greek painting and sculpture as a noble simplicity and quiet grandeur. He cited Laocoön as typical. While being crushed by a serpent, Laocoön does not cry out in agony, as he does in Virgil's poetic description of the scene. Instead, his mouth is scarcely open: "Bodily anguish and moral greatness are diffused in equal measure through the whole structure of the figure, being, as it were, balanced against each other." There is more to be said for Winckelmann's interpretation than admirers of Lessing have admitted, though, of course, such an interpretation should be supplemented by other considerations. At all events, Lessing's reply is to point to the essentially different *media* employed by the visual arts on the one hand and by poetry on the other, and to suggest an important distinction. It is a distinction that is apparent in Schiller's *Naïve and Sentimental Poetry* and that remains common in German esthetic theory throughout the nineteenth and into the twentieth centuries. The visual arts are *spatial*; poetry, however, like music, is *temporal*—it exists in *time*. Hence the visual arts are limited in what they can convey. Some of what poetry can describe or suggest becomes merely ugly when it is portrayed in painting or sculpture. It is in this emphasis on the limits of a particular art that Lessing's *Laokoon* is most closely allied to classical premises.

The *Hamburg Dramaturgy* (1767-68), originally intended as a series of critical essays on performances at the Hamburg National Theater, evolves into a general discussion of the drama. Here Lessing, like Johnson and Reynolds, illustrates the desire of the last major neoclassic critics to return to a broader interpretation of classical premises than that offered by systematized French neoclassicism. In the case of Lessing, as in those of Johnson and Diderot, the primary function of the drama is the truthful and moving portrayal of human nature and of human passions. To some extent, Lessing and Diderot, in maintaining this ideal, verged towards an almost sentimental conception of what should be the proper subject matter of the drama. Nor is even Johnson, at times, wholly free from the same tendency, although it is modified by his exacting sense of poetic form and language, and his central emphasis on "general nature." At all events, like Diderot in France and, perhaps, to some extent, like Johnson in England, Lessing, in his dramatic theory, illustrates what may loosely be called "classical realism"—a realism which is still generalized, and in which a grasp of dramatic structure is still strong, but from which a comparatively easy transition was to be made to the serious romantic criticism of the drama.

From Laocoon

I I

BE IT truth or fable that Love made the first attempt in the imitative arts, thus much is certain: that she never tired of guiding the hand of the great masters of antiquity. For although painting, as the art which reproduces objects upon flat surfaces, is now practised in the broadest sense of that definition, yet the wise Greek set much narrower bounds to it. He confined it strictly to the imitation of beauty. The Greek artist represented nothing that was not beautiful. Even the vulgarly beautiful, the beauty of inferior types, he copied only incidentally for practice or recreation. The perfection of the subject must charm in his work. He was too great to require the beholders to be satisfied with the mere barren pleasure arising from a successful likeness or from consideration of the artist's skill. Nothing in his art was dearer to him or seemed to him more noble than the ends of art.

"Who would want to paint you when no one wants to look at you?" says an old epigrammatist [1] to a misshapen man. Many a modern artist would say, "No matter how misshapen you are, I will paint you. Though people may not like to look at you, they will be glad to look at my picture; not as a portrait of you, but as a proof of my skill in making so close a copy of such a monster."

The fondness for making a display with mere manual dexterity, ennobled by no worth in the subject, is too natural not to have produced among the Greeks a Pauson and a Pyreicus. They had such painters, but meted out to them strict justice. Pauson, who confined himself to the beauties of ordinary nature, and whose depraved taste liked best to represent the imperfections and deformities of humanity, lived in the most abandoned poverty; and Pyreicus, who painted barbers' rooms, dirty workshops, donkeys, and kitchen herbs, with all the diligence of a Dutch painter, as if such things were rare or attractive

in nature, acquired the surname of Rhyparographer,[2] the dirt-painter. The rich voluptuaries, indeed, paid for his works their weight in gold, as if by this fictitious valuation to atone for their insignificance.

Even the magistrates considered this subject a matter worthy their attention, and confined the artist by force within his proper sphere. The law of the Thebans commanding him to make his copies more beautiful than the originals, and never under pain of punishment less so, is well known. This was no law against bunglers, as has been supposed by critics generally, and even by Junius himself,[3] but was aimed against the Greek Ghezzi, and condemned the unworthy artifice of obtaining a likeness by exaggerating the deformities of the model. It was, in fact, a law against caricature.

From this same conception of the beautiful came the law of the Olympic judges. Every conqueror in the Olympic games received a statue, but a portrait-statue was erected only to him who had been thrice victor. Too many indifferent portraits were not allowed among works of art. For although a portrait admits of being idealized, yet the likeness should predominate. It is the ideal of a particular person, not the ideal of humanity.

We laugh when we read that the very arts among the ancients were subject to the control of civil law; but we have no right to laugh. Laws should unquestionably usurp no sway over science, for the object of science is truth. Truth is a necessity of the soul, and to put any restraint upon the gratification of this essential want is tyranny. The object of art, on the contrary, is pleasure, and pleasure is not indispensable. What kind and what degree of pleasure shall be permitted may justly depend on the law-giver.

The plastic arts especially, besides the inevitable influence which they exercise on the character of a nation, have power to work one effect which demands the careful attention of the law. Beautiful statues fashioned from beautiful

---

Laocoon. First published in 1766; translated by E. Frothingham. Chapter II is here printed complete, and Chs. III and XVI printed in part.

[1] Antiochus, Anthol. lib. ii, cap. 4. [Lessing.]

[2] Plinius, lib. xxx, sect. 37. [Lessing.]

[3] De Pictura vet. lib. ii, cap. iv, sect. 1. [Lessing.]

men reacted upon their creators, and the state was indebted for its beautiful men to beautiful statues. With us the susceptible imagination of the mother seems to express itself only in monsters.

From this point of view I think I detect a truth in certain old stories which have been rejected as fables. The mothers of Aristomenes, of Aristodamas, of Alexander the Great, Scipio, Augustus, and Galerius, each dreamed during pregnancy that she was visited by a serpent. The serpent was an emblem of divinity. Without it Bacchus, Apollo, Mercury, and Hercules were seldom represented in their beautiful pictures and statues. These honorable women had been feasting their eyes upon the god during the day, and the bewildering dream suggested to them the image of the snake. Thus I vindicate the dream, and show up the explanation given by the pride of their sons and by unblushing flattery. For there must have been some reason for the adulterous fancy always taking the form of a serpent.

But I am wandering from my purpose, which was simply to prove that among the ancients beauty was the supreme law of the imitative arts. This being established, it follows necessarily that whatever else these arts may aim at must give way completely if incompatible with beauty, and, if compatible, must at least be secondary to it.

I will confine myself wholly to expression. There are passions and degrees of passion whose expression produces the most hideous contortions of the face, and throws the whole body into such unnatural positions as to destroy all the beautiful lines that mark it when in a state of greater repose. These passions the old artists either refrained altogether from representing, or softened into emotions which were capable of being expressed with some degree of beauty.

Rage and despair disfigured none of their works. I venture to maintain that they never represented a fury. Wrath they tempered into severity. In poetry we have the wrathful Jupiter, who hurls the thunderbolt; in art he is simply the austere.

Anguish was softened into sadness. Where that was impossible, and where the representation of intense grief would belittle as well as disfigure, how did Timanthes manage? There is a well-known picture by him of the sacrifice of Iphigenia, wherein he gives to the countenance of every spectator a fitting degree of sadness, but veils the face of the father, on which should have been depicted the most intense suffering. This has been the subject of many petty criticisms. "The artist," says one,[4] "had so exhausted himself in representations of sadness that he despaired of depicting the father's face worthily." "He hereby confessed," says another,[5] "that the bitterness of extreme grief cannot be expressed by art." I, for my part, see in this no proof of incapacity in the artist or his art. In proportion to the intensity of feeling, the expression of the features is intensified, and nothing is easier than to express extremes. But Timanthes knew the limits which the graces have imposed upon his art. He knew that the grief befitting Agamemnon, as father, produces contortions which are essentially ugly. He carried expression as far as was consistent with beauty and dignity. Ugliness he would gladly have passed over, or have softened, but since his subject admitted of neither, there was nothing left him but to veil it. What he might not paint he left to be imagined. That concealment was in short a sacrifice to beauty; an example to show, not how expression can be carried beyond the limits of art, but how it should be subjected to the first law of art, the law of beauty.

Apply this to the Laocoon and we have the cause we were seeking. The master was striving to attain the greatest beauty under the given conditions of bodily pain. Pain, in its disfiguring extreme, was not compatible with beauty, and must therefore be softened. Screams must be reduced to sighs, not because screams would betray weakness, but because they would deform the countenance to a repulsive degree. Imagine Laocoon's mouth open, and judge. Let him scream, and see. It was, before, a figure to inspire compassion in its beauty and suffering. Now it is ugly, abhorrent, and we gladly avert our eyes from a painful spectacle, destitute of the beauty which alone could turn our pain into the sweet feeling of pity for the suffering object.

The simple opening of the mouth, apart from the violent and repulsive contortions it causes in the other parts of the face, is a blot on a painting

[4] Plinius, lib. xxxv, sect. 35. [Lessing.]
[5] Valerius Maximus, lib. viii, cap. 2. [Lessing.]

and a cavity in a statue productive of the worst possible effect. Montfaucon showed little taste when he pronounced the bearded face of an old man with wide open mouth, to be a Jupiter delivering an oracle.[6] Cannot a god foretell the future without screaming? Would a more becoming posture of the lips cast suspicion upon his prophecies? Valerius cannot make me believe that Ajax was painted screaming in the above-mentioned picture of Timanthes. Far inferior masters, after the decline of art, do not in a single instance make the wildest barbarian open his mouth to scream, even though in mortal terror of his enemy's sword.[7]

This softening of the extremity of bodily suffering into a lesser degree of pain is apparent in the works of many of the old artists. Hercules, writhing in his poisoned robe, from the hand of an unknown master, was not the Hercules of Sophocles, who made the Locrian rocks and the Euboean promontory ring with his horrid cries. He was gloomy rather than wild. The Philoctetes of Pythagoras Leontinus seemed to communicate his pain to the beholder, an effect which would have been destroyed by the slightest disfigurement of the features. It may be asked how I know that this master made a statue of Philoctetes. From a passage in Pliny, which ought not to have waited for my emendation, so evident is the alteration or mutilation it has undergone.[8]

III

But, as already observed, the realm of art has in modern times been greatly enlarged. Its imitations are allowed to extend over all visible nature, of which beauty constitutes but a small part. Truth and expression are taken as its first law. As nature always sacrifices beauty to higher ends, so should the artist subordinate it to his general purpose, and not pursue it further than truth and expression allow. Enough that truth and expression convert what is unsightly in nature into a beauty of art.

Allowing this idea to pass unchallenged at present for whatever it is worth, are there not other independent considerations which should set bounds to expression, and prevent the artist from choosing for his imitation the culminating point of any action?

The single moment of time to which art must confine itself, will lead us, I think, to such considerations. Since the artist can use but a single moment of ever-changing nature, and the painter must further confine his study of this one moment to a single point of view, while their works are made not simply to be looked at, but to be contemplated long and often, evidently the most fruitful moment and the most fruitful aspect of that moment must be chosen. Now that only is fruitful which allows free play to the imagination. The more we see the more we must be able to imagine; and the more we imagine, the more we must think we see. But no moment in the whole course of an action is so disadvantageous in this respect as that of its culmination. There is nothing beyond, and to present the uttermost to the eye is to bind the wings of Fancy, and compel her, since she cannot soar beyond the impression made on the senses, to employ herself with feebler images, shunning as her limit the visible fulness already expressed. When, for instance, Laocoon sighs, imagination can hear him cry; but if he cry, imagination can neither mount a step higher, nor fall a step lower, without seeing him in a more endurable, and therefore less interesting, condition. We hear him merely groaning, or we see him already dead.

Again, since this single moment receives from art an unchanging duration, it should express nothing essentially transitory. All phenomena, whose nature it is suddenly to break out and as suddenly to disappear, which can remain as they are but for a moment; all such phenomena, whether agreeable or otherwise, acquire through the perpetuity conferred upon them by art such an unnatural appearance, that the impression they produce becomes weaker with every fresh observation, till the whole subject at last wearies or disgusts us. La Mettrie, who had himself painted and engraved as a second Democritus, laughs only the first time we look at him. Looked at again, the philosopher becomes a buffoon, and his laugh a grimace. So it is with a cry. Pain, which is so violent as to extort a scream, either soon abates or it must destroy the sufferer. Again, if a man of firmness and endurance cry, he does not do so unceasingly, and only this ap-

---

[6] Antiquit. expl. T. i, p. 50. [Lessing.]

[7] Bellorii Admiranda, Tab. 11, 12. [Lessing.]

[8] Pliny, lib. 34, sect. 19. [Lessing.]

parent continuity in art makes the cry degenerate into womanish weakness or childish impatience. This, at least, the sculptor of the Laocoon had to guard against, even had a cry not been an offence against beauty, and were suffering without beauty a legitimate subject of art. . . .

XVI

But I will try to prove my conclusions by starting from first principles.

I argue thus. If it be true that painting employs wholly different signs or means of imitation from poetry,—the one using forms and colors in space, the other articulate sounds in time,—and if signs must unquestionably stand in convenient relation with the thing signified, then signs arranged side by side can represent only objects existing side by side, or whose parts so exist, while consecutive signs can express only objects which succeed each other, or whose parts succeed each other, in time.

Objects which exist side by side, or whose parts so exist, are called bodies. Consequently bodies with their visible properties are the peculiar subjects of painting.

Objects which succeed each other, or whose parts succeed each other in time, are actions. Consequently actions are the peculiar subjects of poetry.

All bodies, however, exist not only in space, but also in time. They continue, and, at any moment of their continuance, may assume a different appearance and stand in different relations. Every one of these momentary appearances and groupings was the result of a preceding, may become the cause of a following, and is therefore the centre of a present, action. Consequently painting can imitate actions also,

but only as they are suggested through forms.

Actions, on the other hand, cannot exist independently, but must always be joined to certain agents. In so far as those agents are bodies or are regarded as such, poetry describes also bodies, but only indirectly through actions.

Painting, in its coexistent compositions, can use but a single moment of an action, and must therefore choose the most pregnant one, the one most suggestive of what has gone before and what is to follow.

Poetry, in its progressive imitations, can use but a single attribute of bodies, and must choose that one which gives the most vivid picture of the body as exercised in this particular action.

Hence the rule for the employment of a single descriptive epithet, and the cause of the rare occurrence of descriptions of physical objects.

I should place less confidence in this dry chain of conclusions, did I not find them fully confirmed by Homer, or, rather, had they not been first suggested to me by Homer's method. These principles alone furnish a key to the noble style of the Greek, and enable us to pass just judgment on the opposite method of many modern poets who insist upon emulating the artist in a point where they must of necessity remain inferior to him.

I find that Homer paints nothing but progressive actions. All bodies, all separate objects, are painted only as they take part in such actions, and generally with a single touch. No wonder, then, that artists find in Homer's pictures little or nothing to their purpose, and that their only harvest is where the narration brings together in a space favorable to art a number of beautiful shapes in graceful attitudes, however little the poet himself may have painted shapes, attitudes, or space. . . .

From the Hamburg Dramaturgy

THE NAMES of princes and heroes can lend pomp and majesty to a play, but they contribute nothing to our emotion. The misfortunes of those whose circumstances most

resemble our own, must naturally penetrate most deeply into our hearts, and if we pity kings, we pity them as human beings, not as kings. Though their position often renders their misfortunes more important, it does not make them more interesting. Whole nations may be involved in

Hamburg Dramaturgy. Published in 1767-68; translated by E. C. Beasley and H. Zimmern.

them, but our sympathy requires an individual object and a state is far too much an abstract conception to touch our feelings.

"We wrong the human heart," says Marmontel, "we misread nature, if we believe that it requires titles to rouse and touch us. The sacred names of friend, father, lover, husband, son, mother, of mankind in general, these are far more pathetic than aught else and retain their claims for ever. What matters the rank, the surname, the genealogy of the unfortunate man whose easy good nature towards unworthy friends has involved him in gambling and who loses over this his wealth and honour and now sighs in prison distracted by shame and remorse? If asked, who is he? I reply: He was an honest man and to add to his grief he is a husband and a father; his wife whom he loves and who loves him is suffering extreme need and can only give tears to the children who clamour for bread. Show me in the history of heroes a more touching, a more moral, indeed a more tragic situation! And when at last this miserable man takes poison and then learns that Heaven had willed his release, what is absent, in this painful terrible moment, when to the horrors of death are added the tortures of imagination, telling him how happily he could have lived, what I say is absent to render the situation worthy of a tragedy? The wonderful, will be replied. What! is there not matter wonderful enough in this sudden change from honour to shame, from innocence to guilt, from sweet peace to despair; in brief, in the extreme misfortune into which mere weakness has plunged him!"

But no matter how much their Diderots and Marmontels preach this to the French, it does not seem as though domestic tragedies were coming into vogue among them. The nation is too vain, too much enamoured of titles and other external favours; even the humblest man desires to consort with aristocrats and considers the society of his equals as bad society. True, a happy genius can exert great influence over his nation. Nature has nowhere resigned her rights and she is perhaps only waiting there for the poet who is to exhibit her in all her truth and strength.

The objections raised by the above critic against the German "Sara" are in part not without foundation. Yet I fancy the author would rather retain all its faults than take the trouble of entirely rewriting the play. He recalls what Voltaire said on a similar occasion: "We cannot do all that our friends advise. There are such things as necessary faults. To cure a humpbacked man of his hump we should have to take his life. My child is humpbacked, but otherwise it is quite well." (No. 14.)

Genius is only busied with events that are rooted in one another, that form a chain of cause and effect. To reduce the latter to the former, to weigh the latter against the former, everywhere to exclude chance, to cause everything that occurs to occur so that it could not have happened otherwise, this is the part of genius when it works in the domains of history and converts the useless treasures of memory into nourishment for the soul. Wit on the contrary, that does not depend on matters rooted in each other, but on the similar or dissimilar, if it ventures on a work that should be reserved to genius alone, detains itself with such events that have not further concern with one another except that they have occurred at the same time. To connect these, to interweave and confuse their threads so that we lose the one at every moment in following out the other and are thrown from one surprise into another, this is the part of wit and this only. From the incessant crossing of such threads of opposed colours results a texture, which is to art what weavers call *changeant*: a material of which we cannot say whether it be blue or red, green or yellow; it is both, it seems this from one side, that from another, a plaything of fashion, a juggling trick for children.

Now judge whether the great Corneille has used his theme like a genius or like a wit. For this judgment nothing else is required but the application of the axiom, disputed by none: Genius loves simplicity, and wit complication. (No. 30.)

OLIVER GOLDSMITH   (1730?-1774)

GOLDSMITH's critical essays are in the English tradition of liberal neo-classicism. On the one hand, he showed a continued antagonism to the mechanical use of hard and fast rules. Yet on the other he takes for granted, in a broad sense, the neoclassic values of decorum, probability, unity of outline, clarity and propriety of style, and the general type rather than the particular individual. The essay on *Sentimental and Laughing Comedy* (1773) has another neoclassic characteristic: it reasserts the classical distinction of genres at a time when this distinction was beginning to disintegrate in many ways. What Goldsmith reapplied is the traditional distinction between tragedy and comedy. Each, in classical theory, is concerned with different sorts of characters. Tragedy is possible only if the character has some mental or emotional largeness. Moreover, he must have a high enough position of some sort if the tragic fall or disintegration is to be important and affecting. Comedy, on the other hand, is concerned with lower, less significant figures. It does not seek to glorify or sentimentalize them, but to see them as they are and to "expose the vices and follies" they commit.

Goldsmith, in reapplying this distinction, was not attacking English tragicomedy—the mixture of tragic and comic scenes in the same play, such as we find in Shakespeare. He was attacking a new kind of drama that was neither tragedy nor comedy. For the eighteenth century was witnessing the rapid growth of "sentimental" comedy, a form that has since tended to become the staple diet of theater-goers, especially with the advent of motion pictures in the twentieth century. Its theme is mainly romantic love. It deals with ordinary, or even "low" characters, as indeed comedy should; but instead of exposing their "vices and follies," it approves and even glorifies them. Its action is drawn from the more trifling ups-and-downs of casual or domestic life. It exploits the sentimental feelings of the observer—leaving

OLIVER GOLDSMITH. The son of an Irish clergyman, Goldsmith was educated at Trinity College, Dublin, and studied medicine at Edinburgh and Leyden. After wandering about Europe (1755-56), he worked in London as a hack writer, gradually became known in literary circles, and was one of the original members of the famous club over which Johnson presided. Goldsmith wrote prolifically; he also showed talent in a wide range of genres: the familiar essay, poetry, the novel, drama, history, and criticism. His play, *She Stoops to Conquer* (1773), partly exemplifies his theory of comedy.

Two nineteenth-century editions of the *Works* (ed. P. Cunningham, 4 vols., 1854; and ed. J. W. M. Gibbs, 5 vols., 1884-86) have been superseded by the edition of Arthur Friedman (5 vols., Oxford, 1966). Helpful commentary is largely confined to general works on the critical theory of the period (see above, p. 12). Also useful are Robert Hopkins, *The True Genius of Oliver Goldsmith* (Baltimore, 1969); and Ricardo Quintana, *Oliver Goldsmith: a Georgian Study* (1967).

one, as Coleridge later said, in "a hot huddle of indefinite sensations"—without taking a subject strong enough to bring about the Aristotelian *katharsis* of genuine tragedy. On the other hand, it has nothing in common with comedy except that it does not end unhappily. As Goethe said of the modern theater, "No one is killed, and everyone gets married." Goldsmith's brief but spirited essay, written at the close of the classical tradition, is an attempt to redirect comedy to its original aim and function.

Essay on the Theatre; or, A Comparison Between Sentimental and Laughing Comedy

THE THEATRE, like all other amusements, has its fashions and its prejudices; and when satiated with its excellence, mankind begin to mistake change for improvement. For some years tragedy was the reigning entertainment; but of late it has entirely given way to comedy, and our best efforts are now exerted in these lighter kinds of composition. The pompous train, the swelling phrase, and the unnatural rant, are displaced for that natural portrait of human folly and frailty, of which all are judges, because all have sat for the picture.

But, as in describing nature, it is presented with a double face, either of mirth or sadness, our modern writers find themselves at a loss which chiefly to copy from; and it is now debated, whether the exhibition of human distress is likely to afford the mind more entertainment than that of human absurdity?

Comedy is defined by Aristotle to be a picture of the frailties of the lower part of mankind, to distinguish it from tragedy, which is an exhibition of the misfortunes of the great. When comedy therefore ascends to produce the characters of princes or generals upon the stage, it is out of its walk, since low life and middle life are entirely its object. The principal question therefore is, whether in describing low or middle life, an exhibition of its follies be not preferable to a detail of its calamities? Or, in other words, which deserves the preference, the weeping sentimental comedy, so much in fashion at present, or the laughing and even low comedy, which seems to have been last exhibited by Vanbrugh and Cibber? [1]

If we apply to authorities, all the great masters in the dramatic art have but one opinion. Their rule is, that as tragedy displays the calamities of the great, so comedy should excite our laughter, by ridiculously exhibiting the follies of the lower part of mankind. Boileau, one of the best modern critics, asserts, that comedy will not admit of tragic distress:

Le Comique, ennemi des soupirs et des pleurs,
N'admet point dans ses vers de tragiques douleurs. [2]

Nor is this rule without the strongest foundation in nature, as the distresses of the mean by no means affect us so strongly as the calamities of the great. When tragedy exhibits to us some great man fallen from his height, and struggling with want and adversity, we feel his situation in the same manner as we suppose he himself must feel, and our pity is increased in proportion to the height from which he fell. On the contrary, we do not so strongly sympathize with one born in humbler circumstances, and encountering accidental distress: so that while we melt for Belisarius,[3] we scarcely give halfpence to the beggar, who accosts us in the street. The

Essay on the Theatre. First printed in the *Westminster Magazine*, January, 1773.

[1] Sir John Vanbrugh (1664-1726), the English dramatist, and Colley Cibber (1671-1757), playwright and poet laureate. The play is *The Provoked Husband* (1728).

[2] "Comedy, the enemy of sighs and tears, does not admit tragic griefs into its verses" (*L'Art Poétique*, III, 401-02).

[3] A Roman commander who was blinded, after being accused of conspiracy, and forced to wander as a beggar through the streets of Constantinople; the hero of Marmontel's romance, *Belisaire* (1767).

one has our pity, the other our contempt. Distress therefore is the proper object of tragedy, since the great excite our pity by their fall; but not equally so of comedy, since the actors employed in it are originally so mean, that they sink but little by their fall.

Since the first origin of the stage, tragedy and comedy have run in distinct channels, and never till of late encroached upon the provinces of each other. Terence, who seems to have made the nearest approaches, always judiciously stops short before he comes to the downright pathetic; and yet he is even reproached by Caesar for wanting the *vis comica*. All the other comic writers of antiquity aim only at rendering folly or vice ridiculous, but never exalt their characters into buskined pomp, or make what Voltaire humourously calls a *tradesman's tragedy*.

Yet notwithstanding this weight of authority, and the universal practice of former ages, a new species of dramatic composition has been introduced under the name of *sentimental* comedy, in which the virtues of private life are exhibited, rather than the vices exposed; and the distresses rather than the faults of mankind make our interest in the piece. These comedies have had of late great success, perhaps from their novelty, and also from their flattering every man in his favourite foible. In these plays almost all the characters are good, and exceedingly generous; they are lavish enough of their *tin* money on the stage; and though they want humour, have abundance of sentiment and feeling. If they happen to have faults or foibles, the spectator is taught not only to pardon, but to applaud them, in consideration of the goodness of their hearts; so that folly, instead of being ridiculed, is commended, and the comedy aims at touching our passions without the power of being truly pathetic. In this manner we are likely to lose one great source of entertainment on the stage; for while the comic poet is invading the province of the tragic muse, he leaves her lovely sister quite neglected. Of this, however, he is no way solicitous, as he measures his fame by his profits.

But it will be said, that the theatre is formed to amuse mankind, and that it matters little, if this end be answered, by what means it is obtained. If mankind find delight in weeping at comedy, it would be cruel to abridge them in that or any other innocent pleasure. If those pieces are denied the name of comedies, yet call them by any other name, and if they are delightful, they are good. Their success, it will be said, is a mark of their merit, and it is only abridging our happiness to deny us an inlet to amusement.

These objections, however, are rather specious than solid. It is true, that amusement is a great object of the theatre; and it will be allowed, that these sentimental pieces do often amuse us; but the question is, whether the true comedy would not amuse us more? The question is, whether a character supported throughout a piece with its ridicule still attending, would not give us more delight than this species of bastard tragedy, which only is applauded because it is new?

A friend of mine, who was sitting unmoved at one of these sentimental pieces, was asked how he could be so indifferent? "Why, truly," says he, "as the hero is but a tradesman, it is indifferent to me whether he be turned out of his counting-house on Fish-Street Hill, since he will still have enough left to open shop in St. Giles's."

The other objection is as ill-grounded; for though we should give these pieces another name, it will not mend their efficacy. It will continue a kind of *mulish* production, with all the defects of its opposite parents, and marked with sterility. If we are permitted to make comedy weep, we have an equal right to make tragedy laugh, and to set down in blank verse the jests and repartees of all the attendants in a funeral procession.

But there is one argument in favour of sentimental comedy which will keep it on the stage, in spite of all that can be said against it. It is of all others the most easily written. Those abilities that can hammer out a novel, are fully sufficient for the production of a sentimental comedy. It is only sufficient to raise the characters a little; to deck out the hero with a riband, or give the heroine a title; then to put an insipid dialogue, without character or humour, into their mouths, give them mighty good hearts, very fine clothes, furnish a new set of scenes, make a pathetic scene or two, with a sprinkling of tender melancholy conversation through the whole; and there is no doubt but all the ladies will cry and all the gentlemen applaud.

Humour at present seems to be departing from the stage, and it will soon happen that our comic players will have nothing left for it but a fine coat and a song. It depends upon the audience whether they will actually drive those poor merry creatures from the stage, or sit at a play as gloomy as at the tabernacle. It is not easy to recover an art when once lost; and it will be but a just punishment, that when, by our being too fastidious, we have banished humour from the stage, we should ourselves be deprived of the art of laughing.

SIR JOSHUA REYNOLDS   (1723-1792)

THE DISCOURSES Reynolds delivered as president of the Royal Academy from 1769 to 1790 were primarily addressed to the young students there. They deal less with the technical aspects of painting and sculpture than with the general principles of art. In doing so, they bring together almost all the approaches to art that prevailed at the time. Reynolds's critical position not only rests upon the neoclassic principles of "general nature," the moral aim of art, and the importance of tradition. It also includes the romantic values of emotional immediacy, imaginative intuition, and a controlled use of particular details. It shows as well a romantic interest in the psychological reactions that make up taste. Altogether, Reynolds's *Discourses* offer the most representative single embodiment in English of eighteenth-century critical principles.

Like Johnson, Reynolds assumed the classical premise that the end of art is to enlarge man's mental and moral nature. Hence, to begin with, it is humanistic: the highest art deals with human beings, not landscape or animal life, though these may show technical skill and sensitivity to line and color. Moreover, in portraying human beings, art should seek to "imitate" the ideal by presenting a *completed* and generalized model. A realistic fidelity to purely individual features and details is not "nature"; for "how can that be the nature of man, in which no two individuals are the same?" But

SIR JOSHUA REYNOLDS. After being educated by his father, a clergyman and teacher, Reynolds studied art in London and then for four years in Italy; on his return (1752) he quickly became noted as the foremost portrait painter of England. His intelligence and kindly, understanding nature brought him a wide and cultivated acquaintance. He was one of the founders of Johnson's Club, and in 1769 he became the first president of the Royal Academy.

Editions of the *Discourses* include those of E. G. Johnson (1891), R. Fry (1905), A. Dobson (1907), L. Dimier (1909), R. R. Wark (San Marino, 1959), and the *Works* (ed. Beechey, 2 vols., 1835). For commentary, see especially F. W. Hilles, *The Literary Career of Sir Joshua Reynolds* (1936). Other discussions are found in W. J. Bate, "Johnson and Reynolds: the Premise of General Nature," in *From Classic to Romantic* (1946); M. Macklem, "Reynolds and the Ambiguities of Neoclassical Criticism," *Philological Quarterly*, XXXI (1952), 383-98; E. Olson's Introd. to a joint edition of Longinus and Reynolds (1945); and W. D. Templeman, "Sir Joshua Reynolds on the Picturesque," *Modern Language Notes*, XLVII (1933).

if Reynolds began by emphasizing that art is concerned with the *ethos*—the universal character—rather than the particular, his later *Discourses* increasingly imply that the greatest art is that which successfully unites the universal and the particular. We do not feel the ideal vitally unless it has been presented in terms of particulars. Reynolds's increasing preference for Michelangelo above other artists is an illustration. For Michelangelo, through individualized expression, evokes an emotional and sympathetic response from the observer that could not have been aroused by a purely generalized decorum, while at the same time he retains the ideal as a controlling guide. He thus differs from the severe classicist by calling forth a more energetic, personal, and emotionally immediate feeling.

Reynolds thus combined and reconciled classical and broadly romantic values in his conception of the function of art. He did so even more in his conception of what comprises "taste." The first and most essential element in taste is "the knowledge of what is truly nature": the rational grasp of the uniform and fixed principles of nature. To this extent, there is a stable and uniform "standard of taste"—conformity to nature—and it is based on "reason." But more enters into taste than this. Art, after all, is not the same thing as mathematics. It is broadly humanistic; it deals with things, not absolute and abstractly demonstrable, but learned tentatively and by experience. Hence the need to widen one's experience as much as possible by noting empirically what standards, ideals, or opinions have tended to persist most vitally among other cultivated ages and societies. In a general way, we may assume that "what has pleased, and continues to please, is likely to please again." We can profit especially, therefore, from studying great works that have appealed to the cultivated people of different periods and nations. Through them, "the accumulated experience of mankind may at once be acquired."

The so-called "rules" of art comprise, at their best, generalizations of the past experience of mankind with the various arts. In his attitude toward the "rules" of art, Reynolds was far from advocating their mechanical use. Indeed, genius begins "where known vulgar and trite rules have no longer any place"—where whatever knowledge those rules can give has been assimilated in such a way that they are felt in their cumulative force rather than applied with deliberate, piecemeal method. As with the rules, so with the imitation of great artists of the past. "The great use of studying our predecessors," he said, "is to *open* the mind"—to get it out of its own subjective channels of thinking and feeling, and enlarge its receptivity. The extreme self-expressionist, who believes that all great art is the result of inspiration or sheer native capacity, forgets that, being imitative animals, we have to imitate something; and he will "soon be reduced, from mere barrenness, to the poorest of all imitations; he will be obliged to imitate himself." Reynolds would have agreed with Goethe that "a subjective nature has soon talked out his little internal material, and is at last ruined by mannerism." It is noteworthy in this connection that the greatest artists of the Renaissance, such as Raphael and Michelangelo, neglected no opportunity to learn as much from ancient Greek art as possible, and from the beginning studied art through an earnest but liberal imitation.

But Reynolds repeatedly distinguished this formative and educational method of imitating from the mere passive copying of "a particular thought, an action, attitude, or figure." Mere copying, as well as rule-mongering and the love of method for its own sake are, in art, a species of "idleness." "A provision of endless apparatus," he wisely said, "a bustle of infinite inquiry and research, or even the mere mechanical labour of copying, may be employed to evade and shuffle off real labour—the real labour of thinking." Unless the imaginative judgment is continually used, it "by degrees loses its power of becoming active when exertion is necessary." What is needed is a strong, sympathetic mental grasp of general ideals and principles and general technical devices as exemplified in the greatest works; it is acquired mainly through imaginatively "contemplating and brooding over the ideas of great geniuses, till you find yourself warmed by the contact." Here Reynolds was very close to Longinus. And like Longinus, he was confident that through this selective and sympathetic imitation the mind acquires a new and greater independence. For it is not now left the prey of personal whim or whatever temporary fashions dominate the environment.

In his later *Discourses* especially, Reynolds plainly tried to stress the point that knowledge of whatever sort is of genuine value only to the degree that one has assimilated it and immediately reacts in accordance with it. We may recall Aristotle's definition of virtue as "rejoicing and loving and hating aright," and his belief that we attain it by forming the active "power" of judging and "taking delight" in the good. So the kind of knowledge special to art—knowledge of "the general idea of nature" attainable through reason and through ways of thinking and feeling caught from great predecessors, as well as the knowledge of the technical demands of a given art and of general rules applicable to it—does not vitally affect taste or genius if it is external to the artist, existing on the shelf of his memory for reference or consultation, but only if it becomes "a part of himself" and is "woven into his mind." In order to reassert this classical principle as broadly as possible, the criticism of the middle and later eighteenth century felt the need of a new terminology. For, as in the general "commerce of life," the ability needed is a kind of "sagacity" that draws upon the "accumulated experience of our whole life," but which supersedes "the slow progress of deduction," and "goes at once, by what *appears* a kind of intuition, to the conclusion." The word "reason" had come to connote abstract deliberation, and to be applied, as Reynolds suggested in one of his last *Discourses* (XIII, 1786) to "partial, confined, argumentative theories."

Reynolds, like the romantic critics of his own day and later, found a substitute in the word "imagination," with its suggestion of a more immediate act of mind. Hence Reynolds's statement, in this same discourse, that the imagination—as distinct from "principles falsely called rational"—is in art the final "residence of truth." With Reynolds, the door stands open to what is best and most durable in the romantic theory of the imagination. That one can say this of the most representative of English neoclassic critics is one more illustration of the extent to which the classical tradition, at the close of its long history, has recovered its original flexibility and liberality.

From Discourse VI

THE TRAVELLERS into the East tell us that when the ignorant inhabitants of those countries are asked concerning the ruins of stately edifices yet remaining amongst them, the melancholy monuments of their former grandeur and long-lost science, they always answer that they were built by magicians. The untaught mind finds a vast gulf between its own powers, and those works of complicated art, which it is utterly unable to fathom; and it supposes that such a void can be passed only by supernatural powers.

And, as for artists themselves, it is by no means their interest to undeceive such judges, however conscious they may be of the very natural means by which their extraordinary powers were acquired; though our art, being intrinsically imitative, rejects this idea of inspiration, more perhaps than any other.

It is to avoid this plain confession of truth, as it should seem, that this imitation of masters, indeed almost all imitation, which implies a more regular and progressive method of attaining the ends of painting, has ever been particularly inveighed against with great keenness, both by ancient and modern writers.

To derive all from native power, to owe nothing to another, is the praise which men who do not much think on what they are saying bestow sometimes upon others, and sometimes on themselves; and their imaginary dignity is naturally heightened by a supercilious censure of the low, the barren, the grovelling, the servile

Discourse VI. Delivered in 1774.

imitator. It would be no wonder if a student, frightened by these terrific and disgraceful epithets with which the poor imitators are so often loaded, should let fall his pencil in mere despair (conscious as he must be how much he has been indebted to the labours of others, how little, how very little of his art was born with him); and consider it as hopeless to set about acquiring by the imitation of any human master what he is taught to suppose is matter of inspiration from heaven.

Some allowance must be made for what is said in the gaiety of rhetoric. We cannot suppose that anyone can really mean to exclude all imitation of others. A position so wild would scarce deserve a serious answer; for it is apparent, if we were forbid to make use of the advantages which our predecessors afford us, the art would be always to begin, and consequently remain always in its infant state; and it is a common observation that no art was ever invented and carried to perfection at the same time. . . .

What we now call genius begins, not where rules, abstractedly taken, end; but where known vulgar and trite rules have no longer any place. It must of necessity be that even works of genius, like every other effect, as they must have their cause, must likewise have their rules; it cannot be by chance that excellences are produced with any constancy or any certainty, for this is not the nature of chance; but the rules by which men of extraordinary parts, and such as are called men of genius, work, are either such as they discover by their own peculiar observations, or of such a nice texture as not easily to admit being expressed in words; especially as artists are not very frequently skilful in that mode of communicating ideas. Unsubstantial, however, as these rules may seem, and difficult as it may be to convey them in writing, they are still seen and felt in the mind of the artist; and he works from them with as much certainty as if they were embodied, as I may say, upon paper. It is true, these refined principles cannot be always made palpable, like the more gross rules of art; yet it does not follow, but that the mind may be put in such a train that it shall perceive, by a kind of scientific sense, that propriety, which words, particularly words of unpractised writers, such as we are, can but very feebly suggest.

Invention is one of the great marks of genius; but if we consult experience, we shall find that it is by being conversant with the inventions of others that we learn to invent; as by reading the thoughts of others we learn to think.

Whoever has so far formed his taste as to be able to relish and feel the beauties of the great masters has gone a great way in his study; for, merely from a consciousness of this relish of the right, the mind swells with an inward pride, and is almost as powerfully affected as if it had itself produced what it admires. Our hearts, frequently warmed in this manner by the contact of those whom we wish to resemble, will undoubtedly catch something of their own way of thinking; and we shall receive in our own bosoms some radiation at least of their fire and splendour.[1] That disposition, which is so strong in children, still continues with us, of catching involuntarily the general air and manner of those with whom we are most conversant; with this difference only, that a young mind is naturally pliable and imitative; but in a more advanced state it grows rigid, and must be warmed and softened before it will receive a deep impression.

From these considerations, which a little of your own reflection will carry a great way further, it appears, of what great consequence it is that our minds should be habituated to the contemplation of excellence; and that, far from being contented to make such habits the discipline of our youth only, we should, to the last moment of our lives, continue a settled inter-

course with all the true examples of grandeur. Their inventions are not only the food of our infancy, but the substance which supplies the fullest maturity of our vigour.

The mind is but a barren soil; a soil which is soon exhausted, and will produce no crop, or only one, unless it be continually fertilised and enriched with foreign matter.

When we have had continually before us the great works of art to impregnate our minds with kindred ideas, we are then, and not till then, fit to produce something of the same species. We behold all about us with the eyes of those penetrating observers whose works we contemplate; and our minds, accustomed to think the thoughts of the noblest and brightest intellects, are prepared for the discovery and selection of all that is great and noble in nature. The greatest natural genius cannot subsist on its own stock: he who resolves never to ransack any mind but his own will be soon reduced, from mere barrenness, to the poorest of all imitations; he will be obliged to imitate himself, and to repeat what he has before often repeated. When we know the subject designed by such men, it will never be difficult to guess what kind of work is to be produced.

It is vain for painters or poets to endeavour to invent without materials on which the mind may work, and from which invention must originate. Nothing can come of nothing.

Homer is supposed to be possessed of all the learning of his time; and we are certain that Michael Angelo and Raffaelle were equally possessed of all the knowledge in the art which had been discovered in the works of their predecessors.

A mind enriched by an assemblage of all the treasures of ancient and modern art will be more elevated and fruitful in resources, in proportion to the number of ideas which have been carefully collected and thoroughly digested. There can be no doubt but that he who has the most materials has the greatest means of invention; and if he has not the power of using them, it must proceed from a feebleness of intellect, or from the confused manner in which those collections have been laid up in his mind.

The addition of other men's judgment is so far from weakening our own, as is the opinion of many, that it will fashion and consolidate

[1] See Longinus, above, p. 68.

those ideas of excellence which lay in embryo, feeble, ill-shaped, and confused, but which are finished and put in order by the authority and practice of those whose works may be said to have been consecrated by having stood the test of ages. . . .

Discourse XIII

Delivered to the Students of the Royal Academy, on the Distribution of the Prizes, December 11, 1786

Art not merely Imitation, but under the Direction of the Imagination. In what Manner Poetry, Painting, Acting, Gardening, and Architecture depart from Nature

GENTLEMEN,

To discover beauties, or to point out faults, in the works of celebrated masters, and to compare the conduct of one artist with another, is certainly no mean or inconsiderable part of criticism; but this is still no more than to know the art through the artist. This test of investigation must have two capital defects; it must be narrow, and it must be uncertain. To enlarge the boundaries of the art of painting, as well as to fix its principles, it will be necessary, that *that* art and *those* principles should be considered in their correspondence with the principles of the other arts which, like this, address themselves primarily and principally to the imagination. When those connected and kindred principles are brought together to be compared, another comparison will grow out of this; that is, the comparison of them all with those of human nature, from whence arts derive the materials upon which they are to produce their effects.

When this comparison of art with art, and of all arts with the nature of man, is once made with success, our guiding lines are as well ascertained and established, as they can be in matters of this description.

This, as it is the highest style of criticism, is at the same time the soundest; for it refers to the eternal and immutable nature of things.

You are not to imagine that I mean to open to you at large, or to recommend to your research, the whole of this vast field of science. It is certainly much above my faculties to reach it; and though it may not be above yours to comprehend it fully, if it were fully and properly brought before you, yet perhaps the most perfect criticism requires habits of speculation and abstraction, not very consistent with the employment which ought to occupy and the habits of mind which ought to prevail in a practical artist. I only point out to you these things, that when you do criticise (as all who work on a plan will criticise more or less), your criticism may be built on the foundation of true principles; and that though you may not always travel a great way, the way that you do travel may be the right road.

I observe, as a fundamental ground, common to all the arts with which we have any concern in this discourse, that they address themselves only to two faculties of the mind, its imagination and its sensibility.

All theories which attempt to direct or to control the art, upon any principles falsely called rational, which we form to ourselves upon a supposition of what ought in reason to be the end or means of art, independent of the known first effect produced by objects on the imagination, must be false and delusive. For though it may appear bold to say it, the imagination is here the residence of truth. If the imagination be affected, the conclusion is fairly drawn; if it be not affected, the reasoning is erroneous, because the end is not obtained; the effect itself being the test, and the only test, of the truth and efficacy of the means.

There is in the commerce of life, as in art, a sagacity which is far from being contradictory to right reason, and is superior to any occasional exercise of that faculty; which supersedes it; and does not wait for the slow progress of deduction, but goes at once, by what appears a kind of intuition, to the conclusion. A man endowed with this faculty feels and acknowledges the truth, though it is not always in his power, perhaps, to give a reason for it; because he cannot recollect and bring before him all the materials that gave birth to his opinion; for very many and very intricate considerations may unite to form the principle, even of small and minute parts, involved in, or dependent on, a great system of things: though these in process of time are forgotten, the right impression still remains fixed in his mind.

This impression is the result of the accumulated experience of our whole life, and has been collected, we do not always know how, or when. But this mass of collective observation, however acquired, ought to prevail over that reason, which, however powerfully exerted on any particular occasion, will probably comprehend but a partial view of the subject; and our conduct in life as well as in the arts is, or ought to be, generally governed by this habitual reason: it is our happiness that we are enabled to draw on such funds. If we were obliged to enter into a theoretical deliberation on every occasion, before we act, life would be at a stand, and art would be impracticable.

It appears to me, therefore, that our first thoughts, that is, the effect which anything produces on our minds, on its first appearance, is never to be forgotten; and it demands for that reason, because it is the first, to be laid up with care. If this be not done, the artist may happen to impose on himself by partial reasoning; by a cold consideration of those animated thoughts which proceed, not perhaps from caprice or rashness (as he may afterwards conceit), but from the fulness of his mind, enriched with the copious stores of all the various inventions which he had ever seen, or had ever passed in his mind. These ideas are infused into his design, without any conscious effort; but if he be not on his guard, he may reconsider and correct them, till the whole matter is reduced to a commonplace invention.

This is sometimes the effect of what I mean to caution you against; that is to say, an unfounded distrust of the imagination and feeling, in favour of narrow, partial, confined, argumentative theories; and of principles that seem to apply to the design in hand; without considering those general impressions on the fancy in which real principles of *sound reason*, and of much more weight and importance, are involved, and, as it were, lie hid, under the appearance of a sort of vulgar sentiment.

Reason, without doubt, must ultimately deter-

mine everything; at this minute it is required to inform us when that very reason is to give way to feeling.

Though I have often spoken of that mean conception of our art which confines it to mere imitation, I must add, that it may be narrowed to such a mere matter of experiment, as to exclude from it the application of science, which alone gives dignity and compass to any art. But to find proper foundations for science is neither to narrow nor to vulgarise it; and this is sufficiently exemplified in the success of experimental philosophy. It is the false system of reasoning, grounded on a partial view of things, against which I would most earnestly guard you. And I do it the rather, because those narrow theories, so coincident with the poorest and most miserable practice, and which are adopted to give it countenance, have not had their origin in the poorest minds, but in the mistakes, or possibly in the mistaken interpretations, of great and commanding authorities. We are not therefore in this case misled by feeling, but by false speculation.

When such a man as Plato speaks of painting as only an imitative art, and that our pleasure proceeds from observing and acknowledging the truth of the imitation, I think he misleads us by a partial theory. It is in this poor, partial, and so far false view of the art, that Cardinal Bembo has chosen to distinguish even Raffaelle himself, whom our enthusiasm honours with the name of Divine. The same sentiment is adopted by Pope in his epitaph on Sir Godfrey Kneller; and he turns the panegyric solely on imitation, as it is a sort of deception.

I shall not think my time misemployed, if by any means I may contribute to confirm your opinion of what ought to be the object of your pursuit; because, though the best critics must always have exploded this strange idea, yet I know that there is a disposition towards a perpetual recurrence to it, on account of its simplicity and superficial plausibility. For this reason I shall beg leave to lay before you a few thoughts on this subject; to throw out some hints that may lead your minds to an opinion (which I take to be the truth), that painting is not only to be considered as an imitation, operating by deception, but that it is, and ought to be, in many points of view, and strictly speaking, no imitation at all of external nature. Perhaps it ought to be as far removed from the vulgar idea of imitation, as the refined civilised state in which we live, is removed from a gross state of nature; and those who have not cultivated their imaginations, which the majority of mankind certainly have not, may be said, in regard to arts, to continue in this state of nature. Such men will always prefer imitation to that excellence which is addressed to another faculty that they do not possess; but these are not the persons to whom a painter is to look, any more than a judge of morals and manners ought to refer controverted points upon those subjects to the opinions of people taken from the banks of the Ohio, or from New Holland.

It is the lowest style only of arts, whether of painting, poetry, or music, that may be said, in the vulgar sense, to be naturally pleasing. The higher efforts of those arts, we know by experience, do not affect minds wholly uncultivated. This refined taste is the consequence of education and habit; we are born only with a capacity of entertaining this refinement, as we are born with a disposition to receive and obey all the rules and regulations of society; and so far it may be said to be natural to us, and no further.

What has been said, may show the artist how necessary it is, when he looks about him for the advice and criticism of his friends, to make some distinction of the character, taste, experience, and observation in this art of those from whom it is received. An ignorant uneducated man may, like Apelles's critic, be a competent judge of the truth of the representation of a sandal; or to go somewhat higher, like Molière's old woman, may decide upon what is nature, in regard to comic humour; but a critic in the higher style of art ought to possess the same refined taste, which directed the artist in his work.

To illustrate this principle by a comparison with other arts, I shall now produce some instances to show, that they, as well as our own art, renounce the narrow idea of nature, and the narrow theories derived from that mistaken principle, and apply to that reason only which informs us not what imitation is,—a natural representation of a given object,—but what it is natural for the imagination to be delighted with.

And perhaps there is no better way of acquiring this knowledge, than by this kind of analogy: each art will corroborate and mutually reflect the truth on the other. Such a kind of juxtaposition may likewise have this use, that whilst the artist is amusing himself in the contemplation of other arts, he may habitually transfer the principles of those arts to that which he professes; which ought to be always present in his mind, and to which everything is to be referred.

So far is art from being derived from, or having any immediate intercourse with, particular nature as its model, that there are many arts that set out with a professed deviation from it.

This is certainly not so exactly true in regard to painting and sculpture. Our elements are laid in gross common nature,—an exact imitation of what is before us: but when we advance to the higher state, we consider this power of imitation, though first in the order of acquisition, as by no means the highest in the scale of perfection.

Poetry addresses itself to the same faculties and the same dispositions as painting, though by different means. The object of both is to accommodate itself to all the natural propensities and inclinations of the mind. The very existence of poetry depends on the licence it assumes of deviating from actual nature, in order to gratify natural propensities by other means, which are found by experience full as capable of affording such gratification. It sets out with a language in the highest degree artificial, a construction of measured words, such as never is, nor ever was used by man. Let this measure be what it may, whether hexameter or any other metre used in Latin or Greek—or rhyme, or blank verse varied with pauses and accents, in modern languages,— they are all equally removed from nature, and equally a violation of common speech. When this artificial mode has been established as the vehicle of sentiment, there is another principle in the human mind, to which the work must be referred, which still renders it more artificial, carries it still further from common nature, and deviates only to render it more perfect. That principle is the sense of congruity, coherence, and consistency, which is a real existing principle in man; and it must be gratified. Therefore having once adopted a style and a measure not found in common discourse, it is required that the sentiments also should be in the same proportion elevated above common nature, from the necessity of there being an agreement of the parts among themselves, that one uniform whole may be produced.

To correspond therefore with this general system of deviation from nature, the manner in which poetry is offered to the ear, the tone in which it is recited, should be as far removed from the tone of conversation, as the words of which that poetry is composed. This naturally suggests the idea of modulating the voice by art, which I suppose may be considered as accomplished to the highest degree of excellence in the recitative of the Italian Opera; as we may conjecture it was in the chorus that attended the ancient drama. And though the most violent passions, the highest distress, even death itself, are expressed in singing or recitative, I would not admit as sound criticism the condemnation of such exhibitions on account of their being unnatural.

If it is natural for our senses, and our imaginations, to be delighted with singing, with instrumental music, with poetry, and with graceful action, taken separately (none of them being in the vulgar sense natural, even in that separate state); it is conformable to experience, and therefore agreeable to reason as connected with and referred to experience, that we should also be delighted with this union of music, poetry, and graceful action, joined to every circumstance of pomp and magnificence calculated to strike the senses of the spectator. Shall reason stand in the way, and tell us that we ought not to like what we know we do like, and prevent us from feeling the full effect of this complicated exertion of art? This is what I would understand by poets and painters being allowed to dare everything; for what can be more daring, than accomplishing the purpose and end of art, by a complication of means, none of which have their archetypes in actual nature?

So far therefore is servile imitation from being necessary, that whatever is familiar, or in any way reminds us of what we see and hear every day, perhaps does not belong to the higher provinces of art, either in poetry or painting. The mind is to be transported, as Shakspeare expresses it, *beyond the ignorant present* to ages past. Another and a higher order of

beings is supposed; and to those beings everything which is introduced into the work must correspond. Of this conduct, under these circumstances, the Roman and Florentine schools afford sufficient examples. Their style by this means is raised and elevated above all others; and by the same means the compass of art itself is enlarged.

We often see grave and great subjects attempted by artists of another school; who, though excellent in the lower class of art, proceeding on the principles which regulate that class, and not recollecting, or not knowing, that they were to address themselves to another faculty of the mind, have become perfectly ridiculous.

The picture which I have at present in my thoughts is a sacrifice of Iphigenia, painted by Jan Steen, a painter of whom I have formerly had occasion to speak with the highest approbation; and even in this picture, the subject of which is by no means adapted to his genius, there is nature and expression; but it is such expression, and the countenances are so familiar, and consequently so vulgar, and the whole accompanied with such finery of silks and velvets, that one would be almost tempted to doubt, whether the artist did not purposely intend to burlesque his subject.

Instances of the same kind we frequently see in poetry. Parts of Hobbes's translation of Homer are remembered and repeated merely for the familiarity and meanness of their phraseology, so ill corresponding with the ideas which ought to have been expressed, and, as I conceive, with the style of the original.

We may proceed in the same manner through the comparatively inferior branches of art. There are in works of that class, the same distinction of a higher and a lower style; and they take their rank and degree in proportion as the artist departs more, or less, from common nature, and makes it an object of his attention to strike the imagination of the spectator by ways belonging specially to art,—unobserved and untaught out of the school of its practice.

If our judgments are to be directed by narrow, vulgar, untaught, or rather ill-taught reason, we must prefer a portrait by Denner or any other high finisher, to those of Titian or Vandyck; and a landscape of Vanderheyden to those of Titian or Rubens; for they are certainly more exact representations of nature.

If we suppose a view of nature represented with all the truth of the *camera obscura*, and the same scene represented by a great artist, how little and mean will the one appear in comparison of the other, where no superiority is supposed from the choice of the subject. The scene shall be the same, the difference only will be in the manner in which it is presented to the eye. With what additional superiority then will the same artist appear when he has the power of selecting his materials, as well as elevating his style? Like Nicolas Poussin, he transports us to the environs of ancient Rome, with all the objects which a literary education makes so precious and interesting to man: or, like Sebastian Bourdon, he leads us to the dark antiquity of the Pyramids of Egypt; or, like Claude Lorrain, he conducts us to the tranquillity of arcadian scenes and fairyland.

Like the history-painter, a painter of landscapes in this style and with this conduct sends the imagination back into antiquity; and, like the poet, he makes the elements sympathise with his subject; whether the clouds roll in volumes, like those of Titian or Salvator Rosa, or, like those of Claude, are gilded with the setting sun; whether the mountains have sudden and bold projections, or are gently sloped; whether the branches of his trees shoot out abruptly in right angles from their trunks, or follow each other with only a gentle inclination. All these circumstances contribute to the general character of the work, whether it be of the elegant, or of the more sublime kind. If we add to this the powerful materials of lightness and darkness, over which the artist has complete dominion, to vary and dispose them as he pleases; to diminish, or increase them, as will best suit his purpose, and correspond to the general idea of his work; a landscape thus conducted, under the influence of a poetical mind, will have the same superiority over the more ordinary and common views, as Milton's *Allegro* and *Penseroso* have over a cold prosaic narration or description; and such a picture would make a more forcible impression on the mind than the real scenes, were they presented before us.

If we look abroad to other arts, we may observe the same distinction, the same division into two classes; each of them acting under the influence of two different principles, in which the one follows nature, the other varies it, and sometimes departs from it.

The theatre, which is said *to hold the mirror up to nature,* comprehends both those sides. The lower kind of comedy or farce, like the inferior style of painting, the more naturally it is represented, the better; but the higher appears to me to aim no more at imitation, so far as it belongs to anything like deception, or to expect that the spectators should think that the events there represented are really passing before them, than Raffaelle in his cartoons, or Poussin in his sacraments, expected it to be believed, even for a moment, that what they exhibited were real figures.

For want of this distinction, the world is filled with false criticism. Raffaelle is praised for naturalness and deception, which he certainly has not accomplished, and as certainly never intended; and our late great actor, Garrick, has been as ignorantly praised by his friend Fielding; who doubtless imagined he had hit upon an ingenious device, by introducing in one of his novels (otherwise a work of the highest merit) an ignorant man, mistaking Garrick's representation of a scene in Hamlet for reality. A very little reflection will convince us, that there is not one circumstance in the whole scene that is of the nature of deception. The merit and excellence of Shakspeare, and of Garrick, when they were engaged in such scenes, is of a different and much higher kind. But what adds to the falsity of this intended compliment is that the best stage-representation appears even more unnatural to a person of such a character, who is supposed never to have seen a play before, than it does to those who have had a habit of allowing for those necessary deviations from nature which the art requires.

In theatric representation, great allowances must always be made for the place in which the exhibition is represented; for the surrounding company, the lighted candles, the scenes visibly shifted in your sight, and the language of blank verse, so different from common English; which merely as English must appear surprising in the mouths of Hamlet, and all the court and natives of Denmark. These allowances are made; but their being made puts an end to all manner of deception: and further, we know that the more low, illiterate, and vulgar any person is, the less he will be disposed to make these allowances, and of course to be deceived by any imitation; the things in which the trespass against nature and common probability is made in favour of the theatre being quite within the sphere of such uninformed men.

Though I have no intention of entering into all the circumstances of unnaturalness in theatrical representations, I must observe, that even the expression of violent passion is not always the most excellent in proportion as it is the most natural; so great terror and such disagreeable sensations may be communicated to the audience, that the balance may be destroyed by which pleasure is preserved, and holds its predominance in the mind: violent distortion of action, harsh screamings of the voice, however great the occasion, or however natural on such occasion, are therefore not admissible in the theatric art. Many of these allowed deviations from nature arise from the necessity which there is, that everything should be raised and enlarged beyond its natural state; that the full effect may come home to the spectator, which otherwise would be lost in the comparatively extensive space of the theatre. Hence the deliberate and stately step, the studied grace of action, which seems to enlarge the dimensions of the actor, and alone to fill the stage. All this unnaturalness, though right and proper in its place, would appear affected and ridiculous in a private room; *quid enim deformius, quam scenam in vitam transferre?* [1]

And here I must observe, and I believe it may be considered as a general rule, that no art can be engrafted with success on another art. For though they all profess the same origin, and to proceed from the same stock, yet each has its own peculiar modes both of imitating nature, and of deviating from it, each for the accomplishment of its own particular purpose. These deviations, more especially, will not bear transplantation to another soil.

If a painter should endeavour to copy the theatrical pomp and parade of dress and attitude, instead of that simplicity, which is not a

greater beauty in life than it is in painting, we should condemn such pictures, as painted in the meanest style.

So also gardening, as far as gardening is an art, or entitled to that appellation, is a deviation from nature; for if the true taste consists, as many hold, in banishing every appearance of art, or any traces of the footsteps of man, it would then be no longer a garden. Even though we define it "Nature to advantage dress'd," and in some sense is such, and much more beautiful and commodious for the recreation of man; it is, however, when so dressed, no longer a subject for the pencil of a landscape-painter, as all landscape-painters know, who love to have recourse to nature herself, and to dress her according to the principles of their own art; which are far different from those of gardening, even when conducted according to the most approved principles; and such as a landscape-painter himself would adopt in the disposition of his own grounds, for his own private satisfaction.

I have brought together as many instances as appear necessary to make out the several points which I wished to suggest to your consideration in this discourse, that your own thoughts may lead you further in the use that may be made of the analogy of the arts, and of the restraint which a full understanding of the diversity of many of their principles ought to impose on the employment of that analogy.

The great end of all those arts is, to make an impression on the imagination and the feeling. The imitation of nature frequently does this. Sometimes it fails, and something else succeeds. I think therefore the true test of all the arts is not solely whether the production is a true copy of nature, but whether it answers the end of art, which is to produce a pleasing effect upon the mind.

It remains only to speak a few words of architecture, which does not come under the denomination of an imitative art. It applies itself, like music (and I believe we may add poetry), directly to the imagination, without the intervention of any kind of imitation.

There is in architecture, as in painting, an inferior branch of art, in which the imagination appears to have no concern. It does not, however, acquire the name of a polite and liberal art, from its usefulness, or administering to our

[1] "For what [would be] more unbecoming than to transfer a scene from drama to actual life?"

wants or necessities, but from some higher principle: we are sure that in the hands of a man of genius it is capable of inspiring sentiment, and of filling the mind with great and sublime ideas.

It may be worth the attention of artists to consider what materials are in their hands, that may contribute to this end; and whether this art has it not in its power to address itself to the imagination with effect, by more ways than are generally employed by architects.

To pass over the effect produced by that general symmetry and proportion, by which the eye is delighted, as the ear is with music, architecture certainly possesses many principles in common with poetry and painting. Among those which may be reckoned as the first is that of affecting the imagination by means of association of ideas. Thus, for instance, as we have naturally a veneration for antiquity, whatever building brings to our remembrance ancient customs and manners, such as the castles of the barons of ancient chivalry, is sure to give this delight. Hence it is that *towers and battlements* [2] are so often selected by the painter and the poet, to make a part of the composition of their ideal landscape; and it is from hence in a great degree, that in the buildings of Vanbrugh, who was a poet as well as an architect, there is a greater display of imagination than we shall find perhaps in any other, and this is the ground of the effect we feel in many of his works, notwithstanding the faults with which many of them are justly charged. For this purpose, Vanbrugh appears to have had recourse to some of the principles of the Gothic architecture; which, though not so ancient as the Grecian, is more so to our imagination, with which the artist is more concerned than with absolute truth.

The barbaric splendour of those Asiatic buildings, which are now publishing by a member of this Academy, may possibly, in the same manner, furnish an architect, not with models to copy, but with hints of composition and general effect, which would not otherwise have occurred.

It is, I know, a delicate and hazardous thing (and as such I have already pointed it out), to carry the principles of one art to another, or even to reconcile in one object the various modes

of the same art, when they proceed on different principles. The sound rules of the Grecian architecture are not to be lightly sacrificed. A deviation from them, or even an addition to them, is like a deviation or addition to, or from, the rules of other arts,—fit only for a great master, who is thoroughly conversant in the nature of man, as well as all combinations in his own art.

It may not be amiss for the architect to take advantage *sometimes* of that to which I am sure the painter ought always to have his eyes open, I mean the use of accidents; to follow when they lead, and to improve them, rather than always to trust to a regular plan. It often happens that additions have been made to houses, at various times, for use or pleasure. As such buildings depart from regularity, they now and then acquire something of scenery by this accident, which I should think might not unsuccessfully be adopted by an architect, in an original plan, if it does not too much interfere with convenience. Variety and intricacy is a beauty and excellence in every other of the arts which address the imagination; and why not in architecture?

The forms and turnings of the streets of London, and other old towns, are produced by accident, without any original plan or design; but they are not always the less pleasant to the walker or spectator, on that account. On the contrary, if the city had been built on the regular plan of Sir Christopher Wren, the effect might have been, as we know it is in some new parts of the town, rather unpleasing; the uniformity might have produced weariness, and a slight degree of disgust.

I can pretend to no skill in the detail of architecture. I judge now of the art, merely as a painter. When I speak of Vanbrugh, I mean to speak of him in the language of our art. To speak then of Vanbrugh in the language of a painter, he had originality of invention, he understood light and shadow, and had great skill in composition. To support his principal object he produced his second and third groups or masses; he perfectly understood in his art what is the most difficult in ours, the conduct of the background, by which the design and invention is set off to the greatest advantage. What the background is in painting, in architecture is the real ground on which the building is erected; and no architect took greater care than he that

[2] Towers and battlements it sees
Bosom'd high in tufted trees.—MILTON,
"L'Allegro." [Reynolds.]

his work should not appear crude and hard: that is, it did not abruptly start out of the ground without expectation or preparation.

This is a tribute which a painter owes to an architect who composed like a painter; and was defrauded of the due reward of his merit by the wits of his time, who did not understand the principles of composition in poetry better than he; and who knew little or nothing of what he understood perfectly, the general ruling principles of architecture and painting. His fate was that of the great Perrault; both were the objects of the petulant sarcasms of factious men of letters; and both have left some of the fairest ornaments which to this day decorate their several countries; the façade of the Louvre, Blenheim, and Castle Howard.

Upon the whole, it seems to me, that the object and intention of all the arts is to supply the natural imperfection of things, and often to gratify the mind by realising and embodying what never existed but in the imagination.

It is allowed on all hands, that facts and events, however they may bind the historian, have no dominion over the poet or the painter. With us, history is made to bend and conform to this great idea of art. And why? Because these arts, in their highest province, are not addressed to the gross senses, but to the desires of the mind, to that spark of divinity which we have within, impatient of being circumscribed and pent up by the world which is about us. Just so much as our art has of this, just so much of dignity, I had almost said of divinity, it exhibits; and those of our artists who possessed this mark of distinction in the highest degree acquired from thence the glorious appellation of Divine.

II. THE DEVELOPMENT OF MODERN CRITICISM: ROMANTICISM AND AFTER

INTRODUCTION

THE MOST complete single transition in the history of criticism is that which gradually took place between the beginning and the close of the eighteenth century. For this period witnessed the subsiding of the classical tradition which, in one way or another, had until then dominated European conceptions of art. What arose in its place, during the later eighteenth and early nineteenth centuries, was no one central approach or guiding concern, but rather a variety of different critical premises and aims. Some of these repeated or reinterpreted classical values; others were relatively new. Some have persisted to the present day, while others were short-lived and rapidly gave way to different attitudes. Indeed, this transition period in the history of criticism is characterized by no quality so much as by its bewildering variety and assertive individualism. With the close of the classical tradition, critical thought moves in many directions like spokes pointing outward from the hub of a wheel; however, thus far no rim encases and reunites these emerging thrusts into a coherent whole. But if we cannot circumscribe this modern movement, of which romanticism comprises the first stage, we can at least note certain common tendencies throughout this movement. It will probably be most fruitful to describe these tendencies, not by generation or half century, but topically, suggesting their range and persistence in each case down to the present day, and devoting more attention to what underlay them at their start, and to their general guiding aims, than to the complex forms into which these tendencies were later elaborated. And though many of these tendencies depart from the classical tradition only through shifts of emphasis rather than through direct opposition, we may see them most clearly by contrast with that tradition.

I

To begin with, there was a natural antagonism, beginning in the late seventeenth century, to extreme neoclassic theory itself. The mere rigidity of the systematized neoclassic "rules" provoked an opposite reaction, and it was argued that taste was determined, not by rational regulations, but by purely individual feeling. As has been stated earlier, in the Introduction to the Classical Tradition, this reaction was particularly strong in England, partly because English thought has always been individualistic, and partly because the English possessed an impressive body of literature written before neoclassic theory became a controlling force. But most statements defending individual feeling as the basis of taste were only vague assertions, often as extreme in one direction as was the mechanical application of rules in the other. They took on dignity and persuasiveness only as they drew encouragement and suggestions from the great authority of Longinus' *On the Sublime*. However, the general eighteenth-century interest in the "sublime" was not merely a romantic phenomenon, confined to writers reacting against neoclassic "rules." It was an intrinsic attribute of English neoclassicism itself.

This protest on behalf of individual feeling was greatly strengthened in the early and middle eighteenth century by British moral philosophy. In reply to Thomas Hobbes's assertion that man is by nature selfish, the Earl of Shaftesbury had written eloquently, in his *Characteristics* (1711), that man was endowed with an innate "moral sense" that was itself directed to the good. Whatever Shaftesbury himself meant by this term, writers who followed him—and he was widely read for over three-quarters of a century after his death—understood the "moral sense" to be an emotional capacity. In effect, it meant for many of them that man reacts to what is good, including beauty, through *feeling*. We may note the great wave of conscious sentimentality that moved through the eighteenth century, particularly in later novels, like Henry Mackenzie's *Man of Feeling* (1771). Long didactic poems were also written, eulogizing man's emotional ability to respond to the ordered and harmonious beauty of the universe. To all such writing, the followers of Shaftesbury gave a quasi-philosophical sanction.

The point to be stressed is that, however complex its sources, there was by the close of the eighteenth century a widespread confidence that, as Goethe's Faust said, "Feeling is all." If the eighteenth century began with the belief that man's distinctive nature is his *reason,* it ended with a common belief that what is "natural" in man is his *feelings.* This assumption took various forms. First, it encouraged an emphasis on such qualities in art as *spontaneity, immediacy,* and *originality.* If what is best and most "natural" in man is his emotional character, then, in art, what is to be prized is the original and outgoing expression of his feelings. "Poetry," said Wordsworth, "is the history, or science of the feelings"; and it is the "heart" that seeks "the light of truth." The belief that art is ideally a form of "self-expression" took rise at this time, as an extreme aspect of romanticism, and it continued, in one way or another, throughout the nineteenth and, to some extent, even the twentieth century. Related to it was the eighteenth-century cult of "originality" and "genius," as seen in such works as William Duff's *Essay on Original Genius* (1767), and the romantic dichotomy of "imaginative" and "rational" art as a dichotomy between "naturalness" and "artificiality." Here, too, the values in question are still current at the present day.

Various themes in literature and in art generally illustrate this new idea of the "natural" man. We may think, for example, of the glorification of the child, in the poems of Wordsworth and Blake, as being "natural" and as yet uncorrupted by the demands of life. A more pervasive theme is shown in the treatment of simple, rural life, especially in the literature and painting of the later eighteenth century, and culminating in the poems of Wordsworth, where the "natural" man is seen as the man who lives in closest communion with external nature rather than passing his days in the "artificial" life of the city. A more extreme illustration is the cult, most familiarly identified with Jean Jacques Rousseau and so frequently attacked by Samuel Johnson, of the "noble savage," who has remained unspoiled by civilized life. All these themes, especially the last, have been labeled as "romantic primitivism," and the term is a deserved as well as convenient description of them in their more extreme form. Third, if man's feelings are naturally directed to the good, then whatever political or social conditions thwart their expression become hindrances to progress. Hence, much of the romantic philosophy is revolutionary. Its effect, through Rousseau, on the French Revolution is the outstanding illustration.

But even at the height of the romantic movement a simple trust in "natural" sentiment was not a basic premise of serious literary criticism, although it came close to being so, for a while, in French romantic writing. Such an attitude is relevant mainly because it helps to indicate the atmosphere in which criticism was written. By itself and as a mere reaction to neoclassic formalism, the idea of "natural" sentiment would not have colored the romantic theory of literature as much as it did without encouragement from a more fundamental change in ideas—a change that also had its beginnings more in England than anywhere else. The romantic "regeneration of literature in the eighteenth century," said Friedrich Schlegel at its close, "received its principal ruling direction from the poetry and criticism of the English." But in other ways as well, including philosophy, "in the eighteenth century the English were the first people of Europe." And in the development of which Schlegel speaks, the principal influence was that of British empirical philosophy.

II

The classical theory of art as an *imitation of nature* was governed by the conception of what nature was. Underlying this theory was a confidence in a rationally ordered universe: the belief that the general, pervading forms that characterize this order constitute the essential reality of nature, and these forms, conceived by reason, are what art seeks to imitate or reduplicate within its own medium. But by the later seventeenth century, British empirical philosophy had revived the ancient argument (itself a creation of Greek naturalistic thought) that the reality of nature is to be found in the particular, concrete world; that what are called "universals" are not objectively existing forms at all, but are merely "generalizations" that we make up when we see two or more things that happen to seem alike. Thomas Hobbes and especially John Locke further substantiated this empirical argument by turning upon the human mind itself and studying its way of reacting. According to these philosophers, what we learn we acquire, not through some abstract rational insight into "universal" or objective forms, but only through concrete *experience:* through our senses, that is, and then through combining our sensations. By the middle of the eighteenth century, this argument was carried even further by the greatest of British empiricists, David Hume. For Hume argues that if we believe only what *experience* teaches us—and we have no justification, no concrete proof that we should believe anything else—then we cannot actually see or directly sense any real faculty such as reason at all. All we can see, when we look into our own minds, are bundles of the different sensations that have entered it. Without touching upon the subtleties, pro or con, to this argument, it is sufficient to say that the influence of Hume, during the hundred years after his death, was enormous. Not only were objective forms and principles now questioned, but even the validity of human reason itself. Can we, indeed, know any reality at all except our own subjective *feelings*—feelings that may very well not correspond in any way to outside reality? The history of philosophy during the nineteenth and, to some extent, the twentieth centuries has been an attempt to overcome the difficulties that arose from the empirical philosophy.

The effect on the theory of art, over a period of time, was far-reaching. The classical conception of art as an "imitation of nature" seemed less impressive to many critics when there was so little agreement about what nature was, and when it seemed probable that man's mind had no means of knowing what nature was anyway. Critical theory did not, however, fall into a complete skeptical relativism. On the contrary, in eighteenth-century England, this empirical-mindedness served to liberalize neoclassic theory in the most salutary way. For under the stress of this new challenge, neoclassical critics were led to survey the literature of great eras in the past with more open minds in order to discover what had been concretely proved to be most effective; and by rendering it less systematized and rigid,

the exponents of the classical tradition restored to it something of its original flexibility while still clinging to the belief that the mind is fully able to ascertain general principles. Yet the very uncertainty of the new philosophical outlook became increasingly reflected in the conceptions of the aim and function of art. Critics themselves adopted the method of empirical investigation. Criticism became more *particularized,* and directed itself to specific problems of literature: to problems of style, to the history of literature, to the use of particular details in a work of art. Above all, critical theory followed the lead of formal empirical psychology, and turned upon the mind itself, hoping, through psychological analysis, to discover at least some common principles of human feeling and human reaction by which some standard of taste could be roughly determined.

III

The modern movement, then, may in one of its aspects be described as a protest on behalf of *concreteness.* In both science and art, it began by being broadly *naturalistic:* not the universal or general, but the specific, the particular, was the more compelling concern. One need not search far for obvious illustrations in literature itself. While classical poetry had sought to lift imagery to a general plane, poetry from the romantic period to the present day has sought to make it specific. Where the classical poet sought at times to "divest himself," as Johnson said, "of the prejudices of his age and country," the romantic deliberately cultivated the local—in folklore, in nationalistic themes, or in "local color." Again, while the classicist emphasized the total structure and outline of a poem, the romantic, as Arnold pointed out, stressed the part, the detail, such as character portrayal, imagery, or language. In nothing is this shift of attitude so clearly apparent as in the altered approach to the drama, where character rather than plot became the primary concern of such men as Coleridge, the Schlegels, or Hazlitt. This concern was especially strong in late eighteenth- and in nineteenth-century Shakespearean criticism. And though, in reaction against the earlier, romantic stages of the modern movement, there has recently been some reversal to the classical concern with plot, the stress on character largely remains, particularly in the English-speaking countries, in whose literary tradition character portrayal has always been a dominant concern of the writer himself. Finally, in the portraying of character itself, not the general, the "type," so much as the unique and the individual have been the focus of attention.

Paralleling this concentration on the particular has been a common romantic, and perhaps generally modern, conception of art as *expression:* as the intense and vital capturing of the unique character—or, to use Gerard Manley Hopkins's term—the "inscape" of the object. No nineteenth-century critic held this as a more central concept than did Hazlitt, and it was taken over from Hazlitt and vividly if briefly phrased in the letters of Keats. The aim of art, in short, is to capture the fluid, almost intangible nature or "identity" of its object—the highest and most challenging object being human character itself—and to disclose and present it in its unique individuality, so that the "beauty" of the object will emerge as a by-product of its intensely conceived character. "This," as Keats said, "is the very thing in which consists poetry." And, in slightly altered and less energetic ways, this conception of art was to persist through the nineteenth century and into the twentieth, either in the restricted form of "Impressionism" and the more imaginative sorts of realism or else as a more general value. But it received no really new or distinguished treatment after the middle nineteenth century. For the "naturalism" and "realism" that were postulated as ideals in serious criticism after the romantic movement were of a barer, more thoroughgoing sort, without the element of impassioned expression involved. As in the extreme case of Zola especially, naturalism joined hands with the aims and dispassionate methods of laboratory science.

I V

The particularized interests and naturalistic criteria of the late eighteenth century and afterwards focused on *methods* of studying literature as well as on the end and general theory of art. The eighteenth century saw the rise of the analytic study of versification and of prose rhetoric, though this interest subsided at the beginning of the nineteenth century and remained largely dormant until the past two generations. But a method of approach that has been continually developed is the historical study of literature and the specific relating of literature to its local setting. Instances of a historical approach occurred here and there before the eighteenth century. But with the publication of Giovanni Battista Vico's *New Science* (1725) in Italy, this approach began to be definitely exploited. In England, critics like Thomas Blackwell, in his *Enquiry into the Life and Writings of Homer* (1735), looked to the historical circumstances of the writer; theories of cultural history were tentatively sketched. But much of the English investigation—as in Thomas Warton's study of Spenser (1754) and his famous *History of English Poetry* (1774–81)—became rapidly more particularized and less theoretical.

It was in Germany, more than any other country, that the historical study of literature in relation to its general cultural background was carried furthest. Near the close of the eighteenth century in Germany, J. G. Herder's boldly systematic and imaginative interpretation of history ushered in the new field of *Kulturgeschichte,* or "cultural history." The German interest in the philosophy of cultural history was often to remain on an abstract and theoretical plane, from Hegel and his immediate followers down through Spengler's *Decline of the West* a century later. It was also to be permeated with a naïve and aggressive romantic nationalism. But this concern with *Kulturgeschichte* succeeded most impressively where, to its interest in finding an organic and over-all connection in cultural history, it joined a patient knowledge of detail and a sympathetic openness to the psychology or character of mind pervading the particular people or epoch under consideration. These qualities were actively present in the work of A. W. Schlegel and his younger brother, Friedrich, early in the nineteenth century. The use of psychology in German historical criticism became more particularized and penetrating after the close of the nineteenth century, especially as psychology was related to the theory of genres. But the virtues of this later criticism are a continuation of those of the Schlegels, who, more than any other critics, served as its initial impetus and guide.

In addition to developing the history of ideas, either on an abstract or on a more concretely critical plane, the new historical study of literature made tentative steps toward regarding art in the light of its specifically social background. Earlier excursions into the subject by eighteenth-century English and French writers, supplemented by the direct influence of Herder, were carried further by Madame de Staël at the beginning of the nineteenth century, especially in her study of the relation of literature to social institutions; and Taine, some fifty years later, brilliantly if prematurely tried to systematize this approach in a thoroughgoing way.

If, however, this challenging field still remains to be fully exploited, other varieties of the detailed historical study of literature have been energetically pursued throughout the nineteenth century to the present day. The semibiographical approach of Sainte-Beuve has found distinguished successors. The historical study of types or genres, most familiarly associated with Ferdinand Brunetière, represents a second fruitful use of history for critical purposes. A third is the historical study of language, and the clarification and establishment of texts. A fourth, found especially in English and American histories of the past half century, has approached literary history in terms of the common themes, presuppositions, political interests, and popular taste of a given period. The historical and biographical approach to literature has been developed to such an extent that it has become an almost independent concern, and an artificial dichotomy within the past generation began to rise between it and literary criticism. The most challenging task now awaiting critical theory is perhaps one of synthesis rather than further particularized investigation: a synthesis that will assimilate the fruits of historical study, and that will in turn render historical investigation more critically alert and more broadly humanistic in its aim.

V

In the development of modern criticism, no new approach to literature or art in general was so quickly exploited as the relating of psychology to criticism. This use of psychology to throw light upon the nature of art was almost solely the product of England. Nor was the English leadership in descriptive psychological criticism to be supplanted until, after the first third of the nineteenth century, English criticism abandoned this approach, and left it prey to the academic experimental laboratories and the often unimaginative theorizing of the German universities. The latter began to make a fruitful contribution to the subject only by the close of the nineteenth century. It may even be questioned whether in one respect at least—the descriptive theory of the imagination—the psychology of art has advanced since the middle nineteenth century.

As early as the time of Joseph Addison (1712), practicing critics had, of course, begun to apply the conclusions of empirical psychology to the literary imagination. Addison himself (in the *Spectator* series) contributed directly to this tendency, though not so much in England, where it was already on the way, as on the Continent. Especially to his followers, the eighteenth-century Swiss critics, Bodmer and Breitinger, he first suggested a fruitful use of empirical psychology as yet unknown to Continental criticism. In England itself, after the mid-eighteenth century, the psychological doctrine of the "association of ideas," first systematized by David Hartley (1749), became a frequently used lever with which to raise if not settle critical problems. Such titles as James Beattie's *Essays on Poetry and Music, as They Affect the Mind* (1776), or Edmund Burke's famous *Origin of Our Ideas of the Sublime and Beautiful* (1757) at once suggest the focus of interest.

To attempt to evolve standards of taste by basing them on an analysis of the human mind and emotions is a process far from certain of success. Much of this psychological inquiry tended, therefore, to increase critical relativism, and at times all evaluation was argued to be a subjective matter, based on personal sentiment or habit. But more definite results arose from this interest in applying psychology to criticism, perhaps the most notable being the development of the theory of the *imagination*. Already, in the "associationist" psychology of the eighteenth century, attempts had been made to show that the imagination is able to do more than merely combine different sensations—to join the image of wings, for example, to the image of a horse, and thus picture a winged horse. In addition, it could so coalesce various elements, and blend them into a unity, that the result would be a new, organically different entity—as a word, for example, is more than simply its particular letters put together, or as the color white, though composed of all the colors of the spectrum, is different from each of them. The English theory of the creative imagination, based on empirical analysis, is best exemplified in the writing of Hazlitt and Wordsworth, while to Coleridge the imaginative process includes even further functions of mind. This general conception of the imagination, though it has not been elaborated since the romantic period, has continued to the present time; and "creative" as a term of high approval has lost none of its intriguing appeal.

A more distinctively romantic aspect of the theory of the imagination—and one of the outstanding contributions of English critical theory—was that which stressed the sympathetic ability of the imagination to identify itself with its object. The mind, as if by infection, takes on the character of what we contemplate. The more vital the attention, the more identified we become. We ourselves, as one eighteenth-century critic said, start back on seeing a man on the edge of a precipice; people playing at bowls writhe their bodies; and a spacious horizon, through our identification with it, gives us a feeling of liberty. Earlier in the eighteenth century, the attempt had been made to ascribe moral feeling to *sympathy*. Hume had already suggested as much; and his friend, Adam Smith, tried to found an entire *Theory of Moral Sentiments* (1759) on the principle of sympathy. Psychological analysis joined with this assumption to evolve a theory of the imagination that was eminently adaptable to criticism, especially the criticism of Shakespeare and the drama. Developed most fully by Hazlitt, and echoed by Keats in his term "negative capability," this was a concept of the imagination by which few English critics were untouched. A general sentiment congenial with it persisted. But the idea, in a specifically critical sense, largely disappeared until at the close of the nineteenth century it was rediscovered, interpreted in a more subjective way, and systematized into the theory of *Einfühlung*—or "empathy"—by the German esthetician, Theodor Lipps; while, in a more directly concrete way, the idea of imaginative identification was suggestively applied in Russia to the theory of acting by Konstantin Stanislavsky.

Aside from producing the theory of the imagination, the romantic interest in psychology led to a shift in the qualities desired in art. Perhaps the most pervasive result is the romantic and generally modern prizing of *suggestiveness*. If one is approaching art in a psychological way, and takes as the end of art the producing of a certain reaction or a given activity of mind, then one may hold up, as desirable qualities in art, whatever excites that reaction or activity. And if, for example, one of the pleasures that arise from the imagination is, as Addison and later Hazlitt said, the activity of *comparing* an imitation with the original object, then one is led to look for characteristics that arouse this activity of comparing. An imitation that is too close incites no such reaction; some difference between it and the original is necessary. Imitation fruits and flowers, said Adam Smith, please less than a mere picture of them, and painted statues, like wax figures, please less than unpainted ones. In a similar way, too clear a presentation in poetry leaves the reader passive. "Nothing more powerfully excites any affection," said Hume, "than to conceal some part of its object, by throwing it into a kind of shade, which . . . leaves still some work for the imagination." Hence the power of poetry, as Coleridge added, is not attained through detailed description, but by instilling "energy into the mind, which compels the imagination to produce the picture."

Through suggestion, in other words, art may incite a more energetic response, in which the reader or observer himself actively *creates*. This premise was developed in more than one direction. The nineteenth-century cult of "wonder," "strangeness," and "magic" is one example; the more involved poetic symbolism of the late nineteenth century in France and of the present day in England and America offers another. The end in either case is—as distinct from the classical ideal of art—to awaken and lead into play the subjective activity of the reader's own mind. The difference is that the romantic use of suggestion, however brilliant, was capable of later degenerating into a cult of subjective emotional revery for its own sake; whereas more recent and exacting uses of poetic suggestion, however effective when held within bounds, are capable of degenerating into a deliberate obscurity that has become stereotyped and commonplace, but which is still so shy and self-conscious as to give, as Johnson said of the "unities" of time and place, "more trouble to the poet, than pleasure to the auditor."

The effect of psychology on modern criticism, then, though strong and pervasive, has been to create a general shift in emphasis, and to induce a more sophisticated and conscious outlook, rather than to offer a new systematic procedure. Indeed, its most specific single achievement, the theory of the imagination, is almost wholly the product, as was stated earlier, of the romantic movement alone. This may be possibly explained by the rapid growth of specialization during the past century. Psychologists, trained solely according to professionally imposed standards, are no longer educated in such a way as to be acquainted with the problems involved in creating or responding to art. Conversely, at least until very recently, literary critics have been able to profit relatively little from the development of psychology during the past century; that development has been clinical and quasi-medical rather than concretely concerned with the mental processes involved in creative or imaginative thinking. Accordingly, critics have been forced to rely on individual introspection, and to revert to the scattered insights recorded by romantic writers like Coleridge, who combined an eager theoretical interest in psychology with a gifted imagination that could offer the concrete example of direct experience with poetry. The systematic study of psychology, however, did become profitably used in Germany at the close of the nineteenth century, especially as a supplement to the study of cultural history and of art forms. Finally, the recent revival, in England and America, of interest in applying psychology to criticism has fallen roughly into two categories. One is the attempt, in approaching either a writer or a particular work, to employ the methods and terminology of psychoanalysis. The other is a returning interest in the psychology of the imagination, and the desire—most familiarly associated with I. A. Richards—to relate it to the study of semantics and of the associational power of words, images, and metaphor.

VI

Both the *naturalistic* approach of modern criticism—its concern with the concrete and the particular—and its general interest in the imagination, interweave with another characteristic of the modern movement in criticism, particularly during the romantic period itself. This characteristic may be described as the *organic* view of nature, the belief that the essential reality of nature is not to be found through its specific parts, fixed concepts, and static principles. Rather it resides in the dynamic process or activity in which the parts are brought together into an *organic unity* and in which the general principle and the concrete become one, each evolving through and by means of the other. Indeed, the romantic theory of the imagination partly rests on the organic conception of nature. Reason analyzes, divides, and stratifies reality into static concepts. In doing so, it distorts reality, and loses the inner life, the organically evolving process that animates nature. The imagination, on the other hand, is able, by a sympathetic identification, to grasp things in their living process: to sense their qualities and nuances, not as distinct entities, but as an indivisible part of the concrete totality from which they emerge. Thus the activity of the imagination appeared, for example, to Wordsworth, Hazlitt, and Keats.

But the most thorough treatment of the organic philosophy of both nature and art took place in the late eighteenth and early nineteenth century in Germany. The inveterate individualism of the English, their tendency to rely on their own feelings and experience, and above all the development of English empirical psychology were certainly—as Friedrich Schlegel implied—the initial sources of the romantic movement. But this very empiricism has always prevented English thought from trusting in conclusive and thoroughgoing systems of philosophy. In Germany, F. W. von Schelling, in particular, developed a philosophy—or series of philosophies—according to which the universe is viewed as a vast field of evolving activity; and art is the means by which man most vitally participates in this process and comes to realize it. In art, form and content—the general principle and the concrete—organically combine, each sustaining and permitting the development of the other. Art thus duplicates nature, in which this unifying activity is the central and guiding principle.

After Kant, the new German philosophy of romanticism, including that of Schelling at times, tended to become subjective—in some cases, extremely so. Among literary critics, Schiller, in his *Aesthetical Letters,* came close to illustrating this subjectivism. In Goethe, however, and especially in the two Schlegels, the organic philosophy of German romanticism was informed and broadened by a sympathetic knowledge of classical art and was professedly objective. But it was an Englishman, Coleridge, who tried most openly to combine the organic vitalism prized by the German romantics with the traditional objective rationalism of classical thought. If he did not succeed in unifying them systematically, it is partly because he was too openly empirical and aware of exceptions to be able to arrive at any one system quickly, and therefore felt compelled to keep gathering diverse elements to be synthesized.

In almost all these cases, the organic philosophy is also characterized by *transcendentalism.* This very loose term may be used in at least two general ways. Applied specifically to the philosophy of Kant and his followers, transcendentalism either means that there is a reality beyond our experience that we can never know, or else it may refer to the way the human mind works,—namely, "transcending" our experience, and imposing a certain order on that experience. But the term may also be used in a sense other than those senses it has for Kant. It may imply a belief in an ultimate reality that "transcends" the concrete, material world. It is especially in this latter sense that the critical work of Coleridge, and even Shelley's neo-Platonic *Defence of Poetry* (1821), show a "transcendental" as well as an organic sense of values.

With or without the "transcendental" element, the organic philosophy, after a lag throughout the middle and later nineteenth century, has continued to the present day. In the philosophy of our own generation, it has been associated with the creative evolutionist theory of Henri Bergson, and, above all, with the majestic and imaginatively open philosophy of Alfred North Whitehead, who himself looked back on the whole romantic movement as "a protest on behalf of the organic view of nature." The organic philosophy, as we find it developed in the romantic period, is eminently characteristic of modern thought. But it is not necessarily "unclassical" for that reason. Indeed, like most of the basic philosophical outlooks found in Western thought, it was first advanced by the Greeks. And classical art is almost directly founded on what is in some respects an organic theory of nature. The emphasis on the *whole*, on the total and completed structure with which art duplicates nature, is altogether organic. The difference is that, in modern thought, the emphasis is joined with *vitalism:* it thinks of the organic, that is, in terms of a living and evolving *process*—although here, too, it should be remembered that no philosopher has ever regarded nature more in terms of *activity* than did Aristotle. The modern outlook, especially in its romantic stage, is perhaps more accurately viewed as an *organic vitalism*.

In literary criticism itself, organic values have once again become pronounced, and have shown themselves especially in the criticism of form and style. They are most apparent in the historical study of genres, where, as in the work of Brunetière, a form is regarded in evolutionary terms, with a quasi-biological development and decay of its own, or, as in German criticism after the close of the nineteenth century, art forms are viewed as expressions of the psychological and social character of a given culture. A more specifically stylistic concern with formal unity is found in the "Russian Formalists," after World War I, especially in their emphasis on rhythmic patterns in versification and on the uniqueness of these patterns to particular schools or writers. In England and America, recent criticism has also applied the organic criterion to style rather than to the nature of what is being rendered in the poem. It has thus given a new interpretation to the thesis of a romantic theorist like Coleridge that expression and subject, form and content, are not distinct. The organic quality desired, that is to say, is the interconnection within the *medium* of art itself—the mutual sustaining and interfusing of words in a poem, for example, toward a unified imaginative impact. In Coleridge, on the other hand, the classical conception of art as an "imitation" of nature is still assumed. The organic character of art, therefore, is of value because, through it as a medium, the artist can capture and duplicate, with impressive power, the significant organic processes of nature. From the Coleridgean point of view, a work of art should be organic because it is *dependent* on so many things outside itself, above all on the vital organic character of its subject. In more recent English and American criticism, the work of art is often regarded as organic because it is *independent*, with a virtually self-sufficient life of its own.

During the past thirty years in England and America, particularly with the revival of interest in "metaphysical" poetry, the organic approach to form has focused, with provocative results, on metaphor, imagery, and integrated associational compactness as they are found in actual poems. Especially among the group of "New Critics," who have developed positions expounded by T. E. Hulme, T. S. Eliot, and I. A. Richards, the principle of contextual structure—of the internal coordination and emerging unity of texture—in a poem has been pursued with brilliant and searching thoroughness. Through such a concentration, their concern has been deliberately, perhaps necessarily, restricted. The poem, though itself regarded organically as a unit, is considered chiefly in its possible organic connection with specific psychological and semantic criteria selected in advance. Whatever the theoretical stand, therefore, on the necessary interplay of form and content, in actual practice this approach has stressed the medium of art without an equal emphasis on the value and range of what is being organized. It is a concern—to cite once again Aristotle's two "instincts" on which poetry is based—with *harmonia*, or the unifying principle of experience, without a corresponding stress on *mimesis*, or the massiveness and significance of the content of experience. The possible limitations that emerge from concentrating on the bare text are those that disclose themselves in any approach verging toward a strict formalism. The poem certainly is conceived as a coalesced totality. The question still remains whether it is being considered as a totality from which certain relevant and valuable elements have been deliberately excluded. The question, in other words, is whether such an organic approach is sufficiently organic. On the other hand, the justification of this deliberate limiting of what is being considered is that this approach is openly concerned with critical evaluation as an end. It has thus served as a salutary corrective to a highly developed biographical and historical study of literature that has at times almost lost sight of the concrete work of art. As such, it marks a reversion to the comparatively unhistorical approach of classical and neoclassical criticism, which was also directly concerned with ends. The recent critical concentration on particular texts has a superior psychological subtlety; but where it—or indeed any other form of criticism—may profit most from the example of the classical tradition is in assuring itself constantly that the direct ends desired are sufficiently capacious and humane.

The development of modern formalistic criticism as a whole, then, may be partly viewed as an offshoot of the organic view of art, even when—as in the extreme case of T. E. Hulme—the organic view of nature is itself openly rejected. Hulme, for example, condemns the belief in an "organic" nature as a happy, deluded pantheism, and he advocates an art of rigid, abstract, and "inorganic" forms. Yet he applies the organic criterion to the structure and interconnection in the work of art itself, judges the success of a work by the closeness with which subject and expression, form and content, are mutually interfused, and, following the German theorist, Wilhelm Worringer, supports his division of art into the two categories of "vital" and abstract or "geometrical" art by viewing them as the organic products of two entirely different outlooks, or tempers of mind, Hulme's own rather paradoxical preference being for an art that is an organic expression of an inorganic conception of nature.

VII

The modern critical movement since the later eighteenth century, then, is characterized by no quality so much as by its diversity. And this introduction has been able only to suggest the more general premises and aims of this diverse body of criticism. Yet it should be remembered that they have all tended to cross and combine with each other until, at the present time, there seem to be few possible points of view in criticism that are not somewhere espoused by someone. The result, for modern critical theory, has been an increased *relativism*. There is less confidence in the possibility of any objective way of criticizing and evaluating art. When such a confidence has been expressed, throughout the nineteenth and twentieth centuries, it has often been dogmatic and intolerant, perhaps because it is not a genuine confidence after all but merely one way of reacting defensively to an environment in some ways hostile but mainly indifferent. We may think, for example, of the extreme naturalism that has taken the physical sciences as an ideal; the "art-for-art's-sake" movement of the late nineteenth century; the neohumanism of Irving Babbitt; the academic concentration on the biographical and historical study of literature; and even the growing textual academicism that has followed the revival of "metaphysical" poetry. On the other hand, during the nineteenth century, any exclusive and dogmatic method of interpreting art lasted only briefly; and if any from the last half century should prove to be longer-lived, at least no one attitude has been pervasive or dominant. Except where this relativism has itself become a dogma, with the abandonment of any attempt to evaluate art in the light of general human aims, the result of diversified critical activity has been healthful. The desire to explore as many avenues of approach as possible has inevitably provided a broader horizon, at least to those capable of using additional knowledge without losing sight of primary aims. On the other hand, with such abundant information and divergent techniques available, art itself has become self-conscious, during the past century and a half, to a degree never before equaled. Self-consciousness is a mixed blessing. It provides a challenge—a challenge which the Greeks would have understood and welcomed. But it may also, as Edward Young said in the middle eighteenth century, induce a paralysis. So much care, that is, may be devoted to each step one takes that the procedure may engross all one's attention. The end may be lost through over-concern with the means. The practicing artist, the student, the critic are all liable to the danger. We may re-member Taine's ominous prediction that the day will come when the study of the history of literature will replace the reading of literature itself.

The diversity of modern criticism has been increased by the direct impact of the challenging prestige and methods of science. Criticism has reacted variously to this impact. One reaction was simply to adopt a similar analytic rigor, either by trying to evolve hard-and-fast theoretical systems, or else, more frequently, by devoting attention exclusively to atomistic, piecemeal research. Modern historical, sociological, and formalistic criticism represent, at their best, the impressive if incomplete success of this reaction. A second result of the impact of science has been the deliberate retreat from it into an aloof but half-hearted belief in "art-for-art's-sake," whether of the "simple," nineteenth-century sort, or of the "complex," twentieth-century variety. A third reaction has been the attempt to reassert once again the classical function of humane arts and letters, as the Renaissance had earlier done with such sudden and fruitful results to itself and to Western culture as a whole. This reaction, most familiarly associated in England and America with Matthew Arnold and the classical values he tried to revive, has often tended, because of its defensive feeling, to narrow its ground. But the attempt to reassert such ideals, and to adapt criticism to them, has been successful only to the degree that criticism has lived up to its own initial precept and become *humanistic:* only to the degree that it has been joined, that is, with the constant desire to be as flexibly open and informed as possible. Such, indeed, was the original classical ideal: the active and integrated employment of the total mind. The criticism of art in general, as was emphasized at the outset of this volume, is one of the many creations of Greek thought, resulting, as a by-product, from the attempt to fulfill this ideal. The present richness and variety of criticism, in knowledge and approach, can be most profitably exploited by frequently recurring to the ideals of the classical spirit to which criticism owes its very existence and original inspiration. Criticism will come closest to this spirit to the degree that it continues to experiment and to tap all available resources open-mindedly, but without losing its grasp of the primary human ends.

BIBLIOGRAPHICAL NOTE

Except for anthologies devoted to recent and especially contemporary American criticism, collections of modern critical writing are both rare and, in their selections, brief. General anthologies include: *Criticism: the Foundations of Modern Literary Judgment* (ed. Mark Schorer, J. Miles, and G. McKenzie, 1948); *Literary Criticism: From Pope to Croce* (ed. G. W. Allen and H. H. Clark, 1941); and *Literary Criticism: an Introductory Reader* (ed. Lionel Trilling, 1970). More restricted collections include *Critical Essays of the Early Nineteenth Century* (ed. R. Alden, 1921); *English Critical Essays of the Nineteenth Century* (ed. E. D. Jones, 1922); *Specimens of Modern English Criticism* (ed. W. T. Brewster, 1908); *American Critical Essays* (ed. Norman Foerster, 1930); and, largely for the twentieth century, *The New Criticism* (ed. E. B. Burgum, 1930). For recent American criticism, the following collections, arranged chronologically, are available: *Criticism in America* (ed. J. E. Spingarn, 1924); *Contemporary American Criticism* (ed. J. C. Bowman, 1926); *American Criticism: 1926* (ed. W. A. Drake, 1926); *After the Genteel Tradition* (ed. Malcolm Cowley, 1937); *Literary Opinion in America* (ed. Morton Zabel, 1937); and *Critiques and Essays in Criticism, 1928-1940* (ed. R. W. Stallman, 1949), which also includes some contemporary English criticism.

Though discussion of particular critics in the modern period is both abundant and helpful, general commentary in English on criticism as a whole since the later eighteenth century is less so; and what there is naturally stresses English and American criticism. Besides George Saintsbury's *History of Criticism* (1900-04), Vol. III, other general works include René Wellek and Austin Warren, *The Theory of Literature* (1949), concerned mainly with recent works but helpful for the study of criticism in every way; the articles on criticism in the *Dictionary of World Literature* (ed. J. T. Shipley, 1943); and Augustus Ralli, *History of Shakespearian Criticism* (2 vols., 1932). A comprehensive history of criticism is W. K. Wimsatt and Cleanth Brooks, *Literary Criticism* (1957), and four of five volumes have been published of René Wellek's detailed *History of Modern Criticism* (1955-   ). Nineteenth-century French critics are brilliantly discussed in Irving Babbitt, *Masters of Modern French Criticism* (1912). For England, there is also Saintsbury's *History of English Criticism* (1911), which consists of the chapters on English critics in his general *History of Criticism*. For American critical theory from Poe to the 1920's, see Norman Foerster, *American Criticism* (1928). For different topics or periods, from the beginning of the romantic movement to the present day, largely in England and America, see M. H. Abrams, *The Mirror and the Lamp: Romantic Theory and the Critical Tradition* (1953); Irving Babbitt, *The New Laokoon* (1910) and *Rousseau and Romanticism* (1919); W. J. Bate, *From Classic to Romantic: Premises of Taste in Eighteenth-Century England* (1946) and *The Burden of the Past and the English Poet* (Cambridge, Mass., 1970); M. C. Beardsley, *Aesthetics from Classical Greece to the Present: a Short History* (1966); W. C. Booth, *The Rhetoric of Fiction* (1961); Bernard Bosanquet, *A History of Aesthetic* (2d ed., 1940); John Casey, *The Language of Criticism* (1966); W. Charvat, *Origins of American Critical Thought, 1810-1835* (1936); A. F. B. Clark, *Boileau and the French Classical Critics in England, 1660-1830* (Paris, 1925); R. S. Crane, *The Language of Criticism and the Structure of Poetry* (Toronto, 1953) and *The Idea of the Humanities* (2 vols., Chicago, 1967); Anton Ehrenzweig, *The Hidden Order of Art: a Study in the Psychology of the Artistic Imagination* (1967); Richard Foster, *The New Romantics: a Reappraisal of the New Criticism* (Bloomington, Ind., 1962); Helen Gardner, *The Business of Criticism* (Oxford, 1959); K. Gilbert and H. Kuhn, *A History of Aesthetics* (1939); G. J. and N. M. Goldberg, *The Modern Critical Spectrum* (Englewood Cliffs, 1962); E. H. Gombrich, *Art and Illusion* (1960); Andor Gomme, *Attitudes to Criticism* (Carbondale, Ill., 1966); Paul Goodman, *The Structure of Literature* (Chicago, 1954); William Greene, *The Choices of Criticism* (Cambridge, Mass., 1965); V. M. Hamm, *The Pattern of Criticism* (Milwaukee, 1960); O. B. Hardison, Jr. (ed.), *Modern Continental Literary Criticism* (1962); E. D. Hirsch, Jr., *Validity in Interpretation* (1967); Graham Hough, *An Essay on Criticism* (1966); S. E. Hyman, *The Armed Vision* (1948); Arthur Koestler, *The Act of Creation* (1964); Murray Krieger, *The New Apologists for Poetry* (Minneapolis, 1956) and *The Play and Place of Criticism* (Baltimore, 1967); L. T. Lemon, *The Partial Critics* (1965); Harry Levin, *Contexts of Criticism* (Cambridge, Mass., 1957) and *Refractions: Essays in Comparative Literature* (1966); A. Flores (ed.), *Literature and Marxism: a Controversy by Soviet Critics* (1938); J. Maritain, *Creative Intuition in*

Art and Poetry (1955); E. R. Marks, *The Poetics of Reason: English Neoclassical Criticism* (1968); Alexandre Maurocordato, *La Critique Classique en Angleterre* (Paris, 1964); Elder Olson, *Tragedy and the Theory of Drama* (Detroit, 1961); Harold Osborne, *Aesthetics and Criticism* (1955); Renato Poggioli, *The Theory of the Avant-Garde* (Cambridge, Mass., 1968); J. C. Ransom, *The New Criticism* (1941); Herbert Read, *Icon and Idea* (1955) and *The Nature of Literature* (1956); William Righter, *Logic and Criticism* (1963); J. T. Shipley, *The Quest for Literature: a Survey of Literary Criticism and the Theories of the Literary Forms* (1931); Walter Stein, *Criticism as Dialogue* (Cambridge, 1969); George Steiner, *The Death of Tragedy* (1961) and *Language and Silence* (1967); P. R. Sullivan (ed.), *The Critical Matrix* (Washington, D.C., 1961); Wylie Sypher, *Loss of the Self in Modern Literature and Art* (1962); Lionel Trilling, *Beyond Culture* (1965); J. B. Vickery (ed.), *Myth and Literature: Contemporary Theory and Practice* (Lincoln, 1966); Eliseo Vivas, *Creation and Discovery* (1955) and "A Semantics for Humanists," *Sewanee Review*, LXIII (1955); Dorothy Walsh, *Literature and Knowledge* (Middleton, Conn., 1969); A. H. Warren, *English Poetic Theory, 1825-65* (1950); George Watson, *The Literary Critics: a Study of English Descriptive Criticism* (1962) and *The Study of Literature: a New Rationale of Literary History* (1967); René Wellek, *The Rise of English Literary History* (1941) and *Concepts of Criticism* (ed. S. G. Nichols, Jr., 1963); Philip Wheelwright, *The Burning Fountain* (Bloomington, Ind., 1954); John Wild (ed.), *The Return to Reason* (Chicago, 1953); Raymond Williams, *Modern Tragedy* (1966); W. K. Wimsatt, Jr. (with M. C. Beardsley), *The Verbal Icon* (Lexington, Ky., 1954) and *Hateful Contraries: Studies in Literature and Criticism* (Lexington, Ky., 1966); Yvor Winters, *The Function of Criticism* (Denver, 1957); Morton Zabel, "The Condition of American Criticism," *English Journal*, College Ed., XVIII (1939).

1. Romantic Individualism:
The Imagination and Emotion

WILLIAM HAZLITT   (1778-1830)

WITH the exception of two brief but promising excursions into philosophy, Hazlitt wrote little of importance till he was past thirty. When he was not reading widely, especially in literature and philosophy, he was trying, without much success, to become a painter; and he retained a strong critical interest in painting throughout his life. His prolific writing, belonging to a period of little more than twenty years, falls roughly into three categories: (1) his familiar essays on miscellaneous subjects, which—together with those of Charles Lamb and Leigh Hunt—served as a model for the later Victorian use of the familiar essay; (2) his discussions of political, economic, and social subjects, such as his writings on Bentham, Malthus, Godwin, and his life of Napoleon (more than any other major writer of the period, Hazlitt retained throughout his life an intense and well-informed political liberalism); and (3), what is certainly most durable and valuable in his writings, his literary criticism as it is found in his numerous reviews, articles, and lectures.

There is an appearance of hastiness in almost everything Hazlitt wrote, as though the printer's boy were at the door awaiting the sheets as they came from his pen. For Hazlitt was forced to live by writing for the press; he was one of the greatest of journalists, and dashed off articles and reviews in order to make ends meet. He planned to write during his leisure more serious works

WILLIAM HAZLITT. The son of a Nonconformist minister, Hazlitt had an irregular education except for a brief period at the Unitarian College in Hackney. As a result, Hazlitt was needlessly on the defensive at times. As a person he was honest, impulsive, occasionally tart and surly; his background and early idols belonged to the practical and dissenting side of England at that time—the side of England that is traditionally liberal in politics and religion, pragmatic in morals, and empirically skeptical in psychology.

The standard editions of Hazlitt are the *Collected Works* (ed. A. R. Waller and A. Glover, 1902-04), and the more comprehensive *Complete Works* (21 vols., ed. P. P. Howe, 1930-33). There are numerous selected editions, of debatable representativeness, the most ample being *Hazlitt on English Literature* (ed. Jacob Zeitlin, 1913) and *Selected Essays* (ed. Geoffrey Keynes, 1930). Discussions of his criticism (aside from those in the biographies by P. P. Howe [1922], C. M. Maclean [1944], and Herschel Baker [1962]) may be found in W. P. Albrecht, *Hazlitt and the Creative Imagination* (Lawrence, Kans., 1965); John Bullitt, "Hazlitt and the Romantic Conception of the Imagination," *Philological Quarterly*, XXIV (1945), 343-61; and S. P. Chase, "Hazlitt as a Critic of Art," *Publications of the Modern Language Association*, XXXIX (1924), 179-202. There is also some general discussion, of doubtful help, in Elizabeth Schneider, *The Aesthetics of William Hazlitt* (Philadelphia, 1933).

that were never undertaken. Yet one feels that, if financial circumstances had permitted, these projected works—unlike those of Coleridge—would have actually been written. As a result, though Hazlitt was one of the most prolific of all critics, there is no single work devoted to any one dominant principle or aspect of his criticism; and in order to cull his views, one must go through some scores of articles, reviews, and lectures, written under financial pressure and aimed at an immediate market. No critic could be better served by a judicious anthology of his writing—an anthology several times larger than the brief space that can be devoted to him in this volume; and it is difficult to represent, by a few essays or lectures, the critic whose "depth of taste" Keats praised so highly. Even in his best writing, Hazlitt seems to have felt forced to pad in order to fill out space rapidly; one of his most frequent tricks was simply to introduce long quotations unnecessarily. In the present volume lengthy quotations and other padding have usually been omitted in order to leave space for a broader indication of his range than would otherwise have been possible. Five of his essays are presented in their entirety, however.

Because of his comparative diffuseness, Hazlitt's virtues as a critic are not quickly grasped from reading a few essays; he has therefore been less read since his death than more condensed but less significant critics, and his importance has thus tended to be underrated. Yet Hazlitt is easily the most representative critic in English romanticism, and this representativeness is shown in several ways. (1) Like the majority of romantic critics, he was strongly interested in the way in which the human mind and emotions react in creating or responding to art. (2) Like Wordsworth and Coleridge, he was much concerned with moral theory and its relation to psychology. (3) More than any other major English critic of any period, Hazlitt dwelt upon and accepted the romantic values of "gusto" and emotional excitement in art. Yet (4) he also saw, with perhaps a clearer eye than his contemporaries, the dangers of emotional subjectivism, and the degree to which his own age was moving toward it in literature and the other arts. Hence the moderation of English thought, in all periods, is typified by Hazlitt. The extreme romantic was as rare in England as the extreme neoclassicist had been.

Hazlitt's criticism moved in and around subjects other than those concerned with abstract esthetic theory. When he turned, for example, to such problems as the nature of the comic, he wrote with more practical understanding than the seriously speculative Coleridge, not to mention Continental critics of the time. The result is a less rarified, a more ample and empirical approach, which never loses its grasp on specific works of literature and art. With the exception of Wordsworth and Keats—neither of whom is essentially a critic—Hazlitt, in his moral, critical, and psychological premises, represents more than any other writer of his time a union of eighteenth-century English empiricism and emotional intuitionalism, a combination which—with its distrust of abstraction, its confidence in concrete nature, its values of sympathy and emotional immediacy—had encouraged the disintegration of classical rationalism and sustained the development of European romanticism as a whole. In Hazlitt, as in English romanticism generally, these attitudes center in a conception of the imagination.

2

The various principles and assumptions that run through Hazlitt's criticism were nowhere collected by him in one place and then unified by any one comprehensive but specific standpoint. But there is one point of view which permeates and colors many of his other principles, and gives a certain unity to his criticism: that is, his conception of the sympathetic character of the imagination, and his belief in the absolute dependence of great art upon it. Earlier in this volume (see above, p. 274) there was some mention of the increasing importance of sympathy both in English criticism and in English moral philosophy during the later eighteenth century. Through identifying ourselves with others, by an act of the imagination, we come to understand them; we suffer as they do; moral feeling comes from developing this capacity. In art, an intense awareness of the object, an absorption in it, arises from sympathetic identification. Not only human characters, as in a drama, but imagery vividly presented, line and color in a painting, the rhythmic flow of music, all arouse an identification that lifts the reader, observer, or hearer beyond himself. Hazlitt carried the conception of the sympathetic imagination further than any other critic. His first work, written when he was quite young—an *Essay on the Principles of Human Action* (1805)—tries to establish sympathy as the basis of all moral action. It is an answer to the belief of Thomas Hobbes and his followers that all men are basically selfish, that self-love is the mainspring of human action: if we act generously, for example, it is because we wish to be praised, we wish to get along with people, we wish to think well of ourselves, etc. Hazlitt's answer is that we have no innately implanted love of ourselves—or of others, for that matter. Suppose that I love myself, that I want to do something to help myself or avoid pain in the future. How can I know and "love" my own identity? I know my past and present identity through memory and sensation. If a child burns his finger, he knows only through *sensation* that it is he and not someone else who feels the pain. In a similar way, he knows only through *memory* that it was he, and not someone else, who felt pain in the past. If our identities until now depend on sensation and memory, what can give me an interest in my future sensations? Sensation and memory are not enough; I can picture my future identity only in my *imagination*. The child who has been burned will recoil from the fire, with its prospect of future pain, only because, through his imagination, he "projects himself forward into the future, and identifies himself with his future being."

Now this sympathetic, identifying ability is able to turn in any direction. It does not *have* to turn in one way—toward oneself, for example—more than another. The same ability that enables a person to "throw himself into the future," and anticipate events that do not yet exist, also enables him to enter into the feelings of others. I therefore "could not love myself, if I were not capable of loving others." If stronger ideas than those of one's own identity are present in the mind, the identifying imagination can as easily turn to them. Knowledge may broaden and direct sympathy, and habituate it to ideas other than that of our own identity. The more we know of what another is undergoing, the more we sympathize; and long acquaintance increases sympathy—if certain qualities in the other person, or monotony, have not weighed against it. If the child is insensible to the good of others, it is not from self-love, but from lack of knowing any better. Self-centeredness in an adult results from a long, habitual narrowing of the mind to one's own feelings and interests. Greatness in art, philosophy, or moral action—the "heroic" in any sense—all involve losing the sense "of our personal identity in some object dearer to us than ourselves."

Hazlitt's small book on the *Principles of Human Action* is a more ingenious argument than this summary would indicate, and the critical principles in his later writing emanate from the problem of sympathetic identification. This is especially true of his criticism of Shakespeare, who was "the least of an egotist that it was possible to be." Through imaginative participation, Shakespeare could follow in others "the germs of every faculty and feeling . . . into all their conceivable ramifications, through every change of fortune, or conflict of passion, or turn of thought. . . . He had only to think of anything in order to become that thing, with all the circumstances belonging to it." In his second essay "On Genius and Common Sense," Hazlitt contrasts the character of Shakespeare with "genius in ordinary." The ordinary genius is "exclusive and self-willed"; he dominates by projecting his own identity. "It is just the reverse of the chameleon; for it does not borrow but lend its color to all about it." Shakespeare, on the other hand, is "the Proteus of human intellect." By taking on the character of what was outside himself, he achieved an added objectivity. For this reason Shakespeare is not only one of the greatest poets "but one of the greatest moralists." Not that he was didactic, in the usual sense. In fact, his sympathy at times was shed "equally on the bad and the good." But this sympathetic identification in the greatest art acts morally in raising, expanding, and developing the sympathy of the reader. Tragedy at its best, for example, "substitutes imaginary sympathy for mere selfishness. It gives us a high and permanent interest beyond ourselves."

3

Hazlitt's conception of the sympathetic imagination interweaves with his other critical attitudes at almost every point. For example, it underlies his conception of the drama as the most objective and therefore the highest form of poetry. As contrasted with lyric verse, the aim of the drama can never be to express the subjective feelings of the poet, but rather to represent human life. Hazlitt's position led him to feel, at times, that the French mind often fails to "identify itself with anything, but always has its own consciousness." This premise also underlies the harsher criticism of his own contemporaries, especially Wordsworth, Byron, and Shelley. He sensed an increasing obtrusion of the poet's own personal feelings and interests, and a tendency to lose the "chameleon" form of genius.

The sympathetic identification he believed so essential in art especially underlies his stress on what he called "gusto." As generally used by Hazlitt, "gusto" seems to imply a strong excitement of the imagination by which, geared to its highest activity, it seizes and draws out the dynamic and living character of its object into telling expression. This emphasis on strong emotion in art is, of course, characteristically romantic. But the stress is on emotion turned *outward* toward its object, to the external world, not on subjective emotion directed inward. Strong emotion, for Hazlitt, is necessary if there is to be sympathetic identification, and hence the understanding which that identification brings. In a state of strong excitement, the imagination so grasps its object that the various elements and qualities of that object become animated into a living unity. "Gusto," in other words, is the state in which the imagination's fusing power comes into play through a strong sympathetic excitement. In doing so, it brings into focus and unifies, for example, all the senses. This is not "synesthesia" in the ordinary sense, but it is so living a grasp of the separate sense impressions by the imagination that all the senses are brought into focus, interpreting and substantiating each other. Hence Hazlitt's remark that Claude Lorrain's landscapes lack gusto because "they do not interpret one sense by another . . . his eye wanted imagination. . . . He saw the atmosphere but did not feel it." Chaucer's descriptions of natural scenery have gusto, and give "the very feeling of the air, the coolness or moisture of the ground."

This conception of "gusto" should be taken into consideration in approaching Hazlitt's essay "On Poetry in General," where he says, for example, that "Poetry is only the highest eloquence of passion, the most vivid form of expression that can be given to our conception of anything, whether pleasurable or painful, mean or dignified, delightful or distressing." This does not, we repeat, imply the extreme romantic contention that "feeling is all"— that the end of poetry is self-expression, or the boiling over of one's inner lava. Irving Babbitt said that, after the romantic movement, Aristotle's theory of *katharsis* degenerated into a *katharsis* not for the reader but for the artist; and he cited H. L. Mencken's remark that, in writing a symphony, the composer achieves "the same grateful feeling that a hen achieves every time she lays an egg." In stating that poetry is the "highest eloquence of passion," Hazlitt is maintaining something very different. He is stressing a passionate and objective understanding of what is beyond the personal and subjective. In those who lack sufficient imagination, feeling is localized largely in self. But in those who possess it, the imagination can broaden and direct feeling, lifting it beyond self, and riveting it to other objects. Hence he took issue with Mme. de Staël's remark that imagination was the dominant faculty of Rousseau's mind; Rousseau had only an "extreme sensibility," and that was centered almost exclusively in his own impressions.

Hazlitt, in fact, seemed to find a marked absence of objective imagination in the English poetry of his own day. In reviewing Wordsworth's *Excursion*, he divided poetry roughly into two classes: the poetry of imagination, and that of sentiment. Poetry should ideally combine the two. He cites Chaucer, Shakespeare, and Milton as examples of such a combination. Cowley and Young show a certain kind of imaginative activity divorced from feeling; while Wordsworth has the feeling without a corresponding strength of imagination. The point seems a suggestive anticipation of T. S. Eliot's remarks on the "dissociation of sensibility" that took place after the mid-seventeenth century. Combining much feeling and little objective imagination, said Hazlitt, Wordsworth's *Excursion* "is less a poem on the country than on the love of the country." It describes the feelings associated with objects rather than portraying the objects themselves. "There is, in fact, in Mr. Wordsworth's mind, . . . a systematic unwillingness to share the palm with his subject." Both Wordsworth and Rousseau "wind their being round whatever object occurs to them." Coleridge's verse, except for the "Ancient Mariner," lacks body: "Christabel" reminds Hazlitt of "moon-beams playing on a charnel-house, or flowers strewn on a dead body," and "Kubla Khan" proves only that "Mr. Coleridge can write better nonsense verses than anyone else in England." Byron has passion; but it is subservient to his own mood. "There is nothing less poetical than this sort of unaccommodating selfishness. . . . It is like a cancer, eating into the heart of poetry."

Hazlitt, then, despite his stress on emotional "gusto," stood opposed to the extreme offshoots of the doctrine of "original genius" and self-expression in art. No critic has urged originality more fervently. On the other hand, the mere expression of subjective feeling is very easy, and what is really rare and original is the ability to uncover and express the living reality of nature and human nature. The writings of Hazlitt probably contain the most consistent onslaught, since the broad neoclassicism of Johnson and Reynolds, on the belief in art as self-expression. In modern poetry, as he states in his lecture "On Shakespeare and Milton," there seems to be a widespread "experiment to reduce poetry to a mere effusion of natural sensibility," or surround "the meanest objects with the . . . devouring egotism of the writers' own minds." Milton and Shakespeare "owe their power over the human mind to their having had a deeper sense than others of what was grand in the objects of nature, or affecting in the events of human life. But to the men I speak of there is nothing interesting . . . but themselves." Hazlitt, it should be noted, is here opposing the occasional romantic belief that any subject will serve equally well in art if the artist is sufficiently affected by it and treats it with enough technical skill. This belief was to develop throughout the nineteenth century, and be encouraged by critics at the beginning of the twentieth century. To Hazlitt, this was essentially a form of subjectivism. As he stated in his lecture "On the Living Poets," "A thorough adept in this school of poetry and philanthropy is jealous of all excellence but his own. He does not even like to share his reputation with his subject . . . he sympathizes only with what can enter into no competition with him . . ."

4

Hence art is not an expression of the artist himself. Its aim is to express a heightened and perceptive grasp of objective reality. To Hazlitt, who is very English in being empirically minded, this reality is to be found in the concrete, particularized world about us. Indeed, Hazlitt is entirely in the tradition of John Locke, whose philosophy, as repeated and developed by his followers, gave critical support to the growth of romantic naturalism during the latter half of the eighteenth century. Universal forms do not exist outside the mind. We simply put together particular things, note similarities, and then make generalizations. We not only learn to think by beginning with concrete particulars; but general terms mean very little to us unless an awareness of the concrete lingers on to give them body and force. Art is especially a means of realizing truth in its full concreteness and of communicating it with vitality and penetration. In Hazlitt's words the arts "resemble Antaeus in his struggle with Hercules, who was strangled when he was raised above the ground, and only revived and recovered his strength when he touched his mother earth." When art, in any way, departs from concrete reality, it loses truth and force. One such departure is to exploit art for self-expression. Another is to use it as a way of exhibiting technical skill. Was Raphael, in painting his pictures of the Madonna and Child, "thinking most of the subject or himself? Do you suppose that Titian, when he painted a landscape, was pluming himself on being thought the finest colourist in the world, or making himself so by looking at nature?" One may, that is, neglect the subject and concentrate on the potentialities of the esthetic medium—a tendency that was to increase during the century after Hazlitt. For example,

Turner's landscapes are "too much abstractions of aerial perspective, and representations not so properly of the objects of nature as of the medium through which they are seen. They are the triumph of the knowledge of the artist . . . over the barrenness of the subject." The stricter neoclassic emphasis on types and classes in dramatic characters represents another abstraction from concrete reality. A walking type is not concretely true; it is an abstraction of various elements from the concrete truth.

Similarly, the diction of poetry must evolve from the concrete image. One of Hazlitt's reasons for preferring English poetry to French was his feeling that the French poetry up to his own day often lacked the necessary ballast of concrete imagery—that it lacked "natural bones or substance. Ours constantly clings to the concrete, and has a *purchase* upon matter." English thought and writing in the late Renaissance, particularly during the early seventeenth century, has this "clinging to the concrete" to a marked degree. The minds of these thinkers and writers, as Hazlitt stated in an essay called the "British Senate"—again reminding us of T. S. Eliot's later discussion of the "sensibility" found in English writing before the Restoration—"were stored with facts and images almost to excess; there was a tenacity and firmness in them that kept fast hold of the impressions of things. . . . Facts and feelings went hand in hand . . ." Ideas were not yet "squeezed" out of the concrete to fly like ghosts through a "vacuum of abstract reasoning, and sentimental refinement."

5

The arts, then, rest on concrete nature. But Hazlitt would insist that actual concreteness is never static. Static or fixed objects, qualities, or generalizations are simply the artificial creation of our categorizing faculty, reason. Nature, in its actuality, is characterized by flux, by the interweaving of relationships, by elements mutually modifying each other. Art tries to arrest and express this evolving concreteness, and give it qualitative value. It does this by going beyond the separate sense impressions, and by evoking a sympathetic gusto or intensity that centralizes the various isolated impressions of the senses into a unified and living conception. Hence, as Hazlitt says in "On Poetry in General," "Poetry puts a spirit of life and motion into the universe. It describes the flowing, not the fixed." In doing so, art does not declare and stamp a form upon the mind so much as it tries, by *suggestion*, to encourage the mind, through its *own* imaginative activity, to fill out nuances and relations, and thus realize them more vividly. This is the value of suggestive "imitation" in art. It stimulates the mind to greater activity by encouraging it to compare the imitation with the original object, and thus "excites a more intense perception of truth." The principles of connection and interrelation between the various elements of nature—the relation between the parts of an object as they combine to make up the identity and totality of that object; the connection between various objects and forms as they make up larger patterns of meaning or form; the mutual interaction of various passions, feelings, and thoughts in the human character, and their modifying of each other—constitute a primary aspect of concrete truth. Art, in its highest function, tries to lay bare and communicate the value and meaning of this interrelation as it evolves in its concrete setting. To seize suggestively upon it in what Hazlitt calls an "excess of power," and communicate it with intense gusto and force, constitutes "sublimity." "Beauty," on the other hand, is the harmonizing of different objects and qualities. Moreover, "truth," grasped in a vivid way, may justly be called beautiful or sublime "since all things are connected, and all things modify one another in nature." In other words, beauty, to Hazlitt, may be described as the truthful blending and harmonizing of elements and qualities into a vital significance, and the sublime may be described as their truthful heightening. It might be added that the comic, in one of its aspects, consists in the knocking out of interconnection.

Hazlitt's critical writing, then, supports one of the most characteristic of the romantic esthetic values: the conception of art as intense naturalistic expression—that is, the sympathetic and objective expression of the particular and concrete. With this as its aim, art fulfills a higher function in proportion as its object is more meaningful to human life and more expressive of it. Hence its highest object—at least in poetry and painting—is human character. Other things being equal, "The historical painter is superior to the flower painter." Above all, dramatic poetry is ideally capable of expressing human character. Like Coleridge, or like the youthful Keats underlining passages in Shakespeare, Hazlitt had the characteristic romantic delight in Shakespeare's ability to unveil character in a single passage or even a single line—in "flashes of passion" that offer a "revelation as it were of the whole extent of our being." Thus he cites Cleopatra conjecturing what Antony is doing in his absence. Her confidence that he is thinking about her, and her self-centered indolence, are disclosed in her sensuous musing, "He's speaking now, or murmuring—'Where's my serpent of old Nile?'" Or again, when Macduff hears of the murder of his wife and children, Malcolm says to him: "What! man, ne'er pull your hat upon your brows; give sorrow words. . . ." In this friendly statement, Macduff's character is immediately revealed— his quiet reserve, and the silence with which he reacts to an intense anguish. Such sudden disclosure of character is one of the marks of dramatic genius. Another is the grasp of a human character, not as a collection of separate impulses, emotions, or reactions, but as an organic, if fluctuating, whole, in which the various thoughts and feelings of the character react upon and modify each other as they do in actual life. Thus Chaucer's characters— compared with those of Shakespeare, at least—"are too little varied in themselves," however distinct they may be from each other: "In Chaucer we perceive a fixed essence of character. In Shakespeare there is a continual composition and decomposition of its elements, a fermentation of every particle in the whole mass, by its alternate affinity or antipathy to other principles which are brought in contact with it."

Dramatic tragedy is the best adapted of all the arts to express the intricate and dynamic truth of human character as it is evolved by and spends itself upon incident and situation. In tragedy the interrelations between the various thoughts and feelings of a given character are intensified; the more they are intensified, the greater our sympathetic identification. Comedy is the reverse. It does not confirm or enforce connections, but loosens and relaxes them. It thus "disconnects our sympathy"; objects are viewed with detachment, and the impulses of a character appear unmotivated. Hazlitt, in a sense, anticipated Henri Bergson's belief that the comic is incongruity viewed with a momentary anesthesia of the heart: the speech and gestures of a person then seem to lack motive, become incongruous and hence, Bergson adds, "mechanical." When introduced in tragedy, side by side with intense sympathy, the detachment of comedy can offer an additional dimension. *King Lear* especially illustrates the effect that can come from the combination.

The drama can develop successfully only when the imagination has been habitually nourished on actual life. Like some other English critics of the period, especially Francis Jeffrey and John Wilson, Hazlitt seems to have felt that the conditions for poetic drama had become less favorable since the mid-seventeenth century. Wilson had said that with the growth of specialized, commercial life the imagination had become divorced from daily existence. Youthful poets had been nourished on the reading of poetry. Hence they wrote lyrical verse—verse either "sentimental" or in other ways "abstracted" from life—or else they turned to life and tried to picture it realistically, but could not use it imaginatively. Hazlitt, who often attacked the belief that the arts became progressively better, took a similar attitude. The primary aspects of nature and human nature are no longer treated with grandeur and freshness. By reading and watching dramas, the sensibilities of writers have become refined, abstract, and self-conscious. They have already been habitually exposed to what Aristotle calls a *katharsis*—a *katharsis* that "substitutes an artificial and intellectual interest for real passion." Like comedy, tragedy "must therefore defeat itself; for its patterns must be drawn from the living models. . . ." And its materials cannot easily be found among a people "who are the habitual spectators of tragedy, whose interests and passions are not their own. . . ."

6

The sympathetic grasp of concrete reality, and the transmitting of it through a given medium of art, is the product not of rules and logical reason but of the imagination. Hazlitt admitted that certain broad rules naturally have a place in all art. But these are not so much rules deliberately and consciously followed as they are injunctions learned by experience and good sense, and as such are automatically *felt* in the actual process of creating or responding to art. What is needed, then, is the ability to absorb knowledge and experience, and the ability to apply them automatically, with instinctive immediacy. The logical reason is not a direct realizing of the concrete. In fact, it abstracts *from* the concrete. It categorizes; somewhat like a minting machine, it stamps out and coins static and definite concepts; and with these as its counters—in place of the fluid, living process of actual nature—it proceeds piecemeal, step by step, instead of with a total and immediate comprehension. Hazlitt's standpoint may be called characteristically romantic. His point, in effect, is similar to that of the late Professor Whitehead in his remarks on the "fallacy of misplaced concreteness." Abstraction, says Whitehead, fails by its very nature to conceive the whole truth. It is an act of mind which draws out or abstracts from reality only certain elements, and then combines them for special purposes of thought. The danger of "misplaced concreteness" is that one may mistakenly regard an abstraction as equivalent to the concrete truth. Hazlitt discusses this in an early philosophical essay, and describes abstraction as a kind of "short-cut" in thinking—a trick to supply our lack of complete comprehension. Abstractions are necessary; thinking is impossible without them. What is needed is to anchor them as much as possible in the concrete reality.

The ability to absorb experience and apply it immediately and relevantly to concrete objects and circumstances is the principal characteristic of what Hazlitt calls the imagination. Sympathetic identification is its most successful form of applying knowledge and experience, and of attaining a strongly felt understanding. Sir Joshua Reynolds stated that the ability needed in art was not so much "reason" in the ordinary sense, with its confidence in rules, but—as in life itself—a "sagacity" that supersedes "the slow progress of deduction," and "goes at once, by what appears a kind of intuition, to the conclusion": a sagacity drawing upon "the accumulated experience of our whole life." In his essay "On Genius and Common Sense," Hazlitt repeated and expanded what Reynolds said. "In art, in taste, in life, in speech, you decide from feeling, and not from reason; that is, from the impression of a number of things on the mind, which impression is true and well-founded, though you may not be able to analyse or account for it in the several particulars. In a gesture you use, in a look you see, in a tone you hear, you judge of the expression, propriety, and meaning from habit, from innumerable instances of like gestures, looks, and tones, in innumerable other circumstances, variously modified, which are too many and too refined to be all distinctly recollected, but which do not therefore operate the less powerfully. . . ."

The imagination acts, then, not by retaining in memory all the separate particles of our knowledge, employing them one by one, but by having transformed them all into what might be called a *readiness of response*. To discover this ability, to describe its working, to justify confidence in it, had been the unique achievement of English psychological criticism during the eighteenth century, particularly the latter half of that century. Where it is most successful and informative, the romantic conception of the imagination simply assumes and expands the theory of mind that was developed during the eighteenth century by English empirical psychology—a theory of mind that had supported and had developed along with the empirical emphasis on concrete, particularized nature. Of its application to romantic values in literary criticism, Hazlitt is the most notable example.

Why the Arts Are Not Progressive

I T IS often made a subject of complaint and surprise, that the arts in this country, and in modern times, have not kept pace with the general progress of society and civilisation in other respects, and it has been proposed to remedy the deficiency by more carefully availing ourselves of the advantages which time and circumstances have placed within our reach, but which we have hitherto neglected, the study of the antique, the formation of academies, and the distribution of prizes.

First, the complaint itself, that the arts do not attain that progressive degree of perfection which might reasonably be expected from them, proceeds on a false notion, for the analogy appealed to in support of the regular advances of art to higher degrees of excellence, totally fails; it applies to science, not to art. Secondly, the expedients proposed to remedy the evil by adventitious means are only calculated to confirm it. The arts hold immediate communication with nature, and are only derived from that source. When that original impulse no longer exists, when the inspiration of genius is fled, all the attempts to recall it are no better than the tricks of galvanism to restore the dead to life. The arts may be said to resemble Antaeus in his struggle with Hercules, who was strangled when

Why the Arts Are Not Progressive. From the *Round Table*; first printed in part in the *Morning Chronicle*, Jan. 11 and 15, 1814, and in the *Champion*, Sept. 11, 1814.

he was raised above the ground, and only revived and recovered his strength when he touched his mother earth.

Nothing is more contrary to the fact than the supposition that in what we understand by the *fine arts*, as painting and poetry, relative perfection is only the result of repeated efforts, and that what has been once well done constantly leads to something better. What is mechanical, reducible to rule, or capable of demonstration, is progressive, and admits of gradual improvement: what is not mechanical or definite, but depends on genius, taste, and feeling, very soon becomes stationary or retrograde, and loses more than it gains by transfusion. The contrary opinion is, indeed, a common error, which has grown up, like many others, from transferring an analogy of one kind to something quite distinct, without thinking of the difference in the nature of the things, or attending to the difference of the results. For most persons, finding what wonderful advances have been made in biblical criticism, in chemistry, in mechanics, in geometry, astronomy, etc.—*i.e.*, in things depending on mere inquiry and experiment, or on absolute demonstration, have been led hastily to conclude, that there was a general tendency in the efforts of the human intellect to improve by repetition, and in all other arts and institutions to grow perfect and mature by time. We look back upon the theological creed of our ancestors, and their discoveries in natural philosophy, with a smile of pity; science, and the arts connected with it, have all had their infancy, their youth, and manhood, and seem to have in them no principle of limitation or decay; and, inquiring no farther about the matter, we infer, in the height of our self-congratulation, and in the intoxication of our pride, that the same progress has been, and will continue to be, made in all other things which are the work of man. The fact, however, stares us so plainly in the face, that one would think the smallest reflection must suggest the truth, and overturn our sanguine theories. The greatest poets, the ablest orators, the best painters, and the finest sculptors that the world ever saw, appeared soon after the birth of these arts, and lived in a state of society which was, in other respects, comparatively barbarous. Those arts, which depend on individual genius and incommunicable power, have always leaped at once from infancy to manhood, from the first rude dawn of invention to their meridian height and dazzling lustre, and have in general declined ever after. This is the peculiar distinction and privilege of each, of science and of art; of the one, never to attain its utmost summit of perfection, and of the other, to arrive at it almost at once. Homer, Chaucer, Spenser, Shakspeare, Dante, and Ariosto (Milton alone was of a later age, and not the worse for it), Raphael, Titian, Michael Angelo, Correggio, Cervantes, and Boccaccio— all lived near the beginning of their arts—perfected, and all but created them. These giant sons of genius stand, indeed, upon the earth, but they tower above their fellows, and the long line of their successors does not interpose anything to obstruct their view, or lessen their brightness. In strength and stature they are unrivalled, in grace and beauty they have never been surpassed. In after-ages, and more refined periods, (as they are called), great men have arisen one by one, as it were by throes and at intervals: though in general the best of these cultivated and artificial minds were of an inferior order, as Tasso and Pope among poets, Guido and Vandyke among painters. But in the earliest stages of the arts, when the first mechanical difficulties had been got over, and the language as it were acquired, they rose by clusters and in constellations, never to rise again.

The arts of painting and poetry are conversant with the world of thought within us, and with the world of sense without us—with what we know, and see, and feel intimately. They flow from the sacred shrine of our own breasts, and are kindled at the living lamp of nature. The pulse of the passions assuredly beat as high, the depths and soundings of the human heart were as well understood three thousand years ago, as they are at present; the face of nature and "the human face divine," shone as bright then as they have ever done. It is this light, reflected by true genius on art, that marks out its path before it, and sheds a glory round the Muses' feet, like that which "circled Una's angel face,

And made a sunshine in the shady place." [1]

Nature is the soul of art. There is a strength in the imagination that reposes entirely on nature, which nothing else can supply. There is in the old poets and painters a vigour and grasp of mind, a full possession of their subject, a confidence and firm faith, a sublime simplicity, an elevation of thought, proportioned to their depth of feeling, an increasing force and impetus, which moves, penetrates, and kindles all that comes in contact with it, which seems, not theirs, but given to them. It is this reliance on the power of nature which has produced those masterpieces by the Prince of Painters, in which expression is all in all, where one spirit, that of truth, pervades every part, brings down heaven to earth, mingles cardinals and popes with angles and apostles, and yet blends and harmonises the whole by the true touches and intense feeling of what is beautiful and grand in nature. It was the same trust in nature that enabled Chaucer to describe the patient sorrow of Griselda; or the delight of that young beauty in the Flower and the Leaf, shrouded in her bower, and listening, in the morning of the year, to the singing of the nightingale, while her joy rises with the rising song, and gushes out afresh at every pause, and is borne along with the full tide of pleasure, and still increases and repeats and prolongs itself, and knows no ebb. It is thus that Boccaccio, in the divine story of the Hawk, has represented Frederigo Alberigi

[1] *Faerie Queene*, I, iii, 4.

steadily contemplating his favourite Falcon (the wreck and remnant of his fortune), and glad to see how fat and fair a bird she is, thinking what a dainty repast she would make for his Mistress, who had deigned to visit him in his low cell. So Isabella mourns over her pot of Basile, and never asks for any thing but that. So Lear calls out for his poor fool, and invokes the heavens, for they are old like him. So Titian impressed on the countenance of that young Neapolitan noble-man in the Louvre, a look that never passed away. So Nicolas Poussin describes some shep-herds wandering out in a morning of the spring, and coming to a tomb with this inscription, "I ALSO WAS AN ARCADIAN."

In general, it must happen in the first stages of the Arts, that as none but those who had a natural genius for them would attempt to prac-tise them, so none but those who had a natural taste for them would pretend to judge of or criticise them. This must be an incalculable ad-vantage to the man of true genius, for it is no other than the privilege of being tried by his peers. In an age when connoisseurship had not become a fashion; when religion, war, and in-trigue, occupied the time and thoughts of the great, only those minds of superior refinement would be led to notice the works of art, who had a real sense of their excellence; and in giving way to the powerful bent of his own genius, the painter was most likely to consult the taste of his judges. He had not to deal with pretenders to taste, through vanity, affectation, and idle-ness. He had to appeal to the higher faculties of the soul; to that deep and innate sensibility to truth and beauty, which required only a proper object to have its enthusiasm excited; and to that independent strength of mind, which, in the midst of ignorance and barbarism, hailed and fostered genius, wherever it met with it. Titian was patronised by Charles V, Count Castiglione was the friend of Raphael. These were true patrons, and true critics; and as there were no others, (for the world, in general, merely looked on and wondered), there can be little doubt, that such a period of dearth of factitious patron-age would be the most favourable to the full development of the greatest talents, and the attainment of the highest excellence.

The diffusion of taste is not the same thing as the improvement of taste; but it is only the former of these objects that is promoted by public institutions and other artificial means. The number of candidates for fame, and of pretenders to criticism, is thus increased beyond all proportion, while the quantity of genius and feeling remains the same; with this difference, that the man of genius is lost in the crowd of competitors, who would never have become such but from encouragement and example; and that the opinion of those few persons whom nature intended for judges, is drowned in the noisy suffrages of shallow smatterers in taste. The principle of universal suffrage, however ap-plicable to matters of government, which con-cern the common feelings and common interests of society is by no means applicable to matters of taste, which can only be decided upon by the most refined understandings. The highest efforts of genius, in every walk of art can never be properly understood by the generality of man-kind: There are numberless beauties and truths which lie far beyond their comprehension. It is only as refinement and sublimity are blended with other qualities of a more obvious and grosser nature, that they pass current with the world. Taste is the highest degree of sensibility, or the impression made on the most cultivated and sensible of minds, as genius is the result of the highest powers both of feeling and invention. It may be objected, that the public taste is ca-pable of gradual improvement, because, in the end, the public do justice to works of the great-est merit. This is a mistake. The reputation ultimately, and often slowly affixed to works of genius is stamped upon them by authority, not by popular consent or the common sense of the world. We imagine that the admiration of the works of celebrated men has become common, because the admiration of their names has be-come so. But does not every ignorant connois-seur pretend the same veneration, and talk with the same vapid assurance of Michael Angelo, though he has never seen even a copy of any of his pictures, as if he had studied them ac-curately,—merely because Sir Joshua Reynolds has praised him? Is Milton more popular now than when the *Paradise Lost* was first published? Or does he not rather owe his reputation to the judgment of a few persons in every successive period, accumulating in his favour, and overpowering by its weight the public indifference? Why is Shakspeare popular? Not from his re- finement of character or sentiment, so much as from his power of telling a story, the variety and invention, the tragic catastrophe and broad farce of his plays. Spenser is not yet understood. Does not Boccaccio pass to this day for a writer of ribaldry, because his jests and lascivious tales were all that caught the vulgar ear, while the story of the Falcon is forgotten!

On Modern Comedy

THE QUESTION which has often been asked, *Why there are so few good modern Com- edies?* appears in a great measure to an- swer itself. It is because so many excellent Comedies have been written, that there are none written at present. Comedy naturally wears itself out—destroys the very food on which it lives; and by constantly and successfully exposing the follies and weaknesses of mankind to ridicule, in the end leaves itself nothing worth laughing at. It holds the mirror up to nature; and men, seeing their most striking peculiarities and de- fects pass in gay review before them, learn either to avoid or conceal them. It is not the criticism which the public taste exercises upon the stage, but the criticism which the stage exercises upon public manners, that is fatal to comedy, by ren- dering the subject-matter of it tame, correct, and spiritless. We are drilled into a sort of stupid decorum, and forced to wear the same dull uni- form of outward appearance; and yet it is asked, why the Comic Muse does not point, as she was wont, at the peculiarities of our gait and ges- ture, and exhibit the picturesque contrast of our dress and costume, in all that graceful variety in which she delights. The genuine source of comic writing,

Where it must live, or have no life at all,[1]

is undoubtedly to be found in the distinguishing peculiarities of men and manners. Now, this dis- tinction can subsist, so as to be strong, pointed, and general, only while the manners of different classes are formed immediately by their particu- lar circumstances, and the characters of individ- uals by their natural temperament and situation, without being everlastingly modified and neu-

On Modern Comedy. From the *Round Table;* first printed in the *Examiner,* Aug. 20, 1815.

[1] Othello, II, 4.

tralised by intercourse with the world—by knowledge and education. In a certain stage of society, men may be said to vegetate like trees, and to become rooted to the soil in which they grow. They have no idea of anything beyond themselves and their immediate sphere of ac- tion; they are, as it were, circumscribed, and defined by their particular circumstances; they are what their situation makes them, and noth- ing more. Each is absorbed in his own profes- sion or pursuit, and each in his turn contracts that habitual peculiarity of manners and opin- ions, which makes him the subject of ridicule to others, and the sport of the Comic Muse. Thus the physician is nothing but a physician, the lawyer is a mere lawyer, the scholar degenerates into a pedant, the country squire is a different species of being from the fine gentleman, the citizen and the courtier inhabit a different world, and even the affectation of certain characters, in aping the follies or vices of their betters, only serves to show the immeasurable distance which custom or fortune has placed between them. Hence the early comic writers, taking advantage of this mixed and solid mass of ignorance, folly, pride, and prejudice, made those deep and last- ing incisions into it,—have given those sharp and nice touches, that bold relief to their char- acters,—have opposed them in every variety of contrast and collision, of conscious self-satisfac- tion and mutual antipathy, with a power which can only find full scope in the same rich and in- exhaustible materials. But in proportion as comic genius succeeds in taking off the mask from ig- norance and conceit, as it teaches us to "see our- selves as others see us,"—in proportion as we are brought out on the stage together, and our prejudices clash one against the other, our sharp angular points wear off; we are no longer rigid in absurdity, passionate in folly, and we prevent the ridicule directed at our habitual foibles, by laughing at them ourselves.

If it be said, that there is the same fund of absurdity and prejudice in the world as ever—that there are the same unaccountable perversities lurking at the bottom of every breast,—I should answer, be it so: but at least we keep our follies to ourselves as much as possible—we palliate, shuffle, and equivocate with them—they sneak into bycorners, and do not, like Chaucer's *Canterbury Pilgrims,* march along the highroad, and form a procession—they do not entrench themselves strongly behind custom and precedent—they are not embodied in professions and ranks in life—they are not organised into a system—they do not openly resort to a standard, but are a sort of straggling nondescripts, that, like *Wart,* "present no mark to the foeman." [2] As to the gross and palpable absurdities of modern manners, they are too shallow and barefaced, and those who affect, are too little *serious* in them, to make them worth the detection of the Comic Muse. They proceed from an idle, impudent affectation of folly in general, in the dashing *bravura* style, not from an infatuation with any of its characteristic modes. In short, the proper object of ridicule is *egotism;* and a man cannot be a very great egotist who every day sees himself represented on the stage. We are deficient in Comedy, because we are without characters in real life—as we have no historical pictures, because we have no faces proper for them.

It is, indeed, the evident tendency of all literature to generalise and *dissipate* character, by giving men the same artificial education, and the same common stock of ideas; so that we see all objects from the same point of view, and through the same reflected medium;—we learn to exist, not in ourselves, but in books;—all men become alike mere readers—spectators, not actors in the scene, and lose all proper personal identity. The templar, the wit, the man of pleasure, and the man of fashion, the courtier and the citizen, the knight and the squire, the lover and the miser—*Lovelace, Lothario, Will Honeycomb,* and *Sir Roger de Coverley, Sparkish* and *Lord Foppington, Western* and *Tom Jones, My Father,* and *My Uncle Toby, Millamant* and *Sir Sampson Legend, Don Quixote* and *Sancho, Gil*

Blas and *Guzman d'Alfarache, Count Fathom* and *Joseph Surface,*—have all met, and exchanged common-places on the barren plains of the *haute littérature*—toil slowly on to the Temple of Science, seen a long way off upon a level, and end in one dull compound of politics, criticism, chemistry, and metaphysics!

We cannot expect to reconcile opposite things. If, for example, any of us were to put ourselves into the stage-coach from Salisbury to London, it is more than probable we should not meet with the same number of odd accidents, or ludicrous distresses on the road, that befell *Parson Adams;* but why, if we get into a common vehicle, and submit to the conveniences of modern travelling, should we complain of the want of adventures? Modern manners may be compared to a modern stage-coach: our limbs may be a little cramped with the confinement, and we may grow drowsy; but we arrive safe, without any very amusing or very sad accident, at our journey's end.

Again, the alterations which have taken place in conversation and dress in the same period, have been by no means favourable to Comedy. The present prevailing style of conversation is not personal, but critical and analytical. It consists almost entirely in the discussion of general topics, in dissertations on philosophy or taste: and Congreve would be able to derive no better hints from the conversations of our toilettes or drawing-rooms, for the exquisite raillery or poignant repartee of his dialogues, than from a deliberation of the Royal Society. In the same manner, the extreme simplicity and graceful uniformity of modern dress, however favourable to the arts, has certainly stript Comedy of one of its richest ornaments and most expressive symbols. The sweeping pall and buskin, and nodding plume, were never more serviceable to Tragedy, than the enormous hoops and stiff stays worn by the belles of former days were to the intrigues of Comedy. They assisted wonderfully in heightening the mysteries of the passion, and adding to the intricacy of the plot. Wycherley and Vanbrugh could not have spared the dresses of Vandyke. These strange fancydresses, perverse disguises, and counterfeit shapes, gave an agreeable scope to the imagination. "That sevenfold fence" [3] was a sort of foil to the lusciousness of

[2] Shadow, not Wart (*Henry IV,* Pt. 2, III, 2).

[3] *Antony and Cleopatra,* IV, 14.

the dialogue, and a barrier against the sly encroachments of *double entendre*. The greedy eye and bold hand of indiscretion were repressed, which gave a greater licence to the tongue. The senses were not to be gratified in an instant. Love was entangled in the folds of the swelling handkerchief, and the desires might wander for ever round the circumference of a quilted petticoat, or find a rich lodging in the flowers of a damask stomacher. There was room for years of patient contrivance, for a thousand thoughts, schemes, conjectures, hopes, fears, and wishes. There seemed no end of difficulties and delays; to overcome so many obstacles was the work of ages. A mistress was an angel concealed behind whalebone, flounces, and brocade. What an undertaking to penetrate through the disguise! What an impulse must it give to the blood, what a keenness to the invention, what a volubility to the tongue! "Mr. Smirk, you are a brisk man," was then the most significant commendation. But now-a-days —a woman can be *but undressed!*

The same account might be extended to Tragedy. Aristotle has long since said, that Tragedy purifies the mind by terror and pity; that is, substitutes an artificial and intellectual interest for real passion. Tragedy, like Comedy, must therefore defeat itself; for its patterns must be drawn from the living models within the breast, from feeling or from observation; and the materials of Tragedy cannot be found among a people, who are the habitual spectators of Tragedy, whose interests and passions are not their own, but ideal, remote, sentimental, and abstracted. It is for this reason chiefly, we conceive, that the highest efforts of the Tragic Muse are in general the earliest; where the strong impulses of nature are not lost in the refinements and glosses of art;

where the writers themselves, and those whom they saw about them, had "warm hearts of flesh and blood beating in their bosoms, and were not embowelled of their natural entrails, and stuffed with paltry blurred sheets of paper."[4] Shakspeare, with all his genius, could not have written as he did, if he had lived in the present times. Nature would not have presented itself to him in the same freshness and vigour; he must have seen it through all the refractions of successive dullness, and his powers would have languished in the dense atmosphere of logic and criticism. "Men's minds," he somewhere says, "are parcel of their fortunes";[5] and his age was necessary to him. It was this which enabled him to grapple at once with Nature, and which stamped his characters with her image and superscription.[6]

[4] Loosely quoted from Burke, *Reflections on the Revolution in France, Select Works* (ed. Payne, 1842), II, 101.

[5] *Antony and Cleopatra*, III, 13.

[6] "The age we live in is critical, didactic, paradoxical, romantic, but it is not dramatic. . . . If a bias to abstraction is evidently, then, the reigning spirit of the age, dramatic poetry must be allowed to be most irreconcilable with this spirit; it is essentially individual and concrete, both in form and in power. It is the closest imitation of nature; it has a body of truth; it is 'a counterfeit presentment' of reality; for it brings forward certain characters to act and speak for themselves, in the most trying and singular circumstances. It is not enough for them to declaim on certain general topics, however forcibly or learnedly—this is merely oratory . . . nor is it sufficient for the poet to furnish the colours and forms of style and fancy out of his own store, however inexhaustible; for if he merely makes them express his own feelings, and idle diffusions of his own breast, he had better speak in his own person without any of those troublesome 'interlocutions between Lucius and Caius.'" ("The Drama: No. IV," *London Magazine*, April, 1820, *Complete Works*, XVIII, 302-05.)

On Imitation

OBJECTS in themselves disagreeable or indifferent, often please in the imitation. A brick-floor, a pewter-table, an ugly cur barking, a Dutch boor smoking or playing at skittles, the inside of a shambles, a fishmonger's or a greengrocer's stall, have been made very in-

On Imitation. From the *Round Table;* first printed in the *Examiner*, Feb. 18, 1816.

teresting as pictures by the fidelity, skill, and spirit, with which they have been copied. One source of the pleasure thus received is undoubtedly the surprise or feeling of admiration, occasioned by the unexpected coincidence between the imitation and the object. The deception, however, not only pleases at first sight, or from mere novelty; but it continues to please upon farther acquaintance, and in proportion to the insight we acquire into the distinctions of nature and of art. By far the most numerous class of connoisseurs are the admirers of pictures of *still life*, which have nothing but the elaborateness of the execution to recommend them. One chief reason, it should seem then, why imitation pleases, is, because, by exciting curiosity, and inviting a comparison between the object and the representation, it opens a new field of inquiry, and leads the attention to a variety of details and distinctions not perceived before.[1] This latter source of the pleasure derived from imitation has never been properly insisted on.

The anatomist is delighted with a coloured plate, conveying the exact appearance of the progress of certain diseases, or of the internal parts and dissections of the human body. We have known a Jennerian Professor as much enraptured with a delineation of the different stages of vaccination, as a florist with a bed of tulips, or an auctioneer with a collection of Indian shells. But in this case, we find that not only the imitation pleases,—the objects themselves give as much pleasure to the professional inquirer, as they would pain to the uninitiated. The learned amateur is struck with the beauty of the coats of the stomach laid bare, or contemplates with eager curiosity the transverse section of the brain, divided on the new Spurzheim principles.[2] It is here, then, the number of the parts, their distinctions, connections, structure, uses; in short, an entire new set of ideas, which occupies the mind of the student, and overcomes the sense

of pain and repugnance, which is the only feeling that the sight of a dead and mangled body presents to ordinary men. It is the same in art as in science. The painter of still life, as it is called, takes the same pleasure in the object as the spectator does in the imitation; because by habit he is led to perceive all those distinctions in nature, to which other persons never pay any attention till they are pointed out to them in the picture. The vulgar only see nature as it is reflected to them from art; the painter sees the picture in nature, before he transfers it to the canvass. He refines, he analyses, he remarks fifty things, which escape common eyes; and this affords a distinct source of reflection and amusement to him, independently of the beauty or grandeur of the objects themselves, or of their connection with other impressions besides those of sight. The charm of the Fine Arts, then, does not consist in any thing peculiar to imitation, even where only imitation is concerned, since *there*, where art exists in the highest perfection, namely, in the mind of the artist, the object excites the same or greater pleasure, before the imitation exists. Imitation renders an object, displeasing in itself, a source of pleasure, not by repetition of the same idea, but by suggesting new ideas, by detecting new properties, and endless shades of difference, just as a close and continued contemplation of the object itself would do. Art shows us nature, divested of the medium of our prejudices. It divides and decompounds objects into a thousand curious parts, which may be full of variety, beauty, and delicacy in themselves, though the object to which they belong may be disagreeable in its general appearance, or by association with other ideas. A painted marigold is inferior to a painted rose only in form and colour: it loses nothing in point of smell. Yellow hair is perfectly beautiful in a picture. To a person lying with his face close to the ground in a summer's day, the blades of spear-grass will appear like tall forest trees, shooting up into the sky; as an insect seen through a microscope is magnified into an elephant. Art is the microscope of the mind, which sharpens the wit as the other does the sight; and converts every object into a little universe in itself. Art may be said to draw aside the veil from nature. To those who are perfectly unskilled in the practice, unimbued with the principles of art, most objects present

---

[1] *Cf*. Addison, *Spectator*, No. 416. The same point is frequently made in English critical writing throughout the eighteenth century. Locke had defined "wit" as the assembling, comparing, and joining of ideas. Imitation appeals to this faculty by inciting the mind to make comparisons. Hence the increasing romantic stress on "suggestiveness" (see above, p. 274), which arose as one of the by-products of British empirical psychology: if the imitation is too close, the imagination is passive; but if fewer details are offered, the imagination is stimulated by more far-reaching comparisons and is led into a more active state where it participates creatively in the artist's conception. This standpoint, of course, strongly colors modern esthetic theory, and particularly underlies present-day critical attitudes toward poetic imagery and metaphor.

[2] See "On Dr. Spurzheim's Theory," in Hazlitt's *Plain Speaker*. J. G. Spurzheim (1776-1832) was a phrenologist.

only a confused mass. The pursuit of art is liable to be carried to a contrary excess, as where it produces a rage for the *picturesque*. You cannot go a step with a person of this class, but he stops you to point out some choice bit of landscape, or fancied improvement, and teazes you almost to death with the frequency and insignificance of his discoveries!

It is a common opinion, (which may be worth noticing here), that the study of physiognomy has a tendency to make people satirical, and the knowledge of art to make them fastidious in their taste. Knowledge may, indeed, afford a handle to ill-nature; but it takes away the principal temptation to its exercise, by supplying the mind with better resources against *ennui*. Idiots are always mischievous; and the most superficial persons are the most disposed to find fault, because they understand the fewest things. The English are more apt than any other nation to treat foreigners with contempt, because they seldom see anything but their own dress and manners; and it is only in petty provincial towns that you meet with persons who pride themselves on being satirical. In every country place in England there are one or two persons of this description who keep the whole neighbourhood in terror. It is not to be denied that the study of the *ideal* in art, if separated from the study of nature, may have the effect above stated, of producing dissatisfaction and contempt for everything but itself, as all affectation must; but to the genuine artist, truth, nature, beauty, are almost different names for the same thing.

Imitation interests, then, by exciting a more intense perception of truth, and calling out the powers of observation and comparison: wherever this effect takes place the interest follows of course, with or without the imitation, whether the object is real or artificial. The gardener delights in the streaks of a tulip, or "pansy freak'd with jet"; the mineralogist in the varieties of certain strata, because he understands them. Knowledge is pleasure as well as power. A work of art has in this respect no advantage over a work of nature, except inasmuch as it furnishes an additional stimulus to curiosity. Again, natural objects please in proportion as they are uncommon, by fixing the attention more steadily on their beauties or differences. The same principle of the effect of novelty in exciting the attention,

may account, perhaps, for the extraordinary discoveries and lies told by travellers, who, opening their eyes for the first time in foreign parts, are startled at every object they meet.

Why the excitement of intellectual activity pleases, is not here the question; but that it does so, is a general and acknowledged law of the human mind. We grow attached to the mathematics only from finding out their truth; and their utility chiefly consists (at present) in the contemplative pleasure they afford to the student. Lines, points, angles, squares, and circles are not interesting in themselves; they become so by the power of mind exerted in comprehending their properties and relations. People dispute for ever about Hogarth. The question has not in one respect been fairly stated. The merit of his pictures does not so much depend on the nature of the subject, as on the knowledge displayed of it, on the number of ideas they excite, on the fund of thought and observation contained in them. They are to be looked on as works of science; they gratify our love of truth; they fill up the void of the mind: they are a series of plates of natural history, and also of that most interesting part of natural history, the history of man. The superiority of high art over the common or mechanical consists in combining truth of imitation with beauty and grandeur of subject. The historical painter is superior to the flower-painter, because he combines or ought to combine human interests and passions with the same power of imitating external nature; or, indeed, with greater, for the greatest difficulty of imitation is the power of imitating expression. The difficulty of copying increases with our knowledge of the object; and that again with the interest we take in it. The same argument might be applied to shew that the poet and painter of imagination are superior to the mere philosopher or man of science, because they exercise the powers of reason and intellect combined with nature and passion. They treat of the highest categories of the human soul, pleasure and pain.

From the foregoing train of reasoning, we may easily account for the too great tendency of art to run into pedantry and affectation. There is "a pleasure in art which none but artists feel." They see beauty where others see nothing of the sort, in wrinkles, deformity, and old age. They see it in Titian's Schoolmaster as well as in

Raphael's Galatea; in the dark shadows of Rembrandt as well as in the splendid colours of Rubens; in an angel's or in a butterfly's wings. They see with different eyes from the multitude. But true genius, though it has new sources of pleasure opened to it, does not lose its sympathy with humanity. It combines truth of imitation with effect, the parts with the whole, the means with the end. The mechanic artist sees only that which nobody else sees, and is conversant only with the technical language and difficulties of his art. A painter, if shewn a picture, will generally dwell upon the academic skill displayed in it, and the knowledge of the received rules of composition. A musician, if asked to play a tune, will select that which is the most difficult and the least intelligible. The poet will be struck with the harmony of versification, or the elaborateness of the arrangement in a composition. The conceits in Shakspeare were his greatest delight; and improving upon this perverse method of judging, the German writers, Goethe and Schiller, look upon Werter and The Robbers as the worst of all their works, because they are the most popular. Some artists among ourselves have carried the same principle to a singular excess.[3] If professors themselves are liable to this kind of pedantry, connoisseurs and dilettanti, who have less sensibility and more affectation, are almost wholly swayed by it. They see nothing in a picture but the execution. They are proud of their knowledge in proportion as it is a secret. The worst judges of pictures in the United Kingdom are, first, picture-dealers; next, perhaps, the Directors of the British Institution; and after them, in all probability, the Members of the Royal Academy.

[3] "We here allude particularly to Turner, the ablest landscape painter now living, whose pictures are, however, too much abstractions of aerial perspective, and representations not so properly of the objects of nature as of the medium through which they are seen. They are the triumph of the knowledge of the artist, and of the power of the pencil over the barrenness of the subject. They are pictures of the elements of air, earth, and water. The artist delights to go back to the first chaos of the world, or to that state of things when the waters were separated from the dry land, and light from darkness, but as yet no living thing nor tree bearing fruit was seen upon the face of the earth. All is 'without form and void.' Some one said of his landscapes that they were *pictures of nothing, and very like.*" [Hazlitt's note.]

From On the Character of Rousseau

MADAME DE STAEL, in her Letters on the Writings and Character of Rousseau, gives it as her opinion, "that the imagination was the first faculty of his mind, and that this faculty even absorbed all the others." And she farther adds, "Rousseau had great strength of reason on abstract questions, or with respect to objects, which have no reality but in the mind." Both these opinions are radically wrong. Neither imagination nor reason can properly be said to have been the original predominant faculties of his mind. The strength both of imagination and reason, which he possessed, was borrowed from the excess of another faculty; and the weakness and poverty of reason and imagination, which are to be found in his works, may be traced to the same source, namely, that these faculties in him were artificial, secondary, and

On the Character of Rousseau. From the *Round Table;* first printed in the *Examiner,* Apr. 14, 1816.

dependent, operating by a power not theirs, but lent to them. The only quality which he possessed in an eminent degree, which alone raised him above ordinary men, and which gave to his writings and opinions an influence greater, perhaps, than has been exerted by any individual in modern times, was extreme sensibility, or an acute and even morbid feeling of all that related to his own impressions, to the objects and events of his life. He had the most intense consciousness of his own existence. No object that had once made an impression on him was ever after effaced. Every feeling in his mind become a passion. His craving after excitement was an appetite and a disease. His interest in his own thoughts and feelings was always wound up to the highest pitch; and hence the enthusiasm which he excited in others. . . . Hence the tenaciousness of his logic, the acuteness of his observations, the refinement and the inconsistency of his reasoning. Hence, his keen penetration, and his strange want of comprehension of mind: for the same intense feeling which enabled him to discern the first principles of things, and seize some one view of a subject in all its ramifications, prevented him from admitting the operation of other causes which interfered with his favourite purpose, and involved him in endless wilful contradictions. Hence his excessive egotism, which filled all objects with himself, and would have occupied the universe with his smallest interest. Hence his jealousy and suspicion of others; for no attention, no respect or sympathy, could come up to the extravagant claims of his self-love. Hence his dissatisfaction with himself and with all around him; for nothing could satisfy his ardent longings after good, his restless appetite of being. Hence in part also his quarrel with the artificial institutions and distinctions of society, which opposed so many barriers to the unrestrained indulgence of his will, and allured his imagination to scenes of pastoral simplicity or of savage life, where the passions were either not excited or left to follow their own impulse,—where the petty vexations and irritating disappointments of common life had no place,—and where the tormenting pursuits of arts and sciences were lost in pure animal enjoyment, or indolent repose. Thus he describes the first savage wandering for ever under the shade of magnificent forests, or by the side of mighty rivers, smit with the unquenchable love of nature! . . .

Rousseau, in all his writings, never once lost sight of himself. He was the same individual from first to last. The spring that moved his passions never went down, the pulse that agitated his heart never ceased to beat. It was this strong feeling of interest, accumulating in his mind, which overpowers and absorbs the feelings of his readers. He owed all his power to sentiment. The writer who most nearly resembles him in our own times is the author of the *Lyrical Ballads*. We see no other difference between them, than that the one wrote in prose and the other in poetry; and that prose is perhaps better adapted to express those local and personal feelings, which are inveterate habits in the mind, than poetry, which embodies its imaginary creations. We conceive that Rousseau's exclamation, *"Ah, voila de la pervenche,"* [1] comes more home to the mind than Mr. Wordsworth's discovery of the linnet's nest "with five blue eggs," [2] or than his address to the cuckoo, beautiful as we think it is; and we will confidently match the Citizen of Geneva's adventures on the Lake of Bienne against the Cumberland Poet's floating dreams on the Lake of Grasmere. Both create an interest out of nothing, or rather out of their own feelings; both weave numberless recollections into one sentiment; both wind their own being round whatever object occurs to them. But Rousseau, as a prose-writer, gives only the habitual and personal impression. Mr. Wordsworth, as a poet, is forced to lend the colours of imagination to impressions which owe all their force to their identity with themselves, and tries to paint what is only to be felt. Rousseau, in a word, interests you in certain objects by interesting you in himself: Mr. Wordsworth would persuade you that the most insignificant objects are interesting in themselves, because he is interested in them. . . .

[1] "Ah! there are periwinkles . . ." (*Confessions*, I, 6).

[2] Wordsworth's "The Sparrow's Nest."

On Gusto

GUSTO in art is power or passion defining any object. It is not so difficult to explain this term in what relates to expression (of which it may be said to be the highest degree) as in what relates to things without expression, to the natural appearances of objects, as mere colour or form. In one sense, however,

On Gusto. From the *Round Table;* first printed in the *Examiner*, May 26, 1816.

there is hardly any object entirely devoid of expression, without some character of power belonging to it, some precise association with pleasure or pain: and it is in giving this truth of character from the truth of feeling, whether in the highest or the lowest degree, but always in the highest degree of which the subject is capable, that gusto consists.

There is a gusto in the colouring of Titian.

Not only do his heads seem to think—his bodies seem to feel. This is what the Italians mean by the *morbidezza* of his flesh-colour. It seems sensitive and alive all over; not merely to have the look and texture of flesh, but the feeling in itself. For example, the limbs of his female figures have a luxurious softness and delicacy, which appears conscious of the pleasure of the beholder. As the objects themselves in nature would produce an impression on the sense, distinct from every other object, and having something divine in it, which the heart owns and the imagination consecrates, the objects in the picture preserve the same impression, absolute, unimpaired, stamped with all the truth of passion, the pride of the eye, and the charm of beauty. Rubens makes his flesh-colour like flowers; Albano's [1] is like ivory; Titian's is like flesh, and like nothing else. It is as different from that of other painters, as the skin is from a piece of white or red drapery thrown over it. The blood circulates here and there, the blue veins just appear, the rest is distinguished throughout only by that sort of tingling sensation to the eye, which the body feels within itself. This is gusto. Vandyke's flesh-colour, though it has great truth and purity, wants gusto. It has not the internal character, the living principle in it. It is a smooth surface,. not a warm, moving mass. It is painted without passion, with indifference. The hand only had been concerned. The impression slides off from the eye, and does not, like the tones of Titian's pencil, leave a sting behind it in the mind of the spectator. The eye does not acquire a taste or appetite for what it sees. In a word, gusto in painting is where the impression made on one sense excites by affinity those of another.

Michael Angelo's forms are full of gusto. They everywhere obtrude the sense of power upon the eye. His limbs convey an idea of muscular strength, of moral grandeur, and even of intellectual dignity: they are firm, commanding, broad, and massy, capable of executing with ease the determined purposes of the will. His faces have no other expression than his figures, conscious power and capacity. They appear only to think what they shall do, and to know that they can do it. This is what is meant by saying that his style is hard and masculine. It is the reverse

of Correggio's, which is effeminate. That is, the gusto of Michael Angelo consists in expressing energy of will without proportionable sensibility, Correggio's in expressing exquisite sensibility without energy of will. In Correggio's faces as well as figures we see neither bones nor muscles, but then what a soul is there, full of sweetness and of grace—pure, playful, soft, angelical! There is sentiment enough in a hand painted by Correggio to set up a school of history painters. Whenever we look at the hands of Correggio's women or of Raphael's, we always wish to touch them.

Again, Titian's landscapes have a prodigious gusto, both in the colouring and forms. We shall never forget one that we saw many years ago in the Orleans Gallery of Acteon hunting. It had a brown, mellow, autumnal look. The sky was of the colour of stone. The winds seemed to sing through the rustling branches of the trees, and already you might hear the twanging of bows resound through the tangled mazes of the wood. Mr. West,[2] we understand, has this landscape. He will know if this description of it is just. The landscape back-ground of the St. Peter Martyr is another well known instance of the power of this great painter to give a romantic interest and an appropriate character to the objects of his pencil, where every circumstance adds to the effect of the scene,—the bold trunks of the tall forest trees, the trailing ground plants, with that tall convent spire rising in the distance, amidst the blue sapphire mountains and the golden sky.

Rubens has a great deal of gusto in his Fauns and Satyrs, and in all that expresses motion, but in nothing else. Rembrandt has it in everything; everything in his pictures has a tangible character. If he puts a diamond in the ear of a burgomaster's wife, it is of the first water; and his furs and stuffs are proof against a Russian winter. Raphael's gusto was only in expression; he had no idea of the character of anything but the human form. The dryness and poverty of his style in other respects is a phenomenon in the art. His trees are like sprigs of grass stuck in a book of botanical specimens. Was it that Raphael never had time to go beyond the walls of Rome? That he was always in the streets, at church, or

[1] Francesco Albani (1578-1660).

[2] Benjamin West (1738-1820), President of the Royal Academy.

in the bath? He was not one of the Society of Arcadians.

Claude's landscapes, perfect as they are, want gusto. This is not easy to explain. They are perfect abstractions of the visible images of things; they speak the visible language of nature truly. They resemble a mirror or a microscope. To the eye only they are more perfect than any other landscapes that ever were or will be painted; they give more of nature, as cognisable by one sense alone; but they lay an equal stress on all visible impressions. They do not interpret one sense by another; they do not distinguish the character of different objects as we are taught, and can only be taught, to distinguish them by their effect on the different senses. That is, his eye wanted imagination: it did not strongly sympathise with his other faculties. He saw the atmosphere, but he did not feel it. He painted the trunk of a tree or a rock in the foreground as smooth—with as complete an abstraction of the gross, tangible impression, as any other part of the picture. His trees are perfectly beautiful, but quite immovable; they have a look of enchantment. In short, his landscapes are unequalled imitations of nature, released from its subjection to the elements, as if all objects were become a delightful fairy vision, and the eye had rarefied and refined away the other senses.

The gusto in the Greek statues is of a very singular kind. The sense of perfect form nearly occupies the whole mind, and hardly suffers it to dwell on any other feeling. It seems enough for them *to be,* without acting or suffering. Their forms are ideal, spiritual. Their beauty is power. By their beauty they are raised above the frailties of pain or passion; by their beauty they are deified.

The infinite quantity of dramatic invention in Shakspeare takes from his gusto. The power he delights to show is not intense, but discursive. He never insists on anything as much as he might, except a quibble. Milton has great gusto. He repeats his blows twice; grapples with and exhausts his subject. His imagination has a double relish of its objects, an inveterate attachment to the things he describes, and to the words describing them.

> —Or where Chineses drive
> With sails and wind their *cany* waggons *light.*

Wild above rule or art, *enormous* bliss.[3]

There is a gusto in Pope's compliments, in Dryden's satires, and Prior's tales; and among prose writers Boccaccio and Rabelais had the most of it. We will only mention one other work which appears to us to be full of gusto, and that is the *Beggar's Opera.* If it is not, we are altogether mistaken in our notions on this delicate subject.

[3] *Paradise Lost,* III, 438-39; V, 297.

From On Poetry in General

THE BEST general notion which I can give of poetry is, that it is the natural impression of any object or event, by its vividness exciting an involuntary movement of imagination and passion, and producing, by sympathy, a certain modulation of the voice, or sounds, expressing it.

In treating of poetry, I shall speak first of the subject-matter of it, next of the forms of expression to which it gives birth, and afterwards of its connexion with harmony of sound.

Poetry is the language of the imagination and the passions. It relates to whatever gives immediate pleasure or pain to the human mind. It comes home to the bosoms and businesses of men; for nothing but what so comes home to them in the most general and intelligible shape, can be a subject for poetry. Poetry is the universal language which the heart holds with nature and itself. He who has a contempt for poetry, cannot have much respect for himself, or for anything else. It is not a mere frivolous accomplishment (as some persons have been led to imagine), the trifling amusement of a few idle readers or leisure hours—it has been the study and delight of mankind in all ages. Many people suppose that poetry is something to be found only in books, contained in lines of ten syllables, with

On Poetry in General. From Lecture I, in *Lectures on the English Poets* (1818).

like endings: but wherever there is a sense of beauty, or power, or harmony, as in the motion of a wave of the sea, in the growth of a flower that "spreads its sweet leaves to the air, and dedicates its beauty to the sun,"—*there* is poetry, in its birth. If history is a grave study, poetry may be said to be a graver: its materials lie deeper, and are spread wider. History treats, for the most part, of the cumbrous and unwieldy masses of things, the empty cases in which the affairs of the world are packed, under the heads of intrigue or war, in different states, and from century to century: but there is no thought or feeling that can have entered into the mind of man, which he would be eager to communicate to others, or which they would listen to with delight, that is not a fit subject for poetry. It is not a branch of authorship: it is "the stuff of which our life is made." The rest is "mere oblivion," a dead letter: for all that is worth remembering in life, is the poetry of it. Fear is poetry, hope is poetry, love is poetry, hatred is poetry; contempt, jealousy, remorse, admiration, wonder, pity, despair, or madness, are all poetry. Poetry is that fine particle within us, that expands, rarefies, refines, raises our whole being: without it "man's life is poor as beast's." Man is a poetical animal: and those of us who do not study the principles of poetry, act upon them all our lives, like Molière's *Bourgeois Gentilhomme*, who had always spoken prose without knowing it. The child is a poet in fact, when he first plays at hide-and-seek, or repeats the story of Jack the Giant-killer; the shepherd-boy is a poet, when he first crowns his mistress with a garland of flowers; the countryman, when he stops to look at the rainbow; the city-apprentice, when he gazes after the Lord Mayor's show; the miser, when he hugs his gold; the courtier, who builds his hopes upon a smile; the savage, who paints his idol with blood; the slave, who worships a tyrant, or the tyrant, who fancies himself a god; —the vain, the ambitious, the proud, the choleric man, the hero and the coward, the beggar and the king, the rich and the poor, the young and the old, all live in a world of their own making; and the poet does no more than describe what all the others think and act. . . .

Poetry then is an imitation of nature, but the imagination and the passions are a part of man's nature. We shape things according to our wishes and fancies, without poetry; but poetry is the most emphatical language that can be found for those creations of the mind "which ecstasy is very cunning in." Neither a mere description of natural objects, nor a mere delineation of natural feelings, however distinct or forcible, constitutes the ultimate end and aim of poetry, without the heightenings of the imagination. The light of poetry is not only a direct but also a reflected light, that while it shows us the object, throws a sparkling radiance on all around it: the flame of the passions, communicated to the imagination, reveals to us, as with a flash of lightning, the inmost recesses of thought, and penetrates our whole being. Poetry represents forms chiefly as they suggest other forms; feelings, as they suggest forms or other feelings. Poetry puts a spirit of life and motion into the universe. It describes the flowing, not the fixed. It does not define the limits of sense, or analyse the distinctions of the understanding, but signifies the excess of the imagination beyond the actual or ordinary impression of any object or feeling. The poetical impression of any object is that uneasy, exquisite sense of beauty or power that cannot be contained within itself; that is impatient of all limit; that (as flame bends to flame) strives to link itself to some other image of kindred beauty or grandeur; to enshrine itself, as it were, in the highest forms of fancy, and to relieve the aching sense of pleasure by expressing it in the boldest manner, and by the most striking examples of the same quality in other instances. Poetry, according to Lord Bacon, for this reason, "has something divine in it, because it raises the mind and hurries it into sublimity, by conforming the shows of things to the desires of the soul, instead of subjecting the soul to external things, as reason and history do." [1] It is strictly the language of the imagination; and the imagination is that faculty which represents objects, not as they are in themselves, but as they are moulded by other thoughts and feelings, into an infinite variety of shapes and combinations of power. This language is not the less true to nature, because it is false in point of fact; but so much the more true and natural, if it conveys the impression which the object under the influence of passion makes on the mind. Let an object, for instance, be pre-

[1] *Advancement of Learning*, II, Ch. 4.

sented to the senses in a state of agitation or fear —and the imagination will distort or magnify the object, and convert it into the likeness of whatever is most proper to encourage the fear. "Our eyes are made the fools" of our other faculties. This is the universal law of the imagination . . . We compare a man of gigantic stature to a tower: not that he is anything like so large, but because the excess of his size beyond what we are accustomed to expect, or the usual size of things of the same class, produces by contrast a greater feeling of magnitude and ponderous strength than another object of ten times the same dimensions. The intensity of the feeling makes up for the disproportion of the objects. Things are equal to the imagination, which have the power of affecting the mind with an equal degree of terror, admiration, delight, or love. When Lear calls upon the heavens to avenge his cause, "for they are old like him," there is nothing extravagant or impious in this sublime identification of his age with theirs; for there is no other image which could do justice to the agonizing sense of his wrongs and his despair!

Poetry is the high-wrought enthusiasm of fancy and feeling. As in describing natural objects, it impregnates sensible impressions with the forms of fancy, so it describes the feelings of pleasure or pain, by blending them with the strongest movements of passion, and the most striking forms of nature. Tragic poetry, which is the most impassioned species of it, strives to carry on the feeling to the utmost point of sublimity or pathos, by all the force of comparison or contrast; loses the sense of present suffering in the imaginary exaggeration of it; exhausts the terror or pity by an unlimited indulgence of it; grapples with impossibilities in its desperate impatience of restraint; throws us back upon the past, forward into the future; brings every moment of our being or object of nature in startling review before us; and in the rapid whirl of events, lifts us from the depths of woe to the highest contemplations on human life. When Lear says of Edgar, "Nothing but his unkind daughters could have brought him to this"; what a bewildered amazement, what a wrench of the imagination, that cannot be brought to conceive of any other cause of misery than that which has bowed it down, and absorbs all other sorrow in its own! His sorrow, like a flood, sup-

plies the sources of all other sorrow. Again, when he exclaims in the mad scene, "The little dogs and all, Tray, Blanche, and Sweetheart, see, they bark at me!" it is passion lending occasion to imagination to make every creature in league against him, conjuring up ingratitude and insult in their least looked-for and most galling shapes, searching every thread and fibre of his heart, and finding out the last remaining image of respect or attachment in the bottom of his breast, only to torture and kill it! . . .

One mode in which the dramatic exhibition of passion excites our sympathy without raising our disgust is, that in proportion as it sharpens the edge of calamity and disappointment, it strengthens the desire of good. It enhances our consciousness of the blessing, by making us sensible of the magnitude of the loss. The storm of passion lays bare and shows us the rich depths of the human soul: the whole of our existence, the sum total of our passions and pursuits, of that which we desire and that which we dread, is brought before us by contrast; the action and reaction are equal; the keenness of immediate suffering only gives us a more intense aspiration after, and a more intimate participation with the antagonist world of good; makes us drink deeper of the cup of human life; tugs at the heart-strings; loosens the pressure about them; and calls the springs of thought and feeling into play with tenfold force.

Impassioned poetry is an emanation of the moral and intellectual part of our nature, as well as of the sensitive—of the desire to know, the will to act, and the power to feel; and ought to appeal to these different parts of our constitution, in order to be perfect. The domestic or prose tragedy, which is thought to be the most natural, is in this sense the least so, because it appeals almost exclusively to one of these faculties, our sensibility. The tragedies of Moore and Lillo, for this reason, however affecting at the time, oppress and lie like a dead weight upon the mind, a load of misery which it is unable to throw off: the tragedy of Shakespeare, which is true poetry, stirs our inmost affections; abstracts evil from itself by combining it with all the forms of imagination, and with the deepest workings of the heart, and rouses the whole man within us.

The pleasure, however, derived from tragic

poetry, is not anything peculiar to it as poetry, as a fictitious and fanciful thing. It is not an anomaly of the imagination. It has its source and groundwork in the common love of strong excitement. As Mr. Burke observes, people flock to see a tragedy; [2] but if there were a public execution in the next street, the theatre would very soon be empty. It is not then the difference between fiction and reality that solves the difficulty. Children are satisfied with the stories of ghosts and witches in plain prose: nor do the hawkers of full, true, and particular accounts of murders and executions about the streets, find it necessary to have them turned into penny ballads, before they can dispose of these interesting and authentic documents. The grave politician drives a thriving trade of abuse and calumnies poured out against those whom he makes his enemies for no other end than that he may live by them. The popular preacher makes less frequent mention of heaven than of hell. Oaths and nicknames are only a more vulgar sort of poetry or rhetoric. We are as fond of indulging our violent passions as of reading a description of those of others. We are as prone to make a torment of our fears, as to luxuriate in our hopes of good. If it be asked, Why we do so? the best answer will be, Because we cannot help it. The sense of power is as strong a principle in the mind as the love of pleasure. Objects of terror and pity exercise the same despotic control over it as those of love or beauty. It is as natural to hate as to love, to despise as to admire, to express our hatred or contempt, as our love or admiration.

> Masterless passion sways us to the mood
> Of what it likes or loathes.

Not that we like what we loathe; but we like to indulge our hatred and scorn of it; to dwell upon it, to exasperate our idea of it by every refinement of ingenuity and extravagance of illustration; to make it a bugbear to ourselves, to

point it out to others in all the splendour of deformity, to embody it to the senses, to stigmatize it by name, to grapple with it in thought, in action, to sharpen our intellect, to arm our will against it, to know the worst we have to contend with, and to contend with it to the utmost. Poetry is only the highest eloquence of passion, the most vivid form of expression that can be given to our conception of anything, whether pleasurable or painful, mean or dignified, delightful or distressing. It is the perfect coincidence of the image and the words with the feeling we have, and of which we cannot get rid in any other way, that gives an instant "satisfaction to the thought." This is equally the origin of wit and fancy, of comedy and tragedy, of the sublime and pathetic. When Pope says of the Lord Mayor's show,—

> Now night descending, the proud scene is o'er,
> But lives in Settle's numbers one day more! [3]

—when Collins makes Danger, "with limbs of giant mould,"

> ——Throw him on the steep
> Of some loose hanging rock asleep:

when Lear calls out in extreme anguish,

> Ingratitude, thou marble-hearted fiend,
> How much more hideous shew'st in a child
> Than the sea-monster!

—the passion of contempt in the one case, of terror in the other, and of indignation in the last, is perfectly satisfied. We see the thing ourselves, and show it to others as we feel it to exist, and as, in spite of ourselves, we are compelled to think of it. The imagination, by thus embodying and turning them to shape, gives an obvious relief to the indistinct and importunate cravings of the will.—We do not wish the thing to be so; but we wish it to appear such as it is. For knowledge is conscious power; and the mind is no longer, in this case, the dupe, though it may be the victim of vice or folly. . . .

[2] *Sublime and Beautiful,* Pt. I, Sec. 15.

[3] *Dunciad,* I, 89-90.

On Shakespeare and Milton

THE STRIKING peculiarity of Shakespeare's mind was its generic quality, its power of communication with all other minds—so that it contained a universe of thought and feeling within itself, and had no one peculiar bias, or exclusive excellence more than another. He was just like any other man, but that he was like all other men. He was the least of an egotist that it was possible to be. He was nothing in himself; but he was all that others were, or that they could become. He not only had in himself the germs of every faculty and feeling, but he could follow them by anticipation, intuitively, into all their conceivable ramifications, through every change of fortune or conflict of passion, or turn of thought. He had "a mind reflecting ages past," and present:—all the people that ever lived are there. There was no respect of persons with him. His genius shone equally on the evil and on the good, on the wise and the foolish, the monarch and the beggar: "All corners of the earth, kings, queens, and states, maids, matrons, nay, the secrets of the grave," are hardly hid from his searching glance. He was like the genius of humanity, changing places with all of us at pleasure, and playing with our purposes as with his own. He turned the globe round for his amusement, and surveyed the generations of men, and the individuals as they passed, with their different concerns, passions, follies, vices, virtues, actions, and motives—as well those that they knew, as those which they did not know, or acknowledge to themselves. The dreams of childhood, the ravings of despair, were the toys of his fancy. Airy beings waited at his call, and came at his bidding. Harmless fairies "nodded to him, and did him curtesies": and the night-hag bestrode the blast at the command of "his so potent art." The world of spirits lay open to him, like the world of real men and women: and there is the same truth in his delineations of the one as of the other; for if the preternatural characters he describes could be supposed to exist, they would speak, and feel, and act, as he makes them. He

On Shakespeare and Milton. From Lecture III, in *Lectures on the English Poets* (1818).

had only to think of anything in order to become that thing, with all the circumstances belonging to it. When he conceived of a character, whether real or imaginary, he not only entered into all its thoughts and feelings, but seemed instantly, and as if by touching a secret spring, to be surrounded with all the same objects, "subject to the same skyey influences," the same local, outward, and unforeseen accidents which would occur in reality. Thus the character of Caliban not only stands before us with a language and manners of its own, but the scenery and situation of the enchanted island he inhabits, the traditions of the place, its strange noises, its hidden recesses, "his frequent haunts and ancient neighbourhood," are given with a miraculous truth of nature, and with all the familiarity of an old recollection. The whole "coheres semblably together" in time, place, and circumstance. In reading this author, you do not merely learn what his characters say,—you see their persons. By something expressed or understood, you are at no loss to decipher their peculiar physiognomy, the meaning of a look, the grouping, the by-play, as we might see it on the stage. A word, an epithet paints a whole scene, or throws us back whole years in the history of the person represented. So (as it has been ingeniously remarked) when Prospero describes himself as left alone in the boat with his daughter, the epithet which he applies to her, "Me and thy *crying* self," flings the imagination instantly back from the grown woman to the helpless condition of infancy, and places the first and most trying scene of his misfortunes before us, with all that he must have suffered in the interval. How well the silent anguish of Macduff is conveyed to the reader, by the friendly expostulation of Malcolm—"What! man, ne'er pull your hat upon your brows!" Again, Hamlet, in the scene with Rosencrans and Guildenstern, somewhat abruptly concludes his fine soliloquy on life by saying, "Man delights not me, nor woman neither, though by your smiling you seem to say so." Which is explained by their answer—"My lord, we had no such stuff in our thoughts. But we smiled to think, if you delight not in man, what lenten entertainment the players shall receive from you, whom we met on the way":—as if while Hamlet was making this speech, his two old schoolfellows from Wittenberg had been really standing by, and he had seen them smiling by stealth, at the idea of the players crossing their minds. It is not "a combination and a form" of words, a set speech or two, a preconcerted theory of a character, that will do this: but all the persons concerned must have been present in the poet's imagination, as at a kind of rehearsal; and whatever would have passed through their minds on the occasion, and have been observed by others, passed through his, and is made known to the reader. . . . The account of Ophelia's death begins thus:

There is a willow hanging o'er a brook,
That shows its hoary leaves in the glassy stream.—

Now this is an instance of the same unconscious power of mind which is as true to nature as itself. The leaves of the willow are, in fact, white underneath, and it is this part of them which would appear "hoary" in the reflection in the brook. The same sort of intuitive power, the same faculty of bringing every object in nature, whether present or absent, before the mind's eye, is observable in the speech of Cleopatra, when conjecturing what were the employments of Antony in his absence:—"He's speaking now, or murmuring, where's my serpent of old Nile?" How fine to make Cleopatra have this consciousness of her own character, and to make her feel that it is this for which Antony is in love with her! She says, after the battle of Actium, when Antony has resolved to risk another fight, "It is my birthday; I had thought to have held it poor: but since my lord is Antony again, I will be Cleopatra." What other poet would have thought of such a casual resource of the imagination, or would have dared to avail himself of it? The thing happens in the play as it might have happened in fact.—That which, perhaps, more than anything else distinguishes the dramatic productions of Shakespeare from all others, is this wonderful truth and individuality of conception. Each of his characters is as much itself, and as absolutely independent of the rest, as well as of the author, as if they were living persons, not fictions of the mind. The poet may be said, for the time, to identify himself with the character he wishes to represent, and to pass from one to another, like the same soul successively animating different bodies. By an art like that of the ventriloquist, he throws his imagination out of himself, and makes every word appear to proceed from the mouth of the person in whose name it is given. His plays alone are properly expressions of the passions, not descriptions of them. His characters are real beings of flesh and blood; they speak like men, not like authors. One might suppose that he had stood by at the time, and overheard what passed. As in our dreams we hold conversations with ourselves, make remarks, or communicate intelligence, and have no idea of the answer which we shall receive, and which we ourselves make, till we hear it: so the dialogues in Shakespeare are carried on without any consciousness of what is to follow, without any appearance of preparation or premeditation. The gusts of passion come and go like sounds of music borne on the wind. Nothing is made out by formal inference and analogy, by climax and antithesis: all comes, or seems to come, immediately from nature. Each object and circumstance exists in his mind, as it would have existed in reality: each several train of thought and feeling goes on of itself, without confusion or effort. In the world of his imagination, everything has a life, a place, and being of its own!

Chaucer's characters are sufficiently distinct from one another, but they are too little varied in themselves, too much like identical propositions. They are consistent, but uniform; we get no new idea of them from first to last; they are not placed in different lights, nor are their subordinate *traits* brought out in new situations; they are like portraits or physiognomical studies, with the distinguishing features marked with inconceivable truth and precision, but that preserve the same unaltered air and attitude. Shakespeare's are historical figures, equally true and correct, but put into action, where every nerve and muscle is displayed in the struggle with others, with all the effect of collision and contrast, with every variety of light and shade. Chaucer's characters are narrative, Shakespeare's dramatic, Milton's epic. That is, Chaucer told only as much of his story as he pleased, as was required for a particular purpose. He answered for his characters himself. In Shakespeare they are introduced upon the stage, are liable to be asked all sorts of questions, and are forced to answer for themselves. In Chaucer we perceive a fixed essence of character. In Shakespeare there is a continual composition and decomposition of its elements, a fermentation of every particle in the whole mass, by its alternate affinity or antipathy to other principles which are brought in contact with it. Till the experiment is tried, we do not know the result, the turn which the character will take in its new circumstances. Milton took only a few simple principles of character, and raised them to the utmost conceivable grandeur, and refined them from every base alloy. His imagination, "nigh sphered in Heaven," claimed kindred only with what he saw from that height, and could raise to the same elevation with itself. He sat retired and kept his state alone, "playing with wisdom"; while Shakespeare mingled with the crowd, and played the host, "to make society the sweeter welcome."

The passion in Shakespeare is of the same nature as his delineation of character. It is not some one habitual feeling or sentiment preying upon itself, growing out of itself, and moulding everything to itself; it is passion modified by passion, by all the other feelings to which the individual is liable, and to which others are liable with him; subject to all the fluctuations of caprice and accident; calling into play all the resources of the understanding and all the energies of the will; irritated by obstacles or yielding to them; rising from small beginnings to its utmost height; now drunk with hope, now stung to madness, now sunk in despair, now blown to air with a breath, now raging like a torrent. The human soul is made the sport of fortune, the prey of adversity: it is stretched on the wheel of destiny, in restless ecstasy. The passions are in a state of projection. Years are melted down to moments, and every instant teems with fate. We know the results, we see the process. Thus after Iago has been boasting to himself of the effect of his poisonous suggestions on the mind of Othello, "which, with a little act upon the blood, will work like mines of sulphur," he adds—

Look where he comes! not poppy, nor mandragora,
Nor all the drowsy syrups of the East,
Shall ever medicine thee to that sweet sleep
Which thou ow'dst yesterday.—

And he enters at this moment, like the crested serpent, crowned with his wrongs and raging for revenge! The whole depends upon the turn of a thought. A word, a look, blows the spark of jealousy into a flame; and the explosion is immediate and terrible as a volcano. The dialogues in *Lear*, in *Macbeth*, that between Brutus and Cassius, and nearly all those in Shakespeare, where the interest is wrought up to its highest pitch, afford examples of this dramatic fluctuation of passion. The interest in Chaucer is quite different; it is like the course of a river, strong, and full, and increasing. In Shakespeare, on the contrary, it is like the sea, agitated this way and that, and loud-lashed by furious storms; while in the still pauses of the blast, we distinguish only the cries of despair, or the silence of death! Milton, on the other hand, takes the imaginative part of passion—that which remains after the event, which the mind reposes on when all is over, which looks upon circumstances from the remotest elevation of thought and fancy, and abstracts them from the world of action to that of contemplation. The objects of dramatic poetry affect us by sympathy, by their nearness to ourselves, as they take us by surprise, or force us upon action, "while rage with rage doth sympathize": the objects of epic poetry affect us through the medium of the imagination, by magnitude and distance, by their permanence and universality. The one fill us with terror and pity, the other with admiration and delight. There are certain objects that strike the imagination, and inspire awe in the very idea of them, independently of any dramatic interest, that is, of any connexion with the vicissitudes of human life. For instance, we cannot think of the pyramids of Egypt, of a Gothic ruin, or an old Roman encampment, without a certain emotion, a sense of power and sublimity coming over the mind. The heavenly bodies that hang over our heads wherever we go, and "in their untroubled element shall shine when we are laid in dust, and all our cares forgotten," affect us in the same way. Thus Satan's address to the Sun [1] has an epic, not a dramatic interest; for though the second person in the dialogue makes no answer and feels no concern, yet the eye of that vast luminary is upon him, like the eye of heaven, and seems con-

[1] *Paradise Lost*, IV, 31 ff.

scious of what he says, like a universal presence. Dramatic poetry and epic, in their perfection, indeed, approximate to and strengthen one another. Dramatic poetry borrows aid from the dignity of persons and things, as the heroic does from human passion, but in theory they are distinct.—When Richard II calls for the looking-glass to contemplate his faded majesty in it, and bursts into that affecting exclamation: "Oh, that I were a mockery-king of snow, to melt away before the sun of Bolingbroke," we have here the utmost force of human passion, combined with the ideas of regal splendour and fallen power. When Milton says of Satan:

> ————His form had not yet lost
> All her original brightness, nor appear'd
> Less than archangel ruin'd, and th' excess
> Of glory obscur'd;— [2]

the mixture of beauty, or grandeur, and pathos, from the sense of irreparable loss, of never-ending, unavailing regret, is perfect.

The great fault of a modern school of poetry is, that it is an experiment to reduce poetry to a mere effusion of natural sensibility; or what is worse, to divest it both of imaginary splendour and human passion, to surround the meanest objects with the morbid feelings and devouring egotism of the writers' own minds. Milton and Shakespeare did not so understand poetry. They gave a more liberal interpretation both to nature and art. They did not do all they could to get rid of the one and the other, to fill up the dreary void with the Moods of their own Minds.[3] They owe their power over the human mind to their having had a deeper sense than others of what was grand in the objects of nature, or affecting in the events of human life. But to the men I speak of there is nothing interesting, nothing heroical, but themselves. To them the fall of gods or of great men is the same. They do not enter into the feeling. They cannot understand the terms. They are even debarred from the last poor, paltry consolation of an unmanly triumph over fallen greatness; for their minds reject, with a convulsive effort and intolerable loathing, the very idea that there ever was, or was thought to

be, anything superior to themselves. All that has ever excited the attention or admiration of the world, they look upon with the most perfect indifference; and they are surprised to find that the world repays their indifference with scorn. "With what measure they mete, it has been meted to them again."—

Shakespeare's imagination is of the same plastic kind as his conception of character or passion. "It glances from heaven to earth, from earth to heaven." Its movement is rapid and devious. It unites the most opposite extremes; or, as Puck says, in boasting of his own feats, "puts a girdle round about the earth in forty minutes." He seems always hurrying from his subject, even while describing it; but the stroke, like the lightning's, is sure as it is sudden. He takes the widest possible range, but from that very range he has his choice of the greatest variety and aptitude of materials. He brings together images the most alike, but placed at the greatest distance from each other; that is, found in circumstances of the greatest dissimilitude. From the remoteness of his combinations, and the celerity with which they are effected, they coalesce the more indissolubly together. The more the thoughts are strangers to each other, and the longer they have been kept asunder, the more intimate does their union seem to become. . . .

It remains to speak of the faults of Shakespeare. They are not so many or so great as they have been represented; what there are, are chiefly owing to the following causes:—The universality of his genius was, perhaps, a disadvantage to his single works; the variety of his resources, sometimes diverting him from applying them to the most effectual purposes. He might be said to combine the powers of Aeschylus and Aristophanes, of Dante and Rabelais, in his own mind. If he had been only half what he was, he would perhaps have appeared greater. The natural ease and indifference of his temper made him sometimes less scrupulous than he might have been. He is relaxed and careless in critical places; he is in earnest throughout only in *Timon, Macbeth,* and *Lear.* Again, he had no models of acknowledged excellence constantly in view to stimulate his efforts, and by all that appears, no love of fame. He wrote for the "great vulgar and the small," in his time, not for posterity. If Queen Elizabeth and the maids of hon-

---

[2] *Ibid.*, I, 591-94.

[3] Hazlitt is thinking of the phrase used by Wordsworth as a title ("Moods of my own Mind") of one of the sections of his *Poems* (1807).

our laughed heartily at his worst jokes, and the catcalls in the gallery were silent at his best passages, he went home satisfied, and slept the next night well. He did not trouble himself about Voltaire's criticisms. He was willing to take advantage of the ignorance of the age in many things; and if his plays pleased others, not to quarrel with them himself. His very facility of production would make him set less value on his own excellences, and not care to distinguish nicely between what he did well or ill. His blunders in chronology and geography do not amount to above half a dozen, and they are offences against chronology and geography, not against poetry. As to the unities, he was right in setting them at defiance. He was fonder of puns than became so great a man. His barbarisms were those of his age. His genius was his own. He had no objection to float down with the stream of common taste and opinion: he rose above it by his own buoyancy, and an impulse which he could not keep under, in spite of himself or others, and "his delights did show most dolphin-like." . . .

Shakespeare discovers in his writings little religious enthusiasm, and an indifference to personal reputation; he had none of the bigotry of his age, and his political prejudices were not very strong. In these respects, as well as in every other, he formed a direct contrast to Milton. Milton's works are a perpetual invocation to the Muses; a hymn to Fame. He had his thoughts constantly fixed on the contemplation of the Hebrew theocracy, and of a perfect commonwealth; and he seized the pen with a hand just warm from the touch of the ark of faith. His religious zeal infused its character into his imagination; so that he devotes himself with the same sense of duty to the cultivation of his genius, as he did to the exercise of virtue, or the good of his country. The spirit of the poet, the patriot, and the prophet, vied with each other in his breast. His mind appears to have held equal communion with the inspired writers, and with the bards and sages of ancient Greece and Rome;—

Blind Thamyris, and blind Maeonides,
And Tiresias, and Phineus, prophets old.

He had a high standard, with which he was always comparing himself, nothing short of which could satisfy his jealous ambition. He thought of nobler forms and nobler things than those he found about him. He lived apart, in the solitude of his own thoughts, carefully excluding from his mind whatever might distract its purposes or alloy its purity, or damp its zeal. "With darkness and with dangers compassed round," he had the mighty models of antiquity always present to his thoughts, and determined to raise a monument of equal height and glory, "piling up every stone of lustre from the brook," for the delight and wonder of posterity. He had girded himself up, and as it were, sanctified his genius to this service from his youth. . . .

Milton, therefore, did not write from casual impulse, but after a severe examination of his own strength, and with a resolution to leave nothing undone which it was in his power to do. He always labours, and almost always succeeds. He strives hard to say the finest things in the world, and he does say them. He adorns and dignifies his subject to the utmost: he surrounds it with every possible association of beauty or grandeur, whether moral, intellectual, or physical. He refines on his descriptions of beauty; loading sweets on sweets, till the sense aches at them; and raises his images of terror to a gigantic elevation, that "makes Ossa like a wart." In Milton, there is always an appearance of effort: in Shakespeare, scarcely any.

Milton has borrowed more than any other writer, and exhausted every source of imitation, sacred or profane; yet he is perfectly distinct from every other writer. He is a writer of centos, and yet in originality scarcely inferior to Homer. The power of his mind is stamped on every line. The fervour of his imagination melts down and renders malleable, as in a furnace, the most contradictory materials. In reading his works, we feel ourselves under the influence of a mighty intellect, that the nearer it approaches to others, becomes more distinct from them. The quantity of art in him shows the strength of his genius: the weight of his intellectual obligations would have oppressed any other writer. Milton's learning has the effect of intuition. He describes objects, of which he could only have read in books, with the vividness of actual observation. His imagination has the force of nature. . . .

We might be tempted to suppose that the vividness with which he describes visible objects, was owing to their having acquired an unusual degree of strength in his mind, after the privation of his sight; but we find the same palpableness and truth in the descriptions which occur in his early poems. In *Lycidas* he speaks of "the great vision of the guarded mount," with that preternatural weight of impression with which it would present itself suddenly to "the pilot of some small night-foundered skiff." . . . There is also the same depth of impression in his descriptions of the objects of all the different senses, whether colours, or sounds, or smells—the same absorption of his mind in whatever engaged his attention at the time. It has been indeed objected to Milton, by a common perversity of criticism, that his ideas were musical rather than picturesque, as if because they were in the highest degree musical, they must be (to keep the sage critical balance even, and to allow no one man to possess two qualities at the same time) proportionably deficient in other respects. But Milton's poetry is not cast in any such narrow, common-place mould; it is not so barren of resources. His worship of the Muse was not so simple or confined. A sound arises "like a steam of rich distilled perfumes"; we hear the pealing organ, but the incense on the altars is also there, and the statues of the gods are ranged around! The ear indeed predominates over the eye, because it is more immediately affected, and because the language of music blends more immediately with, and forms a more natural accompaniment to, the variable and indefinite associations of ideas conveyed by words. But where the associations of the imagination are not the principal thing, the individual object is given by Milton with equal force and beauty. The strongest and best proof of this, as a characteristic power of his mind, is, that the persons of Adam and Eve, of Satan, &c. are always accompanied, in our imagination, with the grandeur of the naked figure; they convey to us the ideas of sculpture. . . .

Again, nothing can be more magnificent than the portrait of Beelzebub:

> With Atlantean sholders fit to bear
> The weight of mightiest monarchies:

Or the comparison of Satan, as he "lay floating many a rood," to "that sea beast,"

> Leviathan, which God of all his works
> Created hugest that swim the ocean-stream!

What a force of imagination is there in this last expression! What an idea it conveys of the size of that hugest of created beings, as if it shrunk up the ocean to a stream, and took up the sea in its nostrils as a very little thing! Force of style is one of Milton's greatest excellences. Hence, perhaps, he stimulates us more in the reading, and less afterwards. The way to defend Milton against all impugners, is to take down the book and read it.

Milton's blank verse is the only blank verse in the language (except Shakespeare's) that deserves the name of verse. Dr. Johnson, who had modelled his ideas of versification on the regular sing-song of Pope, condemns the *Paradise Lost* as harsh and unequal. I shall not pretend to say that this is not sometimes the case; for where a degree of excellence beyond the mechanical rules of art is attempted, the poet must sometimes fail. But I imagine that there are more perfect examples in Milton of musical expression, or of an adaptation of the sound and movement of the verse to the meaning of the passage, than in all our other writers, whether of rhyme or blank verse, put together (with the exception already mentioned). Spenser is the most harmonious of our stanza writers, as Dryden is the most sounding and varied of our rhymists. But in neither is there anything like the same ear for music, the same power of approximating the varieties of poetical to those of musical rhythm, as there is in our great epic poet. The sound of his lines is moulded into the expression of the sentiment, almost of the very image. They rise or fall, pause or hurry rapidly on, with exquisite art, but without the least trick or affectation, as the occasion seems to require. . . .

On Wit and Humor

MAN IS the only animal that laughs and weeps; for he is the only animal that is struck with the difference between what things are, and what they ought to be. We weep at what thwarts or exceeds our desires in serious matters: we laugh at what only disappoints our expectations in trifles. We shed tears from sympathy with real and necessary distress; as we burst into laughter from want of sympathy with that which is unreasonable and unnecessary, the absurdity of which provokes our spleen or mirth, rather than any serious reflections on it.

To explain the nature of laughter and tears is to account for the condition of human life; for it is in a manner compounded of these two! It is a tragedy or a comedy—sad or merry, as it happens. The crimes and misfortunes that are inseparable from it shock and wound the mind when they once seize upon it, and when the pressure can no longer be borne, seek relief in tears: the follies and absurdities that men commit, or the odd accidents that befall them, afford us amusement from the very rejection of these false claims upon our sympathy and end in laughter. If everything that went wrong, if every vanity or weakness in another gave us a sensible pang, it would be hard indeed: but as long as the disagreeableness of the consequences of a sudden disaster is kept out of sight by the immediate oddity of the circumstances, and the absurdity or unaccountableness of a foolish action is the most striking thing in it, the ludicrous prevails over the pathetic, and we receive pleasure instead of pain from the farce of life which is played before us, and which discomposes our gravity as often as it fails to move our anger or our pity!

Tears may be considered as the natural and involuntary resource of the mind overcome by some sudden and violent emotion before it has had time to reconcile its feelings to the change of circumstances: while laughter may be defined to be the same sort of convulsive and involuntary movement, occasioned by mere surprise or contrast (in the absence of any more serious emotion), before it has time to reconcile its belief to contradictory appearances. If we hold a mask before our face and approach a child with this disguise on, it will at first, from the oddity and incongruity of the appearance, be inclined to laugh; if we go nearer to it, steadily, and without saying a word, it will begin to be alarmed and be half inclined to cry: if we suddenly take off the mask, it will recover from its fears and burst out a-laughing; but if, instead of presenting the old well-known countenance, we have concealed a satyr's head or some frightful caricature behind the first mask, the suddenness of the change will not in this case be a source of merriment to it, but will convert its surprise into an agony of consternation, and will make it scream out for help, even though it may be convinced that the whole is a trick at bottom.

The alternation of tears and laughter, in this little episode in common life, depends almost entirely on the greater or less degree of interest attached to the different changes of appearance. The mere suddenness of the transition, the mere balking our expectations and turning them abruptly into another channel, seems to give additional liveliness and gaiety to the animal spirits; but the instant the change is not only sudden, but threatens serious consequences or calls up the shape of danger, terror supersedes our disposition to mirth, and laughter gives place to tears. It is usual to play with infants, and make them laugh by clapping your hands suddenly before them; but, if you clap your hands too loud, or too near their sight, their countenances immediately change, and they hide them in the nurse's arms. Or suppose the same child grown up a little older comes to a place, expecting to meet a person it is particularly fond of, and does not find that person there, its countenance suddenly falls, its lips begin to quiver, its cheek turns pale, its eye glistens, and it vents its little sorrow (grown too big to be concealed) in a flood of tears. Again, if the child meets the same

On Wit and Humor. From Lecture I, in Lectures on the English Comic Writers (1819).

person unexpectedly after long absence, the same effect will be produced by an excess of joy, with different accompaniments; that is, the surprise and the emotion excited will make the blood come into his face, his eyes sparkle, his tongue falter or be mute; but in either case the tears will gush to his relief and lighten the pressure about his heart. On the other hand, if a child is playing at hide-and-seek or blindman's buff with persons it is ever so fond of, and either misses them where it had made sure of finding them or suddenly runs up against them where it had least expected it, the shock or additional impetus given to the imagination by the disappointment or the discovery, in a matter of this indifference, will only vent itself in a fit of laughter.[1] The transition here is not from one thing of importance to another, or from a state of indifference to a state of strong excitement, but merely from one impression to another that we did not at all expect and when we had expected just the contrary. The mind having been led to form a certain conclusion, and the result producing an immediate solution of continuity in the chain of our ideas, this alternate excitement and relaxation of the imagination, the object also striking upon the mind more vividly in its loose unsettled state, and before it has had time to recover and collect itself, causes that alternate excitement and relaxation, or irregular convulsive movement of the muscular and nervous system, which constitutes physical laughter. The *discontinuous* in our sensations produces a correspondent jar and discord in the frame. . . .

To understand or define the ludicrous, we must first know what the serious is. Now the serious is the habitual stress which the mind lays upon the expectation of a given order of events, following one another with a certain regularity and weight of interest attached to them. When this stress is increased beyond its usual pitch of intensity so as to overstrain the feelings by the violent opposition of good to bad, or of objects to our desires, it becomes the pathetic or tragical. The ludicrous or comic is the unexpected loosening or relaxing this stress

[1] "A child that has hid itself out of the way in sport is under a great temptation to laugh at the unconsciousness of others as to its situation. A person concealed from assassins is in no danger of betraying his situation by laughing." [Hazlitt.]

below its usual pitch of intensity, by such an abrupt transposition of the order of our ideas as, taking the mind unawares, throws it off its guard, startles it into a lively sense of pleasure, and leaves no time nor inclination for painful reflections.

The essence of the laughable then is the incongruous, the disconnecting one idea from another, or the jostling of one feeling against another. The first and most obvious cause of laughter is to be found in the simple succession of events, as in the sudden shifting of a disguise, or some unlooked-for accident, without any absurdity of character or situation. The accidental contradiction between our expectations and the event can hardly be said, however, to amount to the ludicrous: it is merely laughable. The ludicrous is where there is the same contradiction between the object and our expectations, heightened by some deformity or inconvenience, that is, by its being contrary to what is customary or desirable; as the ridiculous, which is the highest degree of the laughable, is that which is contrary not only to custom but to sense and reason, or is a voluntary departure from what we have a right to expect from those who are conscious of absurdity and propriety in words, looks, and actions.

Of these different kinds or degrees of the laughable, the first is the most shallow and short-lived; for the instant the immediate surprise of a thing's merely happening one way or another is over, there is nothing to throw us back upon our former expectation, and renew our wonder at the event a second time. The second sort, that is, the ludicrous arising out of the improbable or distressing, is more deep and lasting either because the painful catastrophe excites a greater curiosity or because the old impression, from its habitual hold on the imagination, still recurs mechanically so that it is longer before we can seriously make up our minds to the unaccountable deviation from it. The third sort, or the ridiculous arising out of absurdity as well as improbability, that is, where the defect or weakness is of a man's own seeking, is the most refined of all, but not always so pleasant as the last because the same contempt and disapprobation which sharpens and subtilizes our sense of the impropriety, adds a severity to it inconsistent with perfect ease and enjoyment. This last species is properly the province of satire. The principle of contrast is, however, the same in all the stages, in the simply laughable, the ludicrous, the ridiculous; and the effect is only the more complete, the more durably and pointedly this principle operates.

To give some examples in these different kinds. We laugh, when children, at the sudden removing of a pasteboard mask; we laugh, when grown up, more gravely at the tearing off the mask of deceit. We laugh at absurdity; we laugh at deformity. We laugh at a bottlenose in a caricature; at a stuffed figure of an alderman in a pantomime; and at the tale of Slaukenbergius.[2] A giant standing by a dwarf makes a contemptible figure enough. Rosinante and Dapple[3] are laughable from contrast, as their masters from the same principle make two for a pair. We laugh at the dress of foreigners, and they at ours. Three chimney sweepers, meeting three Chinese in Lincoln's-Inn Fields, they laughed at one another till they were ready to drop down. Country people laugh at a person because they never saw him before. Anyone dressed in the height of the fashion, or quite out of it, is equally an object of ridicule. One rich source of the ludicrous is distress with which we cannot sympathize from its absurdity or insignificance. Women laugh at their lovers. We laugh at a damned author, in spite of our teeth, and though he may be our friend. "There is something in the misfortunes of our best friends that pleases us."[4] We laugh at people on the top of a stagecoach, or in it, if they seem in great extremity. It is hard to hinder children from laughing at a stammerer, at a Negro, at a drunken man, or even at a madman. We laugh at mischief. We laugh at what we do not believe. We say that an argument, or an assertion that is very absurd, is quite ludicrous. We laugh to show our satisfaction with ourselves, or our contempt for those about us, or to conceal our envy or our ignorance. We laugh at fools, and at those who pretend to be wise—at extreme simplicity, awkwardness, hypocrisy, and affectation. "They were talking of me," says Scrub, "for they laughed *consumedly*." Lord Foppington's

insensibility to ridicule and airs of ineffable self-conceit are no less admirable; and Joseph Surface's[5] cant maxims of morality, when once disarmed of their power to do hurt, become sufficiently ludicrous. We laugh at that in others which is a serious matter to ourselves; because our self-love is stronger than our sympathy, sooner takes the alarm, and instantly turns our heedless mirth into gravity, which only enhances the jest to others. Someone is generally sure to be the sufferer by a joke. What is sport to one, is death to another. It is only very sensible or very honest people who laugh as freely at their own absurdities as at those of their neighbors. In general the contrary rule holds, and we only laugh at those misfortunes in which we are spectators, not sharers. The injury, the disappointment, shame, and vexation that we feel put a stop to our mirth; while the disasters that come home to us and excite our repugnance and dismay are an amusing spectacle to others. The greater resistance we make, and the greater the perplexity into which we are thrown, the more lively and piquant is the intellectual display of cross purposes to the bystanders. Our humiliation is their triumph. We are occupied with the disagreeableness of the result instead of its oddity or unexpectedness. Others see only the conflict of motives and the sudden alternation of events; we feel the pain as well, which more than counterbalances the speculative entertainment we might receive from the contemplation of our abstract situation. . . .

Misunderstandings (*mal-entendus*), where one person means one thing, and another is aiming at something else, are another great source of comic humor, on the same principle of ambiguity and contrast. There is a high-wrought instance of this in the dialogue between Aimwell and Gibbet, in the *Beaux' Stratagem*, where Aimwell mistakes his companion for an officer in a marching regiment, and Gibbet takes it for granted that the gentleman is a highwayman. The alarm and consternation occasioned by someone saying to him in the course of common conversation, "I apprehend you," is the most ludicrous thing in that admirably natural and powerful performance, Mr. Emery's *Robert*

---

[2] *Tristram Shandy*, Bk. IV.

[3] Rosinante was Don Quixote's horse; Dapple was Sancho Panza's donkey.

[4] La Rochefoucauld, maxim no. 99.

[5] Characters in Farquhar's *Beaux' Stratagem*, Vanbrugh's *Relapse*, and Sheridan's *School for Scandal*, respectively.

Tyke.[6] Again, unconsciousness in the person himself of what he is about, or of what others think of him, is also a great heightener of the sense of absurdity. It makes it come the fuller home upon us from his insensibility to it. His simplicity sets off the satire and gives it a finer edge. It is a more extreme case still where the person is aware of being the object of ridicule, and yet seems perfectly reconciled to it as a matter of course. So wit is often the more forcible and pointed for being dry and serious, for it then seems as if the speaker himself had no intention in it, and we were the first to find it out. Irony, as a species of wit, owes its force to the same principle. In such cases it is the contrast between the appearance and the reality, the suspense of belief and the seeming incongruity, that gives point to the ridicule, and makes it enter the deeper when the first impression is overcome. Excessive impudence, as in the *Liar,*[7] or excessive modesty, as in the hero of *She Stoops to Conquer;* or a mixture of the two, as in the *Busybody,*[8] are equally amusing. Lying is a species of wit and humor. To lay anything to a person's charge from which he is perfectly free shows spirit and invention; and the more incredible the effrontery, the greater is the joke.

There is nothing more powerfully humorous than what is called *keeping* in comic character, as we see it very finely exemplified in Sancho Panza and Don Quixote. The proverbial phlegm and the romantic gravity of these two celebrated persons may be regarded as the height of this kind of excellence. The deep feeling of character strengthens the sense of the ludicrous. Keeping in comic character is consistency in absurdity, a determined and laudable attachment to the incongruous and singular. The regularity completes the contradiction; for the number of instances of deviation from the right line, branching out in all directions, shows the inveteracy of the original bias to any extravagance or folly, the natural improbability, as it were, increasing every time with the multiplication of chances for a return to common sense, and in the end mounting up to an incredible and unaccountably ridiculous height, when we find our expectations as invariably baffled. The most curious problem

of all is this truth of absurdity to itself. That reason and good sense should be consistent is not wonderful; but that caprice and whim and fantastical prejudice should be uniform and infallible in their results is the surprising thing. But while this characteristic clue to absurdity helps on the ridicule, it also softens and harmonizes its excesses; and the ludicrous is here blended with a certain beauty and decorum, from this very truth of habit and sentiment, or from the principle of similitude in dissimilitude. The devotion to nonsense, and enthusiasm about trifles, is highly affecting as a moral lesson; it is one of the striking weaknesses and greatest happinesses of our nature. That which excites so lively and lasting an interest in itself, even though it should not be wisdom, is not despicable in the sight of reason and humanity. We cannot suppress the smile on the lip; but the tear should also stand ready to start from the eye. The history of hobbyhorses is equally instructive and delightful; and, after the pair I have just alluded to, my Uncle Toby's is one of the best and gentlest that "ever lifted leg!" The inconveniences, odd accidents, falls, and bruises to which they expose their riders contribute their share to the amusement of the spectators; and the blows and wounds that the Knight of the Sorrowful Countenance received in his may perilous adventures have applied their healing influence to many a hurt mind. In what relates to the laughable, as it arises from unforeseen accidents or self-willed scrapes, the pain, the shame, the mortification, and utter helplessness of situation add to the joke, provided they are momentary or overwhelming only to the imagination of the sufferer. . . .

Humor is the describing the ludicrous as it is in itself; wit is the exposing it, by comparing or contrasting it with something else. Humor is, as it were, the growth of nature and accident; wit is the product of art and fancy. Humor, as it is shown in books, is an imitation of the natural or acquired absurdities of mankind, or of the ludicrous in accident, situation, and character: wit is the illustrating and heightening the sense of that absurdity by some sudden and unexpected likeness or opposition of one thing to another, which sets off the quality we laugh at or despise in a still more contemptible or striking point of view. Wit, as distinguished from poetry,

[6] In Thomas Morton's *School of Reform* (1805).
[7] Samuel Foote, *The Liar* (1762).
[8] Susannah Centilivre, *The Busybody* (1709).

is the imagination or fancy inverted, and so applied to given objects as to make the little look less, the mean more light and worthless; or to divert our admiration or wean our affections from that which is lofty and impressive, instead of producing a more intense admiration and exalted passion, as poetry does. Wit may sometimes, indeed, be shown in compliments as well as satire, as in the common epigram—

> Accept a miracle, instead of wit:
> See two dull lines with Stanhope's pencil writ.[9]

But then the mode of paying it is playful and ironical, and contradicts itself in the very act of making its own performance an humble foil to another's. Wit hovers round the borders of the light and trifling, whether in matters of pleasure or pain; for, as soon as it describes the serious seriously, it ceases to be wit, and passes into a different form. Wit is, in fact, the eloquence of indifference, or an ingenious and striking exposition of those evanescent and glancing impressions of objects which affect us more from surprise or contrast to the train of our ordinary and literal preconceptions, than from anything in the objects themselves exciting our necessary sympathy or lasting hatred. The favorite employment of wit is to add littleness to littleness, and heap contempt on insignificance by all the arts of petty and incessant warfare; or, if it ever affects to aggrandize and use the language of hyperbole, it is only to betray into derision by a fatal comparison, as in the mock-heroic; or, if it treats of serious passion, it must do it so as to lower the tone of intense and high-wrought sentiment by the introduction of burlesque and familiar circumstances. To give an instance or two. Butler, in his *Hudibras*, compares the change of night into day, to the change of color in a boiled lobster:

> The sun had long since, in the lap
> Of Thetis, taken out his nap;
> And, like a lobster boiled, the morn
> From black to red, began to turn:
> When Hudibras, whom thoughts and aching
> 'Twixt sleeping kept all night, and waking,
> Began to rub his drowsy eyes,
> And from his couch prepared to rise,
> Resolving to dispatch the deed
> He vowed to do with trusty speed.[10]

[9] Spence, *Anecdotes* (1820), p. 378.
[10] *Hudibras*, II, ii, 29-38.

Compare this with the following stanzas in Spenser, treating of the same subject:

> By this the Northern waggoner had set
> His seven-fold team behind the stedfast star,
> That was in ocean waves yet never wet,
> But firm is fixed and sendeth light from far
> To all that in the wide deep wand'ring are:
> And cheerful Chanticleer with his note shrill,
> Had warned once that Phoebus' fiery car
> In haste was climbing up the eastern hill,
> Full envious that night so long his room did fill.[11]

. . . I need not multiply examples of this sort. Wit or ludicrous invention produces its effect oftenest by comparison, but not always. It frequently effects its purposes by unexpected and subtle distinctions. For instance, in the first kind, Mr. Sheridan's description of Mr. Addington's administration as the fag end of Mr. Pitt's, who had remained so long on the treasury bench that, like Nicias in the fable, "he left the sitting part of the man behind him,"[12] is as fine an example of metaphorical wit as any on record. The same idea seems, however, to have been included in the old well-known nickname of the *Rump* Parliament. Almost as happy an instance of the other kind of wit, which consists in sudden retorts, in turns upon an idea, and diverting the train of your adversary's argument abruptly and adroitly into another channel, may be seen in the sarcastic reply of Porson, who, hearing someone observe that "certain modern poets would be read and admired when Homer and Vergil were forgotten," made answer—"And not till then!" Sir Robert Walpole's definition of the gratitude of place-expectants, "that it is a lively sense of *future* favors," is no doubt wit, but it does not consist in the finding out any coincidence or likeness, but in suddenly transposing the order of time in the common account of this feeling, so as to make the professions of those who pretend to it correspond more with their practice. It is filling up a blank in the human heart with a word that explains its hollowness at once. Voltaire's saying, in answer to a stranger who was observing how tall his trees grew, "that they had nothing else to do," was a quaint mixture of wit and humor, making it out as if they really led a lazy, laborious life; but there was

[11] *The Faerie Queene*, I, ii, 1.
[12] Speech on the Definitive Treaty of Peace (May 14, 1794).

here neither allusion or metaphor. Again, that master stroke in *Hudibras* is sterling wit and profound satire, where speaking of certain religious hypocrites he says, that they

> Compound for sins they are inclined to,
> By damning those they have no mind to; [13]

but the wit consists in the truth of the character, and in the happy exposure of the ludicrous contradiction between the pretext and the practice; between their lenity towards their own vices, and their severity to those of others. The same principle of nice distinction must be allowed to prevail in those lines of the same author, where he is professing to expound the dreams of judicial astrology.

> There's but the twinkling of a star
> Betwixt a man of peace and war;
> A thief and justice, fool and knave,
> A huffing officer and a slave;
> A crafty lawyer and pickpocket,
> A great philosopher and a blockhead;
> A formal preacher and a player,
> A learned physician and manslayer. [14]

The finest piece of wit I know of, is in the lines of Pope on the Lord Mayor's show—

> Now night descending, the proud scene is o'er,
> But lives in Settle's numbers one day more. [15]

This is certainly as mortifying an inversion of the idea of poetical immortality as could be thought of; it fixes the *maximum* of littleness and insignificance: but it is not by likeness to anything else that it does this, but by literally taking the lowest possible duration of ephemeral reputation, marking it (as with a slider) on the scale of endless renown, and giving a rival credit for it as his loftiest praise. In a word, the shrewd separation or disentangling of ideas that seem the same, or where the secret contradiction is not sufficiently suspected and is of a ludicrous and whimsical nature, is wit just as much as the bringing together those that appear at first sight totally different. There is then no sufficient ground for admitting Mr. Locke's celebrated definition of wit, which he makes to consist in the finding out striking and unexpected resemblances in things so as to make

pleasant pictures in the fancy, while judgment and reason, according to him, lie the clean contrary way, in separating and nicely distinguishing those wherein the smallest difference is to be found.

On this definition Harris, the author of *Hermes*, [16] has very well observed that the demonstrating the equality of the three angles of a right-angled triangle to two right ones, would, upon the principle here stated, be a piece of wit instead of an act of the judgment or understanding, and Euclid's *Elements* a collection of epigrams. On the contrary it has appeared that the detection and exposure of difference, particularly where this implies nice and subtle observation, as in discriminating between pretense and practice, between appearance and reality, is common to wit and satire with judgment and reasoning, and certainly the comparing and connecting our ideas together is an essential part of reason and judgment, as well as of wit and fancy. Mere wit, as opposed to reason or argument, consists in striking out some casual and partial coincidence which has nothing to do, or at least implies no necessary connection with the nature of the things, which are forced into a seeming analogy by a play upon words, or some irrelevant conceit, as in puns, riddles, alliteration, etc. The jest, in all such cases, lies in the sort of mock-identity, or nominal resemblance, established by the intervention of the same words expressing different ideas, and countenancing as it were, by a fatality of language, the mischievous insinuation which the person who has the wit to take advantage of it wishes to convey. So when the disaffected French wits applied to the new order of the *Fleur du lys* the *double entendre* of *Compagnons d'Ulysse*, or companions of Ulysses, meaning the animal into which the fellow travelers of the hero of the *Odyssey* were transformed, this was a shrewd and biting intimation of a galling truth (if truth it were) by a fortuitous concourse of letters of the alphabet, jumping in "a foregone conclusion," but there was no proof of the thing, unless it was self-evident. And, indeed, this may be considered as the best defense of the contested maxim—That *ridicule is the test of truth*; viz., that it does not contain or attempt a formal

---

[13] *Hudibras*, I, i, 215-16.
[14] *Ibid.*, II, iii, 957-64.
[15] *Dunciad*, I, 89-90.

[16] James Harris, *Hermes, or a Philosophical Inquiry concerning Universal Grammar* (1751).

proof of it, but owes its power of conviction to the bare suggestion of it, so that if the thing when once hinted is not clear in itself, the satire fails of its effect and falls to the ground. The sarcasm here glanced at the character of the new or old French noblesse may not be well founded; but it is so like truth, and "comes in such a questionable shape," backed with the appearance of an identical proposition, that it would require a long train of facts and labored arguments to do away the impression, even if we were sure of the honesty and wisdom of the person who undertook to refute it. A flippant jest is as good a test of truth as a solid bribe . . . Ridicule is necessarily built on certain supposed facts, whether true or false, and on their inconsistency with certain acknowledged maxims, whether right or wrong. It is, therefore, a fair test, if not of philosophical or abstract truth, at least of what is truth according to public opinion and common sense; for it can only expose to instantaneous contempt that which is condemned by public opinion, and is hostile to the common sense of mankind. Or to put it differently, it is the test of the quantity of truth that there is in our favorite prejudices. To show how nearly allied wit is thought to be to truth, it is not unusual to say of any person—"Such a one is a man of sense, for though he said nothing, he laughed in the right place." Alliteration comes in here under the head of a certain sort of verbal wit; or, by pointing the expression, sometimes points the sense. Mr. Grattan's wit or eloquence (I don't know by what name to call it) would be nothing without this accompaniment. Speaking of some ministers whom he did not like, he said, "Their only means of government are the guinea and the gallows." There can scarcely, it must be confessed, be a more effectual mode of political conversion than one of these applied to a man's friends, and the other to himself. The fine sarcasm of Junius on the effect of the supposed ingratitude of the Duke of Grafton at court—"The instance might be painful, but the principle would please" [17]—notwithstanding the profound insight into human nature it implies, would hardly pass for wit without the alliteration, as some poetry would hardly be acknowledged as such without the rhyme to

[17] Junius, Letter 49.

clench it. A quotation or a hackneyed phrase dextrously turned or wrested to another purpose has often the effect of the liveliest wit. An idle fellow who had only fourpence left in the world, which had been put by to pay for the baking some meat for his dinner, went and laid it out to buy a new string for a guitar. An old acquaintance, on hearing this story, repeated those lines out of the "Allegro"—

> And ever against *eating* cares
> Lap me in soft Lydian airs.

The reply of the author of the periodical paper called the *World* to a lady at church, who, seeing him look thoughtful, asked what he was thinking of—"The next World"—is a perversion of an established formula of language, something of the same kind. Rhymes are sometimes a species of wit, where there is an alternate combination and resolution or decomposition of the elements of sound, contrary to our usual division and classification of them in ordinary speech, not unlike the sudden separation and reunion of the component parts of the machinery in a pantomime. The author who excels infinitely the most in this way is the writer of *Hudibras*. He also excels in the invention of single words and names which have the effect of wit by sounding big, and meaning nothing:—"full of sound and fury, signifying nothing." But of the artifices of this author's burlesque style I shall have occasion to speak hereafter. It is not always easy to distinguish between the wit of words and that of things; "For thin partitions do their bounds divide." Some of the late Mr. Curran's bons mots or *jeux d'esprit* might be said to owe their birth to this sort of equivocal generation, or were a happy mixture of verbal wit and a lively and picturesque fancy of legal acuteness in detecting the variable applications of words, and of a mind apt at perceiving the ludicrous in external objects. "Do you see anything ridiculous in this wig?" said one of his brother judges to him. "Nothing but the head" was the answer. Now here instantaneous advantage was taken of the slight technical ambiguity in the construction of language, and the matter-of-fact is flung into the scale as a thumping makeweight. After all, verbal and accidental strokes of wit, though the most surprising and laughable, are not the best and most lasting. That wit is the most refined and effectual which is founded on the detection of unexpected likeness or distinction in things, rather than in words. It is more severe and galling—that is, it is more unpardonable though less surprising, in proportion as the thought suggested is more complete and satisfactory from its being inherent in the nature of the things themselves. *Haeret lateri lethalis arundo.*[18] Truth makes the greatest libel; and it is that which bars the darts of wit. The Duke of Buckingham's saying, "Laws are not, like women, the worse for being old,"[19] is an instance of a harmless truism and the utmost malice of wit united. This is, perhaps, what has been meant by the distinction between true and false wit. Mr. Addison, indeed, goes so far as to make it the exclusive test of true wit that it will bear translation into another language[20]—that is to say, that it does not depend at all on the form of expression. But this is by no means the case. Swift would hardly have allowed of such a straitlaced theory to make havoc with his darling conundrums, though there is no one whose serious wit is more that of things, as opposed to a mere play either of words or fancy. I ought, I believe, to have noticed before, in speaking of the difference between wit and humor, that wit is often pretended absurdity, where the person overacts or exaggerates a certain part with a conscious design to expose it as if it were another person, as when Mandrake in the *Twin Rivals* says, "This glass is too big, carry it away, I'll drink out of the bottle."[21] On the contrary, when Sir Hugh Evans says, very innocently, " 'Od's plessed will, I will not be absence at the grace,"[22] though there is here a great deal of humor, there is no wit. This kind of wit of the humorist, where the person makes a butt of himself and exhibits his own absurdities or foibles purposely in the most pointed and glaring lights, runs through the whole of the character of Falstaff and is, in truth, the principle on which it is founded. It is an irony directed against one's self. Wit is, in fact, a voluntary act of the mind or exercise of the invention, showing the absurd and ludicrous con-

sciously, whether in ourselves or another. Cross-readings, where the blunders are designed, are wit; but, if anyone were to light upon them through ignorance or accident, they would be merely ludicrous.

It might be made an argument of the intrinsic superiority of poetry or imagination to wit, that the former does not admit of mere verbal combinations. Whenever they do occur, they are uniformly blemishes. It requires something more solid and substantial to raise admiration or passion. The general forms and aggregate masses of our ideas must be brought more into play to give weight and magnitude. Imagination may be said to be the finding out something similar in things generally alike, or with like feelings attached to them; while wit principally aims at finding out something that seems the same, or amounts to a momentary deception where you least expected it, namely, in things totally opposite. The reason why more slight and partial, or merely accidental and nominal resemblances serve the purposes of wit, and indeed characterize its essence as a distinct operation and faculty of the mind, is that the object of ludicrous poetry is naturally to let down and lessen; and it is easier to let down than to raise up; to weaken than to strengthen; to disconnect our sympathy from passion and power than to attach and rivet it to any object of grandeur or interest; to startle and shock our preconceptions by incongruous and equivocal combinations than to confirm, enforce, and expand them by powerful and lasting associations of ideas, or striking and true analogies. A slight cause is sufficient to produce a slight effect. To be indifferent or skeptical requires no effort; to be enthusiastic and in earnest requires a strong impulse and collective power. Wit and humor (comparatively speaking, or taking the extremes to judge of the gradations by) appeal to our indolence, our vanity, our weakness, and insensibility; serious and impassioned poetry appeals to our strength, our magnanimity, our virtue, and humanity. . . .

Lear and the Fool are the sublimest instance I know of passion and wit united, or of imagination unfolding the most tremendous sufferings, and of burlesque on passion playing with it, aiding and relieving its intensity by the most pointed, but familiar and indifferent illustrations of the same thing in different objects, and on a

[18] *Aeneid, IV*, 73: "Fast in her side clings the deadly reed."

[19] Speech on the Dissolution of Parliament (1676).

[20] *Spectator*, no. 61.

[21] Farquhar, *Twin Rivals*, II, ii.

[22] *Merry Wives of Windsor*, I, i, 276.

meaner scale. The Fool's reproaching Lear with "making his daughters his mothers," his snatches of proverbs and old ballads, "The hedge sparrow fed the cuckoo so long that it had its head bit off by its young," and "Whoop jug, I know when the horse follows the cart," are a running commentary of trite truisms, pointing out the extreme folly of the infatuated old monarch and in a manner reconciling us to its inevitable consequences.

Lastly, there is a wit of sense and observation, which consists in the acute illustration of good sense and practical wisdom, by means of some far-fetched conceit or quaint imagery. The matter is sense, but the form is wit. Thus the lines in Pope—

> 'Tis with our judgments as our watches, none
> Go just alike; yet each believes his own— [23]

are witty, rather than poetical; because the truth they convey is a mere dry observation on human life, without elevation or enthusiasm, and the illustration of it is of that quaint and familiar kind that is merely curious and fanciful. Cowley is an instance of the same kind in almost all his writings. Many of the jests and witticisms in the best comedies are moral aphorisms and rules for the conduct of life, sparkling with wit and fancy in the mode of expression. The ancient philosophers also abounded in the same kind of wit, in telling home truths in the most unexpected manner. In this sense Aesop was the greatest wit and moralist that ever lived. Ape and slave, he looked askance at human nature, and beheld its weaknesses and errors transferred to another species. Vice and virtue were to him as plain as any objects of sense. He saw in man a talking, absurd, obstinate, proud, angry animal; and clothed these abstractions with wings, or a beak, or tail, or claws, or long ears, as they appeared embodied in these hieroglyphics in the brute creation. . . .

I shall conclude this imperfect and desultory sketch of wit and humor with Barrow's celebrated description of the same subject. He says:

But first it may be demanded, what the thing we speak of is, or what this facetiousness doth import; to which question I might reply, as Democritus did to him that asked the definition of a man—'tis that which we all see and know; and one better apprehends what it is by acquaintance than I can inform him by description. It is, indeed, a thing so versatile and multiform, appearing in so many shapes, so many postures, so many garbs, so variously apprehended by several eyes and judgments, that it seemeth no less hard to settle a clear and certain notice thereof than to make a portrait of Proteus or to define the figure of fleeting air. Sometimes it lieth in pat allusion to a known story, or in seasonable application of a trivial saying, or in forging an apposite tale; sometimes it playeth in words and phrases, taking advantage from the ambiguity of their sense, or the affinity of their sound; sometimes it is wrapped in a dress of luminous expression; sometimes it lurketh under an odd similitude. Sometimes it is lodged in a sly question, in a smart answer, in a quirkish reason, in a shrewd intimation, in cunningly diverting or cleverly restoring an objection; sometimes it is couched in a bold scheme of speech, in a tart irony, in a lusty hyperbole, in a startling metaphor, in a plausible reconciling of contradictions, or in acute nonsense; sometimes a scenical representation of persons or things, a counterfeit speech, a mimical look or gesture passeth for it; sometimes an affected simplicity, sometimes a presumptuous bluntness giveth it being; sometimes it riseth only from a lucky hitting upon what is strange, sometimes from a crafty wresting obvious matter to the purpose; often it consisteth in one knows not what and springeth up one can hardly tell how. Its ways are unaccountable and inexplicable, being answerable to the numberless rovings of fancy and windings of language. It is, in short, a manner of speaking out of the simple and plain way (such as reason teacheth and knoweth things by), which by a pretty surprising uncouthness in conceit or expression doth affect and amuse the fancy, showing in it some wonder and breathing some delight thereto. It raiseth admiration, as signifying a nimble sagacity of apprehension, a special felicity of invention, a vivacity of spirit, and reach of wit more than vulgar: it seeming to argue a rare quickness of parts that one can fetch in remote conceits applicable; a notable skill that he can dextrously accommodate them to a purpose before him, together with a lively briskness of humor, not apt to damp those sportful flashes of imagination. (Whence in Aristotle such persons are termed ἐπιδέξιοι, dextrous men and εὔτροποι, men of facile or versatile manners, who can easily turn themselves to all things, or turn all things to themselves.) It also procureth delight by gratifying curiosity with its rareness or semblance of difficulty (as monsters, not

[23] *Essay on Criticism*, ll. 9-10.

for their beauty but their rarity; as juggling tricks, not for their use but their abstruseness, are beheld with pleasure); by diverting the mind from its road of serious thoughts; by instilling gaiety and airiness of spirit; by provoking to such dispositions of spirit, in way of emulation or complaisance, and by seasoning matter, otherwise distasteful or insipid, with an unusual and thence grateful tang.[24]

[24] Isaac Barrow, Sermon 14.

On Genius and Common Sense

WE HEAR it maintained by people of more gravity than understanding, that genius and taste are strictly reducible to rules, and that there is a rule for every thing. So far is it from being true that the finest breath of fancy is a definable thing, that the plainest common sense is only what Mr. Locke would have called a *mixed mode,* subject to a particular sort of acquired and undefinable tact. It is asked, "If you do not know the rule by which a thing is done, how can you be sure of doing it a second time?" And the answer is, "If you do not know the muscles by the help of which you walk, how is it you do not fall down at every step you take?" In art, in taste, in life, in speech, you decide from feeling, and not from reason; that is, from the impression of a number of things on the mind, which impression is true and well-founded, though you may not be able to analyse or account for it in the several particulars. In a gesture you use, in a look you see, in a tone you hear, you judge of the expression, propriety, and meaning from habit, not from reason or rules; that is to say, from innumerable instances of like gestures, looks, and tones, in innumerable other circumstances, variously modified, which are too many and too refined to be all distinctly recollected, but which do not therefore operate the less powerfully upon the mind and eye of taste. Shall we say that these impressions

On Genius and Common Sense. From *Table Talk, or Original Essays on Men and Manners* (1821-22). Of all Hazlitt's more popular essays, this and the following essay are the best brief statement of his conception of the process of mind which underlies most nonabstract thinking, and on which the imagination builds. He is discussing the ability to absorb experience and knowledge into a formative reaction—into a schooled, enlarged and matured *feeling* which is capable of responding immediately (and, to that extent might be called "intuitive"), and which—because it draws upon so many scattered experiences and acts so rapidly—is not susceptible of abstract "rules" and methodizing.

(the immediate stamp of nature) do not operate in a given manner till they are classified and reduced to rules, or is not the rule itself grounded upon the truth and certainty of that natural operation? How then can the distinction of the understanding as to the manner in which they operate be necessary to their producing their due and uniform effect upon the mind? If certain effects did not regularly arise out of certain causes in mind as well as matter, there could be no rule given for them: nature does not follow the rule, but suggests it. Reason is the interpreter and critic of nature and genius, not their lawgiver and judge. He must be a poor creature indeed whose practical convictions do not in almost all cases outrun his deliberate understanding, or who does not feel and know much more than he can give a reason for.—Hence the distinction between eloquence and wisdom, between ingenuity and common sense. A man may be dextrous and able in explaining the grounds of his opinions, and yet may be a mere sophist, because he only sees one half of a subject. Another may feel the whole weight of a question, nothing relating to it may be lost upon him, and yet he may be able to give no account of the manner in which it affects him, or to drag his reasons from their silent lurking-places. This last will be a wise man, though neither a logician nor rhetorician. Goldsmith was a fool to Dr. Johnson in argument; that is, in assigning the specific grounds of his opinions: Dr. Johnson was a fool to Goldsmith in the fine tact, the airy, intuitive faculty with which he skimmed the surfaces of things, and unconsciously formed his opinions. Common sense is the just result of the sum-total of such unconscious impressions in the ordinary occurrences of life, as they are treasured up in the memory, and called out by the occasion. Genius and taste depend much upon the same principle exercised on loftier ground and in more unusual combinations.

I am glad to shelter myself from the charge of affection or singularity in this view of an often debated but ill-understood point, by quoting a passage from Sir Joshua Reynolds's Discourses, which is full, and, I think, conclusive to the purpose. He says:

I observe, as a fundamental ground common to all the Arts with which we have any concern in this Discourse, that they address themselves only to two faculties of the mind, its imagination and its sensibility.

All theories which attempt to direct or to control the Art, upon any principles falsely called rational, which we form to ourselves upon a supposition of what ought in reason to be the end or means of Art, independent of the known first effect produced by objects on the imagination, must be false and delusive. For though it may appear bold to say it, the imagination is here the residence of truth. If the imagination be affected, the conclusion is fairly drawn; if it be not affected, the reasoning is erroneous, because the end is not obtained; the effect itself being the test, and the only test, of the truth and efficacy of the means.

There is in the commerce of life, as in Art, a sagacity which is far from being contradictory to right reason, and is superior to any occasional exercise of that faculty; which supersedes it; and does not wait for the slow progress of deduction, but goes at once, by what appears a kind of intuition, to the conclusion. A man endowed with this faculty feels and acknowledges the truth, though it is not always in his power, perhaps, to give a reason for it; because he cannot recollect and bring before him all the materials that gave birth to his opinion; for very many and very intricate considerations may unite to form the principle, even of small and minute parts, involved in, or dependent on, a great system of things:—though these in process of time are forgotten, the right impression still remains fixed in his mind.

This impression is the result of the accumulated experience of our whole life, and has been collected, we do not always know how, or when. But this mass of collective observation, however acquired, ought to prevail over that reason, which, however powerfully exerted on any particular occasion, will probably comprehend but a partial view of the subject; and our conduct in life, as well as in the arts, is or ought to be generally governed by this habitual reason: it is our happiness that we are enabled to draw on such funds. If we were obliged to enter into a theoretical deliberation on every occasion before we act, life would be at a stand, and Art would be impracticable.

It appears to me therefore [continues Sir Joshua] that our first thoughts, that is, the effect which any thing produces on our minds, on its first appearance, is never to be forgotten; and it demands for that reason, because it is the first, to be laid up with care. If this be not done, the artist may happen to impose on himself by partial reasoning; by a cold consideration of those animated thoughts which proceed, not perhaps from caprice or rashness (as he may afterwards conceit), but from the fulness of his mind, enriched with the copious stores of all the various inventions which he had ever seen, or had ever passed in his mind. These ideas are infused into his design, without any conscious effort; but if he be not on his guard, he may reconsider and correct them, till the whole matter is reduced to a common-place invention.

This is sometimes the effect of what I mean to caution you against; that is to say, an unfounded distrust of the imagination and feeling, in favour of narrow, partial, confined, argumentative theories, and of principles that seem to apply to the design in hand; without considering those general impressions on the fancy in which real principles of *sound reason*, and of much more weight and importance, are involved, and, as it were, lie hid under the appearance of a sort of vulgar sentiment. Reason, without doubt, must ultimately determine every thing; at this minute it is required to inform us when that very reason is to give way to feeling.[1]

Mr. Burke, by whom the foregoing train of thinking was probably suggested, has insisted on the same thing, and made rather a perverse use of it in several parts of his Reflections on the French Revolution; and Windham in one of his Speeches has clenched it into an aphorism— "There is nothing so true as habit." Once more I would say, common sense is tacit reason. Conscience is the same tacit sense of right and wrong, or the impression of our moral experience and moral apprehensions on the mind, which, because it works unseen, yet certainly, we suppose to be an instinct, implanted in the mind; as we sometimes attribute the violent operations of our passions, of which we can neither trace the source nor assign the reason, to the instigation of the Devil!

I shall here try to go more at large into this

[1] *Discourse* XIII, vol. ii, pp. 113-17. [Hazlitt.] See above, pp. 258-59.

subject, and to give such instances and illustrations of it as occur to me.

One of the persons who had rendered themselves obnoxious to Government, and been included in a charge for high treason in the year 1794, had retired soon after into Wales to write an epic poem and enjoy the luxuries of a rural life. In his peregrinations through that beautiful scenery, he had arrived one fine morning at the inn at Llangollen, in the romantic valley of that name. He had ordered his breakfast, and was sitting at the window in all the dalliance of expectation, when a face passed of which he took no notice at the instant—but when his breakfast was brought in presently after, he found his appetite for it gone, the day had lost its freshness in his eye, he was uneasy and spiritless; and without any cause that he could discover, a total change had taken place in his feelings. While he was trying to account for this odd circumstance, the same face passed again—it was the face of Taylor the spy; and he was no longer at a loss to explain the difficulty. He had before caught only a transient glimpse, a passing side-view of the face; but though this was not sufficient to awaken a distinct idea in his memory, his feelings, quicker and surer, had taken the alarm; a string had been touched that gave a jar to his whole frame, and would not let him rest, though he could not at all tell what was the matter with him. To the flitting, shadowy, half-distinguished profile that had glided by his window was linked unconsciously and mysteriously, but inseparably, the impression of the trains that had been laid for him by this person;—in this brief moment, in this dim, illegible shorthand of the mind he had just escaped the speeches of the Attorney and Solicitor-General over again; the gaunt figure of Mr. Pitt glared by him; the walls of a prison enclosed him; and he felt the hands of the executioner near him, without knowing it till the tremor and disorder of his nerves gave information to his reasoning faculties that all was not well within. That is, the same state of mind was recalled by one circumstance in the series of association that had been produced by the whole set of circumstances at the time, though the manner in which this was done was not immediately perceptible. In other words, the feeling of pleasure or pain, of good or evil, is revived, and acts instantaneously upon the mind, before

we have time to recollect the precise objects which have originally given birth to it. The incident here mentioned was merely, then, one case of what the learned understand by the *association of ideas:* but all that is meant by feeling or common sense is nothing but the different cases of the association of ideas, more or less true to the impression of the original circumstances, as reason begins with the more formal developement of those circumstances, or pretends to account for the different cases of the association of ideas. But it does not follow that the dumb and silent pleading of the former (though sometimes, nay often mistaken) is less true than that of its babbling interpreter, or that we are never to trust its dictates without consulting the express authority of reason. Both are imperfect, both are useful in their way, and therefore both are best together, to correct or to confirm one another. It does not appear that in the singular instance above mentioned, the sudden impression on the mind was superstition or fancy, though it might have been thought so, had it not been proved by the event to have a real physical and moral cause. Had not the same face returned again, the doubt would never have been properly cleared up, but would have remained a puzzle ever after, or perhaps have been soon forgot.—By the law of association, as laid down by physiologists, any impression in a series can recal any other impression in that series without going through the whole in order: so that the mind drops the intermediate links, and passes on rapidly and by stealth to the more striking effects of pleasure or pain which have naturally taken the strongest hold of it.[2] By doing this habitually and skilfully with respect to the various impressions and circumstances with which our experience makes us acquainted, it forms a series of unpremeditated conclusions on almost all subjects that can be brought before it, as just as they are of ready

[2] Thus if a given series of steps (A, B, C, and D) produces a certain conclusion (E), the intervening steps may "lapse," and the mere sight or thought of the first (A) will bring us at once to the conclusion (E), as if with a sudden intuition. It is this ability that allows us to resolve our various isolated experiences into a single, total apprehension of a thing. Hazlitt, here, is particularly indebted to the eighteenth-century associationist, Abraham Tucker, whose *Light of Nature Pursued* (1768-78) he abridged and edited (1807) as a young man.

application to human life; and common sense is the name of this body of unassuming but practical wisdom. Common sense, however, is an impartial, instinctive result of truth and nature, and will therefore bear the test and abide the scrutiny of the most severe and patient reasoning. It is indeed incomplete without it. By ingrafting reason on feeling, we "make assurance double sure."

'Tis the last key-stone that makes up the arch—
Then stands it a triumphal mark! Then men
Observe the strength, the height, the why and when
It was erected: and still walking under,
Meet some new matter to look up, and wonder.

But reason, not employed to interpret nature, and to improve and perfect common sense and experience, is, for the most part, a building without a foundation.—The criticism exercised by reason then on common sense may be as severe as it pleases, but it must be as patient as it is severe. Hasty, dogmatical, self-satisfied reason is worse than idle fancy, or bigotted prejudice. It is systematic, ostentatious in error, closes up the avenues of knowledge, and "shuts the gates of wisdom on mankind." It is not enough to shew that there is no reason for a thing, that we do not see the reason of it: if the common feeling, if the involuntary prejudice sets in strong in favour of it, if, in spite of all we can do, there is a lurking suspicion on the side of our first impressions, we must try again, and believe that truth is mightier than we. So, in offering a definition of any subject, if we feel a misgiving that there is any fact or circumstance omitted, but of which we have only a vague apprehension, like a name we cannot recollect, we must ask for more time, and not cut the matter short by an arrogant assumption of the point in dispute. Common sense thus acts as a check-weight on sophistry, and suspends our rash and superficial judgments. On the other hand, if not only no reason can be given for a thing, but every reason is clear against it, and we can account from ignorance, from authority, from interest, from different causes, for the prevalence of an opinion or sentiment, then we have a right to conclude that we have mistaken a prejudice for an instinct, or have confounded a false and partial impression with the fair and unavoidable inference from general observation. Mr. Burke said that we

ought not to reject every prejudice, but should separate the husk of prejudice from the truth it encloses, and so try to get at the kernel within; and thus far he was right.[3] But he was wrong in insisting that we are to cherish our prejudices, "because they are prejudices:" for if they are all well-founded, there is no occasion to inquire into their origin or use; and he who sets out to philosophise upon them, or make the separation Mr. Burke talks of in this spirit and with this previous determination, will be very likely to mistake a maggot or a rotten canker for the precious kernel of truth, as was indeed the case with our political sophist.

There is nothing more distinct than common sense and vulgar opinion. Common sense is only a judge of things that fall under common observation, or immediately come home to the business and bosoms of men. This is of the very essence of its principle, the basis of its pretensions. It rests upon the simple process of feeling, it anchors in experience. It is not, nor it cannot be, the test of abstract, speculative opinions. But half the opinions and prejudices of mankind, those which they hold in the most unqualified approbation and which have been instilled into them under the strongest sanctions, are of this latter kind, that is, opinions, not which they have ever thought, known, or felt one tittle about, but which they have taken up on trust from others, which have been palmed on their understandings by fraud or force, and which they continue to hold at the peril of life, limb, property, and character, with as little warrant from common sense in the first instance as appeal to reason in the last. The *ultima ratio regum* proceeds upon a very different plea. Common sense is neither priestcraft nor state-policy. Yet "there's the rub that makes absurdity of so long life;" and, at the same time, gives the sceptical philosophers the advantage over us. Till nature has fair play allowed it, and is not adulterated by political and polemical quacks (as it so often has been), it is impossible to appeal to it as a defence against the errors and extravagances of mere reason. If we talk of common sense, we are twitted with vulgar prejudice, and asked how we distinguish the one from the other: but common

3 *Reflections on the Revolution in France*, in *Select Works* (ed. E. J. Payne, 1842), II, 102.

and received opinion is indeed "a compost heap" of crude notions, got together by the pride and passions of individuals, and reason is itself the thrall or manumitted slave of the same lordly and besotted masters, dragging its servile chain, or committing all sorts of Saturnalian licences, the moment it feels itself freed from it.—If ten millions of Englishmen are furious in thinking themselves right in making war upon thirty millions of Frenchmen, and if the last are equally bent upon thinking the others always in the wrong, though it is a common and national prejudice, both opinions cannot be the dictate of good sense: but it may be the infatuated policy of one or both governments to keep their subjects always at variance. If a few centuries ago all Europe believed in the infallibility of the Pope, this was not an opinion derived from the proper exercise or erroneous direction of the common sense of the people: common sense had nothing to do with it—they believed whatever their priests told them. England at present is divided into Whigs and Tories, Churchmen and Dissenters: both parties have numbers on their side; but common sense and party-spirit are two different things. Sects and heresies are upheld partly by sympathy, and partly by the love of contradiction: if there was nobody of a different way of thinking, they would fall to pieces of themselves. If a whole court say the same thing, this is no proof that they think it, but that the individual at the head of the court has said it: if a mob agree for a while in shouting the same watch-word, this is not to me an example of the *sensus communis;* they only repeat what they have heard repeated by others. If indeed a large proportion of the people are in want of food, of clothing, of shelter, if they are sick, miserable, scorned, oppressed, and if each feeling it in himself, they all say so with one voice and one heart, and lift up their hands to second their appeal, this I should say was but the dictate of common sense, the cry of nature. But to waive this part of the argument, which it is needless to push farther, I believe that the best way to instruct mankind is not by pointing out to them their mutual errors, but by teaching them to think rightly on indifferent matters, where they will listen with patience in order to be amused, and where they do not consider a definition or a syllogism as the greatest injury you can offer them.

There is no rule for expression. It is got at solely by *feeling*, that is, on the principle of the association of ideas, and by transferring what has been found to hold good in one case (with the necessary modifications) to others. A certain look has been remarked strongly indicative of a certain passion or trait of character, and we attach the same meaning to it or are affected in the same pleasurable or painful manner by it, where it exists in a less degree, though we can define neither the look itself nor the modification of it. Having got the general clue, the exact result may be left to the imagination to vary, to extenuate or aggravate it according to circumstances. In the admirable profile of Oliver Cromwell after ——, the drooping eye-lids, as if drawing a veil over the fixed, penetrating glance, the nostrils somewhat distended, and lips compressed so as hardly to let the breath escape him, denote the character of the man for high-reaching policy and deep designs as plainly as they can be written. How is it that we decipher this expression in the face? First, by feeling it: and how is it that we feel it? Not by pre-established rules, but by the instinct of analogy, by the principle of association, which is subtle and sure in proportion as it is variable and indefinite. A circumstance, apparently of no value, shall alter the whole interpretation to be put upon an expression or action; and it shall alter it thus powerfully because in proportion to its very insignificance it shews a strong general principle at work that extends in its ramifications to the smallest things. This in fact will make all the difference between minuteness and subtlety or refinement; for a small or trivial effect may in given circumstances imply the operation of a great power. Stillness may be the result of a blow too powerful to be resisted; silence may be imposed by feelings too agonising for utterance. The minute, the trifling and insipid, is that which is little in itself, in its causes and its consequences: the subtle and refined is that which is slight and evanescent at first sight, but which mounts up to a mighty sum in the end, which is an essential part of an important whole, which has consequences greater than itself, and where more is meant than meets the eye or ear. We complain sometimes of littleness in a Dutch picture, where there are a vast number of distinct parts and objects, each small in itself, and leading to nothing else. A sky of Claude's cannot fall under this censure, where one imperceptible gradation is as it were the scale to another, where the broad arch of heaven is piled up of endlessly intermediate gold and azure tints, and where an infinite number of minute, scarce noticed particulars blend and melt into universal harmony. The subtlety in Shakespear, of which there is an immense deal every where scattered up and down, is always the instrument of passion, the vehicle of character. The action of a man pulling his hat over his forehead is indifferent enough in itself, and, generally speaking, may mean any thing or nothing: but in the circumstances in which Macduff is placed, it is neither insignificant nor equivocal.

What! man, ne'er pull your hat upon your brows, &c.[4]

It admits but of one interpretation or inference, that which follows it:—

Give sorrow words: the grief that does not speak,
Whispers the o'er-fraught heart, and bids it break.

The passage in the same play, in which Duncan and his attendants are introduced commenting on the beauty and situation of Macbeth's castle, though familiar in itself, has been often praised for the striking contrast it presents to the scenes which follow.—The same look in different circumstances may convey a totally different expression. Thus the eye turned round to look at you without turning the head indicates generally slyness or suspicion: but if this is combined with large expanded eye-lids or fixed eye-brows, as we see it in Titian's pictures, it will denote calm contemplation or piercing sagacity, without any thing of meanness or fear of being observed. In other cases, it may imply merely indolent enticing voluptuousness, as in Lely's portraits of women. The languor and weakness of the eye-lids gives the amorous turn to the expression. How should there be a rule for all this beforehand, seeing it depends on circumstances ever varying, and scarce discernible but by their effect on the mind? Rules are applicable to abstractions, but expression is concrete and individual. We know the meaning of certain looks,

and we feel how they modify one another in conjunction. But we cannot have a separate rule to judge of all their combinations in different degrees and circumstances, without foreseeing all those combinations, which is impossible: or, if we did foresee them, we should only be where we are, that is, we could only make the rule as we now judge without it, from imagination and the feeling of the moment. The absurdity of reducing expression to a preconcerted system was perhaps never more evidently shewn than in a picture of the Judgment of Solomon by so great a man as N. Poussin, which I once heard admired for the skill and discrimination of the artist in making all the women, who are ranged on one side, in the greatest alarm at the sentence of the judge, while all the men on the opposite side see through the design of it. Nature does not go to work or cast things in a regular mould in this sort of way. I once heard a person remark of another—"He has an eye like a vicious horse." This was a fair analogy. We all, I believe, have noticed the look of an horse's eye, just before he is going to bite or kick. But will any one, therefore, describe to me exactly what that look is? It was the same acute observer that said of a self-sufficient prating music-master—"He talks on all subjects *at sight*"—which expressed the man at once by an allusion to his profession. The coincidence was indeed perfect. Nothing else could compare to the easy assurance with which this gentleman would volunteer an explanation of things of which he was most ignorant; but the *nonchalance* with which a musician sits down to a harpsichord to play a piece he has never seen before. My physiognomical friend would not have hit on this mode of illustration without knowing the profession of the subject of his criticism; but having this hint given him, it instantly suggested itself to his "sure trailing." The manner of the speaker was evident; and the association of the music-master sitting down to play at sight, lurking in his mind, was immediately called out by the strength of his impression of the character. The feeling of character, and the felicity of invention in explaining it, were nearly allied to each other. The first was so wrought up and running over, that the transition to the last was easy and unavoidable. When Mr. Kean was so much praised for the action of Richard in his last struggle with his triumphant antagonist, where he stands, after his sword is wrested from him, with his hands stretched out, "as if his will could not be disarmed, and the very phantoms of his despair had a withering power," he said that he borrowed it from seeing the last efforts of Painter in his fight with Oliver. This assuredly did not lessen the merit of it. Thus it ever is with the man of real genius. He has the feeling of truth already shrined in his own breast, and his eye is still bent on nature to see how she expresses herself. When we thoroughly understand the subject, it is easy to translate from one language into another. Raphael, in muffling up the figure of Elymas the Sorcerer in his garments, appears to have extended the idea of blindness even to his clothes. Was this design? Probably not; but merely the feeling of analogy thoughtlessly suggesting this device, which being so suggested was retained and carried on, because it flattered or fell in with the original feeling. The tide of passion, when strong, over-flows and gradually insinuates itself into all nooks and corners of the mind. Invention (of the best kind) I therefore do not think so distinct a thing from feeling, as some are apt to imagine. The springs of pure feeling will rise and fill the moulds of fancy that are fit to receive it. There are some striking coincidences of colour in well-composed pictures, as in a straggling weed in the foreground streaked with blue or red to answer to a blue or red drapery, to the tone of the flesh or an opening in the sky:—not that this was intended, or done by rule (for then it would presently become affected and ridiculous), but the eye being imbued with a certain colour, repeats and varies it from a natural sense of harmony, a secret craving and appetite for beauty, which in the same manner soothes and gratifies the eye of taste, though the cause is not understood. *Tact, finesse,* is nothing but the being completely aware of the feeling belonging to certain situations, passions, &c. and the being consequently sensible to their slightest indications or movements in others. One of the most remarkable instances of this sort of faculty is the following story, told of Lord Shaftesbury, the grandfather of the author of the Characteristics. He had been to dine with Lady Clarendon and her daughter, who was at that time privately married to the Duke of York (afterwards James II.) and as he returned home with another nobleman who had accompanied him, he suddenly turned to him, and said, "Depend upon it, the Duke has married Hyde's daughter." His companion could not comprehend what he meant; but on explaining himself, he said, "Her mother behaved to her with an attention and a marked respect that it is impossible to account for in any other way; and I am sure of it." His conjecture shortly afterwards proved to be the truth. This was carrying the prophetic spirit of common sense as far as it could go.—

The Same Subject Continued

GENIUS or originality is, for the most part, *some strong quality in the mind, answering to and bringing out some new and striking quality in nature.*

Imagination is, more properly, the power of carrying on a given feeling into other situations, which must be done best according to the hold which the feeling itself has taken of the mind.[1] In new and unknown combinations, the impression must act by sympathy, and not by rule; but there can be no sympathy, where there is no passion, no original interest. The personal interest may in some cases oppress and circumscribe the imaginative faculty, as in the instance of Rousseau: but in general the strength and consistency of the imagination will be in proportion to the strength and depth of feeling; and it is rarely that a man even of lofty genius will be able to do more than carry on his own feelings and character, or some prominent and ruling passion, into fictitious and uncommon situations. Milton has by allusion embodied a great part of his political and personal history in the chief characters and incidents of Paradise Lost. He has, no doubt, wonderfully adapted and heightened them, but the elements are the same; you trace

[1] I do not here speak of the figurative or fanciful exercise of the imagination, which consists in finding out some striking object or image to illustrate another. [Hazlitt.]

the bias and opinions of the man in the creations of the poet. Shakespear (almost alone) seems to have been a man of genius, raised above the definition of genius. "Born universal heir to all humanity," he was "as one, in suffering all who suffered nothing;" with a perfect sympathy with all things, yet alike indifferent to all: who did not tamper with nature or warp her to his own purposes; who "knew all qualities with a learned spirit," instead of judging of them by his own predilections; and was rather "a pipe for the Muse's finger to play what stop she pleased," than anxious to set up any character or pretensions of his own. His genius consisted in the faculty of transforming himself at will into whatever he chose: his originality was the power of seeing every object from the exact point of view in which others would see it. He was the Proteus of human intellect. Genius in ordinary is a more obstinate and less versatile thing. It is sufficiently exclusive and self-willed, quaint and peculiar. It does some one thing by virtue of doing nothing else: it excels in some one pursuit by being blind to all excellence but its own. It is just the reverse of the cameleon; for it does not borrow, but lend its colour to all about it: or like the glow-worm, discloses a little circle of gorgeous light in the twilight of obscurity, in the night of intellect, that surrounds it. So did Rembrandt. If ever there was a man of genius, he was one, in the proper sense of the term. He lived in and revealed to others a world of his own, and might be said to have invented a new view of nature. He did not discover things *out of* nature, in fiction or fairy land, or make a voyage to the moon "to descry new lands, rivers, or mountains in her spotty globe," but saw things *in* nature that every one had missed before him, and gave others eyes to see them with. This is the test and triumph of originality, not to shew us what has never been, and what we may therefore very easily never have dreamt of, but to point out to us what is before our eyes and under our feet, though we have had no suspicion of its existence, for want of sufficient strength of intuition, of determined grasp of mind to seize and retain it. Rembrandt's conquests were not over the *ideal*, but the real. He did not contrive a new story or character, but we nearly owe to him a fifth part of painting, the knowledge of *chiaroscuro*—a distinct power

and element in art and nature. He had a steadiness, a firm keeping of mind and eye, that first stood the shock of "fierce extremes" in light and shade, or reconciled the greatest obscurity and the greatest brilliancy into perfect harmony; and he therefore was the first to hazard this appearance upon canvas, and give full effect to what he saw and delighted in. He was led to adopt this style of broad and startling contrast from its congeniality to his own feelings: his mind grappled with that which afforded the best exercise to its master-powers: he was bold in act, because he was urged on by a strong native impulse. Originality is then nothing but nature and feeling working in the mind. A man does not affect to be original: he is so, because he cannot help it, and often without knowing it. This extraordinary artist indeed might be said to have had a particular organ for colour. His eye seemed to come in contact with it as a feeling, to lay hold of it as a substance, rather than to contemplate it as a visual object. The texture of his landscapes is "of the earth, earthy"—his clouds are humid, heavy, slow; his shadows are "darkness that may be felt," a "palpable obscure;" his lights are lumps of liquid splendour! There is something more in this than can be accounted for from design or accident: Rembrandt was not a man made up of two or three rules and directions for acquiring genius.

I am afraid I shall hardly write so satisfactory a character of Mr. Wordsworth, though he, too, like Rembrandt, has a faculty of making something out of nothing, that is, out of himself, by the medium through which he sees and with which he clothes the barrenest subject. Mr. Wordsworth is the last man to "look abroad into universality," if that alone constituted genius: he looks at home into himself, and is "content with riches fineless." He would in the other case be "poor as winter," if he had nothing but general capacity to trust to. He is the greatest, that is, the most original poet of the present day, only because he is the greatest egotist. He is "self-involved, not dark." He sits in the centre of his own being, and there "enjoys bright day." He does not waste a thought on others. Whatever does not relate exclusively and wholly to himself, is foreign to his views. He contemplates a whole-length figure of himself, he looks along the unbroken line of his personal identity. He thrusts aside all other objects, all other interests with scorn and impatience, that he may repose on his own being, that he may dig out the treasures of thought contained in it, that he may unfold the precious stores of a mind for ever brooding over itself. His genius is the effect of his individual character. He stamps that character, that deep individual interest, on whatever he meets. The object is nothing but as it furnishes food for internal meditation, for old associations. If there had been no other being in the universe, Mr. Wordsworth's poetry would have been just what it is. If there had been neither love nor friendship, neither ambition nor pleasure nor business in the world, the author of the Lyrical Ballads need not have been greatly changed from what he is—might still have "kept the noiseless tenour of his way," retired in the sanctuary of his own heart, hallowing the Sabbath of his own thoughts. With the passions, the pursuits, and imaginations of other men, he does not profess to sympathise, but "finds tongues in the trees, books in the running brooks, sermons in stones, and good in every thing." With a mind averse from outward objects, but ever intent upon its own workings, he hangs a weight of thought and feeling upon every trifling circumstance connected with his past history. The note of the cuckoo sounds in his ear like the voice of other years; the daisy spreads its leaves in the rays of boyish delight, that stream from his thoughtful eyes; the rainbow lits its proud arch in heaven but to mark his progress from infancy to manhood; an old thorn is buried, bowed down under the mass of associations he has wound about it; and to him, as he himself beautifully says,

——The meanest flow'r that blows can give
Thoughts that do often lie too deep for tears.[2]

It is this power of habitual sentiment, or of transferring the interest of our conscious existence to whatever gently solicits attention, and is a link in the chain of association, without rousing our passions or hurting our pride, that is the striking feature in Mr. Wordsworth's mind and

[2] "Intimations of Immortality," ll. 201-02.

poetry. Others have felt and shown this power before, as Withers, Burns, &c. but none have felt it so intensely and absolutely as to lend to it the voice of inspiration, as to make it the foundation of a new style and school in poetry. His strength, as it so often happens, arises from the excess of his weakness. But he has opened a new avenue to the human heart, has explored another secret haunt and nook of nature, "sacred to verse, and sure of everlasting fame." Compared with his lines, Lord Byron's stanzas are but exaggerated commonplace, and Walter Scott's poetry (not his prose) old wives' fables. . . .

Originality is the seeing nature differently from others, and yet as it is in itself. It is not singularity or affectation, but the discovery of new and valuable truth. All the world do not see the whole meaning of any object they have been looking at. Habit blinds them to some things: short-sightedness to others. Every mind is not a gauge and measure of truth. Nature has her surface and her dark recesses. She is deep, obscure, and infinite. It is only minds on whom she makes her fullest impressions that can penetrate her shrine or unveil her *Holy of Holies*. It is only those whom she has filled with her spirit that have the boldness or the power to reveal her mysteries to others. But nature has a thousand aspects, and one man can only draw out one of them. Whoever does this, is a man of genius. One displays her force, another her refinement, one her power of harmony, another her suddenness of contrast, one her beauty of form, another her splendour of colour. Each does that for which he is best fitted by his particular genius, that is to say, by some quality of mind in which the quality of the object sinks deepest, where it finds the most cordial welcome, is perceived to its utmost extent, and where again it forces its way out from the fulness with which it has taken possession of the mind of the student. The imagination gives out what it has first absorbed by congeniality of temperament, what it has attracted and moulded into itself by elective affinity, as the loadstone draws and impregnates iron. . . .

WILLIAM WORDSWORTH (1770-1850)

THE *Lyrical Ballads* (1798) and Wordsworth's famous preface to the second edition (1800) of that book have frequently been cited as signposts dividing eighteenth- and nineteenth-century English literature. Actually Wordsworth, in many respects, simply used and built upon attitudes common in eighteenth-century English thought. Even his conception of nature may be viewed as a development in a tradition that goes back to the Earl of Shaftesbury at the beginning of the eighteenth century: in Shaftesbury's Deism, God is regarded as revealing Himself through the harmonious beauty of nature, and man's moral character is formed and developed by participating in this harmony. Throughout the eighteenth century the theme was treated in many blank verse poems of the same mixed genre (half descriptive, half didactic) that Wordsworth himself was later to use in the *Prelude* and the *Excursion*. But even more particularly in his psychology Wordsworth continued eighteenth-century English premises and beliefs. His conception of the imagination and of the mind generally was largely based on the doctrine of the association of ideas that had been developed in England during the eighteenth century. Even those psychological findings that tended to modify Wordsworth's use of this doctrine had also become common in English and Scottish philosophy and criticism during the preceding fifty years. In fact, it is largely in his theory and use of poetic language that Wordsworth departs from the practice and critical theory of eighteenth-century poetry, and even in this respect he was not completely unique. In the expanded preface to the second edition of the *Lyrical Ballads* the primary problem seems to be the proper language of poetry. His later, less familiar preface to his collected poems (1815) is devoted almost solely to discussing the imagination.

Wordsworth's critical and moral views were closely interwoven. Together they illustrate his answer to the problem that has always faced moralists and

WILLIAM WORDSWORTH. After his childhood in the Lake Country of northern England, Wordsworth attended Cambridge (1787-90), visited the Continent, and on his return lived as a neighbor of Coleridge and collaborated with him on the *Lyrical Ballads*. He completed most of his important poetry by 1810, settled in Grasmere (1813), in the midst of the Lake Country, and became Poet Laureate during his last years (1843-50).

Editions of Wordsworth's criticism include *Prose Works* (ed. A. B. Grosart, 1876; and ed. Wm. Knight, 1896); *Literary Criticism* (ed. N. C. Smith, 1905; and ed. P. M. Zall, Lincoln, 1966); and *Wordsworth's Preface to Lyrical Ballads* (ed. W. J. B. Owen, Copenhagen, 1957). Among relevant commentary may be mentioned R. D. Havens, *The Mind of a Poet: a Study of Wordsworth's Thought with Particular Reference to* The Prelude (Baltimore, 1941); J. A. Heffernan, *Wordsworth's Theory of Poetry* (Ithaca, 1969); W. J. B. Owen, *Wordsworth as Critic* (Toronto, 1969); and David Perkins, *Wordsworth and the Poetry of Sincerity* (Cambridge, Mass., 1964).

critics but was especially pressing after the classical tradition had subsided:
What is most basic and essential in human nature? What, fundamentally, *is*
human nature? And what is there in the environment or universe about us
that is most "naturally" fitted to nourish and develop this basic quality? In
facing these problems Wordsworth evolved for himself the primitivist answer
that what is most basic, distinctive, and valuable in man is an instinctive emotional and imaginative capacity that responds to the beauty, good, and order
in the concrete world of nature. Man, to the extent that he lives in close communication with the natural world, is man as he should be. The primary aim
of Wordsworth's poetry is to portray man in that state, and to show the influence of that natural environment on him. Therefore, Wordsworth selected
"incidents and situations from common life," and tried to trace in them "the
primary laws of our nature, chiefly as far as regards the manner in which
we associate ideas in a state of excitement"—thus showing how external nature, by causing ideas to assume a certain course, would be molding and
developing man's mental and emotional character. "Humble and rustic life
was generally chosen"; for there "the essential passions of the heart" are
less restrained, simpler, and more "durable"; they may therefore be "more
accurately contemplated"; and also in this state "the passions of men are
incorporated with the beautiful and permanent forms of Nature." Wordsworth's approach to his rural characters, in short, may be described as *romantic naturalism.* In taking particular characters, unidealized, unequated
with what Johnson called "rational nature, or at least the whole circle of
polished life," and portraying them in close relationship with their environment, Wordsworth is "naturalistic"; by associating them with feelings of
tenderness and profundity, by finding in them poetic beauty, his naturalism
becomes "romantic." The position, as Hazlitt and Keats were aware, has
liabilities; the reactions of the poet may be out of all proportion to the
significance of the subject, the subject serving merely as a vessel into which
he has poured his own personal feelings. Wordsworth himself was uneasy
lest "giving to things a false importance, I may have sometimes written upon
unworthy subjects."

What is essential and "natural" in man, then, is his developed response
to the ordered meaning and permanent forms of concrete nature. Wordsworth's theory of the proper language of poetry is closely related to this
central premise. Urban life, the fashions of society, the technical character
of specific occupations, all foster associations in us that are accidental and
temporary rather than basic and permanent, and these associations color our
language. In its most lasting idiom, language is found among people whose
associations and emotions have been molded by "the permanent forms of Nature," who "hourly communicate with the best objects, from which the best
part of language is originally derived." Their language is "less under the
influence of social vanity," and, "arising out of repeated experience and

regular feelings, is a more permanent, and a far more philosophical language, than that which is frequently substituted for it by Poets . . ." In referring disparagingly to a language peculiar to poets, Wordsworth was thinking primarily of the abstractions and poetic diction of much neoclassic verse. But his aim here is as characteristic of the classical tradition as it is of the early (if not later) stages of romanticism. Both Wordsworth and the neoclassicist regarded immediacy of communication as desirable. Both held up permanence in language as an end. They differed, however, in their conceptions of the means by which permanence is attained. To the neoclassicist, a generalized poetic diction could be made permanent by being adapted to persisting rational concepts, and by being lifted above the fluctuating speech of daily life. To Wordsworth, such a generalized diction lacked roots; language becomes more permanent to the degree that it is closely anchored to enduring objects in the concrete world.

Poetry, then, according to Wordsworth, has as its subject the permanent and primary aspects of nature, and the manner in which they influence the permanent and essential qualities of human nature. It grasps and communicates its insight in terms of *value*; it is, in a sense, the qualitative distillation of truth, rendered vital and meaningful to human emotions. Hence his remark that poetry is "the breath and finer spirit of all knowledge; it is the impassioned expression which is in the countenance of all Science." In other words, the value, meaning, and beauty of things are not a quantitative matter; they cannot be grasped by the analytic process of mind that weighs, measures, and divides ("we murder to dissect"), or fitted to the abstractions stamped out by our "meddling intellect"—by that "false secondary power," as he says in the *Prelude*, "By which we multiply distinctions." The fluid, vital reality of nature is lost in such a dissecting process; analysis discloses only the isolated, quantitative parts of a thing—"In disconnection, dead and spiritless"—not the living totality. The analytic reason is really a subjective intrusion on the part of the mind; it comes between reality and us, distorting what is actually there to fit its own subjective categories and abstractions. Wordsworth, in short, continued the tendency of later eighteenth-century criticism to equate "reason" with logical abstraction and thus to find it an unsatisfactory term for the process of mind needed to grasp reality in its full concreteness; and he also followed suit in turning to the word "imagination" for the process of mind desired. Indeed, the creative imagination, and the manner in which it works, is the pivotal problem in Wordsworth's esthetic theory, as it is in almost all romantic criticism—especially English romantic criticism—though his statements about it in the famous "Preface" are less significant than those in his verse, particularly in the *Prelude*, or those prefixed to the 1815 edition of his poems.

We have, then, in the imagination, an ability to draw upon all the resources of the mind: to centralize and unify sense impressions, to combine them with intuitions of form and value, and with realizations won from past experience. Through the imagination we have the capacity to grasp things as they really are—as living and meaningful totalities rather than as collections of isolated parts and fragments—and then to convert these total conceptions into active responses or feelings. Now the word "feeling" appears very frequently in Wordsworth, as it does in many other romantic writers; but it does not always mean the same thing, even though the late Irving Babbitt tended to think so. As the term is used in more sober romantic criticism, it is not to be confused with mere impulse. It tends, rather, to imply a more intense awareness and often a broader use of experience than can be obtained through analysis and abstraction. As such, the term may often signify, as it does for Wordsworth, the vivid, immediate experiences we have, from which ideas are afterwards drawn out and formed. In other words, "thought" is a later, vestigial "representative" of feeling. It is necessary that feeling be vivid if the ideas, the generalizations, screened out from it are to be vital and applicable. Though feeling furnishes, so to speak, the groundwork of understanding, this sifting of ideas from elementary feelings is only the first step in the development of mind that so interested Wordsworth and that serves as a central theme in his longer poems. For "our continued influxes of feeling are modified and directed by our thoughts, which are indeed the representatives of all our past feelings"; and the second step in the process is that ideas acquired by experience and matured by reflection should modify and direct feeling— should again *become* feeling, but feeling that is now enlarged and developed. The "emotion recollected in tranquillity" has undergone such a process. Thus, although poetry "is the spontaneous overflow of powerful feelings," those feelings must have been educated by thought—an education carried on "till at length, if we be originally possessed of much sensibility, such habits of mind will be produced" that we can confidently obey "blindly and mechanically the impulses of those habits . . ." This development is naturally moral, in a broad sense: man's emotional awareness is sharpened, purified, and regulated. Above all, sympathy is increased and broadened. The eye is taught to catch "the moral intimations of the sky," and objects of nature, "where no brotherhood exists to *passive* minds," are seen to have "affinities" with ourselves. The heart thus comes to participate "In the great social principle of life / Coercing all things into sympathy."

Feeling, then, is not only the groundwork of thought. It also characterizes thought in its final stage—thought transmuted back into formative and persuasive habits of reacting. Wordsworth, in taking this point of view, is drawing upon a principle of the doctrine called the "association of ideas" and developed by David Hartley and other eighteenth-century English writers. According to this doctrine ideas, originally evolved or abstracted from elementary feelings and impressions, may coalesce into convictions and be resolved into automatic habits of reacting that are vivid and immediate enough to be called "feelings." And to the capacity that unifies and guides this educated sensibility Wordsworth, like other writers of the period, applied the word "imagination." Far from being used to imply mere image-making, it is meant as "but another name" for "Reason in her most exalted mood." Yet since "reason" carries the limited connotation of an analytic and abstracting procedure, a more fluid term is needed to suggest the power to combine impressions, guide emotional response, detect nuances of relationship, and realize sympathies to which logical abstraction is impervious. Accordingly the term "imagination," as Wordsworth said, "has been overstrained, from impulses honourable to mankind, to meet the demands of the faculty which is perhaps the noblest of our nature."

Preface to the Second Edition of the *Lyrical Ballads*

THE FIRST Volume of these Poems has already been submitted to general perusal. It was published, as an experiment, which, I hoped, might be of some use to ascertain, how far, by fitting to metrical arrangement a selection of the real language of men in a state of vivid sensation, that sort of pleasure and that quantity of pleasure may be imparted, which a Poet may rationally endeavour to impart.

I had formed no very inaccurate estimate of the probable effect of those Poems: I flattered myself that they who should be pleased with them would read them with more than common pleasure: and, on the other hand, I was well aware, that by those who should dislike them, they would be read with more than common dislike. The result has differed from my expectation in this only, that a greater number have been pleased than I ventured to hope I should please.

Several of my Friends are anxious for the success of these Poems, from a belief, that, if the views with which they were composed were indeed realized, a class of Poetry would be produced, well adapted to interest mankind permanently, and not unimportant in the quality, and in the multiplicity of its moral relations: and on this account they have advised me to prefix a systematic defence of the theory upon which the Poems were written. But I was unwilling to undertake the task, knowing that on this occasion the Reader would look coldly upon my argu-

Lyrical Ballads. Published 1800.

ments, since I might be suspected of having been principally influenced by the selfish and foolish hope of *reasoning* him into an approbation of these particular Poems: and I was still more unwilling to undertake the task, because, adequately to display the opinions, and fully to enforce the arguments, would require a space wholly disproportionate to a preface. For, to treat the subject with the clearness and coherence of which it is susceptible, it would be necessary to give a full account of the present state of the public taste in this country, and to determine how far this taste is healthy or depraved; which, again, could not be determined, without pointing out in what manner language and the human mind act and re-act on each other, and without retracing the revolutions, not of literature alone, but likewise of society itself. I have therefore altogether declined to enter regularly upon this defence; yet I am sensible, that there would be something like impropriety in abruptly obtruding upon the Public, without a few words of introduction, Poems so materially different from those upon which general approbation is at present bestowed.

It is supposed, that by the act of writing in verse an Author makes a formal engagement that he will gratify certain known habits of association; that he not only thus apprises the Reader that certain classes of ideas and expressions will be found in his book, but that others will be carefully excluded. This exponent or symbol held forth by metrical language must in different eras of literature have excited very different expectations: for example, in the age of Catullus, Terence, and Lucretius, and that of Statius or Claudian; and in our own country, in the age of Shakespeare and Beaumont and Fletcher, and that of Donne and Cowley, or Dryden, or Pope. I will not take upon me to determine the exact import of the promise which, by the act of writing in verse, an Author in the present day makes to his reader: but it will undoubtedly appear to many persons that I have not fulfilled the terms of an engagement thus voluntarily contracted. They who have been accustomed to the gaudiness and inane phraseology of many modern writers, if they persist in reading this book to its conclusion, will, no doubt, frequently have to struggle with feelings of strangeness and awkwardness: they will look round for poetry, and will be induced to inquire by what species of courtesy these attempts can be permitted to assume that title. I hope therefore the reader will not censure me for attempting to state what I have proposed to myself to perform; and also (as far as the limits of a preface will permit) to explain some of the chief reasons which have determined me in the choice of my purpose: that at least he may be spared any unpleasant feeling of disappointment, and that I myself may be protected from one of the most dishonourable accusations which can be brought against an Author; namely, that of an indolence which prevents him from endeavouring to ascertain what is his duty, or, when his duty is ascertained, prevents him from performing it.

The principal object, then, proposed in these Poems was to choose incidents and situations from common life, and to relate or describe them, throughout, as far as was possible in a selection of language really used by men, and, at the same time, to throw over them a certain colouring of imagination, whereby ordinary things should be presented to the mind in an unusual aspect; and, further, and above all, to make these incidents and situations interesting by tracing in them, truly though not ostentatiously, the primary laws of our nature: chiefly, as far as regards the manner in which we associate ideas in a state of excitement. Humble and rustic life was generally chosen, because, in that condition, the essential passions of the heart find a better soil in which they can attain their maturity, are less under restraint, and speak a plainer and more emphatic language; because in that condition of life our elementary feelings co-exist in a state of greater simplicity, and, consequently, may be more accurately contemplated, and more forcibly communicated; because the manners of rural life germinate from those elementary feelings, and, from the necessary character of rural occupations, are more easily comprehended, and are more durable; and, lastly, because in that condition the passions of men are incorporated with the beautiful and permanent forms of nature. The language, too, of these men has been adopted (purified indeed from what appear to be its real defects, from all lasting and rational causes of dislike or disgust) because such men hourly communicate with the best objects from which the best part of language is originally derived; and because, from their rank in society and the sameness and narrow circle of their intercourse, being less under the influence of social vanity, they convey their feelings and notions in simple and unelaborated expressions. Accordingly, such a language, arising out of repeated experience and regular feelings, is a more permanent, and a far more philosophical language, than that which is frequently substituted for it by Poets, who think that they are conferring honour upon themselves and their art, in proportion as they separate themselves from the sympathies of men, and indulge in arbitrary and capricious habits of expression, in order to furnish food for fickle tastes, and fickle appetites, of their own creation.[1]

I cannot, however, be insensible to the present outcry against the triviality and meanness, both of thought and language, which some of my contemporaries have occasionally introduced into their metrical compositions; and I acknowledge that this defect, where it exists, is more dishonourable to the Writer's own character than false refinement or arbitrary innovation, though I should contend at the same time, that it is far less pernicious in the sum of its consequences. From such verses the Poems in these volumes will be found distinguished at least by one mark of difference, that each of them has a worthy

[1] It is worth while here to observe, that the affecting parts of Chaucer are almost always expressed in language pure and universally intelligible even to this day. [Wordsworth.]

purpose. Not that I always began to write with a distinct purpose formally conceived; but habits of meditation have, I trust, so prompted and regulated my feelings, that my descriptions of such objects as strongly excite those feelings, will be found to carry along with them a *purpose.* If this opinion be erroneous, I can have little right to the name of a Poet. For all good poetry is the spontaneous overflow of powerful feelings: and though this be true, Poems to which any value can be attached were never produced on any variety of subjects but by a man who, being possessed of more than usual organic sensibility, had also thought long and deeply. For our continued influxes of feeling are modified and directed by our thoughts, which are indeed the representatives of all our past feelings; and, as by contemplating the relation of these general representatives to each other, we discover what is really important to men, so, by the repetition and continuance of this act, our feelings will be connected with important subjects, till at length, if we be originally possessed of much sensibility, such habits of mind will be produced, that, by obeying blindly and mechanically the impulses of those habits, we shall describe objects, and utter sentiments, of such a nature, and in such connexion with each other, that the understanding of the Reader must necessarily be in some degree enlightened, and his affections strengthened and purified.

It has been said that each of these Poems has a purpose. Another circumstance must be mentioned which distinguishes these Poems from the popular Poetry of the day; it is this, that the feeling therein developed gives importance to the action and situation, and not the action and situation to the feeling.

A sense of false modesty shall not prevent me from asserting, that the Reader's attention is pointed to this mark of distinction, far less for the sake of these particular Poems than from the general importance of the subject. The subject is indeed important! For the human mind is capable of being excited without the application of gross and violent stimulants; and he must have a very faint perception of its beauty and dignity who does not know this, and who does not further know, that one being is elevated above another, in proportion as he possesses this capability. It has therefore appeared to me,

that to endeavour to produce or enlarge this capability is one of the best services in which, at any period, a Writer can be engaged; but this service, excellent at all times, is especially so at the present day. For a multitude of causes, unknown to former times, are now acting with a combined force to blunt the discriminating powers of the mind, and, unfitting it for all voluntary exertion, to reduce it to a state of almost savage torpor. The most effective of these causes are the great national events which are daily taking place,[2] and the increasing accumulation of men in cities, where the uniformity of their occupations produces a craving for extraordinary incident, which the rapid communication of intelligence hourly gratifies. To this tendency of life and manners the literature and theatrical exhibitions of the country have conformed themselves. The invaluable works of our elder writers, I had almost said the works of Shakespeare and Milton, are driven into neglect by frantic novels,[3] sickly and stupid German Tragedies, and deluges of idle and extravagant stories in verse.—When I think upon this degrading thirst after outrageous stimulation, I am almost ashamed to have spoken of the feeble endeavour made in these volumes to counteract it; and, reflecting upon the magnitude of the general evil, I should be oppressed with no dishonourable melancholy, had I not a deep impression of certain inherent and indestructible qualities of the human mind, and likewise of certain powers in the great and permanent objects that act upon it, which are equally inherent and indestructible; and were there not added to this impression a belief, that the time is approaching when the evil will be systematically opposed, by men of greater powers, and with far more distinguished success.

Having dwelt thus long on the subjects and aim of these Poems, I shall request the Reader's permission to apprise him of a few circumstances relating to their *style,* in order, among other reasons, that he may not censure me for not having performed what I never attempted. The Reader will find that personifications of abstract ideas rarely occur in these volumes; and

[2] Particularly the war with France.
[3] That is, "Gothic novels," such as Ann Radcliffe's *Mysteries of Udolpho* (1794) or M. G. Lewis's *The Monk* (1796).

are utterly rejected, as an ordinary device to elevate the style, and raise it above prose. My purpose was to imitate, and, as far as possible, to adopt the very language of men; and assuredly such personifications do not make any natural or regular part of that language. They are, indeed, a figure of speech occasionally prompted by passion, and I have made use of them as such; but have endeavoured utterly to reject them as a mechanical device of style, or as a family language which Writers in metre seem to lay claim to by prescription. I have wished to keep the Reader in the company of flesh and blood, persuaded that by so doing I shall interest him. Others who pursue a different track will interest him likewise; I do not interfere with their claim, but wish to prefer a claim of my own. There will also be found in these volumes little of what is usually called poetic diction; as much pains has been taken to avoid it as is ordinarily taken to produce it; this has been done for the reason already alleged, to bring my language near to the language of men; and further, because the pleasure which I have proposed to myself to impart, is of a kind very different from that which is supposed by many persons to be the proper object of poetry. Without being culpably particular, I do not know how to give my Reader a more exact notion of the style in which it was my wish and intention to write, than by informing him that I have at all times endeavoured to look steadily at my subject; consequently, there is I hope in these Poems little falsehood of description, and my ideas are expressed in language fitted to their respective importance. Something must have been gained by this practice, as it is friendly to one property of all good poetry, namely, good sense: but it has necessarily cut me off from a large portion of phrases and figures of speech which from father to son have long been regarded as the common inheritance of Poets. I have also thought it expedient to restrict myself still further, having abstained from the use of many expressions, in themselves proper and beautiful, but which have been foolishly repeated by bad Poets, till such feelings of disgust are connected with them as it is scarcely possible by any art of association to overpower.

If in a poem there should be found a series of lines, or even a single line, in which the language, though naturally arranged, and according to the strict laws of metre, does not differ from that of prose, there is a numerous class of critics, who, when they stumble upon these prosaisms, as they call them, imagine that they have made a notable discovery, and exult over the Poet as over a man ignorant of his own profession. Now these men would establish a canon of criticism which the Reader will conclude he must utterly reject, if he wishes to be pleased with these volumes. And it would be a most easy task to prove to him, that not only the language of a large portion of every good poem, even of the most elevated character, must necessarily, except with reference to the metre, in no respect differ from that of good prose, but likewise that some of the most interesting parts of the best poems will be found to be strictly the language of prose when prose is well written. The truth of this assertion might be demonstrated by innumerable passages from almost all the poetical writings, even of Milton himself. To illustrate the subject in a general manner, I will here adduce a short composition of Gray, who was at the head of those who, by their reasonings, have attempted to widen the space of separation betwixt Prose and Metrical composition, and was more than any other man curiously elaborate in the structure of his own poetic diction.

In vain to me the smiling mornings shine,
And reddening Phoebus lifts his golden fire:
The birds in vain their amorous descant join,
Or cheerful fields resume their green attire.
These ears, alas! for other notes repine;
A different object do these eyes require;
My lonely anguish melts no heart but mine;
And in my breast the imperfect joys expire;
Yet morning smiles the busy race to cheer,
And new-born pleasure brings to happier men;
The fields to all their wonted tribute bear;
To warm their little loves the birds complain.
I fruitless mourn to him that cannot hear,
And weep the more because I weep in vain.[4]

It will easily be perceived, that the only part of this Sonnet which is of any value is the lines printed in Italics; it is equally obvious, that, except in the rhyme, and in the use of the single word "fruitless" for fruitlessly, which is so far a

[4] "Sonnet on the Death of Mr. Richard West."

defect, the language of these lines does in no respect differ from that of prose.

By the foregoing quotation it has been shown that the language of Prose may yet be well adapted to Poetry; and it was previously asserted, that a large portion of the language of every good poem can in no respect differ from that of good Prose. We will go further. It may be safely affirmed, that there neither is, nor can be, any *essential* difference between the language of prose and metrical composition. We are fond of tracing the resemblance between Poetry and Painting, and, accordingly, we call them Sisters: but where shall we find bonds of connexion sufficiently strict to typify the affinity betwixt metrical and prose composition? They both speak by and to the same organs; the bodies in which both of them are clothed may be said to be of the same substance, their affections are kindred, and almost identical, not necessarily differing even in degree; Poetry [5] sheds no tears "such as Angels weep," but natural and human tears; she can boast of no celestial ichor that distinguishes her vital juices from those of prose; the same human blood circulates through the veins of them both.

If it be affirmed that rhyme and metrical arrangement of themselves constitute a distinction which overturns what has just been said on the strict affinity of metrical language with that of prose, and paves the way for other artificial distinctions which the mind voluntarily admits, I answer that the language of such Poetry as is here recommended is, as far as is possible, a selection of the language really spoken by men; that this selection, wherever it is made with true taste and feeling, will of itself form a distinction far greater than would at first be imagined, and will entirely separate the composition from the vulgarity and meanness of ordinary life; and, if metre be superadded thereto, I believe that a

[5] I here use the word "Poetry" (though against my own judgement) as opposed to the word Prose, and synonymous with metrical composition. But much confusion has been introduced into criticism by this contradistinction of Poetry and Prose, instead of the more philosophical one of Poetry and Matter of Fact, or Science. The only strict antithesis to Prose is Metre; nor is this, in truth, a *strict* antithesis, because lines and passages of metre so naturally occur in writing prose, that it would be scarcely possible to avoid them, even were it desirable. [Wordsworth.]

dissimilitude will be produced altogether sufficient for the gratification of a rational mind. What other distinction would we have? Whence is it to come? And where is it to exist? Not, surely, where the Poet speaks through the mouths of his characters: it cannot be necessary here, either for elevation of style, or any of its supposed ornaments: for, if the Poet's subject be judiciously chosen, it will naturally, and upon fit occasion, lead him to passions the language of which, if selected truly and judiciously, must necessarily be dignified and variegated, and alive with metaphors and figures. I forbear to speak of an incongruity which would shock the intelligent Reader, should the Poet interweave any foreign splendour of his own with that which the passion naturally suggests: it is sufficient to say that such addition is unnecessary. And, surely, it is more probable that those passages, which with propriety abound with metaphors and figures, will have their due effect, if, upon other occasions where the passions are of a milder character, the style also be subdued and temperate.

But, as the pleasure which I hope to give by the Poems now presented to the Reader must depend entirely on just notions upon this subject, and, as it is in itself of high importance to our taste and moral feelings, I cannot content myself with these detached remarks. And if, in what I am about to say, it shall appear to some that my labour is unnecessary, and that I am like a man fighting a battle without enemies, such persons may be reminded, that, whatever be the language outwardly holden by men, a practical faith in the opinions which I am wishing to establish is almost unknown. If my conclusions are admitted, and carried as far as they must be carried if admitted at all, our judgements concerning the works of the greatest Poets both ancient and modern will be far different from what they are at present, both when we praise, and when we censure: and our moral feelings influencing and influenced by these judgements will, I believe, be corrected and purified.

Taking up the subject, then, upon general grounds, let me ask, what is meant by the word Poet? What is a Poet? To whom does he address himself? And what language is to be expected from him?—He is a man speaking to men: a man, it is true, endowed with more lively sensibility, more enthusiasm and tenderness, who has a greater knowledge of human nature, and a more comprehensive soul, than are supposed to be common among mankind; a man pleased with his own passions and volitions, and who rejoices more than other men in the spirit of life that is in him; delighting to contemplate similar volitions and passions as manifested in the goings-on of the Universe, and habitually impelled to create them where he does not find them. To these qualities he has added a disposition to be affected more than other men by absent things as if they were present; an ability of conjuring up in himself passions, which are indeed far from being the same as those produced by real events, yet (especially in those parts of the general sympathy which are pleasing and delightful) do more nearly resemble the passions produced by real events, than anything which, from the motions of their own minds merely, other men are accustomed to feel in themselves:—whence, and from practice, he has acquired a greater readiness and power in expressing what he thinks and feels, and especially those thoughts and feelings which, by his own choice, or from the structure of his own mind, arise in him without immediate external excitement.

But whatever portion of this faculty we may suppose even the greatest Poet to possess, there cannot be a doubt that the language which it will suggest to him, must often, in liveliness and truth, fall short of that which is uttered by men in real life, under the actual pressure of those passions, certain shadows of which the Poet thus produces, or feels to be produced, in himself.

However exalted a notion we would wish to cherish of the character of a Poet, it is obvious, that while he describes and imitates passions, his employment is in some degree mechanical, compared with the freedom and power of real and substantial action and suffering. So that it will be the wish of the Poet to bring his feelings near to those of the persons whose feelings he describes, nay, for short spaces of time, perhaps, to let himself slip into an entire delusion, and even confound and identify his own feelings with theirs; modifying only the language which is thus suggested to him by a consideration that he describes for a particular purpose, that of giving pleasure. Here, then, he will apply

the principle of selection which has been already insisted upon. He will depend upon this for removing what would otherwise be painful or disgusting in the passion; he will feel that there is no necessity to trick out or to elevate nature: and, the more industriously he applies this principle, the deeper will be his faith that no words, which *his* fancy or imagination can suggest, will be to be compared with those which are the emanations of reality and truth.

But it may be said by those who do not object to the general spirit of these remarks, that, as it is impossible for the Poet to produce upon all occasions language as exquisitely fitted for the passion as that which the real passion itself suggests, it is proper that he should consider himself as in the situation of a translator, who does not scruple to substitute excellencies of another kind for those which are unattainable by him; and endeavours occasionally to surpass his original, in order to make some amends for the general inferiority to which he feels that he must submit. But this would be to encourage idleness and unmanly despair. Further, it is the language of men who speak of what they do not understand; who talk of Poetry as of a matter of amusement and idle pleasure; who will converse with us as gravely about a *taste* for Poetry, as they express it, as if it were a thing as indifferent as a taste for rope-dancing or Frontiniac or Sherry. Aristotle, I have been told, has said, that Poetry is the most philosophic of all writing: [6] it is so: its object is truth, not individual and local, but general, and operative; not standing upon external testimony, but carried alive into the heart by passion; truth which is its own testimony, which gives competence and confidence to the tribunal to which it appeals, and receives them from the same tribunal. Poetry is the image of man and nature. The obstacles which stand in the way of the fidelity of the Biographer and Historian, and of their consequent utility, are incalculably greater than those which are to be encountered by the Poet who comprehends the dignity of his art. The Poet writes under one restriction only, namely, the necessity of giving immediate pleasure to a human Being possessed of that information which

[6] Not quite accurate; Aristotle states that it is "*more* philosophical" than "history" (that is, than straightforward particularized description).

may be expected from him, not as a lawyer, a physician, a mariner, an astronomer, or a natural philosopher, but as a Man. Except this one restriction, there is no object standing between the Poet and the image of things; between this, and the Biographer and Historian, there are a thousand.

Nor let this necessity of producing immediate pleasure be considered as a degradation of the Poet's art. It is far otherwise. It is an acknowledgement of the beauty of the universe, an acknowledgement the more sincere, because not formal, but indirect; it is a task light and easy to him who looks at the world in the spirit of love: further, it is a homage paid to the native and naked dignity of man, to the grand elementary principle of pleasure, by which he knows, and feels, and lives, and moves. We have no sympathy but what is propagated by pleasure: I would not be misunderstood; but wherever we sympathize with pain, it will be found that the sympathy is produced and carried on by subtle combinations with pleasure. We have no knowledge, that is, no general principles drawn from the contemplation of particular facts, but what has been built up by pleasure, and exists in us by pleasure alone. The Man of science, the Chemist and Mathematician, whatever difficulties and disgusts they may have had to struggle with, know and feel this. However painful may be the objects with which the Anatomist's knowledge is connected, he feels that his knowledge is pleasure; and where he has no pleasure he has no knowledge. What then does the Poet? He considers man and the objects that surround him as acting and re-acting upon each other, so as to produce an infinite complexity of pain and pleasure; he considers man in his own nature and in his ordinary life as contemplating this with a certain quantity of immediate knowledge, with certain convictions, intuitions, and deductions, which from habit acquire the quality of intuitions; he considers him as looking upon this complex scene of ideas and sensations, and finding everywhere objects that immediately excite in him sympathies which, from the necessities of his nature, are accompanied by an overbalance of enjoyment.

To this knowledge which all men carry about with them, and to these sympathies in which,

without any other discipline than that of our daily life, we are fitted to take delight, the Poet principally directs his attention. He considers man and nature as essentially adapted to each other, and the mind of man as naturally the mirror of the fairest and most interesting properties of nature. And thus the Poet, prompted by this feeling of pleasure, which accompanies him through the whole course of his studies, converses with general nature, with affections akin to those, which, through labour and length of time, the Man of science has raised up in himself, by conversing with those particular parts of nature which are the objects of his studies. The knowledge both of the Poet and the Man of science is pleasure; but the knowledge of the one cleaves to us as a necessary part of our existence, our natural and unalienable inheritance; the other is a personal and individual acquisition, slow to come to us, and by no habitual and direct sympathy connecting us with our fellow-beings. The Man of science seeks truth as a remote and unknown benefactor; he cherishes and loves it in his solitude: the Poet, singing a song in which all human beings join with him, rejoices in the presence of truth as our visible friend and hourly companion. Poetry is the breath and finer spirit of all knowledge; it is the impassioned expression which is in the countenance of all Science. Emphatically may it be said of the Poet, as Shakespeare hath said of man, "that he looks before and after." He is the rock of defence for human nature; an upholder and preserver, carrying everywhere with him relationship and love. In spite of difference of soil and climate, of language and manners, of laws and customs: in spite of things silently gone out of mind, and things violently destroyed; the Poet binds together by passion and knowledge the vast empire of human society, as it is spread over the whole earth, and over all time. The objects of the Poet's thoughts are everywhere; though the eyes and senses of man are, it is true, his favourite guides, yet he will follow wheresoever he can find an atmosphere of sensation in which to move his wings. Poetry is the first and last of all knowledge—it is as immortal as the heart of man. If the labours of Men of science should ever create any material revolution, direct or indirect, in our condition, and in the impressions which we habitually receive, the Poet will sleep then no more than at present; he will be ready to follow the steps of the Man of science, not only in those general indirect effects, but he will be at his side, carrying sensation into the midst of the objects of the science itself. The remotest discoveries of the Chemist, the Botanist, or Mineralogist, will be as proper objects of the Poet's art as any upon which it can be employed, if the time should ever come when these things shall be familiar to us, and the relations under which they are contemplated by the followers of these respective sciences shall be manifestly and palpably material to us as enjoying and suffering beings. If the time should ever come when what is now called science, thus familiarized to men, shall be ready to put on, as it were, a form of flesh and blood, the Poet will lend his divine spirit to aid the transfiguration, and will welcome the Being thus produced, as a dear and genuine inmate of the household of man.—It is not, then, to be supposed that any one, who holds that sublime notion of Poetry which I have attempted to convey, will break in upon the sanctity and truth of his pictures by transitory and accidental ornaments, and endeavour to excite admiration of himself by arts, the necessity of which must manifestly depend upon the assumed meanness of his subject.

What has been thus far said applies to Poetry in general; but especially to those parts of composition where the Poet speaks through the mouths of his characters; and upon this point it appears to authorize the conclusion that there are few persons of good sense, who would not allow that the dramatic parts of composition are defective, in proportion as they deviate from the real language of nature, and are coloured by a diction of the Poet's own, either peculiar to him as an individual Poet or belonging simply to Poets in general; to a body of men who, from the circumstance of their compositions being in metre, it is expected will employ a particular language.

It is not, then, in the dramatic parts of composition that we look for this distinction of language; but still it may be proper and necessary where the Poet speaks to us in his own person and character. To this I answer by referring the Reader to the description before given of a Poet. Among the qualities there

enumerated as principally conducing to form a Poet, is implied nothing differing in kind from other men, but only in degree. The sum of what was said is, that the Poet is chiefly distinguished from other men by a greater promptness to think and feel without immediate external excitement, and a greater power in expressing such thoughts and feelings as are produced in him in that manner. But these passions and thoughts and feelings are the general passions and thoughts and feelings of men. And with what are they connected? Undoubtedly with our moral sentiments and animal sensations, and with the causes which excite these; with the operations of the elements, and the appearances of the visible universe; with storm and sunshine, with the revolutions of the seasons, with cold and heat, with loss of friends and kindred, with injuries and resentments, gratitude and hope, with fear and sorrow. These, and the like, are the sensations and objects which the Poet describes, as they are the sensations of other men, and the objects which interest them. The Poet thinks and feels in the spirit of human passions. How, then, can his language differ in any material degree from that of all other men who feel vividly and see clearly? It might be *proved* that it is impossible. But supposing that this were not the case, the Poet might then be allowed to use a peculiar language when expressing his feelings for his own gratification, or that of men like himself. But Poets do not write for Poets alone, but for men. Unless therefore we are advocates for that admiration which subsists upon ignorance, and that pleasure which arises from hearing what we do not understand, the Poet must descend from this supposed height; and, in order to excite rational sympathy, he must express himself as other men express themselves. To this it may be added, that while he is only selecting from the real language of men, or, which amounts to the same thing, composing accurately in the spirit of such selection, he is treading upon safe ground, and we know what we are to expect from him. Our feelings are the same with respect to metre; for, as it may be proper to remind the Reader, the distinction of metre is regular and uniform, and not, like that which is produced by what is usually called POETIC DICTION, arbitrary, and subject to infinite caprices upon which no calculation whatever can be made. In the one case, the Reader is utterly at the mercy of the Poet, respecting what imagery or diction he may choose to connect with the passion; whereas, in the other, the metre obeys certain laws, to which the Poet and Reader both willingly submit because they are certain, and because no interference is made by them with the passion, but such as the concurring testimony of ages has shown to heighten and improve the pleasure which co-exists with it.

It will now be proper to answer an obvious question, namely, Why, professing these opinions, have I written in verse? To this, in addition to such answer as is included in what has been already said, I reply, in the first place, Because, however I may have restricted myself, there is still left open to me what confessedly constitutes the most valuable object of all writing, whether in prose or verse; the great and universal passions of men, the most general and interesting of their occupations, and the entire world of nature before me—to supply endless combinations of forms and imagery. Now, supposing for a moment that whatever is interesting in these objects may be as vividly described in prose, why should I be condemned for attempting to superadd to such description the charm which, by the consent of all nations, is acknowledged to exist in metrical language? To this, by such as are yet unconvinced, it may be answered that a very small part of the pleasure given by Poetry depends upon the metre, and that it is injudicious to write in metre, unless it be accompanied with the other artificial distinctions of style with which metre is usually accompanied, and that, by such deviation, more will be lost from the shock which will thereby be given to the Reader's associations than will be counterbalanced by any pleasure which he can derive from the general power of numbers.[7] In answer to those who still contend for the necessity of accompanying metre with certain appropriate colours of style in order to the accomplishment of its appropriate end, and who also, in my opinion, greatly underrate the power of metre in itself, it might, perhaps, as far as relates to these Volumes, have been almost

sufficient to observe, that poems are extant, written upon more humble subjects, and in a still more naked and simple style, which have continued to give pleasure from generation to generation. Now, if nakedness and simplicity be a defect, the fact here mentioned affords a strong presumption that poems somewhat less naked and simple are capable of affording pleasure at the present day; and, what I wished *chiefly* to attempt, at present, was to justify myself for having written under the impression of this belief.

But various causes might be pointed out why, when the style is manly, and the subject of some importance, words metrically arranged will long continue to impart such a pleasure to mankind as he who proves the extent of that pleasure will be desirous to impart. The end of Poetry is to produce excitement in co-existence with an overbalance of pleasure; but, by the supposition, excitement is an unusual and irregular state of the mind; ideas and feelings do not, in that state, succeed each other in accustomed order. If the words, however, by which this excitement is produced be in themselves powerful, or the images and feelings have an undue proportion of pain connected with them, there is some danger that the excitement may be carried beyond its proper bounds. Now the co-presence of something regular, something to which the mind has been accustomed in various moods and in a less excited state, cannot but have great efficacy in tempering and restraining the passion by an intertexture of ordinary feeling, and of feeling not strictly and necessarily connected with the passion. This is unquestionably true; and hence, though the opinion will at first appear paradoxical, from the tendency of metre to divest language, in a certain degree, of its reality, and thus to throw a sort of half-consciousness of unsubstantial existence over the whole composition, there can be little doubt but that more pathetic situations and sentiments, that is, those which have a greater proportion of pain connected with them, may be endured in metrical composition, especially in rhyme, than in prose. The metre of the old ballads is very artless; yet they contain many passages which would illustrate this opinion; and, I hope, if the following Poems be attentively perused, similar instances will be found in them. This opinion may be further illustrated by ap-

---

[7] That is, versification, especially meter: the sheer *sound* of verse as distinct from imagery, metaphor, and other elements of poetry.

pealing to the Reader's own experience of the reluctance with which he comes to the re-perusal of the distressful parts of *Clarissa Harlowe,* or the *Gamester;* [8] while Shakespeare's writings, in the most pathetic scenes, never act upon us, as pathetic, beyond the bounds of pleasure—an effect which, in a much greater degree than might at first be imagined, is to be ascribed to small, but continual and regular impulses of pleasurable surprise from the metrical arrangement.—On the other hand (what it must be allowed will much more frequently happen) if the Poet's words should be incommensurate with the passion, and inadequate to raise the Reader to a height of desirable excitement, then (unless the Poet's choice of his metre has been grossly injudicious), in the feelings of pleasure which the Reader has been accustomed to connect with metre in general, and in the feeling, whether cheerful or melancholy, which he has been accustomed to connect with that particular movement of metre, there will be found something which will greatly contribute to impart passion to the words, and to effect the complex end which the Poet proposes to himself.

If I had undertaken a SYSTEMATIC defence of the theory here maintained, it would have been my duty to develop the various causes upon which the pleasure received from metrical language depends. Among the chief of these causes is to be reckoned a principle which must be well known to those who have made any of the Arts the object of accurate reflection; namely, the pleasure which the mind derives from the perception of similitude in dissimilitude. This principle is the great spring of the activity of our minds, and their chief feeder. From this principle the direction of the sexual appetite, and all the passions connected with it, take their origin: it is the life of our ordinary conversation; and upon the accuracy with which similitude in dissimilitude, and dissimilitude in similitude are perceived, depend our taste and our moral feelings. It would not be a useless employment to apply this principle to the consideration of metre, and to show that metre is hence enabled to afford much pleasure, and to point out in what manner that pleasure is produced.

[8] A play (1753) by Edward Moore, intended as a tragedy and designed to show the hazards of gambling.

But my limits will not permit me to enter upon this subject, and I must content myself with a general summary.

I have said that poetry is the spontaneous overflow of powerful feelings: it takes its origin from emotion recollected in tranquillity: the emotion is contemplated till, by a species of reaction, the tranquillity gradually disappears, and an emotion, kindred to that which was before the subject of contemplation, is gradually produced, and does itself actually exist in the mind. In this mood successful composition generally begins, and in a mood similar to this it is carried on; but the emotion, of whatever kind, and in whatever degree, from various causes, is qualified by various pleasures, so that in describing any passions whatsoever, which are voluntarily described, the mind will, upon the whole, be in a state of enjoyment. If Nature be thus cautious to preserve in a state of enjoyment a being so employed, the Poet ought to profit by the lesson held forth to him, and ought especially to take care, that, whatever passions he communicates to his Reader, those passions, if his Reader's mind be sound and vigorous, should always be accompanied with an overbalance of pleasure. Now the music of harmonious metrical language, the sense of difficulty overcome, and the blind association of pleasure which has been previously received from works of rhyme or metre of the same or similar construction, an indistinct perception perpetually renewed of language closely resembling that of real life, and yet, in the circumstance of metre, differing from it so widely—all these imperceptibly make up a complex feeling of delight, which is of the most important use in tempering the painful feeling always found intermingled with powerful descriptions of the deeper passions. This effect is always produced in pathetic and impassioned poetry; while, in lighter compositions, the ease and gracefulness with which the Poet manages his numbers are themselves confessedly a principal source of the gratification of the Reader. All that it is *necessary* to say, however, upon this subject, may be effected by affirming, what few persons will deny, that, of two descriptions, either of passions, manners, or characters, each of them equally well executed, the one in prose and the other in verse, the verse will be read a hundred times where the prose is read once.

Having thus explained a few of my reasons for writing in verse, and why I have chosen subjects from common life, and endeavoured to bring my language near to the real language of men, if I have been too minute in pleading my own cause, I have at the same time been treating a subject of general interest; and for this reason a few words shall be added with reference solely to these particular poems, and to some defects which will probably be found in them. I am sensible that my associations must have sometimes been particular instead of general, and that, consequently, giving to things a false importance, I may have sometimes written upon unworthy subjects; but I am less apprehensive on this account, than that my language may frequently have suffered from those arbitrary connexions of feelings and ideas with particular words and phrases, from which no man can altogether protect himself. Hence I have no doubt, that, in some instances, feelings, even of the ludicrous, may be given to my Readers by expressions which appeared to me tender and pathetic. Such faulty expressions, were I convinced they were faulty at present, and that they must necessarily continue to be so, I would willingly take all reasonable pains to correct. But it is dangerous to make these alterations on the simple authority of a few individuals, or even of certain classes of men; for where the understanding of an Author is not convinced, or his feelings altered, this cannot be done without great injury to himself: for his own feelings are his stay and support; and, if he set them aside in one instance, he may be induced to repeat this act till his mind shall lose all confidence in itself, and become utterly debilitated. To this it may be added, that the critic ought never to forget that he is himself exposed to the same errors as the Poet, and, perhaps, in a much greater degree: for there can be no presumption in saying of most readers, that it is not probable they will be so well acquainted with the various stages of meaning through which words have passed, or with the fickleness or stability of the relations of particular ideas to each other; and, above all, since they are so much less interested in the subject, they may decide lightly and carelessly.

Long as the Reader has been detained, I hope he will permit me to caution him against a mode of false criticism which has been applied to Poetry, in which the language closely resembles that of life and nature. Such verses have been triumphed over in parodies, of which Dr. Johnson's stanza is a fair specimen:—

> I put my hat upon my head
> And walked into the Strand,
> And there I met another man
> Whose hat was in his hand.

Immediately under these lines let us place one of the most justly-admired stanzas of the "Babes in the Wood."

> These pretty Babes with hand in hand
> Went wandering up and down;
> But never more they saw the Man
> Approaching from the Town.

In both these stanzas the words, and the order of the words, in no respect differ from the most unimpassioned conversation. There are words in both, for example, "the Strand," and "the Town," connected with none but the most familiar ideas; yet the one stanza we admit as admirable, and the other as a fair example of the superlatively contemptible. Whence arises this difference? Not from the metre, not from the language, not from the order of the words; but the *matter* expressed in Dr. Johnson's stanza is contemptible. The proper method of treating trivial and simple verses, to which Dr. Johnson's stanza would be a fair parallelism, is not to say, this is a bad kind of poetry, or, this is not poetry; but, this wants sense; it is neither interesting in itself, nor can *lead* to anything interesting; the images neither originate in that sane state of feeling which arises out of thought, nor can excite thought or feeling in the Reader. This is the only sensible manner of dealing with such verses. Why trouble yourself about the species till you have previously decided upon the genus? Why take pains to prove that an ape is not a Newton, when it is self-evident that he is not a man?

One request I must make of my reader, which is, that in judging these Poems he would decide by his own feelings genuinely, and not by reflection upon what will probably be the judgement of others. How common is it to hear a person say, I myself do not object to this style of composition, or this or that expression, but, to such and such classes of people it will appear mean or ludicrous! This mode of criticism, so destructive of all sound unadulterated judgement, is almost universal: let the Reader then abide, independently, by his own feelings, and, if he finds himself affected, let him not suffer such conjectures to interfere with his pleasure.

If an Author, by any single composition, has impressed us with respect for his talents, it is useful to consider this as affording a presumption, that on other occasions where we have been displeased, he, nevertheless, may not have written ill or absurdly; and further, to give him so much credit for this one composition as may induce us to review what has displeased us, with more care than we should otherwise have bestowed upon it. This is not only an act of justice, but, in our decisions upon poetry especially, may conduce, in a high degree, to the improvement of our own taste; for an *accurate* taste in poetry, and in all the other arts, as Sir Joshua Reynolds has observed, is an *acquired* talent, which can only be produced by thought and a long-continued intercourse with the best models of composition. This is mentioned, not with so ridiculous a purpose as to prevent the most inexperienced Reader from judging for himself, (I have already said that I wish him to judge for himself;) but merely to temper the rashness of decision, and to suggest, that, if Poetry be a subject on which much time has not been bestowed, the judgement may be erroneous; and that, in many cases, it necessarily will be so.

Nothing would, I know, have so effectually contributed to further the end which I have in view, as to have shown of what kind the pleasure is, and how that pleasure is produced, which is confessedly produced by metrical composition essentially different from that which I have here endeavoured to recommend: for the Reader will say that he has been pleased by such composition; and what more can be done for him? The power of any art is limited; and he will suspect, that, if it be proposed to furnish him with new friends, that can be only upon condition of his abandoning his old friends. Besides, as I have said, the Reader is himself conscious of the pleasure which he has received from such composition, composition to which he has peculiarly attached the endearing name of Poetry; and all men feel an habitual gratitude, and something of an honourable bigotry, for the objects which have long continued to please them: we not only wish to be pleased, but to be pleased in that particular way in which we have been accustomed to be pleased. There is in these feelings enough to resist a host of arguments; and I should be the less able to combat them successfully, as I am willing to allow, that in order entirely to enjoy the Poetry which I am recommending, it would be necessary to give up much of what is ordinarily enjoyed. But, would my limits have permitted me to point out how this pleasure is produced, many obstacles might have been removed, and the Reader assisted in perceiving that the powers of language are not so limited as he may suppose; and that it is possible for poetry to give other enjoyments, of a purer, more lasting, and more exquisite nature. This part of the subject has not been altogether neglected, but it has not been so much my present aim to prove, that the interest excited by some other kinds of poetry is less vivid, and less worthy of the nobler powers of the mind, as to offer reasons for presuming, that if my purpose were fulfilled, a species of poetry would be produced, which is genuine poetry; in its nature well adapted to interest mankind permanently, and likewise important in the multiplicity and quality of its moral relations.

From what has been said, and from a perusal of the Poems, the Reader will be able clearly to perceive the object which I had in view: he will determine how far it has been attained; and, what is a much more important question, whether it be worth attaining: and upon the decision of these two questions will rest my claim to the approbation of the Public.

JOHN KEATS   (1795-1821)

T HE SCATTERED remarks of Keats on poetry and the imagination are
among the most suggestive and searching left by any poet. As T. S. Eliot
has said, "There is hardly one statement of Keats about poetry which
. . . will not be found to be true; and what is more, true for greater and
more mature poetry than anything that Keats ever wrote." Keats's early death
prevented him from evolving a unified outlook. But one may infer his critical
values from his letters and marginalia; and these values appear as a gifted
extension and development of Hazlitt, whose "depth of Taste" the youthful
Keats considered one of the three most praiseworthy phenomena in the England of his own age.

The basic premise of Keats's conception of the poet is seen in his "negative
capability" letter (Dec. 21, 1817). Here he tells of meeting a group of
clever literary men, each absorbed in his own "identity," and affectedly intent on saying "things which make one start." Probably in reaction to them,
he became convinced that what is most needed for a "Man of Achievement,
especially in Literature," is the ability to negate or lose one's identity in
something larger than oneself—a sympathetic openness to the concrete reality without, an imaginative identification, a relishing and understanding
of it. It is this capacity which "Shakespeare possessed so enormously," and
which Keats, like Hazlitt, felt was lacking in much of the poetry of his own
day. This desired awareness is not to be attained through logical analysis. In
fact, "consequitive reasoning" can also be a subjective obtrusion of one's own
identity—a barrier between oneself and reality. It too often reflects a love
of system for its own sake, a confidence in mere abstractions, and can easily
result in a distorting of fluid, organic reality to fit the artificial patterns, the
rigid, predetermined molds of abstract concepts.

The object of poetry for Keats is the "identity"—the nature or "truth"—
of individual, concrete reality, or what Gerard Manley Hopkins later called

JOHN KEATS. Keats, after attending Enfield School (1803-11), served for a while as an apprentice to an apothecary-surgeon, and then as a medical student. He became acquainted with Leigh
Hunt and the literary circle in which Hunt moved, and, after an extremely rapid development
of his poetic ability, died of tuberculosis at the early age of twenty-five.
    The most complete collection of his works, including his periodical writing and his marginalia,
is the "Hampstead Edition," *Poetical Works and Other Writings* (ed. H. B. Forman; rev. M. B.
Forman, 1938); the standard edition of his *Letters* is that of H. E. Rollins (2 vols., Cambridge,
Mass., 1958). Commentary dealing with his attitude towards poetry and related interests includes:
W. J. Bate, *Negative Capability* (Cambridge, Mass., 1939) and especially *John Keats* (Cambridge,
Mass., 1963); J. M. Murry, *Keats and Shakespeare* (Oxford, 1925); C. F. E. Spurgeon, *Keats's
Shakespeare* (Oxford, 1928); C. D. Thorpe, *The Mind of John Keats* (Oxford, 1926).

"inscape." And the aim of poetry is the intense expression of this reality, of this energetic fulfillment of identity, caught in its concrete moment of unfolding, and felt and understood by the poet through sympathetic identification. In this state of intense awareness, the "true" is seen as the "beautiful." For with this "swelling into reality" of the character and identity (or "truth") of the object, its essential form and function (or "beauty") are grasped and relished by the imagination in their full significance. There are abundant but scattered indications, however, that Keats at length felt poetry would have to justify itself on broader grounds than this: a feeling that the impassioned expression of concrete reality, though necessary, is not enough. To speculate on the direction his thought might ultimately have taken offers one of the most alluring opportunities for conjecture in literary history.

From the Letters

[*The manner and subject of poetry*]

[February 27, 1818] In Poetry I have a few Axioms, and you will see how far I am from their Centre. 1st. I think Poetry should surprise by a fine excess and not by Singularity—it should strike the Reader as a wording of his own highest thoughts, and appear almost a Remembrance— 2nd. Its touches of Beauty should never be half way thereby making the reader breathless instead of content: the rise, the progress, the setting of imagery should like the Sun come natural to him—shine over him and set soberly although in magnificence leaving him in the Luxury of twilight—but it is easier to think what Poetry should be than to write it—and this leads me on to another axiom. That if Poetry comes not as naturally as the Leaves to a tree it had better not come at all.

[March 19, 1819] The greater part of Men make their way with the same instinctiveness, the same unwandering eye from their purposes, the same animal eagerness as the Hawk. The Hawk wants a Mate, so does the Man—look at them both; they set about it and procure one in the same manner—they want both a nest and they both set about one in the same manner—they get their food in the same manner— The noble animal Man for his amusement smokes his pipe —the Hawk balances about the Clouds—that is the only difference of their leisures. This it is that makes the Amusement of Life—to a specula-

tive Mind. I go among the Fields and catch a glimpse of a Stoat or a fieldmouse peeping out of the withered grass—the creature hath a purpose and its eyes are bright with it. I go amongst the buildings of a city and I see a Man hurrying along—to what? the Creature has a purpose and his eyes are bright with it. But then, as Wordsworth says, "we have all one human heart"—there is an electric fire in human nature tending to purify—so that among these human creatures there is continually some birth of a new heroism. . . . Even here, though I myself am pursuing the same instinctive course as the veriest human animal you can think of (I am, however, young, writing at random), straining at particles of light in the midst of a great darkness, without knowing the bearing of any one assertion, of any one opinion—yet may I not in this be free from sin? May there not be superior beings amused with any graceful, though instinctive attitude my mind may fall into, as I am entertained with the alertness of a Stoat or the anxiety of a Deer? Though a quarrel in the Streets is a thing to be hated, the energies displayed in it are fine; the commonest Man shows a grace in his quarrel— By a superior being our reasonings may take the same tone—though erroneous they may be fine.[1]—This is the very thing in which consists poetry; and if so it is

---

[1] Cf. Hazlitt's remark that the object of the drama is to trace man's passions "whether erroneous or not" ("On the German Drama," *Works*, VI, 362).

not so fine a thing as philosophy— For the same reason that an eagle is not so fine a thing as a truth.

[Imagination and the character of the poet]

[November 22, 1817] Men of Genius are great as certain etherial Chemicals operating on the Mass of neutral intellect—but they have not any individuality, any determined Character. . . . I am certain of nothing but of the holiness of the Heart's affections and the truth of Imagination— What the imagination seizes as Beauty must be truth . . . The Imagination may be compared to Adam's dream—he awoke and found it truth. I am the more zealous in this affair, because I have never yet been able to perceive how anything can be known for truth by consequitive reasoning—and yet it must be. Can it be that even the greatest Philosopher ever arrived at his goal without putting aside numerous objections?

[December 21, 1817] The excellence of every art is its intensity, capable of making all disagreeables evaporate, from their being in close relationship with Beauty and Truth.[2] Examine "King Lear," and you will find this exemplified throughout . . . Several things dove-tailed in my mind, and at once it struck me what quality went to form a Man of Achievement, especially in Literature, and which Shakespeare possessed so enormously—I mean *Negative Capability*, that is, when a man is capable of being in uncertainties, mysteries, doubts, without any irritable reaching after fact and reason—Coleridge, for instance, would let go by a fine isolated verisimilitude caught from the Penetralium of mystery, from being incapable of remaining content with half-knowledge. This pursued through volumes would perhaps take us no further than this, that with a great poet the sense of Beauty overcomes every other consideration, or rather obliterates all consideration.[3]

[October 27, 1818] As to the poetical Character itself (I mean that sort of which, if I am anything, I am a Member; that sort distinguished from the Wordsworthian or egotistical sublime; which is a thing per se and stands alone) it is not itself—it has no self—it is everything and nothing— It has no character—it enjoys light and shade; it lives in gusto, be it foul or fair, high or low, rich or poor, mean or elevated— It has as much delight in conceiving an Iago as an Imogen. What shocks the virtuous philosopher, delights the camelion Poet.[4] It does no harm from its relish of the dark side of things any more than from its taste for the bright one; because they both end in speculation.

---

[2] "Intensity" here, and frequently elsewhere in Keats, seems to have a meaning similar to Hazlitt's term "gusto" (see above, p. 301). In a state of intense imaginative gusto, the nature and "identity" of an object is grasped so vividly that only those associations or qualities that are strictly relevant to its central significance appear; the irrelevant or discordant aspects (the "disagreeables") "evaporate"; and the meaning and character of the object (its "truth") is expressed with so vital a grace that it is also seen as "beauty."

[3] The two foregoing sentences might be interpreted thus: In our life of uncertainties, where no one system or formula can explain everything, what is needed is an imaginative openness of mind and heightened receptivity to reality in its full (though elusive) concreteness. This, however, involves negating one's own *ego*, or submerging the self-centered consciousness of one's own identity, in favor of something more important: an awareness and savor of the reality outside us. To be dissatisfied with the insights achieved thus, to discard them unless they can be wrenched into part of a systematic structure of one's own making, is an egoistic assertion of one's own identity. But for a great poet, a sympathetic readiness and an absorption in the essential significance of his object—caught and relished in an awareness of its "beauty"—overcome considerations irrelevant to the central insight (considerations which an "irritable reaching after fact and reason" might otherwise itch to pursue); indeed it "obliterates" all deliberate consideration, all "consequitive reasoning."

[4] Richard Woodhouse, the friend to whom Keats's letter is addressed, wrote the following comment on it: "I believe him to be right with regard to his own Poetical Character— And I perceive clearly the distinction he draws between himself & those of the Wordsworth School. . . . The highest order of Poet . . . will have so high an imag[ination] that he will be able to throw his own soul into any object he sees or imagines, so as to see, feel, be sensible of, & express, all that the object itself wo[ul]d see, feel, be sensible of, or express—& he will speak out of that object so that his own self will with the Exception of the Mechanical part be "annihilated."—And it is the excess of this power that I suppose Keats to speak, when he says he has no identity— As a poet, and when the fit is upon him, this is true— . . . He has affirmed that he can conceive of a billiard Ball that it may have a sense of delight from its own roundness, smoothness, volubility, & the rapidity of its motion" (Woodhouse's *Scrapbook*; printed in *The Keats Circle* [ed. H. E. Rollins, Cambridge, Mass., 1948], I, 58).

A Poet is the most unpoetical of any thing in existence; because he has no Identity—he is continually infor[ming] and filling some other Body— The Sun, the Moon, the Sea and Men and Women who are creatures of impulse are poetical and have about them an unchangeable attribute—the poet has none; no identity—he is certainly the most unpoetical of all God's Creatures. If then he has no self, and if I am a Poet, where is the Wonder that I should say I would write no more? Might I not at that very instant have been cogitating on the Characters of Saturn and Ops? It is a wretched thing to confess; but is a very fact that not one word I ever utter can be taken for granted as an opinion growing out of my identical nature—how can it, when I have no nature? When I am in a room with People if I ever am free from speculating on creations of my own brain, then not myself goes home to myself: but the identity of every one in the room begins to press upon me [so] that I am in a very little time annihilated—not only among Men; it would be the same in a Nursery of children.

[*Wordsworth*]

[February 3, 1818] It may be said that we ought to read our Contemporaries—that Wordsworth &c. should have their due from us. But, for the sake of a few fine imaginative or domestic passages, are we to be bullied into a certain Philosophy engendered in the whims of an Egotist.[5]—Every man has his speculations, but every man does not brood and peacock over

[5] Cf. Hazlitt's remarks on Wordsworth, above, p. 301.

them till he makes a false coinage and deceives himself. Many a man can travel to the very bourne of Heaven, and yet want confidence to put down his half-seeing. Sancho will invent a Journey heavenward as well as anybody. We hate poetry that has a palpable design upon us—and if we do not agree, seems to put its hand in its breeches pocket. Poetry should be great and unobtrusive, a thing which enters into one's soul, and does not startle it or amaze it with itself, but with its subject.—How beautiful are the retired flowers! how would they lose their beauty were they to throng into the highway crying out, "admire me I am a violet!—dote upon me I am a primrose!" Modern poets differ from the Elizabethans in this. Each of the moderns like an Elector of Hanover governs his petty state, and knows how many straws are swept daily from the Causeways in all his dominions and has a continual itching that all the Housewives should have their coppers well scoured: the antients were Emperors of vast Provinces, they had only heard of the remote ones and scarcely cared to visit them.—I will cut all this—I will have no more of Wordsworth or Hunt in particular. . . . Old Matthew spoke to [Wordsworth] some years ago on some nothing, and because he happens in an Evening Walk to imagine the figure of the Old Man—he must stamp it down in black and white, and it is henceforth sacred—I don't mean to deny Wordsworth's grandeur and Hunt's merit, but I mean to say we need not be teazed with grandeur and merit when we can have them uncontaminated and unobtrusive.

EDGAR ALLAN POE   (1809-1849)

Poe is significant for his position as an innovator in the history of American criticism. Moreover, his pronouncements on the short story and his suggestive study of versification ("The Rationale of Verse") have important intrinsic value. Nevertheless, his general critical outlook, when viewed in the perspective of Western criticism as a whole, is mainly significant as one of the more extreme examples of a romantic tendency of thought —the tendency to stress imaginative and emotional intensity as the basic criterion in poetry. Poe proclaimed the imagination as the "soul" of poetry; this is perhaps his central thesis. But, unlike Hazlitt, Poe never tried to indicate exactly what the imagination is, or how it works as a psychological process. It is possible to feel that for him the term was not so inclusive as it was for such critics as Hazlitt or Coleridge, and that Poe's use of the word, despite a careful tracing by two of his critics, is less valuable as critical analysis than as a symptom of the conventional romantic connotations associated with the term.

As his essay "The Poetic Principle" indicates, the qualities for which Poe looked in poetry are visionary magic, suggestive strangeness, brevity, and immediate emotional impact. Hence his characteristic assertion that "a long poem does not exist" since emotional excitement cannot always be retained to the highest degree. The statement is characteristic of a general romantic tendency, in the nineteenth century, to narrow the word "poetry" until it suggested merely short, lyric verse, or even isolated lines of verse. This viewpoint tends to date "The Poetic Principle" and make it interesting chiefly as a signpost pointing the way to late nineteenth-century estheticism. For Poe, in reacting against the crude and unsophisticated moral didacticism in the American periodical criticism of his day, swung over to an opposite position only slightly more sophisticated, and one which, despite his own technical accomplishments as a craftsman, scarcely bears serious comparison with

EDGAR ALLAN POE. Born of a theatrical family in Boston and left an orphan at an early age, Poe was adopted and brought up by John Allan, a Virginia tobacco-exporter. He attended school in England, was a student for a short while at the University of Virginia, entered the army (1827) for two years, and was later a military cadet at West Point (1830-31), from which he was dismissed for disregarding rules. He henceforth led a somewhat irregular life. In addition to writing verse and his gifted short stories, he edited various journals, and took an active interest in practical literary criticism.

Complete Works (ed. J. A. Harrison, 1902); Selections from the Critical Writings (ed. F. C. Prescott, 1909). For discussion, see: M. Alterton, Origins of Poe's Critical Theory, Univ. of Iowa Humanistic Studies, 11 (1925), No. 3; M. Alterton and H. Craig, Edgar Allan Poe (1935); Charles Baudelaire, Baudelaire on Poe: Critical Papers (ed. L. and F. E. Hyslop, State College, Pa., 1952); J. Chiari, Symbolism from Poe to Mallarmé (1956); Norman Foerster, American Criticism (1928); J. W. Krutch, Edgar Allan Poe (1926); and E. W. Parks, Edgar Allan Poe as Literary Critic (Athens, Ga., 1964).

the contributions of the major English and German critics of the later eighteenth and early nineteenth centuries, with whom he is ocasionally associated.

Poe has, for example, been bracketed as a disciple of Coleridge. Actually, he has little in common with Coleridge except for certain broad similarities that apply to many romantic critics, and except for the fact that he took over the externals and terminology of a few of Coleridge's points. Thus beauty, for Coleridge, was an "imitation" of truth, the transmitting of truth into a special medium and under special circumstances. And if Coleridge said that "the immediate" end of Poetry is pleasure rather than truth, he made it very plain that the *ultimate* end of poetry is truth, and that the "immediate" pleasure desired is a pleasure that rests on it. Poe, in "The Poetic Principle," seems hardly to note the difference between maintaining that the "ultimate object" of poetry is "truth" and the naïve demand that every poem should have a "moral." If Coleridge opposed a crude didacticism by a more enlightened analysis, Poe opposed it simply by postulating "beauty" (which he did not really succeed in defining) as something that can exist quite apart from truth, and considered any critic "theory-mad" who tries to reconcile "the obstinate oils and waters of Poetry and Truth." Poe's standpoint illustrates an attitude that is one of the by-products of romanticism—an attitude that was to affect literary criticism down to the first World War, and to affect much more the history of poetical taste and general reaction to poetry from the early nineteenth century to the present day.

The Poetic Principle

IN SPEAKING of the Poetic Principle, I have no design to be either thorough or profound. While discussing, very much at random, the essentiality of what we call Poetry, my principal purpose will be to cite for consideration, some few of those minor English or American poems which best suit my own taste, or which, upon my own fancy, have left the most definite impression. By "minor poems" I mean, of course, poems of little length. And here, in the beginning, permit me to say a few words in regard to a somewhat peculiar principle which, whether rightfully or wrongfully, has always had its influence in my own critical estimate of the poem. I hold that a long poem does not exist. I maintain that the phrase, "a long poem," is simply a flat contradiction in terms.

I need scarcely observe that a poem deserves

The Poetic Principle. First published in 1848.

its title only inasmuch as it excites, by elevating the soul. The value of the poem is in the ratio of this elevating excitement. But all excitements are, through a psychal necessity, transient. That degree of excitement which would entitle a poem to be so called at all, cannot be sustained throughout a composition of any great length. After the lapse of half an hour, at the very utmost, it flags—fails—a revulsion ensues—and then the poem is, in effect, and in fact, no longer such.

There are, no doubt, many who have found difficulty in reconciling the critical dictum that the "Paradise Lost" is to be devoutly admired throughout, with the absolute impossibility of maintaining for it, during perusal, the amount of enthusiasm which that critical dictum would demand. This great work, in fact, is to be regarded as poetical, only when, losing sight of that vital requisite in all works of Art, Unity, we view it merely as a series of minor poems.

If, to preserve its Unity—its totality of effect or impression—we read it (as would be necessary) at a single sitting, the result is but a constant alternation of excitement and depression. After a passage of what we feel to be true poetry, there follows, inevitably, a passage of platitude which no critical prejudgment can force us to admire; but if, upon completing the work, we read it again, omitting the first book (that is to say, commencing with the second), we shall be surprised at now finding that admirable which we before condemned—that damnable which we had previously so much admired. It follows from all this that the ultimate, aggregate, or absolute effect of even the best epic under the sun is a nullity;—and this is precisely the fact.

In regard to the "Iliad," we have, if not positive proof, at least very good reason for believing it intended as a series of lyrics; but, granting the epic intention, I can say only that the work is based in an imperfect sense of art. The modern epic is, of the supposititious ancient model, but an inconsiderate and blindfold imitation. But the day of these artistic anomalies is over. If, at any time, any very long poems *were* popular in reality—which I doubt—it is at least clear that no very long poem will ever be popular again.

That the extent of a poetical work is, *ceteris paribus*, the measure of its merit, seems undoubtedly, when we thus state it, a proposition sufficiently absurd—yet we are indebted for it to the Quarterly Reviews. Surely there can be nothing in mere size, abstractly considered—there can be nothing in mere bulk, so far as a volume is concerned which has so continuously elicited admiration from these saturnine pamphlets! A mountain, to be sure, by the mere sentiment of physical magnitude which it conveys, does impress us with a sense of the sublime—but no man is impressed after *this* fashion by the material grandeur of even "The Columbiad." Even the Quarterlies have not instructed us to be so impressed by it. *As yet*, they have not *insisted* on our estimating Lamartine by the cubic foot, or Pollok by the pound—but what else are we to, *infer* from their continual prating about "sustained effort"? If, by "sustained effort," any little gentleman has accomplished an epic, let us frankly commend him

for the effort,—if this indeed be a thing commendable,—but let us forbear praising the epic on the effort's account. It is to be hoped that common sense, in the time to come, will prefer deciding upon a work of Art, rather by the impression it makes—by the effect it produces—than by the time it took to impress the effect, or by the amount of "sustained effort" which had been found necessary in effecting the impression. The fact is, that perseverance is one thing and genius quite another; nor can all the Quarterlies in Christendom confound them. By and by, this proposition, with many which I have been just urging, will be received as self-evident. In the mean time, by being generally condemned as falsities they will not be essentially damaged as truths.

On the other hand, it is clear that a poem may be improperly brief. Undue brevity degenerates into mere epigrammatism. A *very* short poem, while now and then producing a brilliant or vivid, never produces a profound or enduring, effect. There must be the steady pressing down of the stamp upon the wax. . . .

While the epic mania—while the idea that, to merit in poetry, prolixity is indispensable—has, for some years past, been gradually dying out of the public mind, by mere dint of its own absurdity, we find it succeeded by a heresy too palpably false to be long tolerated, but one which, in the brief period it has already endured, may be said to have accomplished more in the corruption of our Poetical Literature than all its other enemies combined. I allude to the heresy of *The Didactic*. It has been assumed, tacitly and avowedly, directly and indirectly, that the ultimate object of all Poetry is Truth. Every poem, it is said, should inculcate a moral; and by this moral is the poetical merit of the work to be adjudged. We Americans especially have patronized this happy idea; and we Bostonians, very especially, have developed it in full. We have taken it into our heads that to write a poem simply for the poem's sake, and to acknowledge such to have been our design, would be to confess ourselves radically wanting in the true Poetic dignity and force:—but the simple fact is, that, would we but permit ourselves to look into our own souls, we should immediately there discover that under the sun there neither exists nor *can* exist any work more thoroughly dignified—more supremely noble than this very poem—this poem *per se*—this poem which is a poem and nothing more—this poem written solely for the poem's sake.

With as deep a reverence for the True as ever inspired the bosom of man, I would, nevertheless, limit in some measure its modes of inculcation. I would limit to enforce them. I would not enfeeble them by dissipation. The demands of Truth are severe; she has no sympathy with the myrtles. All *that* which is so indispensable in Song, is precisely all *that* with which *she* has nothing whatever to do. It is but making her a flaunting paradox to wreathe her in gems and flowers. In enforcing a truth we need severity rather than efflorescence of language. We must be simple, precise, terse. We must be cool, calm, unimpassioned. In a word, we must be in that mood, which, as nearly as possible, is the exact converse of the poetical. He must be blind, indeed, who does not perceive the radical and chasmal differences between the truthful and the poetical modes of inculcation. He must be theory-mad beyond redemption who, in spite of these differences, shall still persist in attempting to reconcile the obstinate oils and waters of Poetry and Truth.

Dividing the world of mind into its three most immediately obvious distinctions, we have the Pure Intellect, Taste, and the Moral Sense. I place Taste in the middle, because it is just this position which in the mind it occupies. It holds intimate relations with either extreme, but from the Moral Sense is separated by so faint a difference that Aristotle has not hesitated to place some of its operations among the virtues themselves. Nevertheless, we find the *offices* of the trio marked with a sufficient distinction. Just as the intellect concerns itself with Truth, so Taste informs us of the Beautiful, while the Moral Sense is regardful of Duty. Of this latter, while Conscience teaches the obligation, and Reason the expediency, Taste contents herself with displaying the charms:—waging war upon Vice solely on the ground of her deformity—her disproportion—her animosity to the fitting, to the appropriate, to the harmonious—in a word, to Beauty. . . .

The Poetic Sentiment, of course, may develop itself in various modes—in Painting, in Sculpture, in Architecture, in the Dance—very especially in Music,—and very peculiarly and with a wide field, in the composition of the Landscape Garden. Our present theme, however, has regard only to its manifestation in words. And here let me speak briefly on the topic of rhythm. Contenting myself with the certainty that Music, in its various modes of metre, rhythm, and rhyme, is of so vast a moment in Poetry as never to be wisely rejected—is so vitally important an adjunct, that he is simply silly who declines its assistance, I will not now pause to maintain its absolute essentiality. It is in Music, perhaps, that the soul most nearly attains the great end for which, when inspired by the Poetic Sentiment, it struggles—the creation of supernal Beauty. It *may* be, indeed, that here this sublime end is, now and then, attained *in fact*. We are often made to feel, with a shivering delight, that from an earthly harp are stricken notes which *cannot* have been unfamiliar to the angels. And thus there can be little doubt that in the union of Poetry with Music in its popular sense, we shall find the widest field for the Poetic development. The old Bards and Minnesingers had advantages which we do not possess—and Thomas Moore, singing his own songs, was, in the most legitimate manner, perfecting them as poems.

To recapitulate, then:—I would define, in brief, the Poetry of words as *The Rhythmical Creation of Beauty*. Its sole arbiter is Taste. With the Intellect or with the Conscience, it has only collateral relations. Unless incidentally, it has no concern whatever either with Duty or with Truth.

A few words, however, in explanation. *That* pleasure which is at once the most pure, the most elevating, and the most intense, is derived, I maintain, from the contemplation of the Beautiful. In the contemplation of Beauty we alone find it possible to attain that pleasurable elevation, or excitement *of the soul*, which we recognize as the Poetic Sentiment, and which is so easily distinguished from Truth, which is the satisfaction of Reason, or from Passion, which is the excitement of the Heart. I make Beauty, therefore,—using the word as inclusive of the sublime,—I make Beauty the province of the poem, simply because it is an obvious rule of Art that effects should be made to spring as directly as possible from their causes:—no one as yet having been weak enough to deny that the peculiar elevation in question is at least *most readily* attainable in the poem. It by no means follows, however, that the incitements of Passion, or the precepts of Duty, or even the lessons of Truth, may not be introduced into a poem, and with advantage; for they may subserve, incidentally, in various ways, the general purposes of the work:—but the true artist will always contrive to tone them down in proper subjection to that *Beauty* which is the atmosphere and the real essence of the poem. . . .

2. *Romantic Transcendentalism,*
and the Organic View of Nature

SAMUEL TAYLOR COLERIDGE (1772-1834)

T HE CHARACTER and value of Coleridge's writings are among the baffling problems in the history of literature. It is generally felt that he never fulfilled his promise, and there remains the debatable question of how much capacity he actually possessed. His own contemporaries felt the same admiration and misgivings that readers have since expressed. Men of talent spoke of Coleridge's genius and of the wonder with which people heard him. But his discourse became vaguer as the years passed; relatively little of what reached print was very coherent, and his admirers began to regard him with the same nostalgia with which his old school friend, Charles Lamb, viewed Coleridge's boyhood:

> Come back into memory, like as thou wert in the day-spring of thy fancies, with hope like a fiery column before thee—the dark pillar not yet turned—Samuel Taylor Coleridge—Logician, Metaphysician, Bard!—How have I seen the casual passer through the Cloisters, stand still, intranced with admiration (while he weighed the disproportion between the *speech* and the *garb* of the young Mirandula), to hear thee unfold . . . the mysteries of Jamblichus, or Plotinus (for even in those years thou waxedest not pale at such philosophic draughts), or reciting Homer in his Greek, or Pindar—while the walls of the old Grey Friars re-echoed to the accents of the *inspired charity-boy!*

Coleridge inspired the feeling, at first, that he was always on the point of doing something transcendent in metaphysics and esthetics; later, the feeling that he could have done so at one time. As the Victorian age got under way, he then passed into the realm of legend. However, during the last half cen-

SAMUEL TAYLOR COLERIDGE. Left fatherless at an early age, Coleridge entered the school at Christ's Hospital as a charity student, showed remarkable precocity, and quickly developed his lifelong habits of reading widely and discoursing to astonished auditors. After attending Cambridge, he met Robert Southey, and became interested for a while in the "pantisocratic" scheme for establishing an ideal community in America. His acquaintance with Wordsworth (1795) had more concrete results; together they worked on the *Lyrical Ballads* (1798), and then journeyed to the Continent. Before 1802 most of his poetry, including his plays, had been written. After studying metaphysics in Germany, Coleridge returned, became connected for a while with the *Morning Post,* lectured and wrote on politics, religion, and poetry, and was given an annuity by his friends, Josiah and Thomas Wedgwood. His life had been desultory since he left Cambridge: even before his trip to the Continent he had worked as a lecturer, journalist, preacher, and had even tried farming. During the next fifteen years, despite his increasing addiction to opium, he wrote and lectured prolifically; he finally overcame the opium habit to some extent, was assisted

tury the publication of long-forgotten works has at least tended to substantiate the range of his mind and the scattered brilliance of his insights. Closely as some of his works have been examined, his prose writings as a whole still constitute one of the most challenging unexplored territories in the history of critical thinking.

Yet to interpret Coleridge's criticism has been a scholarly pastime for over a century, and particularly within the last forty years or so. Certainly one of the reasons for his attractiveness is his attempt to combine so many different attitudes and to pursue so many problems. It is always possible, therefore, for one to find statements by Coleridge that are congenial with one's own personal beliefs. Because of the fragmentary and elusive quality of much of his writing, there is the constant temptation to abstract his statements from their context and develop them in whatever way one wishes, rather than to reconcile them with other attitudes of Coleridge and then try to discern a common basis and a common aim underlying all his critical attitudes. Another temptation—at least for scholars—has been to concentrate too exclusively on source-hunting. Certainly Coleridge's criticism provides a happy hunting ground for this purpose. In his early years he fell under the influence of David Hartley and the doctrine of the association of ideas, and later under the influence of Berkeley, Spinoza, the Neoplatonism of Plotinus and Jakob Boehme, and the German philosophy of his own day, especially that of Kant and Schelling. From these philosophers and from others Coleridge borrowed terms, phrases, and ideas with embarrassing freedom. But it would be a mistake to assume that if Coleridge took over a particular term or idea from Kant, for example, we have then only to turn to Kant for the explanation of what Coleridge was trying to say on this subject. Actually, he tended to take over terms or concepts from others because they seemed, for the time being, to help fill out or to fit in with more

---

financially by friends, and spent the rest of his life studying, writing occasionally, and talking with admiring visitors.

Although there is no definitive edition, there is a substantial collection in the *Complete Works* (ed. W. G. T. Shedd, 1858), and the following works contain his literary criticism: *Biographia Literaria* (ed. J. Shawcross, Oxford, 1907); *Literary Remains* (ed. H. N. Coleridge, 1836-39); *Anima Poetae* (ed. E. H. Coleridge, 1895); *Specimens of the Table-Talk* (ed. H. N. Coleridge, 1835); *Shakespearian Criticism* (ed. T. M. Raysor, Cambridge, Mass., 1930); *Miscellaneous Criticism* (ed. Raysor, Cambridge, Mass., 1936). Other relevant works include: *Letters* (ed. Earl L. Griggs, Oxford, 1956-59); *Notebooks* (ed. Kathleen Coburn, 1957-62 [in progress]); *Coleridge on Logic and Learning* (ed. Alice Snyder, New Haven, 1929); *Treatise on Method* (ed. Alice Snyder, 1934); *Philosophical Lectures* (ed. K. Coburn, Philosophical Library, 1949). Commentary, dealing with his criticism, includes: the introduction and notes to Shawcross's edition of the *Biographia Literaria*, still heavily relied upon by critics of Coleridge; J. A. Appleyard, *Coleridge's Philosophy of Literature* (Cambridge, Mass., 1965); W. J. Bate, *Coleridge* (1968); R. H. Fogle, *The Idea of Coleridge's Criticism* (Berkeley, 1962); J. R. de J. Jackson, *Method and Imagination in Coleridge's Criticism* (Cambridge, Mass., 1969); J. H. Muirhead, *Coleridge as Philosopher* (1930); and I. A. Richards, *Coleridge on Imagination* (1934), possibly more valuable as a document in Richards's criticism than as an examination of Coleridge.

general ideas of his own—ideas that were quite different, in some cases, from those of the original writer. To take his borrowings as a starting point is not only futile but misleading. The student should refuse to be intimidated by the accretion of source studies that have barnacled over Coleridge's criticism, and should try to approach him as directly as possible.

2

Art, for Coleridge, is the "imitator" of nature; it tries to offer an "abridgement" of reality. In speaking of an imitation one cannot get very far without first understanding what it imitates. The interpretation of Coleridge's critical writing suggested here is that it comprises an attempt—a challenging but incomplete and uneven attempt—to combine the concreteness and the organic vitalism that the romantic movement prized, with the traditional values of classical rationalism and idealism; to support this union with a metaphysical basis; to outline a psychology appropriate to it; and then to apply it to the understanding and evaluating of art.

On the one hand, therefore, we have Coleridge emphasizing the natural, concrete world, not as a shadow of the ideal, still less as a subjective creation of one's own mind, but as an actual, vital, and organic unfolding of process. Accordingly, art—as the "mediator" between nature and man, as the explainer and transmitter of reality into terms of human feelings and reactions —must not lose its grasp of the concretely organic and become merely abstract. Much of Coleridge's preference for Shakespeare over the classical dramatists rests on this point. On the other hand, concrete life cannot exist apart from universal form. What makes a plant a plant, for example,— what distinguishes the plant from the soil, water, and sunlight of which it is composed—is the controlling *form* that funnels, unifies, and spins out these materials, so to speak, into a different thing, guiding and shaping them into a new individuality. And the finished, particular plant, therefore, is nothing except as it draws its character and existence from the form; it has no function apart from the form, the universal, any more than the lungs can have a function or significance apart from the atmosphere they breathe.

The reality that we call "nature," in short, is neither to be found in the particular, the concrete, by itself, apart from the form, nor in the universal by itself. Instead, the reality of nature is to be found in a *process*, or *activity*, in which the universal and the particular fulfill each other. The universal gives to the particular its form, thus permitting it to flower into existence and become what it is. In a similar way, the universal must have the particular in order to fulfill *itself*. It cannot perform its function as a controlling form unless there is something being acted upon, something to *be* controlled and formed. In a sense, Coleridge's standpoint is very much like Aristotle's principle that form and matter exist only through each other. Yet Coleridge is always maintaining that he is a Platonist, not an Aristotelian. In fact, his basic aim seems to have been to try to reconcile the concrete, organic natural-ism in which he believed with the Platonic doctrine that universal forms or "ideas" have an absolute existence of their own and can be known by man through reason. That is partly why he toyed with as many different philoso-phers as he did, hoping that each, in turn, might suggest how to reconcile these two convictions. The whole problem of Coleridge's Platonism leads to many complications. But we might loosely summarize his position as follows: universal forms or "ideas" do exist by themselves, as Plato said, and can be known by reason; but they become "real," they fulfill their potentiality and become truly themselves, only as they have something with and through which to work—only as they are functioning as creative and guiding prin-ciples. Unity, for example, exists as a universal form; but it cannot realize itself completely unless it is in the process of unifying opposition—of unify-ing what is diverse. Here Coleridge was much influenced by the Neoplatonism of Plotinus and Jakob Boehme.

3

Nature, then, should be regarded as concrete activity, organically evolving in accordance with universal forms. Hence Coleridge's emphasis on thinking in terms of "an *act*, instead of a *thing* or a *substance*." Art, therefore, as the "imitator" of nature, takes neither the form alone nor the concrete, indi-vidual thing alone as its model. It is directed to the focal point in which each substantiates and permits the other to realize itself. Art imitates a *process*; it tries to reveal the universal at work "within the thing, that which is active through form and figure"—to "interpret and understand the symbol, that the wings of the air-sylph are forming within the skin of the caterpillar." This is the central theme in Coleridge's Shakespearean criticism—that Shakespeare had "the *universal* which is potentially in each *particular*, opened out to him . . . not as an abstraction of observation of a variety of men, but as the substance capable of endless modifications." Shakespeare thus contrasts with Beaumont and Fletcher, whose dramatic characters are types pieced together from observing different men. It is as though one might "fit together a quarter of an orange, a quarter of an apple, and the like of a lemon and a pomegranate, and make it look like one round diverse colored fruit. But nature, who works *from within by evolution and assimilation* ac-cording to a law, cannot do it. Nor could Shakespeare, for he too worked in the spirit of nature, by *evolving the germ within* . . ."

Art, then, imitates the essential process of nature, the reconciliation of uni-versal and particular. But it does not do so by directly "copying" its model, which would be an "idle rivalry" with nature. It does so by *translating* its insight into a given medium: into two-dimensional line and color in a paint-ing, for example; into the unifying of sounds by rhythm and harmony in music; or, in a drama, into words, metaphors, verse-rhythms, and the interplay of characters and incidents, rounded and harmonized to an ordered end. In all such instances, art is characterized by a process of unified order emerging through what Coleridge calls "multëity"—a "fusion to force many into one." Therefore, in portraying its object, art does not offer a dead "copy"; but it duplicates the active principle of nature by presenting, within its *own* given medium, the same process of form organically controlling the diverse, concrete details. It is in this sense that Coleridge states that the symbols in art should be "living," that they should actively contain within themselves "the germinal causes in Nature," and that a true symbol "always partakes of the reality that it renders intelligible."

By thus translating and "abridging" reality into symbols that strike home to the human mind and heart, art serves as the "mediator" between nature and man. It achieves the "beautiful." Now beauty is not a mere subjective state of mind; this is the central point of the three essays, *On the Principles of Genial Criticism.* Rather, beauty arises only when what is being conceived is a universal form emerging through concrete diversity or "multëity." On the other hand, beauty is not truth, as it was for Keats. Beauty is a *way of approaching* the true and the good: it is a way of rendering truth *realizable* to the total mind, through the medium of humanly persuasive symbols. "Beauty is the shorthand hieroglyphic of Truth—the mediator between Truth and Feeling, the Head and the Heart." It is a means, in other words, rather than an ultimate end: "As light to the eye, even such is beauty to the mind . . . [a] *calling on* the soul."

4

No aspect of Coleridge's criticism has so intrigued modern readers as his theory of the imagination. Discussion of it, however, has too often been confined merely to stating that the imagination, for Coleridge, "fuses" things together, and is "creative." The same remark could be made of any number of other critics. The important point is what it "fuses," and what—and how far—it "creates." Coleridge's actual remarks on the imagination, however, are surprisingly few, brief, and scattered. Perhaps the least satisfactory discussion is the one most frequently quoted: a page (see p. 387) that concludes Chapter 13 of the *Biographia Literaria,* with its unclear distinction between "primary" and "secondary" imagination. He had considered publishing here, Coleridge tells us, a hundred-page discussion of the imagination, and it is led up to with much fanfare. But he decided to omit it because it would be "unintelligible" and printed only the conclusion. The reader may pardonably feel that this famous concluding passage is hardly more than an empty April-fool purse in his path. For it says very little indeed.

Coleridge's general theory of mind, in fact, should be approached, not as an independent subject by itself, but as a corollary to the more basic conceptions summarized in the last section above. In his psychology, the cornerstone—at least the premise that he continued to stress most strongly —is his distinction between "reason" and "understanding." The understanding is directed toward the concrete world—to the world we know through our senses. It classifies our sense impressions, and our associations and feeling drawn from these impressions; it abstracts and generalizes on the basis of them. Reason, on the other hand, is the direct insight into the universal. The distinction, as Coleridge says, is similar in a general way to that of the Platonic tradition, particularly common in the Renaissance, between "discursive" reason, which generalizes from sense-impressions, and "intuitive reason." [1]

Thus, in order to explain the means by which the mind conceives both the ultimate universal forms and at the same time the concrete, particular world, Coleridge postulated two different aspects of mind directed to each: reason, on the one hand, and the senses and understanding on the other. But thus to divide the mind into two separate capacities violated his own organic conception of nature. For nature is neither the universal nor the particular, but a process in which each declares and sustains the other. If the human mind were to realize this process, therefore, it could do so only through a "completing power," as he called it, which would join together what is grasped by the different aspects of the mind. This "completing power" of the mind he called the "imagination." In short, the material world has, in the human mind, a corresponding capacity in the senses and understanding. The universal has its counterpart in reason. And the creative activity of nature, which unites universal and particular, has *its* counterpart in the imagination, which "fuses" together the insights of reason with the impressions of the senses and the conceptions of the understanding. In order to stress this unique function of the imagination, Coleridge developed a distinction between "fancy" and "imagination," which was at one time mistakenly thought to have had a "German" source. But the distinction is of English origin, and had already become familiar in English criticial terminology during the later eighteenth century. Its importance has probably been overrated; as Coleridge himself said, his "grievous fault" was that he was too much inclined to make and labor distinctions. What he was trying to do was to cut off the term "imagination" from its older meaning of an

---

[1] This distinction is often considered to be the same as that made by Kant between *Vernunft* (reason) and *Verstand* (understanding). Kant's distinction had much to do with that of Coleridge. Coleridge's theory of "understanding," moreover, is very similar to Kant's. The difference comes in the conception of "reason." For Kant, the ultimate "ideas" by which reason arranges and synthesizes the judgments of understanding are merely necessary hypotheses rather than realities known to exist outside the mind; whereas, for Coleridge, they do so exist, and are actually known by reason. It was largely on this ground that Coleridge distinguished his own thought from most of the German philosophy of the period.

"image-making" faculty that simply reproduces and combines images derived from sense impressions.

In anchoring and "incorporating the reason in images of sense," and at the same time elevating and "organizing . . . the flux of the senses by the permanent and self-circling energies of the reason," the imagination creates a dynamic and emerging balance of "the general, with the concrete; the idea, with the image; the individual with the representative," and thus achieves a true insight that duplicates the reality to which it is turned. To this extent, the imagination is like the creative impulse of nature itself. Hence Coleridge's remark that the imagination is "a repetition in the finite mind of the eternal act of creation" (he does not mean that it spins something out of nothing); and to this extent the imagination serves as "the living Power and prime agent of all human Perception." But the imagination has another basic function. For this creative activity interpenetrates all forms of human response. It not only joins reason with the senses and understanding, but, in permeating the "whole man," it can transmute the realization it has attained into emotional persuasion and mold and develop human feeling accordingly. The imagination converts its awareness, in other words, into "beauty"— "the mediator between Truth and Feeling, the Head and the Heart," into a *"calling on* the soul." This, in effect, is the ideal aim of art, as it draws upon the total function of the imagination: by employing "symbols" that convey truth to feeling, by infiltrating its insight into habitual motivations and harmonizing it "with that which is exclusively human," art can ideally serve as "the mediatress between, and reconciler of, nature and man." Art is ultimately to be valued, therefore, to the degree that it succeeds in attaining this end. Far from being an "expression of feeling," in the more extreme romantic sense, art seeks to inform, broaden, and develop feeling—to arouse "that sublime faculty by which a great mind becomes that on which it meditates." Indeed, feeling is nothing except as it is drawn outward into sympathetic participation, and takes on the character of what it conceives. It should be noted that the English romantic conception of the sympathetic imagination, to which Hazlitt gave the fullest expression, is a fundamental premise of Coleridge, particularly in his criticism of Shakespeare.

The scattered, critical fragments of this brilliant and often exasperating writer thus form a challenging pattern of thought that ultimately leads back to the greatest of classical premises: the conviction that truth is formative. *"The heart,"* as Coleridge wrote in what is perhaps the most profoundly suggestive of his remarks—"The *heart* should have *fed* upon the *truth,* as insects on a leaf, till it be tinged with the colour, and show its food in every . . . minutest fibre." Art, by infiltrating awareness into one's total response, by instilling a broadened realization into one's habitual ways of reacting and evaluating, thus "reconciles" man to reality, and by "assimilating him to Nature," is formative. It develops in man the imaginative capacity that serves as "the mediator between Truth and Feeling, the Head and the Heart," thus ministering to that end in which the "mind becomes that on which it meditates," and "truth . . . changes by domestication into power," into active fulfillment.

On the Principles of Genial Criticism concerning the Fine Arts[1]

PRELIMINARY ESSAY

IT WILL not appear complimentary to liken the Editors of Newspapers, in one respect, to galley-slaves; but the likeness is not the less apt on that account, and a simile is not expected *to go on all fours*. When storms blow high in the political atmosphere, the events of the day fill the sails, and the writer may draw in his oars, and let his brain rest; but when calm weather returns, then comes too "the tug of toil," hard work and little speed. Yet he not only sympathizes with the public joy, as a man and a citizen, but will seek to derive some advantages even for his editorial functions, from the cessation of battles and revolutions.[2] He cannot indeed hope to excite the same keen and promiscuous sensation as when he had to announce events, which by the mere bond of interest brought home the movements of monarchs and empires to every individual's counting-house and fire-side; but he consoles himself by the reflec-

tion, that these troublesome times occasioned thousands to acquire a habit, and almost a necessity, of reading, which it now becomes his object to retain by the gradual substitution of a milder stimulant, which though less intense is more permanent, and by its greater divergency no less than duration, even more pleasureable.— And how can he hail and celebrate the return of peace more worthily or more appropriately, than by exerting his best faculties to direct the taste and affections of his readers to the noblest works of peace? The tranquillity of nations permits our patriotism to repose. We are now allowed to think and feel as men, for all that may confer honor on human nature; not ignorant, meantime, that the greatness of a nation is by no distant links connected with the celebrity of its individual citizens—that whatever raises our country in the eyes of the civilized world, will make that country dearer and more venerable to its inhabitants, and thence actually more powerful, and more worthy of love and veneration. Add too (what in a great commercial city will not be deemed trifling or inappertinent) the certain reaction of the Fine Arts on the more immediate utilities of life. The transfusion of the fairest forms of Greece and Rome into the articles of hourly domestic use by Mr. Wedgwood; the impulse given to our engravings by Boydell;[3] the superior beauty of our patterns in the cotton manufactory, of our furniture and musical instruments, hold as honorable a rank in our archives of trade, as in those of taste.

Regarded from these points of view, painting and statuary call on our attention with superior claims. All the fine arts are different species of

---

[1] *On the Principles of Genial Criticism.* These three essays, which Coleridge himself felt were "the best things" he had yet written and which probably comprise his most important single contribution to the general criticism of art, were published in *Felix Farley's Bristol Journal* (August and September, 1814). He kept no copy, and in later years spoke of his regret at losing "those essays on beauty, which I wrote for a Bristol newspaper." There is something a little grotesque in these suggestive essays appearing in such an unlikely place. And it is characteristically Coleridgean that he started to write them in order to draw public attention to Washington Allston, an American painter whom Coleridge knew and liked and whose paintings were being exhibited in Bristol; but as Coleridge warmed to his subject, he quickly—and fortunately—forgot his original purpose, and after inserting a remark on poor Allston near the close of the first essay, remembered to mention him briefly only twice thereafter.

[2] The essays were written during a lull in the Napoleonic Wars.

[3] John Boydell, who had died a few years before, published prints and engravings.

poetry.[4] The same spirit speaks to the mind through different senses by manifestations of itself, appropriate to each. They admit therefore of a natural division into poetry of language (poetry in the emphatic sense, because less subject to the accidents and limitations of time and space); poetry of the ear, or music; and poetry of the eye, which is again subdivided into plastic poetry, or statuary, and graphic poetry, or painting. The common essence of all consists in the excitement of emotion for the immediate purpose of pleasure through the medium of beauty;[5] herein contra-distinguishing poetry from science, the immediate object and primary purpose of which is truth and possible utility. (The sciences indeed may and will give a high and pure pleasure; and the Fine Arts may lead to important truth, and be in various ways useful in the ordinary meaning of the word; but these are not the direct and characteristic ends, and we define things by their peculiar, not their common properties.)

Of the three sorts of poetry each possesses both exclusive and comparative advantages. The last (i.e. the plastic and graphic) is more permanent, and incomparably less dependent,[6] than the second, i.e. music; and though yielding in both these respects to the first, yet it regains its balance and equality of rank by the universality of its language. Michael Angelo and Raphael are for all beholders; Dante and Ariosto only for the readers of Italian. Hence though the title of these essays proposes, as their subject, the Fine Arts in general, which as far as the main principles are in question, will be realized in proportion to the writer's ability; yet the application and illustration of them will be confined to those of Painting and Statuary, and of these, chiefly to the former,

[4] Poetry in its broadest and original sense: imaginative creation.

[5] The key word here, as Coleridge later says (p. 366, below), is *immediate*. The *ultimate* aim of art, however, certainly involves truth. For genuine satisfaction can be secured and retained only through the awareness of truth or reality. And beauty is to be found in the heightened awareness of what is real and therefore significant; it is "the shorthand hieroglyphic of truth." It is in this sense that art excites emotion for the "*immediate* purpose of pleasure through the medium of beauty."

[6] That is, music has to depend upon performers and instruments, and is not generally available without having them first as a medium.

Which, like a second and more lovely nature,
Turns the blank canvas to a magic mirror;
That makes the absent present, and to shadows
Gives light, depth, substance, bloom, yea, thought
    and motion.[7]

To this disquisition two obstacles suggest themselves—that enough has been already written on the subject (this we may suppose an objection on the part of the reader) and the writer's own feeling concerning the grandeur and delicacy of the subject itself. As to the first, he would consider himself as having grossly failed in his duty to the public, if he had not carefully perused all the works on the Fine Arts known to him; and let it not be rashly attributed to self-conceit, if he dares avow his conviction that much remains to be done; a conviction indeed, which every author must entertain, who, whether from disqualifying ignorance or utter want of thought, does not act with the full consciousness of acting to no wise purpose. The works, that have hitherto appeared, have been either technical, and useful only to the Artist himself (if indeed useful at all) or employed in explaining by the laws of association the effects produced on the spectator by such and such impressions. In the latter, as in Alison, &c.,[8] much has been said well and truly; but the principle itself is too vague for practical guidance.—Association in philosophy is like the term stimulus in medicine; explaining everything, it explains nothing; and above all, leaves itself unexplained. It is an excellent charm to enable a man to talk *about* and *about* any thing he likes, and to make himself and his hearers as wise as before. Besides, the specific object of the present attempt is to enable the spectator to judge in the same spirit in which the Artist produced, or ought to have produced.

To the second objection, derived from the author's own feelings, he would find himself embarrassed in the attempt to answer, if the peculiar advantages of the subject itself did not aid him. His illustrations of his principles do

[7] Coleridge's play, *Remorse*, II, ii.

[8] Archibald Alison, in his *Essays on Taste* (1790), bases the imagination and all other mental functions on the association of ideas. See above, p. 273. Many of the problems of associationism, like those in modern psychology and sociology, were felt to be settled by the mere use of jargon ("like the term stimulus in medicine; explaining everything, it explains nothing").

not here depend on his own ingenuity—he writes for those, who can consult their own eyes and judgements. The various collections, as of Mr. Acraman (the father of the Fine Arts in this city [9]), of Mr. Davis, Mr. Gibbons, &c.; to which many of our readers either will have had, or may procure, access; and the admirable works exhibiting now by Allston; whose great picture, with his Hebe, landscape, and sea-piece, would of themselves suffice to elucidate the fundamental doctrines of color, ideal form, and grouping; assist the reasoner in the same way as the diagrams aid the geometrician, but far more and more vividly. The writer therefore concludes this his preparatory Essay by two postulates, the only ones he deems necessary for his complete intelligibility: the first, that the reader would steadily look into his own mind to know whether the principles stated are ideally true; the second, to look at the works or parts of the works mentioned, as illustrating or exemplifying the principle, to judge whether or how far it has been realized.

ESSAY SECOND

In Mathematics the definitions, of necessity, precede not only the demonstrations, but likewise the postulates and axioms: they are the rock, which at once forms the foundation and supplies the materials of the edifice. Philosophy, on the contrary, concludes with the definition: it is the result, the compendium, the remembrancer of all the preceding facts and inferences. Whenever, therefore, it appears in the front, it ought to be considered as a faint outline, which answers all its intended purposes, if only it circumscribe the subject, and direct the reader's anticipation toward the one road, on which he is to travel.

Examined from this point of view, the definition of poetry, in the preliminary Essay, as the regulative idea of all the Fine Arts, appears to me after many experimental applications of it to general illustrations and to individual instances, liable to no just *logical* reversion, or complaint: "the excitement of emotion for the purpose of *immediate* pleasure, through the medium of beauty."—But like all previous statements in Philosophy (as distinguished from Mathematics) it has the inconvenience of pre-

suming conceptions which do not perhaps consciously or distinctly exist. Thus, the former part of my definition might appear equally applicable to any object of our animal appetites, till by after-reasonings the attention has been directed to the full force of the word *"immediate"*; [10] and till the mind, by being led to refer discriminatingly to its own experience, has become conscious that all objects of mere desire constitute an interest (i.e. aliquid quod est inter hoc et aliud, or that which is between the agent and his motive), and which is therefore valued only as the means to the end. To take a trivial but unexceptionable instance, the venison is agreeable because it gives pleasure; while the Apollo Belvedere is not beautiful because it pleases, but it pleases us because it is beautiful.[11] The term, pleasure, is unfortunately so comprehensive, as frequently to become equivocal: and yet it is hard to discover a substitute. *Complacency*, which would indeed better express the intellectual nature of the enjoyment essentially involved in the sense of the beautiful, yet seems to preclude all emotion: and *delight*, on the other hand, conveys a comparative *degree* of pleasureable emotion, and is therefore unfit for a *general* definition, the object of which is to abstract the

[10] See above, note 4.

[11] Though Coleridge confuses his statement by saying hastily that "the venison is agreeable because it gives pleasure," his general point here, to judge from other remarks about beauty, seems simply this: Pleasure is not itself a specific "emotion," or reaction, or a single quality or characteristic. Instead, it is a *result*, or by-product, that comes from many different *kinds* of experiences. There are many different kinds of pleasures, therefore. Some pleasures arise when an experience appeals to only a *limited* part of the mind, or to a limited reaction or sensation. For this and for other reasons, they may be quite limited in their range of satisfaction, as well as quickly over. Venison may give a pleasure of this sort, not because it is beautiful, but because it may appeal to the sense of taste—at least the taste of some people—during the time it is consumed, provided it not be eaten too frequently. Other pleasures, however, may arise when a more complex and extensive range of experience and awareness is brought into play. And these pleasures increase in quality and also become more permanent to the degree that more facets of the mind are opened out and brought into activity, and to the degree that experiences become enlightened, guided, given order, or are seen to have value or meaning. Beauty thus gives pleasure by presenting what is valuable and true in such a way as to secure effective emotional response; it "pleases us *because* it is beautiful."

[9] Bristol.

kind. For this reason, we added the words "through the medium of beauty." But here the same difficulty recurs from the promiscuous use of the term, Beauty. Many years ago, the writer, in company with an accidental party of travellers, was gazing on a cataract of great height, breadth, and impetuosity, the summit of which appeared to blend with the sky and clouds, while the lower part was hidden by rocks and trees; and on his observing, that it was, in the strictest sense of the word, a sublime object, a lady present assented with warmth to the remark, adding— "Yes! and it is not only sublime, but beautiful and absolutely pretty."

And let not these distinctions be charged on the writer, as obscurity and needless sublety; for it is in the nature of all disquisitions on matters of taste, that the reasoner must appeal for his very premises to facts of feeling and of inner sense, which all men do not possess, and which many, who do possess and even act upon them, yet have never reflectively adverted to, have never made them objects of a full and distinct consciousness. The geometrician refers to certain figures in space, and to the power of describing certain lines, which are intuitive to all men, as men; and therefore his demonstrations are throughout *compulsory.* The moralist and the philosophic critic lay claim to no *positive,* but only to a *conditional* necessity. It is not necessary, that A or B should judge *at all* concerning poetry; but *if* he does, in order to a just taste, such and such faculties *must have* been developed in his mind. If a man, upon questioning his own experience, can detect no difference in *kind* between the enjoyment derived from the eating of turtle, and that from the perception of a new truth; if in *his* feelings a taste *for* Milton is essentially the same as the taste *of* mutton, he may still be a sensible and a valuable member of society; but it would be desecration to argue with him on the Fine Arts; and should he himself dispute on them, or even publish a book (and such books *have* been perpetrated within the memory of man) we can answer him only by silence, or a courteous waiving of the subject. To tell a blind man, declaiming concerning light and color, "you should wait till you have got eyes to see with," would indeed be telling the truth, but at the same time be acting a useless as well as an inhuman part. An English critic, who as-

sumes and proceeds on the identity in kind of the pleasures derived from the palate and from the intellect, and who literally considers *taste* to mean one and the same thing, whether it be the taste of venison, or a taste for Virgil, and who, in strict consistence with his principles, passes sentence on Milton as a tiresome poet, because he finds nothing *amusing* in the Paradise Lost (i.e. damnat Musas, quia animum a musis non divertunt) [12]—this taste-meter to the fashionable world gives a ludicrous portrait of an African belle, and concludes with a triumphant exclamation, "such is the ideal of beauty in Dahoma!" Now it is curious, that a very intelligent traveller, describing the low state of the human mind in this very country, gives as an instance, that in their whole language they have no word for beauty, or the beautiful; but say either it is nice, or it is good; doubtless, says he, because this very sense is as yet dormant, and the idea of beauty as little developed in their minds, as in that of an infant.—I give the substance of the meaning, not the words; as I quote both writers from memory.

There are few mental exertions more instructive, or which are capable of being rendered more entertaining, than the attempt to establish and exemplify the distinct meaning of terms, often confounded in common use, and considered as mere synonyms. Such are the words, Agreeable, Beautiful, Picturesque, Grand, Sublime: and to attach a distinct and separate sense to each of these, is a previous step of indispensable necessity to a writer, who would reason intelligibly, either to himself or to his readers, concerning the works of poetic genius, and the sources and the nature of the pleasure derived from them. But more especially on the essential difference of the beautiful and the agreeable, rests fundamentally the whole question, which assuredly must possess no vulgar or feeble interest for all who regard the dignity of their own nature: whether the noblest productions of human genius (such as the Iliad, the works of Shakspeare and Milton, the Pantheon, Raphael's Gallery, and Michael Angelo's Sistine Chapel, the Venus de Medici and the Apollo Belvedere, involving, of course, the human forms that ap-

[12] "He condemns the Muses because they do not divert his mind from the arts."

proximate to them in actual life) delight us merely by chance, from accidents of local associations—in short, please us because they please us (in which case it would be impossible either to praise or to condemn any man's taste, however opposite to our own, and we could be no more justified in assigning a corruption or absence of just taste to a man, who should prefer Blackmore to Homer or Milton, or the Castle Spectre to Othello,[13] than to the same man for preferring a black-pudding to a sirloin of beef); or whether there exists in the constitution of the human soul a sense, and a regulative principle, which may indeed be stifled and latent in some, and be perverted and denaturalized in others, yet is nevertheless universal in a given state of intellectual and moral culture; which is independent of local and temporary circumstances, and dependent only on the degree in which the faculties of the mind are developed; and which, consequently, it is our duty to cultivate and improve, as soon as the sense of its actual existence dawns upon us.

The space allotted to these Essays obliges me to defer this attempt to the following week: and I will now conclude by requesting the candid reader not altogether to condemn this second Essay, without having considered, that the ground-works of an edifice cannot be as sightly as the superstructure, and that the philosopher, unlike the architect, must lay his foundations in sight; unlike the musician, must tune his instruments in the hearing of his audience. TASTE is the intermediate faculty which connects the active with the passive powers of our nature, the intellect with the senses; and its appointed function is to elevate the *images* of the latter, while it realizes the *ideas* of the former.[14] We must therefore have learned what is peculiar to each, before we can understand that "Third something," which is formed by a harmony of both.

ESSAY THIRD

PEDANTRY consists in the use of words unsuitable to the time, place, and company. The language of the market would be as pedantic in the schools as that of the schools in the market. The mere man of the world, who insists that in a philosophic investigation of principles and general laws, no other terms should be used, than occur in common conversation, and with no greater definiteness, is at least as much a *pedant* as the man of learning, who, perhaps overrating the acquirements of his auditors, or deceived by his own familiarity with technical phrases, talks at the winetable with his eye fixed on his study or laboratory; even though, instead of desiring his wife to make the tea, he should bid her add to the usual quantum sufficit of Thea Sinensis the Oxyd of Hydrogen, saturated with Calorique. If (to use the old metaphor) both smell of the shop, yet the odour from the Russia-leather bindings of the good old *authentic-looking* folios and quartos is less annoying than the steams from the tavern or tallow-vat. Nay, though the pedantry should originate in vanity, yet a good-natured man would more easily tolerate the Fox-brush of ostentatious erudition ("the fable is somewhat musty") than the Sans-culotterie of a contemptuous ignorance, that assumes a merit from mutilation by a self-consoling grin at the pompous incumbrance of tails.

In a philosophic disquisition, besides the necessity of confining many words of ordinary use to one definite sense, the writer has to make his choice between two difficulties, whenever his purpose requires him to wean his reader's attention from the *degrees* of things, which alone form the dictionary of common life, to the *kind*, independent of *degree*: as when, for instance, a chemist discourses on the heat in ice, or on latent or fixed light. In this case, he must either use old words with new meanings, the plan adopted by Dr. Darwin in his Zoonomia,[15] or he must borrow from the schools, or himself coin a nomenclature exclusively appropriated to his subject, after the example of the French chemists, and indeed of all eminent natural philosophers and historians in all countries. There seems to me little ground for hesitation as to which of the two shall be preferred: it being

---

[13] Sir Richard Blackmore, a minor poet of the early eighteenth-century, attempted to write heroic and philosophical poetry. *The Castle Spectre* was a drama by M. G. Lewis, better known for his lurid novel, *The Monk*.

[14] See above, p. 363.

[15] In his *Zoönomia* (1794-96), Erasmus Darwin, grandfather of the great naturalist, Charles Darwin, applied to biological instincts some of the principles of the doctrine of association or ideas, and developed a theory of evolution in accordance with them.

clear, that the former is a twofold exertion of mind in one and the same act. The reader is obliged, not only to recollect the new definition, but—which is incomparably more difficult and perplexing—to unlearn and keep out of view the old and habitual meaning: an evil, for which the *semblance* of eschewing pedantry is a very poor and inadequate compensation. I have, therefore, in two or three instances ventured on a disused or scholastic term, where without it I could not have avoided confusion or ambiguity. Thus, to express in one word what belongs to the senses or the recipient and more passive faculty of the soul, I have re-introduced the word *sensuous,* used, among many others of our elder writers, by Milton, in his exquisite definition of poetry, as "simple, sensuous, passionate": because the term *sensual* is seldom used at present, except in a bad sense, and *sensitive* would convey a different meaning. Thus too I have restored the words, *intuition* and *intuitive,* to their original sense—"an intuition," says Hooker, "that is, a direct and immediate beholding or presentation of an object to the mind through the senses or the imagination." —Thus geometrical truths are all intuitive, or accompanied by an intuition. Nay, in order to express *"the many,"* as simply contra-distinguished from *"the one,"* I have hazarded the smile of the reader, by introducing to his acquaintance, from the forgotten terminology of the old schoolmen, the phrase, *multëity,* because I felt that I could not substitute *multitude,* without more or less connecting with it the notion of "a *great* many." Thus the Philosopher of the later Platonic, or Alexandrine school, named the triangle the first-born of beauty, it being the first and simplest symbol of *multëity in unity.* These are, I believe, the only liberties of this kind which I have found it necessary to attempt in the present essay: partly, because its object will be attained sufficiently for my present purpose, by attaching a clear and distinct meaning to the different terms used by us, in our appreciation of works of art, and partly because I am about to put to the press a large volume on the Logos,[16] or the communicative

intelligence in nature and in man, together with, and as preliminary to, a Commentary on the Gospel of St. John; and in this work I have labored to give real and adequate definitions of all the component faculties of our moral and intellectual being, exhibiting constructively the origin, development, and destined functions of each. And now with silent wishes that these explanatory pre-notices may be attributed to their true cause, a sense of respect for the understanding of my reflecting readers, I proceed to my promised and more amusing task, that of establishing, illustrating, and exemplifying the distinct powers of the different modes of pleasure excited by the works of nature or of human genius with their exponent and appropriable terms. "Harum indagatio subtilitatum etsi non est utilis ad machinas farinarias conficiendas, exuit animum tamen inscitiae rubigine, acuitque ad alia."—*Scaliger, Exerc.* 307, § 3.[17]

AGREEABLE.—We use this word in two senses; in the first for whatever agrees with our nature, for that which is congruous with the primary constitution of our senses. Thus green is naturally agreeable to the eye. In this sense the word expresses, at least involves, a pre-established harmony between the organs and their appointed objects. In the second sense, we convey by the word *agreeable,* that the thing has by force of habit (thence called a second nature) been made to agree with us; or that it has become agreeable to us by its recalling to our minds some one or more things that were dear and pleasing to us; or lastly, on account of some after pleasure or advantage, of which it has been the constant cause or occasion. Thus by force of custom men *make* the taste of tobacco, which was at first hateful to the palate, agreeable to them; thus too, as our Shakspeare observes,

> Things base and vile, holding no quality,
> Love can transpose to form and dignity—

the crutch that had supported a revered parent, after the first anguish of regret, becomes agreeable

---

[16] One of the great works which Coleridge often promised but which, as Hazlitt said in his review of the *Biographia Literaria,* exist only as promises. According to a letter of Coleridge, written at this time, he even

states that the "large volume on the LOGOS" is in the process of being printed. Some fragments, which were apparently to be a part of it, survive, including a sizable manuscript on logic.

[17] "The investigation of this fine point, even though it is not useful for making food-producing machines, strips off the mold of ignorance from the mind, and sharpens it for other things."

to the affectionate child; and I once knew a very sensible and accomplished Dutch gentleman, who, spite of his own sense of the ludicrous nature of the feeling, was more delighted by the first grand concert of frogs he heard in this country, than he had been by Catalina singing in the compositions of Cimarosa.[18] The last clause needs no illustrations, as it comprises all the objects that are agreeable to us, only because they are the means by which we gratify our smell, touch, palate, and mere bodily feeling.

The BEAUTIFUL, contemplated in its essentials, that is, in *kind* and not in *degree*, is that in which the *many*, still seen as many, becomes one. Take a familiar instance, one of a thousand. The frost on a window-pane has by accident crystallized into a striking resemblance of a tree or a seaweed. With what pleasure we trace the parts, and their relations to each other, and to the whole! Here is the stalk or trunk, and here the branches or sprays—sometimes even the buds or flowers. Nor will our pleasure be less, should the caprice of the crystallization represent some object disagreeable to us, provided only we can see or fancy the component parts each in relation to each, and all forming a whole. A lady would see an admirably painted tiger with pleasure, and at once pronounce it beautiful,— nay, an owl, a frog, or a toad, who would have shrieked or shuddered at the sight of the things themselves. So far is the Beautiful from depending wholly on association, that it is frequently produced by the mere removal of associations. Many a sincere convert to the beauty of various insects, as of the dragon-fly, the fangless snake, &c., has Natural History made, by exploding the terror or aversion that had been connected with them.

The most general definition of beauty, therefore, is—that I may fulfil my threat of plaguing my readers with hard words—Multëity in Unity. Now it will be always found, that whatever is the definition of the *kind*, independent of degree, becomes likewise the definition of the highest degree of that kind. An old coach-wheel lies in the coachmaker's yard, disfigured with tar and dirt (I purposely take the most trivial instances) —if I turn away my attention from these, and regard the *figure* abstractly, "still," I might say

18 An Italian composer of the later eighteenth century.

to my companion; "there is beauty in that wheel, and you yourself would not only admit, but would feel it, had you never seen a wheel before. See how the rays proceed from the centre to the circumferences, and how many different images are distinctly comprehended at one glance, as forming one whole, and each part in some harmonious relation to each and to all." But imagine the polished golden wheel of the chariot of the Sun, as the poets have described it: then the figure, and the real thing so figured, exactly coincide. There is nothing heterogeneous, nothing to abstract from: by its perfect smoothness and circularity in width, each part is (if I may borrow a metaphor from a sister sense) as perfect a melody, as the whole is a complete harmony. This, we should say, is beautiful throughout. Of all "the many," which I actually see, each and all are really reconciled into unity: while the effulgence from the whole coincides with, and seems to represent, the effluence of delight from my own mind in the intuition of it.

It seems evident then, first, that beauty is harmony, and subsists only in composition, and secondly, that the first species of the Agreeable can alone be a component part of the beautiful, that namely which is naturally consonant with our senses by the pre-established harmony between nature and the human mind; [19] and thirdly, that even of this species, those objects only can be admitted (according to rule the first) which belong to the eye and ear, because they alone are susceptible of distinction of parts. Should an Englishman gazing on a mass of cloud rich with the rays of the rising sun exclaim, even without distinction of, or reference to its form, or its relation to other objects, how beautiful! I should have no quarrel with him. First, because by the law of association there is in all visual beholdings at least an indistinct subsumption of

19 That is, (1) beauty does not characterize a single element but rather a harmonizing of *different* ones, and exists only "in composition"—when different elements are *arranged*, or *brought together*. (2) Beauty is agreeable. But not everything that is agreeable is beauty. What is agreeable is not beauty if, for example, it pleases *only* because it fits in with habits of association that were picked up through the accidents of environment. Nor is an agreeable object beautiful if it pleases us merely by reminding us of something of which we were or are fond (the crutch of a lame parent to whose memory one is devoted). Compare the discussion of "stock responses" by I. A. Richards, below, pp. 575-78.

form and relation: and, secondly, because even in the coincidence between the sight and the object there is an approximation to the reduction of the many into one.[20] But who, that heard a Frenchman call the flavor of a leg of mutton a beautiful taste, would not immediately recognize him for a Frenchman, even though there should be neither grimace or characteristic nasal twang? The result, then, of the whole is that the shapely (i.e. *formosus*) joined with the naturally agreeable, constitutes what, speaking accurately, we mean by the word beautiful (i.e. *pulcher*).

But we are conscious of faculties far superior to the highest impressions of sense; we have life and free-will.—What then will be the result, when the Beautiful, arising from regular form, is so modified by the perception of life and spontaneous action, as that the latter only shall be the object of our conscious *perception*, while the former merely acts, and yet does effectively act, on our feelings? With pride and pleasure I reply by referring my reader to the group in Mr. Allston's grand picture of the "Dead Man reviving from the touch of the bones of the Prophet Elisha," beginning with the slave at the head of the reviving body, then proceeding to the daughter clasping her swooning mother; to the mother, the wife of the reviving man; then to the soldier behind who supports her; to the two figures eagerly conversing: and lastly, to the exquisitely graceful girl who is bending downward, and whose hand nearly touches the thumb of the slave! You will find, what you had not suspected, that you have here before you a circular group. But by what variety of life, motion, and passion is all the stiffness, that would result from an obvious regular figure, swallowed up, and the figure of the group as much concealed by the action and passion, as the skeleton, which gives the form of the human body, is hidden by the flesh and its endless outlines! [21]

In Raphael's admirable Galatea (the print of which is doubtless familiar to most of my readers) the circle is perceived at first sight; but with what multiplicity of rays and chords within the area of the circular group, with what elevations and depressions of the circumference, with what an endless variety and sportive wildness in the component figure, and in the junctions of the figures, is the balance, the perfect reconciliation, effected between these two conflicting principles of the FREE LIFE, and of the confining FORM! How entirely is the stiffness that would have resulted from the obvious regularity of the latter, *fused* and (if I may hazard so bold a metaphor) almost *volatilized* by the interpenetration and electrical flashes of the former.

But I shall recur to this consummate work for more specific illustrations hereafter: and have indeed in some measure offended already against the laws of method, by anticipating materials which rather belong to a more advanced stage of the disquisition. It is time to recapitulate, as briefly as possible, the arguments already advanced, and having summed up the result, to leave behind me this, the only portion of these essays, which, as far as the subject itself is concerned, will demand any *effort* of attention from a reflecting and intelligent reader. And let me be permitted to remind him, that the distinctions,

---

[20] Though the Englishman believes he is admiring only the *color* of the clouds, he could not do so unless the colored clouds were *limited* and marked off as a unit occupying a certain space (that is, had a shape, or form). Otherwise the whole sky and everything else would be the same color, in fact the same thing. Then, without anything to contrast it with, this color could not even be distinguished—unless it were seen suddenly, for a short time, and then contrasted with colors previously seen (and even in that case, there is a limitation or form in *time*, if not space, that marks off the perception of that color as a distinct unit). Secondly, the mere act of seeing represents a bringing together of diversity, a combining of more than one, into a unity. For there is the spectator, on the one hand, and on the other hand there is the object. The process of perceiving is impossible without both, and therefore involves a bringing together, or unification, of two different things (the spectator and the object) into one act (the act of perceiving).

[21] The passage exemplifies Coleridge's frequent emphasis on "organic" form in art. As distinct from the sort of formalism that simply stamps its pattern or arrangement upon objects, distorting them to fit a preconceived shape or order, art, according to Coleridge, should draw out the form organically from the object or materials; the form has no real function or vital existence until it is given substance by the materials, and sustains and works through them. Form simply imposed on the object is "the death or imprisonment of the thing." (See "On Poesy or Art," below, p. 398.) Egyptian art, with its stiff pyramids and angular lines, would be an example of this, when contrasted with Greek art (Coleridge's "Fragment of an Essay on Beauty"). Compare the discussion by T. E. Hulme, below, pp. 562-64.

which it is my object to prove and elucidate, have not merely a foundation in nature and the noblest faculties of the human mind, but are likewise the very ground-work, nay, an indispensable condition, of all *rational* enquiry concerning the Arts. For it is self-evident, that whatever may be judged of differently by different persons, in the very same degree of moral and intellectual cultivation, extolled by one and condemned by another, without any error being assignable to either, can never be an object of general principles: and *vice versâ*, that whatever can be brought to the test of general principles presupposes a distinct origin from these pleasures and tastes, which, for the wisest purposes, are made to depend on local and transitory fashions, accidental associations, and the peculiarities of individual temperament: to all which the philosopher, equally with the well-bred man of the world, applies the old adage, *de gustibus non est disputandum*. Be it, however, observed that "de gustibus" is by no means the same as "de gustu," nor will it escape the scholar's recollection, that taste, in its metaphorical use, was first adopted by the Romans, and unknown to the less luxurious Greeks, who designated this faculty, sometimes by the word αἴσθησις, and sometimes by φιλοκαλία—"ἀνδρῶν τῶν καθ' ἡμᾶς φιλοκαλώτατος γεγονώς—i.e. endowed by nature with the most exquisite taste of any man of our age," says Porphyry of his friend, Castricius. Still, this metaphor, borrowed from the pregustatores of the old Roman Banquets, is singularly happy and appropriate. In the palate, the perception of the object and its qualities is involved in the *sensation*, in the mental taste it is involved in the *sense*. We have a *sensation* of sweetness, in a healthy palate, from honey; a *sense* of beauty, in an uncorrupted taste, from the view of the rising or setting sun.

RECAPITULATION. *Principle the First*. That which has become, or which has been *made* agreeable to us, from causes not contained in its own nature, or in its original conformity to the human organs and faculties; that which is not pleasing for its own sake, but by connection or association with some other thing, separate or separable from it, is neither beautiful, nor capable of being a component part of Beauty: though it may greatly increase the sum of our pleasure, when it does not interfere with the

beauty of the object, nay, even when it detracts from it. A moss-rose, with a sprig of myrtle and jasmine, is not more *beautiful* from having been plucked from the garden, or presented to us by the hand of the woman we love, but is abundantly more delightful. The total pleasure received from one of Mr. Bird's finest pictures may, without any impeachment of our taste, be the greater from his having introduced into it the portrait of one of our friends, or from our pride in him as our townsman, or from our knowledge of his personal qualities; but the amiable artist would rightly consider it a coarse compliment, were it affirmed, that the *beauty* of the piece, or its merit as a work of genius, was the more perfect on this account. I am conscious that I look with a stronger and more pleasureable emotion at Mr. Allston's large landscape, in the spirit of Swiss scenery, from its having been the occasion of my first acquaintance with him in Rome. This may or may not be a compliment to *him*; but the true compliment to the picture was made by a lady of high rank and cultivated taste, who declared, in my hearing, that she never stood before that landscape without seeming to feel the breeze blow out of it upon her. But the most striking instance is afforded by the portrait of a departed or absent friend or parent; which is endeared to us, and more delightful, from some awkward position of the limbs, which had defied the contrivances of art to render it picturesque, but which was the characteristic habit of the original.

Principle the Second. That which is naturally agreeable and consonant to human nature, so that the exceptions may be attributed to disease or defect; that, the pleasure from which is contained in the immediate impression; cannot, indeed, with strict propriety, be called beautiful, exclusive of its relations, but one among the component parts of beauty, in whatever instance it is susceptible of existing as a part of a whole.[22] This, of course, excludes the mere objects of the

[22] That is, beauty is not a biological reaction; it cannot be found solely in a simple, isolated sensation, as in a single touch of anything, however pleasant. Edmund Burke, for example, in his noted essay, *On the Sublime and Beautiful* (1756), had instanced "smoothness" as a major source of beauty. To this, a later critic, Richard Payne Knight, aptly replied that if one stroked a feeling-board, smoothly planed and polished for the purpose, any belief that it was beautiful would quickly pass.

taste, smell, and feeling, though the sensation from these, especially from the latter when organized into touch, may secretly, and without our consciousness, enrich and vivify the perceptions and images of the eye and ear; which alone are true organs of sense, their sensations in a healthy or uninjured state being too faint to be noticed by the mind. We may, indeed, in common conversation, call purple a beautiful color, or the tone of a single note on an excellent pianoforte a beautiful tone; but if we were questioned, we should agree that a rich or delightful color; a rich, or sweet, or clear tone; would have been more appropriate—and this with less hesitation in the latter instance than in the former, because the single tone is more manifestly of the nature of a *sensation*, while color is the medium which seems to blend sensation and perception, so as to hide, as it were, the former in the latter; the direct opposite of which takes place in the lower senses of feeling, smell, and taste. (In strictness, there is even in these an ascending scale. The smell is less sensual and more sentient than mere feeling, the taste than the smell, and the eye than the ear: but between the ear and the taste exists the chasm or break, which divides the beautiful and the elements of beauty from the merely agreeable.) When I reflect on the manner in which smoothness, richness of sound, &c., enter into the formation of the beautiful, I am induced to suspect that they act negatively rather than positively. Something there must be to realize the form, something in and by which the *forma informans* reveals itself: and these, less than any that could be substituted, and in the least possible degree, distract the attention, in the least possible degree obscure the idea, of which they (composed into outline and surface) are the symbol. An illustrative hint may be taken from a pure crystal, as compared with an opaque, semi-opaque or clouded mass, on the one hand, and with a perfectly transparent body, such as the air, on the other. The crystal is lost in the light, which yet it contains, embodies, and gives a shape to; but which passes shapeless through the air, and, in the ruder body, is either quenched or dissipated.[23]

Principle the Third. The safest definition, then, of Beauty, as well as the oldest, is that of Pythagoras: THE REDUCTION OF MANY TO ONE— or, as finely expressed by the sublime disciple of Ammonius, τὸ ἄμερες ὄν, ἐν πολλοῖς φανταζόμενον,[24] of which the following may be offered as both paraphrase and corollary. *The sense of beauty subsists in simultaneous intuition of the relation of parts, each to each, and of all to a whole: exciting an immediate and absolute complacency, without intervenence, therefore, of any interest, sensual or intellectual.* The BEAUTIFUL is thus at once distinguished both from the AGREEABLE, which is beneath it, and from the GOOD, which is above it: for both these have an interest necessarily attached to them: both act on the WILL, and excite a desire for the actual existence of the image or idea contemplated: while the sense of beauty rests gratified in the mere contemplation or intuition, regardless whether it be a fictitious Apollo, or a real Antinous.

The Mystics meant the same, when they define beauty as the subjection of matter to spirit so as to be transformed into a symbol, in and through which the spirit reveals itself; and declare *that* the *most* beautiful, where the most obstacles to a full manifestation have been most perfectly overcome. I would that the readers, for whom alone I write (*intelligibilia enim, non intellectum adfero*) [25] had Raphael's Galatea, or his School of Athens, before them! or that the Essay might be read by some imaginative student, warm from admiration of the King's College Chapel at Cambridge, or of the exterior and interior of York Cathedral! I deem the sneers of a host of petty critics, unalphabeted in the life and truth of things, and

[23] The preceding four sentences might be paraphrased as follows: Such qualities as smoothness, richness of tone, etc., which are agreeable in themselves, but are not beauty, can become a *part* of beauty. They do so, however, not by making any positive, substantial contribution, but by offering as little interference as possible to more basic elements—by fitting in, as a kind of lens or window through which the form can penetrate. Now the active, unifying form needs such concrete objects and their qualities through which to work and show itself. Otherwise it would be like light passing through air without shape. But these objects and qualities must be *congenial* to the form—as when a crystal is held up to light—and able to serve as its vessel or symbol. Otherwise, the form is simply obstructed or quenched, as when light meets an opaque body.

[24] "The undivided being, which is imagined issuing through multiplicity."

[25] "For I offer intelligible things, not the mind capable of understanding them."

as devoid of sound learning as of intuitive taste, well and wisely hazarded for the prospect of communicating the pleasure, which to such minds the following passage of Plotinus will not fail to give—Plotinus, a name venerable even to religion with the great Cosmus, Lorenzo de Medici, Ficinus, Politian, Leonardo da Vinci, and Michael Angelo, but now known only as a name to the majority even of our most learned Scholars!—Plotinus, difficult indeed, but under a rough and austere rind concealing fruit worthy of Paradise; and if obscure, "*at tenet umbra Deum!*" Ὅταν οὖν καὶ ἡ αἴσθησις τὸ ἐν σώμασιν εἶδος ἴδη συνδησάμενον καὶ κρατῆσαν τῆς φύσεως τῆς ἐναντίας, καὶ μορφὴν ἐπ᾽ ἄλλαις μορφαῖς ἐκπρεπῶς ἐποχουμένην, συνελοῦσα ἀφρόον αὐτὸ τὸ πολλαχῆ ἀνήνεγκέ τε καὶ ἔδωκε τῷ ἔνδον σύμφωνον καὶ οὖν ἁρμόττον καὶ φίλον.[26] A divine passage, faintly represented in the following lines, written many years ago by the writer, though without reference to, or recollection of, the above.

O lady! we *receive* but what we *give*,
And in *our* life alone does nature live!
Ours is her wedding-garment, ours her shroud!
And would we aught behold of higher worth,
Than that inanimate cold world allow'd
To the poor, loveless, ever-anxious crowd:
Ah! from the soul itself must issue forth
A light, a glory, a fair luminous cloud,
⠀⠀Enveloping the earth!
And from the soul itself must there be sent
A sweet and powerful voice, of its own birth,
⠀Of all sweet sounds the life and element!
O pure of heart! thou need'st not ask of me,
⠀What this strong music in the soul may be;
⠀⠀What and wherein it doth subsist,
This light, this glory, this fair luminous mist,
⠀⠀This beautiful, and beauty-making power!
Joy, O beloved! joy, that ne'er was given,
⠀Save to the pure and in their purest hour,
Life of our life, the parent and the birth,
Which, wedding nature to us, gives in dower
⠀⠀A new heaven and new earth,

[26] "When the mind perceives the form intertwining itself through the concrete, and conquering the material reality opposed to it: then, after perceiving the dominating form, visibly emerging, the mind—collecting together the diverse materials into a harmonized union—bestows this form it has perceived back upon the object —a form quite in keeping with the character of the inner principle [actually there] in the object" (Plotinus, *Ennead,* I, 6).

Undreamt of by the sensual and the proud—
This is the strong voice, this the luminous cloud!
⠀⠀Our inmost selves rejoice:
And thence flows all that glads or ear or sight,
All melodies the echoes of that voice,
All colors a suffusion from that light,
And its celestial tint of yellow-green:
And still I gaze—and with how blank an eye!
And those thin clouds above, in flakes and bars,
That give away their motion to the stars;
Those stars, that glide behind them or between,
Now sparkling, now bedimm'd, but always seen;
Yon crescent moon, that seems as if it grew
In its own starless, cloudless lake of blue—
I see them all, so excellently fair!
I see, not feel, how beautiful they are.[27]
⠀⠀⠀⠀⠀⠀⠀⠀⠀S. T. C. MS. Poem.

SCHOLIUM. We have sufficiently distinguished the beautiful from the agreeable, by the sure criterion, that, when we find an object agreeable, the *sensation* of pleasure always precedes the judgement, and is its determining cause. We *find* it agreeable. But when we declare an object beautiful, the contemplation or intuition of its beauty precedes the *feeling* of complacency, in order of nature at least: nay, in great depression of spirits may even exist without sensibly producing it.—

A grief without a pang, void, dark, and drear!
A stifled, drowsy, unimpassion'd grief,
⠀⠀That finds no natural outlet, no relief
⠀⠀⠀In word, or sigh, or tear!
O dearest lady! in this heartless mood,
To other thoughts by yon sweet throstle woo'd!
All this long eve, so balmy and serene,
Have I been gazing at the western sky.

Now the least reflection convinces us that our sensations, whether of pleasure or of pain, are the incommunicable parts of our nature; such as can be reduced to no universal rule; and in which therefore we have no right to expect that others should agree with us, or to blame them for disagreement. That the Greenlander prefers train oil [28] to olive oil, and even to wine, we explain at once by our knowledge of the climate and productions to which he has been habituated. Were the man as enlightened as Plato, his palate would still find that most agreeable to which it had been most accustomed. But when the Iro-

[27] These and the next quoted lines are from Coleridge's *Dejection: an Ode* (1802).
[28] Whale, not locomotive, oil.

quois Sachem, after having been led to the most perfect specimens of architecture in Paris, said that he saw nothing so beautiful as the cook's shops, we attribute this without hesitation to savagery of intellect, and infer with certainty that the sense of the beautiful was either altogether dormant in his mind, or at best very imperfect. The Beautiful, therefore, not originating in the sensations, must belong to the intellect: and therefore we *declare* an object beautiful, and feel an inward right to *expect* that others should coincide with us. But we feel no right to *demand* it: and this leads us to that, which hitherto we have barely touched upon, and which we shall now attempt to illustrate more fully, namely, to the distinction of the Beautiful from the Good.

Let us suppose Milton in company with some stern and prejudiced Puritan, contemplating the front of York Cathedral, and at length expressing his admiration of its beauty. We will suppose it too at that time of his life, when his religious opinions, feelings, and prejudices most nearly coincided with those of the rigid Anti-prelatists.— P. Beauty; I am sure, it is not the beauty of holiness. M. True; but yet it is beautiful.—P. It delights not me. What is it good for? Is it of any use but to be stared at?—M. Perhaps not! but still it is beautiful.—P. But call to mind the pride and wanton vanity of those cruel shavelings, that wasted the labor and substance of so many thousand poor creatures in the erection of this haughty pile.—M. I do. But still it is very beautiful.—P. Think how many score of places of worship, incomparably better suited both for prayer and preaching, and how many faithful ministers might have been maintained, to the blessing of tens of thousands, to them and their children's children, with the treasures lavished on this worthless mass of stone and cement.—M. Too true! but nevertheless it is *very* beautiful.— P. And it is not merely useless; but it feeds the pride of the prelates, and keeps alive the popish and carnal spirit among the people.—M. Even so! and I presume not to question the wisdom, nor detract from the pious zeal, of the first Reformers of Scotland, who for these reasons destroyed so many fabrics, scarce inferior in beauty to this now before our eyes. But I did not call it *good*, nor have I told thee, brother! that if this were levelled with the ground, and existed only in the works of the modeller or engraver, that I should desire to reconstruct it. The GOOD consists in the congruity of a thing with the laws of the reason and the nature of the will, and in its fitness to determine the latter to actualize the former: and it is always discursive. The Beautiful arises from the perceived harmony of an object, whether sight or sound, with the inborn and constitutive rules of the judgement and imagination: and it is always intuitive. As light to the eye, even such is beauty to the mind, which cannot but have complacency in whatever is perceived as pre-configured to its living faculties. Hence the Greeks called a beautiful object καλόν quasi καλοῦν, i.e. *calling on* the soul, which receives instantly, and welcomes it as something connatural. Πάλιν οὖν ἀναλαβόντες, λέγωμεν τί δῆτα ἐστὶ τὸ ἐν τοῖς σώμασι καλόν. Πρῶτον ἔστι μὲν γάρ τι καὶ βολῇ τῇ πρώτῃ αἰσθητὸν γινόμενον, καὶ ἡ ψυχὴ ὥσπερ συνεῖσα λέγει, καὶ ἐπιγνοῦσα ἀποδέχεται, καὶ οἷον συναρμόττεται. Πρὸς δὲ τὸ αἰσχρὸν προσβαλοῦσα ἀνίλλεται, καὶ ἀρνεῖται καὶ ἀνανεύει ἐπ' αὐτοῦ οὐ συμφωνοῦσα, καὶ ἀλλοτριουμένη.[29]— PLOTIN: Ennead. I. Lib. 6.

[29] "To return, then: let us state what physical beauty [the beauty in objects] is. It is something perceived esthetically, in the first impression of it. And the soul, as if understanding it, responds to it, and is drawn, as it were, into harmony with it. On the other hand, in confronting the ugly, the soul shrinks back, refusing and rejecting it because of the lack of harmony with it, and a feeling of estrangement." Coleridge has no etymological basis for his interpretation of καλόν as a "calling on"; but the term is suggestive of his own conception of beauty.

From Biographia Literaria

CHAPTER XIV

Occasion of the Lyrical Ballads, and the objects originally proposed—Preface to the second edition—The ensuing controversy, its causes and acrimony—Philosophic definitions of a poem and poetry with scholia.

DURING the first year [1] that Mr. Wordsworth and I were neighbors, our conversations turned frequently on the two cardinal points of poetry, the power of exciting the sympathy of the reader by a faithful adherence to the truth of nature, and the power of giving the interest of novelty by the modifying colors of imagination. The sudden charm, which accidents of light and shade, which moon-light or sun-set diffused over a known and familiar landscape, appeared to represent the practicability of combining both. These are the poetry of nature. The thought suggested itself (to which of us I do not recollect) that a series of poems might be composed of two sorts. In the one, the incidents and agents were to be, in part at least, supernatural; and the excellence aimed at was to consist in the interesting of the affections by the dramatic truth of such emotions, as would naturally accompany such situations, supposing them real. And real in *this* sense they have been to every human being who, from whatever source of delusion, has at any time believed himself under supernatural agency. For the second class, subjects were to be chosen from ordinary life; the characters and incidents were to be such, as will be found in every village and its vicinity, where there is a meditative and feeling mind to seek after them, or to notice them, when they present themselves.

In this idea originated the plan of the "Lyrical Ballads"; in which it was agreed, that my endeavours should be directed to persons and characters supernatural, or at least romantic; yet so as to transfer from our inward nature a human interest and a semblance of truth suffi-

Biographia Literaria. Published in 1817.

[1] In 1797.

cient to procure for these shadows of imagination that willing suspension of disbelief for the moment, which constitutes poetic faith. Mr. Wordsworth, on the other hand, was to propose to himself as his object, to give the charm of novelty to things of every day, and to excite a feeling analogous to the supernatural, by awakening the mind's attention from the lethargy of custom, and directing it to the loveliness and the wonders of the world before us; an inexhaustible treasure, but for which, in consequence of the film of familiarity and selfish solicitude we have eyes, yet see not, ears that hear not, and hearts that neither feel nor understand.

With this view I wrote "The Ancient Mariner," and was preparing among other poems, "The Dark Ladie," and the "Christabel," in which I should have more nearly realized my ideal, than I had done in my first attempt. But Mr. Wordsworth's industry had proved so much more successful, and the number of his poems so much greater, that my compositions, instead of forming a balance, appeared rather an interpolation of heterogeneous matter. Mr. Wordsworth added two or three poems written in his own character, in the impassioned, lofty, and sustained diction, which is characteristic of his genius. In this form the "Lyrical Ballads" were published; and were presented by him, as an *experiment*, whether subjects, which from their nature rejected the usual ornaments and extra-colloquial style of poems in general, might not be so managed in the language of ordinary life as to produce the pleasureable interest, which it is the peculiar business of poetry to impart. To the second edition he added a preface of considerable length; in which, notwithstanding some passages of apparently a contrary import, he was understood to contend for the extension of this style to poetry of all kinds, and to reject as vicious and indefensible all phrases and forms of style that were not included in what he (unfortunately, I think, adopting an equivocal expression) called the language of *real* life. From this preface, prefixed to poems in which it was impossible to deny the presence of original genius, however mistaken its direction might be deemed, arose the whole long-continued controversy.[2] For from the conjunction of perceived power with supposed heresy I explain the inveteracy and in some instances, I grieve to say, the acrimonious passions, with which the controversy has been conducted by the assailants.

Had Mr. Wordsworth's poems been the silly, the childish things, which they were for a long time described as being; had they been really distinguished from the compositions of other poets merely by meanness of language and inanity of thought; had they indeed contained nothing more than what is found in the parodies and pretended imitations of them; they must have sunk at once, a dead weight, into the slough of oblivion, and have dragged the preface along with them. But year after year increased the number of Mr. Wordsworth's admirers. They were found too not in the lower classes of the reading public, but chiefly among young men of strong sensibility and meditative minds; and their admiration (inflamed perhaps in some degree by opposition) was distinguished by its intensity, I might almost say, by its *religious* fervor. These facts, and the intellectual energy of the author, which was more or less consciously felt, where it was outwardly and even boisterously denied, meeting with sentiments of aversion to his opinions, and of alarm at their consequences, produced an eddy of criticism, which would of itself have borne up the poems by the violence, with which it whirled them round and round. With many parts of this preface, in the sense attributed to them, and which the words undoubtedly seem to authorize, I never concurred; but on the contrary objected to them as erroneous in principle, and as contradictory (in appearance at least) both to other parts of the same preface, and to the author's own practice in the greater number of the poems themselves. Mr. Wordsworth in his recent collection has, I find, degraded this prefatory disquisition to the end of his second volume, to be read or not at the reader's choice. But he has not, as far as I can discover, announced any change in his poetic creed. At all events, considering it as the source of a controversy, in which I have been honored more than I deserve

[2] The controversy over Wordsworth's theory of poetic diction.

by the frequent conjunction of my name with his, I think it expedient to declare once for all, in what points I coincide with his opinions, and in what points I altogether differ. But in order to render myself intelligible I must previously, in as few words as possible, explain my ideas, first, of a POEM; and secondly, of POETRY itself, in *kind,* and in *essence.*

The office of philosophical *disquisition* consists in just *distinction;* while it is the privilege of the philosopher to preserve himself constantly aware, that distinction is not division. In order to obtain adequate notions of any truth, we must intellectually separate its distinguishable parts; and this is the technical *process* of philosophy. But having so done, we must then restore them in our conceptions to the unity, in which they actually co-exist; and this is the *result* of philosophy. A poem contains the same elements as a prose composition; the difference therefore must consist in a different combination of them, in consequence of a different object being proposed. According to the difference of the object will be the difference of the combination. It is possible, that the object may be merely to facilitate the recollection of any given facts or observations by artificial arrangement; and the composition will be a poem, merely because it is distinguished from prose by metre, or by rhyme, or by both conjointly. In this, the lowest sense, a man might attribute the name of a poem to the well-known enumeration of the days in the several months;

> Thirty days hath September,
> April, June, and November, &c.

and others of the same class and purpose. And as a particular pleasure is found in anticipating the recurrence of sounds and quantities, all compositions that have this charm super-added, whatever be their contents, *may* be entitled poems.

So much for the superficial *form.* A difference of object and contents supplies an additional ground of distinction. The immediate purpose may be the communication of truths; either of truth absolute and demonstrable, as in works of science; or of facts experienced and recorded, as in history. Pleasure, and that of the highest and most permanent kind, may *result* from the *attainment* of the end; but it is not itself the immediate end. In other works the communication of pleasure may be the immediate purpose; and though truth, either moral or intellectual, ought to be the *ultimate* end, yet this will distinguish the character of the author, not the class to which the work belongs. Blest indeed is that state of society, in which the immediate purpose would be baffled by the perversion of the proper ultimate end; in which no charm of diction or imagery could exempt the Bathyllus even of an Anacreon, or the Alexis of Virgil, from disgust and aversion!

But the communication of pleasure may be the immediate object of a work not metrically composed; and that object may have been in a high degree attained, as in novels and romances. Would then the mere superaddition of metre, with or without rhyme, entitle *these* to the name of poems? The answer is, that nothing can permanently please, which does not contain in itself the reason why it is so, and not otherwise. If metre be superadded, all other parts must be made consonant with it. They must be such, as to justify the perpetual and distinct attention to each part, which an exact correspondent recurrence of accent and sound are calculated to excite. The final definition then, so deduced, may be thus worded. A poem is that species of composition, which is opposed to works of science, by proposing for its *immediate* object pleasure, not truth; [3] and from all other species (having *this* object in common with it) it is discriminated by proposing to itself such delight from the *whole*, as is compatible with a distinct gratification from each component *part*.

Controversy is not seldom excited in consequence of the disputants attaching each a different meaning to the same word; and in few instances has this been more striking, than in disputes concerning the present subject. If a man chooses to call every composition a poem, which is rhyme, or measure, or both, I must leave his opinion uncontroverted. The distinction is at least competent to characterize the writer's intention. If it were subjoined, that the whole is likewise entertaining or affecting, as a tale, or as a series of interesting reflections, I of course admit this as another fit ingredient of a poem, and an additional merit. But if the definition sought for be that of a *legitimate* poem, I answer, it must be one, the parts of which mutually support and explain each other; all in their proportion harmonizing with, and supporting the purpose and known influences of metrical arrangement. The philosophic critics of all ages coincide with the ultimate judgement of all countries, in equally denying the praises of a just poem, on the one hand, to a series of striking lines or distiches, each of which, absorbing the whole attention of the reader to itself, disjoins it from its context, and makes it a separate whole, instead of an harmonizing part; and on the other hand, to an unsustained composition, from which the reader collects rapidly the general result, unattracted by the component parts. The reader should be carried forward, not merely or chiefly by the mechanical impulse of curiosity, or by a restless desire to arrive at the final solution; but by the pleasureable activity of mind excited by the attractions of the journey itself. Like the motion of a serpent, which the Egyptians made the emblem of intellectual power; or like the path of sound through the air; at every step he pauses and half recedes, and from the retrogressive movement collects the force which again carries him onward. "Praecipitandus est *liber* spiritus," [4] says Petronius Arbiter most happily. The epithet, *liber*, here balances the preceding verb; and it is not easy to conceive more meaning condensed in fewer words.

But if this should be admitted as a satisfactory character of a poem, we have still to seek for a definition of poetry. The writings of PLATO, and Bishop TAYLOR, and the "Theoria Sacra" of BURNET, furnish undeniable proofs that poetry of the highest kind may exist without metre, and even without the contra-distinguishing objects of a poem. The first chapter of Isaiah (indeed a very large portion of the whole book) is poetry in the most emphatic sense; yet it would be not less irrational than strange to assert, that pleasure, and not truth, was the immediate object of the prophet. In short, whatever *specific* import we attach to the word, poetry, there will be found involved in it, as a necessary consequence, that a poem of any length neither can be, or ought to be, all poetry. Yet if an harmonious whole is to be produced, the remaining parts must be preserved *in keeping* with the poetry;

---

[3] For a discussion and qualification of this point, see "On the Principles of Genial Criticism," above, p. 366.

[4] "The free spirit should be urged on."

and this can be no otherwise effected than by such a studied selection and artificial arrangement, as will partake of *one*, though not a *peculiar* property of poetry. And this again can be no other than the property of exciting a more continuous and equal attention than the language of prose aims at, whether colloquial or written.

My own conclusions on the nature of poetry, in the strictest use of the word, have been in part anticipated in the preceding disquisition on the fancy and imagination.[5] What is poetry? is so nearly the same question with, what is a poet? that the answer to the one is involved in the solution of the other. For it is a distinction resulting from the poetic genius itself, which sustains and modifies the images, thoughts, and emotions of the poet's own mind.

The poet, described in *ideal* perfection, brings the whole soul of man into activity, with the subordination of its faculties to each other, according to their relative worth and dignity.[6] He diffuses a tone and spirit of unity, that blends, and (as it were) *fuses*, each into each, by that synthetic and magical power, to which we have exclusively appropriated the name of imagination. This power, first put in action by the will and understanding, and retained under their irremissive, though gentle and unnoticed, controul (*laxis effertur habenis*) [7] reveals itself in the balance or reconciliation of opposite or discordant qualities: of sameness, with difference; of the general, with the concrete; the idea, with the image; the individual, with the representative; the sense of novelty and freshness, with old and familiar objects; a more than usual state of emotion, with more than usual order; judgement ever awake and steady self-possession, with enthusiasm and feeling profound or vehement; and while it blends and harmonizes the natural and the artificial, still subordinates art to nature; the manner to the matter; and our admiration of the poet to our sympathy with the poetry. "Doubtless," as Sir John Davies [8] observes of the soul (and his words may with slight alteration be applied, and even more appropriately, to the poetic IMAGINATION)

Doubtless this could not be, but that she turns
Bodies to spirit by sublimation strange,
As fire converts to fire the things it burns,
As we our food into our nature change.

From their gross matter she abstracts their forms,
And draws a kind of quintessence from things;
Which to her proper nature she transforms,
To bear them light on her celestial wings.

Thus does she, when from individual states
She doth abstract the universal kinds;
Which then re-clothed in divers names and fates
Steal access through our senses to our minds.

Finally, GOOD SENSE is the BODY of poetic genius,[9] FANCY its DRAPERY, MOTION its LIFE, and IMAGINATION the SOUL that is everywhere, and in each; and forms all into one graceful and intelligent whole.

CHAPTER XVII

Examination of the tenets peculiar to Mr. Wordsworth—Rustic life (above all, low and rustic life) especially unfavorable to the formation of a human diction—The best parts of language the product of philosophers, not of clowns or shepherds—Poetry essentially ideal and generic—The language of Milton as much the language of real life, yea, incomparably more so than that of the cottager.

As far then as Mr. Wordsworth in his preface contended, and most ably contended, for a reformation in our poetic diction, as far as he has evinced the truth of passion, and the *dramatic* propriety of those figures and metaphors in the original poets, which, stripped of their justifying reasons, and converted into mere artifices of connection or ornament, constitute the characteristic falsity in the poetic style of the moderns; and as far as he has, with equal acuteness and clearness, pointed out the process by which this

---

[5] He refers to the brief passage printed below, p. 387.
[6] See above, p. 362.
[7] "Is carried along with loose reins."
[8] In his poem, *Of the Soul of Man*, sec. 4.

[9] "The sum total of all intellectual excellence is good sense and method. When these have passed into the instinctive readiness of habit, when the wheel revolves so rapidly that we cannot see it revolve at all, then we call the combination Genius. But in all modes alike, and in all professions, the two sole component parts even of *Genius*, are GOOD SENSE and METHOD" (Letter to Lady Beaumont, June, 1814). Compare Hazlitt's essays "On Genius and Common Sense," above, pp. 322-30.

change was effected, and the resemblances between that state into which the reader's mind is thrown by the pleasurable confusion of thought from an unaccustomed train of words and images; and that state which is induced by the natural language of empassioned feeling; he undertook a useful task, and deserves all praise, both for the attempt and for the execution. The provocations to this remonstrance in behalf of truth and nature were still of perpetual recurrence before and after the publication of this preface. I cannot likewise but add, that the comparison of such poems of merit, as have been given to the public within the last ten or twelve years, with the majority of those produced previously to the appearance of that preface, leave no doubt on my mind, that Mr. Wordsworth is fully justified in believing his efforts to have been by no means ineffectual. Not only in the verses of those who have professed their admiration of his genius, but even of those who have distinguished themselves by hostility to his theory, and depreciation of his writings, are the impressions of his principles plainly visible. It is possible, that with these principles others may have been blended, which are not equally evident; and some which are unsteady and subvertible from the narrowness or imperfection of their basis. But it is more than possible, that these errors of defect or exaggeration, by kindling and feeding the controversy, may have conduced not only to the wider propagation of the accompanying truths, but that, by their frequent presentation to the mind in an excited state, they may have won for them a more permanent and practical result. A man will borrow a part from his opponent the more easily, if he feels himself justified in continuing to reject a part. While there remain important points in which he can still feel himself in the right, in which he still finds firm footing for continued resistance, he will gradually adopt those opinions, which were the least remote from his own convictions, as not less congruous with his own theory than with that which he reprobates. In like manner with a kind of instinctive prudence, he will abandon by little and little his weakest posts, till at length he seems to forget that they had ever belonged to him, or affects to consider them at most as accidental and "petty annexments," the removal of which leaves the citadel unhurt and unendangered.

My own differences from certain supposed parts of Mr. Wordsworth's theory ground themselves on the assumption, that his words had been rightly interpreted, as purporting that the proper diction for poetry in general consists altogether in a language taken, with due exceptions, from the mouths of men in real life, a language which actually constitutes the natural conversation of men under the influence of natural feelings. My objection is, first, that in *any* sense this rule is applicable only to *certain* classes of poetry; secondly, that even to these classes it is not applicable, except in such a sense, as hath never by any one (as far as I know or have read) been denied or doubted; and lastly, that as far as, and in that degree in which it is *practicable*, yet as a *rule* it is useless, if not injurious, and therefore either need not, or ought not to be practised. The poet informs his reader, that he had generally chosen *low and rustic* life; but not *as* low and rustic, or in order to repeat that pleasure of doubtful moral effect, which persons of elevated rank and of superior refinement oftentimes derive from a happy *imitation* of the rude unpolished manners and discourse of their inferiors. For the pleasure so derived may be traced to three exciting causes. The first is the naturalness, in *fact*, of the things represented. The second is the apparent naturalness of the *representation*, as raised and qualified by an imperceptible infusion of the author's own knowledge and talent, which infusion does, indeed, constitute it an *imitation* as distinguished from a mere *copy*.[1] The third cause may be found in the reader's conscious feeling of his superiority awakened by the contrast presented to him; even as for the same purpose the kings and great barons of yore retained sometimes *actual* clowns and fools, but more frequently shrewd and witty fellows in that *character*. These, however, were not Mr. Wordsworth's objects. *He* chose low and rustic life, "because in that condition the essential passions of the heart find a better soil, in which they can attain their maturity, are less under restraint, and speak a plainer and more emphatic language; because in that condition of life our elementary

[1] For a discussion of the distinction between "imitation" and "copy," which is a favorite theme of Coleridge, see "On Poesy or Art," below, p. 395.

feelings coexist in a state of greater simplicity, and consequently may be more accurately contemplated, and more forcibly communicated; because the manners of rural life germinate from those elementary feelings; and from the necessary character of rural occupations are more easily comprehended, and are more durable; and lastly, because in that condition the passions of men are incorporated with the beautiful and permanent forms of nature."

Now it is clear to me, that in the most interesting of the poems, in which the author is more or less dramatic, as "the Brothers," "Michael," "Ruth," "the Mad Mother," [2] &c., the persons introduced are by no means taken *from low or rustic life* in the common acceptation of those words; and it is not less clear, that the sentiments and language, as far as they can be conceived to have been really transferred from the minds and conversation of such persons, are attributable to causes and circumstances not necessarily connected with "their occupations and abode." The thoughts, feelings, language, and manners of the shepherd-farmers in the vales of Cumberland and Westmoreland, as far as they are actually adopted in those poems, may be accounted for from causes, which will and do produce the same results in *every* state of life, whether in town or country. As the two principal I rank that INDEPENDENCE, which raises a man above servitude, or daily toil for the profit of others, yet not above the necessity of industry and a frugal simplicity of domestic life; and the accompanying unambitious, but solid and religious, EDUCATION, which has rendered few books familiar, but the Bible, and the liturgy or hymn book. To this latter cause, indeed, which is so far *accidental*, that it is the blessing of particular countries and a particular age, not the product of particular places or employments, the poet owes the show of probability, that his personages might really feel, think, and talk with any tolerable resemblance to his representation. It is an excellent remark of Dr. Henry More's, (Enthusiasmus triumphatus, Sec. XXXV.), that "a man of confined education, but of good parts, by constant reading of the Bible will naturally form a more winning and commanding rhetoric than those that are learned; the intermixture of

tongues and of artificial phrases debasing *their* style."

It is, moreover, to be considered that to the formation of healthy feelings, and a reflecting mind, *negations* involve impediments not less formidable than sophistication and vicious intermixture. I am convinced, that for the human soul to prosper in rustic life a certain vantage-ground is pre-requisite. It is not every man that is likely to be improved by a country life or by country labors. Education, or original sensibility, or both, must pre-exist, if the changes, forms, and incidents of nature are to prove a sufficient stimulant. And where these are not sufficient, the mind contracts and hardens by want of stimulants: and the man becomes selfish, sensual, gross, and hard-hearted. Let the management of the POOR LAWS in Liverpool, Manchester, or Bristol be compared with the ordinary dispensation of the poor rates in agricultural villages, where the *farmers* are the overseers and guardians of the poor. If my own experience have not been particularly unfortunate, as well as that of the many respectable country clergymen with whom I have conversed on the subject, the result would engender more than scepticism concerning the desireable influences of low and rustic life in and for itself. Whatever may be concluded on the other side, from the stronger local attachments and enterprising spirit of the Swiss, and other mountaineers, applies to a particular mode of pastoral life, under forms of property that permit and beget manners truly republican, not to rustic life in general, or to the absence of artificial cultivation. On the contrary the mountaineers, whose manners have been so often eulogized, are in general better educated and greater readers than men of equal rank elsewhere. But where this is not the case, as among the peasantry of North Wales, the ancient mountains, with all their terrors and all their glories, are pictures to the blind, and music to the deaf.

I should not have entered so much into detail upon this passage, but here seems to be the point, to which all the lines of difference converge as to their source and centre. (I mean, as far as, and in whatever respect, my poetic creed *does* differ from the doctrines promulged in this preface.) I adopt with full faith the principle

<hr>

[2] Entitled "Her eyes are wild" in later editions.

of Aristotle, that poetry as poetry is essentially [3] *ideal,* that it avoids and excludes all *accident;* that its apparent individualities of rank, character, or occupation must be *representative* of a class; and that the *persons* of poetry must be clothed with *generic* attributes, with the *common* attributes of the class: not with such as one gifted individual might *possibly* possess, but such as from his situation it is most probable before-hand that he *would* possess. If my premises are right and my deductions legitimate, it follows that there can be no *poetic* medium between the swains of Theocritus and those of an imaginary golden age.[4]

The characters of the vicar and the shepherd-mariner in the poem of "The Brothers," that of the shepherd of Greenhead Ghyll in the "Michael," have all the verisimilitude and representative quality, that the purposes of poetry can require. They are persons of a known

[3] Say not that I am recommending abstractions; for these class-characteristics which constitute the instructiveness of a character, are so modified and particularized in each person of the Shakespearean Drama, that life itself does not excite more distinctly that sense of individuality which belongs to real existence. Paradoxical as it may sound, one of the essential properties of Geometry is not less essential to dramatic excellence; and Aristotle has accordingly required of the poet an involution of the universal in the individual. The chief differences are, that in Geometry it is the universal truth, which is uppermost in the consciousness; in poetry the individual form, in which the truth is clothed. With the ancients, and not less with the elder dramatists of England and France, both comedy and tragedy were considered as kinds of poetry. They neither sought in comedy to make us laugh merely; much less to make us laugh by wry faces, accidents of jargon, *slang* phrases for the day, or the clothing of common-place morals drawn from the shops or mechanic occupations of their characters. Nor did they condescend in tragedy to wheedle away the applause of the spectators, by representing before them facsimiles of their own mean selves in all their existing meanness, or to work on the sluggish sympathies by a pathos not a whit more respectable than the maudlin tears of drunkenness. Their tragic scenes were meant to *affect* us indeed; but yet within the bounds of pleasure, and in union with the activity both of our understanding and imagination. They wished to transport the mind to a sense of its possible greatness, and to implant the germs of that greatness, during the temporary oblivion of the worthless "thing we are," and of the peculiar state in which each man *happens* to be, suspending our individual recollections and lulling them to sleep amid the music of nobler thoughts.—Friend, Pages 251, 252. [Coleridge.]

[4] Theocritus took his swains from real life.

and abiding class, and their manners and sentiments the natural product of circumstances common to the class. Take "Michael" for instance:

An old man stout of heart, and strong of limb:
His bodily frame had been from youth to age
Of an unusual strength: his mind was keen,
Intense, and frugal, apt for all affairs,
And in his shepherd's calling he was prompt
And watchful more than ordinary men.
Hence he had learnt the meaning of all winds,
Of blasts of every tone; and oftentimes
When others heeded not, he heard the South
Make subterraneous music, like the noise
Of bagpipers on distant Highland hills.
The shepherd, at such warning, of his flock
Bethought him, and to himself would say,
The winds are now devising work for me!
And truly at all times the storm, that drives
The traveller to a shelter, summon'd him
Up to the mountains. He had been alone
Amid the heart of many thousand mists,
That came to him and left him on the heights.
So liv'd he, till his eightieth year was pass'd.
And grossly that man errs, who should suppose
That the green vallies, and the streams and rocks,
Were things indifferent to the shepherd's thoughts.
Fields, where with chearful spirits he had breath'd
The common air; the hills, which he so oft
Had climb'd with vigorous steps; which had im-
    press'd
So many incidents upon his mind
Of hardship, skill or courage, joy or fear;
Which, like a book, preserved the memory
Of the dumb animals, whom he had sav'd,
Had fed or shelter'd, linking to such acts,
So grateful in themselves, the certainty
Of honorable gain; these fields, these hills
Which were his living being, even more
Than his own blood—what could they less? had
    laid
Strong hold on his affections, were to him
A pleasureable feeling of blind love,
The pleasure which there is in life itself.

On the other hand, in the poems which are pitched at a lower note, as the "Harry Gill," "Idiot Boy," the *feelings* are those of human nature in general; though the poet has judiciously laid the *scene* in the country, in order to place *himself* in the vicinity of interesting images, without the necessity of ascribing a sentimental perception of their beauty to the persons of his drama. In the "Idiot Boy," indeed, the mother's character is not so much a real and native product of a "situation where the essential pasisons of the heart find a better soil, in which they can attain their maturity and speak a plainer and more emphatic language," as it is an impersonation of an instinct abandoned by judgement. Hence the two following charges seem to me not wholly groundless: at least, they are the only plausible objections, which I have heard to that fine poem. The one is, that the author has not, in the poem itself, taken sufficient care to preclude from the reader's fancy the disgusting images of *ordinary morbid idiocy,* which yet it was by no means his intention to represent. He has even by the "burr, burr, burr," uncounteracted by any preceding description of the boy's beauty, assisted in recalling them. The other is, that the idiocy of the *boy* is so evenly balanced by the folly of the *mother,* as to present to the general reader rather a laughable burlesque on the blindness of anile dotage, than an analytic display of maternal affection in its ordinary workings.

In the "Thorn" the poet himself acknowledges in a note the necessity of an introductory poem, in which he should have pourtrayed the character of the person from whom the words of the poem are supposed to proceed: a superstitious man moderately imaginative, of slow faculties and deep feelings, "a captain of a small trading vessel, for example, who, being past the middle age of life, had retired upon an annuity, or small independent income, to some village or country town of which he was not a native, or in which he had not been accustomed to live. Such men having nothing to do become credulous and talkative from indolence." But in a poem, still more in a lyric poem (and the NURSE in Shakespeare's Romeo and Juliet alone prevents me from extending the remark even to dramatic *poetry,* if indeed the Nurse itself can be deemed altogether a case in point) it is not possible to imitate truly a dull and garrulous discourser, without repeating the effects of dullness and garrulity. However this may be, I dare assert, that the parts (and these form the far larger portion of the whole) which might as well or still better have proceeded from the poet's own imagination, and have been spoken in his own character, are those which have given, and which will continue to give, universal delight; and that the passages exclusively appropriate to the supposed narrator, such as the last couplet of the third stanza; [5] the seven last lines of the tenth; [6] and the five following stanzas, with the

[5] "I've measured it from side to side;
'Tis three feet long, and two feet wide." [Coleridge.]

[6]   "Nay, rack your brain—'tis all in vain,
I'll tell you every thing I know;
But to the Thorn, and to the Pond
Which is a little step beyond,
I wish that you would go:
Perhaps when you are at the place,
You something of her tale may trace.
I'll give you the best help I can:
Before you up the mountain go,
Up to the dreary mountain-top,
I'll tell you all I know.
'Tis now some two-and-twenty years
Since she (her name is Martha Ray)
Gave, with a maiden's true good will,
Her company to Stephen Hill;
And she was blithe and gay,
And she was happy, happy still
Whene'er she thought of Stephen Hill.

And they had fix'd the wedding-day,
The morning that must wed them both;
But Stephen to another maid
Had sworn another oath;
And, with this other maid, to church
Unthinking Stephen went—
Poor Martha! on that woeful day
A pang of pitiless dismay
Into her soul was sent;
A fire was kindled in her breast,
Which might not burn itself to rest.

They say, full six months after this,
While yet the summer leaves were green,
She to the mountain-top would go,
And there was often seen.
'Tis said a child was in her womb,
As now to any eye was plain;
She was with child, and she was mad;
Yet often she was sober sad
From her exceeding pain.
Oh me! ten thousand times I'd rather
That he had died, that cruel father!

.   .   .   .   .

Last Christmas when we talked of this,
Old farmer Simpson did maintain,
That in her womb the infant wrought
About its mother's heart, and brought
Her senses back again:
And, when at last her time drew near,
Her looks were calm, her senses clear.
No more I know, I wish I did,
And I would tell it all to you:
For what became of this poor child
There's none that ever knew:
And if a child was born or no,

exception of the four admirable lines at the commencement of the fourteenth, are felt by many unprejudiced and unsophisticated hearts, as sudden and unpleasant sinkings from the height to which the poet had previously lifted them, and to which he again re-elevates both himself and his reader.

If then I am compelled to doubt the theory, by which the choice of *characters* was to be directed, not only *à priori*, from grounds of reason, but both from the few instances in which the poet himself *need* be supposed to have been governed by it, and from the comparative inferiority of those instances; still more must I hesitate in my assent to the sentence which immediately follows the former citation; and which I can neither admit as particular fact, or as general rule. "The language too of these men is adopted (purified indeed from what appear to be its real defects, from all lasting and rational causes of dislike or disgust) because such men hourly communicate with the best objects from which the best part of language is originally derived; and because, from their rank in society and the sameness and narrow circle of their intercourse, being less under the action of social vanity, they convey their feelings and notions in simple and unelaborated expressions." To this I reply; that a rustic's language, purified from all provincialism and grossness, and so far reconstructed as to be made consistent with the rules of grammar (which are in essence no other than the laws of universal logic, applied to psychological materials) will not differ from the language of any other man of common-sense, however learned or refined he may be, except as far as the notions, which the rustic has to convey, are fewer and more indiscriminate. This will become still clearer, if we add the consideration (equally important though less obvious) that the rustic, from the more imperfect development of his faculties, and from the lower state of their cultivation, aims almost solely to convey *insulated facts*, either those of his scanty

There's no one that could ever tell;
And if 'twas born alive or dead,
There's no one knows, as I have said:
But some remember well,
That Martha Ray about this time
Would up the mountain often climb."

[Coleridge.]

experience or his traditional belief; while the educated man chiefly seeks to discover and express those *connections* of things, or those relative *bearings* of fact to fact, from which some more or less general law is deducible. For *facts* are valuable to a wise man, chiefly as they lead to the discovery of the indwelling *law*, which is the true *being* of things, the sole solution of their modes of existence, and in the knowledge of which consists our dignity and our power.

As little can I agree with the assertion, that from the objects with which the rustic hourly communicates the best part of language is formed. For first, if to communicate with an object implies such an acquaintance with it, as renders it capable of being discriminately reflected on; the distinct knowledge of an uneducated rustic would furnish a very scanty vocabulary. The few things, and modes of action, requisite for his bodily conveniences, would alone be individualized; while all the rest of nature would be expressed by a small number of confused general terms. Secondly, I deny that the words and combinations of words derived from the objects, with which the rustic is familiar, whether with distinct or confused knowledge, can be justly said to form the *best* part of language. It is more than probable, that many classes of the brute creation possess discriminating sounds, by which they can convey to each other notices of such objects as concern their food, shelter, or safety. Yet we hesitate to call the aggregate of such sounds a language, otherwise than metaphorically. The best part of human language, properly so called, is derived from reflection on the acts of the mind itself. It is formed by a voluntary appropriation of fixed symbols to internal acts, to processes and results of imagination, the greater part of which have no place in the consciousness of uneducated man; though in civilized society, by imitation and passive remembrance of what they hear from their religious instructors and other superiors, the most uneducated share in the harvest which they neither sowed or reaped. If the history of the phrases in hourly currency among our peasants were traced, a person not previously aware of the fact would be surprised at finding so large a number, which three or four centuries ago were the exclusive property of the universities and the schools; and, at the commencement of the Reformation, had been transferred from the school to the pulpit, and thus gradually passed into common life. The extreme difficulty, and often the impossibility, of finding words for the simplest moral and intellectual processes of the languages of uncivilized tribes has proved perhaps the weightiest obstacle to the progress of our most zealous and adroit missionaries. Yet these tribes are surrounded by the same nature as our peasants are; but in still more impressive forms; and they are, moreover, obliged to *particularize* many more of them. When, therefore, Mr. Wordsworth adds, "accordingly, such a language" (meaning, as before, the language of rustic life purified from provincialism) "arising out of repeated experience and regular feelings, is a more permanent, and a far more philosophical language, than that which is frequently substituted for it by poets, who think they are conferring honor upon themselves and their art in proportion as they indulge in arbitrary and capricious habits of expression:" it may be answered, that the language, which he has in view, can be attributed to rustics with no greater right, than the style of Hooker or Bacon to Tom Brown or Sir Roger L'Estrange.[7] Doubtless, if what is peculiar to each were omitted in each, the result must needs be the same. Further, that the poet, who uses an illogical diction, or a style fitted to excite only the low and changeable pleasure of wonder by means of groundless novelty, substitutes a language of *folly* and *vanity*, not for that of the *rustic*, but for that of *good sense* and *natural feeling*.

Here let me be permitted to remind the reader, that the positions, which I controvert, are contained in the sentences—"*a selection of the* REAL *language of men;*"—"*the language of these men*" (i.e. men in low and rustic life) "*I propose to myself to imitate, and, as far as is possible, to adopt the very language of men.*" "*Between the language of prose and that of metrical composition, there neither is, nor can be any essential difference.*" It is against these exclusively that my opposition is directed.

I object, in the very first instance, to an

equivocation in the use of the word "real." Every man's language varies, according to the extent of his knowledge, the activity of his faculties, and the depth or quickness of his feelings. Every man's language has, first its *individualities;* secondly, the common properties of the *class* to which he belongs; and thirdly, words and phrases of *universal* use. The language of Hooker, Bacon, Bishop Taylor, and Burke differs from the common language of the learned class only by the superior number and novelty of the thoughts and relations which they had to convey. The language of Algernon Sidney differs not at all from that, which every well-educated gentleman would wish to write, and (with due allowances for the undeliberateness, and less connected train, of thinking natural and proper to conversation) such as he would wish to talk. Neither one nor the other differ half so much from the general language of cultivated society, as the language of Mr. Wordsworth's homeliest composition differs from that of a common peasant. For "real" therefore, we must substitute *ordinary*, or *lingua communis*. And this, we have proved, is no more to be found in the phraseology of low and rustic life than in that of any other class. Omit the peculiarities of each, and the result of course must be common to all. And assuredly the omissions and changes to be made in the language of rustics, before it could be transferred to any species of poem, except the drama or other professed imitation, are at least as numerous and weighty, as would be required in adapting to the same purpose the ordinary language of tradesmen and manufacturers. Not to mention, that the language so highly extolled by Mr. Wordsworth varies in every county, nay in every village, according to the accidental character of the clergyman, the existence or non-existence of schools; or even, perhaps, as the exciseman, publican, or barber, happen to be, or not to be, zealous politicians, and readers of the weekly newspaper *pro bono publico*. Anterior to cultivation, the lingua communis of every country, as Dante has well observed, exists every where in parts, and no where as a whole.

Neither is the case rendered at all more tenable by the addition of the words, *in a state of excitement.* For the nature of a man's words, where he is strongly affected by joy, grief, or

---

[7] Tom Brown was a minor satirist and hack writer of the late seventeenth and early eighteenth centuries; L'Estrange, a prolific and in some ways gifted writer of the same period, was one of the earliest English journalists.

anger, must necessarily depend on the number and quality of the general truths, conceptions and images, and of the words expressing them, with which his mind had been previously stored. For the property of passion is not to *create;* but to set in increased activity. At least, whatever new connections of thoughts or images, or (which is equally, if not more than equally, the appropriate effect of strong excitement) whatever generalizations of truth or experience, the heat of passion may produce; yet the terms of their conveyance must have pre-existed in his former conversations, and are only collected and crowded together by the unusual stimulation. It is indeed very possible to adopt in a poem the unmeaning repetitions, habitual phrases, and other blank counters, which an unfurnished or confused understanding interposes at short intervals, in order to keep hold of his subject, which is still slipping from him, and to give him time

for recollection; or in mere aid of vacancy, as in the scanty companies of a country stage the same player pops backwards and forwards, in order to prevent the appearance of empty spaces, in the procession of Macbeth, or Henry VIIIth. But what assistance to the poet, or ornament to the poem, these can supply, I am at a loss to conjecture. Nothing assuredly can differ either in origin or in mode more widely from the *apparent* tautologies of intense and turbulent feeling, in which the passion is greater and of longer endurance than to be exhausted or satisfied by a single representation of the image or incident exciting it. Such repetitions I admit to be a beauty of the highest kind; as illustrated by Mr. Wordsworth himself from the song of Deborah. *"At her feet he bowed, he fell, he lay down; at her feet he bowed, he fell; where he bowed, there he fell down dead."* [8]

[8] *Judges,* 5:27.

The Imagination [1]

(I) The histories and political economy of the present and preceding century partake in

[1] The following three brief fragments comprise most of what Coleridge has to say *explicitly* about the imagination. These fragments are included only because Coleridge's remarks on the imagination have become some of the most famous, if mysterious, *dicta* in the history of criticism. Number I is from the *Statesman's Manual* (1816). It contains, in its second sentence, Coleridge's clearest and most comprehensive definition of the imaginative process. Number II is from the *Biographia Literaria* (1817), Ch. IV. Number III is the famous close of Ch. XIII of the *Biographia Literaria.* It is this chapter that was to have been devoted to a full analysis of the "Imagination, or esemplastic power"— an analysis, Coleridge tells us, more than a hundred pages in length. Instead, the chapter prints a "judicious letter" to Coleridge, supposedly from a friend but actually written by Coleridge himself, advising him to omit his analysis. For to *"unprepared* minds your speculations on the esemplastic power would be utterly unintelligible." We are at once reassured, however, that "In that greater work to which you have devoted so many years . . . it will be in its proper place." Whether the discussion was really laid aside for the *magnum opus,* or whether it was simply never written to begin with, these two paragraphs are all there is of it. For general discussion of Coleridge's theory of the imagination, see the introduction, above, pp. 362-64.

the general contagion of its mechanistic philosophy, and are the product of an unenlivened generalizing understanding. In the Scriptures they are the living educts of the imagination; of that reconciling and mediatory power, which incorporating the reason in images of the sense, and organizing (as it were) the flux of the senses by the permanence and self-circling energies of the reason, gives birth to a system of symbols, harmonious in themselves, and consubstantial with the truths of which they are the conductors. These are the *wheels* which Ezekiel beheld, when the hand of the Lord was upon him, and he saw the visions of God as he sate among the captives by the river of Chebar. *Whithersoever the Spirit was to go, the* wheels *went, and thither was their spirit to go:—for the spirit of the living creature was in the* wheels *also.*

(II) Repeated meditations led me first to suspect, (and a more intimate analysis of the human faculties, their appropriate marks, functions, and effects matured my conjecture into full conviction,) that fancy and imagination were two distinct and widely different faculties,[2] instead of being, according to the general belief, either two names with one meaning, or, at furthest, the lower and higher degree of one and the same power. It is not, I own, easy to conceive a more opposite translation of the Greek *Phantasia* than the Latin Imaginatio; but it is equally true that in all societies there exists an instinct of growth, a certain collective, unconscious good sense working progressively to desynonymize those words originally of the same meaning, which the conflux of dialects had supplied to the more homogeneous languages, as the Greek and German: and which the same cause, joined with accidents of translation from original works of different countries, occasion in mixt languages like our own. The first and most important point to be proved is, that two conceptions perfectly distinct are confused under one and the same word, and (this done) to appropriate that word exclusively to one meaning, and the synonyme (should there be one) to the other. But if (as will be often the case in the arts and sciences) no synonyme exists, we must either invent or borrow a word. In the present instance the appropriation has already begun, and been legitimated in the derivative adjective: Milton had a highly *imaginative*, Cowley, a very *fanciful* mind. If therefore I should succeed in establishing the actual existences of two faculties generally different, the nomenclature would be at once determined. To the faculty by which I had characterized Milton, we should confine the term *imagination;* while the other would be contradistinguished as *fancy*. Now were it once fully ascertained, that this division is no less grounded in nature, than that of delirium from mania, or Otway's

Lutes, lobsters, seas of milk, and ships of amber,

from Shakespeare's

What! have his daughters brought him to this
    pass? [3]

or from the preceding apostrophe to the elements; the theory of the fine arts, and of poetry in particular, could not, I thought, but derive some addition and important light. It would in its immediate effects furnish a torch of guidance to the philosophical critic; and ultimately to the poet himself. In energetic minds, truth soon changes by domestication into power; and from directing in the discrimination and appraisal of the product, becomes influencive in the production. To admire on principle, is the only way to imitate without loss of originality.

(III) The IMAGINATION then, I consider either as primary, or secondary. The primary IMAGINATION I hold to be the living Power and prime Agent of all human Perception, and as a repetition in the finite mind of the eternal act of creation in the infinite I AM. The secondary Imagination I consider as an echo of the former, co-existing with the conscious will, yet still as identical with the primary in the *kind* of its agency, and differing only in *degree*, and in the *mode* of its operation. It dissolves, diffuses, dissipates, in order to recreate; or where this process is rendered impossible, yet still at all events it struggles to idealize and to unify. It is essentially *vital*, even as all objects (*as* objects) are essentially fixed and dead.

FANCY, on the contrary, has no other counters to play with, but fixities and definites. The Fancy is indeed no other than a mode of Memory emancipated from the order of time and space; while it is blended with, and modified by that empirical phenomenon of the will, which we express by the word CHOICE. But equally with the ordinary memory the Fancy must receive all its materials ready made from the law of association.[4]

---

[2] Coleridge, in this famous distinction, is building upon distinctions between the terms found in eighteenth-century English critical and philosophical writing. (See J. Bullitt and W. J. Bate, "Distinctions between Fancy and Imagination," *Modern Language Notes*, LX [1945], 8-15.)

[3] Otway's *Venice Preserved*, V, ii, 151; *King Lear*, III, iv, 63.

[4] For other remarks on the imagination, see especially above, p. 379.

Shakespeare as a Poet Generally

CLOTHED in radiant armour, and authorized by titles sure and manifold, as a poet, Shakespeare came forward to demand the throne of fame, as the dramatic poet of England. His excellencies compelled even his contemporaries to seat him on that throne, although there were giants in those days contending for the same honour. Hereafter, I would fain endeavour to make out the title of the English drama as created by, and existing in, Shakespeare, and its right to the supremacy of dramatic excellence in general. But he had shown himself a poet, previously to his appearance as a dramatic poet; and had no *Lear*, no *Othello*, no *Henry IV*, no *Twelfth Night* ever appeared, we must have admitted that Shakespeare possessed the chief, if not every, requisite of a poet—deep feeling and exquisite sense of beauty, both as exhibited to the eye in the combinations of form, and to the ear in sweet and appropriate melody; that these feelings were under the command of his own will; that in his very first productions he projected his mind out of his own particular being, and felt, and made others feel, on subjects no way connected with himself, except by force of contemplation and that sublime faculty by which a great mind becomes that on which it meditates.[1] To this must be added that affectionate love of nature and natural objects, without which no man could have observed so steadily, or painted so truly and passionately, the very minutest beauties of the external world:

And when thou hast on foot the purblind hare,
Mark the poor wretch; to overshoot his troubles,
How he outruns the wind, and with what care
He cranks and crosses with a thousand doubles;
The many musits through the which he goes
Are like a labyrinth to amaze his foes.

Shakespeare as a Poet Generally. First published in *Literary Remains* (ed. H. N. Coleridge, 1836). This and the following lecture may have been delivered in 1818 as one of a course of lectures; but it is equally, if not more, probable that it was delivered as far back as 1808. By far the most complete collection of Coleridge's writings on Shakespeare is *Coleridge's Shakespearean Criticism* (ed. T. M. Raysor, Cambridge, Mass., 2v., 1930).

[1] See above, pp. 363-64.

Sometimes he runs among the flock of sheep,
To make the cunning hounds mistake their smell;
And sometime where earth-delving conies keep,
To stop the loud pursuers in their yell;
And sometime sorteth with a herd of deer:
Danger deviseth shifts, wit waits on fear.

For there his smell with others' being mingled,
The hot scent-snuffing hounds are driven to doubt,
Ceasing their clamorous cry, till they have singled,
With much ado, the cold fault cleanly out,
Then do they spend their mouths; echo replies,
As if another chase were in the skies.

By this poor Wat, far off, upon a hill,
Stands on his hinder legs with listening ear,
To hearken if his foes pursue him still:
Anon their loud alarums he doth hear,
And now his grief may be compared well
To one sore-sick, that hears the passing-bell.

Then shalt thou see the dew-bedabbled wretch
Turn, and return, indenting with the way:
Each envious briar his weary legs doth scratch,
Each shadow makes him stop, each murmur stay.
For misery is trodden on by many,
And being low, never relieved by any.—*Venus and
   Adonis*

And the preceding description:—

But, lo! from forth a copse that neighbours by,
A breeding jennet, lusty, young and proud, etc.

is much more admirable, but in parts less fitted for quotation.

Moreover, Shakespeare had shown that he possessed fancy, considered as the faculty of bringing together images, dissimilar in the main, by some one point or more of likeness, as in such a passage as this:

Full gently now she takes him by the hand,
A lily prisoned in a jail of snow,
Or ivory in an alabaster band;
So white a friend ingirts so white a foe!—*Ib.*

And still mounting the intellectual ladder, he had as unequivocally proved the indwelling in his mind of imagination, or the power by which one image or feeling is made to modify many others, and by a sort of fusion to force many into one—that which afterwards showed itself in such might and energy in *Lear*, where the deep anguish of a father spreads the feeling of ingratitude and cruelty over the very elements of heaven; and which, combining many circumstances into one moment of consciousness, tends to produce that ultimate end of all human thought and human feeling, unity, and thereby the reduction of the spirit to its principle and fountain, who is alone truly one. Various are the workings of this, the greatest, faculty of the human mind, both passionate and tranquil. In its tranquil and purely pleasurable operation it acts chiefly by creating out of many things, as they would have appeared in the description of an ordinary mind, detailed in unimpassioned succession, a oneness, even as nature, the greatest of poets, acts upon us when we open our eyes upon an extended prospect. Thus the flight of Adonis in the dusk of the evening:

Look! how a bright star shooteth from the sky;
So glides he in the night from Venus' eye!

How many images and feelings are here brought together, without effort and without discord, in the beauty of Adonis, the rapidity of his flight, the yearning, yet hopelessness, of the enamoured gazer, while a shadowy ideal character is thrown over the whole! Or this power acts by impressing the stamp of humanity, and of human feelings, on inanimate or mere natural objects:

Lo! here the gentle lark, weary of rest,
From his moist cabinet mounts up on high,
And wakes the morning, from whose silver breast
The sun ariseth in his majesty,
Who doth the world so gloriously behold,
The cedar-tops and hills seem burnish'd gold.

Or again, it acts by so carrying on the eye of the reader as to make him almost lose the consciousness of words, to make him see everything flashed, as Wordsworth has grandly and appropriately said:

Flashed upon that inward eye
Which is the bliss of solitude;—

and this without exciting any painful or laborious attention, without any anatomy of description, (a fault not uncommon in descriptive poetry) but with the sweetness and easy movement of nature. This energy is an absolute essential of poetry, and of itself would constitute a poet, though not one of the highest class; it is, however, a most hopeful symptom, and the *Venus and Adonis* is one continued specimen of it.

In this beautiful poem there is an endless activity of thought in all the possible associations of thought with thought, thought with feeling, or with words, of feelings with feelings, and of words with words.

Even as the sun, with purple-colour'd face,
Had ta'en his last leave of the weeping morn,
Rose-cheek'd Adonis hied him to the chase:
Hunting he loved, but love he laugh'd to scorn.
Sick-thoughted Venus makes amain unto him,
And like a bold-faced suitor 'gins to woo him.

Remark the humanizing imagery and circumstances of the first two lines, and the activity of thought in the play of words in the fourth line. The whole stanza presents at once the time, the appearance of the morning, and the two persons distinctly characterized, and in six simple verses puts the reader in possession of the whole argument of the poem.

Over one arm the lusty courser's rein,
Under the other was the tender boy,
Who blush'd and pouted in a dull disdain,
With leaden appetite, unapt to toy,
She red and hot, as coals of glowing fire,
He red for shame, but frosty to desire:

This stanza and the two following afford good instances of that poetic power, which I mentioned above, of making everything present to the imagination—both the forms, and the passions which modify those forms, either actually, as in the representations of love, or anger, or other human affections: or imaginatively, by the different manner in which inanimate objects, or objects unimpassioned themselves, are caused to be seen by the mind in moments of strong excitement, and according to the kind of the excitement, whether of jealousy, or rage, or love, in the only appropriate sense of the word, or of the lower impulses of our nature, or finally of the poetic feeling itself. It is, perhaps, chiefly in the power of producing and reproducing the latter that the poet stands distinct.

The subject of the *Venus and Adonis* is unpleasing; but the poem itself is for that very reason the more illustrative of Shakespeare.

There are men who can write passages of deepest pathos, and even sublimity, on circumstances personal to themselves and stimulative of their own passions; but they are not, therefore, on this account poets. Read that magnificent burst of woman's patriotism and exultation, Deborah's song of victory; it is glorious, but nature is the poet there. It is quite another matter to become all things, and yet remain the same, to make the changeful god be felt in the river, the lion, and the flame; this it is, that is the true imagination. Shakespeare writes in this poem as if he were of another planet, charming you to gaze on the movements of Venus and Adonis as you would on the twinkling dances of two vernal butterflies.

Finally, in this poem and the *Rape of Lucrece,* Shakespeare gave ample proof of his possession of a most profound, energetic, and philosophical mind, without which he might have pleased, but could not have been a great dramatic poet. Chance and the necessity of his genius combined to lead him to the drama, his proper province; in his conquest of which we should consider both the difficulties which opposed him, and the advantages by which he was assisted.

Shakespeare's Judgment Equal to His Genius

THUS, then, Shakespeare appears, from his *Venus and Adonis* and *Rape of Lucrece* alone, apart from all his great works, to have possessed all the conditions of the true poet. Let me now proceed to destroy, as far as may be in my power, the popular notion that he was a great dramatist by mere instinct, that he grew immortal in his own despite, and sank below men of second or third-rate power when he attempted aught beside the drama—even as bees construct their cells and manufacture their honey to admirable perfection; but would in vain attempt to build a nest. Now this mode of reconciling a compelled sense of inferiority with a feeling of pride began in a few pedants, who, having read that Sophocles was the great model of tragedy, and Aristotle the infallible dictator of its rules, and finding that the *Lear, Hamlet, Othello,* and other masterpieces were neither in imitation of Sophocles nor in obedience to Aristotle—and, not having (with one or two exceptions) the courage to affirm, that the delight which their country received from generation to generation, in defiance of the alterations of circumstances and habits, was wholly groundless—took upon them, as a happy medium and refuge, to talk of Shakespeare as a sort of beautiful *lusus naturae,* a delightful monster, wild, indeed, and without taste or judgment, but like the inspired idiots so much venerated in the East, uttering, amid the strangest follies, the sublimest truths. In nine places out of ten in which I find his awful name mentioned, it is with some epithet of "wild," "irregular," "pure child of nature," etc. If all this be true, we must submit to it; though to a thinking mind it cannot but be painful to find any excellence, merely human, thrown out of all human analogy, and thereby leaving us neither rules for imitation, nor motives to imitate; but, if false, it is a dangerous falsehood; for it affords a refuge to secret self-conceit, enables a vain man at once to escape his reader's indignation by general swollen panegyrics, and merely by his *ipse dixit* to treat as contemptible what he has not intellect enough to comprehend, or soul to feel, without assigning any reason, or referring his opinion to any demonstrative principle; thus leaving Shakespeare as a sort of Grand Lama, adored indeed, and his very excrements prized as relics, but with no authority or real influence. I grieve that every late voluminous edition of his works would enable me to substantiate the present charge with a variety of facts, one-tenth of which would of themselves exhaust the time allotted to me. Every critic, who has or has not made a collection of black letter books—in itself a useful and respectable amusement—puts on the seven-league boots of self-opinion, and strides at once from an illustrator into a supreme judge, and blind and deaf, fills his three-ounce phial at the waters of Niagara; and determines positively the greatness of the cataract to be neither more nor less than his three-ounce phial has been able to receive.

I think this a very serious subject. It is my earnest desire—my passionate endeavour—to enforce at various times and by various arguments and instances the close and reciprocal connection of just taste with pure morality. Without that acquaintance with the heart of man, or that docility and childlike gladness to be made acquainted with it, which those only can have, who dare look at their own hearts—and that with a steadiness which religion only has the power of reconciling with sincere humility; without this, and the modesty produced by it, I am deeply convinced that no man, however wide his erudition, however patient his antiquarian researches, can possibly understand, or be worthy of understanding, the writings of Shakespeare.

Assuredly, that criticism of Shakespeare will alone be genial which is reverential. The Englishman, who without reverence, a proud and affectionate reverence, can utter the name of William Shakespeare, stands disqualified for the office of critic. He wants one at least of the very senses, the language of which he is to employ, and will discourse, at best, but as a blind man, while the whole harmonious creation of light and shade with all its subtle interchange of deepening and dissolving colours rises in silence to the silent *fiat* of the uprising Apollo. However inferior in ability I may be to some who have followed me, I own I am proud that I was the first in time who publicly demonstrated to the full extent of the position, that the supposed irregularity and extravagancies of Shakespeare were the mere dreams of a pedantry that arraigned the eagle because it had not the dimensions of the swan. In all the successive courses of lectures delivered by me, since my first attempt at the Royal Institution, it has been, and it still remains, my object, to prove that in all points from the most important to the most minute, the judgment of Shakespeare is commensurate with his genius, nay, that his genius reveals itself in his judgment, as in its most exalted form. And the more gladly do I recur to this subject from the clear conviction, that to judge aright, and with distinct consciousness of the grounds of our judgment, concerning the works of Shakespeare, implies the power and the means of judging rightly of all other works of intellect, those of abstract science alone excepted.

It is a painful truth that not only individuals, but even whole nations, are ofttimes so enslaved to the habits of their education and immediate circumstances, as not to judge disinterestedly even on those subjects, the very pleasure arising from which consists in its disinterestedness, namely, on subjects of taste and polite literature. Instead of deciding concerning their own modes and customs by any rule of reason, nothing appears rational, becoming, or beautiful to them, but what coincides with the peculiarities of their education. In this narrow circle, individuals may attain to exquisite discrimination, as the French critics have done in their own literature; but a true critic can no more be such without placing himself on some central point, from which he may command the whole, that is, some general rule, which, founded in reason, or the faculties common to all men, must therefore apply to each, than an astronomer can explain the movements of the solar system without taking his stand in the sun. And let me remark, that this will not tend to produce despotism, but, on the contrary, true tolerance, in the critic. He will, indeed, require, as the spirit and substance of a work, something true in human nature itself, and independent of all circumstances; but in the mode of applying it, he will estimate genius and judgment according to the felicity with which the imperishable soul of intellect shall have adapted itself to the age, the place, and the existing manners. The error he will expose lies in reversing this, and holding up the mere circumstances as perpetual, to the utter neglect of the power which can alone animate them. For art cannot exist without, or apart from, nature; and what has man of his own to give to his fellow-man, but his own thoughts and feelings, and his observations so far as they are modified by his own thoughts or feelings?

Let me, then, once more submit this question to minds emancipated alike from national, or party, or sectarian prejudice. Are the plays of Shakespeare works of rude uncultivated genius, in which the splendour of the parts compensates, if aught can compensate, for the barbarous shapelessness and irregularity of the whole? Or is the form equally admirable with the matter, and the judgment of the great poet not less deserving our wonder than his genius? Or, again, to repeat the question in other words: Is Shakespeare a great dramatic poet on account only of those beauties and excellencies which he possesses in common with the ancients, but with diminished claims to our love and honour to the full extent of his differences from them? Or are these very differences additional proofs of poetic wisdom, at once results and symbols of living power as contrasted with lifeless mechanism— of free and rival originality as contradistinguished from servile imitation, or, more accurately, a blind copying of effects, instead of a true imitation of the essential principles? Imagine not that I am about to oppose genius to rules. No! the comparative value of these rules is the very cause to be tried. The spirit of poetry, like all other living powers, must of necessity circumscribe itself by rules, were it only to unite power with beauty. It must embody in order to reveal itself; but a living body is of necessity an organized one; and what is organization but the connection of parts in and for a whole, so that each part is at once end and means? This is the discovery of criticism; it is a necessity of the human mind; and all nations have felt and obeyed it, in the invention of metre, and measured sounds, as the vehicle and *involucrum* of poetry, itself a fellow-growth from the same life, even as the bark is to the tree!

No work of true genius dares want its appropriate form, neither indeed is there any danger of this. As it must not, so genius cannot, be lawless: for it is even this that constitutes it genius —the power of acting creatively under laws of its own origination. How then comes it that not only single *Zoili*, but whole nations have combined in unhesitating condemnation of our great dramatist, as a sort of African nature, rich in beautiful monsters, as a wild heath where islands of fertility look the greener from the surrounding waste, where the loveliest plants now shine out among unsightly weeds, and now are choked by their parasitic growth, so intertwined that we cannot disentangle the weed without snapping the flower? In this statement I have had no reference to the vulgar abuse of Voltaire, save as far as his charges are coincident with the decisions of Shakespeare's own commentators and (so they would tell you) almost idolatrous admirers. The true ground of the mistake lies in the confounding mechanical regularity with organic form. The form is mechanic, when on any given material we impress a pre-determined form, not neces-

sarily arising out of the properties of the material; as when to a mass of wet clay we give whatever shape we wish it to retain when hardened. The organic form, on the other hand, is innate; it shapes, as it developes, itself from within, and the fulness of its development is one and the same with the perfection of its outward form. Such as the life is, such is the form. Nature, the prime genial artist, inexhaustible in diverse powers, is equally inexhaustible in forms, each exterior is the physiognomy of the being within its true image reflected and thrown out from the concave mirror: and even such is the appropriate excellence of her chosen poet, of our own Shakespeare, himself a nature humanized, a genial understanding, directing self-consciously a power and an implicit wisdom deeper even than our consciousness.

I greatly dislike beauties and selections in general; but as proof positive of his unrivalled excellence, I should like to try Shakespeare by this criterion. Make out your amplest catalogue of all the human faculties, as reason or the moral law, the will, the feeling of the coincidence of the two (a feeling *sui generis et demonstratio demonstrationum*) called the conscience, the understanding, or prudence, wit, fancy, imagination, judgment, and then of the objects on which these are to be employed, as the beauties, the terrors, and the seeming caprices of nature, the capabilities, that is, the actual and the ideal, of the human mind, conceived as an individual or as a social being, as in innocence or in guilt, in a play-paradise or in a war-field of temptation; and then compare with Shakespeare under each of these heads all or any of the writers in prose and verse that have ever lived! Who, that is competent to judge, doubts the result? And ask your own hearts, ask your own common-sense to conceive the possibility of this man being—I say not, the drunken savage of that wretched sciolist, whom Frenchmen, to their shame, have honoured before their elder and better worthies—but the anomalous, the wild, the irregular, genius of our daily criticism! What! are we to have miracles in sport?—Or, I speak reverently, does God choose idiots by whom to convey divine truths to man?

On Poesy or Art [1]

MAN communicates by articulation of sounds, and paramountly by the memory in the ear; nature by the impression of bounds and surfaces on the eye, and through the eye it gives significance and appropriation, and thus the conditions of memory, or the capability of being remembered, to sounds, smells, &c. Now Art, used collectively for painting, sculpture, architecture and music, is the mediatress between, and reconciler of, nature and man. It is, therefore, the power of humanizing nature, of infusing the thoughts and passions of man into everything which is the object of his contemplation; color, form, motion, and sound, are the elements which it combines, and it stamps them into unity in the mould of a moral idea. [2]

The primary art is writing;—primary, if we regard the purpose abstracted from the different modes of realizing it, those steps of progression of which the instances are still visible in the lower degrees of civilization. First, there is mere gesticulation; then rosaries or *wampum*; then picture-language; then hieroglyphics, and finally alphabetic letters. These all consist of a translation of man into nature, of a substitution of the visible for the audible.

The so called music of savage tribes as little deserves the name of art for the understanding, as the ear warrants it for music. Its lowest state is a mere expression of passion by the sounds

---

[1] *On Poesy or Art.* This essay, first printed after his death in Coleridge's *Literary Remains*, was given as a lecture in 1818. It is inserted in order to give an example of those more fragmentary critical writings of Coleridge that are so famous for both their suggestive insights and their obscurity. Of these fragments, "On Poesy or Art" is possibly the most lucid and certainly the most central. In fact, with the exception of the essays "On the Principles of Genial Criticism," it is probably—despite its hieroglyphic character—the most significant single example of Coleridge's excursions into a quasi-metaphysical criticism of art. The essay is also important as the most extreme instance in which Coleridge closely followed the great German philosopher of romanticism, Friedrich Wilhelm von Schelling, particularly his provocative "On the Relation of the Formative Arts to Nature." To the charge of plagiarism, it is at least a partial answer to point out that the essay consists of notes to be developed in a lecture. It would not have been published thus by Coleridge; he was never, in his printed work, reluctant to introduce, *as quotations*, passages he liked or that seemed to coincide with his convictions. His legendary memory for whatever he read, and his habitual assimilation of it into his own thought, should also be kept in mind; and one may perhaps allow it to have unfolded more spontaneously in a mere outline of a lecture, without expecting a conscious checking of it from Coleridge, than in an essay prepared for publication. This is not the place to touch on the complicated problem of the similarity of Coleridge's thought to Schelling's, which so eminent an authority as Professor René Wellek regards as quite marked. In the opinion of the editor, however, the similarity is to be found more in certain specific points of view than in ultimate aim, and the general direction of Coleridge's thinking was toward an objective rationalism, in the Platonic tradition,—a more clear-cut objectivism than is to be found in Schelling.

[2] This rather abrupt opening, and the two following paragraphs, might be paraphrased as follows: Men communicate with each other by sounds, particularly words. We learn about nature, however, primarily through our eyes; and what we see gives order and point to what we pick up about nature through our other senses. Now art seeks to present nature to man in the most meaningful way possible. It draws upon both sight and sound, therefore; it puts what it portrays in such a way as to strike home to man's feelings, and also gives it meaning to the *mind* by presenting it in the light of thought and ideals. Art, by doing this, is thus a coming together of nature and man—a mediator between them. Now the kind of thing art tries to do is shown, in its most basic form, by writing (that is, *visible signs* or *symbols*—whether in the forms of gestures, picture-language, or alphabetic letters). For here especially what man is trying to do is to take his own thoughts and feelings and translate them into forms that are visible. He is *creating symbols*, in other words, visible signs, like the forms we see in nature, and through which we learn about nature, but which are now being used to represent *human* thoughts and feelings. Consequently, language—particularly written language—is a more distinctively human medium than are the sounds used by music or the forms or colors used by the visual arts (which, as contrasted with language, are more directly taken over from nature). That is, articulate speech, particularly written speech, is more *symbolic*, more creative; the human mind has entered more into the making of it as a medium of communication. Thus, in that "union or reconciliation" of nature and man which art tries to bring about, poetry especially, of all the arts, represents more of a reaching out on the part of the human mind—more of a coming forward to meet nature, so to speak.

which the passion itself necessitates; [3]—the highest amounts to no more than a voluntary reproduction of these sounds in the absence of the occasioning causes, so as to give the pleasure of contrast,—for example, by the various outcries of battle in the song of security and triumph. Poetry also is purely human; for all its materials are from the mind, and all its products are for the mind. But it is the apotheosis of the former state, in which by excitement of the associative power passion itself imitates order, and the order resulting produces a pleasureable passion, and thus it elevates the mind by making its feelings the object of its reflexion. So likewise, whilst it recalls the sights and sounds that had accompanied the occasions of the original passions, poetry impregnates them with an interest not their own by means of the passions, and yet tempers the passion by the calming power which all distinct images exert on the human soul. In this way poetry is the preparation for art, inasmuch as it avails itself of the forms of nature to recall, to express, and to modify the thoughts and feelings of the mind. Still, however, poetry can only act through the intervention of articulate speech, which is so peculiarly human, that in all languages it constitutes the ordinary phrase by which man and nature are contradistinguished. It is the original force of the word "brute," and even "mute" and "dumb" do not convey the absence of sound, but the absence of articulated sounds.

As soon as the human mind is intelligibly addressed by an outward image exclusively of articulate speech, so soon does art commence. But please to observe that I have laid particular stress on the words "human mind,"—meaning to exclude thereby all results common to man and all other sentient creatures, and consequently confining myself to the effect produced by the congruity of the animal impression with the reflective powers of the mind; so that not the thing presented, but that which is re-presented by the thing, shall be the source of the pleasure.

In this sense nature itself is to a religious observer the art of God; and for the same cause art itself might be defined as of a middle quality between a thought and a thing, or, as I said before, the union and reconciliation of that which is nature with that which is exclusively human. It is the figured language of thought, and is distinguished from nature by the unity of all the parts in one thought or idea. Hence nature itself would give us the impression of a work of art, if we could see the thought which is present at once in the whole and every part; and a work of art will be just in proportion as it adequately conveys the thought, and rich in proportion to the variety of parts which it holds in unity.

If, therefore, the term "mute" be taken as opposed not to sound but to articulate speech, the old definition of painting will in fact be the true and best definition of the Fine Arts in general, that is, *muta poesis,* mute poesy, and so of course poesy. And, as all languages perfect themselves by a gradual process of desynonymizing words originally equivalent, I have cherished the wish to use the word "poesy" as the generic or common term, and to distinguish that species of poesy which is not *muta poesis* by its usual name "poetry"; while of all the other species which collectively form the Fine Arts, there would remain this as the common definition,—that they all, like poetry, are to express intellectual purposes, thoughts, conceptions, and sentiments which have their origin in the human mind,[4]—not, however, as poetry does, by means of articulate speech, but as nature or the divine art does, by form, color, magnitude, proportion, or by sound, that is, silently or musically.

[3] That is, it is hardly mediating between nature and man, but is simply the outpouring and channeling of feeling through sound, either at the moment of excitement or deliberately reproduced later. The statement may be contrasted with the extreme romantic conception of art as "self-expression" that was particularly popular around the close of the nineteenth century.

[4] Despite what may seem implied by the cryptic phrasing here, art, for Coleridge, does not project or stamp human feelings and thoughts upon nature; it is not a subjective reading into nature of qualities or forms that are not there (though art may arouse in us *feelings* that are not in nature, and may bring *them* to bear on the object it is portraying). Instead, the laws of human reason have, in a phrase used later in the essay, "the same ground with nature": they duplicate or echo those laws that underlie the objective forms of nature; and through reason these forms are *known,* not *invented.* These insights of reason (together with emotions and reactions to them which, however, are purely human) are then brought forward by the imagination and joined to the material objects in nature; and it is in this sense that the imaginative process of meeting nature, in order to effect the "union or reconciliation," takes its "origin in the human mind."

Well! it may be said—but who has ever thought otherwise? We all know that art is the imitatress of nature. And, doubtless, the truths which I hope to convey would be barren truisms, if all men meant the same by the words "imitate" and "nature." But it would be flattering mankind at large, to presume that such is the fact. First, to imitate. The impression on the wax is not an imitation, but a copy, of the seal; the seal itself is an imitation.[5] But, further, in order to form a philosophic conception, we must seek for the kind, as the heat in ice, invisible light, &c., whilst, for practical purposes, we must have reference to the degree.[6] It is sufficient that philosophically we understand that in all imitation two elements must coexist, and not only

coexist, but must be perceived as coexisting. These two constituent elements are likeness and unlikeness, or sameness and difference, and in all genuine creations of art there must be a union of these disparates. The artist may take his point of view where he pleases, provided that the desired effect be perceptibly produced,— that there be likeness in the difference, difference in the likeness, and a reconcilement of both in one. If there be likeness to nature without any check of difference, the result is disgusting, and the more complete the delusion, the more loathsome the effect. Why are such simulations of nature, as wax-work figures of men and women, so disagreeable? Because, not finding the motion and the life which we expected, we are shocked as by a falsehood, every circumstance of detail, which before induced us to be interested, making the distance from truth more palpable. You set out with a supposed reality and are disappointed and disgusted with the deception; whilst, in respect to a work of genuine imitation, you begin with an acknowledged total difference, and then every touch of nature gives you the pleasure of an approximation to truth. The fundamental principle of all this is undoubtedly the horror of falsehood and the love of truth inherent in the human breast. The Greek tragic dance rested on these principles, and I can deeply sympathize in imagination with the Greeks in this favorite part of their theatrical exhibitions, when I call to mind the pleasure I felt in beholding the combat of the Horatii and Curiatii most exquisitely danced in Italy to the music of Cimarosa.

Secondly, as to nature. We must imitate nature! yes, but what in nature,—all and every thing? No, the beautiful in nature. And what then is the beautiful? What is beauty? It is, in the abstract, the unity of the manifold, the coalescence of the diverse; in the concrete, it is the union of the shapely (*formosum*) with the vital.[7] In the dead organic it depends on regularity of

[5] One of Coleridge's favorite distinctions is that between "imitation" and "copy." A true imitation, as distinct from a copy, will have different materials with which to work; and the form that is drawn out from those materials will, in some ways, also be different from that of the original. Thus, if an animal is carved in profile onto a seal, not only are the materials different— metal instead of bone, flesh, and skin, and a two-dimensional plane instead of three dimensions—but the form also (except for the similarity in the outline of the profile) may in many ways be different because of circumstances determined by the nature of the *materials*. In this sense, a true "imitation" or "symbol" has a unity or form of its *own*, emerging through a "multëity" also its own; and it may thus be described as "dynamic," "living," or as an active representation rather than a passive "copy." (See Coleridge's discussion of the symbol, p. 386.) Because an imitation starts with an acknowledged difference, we then—as we note similarities in it with the original—work from diversity up to similarity (or unity); this process of *unity working through diversity* is not only a characteristic of what is beautiful in nature, as well as of an "imitation" of it, but also, on a third level, it characterizes that act of mind by which we compare the imitation and the original. But if we see a "copy"—which is never as good as the original, and can never compete with nature herself on her own grounds—then this process of moving from diversity to similarity is turned around, and we move backwards. We *start* with similarity (the unity between the original and the copy), and then begin to note the differences, as in Coleridge's example of seeing wax figures.

[6] See "On the Principles of Genial Criticism," above, pp. 368-69. For ordinary purposes, we regard as differences in *kind* what are really only differences in *degree* (for example, we assume that 100° is "hot," and that ice is "cold," though there may be 32° of heat in it). It is unphilosophical to confuse together *kind* and *degree*. The difference between "imitation" and "copy" is not a mere difference in degree—a copy being simply closer— but it is instead a difference in kind.

[7] *In the abstract.* That is, *abstractly considered*, beauty may be defined as the unifying of "multëity" or the "diverse." When it is found existing concretely—in actual objects of nature or works of art—it is marked by the presence of form ("the shapely") organically modifying, developing, and giving direction to particular things ("multëity") that are *vital*—that are functioning actively in response to the form (and without which the form itself cannot be fulfilled).

form, the first and lowest species of which is the triangle with all its modifications, as in crystals, architecture, &c.; in the living organic it is not mere regularity of form, which would produce a sense of formality; neither is it subservient to any thing beside itself. It may be present in a disagreeable object, in which the proportion of the parts constitutes a whole; it does not arise from association, as the agreeable does, but sometimes lies in the rupture of association; it is not different to different individuals and nations, as has been said, nor is it connected with the ideas of the good, or the fit, or the useful. The sense of beauty is intuitive, and beauty itself is all that inspires pleasure without, and aloof from, and even contrarily to, interest.

If the artist copies the mere nature, the *natura naturata*, what idle rivalry! If he proceeds only from a given form, which is supposed to answer to the notion of beauty, what an emptiness, what an unreality there always is in his productions, as in Cipriani's pictures! Believe me, you must master the essence, the *natura naturans*, which presupposes a bond between nature in the higher sense and the soul of man.[8]

The wisdom in nature is distinguished from that in man by the co-instantaneity of the plan and the execution; the thought and the product are one, or are given at once; but there is no reflex act, and hence there is no moral responsibility. In man there is reflexion, freedom, and choice; he is, therefore, the head of the visible creation. In the objects of nature are presented, as in a mirror, all the possible elements, steps, and processes of intellect antecedent to consciousness, and therefore to the full development of the intelligential act; and man's mind is the very focus of all the rays of intellect which are scattered throughout the images of nature. Now so to place these images, totalized, and fitted to the limits of the human mind, as to elicit from, and to superinduce upon, the forms themselves

the moral reflexions to which they approximate, to make the external internal, the internal external, to make nature thought, and thought nature,—this is the mystery of genius in the Fine Arts. Dare I add that the genius must act on the feeling, that body is but a striving to become mind,—that it is mind in its essence! [9]

In every work of art there is a reconcilement of the external with the internal; the conscious is so impressed on the unconscious as to appear in it; as compare mere letters inscribed on a tomb with figures themselves constituting the tomb. He who combines the two is the man of genius; and for that reason he must partake of both. Hence there is in genius itself an unconscious activity; nay, that is the genius in the man of genius. And this is the true exposition of the rule that the artist must first eloign himself from nature in order to return to her with full effect. Why this? Because if he were to begin by mere painful copying, he would produce masks only, not forms breathing life. He must out of his own mind create forms according to the severe laws of the intellect, in order to generate in himself that co-ordination of freedom and law, that involution of obedience in the prescript, and of the prescript in the impulse to obey, which assimilates him to nature, and enables him to understand her. He merely absents himself for a season from her, that his own spirit, which has the same ground with nature, may learn her unspoken language in its main radicals, before he approaches to her endless compositions of them. Yes, not to acquire cold notions—lifeless technical rules—but living and life-producing ideas, which shall contain their own evidence, the certainty that they are essentially one with the germinal causes in nature,—his consciousness being the focus and mirror of both,—for

---

[8] The standpoint is opposed both to complete naturalism and to abstractionism in art. If the artist simply copies the *natura naturata*, he is fighting a losing battle with nature. If, on the other hand, he takes some abstract form for beauty, and tries to *project* it upon his object, the form will still be bodiless and unreal. What must be mastered are the living forms that work organically through nature according to principles which are the same as those that characterize human reason itself.

[9] By having consciousness and the ability to reflect and choose, man's mind serves as a focal point at which the unfolding processes of nature can become awake, so to speak, and achieve, through awareness, the ability to see, distinguish, and know themselves. In this sense, whatever awareness is attained by the human mind may be regarded as a *completing* of nature, as a coming of nature to a head and a *flowering out* of it into a *self-consciousness that is able to evaluate and select* and is therefore morally responsible. Genius in art is found in the ability to weld the processes of nature ("the external") to the completing thought and moral evaluating of the mind ("the internal") in such a way that they become entirely one.

this does the artist for a time abandon the external real in order to return to it with a complete sympathy with its internal and actual. For of all we see, hear, feel and touch the substance is and must be in ourselves; and therefore there is no alternative in reason between the dreary (and thank heaven! almost impossible) belief that every thing around us is but a phantom, or that the life which is in us is in them likewise; and that to know is to resemble, when we speak of objects out of ourselves, even as within ourselves to learn is, according to Plato, only to recollect; [10]—the only effective answer to which, that I have been fortunate to meet with, is that which Pope has consecrated for future use in the line—

And coxcombs vanquish Berkeley with a grin! [11]

The artist must imitate that which is within the thing, that which is active through form and figure, and discourses to us by symbols—the *Natur-geist*, or spirit of nature, as we unconsciously imitate those whom we love; for so only can he hope to produce any work truly natural in the object and truly human in the effect. The idea which puts the form together cannot itself be the form. It is above form, and is its essence, the universal in the individual, or the individuality itself,—the glance and the exponent of the indwelling power.[12]

[10] The substance of what we perceive is in us. But it is not *solely* in us, with everything else a mere phantom. Instead, it is a case of the forms that characterize nature *also* characterizing our minds. Therefore, when we perceive and come to know them in nature, we may be said to be in a state of approximating and resembling them. What was already there, in nature, has simply become *conscious*, so to speak; just as to learn is, according to Plato, to have forms—which were previously implanted in our own nature—come awake into active thinking.

[11] John Brown, "Essay on Satire, Occasioned by the Death of Mr. Pope," II, 224. Cf. the end of Ch. 8, *Biographia Literaria:* ". . . the supporters of the Ptolemaic system might have rebuffed the Newtonian, and pointing to the sky with a self-complacent grin have appealed to *common sense*, whether the sun did not move and the earth stand still."

[12] The "idea" is the "essence" of form and also "the individuality itself": form becomes form—it fulfills its function as a shaping and guiding agent—only if there is *something to be formed*. The "idea" that brings the form to bear upon something to be formed (that makes form active and formative, in other words, by bringing it into play) is not only above form; it is the "essence"

Each thing that lives has its moment of self-exposition, and so has each period of each thing, if we remove the disturbing forces of accident. To do this is the business of ideal art, whether in images of childhood, youth, or age, in man or in woman. Hence a good portrait is the abstract of the personal; it is not the likeness for actual comparison, but for recollection. This explains why the likeness of a very good portrait is not always recognized; because some persons never abstract, and amongst these are especially to be numbered the near relations and friends of the subject, in consequence of the constant pressure and check exercised on their minds by the actual presence of the original. And each thing that only appears to live has also its possible position of relation to life, as nature herself testifies, who where she cannot be, prophesies her being in the crystallized metal, or the inhaling plant.

The charm, the indispensable requisite, of sculpture is the unity of effect. But painting rests in a material remoter from nature, and its compass is therefore greater. Light and shade give external, as well as internal, being even with all its accidents, whilst sculpture is confined to the latter. And here I may observe that the subjects chosen for works of art, whether in sculpture or painting, should be such as really are capable of being expressed and conveyed within the limits of those arts. Moreover they ought to be such as will affect the spectator by their truth, their beauty, or their sublimity, and therefore they may be addressed to the judgement, the senses, or the reason. The peculiarity of the impression which they may make, may be derived either from color and form, or from proportion and fitness, or from the excitement of the moral feelings; or all these may be combined. Such works as do combine these sources of effect must have the preference in dignity.

of form—it is what permits that form to fulfill and be itself; it is the universal made active in the finite and individual. In fact, in the process of fulfilling the form by bringing the universal to focus in the individual, it also simultaneously gives form to the individual and thus permits the individual to come into being for a "moment of self-exposition" and achieve its individuality. Hence Coleridge, who often seems to anticipate the great modern metaphysician, Whitehead, defines life as "the principle of *individuation*." (*Theory of Life*, published as Appendix C in *Aids to Reflection*.)

Imitation of the antique may be too exclusive, and may produce an injurious effect on modern sculpture;—1st, generally, because such an imitation cannot fail to have a tendency to keep the attention fixed on externals rather than on the thought within;—2ndly, because, accordingly, it leads the artist to rest satisfied with that which is always imperfect, namely, bodily form, and circumscribes his views of mental expression to the ideas of power and grandeur only;—3rdly, because it induces an effort to combine together two incongruous things, that is to say, modern feelings in antique forms;—4thly, because it speaks in a language, as it were, learned and dead, the tones of which, being unfamiliar, leave the common spectator cold and unimpressed;—and lastly, because it necessarily causes a neglect of thoughts, emotions and images of profounder interest and more exalted dignity, as motherly, sisterly, and brotherly love, piety, devotion, the divine become human,—the Virgin, the Apostle, the Christ. The artist's principle in the statue of a great man should be the illustration of departed merit; and I cannot but think that a skilful adoption of modern habiliments would, in many instances, give a variety and force of effect which a bigoted adherence to Greek or Roman costume precludes. It is, I believe, from artists finding Greek models unfit for several important modern purposes, that we see so many allegorical figures on monuments and elsewhere. Painting was, as it were, a new art, and being unshackled by old models it chose its own subjects, and took an eagle's flight. And a new field seems opened for modern sculpture in the symbolical expression of the ends of life, as in Guy's monument, Chantrey's children in Worcester Cathedral, &c.[13]

Architecture exhibits the greatest extent of the difference from nature which may exist in works of art. It involves all the powers of design, and is sculpture and painting inclusively. It shews the greatness of man, and should at the same time teach him humility.

Music is the most entirely human of the fine arts, and has the fewest *analoga* in nature. Its first delightfulness is simple accordance with the ear; but it is an associated thing, and recalls the deep emotions of the past with an intellectual sense of proportion. Every human feeling is greater and larger than the exciting cause,—a proof, I think, that man is designed for a higher state of existence; and this is deeply implied in music, in which there is always something more and beyond the immediate impression.

With regard to works in all the branches of the fine arts, I may remark that the pleasure arising from novelty must of course be allowed its due place and weight. This pleasure consists in the identity of two opposite elements, that is to say—sameness and variety. If in the midst of the variety there be not some fixed object for the attention, the unceasing succession of the variety will prevent the mind from observing the difference of the individual objects; and the only thing remaining will be the succession, which will then produce precisely the same effect as sameness. This we experience when we let the trees or hedges pass before the fixed eye during a rapid movement in a carriage, or, on the other hand, when we suffer a file of soldiers or ranks of men in procession to go on before us without resting the eye on any one in particular. In order to derive pleasure from the occupation of the mind, the principle of unity must always be present, so that in the midst of the multeity the centripetal force be never suspended, nor the sense be fatigued by the predominance of the centrifugal force. This unity in multeity I have elsewhere stated as the principle of beauty. It is equally the source of pleasure in variety, and in fact a higher term including both. What is the seclusive or distinguishing term between them? [14]

Remember that there is a difference between form as proceeding, and shape as superinduced; —the latter is either the death or the imprisonment of the thing;—the former is its self-witnessing and self-effected sphere of agency. Art would or should be the abridgment of nature. Now the fulness of nature is without character, as water is purest when without taste, smell, or color; but this is the highest, the apex only,—

---

[13] Thomas Guy (1645?-1742), founder of Guy's Hospital, London. The "Sleeping Children" by Sir Francis Chantrey, a sculptor of Coleridge's time, are in Lichfield Cathedral, not Worcester.

[14] The difference between beauty and the pleasure derived from sameness in variety is that, in *beauty*, the form arises *organically* from the diverse multëity of the materials. Mere sameness in variety, however, may give pleasure even though it is not an organic unifying of the diverse but is simply a uniformity *imposed* on it from without. See "On the Principles of Genial Criticism," above, p. 371, n. 21.

it is not the whole.[15] The object of art is to give the whole *ad hominem;* hence each step of nature hath its ideal, and hence the possibility of a climax up to the perfect form of a harmonized chaos.

To the idea of life victory or strife is necessary; as virtue consists not simply in the absence of vices, but in the overcoming of them. So it is in beauty.[16] The sight of what is subordinated and conquered heightens the strength and the pleasure; and this should be exhibited by the artist either inclusively in his figure, or else out of it, and beside it to act by way of supplement and contrast. And with a view to this, remark the seeming identity of body and mind in infants, and thence the loveliness of the former; the commencing separation in boyhood, and the struggle of equilibrium in youth: thence onward the body is first simply indifferent; then demanding the translucency of the mind not to be worse than indifferent; and finally all that presents the body as body becoming almost of an excremental nature.

[15] The ultimate forms of nature, when they are abstracted from their function as controlling agents, lack the character, the definite outlines, that arise from limitation—from being brought to focus, in other words, into specific individuality. But this ultimate "apex" is not the "whole" of nature; the "whole" includes the process Coleridge elsewhere described as "totality dawning into individuation." The aim of art is to render this *whole*, this *active process*, meaningful *ad hominem* —that is, meaningful to human nature, to human feelings.

[16] "Something there must be to realize the form, something in and by which the *forma informans* reveals itself" (see "Genial Criticism," above, p. 373). This realizing of the form implies activity; and this activity further implies the presence of something being *acted upon*. Beauty is not the final unity, but is to be found in the process of *unifying*, and therefore necessitates the existence of something *being* unified.

JOHANN WOLFGANG VON GOETHE   (1749-1832)

THE CRITICAL observations of Goethe have a unique value. For no practicing imaginative writer of equal importance—or at least of equal world renown—has ever really entered the field of criticism. This may be readily explained by the fact that, almost alone among writers of world reputation, Goethe wrote after the mid-eighteenth century.

In the history of a cultural tradition, a developed literary criticism is always a fairly late genre or branch of writing. It is so almost by definition.

JOHANN WOLFGANG VON GOETHE. After studying law as a youth, Goethe settled in Weimar at the invitation of its Duke (1775). He held various governmental positions, gave part of his time to independent scientific research, devoted himself as well to literature and philosophy, and, through his prolific writing in several genres, became idolized throughout Germany and the whole of western Europe.

The standard translation of Eckermann's *Conversations of Goethe* is that of John Oxenford (1850; and several later editions). Excerpts from this translation, together with translations of some of Goethe's critical essays, may be found in *Goethe's Literary Essays* (ed. J. E. Spingarn, 1921), and there is also *Conversations with Goethe* (tr. G. O'Brien and annotated with an introduction by H. Kohn, 1964). For commentary in English, see especially Karl Viëtor, *Goethe, the Thinker* (Cambridge, Mass., 1950); Henry Hatfield, *Aesthetic Paganism in German Literature* (Cambridge, Mass., 1964) and *Goethe: a Critical Introduction* (Norfolk, Conn., 1963); and E. M. Wilkinson and L. A. Willoughby, *Goethe: Poet and Thinker* (1962). For more general background, see W. H. Bruford, *Culture and Society in Classical Weimar, 1775-1806* (Cambridge, 1962).

For criticism implies an increased self-consciousness, and also the previous —and perhaps well-established—existence of literary works and literary traditions on which and through which to employ itself. The flowering of literary criticism as we think of it, with an increase in subtlety, method, and variety of approach, largely began in the eighteenth century; and with it came a far more widespread interest in criticism on the part of practicing writers also.

From the critical reviews, essays, and scattered observations of Goethe, there emerges a broad and enlightened conception of literature in which the romantic concern with the organic process of nature is joined with a classical confidence in objective form and value and in their formative molding of the human mind and character. It is not a conception of literature that is critically analyzed or developed by Goethe in any detail. Instead it appears as a general criterion of values that underlies his approach to specific writers and literary problems. The penetration and sanity of Goethe's criticism are perhaps shown less well by his various essays and reviews than by the mature and condensed insights found in the famous *Conversations of Goethe in the Last Years of his Life,* collected by his devoted if somewhat humorless admirer, J. P. Eckermann.

From Conversations of Goethe

[*The Formative Influence of the Classical*]

[April 1, 1827] The conversation then turned upon dramatic authors in general, and upon the important influence they exerted, and could exert, upon the people.

"A great dramatic poet," said Goethe, "if he is at the same time productive, and is actuated by a strong noble purpose in all his works, may make the soul of his pieces become the soul of the people. I should think this was something well worth the trouble. From Corneille proceeded an influence capable of forming heroes. This was something for Napoleon, who had need of an heroic people; on which account he said of Corneille, that if he were still living he would make a prince of him. A dramatic poet who knows his vocation should therefore work incessantly at its higher development, so that his influence on the people may be noble and beneficial.

Conversations of Goethe. By J. P. Eckermann (1836-48, tr. John Oxenford).

"Not contemporaries and competitors ought to be the objects of study; but the great men of antiquity, whose works have for centuries received equal homage and consideration. Indeed, a man of really superior endowments will feel the necessity of this; need for an intercourse with great predecessors is the sure sign of a higher talent. Study Molière, study Shakespeare; but, above all things, the old Greeks, and always the Greeks."

"For highly-endowed natures," remarked I, "the study of the authors of antiquity may be invaluable; but in general it appears to have little influence upon personal character. If this were the case, all philologists and theologians would be the most excellent of men. But this is by no means so; such connoisseurs of the ancient Greek and Latin authors are able people or pitiful creatures, according to the good or bad qualities given them by God or inherited from their parents."

"There is nothing to be said against that," returned Goethe; "but it must not therefore be said that the study of the authors of antiquity is entirely without effect upon character. A worthless man will always remain worthless; and a little mind will not, by daily intercourse with the great minds of antiquity, become one inch greater. But a noble man, in whose soul God has placed the capability for future greatness of character and elevation of mind, will, through knowledge of and familiar intercourse with the elevated natures of ancient Greeks and Romans, develop to the utmost, and every day make a visible approach to similar greatness."

[*The Subject Matter of Poetry*]

[September 18, 1823] "The world is so great and rich, and life so full of variety, that you can never want occasions for poems. But they must all be occasional poems; that is to say, reality must give both impulse and material for their production. A particular case becomes universal and poetic by the very circumstance that it is treated by a poet. All my poems are occasional poems, suggested by real life, and having therein a firm foundation. I attach no value to poems snatched out of the air.

"Let no one say that reality wants poetical interest; for in this the poet proves his vocation, that he has the art to win from a common subject an interesting side. Reality must give the motive, the points to be expressed, the kernel, as I may say; but to work out of it a beautiful, animated whole belongs to the poet. You know Fürnstein, called the Poet of Nature; he has written the prettiest poem possible on the cultivation of hops. I have now proposed to him to make songs for the different crafts of working men, particularly a weaver's song, and I am sure he will do it well, for he has lived among such people from his youth; he understands the subject thoroughly, and is therefore master of his material. That is exactly the advantage of small works; you need only choose those subjects of which you are master. With a great poem, this cannot be: no part can be evaded; all which belongs to the animation of the whole, and is interwoven into the plan, must be represented with precision. In youth, however, the knowledge of things is only one-sided. A great work requires many-sidedness, and on that rock the young author splits. . . ."

[Nov. 24, 1824] "The majority of our young poets," said Goethe, "have no fault but this, that their subjectivity is not important, and that they cannot find matter in the objective. At best, they only find a material which is similar to themselves, which corresponds to their own subjectivity; but as for taking the material on its own account, merely because it is poetical, even when it is repugnant to their subjectivity, such a thing is never thought of."

[*The Influence of Environment*]

[May 3, 1827] "If a talent is to be speedily and happily developed, the great point is that a great deal of intellect and sound culture should be current in a nation.

"We admire the tragedies of the ancient Greeks; but, to take a correct view of the case, we ought rather to admire the period and the nation in which their production was possible than the individual authors; for though these pieces differ a little from each other, and one of these poets appears somewhat greater and more finished than the other, still, taking all things together, only one decided character runs through the whole.

"This is the character of grandeur, fitness, soundness, human perfection, elevated wisdom, sublime thought, clear, concrete vision, and whatever other qualities one might enumerate. But when we find all these qualities not only in the dramatic works that have come down to us, but also in lyrical and epic works, in the philosophers, the orators, and the historians, and in an equally high degree in the works of plastic art that have come down to us, we must feel convinced that such qualities did not merely belong to individuals, but were the current property of the nation and the whole period."

[*Originality*]

[December 16, 1828] "The Germans," said Goethe, "cannot cease to be Philistines. They are now squabbling about some verses, which are printed both in Schiller's works and mine, and fancy it is important to ascertain which really belong to Schiller and which to me; as if anything could be gained by such investigation—as if the existence of such things were not enough. Friends like Schiller and myself, intimate for years, with the same interests, in habits of daily intercourse, and under reciprocal obligations, live so completely in one another that it is hardly possible to decide to which of the two the particular thoughts belong. We have made many distichs together; sometimes I gave the thought, and Schiller made the verse; sometimes the contrary was the case; sometimes he made one line, and I the other. What matters the mine and thine? One must be a thorough Philistine, indeed, to attach the slightest importance to the solution of such questions. . . .

"We are indeed born with faculties; but we owe our development to a thousand influences of the great world, from which we appropriate to ourselves what we can, and what is suitable to us. I owe much to the Greeks and French; I am infinitely indebted to Shakespeare, Sterne, and Goldsmith; but in saying this I do not exhaust the sources of my culture; that would be an endless as well as an unnecessary task. We might as well question a strong man about the oxen, sheep, and swine which he has eaten and which have given him strength. What is important is to have a soul which loves truth and receives it wherever it finds it.

"Besides, the world is now so old, so many eminent men have lived and thought for thousands of years, that there is little new to be discovered or expressed. Even my theory of colors is not entirely new. Plato, Leonardo da Vinci, and many other excellent men have before me found and expressed the same thing in a detached form: my merit is that I have found it also, that I have said it again, and that I have striven to bring the truth once more into a confused world.

"The truth must be repeated over and over again, because error is repeatedly preached among us, not only by individuals but by the masses. In periodicals and cyclopedias, in schools and universities, everywhere, in fact, error prevails, and is quite easy in the feeling that it has a decided majority on its side."

[May 12, 1825] "People are always talking about originality; but what do they mean? As soon as we are born, the world begins to work upon us, and this goes on to the end. And, after all, what can we call our own except energy, strength, and will? If I could give an account of all that I owe to great predecessors

and contemporaries, there would be but a small balance in my favor.

"However, the time of life in which we are subjected to a new and important personal influence is, by no means, a matter of indifference. That Lessing, Winckelmann, and Kant were older than I, and that the first two acted upon my youth, the latter on my advanced age—this circumstance was for me very important. Again, that Schiller was so much younger than I, and engaged in his freshest strivings just as I began to be weary of the world—just, too, as the brothers von Humboldt and Schlegel were beginning their career under my eye—was of the greatest importance. I derived from it unspeakable advantages."

[April 15, 1829] "What seduces young people," said Goethe, "is this. We live in a time in which so much culture is diffused that it has communicated itself, as it were, to the atmosphere which a young man breathes. Poetical and philosophic thoughts live and move within him, he has sucked them in with his very breath, but he thinks they are his own property and utters them as such. But after he has restored to the time what he has received from it, he remains poor. He is like a fountain which plays for a while with the water with which it is supplied, but which ceases to flow as soon as the liquid treasure is exhausted."

[Classic and Romantic]

[April 2, 1829] "A new expression occurs to me," said Goethe, "which does not ill define the state of the case. I call the classic *healthy*, the romantic *sickly*. In this sense, the *Nibelungenlied* is as classic as the Iliad, for both are vigorous and healthy. Most modern productions are romantic—not because they are new; but because they are weak, morbid, and sickly. And the antique is classic—not because it is old; but because it is strong, fresh, joyous, and healthy. If we distinguish 'classic' and 'romantic' by these qualities, it will be easy to see our way."

[April 5, 1829] Goethe also told me about a tragedy by a young poet. "It is a pathological work," said he; "a superfluity of sap is bestowed on some parts that do not require it, and drawn out of those standing in need of it. The subject was good, but the scenes I expected were not there; while others that I did not expect were elaborated with assiduity and love. This is what I call pathological, or even 'romantic'—if you would rather speak after our new theory."

[March 21, 1830] "The idea of the distinction between classical and romantic poetry, which is now spread over the whole world and occasions so many quarrels and divisions, came originally from Schiller and myself. I laid down the maxim of objective treatment in poetry, and would allow no other; but Schiller, who worked quite in the subjective way, deemed his own fashion the right one, and to defend himself against me, wrote the treatise upon *Naïve and Sentimental Poetry.* He proved to me that I myself, against my will, was romantic, and that my *Iphigenia,* through the predominance of sentiment, was by no means so classical and so much in the antique spirit as some people supposed.

"The Schlegels took up this idea, and carried it further, so that it has now been diffused over the whole world; and everyone talks about classicism and romanticism—of which nobody thought fifty years ago."

[Modern Subjectivism]

[January 29, 1826] "If a person learns to sing," continued Goethe, "all the notes that are within his natural compass are easy to him, whilst those beyond the compass are at first extremely difficult. But, to be a vocalist, he must have them all at command. Just so with the poet—he deserves not the name while he only speaks out his few subjective feelings; but as soon as he can appropriate to himself, and express, the world, he is a poet. Then he is inexhaustible, and can be always new; while a subjective nature has soon talked out his little internal material, and is at last ruined by mannerism. People always talk of the study of the ancients; but what does that mean, except that it says, turn your attention to the real world, and try to express it—for that is what the ancients did."

Goethe arose and walked to and fro, while I remained seated at the table as he likes to see me. He stood a moment at the stove; and then, like one who has reflected, came to me, and, with his finger on his lips, said:

"I will now tell you something you will often find confirmed in your experience. All eras in a state of decline and dissolution are subjective; on the other hand, all progressive eras have an objective tendency. Our present time is retrograde, for it is subjective: we see this not merely in poetry, but also in painting, and much besides. Every healthy effort, on the contrary, is directed from the inward to the outward world; as you see in all great eras, which were really in a state of progression and all of an objective nature."

[February 12, 1831] "These are really good things," said Goethe. "You have before you the works of very fair talents, who have learned something, and have acquired no little taste and art. Still, something is wanting in all these pictures—the *Manly.* Take notice of this word, and underscore it. The pictures lack a certain urgent power; which in former ages was generally expressed, but in which the present age is deficient, and that with respect not only to painting but to all the other arts also. We have a more weakly race, of which we cannot say whether it is so by its origin, or by a more weakly training and diet. . . .

"Certainly," said Goethe, "personality is everything in art and poetry; yet there are many weak personages among the modern critics who do not admit this, but look upon a great personality in a work of poetry or art merely as a kind of trifling appendage.

"However, to feel and respect a great personality one must be something oneself. All who denied the sublime to Euripides were either poor wretches incapable of comprehending such sublimity, or shameless charlatans who by their presumption wished to make more of themselves—and really did make more of themselves than they were."

[Byron]

[February 24, 1825] "Lord Byron," continued Goethe, "is to be regarded as a man, as an Englishman, and as a great talent. His good qualities belong chiefly to the man, his bad to the Englishman and the peer, his talent is incommensurable.

"All Englishmen are, as such, without reflection, properly so called; distractions and party spirit will not permit them to perfect themselves in quiet. But they are great as practical men.

"Thus, Lord Byron could never attain reflection on himself, and on this account his maxims in general are not successful, as is shown by his creed, 'much money, no authority,' for much money always paralyses authority.

"But where he will create, he always succeeds; with him inspiration supplies the place of reflection. He was obliged to go on poetizing; and then everything that came from the man, especially from his heart, was excellent. He produced his best things as women do pretty children, without thinking about it or knowing how it was done.

"He is a great talent, a born talent, and I never saw the true poetical power greater in any man. In the apprehension of external objects, and a clear penetration into past situations, he is quite as great as Shakespeare. But, as a pure individuality, Shakespeare is his superior. This was felt by Byron; and on this account he does not say much of Shakespeare, although he knows whole passages by heart. He would willingly have denied him altogether; for Shakespeare's cheerfulness is in his way, and he feels that he is no match for it. Pope he does not deny, for he had no cause to fear him: on the contrary, he mentions him, and shows him respect when he can; for he knows well enough that Pope is a mere foil to himself."

Goethe seemed inexhaustible on the subject of Byron. After a few digressions, he proceeded thus:

"His high rank as an English peer was very injurious to Byron; for every talent is oppressed by the outer world—how much more, then, when there is such high birth and so great a fortune? A middle rank is much more favourable to talent, so we find all great artists and poets in the middle classes. Byron's predilection for the unbounded could not have been nearly so dangerous with more humble birth and smaller means. As it was, he was able to put every fancy into practice, and this involved him in innumerable scrapes. Besides, how could one of such high rank be inspired with awe and respect by any rank whatever? He spoke out whatever he felt, and this brought him into ceaseless conflict with the world."

[July 5, 1827] "I could not," said Goethe [speaking of Byron], "make use of any man as the representative of the modern poetical era except him, who undoubtedly is the greatest genius of our century. Again, Byron is neither antique nor romantic, but like the present day itself. This was the sort of man I required. Then he suited me on account of his unsatisfied nature and his warlike tendency, which led to his death at Missolonghi. A treatise upon Byron would be neither convenient nor advisable; but I shall not fail to pay him honour and to allude to him at proper times."

[*Molière*]

[May 12, 1825] "Molière," said Goethe, "is so great that he astonishes anew every time he is read. He is a man by himself—his pieces border on tragedy; they are apprehensive; and nobody has the courage to imitate them. His *Miser*, where the vice destroys all the natural piety between father and son, is especially great, and in a high sense tragic. But when, in a German paraphrase, the son is changed into a relation, the whole is weakened and loses its significance. They feared to show the vice in its true nature as he did; but what is tragic there, or indeed anywhere, except what is intolerable?

"I read some pieces of Molière's every year—just as, from time to time, I contemplate the engravings after the great Italian masters. For we little men are not able to retain the greatness of such things within ourselves; we must therefore return to them from time to time, and renew our impressions."

[*English Literature*]

[December 3, 1824] "The great point," he continued, "is to make a capital that will not be exhausted. This you will acquire by the study of the English language and literature, which you have already begun. Keep to that, and continually make use of the advantages you now possess in the acquaintance of the young Englishmen. You studied the ancient languages but little during your youth; therefore, seek now a stronghold in the literature of so able a nation as the English. And, besides, our own literature is chiefly the offspring of theirs! Whence have we our novels, our tragedies, but from Goldsmith, Fielding, and Shakespeare? And in our own day, where will you find in Germany three literary heroes who can be placed on a level with Lord Byron, Moore, and Walter Scott? Once more, ground yourself in English, concentrate your powers for something good, and give up everything that can produce no result of consequence and is not suited to you."

FRIEDRICH VON SCHILLER   (1759-1805)

THE CONCEPTION of beauty outlined in Schiller's *Aesthetic Letters* somewhat foreshadowed that of Coleridge, though Schiller anticipated few of Coleridge's other basic ideas. Beauty, said Schiller, following Kant, is to be found in the union of "life in its widest acceptation" (the concrete world) with the confining and regulating "form." Beauty, that is, arises when a form, satisfying to the reason, is seen emerging from or interwined with concrete things. Now "life"—that is, nature, the vital world of material energy and body—is known to us through our senses. But the "form" by which this amorphous welter of life is subdued and unified is a form that comes from the mind of man. It is man's mind, in other words, that "gives a form to matter . . . by placing the diversity of the world under the unity of the Ego" (Letter XI).

It is here, incidentally, that Coleridge later departed not only from Schiller, but also from many other German writers of the period. For though many of their attitudes were congenial to him, he felt that their approach tended ultimately to "degenerate into a crude egoismus"; and the crucial point on which Coleridge tried to distinguish himself from them was in his Platonic emphasis that form exists independently of man's mind and can be *known*—as distinct from being projected outward—by reason.

For Schiller, then, beauty arises when the "formal instinct" of the mind is brought into harmonious balance with the external objects that we grasp

FRIEDRICH VON SCHILLER. Though compelled against his will to study law and then medicine, and afterwards to serve for a while as an army surgeon, Schiller early became interested in history, philosophy, and literature, and first gained a literary reputation for his tragedy, *The Robbers* (1781). After leading an insecure life in various places and writing prolifically, he became a professor at Jena (1789-93), and then moved to Weimar (1799).

Translations of Schiller's *Works* (1889) and of the *Aesthetical and Philosophical Essays* (1875) are available in the Bohn Library series. There is also *On the Aesthetic Education of Man* (ed. E. M. Wilkinson and L. A. Willoughby, Oxford, 1967), and *Naïve and Sentimental Poetry* and *On the Sublime* (ed. J. A. Elias, 1966). Commentaries include: A. L. Carter, *Parallel Themes and Their Treatment in Schiller and Shaftesbury* (Philadelphia, 1919); S. S. Kerry, *Schiller's Writings on Aesthetics* (Manchester, 1961); Thomas Mann, "On Schiller," *Last Essays* (1959); R. D. Miller, *Schiller and the Ideal of Freedom* (Harrowgate, 1959); F. Norman (ed.), *Schiller Bicentenary Lectures* (1960); and E. C. Wilm, *The Philosophy of Schiller in Its Historical Relations* (Boston, 1912).

through our senses. And it is in this state of balance, where the "formal instinct" of the reason and the "sensuous instinct" interpenetrate and sustain each other, that a third instinct is appealed to and satisfied. Schiller calls this third capacity "the instinct for *play*," and, using it as a premise, derives from it the famous "play theory of art." Schiller intended by the term "play" to suggest a free activity or interplay of mental and emotional "forces" to the fullest possible extent. He was not implying, as is sometimes thought, that art is a mere game—unless one chooses to stretch the word "game" far beyond the connotation it has for most people. In the union of the "formal" and the "sensuous instinct," one can join "the highest degree of self-spontaneity (autonomy) and of freedom with the fullest plenitude of existence, and instead of abandoning himself to the world so as to get lost in it, he will rather absorb it in himself, with all the infinitude of its phenomena, and subject it to the unity of his reason" (Letter XIII). But, as Schiller goes on to say, one can fail to attain this ideal state in two ways. The "intensity" that should be reserved for the active, form-conceiving reason can be handed over to the senses (which should be "passively" open and receptive to external nature and should absorb it as much as possible), and one can thus degenerate into animal or "material impulsion." Similarly, if the "formal instinct" of the mind obtrudes itself in such a way as to block the open receptivity of the senses, then what one acquires by sense experience will have first been stamped into a pattern by the interfering intellect, and the real nature and variety of concrete life will no longer be available as an external stimulus to challenge and refresh the mind. Accordingly, man is "completely a man only when he plays"—only when the formal and the sensuous instinct are both kept freely active and balanced in concert. And the object of the *play instinct*—that is, beauty—is neither form, arising out of the mind, nor the changing flux of life that our senses bring us. Instead, the object of the *play instinct* is form shaping life—or, in other words, what Schiller calls "living form." It is this living form, in which the mind and the external object are brought together into harmony, that art tries to achieve.

The essay "On Simple [or Naïve] and Sentimental Poetry" (1795) is concerned with the differences between ancient and modern poetry—or, more properly, the differences between poetry written during the earlier stages of a culture and the less direct, less boldly imaginative, but more reflective and sophisticated poetry of later epochs: the poetry of Homer, for example, compared with the later poetry of classical antiquity, or the poetry of Shakespeare, contrasted with poetry since the late Renaissance. As such, the essay may be viewed as a notable by-product of one of the most crucial problems in later eighteenth-century criticism, a problem that had already arisen in England, in particular, a hundred years before: namely, what had happened to European poetry since the mid-seventeenth century? Had there, for example, been a "decline" in available genius; or was the "decline" of poetry a sign of the exhaustion of genres, of a growing self-consciousness, or of an increasingly complicated life generally? (See above, p. 290.) Schiller's essay is more a symptom of the importance and interest of the problem than an attempt to analyze it. In fact, his particular purpose was to justify modern reflective or "sentimental" poetry—to show that because of more complex conditions an increased self-consciousness was inevitable, and because modern poetry had the harder task one could not fairly judge it by classical criteria. "I laid down the maxim of objective treatment in poetry," said Goethe, "and would allow no other; but Schiller, who worked quite in the subjective way, deemed his own fashion the right one, and to defend himself against me wrote the treatise *On Naïve and Sentimental Poetry*. He proved to me that I myself, against my will, was romantic. . . ."

From Aesthetical Letters

LETTER XV

THE OBJECT of the sensuous instinct, expressed in a universal conception, is named Life in the widest acceptation: a conception that expresses all material existence and all that is immediately present in the senses. The object of the formal instinct, expressed in a universal conception, is called shape or form, as well in an exact as in an inexact acceptation; a conception that embraces all formal qualities of things and all relations of the same to the thinking powers. The object of the play instinct, represented in a general statement, may therefore bear the name of *living form*; a term that serves to describe all aesthetic qualities of phaenomena, and what people style, in the widest sense, *beauty*.

Beauty is neither extended to the whole field of all living things nor merely enclosed in this field. A marble block, though it is and remains lifeless, can nevertheless become a living form by the architect and sculptor; a man, though he lives and has a form, is far from being a living form on that account. For this to be the case, it is necessary that his form should be life, and that his life should be a form. As long as we only think of his form, it is lifeless, a mere abstraction; as long as we only feel his life, it is

Aesthetical Letters. First printed in 1795; anon. Eng. translation, in *Essays Aesthetical and Philosophical* (Bohn Library, 1875).

without form, a mere impression. It is only when his form lives in our feeling, and his life in our understanding, he is the living form, and this will everywhere be the case where we judge him to be beautiful.

But the genesis of beauty is by no means declared because we know how to point out the component parts, which in their combination produce beauty. For to this end it would be necessary to comprehend that *combination itself*, which continues to defy our exploration, as well as all mutual operation between the finite and the infinite. The reason, on transcendental grounds, makes the following demand: There shall be a communion between the formal impulse—that is, there shall be a play instinct—because it is only the unity of reality with the form, of the accidental with the necessary, of the passive state with freedom, that the conception of humanity is completed. Reason is obliged to make this demand, because her nature impels her to completeness and to the removal of all bounds; while every exclusive activity of one or the other impulse leaves human nature incomplete and places a limit in it. Accordingly, as soon as reason issues the mandate, "a humanity shall exist," it proclaims at the same time the law, "there shall be a beauty." Experience can answer us if there is a beauty, and we shall know it as soon as she has taught us if a humanity can exist. But neither reason nor experience can tell us how beauty can be, and how a humanity is possible.

We know that man is neither exclusively matter nor exclusively spirit. Accordingly, beauty, as the consummation of humanity, can neither be exclusively mere life, as has been asserted by sharp-sighted observers, who kept too close to the testimony of experience, and to which the taste of the time would gladly degrade it; nor can beauty be merely form, as has been judged by speculative sophists, who departed too far from experience, and by philosophic artists, who were led too much by the necessity of art in explaining beauty; it is rather the common object of both impulses, that is, of the play instinct. The use of language completely justifies this name, as it is wont to qualify with the word play what is neither subjectively nor objectively accidental, and yet does not impose necessity either externally or internally. As the mind in the intuition of the beautiful finds itself in a happy medium between law and necessity, it is because it divides itself between both, emancipated from the pressure of both. . . .

LETTER XVI

From the antagonism of the two impulses, and from the association of two opposite principles, we have seen beauty to result, of which the highest ideal must therefore be sought in the perfect union and equilibrium possible of the reality and of the form. But this equilibrium remains always an idea that reality can never completely reach. In reality, there will always remain a preponderance of one of these elements over the other, and the highest point to which experience can reach will consist in an oscillation between two principles, when sometimes reality and at others form will have the advantage. Ideal beauty is therefore eternally one and indivisible, because there can only be one single equilibrium; on the contrary, experimental beauty will be eternally double, because in the oscillation the equilibrium may be destroyed in two ways—this side and that.

I have called attention in the foregoing letters to a fact that can also be rigorously deduced from the considerations that have engaged our attention to the present point; this fact is that an exciting and also a moderating action may be expected from the beautiful. The *tempering* action is directed to keep within proper limits the sensuous and the formal impulsions; the *exciting*, to maintain both of them in their full force. But these two modes of action of beauty ought to be completely identified in the idea. The beautiful ought to temper while uniformly exciting the two natures, and it ought also to excite while uniformly moderating them. This result flows at once from the idea of a correlation, in virtue of which the two terms mutually imply each other, and are the reciprocal condition one of the other, a correlation of which the purest product is beauty. But experience does not offer an example of so perfect a correlation. In the field of experience it will always happen more or less that excess on the one side will give rise to deficiency on the other, and deficiency will give birth to excess. . . .

From On Simple and Sentimental Poetry

THERE are moments in life when nature inspires us with a sort of love and respectful emotion, not because she is pleasing to our senses, or because she satisfies our mind or our taste (it is often the very opposite that happens), but merely because *she is nature*. This feeling is often elicited when nature is considered in her plants, in the mineral kingdom, in rural districts; also in the case of human nature, in the case of children, and in the manners of country people and of the primitive races. Every man of refined feeling, provided he has a soul, experiences this feeling when he walks out under the open sky, when he lives in the country, or when he stops to contemplate the monuments of early ages; in short, when escaping from factitious situations and relations, he finds himself suddenly face to face with nature. This interest, which is often exalted in us so as to become a

On Simple and Sentimental Poetry. 1795; anon. Eng. translation, *Essays Aesthetical and Philosophical* (Bohn Library, 1875).

want, is the explanation of many of our fancies for flowers and for animals, our preference for gardens laid out in a natural style, our love of walks, of the country and those who live there, of a great number of objects proceeding from a remote antiquity, etc. It is taken for granted that no affectation exists in the matter, and moreover that no accidental interest comes into play. But this sort of interest which we take in nature is only possible under two conditions. First the object that inspires us with this feeling must be really *nature,* or something we take for nature; secondly, this object must be in the full sense of the word *simple,* that is, presenting the entire contrast of nature with art, all the advantage remaining on the side of nature. Directly this second condition is united to the first, but no sooner, nature assumes the character of simplicity. . . .

If we think of that beautiful nature which surrounded the ancient Greeks, if we remember how intimately that people, under its blessed sky, could live with that free nature; how their mode of imagining, and of feeling, and their manners, approached far nearer than ours to the simplicity of nature, how faithfully the works of their poets express this; we must necessarily remark, as a strange fact, that so few traces are met among them of that *sentimental* interest that we moderns ever take in the scenes of nature and in natural characters. I admit that the Greeks are superiorly exact and faithful in their descriptions of nature. They reproduce their details with care, but we see that they take no more interest in them and no more heart in them than in describing a vestment, a shield, armour, a piece of furniture, or any production of the mechanical arts. In their love for the object it seems that they make no difference between what exists in itself and what owes its existence to art, to the human will. It seems that nature interests their minds and their curiosity more than moral feeling. They do not attach themselves to it with that depth of feeling, with that gentle melancholy, that characterise the moderns. Nay, more, by personifying nature in its particular phenomena, by deifying it, by representing its effects as the acts of free being, they take from it that character of calm necessity which is precisely what makes it so attractive to us. Their impatient imagination only traverses nature to pass beyond it to the drama of human life. It only takes pleasure in the spectacle of what is living and free; it requires characters, acts, the accidents of fortune and of manners; and whilst it happens with *us,* at least in certain moral dispositions, to curse our prerogative, this free will, which exposes us to so many combats with ourselves, to so many anxieties and errors, and to wish to exchange it for the condition of beings destitute of reason, for that fatal existence that no longer admits of any choice, but which is so calm in its uniformity,—while we do this, the Greeks, on the contrary, only have their imagination occupied in retracing human nature in the inanimate world, and in giving to the will an influence where blind necessity rules.

Whence can arise this difference between the spirit of the ancients and the modern spirit? How comes it that, being, for all that relates to nature, incomparably below the ancients, we are superior to them precisely on this point, that we render a more complete homage to nature; that we have a closer attachment to it; and that we are capable of embracing even the inanimate world with the most ardent sensibility? It is because nature, in our time, is no longer in man, and that we no longer encounter it in its primitive truth, except out of humanity, in the inanimate world. It is not because we are more *conformable to nature*—quite the contrary; it is because in our social relations, in our mode of existence, in our manners, we are in *opposition with nature.* This is what leads us, when the instinct of truth and of simplicity is awakened— this instinct which, like the moral aptitude from which it proceeds, lives incorruptible and indelible in every human heart—to procure for it in the physical world the satisfaction which there is no hope of finding in the moral order. This is the reason why the feeling that attaches us to nature is connected so closely with that which makes us regret our infancy, for ever flown, and our primitive innocence. Our childhood is all that remains of nature in humanity, such as civilisation has made it, of untouched, unmutilated nature. It is, therefore, not wonderful, when we meet out of us the impress of nature, that we are always brought back to the idea of our childhood. . . .

It is in the fundamental idea of poetry that the poet is everywhere the *guardian* of nature.

When he can no longer entirely fill this part, and has already in himself suffered the deleterious influence of arbitrary and factitious forms, or has had to struggle against this influence, he presents himself as the *witness* of nature and as its avenger. The poet will, therefore, be the *expression* of nature itself, or his part will be to *seek* it, if men have lost sight of it. Hence arise two kinds of poetry, which embrace and exhaust the entire field of poetry. All poets—I mean those who are really so—will belong, according to the time when they flourish, according to the accidental circumstances that have influenced their education generally, and the different dispositions of mind through which they pass, will belong, I say, to the order of the *sentimental* poetry or to *simple* poetry.

The poet of a young world, simple and inspired, as also the poet who at an epoch of artificial civilisation approaches nearest to the primitive bards, is austere and prudish, like the virginal Diana in her forests. Wholly unconfiding, he hides himself from the heart that seeks him, from the desire that wishes to embrace him. It is not rare for the dry truth with which he treats his subject to resemble insensibility. The whole object possesses him, and to reach his heart it does not suffice, as with metals of little value, to stir up the surface; as with pure gold, you must go down to the lowest depths. Like the Deity behind this universe, the simple poet hides himself behind his work; he is *himself* his work, and his work is *himself*. A man must be no longer worthy of the work, nor understand it, or be tired of it, to be even anxious to learn who is its author.

Such appears to us, for instance, Homer in antiquity, and Shakespeare among moderns: two natures infinitely different and separated in time by an abyss, but perfectly identical as to this trait of character. When, at a very youthful age, I became first acquainted with Shakespeare, I was displeased with his coldness, with his insensibility, which allows him to jest even in the most pathetic moments, to disturb the impression of the most harrowing scenes in "Hamlet," in "King Lear," and in "Macbeth," &c., by mixing with them the buffooneries of a madman. I was revolted by his insensibility, which allowed him to pause sometimes at places where my sensibility would bid me hasten and bear me along, and which sometimes carried him away with indifference when my heart would be so happy to pause. Though I was accustomed, by the practice of modern poets, to seek at once the poet in his works, to meet *his* heart, to reflect *with him* in his theme—in a word, to see the object in the subject—I could not bear that the poet could in Shakespeare never be seized, that he would never give me an account of himself. For some years Shakespeare had been the object of my study and of all my respect, before I had learnt to love his personality. I was not yet able to comprehend nature at first hand. All that my eyes could bear was its image only, reflected by the understanding and arranged by rules; and on this score the sentimental poetry of the French, or that of the Germans of 1750 to 1780, was what suited me best. For the rest, I do not blush at this childish judgment; adult critics pronounced in that day in the same way, and carried their simplicity so far as to publish their decisions to the world. . . .

The poets of this order,—the genuinely simple poets, are scarcely any longer in their place in this artificial age. Accordingly they are scarcely possible in it, or at least they are only possible on the condition of *traversing* their age, like *scared persons*, at a *running* pace, and of being preserved by a happy star from the influence of their age, which would mutilate their genius. Never, for aye and for ever, will society produce these poets; but out of society they still appear sometimes at intervals, rather, I admit, as strangers, who excite wonder, or as ill-trained children of nature, who give offence. These apparitions, so very comforting for the artist who studies them, and for the real connoisseur, who knows how to appreciate them, are, as a general conclusion, in the age when they are begotten, to a very small degree prosperous. The seal of empire is stamped on their brow, and we, we ask the Muses to cradle us, to carry us in their arms. The critics, as regular constables of art, detest these poets as *disturbers of rules or of limits*. Homer himself may have been only indebted to the testimony of ten centuries for the reward these aristarchs are kindly willing to concede him. Moreover, they find it a hard matter to maintain their rules against his example, or his authority against their rules.

SENTIMENTAL POETRY

I have previously remarked that the poet *is* nature, or he *seeks* nature. In the former case, he is a simple poet, in the second case, a sentimental poet.

The poetic spirit is immortal, nor can it disappear from humanity; it can only disappear with humanity itself, or with the aptitude to be a man, a human being. And actually, though man by the freedom of his imagination and of his understanding departs from simplicity, from truth, from the necessity of nature, not only a road always remains open to him to return to it, but, moreover, a powerful and indestructible instinct, the moral instinct, brings him incessantly back to nature; and it is precisely the poetical faculty that is united to this instinct by the ties of the closest relationship. Thus man does not lose the poetic faculty directly he parts with the simplicity of nature; only this faculty acts out of him in another direction. . . .

As long as man dwells in a state of pure nature (I mean pure and not coarse nature), all his being acts at once like a simple sensuous unity, like a harmonious whole. The senses and reason, the receptive faculty and the spontaneously active faculty, have not been as yet separated in their respective functions: *à fortiori* they are not yet in contradiction with each other. Then the feelings of man are not the formless play of chance; nor are his thoughts an empty play of the imagination, without any value. His feelings proceed from the law of necessity; his *thoughts* from *reality*. But when man enters the state of civilisation, and art has fashioned him, this *sensuous* harmony which was in him disappears, and henceforth he can only manifest himself as a *moral unity*, that is, as aspiring to unity. The harmony that existed as a *fact* in the former state, the harmony of feeling and thought, only exists now in an *ideal* state. It is no longer in him, but out of him; it is a conception of thought which he must begin by realising in himself; it is no longer a fact, a reality of his life. Well, now let us take the idea of poetry, which is nothing else than *expressing humanity as completely as possible,* and let us apply this idea to these two states. We shall be brought to infer that, on the one hand, in the state of natural simplicity, when all the faculties of man are exerted together, his being still manifests itself in a harmonious unity, where, consequently, the *totality* of his nature expresses itself in reality itself, the part of the *poet* is necessarily to imitate the real as completely as is possible. In the state of civilisation, on the contrary, when this harmonious competition of the whole of human nature is no longer anything but an idea, the part of the poet is necessarily to raise reality to the ideal, or what amounts to the same thing, *to represent the ideal*. And, actually, these are the only two ways in which, in general, the poetic genius can manifest itself. Their great difference is quite evident, but though there be great opposition between them, a higher idea exists that embraces both, and there is no cause to be astonished if this idea coincides with the very idea of humanity.

This is not the place to pursue this thought any further, as it would require a separate discussion to place it in its full light. But if we only compare the modern and ancient poets together, not according to the accidental forms which they may have employed, but according to their spirit, we shall be easily convinced of the truth of this thought. The thing that touches us in the ancient poets is nature; it is the truth of sense, it is a present and a living reality: modern poets touch us through the medium of ideas.

The path followed by modern poets is moreover that necessarily followed by man generally, individuals as well as the species. Nature reconciles man with himself; art divides and disunites him; the ideal brings him back to unity. Now, the ideal being an infinite that he never succeeds in reaching, it follows that civilised man can never become perfect in his kind, while the man of nature can become so in his. Accordingly in relation to perfection one would be infinitely below the other, if we only considered the relation in which they are both to their own kind and to their maximum. If, on the other hand, it is the kinds that are compared together, it is ascertained that the end to which man tends by civilisation is infinitely superior to that which he reaches through nature. Thus one has his reward, because having for object a finite magnitude, he completely reaches this object: the merit of the other is to approach an object that is of infinite magnitude. Now, as there are only degrees, and as there is only progress in the second of these evolutions, it follows that the relative merit of the man engaged in the ways of civilisation is never determinable in general, though this man, taking the individuals separately, is necessarily at a disadvantage, compared with the man in whom nature acts in all its perfection. But we know also that humanity cannot reach its final end except by progress, and that the man of nature cannot make progress save through culture, and consequently by passing himself through the way of civilisation. Accordingly there is no occasion to ask with which of the two the advantage must remain, considering this last end.

All that we say here of the different forms of humanity may be applied equally to the two orders of poets who correspond to them.

Accordingly it would have been desirable not to compare at all the ancient and the modern poets, the simple and the sentimental poets, or only to compare them by referring them to a higher idea (since there is really only one) which embraces both. For, sooth to say, if we begin by forming a specific idea of poetry, merely from the ancient poets, nothing is easier, but also nothing is more vulgar, than to depreciate the moderns by this comparison. If persons wish to confine the name of poetry to that which has in all times produced the same impression of simple nature, this places them in the necessity of contesting the title of poet in the moderns precisely in that which constitutes their highest beauties, their greatest originality and sublimity; for precisely in the points where they excel the most, it is the child of civilisation whom they address, and they have nothing to say to the simple child of nature.

To the man who is not disposed beforehand to issue from reality in order to enter the field of the ideal, the richest and most substantial poetry is an empty appearance, and the sublimest flights of poetic inspiration are an exaggeration. Never will a reasonable man think of placing alongside Homer, in his grandest episodes, any of our modern poets; and it has a discordant and ridiculous effect to hear Milton or Klopstock honoured with the name of "a new Homer." But take in modern poets what characterizes them, what makes their special merit, and try to compare any ancient poet with them in this point, they will not be able to support the comparison any better, and Homer less than any other. I should express it thus: the power of the ancients consists in compressing objects into the finite, and the moderns excel in the art of the infinite.

What we have said here may be extended to the fine arts in general, except certain restrictions that are self-evident. If then the strength of the artists of antiquity consists in determining and limiting objects, we must no longer wonder that in the field of the plastic arts the ancients remain so far superior to the moderns, nor especially that poetry and the plastic arts with the moderns, compared respectively with what they were among the ancients, do not offer the same relative value. This is because an object that addresses itself to the eyes is only perfect in proportion as the object is clearly limited in it; whilst a work that is addressed to the imagination can also reach the perfection which is proper to it by means of the ideal and the infinite. This is why the superiority of the moderns in what relates to ideas is not of great aid to them in the plastic arts, where it is necessary for them to *determine in space,* with the greatest precision, the image which their imagination has conceived, and where they must therefore measure themselves with the ancient artist just on a point where his superiority cannot be contested. In the matter of poetry it is another affair, and if the advantage is still with the ancients on that ground, as respects the simplicity of forms —all that can be represented by sensuous features, all that is something *bodily*—yet, on the other hand, the moderns have the advantage over the ancients as regards fundamental wealth, and all that can neither be represented nor translated by sensuous signs, in short, for all that is called mind and idea in the works of art. . . .

AUGUST WILHELM VON SCHLEGEL   (1767-1845)
FRIEDRICH VON SCHLEGEL   (1772-1829)

PERHAPS more than anyone else, A. W. von Schlegel and his younger brother, Friedrich, served as the chief critical spokesmen for German romanticism. This is equivalent to saying that they occupied a central position in the European romantic movement as a whole. For although the English poet-critics possessed a more sensitive grasp of the concrete problems of poetic style, and although English empirical psychology had already carried further the actual descriptive analysis of the imagination and the poetic process, it was Germany that offered the broadest philosophical basis for romanticism.

The writings of the Schlegels are strongly permeated by the sense of history that had been growing throughout the eighteenth century—an interested awareness of history that was still not too timid to make generalizations. In the Schlegels, as in other German critics especially, this historical sense is also colored by the feeling of nationalism that had accompanied the growth of the romantic movement generally, stimulating a belief in inherent national peculiarities and an interest in cultural origins and folklore —an approach in which the influence of Herder had an important place. Above all, the Schlegels voiced the romantic emphasis on the organic nature of reality. Indeed, it is basically in terms of the organic that they made

A. W. VON SCHLEGEL. The son of a Lutheran pastor, A. W. von Schlegel was educated in Hanover and at the University of Göttingen, became a professor at Jena (1798), began his translation of Shakespeare, and with his brother made the *Athenaeum* into what was virtually the official organ for German romanticism. He lectured at Berlin and Vienna and became a professor at Bonn (1818).

Among standard texts of his works are the *Sämtliche Werke* (ed. E. Böcking, Leipzig, 1846-47) and *Kritische Schriften und Briefe* (ed. E. Lohner, 1962-   ) ; critical editions of the *Athenaeum* (ed. F. Baader, Berlin, 1905) and a photocopy edition with a *Nachwort* by E. Behler, Vol. III (Stuttgart, 1960) ; and the English translation of *A Course of Lectures on Dramatic Art and Literature* (tr. J. Black, 1815; rev. by A. J. W. Morrison, 1846). Commentaries include: C. H. Alt, *Schiller und die Brüder Schlegel* (Weimar, 1904) ; O. L. Brandt, *A. W. Schlegel* (Berlin, 1919) ; and Bernard von Brentano, *August Wilhelm Schlegel* (Stuttgart, 1949).

FRIEDRICH VON SCHLEGEL. Turning to literature after the study of law, Friedrich von Schlegel lectured at Jena, contributed significant essays to the *Athenaeum*, and then went to Paris (1802), where he lectured on philosophy and studied oriental literature. He later (1809) held official positions in Austria, where he continued to lecture and write.

Texts of Friedrich von Schlegel include *Sämtliche Werke* (Vienna, 1846) ; the *Athenaeum* (cited above) ; *Kritische Friedrich Schlegel Ausgabe* (ed. E. Behler, *et al.*, 22 vols., Paderborn-Darmstadt, 1958-   ) ; an English translation of *Lectures on the History of Literature, Ancient and Modern* (tr. J. G. Lockhart, 1818, with later reprintings) ; *Literary Notebooks, 1797-1801* (ed. H. Eichner, 1957) ; and *Dialogue on Poetry and Literary Aphorisms* (ed. E. Behler and R. Struc, University Park, Pa., 1968). Among discussions of his work are: C. Enders, *Friedrich Schlegel* (Leipzig, 1913) ; A. Schlagdenhauffer, *F. Schlegel et son groupe* (Strasbourg, 1934) ; and Wellek (cited above), pp. 5-35.

their famous dichotomy between the classic and romantic, a dichotomy to which much eighteenth-century criticism had already pointed. The classical is concerned with fixed types and a finished order, viewed in the light of rational ideals. The romantic attitude, on the other hand, seeks a more essential truth: it is directed to the changing and developing process that characterizes life, and, through imaginative feeling, it tries to grasp the ramifications and outlets of this creative energy not as separate but as organic parts of the process of nature. The critical outlook of the Schlegels is, by their own definition, romantic. But it also contains a genuine and even penetrating understanding of classical values, even though these values do not serve as explicit aims, as they do for Coleridge; nor is there an attempt to offer a metaphysical basis by which these values can be strictly reconciled with the romantic belief in organic process.

The wide interests of A. W. von Schlegel are indicated by the variety of the translations he made—translations of Shakespeare, Calderon, Spanish and Portuguese lyrics, and even the Sanskrit *Bhagavad-Gita*—as well as by his critical writings, which include his four series of lectures: *On the Present State of Literature and the Fine Arts* (1802), *On Dramatic Art and Literature* (1809-11), *On the History of German Language and Poetry* (1818-19), and *The Theory and History of the Fine Arts* (1827). Schlegel's broad learning and his ability to draw upon it with imaginative critical insight are probably best exemplified in the *Lectures on Dramatic Art and Literature*. Of this series, the lectures of most general interest, at least to an English-speaking reader, are the celebrated ones on Shakespeare. For Schlegel, as for most of the English critics, Shakespeare's supremacy as a dramatist appears most in his understanding of human nature and in his power to portray character. Shakespeare is unrivaled in laying bare the active progress, development, and interplay of feelings in a given character, or in depicting the reaction of different characters to each other. He reveals the passions and reactions of his characters, not as fixed traits of mind, but as organically connected aspects or outlets of their natures, fluctuating and adapting themselves to changing occasions, and modifying each other as they come into play. But Schlegel also made clear that other elements besides character are important in the poetic drama: the organic structure of the play as a whole, the need for conventions and devices appropriate to the drama as a unified work of art, and qualities of language and versification desirable in dramatic poetry.

Friedrich von Schlegel's approach to literature was perhaps less generally erudite, but it was equally comprehensive in its historical outlook, and at times more imaginatively suggestive. These qualities are abundantly present in his *Lectures on the History of Literature, Ancient and Modern*. His historical view of literature carries further the sociological approach found earlier in English criticism, as in the books on Homer by Thomas Blackwell (1735) and by Robert Wood (1769). Schlegel interpreted literature in its widest sense as virtually everything written, with belles-lettres serving as the most sensitive end-result or focal mirror of a society's character, beliefs, and ideals. Hence his emphasis, in the selection offered here, on the extent to which literature, broadly considered, enters in every way into the intellectual life of man, and his thesis that nations or peoples can be best understood and evaluated by the character of their literature. Hence also his attempt to connect the study of belles-lettres with general intellectual history. His success in doing this is particularly shown in his shrewd observations on English thought and its influence during the eighteenth century in preparing the way for European romanticism. Underlying his approach to literary history is a view of poetry that reflects both his stress on the organic process of concrete nature and his attempt to retain the classical confidence in universal and ultimate values. For the end of poetry, he believed, is to present the "eternal"; but the "eternal," he added, can be shown only through a "veil"—the veil of concrete nature. In attempting to disclose the universal in the present and actual, poetry must work within the traditions and beliefs of a particular nation or culture. It is the task of literary history to discover those traditions and beliefs, and to discover the extent to which universal values are mirrored within them and are permitted to become articulate through the potentialities of the written word.

A. W. VON SCHLEGEL

Shakespeare

THE ENGLISH critics are unanimous in their praise of the truth and uniform consistency of [Shakespeare's] characters, of his heart-rending pathos, and his comic wit. Moreover, they extol the beauty and sublimity of his separate descriptions, images, and expressions. This last is the most superficial and cheap mode of criticising works of art. Johnson compares him who should endeavour to recommend this poet by passages unconnectedly torn from his works, to the pedant in Hierocles, who exhibited a brick as a sample of his house. And yet how little, and how very unsatisfactorily does he himself speak of the pieces considered as a whole! Let any man, for instance, bring to-

gether the short characters which he gives at the close of each play, and see if the aggregate will amount to that sum of admiration which he himself, at his outset, has stated as the correct standard for the appreciation of the poet. It was, generally speaking, the prevailing tendency of the time which preceded our own, (and which has shown itself particularly in physical science,) to consider everything having life as a mere accumulation of dead parts, to separate what exists only in connexion and cannot otherwise be conceived, instead of penetrating to the central point and viewing all the parts as so many irradiations from it. . . .

Shakspeare's knowledge of mankind has become proverbial: in this his superiority is so great, that he has justly been called the master of the human heart. A readiness to remark the mind's fainter and involuntary utterances, and

Shakespeare. From Lecture XXIII, in *Lectures on Dramatic Art and Literature* (1809-11; tr. John Black, 1815). The selection here is from the translation of Black, revised by A. J. W. Morrison (1846).

the power to express with certainty the meaning of these signs, as determined by experience and reflection, constitutes "the observer of men;" but tacitly to draw from these still further conclusions, and to arrange the separate observations according to grounds of probability, into a just and valid combination, this, it may be said, is to know men. The distinguishing property of the dramatic poet who is great in characterization, is something altogether different here, and which, (take it which way we will,) either includes in it this readiness and this acuteness, or dispenses with both. It is the capability of transporting himself so completely into every situation, even the most unusual, that he is enabled, as plenipotentiary of the whole human race, without particular instructions for each separate case, to act and speak in the name of every individual. It is the power of endowing the creatures of his imagination with such self-existent energy, that they afterwards act in each conjuncture according to general laws of nature: the poet, in his dreams, institutes, as it were, experiments which are received with as much authority as if they had been made on waking objects. The inconceivable element herein, and what moreover can never be learned, is, that the characters appear neither to do nor to say any thing on the spectator's account merely; and yet that the poet simply, by means of the exhibition, and without any subsidiary explanation, communicates to his audience the gift of looking into the inmost recesses of their minds. Hence Goethe has ingeniously compared Shakspeare's characters to watches with crystalline plates and cases, which, while they point out the hours as correctly as other watches, enable us at the same time to perceive the inward springs whereby all this is accomplished.

Nothing, however, is more foreign to Shakspeare than a certain anatomical style of exhibition, which laboriously enumerates all the motives by which a man is determined to act in this or that particular manner. This rage of supplying motives, the mania of so many modern historians, might be carried at length to an extent which would abolish every thing like individuality, and resolve all character into nothing but the effect of foreign or external influences whereas we know that it often announces itself most decidedly in earliest infancy. After all, a man acts so because he is so. And what each man is, that Shakspeare reveals to us most immediately: he demands and obtains our belief, even for what is singular and deviates from the ordinary course of nature. Never perhaps was there so comprehensive a talent for characterization as Shakspeare. It not only grasps every diversity of rank, age, and sex, down to the lispings of infancy; not only do the king and the beggar, the hero and the pickpocket, the sage and the idiot, speak and act with equal truthfulness; not only does he transport himself to distant ages and foreign nations, and portray with the greatest accuracy (a few apparent violations of costume excepted) the spirit of the ancient Romans, of the French in the wars with the English, of the English themselves during a great part of their history, of the Southern Europeans (in the serious part of many comedies), the cultivated society of the day, and the rude barbarism of a Norman fore-time; his human characters have not only such depth and individuality that they do not admit of being classed under common names, and are inexhaustible even in conception: no, this Prometheus not merely forms men, he opens the gates of the magical world of spirits, calls up the midnight ghost, exhibits before us the witches with their unhallowed rites, peoples the air with sportive fairies and sylphs; and these beings, though existing only in the imagination, nevertheless possess such truth and consistency, that even with such misshapen abortions as Caliban, he extorts the assenting conviction, that were there such beings they would so conduct themselves.[1] In a word, as he carries a bold and pregnant fancy into the kingdom of nature, on the other hand, he carries nature into the regions of fancy, which lie beyond the confines of reality. We are lost in astonishment at the close intimacy he brings us into with the extraordinary, the wonderful, and the unheard-of.

Pope and Johnson appear strangely to contradict each other, when the first says, "all the

---

[1] Compare Johnson (*Preface to Shakespeare*, above): "Shakespeare approximates the remote, and familiarizes the wonderful; the event which he represents will not happen, but, if it were possible, its effects would probably be such as he has assigned . . . he has not only shewn human nature as it acts in real exigencies, but as it would be found in trials, to which it cannot be exposed."

characters of Shakspeare are individuals," and the second, "they are species." And yet perhaps these opinions may admit of reconciliation. Pope's expression is unquestionably the more correct. A character which should be merely a personification of a naked general idea could neither exhibit any great depth nor any great variety. The names of genera and species are well known to be merely auxiliaries for the understanding, that we may embrace the infinite variety of nature in a certain order. The characters which Shakspeare has so thoroughly delineated have undoubtedly a number of individual peculiarities, but at the same time they possess a significance which is not applicable to them alone: they generally supply materials for a profound theory of their most prominent and distinguishing property. But even with the above correction, this opinion must still have its limitations. Characterization is merely one ingredient of the dramatic art, and not dramatic poetry itself. It would be improper in the extreme, if the poet were to draw our attention to superfluous traits of character, at a time when it ought to be his endeavour to produce other impressions. Whenever the musical or the fanciful preponderates, the characteristical necessarily falls into the background. Hence many of the figures of Shakspeare exhibit merely external designations, determined by the place which they occupy in the whole: they are like secondary persons in a public procession, to whose physiognomy we seldom pay much attention; their only importance is derived from the solemnity of their dress and the duty in which they are engaged. Shakspeare's messengers, for instance, are for the most part mere messengers, and yet not common, but poetical messengers: the messages which they have to bring is the soul which suggests to them their language. Other voices, too, are merely raised to pour forth these as melodious lamentations or rejoicings, or to dwell in reflection on what has taken place; and in a serious drama without chorus this must always be more or less the case, if we would not have it prosaical.

If Shakspeare deserves our admiration for his characters, he is equally deserving of it for his exhibition of passion, taking this word in its widest signification, as including every mental condition, every tone, from indifference or famil-

iar mirth to the wildest rage and despair. He gives us the history of minds; he lays open to us, in a single word, a whole series of their anterior states. His passions do not stand at the same height, from first to last, as is the case with so many tragic poets, who, in the language of Lessing, are thorough masters of the legal style of love. He paints, with inimitable veracity, the gradual advance from the first origin; "he gives," as Lessing says, "a living picture of all the slight and secret artifices by which a feeling steals into our souls, of all the imperceptible advantages which it there gains, of all the stratagems by which it makes every other passion subservient to itself, till it becomes the sole tyrant of our desires and our aversions." Of all the poets, perhaps, he alone has portrayed the mental diseases, melancholy, delirium, lunacy, with such inexpressible and, in every respect, definite truth, that the physician may enrich his observations from them in the same manner as from real cases.

And yet Johnson has objected to Shakspeare that his pathos is not always natural and free from affectation. There are, it is true, passages, though comparatively speaking very few, where his poetry exceeds the bounds of actual dialogue, where a too soaring imagination, a too luxuriant wit, rendered a complete dramatic forgetfulness of himself impossible. With this exception, the censure originated in a fanciless way of thinking, to which everything appears unnatural that does not consort with its own tame insipidity. Hence an idea has been formed of simple and natural pathos, which consists in exclamations destitute of imagery and nowise elevated above every-day life. But energetical passions electrify all the mental powers, and will consequently, in highly-favoured natures, give utterance to themselves in ingenious and figurative expressions. It has been often remarked that indignation makes a man witty; and as despair occasionally breaks out into laughter, it may sometimes also give vent to itself in antithetical comparisons.

Besides, the rights of the poetical form have not been duly weighed. Shakspeare, who was always sure of his power to excite, when he wished, sufficiently powerful emotions, has occasionally, by indulging in a freer play of fancy, purposely tempered the impressions when too painful, and immediately introduced a musical softening of our sympathy. He had not those rude ideas of his art which many moderns seem to have, as if the poet, like the clown in the proverb, must strike twice on the same place. An ancient rhetorician delivered a caution against dwelling too long on the excitation of pity; for nothing, he said, dries so soon as tears; and Shakspeare acted conformably to this ingenious maxim without having learned it. The paradoxical assertion of Johnson that "Shakspeare had a greater talent for comedy than tragedy, and that in the latter he has frequently displayed an affected tone," is scarcely deserving of lengthy notice. For its refutation, it is unnecessary to appeal to the great tragical compositions of the poet, which, for overpowering effect, leave far behind them almost everything that the stage has seen besides; a few of their less celebrated scenes would be quite sufficient. What to many readers might lend an appearance of truth to this assertion are the verbal witticisms, that playing upon words, which Shakspeare not unfrequently introduces into serious and sublime passages, and even into those also of a peculiarly pathetic nature.

I have already stated the point of view in which we ought to consider this sportive play upon words. I shall here, therefore, merely deliver a few observations respecting the playing upon words in general, and its poetical use. A thorough investigation would lead us too far from our subject, and too deeply into considerations on the essence of language, and its relation to poetry, or rhyme, &c.

There is in the human mind a desire that language should exhibit the object which it denotes, sensibly, by its very sound, which may be traced even as far back as in the first origin of poetry. As, in the shape in which language comes down to us, this is seldom perceptibly the case, an imagination which has been powerfully excited is fond of laying hold of any congruity in sound which may accidentally offer itself, that by such means he may, for the nonce, restore the lost resemblance between the word and the thing. For example, how common was it and is it to seek in the name of a person, however arbitrarily bestowed, a reference to his qualities and fortunes,—to convert it purposely into a significant name. Those who cry out against the play upon words as an unnatural and

affected invention, only betray their own ignorance of original nature. A great fondness for it is always evinced among children, as well as with nations of simple manners, among whom correct ideas of the derivation and affinity of words have not yet been developed, and do not, consequently, stand in the way of this caprice. In Homer we find several examples of it; the Books of Moses, the oldest written memorial of the primitive world, are, as is well known, full of them. On the other hand, poets of a very cultivated taste, like Petrarch, or orators, like Cicero, have delighted in them. Whoever, in *Richard the Second,* is disgusted with the affecting play of words of the dying John of Gaunt on his own name, should remember that the same thing occurs in the *Ajax* of Sophocles. We do not mean to say that all playing upon words is on all occasions to be justified. This must depend on the disposition of mind, whether it will admit of such a play of fancy, and whether the sallies, comparisons and allusions, which lie at the bottom of them, possess internal solidity. Yet we must not proceed upon the principle of trying how the thought appears after it is deprived of the resemblance in sound, any more than we are to endeavour to feel the charm of rhymed versification after depriving it of its rhyme. The laws of good taste on this subject must, moreover, vary with the quality of the languages. In those which possess a great number of homonymes, that is, words possessing the same, or nearly the same, sound, though quite different in their derivation and signification, it is almost more difficult to avoid, than to fall on such verbal play. It has, however, been feared, lest a door might be opened to puerile witticism, if they were not rigorously proscribed. But I cannot, for my part, find that Shakspeare had such an invincible and immoderate passion for this verbal witticism. It is true, he sometimes makes a most lavish use of this figure; at others, he has employed it very sparingly; and at times (for example, in *Macbeth*),[2] I do not believe a vestige of it is to be found. Hence, in respect to the use or the rejection of the play upon words, he must have been guided by the measure of the objects, and the different style in

[2] Yet *Macbeth* (II, ii, 56-57) contains one of the best-known examples: Lady Macbeth's "I'll *gild* the faces of the grooms withal, for it must seem their *guilt.*"

which they required to be treated, and probably have followed here, as in every thing else, principles which, fairly examined, will bear a strict examination.

The objection that Shakspeare wounds our feelings by the open display of the most disgusting moral odiousness, unmercifully harrows up the mind, and tortures even our eyes by the exhibition of the most insupportable and hateful spectacles, is one of greater and graver importance. He has, in fact, never varnished over wild and blood-thirsty passions with a pleasing exterior—never clothed crime and want of principle with a false show of greatness of soul; and in that respect he is every way deserving of praise. Twice he has portrayed downright villains, and the masterly way in which he has contrived to elude impressions of too painful a nature may be seen in Iago and Richard the Third. I allow that the reading, and still more the sight, of some of his pieces, is not advisable to weak nerves, any more than was the *Eumenides* of Aeschylus; but is the poet, who can only reach an important object by a bold and hazardous daring, to be checked by considerations for such persons? If the effeminacy of the present day is to serve as a general standard of what tragical composition may properly exhibit to human nature, we shall be forced to set very narrow limits indeed to art, and the hope of anything like powerful effect must at once and for ever be renounced. If we wish to have a grand purpose, we must also wish to have the grand means, and our nerves ought in some measure to accommodate themselves to painful impressions, if, by way of requital, our mind is thereby elevated and strengthened. The constant reference to a petty and puny race must cripple the boldness of the poet. Fortunately for his art, Shakspeare lived in an age extremely susceptible of noble and tender impressions, but which had yet inherited enough of the firmness of a vigorous olden time, not to shrink with dismay from every strong and forcible painting. We have lived to see tragedies of which the castastrophe consists in the swoon of an enamoured princess: if Shakspeare falls occasionally into the opposite extreme, it is a noble error, originating in the fulness of a gigantic strength. And this tragical Titan, who storms the heavens and threatens to tear the world from off its

hinges, who, more terrible than Aeschylus, makes our hair to stand on end, and congeals our blood with horror, possessed at the same time the insinuating loveliness of the sweetest poesy; he toys with love like a child, and his songs die away on the ear like melting sighs. He unites in his soul the utmost elevation and the utmost depth; and the most opposite and even apparently irreconcilable properties subsist in him peaceably together. The world of spirits and nature have laid all their treasures at his feet: in strength a demi-god, in profundity of view a prophet, in all-seeing wisdom a guardian spirit of a higher order, he lowers himself to mortals as if unconscious of his superiority, and is as open and unassuming as a child.

If the delineation of all his characters, separately considered, is inimitably bold and correct, he surpasses even himself in so combining and contrasting them, that they serve to bring out each other's peculiarities. This is the very perfection of dramatic characterization: for we can never estimate a man's true worth if we consider him altogether abstractedly by himself; we must see him in his relations with others; and it is here that most dramatic poets are deficient. Shakspeare makes each of his principal characters the glass in which the others are reflected, and by like means enables us to discover what could not be immediately revealed to us. What in others is most profound, is with him but surface. Ill-advised should we be were we always to take men's declarations respecting themselves and others for sterling coin. Ambiguity of design with much propriety he makes to overflow with the most praiseworthy principles; and sage maxims are not unfrequently put in the mouth of stupidity, to show how easily such commonplace truisms may be acquired. Nobody ever painted so truthfully as he has done the facility of self-deception, the half self-conscious hypocrisy towards ourselves, with which even noble minds attempt to disguise the almost inevitable influence of selfish motives in human nature. This secret irony of the characterization commands admiration as the profound abyss of acuteness and sagacity; but it is the grave of enthusiasm. We arrive at it only after we have had the misfortune to see human nature through and through; and when no choice remains but to adopt the melancholy truth, that "no virtue or greatness is altogether pure and genuine," or the dangerous error that "the highest perfection is attainable." Here we therefore may perceive in the poet himself, notwithstanding his power to excite the most fervent emotions, a certain cool indifference, but still the indifference of a superior mind, which has run through the whole sphere of human existence and survived feeling.

The irony in Shakspeare has not merely a reference to the separate characters, but frequently to the whole of the action. Most poets who portray human events in a narrative or dramatic form take themselves a part, and exact from their readers a blind approbation or condemnation of whatever side they choose to support or oppose. The more zealous this rhetoric is, the more certainly it fails of its effect. In every case we are conscious that the subject itself is not brought immediately before us, but that we view it through the medium of a different way of thinking. When, however, by a dexterous manoeuvre, the poet allows us an occasional glance at the less brilliant reverse of the medal, then he makes, as it were, a sort of secret understanding with the select circle of the more intelligent of his readers or spectators; he shows them that he had previously seen and admitted the validity of their tacit objections; that he himself is not tied down to the represented subject, but soars freely above it; and that, if he chose, he could unrelentingly annihilate the beautiful and irresistibly attractive scenes which his magic pen has produced. No doubt, wherever the proper tragic enters, every thing like irony immediately ceases; but from the avowed raillery of Comedy, to the point where the subjection of mortal beings to an inevitable destiny demands the highest degree of seriousness, there are a multitude of human relations which unquestionably may be considered in an ironical view, without confounding the eternal line of separation between good and evil. This purpose is answered by the comic characters and scenes which are interwoven with the serious parts in most of those pieces of Shakspeare where romantic fables or historical events are made the subject of a noble and elevating exhibition. Frequently an intentional parody of the serious part is not to be mistaken in them; at other times the connexion is more arbitrary and loose, and the more so the more marvellous the invention of the whole, and the more entirely it is become a light revelling of the fancy. The comic intervals everywhere serve to prevent the pastime from being converted into a business, to preserve the mind in the possession of its serenity, and to keep off that gloomy and inert seriousness which so easily steals upon the sentimental, but not tragical, drama. Most assuredly Shakspeare did not intend thereby, in defiance to his own better judgment, to humour the taste of the multitude: for in various pieces, and throughout considerable portions of others, and especially when the castastrophe is approaching, and the mind consequently is more on the stretch and no longer likely to give heed to any amusement which would distract their attention, he has abstained from all such comic intermixtures. It was also an object with him, that the clowns or buffoons should not occupy a more important place than that which he had assigned them: he expressly condemns the extemporizing with which they loved to enlarge their parts. Johnson founds the justification of the species of drama in which seriousness and mirth are mixed, on this, that in real life the vulgar is found close to the sublime, that the merry and the sad usually accompany and succeed one another. But it does not follow that because both are found together, therefore they must not be separable in the compositions of art. The observation is in other respects just, and this circumstance invests the poet with a power to adopt this procedure, because every thing in the drama must be regulated by the conditions of theatrical probability; but the mixture of such dissimilar, and apparently contradictory, ingredients, in the same works can only be justifiable on principles reconcilable with the views of art, which I have already described. In the dramas of Shakspeare the comic scenes are the antechamber of the poetry, where the servants remain; these prosaic attendants must not raise their voices so high as to deafen the speakers in the presence-chamber; however, in those intervals when the ideal society has retired they deserve to be listened to; their bold raillery, their presumption of mockery, may afford many an insight into the situation and circumstances of their masters. . . .

I have still a few observations to make on the diction and versification of our poet. The language is here and there somewhat obsolete, but on the whole much less so than in most of the contemporary writers, a sufficient proof of the goodness of his choice. Prose had as yet been but little cultivated, as the learned generally wrote in Latin: a favourable circumstance for the dramatic poet; for what has he to do with the scientific language of books? He had not only read, but studied the earlier English poets; but he drew his language immediately from life itself, and he possessed a masterly skill in blending the dialogical element with the highest poetical elevation. I know not what certain critics mean, when they say Shakspeare is frequently ungrammatical. To make good their assertion, they must prove that similar constructions never occur in his contemporaries, the direct contrary of which can, however, be easily shown. In no language is every thing determined on principle; much is always left to the caprice of custom, and if this has since changed, is the poet to be made answerable for it? The English language had not then attained to that correct insipidity which has been introduced into the more recent literature of the country, to the prejudice, perhaps, of its originality. As a field when first brought under the plough produces, along with the fruitful shoots, many luxuriant weeds, so the poetical diction of the day ran occasionally into extravagance, but an extravagance originating in the exuberance of its vigour. We may still perceive traces of awkwardness, but nowhere of a laboured and spiritless display of art. In general Shakspeare's style yet remains the very best model, both in the vigorous and sublime, and the pleasing and tender. In his sphere he has exhausted all the means and appliances of language. On all he has impressed the stamp of his mighty spirit. His images and figures, in their unsought, nay, uncapricious singularity, have often a sweetness altogether peculiar. He becomes occasionally obscure from too great fondness for compressed brevity; but still, the labour of poring over Shakspeare's lines will invariably meet an ample requital.

The verse in all his plays is generally the rhymeless Iambic of ten or eleven syllables, occasionally only intermixed with rhymes, but more frequently alternating with prose. No one piece is written entirely in prose; for even in those which approach the most to the pure Comedy, there is always something added which gives them a more poetical hue than usually belongs to this species. Many scenes are wholly in prose, in others verse and prose succeed each other alternately. This can only appear an impropriety in the eyes of those who are accustomed to consider the lines of a drama like so many soldiers drawn up rank and file on a parade, with the same uniform, arms, and accoutrements, so that when we see one or two we may represent to ourselves thousands as being every way like them.

In the use of verse and prose Shakspeare observes very nice distinctions according to the ranks of the speakers, but still more according to their characters and disposition of mind. A noble language, elevated above the usual tone, is only suitable to a certain decorum of manners, which is thrown over both vices and virtues, and which does not even wholly disappear amidst the violence of passion. If this is not exclusively possessed by the higher ranks, it still, however, belongs naturally more to them than to the lower; and therefore in Shakspeare dignity and familiarity of language, poetry, and prose, are in this manner distributed among the characters. Hence his tradesmen, peasants, soldiers, sailors, servants, but more especially his fools and clowns, speak, almost without exception, in the tone of their actual life. However, inward dignity of sentiment, wherever it is possessed, invariably displays itself with a nobleness of its own, and stands not in need, for that end, of the artificial elegancies of education and custom; it is a universal right of man, of the highest as well as the lowest; and hence also, in Shakspeare, the nobility of nature and morality is ennobled above the artificial nobility of society. Not unfrequently also he makes the very same persons express themselves at times in the sublimest language, and at others in the lowest; and this inequality is in like manner founded in truth. Extraordinary situations, which intensely occupy the head and throw mighty passions into play, give elevation and tension to the soul: it collects together all its powers, and exhibits an unusual energy, both in its operations and in its communications by language. On the other hand, even the greatest men have their moments of remissness, when to a certain degree they forget the dignity of their character in unreserved relaxation. This very tone of mind is necessary before they can receive amusement from the jokes of others, or what surely cannot dishonour even a hero, from passing jokes themselves. Let any person, for example, go carefully through the part of Hamlet. How bold and powerful the language of his poetry when he conjures the ghost of his father, when he spurs himself on to the bloody deed, when he thunders into the soul of his mother! How he lowers his tone down to that of common life, when he has to do with persons whose station demands from him such a line of conduct; when he makes game of Polonius and the courtiers, instructs the player, and even enters into the jokes of the grave-digger. Of all the poet's serious leading characters there is none so rich in wit and humour as Hamlet; hence he it is of all of them that makes the greatest use of the familiar style. Others, again, never do fall into it; either because they are constantly surrounded by the pomp of rank, or because a uniform seriousness is natural to them; or, in short, because through the whole piece they are under the dominion of a passion calculated to excite, and not, like the sorrow of Hamlet, to depress the mind. The choice of the one form or the other is everywhere so appropriate, and so much founded in the nature of the thing, that I ·will venture to assert, even where the poet in the very same speech makes the speaker leave prose for poetry, or the converse, this could not be altered without danger of injuring or destroying some beauty or other. The blank verse has this advantage, that its tone may be elevated or lowered; it admits of approximation to the familiar style of conversation, and never forms such an abrupt contrast as that, for example, between plain prose and the rhyming Alexandrines.

Shakspeare's Iambics are sometimes highly harmonious and full sounding; always varied and suitable to the subject, at one time distinguished by ease and rapidity, at another they move along with ponderous energy. They never fall out of the dialogical character, which may always be traced even in the continued discourses of individuals, excepting when the latter run into the lyrical. They are a complete model of the dramatic use of this species of verse, which, in English, since Milton, has been also used in epic poetry; but in the latter it has assumed a quite different turn. Even the irregularities of

Shakspeare's versification are expressive; a verse broken off, or a sudden change of rhythmus, coincides with some pause in the progress of the thought, or the entrance of another mental disposition. As a proof that he purposely violated the mechanical rules, from a conviction that too symmetrical a versification does not suit with the drama, and on the stage has in the long run a tendency to lull the spectators asleep, we may observe that his earlier pieces are the most diligently versified, and that in the later works, when through practice he must have acquired a greater facility, we find the strongest deviations from the regular structure of the verse. As it served with him merely to make the poetical elevation perceptible, he therefore claimed the utmost possible freedom in the use of it.

The views or suggestions of feeling by which he was guided in the use of rhyme may likewise be traced with almost equal certainty. Not unfrequently scenes, or even single speeches, close with a few rhyming lines, for the purpose of more strongly marking the division, and of giving it more rounding. This was injudiciously imitated by the English tragic poets of a later date; they suddenly elevated the tone in the rhymed lines, as if the person began all at once to speak in another language. The practice was welcomed by the actors from its serving as a signal for clapping when they made their exit. In Shakspeare, on the other hand, the transitions are more easy: all changes of forms are brought about insensibly, and as if of themselves. . . .

In England the manner of handling rhyming verse, and the opinion as to its harmony and elegance, have, in the course of two centuries, undergone a much greater change than is the case with the rhymeless Iambic or blank verse. In the former, Dryden and Pope have become models; these writers have communicated the utmost smoothing to rhyme, but they have also tied it down to a harmonious uniformity. A foreigner, to whom antiquated and new are the same, may perhaps feel with greater freedom the advantages of the more ancient manner. Certain it is, the rhyme of the present day, from the too great confinement of the couplet, is unfit for the drama. We must not estimate the rhyme of Shakspeare by the mode of subsequent times, but by a comparison with his contemporaries or with Spenser. The comparison will, without doubt, turn out to his advantage. Spenser is often diffuse; Shakspeare, though sometimes hard, is always brief and vigorous. He has more frequently been induced by the rhyme to leave out something necessary than to insert anything superfluous. Many of his rhymes, however, are faultless: ingenious with attractive ease, and rich without false brilliancy. The songs interspersed (those, I mean, of the poet himself) are generally sweetly playful and altogether musical; in imagination, while we merely read them, we hear their melody.

The whole of Shakspeare's productions bear the certain stamp of his original genius, but yet no writer was ever farther removed from everything like a mannerism derived from habit or personal peculiarities. Rather is he, such is the diversity of tone and colour, which varies according to the quality of his subjects he assumes, a very Proteus. Each of his compositions is like a world of its own, moving in its own sphere. They are works of art, finished in one pervading style, which revealed the freedom and judicious choice of their author. If the formation of a work throughout, even in its minutest parts, in conformity with a leading idea; if the domination of one animating spirit over all the means of execution, deserves the name of correctness (and this, excepting in matters of grammar, is the only proper sense of the term); we shall then, after allowing to Shakspeare all the higher qualities which demand our admiration, be also compelled, in most cases, to concede to him the title of a correct poet.

FRIEDRICH VON SCHLEGEL

Literature and National Character

[Under the name of literature] I comprehend all those arts and sciences, and all those mental exertions which have human life, and man himself, for their object; but which, manifesting themselves in no external effect, energize only in thought and speech, and without requiring any corporeal matter on which to operate, display intellect as embodied in written language. Under these are included,—first, the art of poetry, and the kindred arts of narration, or history; next, all those higher exertions of pure reason and intellect which have human life, and man himself, for their object, and which have influence upon both; and, last of all, eloquence and wit, whenever these do not escape in the fleeting vehicle of oral communication, but remain displayed in the more substantial and lasting form of written productions. And when I have enumerated these, I imagine I have comprehended almost everything which can enter into the composition of the intellectual life of man. With the single exception of reason—and even reason can scarcely operate without the intervention of language—is there anything more important to man, more peculiar to him, or more inseparable from his nature, than speech? Nature, indeed, could not have bestowed on us a gift more precious than the human voice, which, possessing sounds for the expression of every feeling, and being capable of distinctions as minute, and combinations as intricate, as the most complex instrument of music, is thus enabled to furnish materials so admirable for the formation of artificial language. The greatest and most important discovery of human ingenuity is writing. . . . So inseparable, indeed, are mind and language, so identically one are thought and speech, that although we must always hold reason to be the great characteristic and peculiar attribute of man, yet language also, when we regard its original object and intrinsic dignity, is well entitled to be considered as a component part of the intellectual structure of our being. And although, in strict application and rigid expression, thought and speech always are and always must be regarded as two things metaphysically distinct,—yet there only can we find these two elements in disunion, where one or both have been employed imperfectly or amiss. Nay,

Literature and National Character. From Lecture I, in *Lectures on the History of Literature, Ancient and Modern* (1811; tr. J. G. Lockhart, 1818).

such is the effect of the original union or identity that, in their most extensive varieties of application, they can never be totally disunited, but must always remain inseparable, and everywhere be exerted in combination.

However greatly both of these high gifts, which are so essentially the same,—these, the proudest distinctions of human nature, which have made man what he is,—may be in many instances misdirected and abused; still our innate and indestructible sense of the original dignity of speech and language is sufficiently manifest from the importance which we attach to them, in the formation of all our particular judgments and opinions. What influence the art of speaking has upon our judgment in the affairs of active life, and in all the relations of society,—what power the force of expression everywhere exerts over our thoughts, it would be superfluous to detail. The same considerations which govern us in our judgment of individuals, determine us also in our opinions concerning nations; and we are at once disposed to look upon that people as the most enlightened and the most polished, which makes use of the most clear, precise, appropriate and agreeable medium of expression: insomuch, that we not unfrequently allow ourselves to be biassed even to weakness by the external advantage of diction and utterance, and pay more attention to the vehicle than to the intrinsic value of the thoughts themselves, or the moral character of those from whom they proceed. Nor do we form our opinions in this manner concerning those individuals alone, and those people who reside in our vicinity, or with whom we are personally acquainted; but we apply the same standard to those who are removed to the greatest distance from us, both in time and situation. Let us take, for instance, the example of a people which we have always been accustomed to class under the general epithet of barbarian. So soon as some observing traveller makes himself acquainted with their language, this unfavorable opinion begins essentially to be changed. "Barbarians!" he will say, "they are indeed barbarians, for they are unacquainted with our arts and our refinements, as well as with those moral evils which are so often their consequence; but it is at least impossible to deny that they possess a sound and strong understanding, and a natural acuteness, which we cannot observe without ad-

miration. Their brief replies are most touching, and not unfrequently display a native vein of wit. Their language is powerful and expressive, and possesses the most marked clearness and precision." Thus, in all situations, and in all affairs, we are accustomed and compelled to reason from language to intellect, and from the expression to the thought. But these are only solitary examples in solitary cases.

The true excellence and importance of those arts and sciences which exert and display themselves in writing may be seen, in a more general point of view, in the great influence which they have exerted on the character and fate of nations throughout the history of the world. Here it is that literature appears in all its reach and comprehension, as the epitome of all intellectual capabilities and progressive improvements of mankind. If we look back to the history of our species, and observe what circumstances have given to any one nation the greatest advantages over others, we shall not, I think, hesitate to admit that there is nothing so necessary to the whole improvement, or rather to the whole intellectual existence of a nation, as the possession of a plentiful store of those national recollections and associations, which are lost in a great measure during the dark ages of infant society, but which it forms the great object of the poetical art to perpetuate and adorn. Such national recollections, the noblest inheritance which a people can possess, bestow an advantage which no other riches can supply; for when a people are exalted in their feelings and ennobled in their own estimation, by the consciousness that they have been illustrious in ages that are gone by,—that these recollections have come down to them from a remote and heroic ancestry,—in a word, that they have a *national poetry* of their own, we are willing to acknowledge that their pride is reasonable, and they are raised in our eyes by the same circumstances which gives them elevation in their own. It is not from the extent of its undertakings alone, or from the remarkable nature of the incidents of its history, that we judge of the character and importance of a nation. Many a nation, which has undergone in its time all the varieties of human fortune, has sunk nameless into oblivion, and left behind scarcely a trace of its existence. Others, more fortunate, have transmitted to posterity the memory of their influence, and the fame of their conquests; and yet we scarcely hold the narrative to be worthy of our attention, unless the spirit of the nation has been such as to communicate *its* interests to those undertakings and those incidents which at best occupy but too great a space in the history of the world. Remarkable actions, great events, and strange catastrophies, are not of themselves sufficient to preserve the admiration and determine the judgment of posterity. These are only to be attained by a nation who have given clear proofs that they were not insensible instruments in the hands of destiny, but were themselves conscious of the greatness of their deeds and the singularity of their fortunes. This national consciousness, expressing itself in the works of narrative and illustration, is HISTORY. A people whose days of glory and victory have been celebrated by the pen of a Livy, whose misfortunes and decline have been bequeathed to posterity in the pages of a Tacitus, acquires a strange pre-eminence by the genius of her historians, and is no longer in any danger of being classed with the vulgar multitude of nations, which, occupying no place in the history of human intellect, as soon as they have performed their part of conquest or defeat on the stage of the world, pass away from our view, and sink forever into oblivion. The poet, the painter, or the sculptor, though endued with all the power and all the magic of his art,— though capable of reaching or embodying the boldest flights of imagination;—the philosopher, though he may be able to scrutinize the most hidden depth of human thought, (rare as these attainments may be, and few equals as he may find in the society with which he is surrounded,) can, during the period of his own life, be known and appreciated only by a few. But the sphere of his influence extends with the progress of ages, and his name shines brighter and broader as it grows old. Compared with his, the fame of the legislator, among distant nations, and the celebrity of new institutions, appears uncertain and obscure; while the glory of the conqueror, after a few centuries have sunk into the allwhelming, all-destroying abyss of time, is for ever fading in its lustre, until at length it perhaps affords a subject of exultation to some plodding antiquarian, that he should be able to discover some glimmerings of a name which had once challenged the reverence of the world. It may safely be affirmed, that not only among the moderns, but even in the latter ages of antiquity, the preservation and extension of the fame of Greece were at least as much the work of Homer and Plato, as of Solon and Alexander. The tribute of attention which all the European nations so willingly pay to the history of the Greeks, as the authors and examples of European refinement, is in truth more rightly due to the philosopher and the poet, than to the conqueror and the legislator. The influence which the works and the genius of Homer have of themselves produced on after ages, or rather, indeed, on the general character and improvement of the human race, has alone been far more durable, and for more extensive, than the combined effects of all the institutions of the Athenian, and all the heroic deeds and transcendent victories of the Macedonian. In truth, if Solon and Alexander still continue to be glorious and immortal names, their glory and immortality are to be traced rather to the influence which, by certain accidents, their genius has exerted on the intellectual character and progress of the species, than to the intrinsic value of a system of municipal laws altogether discrepant from our own, or to the establishment of a few dynasties which have long since passed away.

We must not, indeed, expect to find many poets or many philosophers whose genius or whose celebrity have in any degree entitled them to be compared with Homer and Plato. But wherever one is to be found, he, like them, is deservedly valued by posterity as a solitary light in the midst of darkness, a sure index and a common standard, by which we may form an estimate of the intellectual power and refinement of the age and nation which gave him birth.

If to these high advantages of national poetry and national traditions, of a history abounding in subjects of meditation, of refined art, and profound science, we add the gifts of eloquence, of wit, and of a language of society adapted to all the ends of elegant intercourse, but not abused to the purpose of immorality: we have filled up the picture of a polished and intellectual people, and we have a full view of what a perfect and comprehensive literature ought to be. . . .

The Subject-Matter of Poetry: The Ideal and the Actual

To DETERMINE the true and proper relation between poetry, and the past or the present, involves the investigation of the whole depth and essence of the art. In general, in our theories, with the exception of some very general, meaningless, and most commonly false definitions of the art itself, and of the beautiful, the chief subjects of attention are always the mere forms of poetry, things necessary without doubt, but by no means sufficient, to be known. As yet there has scarcely been any theory with regard to the proper subject of poetry, although such a theory would evidently be far the most useful in regard to the effect which poetry is to have upon life. In the preceding discourses I have endeavoured to supply this defect, and to give some glimpses of such a theory, wherever the nature of my topics has furnished me with an opportunity.

With regard to the representation of actual life in poetry, we must, above all things, remember that it is by no means certain that the actual and present are intractable or unworthy subjects of poetical representation, merely because in themselves they appear less noble and uncommon than the past. It is true that in what is near and present, the common and unpoetical come at all times more strongly and more conspicuously into view; while in the remote and the past, they occupy the distance, and leave the foreground to be filled with forms of greatness and sublimity alone. But this difficulty is one which the true poet can easily conquer; his art has no more favourite mode of displaying itself than in lending to things of common-place, and every day occurrence, the brilliancy of a poetic illumination, by extracting from them higher signification, and deeper purpose, and more refined feeling, than we had before suspected them of concealing, or dreamed them to be capable of exciting. Still the precision of the present is at all times binding and confining for the fancy, and when we, by our subject, impose so many fetters upon her, there is always reason to fear,

that she will be inclined to make up for this restraint, by an excess of liberty in regard to language and description.

To make my views upon this point intelligible to you in the shortest way, I need only recall to your recollection what I said some time ago, with regard to subjects of a religious or Christian import. The invisible world, the Deity, and pure intellects, can never, upon the whole, be with propriety represented by us; nature and human beings are the proper and immediate subjects of poetry. But the higher and spiritual world can be everywhere embodied and shadowed forth in our terrestrial materials. In like manner the indirect representation of the actual and the present is the best and most appropriate. The bloom of young life, and the high ecstasies of passion, as well as the maturity of wise reflection, may all be combined with the old traditions of our nation; they will there have more room for exertion, and be displayed in a purer light than the present can command. The oldest poet of the past, Homer, is at the same time to us a describer of the present in its utmost liveliness and freshness. Every true poet carries into the past his own age, and, in a certain sense, himself. The following appears to me to be the true account of the proper relation between poetry and time. The proper business of poetry is to represent only the eternal, that which is, at all places, and in all times, significant and beautiful; but this cannot be accomplished without the intervention of a veil. Poetry requires to have a corporeal habitation, and this she finds in her best sphere, the traditions of a nation, the recollections and past of a people. In her representations of these, however, she introduces the whole wealth of the present, so far as that is susceptible of poetical ornament; she plunges also into the future, because she explains the apparent mysteries of earthly existence, accompanies individual life through all its development, down to its period of termination, and sheds from her magic mirror the light of a higher interpretation upon all things; she embraces all the tenses, the past, the present, and the future, in order to make

The Subject-Matter of Poetry. From Lecture XII, *Lectures on the History of Literature.*

a truly sensible representation of the eternal or the perfect time. Even in a philosophical sense, eternity is no nonentity, no mere negation of time, but rather its entire and undivided fulness, wherein all its elements are united, where the past becomes new and present, and with the present itself, is mingled the abundance of hope, and all the richness of futurity. . . .

It is only in the first and lowest scale of the drama, that I can place those pieces in which we are presented with the visible surface of life alone, the fleeting appearance of the rich picture of the world. It is thus that I view them, even although they display the highest sway of passion in tragedy, or the perfection of all social refinements and absurdities in comedy, so long as the whole business of the play is limited to external appearances, and these things are brought before us merely in perspective, and as pictures for the purposes of drawing our attention, and awakening the sympathy of our passions. The second order of the art is that, where in dramatic representations, together with passion and the pictoric appearance of things, a spirit of more profound sense and thought is predominate over the scene, wherein there is displayed a deep knowledge, not of individuals and their affairs alone, but of our whole species, of the world and of life, in all their manifold shapes, contradictions, and catastrophies, of man and of his being, that darkest of riddles—as such—as a riddle. Were this profound knowledge of us and our nature the only end of dramatic poetry, Shakespeare would not merely deserve to be called the first in his art, but there could scarcely be found a single poet, either among the ancients or the moderns, worthy for a moment to be compared with him. But in my opinion the art of the dramatic poet has, besides all this, yet another and a higher end. The enigma of life should not barely be expressed but solved; the perplexities of the present should indeed be represented, but from them our view should be led to the last development and the final issue. The poet should entwine the future with the present, and lay before our eyes the mysteries of the internal man. This is indeed something quite different from what we commonly demand in a tragedy by the name of catastrophe. There are many celebrated dramatic works wherein that sort of denouement, to which I here allude, is altogether wanting, or which, at least, have only the outward form, but are quite destitute of the internal being and spirit of it. . . .

PERCY BYSSHE SHELLEY   (1792-1822)

SHELLEY assumed various intellectual attitudes throughout his short life, starting as a disciple of eighteenth-century French materialism and ending with a romantic Neoplatonism of his own. His ultimate position, in fact, was a complicated web of attitudes. But however pertinent his various premises are in studying his poetry, it is not necessary to try to disentangle them before approaching his *Defence of Poetry* (1821). It is sufficient to

PERCY BYSSHE SHELLEY. Educated at Eton and Oxford, and expelled from the latter for espousing atheism, Shelley quickly became sensitive to prevailing ideas of many sorts. As time passed, his humanitarianism became broader, more genuine and informed; his personal domestic life became troubled, and is now famous. He occasionally lived abroad (starting in 1814), left England permanently in 1818, settled in Italy, and died by drowning at the age of 29.

Complete Works (ed. R. Ingpen and W. E. Peck, 1926-30); *Literary and Philosophical Criticism*

point out that this famous credo, voicing Shelley's faith in poetry, expresses an attitude quite in keeping with the romantic stress on the organic character of reality and the romantic confidence in the imagination. At the same time it reasserts a transcendental, Platonic idealism—viewing organic nature in the light of ultimate values and absolute, universal forms—and reaches back through Sidney's *Apology for Poetry* to the Renaissance Platonic tradition.

Shelley began by making a common romantic distinction between "reason" and the "imagination." Reason analyzes; it views things—to use Wordsworth's phrase—"in disconnection, dead and spiritless." One may see here an anticipation of the more recent thesis of Henri Bergson: the intellect is almost *spatial* or *geometrical* in character; it measures and divides, as though dealing with *quantitative* things, and distorts reality to fit the molds of its categories. The imagination, said Shelley, thinks in terms of totalities rather than proceeding by artificial analysis; it grasps the inner activity animating the changing, evolving reality outside, reacts to the varying crosslights in it, and captures the qualitative value potential in them. It is in construing this value in terms of ultimate and universal forms that Shelley reached back to the Platonic tradition and transcendentalized his romantic, organic theory of nature. Hence the remark that poetry tries to reveal "the image [the organic concreteness] of life expressed in its eternal truth," and that poets, in disclosing this reality, are the ultimate teachers and "unacknowledged legislators of the world." To this aim, Shelley subjoined another classical tenet: in conveying an awareness of reality in its full value and meaning, poetry is formative and moral in the highest sense. And Shelley gave this tenet a characteristically romantic phrasing by putting it in terms of "sympathy," though the spirit of what he said is essentially classical. The "great secret of morals is love"—it is a "going out of one's own nature," a sympathetic identification with others. Now the "imagination" is the means by which we do this; and poetry enlarges the range and scope of the imagination, gives it knowledge and experience, sharpens its delicacy and readiness to react, and in general strengthens and exercises this fundamental "instrument of moral good."

(ed. J. Shawcross, 1909). There is also *Shelley's Prose or the Trumpet of a Prophecy* (ed. D. C. Clark, Albuquerque, 1964). The *Letters* have been edited by F. L. Jones (2 vols., Oxford, 1964). In addition to N. I. White, *Shelley* (1940), which, though primarily biographical, gives related background, the following may be mentioned: J. E. Baker, *Shelley's Platonic Answer to a Platonic Attack on Poetry* (Iowa City, 1965); Carl H. Grabo, *The Magic Plant: the Growth of Shelley's Thought* (Chapel Hill, 1936); Gerald MacNiece, *Shelley and the Revolutionary Idea* (Cambridge, Mass., 1969); Melvin T. Solve, *Shelley: His Theory of Poetry* (Chicago, 1927); and especially E. R. Wasserman, "Shelley's Last Poetics: a Reconsideration," in *From Sensibility to Romanticism: Essays Presented to Frederick A. Pottle*, ed. F. W. Hilles and Harold Bloom (1965).

A Defence of Poetry

ACCORDING to one mode of regarding those two classes of mental action, which are called reason and imagination, the former may be considered as mind contemplating the relations borne by one thought to another, however produced; and the latter, as mind acting upon those thoughts so as to colour them with its own light, and composing from them, as from elements, other thoughts, each containing within itself the principle of its own integrity. The one is the τὸ ποιεῖν,[1] or the principle of synthesis, and has for its objects those forms which are common to universal nature and existence itself; the other is the τὸ λογίζειν,[2] or principle of analysis, and its action regards the relations of things, simply as relations; considering thoughts, not in their integral unity, but as the algebraical representations which conduct to certain general results. Reason is the enumeration of quantities already known; imagination is the perception of the value of those quantities, both separately and as a whole. Reason respects the differences, and imagination the similitudes of things. Reason is to the imagination as the instrument to the agent, as the body to the spirit, as the shadow to the substance.

Poetry, in a general sense, may be defined to be "the expression of the imagination": and poetry is connate with the origin of man. Man is an instrument over which a series of external and internal impressions are driven, like the alternations of an ever-changing wind over an Aeolian lyre, which move it by their motion to ever-changing melody. But there is a principle within the human being, and perhaps within all sentient beings, which acts otherwise than in the lyre, and produces not melody alone, but harmony, by an internal adjustment of the sounds or motions thus excited to the impressions which excite them. It is as if the lyre could accommodate its chords to the motions of that which strikes them, in a determined proportion of sound; even as the musician can accommodate his voice to the sound of the lyre. A child at play by itself will express its delight by its voice and motions; and every inflexion of tone and every gesture will bear exact relation to a corresponding antitype in the pleasurable impressions which awakened it; it will be the reflected image of that impression; and as the lyre trembles and sounds after the wind has died away, so the child seeks, by prolonging in its voice and motions the duration of the effect, to prolong also a consciousness of the cause. In relation to the objects which delight a child, these expressions are, what poetry is to higher objects. The savage (for the savage is to ages what the child is to years) expresses the emotions produced in him by surrounding objects in a similar manner; and language and gesture, together with plastic or pictorial imitation, become the image of the combined effect of those objects, and of his apprehension of them. Man in society, with all his passions and his pleasures, next becomes the object of the passions and pleasures of man; an additional class of emotions produces an augmented treasure of expressions; and language, gesture, and the imitative arts, become at once the representation and the medium, the pencil and the picture, the chisel and the statue, the chord and the harmony. The social sympathies, or those laws from which, as from its elements, society results, begin to develop themselves from the moment that two human beings coexist; the future is contained within the present, as the plant within the seed; and equality, diversity, unity, contrast, mutual dependence, become the principles alone capable of affording the motives according to which the will of a social being is determined to action, inasmuch as he is social; and constitute pleasure in sensation, virtue in sentiment, beauty in art, truth in reasoning, and love in the intercourse of kind. Hence men, even in the infancy of society, observe a certain order in their words and actions, distinct from that of the objects and the impressions represented by them, all expression being subject to the laws of that from which it proceeds. But let us dismiss

A Defence of Poetry. Written in 1821; first published in 1840.

[1] The creative process.
[2] Analytic reasoning.

those more general considerations which might involve an inquiry into the principles of society itself, and restrict our view to the manner in which the imagination is expressed upon its forms.

In the youth of the world, men dance and sing and imitate natural objects, observing in these actions, as in all others, a certain rhythm or order. And, although all men observe a similar, they observe not the same order, in the motions of the dance, in the melody of the song, in the combinations of language, in the series of their imitations of natural objects. For there is a certain order or rhythm belonging to each of these classes of mimetic representation, from which the hearer and the spectator receive an intenser and purer pleasure than from other: the sense of an approximation to this order has been called taste by modern writers. Every man in the infancy of art observes an order which approximates more or less closely to that from which this highest delight results: but the diversity is not sufficiently marked, as that its gradations should be sensible, except in those instances where the predominance of this faculty of approximation to the beautiful (for so we may be permitted to name the relation between this highest pleasure and its cause) is very great. Those in whom it exists in excess are poets, in the most universal sense of the word; and the pleasure resulting from the manner in which they express the influence of society or nature upon their own minds, communicates itself to others, and gathers a sort of reduplication from that community. Their language is vitally metaphorical; that is, it marks the before unapprehended relations of things and perpetuates their apprehension, until the words which represent them become, through time, signs for portions or classes of thoughts instead of pictures of integral thoughts; and then if no new poets should arise to create afresh the associations which have been thus disorganized, language will be dead to all the nobler purposes of human intercourse. These similitudes or relations are finely said by Lord Bacon to be "the same footsteps of nature impressed upon the various subjects of the world"; [3] and he considers the faculty which perceives them as the storehouse of axioms common to all knowledge. In the infancy of society every author is necessarily a poet, because language itself is poetry; and to be a poet is to apprehend the true and the beautiful, in a word, the good which exists in the relation, subsisting, first between existence and perception, and secondly between perception and expression. Every original language near to its source is in itself the chaos of a cyclic poem: [4] the copiousness of lexicography and the distinctions of grammar are the works of a later age, and are merely the catalogue and the form of the creations of poetry.

But poets, or those who imagine and express this indestructible order, are not only the authors of language and of music, of the dance, and architecture, and statuary, and painting; they are the institutors of laws, and the founders of civil society, and the inventors of the arts of life, and the teachers who draw into a certain propinquity with the beautiful and the true, that partial apprehension of the agencies of the invisible world which is called religion. Hence all original religions are allegorical, or susceptible of allegory, and, like Janus, have a double face of false and true. Poets, according to the circumstances of the age and nation in which they appeared, were called, in the earlier epochs of the world, legislators, or prophets: a poet essentially comprises and unites both these characters. [5] For he not only beholds intensely the present as it is, and discovers those laws according to which present things ought to be ordered, but he beholds the future in the present, and his thoughts are the germs of the flower and the fruit of latest time. Not that I assert poets to be prophets in the gross sense of the word, or that they can foretell the form as surely as they foreknow the spirit of events: such is the pretence of superstition, which would make poetry an attribute of prophecy, rather than prophecy an attribute of poetry. A poet participates in the eternal, the infinite, and the one; as far as relates to his conceptions, time and place and number are not. The grammatical forms which express the moods of time, and the difference of persons, and the distinction of place, are convertible with respect to the highest poetry without injuring it as poetry;

[3] *De Augment. Scient.*, cap. i, lib. iii. [Shelley.]

[4] A "cycle" or series of early heroic poems.

[5] See Sidney, above, pp. 84-86.

and the choruses of Aeschylus, and the book of *Job,* and Dante's *Paradise,* would afford, more than any other writings, examples of this fact, if the limits of this essay did not forbid citation. The creations of sculpture, painting, and music, are illustrations still more decisive. . . .

A poem is the very image of life expressed in its eternal truth. There is this difference between a story and a poem, that a story is a catalogue of detached facts, which have no other connexion than time, place, circumstance, cause and effect; the other is the creation of actions according to the unchangeable forms of human nature, as existing in the mind of the Creator, which is itself the image of all other minds.[6] The one is partial, and applies only to a definite period of time, and a certain combination of events which can never again recur; the other is universal, and contains within itself the germ of a relation to whatever motives or actions have place in the possible varieties of human nature. Time, which destroys the beauty and the use of the story of particular facts, stripped of the poetry which should invest them, augments that of poetry, and for ever develops new and wonderful applications of the eternal truth which it contains. Hence epitomes have been called the moths of just history; they eat out the poetry of it. A story of particular facts is as a mirror which obscures and distorts that which should be beautiful; poetry is a mirror which makes beautiful that which is distorted.

The parts of a composition may be poetical, without the composition as a whole being a poem. A single sentence may be considered as a whole, though it may be found in the midst of a series of unassimilated portions: a single word even may be a spark of inextinguishable thought. And thus all the great historians, Herodotus, Plutarch, Livy, were poets; and although the plan of these writers, especially that of Livy, restrained them from developing this faculty in its highest degree, they made copious and ample amends for their subjection, by filling all the interstices of their subjects with living images.

Having determined what is poetry, and who

[6] Shelley, along lines suggested by Sidney, is here expanding Aristotle's thesis that poetry is "more philosophical" than history because it "tends to express the universal, history the particular."

are poets, let us proceed to estimate its effects upon society.

Poetry is ever accompanied with pleasure: all spirits on which it falls open themselves to receive the wisdom which is mingled with its delight. In the infancy of the world, neither poets themselves nor their auditors are fully aware of the excellence of poetry: for it acts in a divine and unapprehended manner, beyond and above consciousness; and it is reserved for future generations to contemplate and measure the mighty cause and effect in all the strength and splendour of their union. Even in modern times, no living poet ever arrived at the fullness of his fame; the jury which sits in judgement upon a poet, belonging as he does to all time, must be composed of his peers: it must be impanelled by Time from the selectest of the wise of many generations. A poet is a nightingale, who sits in darkness and sings to cheer its own solitude with sweet sounds; his auditors are as men entranced by the melody of an unseen musician, who feel that they are moved and softened, yet know not whence or why. The poems of Homer and his contemporaries were the delight of infant Greece; they were the elements of that social system which is the column upon which all succeeding civilization has reposed. Homer embodied the ideal perfection of his age in human character; nor can we doubt that those who read his verses were awakened to an ambition of becoming like to Achilles, Hector, and Ulysses: the truth and beauty of friendship, patriotism, and persevering devotion to an object, were unveiled to the depths in these immortal creations: the sentiments of the auditors must have been refined and enlarged by a sympathy with such great and lovely impersonations, until from admiring they imitated, and from imitation they identified themselves with the objects of their admiration. Nor let it be objected, that these characters are remote from moral perfection, and that they can by no means be considered as edifying patterns for general imitation. Every epoch, under names more or less specious, has deified its peculiar errors; Revenge is the naked idol of the worship of a semi-barbarous age; and Self-deceit is the veiled image of unknown evil, before which luxury and satiety lie prostrate. But a poet considers the vices of his contemporaries as a temporary dress in which his creations must be arrayed, and which cover without concealing the eternal proportions of their beauty. An epic or dramatic personage is understood to wear them around his soul, as he may the ancient armour or the modern uniform around his body; whilst it is easy to conceive a dress more graceful than either. The beauty of the internal nature cannot be so far concealed by its accidental vesture, but that the spirit of its form shall communicate itself to the very disguise, and indicate the shape it hides from the manner in which it is worn. A majestic form and graceful motions will express themselves through the most barbarous and tasteless costume. Few poets of the highest class have chosen to exhibit the beauty of their conceptions in its naked truth and splendour; and it is doubtful whether the alloy of costume, habit, &c., be not necessary to temper this planetary music for mortal ears.

The whole objection, however, of the immorality of poetry rests upon a misconception of the manner in which poetry acts to produce the moral improvement of man. Ethical science arranges the elements which poetry has created, and propounds schemes and proposes examples of civil and domestic life: nor is it for want of admirable doctrines that men hate, and despise, and censure, and deceive, and subjugate one another. But poetry acts in another and diviner manner. It awakens and enlarges the mind itself by rendering it the receptacle of a thousand unapprehended combinations of thought. Poetry lifts the veil from the hidden beauty of the world, and makes familiar objects be as if they were not familiar; it reproduces all that it represents, and the impersonations clothed in its Elysian light stand thenceforward in the minds of those who have once contemplated them, as memorials of that gentle and exalted content which extends itself over all thoughts and actions with which it coexists. The great secret of morals is love; or a going out of our nature, and an identification of ourselves with the beautiful which exists in thought, action, or person, not our own. A man, to be greatly good, must imagine intensely and comprehensively; he must put himself in the place of another and of many others; the pains and pleasures of his species must become his own. The great instrument of moral good is the imagination; and poetry administers to the effect

by acting upon the cause. Poetry enlarges the circumference of the imagination by replenishing it with thoughts of ever new delight, which have the power of attracting and assimilating to their own nature all other thoughts, and which form new intervals and interstices whose void for ever craves fresh food. Poetry strengthens the faculty which is the organ of the moral nature of man, in the same manner as exercise strengthens a limb. A poet therefore would do ill to embody his own conceptions of right and wrong, which are usually those of his place and time, in his poetical creations, which participate in neither. By this assumption of the inferior office of interpreting the effect, in which perhaps after all he might acquit himself but imperfectly, he would resign a glory in a participation in the cause. There was little danger that Homer, or any of the eternal poets, should have so far misunderstood themselves as to have abdicated this throne of their widest dominion. Those in whom the poetical faculty, though great, is less intense, as Euripides, Lucan, Tasso, Spenser, have frequently affected a moral aim, and the effect of their poetry is diminished in exact proportion to the degree in which they compel us to advert to this purpose.

Homer and the cyclic poets were followed at a certain interval by the dramatic and lyrical poets of Athens, who flourished contemporaneously with all that is most perfect in the kindred expressions of the poetical faculty; architecture, painting, music, the dance, sculpture, philosophy, and, we may add, the forms of civil life. For although the scheme of Athenian society was deformed by many imperfections which the poetry existing in chivalry and Christianity has erased from the habits and institutions of modern Europe; yet never at any other period has so much energy, beauty, and virtue, been developed; never was blind strength and stubborn form so disciplined and rendered subject to the will of man, or that will less repugnant to the dictates of the beautiful and the true, as during the century which preceded the death of Socrates. Of no other epoch in the history of our species have we records and fragments stamped so visibly with the image of the divinity in man. But it is poetry alone, in form, in action, or in language, which has rendered this epoch memorable above all others, and the storehouse of examples to everlasting time. For written poetry existed at that epoch simultaneously with the other arts, and it is an idle inquiry to demand which gave and which received the light, which all, as from a common focus, have scattered over the darkest periods of succeeding time. We know no more of cause and effect than a constant conjunction of events: poetry is ever found to co-exist with whatever other arts contribute to the happiness and perfection of man. I appeal to what has already been established to distinguish between the cause and the effect.

It was at the period here adverted to, that the drama had its birth; and however a succeeding writer may have equalled or surpassed those few great specimens of the Athenian drama which have been preserved to us, it is indisputable that the art itself never was understood or practised according to the true philosophy of it, as at Athens. For the Athenians employed language, action, music, painting, the dance, and religious institutions, to produce a common effect in the representation of the highest idealisms of passion and of power; each division in the art was made perfect in its kind by artists of the most consummate skill, and was disciplined into a beautiful proportion and unity one towards the other. On the modern stage a few only of the elements capable of expressing the image of the poet's conception are employed at once. We have tragedy without music and dancing; and music and dancing without the highest impersonations of which they are the fit accompaniment, and both without religion and solemnity. Religious institution has indeed been usually banished from the stage. Our system of divesting the actor's face of a mask, on which the many expressions appropriated to his dramatic character might be moulded into one permanent and unchanging expression, is favourable only to a partial and inharmonious effect; it is fit for nothing but a monologue, where all the attention may be directed to some great master of ideal mimicry. The modern practice of blending comedy with tragedy, though liable to great abuse in point of practice, is undoubtedly an extension of the dramatic circle; but the comedy should be as in *King Lear*, universal, ideal, and sublime. It is perhaps the intervention of this principle which determines the balance in favour of *King Lear* against the *Oedipus Tyrannus* or the

Agamemnon, or, if you will, the trilogies with which they are connected; unless the intense power of the choral poetry, especially that of the latter, should be considered as restoring the equilibrium. *King Lear,* if it can sustain this comparison, may be judged to be the most perfect specimen of the dramatic art existing in the world; in spite of the narrow conditions to which the poet was subjected by the ignorance of the philosophy of the drama which has prevailed in modern Europe. Calderon, in his religious *Autos,* has attempted to fulfil some of the high conditions of dramatic representation neglected by Shakespeare; such as the establishing a relation between the drama and religion, and the accommodating them to music and dancing; but he omits the observation of conditions still more important, and more is lost than gained by the substitution of the rigidly-defined and ever-repeated idealisms of a distorted superstition for the living impersonations of the truth of human passion. . . .

Poetry is indeed something divine. It is at once the centre and circumference of knowledge; it is that which comprehends all science, and that to which all science must be referred. It is at the same time the root and blossom of all other systems of thought; it is that from which all spring, and that which adorns all; and that which, if blighted, denies the fruit and the seed, and withholds from the barren world the nourishment and the succession of the scions of the tree of life. It is the perfect and consummate surface and bloom of all things: it is as the odour and the colour of the rose to the texture of the elements which compose it, as the form and splendour of unfaded beauty to the secrets of anatomy and corruption. What were virtue, love, patriotism, friendship—what were the scenery of this beautiful universe which we inhabit; what were our consolations on this side of the grave—and what were our aspirations beyond it, if poetry did not ascend to bring light and fire from those eternal regions where the owl-winged faculty of calculation dare not ever soar? Poetry is not like reasoning, a power to be exerted according to the determination of the will. A man cannot say, "I will compose poetry." The greatest poet even cannot say it; for the mind in creation is as a fading coal, which some invisible influence, like an inconstant wind, awakens to transitory brightness; this power arises from within, like the colour of a flower which fades and changes as it is developed, and the conscious portions of our natures are unprophetic either of its approach or its departure. Could this influence be durable in its original purity and force, it is impossible to predict the greatness of the results; but when composition begins, inspiration is already on the decline, and the most glorious poetry that has ever been communicated to the world is probably a feeble shadow of the original conceptions of the poet. I appeal to the greatest poets of the present day, whether it is not an error to assert that the finest passages of poetry are produced by labour and study. The toil and the delay recommended by critics can be justly interpreted to mean no more than a careful observation of the inspired moments, and an artificial connexion of the spaces between their suggestions by the intertexture of conventional expressions; a necessity only imposed by the limitedness of the poetical faculty itself; for Milton conceived the *Paradise Lost* as a whole before he executed it in portions. We have his own authority also for the muse having "dictated" to him the "unpremeditated song." And let this be an answer to those who would allege the fifty-six various readings of the first line of the *Orlando Furioso*. Compositions so produced are to poetry what mosaic is to painting. This instinct and intuition of the poetical faculty is still more observable in the plastic and pictorial arts; a great statue or picture grows under the power of the artist as a child in the mother's womb; and the very mind which directs the hands in formation is incapable of accounting to itself for the origin, the gradations, or the media of the process.

Poetry is the record of the best and happiest moments of the happiest and best minds. We are aware of evanescent visitations of thought and feeling sometimes associated with place or person, sometimes regarding our own mind alone, and always arising unforeseen and departing unbidden, but elevating and delightful beyond all expression: so that even in the desire and regret they leave, there cannot but be pleasure, participating as it does in the nature of its object. It is as it were the interpenetration of a diviner nature through our own; but its footsteps are like those of a wind over the sea, which the coming calm erases, and whose traces remain only, as on the wrinkled sand which paves it. These and corresponding conditions of being are experienced principally by those of the most delicate sensibility and the most enlarged imagination; and the state of mind produced by them is at war with every base desire. The enthusiasm of virtue, love, patriotism, and friendship, is essentially linked with such emotions; and whilst they last, self appears as what it is, an atom to a universe. Poets are not only subject to these experiences as spirits of the most refined organization, but they can colour all that they combine with the evanescent hues of this ethereal world; a word, a trait in the representation of a scene or a passion, will touch the enchanted chord, and reanimate, in those who have ever experienced these emotions, the sleeping, the cold, the buried image of the past. Poetry thus makes immortal all that is best and most beautiful in the world; it arrests the vanishing apparitions which haunt the interlunations of life, and veiling them, or in language or in form, sends them forth among mankind, bearing sweet news of kindred joy to those with whom their sisters abide—abide, because there is no portal of expression from the caverns of the spirit which they inhabit into the universe of things. Poetry redeems from decay the visitations of the divinity in man. . . .

The first part of these remarks has related to poetry in its elements and principles; and it has been shown, as well as the narrow limits assigned them would permit, that what is called poetry, in a restricted sense, has a common source with all other forms of order and of beauty, according to which the materials of human life are susceptible of being arranged, and which is poetry in a universal sense.

The second part [7] will have for its object an application of these principles to the present state of the cultivation of poetry, and a defence of the attempt to idealize the modern forms of manners and opinions, and compel them into a subordination to the imaginative and creative faculty. For the literature of England, an energetic development of which has ever preceded or accompanied a great and free development of the national will, has arisen as it were from

[7] The second part was never written.

a new birth. In spite of the low-thoughted envy which would undervalue contemporary merit, our own will be a memorable age in intellectual achievements, and we live among such philosophers and poets as surpass beyond comparison any who have appeared since the last national struggle for civil and religious liberty. The most unfailing herald, companion, and follower of the awakening of a great people to work a beneficial change in opinion or institution, is poetry. At such periods there is an accumulation of the power of communicating and receiving intense and impassioned conceptions respecting man and nature. The persons in whom this power resides may often, as far as regards many portions of their nature, have little apparent correspondence with that spirit of good of which they are the ministers. But even whilst they deny and abjure, they are yet compelled to serve, the power which is seated on the throne of their own soul. It is impossible to read the compositions of the most celebrated writers of the present day without being startled with the electric life which burns within their words. They measure the circumference and sound the depths of human nature with a comprehensive and all-penetrating spirit, and they are themselves perhaps the most sincerely astonished at its manifestations; for it is less their spirit than the spirit of the age. Poets are the hierophants of an unapprehended inspiration; the mirrors of the gigantic shadows which futurity casts upon the present; the words which express what they understand not; the trumpets which sing to battle, and feel not what they inspire; the influence which is moved not, but moves. Poets are the unacknowledged legislators of the world.

3. *Humanism, Naturalism, and Divergent Tendencies*

MATTHEW ARNOLD (1822-1888)

No ENGLISH or American critic since Coleridge has had a more extensive influence than Matthew Arnold. For his influence has operated in at least three ways. He was, in one sense, something of a spokesman for nineteenth-century poetic taste. Secondly, through Arnold, more cosmopolitan ideas became readily accessible to English-speaking critics and readers; after becoming current, these have passed unobtrusively into much of the criticism of the past forty years, including that which now looks back on Arnold himself as either academically ineffectual or else as an evil spirit representing "romantic" tastes in style. Lastly, much of the modern defence of the central educational value of literature rests—where the defence is impressive—on classical premises resurrected and popularized, however vaguely and sketchily, by Arnold.

Arnold's position is therefore much more complex than it appears to be at first sight. One especially needs to prevent his role as a spokesman for nineteenth-century literary taste from assuming undue importance. It is indeed true that the influence of Arnold, during the later years of the nineteenth and the first two decades of the twentieth centuries, helped to standardize the poetic taste of the period. But this is largely because Anglo-American

MATTHEW ARNOLD. The son of Dr. Thomas Arnold, the famous headmaster of Rugby, Matthew Arnold was educated at Rugby, and later (1841-44) at Balliol College, Oxford, where he won the Newdigate prize for poetry. He became a fellow of Oriel College (1845), and later inspector of schools (1851). Most of his poetry was written before he was thirty-five. He was Professor of Poetry at Oxford (1857-67), while still retaining his post as school inspector, an exacting, drudging task he fulfilled until two years before his death. During the last twenty-five years of his life he wrote, in such free time as he had, an imposing body of critical and general expository prose, and in 1883 went to the United States for a year on a lecture tour.

His *Works* (15 vols., 1903-04), though not complete, is the most comprehensive edition. There is also *The Complete Prose Works of Matthew Arnold* (ed. R. H. Super, 6 vols., Ann Arbor, 1960-68); and *The Note-books* (ed. H. F. Lowry, K. Young, and W. H. Dunn, Oxford, 1952). Selections from the criticism are available in numerous editions. Books dealing with Arnold include W. D. Anderson, *Matthew Arnold and the Classical Tradition* (Ann Arbor, 1965); Vincent Buckley, *Poetry and Morality: Studies on the Criticism of Matthew Arnold, T. S. Eliot, and F. R. Leavis* (1959); D. J. DeLaura, *Hebrew and Hellene in Victorian England: Newman, Arnold, and Pater* (Austin, 1969); D. G. James, *Matthew Arnold and the Decline of English Romanticism* (Oxford, 1961); W. A. Madden, *Matthew Arnold: a Study of the Aesthetic Temperament* (Bloomington, Ind., 1967); William Robbins, *The Ethical Idealism of Matthew Arnold* (1959); and Lionel Trilling, *Matthew Arnold* (1939). See also David Perkins, "Arnold and the Function of Literature," in the *Journal of English Literary History*, XVIII (1951), 287-309, to which I am indebted for suggested interpretations offered here.

writers and critics chose only some of his opinions and tastes to echo and extend. This influence illustrates the more strictly Victorian side of Arnold. This is the Arnold who is now often said to have "re-examined" English poetry in the light of merely nineteenth-century standards, as T. S. Eliot has been said to "re-examine" it later by other standards. It is the Arnold who looked down on the eighteenth century as an "age of prose," who spoke of using isolated lines of poetry as "touchstones," and who valued a vaguely declamatory "poetry of statement," lightly graced by what he called "magic." But the only basis Arnold himself offers for such a confined interpretation is found in scattered remarks, and in one particular essay, "The Study of Poetry," originally written not as a central credo or discussion of aims but only to serve as an introduction—for general readers not too well acquainted with poetry—to the popular collection, Ward's *English Poets* (1880).

Arnold's main significance as a critic lies elsewhere: in his constant support of the dignity of critical thinking; his attempt to lift the view of the English-speaking reader toward a wider, more cosmopolitan range; his reapplication of classical criteria; and, above all, his courageous attempt, in an increasingly hostile environment, to reassert the traditional value of literature. Through him, English criticism, which had subsided into mediocrity after Coleridge and Hazlitt, became reanimated and broadened. It became aware of the alert critical intelligence at work in mid-nineteenth-century France, and was reminded once again of the wide aims of classical theory. As a result, Anglo-American criticism of the twentieth century took on a new range and sophistication. Through Irving Babbitt and Paul Elmer More, some of Arnold's ideas were systematized into the "New Humanism," which turned militantly upon both the romantic art and the scientific naturalism of the nineteenth century. Following Arnold, such critics looked back to some classical values but, unlike Arnold, they interpreted them with a quite unclassical dogmatism and openly didactic bias. Critics of a very different sort from the "New Humanists" took stands which, though some of them were not aware of it, had first been made possible for modern English and American criticism by Arnold. More formalistically minded critics, in England and especially America, drew suggestions from both classical and nineteenth-century French critical sources. Without Arnold, either directly or through such disciples as Irving Babbitt, their attention to such sources might not have spread so rapidly. Arnold's frequently voiced charge that the English are not critically minded became one of the clichés of modern criticism. And despite his strong antagonism to Arnold, the chief critical writer since World War I, T. S. Eliot, found himself—as he took the place of Arnold—following the procedure if by no means the opinions of his predecessor, and employing a prose style strikingly similar in its conscious, urbane simplicity and its occasional irony. Arnold's notable "Function of

Criticism at the Present Time" is paralleled by Eliot's briefer "Function of Criticism," in which Arnold's censure of the Englishman's extreme individualism and antipathy to criticism is repeated by Eliot. Arnold's examination of particular poets—and by no means from just a "nineteenth-century" point of view—is matched by Eliot's examinations of other poets in the light of different stylistic values. Finally, although here the differences between the men are at their widest, Arnold's excursions into more general fields, as in *Culture and Anarchy* (1869), also anticipate similar excursions by Eliot in his *Idea of a Christian Society* and *Notes Toward a Definition of Culture*. The respective conceptions of culture involved in these works offer one of the quickest means of contrasting these two critics.

2

Our concern, however, is not to suggest the rather labyrinthine by-ways of Arnold's influence so much as to indicate briefly the central concern of his critical writing, and the more significant ways in which he ramified and applied it. This central premise is his conception of *culture*, which is most clearly and persuasively defined in his essay, "Sweetness and Light," from *Culture and Anarchy*. Culture, to begin with, is an *activity* of mind. It is not, that is, a body of memorized information, but a quality that characterizes an actual way of living, thinking, and feeling—a quality that consists "in *becoming* something rather than in *having* something, in an inward condition of the mind and spirit, not in an outward set of circumstances." It is the ability, in short, to react in accordance with what is true and valuable. Hence it is necessary to have every aspect of the mind as eager and open as possible in order to be able to descry, as effectively as one can, what *is* true and valuable. This eagerness Arnold termed *curiosity,* or the energetic "desire after the things of the mind simply for their own sakes and for the pleasure of seeing them as they are." To "see things as they are" demands openness as well as eagerness of mind. "Disinterestedness"—the rare ability to rise above sect or clique, the desire to see things in their true nature as distinct from an eager interest to prove a preconceived or indoctrinated idea— "disinterestedness and flexibility" are also fundamental characteristics of culture. They are among the primary virtues that should characterize criticism, too. For the ideal that guides criticism is naturally that of culture in the broadest sense. Otherwise criticism would have little real purpose or dignity, and would simply be one more unessential way of passing the time.

It is to Arnold's credit that he himself, as a practicing critic, was unusually "disinterested." He was not a propagandist for any particular school of Victorian poetry. He did not feel compelled to exalt the nineteenth century as one of the great poetic ages merely because he happened to live in it, nor did he disparage it for the same reason. He was far from being provincially nationalistic. His conception of culture was not confined by the standards or boundaries of any one group. In this respect he differs from some of his more recent detractors who extol critical "disinterestedness" in a theoretical way, but who have approached literature from the point of view of fixed economic, political, historical, or religious interests, or else in terms of restricted stylistic values even more intolerant and exclusive than those which had led Arnold to dismiss eighteenth-century poetry. In fact, Arnold has often been censured precisely because of his disinterestedness. His religious and social attitudes especially have been disparaged for this reason. The former have been considered "flabby" because they were not based on a particular theology, and the latter have been regarded as "aristocratic" and "aloof" because he did not expound a specific political creed. But disinterestedness is always liable to be censured as intellectual flabbiness by critics who are dominated by compelling and rigid preconceptions acquired through accident or despair. In his political and economic outlook, far from being "aristocratic" in the ordinary sense of the term, Arnold prophetically believed that the proletariat would come to control the England of the future, and for that reason he courageously felt that no time should be lost in enlightening and educating it as much as possible. He seems ultimately, however, to have desired a state socialism of sorts, one characteristic of which was that it should be completely classless. Far from being class-minded, therefore, he sensibly felt that the hope of the world was not to be found in either the aristocracy (the "Barbarians"), the prosperous commercial class (the "Philistines"), or the "populace," as they then were. Rather, "culture seeks to do away with classes" and with all artificial forms of "inequality"—an inequality that "materializes the upper class, vulgarizes the middle class, brutalizes the lower class."

3

But it is not enough to "see things as they are," however clearly and flexibly. Human perfection implies that one is really fulfilling knowledge by feeling actively and conducting oneself accordingly. This, as David Perkins has shown in his interpretation of Arnold's classical premises, is the central assumption in Arnold's critical thought. In order to integrate the "total man," emotion must be aroused, brought into play, and then illuminated and led by intelligence. The end, as Mr. Perkins says, is a "union of all the facets of human response in moving towards the same object." "There would be no quarrel between desire and intelligence. For desire would follow, carry out, and complete intelligence by intensifying rational awareness. Value judgments, moreover, would then be felt as an emotion, applied instantaneously, and, in a new experience, would immediately inform our emotional reactions." Hence the Greek belief in the power of art to "awaken and develop one's total capacity for reacting," and Arnold's "own confidence in the humanities, especially poetry, as the most effective means of informing and developing . . . the 'whole man'—that is, man as a total process of desiring, feeling, and thinking. . . ." The central premise, in other words, is simply this: that if the end of human culture is the open sensitivity, the integrated and informed feeling and conduct of the "total man," then, as a matter of sheer common sense, the various pursuits of man should naturally be evaluated and *ranked* to the degree that they lead to this end. On this basis, therefore—on the basis of the Greek ideal of *Eros,* the ideal that in the most complete and active way "good should be forever present to us"— Arnold, in "Literature and Science," followed the great classical justification of the liberal and humane arts, but in a more flexible, less rigorously didactic way than did Sir Philip Sidney. Literature especially, because of the broad range of human life that it can exploit and interpret, can serve as the vital transmitter of experience, inciting the emotional interests of man, instilling knowledge imperceptibly but securely, enlarging the sweep of one's mental and imaginative horizon, and developing sympathetic openness. In doing so, it not only educates in the immediate sense, through the particular insights and experiences that it offers and infiltrates into one's feeling. But it also educates in an *ultimate* sense, through heightening, developing, and organizing the individual as a living, reacting creature. It thus ministers to that *sincerity,* to that final *honesty* of character, in which the mind and the heart are one—in which the heart follows and completes the dictates of the mind, and knowledge, rendered habitual and instinctive, is genuinely felt and acted upon through an enlarged, clearer, more vital state of being. Arnold's criticism is best understood when viewed in the light of this ideal. It not only sustains him in his most valuable and influential role: that of an *apologist* for literature, who tried to reassert essential ends at a time when Western thought—in criticism as in almost everything else—was becoming increasingly absorbed in means for their own sake. But this conception of what is the most valuable function of poetry also underlies the qualities for which Arnold looked in poetry—concreteness, moral import and range, "magic" or suggestiveness of style, and unity of impact—and provides the criteria by which he consistently attempts to evaluate particular poets and works.

4

Literature—or "poetry" in the broadest sense of the term—is uniquely capable of furthering the enlightened activity of mind that Arnold calls culture, first because of the range and diversity of its subject matter, and, second, because it communicates in a formative and effective way through offering what is itself a living experience, rather than through abstract analysis and description. Poetry, broadly interpreted, is "nothing less," said

Arnold, "than the most perfect speech of man." Poetry, that is to say, is the use of language in the most effective, reaching, and suggestively adequate way possible. It emerges when, through verbal expression, man "comes nearest to being able to utter the truth." The range of poetry—taking poetry as a whole rather than thinking of it in terms of any one specific poem—is thus as broad as what human speech itself can cover or suggest. The diversity of experience treated in the various forms of poetry—the drama, the lyric, philosophical verse, the epic, satire—is a concrete indication. Poetry can thus *include* the results, the intellectual insights and conclusions, of science or indeed of any branch of knowledge. Unlike specific sciences, it is not restricted in its subject matter; and it is likely that "the student of humane letters only" will be less "incomplete" than "the student of the natural sciences only."

But aside from the range, variety, and importance of what it can take as its subject, the high and liberal value of poetry especially results through the form in which it can interpret and transmit experience. To begin with, poetry does not merely chronicle specific details. It interprets details in the light of ideals, of aspirations, of knowledge, and of moral evaluation. On the other hand, poetry is rooted in the *concrete:* it is not a branch of theoretical ethics. Poetry joins together both the idea and the concrete. By serving simultaneously as the "interpretess of the natural world" and as the "interpretess of the moral world"—by feeling and conceiving the concrete, that is, in terms of human values—poetry is thus analogous to human experience itself. For in our actual lives, Arnold insists, we are constantly seeing and feeling things in the light of what we regard as their desirability or value: as we experience things, the concrete is not divorced from the idea, from the interpreting and evaluating of it—it is not divorced if we are having a genuine *experience* rather than being confused and bewildered. We are not, indeed, undergoing a meaningful experience if we think and evaluate purely on an abstract plane, isolated from our daily concerns, and then live, perceive, and react on a concrete plane without any relevance to anything we have ever conceived or believed to be valuable. It is in this sense, then, and not with a naïve didactic implication, that poetry can be said to be able to deal with the most fundamental and pressing of all problems—"the question, *how to live.*" To this extent, poetry is "moral" in its function. For "the question, *how to live,*" as Arnold said in his essay on Wordsworth, "is itself a moral idea; and it is the question which most interests every man, and with which, in some way or other, he is perpetually occupied. A large sense is of course to be given to the term *moral.* Whatever bears upon the question, 'how to live,' comes under it." The greatness of English poetry at its best resides in the vigorous imaginative power with which it has related moral ideas to concrete life.

Hence, in estimating and distinguishing the value of particular poems or particular poets, Arnold is led to regard "the noble and profound application of ideas to life" as "the most essential part of poetic greatness." Accordingly, poetry must first of all work within and through the concrete. Arnold's censure of abstract didactic poetry, such as we find in Wordsworth's *Excursion* or in much eighteenth-century verse, and his lack of sympathy with neoclassic poetic style generally, are based on his belief that they lack a sufficient concrete anchorage. His remarks on his own verse-play, *Empedocles on Etna,* indicate a similar viewpoint: it is not a living drama evolving inevitably from a concrete situation. Secondly, the presence of relevant and significant "ideas" is naturally to be expected in poetry of substantial worth. Especially if other elements are—so far as they can be separately noted— more or less equal, then the more significant the ideas and the more pertinent they are to human life, the better the poem. Keats's *Isabella,* for example, may have occasional vivid lines or phrases; but it cannot for that reason, as Keats himself would probably have admitted, take high rank as a poem. But of course neither the concreteness nor the intellectual significance of the "ideas" can be evaluated separately. The unique achievement of "literary genius is a work of *synthesis*"—of joining together these two elements. It is the "noble and profound *application* of ideas to life."

The success of a poem, therefore, depends on the success with which such a combining or synthesizing is attained. This is quite in agreement with the general modern stress on organic unity in style. Where Arnold would differ from more abstractly esthetic critics, however, is in also emphasizing that the synthesis cannot be evaluated in a vacuum; it cannot be evaluated apart from what is *being synthesized.* The "antique symmetry" of Greek style, for example, is meaningful and genuine because it emerges from "fit details strictly combined, in view of a large general result nobly conceived." The more significant the elements and ideas being brought together into the organic unity, the greater the synthesis needed to contain, balance, and reconcile them. *King Lear* and Keats's ode, *To Autumn,* may both be successful examples of a centralizing of various elements into a unified esthetic form or totality. But what is being synthesized in *King Lear* is more vividly applicable to a wider range of human experience: it is at once more universal and more energetically vital; and the synthesis of it into the form it attains is therefore the more powerful, extensive, and valuable. It offers, in short, a more "noble and profound application of ideas to life." Hence Arnold's reservations about nineteenth-century poetry in the Preface to the *Poems* (1853). The great and permanent themes of poetry were being replaced, he felt, both by a subjective concern of the poet with his own feelings for their own sake and also by an increasing technical interest in the "part" rather than the "whole"—in "expression," in language, imagery, or versification. His viewpoint is prophetically applicable to twentieth- as well as nineteenth-century poetry. It is altogether to the credit of Arnold's broad classical premise that, through the perspective it offers, such differences as exist between nineteenth- and twentieth-century poetry do not appear as diametrical opposites but may be seen as in some respects very much alike, or else as different sides of the same coin.

Poetry, then, like every other human pursuit, should be evaluated in the light of man's most basic concern: the active attainment of culture, in the broadest sense, and the total and integrated perfecting of himself and his potentialities as an aware, responsive, and active creature. It is in simultaneously tapping the intellectual, imaginative, and emotional resources of man, and in bringing them to bear on its objects in a unified, harmonious way, that poetry secures its most formative and salutary effect. It brings us into a sympathetic and rounded "contact with the essential nature of these objects," so that we are "no longer bewildered and oppressed by them" but, by assimilating the realization of them into our habitual feelings, become more "in harmony with them; and this feeling calms and satisfies as no other can." Through "magic" of style, we are incited to participate actively and imaginatively in the experience of the poem. In this living identification, we re-create and feel within ourselves the emerging resolution and unity of form that leads out, guides, and gives meaning to its various parts, thus permitting them to fulfill themselves by dawning into "a large general result nobly conceived." Such an experience, continued and gradually broadened in scope, directly subserves the ideal of human culture itself, in which the various aspects of the human character are integrated, sustaining and completing each other by themselves co-operating toward "a large general result nobly conceived."

Preface to *Poems*[1]

EDITION OF 1853

IN TWO small volumes of Poems, published anonymously, one in 1849, the other in 1852, many of the Poems which compose the present volume have already appeared. The rest are now published for the first time.

I have, in the present collection, omitted the Poem from which the volume published in 1852 took its title. I have done so, not because the subject of it was a Sicilian Greek born between

[1] Arnold's 1853 *Preface* is perhaps the best brief statement in the nineteenth century of classical objectivity in poetry. As such, it is an effective refutation of the belief, popular in the 1920's, that Arnold was a Victorian romantic in his literary values. The dramatic poem of which he is speaking is his *Empedocles on Etna*.

two and three thousand years ago, although many persons would think this a sufficient reason. Neither have I done so because I had, in my own opinion, failed in the delineation which I intended to effect. I intended to delineate the feelings of one of the last of the Greek religious philosophers, one of the family of Orpheus and Musaeus, having survived his fellows, living on into a time when the habits of Greek thought and feeling had begun fast to change, character to dwindle, the influence of the Sophists to prevail. Into the feelings of a man so situated there entered much that we are accustomed to consider as exclusively modern; how much, the fragments of Empedocles himself which remain to us are sufficient at least to indicate. What those who are familiar only with the great monuments of early Greek genius suppose to be its exclusive characteristics, have disappeared; the calm, the cheerfulness, the disinterested objectivity have disappeared: the dialogue of the mind with itself has commenced; modern problems have presented themselves; we hear already the doubts, we witness the discouragement, of Hamlet and of Faust.

The representation of such a man's feelings must be interesting, if consistently drawn. We all naturally take pleasure, says Aristotle, in any imitation or representation whatever: this is the basis of our love of Poetry: [2] and we take pleasure in them, he adds, because all knowledge is naturally agreeable to us; not to the philosopher only, but to mankind at large. Every representation therefore which is consistently drawn may be supposed to be interesting, inasmuch as it gratifies this natural interest in knowledge of all kinds. What is *not* interesting, is that which does not add to our knowledge of any kind; that which is vaguely conceived and loosely drawn; a representation which is general, indeterminate, and faint, instead of being particular, precise, and firm.

Any accurate representation may therefore be expected to be interesting; but, if the representation be a poetical one, more than this is demanded. It is demanded, not only that it shall interest, but also that it shall inspirit and rejoice the reader: that it shall convey a charm, and infuse delight. For the Muses, as Hesiod says, were born that they might be "a forgetfulness of evils, and a truce from cares": and it is not enough that the Poet should add to the knowledge of men, it is required of him also that he should add to their happiness. "All Art," says Schiller, "is dedicated to Joy, and there is no higher and no more serious problem, than how to make men happy. The right Art is that alone, which creates the highest enjoyment." [3]

A poetical work, therefore, is not yet justified when it has been shown to be an accurate, and therefore interesting representation; it has to be shown also that it is a representation from which men can derive enjoyment. In presence of the most tragic circumstances, represented in a work of Art, the feeling of enjoyment, as is

well known, may still subsist: the representation of the most utter calamity, of the liveliest anguish, is not sufficient to destroy it: the more tragic the situation, the deeper becomes the enjoyment; and the situation is more tragic in proportion as it becomes more terrible.

What then are the situations, from the representation of which, though accurate, no poetical enjoyment can be derived? They are those in which the suffering finds no vent in action; in which a continuous state of mental distress is prolonged, unrelieved by incident, hope, or resistance; in which there is everything to be endured, nothing to be done. In such situations there is inevitably something morbid, in the description of them something monotonous. When they occur in actual life, they are painful, not tragic; the representation of them in poetry is painful also.

To this class of situations, poetically faulty as it appears to me, that of Empedocles, as I have endeavoured to represent him, belongs; and I have therefore excluded the Poem from the present collection.

And why, it may be asked, have I entered into this explanation respecting a matter so unimportant as the admission or exclusion of the Poem in question? I have done so, because I was anxious to avow that the sole reason for its exclusion was that which has been stated above; and that it has not been excluded in deference to the opinion which many critics of the present day appear to entertain against subjects chosen from distant times and countries: against the choice, in short, of any subjects but modern ones.

"The Poet," it is said, [4] and by an intelligent critic, "the Poet who would really fix the public attention must leave the exhausted past, and draw his subjects from matters of present import, and *therefore* both of interest and novelty."

Now this view I believe to be completely false. It is worth examining, inasmuch as it is a fair sample of a class of critical dicta everywhere current at the present day, having a philosophical form and air, but no real basis in fact; and which are calculated to vitiate the judgment of readers of poetry, while they exert, so far as

---

[2] *Poetics*, IV, above, p. 21.

[3] From Schiller's preface to *Die Braut von Messina*.

[4] In *The Spectator* of April 2nd, 1853. The words quoted were not used with reference to poems of mine. [Arnold.]

they are adopted, a misleading influence on the practice of those who write it.

What are the eternal objects of Poetry, among all nations and at all times? They are actions; human actions; possessing an inherent interest in themselves, and which are to be communicated in an interesting manner by the art of the Poet. Vainly will the latter imagine that he has everything in his own power; that he can make an intrinsically inferior action equally delightful with a more excellent one by his treatment of it; he may indeed compel us to admire his skill, but his work will possess, within itself, an incurable defect.

The Poet, then, has in the first place to select an excellent action; and what actions are the most excellent? Those, certainly, which most powerfully appeal to the great primary human affections: to those elementary feelings which subsist permanently in the race, and which are independent of time. These feelings are permanent and the same; that which interests them is permanent and the same also. The modernness or antiquity of an action, therefore, has nothing to do with its fitness for poetical representation; this depends upon its inherent qualities. To the elementary part of our nature, to our passions, that which is great and passionate is eternally interesting; and interesting solely in proportion to its greatness and to its passion. A great human action of a thousand years ago is more interesting to it than a smaller human action of to-day, even though upon the representation of this last the most consummate skill may have been expended, and though it has the advantage of appealing by its modern language, familiar manners, and contemporary allusions, to all our transient feelings and interests. These, however, have no right to demand of a poetical work that it shall satisfy them; their claims are to be directed elsewhere. Poetical works belong to the domain of our permanent passions: let them interest these, and the voice of all subordinate claims upon them is at once silenced.

Achilles, Prometheus, Clytemnestra, Dido—what modern poem presents personages as interesting, even to us moderns, as these personages of an "exhausted past"? We have the domestic epic dealing with the details of modern life which pass daily under our eyes; we have poems repre-senting modern personages in contact with the problems of modern life, moral, intellectual, and social; these works have been produced by poets the most distinguished of their nation and time; yet I fearlessly assert that *Hermann and Dorothea, Childe Harold,* "Jocelyn," *The Excursion,*[5] leave the reader cold in comparison with the effect produced upon him by the latter books of the *Iliad,* by the *Orestea,* or by the episode of Dido. And why is this? Simply because in the three latter cases the action is greater, the personages nobler, the situations more intense: and this is the true basis of the interest in a poetical work, and this alone.

It may be urged, however, that past actions may be interesting in themselves, but that they are not to be adopted by the modern Poet, because it is impossible for him to have them clearly present to his own mind, and he cannot therefore feel them deeply, nor represent them forcibly. But this is not necessarily the case. The externals of a past action, indeed, he cannot know with the precision of a contemporary; but his business is with its essentials. The outward man of Oedipus or of Macbeth, the houses in which they lived, the ceremonies of their courts, he cannot accurately figure to himself; but neither do they essentially concern him. His business is with their inward man; with their feelings and behaviour in certain tragic situations, which engage their passions as men; these have in them nothing local and casual; they are as accessible to the modern Poet as to a contemporary.

The date of an action, then, signifies nothing: the action itself, its selection and construction, this is what is all-important. This the Greeks understood far more clearly than we do. The radical difference between their poetical theory and ours consists, as it appears to me, in this: that, with them, the poetical character of the action in itself, and the conduct of it, was the first consideration; with us, attention is fixed mainly on the value of the separate thoughts and images which occur in the treatment of an action. They regarded the whole; we regard the parts. With them, the action predominated over the expression of it; with us, the expression predominates over the action. Not that they failed

[5] By Goethe, Byron, Lamartine, and Wordsworth, respectively.

in expression, or were inattentive to it; on the contrary, they are the highest models of expression, the unapproached masters of the *grand style:* [6] but their expression is so excellent because it is so admirably kept in its right degree of prominence; because it is so simple and so well subordinated; because it draws its force directly from the pregnancy of the matter which it conveys. For what reason was the Greek tragic poet confined to so limited a range of subjects? Because there are so few actions which unite in themselves, in the highest degree, the conditions of excellence: and it was not thought that on any but an excellent subject could an excellent Poem be constructed. A few actions, therefore, eminently adapted for tragedy, maintained almost exclusive possession of the Greek tragic stage; their significance appeared inexhaustible; they were as permanent problems, perpetually offered to the genius of every fresh poet. This too is the reason of what appears to us moderns a certain baldness of expression in Greek tragedy; of the triviality with which we often reproach the remarks of the chorus, where it takes part in the dialogue: that the action itself, the situation of Orestes, or Merope, or Alcmaeon, was to stand the central point of interest, unforgotten, absorbing, principal; that no accessories were for a moment to distract the spectator's attention from this; that the tone of the parts was to be perpetually kept down, in order not to impair the grandiose effect of the whole. The terrible old mythic story on which the drama was founded stood, before he entered the theatre, traced in its bare outlines upon the spectator's mind; it stood in his memory, as a group of statuary, faintly seen, at the end of a long and dark vista: then came the Poet, embodying outlines, developing situations, not a word wasted, not a sentiment capriciously thrown in: stroke upon stroke, the drama proceeded: the light deepened upon the group; more and more it revealed itself to the rivetted gaze of the spectator: until at last, when the final words were spoken, it stood before him in broad sunlight, a model of immortal beauty.

This was what a Greek critic demanded; this was what a Greek poet endeavoured to effect. It signified nothing to what time an action be-

longed; we do not find that the *Persae* occupied a particularly high rank among the dramas of Aeschylus, because it represented a matter of contemporary interest: [7] this was not what a cultivated Athenian required; he required that the permanent elements of his nature should be moved; and dramas of which the action, though taken from a long-distant mythic time, yet was calculated to accomplish this in a higher degree than that of the *Persae,* stood higher in his estimation accordingly. The Greeks felt, no doubt, with their exquisite sagacity of taste, that an action of present times was too near them, too much mixed up with what was accidental and passing, to form a sufficiently grand, detached, and self-subsistent object for a tragic poem: such objects belonged to the domain of the comic poet, and of the lighter kinds of poetry. For the more serious kinds, for *pragmatic* [8] poetry, to use an excellent expression of Polybius, they were more difficult and severe in the range of subjects which they permitted. Their theory and practice alike, the admirable treatise of Aristotle, and the unrivalled works of their poets, exclaim with a thousand tongues—"All depends upon the subject; choose a fitting action, penetrate yourself with the feeling of its situations; this done, everything else will follow."

But for all kinds of poetry alike there was one point on which they were rigidly exacting; the adaptability of the subject to the kind of poetry selected, and the careful construction of the poem.

How different a way of thinking from this is ours! We can hardly at the present day understand what Menander meant, when he told a man who inquired as to the progress of his comedy that he had finished it, not having yet written a single line, because he had constructed the action of it in his mind. A modern critic would have assured him that the merit of his piece depended on the brilliant things which arose under his pen as he went along. We have poems which seem to exist merely for the sake of single lines and passages; not for the sake of producing any total-impression. We have critics who seem to direct their attention merely to detached expressions, to the language about the

[6] Discussed in Arnold's *On Translating Homer: Last Words.*

[7] The war between the Greeks and the Persians.

[8] Dealing with the working out of cause and effect in actual experience.

action, not to the action itself. I verily think that the majority of them do not in their hearts believe that there is such a thing as a total-impression to be derived from a poem at all, or to be demanded from a poet; they think the term a commonplace of metaphysical criticism. They will permit the Poet to select any action he pleases, and to suffer that action to go as it will, provided he gratifies them with occasional bursts of fine writing, and with a shower of isolated thoughts and images. That is, they permit him to leave their poetical sense ungratified, provided that he gratifies their rhetorical sense and their curiosity. Of his neglecting to gratify these, there is little danger; he needs rather to be warned against the danger of attempting to gratify these alone; he needs rather to be perpetually reminded to prefer his action to everything else; so to treat this, as to permit its inherent excellences to develop themselves, without interruption from the intrusion of his personal peculiarities: most fortunate, when he most entirely succeeds in effacing himself, and in enabling a noble action to subsist as it did in nature.

But the modern critic not only permits a false practice; he absolutely prescribes false aims.— "A true allegory of the state of one's own mind in a representative history," the Poet is told, "is perhaps the highest thing that one can attempt in the way of poetry."—And accordingly he attempts it. An allegory of the state of one's own mind, the highest problem of an art which imitates actions! No assuredly, it is not, it never can be so: no great poetical work has ever been produced with such an aim. Faust itself, in which something of the kind is attempted, wonderful passages as it contains, and in spite of the unsurpassed beauty of the scenes which relate to Margaret, Faust itself, judged as a whole, and judged strictly as a poetical work, is defective: its illustrious author, the greatest poet of modern times, the greatest critic of all times, would have been the first to acknowledge it; he only defended his work, indeed, by asserting it to be "something incommensurable." [9]

The confusion of the present times is great, the multitude of voices counselling different things bewildering, the number of existing works

[9] Eckermann's *Conversations with Goethe*, Jan. 3, 1830.

capable of attracting a young writer's attention and of becoming his models, immense: what he wants is a hand to guide him through the confusion, a voice to prescribe to him the aim which he should keep in view, and to explain to him that the value of the literary works which offer themselves to his attention is relative to their power of helping him forward on his road towards this aim. Such a guide the English writer at the present day will nowhere find. Failing this, all that can be looked for, all indeed that can be desired, is, that his attention should be fixed on excellent models; that he may reproduce, at any rate, something of their excellence, by penetrating himself with their works and by catching their spirit, if he cannot be taught to produce what is excellent independently.

Foremost among these models for the English writer stands Shakespeare: a name the greatest perhaps of all poetical names; a name never to be mentioned without reverence. I will venture, however, to express a doubt, whether the influence of his works, excellent and fruitful for the readers of poetry, for the great majority, has been of unmixed advantage to the writers of it. Shakespeare indeed chose excellent subjects; the world could afford no better than Macbeth, or Romeo and Juliet, or Othello: he had no theory respecting the necessity of choosing subjects of present import, or the paramount interest attaching to allegories of the state of one's own mind; like all great poets, he knew well what constituted a poetical action; like them, wherever he found such an action, he took it; like them, too, he found his best in past times. But to these general characteristics of all great poets he added a special one of his own; a gift, namely, of happy, abundant, and ingenious expression, eminent and unrivalled: so eminent as irresistibly to strike the attention first in him, and even to throw into comparative shade his other excellences as a poet. Here has been the mischief. These other excellences were his fundamental excellences *as a poet;* what distinguishes the artist from the mere amateur, says Goethe, is *Architectonicè* in the highest sense; that power of execution, which creates, forms, and constitutes: not the profoundness of single thoughts, not the richness of imagery, not the abundance of illustration. But these attractive accessories of a poetical work being more easily seized than the spirit of the whole, and these accessories being possessed by Shakespeare in an unequalled degree, a young writer having recourse to Shakespeare as his model runs great risk of being vanquished and absorbed by them, and, in consequence, of reproducing, according to the measure of his power, these, and these alone. Of this preponderating quality of Shakespeare's genius, accordingly, almost the whole of modern English poetry has, it appears to me, felt the influence. To the exclusive attention on the part of his imitators to this it is in a great degree owing, that of the majority of modern poetical works the details alone are valuable, the composition worthless. In reading them one is perpetually reminded of that terrible sentence on a modern French poet—*il dit tout ce qu'il veut, mais malheureusement il n'a rien à dire.*[10]

Let me give an instance of what I mean. I will take it from the works of the very chief among those who seem to have been formed in the school of Shakespeare: of one whose exquisite genius and pathetic death render him for ever interesting. I will take the poem of "Isabella, or the Pot of Basil," by Keats. I choose this rather than the "Endymion," because the latter work (which a modern critic has classed with *The Faerie Queene!*), although undoubtedly there blows through it the breath of genius, is yet as a whole so utterly incoherent, as not strictly to merit the name of a poem at all. The poem of "Isabella," then, is a perfect treasure-house of graceful and felicitous words and images: almost in every stanza there occurs one of those vivid and picturesque turns of expression, by which the object is made to flash upon the eye of the mind, and which thrill the reader with a sudden delight. This one short poem contains, perhaps, a greater number of happy single expressions which one could quote than all the extant tragedies of Sophocles. But the action, the story? The action in itself is an excellent one; but so feebly is it conceived by the Poet, so loosely constructed, that the effect produced by it, in and for itself, is absolutely null. Let the reader, after he has finished the poem of Keats, turn to the same story in the *Decameron:* he will then feel how pregnant and interesting the same action has become in the hands

of a great artist, who above all things delineates his object; who subordinates expression to that which it is designed to express.

I have said that the imitators of Shakespeare, fixing their attention on his wonderful gift of expression, have directed their imitation to this, neglecting his other excellences. These excellences, the fundamental excellences of poetical art, Shakespeare no doubt possessed them—possessed many of them in a splendid degree; but it may perhaps be doubted whether even he himself did not sometimes give scope to his faculty of expression to the prejudice of a higher poetical duty. For we must never forget that Shakespeare is the great poet he is from his skill in discerning and firmly conceiving an excellent action, from his power of intensely feeling a situation, of intimately associating himself with a character; not from his gift of expression, which rather even leads him astray, degenerating sometimes into a fondness for curiosity of expression, into an irritability of fancy, which seems to make it impossible for him to say a thing plainly, even when the press of the action demands the very directest language, or its level character the very simplest. Mr. Hallam,[11] than whom it is impossible to find a saner and more judicious critic, has had the courage (for at the present day it needs courage) to remark, how extremely and faultily difficult Shakespeare's language often is. It is so: you may find main scenes in some of his greatest tragedies, *King Lear* for instance, where the language is so artificial, so curiously tortured, and so difficult, that every speech has to be read two or three times before its meaning can be comprehended. This over-curiousness of expression is indeed but the excessive employment of a wonderful gift—of the power of saying a thing in a happier way than any other man; nevertheless, it is carried so far that one understands what M. Guizot [12] meant, when he said that Shakespeare appears in his language to have tried all styles except that of simplicity. He has not the severe and scrupulous self-restraint of the ancients, partly no doubt,

[10] "He says all that he wishes, but unfortunately has nothing to say."

[11] Henry Hallam, English historian of literature, author of *Introduction to the Literature of Europe in the Fifteenth, Sixteenth, and Seventeenth Centuries* (1837-39).

[12] François Pierre Guillaume Guizot (1787-1874), the French historian.

because he had a far less cultivated and exacting audience: he has indeed a far wider range than they had, a far richer fertility of thought; in this respect he rises above them: in his strong conception of his subject, in the genuine way in which he is penetrated with it, he resembles them, and is unlike the moderns: but in the accurate limitation of it, the conscientious rejection of superfluities, the simple and rigorous development of it from the first line of his work to the last, he falls below them, and comes nearer to the moderns. In his chief works, besides what he has of his own, he has the elementary soundness of the ancients; he has their important action and their large and broad manner: but he has not their purity of method. He is therefore a less safe model; for what he has of his own is personal, and inseparable from his own rich nature; it may be imitated and exaggerated, it cannot be learned or applied as an art; he is above all suggestive; more valuable, therefore, to young writers as men than as artists. But clearness of arrangement, rigour of development, simplicity of style —these may to a certain extent be learned: and these may, I am convinced, be learned best from the ancients, who although infinitely less suggestive than Shakespeare, are thus, to the artist, more instructive.

What, then, it will be asked, are the ancients to be our sole models? the ancients with their comparatively narrow range of experience, and their widely different circumstances? Not, certainly, that which is narrow in the ancients, nor that in which we can no longer sympathize. An action like the action of the *Antigone* of Sophocles, which turns upon the conflict between the heroine's duty to her brother's corpse and that to the laws of her country, is no longer one in which it is possible that we should feel a deep interest. I am speaking too, it will be 'remembered, not of the best sources of intellectual stimulus for the general reader, but of the best models of instruction for the individual writer. This last may certainly learn of the ancients, better than anywhere else, three things which it is vitally important for him to know:—the all-importance of the choice of a subject; the necessity of accurate construction; and the subordinate character of expression. He will learn from them how unspeakably superior is the effect of the one moral impression left by a great action

treated as a whole, to the effect produced by the most striking single thought or by the happiest image. As he penetrates into the spirit of the great classical works, as he becomes gradually aware of their intense significance, their noble simplicity, and their calm pathos, he will be convinced that it is this effect, unity and profoundness of moral impression, at which the ancient Poets aimed; that it is this which constitutes the grandeur of their works, and which makes them immortal. He will desire to direct his own efforts towards producing the same effect. Above all, he will deliver himself from the jargon of modern criticism, and escape the danger of producing poetical works conceived in the spirit of the passing time, and which partake of its transitoriness.

The present age makes great claims upon us: we owe it service, it will not be satisfied without our admiration. I know not how it is, but their commerce with the ancients appears to me to produce, in those who constantly practise it, a steadying and composing effect upon their judgment, not of literary works only, but of men and events in general. They are like persons who have had a very weighty and impressive experience: they are more truly than others under the empire of facts, and more independent of the language current among those with whom they live. They wish neither to applaud nor to revile their age: they wish to know what it is, what it can give them, and whether this is what they want. What they want, they know very well; they want to educe and cultivate what is best and noblest in themselves: they know, too, that this is no easy task—χαλεπόν, as Pittacus said, χαλεπὸν ἐσθλὸν ἔμμεναι [13]—and they ask themselves sincerely whether their age and its literature can assist them in the attempt. If they are endeavouring to practise any art, they remember the plain and simple proceedings of the old artists, who attained their grand results by penetrating themselves with some noble and significant action, not by inflating themselves with a belief in the pre-eminent importance and greatness of their own times. They do not talk of their mission, nor of interpreting their age, nor of the coming Poet; all this, they know, is the mere delirium of vanity; their business is not to praise their age, but to afford to the men

[13] "It is difficult to be excellent."

who live in it the highest pleasure which they are capable of feeling. If asked to afford this by means of subjects drawn from the age itself, they ask what special fitness the present age has for supplying them: they are told that it is an era of progress, an age commissioned to carry out the great ideas of industrial development and social amelioration. They reply that with all this they can do nothing; that the elements they need for the exercise of their art are great actions, calculated powerfully and delightfully to affect what is permanent in the human soul; that so far as the present age can supply such actions, they will gladly make use of them; but that an age wanting in moral grandeur can with difficulty supply such, and an age of spiritual discomfort with difficulty be powerfully and delightfully affected by them.

A host of voices will indignantly rejoin that the present age is inferior to the past neither in moral grandeur nor in spiritual health. He who possesses the discipline I speak of will content himself with remembering the judgments passed upon the present age, in this respect, by the two men, the one of strongest head, the other of widest culture, whom it has produced; by Goethe and by Niebuhr. It will be sufficient for him that he knows the opinions held by these two great men respecting the present age and its literature; and that he feels assured in his own mind that their aims and demands upon life were such as he would wish, at any rate, his own to be; and their judgment as to what is impeding and disabling such as he may safely follow. He will not, however, maintain a hostile attitude towards the false pretensions of his age; he will content himself with not being overwhelmed by them. He will esteem himself fortunate if he can succeed in banishing from his mind all feelings of contradiction, and irritation, and impatience; in order to delight himself with the contemplation of some noble action of a heroic time, and to enable others, through his representation of it, to delight in it also.

I am far indeed from making any claim, for myself, that I possess this discipline; or for the following Poems, that they breathe its spirit. But I say, that in the sincere endeavour to learn and practise, amid the bewildering confusion of our times, what is sound and true in poetical art, I seemed to myself to find the only sure guidance, the only solid footing, among the ancients. They, at any rate, knew what they wanted in Art, and we do not. It is this uncertainty which is disheartening, and not hostile criticism. How often have I felt this when reading words of disparagement or of cavil: that it is the uncertainty as to what is really to be aimed at which makes our difficulty, not the dissatisfaction of the critic, who himself suffers from the same uncertainty. *Non me tua fervida terrent Dicta: Dii me terrent, et Jupiter hostis.*[14]

Two kinds of *dilettanti,* says Goethe, there are in poetry: he who neglects the indispensable mechanical part, and thinks he has done enough if he shows spirituality and feeling; and he who seeks to arrive at poetry merely by mechanism, in which he can acquire an artisan's readiness, and is without soul and matter. And he adds, that the first does most harm to Art, and the last to himself. If we must be *dilettanti:* if it is impossible for us, under the circumstances amidst which we live, to think clearly, to feel nobly, and to delineate firmly: if we cannot attain to the mastery of the great artists—let us, at least, have so much respect for our Art as to prefer it to ourselves: let us not bewilder our successors: let us transmit to them the practice of Poetry, with its boundaries and wholesome regulative laws, under which excellent works may again, perhaps, at some future time, be produced, not yet fallen into oblivion through our neglect, not yet condemned and cancelled by the influence of their eternal enemy, Caprice.

[14] "Your fervid words do not terrify me. The gods, and Jupiter as my enemy, terrify me" (*Aeneid,* XII, 894-95).

The Function of Criticism at the Present Time

M ANY objections have been made to a proposition which, in some remarks of mine on translating Homer, I ventured to put forth; a proposition about criticism, and its importance at the present day. I said: "Of the literature of France and Germany, as of the intellect of Europe in general, the main effort, for now many years, has been a critical effort; the endeavour, in all branches of knowledge, theology, philosophy, history, art, science, to see the object as in itself it really is." I added, that owing to the operation in English literature of certain causes, "almost the last thing for which one would come to English literature is just that very thing which now Europe most desires,—criticism"; and that the power and value of English literature was thereby impaired. More than one rejoinder declared that the importance I here assigned to criticism was excessive, and asserted the inherent superiority of the creative effort of the human spirit over its critical effort. And the other day, having been led by a Mr. Shairp's [1] excellent notice of Wordsworth [2] to turn again to his biography, I found, in the words of this great man, whom I, for one, must always listen to with the profoundest respect, a sentence passed on the critic's business, which seems to justify every possible disparagement of it. Wordsworth says in one of his letters:

"The writers in these publications" (the Re-

views), "while they prosecute their inglorious employment, cannot be supposed to be in a state of mind very favourable for being affected by the finer influences of a thing so pure as genuine poetry." [3]

And a trustworthy reporter of his conversation quotes a more elaborate judgment to the same effect:

"Wordsworth holds the critical power very low, infinitely lower than the inventive; and he said to-day that if the quantity of time consumed in writing critiques on the works of others were given to original composition, of whatever kind it might be, it would be much better employed; it would make a man find out sooner his own level, and it would do infinitely less mischief. A false or malicious criticism may do much injury to the minds of others; a stupid invention, either in prose or verse, is quite harmless." [4]

It is almost too much to expect of poor human nature, that a man capable of producing some effect in one line of literature, should, for the greater good of society, voluntarily doom himself to impotence and obscurity in another. Still less is this to be expected from men addicted to the composition of the "false or malicious criticism" of which Wordsworth speaks. However, everybody would admit that a false or malicious criticism had better never have been written. Everybody, too, would be willing to admit, as a general proposition, that the critical faculty is lower than the inventive. But is it true that criticism is really, in itself, a baneful and injurious employment; is it true that all time given to writing critiques on the works of others would be much better employed if it were given to original composition, of whatever kind this may be? Is it true that Johnson had better have gone on producing more *Irenes* [5] instead of writing his *Lives of the Poets*; is it certain that

The Function of Criticism at the Present Time. First published in 1864; later included in *Essays in Criticism, First Series* (1865).

[1] J. C. Shairp, Scottish critic, whose essay on Wordsworth appeared in the *North British Review* (August, 1864).

[2] I cannot help thinking that a practice, common in England during the last century, and still followed in France, of printing a notice of this kind,—a notice by a competent critic,—to serve as an introduction to an eminent author's works, might be revived among us with advantage. To introduce all succeeding editions of Wordsworth, Mr. Shairp's notice might, it seems to me, excellently serve; it is written from the point of view of an admirer, nay, of a disciple, and that is right; but then the disciple must be also, as in this case he is, a critic, a man of letters, not, as too often happens, some relation or friend with no qualification for his task except affection for his author. [Arnold.]

[3] To Bernard Barton (Christopher Wordsworth, *Memoirs* [1856], II, 53).

[4] In W. Knight, *Life of Wordsworth* (Edinburgh, 1889), III, 438.

[5] *Irene* (1749) was an unsuccessful tragedy in which Johnson himself took little pride.

Wordsworth himself was better employed in making his Ecclesiastical Sonnets than when he made his celebrated Preface so full of criticism,[6] and criticism of the works of others? Wordsworth was himself a great critic, and it is to be sincerely regretted that he has not left us more criticism; Goethe was one of the greatest of critics, and we may sincerely congratulate ourselves that he has left us so much criticism. Without wasting time over the exaggeration which Wordsworth's judgment on criticism clearly contains, or over an attempt to trace the causes,—not difficult, I think, to be traced,—which may have led Wordsworth to this exaggeration, a critic may with advantage seize an occasion for trying his own conscience, and for asking himself of what real service, at any given moment, the practice of criticism either is or may be made to his own mind and spirit, and to the minds and spirits of others.

The critical power is of lower rank than the creative. True; but in assenting to this proposition, one or two things are to be kept in mind. It is undeniable that the exercise of a creative power, that a free creative activity, is the highest function of man; it is proved to be so by man's finding in it his true happiness. But it is undeniable, also, that men may have the sense of exercising this free creative activity in other ways than in producing great works of literature or art; if it were not so, all but a very few men would be shut out from the true happiness of all men. They may have it in well-doing, they may have it in learning, they may have it even in criticising. This is one thing to be kept in mind. Another is, that the exercise of the creative power in the production of great works of literature or art, however high this exercise of it may rank, is not at all epochs and under all conditions possible; and that therefore labour may be vainly spent in attempting it, which might with more fruit be used in preparing for it, in rendering it possible. This creative power works with elements, with materials; what if it has not those materials, those elements, ready for its use? In that case it must surely wait till they are ready. Now, in literature,—I will limit myself to literature, for it is about literature that the question arises,—the elements with which the creative

[6] See above, pp. 335-46.

power works are ideas; the best ideas on every matter which literature touches, current at the time. At any rate we may lay it down as certain that in modern literature no manifestation of the creative power not working with these can be very important or fruitful. And I say *current* at the time, not merely accessible at the time; for creative literary genius does not principally show itself in discovering new ideas, that is rather the business of the philosopher. The grand work of literary genius is a work of synthesis and exposition, not of analysis and discovery; its gift lies in the faculty of being happily inspired by a certain intellectual and spiritual atmosphere, by a certain order of ideas, when it finds itself in them; of dealing divinely with these ideas, presenting them in the most effective and attractive combinations,—making beautiful works with them, in short. But it must have the atmosphere, it must find itself amidst the order of ideas, in order to work freely; and these it is not so easy to command. This is why great creative epochs in literature are so rare, this is why there is so much that is unsatisfactory in the productions of many men of real genius; because, for the creation of a master-work of literature two powers must concur, the power of the man and the power of the moment, and the man is not enough without the moment; the creative power has, for its happy exercise, appointed elements, and those elements are not in its own control.

Nay, they are more within the control of the critical power. It is the business of the critical power, as I said in the words already quoted, "in all branches of knowledge, theology, philosophy, history, art, science, to see the object as in itself it really is." Thus it tends, at last, to make an intellectual situation of which the creative power can profitably avail itself. It tends to establish an order of ideas, if not absolutely true, yet true by comparison with that which it displaces; to make the best ideas prevail. Presently these new ideas reach society, the touch of truth is the touch of life, and there is a stir and growth everywhere; out of this stir and growth come the creative epochs of literature.

Or, to narrow our range, and quit these considerations of the general march of genius and of society,—considerations which are apt to become too abstract and impalpable,—every one can see that a poet, for instance, ought to know life and the world before dealing with them in poetry; and life and the world being in modern times very complex things, the creation of a modern poet, to be worth much, implies a great critical effort behind it; else it must be a comparatively poor, barren, and short-lived affair. This is why Byron's poetry had so little endurance in it, and Goethe's so much; both Byron and Goethe had a great productive power, but Goethe's was nourished by a great critical effort providing the true materials for it, and Byron's was not; Goethe knew life and the world, the poet's necessary subjects, much more comprehensively and thoroughly than Byron. He knew a great deal more of them, and he knew them much more as they really are.

It has long seemed to me that the burst of creative activity in our literature, through the first quarter of this century, had about it in fact something premature; and that from this cause its productions are doomed, most of them, in spite of the sanguine hopes which accompanied and do still accompany them, to prove hardly more lasting than the productions of far less splendid epochs. And this prematureness comes from its having proceeded without having its proper data, without sufficient materials to work with. In other words, the English poetry of the first quarter of this century, with plenty of energy, plenty of creative force, did not know enough. This makes Byron so empty of matter, Shelley so incoherent, Wordsworth even, profound as he is, yet so wanting in completeness and variety. Wordsworth cared little for books, and disparaged Goethe. I admire Wordsworth, as he is, so much that I cannot wish him different; and it is vain, no doubt, to imagine such a man different from what he is, to suppose that he *could* have been different. But surely the one thing wanting to make Wordsworth an even greater poet than he is,—his thought richer, and his influence of wider application,—was that he should have read more books, among them, no doubt, those of that Goethe whom he disparaged without reading him.

But to speak of books and reading may easily lead to a misunderstanding here. It was not really books and reading that lacked to our poetry at this epoch: Shelley had plenty of reading, Coleridge had immense reading. Pindar and Sophocles,—as we all say so glibly, and often with so little discernment of the real import of what we are saying,—had not many books; Shakespeare was no deep reader. True; but in the Greece of Pindar and Sophocles, in the England of Shakespeare, the poet lived in a current of ideas in the highest degree animating and nourishing to the creative power; society was, in the fullest measure, permeated by fresh thought, intelligent and alive. And this state of things is the true basis for the creative power's exercise, in this it finds its data, its materials, truly ready for its hand; all the books and reading in the world are only valuable as they are helps to this. Even when this does not actually exist, books and reading may enable a man to construct a kind of semblance of it in his own mind, a world of knowledge and intelligence in which he may live and work. This is by no means an equivalent to the artist for the nationally diffused life and thought of the epochs of Sophocles or Shakespeare; but, besides that it may be a means of preparation for such epochs, it does really constitute, if many share in it, a quickening and sustaining atmosphere of great value. Such an atmosphere the many-sided learning and the long and widely combined critical effort of Germany formed for Goethe, when he lived and worked. There was no national glow of life and thought there as in the Athens of Pericles or the England of Elizabeth. That was the poet's weakness. But there was a sort of equivalent for it in the complete culture and unfettered thinking of a large body of Germans. That was his strength. In the England of the first quarter of this century there was neither a national glow of life and thought, such as we had in the age of Elizabeth, nor yet a culture and a force of learning and criticism such as were to be found in Germany. Therefore the creative power of poetry wanted, for success in the highest sense, materials and a basis; a thorough interpretation of the world was necessarily denied to it.

At first sight it seems strange that out of the immense stir of the French Revolution and its age should not have come a crop of works of genius equal to that which came out of the stir of the great productive time of Greece, or out of that of the Renascence, with its powerful episode the Reformation. But the truth is that the stir of the French Revolution took a character which essentially distinguished it from such movements as these. These were, in the main, disinterestedly intellectual and spiritual movements; movements in which the human spirit looked for its satisfaction in itself and in the increased play of its own activity. The French Revolution took a political, practical character. The movement, which went on in France under the old *régime*, from 1700 to 1789, was far more really akin than that of the Revolution itself to the movement of the Renascence; the France of Voltaire and Rousseau told far more powerfully upon the mind of Europe than the France of the Revolution. Goethe reproached this last expressly with having "thrown quiet culture back." Nay, and the true key to how much in our Byron, even in our Wordsworth, is this!—that they had their source in a great movement of feeling, not in a great movement of mind. The French Revolution, however,—that object of so much blind love and so much blind hatred,—found undoubtedly its motive-power in the intelligence of men, and not in their practical sense; this is what distinguishes it from the English Revolution of Charles the First's time. This is what makes it a more spiritual event than our Revolution, an event of much more powerful and world-wide interest, though practically less successful; it appeals to an order of ideas which are universal, certain, permanent. 1789 asked of a thing, Is it rational? 1642 asked of a thing, Is it legal? or, when it went furthest, Is it according to conscience? This is the English fashion, a fashion to be treated, within its own sphere, with the highest respect; for its success, within its own sphere, has been prodigious. But what is law in one place is not law in another; what is law here to-day is not law even here to-morrow; and as for conscience, what is binding on one man's conscience is not binding on another's. The old woman who threw her stool at the head of the surpliced minister in St. Giles's Church at Edinburgh obeyed an impulse to which millions of the human race may be permitted to remain strangers. But the prescriptions of reason are absolute, unchanging, of universal validity; *to count by tens is the easiest way of counting*—that is a proposition of which every one, from here to the Antipodes, feels the force; at least I should say so if we did not live in a country where it is not impossible that any morning we may find a letter in the *Times* declaring that a decimal coinage is an absurdity.

That a whole nation should have been penetrated with an enthusiasm for pure reason, and with an ardent zeal for making its prescriptions triumph, is a very remarkable thing, when we consider how little of mind, or anything so worthy and quickening as mind, comes into the motives which alone, in general, impel great masses of men. In spite of the extravagant direction given to this enthusiasm, in spite of the crimes and follies in which it lost itself, the French Revolution derives from the force, truth, and universality of the ideas which it took for its law, and from the passion with which it could inspire a multitude for these ideas, a unique and still living power; it is,—it will probably long remain,—the greatest, the most animating event in history. And as no sincere passion for the things of the mind, even though it turn out in many respects an unfortunate passion, is ever quite thrown away and quite barren of good, France has reaped from hers one fruit—the natural and legitimate fruit though not precisely the grand fruit she expected: she is the country in Europe where *the people* is most alive.

But the mania for giving an immediate political and practical application to all these fine ideas of the reason was fatal. Here an Englishman is in his element: on this theme we can all go on for hours. And all we are in the habit of saying on it has undoubtedly a great deal of truth. Ideas cannot be too much prized in and for themselves, cannot be too much lived with; but to transport them abruptly into the world of politics and practice, violently to revolutionise this world to their bidding,—that is quite another thing. There is the world of ideas and there is the world of practice; the French are often for suppressing the one and the English the other; but neither is to be suppressed. A member of the House of Commons said to me the other day: "That a thing is an anomaly, I consider to be no objection to it whatever." I venture to think he was wrong; that a thing is an anomaly *is* an objection to it, but absolutely and in the sphere of ideas: it is not necessarily, under such and such circumstances, or at such and such a moment, an objection to it in the sphere of politics and practice. Joubert has said beautifully: "*C'est la force et le droit qui règlent toutes choses dans le monde; la force en attendant le droit.*" (Force and right are the governors of this world; force till right is ready.) *Force till right is ready;* and till right is ready, force, the existing order of things, is justified, is the legitimate ruler. But right is something moral, and implies inward recognition, free assent of the will; we are not ready for right,—*right, so far as we are concerned, is not ready,*—until we have attained this sense of seeing it and willing it. The way in which for us it may change and transform force, the existing order of things, and become, in its turn, the legitimate ruler of the world, should depend on the way in which, when our time comes, we see it and will it. Therefore for other people enamoured of their own newly discerned right, to attempt to impose it upon us as ours, and violently to substitute their right for our force, is an act of tyranny, and to be resisted. It sets at nought the second great half of our maxim, *force till right is ready.* This was the grand error of the French Revolution; and its movement of ideas, by quitting the intellectual sphere and rushing furiously into the political sphere, ran, indeed, a prodigious and memorable course, but produced no such intellectual fruit as the movement of ideas of the Renascence, and created, in opposition to itself, what I may call an *epoch of concentration.* The great force of that epoch of concentration was England; and the great voice of that epoch of concentration was Burke.[7] It is the fashion to treat Burke's writings on the French Revolution as superannuated and conquered by the event; as the eloquent but unphilosophical tirades of bigotry and prejudice. I will not deny that they are often disfigured by the violence and passion of the moment, and that in some directions Burke's view was bounded, and his observation therefore at fault. But on the whole, and for those who can make the needful corrections, what distinguishes these writings is their profound, permanent, fruitful, philosophical truth. They contain the true philosophy of an epoch of concentration, dissipate the heavy atmosphere which its own nature is apt to engender round it, and make its resistance rational instead of mechanical.

But Burke is so great because, almost alone in England, he brings thought to bear upon politics, he saturates politics with thought. It is his accident that his ideas were at the service of an epoch of concentration, not of an epoch of expansion; it is his characteristic that he so lived by ideas, and had such a source of them welling up within him, that he could float even an epoch of concentration and English Tory politics with them. It does not hurt him that Dr. Price[8] and the Liberals were enraged with him; it does not even hurt him that George the Third and the Tories were enchanted with him. His greatness is that he lived in a world which neither English Liberalism nor English Toryism is apt to enter;—the world of ideas, not the world of catchwords and party habits. So far is it from being really true of him that he "to party gave up what was meant for mankind," that at the very end of his fierce struggle with the French Revolution, after all his invectives against its false pretensions, hollowness, and madness, with his sincere convictions of its mischievousness, he can close a memorandum on the best means of combating it, some of the last pages he ever wrote,—the *Thoughts on French Affairs,* in December 1791,—with these striking words:—

"The evil is stated, in my opinion, as it exists. The remedy must be where power, wisdom, and information, I hope, are more united with good intentions than they can be with me. I have done with this subject, I believe, for ever. It has given me many anxious moments for the last two years. *If a great change is to be made in human affairs, the minds of men will be fitted to it; the general opinions and feelings will draw that way. Every fear, every hope will forward it; and then they who persist in opposing this mighty current in human affairs, will appear rather to resist the decrees of Providence itself, than the mere designs of men. They will not be resolute and firm, but perverse and obstinate.*"

That return of Burke upon himself has always seemed to me one of the finest things in English literature, or indeed in any literature. That is what I call living by ideas: when one side of a question has long had your earnest support, when all your feelings are engaged, when you hear all round you no language but one, when your party talks this language like a steam-engine and can imagine no other,—still to be able to think, still to be irresistibly carried, if

---

[7] Burke, to Arnold, was the "greatest English prose-writer."

[8] Richard Price, Nonconformist minister, who had sympathized with the French Revolution.

so it be, by the current of thought to the opposite side of the question, and, like Balaam, to be unable to speak anything *but what the Lord has put in your mouth.* I know nothing more striking, and I must add that I know nothing more un-English.

For the Englishman in general is like my friend the Member of Parliament, and believes, point-blank, that for a thing to be an anomaly is absolutely no objection to it whatever. He is like the Lord Auckland of Burke's day, who, in a memorandum on the French Revolution, talks of certain "miscreants, assuming the name of philosophers, who have presumed themselves capable of establishing a new system of society." The Englishman has been called a political animal, and he values what is political and practical so much that ideas easily become objects of dislike in his eyes, and thinkers, "miscreants," because ideas and thinkers have rashly meddled with politics and practice. This would be all very well if the dislike and neglect confined themselves to ideas transported out of their own sphere, and meddling rashly with practice; but they are inevitably extended to ideas as such, and to the whole life of intelligence; practice is everything, a free play of the mind is nothing. The notion of the free play of the mind upon all subjects being a pleasure in itself, being an object of desire, being an essential provider of elements without which a nation's spirit, whatever compensations it may have for them, must, in the long run, die of inanition, hardly enters into an Englishman's thoughts. It is noticeable that the word *curiosity*,[9] which in other languages is used in a good sense, to mean, as a high and fine quality of man's nature, just this disinterested love of a free play of the mind on all subjects, for its own sake,—it is noticeable, I say, that this word has in our language no sense of the kind, no sense but a rather bad and disparaging one. But criticism, real criticism, is essentially the exercise of this very quality. It obeys an instinct prompting it to try to know the best that is known and thought in the world, irrespectively of practice, politics, and everything of the kind; and to value knowledge and thought as they approach this best, without the intrusion of any other considerations whatever.

[9] For a fuller discussion, see "Sweetness and Light," below, p. 466.

This is an instinct for which there is, I think, little original sympathy in the practical English nature, and what there was of it has undergone a long benumbing period of blight and suppression in the epoch of concentration which followed the French Revolution.

But epochs of concentration cannot well endure for ever; epochs of expansion, in the due course of things, follow them. Such an epoch of expansion seems to be opening in this country. In the first place all danger of a hostile forcible pressure of foreign ideas upon our practice has long disappeared; like the traveller in the fable, therefore, we begin to wear our cloak a little more loosely. Then, with a long peace, the ideas of Europe steal gradually and amicably in, and mingle, though in infinitesimally small quantities at a time, with our own notions. Then, too, in spite of all that is said about the absorbing and brutalising influence of our passionate material progress, it seems to me indisputable that this progress is likely, though not certain, to lead in the end to an apparition of intellectual life; and that man, after he has made himself perfectly comfortable and has now to determine what to do with himself next, may begin to remember that he has a mind, and that the mind may be made the source of great pleasure. I grant it is mainly the privilege of faith, at present, to discern this end to our railways, our business, and our fortune-making; but we shall see if, here as elsewhere, faith is not in the end the true prophet. Our ease, our travelling, and our unbounded liberty to hold just as hard and securely as we please to the practice to which our notions have given birth, all tend to beget an inclination to deal a little more freely with these notions themselves, to canvass them a little, to penetrate a little into their real nature. Flutterings of curiosity, in the foreign sense of the word, appear amongst us, and it is in these that criticism must look to find its account. Criticism first; a time of true creative activity, perhaps,—which, as I have said, must inevitably be preceded amongst us by a time of criticism,—hereafter, when criticism has done its work.

It is of the last importance that English criticism should clearly discern what rule for its course, in order to avail itself of the field now opening to it, and to produce fruit for the future, it ought to take. The rule may be summed up in one word,—*disinterestedness*. And how is criticism to show disinterestedness? By keeping aloof from what is called "the practical view of things"; by resolutely following the law of its own nature, which is to be a free play of the mind on all subjects which it touches. By steadily refusing to lend itself to any of those ulterior, political, practical considerations about ideas, which plenty of people will be sure to attach to them, which perhaps ought often to be attached to them, which in this country at any rate are certain to be attached to them quite sufficiently, but which criticism has really nothing to do with. Its business is, as I have said, simply to know the best that is known and thought in the world, and by in its turn making this known, to create a current of true and fresh ideas. Its business is to do this with inflexible honesty, with due ability; but its business is to do no more, and to leave alone all questions of practical consequences and applications, questions which will never fail to have due prominence given to them. Else criticism, besides being really false to its own nature, merely continues in the old rut which it has hitherto followed in this country, and will certainly miss the chance now given to it. For what is at present the bane of criticism in this country? It is that practical considerations cling to it and stifle it. It subserves interests not its own. Our organs of criticism are organs of men and parties having practical ends to serve, and with them those practical ends are the first thing and the play of mind the second; so much play of mind as is compatible with the prosecution of those practical ends is all that is wanted. An organ like the *Revue des Deux Mondes,* having for its main function to understand and utter the best that is known and thought in the world, existing, it may be said, as just an organ for a free play of the mind, we have not. But we have the *Edinburgh Review,* existing as an organ of the old Whigs, and for as much play of mind as may suit its being that; we have the *Quarterly Review,* existing as an organ of the Tories, and for as much play of mind as may suit its being that; we have the *British Quarterly Review,* existing as an organ of the political Dissenters, and for as much play of mind as may suit its being that; we have the *Times,* existing as an organ of the common, satisfied, well-to-do Englishman, and for as much

play of mind as may suit its being that. And so on through all the various fractions, political and religious, of our society; every fraction has, as such, its organ of criticism, but the notion of combining all fractions in the common pleasure of a free disinterested play of mind meets with no favour. Directly this play of mind wants to have more scope, and to forget the pressure of practical considerations a little, it is checked, it is made to feel the chain. We saw this the other day in the extinction, so much to be regretted, of the *Home and Foreign Review.* Perhaps in no organ of criticism in this country was there so much knowledge, so much play of mind; but these could not save it. The *Dublin Review* subordinates play of mind to the practical business of English and Irish Catholicism, and lives. It must needs be that men should act in sects and parties, that each of these sects and parties should have its organ, and should make this organ subserve the interests of its action; but it would be well, too, that there should be a criticism, not the minister of these interests, not their enemy, but absolutely and entirely independent of them. No other criticism will ever attain any real authority or make any real way towards its end,—the creating a current of true and fresh ideas.

It is because criticism has so little kept in the pure intellectual sphere, has so little detached itself from practice, has been so directly polemical and controversial, that it has so ill accomplished, in this country, its best spiritual work; which is to keep man from a self-satisfaction which is retarding and vulgarising, to lead him towards perfection, by making his mind dwell upon what is excellent in itself, and the absolute beauty and fitness of things. A polemical practical criticism makes men blind even to the ideal imperfection of their practice, makes them willingly assert its ideal perfection, in order the better to secure it against attack; and clearly this is narrowing and baneful for them. If they were reassured on the practical side, speculative considerations of ideal perfection they might be brought to entertain, and their spiritual horizon would thus gradually widen. Sir Charles Adderley [10] says to the Warwickshire farmers:

"Talk of the improvement of breed! Why, the

[10] Sir Charles Adderley and John Arthur Roebuck, whom Arnold satirizes so persistently, were politicians

race we ourselves represent, the men and women, the old Anglo-Saxon race, are the best breed in the whole world. . . . The absence of a too enervating climate, too unclouded skies, and a too luxurious nature, has produced so vigorous a race of people, and has rendered us so superior to all the world."

Mr. Roebuck says to the Sheffield cutlers:

"I look around me and ask what is the state of England? Is not property safe? Is not every man able to say what he likes? Can you not walk from one end of England to the other in perfect security? I ask you whether, the world over or in past history, there is anything like it? Nothing. I pray that our unrivalled happiness may last."

Now obviously there is a peril for poor human nature in words and thoughts of such exuberant self-satisfaction, until we find ourselves safe in the streets of the Celestial City.

Das wenige verschwindet leicht dem Blicke
Der vorwärts sieht, wie viel noch übrig bleibt—[11]

says Goethe; "the little that is done seems nothing when we look forward and see how much we have yet to do." Clearly this is a better line of reflection for weak humanity, so long as it remains on this earthly field of labour and trial. But neither Sir Charles Adderley nor Mr. Roebuck is by nature inaccessible to considerations of this sort. They only lose sight of them owing to the controversial life we all lead, and the practical form which all speculation takes with us. They have in view opponents whose aim is not ideal, but practical; and in their zeal to uphold their own practice against these innovators, they go so far as even to attribute to this practice an ideal perfection. Somebody has been wanting to introduce a six-pound franchise, or to abolish church-rates,[12] or to collect agricultural statistics by force, or to diminish local self-government. How natural, in reply to such proposals, very likely improper or ill-timed, to go a little beyond the mark and to say stoutly, "Such

a race of people as we stand, so superior to all the world! The old Anglo-Saxon race, the best breed in the whole world! I pray that our unrivalled happiness may last! I ask you whether, the world over or in past history, there is anything like it?" And so long as criticism answers this dithyramb by insisting that the old Anglo-Saxon race would be still more superior to all others if it had no church-rates, or that our unrivalled happiness would last yet longer with a six-pound franchise, so long will the strain, "The best breed in the whole world!" swell louder and louder, everything ideal and refining will be lost out of sight, and both the assailed and their critics will remain in a sphere, to say the truth, perfectly unvital, a sphere in which spiritual progression is impossible. But let criticism leave church-rates and the franchise alone, and in the most candid spirit, without a single lurking thought of practical innovation, confront with our dithyramb this paragraph on which I stumbled in a newspaper immediately after reading Mr. Roebuck:

"A shocking child murder has just been committed at Nottingham. A girl named Wragg left the workhouse there on Saturday morning with her young illegitimate child. The child was soon afterwards found dead on Mapperly Hills, having been strangled. Wragg is in custody."

Nothing but that; but, in juxtaposition with the absolute eulogies of Sir Charles Adderley and Mr. Roebuck, how eloquent, how suggestive are those few lines! "Our old Anglo-Saxon breed, the best in the whole world!"—how much that is harsh and ill-favoured there is in this best! *Wragg!* If we are to talk of ideal perfection, of "the best in the whole world," has any one reflected what a touch of grossness in our race, what an original short-coming in the more delicate spiritual perceptions, is shown by the natural growth amongst us of such hideous names,— Higginbottom, Stiggins, Bugg! In Ionia and Attica they were luckier in this respect than "the best race in the world"; by the Ilissus [13] there was no Wragg, poor thing! And "our unrivalled happiness";—what an element of grimness, bareness, and hideousness mixes with it and blurs it; the workhouse, the dismal Mapperly Hills,— how dismal those who have seen them will re-

of the period. Adderley was a Conservative, while Roebuck was a well-known Liberal reformer.

[11] *Iphigenie auf Tauris*, I, ii, 91-92.

[12] A six-pound franchise would be the right to vote possessed by all citizens owning property worth £6 a year or more. Church-rates were taxes imposed by the Church of England.

[13] A river near Athens.

member;—the gloom, the smoke, the cold, the strangled illegitimate child! "I ask you whether, the world over or in past history, there is anything like it?" Perhaps not, one is inclined to answer; but at any rate, in that case, the world is very much to be pitied. And the final touch,— short, bleak and inhuman: *Wragg is in custody.* The sex lost in the confusion of our unrivalled happiness; or (shall I say?) the superfluous Christian name lopped off by the straightforward vigour of our old Anglo-Saxon breed! There is profit for the spirit in such contrasts as this; criticism serves the cause of perfection by establishing them. By eluding sterile conflict, by refusing to remain in the sphere where alone narrow and relative conceptions have any worth and validity, criticism may diminish its momentary importance, but only in this way has it a chance of gaining admittance for those wider and more perfect conceptions to which all its duty is really owed. Mr. Roebuck will have a poor opinion of an adversary who replies to his defiant songs of triumph only by murmuring under his breath, *Wragg is in custody;* but in no other way will these songs of triumph be induced gradually to moderate themselves, to get rid of what in them is excessive and offensive, and to fall into a softer and truer key.

It will be said that it is a very subtle and indirect action which I am thus prescribing for criticism, and that, by embracing in this manner the Indian virtue of detachment and abandoning the sphere of practical life, it condemns itself to a slow and obscure work. Slow and obscure it may be, but it is the only proper work of criticism. The mass of mankind will never have any ardent zeal for seeing things as they are; very inadequate ideas will always satisfy them. On these inadequate ideas reposes, and must repose, the general practice of the world. That is as much as saying that whoever sets himself to see things as they are will find himself one of a very small circle; but it is only by this small circle resolutely doing its own work that adequate ideas will ever get current at all. The rush and roar of practical life will always have a dizzying and attracting effect upon the most collected spectator, and tend to draw him into its vortex; most of all will this be the case where that life is so powerful as it is in England. But it is only by remaining collected, and

refusing to lend himself to the point of view of the practical man, that the critic can do the practical man any service; and it is only by the greatest sincerity in pursuing his own course, and by at last convincing even the practical man of his sincerity, that he can escape misunderstandings which perpetually threaten him.

For the practical man is not apt for fine distinctions, and yet in these distinctions truth and the highest culture greatly find their account. But it is not easy to lead a practical man,—unless you reassure him as to your practical intentions, you have no chance of leading him,—to see that a thing which he has always been used to look at from one side only, which he greatly values, and which, looked at from that side, quite deserves, perhaps, all the prizing and admiring which he bestows upon it,—that this thing, looked at from another side, may appear much less beneficent and beautiful, and yet retain all its claims to our practical allegiance. Where shall we find language innocent enough, how shall we make the spotless purity of our intentions evident enough, to enable us to say to the political Englishman that the British Constitution itself, which, seen from the practical side, looks such a magnificent organ of progress and virtue, seen from the speculative side,—with its compromises, its love of facts, its horror of theory, its studied avoidance of clear thoughts,— that, seen from this side, our august Constitution sometimes looks,—forgive me, shade of Lord Somers!—a colossal machine for the manufacture of Philistines? [14] How is Cobbett [15] to say this and not be misunderstood, blackened as he is with the smoke of a lifelong conflict in the field of political practice? how is Mr. Carlyle to say it and not be misunderstood, after his furious raid into this field with his *Latter-day Pamphlets?* how is Mr. Ruskin, after his pugnacious political economy? I say, the critic must keep out of the region of immediate practice in the political, social, humanitarian sphere if he wants to make

[14] John, Baron Somers (1651-1716), lord chancellor and noted interpreter of the English Constitution. The term *Philistine* is applied by Arnold to the middle-class individual who is primarily interested in making money. See above, p. 440, and the essay "Barbarians, Philistines, and Populace," in *Culture and Anarchy.*

[15] William Cobbett (1762-1835) was a political writer with strong democratic feelings.

a beginning for that more free speculative treatment of things, which may perhaps one day make its benefits felt even in this sphere, but in a natural and thence irresistible manner.

Do what he will, however, the critic will still remain exposed to frequent misunderstandings, and nowhere so much as in this country. For here people are particularly indisposed even to comprehend that without this free disinterested treatment of things, truth and the highest culture are out of the question. So immersed are they in practical life, so accustomed to take all their notions from this life and its processes, that they are apt to think that truth and culture themselves can be reached by the processes of this life, and that it is an impertinent singularity to think of reaching them in any other. "We are all *terrae filii*," [16] cries their eloquent advocate; "all Philistines together. Away with the notion of proceeding by any other course than the course dear to the Philistines; let us have a social movement, let us organise and combine a party to pursue truth and new thought, let us call it *the liberal party*, and let us all stick to each other, and back each other up. Let us have no nonsense about independent criticism, and intellectual delicacy, and the few and the many. Don't let us trouble ourselves about foreign thought; we shall invent the whole thing for ourselves as we go along. If one of us speaks well, applaud him; if one of us speaks ill, applaud him too; we are all in the same movement, we are all liberals, we are all in pursuit of truth." In this way the pursuit of truth becomes really a social, practical, pleasurable affair, almost requiring a chairman, a secretary, and advertisements; with the excitement of an occasional scandal, with a little resistance to give the happy sense of difficulty overcome; but, in general, plenty of bustle and very little thought. To act is so easy, as Goethe says; to think is so hard! It is true that the critic has many temptations to go with the stream, to make one of the party movement, one of these *terrae filii*; it seems ungracious to refuse to be a *terrae filius* when so many excellent people are; but the critic's duty is to refuse, or, if resistance is vain, at least to cry with Obermann: *Périssons en résistant.*[17]

How serious a matter it is to try and resist, I

had ample opportunity of experiencing when I ventured some time ago to criticise the celebrated first volume of Bishop Colenso.[18] The echoes of the storm which was then raised I still, from time to time, hear grumbling round me. That storm arose out of a misunderstanding almost inevitable. It is a result of no little culture to attain to a clear perception that science and religion are two wholly different things. The multitude will for ever confuse them; but happily that is of no great real importance, for while the multitude imagines itself to live by its false science, it does really live by its true religion. Dr. Colenso,[19] however, in his first volume did all he could to strengthen the confusion, and to make it dangerous. He did this with the best intentions, I freely admit, and with the most candid ignorance that this was the natural effect of what he was doing; but, says Joubert, "Ignorance, which in matters of morals extenuates the crime, is itself, intellectual matters, a crime of the first order." I criticised Bishop Colenso's speculative confusion. Immediately there was a cry raised: "What is this? here is a liberal attacking a liberal. Do not you belong to the movement? are you not a friend of truth? Is not Bishop Colenso in pursuit of truth? then speak with proper respect of his book. Dr. Stanley [20] is another friend of truth, and you speak with proper respect of his book; why make these invidious differences? both books are excellent, admirable, liberal; Bishop Colenso's perhaps

[18] So sincere is my dislike to all personal attack and controversy, that I abstain from reprinting, at this distance of time from the occasion which called them forth, the essays in which I criticised Dr. Colenso's book; I feel bound, however, after all that has passed, to make here a final declaration, of my sincere impenitence for having published them. Nay, I cannot forbear repeating yet once more, for his benefit and that of his readers, this sentence from my original remarks upon him. *There is truth of science and truth of religion; truth of science does not become truth of religion till it is made religious.* And I will add: Let us have all the science there is from the men of science; from the men of religion let us have religion. [Arnold.]

[19] John William Colenso, Bishop of Natal, attacked the literal interpretation of the Bible. Arnold, while far from being a literalist himself, rightly thought the book naïve and unscholarly. (See his essay, "The Bishop and the Philosopher," *Macmillan's Magazine*, January, 1863.)

[20] Arthur P. Stanley, whose work Arnold had contrasted with Colenso's.

[16] "Sons of the earth."

[17] "Let us perish while resisting."

the most so, because it is the boldest, and will have the best practical consequences for the liberal cause. Do you want to encourage to the attack of a brother liberal his, and your, and our implacable enemies, the *Church and State Review* or the *Record*,—the High Church rhinoceros and the Evangelical hyaena? Be silent, therefore; or rather speak, speak as loud as ever you can! and go into ecstasies over the eighty and odd pigeons."

But criticism cannot follow this coarse and indiscriminate method. It is unfortunately possible for a man in pursuit of truth to write a book which reposes upon a false conception. Even the practical consequences of a book are to genuine criticism no recommendation of it, if the book is, in the highest sense, blundering. I see that a lady [21] who herself, too, is in pursuit of truth, and who writes with great ability, but a little too much, perhaps, under the influence of the practical spirit of the English liberal movement, classes Bishop Colenso's book and M. Renan's [22] together, in her survey of the religious state of Europe, as facts of the same order, works, both of them, of "great importance"; "great ability, power, and skill"; Bishop Colenso's, perhaps, the most powerful; at least, Miss Cobbe gives special expression to her gratitude that to Bishop Colenso "has been given the strength to grasp, and the courage to teach, truths of such deep import." In the same way, more than one popular writer has compared him to Luther. Now it is just this kind of false estimate which the critical spirit is, it seems to me, bound to resist. It is really the strongest possible proof of the low ebb at which, in England, the critical spirit is, that while the critical hit in the religious literature of Germany is Dr. Strauss's [23] book, in that of France M. Renan's book, the book of Bishop Colenso is the critical hit in the religious literature of England. Bishop Colenso's book reposes on a total misconception of the essential elements of the religious problem, as that problem is now presented for solu-

tion. To criticism, therefore, which seeks to have the best that is known and thought on this problem, it is, however well meant, of no importance whatever. M. Renan's book attempts a new synthesis of the elements furnished to us by the Four Gospels. It attempts, in my opinion, a synthesis, perhaps premature, perhaps impossible, certainly not successful. Up to the present time, at any rate, we must acquiesce in Fleury's sentence on such recastings of the Gospel story: *Quiconque s'imagine la pouvoir mieux écrire, ne l'entend pas.*[24] M. Renan had himself passed by anticipation a like sentence on his own work, when he said: "If a new presentation of the character of Jesus were offered to me, I would not have it; its very clearness would be, in my opinion, the best proof of its insufficiency." His friends may with perfect justice rejoin that at the sight of the Holy Land, and of the actual scene of the Gospel story, all the current of M. Renan's thoughts may have naturally changed, and a new casting of that story irresistibly suggested itself to him; and that this is just a case for applying Cicero's maxim: Change of mind is not inconsistency—*nemo doctus unquam mutationem consilii inconstantiam dixit esse.*[25] Nevertheless, for criticism, M. Renan's first thought must still be the truer one, as long as his new casting so fails more fully to commend itself, more fully (to use Coleridge's happy phrase about the Bible) to *find* us. Still M. Renan's attempt is, for criticism, of the most real interest and importance, since, with all its difficulty, a fresh synthesis of the New Testament *data*—not a making war on them, in Voltaire's fashion, not a leaving them out of mind, in the world's fashion, but the putting a new construction upon them, the taking them from under the old, traditional, conventional point of view and placing them under a new one,—is the very essence of the religious problem, as now presented; and only by efforts in this direction can it receive a solution.

Again, in the same spirit in which she judges Bishop Colenso, Miss Cobbe, like so many earnest liberals of our practical race, both here and in America, herself sets vigorously about a posi-

---

[21] Frances Cobbe, whose *Broken Lights* (1864) is the book of which Arnold is speaking.

[22] Ernest Renan (1823-1890), author of the *Life of Jesus* (1863).

[23] David Friedrich Strauss, whose *Life of Jesus* (1835) had been translated into English by George Eliot (1846).

[24] "Whoever imagines he can write it better does not understand it."

[25] "No learned man has said that it is inconsistent to change one's mind."

tive reconstruction of religion, about making a religion of the future out of hand, or at least setting about making it. We must not rest, she and they are always thinking and saying, in negative criticism, we must be creative and constructive; hence we have such works as her recent *Religious Duty*, and works still more considerable, perhaps, by others, which will be in every one's mind. These works often have much ability; they often spring out of sincere convictions, and a sincere wish to do good; and they sometimes, perhaps, do good. Their fault is (if I may be permitted to say so) one which they have in common with the British College of Health, in the New Road. Every one knows the British College of Health; it is that building with the lion and the statue of the Goddess Hygeia before it; at least I am sure about the lion, though I am not absolutely certain about the Goddess Hygeia. This building does credit, perhaps, to the resources of Dr. Morrison [26] and his disciples; but it falls a good deal short of one's idea of what a British College of Health ought to be. In England, where we hate public interference and love individual enterprise, we have a whole crop of places like the British College of Health; the grand name without the grand thing. Unluckily, creditable to individual enterprise as they are, they tend to impair our taste by making us forget what more grandiose, noble, or beautiful character properly belongs to a public institution. The same may be said of the religions of the future of Miss Cobbe and others. Creditable, like the British College of Health, to the resources of their authors, they yet tend to make us forget what more grandiose, noble, or beautiful character properly belongs to religious constructions. The historic religions, with all their faults, have had this; it certainly belongs to the religious sentiment, when it truly flowers, to have this; and we impoverish our spirit if we allow a religion of the future without it. What then is the duty of criticism here? To take the practical point of view, to applaud the liberal movement and all its works,—its New Road religions of the future into the bargain,— for their general utility's sake? By no means; but to be perpetually dissatisfied with these

works, while they perpetually fall short of a high and perfect ideal.

For criticism, these are elementary laws; but they never can be popular, and in this country they have been very little followed, and one meets with immense obstacles in following them. That is a reason for asserting them again and again. Criticism must maintain its independence of the practical spirit and its aims. Even with well-meant efforts of the practical spirit it must express dissatisfaction, if in the sphere of the ideal they seem impoverishing and limiting. It must not hurry on to the goal because of its practical importance. It must be patient, and know how to wait; and flexible, and know how to attach itself to things and how to withdraw from them. It must be apt to study and praise elements that for the fulness of spiritual perfection are wanted, even though they belong to a power which in the practical sphere may be maleficent. It must be apt to discern the spiritual shortcomings or illusions of powers that in the practical sphere may be beneficent. And this without any notion of favouring or injuring, in the practical sphere, one power or the other; without any notion of playing off, in this sphere, one power against the other. When one looks, for instance, at the English Divorce Court,—an institution which perhaps has its practical conveniences, but which in the ideal sphere is so hideous; an institution which neither makes divorce impossible nor makes it decent, which allows a man to get rid of his wife, or a wife of her husband, but makes them drag one another first, for the public edification, through a mire of unutterable infamy,—when one looks at this charming institution, I say, with its crowded trials, its newspaper reports, and its money compensations, this institution in which the gross unregenerate British Philistine has indeed stamped an image of himself,—one may be permitted to find the marriage theory of Catholicism refreshing and elevating. Or when Protestantism, in virtue of its supposed rational and intellectual origin, gives the law to criticism too magisterially, criticism may and must remind it that its pretensions, in this respect, are illusive and do it harm; that the Reformation was a moral rather than an intellectual event; that Luther's theory of grace no more exactly reflects the mind of the spirit than Bossuet's philosophy of history

[26] James Morison, who called himself the "Hygeist," sold "Morison's Pills" as a cure for everything at the British College of Health.

reflects it; [27] and that there is no more antecedent probability of the Bishop of Durham's stock of ideas being agreeable to perfect reason than of Pope Pius the Ninth's. But criticism will not on that account forget the achievements of Protestantism in the practical and moral sphere; nor that, even in the intellectual sphere, Protestantism, though in a blind and stumbling manner, carried forward the Renascence, while Catholicism threw itself violently across its path.

I lately heard a man of thought and energy contrasting the want of ardour and movement which he now found amongst young men in this country with what he remembered in his own youth, twenty years ago. "What reformers we were then!" he exclaimed; "What a zeal we had! how we canvassed every institution in Church and State, and were prepared to remodel them all on first principles!" He was inclined to regret, as a spiritual flagging, the lull which he saw. I am disposed rather to regard it as a pause in which the turn to a new mode of spiritual progress is being accomplished. Everything was long seen, by the young and ardent amongst us, in inseparable connection with politics and practical life. We have pretty well exhausted the benefits of seeing things in this connection, we have got all that can be got by so seeing them. Let us try a more disinterested mode of seeing them; let us betake ourselves more to the serener life of the mind and spirit. This life, too, may have its excesses and dangers; but they are not for us at present. Let us think of quietly enlarging our stock of true and fresh ideas, and not, as soon as we get an idea or half an idea, be running out with it into the street, and trying to make it rule there. Our ideas will, in the end, shape the world all the better for maturing a little. Perhaps in fifty years' time it will in the English House of Commons be an objection to an institution that it is an anomaly, and my friend the Member of Parliament will shudder in his grave. But let us in the meanwhile rather endeavour that in twenty years' time it may, in English literature, be an objection to a proposition that it is absurd. That will be a

change so vast, that the imagination almost fails to grasp it. *Ab integro saeclorum nascitur ordo.*[28]

If I have insisted so much on the course which criticism must take where politics and religion are concerned, it is because, where these burning matters are in question, it is most likely to go astray. I have wished, above all, to insist on the attitude which criticism should adopt towards things in general; on its right tone and temper of mind. But then comes another question as to the subject-matter which literary criticism should most seek. Here, in general, its course is determined for it by the idea which is the law of its being; the idea of a disinterested endeavour to learn and propagate the best that is known and thought in the world, and thus to establish a current of fresh and true ideas. By the very nature of things, as England is not all the world, much of the best that is known and thought in the world cannot be of English growth, must be foreign; by the nature of things, again, it is just this that we are least likely to know, while English thought is streaming in upon us from all sides, and takes excellent care that we shall not be ignorant of its existence. The English critic of literature, therefore, must dwell much on foreign thought, and with particular heed on any part of it, which, while significant and fruitful in itself, is for any reason specially likely to escape him. Again, judging is often spoken of as the critic's one business, and so in some sense it is; but the judgment which almost insensibly forms itself in a fair and clear mind, along with fresh knowledge, is the valuable one; and thus knowledge, and ever fresh knowledge, must be the critic's great concern for himself. And it is by communicating fresh knowledge, and letting his own judgment pass along with it,—but insensibly, and in the second place, not the first, as a sort of companion and clue, not as an abstract lawgiver,—that the critic will generally do most good to his readers. Sometimes, no doubt, for the sake of establishing an author's place in literature, and his relation to a central standard (and if this is not done, how are we to get at our *best in the world?*) criticism may have to deal with a sub-

---

[27] Luther's doctrine was that grace came only through faith, regardless of one's deeds. Jacques Bossuet, a seventeenth-century French cleric, argued that all historical events had been divinely guided to lead to and benefit the Catholic Church.

[28] "Order is born from the renewal of generations."

ject-matter so familiar that fresh knowledge is out of the question, and then it must be all judgment; an enunciation and detailed application of principles. Here the great safeguard is never to let oneself become abstract, always to retain an intimate and lively consciousness of the truth of what one is saying, and, the moment this fails us, to be sure that something is wrong. Still under all circumstances, this mere judgment and application of principles is, in itself, not the most satisfactory work to the critic; like mathematics, it is tautological, and cannot well give us, like fresh learning, the sense of creative activity.

But stop, some one will say; all this talk is of no practical use to us whatever; this criticism of yours is not what we have in our minds when we speak of criticism; when we speak of critics and criticism, we mean critics and criticism of the current English literature of the day; when you offer to tell criticism its function, it is to this criticism that we expect you to address yourself. I am sorry for it, for I am afraid I must disappoint these expectations. I am bound by my own definition of criticism: *a disinterested endeavour to learn and propagate the best that is known and thought in the world.* How much of current English literature comes into this "best that is known and thought in the world"? Not very much I fear; certainly less, at this moment, than of the current literature of France or Germany. Well, then, am I to alter my definition of criticism, in order to meet the requirements of a number of practising English critics, who, after all, are free in their choice of a business? That would be making criticism lend itself just to one of those alien practical considerations, which, I have said, are so fatal to it. One may say, indeed, to those who have to deal with the mass—so much better disregarded—of current English literature, that they may at all events endeavour, in dealing with this, to try it, so far as they can, by the standard of the best that is known and thought in the world; one may say, that to get anywhere near this standard, every critic should try and possess one great literature, at least, besides his own; and the more unlike his own, the better. But, after all, the criticism I am really concerned with,—the criticism which alone can much help us for the future, the criticism which, through-

out Europe, is at the present day meant, when so much stress is laid on the importance of criticism and the critical spirit,—is a criticism which regards Europe as being, for intellectual and spiritual purposes, one great confederation, bound to a joint action and working to a common result; and whose members have, for their proper outfit, a knowledge of Greek, Roman, and Eastern antiquity, and of one another. Special, local, and temporary advantages being put out of account, that modern nation will in the intellectual and spiritual sphere make most progress, which most thoroughly carries out this program. And what is that but saying that we too, all of us, as individuals, the more thoroughly we carry it out, shall make the more progress?

There is so much inviting us!—what are we to take? what will nourish us in growth towards perfection? That is the question which, with the immense field of life and of literature lying before him, the critic has to answer; for himself first, and afterwards for others. In this idea of the critic's business the essays brought together in the following pages have had their origin; in this idea, widely different as are their subjects, they have, perhaps, their unity.

I conclude with what I said at the beginning: to have the sense of creative activity is the great happiness and the great proof of being alive, and it is not denied to criticism to have it; but then criticism must be sincere, simple, flexible, ardent, ever widening its knowledge. Then it may have, in no contemptible measure, a joyful sense of creative activity; a sense which a man of insight and conscience will prefer to what he might derive from a poor, starved, fragmentary, inadequate creation. And at some epochs no other creation is possible.

Still, in full measure, the sense of creative activity belongs only to genuine creation; in literature we must never forget that. But what true man of letters ever can forget it? It is no such common matter for a gifted nature to come into possession of a current of true and living ideas, and to produce amidst the inspiration of them, that we are likely to underrate it. The epochs of Aeschylus and Shakespeare make us feel their pre-eminence. In an epoch like those is, no doubt, the true life of literature; there is the promised land, towards which criticism can only beckon. That promised land it will not be ours to enter, and we shall die in the wilderness: but to have desired to enter it, to have saluted it from afar, is already, perhaps, the best distinction among contemporaries; it will certainly be the best title to esteem with posterity.

From Sweetness and Light

THE DISPARAGERS of culture make its motive curiosity; sometimes, indeed, they make its motive mere exclusiveness and vanity. The culture which is supposed to plume itself on a smattering of Greek and Latin is a culture which is begotten by nothing so intellectual as curiosity; it is valued either out of sheer vanity and ignorance or else as an engine of social and class distinction, separating its holder, like a badge or title, from other people who have not got it. No serious man would call this *culture*, or attach any value to it, as culture, at all. To find the real ground for the very different estimate which serious people will set upon culture, we must find some motive for culture in the terms of which may lie a real ambiguity; and such a motive the word *curiosity* gives us.

I have before now pointed out that we English do not, like the foreigners, use this word in a good sense as well as in a bad sense.[1] With us the word is always used in a somewhat disapproving sense. A liberal and intelligent eagerness about the things of the mind may be meant by a foreigner when he speaks of curiosity, but with us the word always conveys a certain notion of frivolous and unedifying activity. In the

Sweetness and Light. Culture and Anarchy was first published in 1869, though various chapters had appeared as articles in periodicals during the preceding two years. The present Introduction and first chapter ("Sweetness and Light") were formerly one article entitled "Culture and its Enemies" (1867). "Sweetness and Light" is unquestionably the most central brief statement of Arnold's cultural values. As such, it is of basic importance in the study of his criticism. For Arnold adheres to the classical premise that literature, like the other arts, is of value to the degree that it enlarges and develops man —to the degree that it enables man to fulfill what is best in him. It is because "Sweetness and Light" attempts to suggest what this end is that it is of fundamental value for the study both of Arnold's own criticism and the criticism of the modern humanist movement that stems from Arnold.

[1] See *On the Function of Criticism*, above, p. 457.

Quarterly Review, some little time ago, was an estimate of the celebrated French critic, M. Sainte-Beuve, and a very inadequate estimate it in my judgment was. And its inadequacy consisted chiefly in this: that in our English way it left out of sight the double sense really involved in the word *curiosity*, thinking enough was said to stamp M. Sainte-Beuve with blame if it was said that he was impelled in his operations as a critic by curiosity, and omitting either to perceive that M. Sainte-Beuve himself, and many other people with him, would consider that this was praiseworthy and not blameworthy, or to point out why it ought really to be accounted worthy of blame and not of praise. For as there is a curiosity about intellectual matters which is futile, and merely a disease, so there is certainly a curiosity,—a desire after the things of the mind simply for their own sakes and for the pleasure of seeing them as they are,—which is, in an intelligent being, natural and laudable. Nay, and the very desire to see things as they are implies a balance and regulation of mind which is not often attained without fruitful effort, and which is the very opposite of the blind and diseased impulse of mind which is what we mean to blame when we blame curiosity. Montesquieu [2] says: "The first motive which ought to impel us to study is the desire to augment the excellence of our nature, and to render an intelligent being yet more intelligent." This is the true ground to assign for the genuine scientific passion, however manifested, and for culture, viewed simply as a fruit of this passion; and it is a worthy ground, even though we let the term *curiosity* stand to describe it.

But there is of culture another view, in which not solely the scientific passion, the sheer desire to see things as they are, natural and proper in an intelligent being, appears as the ground of it.

[2] Charles de Montesquieu (1689-1755), the great French political writer of *De l'Esprit des Lois* (1748).

There is a view in which all the love of our neighbour, the impulses towards action, help, and beneficence, the desire for removing human error, clearing human confusion, and diminishing human misery, the noble aspiration to leave the world better and happier than we found it,—motives eminently such as are called social,—come in as part of the grounds of culture, and the main and pre-eminent part. Culture is then properly described not as having its origin in curiosity, but as having its origin in the love of perfection; it is *a study of perfection*. It moves by the force, not merely or primarily of the scientific passion for pure knowledge, but also of the moral and social passion for doing good. As, in the first view of it, we took for its worthy motto Montesquieu's words: "To render an intelligent being yet more intelligent!" so, in the second view of it, there is no better motto which it can have than these words of Bishop Wilson: "To make reason and the will of God prevail!" [3]

Only, whereas the passion for doing good is apt to be overhasty in determining what reason and the will of God say, because its turn is for acting rather than thinking and it wants to be beginning to act; and whereas it is apt to take its own conceptions, which proceed from its own state of development and share in all the imperfections and immaturities of this, for a basis of action; what distinguishes culture is, that it is possessed by the scientific passion as well as by the passion of doing good; that it demands worthy notions of reason and the will of God, and does not readily suffer its own crude conceptions to substitute themselves for them. And knowing that no action or institution can be salutary and stable which is not based on reason and the will of God, it is not so bent on acting and instituting, even with the great aim of diminishing human error and misery ever before its thoughts, but that it can remember that acting and instituting are of little use, unless we know how and what we ought to act and to institute.

This culture is more interesting and more far-reaching than that other, which is founded solely on the scientific passion for knowing. But it needs times of faith and ardour, times when the intellectual horizon is opening and widening all round us, to flourish in. And is not the close and

bounded intellectual horizon within which we have long lived and moved now lifting up, and are not new lights finding free passage to shine in upon us? For a long time there was no passage for them to make their way in upon us, and then it was of no use to think of adapting the world's action to them. Where was the hope of making reason and the will of God prevail among people who had a routine which they had christened reason and the will of God, in which they were inextricably bound, and beyond which they had no power of looking? But now the iron force of adhesion to the old routine,—social, political, religious,—has wonderfully yielded; the iron force of exclusion of all which is new has wonderfully yielded. The danger now is, not that people should obstinately refuse to allow anything but their old routine to pass for reason and the will of God, but either that they should allow some novelty or other to pass for these too easily, or else that they should underrate the importance of them altogether, and think it enough to follow action for its own sake, without troubling themselves to make reason and the will of God prevail therein. Now, then, is the moment for culture to be of service, culture which believes in making reason and the will of God prevail, believes in perfection, is the study and pursuit of perfection, and is no longer debarred, by a rigid invincible exclusion of whatever is new, from getting acceptance for its ideas, simply because they are new.

The moment this view of culture is seized, the moment it is regarded not solely as the endeavour to see things as they are, to draw towards a knowledge of the universal order which seems to be intended and aimed at in the world, and which it is a man's happiness to go along with or his misery to go counter to,—to learn, in short, the will of God,—the moment, I say, culture is considered not merely as the endeavour to *see* and *learn* this, but as the endeavour, also, to make it *prevail*, the moral, social, and beneficent character of culture becomes manifest. The mere endeavour to see and learn the truth for our own personal satisfaction is indeed a commencement for making it prevail, a preparing the way for this, which always serves this, and is wrongly, therefore, stamped with blame absolutely in itself and not only in its caricature and degeneration. But perhaps it

[3] Bishop Thomas Wilson.

has got stamped with blame, and disparaged with the dubious title of curiosity, because in comparison with this wider endeavour of such great and plain utility it looks selfish, petty, and unprofitable.

And religion, the greatest and most important of the efforts by which the human race has manifested its impulse to perfect itself,—religion, that voice of the deepest human experience,—does not only enjoin and sanction the aim which is the great aim of culture, the aim of setting ourselves to ascertain what perfection is and to make it prevail; but also, in determining generally in what human perfection consists, religion comes to a conclusion identical with that which culture,—culture seeking the determination of this question through *all* the voices of human experience which have been heard upon it, of art, science, poetry, philosophy, history, as well as of religion, in order to give a greater fulness and certainty to its solution,—likewise reaches. Religion says: *The kingdom of God is within you;* and culture, in like manner, places human perfection in an *internal* condition, in the growth and predominance of our humanity proper, as distinguished from our animality. It places it in the ever-increasing efficacy and in the general harmonious expansion of those gifts of thought and feeling, which make the peculiar dignity, wealth, and happiness of human nature. As I have said on a former occasion: "It is in making endless additions to itself, in the endless expansion of its powers, in endless growth in wisdom and beauty, that the spirit of the human race finds its ideal. To reach this ideal, culture is an indispensable aid, and that is the true value of culture." Not a having and a resting, but a growing and a becoming, is the character of perfection as culture conceives it; and here, too, it coincides with religion.

And because men are all members of one great whole, and the sympathy which is in human nature will not allow one member to be indifferent to the rest or to have a perfect welfare independent of the rest, the expansion of our humanity, to suit the idea of perfection which culture forms, must be a *general* expansion. Perfection, as culture conceives it, is not possible while the individual remains isolated. The individual is required, under pain of being stunted and enfeebled in his own development if he dis-

obeys, to carry others along with him in his march towards perfection, to be continually doing all he can to enlarge and increase the volume of the human stream sweeping thitherward. And here, once more, culture lays on us the same obligation as religion, which says, as Bishop Wilson has admirably put it, that "to promote the kingdom of God is to increase and hasten one's own happiness."

But, finally, perfection,—as culture from a thorough disinterested study of human nature and human experience learns to conceive it,—is a harmonious expansion of *all* the powers which make the beauty and worth of human nature, and is not consistent with the over-development of any one power at the expense of the rest. Here culture goes beyond religion, as religion is generally conceived by us.

If culture, then, is a study of perfection, and of harmonious perfection, general perfection, and perfection which consists in becoming something rather than in having something, in an inward condition of the mind and spirit, not in an outward set of circumstances,—it is clear that culture, instead of being the frivolous and useless thing which Mr. Bright, and Mr. Frederic Harrison, and many other Liberals are apt to call it, has a very important function to fulfil for mankind. And this function is particularly important in our modern world, of which the whole civilisation is, to a much greater degree than the civilisation of Greece and Rome, mechanical and external, and tends constantly to become more so. But above all in our own country has culture a weighty part to perform, because here that mechanical character, which civilisation tends to take everywhere, is shown in the most eminent degree. Indeed nearly all the characters of perfection, as culture teaches us to fix them, meet in this country with some powerful tendency which thwarts them and sets them at defiance. The idea of perfection as an *inward* condition of the mind and spirit is at variance with the mechanical and material civilisation in esteem with us, and nowhere, as I have said, so much in esteem as with us. The idea of perfection as a *general* expansion of the human family is at variance with our strong individualism, our hatred of all limits to the unrestrained swing of the individual's personality, our maxim of "every man for himself."

Above all, the idea of perfection as a *harmonious* expansion of human nature is at variance with our want of flexibility, with our inaptitude for seeing more than one side of a thing, with our intense energetic absorption in the particular pursuit we happen to be following. So culture has a rough task to achieve in this country. Its preachers have, and are likely long to have, a hard time of it, and they will much oftener be regarded, for a great while to come, as elegant or spurious Jeremiahs than as friends and bene-factors. That, however, will not prevent their doing in the end good service if they per-severe. And, meanwhile, the mode of action they have to pursue, and the sort of habits they must fight against, ought to be made quite clear for every one to see, who may be willing to look at the matter attentively and dispassionately.

Faith in machinery is, I said, our besetting danger; often in machinery most absurdly dis-proportioned to the end which the machinery, if it is to do any good at all, is to serve; but always in machinery, as if it had a value in and for itself. What is freedom but machinery? what is population but machinery? what is coal but machinery? what are railroads but machinery? what is wealth but machinery? what are, even, religious organisations but machinery? Now almost every voice in England is accustomed to speak of these things as if they were precious ends in themselves, and therefore had some of the characters of perfection indisputably joined to them. I have before now noticed Mr. Roe-buck's stock argument for proving the greatness and happiness of England as she is, and for quite stopping the mouths of all gainsayers.[4] Mr. Roebuck is never weary of reiterating this argument of his, so I do not know why I should be weary of noticing it. "May not every man in England say what he likes?"—Mr. Roebuck perpetually asks; and that, he thinks, is quite sufficient, and when every man may say what he likes, our aspirations ought to be satisfied. But the aspirations of culture, which is the study of perfection, are not satisfied, unless what men say, when they may say what they like, is worth saying,—has good in it, and more good than bad. In the same way the *Times*, replying to some foreign strictures on the dress, looks and behaviour of the English abroad, urges that the English ideal is that every one should be free to do and to look just as he likes. But culture indefatigably tries, not to make what each raw person may like the rule by which he fashions himself; but to draw ever nearer to a sense of what is indeed beautiful, graceful, and becoming, and to get the raw person to like that.

And in the same way with respect to railroads and coal. Every one must have observed the strange language current during the late dis-cussions as to the possible failures of our sup-plies of coal. Our coal, thousands of peope were saying, is the real basis of our national great-ness; if our coal runs short, there is an end of the greatness of England. But what *is* greatness? —culture makes us ask. Greatness is a spiritual condition worthy to excite love, interest, and ad-miration; and the outward proof of possessing greatness is that we excite love, interest, and admiration. If England were swallowed up by the sea to-morrow, which of the two, a hundred years hence, would most excite the love, interest, and admiration of mankind,—would most, there-fore, show the evidences of having possessed greatness,—the England of the last twenty years, or the England of Elizabeth, of a time of splen-did spiritual effort, but when our coal, and our industrial operations depending on coal, were very little developed? Well, then, what an un-sound habit of mind it must be which makes us talk of things like coal or iron as constituting the greatness of England, and how salutary a friend is culture, bent on seeing things as they are, and thus dissipating delusions of this kind and fixing standards of perfection that are real!

Wealth, again, that end to which our prodi-gious works for material avantage are directed, —the commonest of commonplaces tells us how men are always apt to regard wealth as a pre-cious end in itself; and certainly they have never been so apt thus to regard it as they are in England at the present time. Never did people believe anything more firmly than nine English-men out of ten at the present day believe that our greatness and welfare are proved by our being so very rich. Now, the use of culture is that it helps us, by means of its spiritual stand-ard of perfection, to regard wealth as but ma-chinery, and not only to say as a matter of words that we regard wealth as but machinery,

[4] See, for example, *On the Function of Criticism,* above, p. 459.

but really to perceive and feel that it is so. If it were not for this purging effect wrought upon our minds by culture, the whole world, the future as well as the present, would inevitably belong to the Philistines. The people who believe most that our greatness and welfare are proved by our being very rich, and who most give their lives and thoughts to becoming rich, are just the very people whom we call Philistines. Culture says: "Consider these people, then, their way of life, their habits, their manners, the very tones of their voice; look at them attentively; observe the literature they read, the things which give them pleasure, the words which come forth out of their mouths, the thoughts which make the furniture of their minds; would any amount of wealth be worth having with the condition that one was to become just like these people by having it?" And thus culture begets a dissatisfaction which is of the highest possible value in stemming the common tide of men's thoughts in a wealthy and industrial community, and which saves the future, as one may hope, from being vulgarised, even if it cannot save the present.

Population, again, and bodily health and vigour, are things which are nowhere treated in such an unintelligent, misleading, exaggerated way as in England. Both are really machinery; yet how many people all around us do we see rest in them and fail to look beyond them! Why, one has heard people, fresh from reading certain articles of the *Times* on the Registrar-General's returns of marriages and births in this country, who would talk of our large English families in quite a solemn strain, as if they had something in itself beautiful, elevating, and meritorious in them; as if the British Philistine would have only to present himself before the Great Judge with his twelve children, in order to be received among the sheep as a matter of right!

But bodily health and vigour, it may be said, are not to be classed with wealth and population as mere machinery; they have a more real and essential value. True; but only as they are more intimately connected with a perfect spiritual condition than wealth or population are. The moment we disjoin them from the idea of a perfect spiritual condition, and pursue them, as we do pursue them, for their own sake and as ends in themselves, our worship of them becomes as

mere worship of machinery, as our worship of wealth or population, and as unintelligent and vulgarising a worship as that is. Every one with anything like an adequate idea of human perfection has distinctly marked this subordination to higher and spiritual ends of the cultivation of bodily vigour and activity. "Bodily exercise profiteth little; but godliness is profitable unto all things," says the author of the Epistle to Timothy. And the utilitarian Franklin says just as explicitly:—"Eat and drink such an exact quantity as suits the constitution of thy body, *in reference to the services of the mind*." [5] But the point of view of culture, keeping the mark of human perfection simply and broadly in view, and not assigning to this perfection, as religion or utilitarianism assigns to it, a special and limited character, this point of view, I say, of culture is best given by these words of Epictetus: —"It is a sign of ἀφυΐα," says he,—that is, of a nature not finely tempered,—"to give yourselves up to things which relate to the body; to make, for instance, a great fuss about exercise, a great fuss about eating, a great fuss about drinking, a great fuss about walking, a great fuss about riding. All these things ought to be done merely by the way: the formation of the spirit and character must be our real concern." [6] This is admirable; and, indeed, the Greek word εὐφυΐα, a finely tempered nature, gives exactly the notion of perfection as culture brings us to conceive it: a harmonious perfection, a perfection in which the characters of beauty and intelligence are both present, which unites "the two noblest of things,"—as Swift, who of one of the two, at any rate, had himself all too little, most happily calls them in his *Battle of the Books*,—"the two noblest of things, *sweetness and light*." [7] The εὐφυής is the man who tends towards sweetness and light; the ἀφυής, on the other hand, is our Philistine. The immense spiritual significance of the Greeks is due to their having been inspired with this central and happy idea of the essential character of human perfection; and Mr. Bright's misconception of culture, as a smattering of Greek and Latin, comes itself, after all, from this wonderful significance of the

---

[5] I *Timothy* 4:8. Franklin's *Poor Richard's Almanack*, December, 1742.

[6] *Encheirodion*, Ch. 41.

[7] See above, p. 9.

Greeks having affected the very machinery of our education, and is in itself a kind of homage to it.

In thus making sweetness and light to be characters of perfection, culture is of like spirit with poetry, follows one law with poetry. Far more than on our freedom, our population, and our industrialism, many amongst us rely upon our religious organisations to save us. I have called religion a yet more important manifestation of human nature than poetry, because it has worked on a broader scale for perfection, and with greater masses of men. But the idea of beauty and of a human nature perfect on all its sides, which is the dominant idea of poetry, is a true and invaluable idea, though it has not yet had the success that the idea of conquering the obvious faults of our animality, and of a human nature perfect on the moral side,—which is the dominant idea of religion,—has been enabled to have; and it is destined, adding to itself the religious idea of a devout energy, to transform and govern the other.

The best art and poetry of the Greeks, in which religion and poetry are one, in which the idea of beauty and of a human nature perfect on all sides adds to itself a religious and devout energy, and works in the strength of that, is on this account of such surpassing interest and instructiveness for us, though it was,—as, having regard to the human race in general, and, indeed, having regard to the Greeks themselves, we must own,—a premature attempt, an attempt which for success needed the moral and religious fibre in humanity to be more braced and developed than it had yet been. But Greece did not err in having the idea of beauty, harmony, and complete human perfection, so present and paramount. It is impossible to have this idea too present and paramount; only, the moral fibre must be braced too. And we, because we have braced the moral fibre, are not on that account in the right way, if at the same time the idea of beauty, harmony, and complete human perfection, is wanting or misapprehended amongst us; and evidently it *is* wanting or misapprehended at present. And when we rely as we do on our religious organisations, which in themselves do not and cannot give us this idea, and think we have done enough if we make them spread and prevail, then, I say, we fall into our common fault of overvaluing machinery. . . .

Culture tends always thus to deal with the men of a system, of disciples, of a school; with men like Comte,[8] or the late Mr. Buckle,[9] or Mr. Mill. However much it may find to admire in these personages, or in some of them, it nevertheless remembers the text: "Be not ye called Rabbi!" and it soon passes on from any Rabbi. But Jacobinism loves a Rabbi; it does not want to pass on from its Rabbi in pursuit of a future and still unreached perfection; it wants its Rabbi and his ideas to stand for perfection, that they may with the more authority recast the world; and for Jacobinism, therefore, culture,—eternally passing onwards and seeking,—is an impertinence and an offence. But culture, just because it resists this tendency of Jacobinism to impose on us a man with limitations and errors of his own along with the true ideas of which he is the organ, really does the world and Jacobinism itself a service.

So, too, Jacobinism, in its fierce hatred of the past and of those whom it makes liable for the sins of the past, cannot away with the inexhaustible indulgence proper to culture, the consideration of circumstances, the severe judgment of actions joined to the merciful judgment of persons. "The man of culture is in politics," cries Mr. Frederic Harrison, "one of the poorest mortals alive!" Mr. Frederic Harrison wants to be doing business, and he complains that the man of culture stops him with a "turn for small fault-finding, love of selfish ease, and indecision in action." Of what use is culture, he asks, except for "a critic of new books or a professor of *belles lettres?*" Why, it is of use because, in presence of the fierce exasperation which breathes, or rather, I may say, hisses through the whole production in which Mr. Frederic Harrison asks that question, it reminds us that the perfection of human nature is sweetness and light. It is of use because, like religion,—that other effort after perfection,—it testifies that,

8 Auguste Comte (1798-1847), French philosopher who founded a movement called "Positivism" (abandoning the inquiry into final causes as useless, and concentrating solely on concrete data).

9 Henry Thomas Buckle, whose vigorous and suggestive *History of Civilization in England* (1857-61) attempted to base the study of history on scientific principles popular at the time.

where bitter envying and strife are, there is confusion and every evil work.

The pursuit of perfection, then, is the pursuit of sweetness and light. He who works for sweetness and light, works to make reason and the will of God prevail. He who works for machinery, he who works for hatred, works only for confusion. Culture looks beyond machinery, culture hates hatred; culture has one great passion, the passion for sweetness and light. It has one even yet greater!—the passion for making them *prevail*. It is not satisfied till we *all* come to a perfect man; it knows that the sweetness and light of the few must be imperfect until the raw and unkindled masses of humanity are touched with sweetness and light. If I have not shrunk from saying that we must work for sweetness and light, so neither have I shrunk from saying that we must have a broad basis, must have sweetness and light for as many as possible. Again and again I have insisted how those are the happy moments of humanity, how those are the marking epochs of a people's life, how those are the flowering times for literature and art and all the creative power of genius, when there is a *national* glow of life and thought, when the whole of society is in the fullest measure permeated by thought, sensible to beauty, intelligent and alive. Only it must be *real* thought and *real* beauty; *real* sweetness and *real* light. Plenty of people will try to give the masses, as they call them, an intellectual food prepared and adapted in the way they think proper for the actual condition of the masses. The ordinary popular literature is an example of this way of working on the masses. Plenty of people will try to indoctrinate the masses with the set of ideas and judgments constituting the creed of their own profession or party. Our religious and political organisations give an example of this way of working on the masses. I condemn neither way; but culture works differently. It does not try to teach down to the level of inferior classes; it does not try to win them for this or that sect of its own, with ready-made judgments and watchwords. It seeks to do away with classes; to make the best that has been thought and known in the world current everywhere; to make all men live in an atmosphere of sweetness and light, where they may use ideas, as it uses them itself, freely, —nourished, and not bound by them.

This is the *social idea*; and the men of culture are the true apostles of equality. The great men of culture are those who have had a passion for diffusing, for making prevail, for carrying from one end of society to the other, the best knowledge, the best ideas of their time; who have laboured to divest knowledge of all that was harsh, uncouth, difficult, abstract, professional, exclusive; to humanise it, to make it efficient outside the clique of the cultivated and learned, yet still remaining the *best* knowledge and thought of the time, and a true source, therefore, of sweetness and light. Such a man was Abelard in the Middle Ages, in spite of all his imperfections; and thence the boundless emotion and enthusiasm which Abelard excited. Such were Lessing and Herder in Germany, at the end of the last century; and their services to Germany were in this way inestimably precious. Generations will pass, and literary monuments will accumulate, and works far more perfect than the works of Lessing and Herder will be produced in Germany; and yet the names of these two men will fill a German with a reverence and enthusiasm such as the names of the most gifted masters will hardly awaken. And why? Because they *humanised* knowledge; because they broadened the basis of life and intelligence; because they worked powerfully to diffuse sweetness and light, to make reason and the will of God prevail. With Saint Augustine they said: "Let us not leave thee alone to make in the secret of thy knowledge, as thou didst before the creation of the firmament, the division of light from darkness; let the children of thy spirit, placed in their firmament, make their light shine upon the earth, mark the division of night and day, and announce the revolution of the times; for the old order is passed, and the new arises; the night is spent, the day is come forth; and thou shalt crown the year with thy blessing, when thou shalt send forth labourers into thy harvest sown by other hands than theirs; when thou shalt send forth new labourers to new seed-times, whereof the harvest shall be not yet."

Wordsworth

I REMEMBER hearing Lord Macaulay say, after Wordsworth's death, when subscriptions were being collected to found a memorial of him, that ten years earlier more money could have been raised in Cambridge alone, to do honour to Wordsworth, than was now raised all through the country. Lord Macaulay had, as we know, his own heightened and telling way of putting things, and we must always make allowance for it. But probably it is true that Wordsworth has never, either before or since, been so accepted and popular, so established in possession of the minds of all who profess to care for poetry, as he was between the years 1830 and 1840, and at Cambridge. From the very first, no doubt, he had his believers and witnesses. But I have myself heard him declare that, for he knew not how many years, his poetry had never brought him in enough to buy his shoe-strings. The poetry-reading public was very slow to recognise him, and was very easily drawn away from him. Scott effaced him with this public, Byron effaced him.

The death of Byron seemed, however, to make an opening for Wordsworth. Scott, who had for some time ceased to produce poetry himself, and stood before the public as a great novelist; Scott, too genuine himself not to feel the profound genuineness of Wordsworth, and with an instinctive recognition of his firm hold on nature and of his local truth, always admired him sincerely, and praised him generously. The influence of Coleridge upon young men of ability was then powerful, and was still gathering strength; this influence told entirely in favour of Wordsworth's poetry. Cambridge was a place where Coleridge's influence had great action, and where Wordsworth's poetry, therefore, flourished especially. But even amongst the general public its sale grew large, the eminence of its author was widely recognised, and Rydal Mount [1] became an object of pilgrimage. I re-member Wordsworth relating how one of the pilgrims, a clergyman, asked him if he had ever written anything besides the *Guide to the Lakes*. Yes, he answered modestly, he had written verses. Not every pilgrim was a reader, but the vogue was established, and the stream of pilgrims came.

Mr. Tennyson's decisive appearance dates from 1842. One cannot say that he effaced Wordsworth as Scott and Byron had effaced him. The poetry of Wordsworth had been so long before the public, the suffrage of good judges was so steady and so strong in its favour, that by 1842 the verdict of posterity, one may almost say, had been already pronounced, and Wordsworth's English fame was secure. But the vogue, the ear and applause of the great body of poetry-readers, never quite thoroughly perhaps his, he gradually lost more and more, and Mr. Tennyson gained them. Mr. Tennyson drew to himself, and away from Wordsworth, the poetry-reading public, and the new generations. Even in 1850, when Wordsworth died, this diminution of popularity was visible, and occasioned the remark of Lord Macaulay which I quoted at starting.

The diminution has continued. The influence of Coleridge has waned, and Wordsworth's poetry can no longer draw succour from this ally. The poetry has not, however, wanted eulogists; and it may be said to have brought its eulogists luck, for almost every one who has praised Wordsworth's poetry has praised it well. But the public has remained cold, or, at least, undetermined. Even the abundance of Mr. Palgrave's fine and skilfully chosen specimens of Wordsworth, in the *Golden Treasury*, surprised many readers, and gave offence to not a few. To tenth-rate critics and compilers, for whom any violent shock to the public taste would be a temerity not to be risked, it is still quite permissible to speak of Wordsworth's poetry, not only with ignorance, but with impertinence. On the Continent he is almost unknown.

I cannot think, then, that Wordsworth has, up to this time, at all obtained his deserts. "Glory,"

Wordsworth. First printed as an introduction to Arnold's selection, *Poems of Wordsworth* (1879); later included in *Essays in Criticism, Second Series* (1888).

[1] Wordsworth's home in Grasmere.

said M. Renan the other day, "glory after all is the thing which has the best chance of not being altogether vanity." Wordsworth was a homely man, and himself would certainly never have thought of talking of glory as that which, after all, has the best chance of not being altogether vanity. Yet we may well allow that few things are less vain than *real* glory. Let us conceive of the whole group of civilised nations as being, for intellectual and spiritual purposes, one great confederation, bound to a joint action and working towards a common result; a confederation whose members have a due knowledge both of the past, out of which they all proceed, and of one another. This was the ideal of Goethe, and it is an ideal which will impose itself upon the thoughts of our modern societies more and more. Then to be recognised by the verdict of such a confederation as a master, or even as a seriously and eminently worthy workman, in one's own line of intellectual or spiritual activity, is indeed glory; a glory which it would be difficult to rate too highly. For what could be more beneficent, more salutary? The world is forwarded by having its attention fixed on the best things; and here is a tribunal, free from all suspicion of national and provincial partiality, putting a stamp on the best things, and recommending them for general honour and acceptance. A nation, again, is furthered by recognition of its real gifts and successes; it is encouraged to develop them further. And here is an honest verdict, telling us which of our supposed successes are really, in the judgment of the great impartial world, and not in our own private judgment only, successes, and which are not.

It is so easy to feel pride and satisfaction in one's own things, so hard to make sure that one is right in feeling it! We have a great empire. But so had Nebuchadnezzar. We extol the "unrivalled happiness" of our national civilisation.[2] But then comes a candid friend, and remarks that our upper class is materialised, our middle class vulgarised, and our lower class brutalised. We are proud of our painting, our music. But we find that in the judgment of other people our painting is questionable, and our music non-existent. We are proud of our men of science. And here it turns out that the world is with us;

we find that in the judgment of other people, too, Newton among the dead, and Mr. Darwin among the living, hold as high a place as they hold in our national opinion.

Finally, we are proud of our poets and poetry. Now poetry is nothing less than the most perfect speech of man, that in which he comes nearest to being able to utter the truth. It is no small thing, therefore, to succeed eminently in poetry. And so much is required for duly estimating success here, that about poetry it is perhaps hardest to arrive at a sure general verdict, and takes longest. Meanwhile, our own conviction of the superiority of our national poets is not decisive, is almost certain to be mingled, as we see constantly in English eulogy of Shakespeare, with much of provincial infatuation. And we know what was the opinion current amongst our neighbours the French—people of taste, acuteness, and quick literary tact—not a hundred years ago, about our great poets. The old *Biographie Universelle* notices the pretension of the English to a place for their poets among the chief poets of the world, and says that this is a pretension which to no one but an Englishman can ever seem admissible. And the scornful, disparaging things said by foreigners about Shakespeare and Milton, and about our national over-estimate of them, have been often quoted, and will be in every one's remembrance.

A great change has taken place, and Shakespeare is now generally recognised, even in France, as one of the greatest of poets. Yes, some anti-Gallican [3] cynic will say, the French rank him with Corneille and with Victor Hugo! But let me have the pleasure of quoting a sentence about Shakespeare, which I met with by accident not long ago in the *Correspondant,* a French review which not a dozen English people, I suppose, look at. The writer is praising Shakespeare's prose. With Shakespeare, he says, "prose comes in whenever the subject, being more familiar, is unsuited to the majestic English iambic." And he goes on: "Shakespeare is the king of poetic rhythm and style, as well as the king of the realm of thought; along with his dazzling prose, Shakespeare has succeeded in giving us the most varied, the most harmonious verse which has ever sounded upon the human

---

[2] See Arnold's quotation from John Roebuck in the *Function of Criticism,* above, p. 459.

[3] Anti-French.

ear since the verse of the Greeks." M. Henry Cochin, the writer of this sentence, deserves our gratitude for it; it would not be easy to praise Shakespeare, in a single sentence, more justly. And when a foreigner and a Frenchman writes thus of Shakespeare, and when Goethe says of Milton, in whom there was so much to repel Goethe rather than to attract him, that "nothing has been ever done so entirely in the sense of the Greeks as *Samson Agonistes*," and that "Milton is in very truth a poet whom we must treat with all reverence," then we understand what constitutes a European recognition of poets and poetry as contradistinguished from a merely national recognition, and that in favour both of Milton and of Shakespeare the judgment of the high court of appeal has finally gone.

I come back to M. Renan's praise of glory, from which I started. Yes, real glory is a most serious thing, glory authenticated by the Amphictyonic Court[4] of final appeal, definitive glory. And even for poets and poetry, long and difficult as may be the process of arriving at the right award, the right award comes at last, the definitive glory rests where it is deserved. Every establishment of such a real glory is good and wholesome for mankind at large, good and wholesome for the nation which produced the poet crowned with it. To the poet himself it can seldom do harm; for he, poor man, is in his grave, probably, long before his glory crowns him.

Wordsworth has been in his grave for some thirty years, and certainly his lovers and admirers cannot flatter themselves that this great and steady light of glory as yet shines over him. He is not fully recognised at home; he is not recognised at all abroad. Yet I firmly believe that the poetical performance of Wordsworth is, after that of Shakespeare and Milton, of which all the world now recognises the worth, undoubtedly the most considerable in our language from the Elizabethan age to the present time. Chaucer is anterior; and on other grounds, too, he cannot well be brought into the comparison. But taking the roll of our chief poetical names, besides Shakespeare and Milton, from the age of Elizabeth downwards, and going through it,—Spenser, Dryden, Pope, Gray, Goldsmith, Cowper, Burns,

[4] The Court of members from the Greek Amphictyony, or league of city-states.

Coleridge, Scott, Campbell, Moore, Byron, Shelley, Keats (I mention those only who are dead), —I think it certain that Wordsworth's name deserves to stand, and will finally stand, above them all. Several of the poets named have gifts and excellences which Wordsworth has not. But taking the performance of each as a whole, I say that Wordsworth seems to me to have left a body of poetical work superior in power, in interest, in the qualities which give enduring freshness, to that which any one of the others has left.

But this is not enough to say. I think it certain, further, that if we take the chief poetical names of the Continent since the death of Molière, and, omitting Goethe, confront the remaining names with that of Wordsworth, the result is the same. Let us take Klopstock, Lessing, Schiller, Uhland, Rückert, and Heine for Germany; Filicaia, Alfieri, Manzoni, and Leopardi for Italy; Racine, Boileau, Voltaire, André Chenier, Béranger, Lamartine, Musset, M. Victor Hugo (he has been so long celebrated that although he still lives I may be permitted to name him) for France. Several of these, again, have evidently gifts and excellences to which Wordsworth can make no pretension. But in real poetical achievement it seems to me indubitable that to Wordsworth, here again, belongs the palm. It seems to me that Wordsworth has left behind him a body of poetical work which wears, and will wear, better on the whole than the performance of any one of these personages, so far more brilliant and celebrated, most of them, than the homely poet of Rydal. Wordsworth's performance in poetry is on the whole, in power, in interest, in the qualities which give enduring freshness, superior to theirs.

This is a high claim to make for Wordsworth. But if it is a just claim, if Wordsworth's place among the poets who have appeared in the last two or three centuries is after Shakespeare, Molière, Milton, Goethe, indeed, but before all the rest, then in time Wordsworth will have his due. We shall recognise him in his place, as we recognise Shakespeare and Milton; and not only we ourselves shall recognise him, but he will be recognised by Europe also. Meanwhile, those who recognise him already may do well, perhaps, to ask themselves whether there are not in the case of Wordsworth certain special obstacles which hinder or delay his due recognition by others, and whether these obstacles are not in some measure removable.

The Excursion and *The Prelude*, his poems of greatest bulk, are by no means Wordsworth's best work. His best work is in his shorter pieces, and many indeed are there of these which are of first-rate excellence. But in his seven volumes the pieces of high merit are mingled with a mass of pieces very inferior to them; so inferior to them that it seems wonderful how the same poet should have produced both. Shakespeare frequently has lines and passages in a strain quite false, and which are entirely unworthy of him. But one can imagine his smiling if one could meet him in the Elysian Fields and tell him so; smiling and replying that he knew it perfectly well himself, and what did it matter? But with Wordsworth the case is different. Work altogether inferior, work quite uninspired, flat and dull, is produced by him with evident unconsciousness of its defects, and he presents it to us with the same faith and seriousness as his best work. Now a drama or an epic fill the mind, and one does not look beyond them; but in a collection of short pieces the impression made by one piece requires to be continued and sustained by the piece following. In reading Wordsworth the impression made by one of his fine pieces is too often dulled and spoiled by a very inferior piece coming after it.

Wordsworth composed verses during a space of some sixty years; and it is no exaggeration to say that within one single decade of those years, between 1798 and 1808, almost all his really first-rate work was produced. A mass of inferior work remains, work done before and after this golden prime, imbedding the first-rate work and clogging it, obstructing our approach to it, chilling, not unfrequently, the high-wrought mood with which we leave it. To be recognised far and wide as a great poet, to be possible and receivable as a classic, Wordsworth needs to be relieved of a great deal of the poetical baggage which now encumbers him. To administer this relief is indispensable, unless he is to continue to be a poet for the few only,—a poet valued far below his real worth by the world.

There is another thing. Wordsworth classified his poems not according to any commonly received plan of arrangement, but according to a scheme of mental physiology. He has poems of the fancy, poems of the imagination, poems of sentiment and reflection, and so on. His categories are ingenious but far-fetched, and the result of his employment of them is unsatisfactory. Poems are separated one from another which possess a kinship of subject or of treatment far more vital and deep than the supposed unity of mental origin, which was Wordsworth's reason for joining them with others.

The tact of the Greeks in matters of this kind was infallible. We may rely upon it that we shall not improve upon the classification adopted by the Greeks for kinds of poetry; that their categories of epic, dramatic, lyric, and so forth, have a natural propriety, and should be adhered to. It may sometimes seem doubtful to which of two categories a poem belongs; whether this or that poem is to be called, for instance, narrative or lyric, lyric or elegiac. But there is to be found in every good poem a strain, a predominant note, which determines the poem as belonging to one of these kinds rather than the other; and here is the best proof of the value of the classification, and of the advantage of adhering to it. Wordsworth's poems will never produce their due effect until they are freed from their present artificial arrangement, and grouped more naturally.

Disengaged from the quantity of inferior work which now obscures them, the best poems of Wordsworth, I hear many people say, would indeed stand out in great beauty, but they would prove to be very few in number, scarcely more than half a dozen. I maintain, on the other hand, that what strikes me with admiration, what establishes in my opinion Wordsworth's superiority, is the great and ample body of powerful work which remains to him, even after all his inferior work has been cleared away. He gives us so much to rest upon, so much which communicates his spirit and engages ours!

This is of very great importance. If it were a comparison of single pieces, or of three or four pieces, by each poet, I do not say that Wordsworth would stand decisively above Gray, or Burns, or Coleridge, or Keats, or Manzoni, or Heine. It is in his ampler body of powerful work that I find his superiority. His good work itself, his work which counts, is not all of it, of course, of equal value. Some kinds of poetry are in themselves lower kinds than others. The ballad kind is a lower kind; the didactic kind, still more, is a lower kind. Poetry of this latter sort counts, too, sometimes, by its biographical interest partly, not by its poetical interest pure and simple; but then this can only be when the poet producing it has the power and importance of Wordsworth, a power and importance which he assuredly did not establish by such didactic poetry alone. Altogether, it is, I say, by the great body of powerful and significant work which remains to him, after every reduction and deduction has been made, that Wordsworth's superiority is proved.

To exhibit this body of Wordsworth's best work, to clear away obstructions from around it, and to let it speak for itself, is what every lover of Wordsworth should desire. Until this has been done, Wordsworth, whom we, to whom he is dear, all of us know and feel to be so great a poet, has not had a fair chance before the world. When once it has been done, he will make his way best, not by our advocacy of him, but by his own worth and power. We may safely leave him to make his way thus, we who believe that a superior worth and power in poetry finds in mankind a sense responsive to it and disposed at last to recognise it. Yet at the outset, before he has been duly known and recognised, we may do Wordsworth a service, perhaps, by indicating in what his superior power and worth will be found to consist, and in what it will not.

Long ago, in speaking of Homer, I said that the noble and profound application of ideas to life is the most essential part of poetic greatness. I said that a great poet receives his distinctive character of superiority from his application, under the conditions immutably fixed by the laws of poetic beauty and poetic truth, from his application, I say, to his subject, whatever it may be, of the ideas

On man, on nature, and on human life,[5]

which he has acquired for himself. The line quoted is Wordsworth's own; and his superiority arises from his powerful use, in his best pieces, his powerful application to his subject, of ideas "on man, on nature, and on human life."

Voltaire, with his signal acuteness, most truly remarked that "no nation has treated in poetry moral ideas with more energy and depth than

[5] Wordsworth's *Recluse*, l. 754.

the English nation." And he adds: "There, it seems to me, is the great merit of the English poets." Voltaire does not mean, by "treating in poetry moral ideas," the composing moral and didactic poems;—that brings us but a very little way in poetry. He means just the same thing as was meant when I spoke above "of the noble and profound application of ideas to life"; and he means the application of these ideas under the conditions fixed for us by the laws of poetic beauty and poetic truth. If it is said that to call these ideas *moral* ideas is to introduce a strong and injurious limitation, I answer that it is to do nothing of the kind, because moral ideas are really so main a part of human life. The question, *how to live*, is itself a moral idea; and it is the question which most interests every man, and with which, in some way or other, he is perpetually occupied. A large sense is of course to be given to the term *moral*. Whatever bears upon the question, "how to live," comes under it.

Nor love thy life, nor hate; but, what thou liv'st,
Live well; how long or short, permit to heaven. [6]

In those fine lines Milton utters, as every one at once perceives, a moral idea. Yes, but so too, when Keats consoles the forward-bending lover on the Grecian Urn, the lover arrested and presented in immortal relief by the sculptor's hand before he can kiss, with the line,

Forever wilt thou love, and she be fair—

he utters a moral idea. When Shakespeare says, that

We are such stuff
As dreams are made of, and our little life
Is rounded with a sleep,[7]

he utters a moral idea.

Voltaire was right in thinking that the energetic and profound treatment of moral ideas, in this large sense, is what distinguishes the English poetry. He sincerely meant praise, not dispraise or hint of limitation; and they err who suppose that poetic limitation is a necessary consequence of the fact, the fact being granted as Voltaire states it. If what distinguishes the greatest poets is their powerful and profound application of ideas to life, which surely no good critic

[6] *Paradise Lost*, XI, 553-54.
[7] Keats, *Ode on a Grecian Urn*, l. 20; Shakespeare, *Tempest*, IV, 1, 156-58.

will deny, then to prefix to the term ideas here the term moral makes hardly any difference, because human life itself is in so preponderating a degree moral.

It is important, therefore, to hold fast to this: that poetry is at bottom a criticism of life; that the greatness of a poet lies in his powerful and beautiful application of ideas to life,—to the question: How to live. Morals are often treated in a narrow and false fashion; they are bound up with systems of thought and belief which have had their day; they are fallen into the hands of pedants and professional dealers; they grow tiresome to some of us. We find attraction, at times, even in a poetry of revolt against them; in a poetry which might take for its motto Omar Khayyam's words: "Let us make up in the tavern for the time which we have wasted in the mosque." Or we find attractions in a poetry indifferent to them; in a poetry where the contents may be what they will, but where the form is studied and exquisite. We delude ourselves in either case; and the best cure for our delusion is to let our minds rest upon that great and inexhaustible word *life*, until we learn to enter into its meaning. A poetry of revolt against moral ideas is a poetry of revolt against *life;* a poetry of indifference towards moral ideas is a poetry of indifference towards *life*.

Epictetus had a happy figure for things like the play of the senses, or literary form and finish, or argumentative ingenuity, in comparison with "the best and master thing" for us, as he called it, the concern, how to live. Some people were afraid of them, he said, or they disliked and undervalued them. Such people were wrong; they were unthankful or cowardly. But the things might also be over-prized, and treated as final when they are not. They bear to life the relation which inns bear to home. "As if a man, journeying home, and finding a nice inn on the road, and liking it, were to stay for ever at the inn! Man, thou hast forgotten thine object; thy journey was not *to* this, but *through* this. 'But this inn is taking.' And how many other inns, too, are taking, and how many fields and meadows! but as places of passage merely. You have an object, which is this: to get home, to do your duty to your family, friends, and fellow-countrymen, to attain inward freedom, serenity, happiness, contentment. Style takes your fancy, argu-

ing takes your fancy, and you forget your home and want to make your abode with them and to stay with them, on the plea that they are taking. Who denies that they are taking? but as places of passage, as inns. And when I say this, you suppose me to be attacking the care for style, the care for argument. I am not; I attack the resting in them, the not looking to the end which is beyond them."

Now, when we come across a poet like Théophile Gautier, we have a poet who has taken up his abode at an inn, and never got farther. There may be inducements to this or that one of us, at this or that moment, to find delight in him, to cleave to him; but after all, we do not change the truth about him,—we only stay ourselves in his inn along with him. And when we come across a poet like Wordsworth, who sings

Of truth, of grandeur, beauty, love and hope.
And melancholy fear subdued by faith,
Of blessed consolations in distress,
Of moral strength and intellectual power,
Of joy in widest commonalty spread—[8]

then we have a poet intent on "the best and master thing," and who prosecutes his journey home. We say, for brevity's sake, that he deals with *life*, because he deals with that in which life really consists. This is what Voltaire means to praise in the English poets,—this dealing with what is really life. But always it is the mark of the greatest poets that they deal with it; and to say that the English poets are remarkable for dealing with it, is only another way of saying, what is true, that in poetry the English genius has especially shown its power.

Wordsworth deals with it, and his greatness lies in his dealing with it so powerfully. I have named a number of celebrated poets above all of whom he, in my opinion, deserves to be placed. He is to be placed above poets like Voltaire, Dryden, Pope, Lessing, Schiller, because these famous personages, with a thousand gifts and merits, never, or scarcely ever, attain the distinctive accent and utterance of the high and genuine poets—

Quique pii vates et Phoebo digna locuti,[9]

---

[8] *Recluse*, ll. 767-71.
[9] "The pious poets who utter what is worthy of Apollo" (*Aeneid*, VI, 662).

at all. Burns, Keats, Heine, not to speak of others in our list, have this accent;—who can doubt it? And at the same time they have treasures of humour, felicity, passion, for which in Wordsworth we shall look in vain. Where, then, is Wordsworth's superiority? It is here; he deals with more of *life* than they do; he deals with *life*, as a whole, more powerfully.

No Wordsworthian will doubt this. Nay, the fervent Wordsworthian will add, as Mr. Leslie Stephen does, that Wordsworth's poetry is precious because his philosophy is sound; that his "ethical system is as distinctive and capable of exposition as Bishop Butler's"; that his poetry is informed by ideas which "fall spontaneously into a scientific system of thought." But we must be on our guard against the Wordsworthians, if we want to secure for Wordsworth his due rank as a poet. The Wordsworthians are apt to praise him for the wrong things, and to lay far too much stress upon what they call his philosophy. His poetry is the reality, his philosophy,—so far, at least, as it may put on the form and habit of "a scientific system of thought," and the more that it puts them on,—is illusion. Perhaps we shall one day learn to make this proposition general, and to say: Poetry is the reality, philosophy the illusion. But in Wordsworth's case, at any rate, we cannot do him justice until we dismiss his formal philosophy.

The Excursion abounds with philosophy, and therefore *The Excursion* is to the Wordsworthian what it never can be to the disinterested lover of poetry,—a satisfactory work. "Duty exists," says Wordsworth, in *The Excursion*; and then he proceeds thus—

. . . Immutably survive,
For our support, the measures and the forms,
Which an abstract Intelligence supplies,
Whose kingdom is, where time and space are not.[10]

And the Wordsworthian is delighted, and thinks that here is a sweet union of philosophy and poetry. But the disinterested lover of poetry will feel that the lines carry us really not a step farther than the proposition which they would interpret; that they are a tissue of elevated but abstract verbiage, alien to the very nature of poetry.

Or let us come direct to the centre of Words-

worth's philosophy, as "an ethical system, as distinctive and capable of systematical exposition as Bishop Butler's"—

. . . One adequate support
For the calamities of mortal life
Exists, one only;—an assured belief
That the procession of our fate, howe'er
Sad or disturbed, is ordered by a Being
Of infinite benevolence and power;
Whose everlasting purposes embrace
All accidents, converting them to good.[11]

That is doctrine such as we hear in church too, religious and philosophic doctrine; and the attached Wordsworthian loves passages of such doctrine, and brings them forward in proof of his poet's excellence. But however true the doctrine may be, it has, as here presented, none of the characters of *poetic* truth, the kind of truth which we require from a poet, and in which Wordsworth is really strong.

Even the "intimations" of the famous "Ode," those corner-stones of the supposed philosophic system of Wordsworth,—the idea of the high instincts and affections coming out in childhood, testifying of a divine home recently left, and fading away as our life proceeds,—this idea, of undeniable beauty as a play of fancy, has itself not the character of poetic truth of the best kind; it has no real solidity. The instinct of delight in Nature and her beauty had no doubt extraordinary strength in Wordsworth himself as a child. But to say that universally this instinct is mighty in childhood, and tends to die away afterwards, is to say what is extremely doubtful. In many people, perhaps with the majority of educated persons, the love of nature is nearly imperceptible at ten years old, but strong and operative at thirty. In general we may say of these high instincts of early childhood, the base of the alleged systematic philosophy of Wordsworth, what Thucydides says of the early achievements of the Greek race: "It is impossible to speak with certainty of what is so remote; but from all that we can really investigate, I should say that they were no very great things."

Finally, the "scientific system of thought" in

[10] IV, 73-76.

[11] IV, 10-17. Bishop Joseph Butler, the great eighteenth-century moral philosopher, was still much read in Arnold's time. His most famous work was his *Analogy of Religion* (1736).

Wordsworth gives us at last such poetry as this, which the devout Wordsworthian accepts—

O for the coming of that glorious time
When, prizing knowledge as her noblest wealth
And best protection, this Imperial Realm,
While she exacts allegiance, shall admit
An obligation, on her part, to *teach*
Them who are born to serve her and obey;
Binding herself by statute to secure,
For all the children whom her soil maintains,
The rudiments of letters, and inform
The mind with moral and religious truth.[12]

Wordsworth calls Voltaire dull, and surely the production of these un-Voltairian lines must have been imposed on him as a judgment! One can hear them being quoted at a Social Science Congress; one can call up the whole scene. A great room in one of our dismal provincial towns; dusty air and jaded afternoon daylight; benches full of men with bald heads and women in spectacles; an orator lifting up his face from a manuscript written within and without to declaim these lines of Wordsworth; and in the soul of any poor child of nature who may have wandered in thither, an unutterable sense of lamentation, and mourning, and woe!

"But turn we," as Wordsworth says, "from these bold, bad men," the haunters of Social Science Congresses. And let us be on our guard, too, against the exhibitors and extollers of a "scientific system of thought" in Wordsworth's poetry. The poetry will never be seen aright while they thus exhibit it. The cause of its greatness is simple, and may be told quite simply. Wordsworth's poetry is great because of the extraordinary power with which Wordsworth feels the joy offered to us in nature, the joy offered to us in the simple primary affections and duties; and because of the extraordinary power with which, in case after case, he shows us this joy, and renders it so as to make us share it.

The source of joy from which he thus draws is the truest and most unfailing source of joy accessible to man. It is also accessible universally. Wordsworth brings us word, therefore, according to his own strong and characteristic line, he brings us word

Of joy in widest commonalty spread.

[12] *Excursion*, IX, 293-302.

Here is an immense advantage for a poet. Wordsworth tells of what all seek, and tells of it at its truest and best source, and yet a source where all may go and draw for it.

Nevertheless, we are not to suppose that everything is precious which Wordsworth, standing even at this perennial and beautiful source, may give us. Wordsworthians are apt to talk as if it must be. They will speak with the same reverence of "The Sailor's Mother," for example, as of "Lucy Gray." They do their master harm by such lack of discrimination. "Lucy Gray" is a beautiful success; "The Sailor's Mother" is a failure. To give aright what he wishes to give, to interpret and render successfully, is not always within Wordsworth's own command. It is within no poet's command; here is the part of the Muse, the inspiration, the God, the "not ourselves." In Wordsworth's case, the accident, for so it may almost be called, of inspiration, is of peculiar importance. No poet, perhaps, is so evidently filled with a new and sacred energy when the inspiration is upon him; no poet, when it fails him, is so left "weak as is a breaking wave." I remember hearing him say that "Goethe's poetry was not inevitable enough." The remark is striking and true; no line in Goethe, as Goethe said himself, but its maker knew well how it came there. Wordsworth is right, Goethe's poetry is not inevitable; not inevitable enough. But Wordsworth's poetry, when he is at his best, is inevitable, as inevitable as Nature herself. It might seem that Nature not only gave him the matter for his poem, but wrote his poem for him. He has no style. He was too conversant with Milton not to catch at times his master's manner, and he has fine Miltonic lines; but he has no assured poetic style of his own, like Milton. When he seeks to have a style he falls into ponderosity and pomposity. In *The Excursion* we have his style, as an artistic product of his own creation; and although Jeffrey completely failed to recognise Wordsworth's real greatness, he was yet not wrong in saying of *The Excursion*, as a work of poetic style: "This will never do." And yet magical as is that power, which Wordsworth has not, of assured and possessed poetic style, he has something which is an equivalent for it.

Every one who has any sense for these things feels the subtle turn, the heightening, which is given to a poet's verse by his genius for style. We can feel it in the

> After life's fitful fever, he sleeps well—

of Shakespeare; in the

> . . . though fall'n on evil days,
> On evil days though fall'n, and evil tongues—

of Milton. It is the incomparable charm of Milton's power of poetic style which gives such worth to *Paradise Regained,* and makes a great poem of a work in which Milton's imagination does not soar high. Wordsworth has in constant possession, and at command, no style of this kind; but he had too poetic a nature, and had read the great poets too well, not to catch, as I have already remarked, something of it occasionally. We find it not only in his Miltonic lines; we find it in such a phrase as this, where the manner is his own, not Milton's—

> . . . the fierce confederate storm
> Of sorrow barricadoed evermore
> Within the walls of cities; [13]

although even here, perhaps, the power of style, which is undeniable, is more properly that of eloquent prose than the subtle heightening and change wrought by genuine poetic style. It is style, again, and the elevation given by style, which chiefly makes the effectiveness of "Laodameia." Still the right sort of verse to choose from Wordsworth, if we are to seize his true and most characteristic form of expression, is a line like this from "Michael"—

> And never lifted up a single stone.

There is nothing subtle in it, no heightening, no study of poetic style, strictly so called, at all; yet it is expression of the highest and most truly expressive kind.

Wordsworth owed much to Burns, and a style of perfect plainness, relying for effect solely on the weight and force of that which with entire fidelity it utters, Burns could show him.

> The poor inhabitant below
> Was quick to learn and wise to know,
> And keenly felt the friendly glow
> And softer flame:

> But thoughtless follies laid him low
> And stain'd his name.[14]

Every one will be conscious of a likeness here to Wordsworth; and if Wordsworth did great things with this nobly plain manner, we must remember, what indeed he himself would always have been forward to acknowledge, that Burns used it before him.

Still Wordsworth's use of it has something unique and unmatchable. Nature herself seems, I say, to take the pen out of his hand, and to write for him with her own bare, sheer, penetrating power. This arises from two causes; from the profound sincereness with which Wordsworth feels his subject, and also from the profoundly sincere and natural character of his subject itself. He can and will treat such a subject with nothing but the most plain, first-hand, almost austere naturalness. His expression may often be called bald, as, for instance, in the poem of "Resolution and Independence"; but it is bald as the bare mountain tops are bald, with a baldness which is full of grandeur.

Wherever we meet with the successful balance, in Wordsworth, of profound truth of subject with profound truth of execution, he is unique. His best poems are those which most perfectly exhibit this balance. I have a warm admiration for "Laodameia" and for the great "Ode"; but if I am to tell the very truth, I find "Laodameia" not wholly free from something artificial, and the great "Ode" not wholly free from something declamatory. If I had to pick out poems of a kind most perfectly to show Wordsworth's unique power, I should rather choose poems such as "Michael," "The Fountain," "The Highland Reaper." And poems with the peculiar and unique beauty which distinguishes these, Wordsworth produced in considerable number; besides very many other poems of which the worth, although not so rare as the worth of these, is still exceedingly high.

On the whole, then, as I said at the beginning, not only is Wordsworth eminent by reason of the goodness of his best work, but he is eminent also by reason of the great body of good work which he has left to us. With the ancients I will not compare him. In many respects the ancients are far above us, and yet there is something

---

[13] *Recluse,* ll. 831-33.

[14] The "Bard's Epitaph" of Burns.

that we demand which they can never give. Leaving the ancients, let us come to the poets and poetry of Christendom. Dante, Shakespeare, Molière, Milton, Goethe, are altogether larger and more splendid luminaries in the poetical heaven than Wordsworth. But I know not where else, among the moderns, we are to find his superiors.

To disengage the poems which show his power, and to present them to the English-speaking public and to the world, is the object of this volume. I by no means say that it contains all which in Wordsworth's poems is interesting. Except in the case of "Margaret," a story composed separately from the rest of *The Excursion,* and which belongs to a different part of England, I have not ventured on detaching portions of poems, or on giving any piece otherwise than as Wordsworth himself gave it. But under the conditions imposed by this reserve, the volume contains, I think, everything, or nearly everything, which may best serve him with the majority of lovers of poetry, nothing which may disserve him.

I have spoken lightly of Wordsworthians; and if we are to get Wordsworth recognised by the public and by the world, we must recommend him not in the spirit of a clique, but in the spirit of disinterested lovers of poetry. But I am a Wordsworthian myself. I can read with pleasure and edification "Peter Bell," and the whole series of *Ecclesiastical Sonnets,* and the address to Mr. Wilkinson's spade, and even the "Thanksgiving Ode";—everything of Wordsworth, I think, except "Vaudracour and Julia." It is not for nothing that one has been brought up in the veneration of a man so truly worthy of homage; that one has seen him and heard him, lived in his neighbourhood, and been familiar with his country. No Wordsworthian has a tenderer affection for this pure and sage master than I, or is less really offended by his defects. But Wordsworth is something more than the pure and sage master of a small band of devoted followers, and we ought not to rest satisfied until he is seen to be what he is. He is one of the very chief glories of English Poetry; and by nothing is England so glorious as by her poetry. Let us lay aside every weight which hinders our getting him recognised as this, and let our one study be to bring to pass, as widely as possible and as truly as possible, his own word concerning his poems: "They will co-operate with the benign tendencies in human nature and society, and will, in their degree, be efficacious in making men wiser, better, and happier." [15]

[15] From "Essay, Supplementary to the Preface" (1815).

From Literature and Science

I AM going to ask whether the present movement for ousting letters from their old predominance in education, and for transferring the predominance in education to the natural sciences, whether this brisk and flourishing movement ought to prevail, and whether it is likely that in the end it really will prevail. An objection may be raised which I will anticipate. My own studies have been almost wholly in letters, and my visits to the field of the natural sciences have been very slight and inadequate, although those sciences have always strongly moved my curiosity. A man of letters, it will per-

Literature and Science. First published in 1882; revised and delivered as a lecture while Arnold was touring the United States, and republished in *Discourses in America* (1885).

haps be said, is not competent to discuss the comparative merits of letters and natural science as means of education. To this objection I reply, first of all, that his incompetence, if he attempts the discussion but is really incompetent for it, will be abundantly visible; nobody will be taken in; he will have plenty of sharp observers and critics to save mankind from that danger. But the line I am going to follow is, as you will soon discover, so extremely simple, that perhaps it may be followed without failure even by one who for a more ambitious line of discussion would be quite incompetent.

Some of you may possibly remember a phrase of mine which has been the object of a good deal of comment; an observation to the effect that in our culture, the aim being *to know our-*

selves and the world, we have, as the means to this end, *to know the best which has been thought and said in the world.*[1] A man of science, who is also an excellent writer and the very prince of debaters, Professor Huxley, in a discourse at the opening of Sir Josiah Mason's college at Birmingham, laying hold of this phrase, expanded it by quoting some more words of mine, which are these: "The civilised world is to be regarded as now being, for intellectual and spiritual purposes, one great confederation, bound to a joint action and working to a common result; and whose members have for their proper outfit a knowledge of Greek, Roman, and Eastern antiquity, and of one another. Special local and temporary advantages being put out of account, that modern nation will in the intellectual and spiritual sphere make most progress, which most thoroughly carries out this programme."

Now on my phrase, thus enlarged, Professor Huxley remarks that when I speak of the above-mentioned knowledge as enabling us to know ourselves and the world, I assert *literature* to contain the materials which suffice for thus making us know ourselves and the world. But it is not by any means clear, says he, that after having learnt all which ancient and modern literatures have to tell us, we have laid a sufficiently broad and deep foundation for that criticism of life, that knowledge of ourselves and the world, which constitutes culture. On the contrary, Professor Huxley declares that he finds himself "wholly unable to admit that either nations or individuals will really advance, if their outfit draws nothing from the stores of physical science. An army without weapons of precision, and with no particular base of operations, might more hopefully enter upon a campaign on the Rhine, than a man, devoid of a knowledge of what physical science has done in the last century, upon a criticism of life."

This shows how needful it is for those who are to discuss any matter together, to have a common understanding as to the sense of the terms they employ,—how needful, and how difficult. What Professor Huxley says, implies just the reproach which is so often brought against the study of *belles lettres,* as they are called: that the study is an elegant one, but slight and

ineffectual; a smattering of Greek and Latin and other ornamental things, of little use for any one whose object is to get at truth, and to be a practical man. So, too, M. Renan[2] talks of the "superficial humanism" of a school-course which treats us as if we were all going to be poets, writers, preachers, orators, and he opposes this humanism to positive science, or the critical search after truth. And there is always a tendency in those who are remonstrating against the predominance of letters in education, to understand by letters *belles lettres,* and by *belles lettres* a superficial humanism, the opposite of science or true knowledge.

But when we talk of knowing Greek and Roman antiquity, for instance, which is the knowledge people have called the humanities, I for my part mean a knowledge which is something more than a superficial humanism, mainly decorative. "I call all teaching *scientific,*" says Wolf,[3] the critic of Homer, "which is systematically laid out and followed up to its original sources. For example: a knowledge of classical antiquity is scientific when the remains of classical antiquity are correctly studied in the original languages." There can be no doubt that Wolf is perfectly right; that all learning is scientific which is systematically laid out and followed up to its original sources, and that a genuine humanism is scientific.

When I speak of knowing Greek and Roman antiquity, therefore, as a help to knowing ourselves and the world, I mean more than a knowledge of so much vocabulary, so much grammar, so many portions of authors in the Greek and Latin languages. I mean knowing the Greeks and Romans, and their life and genius, and what they were and did in the world; what we get from them, and what is its value. That, at least, is the ideal; and when we talk of endeavouring to know Greek and Roman antiquity, as a help to knowing ourselves and the world, we mean endeavouring so to know them as to satisfy this ideal, however much we may still fall short of it.

The same also as to knowing our own and other modern nations, with the like aim of getting to understand ourselves and the world. To know the best that has been thought and said by

[1] See *On the Function of Criticism,* above, p. 457.

[2] See above, p. 462, n. 22.

[3] Friedrich August Wolf, late eighteenth- and early nineteenth-century German scholar of Greek literature.

the modern nations, is to know, says Professor Huxley, "only what modern *literatures* have to tell us; it is the criticism of life contained in modern literature." And yet "the distinctive character of our times," he urges, "lies in the vast and constantly increasing part which is played by natural knowledge." And how, therefore, can a man, devoid of knowledge of what physical science has done in the last century, enter hopefully upon a criticism of modern life?

Let us, I say, be agreed about the meaning of the terms we are using. I talk of knowing the best which has been thought and uttered in the world; Professor Huxley says this means knowing *literature*. Literature is a large word; it may mean everything written with letters or printed in a book. Euclid's *Elements* and Newton's *Principia* are thus literature. All knowledge that reaches us through books is literature. But by literature Professor Huxley means *belles lettres*. He means to make me say, that knowing the best which has been thought and said by the modern nations is knowing their *belles lettres* and no more. And this is no sufficient equipment, he argues, for a criticism of modern life. But as I do not mean, by knowing ancient Rome, knowing merely more or less of Latin *belles lettres*, and taking no account of Rome's military, and political, and legal, and administrative work in the world; and as, by knowing ancient Greece, I understand knowing her as the giver of Greek art, and the guide to a free and right use of reason and to scientific method, and the founder of our mathematics and physics and astronomy and biology,—I understand knowing her as all this, and not merely knowing certain Greek poems, and histories, and treatises, and speeches, —so as to the knowledge of modern nations also. By knowing modern nations, I mean not merely knowing their *belles lettres*, but knowing also what has been done by such men as Copernicus, Galileo, Newton, Darwin. "Our ancestors learned," says Professor Huxley, "that the earth is the centre of the visible universe, and that man is the cynosure of things terrestrial; and more especially was it inculcated that the course of nature had no fixed order, but that it could be, and constantly was, altered." But for us now, continues Professor Huxley, "the notions of the beginning and the end of the world entertained by our forefathers are no longer credible. It is

very certain that the earth is not the chief body in the material universe, and that the world is not subordinated to man's use. It is even more certain that nature is the expression of a definite order, with which nothing interferes." "And yet," he cries, "the purely classical education advocated by the representatives of the humanists in our day gives no inkling of all this!" . . .

The great results of the scientific investigation of nature we are agreed upon knowing, but how much of our study are we bound to give to the processes by which those results are reached? The results have their visible bearing on human life. But all the processes, too, all the items of fact, by which those results are reached and established, are interesting. All knowledge is interesting to a wise man, and the knowledge of nature is interesting to all men. It is very interesting to know, that, from the albuminous white of the egg, the chick in the egg gets the materials for its flesh, bones, blood, and feathers; while, from the fatty yolk of the egg, it gets the heat and energy which enable it at length to break its shell and begin the world. It is less interesting, perhaps, but still it is interesting, to know that when a taper burns, the wax is converted into carbonic acid and water. Moreover, it is quite true that the habit of dealing with facts, which is given by the study of nature, is, as the friends of physical science praise it for being, an excellent discipline. The appeal, in the study of nature, is constantly to observation and experiment; not only is it said that the thing is so, but we can be made to see that it is so. Not only does a man tell us that when a taper burns the wax is converted into carbonic acid and water, as a man may tell us, if he likes, that Charon is punting his ferry-boat on the river Styx, or that Victor Hugo is a sublime poet, or Mr. Gladstone the most admirable of statesmen; but we are made to see that the conversion into carbonic acid and water does actually happen. This reality of natural knowledge it is, which makes the friends of physical science contrast it, as a knowledge of things, with the humanist's knowledge, which is, say they, a knowledge of words. And hence Professor Huxley is moved to lay it down that, "for the purpose of attaining real culture, an exclusively scientific education is at least as effectual as an exclusively literary education." And a certain President of the Section for Mechanical Science in the British Association is, in Scripture phrase, "very bold," and declares that if a man, in his mental training, "has substituted literature and history for natural science, he has chosen the less useful alternative." But whether we go these lengths or not, we must all admit that in natural science the habit gained of dealing with facts is a most valuable discipline, and that every one should have some experience of it.

More than this, however, is demanded by the reformers. It is proposed to make the training in natural science the main part of education, for the great majority of mankind at any rate. And here, I confess, I part company with the friends of physical science, with whom up to this point I have been agreeing. In differing from them, however, I wish to proceed with the utmost caution and diffidence. The smallness of my own acquaintance with the disciplines of natural science is ever before my mind, and I am fearful of doing these disciplines an injustice. The ability and pugnacity of the partisans of natural science makes them formidable persons to contradict. The tone of tentative inquiry, which befits a being of dim faculties and bounded knowledge, is the tone I would wish to take and not to depart from. At present it seems to me, that those who are for giving to natural knowledge, as they call it, the chief place in the education of the majority of mankind, leave one important thing out of their account: the constitution of human nature. But I put this forward on the strength of some facts not at all recondite, very far from it; facts capable of being stated in the simplest possible fashion, and to which, if I so state them, the man of science will, I am sure, be willing to allow their due weight.

Deny the facts altogether, I think, he hardly can. He can hardly deny, that when we set ourselves to enumerate the powers which go to the building up of human life, and say that they are the power of conduct, the power of intellect and knowledge, the power of beauty, and the power of social life and manners,—he can hardly deny that this scheme, though drawn in rough and plain lines enough, and not pretending to scientific exactness, does yet give a fairly true representation of the matter. Human nature is built up by these powers; we have the need for them all. When we have rightly met and adjusted the claims of them all, we shall then be in a fair way for getting soberness and righteousness, with wisdom. This is evident enough, and the friends of physical science would admit it.

But perhaps they may not have sufficiently observed another thing: namely, that the several powers just mentioned are not isolated, but there is, in the generality of mankind, a perpetual tendency to relate them one to another in divers ways. With one such way of relating them I am particularly concerned now. Following our instinct for intellect and knowledge, we acquire pieces of knowledge; and presently, in the generality of men, there arises the desire to relate these pieces of knowledge to our sense for conduct, to our sense for beauty,—and there is weariness and dissatisfaction if the desire is baulked. Now in this desire lies, I think, the strength of that hold which letters have upon us.

All knowledge is, as I said just now, interesting; and even items of knowledge which from the nature of the case cannot well be related, but must stand isolated in our thoughts, have their interest. Even lists of exceptions have their interest. If we are studying Greek accents, it is interesting to know that *pais* and *pas*, and some other-monosyllables of the same form of declension, do not take the circumflex upon the last syllable of the genitive plural, but vary, in this respect, from the common rule. If we are studying physiology, it is interesting to know that the pulmonary artery carries dark blood and the pulmonary vein carries bright blood, departing in this respect from the common rule for the division of labour between the veins and the arteries. But every one knows how we seek naturally to combine the pieces of our knowledge together, to bring them under general rules, to relate them to principles; and how unsatisfactory and tiresome it would be to go on for ever learning lists of exceptions, or accumulating items of fact which must stand isolated.

Well, that same need of relating our knowledge, which operates here within the sphere of our knowledge itself, we shall find operating, also, outside that sphere. We experience, as we go on learning and knowing,—the vast majority of us experience,—the need of relating what we have learnt and known to the sense which we have in us for conduct, to the sense which we have in us for beauty.

A certain Greek prophetess of Mantineia in Arcadia, Diotima by name, once explained to the philosopher Socrates that love, and impulse, and bent of all kinds, is, in fact, nothing else but the desire in men that good should for ever be present to them.[4] This desire for good, Diotima assured Socrates, is our fundamental desire, of which fundamental desire every impulse in us is only some one particular form. And therefore this fundamental desire it is, I suppose,—this desire in men that good should be for ever present to them,—which acts in us when we feel the impulse for relating our knowledge to our sense for conduct and to our sense for beauty. At any rate, with men in general the instinct exists. Such is human nature. And the instinct, it will be admitted, is innocent, and human nature is preserved by our following the lead of its innocent instincts. Therefore, in seeking to gratify this instinct in question, we are following the instinct of self-preservation in humanity.

But, no doubt, some kinds of knowledge cannot be made to directly serve the instinct in question, cannot be directly related to the sense for beauty, to the sense for conduct. These are instrument-knowledges; they lead on to other knowledges, which can. A man who passes his life in instrument-knowledges is a specialist. They may be invaluable as instruments to something beyond, for those who have the gift thus to employ them; and they may be disciplines in themselves wherein it is useful for every one to have some schooling. But it is inconceivable that the generality of men should pass all their mental life with Greek accents or with formal logic. My friend Professor Sylvester,[5] who is one of the first mathematicians in the world, holds transcendental doctrines as to the virtue of mathe-matics, but those doctrines are not for common men. In the very Senate House and heart of our English Cambridge [6] I once ventured, though not without an apology for my profaneness, to hazard the opinion that for the majority of mankind a little of mathematics, even, goes a long way. Of course this is quite consistent with their being of immense importance as an instrument to something else; but it is the few who have the aptitude for thus using them, not the bulk of mankind.

The natural sciences do not, however, stand on the same footing with these instrument-knowledges. Experience shows us that the generality of men will find more interest in learning that, when a taper burns, the wax is converted into carbonic acid and water, or in learning the explanation of the phenomenon of dew, or in learning how the circulation of the blood is carried on, than they find in learning that the genitive plural of *pais* and *pas* does not take the circumflex on the termination. And one piece of natural knowledge is added to another, and others are added to that, and at last we come to propositions so interesting as Mr. Darwin's famous proposition that "our ancestor was a hairy quadruped furnished with a tail and pointed ears, probably arboreal in his habits." [7] Or we come to propositions of such reach and magnitude as those which Professor Huxley delivers, when he says that the notions of our forefathers about the beginning and the end of the world were all wrong, and that nature is the expression of a definite order with which nothing interferes.

Interesting, indeed, these results of science are, important they are, and we should all of us be acquainted with them. But what I now wish you to mark is, that we are still, when they are propounded to us and we receive them, we are still in the sphere of intellect and knowledge. And for the generality of men there will be found, I say, to arise, when they have duly taken in the proposition that their ancestor was "a hairy quadruped furnished with a tail and pointed ears, probably arboreal in his habits," there will be found to arise an invincible desire to relate this proposition to the sense in us for conduct, and to the sense in us for beauty. But this the men

[4] See the great passage in Plato's *Symposium* (201-07), and Werner Jaeger's *Paideia*, II, Ch. 8 ("Eros"). Man desires to possess and assimilate things because he regards them as *good*—at least good for himself. To the degree that his mind is informed and enlarged by knowledge, his emotional, desiring nature is directed to nobler and more truly valuable ends. The end of human education is not only to clarify and to disclose what are true and worthy as ends, but also to *arouse* the *feeling and desiring capacities* of man (to exploit "Eros," or "love") so that man actually assimilates, moves, and grows toward the noble and the good, and becomes like it.

[5] James J. Sylvester, a noted mathematician who taught at Johns Hopkins and Oxford.

[6] Cambridge has traditionally been the center of British mathematics.

[7] *Descent of Man* (1871), Pt. II, Ch. 21.

of science will not do for us, and will hardly even profess to do. They will give us other pieces of knowledge, other facts, about other animals and their ancestors, or about plants, or about stones, or about stars; and they may finally bring us to those great "general conceptions of the universe, which are forced upon us all," says Professor Huxley, "by the progress of physical science." But still it will be *knowledge* only which they give us; knowledge not put for us into relation with our sense for conduct, our sense for beauty, and touched with emotion by being so put; not thus put for us, and therefore, to the majority of mankind, after a certain while, unsatisfying, wearying. . . .

But now, says Professor Huxley, conceptions of the universe fatal to the notions held by our forefathers have been forced upon us by physical science. Grant to him that they are thus fatal, that the new conceptions must and will soon become current everywhere, and that every one will finally perceive them to be fatal to the beliefs of our forefathers. The need of humane letters, as they are truly called, because they serve the paramount desire in men that good should be for ever present to them,—the need of humane letters, to establish a relation between the new conceptions, and our instinct for beauty, our instinct for conduct, is only the more visible. The Middle Age could do without humane letters, as it could do without the study of nature, because its supposed knowledge was made to engage its emotions so powerfully. Grant that the supposed knowledge disappears, its power of being made to engage the emotions will of course disappear along with it,—but the emotions themselves, and their claim to be engaged and satisfied, will remain. Now if we find by experience that humane letters have an undeniable power of engaging the emotions, the importance of humane letters in a man's training becomes not less, but greater, in proportion to the success of modern science in extirpating what it calls "medieval thinking."

Have humane letters, then, have poetry and eloquence, the power here attributed to them of engaging the emotions, and do they exercise it? And if they have it and exercise it, *how* do they exercise it, so as to exert an influence upon man's sense for conduct, his sense for beauty? Finally, even if they both can and do exert an influence upon the senses in question, how are

they to relate to them the results,—the modern results,—of natural science? All these questions may be asked. First, have poetry and eloquence the power of calling out the emotions? The appeal is to experience. Experience shows that for the vast majority of men, for mankind in general, they have the power. Next do they exercise it? They do. But then, *how* do they exercise it so as to affect man's sense for conduct, his sense for beauty? And this is perhaps a case for applying the Preacher's words: "Though a man labour to seek it out, yet he shall not find it; yea, farther, though a wise man think to know it, yet shall he not be able to find it." [8] Why should it be one thing, in its effect upon the emotions, to say, "Patience is a virtue," and quite another thing, in its effect upon the emotions, to say with Homer,

τλητὸν γὰρ Μοῖραι θυμὸν θέσαν ἀνθρώποισιν— [9]

"for an enduring heart have the destinies appointed to the children of men"? Why should it be one thing, in its effect upon the emotions, to say with the philosopher Spinoza, *Felicitas in eo consistit quod homo suum esse conservare potest* —"Man's happiness consists in his being able to preserve his own essence," and quite another thing, in its effect upon the emotions, to say with the Gospel, "What is a man advantaged, if he gain the whole world, and lose himself, forfeit himself?" How does this difference of effect arise? I cannot tell, and I am not much concerned to know; the important thing is that it does arise, and that we can profit by it. But how, finally, are poetry and eloquence to exercise the power of relating the modern results of natural science to man's instinct for conduct, his instinct for beauty? And here again I answer that I do not know *how* they will exercise it, but that they can and will exercise it I am sure. I do not mean that modern philosophical poets and modern philosophical moralists are to come and relate for us, in express terms, the results of modern scientific research to our instinct for conduct, our instinct for beauty. But I mean that we shall find, as a matter of experience, if we know the best that has been thought and uttered in the world, we shall find that the art and poetry and

8 Ecclesiastes, viii, 17. [Arnold.]
9 *Iliad*, xxiv, 49. [Arnold.]

eloquence of men who lived, perhaps, long ago, who had the most limited natural knowledge, who had the most erroneous conceptions about many important matters, we shall find that this art, and poetry, and eloquence, have in fact not only the power of refreshing and delighting us, they have also the power,—such is the strength and worth, in essentials, of their authors' criticism of life,—they have a fortifying, and elevating, and quickening, and suggestive power, capable of wonderfully helping us to relate the results of modern science to our need for conduct, our need for beauty. Homer's conceptions of the physical universe were, I imagine, grotesque; but really, under the shock of hearing from modern science that "the world is not subordinated to man's use, and that man is not the cynosure of things terrestrial," I could, for my own part, desire no better comfort than Homer's line which I quoted just now,

τλητὸν γὰρ Μοῖραι θυμὸν θέσαν ἀνθρώποισιν—

"for an enduring heart have the destinies appointed to the children of men!"

And the more that men's minds are cleared, the more that the results of science are frankly accepted, the more that poetry and eloquence come to be received and studied as what in truth they really are,—the criticism of life by gifted men, alive and active with extraordinary power at an unusual number of points;—so much the more will the value of humane letters, and of art also, which is an utterance having a like kind of power with theirs, be felt and acknowledged, and their place in education be secured.

Let us therefore, all of us, avoid indeed as much as possible any invidious comparison between the merits of humane letters, as means of education, and the merits of the natural sciences. But when some President of a Section for Mechanical Science insists on making the comparison, and tells us that "he who in his training has substituted literature and history for natural science has chosen the less useful alternative," let us make answer to him that the student of humane letters only, will, at least, know also the great general conceptions brought in by modern physical science; for science, as Professor Huxley says, forces them upon us all. But the student of the natural sciences only, will, by our very hypothesis, know nothing of humane letters; not

to mention that in setting himself to be perpetually accumulating natural knowledge, he sets himself to do what only specialists have in general the gift for doing genially. And so he will probably be unsatisfied, or at any rate incomplete, and even more incomplete than the student of humane letters only. . . .

Defuit una mihi symmetria prisca,—"The antique symmetry was the one thing wanting to me," said Leonardo da Vinci; and he was an Italian. I will not presume to speak for the Americans, but I am sure that, in the Englishman, the want of this admirable symmetry of the Greeks is a thousand times more great and crying than in any Italian. The results of the want show themselves most glaringly, perhaps, in our architecture, but they show themselves, also, in all our art. *Fit details strictly combined, in view of a large general result nobly conceived;* that is just the beautiful *symmetria prisca* of the Greeks, and it is just where we English fail, where all our art fails. Striking ideas we have, and well-executed details we have; but that high symmetry which, with satisfying and delightful effect, combines them, we seldom or never have. The glorious beauty of the Acropolis at Athens did not come from single fine things stuck about on that hill, a statue here, a gateway there;—no, it arose from all things being perfectly combined for a supreme total effect. What must not an Englishman feel about our deficiencies in this respect, as the sense for beauty, whereof this symmetry is an essential element, awakens and strengthens within him! what will not one day be his respect and desire for Greece and its *symmetria prisca,* when the scales drop from his eyes as he walks the London streets, and he sees such a lesson in meanness as the Strand, for instance, in its true deformity! But here we are coming to our friend Mr. Ruskin's province, and I will not intrude upon it, for he is its very sufficient guardian.

And so we at last find, it seems, we find flowing in favour of the humanities the natural and necessary stream of things, which seemed against them when we started. The "hairy quadruped furnished with a tail and pointed ears, probably arboreal in his habits," this good fellow carried hidden in his nature, apparently, something destined to develop into a necessity for humane letters. Nay, more; we seem finally to be even led to the further conclusion that our hairy ancestor carried in his nature, also, a necessity for Greek.

And therefore, to say the truth, I cannot really think that humane letters are in much actual danger of being thrust out from their leading place in education, in spite of the array of authorities against them at this moment. So long as human nature is what it is, their attractions will remain irresistible. As with Greek, so with letters generally: they will some day come, we may hope, to be studied more rationally, but they will not lose their place. What will happen will rather be that there will be crowded into education other matters besides, far too many; there will be, perhaps, a period of unsettlement and confusion and false tendency; but letters will not in the end lose their leading place. If they lose it for a time, they will get it back again. We shall be brought back to them by our wants and aspirations. And a poor humanist may possess his soul in patience, neither strive nor cry, admit the energy and brilliancy of the partisans of physical science, and their present favour with the public, to be far greater than his own, and still have a happy faith that the nature of things works silently on behalf of the studies which he loves, and that, while we shall all have to acquaint ourselves with the great results reached by modern science, and to give ourselves as much training in its disciplines as we can conveniently carry, yet the majority of men will always require humane letters; and so much the more, as they have the more and the greater results of science to relate to the need in man for conduct, and to the need in him for beauty.

CHARLES AUGUSTIN SAINTE-BEUVE   (1804-1869)

No CRITIC of the nineteenth century is more distinguished by range, variety, and sensitivity than Sainte-Beuve. If he has been less completely read than he deserves, it is because he does not discuss, as fully as certain other major critics, the general aims of literature or even the general problems of literary history and technique. Instead, he concentrates on particular writers. The analysis of individual writers, however sensitive and acute, obviously means little to the reader who is not already well acquainted with these writers. And few readers are sufficiently familiar with the five hundred or so figures discussed by Sainte-Beuve to be tempted to read extensively in his fifty volumes of criticism. If this is true even of professional students of French literature, it may be understood why Sainte-Beuve, of all the great Continental critics, is the least read by English-speaking students.

CHARLES AUGUSTIN SAINTE-BEUVE. Partly English on his mother's side, Sainte-Beuve attended the Blériot Institution (Boulogne), later studied medicine (1823-27), began writing for the *Globe*, and through his acquaintance with Victor Hugo became a pro-romantic. After writing for other journals, and lecturing (1837-38) on Port-Royal at Lausanne, Switzerland, he was elected to the Academy (1844), served for a year as Professor of French Literature at Liège, and began writing his *Lundis* (1849). His appointment at the Collège de France (1854) was not successful because of the unpopularity of his political views. But he lectured at the Normal School (1858-61), and then began his *Nouveaux Lundis* (1861).

Translations include: *English Portraits* (tr. anon., 1875); *Monday-Chats* (tr. and selected by William Matthews, 1877); *Portraits of Men* (tr. F. Edeveain, 1891); *Essays* (tr. Elizabeth Lee, 1892); *Portraits of the Seventeenth Century* (tr. K. P. Wormeley, 2 vols., 1904); *Portraits of the Eighteenth Century* (tr. K. P. Wormeley and G. B. Ives, 2 vols., 1905); and especially *Causeries du Lundi* (tr. E. J. Trechmann, 8 vols., 1909-11). For commentary in English, see

But granted that the subject matter of his criticism is often unfamiliar to English-speaking students, his approach should not be alien to them. For the unusual flexibility of Sainte-Beuve's mind makes him by far the most cosmopolitan of French critics. He himself states that the greatest fault of the French mind is its rigidity and provincial intolerance: its monocular tendency to view matters in a two-dimensional flatness and then, with abstract logic, quickly work out a conclusion according to a preconceived plan. In his desire for a more imaginatively and empirically rounded conception of his subject, Sainte-Beuve completely avoids the extreme partisanship of so much French critical thought. His empirical individualism, his aloofness from schools and purely abstract issues, are more akin to English criticism at its best. However he is quite unlike the English in the unwearied persistence of his critical thinking, and in his confident trust in the value of criticism.

After a few years as a militant and eager romantic (1824-31), when he was partly under the influence of Victor Hugo, Sainte-Beuve deliberately sought to attain a more objectively detached and judicial outlook. He compared his approach to the analytic study of the scientific naturalist. "Our nineteenth century," he said, "as distinct from the eighteenth, is not dogmatic: it seems to avoid giving an opinion, and does not hurry to arrive at conclusions." It was this characteristic of science, not its rigid categorizing, that Sainte-Beuve sought to emulate. "I analyze," he said. "I botanize; I am a naturalist of minds. What I should like to establish is the natural history of literature." Hence, as he implied in his discussion of his critical method, nothing alien to the life, experience, and art of the writer is alien to the critic. The relation between the work and the author, the author's background—family, nation, historical period, and his period in relation to other ages—all these relations, in widening concentric circles, are necessary for the critic's estimate. Revealing, too, are the writer's weaknesses, which, as Sainte-Beuve shrewdly notes, may be most profitably studied by looking at the writer's disciples, in whom his faults are caricatured. Once he has probed into such matters as these, the critic has only, with imaginative receptivity, to "listen to writers long and carefully." If he will "merely let them disclose themselves in a free way, without hurrying them," he will at last "seize the familiar trick, the telltale smile; the indefinable wrinkle, the secret line of pain hidden in vain beneath the already scanty hair."

The aim, in short, is to understand and evaluate the character of an

especially Matthew Arnold, "Sainte-Beuve," *Essays in Criticism, Third Series,* in *Works* (1903-04), and his article on "Sainte-Beuve" in the *Encyclopaedia Britannica;* Alfred Austin, "Sainte-Beuve's Critical Method," *Cornhill Magazine,* XXXVIII (1878), Irving Babbitt, *Masters of Modern French Criticism* (1912); Ferdinand Brunetière, "Sainte-Beuve," *Monthly Review,* XIX (1905), 125-40; A. G. Lehmann, *Sainte-Beuve: a Portrait of the Critic, 1804-1842* (Oxford, 1962); and Lander MacClintock, *Sainte-Beuve's Critical Theory and Practice after 1849* (1920). For students with knowledge of French, there are Victor Giraud, *Port-Royal de Sainte-Beuve* (Paris, 1956), and Pierre Moreau, *La Critique selon Sainte-Beuve* (Paris, 1964).

author's work with as sympathetic and informed a sensitivity as possible. It is "scientific" to the extent that science itself participates in the ideal of alert receptivity and openness of mind. But it is not "scientific" if, by that term, one means the blithe confidence that humanistic values can be automatically explained and weighed by simply applying the routine investigative methods used in the physical sciences. Least of all is it "scientific" in so far as science itself becomes a fixed and closed dogma. Hence Sainte-Beuve has little in common with the more thoroughgoing naturalism of Taine, although Taine was in a sense his disciple. "In spite of everything," as Sainte-Beuve wrote in explaining his attitude toward Balzac, "I have continued of the classical school." Indeed, the objective and open flexibility of mind urged by Sainte-Beuve may as justly be called "classical" as "scientific." His most mature criticism (1848-69) may be described as a supple critical example and application of two ideals, each of which tempers and sustains the other even though the two may not blend in complete theoretical harmony. One of these ideals is the spirit of modern scientific naturalism, with its passion for exactness and its experimental questioning. But the other ideal is that of classical humanism, which indeed includes exactly these values, but which joins with them the values of moral completeness and integration, of imaginative breadth and emotional harmony, and a prizing of qualities in art which express and develop these values. Sainte-Beuve thus mirrors two currents of mid-nineteenth-century thinking that were becoming increasingly separated from each other. In doing so, he to some extent reconciles them.

From What Is a Classic?

A DELICATE question, to which somewhat diverse solutions might be given according to times and seasons. An intelligent man suggests it to me, and I intend to try, if not to solve it, at least to examine and discuss it face to face with my readers, were it only to persuade them to answer it for themselves, and, if I can, to make their opinion and mine on the point clear. And why, in criticism, should we not, from time to time, venture to treat some of those subjects which are not personal, in which we no longer speak of some one but of some thing? Our neighbours, the English, have well succeeded in making of it a special division of literature under the modest title of "Essays." It is true that

What Is a Classic? First published in 1850; translated by Elizabeth Lee.

in writing of such subjects, always slightly abstract and moral, it is advisable to speak of them in a season of quiet, to make sure of our own attention and of that of others, to seize one of those moments of calm moderation and leisure seldom granted our amiable France; even when she is desirous of being wise and is not making revolutions, her brilliant genius can scarcely tolerate them.

A classic, according to the usual definition, is an old author canonised by admiration, and an authority in his particular style. The word *classic* was first used in this sense by the Romans. With them not all the citizens of the different classes were properly called *classici*, but only those of the chief class, those who possessed an income of a certain fixed sum. Those who possessed a smaller income were described by the term *infra classem*, below the pre-eminent class. The word *classicus* was used in a figurative sense by Aulus Gellius, and applied to writers: a writer of worth and distinction, *classicus assiduusque scriptor*, a writer who is of account, has real property, and is not lost in the proletariate crowd. Such an expression implies an age sufficiently advanced to have already made some sort of valuation and classification of literature.

At first the only true classics for the moderns were the ancients. The Greeks, by peculiar good fortune and natural enlightenment of mind, had no classics but themselves. They were at first the only classical authors for the Romans, who strove and contrived to imitate them. After the great periods of Roman literature, after Cicero and Virgil, the Romans in their turn had their classics, who became almost exclusively the classical authors of the centuries which followed. The middle ages, which were less ignorant of Latin antiquity than is believed, but which lacked proportion and taste, confused the ranks and orders. Ovid was placed above Homer, and Boethius seemed a classic equal to Plato. The revival of learning in the fifteenth and sixteenth centuries helped to bring this long chaos to order, and then only was admiration rightly proportioned. Thenceforth the true classical authors of Greek and Latin antiquity stood out in a luminous background, and were harmoniously grouped on their two heights.

Meanwhile modern literatures were born, and some of the more precocious, like the Italian, already possessed the style of antiquity. Dante appeared, and, from the very first, posterity greeted him as a classic. Italian poetry has since shrunk into far narrower bounds; but, whenever it desired to do so, it always found again and preserved the impulse and echo of its lofty origin. It is no indifferent matter for a poetry to derive its point of departure and classical source in high places; for example, to spring from Dante rather than to issue laboriously from Malherbe. . . .

Example is the best definition. From the time France possessed her age of Louis XIV and could contemplate it at a little distance, she knew, better than by any arguments, what to be classical meant. The eighteenth century, even in its medley of things, strengthened this idea through some fine works, due to its four great men. Read Voltaire's *Age of Louis XIV*, Montesquieu's *Greatness and Fall of the Romans*, Buffon's *Epochs of Nature*, the beautiful pages of reverie and natural description of Rousseau's *Savoyard Vicar*, and say if the eighteenth century, in these memorable works, did not understand how to reconcile tradition with freedom of development and independence. But at the beginning of the present century and under the Empire, in sight of the first attempts of a decidedly new and somewhat adventurous literature, the idea of a classic in a few resisting minds, more sorrowful than severe, was strangely narrowed and contracted. The first Dictionary of the Academy (1694) merely defined a classical author as "a much-approved ancient writer, who is an authority as regards the subject he treats." The Dictionary of the Academy of 1835 narrows that definition still more, and gives precision and even limit to its rather vague form. It describes classical authors as those "who have become *models* in any language whatever," and in all the articles which follow, the expression, *models, fixed rules* for composition and style, *strict rules* of art to which men must conform, continually recur. That definition of *classic* was evidently made by the respectable Academicians, our predecessors, in face and sight of what was then called *romantic*—that is to say, in sight of the enemy. It seems to me time to renounce those timid and restrictive definitions and to free our mind of them.

A true classic, as I should like to hear it defined, is an author who has enriched the human mind, increased its treasure, and caused it to advance a step; who has discovered some moral and not equivocal truth, or revealed some eternal passion in that heart where all seemed known and discovered; who has expressed his thought, observation, or invention, in no matter what form, only provided it be broad and great, refined and sensible, sane and beautiful in itself; who has spoken to all in his own peculiar style, a style which is found to be also that of the whole world, a style new without neologism, new and old, easily contemporary with all time. . . .

Indeed, before determining and fixing the opinions on that matter, I should like every unbiased mind to take a voyage round the world and devote itself to a survey of different literatures in their primitive vigour and infinite variety. What would be seen? Chief of all a Homer, the father of the classical world, less a single distinct individual than the vast living expression of a whole epoch and a semi-barbarous civilisation. In order to make him a true classic, it was necessary to attribute to him later a design, a plan, literary invention, qualities of atticism and urbanity of which he had certainly never dreamed in the luxuriant development of his natural aspirations. And who appear by his side? August, venerable ancients, the Aeschyluses and the Sophocles, mutilated, it is true, and only there to present us with a *débris* of themselves, the survivors of many others as worthy, doubtless, as they to survive, but who have succumbed to the injuries of time. This thought alone would teach a man of impartial mind not to look upon the whole of even classical literatures with a too narrow and restricted view; he would learn that the exact and well-proportioned order which has since so largely prevailed in our admiration of the past was only the outcome of artificial circumstances.

And in reaching the modern world, how would it be? The greatest names to be seen at the beginning of literatures are those which disturb and run counter to certain fixed ideas of what is beautiful and appropriate in poetry. For example, is Shakespeare a classic? Yes, now, for England and the world; but in the time of Pope he was not considered so. Pope and his friends were the only pre-eminent classics; directly after their death they seemed so for ever. At the present time they are still classics, as they deserve to be, but they are only of the second order, and are for ever subordinated and relegated to their rightful place by him who has again come to his own on the height of the horizon.

It is not, however, for me to speak ill of Pope or his great disciples, above all, when they possess pathos and naturalness like Goldsmith: after the greatest they are perhaps the most agreeable writers and the poets best fitted to add charm to life. Once when Lord Bolingbroke was writing to Swift, Pope added a postcript, in which he said—"I think some advantage would result to our age, if we three spent three years together." Men who, without boasting, have the right to say such things must never be spoken of lightly: the fortunate ages, when men of talent could propose such things, then no chimera, are rather to be envied. The ages called by the name of Louis XIV or of Queen Anne are, in the dispassionate sense of the word, the only true classical ages, those which offer protection and a favourable climate to real talent. We know only too well how in our untrammelled times, through the instability and storminess of the age, talents are lost and dissipated. Nevertheless, let us acknowledge our age's part and superiority in greatness. True and sovereign genius triumphs over the very difficulties that cause others to fail: Dante, Shakespeare, and Milton were able to attain their height and produce their imperishable works in spite of obstacles, hardships, and tempests. Byron's opinion of Pope has been much discussed, and the explanation of it sought in the kind of contradiction by which the singer of *Don Juan* and *Childe Harold* extolled the purely classical school and pronounced it the only good one, while himself acting so differently. Goethe spoke the truth on that point when he remarked that Byron, great by the flow and source of poetry, feared that Shakespeare was more powerful than himself in the creation and realisation of his characters. "He would have liked to deny it; the elevation so free from egoism irritated him; he felt when near it that he could not display himself at ease. He never denied Pope, because he did not fear him; he knew that Pope was only a *low wall* by his side."

If, as Byron desired, Pope's school had kept the supremacy and a sort of honorary empire in the past, Byron would have been the first and only poet in his particular style; the height of Pope's wall shuts out Shakespeare's great figure from sight, whereas when Shakespeare reigns and rules in all his greatness, Byron is only second.

In France there was no great classic before the age of Louis XIV; the Dantes and Shakespeares, the early authorities to whom, in times of emancipation, men sooner or later return, were wanting. There were mere sketches of great poets, like Mathurin Regnier, like Rabelais, without any ideal, without the depth of emotion and the seriousness which canonises. Montaigne was a kind of premature classic, of the family of Horace; but for want of worthy surroundings, like a spoiled child, he gave himself up to the unbridled fancies of his style and humour. Hence it happened that France, less than any other nation, found in her old authors a right to de mand vehemently at a certain time literary liberty and freedom, and that it was more difficult for her, in enfranchising herself, to remain classical. However, with Molière and La Fontaine among her classics of the great period, nothing could justly be refused to those who possessed courage and ability.

The important point now seems to me to be to uphold, while extending, the idea and belief. There is no receipt for making classics; this point should be clearly recognised. To believe that an author will become a classic by imitating certain qualities of purity, moderation, accuracy, and elegance, independently of the style and inspiration, is to believe that after Racine the father there is a place for Racine the son; dull and estimable *rôle*, the worst in poetry. Further, it is hazardous to take too quickly and without opposition the place of a classic in the sight of one's contemporaries; in that case there is a good chance of not retaining the position with posterity. . . .

Meanwhile there is no question of sacrificing or depreciating anything. I believe the temple of taste is to be rebuilt; but its reconstruction is merely a matter of enlargement, so that it may become the home of all noble human beings, of all who have permanently increased the sum of the mind's delights and possessions. As for me, who cannot, obviously, in any degree pretend to be the architect or designer of such a temple, I shall confine myself to expressing a few earnest wishes, to submit, as it were, my designs for the edifice. Above all I should desire not to exclude any one among the worthy, each should be in his place there, from Shakespeare, the freest of creative geniuses, and the greatest of classics without knowing it, to Andrieux, the last of classics in little. "There is more than one chamber in the mansions of my Father;" that should be as true of the kingdom of the beautiful here below, as of the kingdom of Heaven. Homer, as always and everywhere, should be first, likest a god; but behind him, like the procession of the three wise kings of the East, would be seen the three great poets, the three Homers, so long ignored by us, who wrote epics for the use of the old peoples of Asia, the poets Valmiki, Vyasa of the Hindoos, and Firdousi of the Persians: in the domain of taste it is well to know that such men exist,

and not to divide the human race. Our homage paid to what is recognised as soon as perceived, we must not stray further; the eye should delight in a thousand pleasing or majestic spectacles, should rejoice in a thousand varied and surprising combinations, whose apparent confusion would never be without concord and harmony. The oldest of the wise men and poets, those who put human morality into maxims, and those who in simple fashion sung it, would converse together in *rare and gentle* speech, and would not be surprised at understanding each other's meaning at the very first word. Solon, Hesiod, Theognis, Job, Solomon, and why not Confucius, would welcome the cleverest moderns. La Rochefoucauld and La Bruyère, who, when listening to them, would say "they knew all that we know, and in repeating life's experiences, we have discovered nothing." On the hill, most easily discernible, and of most accessible ascent, Virgil, surrounded by Menander, Tibullus, Terence, Fénelon, would occupy himself in discoursing with them with great charm and divine enchantment: his gentle countenance would shine with an inner light, and be tinged with modesty; as on the day when entering the theatre at Rome, just as they finished reciting his verses, he saw the people rise with an unanimous movement and pay to him the same homage as to Augustus. Not far from him, regretting the separation from so dear a friend, Horace, in his turn, would preside (as far as so accomplished and wise a poet could preside) over the group of poets of social life who could talk although they sang,—Pope, Boileau, the one become less irritable, the other less fault-finding. Montaigne, a true poet, would be among them, and would give the finishing touch that should deprive that delightful corner of the air of a literary school. There would La Fontaine forget himself, and becoming less volatile would wander no more. Voltaire would be attracted by it, but while finding pleasure in it would not have patience to remain. A little lower down, on the same hill as Virgil, Xenophon, with a simple bearing, looking in no way like a general, but rather resembling a priest of the Muses, would be seen gathering round him the Attics of every tongue and of every nation, the Addisons, Pellissons, Vauvenargues—all who feel the value of an easy persuasiveness, an exquisite simplicity, and a gentle negligence mingled with ornament. In the centre of the place, in the portico of the principal temple (for there would be several in the enclosure), three great men would like to meet often, and when they were together, no fourth, however great, would dream of joining their discourse or their silence. In them would be seen beauty, proportion in greatness, and that perfect harmony which appears but once in the full youth of the world. Their three names have become the ideal of art—Plato, Sophocles, and Demosthenes. Those demi-gods honoured, we see a numerous and familiar company of choice spirits who follow, the Cervantes and Molières, practical painters of life, indulgent friends who are still the first of benefactors, who laughingly embrace all mankind, turn man's experience to gaiety, and know the powerful workings of a sensible, hearty, and legitimate joy. I do not wish to make this description, which if complete would fill a volume, any longer. In the middle ages, believe me, Dante would occupy the sacred heights: at the feet of the singer of Paradise all Italy would be spread out like a garden; Boccaccio and Ariosto would there disport themselves, and Tasso would find again the orange groves of Sorrento. Usually a corner would be reserved for each of the various nations, but the authors would take delight in leaving it, and in their travels would recognise, where we should least expect it, brothers or masters. Lucretius, for example, would enjoy discussing the origin of the world and the reducing of chaos to order with Milton. But both arguing from their own point of view, they would only agree as regards divine pictures of poetry and nature.

Such are our classics; each individual imagination may finish the sketch and choose the group preferred. For it is necessary to make a choice, and the first condition of taste, after obtaining knowledge of all, lies not in continual travel, but in rest and cessation from wandering. Nothing blunts and destroys taste so much as endless journeyings; the poetic spirit is not the *Wandering Jew.* However, when I speak of resting and making choice, my meaning is not that we are to imitate those who charm us most among our masters in the past. Let us be content to know them, to penetrate them, to admire them; but let us, the latecomers, endeavour to be ourselves. Let us have the sincerity and naturalness of our own thoughts, of our own feelings; so much is always possible. To that let us add what is more difficult, elevation, an aim, if possible, towards an exalted goal; and while speaking our own language, and submitting to the conditions of the times in which we live, whence we derive our strength and our defects, let us ask from time to time, our brows lifted towards the heights and our eyes fixed on the group of honoured mortals: *what would they say of us?*

But why speak always of authors and writings? Maybe an age is coming when there will be no more writing. Happy those who read and read again, those who in their reading can follow their unrestrained inclination! There comes a time in life when, all our journeys over, our experiences ended, there is no enjoyment more delightful than to study and thoroughly examine the things we know, to take pleasure in what we feel, and in seeing and seeing again the people we love: the pure joys of our maturity. Then it is that the word classic takes its true meaning, and is defined for every man of taste by an irresistible choice. Then taste is formed, it is shaped and definite; then good sense, if we are to possess it at all, is perfected in us. We have neither more time for experiments, nor a desire to go forth in search of pastures new. We cling to our friends, to those proved by a long intercourse. Old wine, old books, old friends. We say to ourselves with Voltaire in these delightful lines:—"Let us enjoy, let us write, let us live, my dear Horace! . . . I have lived longer than you: my verse will not last so long. But on the brink of the tomb I shall make it my chief care—to follow the lessons of your philosophy—to despise death in enjoying life—to read your writings full of charm and good sense—as we drink an old wine which revives our senses."

In fact, be it Horace or another who is the author preferred, who reflects our thoughts in all the wealth of their maturity, of some one of those excellent and antique minds shall we request an interview at every moment; of some one of them shall we ask a friendship which never deceives, which could not fail us; to some one of them shall we appeal for that sensation of serenity and amenity (we have often need of it) which reconciles us with mankind and with ourselves.

From Tradition in Literature

IT IS [Goethe], the author of *Werther* and *Faust*,—and he knew what he was saying— who stated so justly: "I call the classic *healthy*, and the romantic the *sickly*." Since the classic and even the romantic make up part of tradition, I must linger over this maxim of Goethe's, in order to consider tradition in its complete range and throughout the whole past; and I wish to try to explain to myself in front of you.

The classic, in effect, in its broadest definition and most general character, consists of literatures in their happily flowering and healthy state—literatures in complete accord and harmony with their epoch, with their social frame, with the directing powers and principles of the society, content with themselves. Let us understand carefully: they are content to be a part of their nation, of their time, of the *regime* in which they are born and flourish (joy of mind, it has been said, indicates force of mind; it is as true for literatures as for individuals); these are literatures which are and feel at home, in their true path, not out of their class, not troubled, not taking discomfort as their principle—which has never been a principle of beauty. It is not for me, Sirs, to disparage romantic literatures; I hold myself to the terms of Goethe and historical explanation. We are not born at the time we wish; we cannot choose the moment for being hatched. We cannot avoid, especially in childhood, the general currents circulating throughout the atmosphere, and which blow dryness or humidity, fever or health. And there are currents like these to affect our souls. This feeling of basic contentment, where there is hope, above all, and into which discouragement does not enter—where we say that there is an epoch before us, longer-lived than we, stronger, an age to nourish and judge, in which you have a fair field for a career, an honored and splendid development in full sunlight—this it is that gives the first basis on which arise later, harmonious

works, regular temples and palaces. When one lives in a continual public instability, when we see society change several times, one is then lured not to believe in literary immortality, and therefore acquieses in everything going on. Now, no one can give himself this feeling of security, of a fixed and durable epoch. One must breathe it with the air in the hours of youth. Romantic literatures, which deal above all with violence and adventure, have their virtues, their exploits, their brilliant rôle, but beyond the control of rules. They mount themselves on two or three epochs, never establishing themselves complete in one, restless, searching, eccentric in their nature, either in advance or arrears, and, besides, wilful and wandering.

Classical literature does not complain, moan, nor feel bored. Sometimes one goes through grief beyond it; but beauty is more tranquil.

The classic, I repeat, has this among other qualities, that it loves its own nation and time, and sees nothing more desirable or beautiful; it has a legitimate pride in them. *Activity in serenity* would be its motto. That is true of the age of Pericles, the age of Augustus, the reign of Louis XIV. Let us listen to them speak—the great poets and orators of that time, beneath their beautiful sky, as if beneath a blue dome. Their hymns of praise still sound within our ears. They have developed the art of applause to a high level.

Romanticism, like Hamlet, has nostalgia. It seeks what it does not have, up and beyond the clouds. It dreams, and lives in dreams. In the nineteenth century, it adores the Middle Ages; in the eighteenth, with Rousseau, it was already rebelling. In Goethe's sense, there are romantics of various periods. Chrysostom's youth, Stagirius, and Augustine, in his youth, were sick romantics of this sort, anticipations of René.[1] But they were invalids who could be cured, and Christianity cured them: it drove out the demon. Hamlet, Werther, Childe Harold, the pure Renés, are invalids in order to suffer and sing, to enjoy

---

Tradition in Literature. A lecture delivered at the Ecole Normale (April 12, 1858); *Causeries du Lundi.* Translated by the editor.

[1] The sentimental hero in Chateaubriand's novel of the same name.

their illness, romantics more or less as dilletantes —sickness for the sake of sickness. . . .

It is not our mission or pretence to bring forth [works of permanent worth]; above all, our duty is to preserve them. What is the best and most certain way of maintaining tradition? It is necessary, first of all, to possess it in its entirety, not to concentrate and constrain upon points too close, not to exaggerate it here and disregard it there. It is not necessary to say these things to you, since from the beginning and in differing literatures, the models are familiar and present to you, and your minds are stocked with true conditions for comparing in every kind of literature. Others have established pillars on you as the base: you have the models of true beauty. When one can see, face to face, Plato, Sophocles, or Demosthenes, one is not tempted to accord too much to the moderns, even the most illustrious. This is the drawback for those who know only one language, one literature. Frederick the Great regarded Voltaire as gospel in everything, even as a poet, and conferred on him all the crowns, because he did not know enough to make a comparison. Because of having restricted tradition too much, because of having considered it in such a local and temporary way, and having made it too inelastic, there were many who, at the beginning of this century, called themselves classics, but in the issues that took place at the time were the least justified in doing so.

At each renewing of an age, parts of recent tradition that are believed to be well-founded crumble and fall, in a way, so that the rock, the indestructible marble, only stands out the more in its solidity.

In order to maintain tradition, it is not always enough to connect it fast to the highest and noblest monuments. It is proper to verify it, to control it ceaselessly at the points most relevant, to rejuvenate it even, and keep it in perpetual contact with the living. Here we touch on a rather delicate question. For it is not my concern to introduce names too recent into the course of study, to judge the works of today —which is aside from the present purpose—or to confuse functions and rôles. The professor is not the critic. The critic, if he does what he ought to do (and where are critics of this sort today?), is a sentinel always alert to see who passes. But he does not merely cry "Hail!" He gives aid. Far from resembling a pirate, or rejoicing at shipwrecks, he is sometimes like the shore-pilot who goes to the aid of those surprised by a storm in entering or leaving port. The professor is less under obligation, or rather under obligation to something different. He is more committed to reserve and dignity. He ought not to stray from the consecrated places which it is his charge to show and guard. He cannot, however, entirely escape knowledge of new things, arrivals and approaches announced with pomp—sails which, from time to time, we signal on the horizon as though they were invincible armadas. It is necessary that he know them (at least the principal ones)—that he have his eye, in short, on the next shore and not fall asleep. . . .

Sainte-Beuve on His Own Method

I⊤ IS agreed, then, that today I shall be allowed to enter into some details touching the procedure and method I believe best in examining books and talents.

To me, literature—literary production—is not at all distinct or at least separable from the rest of the man and his nature. I can relish a work; but it is difficult for me to judge it independently

Sainte-Beuve on His Own Method. From "Chateaubriand," *Nouveaux Lundis* (July 22, 1862). Translated by the editor.

of a knowledge of the man himself. I should readily say "The tree is known by his fruit." Literary study, therefore, leads me naturally to moral study.

With the Ancients, one lacks sufficient means of observation. To get back to the man, the work in hand, is impossible in most cases with the true Ancients—with those of whom we have only a half-broken statue. We are therefore reduced to commenting on the work, to admiring and imagining the author through it. We can thus refashion the figures of the poets or the philosophers, the busts of Plato, Sophocles, or Virgil with an elevated, ideal feeling. It is all that the incomplete state of knowledge permits— the dearth of sources, the lack of means of information, and the impossibility of return. A great river, which in most cases one cannot ford, separates us from the great men of antiquity; we salute from one bank to another.

With the moderns it is entirely different; and the critic who regulates his method according to the means available, has here other duties. To know a man, and know him well moreover— above all if this man is a striking and celebrated individual, is an important thing, and one that ought not to be disdained.

The moral observation of characters is still [confined] to details, to elements, to the description of individuals or at most of some species. They do not go beyond Theophrastus and La Bruyère. A day will come, which I believe I have glimpsed in the course of my observations,—a day when the science [of criticism] will be established, when the great families of the spirit and their principal divisions will be determined and known. When the principal character of a mind is given, one will be able to deduce several other characteristics. Without doubt, one cannot deal with men exactly as with animals or plants. Man is morally more complex. He has what one calls liberty; and this, in all cases, presupposes a great variety of possible combinations. However, we shall someday be able, I imagine, to establish in a broader way the science of the moralist. Today it is at the point where botany was before Jussieu, and comparative anatomy before Cuvier—in the state of anecdote, that is. For our part, we write simple monographs; we amass detailed observations. But I catch sight of connections, of relations; and a more extended mind—more luminous, and still remaining close to precise detail —will someday be able to disclose the great natural divisions that mark the different groups of minds.

But even when the science of minds shall be organized in the way one may hope from afar, it will always be so delicate and mobile that it will exist only for those who have a natural aptitude and talent for observation. It will always be an *art* which will demand a gifted art-ist, just as medicine demands medical tact in the man who practices it, as philosophy must demand a philosophical sense in those who pretend to be philosophers, as poetry ought to be touched only by a poet.

I presuppose, then, someone who has the sort of talent or facility to understand literary groups or families (since at the moment the question has to do with literature)—someone who distinguishes them at first sight, who seizes on the life and the mind, of whom this ought truly to be the vocation: someone suitable to be a good naturalist in this vast field of minds.

Is it a question of studying a superior man, or one simply distinguished by his productions, —an author whose works we have read and who deserves the labor of a detailed examination? How does one proceed if one wishes to omit nothing important and essential in his subject, if one wishes to go beyond the judgments of outdated rhetoric, to be as little as possible the dupe of phrases, words, beautiful conventional sentiments, and attain truth as one does in a study of external nature? . . .

It is enough to indicate my line of thought, and I shall not abuse it. When one has established as well as one can the origins, the immediate and near kinsmen of an eminent writer, the essential point to determine—after a section devoted to his studies and education—is his first *milieu*, or environment: the first group of friends and contemporaries in which he found himself at the moment when his talent burst forth, took form, and became adult. His talent, indeed, will remain marked by it; and whatever he may do afterwards, he will feel the effects of it always. . . .

Very great individuals rise beyond a group. They themselves make a center, and gather others to them. But it is the group, the association, the alliance and active exchange of ideas, that gives to the man of talent all his *participation in what is outside himself*, all his maturing and value. There are talents that participate in several groups at the same time and which do not cease to range through different environments, either perfecting, transforming, or deforming themselves. In such cases, it is important to note, even in these changes, in these slow or sudden transformations, the hidden and constant spring of action, the persisting motive-force.

Each work of an author examined in this way, in its proper place, after you have put it back into the frame, and surrounded it with all the circumstances which have characterized its birth, acquires its complete meaning—its historical and literary significance. It recaptures its correct degree of originality, novelty, or imitation without incurring risks of judgment—of falsely inventing beauties and admiring amiss, as is inevitable when one clings to mere rhetoric.

With this term "rhetoric," which does not in my mind imply an absolute disapproval, I am quite far from disparaging and excluding judgments of taste—immediate and vital impressions. I do not renounce Quintilian; I mark his limits. To be a disciple of Bacon in literary history and criticism seems to me the need of the time, and an excellent approach in order to judge, first of all, and then to relish with greater certainty. . . .

It is important not only to catch a talent at the moment of its first attempt and first disclosure, when it appears fully shaped and more than adolescent, when it is becoming adult. A second period is no less necessary to note, if one wishes to know the man completely. It is the moment when he begins to decay or disintegrate, to fail or falter. . . . After the first moment when a talent, in its brilliant flowering, becomes a man, a young man splendid and striking, it is necessary to mark this second, unhappy moment when, in aging, he is stunted and made different. . . .

One cannot take too many methods or hints in order to know a man; he is another thing than pure spirit. Unless one has faced a certain number of questions about an author, and until one has answered them—even if only by oneself and in a whisper—one cannot be sure of capturing him completely, even though these questions seem completely unrelated to the character of his writings. What did he think religiously? How was he affected by the sight of nature? How did he act so far as women are concerned? —or in the matter of money? Was he rich—was he poor? What was his regimen, his manner of daily life? etc. In brief, what was his vice or weakness? Every person has one. None of the answers to these questions is unimportant in judging the author of a book—and of the book itself, if the work is not a treatise on pure geometry; especially if it is a literary work, a work into which he enters at all.

Very often an author, while writing, throws himself into an excess or affectation opposed to his flaw, his secret inclination, in order to dissemble or hide it. But it is still there as a visible and recognizable effect, though indirect and masked. It is only too easy to take the opposite way in everything. One only turns around one's weakness. Nothing so much resembles a hollow as a swelling. . . .

Up to a certain point, we can study talents in their moral posterity, in their disciples and typical admirers. That is a final easy and convenient means of observing. These affinities declare or betray themselves freely. Genius is a king who creates his people. Apply this to Lamartine, Hugo, Michelet, Balzac, or Musset. Enthusiastic admirers are something of accomplices. They adore themselves, their virtues and faults, in their great model. Tell me who admires and loves you, and I shall tell you who you are. . . .

HIPPOLYTE-ADOLPHE TAINE (1828-1893)

MORE than any other writer of the nineteenth century, Taine resolutely and systematically applied to the study of literary history the approach and general principles of natural science. The three criteria by which he undertook to analyze and classify a work were "race, moment, and *milieu*"—that is to say, national character, the age or period, and the general social environment. The work of art, in fact, became almost a by-product of these forces. Taine first applied his theory of cultural history in a preface to an essay on the Roman historian, Livy (1856), and, after a series of essays in the *Revue de l'Instruction Publique*, first on literary subjects and then on nineteenth-century French philosophers, he published his *tour de force, The History of English Literature* (1863-67), the introduction to which offers the clearest and most incisive statement of his approach. More general excursions of Taine into esthetic theory were his *Philosophy of Art* (1865) and *The Ideal in Art* (1867). Later, in his *Theory of Intelligence* (1878), Taine turned to psychology. In his *Origins of Contemporary France* (1876-93), left incomplete at his death, he tried to analyze the entire character of the French nation from the late eighteenth century to his own time, with the intention of studying man in one of his major crises.

Montesquieu more than a century before had tried in his *Esprit des Lois* to discover a guiding spirit in a nation's institutions, and the Italian philosopher, Vico, had discussed literature in terms of historical cycles. At the beginning of the nineteenth century, as we have seen, the two Schlegels had suggestively interpreted literature in terms of both national spirit and historical period, balanced and modified, however, by other considerations; and Madame de Staël more deliberately considered the relation of literature to social institutions. But Taine went much farther in systematizing the approach and in adding to these criteria the element of milieu. Taine's critics

HIPPOLYTE-ADOLPHE TAINE. After studying at the Collège Bourbon and the Normal School, Taine taught at Poitiers, where he was soon forced to resign (1851) because of his unpopular views. He later (1864) taught at the School of Fine Arts, and lectured at Oxford (1871).

The History of English Literature is translated by H. Van Laun (Edinburgh, 1871). A French edition of the Introduction has been edited, with an essay on Taine's method, by Irving Babbitt (1898). Helpful commentary on Taine is mainly in French. One may cite especially M. E. Boutmy, *Taine, Scherer, Laboulaye* (1901); P. Nève, *La Philosophie de Taine* (1908); and Sainte-Beuve, *Causeries du Lundi* (March, 1857). Among English commentaries, see Irving Babbitt, *Masters of Modern French Criticism* (1912); A. A. Eustis, *Hippolyte Taine and the Classical Genius* (Berkeley, 1951); S. J. Kahn, *Science and Aesthetic Judgment: a Study in Taine's Critical Method* (1953); and Harry Levin, "Literature as an Institution," *Accent,* VI (1946), 159-68, reprinted below, pp. 674-83.

have occasionally applied to him his own method, and have viewed him as a product of his own nation, age, and milieu—as an extreme example, that is, of the French scientific positivism of the mid-nineteenth century. The weakness of Taine lies in the inflexibility with which he applied his principles. There is a humorless intentness in his process of embalming and pinning down writers, like entomological specimens, in order to ornament his theories; and he moves about through the centuries, as Sainte-Beuve observed, with the set look of a laboratory chemist working among his crucibles. On the other hand, as Professor Harry Levin has said, the Introduction to Taine's *History of English Literature* is probably more justly viewed as "a manifesto than a methodology," and when regarded in this light, Taine's determinism appears as essentially "an intensive application of the intellectual curiosity of his age." Hence his value is that of any writer who systematically opens up and begins to explore a fruitful approach to a subject. A further value lies in his courageous application of his approach so intensively that its limitations—as a single and exclusive method of interpreting literature—are concretely and profitably disclosed, thus suggesting the need for a more experimental and subtle revision of that approach.

From the Introduction to the History of English Literature

HISTORY has been transformed, within a hundred years in Germany, within sixty years in France, and that by the study of their literatures.

It was perceived that a literary work is not a mere individual play of imagination, the isolated caprice of an excited brain, but a transcript of contemporary manners, a manifestation of a certain kind of mind. It was concluded that we might recover, from the monuments of literature, a knowledge of the manner in which men thought and felt centuries ago. The attempt was made, and it succeeded.

Pondering on these modes of feeling and thought, men decided that they were facts of the highest kind. They saw that these facts bore reference to the most important occurrences, that they explained and were explained by them, that it was necessary thenceforth to give them a rank, and a most important rank, in history. This rank they have received, and from that moment history has undergone a complete change: in its

History of English Literature. Published in 1863; translated by H. van Laun (Edinburgh, 1871).

subject matter, its system, its machinery, the appreciation of laws and of causes. It is this change, such as it is and must be, that we shall here endeavor to exhibit.

I

What is your first remark on turning over the great, stiff leaves of a folio, the yellow sheets of a manuscript—a poem, a code of laws, a confession of faith? This, you say, did not come into existence all alone. It is but a mold, like a fossil shell, an imprint, like one of those shapes embossed in stone by an animal which lived and perished. Under the shell there was an animal, and behind the document there was a man. Why do you study the shell, except to bring before you the animal? So you study the document only to know the man. The shell and the document are lifeless wrecks, valuable only as a clue to the entire and living existence. We must get hold of this existence, endeavor to re-create it. It is a mistake to study the document as if it were isolated. This were to treat things like a simple scholar, to fall into the error of the bibliomaniac. Neither mythology nor languages exist in themselves; but only men, who arrange words and imagery according to the necessities of their organs and the original bent of their intellects. A dogma is nothing in itself; look at the people who have made it—a portrait, for instance, of the sixteenth century, say the stern powerful face of an English archbishop or martyr. Nothing exists except through some individual man; it is this individual with whom we must become acquainted. When we have established the parentage of dogmas, or the classification of poems, or the progress of constitutions, or the transformation of idioms, we have only cleared the soil: genuine history is brought into existence only when the historian begins to unravel, across the lapse of time, the living man, toiling, impassioned, entrenched in his customs, with his voice and features, his gestures and his dress, distinct and complete as he from whom we have just parted in the street. Let us endeavor, then, to annihilate as far as possible this great interval of time, which prevents us from seeing man with our eyes, with the eyes of our head. . . . Let us make the past present: in order to judge of a thing, it must be before us; there is no experience in respect of what is absent. Doubtless this reconstruction is always incomplete; it can produce only incomplete judgments; but that we cannot help. It is better to have an imperfect knowledge than none at all; and there is no other means of acquainting ourselves approximately with the events of other days, than to *see* approximately the men of other days.

This is the first step in history; it was made in Europe at the revival of imagination, toward the close of the last century, by Lessing and Walter Scott; a little later in France, by Chateaubriand, Augustin Thierry, Michelet, and others. And now for the second step.

I I

When you consider with your eyes the visible man, what do you look for? The man invisible. The words which enter your ears, the gestures, the motions of his head, the clothes he wears, visible acts and deeds of every kind, are expressions merely; somewhat is revealed beneath them, and that is a soul. An inner man is con-

cealed beneath the outer man; the second does but reveal the first. You look at his house, furniture, dress; and that in order to discover in them the marks of his habits and tastes, the degree of his refinement or rusticity, his extravagance or his economy, his stupidity or his acuteness. You listen to his conversation, and you note the inflections of his voice, the changes in his attitudes; and that in order to judge of his vivacity, his self-forgetfulness or his gaiety, his energy or his constraint. You consider his writings, his artistic productions, his business transactions or political ventures; and that in order to measure the scope and limits of his intelligence, his inventiveness, his coolness, to find out the order, the character, the general force of his ideas, the mode in which he thinks and resolves. All these externals are but avenues converging towards a center; you enter them simply in order to reach that center; and that center is the genuine man, I mean that mass of faculties and feelings which are the inner man. We have reached a new world, which is infinite, because every action which we see involves an infinite association of reasonings, emotions, sensations new and old, which have served to bring it to light, and which, like great rocks deep-seated in the ground, find in it their end and their level. This underworld is a new subject matter, proper to the historian. If his critical education is sufficient, he can lay bare, under every detail of architecture, every stroke in a picture, every phrase in a writing, the special sensation whence detail, stroke, or phrase had issue; he is present at the drama which was enacted in the soul of artist or writer; the choice of a word, the brevity or length of a sentence, the nature of a metaphor, the accent of a verse, the development of an argument—everything is a symbol to him; while his eyes read the text, his soul and mind pursue the continuous development and the ever-changing succession of the emotions and conceptions out of which the text has sprung: in short, he works out its psychology. If you would observe this operation, consider the originator and model of all grand contemporary culture, Goethe, who, before writing *Iphigenia*, employed day after day in making drawings of the most finished statues, and who at last, his eyes filled with the noble forms of ancient scenery, his mind penetrated by the harmonious loveliness of antique life, succeeded in reproducing so exactly in himself the peculiarities of the Greek imagination, that he gives us almost the twin sister of the Antigone of Sophocles, and the goddesses of Phidias. This precise and proved interpretation of past sensations has given to history, in our days, a second birth; hardly anything of the sort was known to the preceding century. They thought men of every race and century were all but identical; the Greek, the barbarian, the Hindoo, the man of the Restoration, and the man of the eighteenth century, as if they had been turned out of a common mould; and all in conformity to a certain abstract conception, which served for the whole human race. They knew man, but not men; they had not penetrated to the soul; they had not seen the infinite diversity and marvellous complexity of souls; they did not know that the moral constitution of a people or an age is as particular and distinct as the physical structure of a family of plants or an order of animals. Now-a-days, history, like zoology, has found its anatomy; and whatever the branch of history to which you devote yourself, philology, linguistic lore, mythology, it is by these means you must strive to produce new fruit. . . . This is the second step; we are in a fair way to its completion. It is the fit work of the contemporary critic. No one has done it so justly and grandly as Sainte-Beuve: in this respect we are all his pupils; his method has revolutionized, in our days, in books, and even in newspapers, every kind of literary, philosophical and religious criticism. From it we must set out in order to begin the further development. I have more than once endeavored to indicate this development; there is here, in my mind, a new path open to history, and I will try to describe it more in detail.

III

When you have observed and noted in man one, two, three, then a multitude of sensations, does this suffice, or does your knowledge appear complete? Is psychology only a series of observations? No; here as elsewhere we must search out the causes after we have collected the facts. No matter if the facts be physical or moral, they all have their causes; there is a cause for ambition, for courage, for truth, as there is for

digestion, for muscular movement, for animal heat. Vice and virtue are products, like vitriol and sugar; and every complex phenomenon arises from other more simple phenomena on which it hangs. Let us then seek the simple phenomena for moral qualities; as we seek them for physical qualities; and let us take the first fact that presents itself: for example, religious music, that of a Protestant church. There is an inner cause which has turned the spirit of the faithful toward these grave and montonous melodies, a cause broader than its effect; I mean the general idea of the true, external worship which man owes to God. It is this which has modeled the architecture of Protestant places of worship, thrown down the statues, removed the pictures, destroyed the ornaments, curtailed the ceremonies, shut up the worshippers in high pews which prevent them from seeing anything, and regulated the thousand details of decoration, posture, and general externals. This again comes from another more general cause, the idea of human conduct in all its comprehensiveness, internal and external, prayers, actions, duties of every kind which man owes to God; it is this which has enthroned the doctrine of grace, lowered the status of the clergy, transformed the sacraments, suppressed various practices, and changed religion from a discipline to a morality. This second idea in its turn depends upon a third still more general, that of moral perfection, such as is met with in the perfect God, the unerring judge, the stern watcher of souls, before whom every soul is sinful, worthy of punishment, incapable of virtue or salvation, except by the power of conscience which He calls forth, and the renewal of heart which He produces. That is the master idea, which consists in erecting duty into an absolute king of human life, and in prostrating all ideal models before a moral model. Here we track the root of man; for to explain this conception it is necessary to consider the race itself, the German and Northman, the structure of his character and mind, his general processes of thought and feeling, the sluggishness and coldness of sensation which prevent his falling easily and headlong under the sway of pleasure, the bluntness of his taste, the irregularity and revolutions of his conception, which arrest in him the birth of fair dispositions and harmonious forms, the disdain of appearances, the desire for truth, the attachment for bare and abstract ideas, which develop in him conscience, at the expense of all else. There the search is at an end; we have arrived at a primitive disposition; at a feature peculiar to all the sensations, and to all the conceptions of a century or a race, at a particularity inseparable from all the motions of his intellect and his heart. Here lie the grand causes, for they are the universal and permanent causes, present at every moment and in every case, everywhere and always acting, indestructible, and finally infallibly supreme, since the accidents which thwart them, being limited and partial, end by yielding to the dull and incessant repetition of their efforts; in such a manner that the general structure of things, and the grand features of events, are their work; and religions, philosophies, poetries, industries, the framework of society and of families, are in fact only the imprints stamped by their seal. . . .

V

Three different sources contribute to produce this elementary moral state—RACE, SURROUNDINGS, and EPOCH. What we call the race are the innate and hereditary dispositions which man brings with him into the world and which, as a rule, are united with the marked differences in the temperament and structure of the body. They vary with various peoples. There is a natural variety of men, as of oxen and horses, some brave and intelligent, some timid and dependent, some capable of superior conceptions and creations, some reduced to rudimentary ideas and inventions, some more specially fitted to special works, and gifted more richly with particular instincts, as we meet with species of dogs better favored than others—these for coursing, those for fighting, those for hunting, these again for house dogs or shepherds' dogs. We have here a distinct force—so distinct that amidst the vast deviations which the other two motive forces produce in him, one can recognize it still; and a race, like the old Aryans, scattered from the Ganges as far as the Hebrides, settled in every clime, and every stage of civilization, transformed by thirty centuries of revolutions, nevertheless manifests in its languages, religions, literatures, philosophies, the community of blood and of intellect which to this day binds its off-

shoots together. Different as they are, their parentage is not obliterated; barbarism, culture and grafting, differences of sky and soil, fortunes good and bad, have labored in vain: the great marks of the original model have remained, and we find again the two or three principal lineaments of the primitive stamp underneath the secondary imprints which time has laid upon them. There is nothing astonishing in this extraordinary tenacity. Although the vastness of the distance lets us but half perceive—and by a doubtful light—the origin of species,[1] the events of history sufficiently illumine the events anterior to history, to explain the almost immovable steadfastness of the primordial marks. When we meet with them, fifteen, twenty, thirty centuries before our era, in an Aryan, an Egyptian, a Chinese, they represent the work of a great many ages, perhaps of several myriads of centuries. For as soon as an animal begins to exist, it has to reconcile itself with its surroundings; it breathes and renews itself, is differently affected according to the variations in air, food, temperature. Different climate and situation bring it various needs and, consequently, a different course of activity; and this, again, a different set of habits; and still again, a different set of aptitudes and instincts. Man, forced to accommodate himself to circumstances, contracts a temperament and a character corresponding to them; and his character, like his temperament, is so much more stable, as the external impression is made upon him by more numerous repetitions, and is transmitted to his progeny by a more ancient descent. So that at any moment we may consider the character of a people as an abridgement of all its preceding actions and sensations; that is, as a quantity and as a weight, not infinite,[2] since everything in nature is finite, but disproportioned to the rest, and almost impossible to lift, since every moment of an almost infinite past has contributed to increase it, and because, in order to raise the scale, one must place in the opposite scale a still greater number of actions and sensations. Such is the first and richest source of these master faculties from which historical events take their rise; and one sees at the outset that, if it be powerful, it

[1] Darwin, *The Origin of Species*; Prosper Lucas, *De L'hérédité*. [Taine.]

[2] Spinoza, *Ethics*, Pt. IV, axiom. [Taine.]

is because this is no simple spring but a kind of lake, a deep reservoir wherein other springs have, for a multitude of centuries, discharged their several streams.

Having thus outlined the interior structure of a race, we must consider the surroundings in which it exists. For man is not alone in the world; nature surrounds him, and his fellow men surround him; accidental and secondary tendencies overlay his primitive tendencies, and physical or social circumstances disturb or confirm the character committed to their charge. Sometimes the climate has had its effect. Though we can follow but obscurely the Aryan peoples from their common fatherland to their final settlements, we can yet assert that the profound differences which are manifest between the German races on the one side, and the Greek and Latin on the other, arise for the most part from the difference between the countries in which they are settled: some in cold moist lands, deep in rugged marshy forests or on the shores of a wild ocean, beset by melancholy or violent sensations, prone to drunkenness and gluttony, bent on a fighting, blood-spilling life; others, again, within the loveliest landscapes, on a bright and pleasant seacoast, enticed to navigation and commerce, exempt from gross cravings of the stomach, inclined from the beginning to social ways, to a settled organization of the state, to feelings and dispositions such as develop the art of oratory, the talent for enjoyment, the inventions of science, letters, arts. . . .

Thus it is with a people as with a plant; the same sap, under the same temperature, and in the same soil, produces, at different steps of its progressive development, different formations, buds, flowers, fruits, seed-vessels, in such a manner that the one which follows must always be preceded by the former, and must spring up from its death. And if now you consider no longer a brief epoch, as our own time, but one of those wide intervals which embrace one or more centuries, like the Middle Ages, or our last classic age, the conclusion will be similar. A certain dominant idea has had sway; men, for two, for five hundred years, have taken to themselves a certain ideal model of man: in the Middle Ages, the knight and the monk; in our classic age, the courtier, the man who speaks well. This creative and universal idea is displayed over the whole

field of action and thought; and, after covering the world with its involuntarily systematic works, it has faded, it has died away, and lo, a new idea springs up, destined to a like domination, and as manifold creations. And here remember that the second depends in part upon the first, and that the first, uniting its effect with those of national genius and surrounding circumstances, imposes on each new creation its bent and direction. . . .

VI

It remains for us to examine how these causes, when applied to a nation or an age, produce their results. As a spring, rising from a height and flowing downwards spreads its streams according to the depth of the descent, stage after stage, until it reaches the lowest level of the soil, so the disposition of intellect or soul impressed on a people by race, circumstances, or epoch, spreads in different proportions and by regular descents, down the diverse orders of facts which make up its civilization. If we arrange the map of a country, starting from the watershed, we find that below this common point the streams are divided into five or six principal basins, then each of these into several secondary basins, and so on, until the whole country with its thousand details is included in the ramifications of this network. So, if we arrange the psychological map of the events and sensations of a human civilization, we find first of all five or six well-defined provinces—religion, art, philosophy, the state, the family, the industries; then in each of these provinces natural departments; and in each of these, smaller territories, until we arrive at the numberless details of life such as may be observed within and around us every day. If now we examine and compare these diverse groups of facts, we find first of all that they are made up of parts, and that all have parts in common. Let us take first the three chief works of human intelligence—religion, art, philosophy. What is a philosophy but a conception of nature and its primordial causes, under the form of abstractions and formularies? What is there at the bottom of a religion or of an art but a conception of this same nature and of these same causes, under form of symbols more or less concise, and personages more or less marked; with this difference, that in the first we believe that they exist, in the second we believe that they do not exist? . . . A civilization forms a body, and its parts are connected with each other like the parts of an organic body. As in an animal, instincts, teeth, limbs, osseous structure, muscular envelope, are mutually connected, so that a change in one produces a corresponding change in the rest, and a clever naturalist can by a process of reasoning reconstruct out of a few fragments almost the whole body; even so in a civilization, religion, philosophy, the organization of the family, literature, the arts, make up a system in which every local change induces a general change, so that an experienced historian, studying some particular part of it, sees in advance and half predicts the character of the rest. There is nothing vague in this interdependence. In the living body the regulator is, first, its tendency to manifest a certain primary type; then its necessity for organs whereby to satisfy its wants, and to be in harmony with itself in order that it may live. In a civilization, the regulator is the presence, in every great human creation, of a productive element, present also in other surrounding creations,—to wit, some faculty, aptitude, disposition, effective and discernible, which, being possessed of its proper character, introduces it into all the operations in which it assists, and, according to its variations, causes all the works in which it co-operates to vary also.

VIII

History now attempts, or rather is very near attempting this method of research. The question propounded now-a-days is of this kind. Given a literature, philosophy, society, art, group of arts, what is the moral condition which produced it? what the conditions of race, epoch, circumstance, the most fitted to produce this moral condition? . . . No one has better taught us [than Stendhal] how to open our eyes and see, to see first the men that surround us and the life that is present, then the ancient and authentic documents, to read between the black and white lines of the pages, to recognize beneath the old impression, under the scribbling of a text, the precise sentiment, the movement of ideas, the state of mind in which they were written. In his writings, in Sainte-Beuve, in the German critics, the reader will see all the wealth that may be drawn from a literary work: when the work is rich, and people know how to interpret it, we find there the psychology of a soul, frequently of an age, now and then of a race. In this light, a great poem, a fine novel, the confessions of a superior man, are more instructive than a heap of historians with their histories. I would give fifty volumes of charters and a hundred volumes of state papers for the memoirs of Cellini, the epistles of St. Paul, the table talk of Luther, or the comedies of Aristophanes. In this consists the importance of literary works: they are instructive because they are beautiful; their utility grows with their perfection; and if they furnish documents it is because they are monuments. The more a book brings sentiments into light, the more it is a work of literature; for the proper office of literature is to make sentiments visible. The more a book represents important sentiments, the higher is its place in literature; for it is by representing the mode of being of a whole nation and a whole age that a writer rallies round him the sympathies of an entire age and of an entire nation. That is why, amid the writings which set before our eyes the sentiments of preceding generations, a literature, and notably a grand literature, is incomparably the best. It resembles those admirable apparatuses of extraordinary sensibility by which physicians disentangle and measure the most recondite and delicate changes of a body. Constitutions, religions, do not approach it in importance; the articles of a code of laws and of a creed only show us the spirit roughly and without delicacy. If there are any writings in which politics and dogma are full of life, it is in the eloquent discourses of the pulpit and the tribune, memoirs, unrestrained confessions; and all this belongs to literature: so that, in addition to itself, it has all the advantage of other works. It is then chiefly by the study of literatures that one may construct a moral history, and advance toward the knowledge of psychological laws, from which events spring.

I intend to write the history of a literature, and to seek in it for the psychology of a people: if I have chosen this nation in particular, it is not without a reason. I had to find a people with a grand and complete literature, and this is rare: there are few nations who have, during their whole existence, really thought and written. Among the ancients, the Latin literature is worth nothing at the outset, then it borrowed and became imitative. Among the moderns, German literature does not exist for nearly two centuries.[3] Italian literature and Spanish literature end at the middle of the seventeenth century. Only ancient Greece, modern France and England, offer a complete series of great significant monuments. I have chosen England, because being still living, and subject to direct examination, it may be better studied than a destroyed civilization, of which we retain but the relics, and because, being different from France, it has in the eyes of a Frenchman a more distinct character. Besides, there is a peculiarity in this civilization, that apart from its spontaneous develop-

[3] From 1550 to 1750. [Taine.]

ment, it presents a forced deviation, it has suffered the last and most effectual of all conquests, and the three grounds whence it has sprung, race, climate, the Norman invasion, may be observed in its remains with perfect exactness; so that we may examine in this history the two most powerful moving springs of human transformation, natural bent and constraining force, and we may examine them without uncertainty or gap, in a series of authentic and unmutilated memorials.

I have to define these primary springs, to exhibit their gradual effects, to explain how they have ended by bringing to light great political, religious, and literary works, and by developing the recondite mechanism whereby the Saxon barbarian has been transformed into the Englishman of to-day.

WALTER PATER (1839-1894)

Among the later nineteenth-century attempts to reassert the value of art, in opposition to the prevailing scientific and economic interests, one of the least enduring proved to be the "Art-for-Art's-sake" movement. It was ineffectual largely because it tended to restrict art even more into a specialized and separate pursuit. The most distinguished English representative of this movement was undoubtedly Walter Pater. Yet when Pater is sympathetically read, he does not really seem typical of the "Art-for-Art's-sake" group. His theoretical position is too moderate, too intelligently qualified. There is, in his *Studies in the History of the Renaissance* (1873), an exquisite Epicureanism, which becomes somewhat more austere in his later *Appreciations* (1889), *Greek Studies* (1895), and *Miscellaneous Studies* (1895). Still, Pater was disconcerted when Oscar Wilde and others ex-

WALTER PATER. Educated at King's School, Canterbury, and at Oxford, Pater became a Fellow of Brasenose College, Oxford (1864), toured Italy (1865), and then settled at Oxford for the next twenty years, where, except for later living in London part of the time each year, he remained until his death.

The standard text is *Works* (10 vols., 1910). Relevant commentary may be found in R. C. Child, *The Aesthetic of Walter Pater* (1940); D. J. DeLaura, *Hebrew and Hellene in Victorian England: Newman, Arnold, and Pater* (Austin, 1969); Ian Fletcher, *Walter Pater* (1959); and G. S. Fraser, "Walter Pater: His Theory of Style, His Style in Practice, His Influence," in *The Art of Victorian Prose*, ed. G. Levine and W. Madden (1968).

tolled him as the leader of the esthetic cult. He was particularly embarrassed that the famous Conclusion to the *Renaissance* should be regarded as a proclamation on behalf of hedonistic paganism, and he suppressed it in the second edition, reprinting it only after his *Marius the Epicurean* (1885) had qualified what his readers believed to be his position. Finally, in his more theoretical statements about art—though he did not develop them very far —Pater touched closely on some of the more general ideals of both classical and romantic theory: the formative power of art to deepen our feeling and consciousness of life; the primary importance of the "imaginative reason"— a term originally used by Arnold—in coalescing the activity of one's total mind; and the organic union of form and content, in which "the end is not distinct from the means . . . the subject from the expression."

The Renaissance

PREFACE

MANY attempts have been made by writers on art and poetry to define beauty in the abstract, to express it in the most general terms, to find a universal formula for it. The value of these attempts has most often been in the suggestive and penetrating things said by the way. Such discussions help us very little to enjoy what has been well done in art or poetry, to discriminate between what is more and what is less excellent in them, or to use words like beauty, excellence, art, poetry, with a more precise meaning than they would otherwise have. Beauty, like all other qualities presented to human experience, is relative; and the definition of it becomes unmeaning and useless in proportion to its abstractness. To define beauty, not in the most abstract, but in the most concrete terms possible, to find, not a universal formula for it, but the formula which expresses most adequately this or that special manifestation of it, is the aim of the true student of aesthetics.

"To see the object as in itself it really is," has been justly said to be the aim of all true criticism whatever; and in aesthetic criticism the first step towards seeing one's object as it really is, is to know one's own impression as it really is, to discriminate it, to realise it distinctly. The objects with which aesthetic criticism deals— music, poetry, artistic and accomplished forms

of human life—are indeed receptacles of so many powers or forces: they possess, like the products of nature, so many virtues or qualities. What is this song or picture, this engaging personality presented in life or in a book, to *me?* What effect does it really produce on me? Does it give me pleasure? and if so, what sort or degree of pleasure? How is my nature modified by its presence, and under its influence? The answers to these questions are the original facts with which the aesthetic critic has to do; and, as in the study of light, of morals, of number, one must realise such primary data for oneself, or not at all. And he who experiences these impressions strongly, and drives directly at the analysis and discrimination of them, has no need to trouble himself with the abstract question what beauty is in itself, or what its exact relation to truth or experience—metaphysical questions, as unprofitable as metaphysical questions elsewhere. He may pass them all by as being, answerable or not, of no interest to him.

The aesthetic critic, then, regards all the objects with which he has to do, all works of art, and the fairer forms of nature and human life, as powers or forces producing pleasurable sensations, each of a more or less peculiar or unique kind. This influence he feels, and wishes to explain, analysing it, and reducing it to its elements. To him, the picture, the landscape, the engaging personality in life or in a book, *La Gioconda,* the hills of Carrara, Pico of Miran-

The Renaissance. Published in 1873.

dola, are valuable for their virtues, as we say, in speaking of a herb, a wine, a gem; for the property each has of affecting one with a special, a unique, impression of pleasure. Our education becomes complete in proportion as our susceptibility to these impressions increases in depth and variety. And the function of the aesthetic critic is to distinguish, analyse, and separate from its adjuncts, the virtue by which a picture, a landscape, a fair personality in life or in a book, produces this special impression of beauty or pleasure, to indicate what the source of that impression is, and under what conditions it is experienced. His end is reached when he has disengaged that virtue, and noted it, as a chemist notes some natural element, for himself and others; and the rule for those who would reach this end is stated with great exactness in the words of a recent critic of Sainte-Beuve: *De se borner à connaître de près les belles choses, et à s'en nourrir en exquis amateurs, en humanistes accomplis.*[1]

What is important, then, is not that the critic should possess a correct abstract definition of beauty for the intellect, but a certain kind of temperament, the power of being deeply moved by the presence of beautiful objects. He will remember always that beauty exists in many forms. To him all periods, types, schools of taste, are in themselves equal. In all ages there have been some excellent workmen, and some excellent work done. The question he asks is always:—In whom did the stir, the genius, the sentiment of the period find itself? where was the receptacle of its refinement, its elevation, its taste? "The ages are all equal," says William Blake, "but genius is always above its age."

Often it will require great nicety to disengage this virtue from the commoner elements with which it may be found in combination. Few artists, not Goethe or Byron even, work quite cleanly, casting off all *débris*, and leaving us only what the heat of their imagination has wholly fused and transformed. Take, for instance, the writings of Wordsworth. The heat of his genius, entering into the substance of his work, has crystallised a part, but only a part,

of it; and in that great mass of verse there is much which might well be forgotten. But scattered up and down it, sometimes fusing and transforming entire compositions, like the stanzas on *Resolution and Independence,* and the Ode on the *Recollections of Childhood,* sometimes, as if at random, depositing a fine crystal here or there, in a matter it does not wholly search through and transform, we trace the action of his unique, incommunicable faculty, that strange, mystical sense of a life in natural things, and of man's life as a part of nature, drawing strength and colour and character from local influences, from the hills and streams, and from natural sights and sounds. Well! that is the *virtue,* the active principle in Wordsworth's poetry; and then the function of the critic of Wordsworth is to follow up that active principle, to disengage it, to mark the degree in which it penetrates his verse.

The subjects of the following studies are taken from the history of the Renaissance, and touch what I think the chief points in that complex, many-sided movement. I have explained in the first of them what I understand by the word, giving it a much wider scope than was intended by those who originally used it to denote only that revival of classical antiquity in the fifteenth century which was but one of many results of a general excitement and enlightening of the human mind, of which the great aim and achievements of what, as Christian art, is often falsely opposed to the Renaissance, were another result. This outbreak of the human spirit may be traced far into the Middle Age itself, with its qualities already clearly pronounced, the care for physical beauty, the worship of the body, the breaking down of those limits which the religious system of the Middle Age imposed on the heart and the imagination. I have taken as an example of this movement, this earlier Renaissance within the Middle Age itself, and as an expression of its qualities, two little compositions in early French; not because they constitute the best possible expression of them, but because they help the unity of my series, inasmuch as the Renaissance ends also in France, in French poetry, in a phase of which the writings of Joachim du Bellay are in many ways the most perfect illustration; the Renaissance thus putting forth in France an aftermath, a

[1] *De se borner,* etc.: "To limit themselves to know lovely things near at hand, and to nourish themselves upon them, like refined amateurs, like accomplished humanists." [Pater.]

wonderful later growth, the products of which have to the full that subtle and delicate sweetness which belongs to a refined and comely decadence; just as its earliest phases have the freshness which belongs to all periods of growth in art, the charm of *ascêsis*,[2] of the austere and serious girding of the loins in youth.

But it is in Italy, in the fifteenth century, that the interest of the Renaissance mainly lies, —in that solemn fifteenth century which can hardly be studied too much, not merely for its positive results in the things of the intellect and the imagination, its concrete works of art, its special and prominent personalities, with their profound aesthetic charm, but for its general spirit and character, for the ethical qualities of which it is a consummate type.

The various forms of intellectual activity which together make up the culture of an age, move for the most part from different starting-points, and by unconnected roads. As products of the same generation they partake, indeed, of a common character, and unconsciously illustrate each other; but of the producers themselves, each group is solitary, gaining what advantage or disadvantage there may be in intellectual isolation. Art and poetry, philosophy and the religious life, and that other life of refined pleasure and action in the open places of the world, are each of them confined to its own circle of ideas, and those who prosecute either of them are generally little curious of the thoughts of others. There come, however, from time to time, eras of more favourable conditions, in which the thoughts of men draw nearer together than is their wont, and the many interests of the intellectual world combine in one complete type of general culture. The fifteenth century in Italy is one of these happier eras; and what is sometimes said of the age of Pericles is true of that of Lorenzo:—it is an age productive in personalities, many-sided, centralised, complete. Here, artists and philosophers and those whom the action of the world has elevated and made keen, do not live in isolation, but breathe a common air, and catch light and heat from each other's thoughts. There is a spirit of general elevation and enlightenment in which all alike communicate. It is the unity of

[2] *ascêsis:* "severe training."

this spirit which gives unity to all the various products of the Renaissance; and it is to this intimate alliance with mind, this participation in the best thoughts which that age produced, that the art of Italy in the fifteenth century owes much of its grave dignity and influence.

I have added an essay on Winckelmann, as not incongruous with the studies which precede it, because Winckelmann, coming in the eighteenth century, really belongs in spirit to an earlier age. By his enthusiasm for the things of the intellect and the imagination for their own sake, by his Hellenism, his life-long struggle to attain to the Greek spirit, he is in sympathy with the humanists of an earlier century. He is the last fruit of the Renaissance, and explains in a striking way its motive and tendencies.

CONCLUSION

To regard all things and principles of things as inconstant modes or fashions has more and more become the tendency of modern thought. Let us begin with that which is without—our physical life. Fix upon it in one of its more exquisite intervals, the moment, for instance, of delicious recoil from the flood of water in summer heat. What is the whole physical life in that moment but a combination of natural elements to which science gives their names? But these elements, phosphorus and lime and delicate fibres, are present not in the human body alone: we detect them in places most remote from it. Our physical life is a perpetual motion of them —the passage of the blood, the wasting and repairing of the lenses of the eye, the modification of the tissues of the brain by every ray of light and sound—processes which science reduces to simpler and more elementary forces. Like the elements of which we are composed, the action of these forces extends beyond us; it rusts iron and ripens corn. Far out on every side of us those elements are broadcast, driven by many forces; and birth and gesture and death and the springing of violets from the grave are but a few out of ten thousand resultant combinations. That clear, perpetual outline of face and limb is but an image of ours, under which we group them—a design in a web, the actual threads of which pass out beyond it. This at least of flame-like our life has, that it is but the concurrence, renewed from moment to moment, of forces parting sooner or later on their ways.

Or if we begin with the inward world of thought and feeling, the whirlpool is still more rapid, the flame more eager and devouring. There it is no longer the gradual darkening of the eye and fading of colour from the wall,—the movement of the shoreside, where the water flows down indeed, though in apparent rest,—but the race of the mid-stream, a drift of momentary acts of sight and passion and thought. At first sight experience seems to bury us under a flood of external objects, pressing upon us with a sharp and importunate reality, calling us out of ourselves in a thousand forms of action. But when reflexion begins to act upon those objects they are dissipated under its influence; the cohesive force seems suspended like a trick of magic; each object is loosed into a group of impressions—colour, odour, texture—in the mind of the observer. And if we continue to dwell in thought on this world, not of objects in the solidity with which language invests them, but of impressions unstable, flickering, inconsistent, which burn and are extinguished with our consciousness of them, it contracts still further; the whole scope of observation is dwarfed to the narrow chamber of the individual mind. Experience, already reduced to a swarm of impressions, is ringed round for each one of us by that thick wall of personality through which no real voice has ever pierced on its way to us, or from us to that which we can only conjecture to be without. Every one of those impressions is the impression of the individual in his isolation, each mind keeping as a solitary prisoner its own dream of a world.

Analysis goes a step farther still, and assures us that that those impressions of the individual mind to which, for each one of us, experience dwindles down, are in perpetual flight; that each of them is limited by time, and that as time is infinitely divisible, each of them is infinitely divisible also; all that is actual in it being a single moment, gone while we try to apprehend it, of which it may ever be more truly said that it has ceased to be than that it is. To such a tremulous wisp constantly reforming itself on the stream, to a single sharp impression, with a sense in it, a relic more or less fleeting, of such moments gone by, what is real in our life fines

itself down. It is with this movement, with the passage and dissolution of impressions, images, sensations, that analysis leaves off—that continual vanishing away, that strange, perpetual weaving and unweaving of ourselves.

Philosophiren, says Novalis, *ist dephlegmatisiren, vivificiren.*[3] The service of philosophy, of speculative culture, towards the human spirit is to rouse, to startle it into sharp and eager observation. Every moment some form grows perfect in hand or face; some tone on the hills or the sea is choicer than the rest; some mood of passion or insight or intellectual excitement is irresistibly real and attractive for us,—for that moment only. Not the fruit of experience, but experience itself, is the end. A counted number of pulses only is given to us of a variegated, dramatic, life. How may we see in them all that is to be seen in them by the finest senses? How shall we pass most swiftly from point to point, and be present always at the focus where the greatest number of vital forces unite in their purest energy?

To burn always with this hard, gemlike flame, to maintain this ecstasy, is success in life. In a sense it might even be said that our failure is to form habits: for, after all, habit is relative to a stereotyped world, and meantime it is only the roughness of the eye that makes any two persons, things, situations, seem alike. While all melts under our feet, we may well catch at any exquisite passion, or any contribution to knowledge that seems by a lifted horizon to set the spirit free for a moment, or any stirring of the senses, strange dyes, strange colours, and curious odours, or work of the artist's hands, or the face of one's friend. Not to discriminate every moment some passionate attitude in those about us, and in the brilliancy of their gifts some tragic dividing of forces on their ways, is, on this short day of frost and sun, to sleep before evening. With this sense of the splendour of our experience and of its awful brevity, gathering all we are into one desperate effort to see and touch, we shall hardly have time to make theories about the things we see and touch. What we have to do is to be for ever curiously testing new opinions and courting new impressions, never

---

[3] *Philosophiren,* etc.: "To philosophize is to throw off inertia, to come to life."

acquiescing in a facile orthodoxy of Comte, or of Hegel, or of our own. Philosophical theories or ideas, as points of view, instruments of criticism, may help us to gather up what might otherwise pass unregarded by us. "Philosophy is the microscope of thought." The theory or idea or system which requires of us the sacrifice of any part of this experience, in consideration of some interest into which we cannot enter, or some abstract theory we have not identified with ourselves, or what is only conventional, has no real claim upon us.

One of the most beautiful passages in the writings of Rousseau is that in the sixth book of the *Confessions*, where he describes the awakening in him of the literary sense. An undefinable taint of death had always clung about him, and now in early manhood he believed himself smitten by mortal disease. He asked himself how he might make as much as possible of the interval that remained; and he was not biassed by anything in his previous life when he decided that it must be by intellectual excitement, which he found just then in the clear, fresh writings of Voltaire. Well! we are all *condamnés*, as Victor Hugo says: we are all under sentence of death but with a sort of indefinite reprieve—*les hommes sont tous condamnés à mort avec des sursis indéfinis:* we have an interval, and then our place knows us no more. Some spend this interval in listlessness, some in high passions, the wisest, at least among "the children of this world," in art and song. For our one chance lies in expanding that interval, in getting as many pulsations as possible into the given time. Great passions may give us this quickened sense of life, ecstasy and sorrow of love, the various forms of enthusiastic activity, disinterested or otherwise, which come naturally to many of us. Only be sure it is passion—that it does yield you this fruit of a quickened, multiplied consciousness. Of this wisdom, the poetic passion, the desire of beauty, the love of art for art's sake, has most; for art comes to you professing frankly to give nothing but the highest quality to your moments as they pass, and simply for those moments' sake.

LEO TOLSTOY   (1828-1910)

Tolstoy's *What Is Art?* is the most distinguished statement in modern criticism of the view that the value of art lies in its obvious social usefulness. The function of art, in other words, is to spread and instill specific social ideals in human minds. The end that Tolstoy envisages is nothing less than the universal Christian brotherhood of man. And this noble ideal, as he urged it in his later writings, becomes the more moving because Tolstoy, in his own life, tried so consistently and concretely to abide by it.

The first half of Tolstoy's *What Is Art?* consists of an introductory survey

LEO TOLSTOY. Born of a noble family and privately educated until he attended the University of Kazan, Count Tolstoy became acquainted with social circles in Moscow and St. Petersburg, but was also interested in helping the serfs. For a while he served in the army, wrote fiction showing the evils of war, and then traveled through western Europe. In his early thirties, Tolstoy returned to his family's estate (1861), made efforts to teach the children of serfs, and wrote his great novels, *War and Peace* (1865-69) and *Anna Karenina* (1875-77). He became increasingly interested in expounding a deeply humanitarian conception of Christianity and combining it with high-minded socialist ideals. His *What is Art?* is one of the writings of this later period when, in addition to living according to his beliefs, he was also trying to explain them.

of traditional theories of art. These, to his mind, are vitiated because they generally aim at what is "beautiful." The word "beauty" was interpreted by Tolstoy in a limited sense: as applying to sensuous pleasure, to egoistic feelings, and to whatever desires are socially encouraged by the particular group of people in question. The inadequacy of previous theories of art reflects the general inadequacy of the so-called great art of the past. Though some of the highest examples of art were admittedly created in ancient Greece, Tolstoy could not forget that Greek society permitted slavery. Hence he felt there was a certain exclusiveness, a limited appeal, in the Greek approach to art. On the other hand, though he regarded the Church doctrine of the Middle Ages as a distortion of true Christianity, he felt that, since art subserved religious ends during this period, it was addressed to all people and thus came nearer his demand. In the Renaissance, however, art became the amusement and pastime, he believed, of the aristocratic and wealthy classes. It catered directly to their prejudices and desires. "From the time that people of the upper classes lost faith in Church Christianity, beauty [i.e., the *pleasure* received from art] became their standard of good and bad art," and therefore "an aesthetic theory naturally sprang up among those upper classes justifying such a conception . . ." But the greatest art has always been addressed to the widest possible audience, and has taken as its subject the highest ideals. From the Renaissance to the present time art has largely neglected its duty to propagate the ideal of universal brotherhood. Michelangelo, Milton, Bach, Beethoven, Goethe,—even Shakespeare—have been undeservedly set up by the "false criticism" of the period from the Renaissance to the end of the nineteenth century as "models worthy of imitation," though their works are merely "brain-spun"—that is, ingenious contrivances of art-for-art's-sake. As a result, a debased and "counterfeit" art, patterned after these models, has become dominant. Idle, sensationalistic novels, self-centered and incomprehensible poetry (especially that of the French Symbolists) and refined, self-conscious music and painting have all subserved three desires or feelings cultivated by the rich classes but really "very insignificant" in human life. They are (1) pride and exclusiveness; (2) romantic love; and (3) weariness and dissatisfaction with life.

One may certainly argue, at least, that serious art has become more restricted in its appeal, and that popular taste has been left to be the prey of a cynical, increasingly mass-produced art with ready-made and standardized formulae. But some of Tolstoy's theoretical adverse criticism, particularly when it deals with the nineteenth century, is more impressive than the

---

The standard English translation is that of Aylmer Maude (1898; rev. 1899), made under Tolstoy's supervision. Despite the fame of the work, specific commentary is sparse, probably because of the obviousness of Tolstoy's point of view. The work is largely self-explanatory, and it can hardly be argued against without assuming entirely different premises. See H. G. Duffield (ed.), *Tolstoy and the Critics: Literature and Aesthetics* (Chicago, 1965); and Thomas Mann, "Goethe and Tolstoy," in *Three Essays* (1929; reprinted in *Essays of Three Decades*, 1947).

specific examples he selected for approval. "Art," he believed, "is a human activity, consisting in this, that one man consciously, by means of external signs, hands on to others feelings he has lived through, and that other people are infected by these feelings, and also experience them." It can, in short, serve as the most active and effective communicator among men, and, as such, art has a high educative function. This premise has, of course, been a common assumption since the beginning of the criticism of art in ancient Greece. What differentiates it here, however, is the narrowness with which it is interpreted by Tolstoy—a narrowness shown both in his restricted idea of the proper subject matter of art and in his belief that the only manner in which art educates is in the most elementary and direct ways. Like Plato, therefore, this high-minded humanitarian would have forbidden, if he could, all art that did not immediately and obviously contribute to the religious and social ideal he had in mind. And again like Plato, Tolstoy took the stand he did partly because he appreciated so vividly the remarkable power of art to shape human character.

From What Is Art?

CHAPTER X

IT IS said that the very best works of art are such that they cannot be understood by the mass, but are accessible only to the elect who are prepared to understand these great works. But if the majority of men do not understand, the knowledge necessary to enable them to understand should be taught and explained to them. But it turns out that there is no such knowledge, that the works cannot be explained, and that those who say the majority do not understand good works of art, still do not explain those works, but only tell us that, in order to understand them, one must read, and see, and hear these same works over and over again. But this is not to explain, it is only to habituate! And people may habituate themselves to anything, even to the very worst things. As people may habituate themselves to bad food, to spirits, tobacco, and opium, just in the same way they may habituate themselves to bad art—and that is exactly what is being done.

What Is Art? 1898; translated by Aylmer Maude. Reprinted by permission of Oxford University Press. Of the three chapters printed here, Ch. XV is given as a whole, and Chs. X and XVI are given in part.

Moreover, it cannot be said that the majority of people lack the taste to esteem the highest works of art. The majority always have understood, and still understand, what we also recognise as being the very best art: the epic of Genesis, the Gospel parables, folk-legends, fairy-tales, and folk-songs are understood by all. How can it be that the majority has suddenly lost its capacity to understand what is high in our art?

Of a speech it may be said that it is admirable, but incomprehensible to those who do not know the language in which it is delivered. A speech delivered in Chinese may be excellent, and may yet remain incomprehensible to me if I do not know Chinese; but what distinguishes a work of art from all other mental activity is just the fact that its language is understood by all, and that it infects all without distinction. The tears and laughter of a Chinese infect me just as the laughter and tears of a Russian; and it is the same with painting and music and poetry, when it is translated into a language I understand. The songs of a Kirghiz or of a Japanese touch me, though in a lesser degree than they touch a Kirghiz or a Japanese. I am also touched by Japanese painting, Indian architecture, and Arabian stories. If I am but little touched by a

Japanese song and a Chinese novel, it is not that I do not understand these productions, but that I know and am accustomed to higher works of art. It is not because their art is above me. Great works of art are only great because they are accessible and comprehensible to everyone. The story of Joseph, translated into the Chinese language, touches a Chinese. The story of Sakya Muni touches us. And there are, and must be, buildings, pictures, statues, and music of similar power. So that, if art fails to move men, it cannot be said that this is due to the spectators' or hearers' lack of understanding; but the conclusion to be drawn may, and should be, that such art is either bad art, or is not art at all.

Art is differentiated from activity of the understanding, which demands preparation and a certain sequence of knowledge (so that one cannot learn trigonometry before knowing geometry), by the fact that it acts on people independently of their state of development and education, that the charm of a picture, of sounds, or of forms, infects any man whatever his plane of development.

The business of art lies just in this—to make that understood and felt which, in the form of an argument, might be incomprehensible and inaccessible. Usually it seems to the recipient of a truly artistic impression that he knew the thing before but had been unable to express it.

And such has always been the nature of good, supreme art; the *Iliad*, the *Odyssey*, the stories of Isaac, Jacob, and Joseph, the Hebrew prophets, the psalms, the Gospel parables, the story of Sakya Muni, and the hymns of the Vedas: all transmit very elevated feelings, and are nevertheless quite comprehensible now to us, educated or uneducated, as they were comprehensible to the men of those times, long ago, who were even less educated than our labourers. People talk about incomprehensibility; but if art is the transmission of feelings flowing from man's religious perception, how can a feeling be incomprehensible which is founded on religion, *i.e.* on man's relation to God? Such art should be, and has actually, always been, comprehensible to everybody, because every man's relation to God is one and the same. And therefore the churches and the images in them were always comprehensible to everyone. The hindrance to understanding the best and highest feelings (as

is said in the gospel) does not at all lie in deficiency of development or learning, but, on the contrary, in false development and false learning. A good and lofty work of art may be incomprehensible, but not to simple, unperverted peasant labourers (all that is highest is understood by them)—it may be, and often is, unintelligible to erudite, perverted people destitute of religion. And this continually occurs in our society, in which the highest feelings are simply not understood. For instance, I know people who consider themselves most refined, and who say that they do not understand the poetry of love to one's neighbor, of self-sacrifice, or of chastity. . . .

CHAPTER XV

ART, in our society, has been so perverted that not only has bad art come to be considered good, but even the very perception of what art really is has been lost. In order to be able to speak about the art of our society, it is, therefore, first of all necessary to distinguish art from counterfeit art.

There is one indubitable indication distinguishing real art from its counterfeit, namely, the infectiousness of art. If a man, without exercising effort and without altering his standpoint, on reading, hearing, or seeing another man's work, experiences a mental condition which unites him with that man and with other people who also partake of that work of art, then the object evoking that condition is a work of art. And however poetical, realistic, effectual, or interesting a work may be, it is not a work of art if it does not evoke that feeling (quite distinct from all other feelings) of joy, and of spiritual union with another (the author) and with others (those who are also infected by it).

It is true that this indication is an *internal* one, and that there are people who have forgotten what the action of real art is, who expect something else from art (in our society the great majority are in this state), and that therefore such people may mistake for this aesthetic feeling the feeling of divertisement and a certain excitement which they receive from counterfeits of art. But though it is impossible to undeceive these people, just as it is impossible to convince a man suffering from "Daltonism" that green is not red, yet, for all that, this indication remains perfectly definite to those whose feeling for art is neither perverted nor atrophied, and it clearly distinguishes the feeling produced by art from all other feelings.

The chief peculiarity of this feeling is that the receiver of a true artistic impression is so united to the artist that he feels as if the work were his own and not someone else's—as if what it expresses were just what he had long been wishing to express. A real work of art destroys, in the consciousness of the receiver, the separation between himself and the artist; nor that alone, but also between himself and all whose minds receive this work of art. In this freeing of our personality from its separation and isolation, in this uniting of it with others, lies the chief characteristic and the great attractive force of art.

If a man is infected by the author's condition of soul, if he feels this emotion and this union with others, then the object which has effected this is art; but if there be no such infection, if there be not this union with the same author and others who are moved by the same work—then it is not art. And not only is infection a sure sign of art, but the degree of infectiousness is also the sole measure of excellence of art.

The stronger the infection the better is the art, as art, speaking now apart from its subject-matter; *i.e.* not considering the quality of the feelings it transmits.

And the degree of the infectiousness of art depends on three conditions:—

(1) On the greater or lesser individuality of the feeling transmitted; (2) on the greater or lesser clearness with which the feeling is transmitted; (3) on the sincerity of the artist, *i.e.* on the greater or lesser force with which the artist himself feels the emotion he transmits.

The more individual the feeling transmitted the more strongly does it act on the receiver; the more individual the state of soul into which he is transferred the more pleasure does the receiver obtain, and therefore the more readily and strongly does he join in it.

The clearness of expression assists infection, because the receiver, who mingles in consciousness with the author, is the better satisfied the more clearly the feeling is transmitted, which, as it seems to him, he has long known and felt,

and for which he has only now found expression.

But most of all is the degree of infectiousness of art increased by the degree of sincerity in the artist. As soon as the spectator, hearer, or reader feels that the artist is infected by his own production, and writes, sings, or plays for himself, and not merely to act on others, this mental condition of the artist infects the receiver; and, contrariwise, as soon as the spectator, reader, or hearer feels that the author is not writing, singing, or playing for his own satisfaction,—does not himself feel what he wishes to express,—but is doing it for him, the receiver, a resistance immediately springs up, and the most individual and the newest feelings and the cleverest technique not only fail to produce any infection, but actually repel.

I have mentioned three condtions of contagiousness in art, but they may be all summed up into one, the last, sincerity, *i.e.* that the artist should be impelled by an inner need to express his feeling. That condition includes the first; for if the artist is sincere he will express the feeling as he experienced it. And as each man is different from everyone else, his feeling will be individual for everyone else; and the more individual it is,—the more the artist has drawn it from the depths of his nature,—the more sympathetic and sincere will it be. And this same sincerity will impel the artist to find a clear expression of the feeling which he wishes to transmit.

Therefore this third condition—sincerity—is the most important of the three. It is always complied with in peasant art, and this explains why such art always acts so powerfully; but it is a condition almost entirely absent from our upper-class art, which is continually produced by artists actuated by personal aims of covetousness or vanity.

Such are the three conditions which divide art from its counterfeits, and which also decide the quality of every work of art apart from its subject-matter.

The absence of any one of these conditions excludes a work from the category of art and relegates it to that of art's counterfeits. If the work does not transmit the artist's peculiarity of feeling, and is therefore not individual, if it is unintelligibly expressed, or if it has not proceeded from the author's inner need for expression—it is not a work of art. If all these conditions are present, even in the smallest degree, then the work, even if a weak one, is yet a work of art.

The presence in various degrees of these three conditions—individuality, clearness, and sincerity—decides the merit of a work of art, as art, apart from subject-matter. All works of art take rank of merit according to the degree in which they fulfil the first, the second, and the third of these conditions. In one the individuality of the feeling transmitted may predominate; in another, clearness of expression; in a third, sincerity; while a fourth may have sincerity and individuality, but be deficient in clearness; a fifth, individuality and clearness, but less sincerity; and so forth, in all possible degrees and combinations.

Thus is art divided from not art, and thus is the quality of art, as art, decided, independently of its subject-matter, *i.e.* apart from whether the feelings it transmits are good or bad.

But how are we to define good and bad art with reference to its subject-matter?

CHAPTER XVI

THE essence of the Christian perception consists in the recognition by every man of his sonship to God, and of the consequent union of men with God and with one another, as is said in the gospel (John 17:21 [1]). Therefore the subject-matter of Christian art is such feeling as can unite men with God and with one another.

The expression *unite men with God and with one another* may seem obscure to people accustomed to the misuse of these words which is so customary, but the words have a perfectly clear meaning nevertheless. They indicate that the Christian union of man (in contradiction to the partial, exclusive union of only some men) is that which unites all without exception.

Art, all art, has this characteristic, that it unites people. Every art causes those to whom the artist's feeling is transmitted to unite in soul with the artist, and also with all who receive the same impression. But non-Christian art, while uniting some people together, makes that very union a cause of separation between these united

people and others; so that union of this kind is often a source, not only of division, but even of enmity toward others. Such is all patriotic art, with its anthems, poems, and monuments; such is all Church art, *i.e.* the art of certain cults, with their images, statues, processions, and other local ceremonies. Such art is belated and non-Christian art, uniting the people of one cult only to separate them yet more sharply from the members of other cults, and even to place them in relations of hostility to each other. Christian art is only such as tends to unite all without exception, either by evoking in them the perception that each man and all men stand in like relation toward God and toward their neighbor, or by evoking in them identical feelings, which may even be the very simplest, provided only that they are not repugnant to Christianity and are natural to everyone without exception.

Good Christian art of our time may be unintelligible to people because of imperfections in its form, or because men are inattentive to it, but it must be such that all men can experience the feelings it transmits. It must be the art, not of some one group of people, nor of one class, nor of one nationality, nor of one religious cult; that is, it must not transmit feelings which are accessible only to a man educated in a certain way, or only to an aristocrat, or a merchant, or only to a Russian, or a native of Japan, or a Roman Catholic, or a Buddhist, etc., but it must transmit feelings accessible to everyone. Only art of this kind can be acknowledged in our time to be good art, worthy of being chosen out from all the rest of art and encouraged.

Christian art, *i.e.* the art of our time, should be catholic in the original meaning of the word, *i.e.* universal, and therefore it should unite all men. And only two kinds of feeling do unite all men: first, feelings flowing from the perception of our sonship to God and of the brotherhood of man; and next, the simple feelings of common life, accessible to everyone without exception—such as the feeling of merriment, of pity, of cheerfulness, of tranquillity, etc. Only these two kinds of feelings can now supply material for art good in its subject-matter.

And the action of these two kinds of art, apparently so dissimilar, is one and the same. The feelings flowing from perception of our sonship to God and of the brotherhood of man—such as

---

[1] "That they may be one; even as thou, Father, art in me, and I in thee, that they also may be in us."

a feeling of sureness in truth, devotion to the will of God, self-sacrifice, respect for and love of man—evoked by Christian religious perception; and the simplest feelings—such as a softened or a merry mood caused by a song or an amusing jest intelligible to everyone, or by a touching story, or a drawing, or a little doll: both alike produce one and the same effect,—the loving union of man with man. Sometimes people who are together are, if not hostile to one another, at least estranged in mood and feeling, till perchance a story, a performance, a picture, or even a building, but oftenest of all, music, unites them all as by an electric flash, and, in place of their former isolation or even enmity, they are all conscious of union and mutual love. Each is glad that another feels what he feels; glad of the communion established, not only between him and all present, but also with all now living who will yet share the same impression; and more than that, he feels the mysterious gladness of a communion which, reaching beyond the grave, unites us with all men of the past who have been moved by the same feelings, and with all men of the future who will yet be touched by them. And this effect is produced both by the religious art which transmits feelings of love to God and one's neighbor, and by universal art, transmitting the very simplest feelings common to all men.

The art of our time should be appraised differently from former art chiefly in this, that the art of our time, *i.e.* Christian art (basing itself on a religious perception which demands the union of man), excludes from the domain of art good in subject-matter everything transmitting exclusive feelings, which do not unite but divide men. It relegates such work to the category of art bad in its subject-matter, while, on the other hand, it includes in the category of art good in subject-matter a section not formerly admitted to deserve to be chosen out and respected, namely, universal art, transmitting even the most trifling and simple feelings if only they are accessible to all men without exception, and therefore unite them. Such art cannot, in our time, but be

esteemed good, for it attains the end which the religious perception of our time, *i.e.* Christianity, sets before humanity.

Christian art either evokes in men those feelings which, through love of God and of one's neighbor, draw them to greater and ever greater union, and make them ready for and capable of such union; or evokes in them those feelings which show them that they are already united in the joys and sorrows of life. And therefore the Christian art of our time can be and is of two kinds: (1) art transmitting feelings flowing from a religious perception of man's position in the world in relation to God and to his neighbor— religious art in the limited meaning of the term; and (2) art transmitting the simplest feelings of common life, but such, always, as are accessible to all men in the whole world—the art of common life—the art of a people—universal art. Only these two kinds of art can be considered good art in our time.

The first, religious art,—transmitting both positive feelings of love to God and one's neighbor, and negative feelings of indignation and horror at the violation of love,—manifests itself chiefly in the form of words, and to some extent also in painting and sculpture; the second kind (universal art), transmitting feelings accessible to all, manifests itself in words, in painting, in sculpture, in dances, in architecture, and, most of all, in music.

If I were asked to give modern examples of each of these kinds of art, then, as examples of the highest art, flowing from love of God and man (both of the higher, positive, and of the lower, negative kind), in literature I should name, "The Robbers," by Schiller; Victor Hugo's "Les Pauvres Gens" and "Les Misérables"; the novels and stories of Dickens,—"The Tale of Two Cities," "The Christmas Carol," "The Chimes," and others; "Uncle Tom's Cabin"; Dostoievsky's works—especially his "Memoirs from the House of Death"; and "Adam Bede," by George Eliot. . . .

4. The Modern Period

T. S. ELIOT   (1888-1965)

THE CRITICAL writing of T. S. Eliot, like that of Coleridge, presents a synthesis of points of view that are frequently urged only separately. Therefore it can hardly be systematized even tentatively, and that, perhaps, is one of its virtues. Most of it, however, may be summarized under three arbitrary headings. A part of it may be described as a general plea for an increased objectivity in poetry. Eliot's more theoretical essays, "Tradition and the Individual Talent" and "The Function of Criticism," would be notable examples. A second and larger part of his criticism is concerned more specifically with problems of form and style, especially in essays that attempt to re-examine particular writers or groups of writers. Examples are the influential essays on "The Metaphysical Poets," "Andrew Marvell," and "John Dryden." The essay "The Modern Mind" is not strictly of this sort. However it occurs at the end of a series of lectures "On the Use of Poetry and the Use of Criticism" which are essentially a re-examination of particular poets and critics, at least partly in terms of form and style. Finally, some of his essays discuss the relation of literature and of criticism to other general subjects, including religion, as in "Arnold and Pater," "The Humanism of Irving Babbitt," and "Religion and Literature."

A stand for objectivity, of course, may be taken in various ways. To Haz-

T. S. ELIOT. Born in St. Louis, Eliot was educated at Harvard (A.B. 1909; A.M. 1910), and, after a year at the Sorbonne, attended Merton College, Oxford (1912-14). He then worked in London as a teacher, bank clerk, and editor. In 1922 he founded and edited the influential *Criterion* magazine, and later became a member of the editorial board of Faber and Faber. In 1927 he became a British subject, was visiting Norton Professor of Poetry, Harvard (1932-33), and in 1948 received the Nobel Prize.

Eliot's critical works include especially: *The Sacred Wood* (1920); *Selected Essays* (1932; rev. 1950); *The Use of Poetry and the Use of Criticism* (Cambridge, Mass., 1933); *After Strange Gods* (1934); *Elizabethan Essays* (1934); *Essays Ancient and Modern* (1936); *The Classics and the Man of Letters* (Oxford, 1942); *On Poetry and Poets* (1957); and *To Criticize the Critic: Eight Essays on Literature* (1965). Relevant commentary includes: R. P. Blackmur, *et al.*, "Mr. Eliot and Notions of Culture," *Partisan Review*, XI (1944), 302-12; Vincent Buckley, *Poetry and Morality: Studies on the Criticism of Matthew Arnold, T. S. Eliot, and F. R. Leavis* (1959); Lewis Freed, *T. S. Eliot: Aesthetics and History* (La Salle, Ill., 1962); Sean Lucy, *T. S. Eliot and the Idea of Tradition* (1960); F. O. Matthiessen, *The Achievement of T. S. Eliot* (1935); John Crowe Ransom, "T. S. Eliot," in *The New Critics* (Norfolk, Conn., 1941); Carol Smith, *T. S. Eliot's Dramatic Theory and Practice* (Princeton, 1963); and Eliseo Vivas, "The Objective Correlative of T. S. Eliot," *American Bookman*, I (1944), 7-18. Also helpful is Northrop Frye, *T. S. Eliot* (1963).

litt, for example, the prime necessity was for the artist to have his eye concentrated on his subject. His aim should be to determine what is essential in it, and to draw out this essential character into intense and impassioned expression. To Eliot, the objectivity desired certainly includes having one's eye on the subject. But the objectivity mainly stressed is rather the submerging of the artist's own personality in the technical process of poetic expression. Both critics are eminent examples of a protest against the extremes of romantic subjectivism. Their positions are not mutually exclusive; they differ, rather, in stress. Hazlitt pointed toward an informed naturalism, in which an open and objectively emotional awareness of concrete reality is fundamental. Eliot's approach is more formalistic: the interest is rather in the formal qualities intrinsic to art as a specific craft—a more pressing concern, to use Aristotle's terms, with *harmonia* than with the object of "imitation." Hence the emphasis, in "Tradition and the Individual Talent," that what counts in a poem is not "any semi-ethical criterion of 'sublimity' in the subject-matter: it is not the 'greatness,' the intensity of the emotions, the components, but the intensity of the artistic process. . . ." Poetry, in this sense, is actually "an escape from emotion" and "an escape from personality."

Art of objective value, then, demands a "continual surrender of himself" by the artist to "something which is more valuable." Eliot believes that an intelligent use of tradition helps both to inform the artist of what is valuable and also to assist him in the active process of attaining it. To follow or conform to tradition does not, of course, involve the copying of the specific materials or techniques of previous works; for these works are of value and help in molding tradition partly because they themselves were not mere copies. He who imitates the *Iliad*, as Edward Young said, does not imitate Homer. What is wanted is a general sense of continuity, a realization of what qualities and approaches have continued to have the most vital effect, and an imaginative, elastic use of this knowledge. "To conform merely," says Eliot, "would be for the new work not really to conform at all; it would not be new, and would therefore not be a work of art." This conception of tradition, as Eliot develops it, is analogous to the British Constitution. For the British Constitution consists of a gradually expanding body of traditional premises, procedures, and values. Moreover, an important part of its tradition has been the tradition of *change*—of adapting itself to changing circumstances. And when these changes are made, in the face of altered circumstances, then the changes themselves enter into the total picture of the history of the British Constitution. They alter that picture by adding further examples. In a similar way, a really *new* work of art, of sufficient quality to have a significant place in the history of literature, constitutes an example of the direction in which literature is capable of going. By adding a new turn to the road, so to speak, it alters the total picture of what that road *is* by illustrating further where the road is going, or where it can go. Hence, "what happens when a new work of art is created is something that happens simultaneously to all the works of art which preceded it. The existing monuments form an ideal order among themselves, which is modified by the introduction of the new . . . work of art . . ."

Eliot's essay on "The Function of Criticism," which should be read as a supplement to "Tradition and the Individual Talent," further emphasizes the need for an elastic use of tradition and for alert critical thinking generally. In doing so, it suggests comparison with Arnold's essay "On the Function of Criticism." For it, too, focuses on the extreme individualistic character of the English, stresses the importance of criticism for the creative writer, and attacks the belief that "the great artist is an unconscious artist" who is able to "muddle through" without the help of criticism. What Arnold called the Englishman's excessive confidence in his "ordinary self"—a term later much used by Eliot's teacher, Irving Babbitt—is echoed in Eliot's discussion of the common English trust in one's "inner voice." Eliot, more than once, has expressed his antagonism to Arnold—an antagonism based partly on different criteria for evaluating poetic style, and partly on the feeling that Arnold slights the importance of religion. Moreover, in his two essays on Irving Babbitt, he has expressed his misgivings about the neohumanist movement which Babbitt and Paul Elmer More developed from Arnold. Still, in his more general and theoretical discussions of literature and criticism, Eliot urges a classical objectivism based on premises and couched in terms that clearly show the strong influence of Arnold, both directly and also indirectly, through Babbitt.

2

The most important qualification for the critic, as Eliot states it in the essay "The Function of Criticism," is "a very highly developed sense of fact." Judgment and taste, in other words—the ability to distinguish what is good from what is not—consist ultimately not in the theory of criticism, nor in the abstract discussion of aims and standards, but in the ability to see, respond, and evaluate when the actual poem is there before you. This sense of fact is one of Eliot's own virtues as a critic. He is himself a member of that impressive line of English poet-critics, including Sidney, Ben Jonson, Dryden, Samuel Johnson, Coleridge, and Arnold, who have insured for English criticism, less theoretically systematic than Continental criticism, a superior empirical concreteness, a firm awareness of poetic style, and a close psychological insight arising from the actual experience of imaginative writing. These qualities, as well as the lack of system, characterize the more particularized criticism of Eliot. What he regards as the English poetic tradition, for example, is nowhere discussed in systematic detail, but it evolves mainly from his studies of specific poets or groups of poets. These studies present the first important re-examination of English poetry since Arnold. It is perhaps inevitable that, just as some of the qualities and aims of poetry brought into focus by Arnold involved a rejection of the neoclassic tradition, so the re-examination by Eliot involved an implicit rejection of the nineteenth century.

In seeking to disclose and emphasize what is best in the tradition of English poetic style, Eliot seems especially to have in mind two general ideals or criteria. One may be described as an urbane classical formalism. The desired qualities are an informed and unillusioned—as distinct from a *disillusioned*—sophistication, a hard clarity of outline and sense of structure, and a deliberate simplicity or even spareness of phrase, with a shrinking from both vagueness and expansive superfluity. Here the encouraging influence of T. E. Hulme on Eliot may be noticed. The second general ideal, and one less easily classified, is a combination of qualities often found in English verse. Indeed, despite certain parallels with the French Symbolist poetry of the nineteenth century, this combination is unique and indigenous to some kinds of English poetry. It is particularly found in the period from about 1590 to the mid-seventeenth century, and received its most extreme development in the "metaphysical" poets of this period. Because of the relatively narrow connotation of the term "metaphysical poetry," we may let the broader phrase, "the English tradition of wit," stand for this desired union of qualities. It is characterized by both an abundance and a marked concreteness of imagery. It is also characterized by a habitual use of metaphor of such reach and extent that, when successfully employed, it has intellectual as well as physical connotations, and thus joins what the seventeenth century called "wit" with emotional power and sensory impact. Eliot's emphasis on "wit" has both reflected and strongly influenced the theory and practice of Anglo-American poetry since the first World War, while the other general criterion—the ideal of classical formalism—has been less closely connected with modern theory and practice.

In the essay on "The Metaphysical Poets" Eliot advances his famous suggestion that "metaphysical" poetry is the logical development from Elizabethan. This general poetic tradition, moreover, of which "metaphysical" verse is a development, is the main trunk line of English poetry. It was characterized by a "mechanism of sensibility" in which thoughts of whatever sort could be melted down, so to speak, into emotional response. In discussing "metaphysical" poetry itself, Eliot particularly prizes the wide range of radically different experiences amalgamated in it. Where he disagrees with Dr. Johnson, who was also attracted by the range, is in maintaining that these experiences, in a poet like Donne, are more successfully unified than Johnson would admit. It is this quality in English poetry, as Eliot believes, that evaporated during the later seventeenth century, when a "dissociation of sensibility set in, from which we have never recovered . . . ." The quality of "wit"—the intellectual acuteness in combining "disparate experience"—went one way in neoclassic poetry after Dryden, dropping its emotional and sensory connection and becoming "wit" in something like the present-day sense—a wit verging toward the comic. Similarly, in Milton, impassioned eloquence, divorced from "wit," went another way, culminating in the romantic verse of the nineteenth and early twentieth centuries.

3

The classical formalism in Eliot is an ideal that colors much of his critical thinking rather than a subject that receives explicit analysis. For example, it pervades his gifted essay on Dryden, in whose poetry he finds the classical and neoclassic virtues of a refined simplicity and naturalness of idiom, an ironic detachment and flexibility, and a firm denotative language. Accordingly, Dryden's is a poetry that stands on its own feet, through its own technical achievement, rather than one that relies for its effect on mere themes of pseudo-sublimity, such as especially appealed later to the stock responses of the nineteenth century. A classical formalism colors, even more, some of Eliot's writings on the drama, particularly his "Dialogue on Dramatic Poetry," in which he deplores the increasing split that has taken place between poetry and the theater, and the modern belief that the more "realistic" a play is, and the farther it is from "poetry," the better it is as a "drama." Eliot urges a more formal and stylized drama, in which "realistic" elements have been subdued in favor of a unified, generalized pattern of action, operating according to fairly fixed conventions. Hence he suggests, in "Four Elizabethan Dramatists," that the strict, stylized drama is really better adapted for theatrical presentation, if one is concerned with the play rather than the personality of the actor. The "realistic" drama, simply because of the danger that the actor's own character will dominate, is the drama that is better read than performed. One may buttress Eliot's argument by pointing to the always fruitful example of Hollywood, where, as a result of its use of a certain kind of realistic drama, its patrons now attend in order to see the performer rather than the play—an interest Hollywood has at last begun to exploit by openly presenting films about the lives of contemporary actors and singers.

4

In combining the values of the English tradition of wit and those associated with classical formalism, Eliot is almost unique among modern critics. A liberal classical interest in form, as distinct from the extreme, abstract formalism with which the last half-century has again become familiar, has not, to be sure, lacked apologists. But this interest has usually been expressed on an even more general plane, with little attention to actual technical problems. Moreover, supporters of a liberal classical interest in form have not been generally sympathetic with the modern revival of the English tradition of wit, any more than most exponents of that revival are really sympathetic with classical poetry, despite paying it a certain lip-service. One could, indeed, argue that the great classical tradition of declamatory and rhetorical verse, with its concern for clarity and immediacy of communication, is far removed in character from much modern verse, in which there is frequently the attempt to concentrate as much image and metaphor as possible, and a tendency to regard any connecting mortar in the form of "poetry of statement" as superfluous "rhetoric." Moreover, in the reaction against Milton during the 1920's and 1930's, much of the adverse criticism of him was equally applicable to classical verse generally.

But if Eliot's values appear, at first glance, to be uneasy bed-fellows, we may remember one of the merits of English criticism. Though, in ignoring what seem to be inconsistencies, it is often wrong-headed, yet at its best it is able to achieve a more capacious and rounded view, and, without systematic theory, to prove itself able to fuse together what is apparently incompatible. English poetry itself, from the early verse of Shakespeare down to the mid-seventeenth century—afterwards, at times, in the verse of Dryden and Pope, and the maturer verse of Keats, for example—frequently presents, in actual practice, a fusion of the diverse qualities that Eliot's criticism expounds. One may even suggest that, among the poet-critics of whom he is the latest representative, Eliot has closest affinity to Samuel Johnson, whom he himself describes as "a very dangerous person to disagree with." For Johnson also prized the qualities that characterized the English tradition of wit. With testy irritation, he felt the absence of fertility and reach of metaphor, and of analytic intellectuality in the verse of Gray, the Wartons, the Miltonic blank-verse writers generally: in the verse that is, which followed the neoclassic conclusion to the English tradition of wit, and which marked the direction much nineteenth-century poetry would take. Like Eliot, he viewed askance the influence of Milton in encouraging, among minor poets, the replacing of meaningful metaphor and thought with sounding phrases and stock rhetorical devices. At the same time, his classical criteria existed side by side with his preferences for a condensed poetry of wit; and though they were often at odds with each other, they were often joined. Johnson did not, of course, urge as a deliberate model the qualities in "metaphysical" poetry praised by Eliot. He was still close to the "metaphysical" poets. He was not trying to resurrect them; rather, he took them more or less for granted, noting their weaknesses as he noted the weaknesses of any other writers when compared with the highest standards. Moreover, he threw his weight more fully behind certain basic classical ideals; and his manner of facing the complexity of life, both in his own tortured nature and in the world of circumstance, took another direction. Still, it is suggestive to note the intellectual similarities between the men, not only in the fusion of the qualities discussed here, but in other respects as well—particularly as they are concerned with general humanistic, moral, and religious values. Though they are in some ways radically different—though their contrasts are perhaps more important than their similarities—Johnson is probably Eliot's closest prototype in the history of English criticism.

Tradition and the Individual Talent

IN ENGLISH writing we seldom speak of tradition, though we occasionally apply its name in deploring its absence. We cannot refer to "the tradition" or to "a tradition"; at most, we employ the adjective in saying that the poetry of So-and-so is "traditional" or even "too traditional." Seldom, perhaps, does the word appear except in a phrase of censure. If otherwise, it is vaguely approbative, with the implication, as to the work approved, of some pleasing archaeological reconstruction. You can hardly make the word agreeable to English ears without this comfortable reference to the reassuring science of archaeology.

Certainly the word is not likely to appear in our appreciations of living or dead writers. Every nation, every race, has not only its own creative, but its own critical turn of mind; and is even more oblivious of the shortcomings and limitations of its critical habits than of those of its creative genius. We know, or think we know, from the enormous mass of critical writing that has appeared in the French language the critical method or habit of the French; we only conclude (we are such unconscious people) that the French are "more critical" than we, and sometimes even plume ourselves a little with the fact, as if the French were the less spontaneous. Perhaps they are; but we might remind ourselves that criticism is as inevitable as breathing, and that we should be none the worse for articulating what passes in our minds when we read a book and feel an emotion about it, for criticizing our own minds in their work of criticism. One of the facts that might come

to light in this process is our tendency to insist, when we praise a poet, upon those aspects of his work in which he least resembles any one else. In these aspects or parts of his work we pretend to find what is individual, what is the peculiar essence of the man. We dwell with satisfaction upon the poet's difference from his predecessors, especially his immediate predecessors; we endeavour to find something that can be isolated in order to be enjoyed. Whereas if we approach a poet without this prejudice we shall often find that not only the best, but the most individual parts of his work may be those in which the dead poets, his ancestors, assert their immortality most vigorously. And I do not mean the impressionable period of adolescence, but the period of full maturity.

Yet if the only form of tradition, of handing down, consisted in following the ways of the immediate generation before us in a blind or timid adherence to its successes, "tradition" should positively be discouraged. We have seen many such simple currents soon lost in the sand; and novelty is better than repetition. Tradition is a matter of much wider significance. It cannot be inherited, and if you want it you must obtain it by great labour. It involves, in the first place, the historical sense, which we may call nearly indispensable to any one who would continue to be a poet beyond his twenty-fifth year; and the historical sense involves a perception, not only of the pastness of the past, but of its presence; [1] the historical sense compels a man to write not merely with his own generation in his bones, but with a feeling that

Tradition and the Individual Talent. First published in 1917. From *Selected Essays, 1917-1932* by T. S. Eliot, copyright, 1932, by Harcourt Brace Jovanovich, Inc. and Faber & Faber Ltd.

[1] A sense, that is, of its relevance now—of the extent to which the past is entering into the content of the present, creating and forming the present into what it is.

the whole of the literature of Europe from Homer and within it the whole of the literature of his own country has a simultaneous existence and composes a simultaneous order. This historical sense, which is a sense of the timeless as well as of the temporal and of the timeless and of the temporal together, is what makes a writer traditional. And it is at the same time what makes a writer most acutely conscious of his place in time, of his own contemporaneity.

No poet, no artist of any art, has his complete meaning alone. His significance, his appreciation is the appreciation of his relation to the dead poets and artists. You cannot value him alone; you must set him, for contrast and comparison, among the dead. I mean this as a principle of aesthetic, not merely historical, criticism. The necessity that he shall conform, that he shall cohere, is not onesided; what happens when a new work of art is created is something that happens simultaneously to all the works of art which preceded it. The existing monuments form an ideal order among themselves, which is modified by the introduction of the new (the really new) work of art among them. The existing order is complete before the new work arrives; for order to persist after the supervention of novelty, the *whole* existing order must be, if ever so slightly, altered; and so the relations, proportions, values of each work of art toward the whole are readjusted; and this is conformity between the old and the new. Whoever has approved this idea of order, of the form of European, of English literature will not find it preposterous that the past should be altered by the present as much as the present is directed by the past. And the poet who is aware of this will be aware of great difficulties and responsibilities.

In a peculiar sense he will be aware also that he must inevitably be judged by the standards of the past. I say judged, not amputated, by them; not judged to be as good as, or worse or better than, the dead; and certainly not judged by the canons of dead critics. It is a judgment, a comparison, in which two things are measured by each other. To conform merely would be for the new work not really to conform at all;[2] it would not be new, and would therefore not be a work of art. And we do not quite

say that the new is more valuable because it fits in; but its fitting in is a test of its value— a test, it is true, which can only be slowly and cautiously applied, for we are none of us infallible judges of conformity. We say: it appears to conform, and is perhaps individual, or it appears individual, and may conform; but we are hardly likely to find that it is one and not the other.

To proceed to a more intelligible exposition of the relation of the poet to the past: he can neither take the past as a lump, an indiscriminate bolus, nor can he form himself wholly on one or two private admirations, nor can he form himself wholly upon one preferred period. The first course is inadmissible, the second is an important experience of youth, and the third is a pleasant and highly desirable supplement. The poet must be very conscious of the main current, which does not at all flow invariably through the most distinguished reputations. He must be quite aware of the obvious fact that art never improves, but that the material of art is never quite the same. He must be aware that the mind of Europe—the mind of his own country—a mind which he learns in time to be much more important than his own private mind—is a mind which changes, and that this change is a development which abandons nothing *en route,* which does not superannuate either Shakespeare, or Homer, or the rock drawing of the Magdalenian draughtsmen. That this development, refinement perhaps, complication certainly, is not, from the point of view of the artist, any improvement. Perhaps not even an improvement from the point of view of the psychologist or not to the extent which we imagine; perhaps only in the end based upon a complication in economics and machinery. But the difference between the present and the past is that the conscious present is an awareness of the past in a way and to an extent which the past's awareness of itself cannot show.

Some one said: "The dead writers are remote from us because we *know* so much more than they did." Precisely, and they are that which we know.

I am alive to a usual objection to what is clearly part of my programme for the *métier*

---

[2] One might illustrate the statement by the remark of Edward Young, which Sir Joshua Reynolds em-

phasized: "He that imitates the . . . *Iliad* does not imitate Homer" (see above, p. 242).

of poetry. The objection is that the doctrine requires a ridiculous amount of erudition (pedantry), a claim which can be rejected by appeal to the lives of poets in any pantheon. It will even be affirmed that much learning deadens or perverts poetic sensibility. While, however, we persist in believing that a poet ought to know as much as will not encroach upon his necessary receptivity and necessary laziness, it is not desirable to confine knowledge to whatever can be put into a useful shape for examinations, drawing-rooms, or the still more pretentious modes of publicity. Some can absorb knowledge, the more tardy must sweat for it. Shakespeare acquired more essential history from Plutarch than most men could from the whole British Museum. What is to be insisted upon is that the poet must develop or procure the consciousness of the past and that he should continue to develop this consciousness throughout his career.

What happens is a continual surrender of himself as he is at the moment to something which is more valuable. The progress of an artist is a continual self-sacrifice, a continual extinction of personality.

There remains to define this process of depersonalization and its relation to the sense of tradition. It is in this depersonalization that art may be said to approach the condition of science. I, therefore, invite you to consider, as a suggestive analogy, the action which takes place when a bit of finely filiated platinum is introduced into a chamber containing oxygen and sulphur dioxide.

I I

Honest criticism and sensitive appreciation are directed not upon the poet but upon the poetry. If we attend to the confused cries of the newspaper critics and the *susurrus* of popular repetition that follows, we shall hear the names of poets in great numbers; if we seek not Bluebook knowledge but the enjoyment of poetry, and ask for a poem, we shall seldom find it. I have tried to point out the importance of the relation of the poem to other poems by other authors, and suggested the conception of poetry as a living whole of all the poetry that has ever been written. The other aspect of this Impersonal theory of poetry is the relation of the poem to its author. And I hinted, by an analogy, that

the mind of the mature poet differs from that of the immature one not precisely in any valuation of "personality," not being necessarily more interesting, or having "more to say," but rather by being a more finely perfected medium in which special, or very varied, feelings are at liberty to enter into new combinations.

The analogy was that of the catalyst. When the two gases previously mentioned are mixed in the presence of a filament of platinum, they form sulphurous acid. This combination takes place only if the platinum is present; nevertheless the newly formed acid contains no trace of platinum, and the platinum itself is apparently unaffected; has remained inert, neutral, and unchanged.[3] The mind of the poet is the shred of platinum. It may partly or exclusively operate upon the experience of the man himself; but, the more perfect the artist, the more completely separate in him will be the man who suffers and the mind which creates; the more perfectly will the mind digest and transmute the passions which are its material.

The experience, you will notice, the elements which enter the presence of the transforming catalyst, are of two kinds: emotions and feelings. The effect of a work of art upon the person who enjoys it is an experience different in kind from any experience not of art. It may be formed out of one emotion, or may be a combination of several; and various feelings, inhering for the writer in particular words or phrases or images, may be added to compose the final result. Or great poetry may be made without the direct use of any emotion whatever: composed out of feelings solely. Canto XV of the *Inferno* (Brunetto Latini) is a working up of the emotion evident in the situation; but the effect, though single as that of any work of art, is obtained by considerable complexity of detail. The last quatrain gives an image, a feeling attaching to an image, which "came," which did not develop

[3] Compare Keats's remark: "Men of Genius are great as certain etherial Chemicals operating on the Mass of neutral intellect—but they have not any individuality, any determined Character" (see above, p. 349). "This is the sort of remark," says Eliot, after citing it, "which, when made by a man so young as Keats, can only be called the result of genius. There is hardly one statement of Keats about poetry, which . . . will not be found to be true . . ." (*The Use of Poetry* [Cambridge, Mass., 1933], p. 93.)

simply out of what precedes, but which was probably in suspension in the poet's mind until the proper combination arrived for it to add itself to. The poet's mind is in fact a receptacle for seizing and storing up numberless feelings, phrases, images, which remain there until all the particles which can unite to form a new compound are present together.

If you compare several representative passages of the greatest poetry you see how great is the variety of types of combination, and also how completely any semi-ethical criterion of "sublimity" misses the mark. For it is not the "greatness," the intensity, of the emotions, the components, but the intensity of the artistic process, the pressure, so to speak, under which the fusion takes place, that counts. The episode of Paolo and Francesca employs a definite emotion, but the intensity of the poetry is something quite different from whatever intensity in the supposed experience it may give the impression of. It is no more intense, furthermore, than Canto XXVI, the voyage of Ulysses, which has not the direct dependence upon an emotion. Great variety is possible in the process of transmutation of emotion: the murder of Agamemnon, or the agony of Othello, gives an artistic effect apparently closer to a possible original than the scenes from Dante. In the *Agamemnon,* the artistic emotion approximates to the emotion of an actual spectator; in *Othello* to the emotion of the protagonist himself. But the difference between art and the event is always absolute; the combination which is the murder of Agamemnon is probably as complex as that which is the voyage of Ulysses. In either case there has been a fusion of elements. The ode of Keats contains a number of feelings which have nothing particular to do with the nightingale, but which the nightingale, partly, perhaps, because of its attractive name, and partly because of its reputation, served to bring together.

The point of view which I am struggling to attack is perhaps related to the metaphysical theory of the substantial unity of the soul: for my meaning is, that the poet has, not a "personality" to express, but a particular medium, which is only a medium and not a personality, in which impressions and experiences combine in peculiar and unexpected ways. Impressions and experiences which are important for the man may take no place in the poetry, and those which become important in the poetry may play quite a negligible part in the man, the personality.

I will quote a passage which is unfamiliar enough to be regarded with fresh attention in the light—or darkness—of these observations:

> And now methinks I could e'en chide myself
> For doating on her beauty, though her death
> Shall be revenged after no common action.
> Does the silkworm expend her yellow labours
> For thee? For thee does she undo herself?
> Are lordships sold to maintain ladyships
> For the poor benefit of a bewildering minute?
> Why does yon fellow falsify highways,
> And put his life between the judge's lips,
> To refine such a thing—keeps horse and men
> To beat their valours for her? . . .[4]

In this passage (as is evident if it is taken in its context) there is a combination of positive and negative emotions: an intensely strong attraction toward beauty and an equally intense fascination by the ugliness which is contrasted with it and which destroys it. This balance of contrasted emotion is in the dramatic situation to which the speech is pertinent, but that situation alone is inadequate to it. This is, so to speak, the structural emotion, provided by the drama. But the whole effect, the dominant tone, is due to the fact that a number of floating feelings, having an affinity to this emotion by no means superficially evident, have combined with it to give us a new art emotion.

It is not in his personal emotions, the emotions provoked by particular events in his life, that the poet is in any way remarkable or interesting. His particular emotions may be simple, or crude, or flat. The emotion in his poetry will be a very complex thing, but not with the complexity of the emotions of people who have very complex or unusual emotions in life. One error, in fact, of eccentricity in poetry is to seek for new human emotions to express; and in this search for novelty in the wrong place it discovers the perverse. The business of the poet is not to find new emotions, but to use the ordinary ones and, in working them up into poetry, to express feelings which are not in actual emotions at all. And emotions which he has never

4 Cyril Tourneur, the *Revenger's Tragedy,* III, 4.

experienced will serve his turn as well as those familiar to him. Consequently, we must believe that "emotion recollected in tranquillity" is an inexact formula. For it is neither emotion, nor recollection, nor, without distortion of meaning, tranquillity. It is a concentration, and a new thing resulting from the concentration, of a very great number of experiences which to the practical and active person would not seem to be experiences at all; it is a concentration which does not happen consciously or of deliberation. These experiences are not "recollected," and they finally unite in an atmosphere which is "tranquil" only in that it is a passive attending upon the event. Of course this is not quite the whole story. There is a great deal, in the writing of poetry, which must be conscious and deliberate. In fact, the bad poet is usually unconscious where he ought to be conscious, and conscious where he ought to be unconscious. Both errors tend to make him "personal." Poetry is not a turning loose of emotion, but an escape from emotion; it is not the expression of personality, but an escape from personality. But, of course, only those who have personality and emotions know what it means to want to escape from these things.

[handwritten: EMOTION = EGO]
[handwritten: DUAL NATURE OF MAN: MAN CAN KNOW REALITY]
[handwritten: (1) BY DIRECT INTUITION]
[handwritten: (2) MAN HAS PHENOMENOLOGICAL EGO]
[handwritten: MAN HAS ETERNAL SELF (CREATING MIND)]

III

ὁ δὲ νοῦς ἴσως Θειότερόν τι καὶ ἀπαθές ἐστιν.[5]

This essay proposes to halt at the frontier of metaphysics or mysticism, and confine itself to such practical conclusions as can be applied by the responsible person interested in poetry. To divert interest from the poet to the poetry is a laudable aim: for it would conduce to a juster estimation of actual poetry, good and bad. There are many people who appreciate the expression of sincere emotion in verse, and there is a smaller number of people who can appreciate technical excellence. But very few know when there is an *[handwritten: ✳]* expression of *significant* emotion, emotion which has its life in the poem and not in the history of the poet. The emotion of art is impersonal. And the poet cannot reach his impersonality without surrendering himself wholly to the work to be done. And he is not likely to know what is to be done unless he lives in what is not merely the present, but the present moment of the past, unless he is conscious, not of what is dead, but of what is already living.

[5] "The mind may be too divine, and therefore unaffected." *[handwritten: ✳ ELIOT CANNOT RECOGNIZE IT.]*

The Metaphysical Poets

BY COLLECTING these poems [1] from the work of a generation more often named than read, and more often read than profitably studied, Professor Grierson has rendered a service of some importance. Certainly the reader will meet with many poems already preserved in other anthologies, at the same time that he discovers poems such as those of Aurelian Townshend or Lord Herbert of Cherbury here included. But the function of such an anthology as this is neither that of Professor Saintsbury's

admirable edition of Caroline poets nor that of the *Oxford Book of English Verse*. Mr. Grierson's book is in itself a piece of criticism and a provocation of criticism; and we think that he was right in including so many poems of Donne, elsewhere (though not in many editions) accessible, as documents in the case of "metaphysical poetry." The phrase has long done duty as a term of abuse or as the label of a quaint and pleasant taste. The question is to what extent the so-called metaphysicals formed a school (in our own time we should say a "movement"), and how far this so-called school or movement is a digression from the main current.

Not only is it extremely difficult to define metaphysical poetry, but difficult to decide what poets practise it and in which of their verses. The poetry of Donne (to whom Marvell and Bishop King are sometimes nearer than any of

The Metaphysical Poets. First published in 1921. From *Selected Essays, 1917-1932* by T. S. Eliot, copyright, 1932, by Harcourt, Brace and Company, Inc. and Faber & Faber Ltd.

[1] *Metaphysical Lyrics and Poems of the Seventeenth Century:* Donne to Butler. Selected and edited, with an Essay, by Herbert J. C. Grierson (Oxford: Clarendon Press. London: Milford). [Eliot.]

the other authors) is late Elizabethan, its feeling often very close to that of Chapman. The "courtly" poetry is derivative from Jonson, who borrowed liberally from the Latin; it expires in the next century with the sentiment and witticism of Prior. There is finally the devotional verse of Herbert, Vaughan, and Crashaw (echoed long after by Christina Rossetti and Francis Thompson) ; Crashaw, sometimes more profound and less sectarian than the others, has a quality which returns through the Elizabethan period to the early Italians. It is difficult to find any precise use of metaphor, simile, or other conceit, which is common to all the poets and at the same time important enough as an element of style to isolate these poets as a group. Donne, and often Cowley, employ a device which is sometimes considered characteristically "metaphysical"; the elaboration (contrasted with the condensation) of a figure of speech to the farthest stage to which ingenuity can carry it. Thus Cowley develops the commonplace comparison of the world to a chess-board through long stanzas (*To Destiny*), and Donne, with more grace, in *A Valediction*, the comparison of two lovers to a pair of compasses. But elsewhere we find, instead of the mere explication of the content of a comparison, a development by rapid association of thought which requires considerable agility on the part of the reader.

> On a round ball
> A workman that hath copies by, can lay
> An Europe, Afrique, and an Asia,
> And quickly make that, which was nothing, All,
> So doth each teare,
> Which thee doth weare,
> A globe, yea, world by that impression grow,
> Till thy tears mixt with mine doe overflow
> This world, by waters sent from thee, my heaven
>   dissolved so.[2]

Here we find at least two connexions which are not implicit in the first figure, but are forced upon it by the poet: from the geographer's globe to the tear, and the tear to the deluge. On the other hand, some of Donne's most successful and characteristic effects are secured by brief words and sudden contrasts:

> A bracelet of bright hair about the bone,

[2] *Valediction: of Weeping*, ll. 10-18.

where the most powerful effect is produced by the sudden contrast of associations of "bright hair" and of "bone." This telescoping of images and multiplied associations is characteristic of the phrase of some of the dramatists of the period which Donne knew: not to mention Shakespeare, it is frequent in Middleton, Webster, and Tourneur, and is one of the sources of the vitality of their language.

Johnson, who employed the term "metaphysical poets," apparently having Donne, Cleveland, and Cowley chiefly in mind, remarks of them that "the most heterogeneous ideas are yoked by violence together." The force of this impeachment lies in the failure of the conjunction, the fact that often the ideas are yoked but not united; and if we are to judge of styles of poetry by their abuse, enough examples may be found in Cleveland to justify Johnson's condemnation. But a degree of heterogeneity of material compelled into unity by the operation of the poet's mind is omnipresent in poetry. We need not select for illustration such a line as:

Notre âme est un trois-mâts cherchant son Icarie; [3]

we may find it in some of the best lines of Johnson himself (*The Vanity of Human Wishes*):

> His fate was destined to a barren strand,
> A petty fortress, and a dubious hand;
> He left a name at which the world grew pale,
> To point a moral, or adorn a tale.

where the effect is due to a contrast of ideas, different in degree but the same in principle, as that which Johnson mildly reprehended. And in one of the finest poems of the age (a poem which could not have been written in any other age), the *Exequy* of Bishop King, the extended comparison is used with perfect success: the idea and the simile become one, in the passage in which the Bishop illustrates his impatience to see his dead wife, under the figure of a journey:

> Stay for me there; I will not faile
> To meet thee in that hollow Vale.
> And think not much of my delay;
> I am already on the way,
> And follow thee with all the speed
> Desire can make, or sorrows breed.

[3] "Our soul is a schooner searching for its Icarus." (Baudelaire, *Le Voyage*, II, 9.)

Each minute is a short degree,
And ev'ry houre a step towards thee.
At night when I betake to rest,
Next morn I rise nearer my West
Of life, almost by eight houres sail,
Than when sleep breath'd his drowsy gale. . . .
But heark! My Pulse, like a soft Drum
Beats my approach, tells *Thee* I come;
And slow howere my marches be,
I shall at last sit down by *Thee*.

(In the last few lines there is that effect of terror which is several times attained by one of Bishop King's admirers, Edgar Poe.) Again, we may justly take these quatrains from Lord Herbert's Ode, stanzas which would, we think, be immediately pronounced to be of the metaphysical school:

So when from hence we shall be gone,
    And be no more, nor you, nor I,
    As one another's mystery,
Each shall be both, yet both but one.

This said, in her up-lifted face,
    Her eyes, which did that beauty crown,
    Were like two starrs, that having faln down,
Look up again to find their place:

While such a moveless silent peace
    Did seize on their becalmed sense,
    One would have thought some influence
Their ravished spirits did possess.[4]

There is nothing in these lines (with the possible exception of the stars, a simile not at once grasped, but lovely and justified) which fits Johnson's general observations on the metaphysical poets in his essay on Cowley. A good deal resides in the richness of association which is at the same time borrowed from and given to the word "becalmed"; but the meaning is clear, the language simple and elegant. It is to be observed that the language of these poets is as a rule simple and pure; in the verse of George Herbert this simplicity is carried as far as it can go—a simplicity emulated without success by numerous modern poets. The *structure* of the sentences, on the other hand, is sometimes far from simple, but this is not a vice; it is a fidelity to thought and feeling. The effect, at its best, is far less artificial than that of an ode by Gray. And as this fidelity induces variety of

thought and feeling, so it induces variety of music. We doubt whether, in the eighteenth century, could be found two poems in nominally the same metre, so dissimilar as Marvell's *Coy Mistress* and Crashaw's *Saint Teresa;* the one producing an effect of great speed by the use of short syllables, and the other an ecclesiastical solemnity by the use of long ones:

Love, thou art absolute sole lord
Of life and death.

If so shrewd and sensitive (though so limited) a critic as Johnson failed to define metaphysical poetry by its faults, it is worth while to inquire whether we may not have more success by adopting the opposite method: by assuming that the poets of the seventeenth century (up to the Revolution) were the direct and normal development of the precedent age; and, without prejudicing their case by the adjective "metaphysical," consider whether their virtue was not something permanently valuable, which subsequently disappeared, but ought not to have disappeared. Johnson has hit, perhaps by accident, on one of their peculiarities, when he observes that "their attempts were always analytic"; he would not agree that, after the dissociation, they put the material together again in a new unity.

It is certain that the dramatic verse of the later Elizabethan and early Jacobean poets expresses a degree of development of sensibility which is not found in any of the prose, good as it often is. If we except Marlowe, a man of prodigious intelligence, these dramatists were directly or indirectly (it is at least a tenable theory) affected by Montaigne. Even if we except also Jonson and Chapman, these two were notably erudite, and were notably men who incorporated their erudition into their sensibility: their mode of feeling was directly and freshly altered by their reading and thought. In Chapman especially there is a direct sensuous apprehension of thought, or a recreation of thought into feeling, which is exactly what we find in Donne:

in this one thing, all the discipline
Of manners and of manhood is contained;
A man to join himself with th' Universe
In his main sway, and make in all things fit
One with that All, and go on, round as it;
Not plucking from the whole his wretched part,

4 *Ode upon . . . Whether Love Should Continue Forever,* ll. 129-40.

And into straits, or into nought revert,
Wishing the complete Universe might be
Subject to such a rag of it as he;
But to consider great Necessity.[5]

We compare this with some modern passage:

No, when the fight begins within himself,
A man's worth something. God stoops o'er his head,
Satan looks up between his feet—both tug—
He's left, himself, i' the middle; the soul wakes
And grows. Prolong that battle through his life! [6]

It is perhaps somewhat less fair, though very tempting (as both poets are concerned with the perpetuation of love by offspring), to compare with the stanzas already quoted from Lord Herbert's Ode the following from Tennyson:

> One walked between his wife and child,
> With measured footfall firm and mild,
> And now and then he gravely smiled.
>   The prudent partner of his blood
>   Leaned on him, faithful, gentle, good,
>   Wearing the rose of womanhood.
> And in their double love secure,
> The little maiden walked demure,
> Pacing with downward eyelids pure.
>   These three made unity so sweet,
>   My frozen heart began to beat,
>   Remembering its ancient heat.[7]

The difference is not a simple difference of degree between poets. It is something which had happened to the mind of England between the time of Donne or Lord Herbert of Cherbury and the time of Tennyson and Browning; it is the difference between the intellectual poet and the reflective poet. Tennyson and Browning are poets, and they think; but they do not feel their thought as immediately as the odour of a rose. A thought to Donne was an experience; it modified his sensibility. When a poet's mind is perfectly equipped for its work, it is constantly amalgamating disparate experience; the ordinary man's experience is chaotic, irregular, fragmentary. The latter falls in love, or reads Spinoza, and these two experiences have nothing to do with each other, or with the noise of the typewriter or the smell of cooking; in the mind of the poet these experiences are always forming new wholes.

We may express the difference by the following theory: The poets of the seventeenth century, the successors of the dramatists of the sixteenth, possessed a mechanism of sensibility which could devour any kind of experience. They are simple, artificial, difficult, or fantastic, as their predecessors were; no less nor more than Dante, Guido Cavalcanti, Guinizelli, or Cino.[8] In the seventeenth century a dissociation of sensibility set in, from which we have never recovered; and this dissociation, as is natural, was aggravated by the influence of the two most powerful poets of the century, Milton and Dryden. Each of these men performed certain poetic functions so magnificently well that the magnitude of the effect concealed the absence of others. The language went on and in some respects improved; the best verse of Collins, Gray, Johnson, and even Goldsmith satisfies some of our fastidious demands better than that of Donne or Marvell or King. But while the language became more refined, the feeling became more crude. The feeling, the sensibility, expressed in the *Country Churchyard* (to say nothing of Tennyson and Browning) is cruder than that in the *Coy Mistress*.

The second effect of the influence of Milton and Dryden followed from the first, and was therefore slow in manifestation. The sentimental age began early in the eighteenth century, and continued. The poets revolted against the ratiocinative, the descriptive; they thought and felt by fits, unbalanced; they reflected. In one or two passages of Shelley's *Triumph of Life*, in the second *Hyperion*, there are traces of a struggle toward unification of sensibility. But Keats and Shelley died, and Tennyson and Browning ruminated.

After this brief exposition of a theory—too brief, perhaps, to carry conviction—we may ask, what would have been the fate of the "metaphysical" had the current of poetry descended in a direct line from them, as it descended in a direct line to them? They would not, certainly, be classified as metaphysical. The possible interests of a poet are unlimited; the more intelligent he is the better; the more intelligent he is

---

[5] *Revenge of Bussy D'Ambois,* IV, 1, 137-46.
[6] Browning, *Bishop Blougram's Apology,* ll. 693-97.
[7] *The Two Voices.* ll. 382-93.

[8] Guido Cavalcanti (1250-1300); Guido Guinicelli (or Guinizelli; 1220-1276); and Cino da Pistoia (1270-1336).

the more likely that he will have interests: our only condition is that he turn them into poetry, and not merely meditate on them poetically. A philosophical theory which has entered into poetry is established, for its truth or falsity in one sense ceases to matter, and its truth in another sense is proved. The poets in question have, like other poets, various faults. But they were, at best, engaged in the task of trying to find the verbal equivalent for states of mind and feeling. And this means both that they are more mature, and that they wear better, than later poets of certainly not less literary ability.

It is not a permanent necessity that poets should be interested in philosophy, or in any other subject. We can only say that it appears likely that poets in our civilization, as it exists at present, must be *difficult*. Our civilization comprehends great variety and complexity, and this variety and complexity, playing upon a refined sensibility, must produce various and complex results. The poet must become more and more comprehensive, more allusive, more indirect, in order to force, to dislocate if necessary, language into his meaning. (A brilliant and extreme statement of this view, with which it is not requisite to associate oneself, is that of M. Jean Epstein, *La Poésie d' aujourd-hui*.) Hence we get something which looks very much like the conceit— we get, in fact, a method curiously similar to that of the "metaphysical poets," similar also in its use of obscure words and of simple phrasing.

O géraniums diaphanes, guerroyeurs sortilèges,
Sacrilèges monomanes!
Emballages, dévergondages, douches! O pressoirs
Des vendanges des grands soirs!
Layettes aux abois,
Thyrses au fond des bois!
Transfusions, représailles,
Relevailles, compresses et l'éternel potion,
Angélus! n'en pouvoir plus
De débâcles nuptiales! de débâcles nuptiales! [9]

The same poet could write also simply:

Elle est bien loin, elle pleure,
Le grand vent se lamente aussi . . . [10]

Jules Laforgue, and Tristan Corbière in many of his poems, are nearer to the "school of Donne" than any modern English poet. But poets more classical than they have the same essential quality of transmuting ideas into sensations, of transforming an observation into a state of mind.

Pour l'enfant, amoureux de cartes et d'estampes,
L'univers est égal à son vaste appétit.
Ah, que le monde est grand à la clarté des lampes!
Aux yeux du souvenir que le monde est petit! [11]

In French literature the great master of the seventeenth century—Racine—and the great master of the nineteenth—Baudelaire—are in some ways more like each other than they are like any one else. The greatest two masters of diction are also the greatest two psychologists, the most curious explorers of the soul. It is interesting to speculate whether it is not a misfortune that two of the greatest masters of diction in our language, Milton and Dryden, triumph with a dazzling disregard of the soul. If we continued to produce Miltons and Drydens it might not so much matter, but as things are it is a pity that English poetry has remained so incomplete. Those who object to the "artificiality" of Milton or Dryden sometimes tell us to "look into our hearts and write." But that is not looking deep enough; Racine or Donne looked into a good deal more than the heart. One must look into the cerebral cortex, the nervous system, and the digestive tracts.

May we not conclude, then, that Donne, Crashaw, Vaughan, Herbert and Lord Herbert, Marvell, King, Cowley at his best, are in the direct current of English poetry, and that their faults should be reprimanded by this standard rather than coddled by antiquarian affection? They have been enough praised in terms which are implicit limitations because they are "metaphysical" or "witty," "quaint" or "obscure," though at their best they have not these attributes

[9] "O translucent geraniums, warriors casting spells, crazed and sacrilegious! Packings, shameless acts, shower baths! O wine-presses for the sale of great entertainments! Boxes at bay, Thyrsus at the bottom of the wood, heady drinks, reprisals, clutching of hands, compresses, and the eternal potion, Angelus! let there be no power more for marital upheavals, for marital upheavals!" (Laforgue, *Derniers Vers*, X, 1-10.)

[10] "She is far away, she weeps; the northwind also weeps. . . ."

[11] "For the child, lover of maps and stamps, the universe is equal to his great appetite. Oh, how large the world is under the bright light of lamps, how small in the eyes of memory." (Baudelaire, *Le Voyage*, I, 1.)

more than other serious poets. On the other hand, we must not reject the criticism of Johnson (a dangerous person to disagree with) without having mastered it, without having assimilated the Johnsonian canons of taste. In reading the celebrated passage in his essay on Cowley we must remember that by wit he clearly means something more serious than we usually mean today; [12] in his criticism of their versification we must remember in what a narrow discipline he was trained, but also how well trained; we must remember that Johnson tortures chiefly the chief offenders, Cowley and Cleveland. It would be a fruitful work, and one requiring a substantial book, to break up the classification of Johnson (for there has been none since) and exhibit these poets in all their difference of kind and of degree, from the massive music of Donne to the faint, pleasing tinkle of Aurelian Townshend— whose *Dialogue between a Pilgrim and Time* is one of the few regrettable omissions from the excellent anthology of Professor Grierson.

[12] See Johnson's *Life of Cowley*, above, p. 218.

Four Elizabethan Dramatists

A PREFACE TO AN UNWRITTEN BOOK

To ATTEMPT to supplement the criticism of Lamb, Coleridge, and Swinburne on these four Elizabethan dramatists — Webster, Tourneur, Middleton, and Chapman—is a task for which I now believe the time has gone by. What I wish to do is to define and illustrate a point of view toward the Elizabethan drama, which is different from that of the nineteenth century tradition. There are two accepted and apparently opposed critical attitudes toward Elizabethan drama, and what I shall endeavour to show is that these attitudes are identical, and that another attitude is possible. Furthermore, I believe that this alternative critical attitude is not merely a possible difference of personal bias, but that it is the inevitable attitude for our time. The statement and explication of a conviction about such an important body of dramatic literature, toward what is in fact the only distinct form of dramatic literature that England has produced, should be something more than an exercise in mental ingenuity or in refinement of taste: it should be something of revolutionary influence on the future of drama. Contemporary literature, like contemporary politics, is confused by the moment-to-moment struggle for existence; but the time arrives when an examination of principles is necessary. I believe that the theatre has reached a point at which a revolution in principles should take place.

The accepted attitude toward Elizabethan drama was established on the publication of Charles Lamb's *Specimens*. By publishing these selections, Lamb set in motion the enthusiasm for poetic drama which still persists, and at the same time encouraged the formation of a distinction which is, I believe, the ruin of modern drama— the distinction between drama and literature. For the *Specimens* made it possible to read the plays as poetry while neglecting their function on the stage. It is for this reason that all modern opinion of the Elizabethans seems to spring from Lamb, for all modern opinion rests upon the admission that poetry and drama are two separate things, which can only be *combined* by a writer of exceptional genius. The difference between the people who prefer Elizabethan drama, in spite of what they admit to be its dramatic defects, and the people who prefer modern drama although acknowledging that it is never good poetry, is comparatively unimportant. For in either case, you are committed to the opinion that a play can be good literature but a bad play and that it may be a good play and bad literature—or else that it may be outside of literature altogether.

On the one hand we have Swinburne, representative of the opinion that plays exist as literature, and on the other hand Mr. William Archer, who with great lucidity and consistency maintains the view that a play need not be literature at all. No two critics of Elizabethan drama

Four Elizabethan Dramatists. First published in 1924. From *Selected Essays, 1917-1932* by T. S. Eliot, copyright, 1932, by Harcourt Brace Jovanovich, Inc. and Faber & Faber Ltd.

could appear to be more opposed than Swinburne and Mr. William Archer; yet their assumptions are fundamentally the same, for the distinction between poetry and drama, which Mr. Archer makes explicit, is implicit in the view of Swinburne; and Swinburne as well as Mr. Archer allows us to entertain the belief that the difference between modern drama and Elizabethan drama is represented by a gain of dramatic technique and the loss of poetry.

Mr. Archer in his brilliant and stimulating book [1] succeeded in making quite clear all of the dramatic faults of Elizabethan drama. What vitiates his analysis is his failure to see why these faults are faults, and not simply different conventions. And he gains his apparent victory over the Elizabethans for this reason, that the Elizabethans themselves admit the same criteria of realism that Mr. Archer asserts. The great vice of English drama from Kyd to Galsworthy has been that its aim of realism was unlimited. In one play, *Everyman,* and perhaps in that one play only, we have a drama within the limitations of art; since Kyd, since *Arden of Feversham,* since *The Yorkshire Tragedy,* there has been no form to arrest, so to speak, the flow of spirit at any particular point before it expands and ends its course in the desert of exact likeness to the reality which is perceived by the most commonplace mind. Mr. Archer confuses faults with conventions; the Elizabethans committed faults and muddled their conventions. In their plays there are faults of inconsistency, faults of incoherency, faults of taste, there are nearly everywhere faults of carelessness. But their great weakness is the same weakness as that of modern drama, it is the lack of a convention. Mr. Archer facilitates his own task of destruction, and avoids offending popular opinion, by making an exception of Shakespeare: but Shakespeare, like all his contemporaries, was aiming in more than one direction. In a play of Aeschylus, we do not find that certain passages are literature and other passages drama; every style of utterance in the play bears a relation to the whole and because of this relation is dramatic in itself. The imitation of life is circumscribed, and the approaches to ordinary speech and withdrawals from ordinary

speech are not without relation and effect upon each other. It is essential that a work of art should be self-consistent, that an artist should consciously or unconsciously draw a circle beyond which he does not trespass: on the one hand actual life is always the material, and on the other hand an abstraction from actual life is a necessary condition to the creation of the work of art.

Let us try to conceive how the Elizabethan drama would appear to us if we had in existence what has never existed in the English language: a drama formed within a conventional scheme—the convention of an individual dramatist, or of a number of dramatists working in the same form at the same time. And when I say convention, I do not necessarily mean any particular convention of subject matter, of treatment, of verse or of dramatic form, of general philosophy of life or any other convention which has already been used. It may be some quite new selection or structure or distortion in subject matter or technique; any form or rhythm imposed upon the world of action. We will take the point of view of persons accustomed to this convention and finding the expression of their dramatic impulses in it. From this point of view such performances as were those of the Phoenix Society are most illuminating. For the drama, the existence of which I suppose, will have its special conventions of the stage and the actor as well as of the play itself. An actor in an Elizabethan play is either too realistic or too abstract in his treatment, whatever system of speech, of expression and of movement he adopts. The play is for ever betraying him. An Elizabethan play was in some ways as different from a modern play, its performance is almost as much a lost art, as if it were a drama of Aeschylus or Sophocles. And in some ways it is more difficult to reproduce. For it is easier to present the effect of something in a firm convention, than the effect of something which was aiming, blindly enough, at something else. The difficulty in presenting Elizabethan plays is that they are liable to be made too modern, or falsely archaic. Why are the asides ridiculous, which Mr. Archer reprehends in *A Woman Killed with Kindness?* Because they are not a convention, but a subterfuge; it is not Heywood who assumes that asides are inaudible, it is

[1] *The Old Drama and the New* (Heinemann, 1923). [Eliot.]

Mrs. Frankford who *pretends* not to hear Wendoll. A convention is not ridiculous: a subterfuge makes us extremely uncomfortable. The weakness of the Elizabethan drama is not its defect of realism, but its attempt at realism; not its conventions, but its lack of conventions.

In order to make an Elizabethan drama give a satisfactory effect as a work of art, we should have to find a method of acting different from that of contemporary social drama, and at the same time to attempt to express all the emotions of actual life in the way in which they actually would be expressed: the result would be something like a performance of *Agamemnon* by the Guitrys. The effect upon actors who attempt to specialise in Shakespearean or other seventeenth-century revivals is unfortunate. The actor is called upon for a great deal that is not his business, and is left to his own devices for things in which he should be trained. His stage personality has to be supplied from and confounded with his real personality. Any one who has observed one of the great dancers of the Russian school will have observed that the man or the woman whom we admire is a being who exists only during the performances, that it is a personality, a vital flame which appears from nowhere, disappears into nothing and is complete and sufficient in its appearance. It is a conventional being, a being which exists only in and for the work of art which is the ballet. A great actor on the ordinary stage is a person who also exists off it and who supplies the rôle which he performs with the person which he is. A ballet is apparently a thing which exists only as acted and would appear to be a creation much more of the dancer than of the choreographer. This is not quite true. It is a development of several centuries into a strict form. In the ballet only that is left to the actor which is properly the actor's part. The general movements are set for him. There are only limited movements that he can make, only a limited degree of emotion that he can express. He is not called upon for his personality. The differences between a great dancer and a merely competent dancer is in the vital flame, that impersonal, and, if you like, inhuman force which transpires between each of the great dancer's movements. So it would be in a strict form of drama; but in realistic drama, which is drama striving steadily to escape the condi-

tions of art, the human being intrudes. Without the human being and without this intrusion, the drama cannot be performed, and this is as true of Shakespeare as it is of Henry Arthur Jones. A play of Shakespeare's and a play of Henry Arthur Jones's are essentially of the same type, the difference being that Shakespeare is very much greater and Mr. Jones very much more skilful. They are both dramatists to be read rather than seen, because it is precisely in that drama which depends upon the interpretation of an actor of genius, that we ought to be on our guard against the actor. The difference is, of course, that without the actor of genius the plays of Mr. Jones are nothing and the plays of Shakespeare are still to be read. But a true acting play is surely a play which does not depend upon the actor for anything but acting, in the sense in which a ballet depends upon the dancer for dancing. Lest any one should fall into a contrary misunderstanding, I will explain that I do not by any means intend the actor to be an automaton, nor would I admit that the human actor can be replaced by a marionette. A great dancer, whose attention is set upon carrying out an appointed task, provides the life of the ballet through his movements; in the same way the drama would depend upon a great trained actor. The advantages of convention for the actor are precisely similar to its advantages for the author. No artist produces great art by a deliberate attempt to express his personality. He expresses his personality indirectly through concentrating upon a task which is a task in the same sense as the making of an efficient engine or the turning of a jug or a table-leg.

The art of the Elizabethans is an impure art. If it be objected that this is a prejudice of the case, I can only reply that one must criticise from some point of view and that it is better to know what one's point of view is. I know that I rebel against most [2] performances of Shakespeare's plays because I want a direct relationship between the work of art and myself, and I want the performance to be such as will not interrupt or alter this relationship any more than it is an alteration or interruption for me to superpose a second inspection of a picture or

[2] A really good performance of Shakespeare, such as the very best productions of the Old Vic and Sadlers' Wells, may add much to our understanding. [Eliot.]

building upon the first. I object, in other words, to the interpretation, and I would have a work of art such that it needs only to be completed and cannot be altered by each interpretation. Now it is obvious that in realistic drama you become more and more dependent upon the actor. And this is another reason why the drama which Mr. Archer desires, as the photograhic and gramophonic record of its time, can never exist. The closer a play is built upon real life, the more the performance by one actor will differ from another, and the more the performances of one generation of actors will differ from those of the next. It is furthermore obvious that what we ask involves a considerable sacrifice of a certain kind of interest. A character in the conventional play can never be as real as is the character in a realistic play while the rôle is being enacted by a great actor who has made the part his own. I can only say that wherever you have a form you make some sacrifice against some gain.

If we examine the faults which Mr. Archer finds in Elizabethan drama, it is possible to come to the conclusion (already indicated) that these faults are due to its tendencies rather than what are ordinarily called its conventions. I mean that no single convention of Elizabethan drama, however ridiculous it may be made to appear, is essentially bad. Neither the soliloquy, nor the aside, nor the ghost, nor the blood-and-thunder, nor absurdity of place or time is in itself absurd. There are, of course, definite faults of bad writing, careless writing, and bad taste. A line-by-line examination of almost any Elizabethan play, including those of Shakespeare, would be a fruitful exercise. But these are not the faults which weaken the foundations. What is fundamentally objectionable is that in the Elizabethan drama there has been no firm principle of what is to be postulated as a convention and what is not. The fault is not with the ghost but with the presentation of a ghost on a plane on which he is inappropriate, and with the confusion between one kind of ghost and another. The three witches in *Macbeth* are a distinguished example of correct supernaturalism amongst a race of ghosts who are too frequently equivocations. It seems to me strictly an error, although an error which is condoned by the success of each passage in itself, that Shakespeare should have introduced into the same play ghosts belonging to such dif-ferent categories as the three sisters and the ghost of Banquo.[3] The aim of the Elizabethans was to attain complete realism without surrendering any of the advantages which as artists they observed in unrealistic conventions.

We shall take up the work of four Elizabethan dramatists and attempt to subject them to an analysis from the point of view which I have indicated. We shall take the objections of Mr. Archer to each one of these dramatists and see if the difficulty does not reside in this confusion of convention and realism, and we must make some attempt also to illustrate the faults as distinguished from the conventions. There were, of course, tendencies toward form. There was a general philosophy of life, if it may be called such, based on Seneca and other influences which we find in Shakespeare as in the others. It is a philosophy which, as Mr. Santayana observed in an essay which passed almost unheeded, may be summarised in the statement that Duncan is in his grave. Even the philosophical basis, the general attitude toward life of the Elizabethans, is one of anarchism, of dissolution, of decay. It is in fact exactly parallel and indeed one and the same thing with their artistic greediness, their desire for every sort of effect together, their unwillingness to accept any limitation and abide by it. The Elizabethans are in fact a part of the movement of progress or deterioration which has culminated in Sir Arthur Pinero and in the present regimen of Europe.[4]

The case of John Webster, and in particular *The Duchess of Malfy*, will provide an interesting example of a very great literary and dramatic genius directed toward chaos. The case of Middleton is an interesting one, because we have from the same hand plays so different as *The Changeling, Women Beware Women, The Roaring Girle,* and *A Game at Chesse.*[5] In the one

[3] This will appear to be an objection as pedantic as that of Thomas Rymer to *Othello.* But Rymer makes out a very good case. [Eliot.]

[4] Mr. Archer calls it progress. He has certain predispositions. "Shakespeare," he says, "was not alive to the great idea which differentiates the present age from all that have gone before—the idea of progress." And he admits speaking of Elizabethan drama in general, that "here and there a certain glimmer of humanitarian feeling is perceptible." [Eliot.]

[5] I agree with Mr. Dugdale Sykes, to whose acute observations I am under a great debt, that certain work

great play of Tourneur's, the discord is less apparent, but not less real. Chapman appears to have been potentially perhaps the greatest artist of all these men: his was the mind which was the most classical, his was the drama which is the most independent in its tendency toward a dramatic form—although it may seem the most formless and the most indifferent to dramatic necessities. If we can establish the same conse-

quence independently by an examination of the Elizabethan philosophy, the Elizabethan dramatic form, and the variations in the rhythms of Elizabethan blank verse as employed by several of the greatest dramatists, we may come to conclusions which will enable us to understand why Mr. Archer, who is the opponent of the Elizabethans, should also be unconsciously their last champion, and why he should be a believer in progress, in the growth of humanitarian feeling, and in the superiority and efficiency of the present age.

attributed to Middleton is not Middleton's, but there appears to be no reason for questioning the authorship of the plays I have just mentioned. [Eliot.]

The Modern Mind

THERE is a sentence in Maritain's *Art and Scholasticism* which occurs to me in this context: "Work such as Picasso's," he says, "shows a fearful progress in self-consciousness on the part of painting."

So far I have drawn a few light sketches to indicate the changes in the self-consciousness of poets thinking about poetry. A thorough history of this "progress in self-consciousness" in poetry and the criticism of poetry would have kinds of criticism to consider which do not fall within the narrow scope of these lectures: the history of Shakespeare criticism alone, in which, for instance, Morgann's Essay on the character of Falstaff and Coleridge's *Lectures on Shakespeare* would be representative moments, would have to be considered in some detail. But we have observed the notable development in self-consciousness in Dryden's Prefaces, and in the first serious attempt, which he made, at a valuation of the English poets. We have seen his work in one direction continued, and a method perfected, by Johnson in his careful estimation of a number of poets, an estimate arrived at by the application of what are on the whole admirably consistent standards. We have found a deeper insight into the nature of the poetic activity in

remarks scattered through the writings of Coleridge and in the Preface of Wordsworth and in the Letters of Keats; and a perception, still immature, of the need to elucidate the social function of poetry in Wordsworth's *Preface* and in Shelley's *Defence*. In the criticism of Arnold we find a continuation of the work of the Romantic poets with a new appraisal of the poetry of the past by a method which, lacking the precision of Johnson's, gropes towards wider and deeper connexions. I have not wished to exhibit this "progress in self-consciousness" as being necessarily *progress* with an association of higher value. For one thing, it cannot be wholly abstracted from the general changes in the human mind in history; and that these changes have any teleological significance is not one of my assumptions.

Arnold's insistence upon order in poetry according to a moral valuation was, for better or worse, of the first importance for his age. When he is not at his best he obviously falls between two stools. Just as his poetry is too reflective, too ruminative, to rise ever to the first rank, so also is his criticism. He is not, on the one hand, quite a pure enough poet to have the sudden illuminations which we find in the criticism of Wordsworth, Coleridge and Keats; and on the other hand he lacked the mental discipline, the passion for exactness in the use of words and for consistency and continuity of reasoning, which distinguishes the philosopher. He sometimes confuses words and meanings: neither as poet nor as philosopher should he have been satisfied with such an utterance as that "poetry is at bottom a criticism of life." A more profound insight into poetry and a more exact use of language than Arnold's are required. The critical method of Arnold, the assumptions of Arnold, remained valid for the rest of his century. In quite diverse developments, it is the criticism of Arnold that sets the tone: Walter Pater, Arthur Symons, Addington Symonds, Leslie Stephen, F. W. H. Myers, George Saintsbury—all the more eminent critical names of the time bear witness to it.

Whether we agree or not with any or all of his conclusions, whether we admit or deny that his method is adequate, we must admit that the work of Mr. I. A. Richards will have been of cardinal importance in the history of literary criticism. Even if his criticism proves to be entirely on the wrong track, even if this modern "self-consciousness" turns out to be only a blind alley, Mr. Richards will have done something in accelerating the exhaustion of the possibilities. He will have helped indirectly to discredit the criticism of persons qualified neither by sensibility nor by knowledge of poetry, from which we suffer daily. There is some hope of greater clarity; we should begin to learn to distinguish the appreciation of poetry from theorising about poetry, and to know when we are not talking about poetry but about something else suggested by it. There are two elements in Richards's scheme, both of considerable importance for its ultimate standing, of which I have the gravest doubts but with which I am not here concerned: his theory of Value and his theory of Education (or rather the theory of Education assumed in or implied by his attitude in *Practical Criticism*). As for psychology and linguistics, that is his field and not mine. I am more concerned here with what seem to me to be a few unexamined assumptions that he has made. I do not know whether he still adheres to certain assertions made in his early essay *Science and Poetry*; but I do not understand that he has yet made any public modification of them. Here is one that is in my mind:

The most dangerous of the sciences is only now beginning to come into action. I am thinking less of Psychoanalysis or of Behaviourism than of the whole subject which includes them. It is very probable that the Hindenburg Line to which the defence of our traditions retired as a result of the onslaughts of the last century will be blown up in the near future. If this should happen a mental

chaos such as man has never experienced may be expected. We shall then be thrown back, as Matthew Arnold foresaw, upon poetry. Poetry is capable of saving us. . . .

I should have felt completely at a loss in this passage, had not Matthew Arnold turned up; and then it seemed to me that I knew a little better what was what. I should say that an affirmation like this was highly characteristic of one type of modern mind. For one of the things that one can say about the modern mind is that it comprehends every extreme and degree of opinion. Here, from the essay, *Art and Scholasticism,* which I have already quoted, is Mr. Maritain:

It is a deadly error to expect poetry to provide the supersubstantial nourishment of man.

Mr. Maritain is a theologian as well as philosopher, and you may be sure that when he says "deadly error" he is in deadly earnest. But if the author of *Anti-Moderne* is hardly to be considered a "modern" man, we can find other varieties of opinion. In a book called *The Human Parrot*, Mr. Montgomery Belgion has two essays, one called *Art and Mr. Maritain* and the other *What is Criticism,* from which you will learn that neither Maritain nor Richards knows what he is talking about. Mr. Richards further maintains that the experience of poetry is not a mystical revelation, and the Abbé Henri Brémond,[1] in *Prayer and Poetry,* is concerned with telling us in what kind and degree it is. On this point Mr. Belgion is apparently in accord with Mr. Richards. And we may be wise to keep in mind a remark of Mr. Herbert Read in *Form in Modern Poetry:* "If a literary critic happens to be also a poet . . . he is liable to suffer from dilemmas which do not trouble the philosophic calm of his more prosaic colleagues."

Beyond a belief that poetry does something of importance, or has something of importance to do, there does not seem to be much agreement. It is interesting that in our time, which has not produced any vast number of important poets, so many people—and there are many more—should be asking questions about poetry. These problems are not those which properly concern poets as poets at all; if poets plunge into the

[1] While preparing this book for press I learn with great regret of the Abbé Brémond's untimely death. It is a great pity that he could not have lived to complete the *Histoire du sentiment religieux en France.* [Eliot.]

discussion, it is probably because they have interests and curiosities outside of writing poetry. We need not summon those who call themselves Humanists (for they have for the most part not been primarily occupied with the nature and function of poetry) to bear witness that we have here the problem of religious faith and its substitutes. Not all contemporary critics, of course, but at least a number who appear to have little else in common, seem to consider that art, specifically poetry, has something to do with religion, though they disagree as to what this something may be. The relationship is not always envisaged so moralistically as it was by Arnold, nor so generally as in the statement by Mr. Richards which I quoted. For Mr. Belgion, for instance,

An outstanding example of poetic allegory is in the final canto of the *Paradiso*, where the poet seeks to give an allegorical account of the Beatific Vision, and then declares his efforts vain. We may read this over and over again, and in the end we shall no more have had a revelation of the nature of the Vision than we had before ever we had heard of either it or Dante.

Mr. Belgion seems to have taken Dante at his word. But what we experience as readers is never exactly what the poet experienced, nor would there be any point in its being, though certainly it has some relation to the poet's experience. What the poet experienced is not poetry but poetic material; the writing of the poetry is a fresh "experience" for him, and the reading of it, by the author or by anyone else, is another thing still. Mr. Belgion, in denying a theory which he attributes to Mr. Maritain, seems to me to make his own mistakes; but it is a religion-analogy which is in question. Mr. Richards is much occupied with the religious problem simply in the attempt to avoid it. In an appendix to the second edition of *Principles of Literary Criticism* he has a note on my own verse, which, being as favourable as I could desire, seems to me very acute. But he observes that Canto XXVI of the *Purgatorio* illuminates my "persistent concern with sex, the problem of our generation, as religion was the problem of the last." I readily admit the importance of Canto XXVI, and it was shrewd of Mr. Richards to notice it; but in his contrast of sex and religion he makes a distinction which is too subtle for me to grasp.

One might think that sex and religion were "problems" like Free Trade and Imperial Preference; it seems odd that the human race should have gone on for so many thousands of years before it suddenly realised that religion and sex, one right after the other, presented problems.

It has been my view throughout—and it is only a commonplace after all—that the development and change of poetry and of the criticism of it is due to elements which enter from outside. I tried to draw attention not so much to the importance of Dryden's "contribution" to literary criticism, as if he were merely adding to a store of quantity, as to the importance of the fact that he should *want* to articulate and expound his views on drama and translation and on the English poetry of the past; and, when we came to Johnson, to call attention to the further development of an historical consciousness which made Johnson *want* to estimate, in more detail, the English poets of his own age and of previous ages; [2] and it seemed to me that Wordsworth's theories about poetry drew their aliment from social sources. To Matthew Arnold we owe the credit of bringing the religious issue explicitly into the discussion of literature and poetry; and with due respect to Mr. Richards, and with Mr. Richards himself as a witness, it does not seem to me that this "issue" has been wholly put aside and replaced by that of "sex." My contemporaries seem to me still to be occupied with it, whether they call themselves churchmen, or agnostics, or rationalists, or social revolutionists. The contrast between the doubts that our contemporaries express, and the questions that they ask and the problems they put themselves, and the attitude of at least a part of the past, was well put by Jacques Rivière in two sentences:

If in the seventeenth century Molière or Racine had been asked why he wrote, no doubt he would have been able to find but one answer; that he wrote "for the entertainment of decent people" (*pour distraire les honnêtes gens*). It is only with the advent of Romanticism that the literary act came to be conceived as a sort of raid on the absolute and its result as a revelation.

Rivière's form of expression is not, to my mind, altogether happy. One might suppose that all

[2] The fact that Johnson was working largely to order only indicates that this historical consciousness was already developed. [Eliot.]

that had happened was that a wilful perversity had taken possession of literary men, a new literary disease called Romanticism. That is one of the dangers of expressing one's meaning in terms of "Romanticism": it is a term which is constantly changing in different contexts, and which is now limited to what appear to be purely literary and purely local problems, now expanding to cover almost the whole of the life of a time and of nearly the whole world. It has perhaps not been observed that in its more comprehensive significance "Romanticism" comes to include nearly everything that distinguishes the last two hundred and fifty years or so from their predecessors, and includes so much that it ceases to bring with it any praise or blame. The change to which Rivière alludes is not a contrast between Molière and Racine on the one hand and more modern French writers on the other; it neither reflects credit upon the former nor implies inferiority in the latter. In the interest of clarity and simplicity I wish myself to avoid employing the terms Romanticism and Classicism, terms which inflame political passions, and tend to prejudice our conclusions. I am only concerned with my contention that the notion of what poetry is for, of what is its function to do, does change, and therefore I quoted Rivière; I am concerned further with criticism as evidence of the conception of the use of poetry in the critics' time, and assert that in order to compare the work of different critics we must investigate their assumptions as to what poetry does and ought to do. Examination of the criticism of our time leads me to believe that we are still in the Arnold period.

I speak of Mr. Richards's views with some diffidence. Some of the problems he discusses are themselves very difficult, and only those are qualified to criticise who have applied themselves to the same specialised studies and have acquired proficiency in this kind of thinking. But here I limit myself to passages in which he does not seem to be speaking as a specialist, and in which I have no advantage of special knowledge either. There are two reasons why the writer of poetry must not be thought to have any great advantage. One is that a discussion of poetry such as this takes us far outside the limits within which a poet may speak with authority; the other is that the poet does many things upon instinct, for

which he can give no better account than anybody else. A poet can try, of course, to give an honest report of the way in which he himself writes: the result may, if he is a good observer, be illuminating. And in one sense, but a very limited one, he knows better what his poems "mean" than can anyone else; he may know the history of their composition, the material which has gone in and come out in an unrecognisable form, and he knows what he was trying to do and what he was meaning to mean. But what a poem means is as much what it means to others as what it means to the author; and indeed, in the course of time a poet may become merely a reader in respect to his own works, forgetting his original meaning—or without forgetting, merely changing. So that, when Mr. Richards asserts that *The Waste Land* effects "a complete severance between poetry and *all* beliefs" I am no better qualified to say No! than is any other reader. I will admit that I think that either Mr. Richards is wrong, or I do not understand his meaning. The statement might mean that it was the first poetry to do what all poetry in the past would have been the better for doing: I can hardly think that he intended to pay me such an unmerited compliment. It might also mean that the present situation is radically different from any in which poetry has been produced in the past: namely, that now there is nothing in which to believe, that Belief itself is dead; and that therefore my poem is the first to respond properly to the modern situation and not call upon Make-Believe. And it is in this connexion, apparently, that Mr. Richards observes that "poetry is capable of saving us."

A discussion of Mr. Richards's theories of knowledge, value and meaning would be by no means irrelevant to this assertion, but it would take us far afield, and I am not the person to undertake it. We cannot of course refute the statement "poetry is capable of saving us" without knowing which one of the multiple definitions of salvation Mr. Richards has in mind.[3] (A good many people behave as if they thought so too: otherwise their interest in poetry is difficult

---

[3] See his *Mencius on the Mind*. There is of course a locution in which we say of someone "he is not one of *us*"; it is possible that the "us" of Mr. Richards's statement represents an equally limited and select number. [Eliot.]

to explain.) I am sure, from the differences of environment, of period, and of mental furniture, that salvation by poetry is not quite the same thing for Mr. Richards as it was for Arnold; but so far as I am concerned these are merely two variants of one theological error.[4] In *Practical Criticism*[5] Mr. Richards provides a recipe which I think throws some light upon his theological ideas. He says:

Something like a technique or ritual for heightening sincerity might well be worked out. When our response to a poem after our best efforts remains uncertain, when we are unsure whether the feelings it excites come from a deep source in our experience, whether our liking or disliking is genuine, is *ours,* or an accident of fashion, a response to surface details or to essentials, we may perhaps help ourselves by considering it in a frame of feelings whose sincerity is beyond our questioning. Sit by the fire (with eyes shut and fingers pressed firmly upon the eyeballs) and consider with as full "realisation" as possible—

five points which follow, and which I shall comment upon one by one. We may observe, in passing, the intense religious seriousness of Mr. Richards's attitude towards poetry.[6] What he proposes—for he hints in the passage above that his sketch might be elaborated—is nothing less than a regimen of Spiritual Exercises. Now for the points.

I. *Man's loneliness (the isolation of the human situation).*

Loneliness is known as a frequent attitude in romantic poetry, and in the form of "lonesomeness" (as I need not remind American readers) is a frequent attitude in contemporary lyrics known as "the blues." But in what sense is Man in general isolated, and from what? What *is* the "human situation"? I can understand the isola-

[4] And different shades of blue. [Eliot.]

[5] Second impression, p. 290. [Eliot.]

[6] This passage is introduced by a long and important discussion of Confucius' conception of "sincerity," which should be read attentively. In passing, it is worthy of remark that Mr. Richards shares his interest in Chinese philosophy with Mr. Ezra Pound and with the late Irving Babbitt. An investigation of an interest common to three apparently quite different thinkers would, I believe, repay the labour. It seems to indicate, at least, a deracination from the Christian tradition. The thought of these three men seems to me to have an interesting similarity. [Eliot.]

tion of the human situation as Plato's Diotima expounds it, or in the Christian sense of the separation of Man from God; but not an isolation which is not a separation from anything in particular.

II. *The facts of birth and of death, in their inexplicable oddity.*

I cannot see why the facts of birth and of death should appear odd in themselves, unless we have a conception of some other way of coming into the world and of leaving it, which strikes us as more natural.

III. *The inconceivable immensity of the Universe.*

It was not, we remember, the "immense spaces" themselves but their *eternal silence* that terrified Pascal. With a definite religious background this is intelligible. But the effect of popular astronomy books (like Sir James Jeans's) upon me is only of the insignificance of vast space.

IV. *Man's place in the perspective of time.*

I confess that I do not find this especially edifying either, or stimulating to the imagination, unless I bring to its contemplation some belief that there is a sense and a meaning in the place of human history in the history of the world. I fear that in many people this subject of meditation can only stimulate the idle wonder and greed for facts which are satisfied by Mr. Wells's compendia.

V. *The enormity (sc. enormousness) of man's ignorance.*

Here again, I must ask, ignorance of what? I am acutely aware, for instance, of my own ignorance of specific subjects on which I want to know more; but Mr. Richards does not, surely, mean the ignorance of any individual man, but of *Man*. But "ignorance" must be relative to the sense in which we take the term "knowledge"; and in *Mencius on the Mind* Mr. Richards has given us a useful analysis of the numerous meanings of "knowledge." Mr. Richards, who has engaged in what I believe will be most fruitful investigations of controversy as systematised misunderstanding, may justly be able to accuse me of perverting his meanings. But his modern substitute for the *Exercises* of St. Ignatius is an appeal to our feelings, and I am only trying to set down how they affect mine. To me Mr. Richards's five points only express a modern emotional attitude which I cannot share, and which finds its most sentimental expression in *A Free Man's Worship*. And as the contemplation of Man's place in the Universe has led Lord Russell to write such bad prose, we may wonder whether it will lead the ordinary aspirant to understanding of good poetry. It is just as likely, I suspect, to confirm him in his taste for the second-rate.

I am willing to admit that such an approach to poetry may help some people: my point is that Mr. Richards speaks as though it were good for everybody. I am perfectly ready to concede the existence of people who feel, think and believe as Mr. Richards does in these matters, if he will only concede that there are some people who do not. He told us in *Science and Poetry:*

For centuries . . . countless pseudo-statements—about God, about the universe, about human nature, the relations of mind to mind, about the soul, its rank and destiny . . . have been believed; now they are gone, irrecoverably; and the knowledge which has killed them is not of a kind upon which an equally fine organisation of the mind can be based.

I submit that this is itself a pseudo-statement, if there is such a thing. But these things are indeed gone, so far as Mr. Richards is concerned, if they are no longer believed by people whose minds Mr. Richards respects: we have no ground for controversy there. I only assert again that what he is trying to do is essentially the same as what Arnold wanted to do: to preserve emotions without the beliefs with which their history has been involved. It would seem that Mr. Richards, on his own showing, is engaged in a rearguard religious action.[7]

Mr. Maritain, with an equally strong conviction that poetry will *not* save us, is equally despondent about the world of today. "Could any weakness," he asks, "be greater than the weakness of our contemporaries?" It is no more, as I have said before, the particular business of the poet as poet to concern himself with Maritain's

attempt to determine the position of poetry in a Christian world than it is to concern himself with Richards's attempt to determine the position of poetry in a pagan world: but these various ambient ideas get in through the pores, and produce an unsettled state of mind. Trotsky, whose *Literature and Revolution* is the most sensible statement of a Communist attitude that I have seen,[8] is pretty clear on the relation of the poet to his environment. He observes:

Artistic creation is always a complicated turning inside out of old forms, under the influence of new stimuli which originate outside of art. In this large sense of the word, art is a handmaiden. It is not a disembodied element feeding on itself, but a function of social man indissolubly tied to his life and environment.

There is a striking contrast between this conception of art as a handmaiden, and that which we have just observed of art as a saviour. But perhaps the two notions are not so opposed as they appear. Trotsky seems, in any case, to draw the commonsense distinction between art and propaganda, and to be dimly aware that the material of the artist is not his beliefs as *held*, but his beliefs as *felt* (so far as his beliefs are part of his material at all); and he is sensible enough to see that a period of revolution is not favourable to art, since it puts pressure upon the poet, both direct and indirect, to make him overconscious of his beliefs as *held*. He would not limit communist poetry to the writing of panegyrics upon the Russian State, any more than I should limit Christian poetry to the composition of hymns; the poetry of Villon is just as "Christian" in this way as that of Prudentius or Adam of St. Victor—though I think it would be a long time before Soviet society could afford to approve a Villon, if one arose.[9] It is probable, how-

---

[7] Somewhat in the spirit of "religion without revelation," of which a greater exponent than Mr. Julian Huxley was Emmanuel Kant. On Kant's attempt (which deeply influenced later German theology) see an illuminating passage in A. E. Taylor's *The Faith of a Moralist*, volume II, chapter ii. [Eliot.]

[8] There were also some interesting articles in *The New Republic* by Mr. Edmund Wilson, in controversy (if I remember correctly) with Mr. Michael Gold. I regret that I cannot give the exact reference. The major part of Trotsky's book is not very interesting for those who are unacquainted with the modern Russian authors: one suspects that most of Trotsky's swans are geese. [Eliot.]

[9] The Roman and Communist idea of an index of prohibited books seems to me perfectly sound in principle. It is a question (*a*) of the goodness and universality of the cause, (*b*) of the intelligence that goes to the application. [Eliot.]

ever, that Russian literature will become increasingly unintelligible, increasingly meaningless, to the peoples of Western Europe unless they develop in the same direction as Russia. Even as things are, in the present chaos of opinion and belief, we may expect to find quite different literatures existing in the same language and the same country. "The unconcealed and palpable influence of the devil on an important part of contemporary literature," says Mr. Maritain, "is one of the significant phenomena of the history of our time." I can hardly expect most of my readers to take this remark seriously; [10] those who do will have very different criteria of criticism from those who do not. Another observation of Mr. Maritain's may be less unacceptable:

By showing us where moral truth and the genuine supernatural are situate, religion saves poetry from the absurdity of believing itself destined to transform ethics and life: saves it from overweening arrogance.

This seems to me to be putting the finger on the great weakness of much poetry and criticism of the nineteenth and twentieth centuries. But between the motive which Rivière attributed to Molière and Racine [11] and the motive of Matthew Arnold bearing on shoulders immense what he thought to be the orb of the poet's fate, there is a serious *via media*.

As the doctrine of the moral and educational value of poetry has been elaborated in different forms by Arnold and Mr. Richards, so the Abbé Brémond presented a modern equivalent for the theory of divine inspiration. The task of *Prayer and Poetry* is to establish the likeness, and the difference of kind and degree, between poetry and mysticism. In his attempt to demonstrate this relation he safeguards himself by just qualifications, and makes many penetrating remarks about the nature of poetry. I will confine myself to two pieces of caution. My first qualm is over the assertion that "the more of a poet any

particular poet is, the more he is tormented by the need of communicating his experience." This is a downright sort of statement which is very easy to accept without examination; but the matter is not so simple as all that. I should say that the poet is tormented primarily by the need to write a poem—and so, I regret to find, are a legion of people who are not poets: so that the line between "need" to write and "desire" to write is by no means easy to draw. And what is the experience that the poet is so bursting to communicate? By the time it has settled down into a poem it may be so different from the original experience as to be hardly recognisable. The "experience" in question may be the result of a fusion of feelings so numerous, and ultimately so obscure in their origins, that even if there be communication of them, the poet may hardly be aware of what he is communicating; and what is there to be communicated was not in existence before the poem was completed. "Communication" will not explain poetry. I will not say that there is not always some varying degree of communication in poetry, or that poetry could exist without any communication taking place. There is room for very great individual variation in the motives of equally good individual poets; and we have the assurance of Coleridge, with the approval of Mr. Housman, that "poetry gives most pleasure when only generally and not perfectly understood." And I think that my first objection to Brémond's theory is related to the second, in which also the question of motive and intention enters. Any theory which relates poetry very closely to a religious or a social scheme of things aims, probably, to *explain* poetry by discovering its natural laws; but it is in danger of *binding* poetry by legislation—and poetry can recognise no such laws. When the critic falls into this error he has probably done what we all do: when we generalise about poetry, as I have said before, we are generalising from the poetry which we best know and best like; not from all poetry, or even all of the poetry which we have read. What is "all poetry"? Everything written in verse which a sufficient number of the best minds have considered to be poetry. By a sufficient number, I mean enough persons of different types, at different times and places, over a space of time, and including foreigners as well as those to

---

[10] With the influence of the devil on contemporary literature I shall be concerned in more detail in another book. [Eliot.]

[11] Which does not seem to me to cover the case. Let us say that it was the primary motive (even in *Athalie*). An exact statement would need much space; for we cannot concern ourselves only with what went on inside the poet's head, but with the general state of society. [Eliot.]

whom the language is native, to cancel every personal bias and eccentricity of taste (for we must all be slightly eccentric in taste to have any taste at all). Now when an account like the Abbé Brémond's is tested by being made itself a test, it tends to reveal some narrowness and exclusiveness; at any rate, a good deal of poetry that I like would be excluded, or given some other name than poetry; just as other writers who like to include much prose as being essentially "poetry" create confusion by including too much. That there is a relation (not necessarily noetic, perhaps merely psychological) between mysticism and some kinds of poetry, or some of the kinds of state in which poetry is produced, I make no doubt. But I prefer not to define, or to test, poetry by means of speculations about its origins; you cannot find a sure test for poetry, a test by which you may distinguish between poetry and mere good verse, by reference to its putative antecedents in the mind of the poet. Brémond seems to me to introduce extra-poetic laws for poetry: such laws as have been frequently made, and constantly violated.

There is another danger in the association of poetry with mysticism besides that which I have just mentioned, and that of leading the reader to look in poetry for religious satisfactions. These were dangers for the critic and the reader; there is also a danger for the poet. No one can read Mr. Yeats's *Autobiographies* and his earlier poetry without feeling that the author was trying to get as a poet something like the exaltation to be obtained, I believe, from hashish or nitrous oxide. He was very much fascinated by self-induced trance states, calculated symbolism, mediums, theosophy, crystal-gazing, folklore and hobgoblins. Golden apples, archers, black pigs and such paraphernalia abounded. Often the verse has an hypnotic charm: but you cannot take heaven by magic, especially if you are, like Mr. Yeats, a very sane person. Then, by a great triumph of development, Mr. Yeats began to write and is still writing some of the most beautiful poetry in the language, some of the clearest, simplest, most direct.[12]

The number of people capable of appreciating "all poetry" is probably very small, if not merely a theoretical limit; but the number of people who can get *some* pleasure and benefit from some poetry is, I believe, very large. A perfectly satisfactory theory which applied to all poetry would do so only at the cost of being voided of all content; the more usual reason for the unsatisfactoriness of our theories and general statements about poetry is that while professing to apply to all poetry, they are really theories about, or generalisations from, a limited range of poetry. Even when two persons of taste like the same poetry, this poetry will be arranged in their minds in slightly different patterns; our individual taste in poetry bears the indelible traces of our individual lives with all their experience pleasurable and painful. We are apt either to shape a theory to cover the poetry that we find most moving, or—what is less excusable—to choose the poetry which illustrates the theory we want to hold. You do not find Matthew Arnold quoting Rochester or Sedley. And it is not merely a matter of individual caprice. Each age demands different things from poetry, though its demands are modified, from time to time, by what some new poet has given. So our criticism, from age to age, will reflect the things that the age demands; and the criticism of no one man and of no one age can be expected to embrace the whole nature of poetry or exhaust all of its uses. Our contemporary critics, like their predecessors, are making particular responses to particular situations. No two readers, perhaps, will go to poetry with quite the same demands. Amongst all these demands from poetry and responses to it there is always some permanent element in common, just as there are standards of good and bad writing independent of what any one of us happens to like and dislike; but every effort to formulate the common element is limited by the limitations of particular men in particular places and at particular times; and these limitations become manifest in the perspective of history.

[12] The best analysis of the weakness of Mr. Yeats's poetry that I know is in Mr. Richards's *Science and Poetry*. But I do not think that Mr. Richards quite appreciated Mr. Yeats's later work. [Eliot.]

IRVING BABBITT   (1865-1933)

BABBITT, indirectly through his influence on other writers and teachers if not through the quality of his own writing, has increasingly emerged as one of the most important English and American critics of the past half century. The amount of writing devoted to him, for example, has been immense, especially during the 1920's and early 1930's. Though much of this material is controversial or even antagonistic, it probably exceeds the amount of commentary dealing with any other modern critic.

Babbitt's central position was fixed and immobile. Yet it is difficult to define; for he himself never positively developed it. Instead, he used it as a starting premise and expounded it negatively, attacking the entire modern movement in science, philosophy, and art from the mid-eighteenth century to the present. Briefly put, this premise is as follows: Man's distinctive nature is separate from the external, natural world, the world of the physical sciences. He is subjected to a "higher" law, a law that human reason can descry. Through the complete mental grasp of universal truths, through the control of his animal nature, through bending his imagination and emotions to his rational hold on truth, he fulfills his own nature, achieves *decorum*—that is, propriety, or a fitting in with universal law—and so becomes "human." This premise, indeed, is theoretically classical. But what is unclassical is the comparative narrowness with which it is interpreted and the complete rigidity with which it is applied. With this premise as a working hypothesis, Joseph Warren Beach has said, Babbitt roamed through the period since the late eighteenth century as through a vast infirmary, noting every sign of disease, some unquestionably real and very serious, others possibly less

IRVING BABBITT. Educated at Harvard (A.B. 1889), Babbitt studied at the Sorbonne (1891-92) at which he afterward lectured, taught briefly at Williams College (1893-94), and returned to Harvard (1894) to teach French and Comparative Literature until his death (1933).

In addition to the works mentioned above, mention should be made, because of its bibliography and index, of *The Spanish Character and Other Essays, with a Bibliography of his Publications and an Index to his Collected Works* (1940). Among the large available commentary, see, besides the personal reminiscenses in *Irving Babbitt, Man and Teacher* (ed. Frederick Manchester and Odell Shepard, 1941), T. S. Eliot, "The Humanism of Irving Babbitt" and "Second Thoughts about Humanism," in *Selected Essays* (1932); Donald MacCampbell, "Irving Babbitt," *Sewanee Review* (April, 1935); P. E. More, "Irving Babbitt," *American Review*, III (1934), 23-40; and G. B. Munson, "Introduction to Irving Babbitt," in *Destinations: a Canvass of American Literature since 1900* (1928), pp. 24-40. Students acquainted with French or German may be referred also to L. J. A. Mercier, *Le Mouvement humaniste aux États-Unis* (1928); and H. Boeschenstein and Victor Lange, *Kulturkritik und Literaturbetrachtung in Amerika* (Breslau, 1938), Chs. 2-3. More recent revaluations have been by Harry Levin, *Irving Babbitt and the Teaching of Literature* (Cambridge, Mass., 1961); and K. F. McKean, *The Moral Measure of Literature* (Denver, 1961).

frightful than he would indicate. Probably no destructive critic ever brought a wider range of reading to bear upon his subject, or marshalled his charges with more energetic and amusing gusto. This side of Babbitt is best shown in his *Rousseau and Romanticism* (1919) and his collection of essays, *On Being Creative* (1932). A more temperate presentation of his ideas is found in his *Literature and the American College* (1908), *The New Laokoön* (1910), and especially his informative *Masters of Modern French Criticism* (1912).

Babbitt's influence was by no means confined to the so-called "New Humanist" movement that he and Paul Elmer More founded and led—a movement that built upon the classical humanism of Matthew Arnold but applied its criteria with a far more rigid moral interpretation and with a less flexible sense of the conventions, esthetic demands, and formal qualities of art. In fact, the "New Humanist" movement of Babbitt and More has hardly continued as an active and co-operative force. The extent of Babbitt's influence is seen less among his immediate disciples than among writers and teachers who, through him, were first introduced to the significance and range of the classical tradition of criticism which he tried, though with a limited outlook, to revive; to the continuity of modern literature as a whole, from the romantic movement to the present day; and to methods and values espoused by great critics of the past. To some extent, Babbitt revolutionized the approach to the history of literary criticism. It was no longer viewed as a series of opinions or expressions of taste but as an articulation of more central attitudes. The modern movement especially, beginning with romanticism, was seen as a product of the eighteenth rather than the nineteenth century, and as closely connected with larger moral and intellectual developments. But Babbitt's more general influence is less tangible. For his students, ranging from some of the "New Humanists" to T. S. Eliot, and also including such diverse political writers as Granville Hicks and Walter Lippmann, varied widely in their points of view. Even the anti-romanticism of the American "New Critics," though their stylistic values are far from Babbitt's, has—indirectly through Eliot—appropriated arguments and attitudes from Babbitt. Perhaps his most important achievement, however, was generally to recall an entire academic and critical generation to consider primary questions. Often his influence appeared in the opposition he aroused; many writers have felt that they had first to answer Babbitt. In doing so, they found themselves facing problems and making distinctions that they might not otherwise have discovered. To a degree unsurpassed by any other writer of the last half century, he made traditional critical issues a vivid and living concern, applicable to almost every aspect of modern life.

Romantic Morality: The Real

THE FUNDAMENTAL thing in Rousseauistic morality is not, as we have seen, the assertion that man is naturally good, but the denial of the "civil war in the cave." Though this denial is not complete in Rousseau himself, nothing is more certain than that his whole tendency is away from this form of dualism. The beautiful soul does the right thing not as a result of effort, but spontaneously, unconsciously and almost inevitably. In fact the beautiful soul can scarcely be said to be a voluntary agent at all. "Nature" acts in him and for him. This minimizing of moral struggle and deliberation and choice, this drift towards a naturalistic fatalism, as it may be termed, is a far more significant thing in Rousseau than his optimism. One may as a matter of fact eliminate dualism in favor of nature and at the same time look on nature as evil. This is precisely what one is likely to do if one sees no alternative to temperamental living, while judging those who live temperamentally not by their "ideal," that is by their feeling of their own loveliness, but by what they actually do. One will become a realist in the sense that came to be attached to this word during the latter part of the nineteenth century. Rousseau himself is often realistic in this sense when he interrupts his Arcadian visions to tell us what actually occurred. In the "Confessions," as I have said, passages that recall Lamartine alternate with passages that recall Zola, and the transition from one type of passage to the other is often disconcertingly sudden. In reading these realistic passages of Rousseau we are led to reflect that his "nature" is not, in practice, so remote from Taine's nature as might at first appear. "What we call *nature*," says Taine, "is this brood of secret passions, often maleficent, generally vulgar, always blind, which tremble and fret within us, ill-covered by the cloak of decency and reason under which we try to disguise them; we think we lead them and they lead us; we

think our actions our own, they are theirs." [1]

The transition from an optimistic to a pessimistic naturalism can be followed with special clearness in the stages by which the sentimental drama of the eighteenth century passes over into the realistic drama of a later period. Petit de Julleville contrasts the beginning and the end of this development as follows: "[In the eighteenth century] to please the public you had to say to it: 'You are all at least at bottom good, virtuous, full of feeling. Let yourselves go, follow your instincts; listen to nature and you will do the right thing spontaneously.' How changed times are! Nowadays [2] any one who wishes to please, to be read and petted and admired, to pass for great and become very rich, should address men as follows: "You are a vile pack of rogues, and profligates, you have neither faith nor law; you are impelled by your instincts alone and these instincts are ignoble. Do not try though to mend matters, that would be of no use at all.' " [3]

The connecting link between these different forms of the drama is naturalistic fatalism, the suppression of moral responsibility for either man's goodness or badness. Strictly speaking, the intrusion of the naturalistic element into the realm of ethical values and the subversion by it of deliberation and choice and of the normal sequence of moral cause and effect is felt from the human point of view not as fate at all, but as chance. Emotional romanticism joins at this point with other forms of romanticism, which all show a proclivity to prefer to strict motivation, to probability in the Aristotelian sense, what is fortuitous and therefore wonderful. This is only another way of saying that the romanticist is moving away from the genuinely dramatic towards melodrama. Nothing is easier than to establish the connection between emotional romanticism and the prodigious efflorescence of melodrama, the irresponsible quest for thrills, that has marked the past century. What perhaps distinguishes this

Romantic Morality: The Real. Chapter V of *Rousseau and Romanticism* (1919); reprinted by permission of Houghton Mifflin Co. Subsequent notes to this essay are those of Babbitt.

[1] *Lit. Ang.*, IV, 130.
[2] About 1885.
[3] *Le Théâtre en France*, 304.

movement from any previous one is the attempt to invest what is at bottom a melodramatic view of life with philosophic and even religious significance. By suppressing the "civil war in the cave" one strikes at the very root of true drama. It does not then much matter from the dramatic point of view whether the burden of responsibility for good or evil of which you have relieved the individual is shifted upon "nature" or society. Shelley, for example, puts the blame for evil on society. "Prometheus Unbound," in which he has developed his conception, is, judged as a play, only an ethereal melodrama. The unaccountable collapse of Zeus, a monster of unalloyed and unmotivated badness, is followed by the gushing forth in man of an equally unalloyed and unmotivated goodness. The whole genius of Hugo, again, as I have said in speaking of his use of antithesis, is melodramatic. His plays may be described as parvenu melodramas. They abound in every variety of startling contrast and strange happening, the whole pressed into the service of "problems" manifold and even of a philosophy of history. At the same time the poverty of ethical insight and true dramatic motivation is dissimulated under profuse lyrical outpourings and purple patches of local color. His Hernani actually glories in not being a responsible agent, but an "unchained and fatal force," and so more capable of striking astonishment into himself and others. Yet the admirers of Hugo would not only promote him to the first rank of poets, but would have us share his own belief that he is a seer and a prophet.

It may be objected that the great dramatists of the past exalt this power of fate and thus diminish moral responsibility. But the very sharpest distinction must be drawn between the subrational fate of the emotional romanticist and the superrational fate of Greek tragedy. The fate of Aeschylean tragedy, for instance, so far from undermining moral responsibility rather reinforces it. It is felt to be the revelation of a moral order of which man's experience at any particular moment is only an infinitesimal fragment. It does not seem, like the subrational fate of the emotional romanticist, the intrusion into the human realm of an alien power whether friendly or unfriendly. This point might be established by a study of the so-called fate drama in Germany (*Schicksaltragödie*), which, though blackly pessimistic, is closely related to the optimistic sentimental drama of the eighteenth century.[4] The German fate drama is in its essence ignoble because its characters are specimens of sensitive morality—incapable, that is, of opposing a firm human purpose to inner impulse or outer impression. The fate that thus wells up from the depths of nature and overwhelms their wills is not only malign and ironical, but as Grillparzer says, makes human deeds seem only "throws of the dice in the blind night of chance."[5] It would be easy to follow similar conceptions of fate down through later literature at least to the novels of Thomas Hardy.

Some of the earlier exponents of the sentimental drama, like Diderot, were not so certain as one might expect that the discarding of traditional decorum in favor of "nature" would result practically in a reign of pure loveliness. At one moment Diderot urges men to get rid of the civil war in the cave in order that they may be Arcadian, like the savages of the South Sea, but at other moments—as in "Rameau's Nephew"—he shows a somewhat closer grip on the problem of what will actually come to pass when a man throws off the conventions of a highly organized civilization and sets out to live temperamentally. Diderot sees clearly that he will be that least primitive of all beings, the Bohemian. Rameau's nephew, in his irresponsibility and emotional instability, in the kaleidoscopic shiftings of his mood, anticipates all the romantic Bohemians and persons of "artistic temperament" who were to afflict the nineteenth century. But he is more than a mere aesthete. At moments we can discern in him the first lineaments of the superman, who knows no law save the law of might. One should recollect that the actual influence of Diderot in France fell in the second rather than in the first half of the nineteenth century—was upon the realists rather than upon the romanticists. The same men that had a cult for Diderot admired the Vautrins and

---

[4] E.g., Lillo's *Fatal Curiosity* (1736) had a marked influence on the rise of the German fate tragedy.

[5]   *Wo ist der, der sagen dürfe,*
          So will ich's, so sei's gemacht,
          Unser Taten sind nur Würfe
          In des Zufalls blinde Nacht.
                              Die Ahnfrau.

the Rastignacs of Balzac and the Julien Sorel of Stendhal. These characters are little Napoleons. They live temperamentally in the midst of a highly organized society, but they set aside its conventions of right and wrong in favor, not of aesthetic enjoyment, but of power.

The ideal of romantic morality, as was seen in the last chapter, is altruism. The real, it should be clear from the examples I have been citing, is always egoism. But egoism may assume very different forms. As to the main forms of egoism in men who have repudiated outer control without acquiring self-control we may perhaps revive profitably the old Christian classification of the three lusts—the lust of knowledge, the lust of sensation, and the lust of power. Goethe indeed may be said to have treated these three main ways of being temperamental in three of his early characters—the lust of knowledge in "Faust," the lust of sensation in "Werther," and the lust of power in "Götz." If we view life solely from the naturalistic level and concern ourselves solely with the world of action, we are justified in neglecting, like Hobbes, the other lusts and putting supreme emphasis on the lust for power. Professor F. J. Mather, Jr., has distinguished between "hard" and "soft" sentimentalists.[6] His distinction might perhaps be brought more closely into line with my own distinctions if I ventured to coin a word and to speak of hard and soft temperamentalists. The soft temperamentalist will prove unable to cope in the actual world with the hard temperamentalist, and is very likely to become his tool. Balzac has very appropriately made Lucien de Rubempré, the romantic poet and a perfect type of a soft temperamentalism, the tool of Vautrin, the superman.

Here indeed is the supreme opposition between the ideal and the real in romantic morality. The ideal to which Rousseau invites us is either the primitivistic anarchy of the "Second Discourse," in which egoism is tempered by "natural pity," or else a state such as is depicted in the "Social Contract," in which egoism is held in check by a disinterested "general will." The preliminary to achieving either of these ideals is that the traditional checks on human nature should be removed. But in exact proportion as this pro-

gramme of emancipation is carried out what emerges in the real world is not the mythical will to brotherhood, but the ego and its fundamental will to power. Give a bootblack half the universe, according to Carlyle, and he will soon be quarreling with the owner of the other half. He will if he is a very temperamental bootblack. Perhaps indeed all other evils in life may be reduced to the failure to check that something in man that is reaching out for more and ever for more. In a society in which the traditional inhibitions are constantly growing weaker, the conflict I have just sketched between the ideal and the real is becoming more and more acute. The soft temperamentalists are overflowing with beautiful professions of brotherly love, and at the same time the hard temperamentalists are reaching out for everything in sight; and inasmuch as the hard temperamentalists operate not in dreamland, but in the real world, they are only too plainly setting the tone. Very often, of course, the same temperamentalist has his hard and his soft side. The triumph of egoism over altruism in the relations between man and man is even more evident in the relations between nation and nation. The egoism that results from the inbreeding of temperament on a national scale runs in the case of the strong nations into imperialism. We have not reflected sufficiently on the fact that the soft temperamentalist Rousseau is more than any other one person the father of *Kultur;* and that the exponents of Kultur in our own day have been revealed as the hardest of hard temperamentalists.

To understand the particular craving that is met by Rousseauistic idealism one would need to go with some care into the psychology of the half-educated man. The half-educated man may be defined as the man who has acquired a degree of critical self-consciousness sufficient to detach him from the standards of his time and place, but not sufficient to acquire the new standards that come with a more thorough cultivation. It was pointed out long ago that the characteristic of the half-educated man is that he is incurably restless; that he is filled with every manner of desire. In contrast with him the uncultivated man, the peasant, let us say, and the man of high cultivation have few and simple desires. Thus Socrates had fewer and simpler desires than the average Athenian. But what is

[6] See *Unpopular Review,* October, 1915.

most noteworthy about the half-educated man is not simply that he harbors many desires and is therefore incurably restless, but that these desires are so often incompatible. He craves various good things, but is not willing to pay the price— not willing to make the necessary renunciations. He pushes to an extreme what is after all a universal human proclivity—the wish to have one's cake and eat it too. Thus, while remaining on the naturalistic level, he wishes to have blessings that accrue only to those who rise to the humanistic or religious levels. He wishes to live in "a universe with the lid off," to borrow a happy phrase from the pragmatist, and at the same time to enjoy the peace and brotherhood that are the fruits of restraint. The moral indolence of the Rousseauist is such that he is unwilling to adjust himself to the truth of the human law; and though living naturalistically, he is loath to recognize that what actually prevails on the naturalistic level is the law of cunning and the law of force. He thus misses the reality of both the human and the natural law and in the pursuit of a vague Arcadian longing falls into sheer unreality. I am indeed overstating the case so far as Rousseau is concerned. He makes plain in the "Emile" that the true law of nature is not the law of love but the law of force. Emile is to be released from the discipline of the human law and given over to the discipline of nature; and this means in practice that he will have "to bow his neck beneath the hard yoke of physical necessity." In so far the "nature" of Emile is no Arcadian dream. Where the Arcadian dreaming begins is when Rousseau assumes that an Emile who has learned the lesson of force from Nature herself, will not pass along this lesson to others, whether citizens of his own or some other country, but will rather display in his dealings with them an ideal fraternity. In the early stages of the naturalistic movement, in Hobbes and Shaftesbury, for example, egoism and altruism, the idea of power and the idea of sympathy, are more sharply contrasted than they are in Rousseau and the later romanticists. Shaftesbury assumes in human nature an altruistic impulse or will to brotherhood that will be able to cope successfully with the will to power that Hobbes declares to be fundamental. Many of the romanticists, as we have seen, combine the cult of power with the cult of brotherhood. Hercules,

as in Shelley's poem, is to bow down before Prometheus, the lover of mankind. The extreme example, however, is probably William Blake. He proclaims himself of the devil's party, he glorifies a free expansion of energy, he looks upon everything that restricts this expansion as synonymous with evil. At the same time he pushes his exaltation of sympathy to the verge of the grotesque.[7]

Such indeed is the jumble of incompatibles in Blake that he would rest an illimitable compassion on the psychology of the superman. For nothing is more certain than that the "Marriage of Heaven and Hell" is among other things a fairly complete anticipation of Nietzsche. The reasons are worth considering why the idea of power and the idea of sympathy which Blake and so many other romanticists hoped to unite have once more come to seem antipodal, why in the late stages of the movement one finds a Nietzsche and a Tolstoy, just as in its early stages one finds a Hobbes and a Shaftesbury. It is plain, first of all, that what brought the two cults together for a time was their common hatred of the past. With the triumph over the past fairly complete, the incompatibility of power and sympathy became increasingly manifest. Nietzsche's attitude is that of a Prometheus whose sympathy for mankind has changed to disgust on seeing the use that they are actually making of their emancipation. Humanitarian sympathy seemed to him to be tending not merely to a subversion, but to an inversion of values, to a positive preference for the trivial and the ignoble. He looked with special loathing on that side of the movement that is symbolized in its homage to the ass. The inevitable flying apart of power and sympathy was further hastened in Nietzsche and others by the progress of evolution. Darwinism was dissipating the Arcadian mist through which nature had been

---

7   A robin redbreast in a cage
     Puts all Heaven in a rage.

     .   .   .

     He who shall hurt the little wren
     Shall never be belov'd by men.
     He who the ox to wrath has mov'd
     Shall never be by woman lov'd.

     .   .   .

     Kill not the moth nor butterfly,
     For the Last Judgment draweth nigh.
     Auguries of Innocence.

viewed by Rousseau and his early followers. The gap is wide between Tennyson's nature "red in tooth and claw" and the tender and pitiful nature of Wordsworth.[8] Nietzsche's preaching of ruthlessness is therefore a protest against the sheer unreality of those who wish to be natural and at the same time sympathetic. But how are we to get a real scale of values to oppose to an indiscriminate sympathy? It is here that Nietzsche shows that he is caught in the same fatal coil of naturalism as the humanitarian. He accepts the naturalistic corruption of conscience which underlies all other naturalistic corruptions. "The will to overcome an emotion," he says, "is ultimately only the will of another or of several other emotions."[9] All he can do with this conception of conscience is to set over against the humanitarian suppression of values a scale of values based on force and not a true scale of values based on the degree to which one imposes or fails to impose on one's temperamental self a human law of vital control. The opposition between a Nietzsche and a Tolstoy is therefore not specially significant; it is only that between the hard and the soft temperamentalist. To be sure Nietzsche can on occasion speak very shrewdly about the evils that have resulted from temperamentalism—especially from the passion for an untrammeled self-expression. But the superman himself is a most authentic descendant of the original genius in whom we first saw this passion dominant. The imagination of the superman, spurning every centre of control, traditional or otherwise, so coöperates with his impulses and desires as to give them "infinitude," that is so as to make them reach out for more and ever for more. The result is a frenzied romanticism.

"Proportionateness is strange to us, let us confess it to ourselves," says Nietzsche. "Our itching is really the itching for the infinite, the immeasurable." How the humanitarian loses proportionateness is plain; it is by his readiness to sacrifice to sympathy the ninety per cent or so of the virtues that imply self-control. The superman would scarcely seem to redress the balance by getting rid of the same restraining virtues in favor of power. He simply oscillates

wildly from the excess of which he is conscious in others or in himself into the opposite excess, at imminent peril in either case to the ethical basis of civilization. The patterns or models that the past had set up for imitation and with reference to which one might rein in his lusts and impose upon them proportionateness are rejected by every type of romantic expansionist, not only as Nietzsche says, because they do not satisfy the yearning for the infinite, but also, as we have seen, because they do not satisfy the yearning for unity and immediacy. Now so far as the forms of the eighteenth century were concerned the romantic expansionist had legitimate grounds for protest. But because the rationalism and artificial decorum of that period failed to satisfy, he goes on to attack the analytical intellect and decorum in general and this attack is entirely illegitimate. It may be affirmed on the contrary that the power by which we multiply distinctions is never so necessary as in an individualistic age, an age that has broken with tradition on the ground that it wishes to be more imaginative and immediate. There are various ways of being imaginative and immediate, and analysis is needed, not to build up some abstract system but to discriminate between the actual data of experience and so to determine which one of these ways it is expedient to follow if one wishes to become wise and happy. It is precisely at such moments of individualistic break with the past that the sophist stands ready to juggle with general terms, and the only protection against such juggling is to define these terms with the aid of the most unflinching analysis. Thus Bergson would have us believe that there are in France two main types of philosophy, a rationalistic type that goes back to Descartes and an intuitive type that goes back to Pascal, and gives us to understand that, inasmuch as he is an intuitionist, he is in the line of descent from Pascal. Monstrous sophistries lurk in this simple assertion, sophistries which if they go uncorrected are enough to wreck civilization. The only remedy is to define the word intuition, to discriminate practically and by their fruits between subrational and superrational intuition. When analyzed and defined in this way subrational intuition will be found to be associated with vital impulse (*élan vital*) and superrational intuition with a power of vital control (*frein*

[8] See *Hart-Leap Well*.
[9] *Beyond Good and Evil*, Ch. IV.

vital) over this impulse; and furthermore it will be clear that this control must be exercised if men are to be drawn towards a common centre, not in dreamland, but in the real world. So far then from its being true that the man who analyzes must needs see things in disconnection dead and spiritless, it is only by analysis that he is, in an individualistic age, put on the pathway of true unity, and also of the rôle of the imagination in achieving this unity. For there is need to discriminate between the different types of imagination no less than between the different types of intuition. One will find through such analysis that the centre of normal human experience that is to serve as a check on impulse (so far at least as it is something distinct from the mere convention of one's age and time) can be apprehended only with the aid of the imagination. This is only another way of saying that the reality that is set above one's ordinary self is not a fixed absolute but can be glimpsed, if at all, only through a veil of illusion and is indeed inseparable from the illusion. This realm of insight cannot be finally formulated for the simple reason that it is anterior to formulae. It must therefore from the point of view of an intellect it transcends seem infinite though in a very different sense from the outer infinite of expansive desire.

This inner or human infinite, so far from being incompatible with decorum, is the source of true decorum. True decorum is only the pulling back and disciplining of impulse to the proportionateness that has been perceived with the aid of what one may term the ethical or generalizing imagination. To dismiss like the romantic expansionist everything that limits or restricts the lust of knowledge or of power or of sensation as arbitrary and artificial is to miss true decorum and at the same time to sink, as a Greek would say, from ethos to pathos. If one is to avoid this error one must, as Hamlet counsels, "in the very torrent, tempest, and (as I may say) whirlwind of passion, acquire and beget a temperance that may give it smoothness." This is probably the best of all modern definitions of decorum simply because it is the most experimental. In general all that has been said about the ethical imagination is not to be taken as a fine-spun theory, but as an attempt however imperfect to give an account of actual experience.

One may report from observation another trait of truly ethical art, art which is at once imaginative and decorous. It is not merely intense, as art that is imaginative at the expense of decorum may very well be, it has a restrained and humanized intensity—intensity on a background of calm. The presence of the ethical imagination whether in art or life is always known as an element of calm.

In art that has the ethical quality, and I am again not setting up a metaphysical theory but reporting from observation, the calm that comes from imaginative insight into the universal is inextricably blended with an element of uniqueness—with a something that belongs to a particular time and place and individual. The truth to the universal, as Aristotle would say, gives the work verisimilitude and the truth to the particular satisfies man's deep-seated craving for novelty; so that the best art unites the probable with the wonderful. But the probable, one cannot insist too often, is won no less than the wonderful with the aid of the imagination and so is of the very soul of art. The romanticist who is ready to sacrifice the probable to the wonderful and to look on the whole demand for verisimilitude as an academic superstition is prone to assume that he has a monopoly of soul and imagination. But the word soul is at least in as much need of Socratic definition as the word intuition. It is possible, for example, with the aid of the ethical imagination so to partake of the ultimate element of calm as to rise to the religious level. The man who has risen to this level has a soul, but it is a soul of peace. Both soul and imagination are also needed to achieve the fine adjustment and mediation of the humanist. It is not enough, however, to have a religious or a humanistic soul if one is to be a creator or even a fully equipped critic of art. For art rests primarily not on ethical but aesthetic perception. This perception itself varies widely according to the art involved. One may, for instance, be musically perceptive and at the same time lack poetic perception. To be a creator in any art one must possess furthermore the technique of this art—something that is more or less separable from its "soul" in any sense of the word. It is possible to put a wildly romantic soul into art, as has often been done in the Far East, and at the same time to be highly conventional or traditional in one's technique. Writers like Mérimée, Renan, and Maupassant again are faithful in the main to the technique of French prose that was worked out during the classical period, but combine with this technique an utterly unclassical "soul."

Rules, especially perhaps rules as to what to avoid, may be of aid in acquiring technique, but are out of place in dealing with the soul of art. There one passes from rules to principles. The only rule, if we are to achieve art that has an ethical soul, is to view life with some degree of imaginative wholeness. Art that has technique without soul in either the classical or romantic sense, and so fails either to inspire elevation or awaken wonder, is likely to be felt as a barren virtuosity. The pseudo-classicist was often unduly minute in the rules he laid down for technique or outer form, as one may say, and then ignored the ethical imagination or inner form entirely, or else set up as a substitute mere didacticism. Since pseudo-classic work of this type plainly lacked soul and imagination, and since the romanticist felt and felt rightly that he himself had a soul and imagination, he concluded wrongly that soul and imagination are romantic monopolies. Like the pseudo-classicist, he inclines to identify high seriousness in art, something that can only come from the exercise of the ethical imagination at its best, with mere preaching, only he differs from the pseudo-classicist in insisting that preaching should be left to divines. One should insist, on the contrary, that the mark of genuinely ethical art, art that is highly serious, is that it is free from preaching. Sophocles is more ethical than Euripides for the simple reason that he views life with more imaginative wholeness. At the same time he is much less given to preaching than Euripides. He does not, as FitzGerald says, interrupt the action and the exhibition of character through action in order to "jaw philosophy."

It is not unusual for the modern artist to seek, like Euripides, to dissimulate the lack of true ethical purpose in his work by agitating various problems. But problems come and go, whereas human nature abides. One may agitate problems without number, and yet lack imaginative insight into the abiding element in human nature. Moreover, not being of the soul of art, the problem that one agitates is in danger of being a clogging intellectualism. Furthermore to seek in problems an equivalent for the definition and purpose that the ethical imagination alone can give is to renew, often in an aggravated form, the neo-classical error. The moralizing of the pseudo-classic dramatist, even though dull and misplaced, was usually sound enough in itself; whereas the moralizing of those who seek nowadays to use the stage as a pulpit, resting as it does on false humanitarian postulates, is in itself dubious. The problem play succeeds not infrequently in being at once dull and indecent.

The problem play is often very superior in technique or outer form to the earlier romantic drama, but it still suffers from the same lack of inner form, inasmuch as its social purpose cannot take the place of true human purpose based on imaginative insight into the universal. The lack of inner form in so much modern drama and art in general can be traced to the original unsoundness of the break with pseudo-classic formalism. To a pseudo-classic art that lacked every kind of perceptiveness the Rousseauist opposed aesthetic perceptiveness, and it is something, one must admit, thus to have discovered the senses. But to his aesthetic perceptiveness he failed, as I have already said, to add ethical perceptiveness because of his inability to distinguish between ethical perceptiveness and mere didacticism, and so when asked to put ethical purpose into art he replied that art should be pursued for its own sake (*l'art pour l'art*) and that "beauty is its own excuse for being." One should note here the transformation that this pure aestheticism brought about in the meaning of the word beauty itself. For the Greek beauty resided in proportion,[10] and proportion can be attained only with the aid of the ethical imagination. With the elimination of the ethical element from the soul of art the result is an imagination that is free to wander wild with the emancipated emotions. The result is likely to be art in which a lively aesthetic perceptiveness is not subordinated to any whole, art that is unstructural, however it may abound in vivid and picturesque details; and a one-sided art of this kind the romanticist does not hesitate to call beautiful. "If we let the reason sleep and are

---

[10] "Beauty resides in due proportion and order," says Aristotle (*Poetics*, Ch. VII).

content to watch a succession of dissolving views," says Mr. Elton of Shelley's "Revolt of Islam," "the poem is seen at once to overflow with beauty." [11] Mere reason is not strictly speaking a sufficient remedy for this unstructural type of "beauty." Thus Chateaubriand's reason is on the side of proportion and all the classical virtues but his imagination is not (and we cannot repeat too often that it is what a man is imaginatively and not what he preaches that really counts). Instead of siding with his reason and aiding it to ethical perception Chateaubriand's imagination is the free playmate of his emotions. "What did I care for all these futilities" (i.e. his functions as cabinet minister), he exclaims, "I who never cared for anything except for my dreams, and even then on condition that they should last only for a night." When a man has once spoken in that vein sensible people will pay little heed to what he preaches; for they will be certain that the driving power of his work and personality is elsewhere. The imagination holds the balance of power between the reason and the perceptions of sense, and Chateaubriand's imagination is plainly on the side of sensuous adventure. This vagabondage of the imagination appears especially in his imagistic trend, in his pursuit of the descriptive detail for its own sake. To set out like Chateaubriand to restore the monarchy and the Christian religion and instead to become the founder of "*l'école des images à tout prix*" is an especially striking form of the contrast in romantic morality between the ideal and the real.

The attempt that we have been studying to divorce beauty from ethics led in the latter part of the eighteenth century to the rise of a nightmare subject,—aesthetics. Shaftesbury indeed, as we have seen already, anticipates the favorite romantic doctrine that beauty is truth and truth beauty, which means in practice to rest both truth and beauty upon a fluid emotionalism. Thus to deal aesthetically with truth is an error of the first magnitude, but it is also an error, though a less serious one, to see only the aesthetic element in beauty. For beauty to be complete must have not only aesthetic perceptiveness but order and proportion; and this brings us back again

to the problem of the ethical imagination and the permanent model or pattern with reference to which it seeks to impose measure and proportion upon sensuous perception and expansive desire. We should not hesitate to say that beauty loses most of its meaning when divorced from ethics even though every aesthete in the world should arise and denounce us as philistines. To rest beauty upon feeling as the very name aesthetics implies, is to rest it upon what is ever shifting. Nor can we escape from this endless mobility with the aid of physical science, for physical science does not itself rise above the naturalistic flux. After eliminating from beauty the permanent pattern and the ethical imagination with the aid of which it is perceived, a man will be ready to term beautiful anything that reflects his ordinary or temperamental self. Diderot is a sentimentalist and so he sees as much beauty in the sentimentalist Richardson as in Homer. If a man is psychically restless he will see beauty only in motion. The Italian futurist Marinetti says that for him a rushing motor car is more beautiful than the Victory of Samothrace. A complete sacrifice of the principle of repose in beauty (which itself arises from the presence of the ethical imagination) to the suggesting of motion such as has been seen in certain recent schools, runs practically into a mixture of charlatanism and madness. "He that is giddy thinks the world goes round," says Shakespeare, and the exponents of certain ultra-modern movements in painting are simply trying to paint their inner giddiness. As a matter of fact the pretension of the aesthete to have a purely personal vision of beauty and then treat as a philistine every one who does not accept it, is intolerable. Either beauty cannot be defined at all or we must say that only is beautiful which seems so to the right kind of man, and the right kind of man is plainly he whose total attitude towards life is correct, who views life with some degree of imaginative wholeness, which is only another way of saying that the problem of beauty is inseparable from the ethical problem. In an absolute sense nobody can see life steadily and see it whole; but we may at least move towards steadiness and wholeness. The aesthete is plainly moving in an opposite direction; he is becoming more and more openly a votary of the god Whirl. His lack of

[11] *A Survey of English Literature, 1780-1830* (1912), II, 191.

inner form is an error not of aesthetics but of general philosophy.

The romantic imagination, the imagination that is not drawn back to any ethical centre and so is free to wander wild in its own empire of chimeras, has indeed a place in life. To understand what this place is one needs to emphasize the distinction between art that has high seriousness and art that is merely recreative. The serious moments of life are moments of tension, of concentration on either the natural or the human law. But Apollo cannot always be bending the bow. Man needs at times to relax, and one way of relaxing is to take refuge for a time in some land of chimeras, to follow the Arcadian gleam. He may then come back to the real world, the world of active effort, solaced and refreshed. But it is only with reference to some ethical centre that we may determine what art is soundly recreative, in what forms of adventure the imagination may innocently indulge. The romanticist should recollect that among other forms of adventure is what Ben Jonson terms "a bold adventure for hell"; and that a not uncommon nostalgia is what the French call *la nostalgie de la boue*—man's nostalgia for his native mud. Because we are justified at times, as Lamb urges, in wandering imaginatively beyond "the diocese of strict conscience," it does not follow that we may, like him, treat Restoration Comedy as a sort of fairyland; for Restoration Comedy is a world not of pure but of impure imagination.

Lamb's paradox, however, is harmless compared with what we have just been seeing in Chateaubriand. With a dalliant imagination that entitles him at best to play a recreative rôle, he sets up as a religious teacher. Michelet again has been described as an "entertainer who believes himself a prophet," and this description fits many other Rousseauists. The aesthete who assumes an apocalyptic pose is an especially flagrant instance of the huddling together of incompatible desires. He wishes to sport with Amaryllis in the shade and at the same time enjoy the honors that belong only to the man who scorns delights and lives laborious days. For the exercise of the ethical imagination, it is hardly necessary to say, involves effort. Perhaps no one has ever surpassed Rousseau himself in the art of which I have already spoken,—

that of giving to moral indolence a semblance of profound philosophy.

One cannot indeed always affirm that the Rousseauist is by the quality of his imagination an entertainer pure and simple. His breaking down of barriers and running together of the planes of being results at times in ambiguous mixtures—gleams of insight that actually seem to minister to fleshliness. One may cite as an example the "voluptuous religiosity" that certain critics have discovered in Wagner.

The romanticist will at once protest against the application of ethical standards to Wagner or any other musician. Music, he holds, is the most soulful of the arts and so the least subject to ethics. For the same reason it is the chief of arts and also—in view of the fact that romanticists have a monopoly of soul—the most romantic. One should not allow to pass unchallenged this notion that because music is filled with soul it is therefore subject to no ethical centre, but should be treated as a pure enchantment. The Greeks were as a matter of fact much concerned with the ethical quality of music. Certain musical modes, the Doric for example, had as they believed a virile "soul," other modes like the Lydian had the contrary ("Lap me in soft Lydian airs"). For the very reason that music is the most appealing of the arts (song, says Aristotle, is the sweetest of all things) they were especially anxious that this art should be guarded from perversion.[12] Without attempting a full discussion of a difficult subject for which I have no competency, it will be enough to point out that the plain song that prevailed in Christian churches for over a thousand years evidently had a very different "soul," a soul that inspired to prayer and peace, from much specifically romantic music that has a soul of restlessness, of infinite indeterminate desire. The result of the failure to recognize this distinction is very often a hybrid art. Berlioz showed a rather peculiar conception of religion when he took pride in the fact that his Requiem (!) Mass frightened one of the listeners into a fit.

The ethical confusion that arises from the romantic cult of "soul" and the closely allied tendency towards a hybrid art—art that lacks

---

[12] Confucius and the Chinese sages were if anything even more concerned than Plato or Aristotle with the ethical quality of music.

high seriousness without being frankly recreative —may also be illustrated from the field of poetry. Many volumes have been published and are still being published on Browning as a philosophic and religious teacher. But Browning can pass as a prophet only with the half-educated person, the person who has lost traditional standards and has at the same time failed to work out with the aid of the ethical imagination some fresh scale of values and in the meanwhile lives impulsively and glorifies impulse. Like the half-educated person, Browning is capable of almost any amount of intellectual and emotional subtlety, and like the half-educated person he is deficient in inner form: that is he deals with experience impressionistically without reference to any central pattern or purpose.[13] It is enough that the separate moments of this experience should each stand forth like

> The quick sharp scratch
> And blue spurt of a lighted match.

One may take as an illustration of this drift towards the melodramatic the "Ring and the Book." The method of this poem is peripheral, that is, the action is viewed not from any centre but as refracted through the temperaments of the actors. The twelve monologues of which the poem is composed illustrate the tendency of romantic writing to run into some "song of myself" or "tale of my heart." The "Ring and the Book" is not only off the centre, but is designed to raise a positive prejudice against everything that is central. Guido, for example, had observed decorum, had done all the conventional things and is horrible. Pompilia, the beautiful soul, had the great advantage of having had an indecorous start. Being the daughter of a drab, she is not kept from heeding the voice of nature. Caponsacchi again shows the beauty of his soul by violating the decorum of the priesthood. This least representative of priests wins our sympathy, not by his Christianity, but by his lyrical intensity:

> O lyric love, half angel and half bird,
> And all a wonder and a wild desire!

Browning here escapes for once from the clogging intellectualism that makes nearly all the

"Ring and the Book" an indeterminate blend of verse and prose, and achieves true poetry though not of the highest type. The hybrid character of his art, due partly to a lack of outer form, to a defective poetical technique, arises even more from a lack of inner form—from an attempt to give a semblance of seriousness to what is at bottom unethical. The aged Pope may well meditate on the revolution that is implied in the substitution of the morality of the beautiful soul for that of St. Augustine. In seeming to accept this revolution Browning's Pope comes near to breaking all records, even in the romantic movement, for paradox and indecorum.

At bottom the war between humanist and romanticist is so irreconcilable because the one is a mediator and the other an extremist. Browning would have us admire his Pompilia because her love knows no limit; but a secular love like hers must know a limit, must be decorous in short, if it is to be distinguished from mere emotional intensity. It is evident that the romantic ideal of art for art's sake meant in the real world art for sensation's sake. The glorification of a love knowing no limit, that a Browning or a Hugo sets up as a substitute for philosophy and even for religion, is therefore closely affiliated in practice with the *libido sentiendi*. "It is hard," wrote Stendhal, in 1817, "not to see what the nineteenth century desires. A love of strong emotions is its true character." The romantic tendency to push every emotion to an extreme, regardless of decorum, is not much affected by what the romanticist preaches or by the problems he agitates. Doudan remarks of a mother who loses her child in Hugo's "Notre Dame de Paris," that "her rage after this loss has nothing to equal it in the roarings of a lioness or tigress who has been robbed of her young. She becomes vulgar by excess of despair. It is the saturnalia of maternal grief. You see that this woman belongs to a world in which neither the instincts nor the passions have that divine aroma which imposes on them some kind of measure—the dignity or decorum that contains a moral principle; . . . When the passions no longer have this check, they should be relegated to the menagerie along with leopards and rhinoceroses, and, strange circumstance, when the passions do recognize this check they produce more effect on the spectators than unregulated outbursts;

---

[13] Like Bishop Blougram's his "interest's on the dangerous edge of things."

they give evidence of more depth." This superlativeness, as one may say, that Hugo displays in his picture of maternal grief is not confined to the emotional romanticist. It appears, for example, among the intellectual romanticists of the seventeenth century and affected the very forms of language. Molière and others ridiculed the adjectives and adverbs with which the *précieuses* sought to express their special type of superlativeness and intensity (*extrêmement, furieusement, terriblement,* etc.). Alfred de Musset's assertion that the chief difference between classicist and romanticist is found in the latter's greater proneness to adjectives is not altogether a jest. It has been said that the pessimist uses few, the optimist many adjectives; but the use of adjectives and above all of superlatives would rather seem to grow with one's expansiveness, and no movement was ever more expansive than that we are studying. Dante, according to Rivarol, is very sparing of adjectives. His sentence tends to maintain itself by the verb and substantive alone. In this as in other respects Dante is at the opposite pole from the expansionist.

The romantic violence of expression is at once a proof of "soul" and a protest against the tameness and smugness of the pseudo-classicist. The human volcano must overflow at times in a lava of molten words. "Damnation!" cries Berlioz, "I could crush a red-hot iron between my teeth." [14] The disproportion between the outer incident and the emotion that the Rousseauist expends on it is often ludicrous. The kind of force that the man attains who sees in emotional intensity a mark of spiritual distinction, and deems moderation identical with mediocrity, is likely to be the force of delirium or fever. What one sees in "Werther," says Goethe himself, is weakness seeking to give itself the prestige of strength; and this remark goes far. There is in some of the romanticists a suggestion not merely of spiritual but of physical anaemia. Still the intensity is often that of a strong but unbridled spirit. Pleasure is pushed to the point where it runs over into pain, and pain to the point where it becomes an auxiliary of pleasure. The *âcre baiser* of the "Nouvelle Héloïse" that so scandalized Voltaire presaged even more than

a literary revolution. The poems of A. de Musset in particular contain an extraordinary perversion of the Christian doctrine of purification through suffering. There is something repellent to the genuine Christian as well as to the worldling in what one is tempted to call Musset's Epicurean cult of pain.

Moments of superlative intensity whether of pleasure or pain must in the nature of the case be brief—mere spasms or paroxysms; and one might apply to the whole school the term paroxyst and spasmodist assumed by certain minor groups during the past century. The Rousseauist is in general loath to rein in his emotional vehemence, to impair the zest with which he responds to the solicitations of sense, by any reference to the "future and sum of time," by any reference, that is, to an ethical purpose. He would enjoy his thrill pure and unalloyed, and this amounts in practice to the pursuit of the beautiful or sensation-crowded moment. Saint-Preux says of the days spent with Julie that a "sweet ecstasy" absorbed "their whole duration and gathered it together in a point like that of eternity. There was for me neither past nor future, and I enjoyed at one and the same time the delights of a thousand centuries." [15] The superlativist one might suppose could go no further. But in the deliberate sacrifice of all ethical values to the beautiful moment Browning has perhaps improved even on Rousseau:

> Truth, that's brighter than gem,
>   Trust, that's purer than pearl,—
> Brightest truth, purest trust in the universe—all
>   were for me
> In the kiss of one girl.

Browning entitles the poem from which I am quoting *Summum Bonum.* The supreme good it would appear is identical with the supreme thrill.

I have already said enough to make clear that the title of this chapter and the last is in a way a misnomer. There is no such thing as romantic morality. The innovations in ethics that are due to romanticism reduce themselves on close scrutiny to a vast system of naturalistic camouflage. To understand how this camouflage has been so successful one needs to connect Rousseauism with the Baconian movement. Sci-

[14] Letter to Joseph d'Ortigue, January 19, 1833.

[15] *Nouvelle Héloïse,* Pt. III, Lettre VI.

entific progress had inspired man with a new confidence in himself at the same time that the positive and critical method by which it had been achieved detached him from the past and its traditional standards of good and evil. To break with tradition on sound lines one needs to apply the utmost keenness of analysis not merely to the natural but to the human law. But man's analytical powers were very much taken up with the new task of mastering the natural law, so much so that he seemed incapable of further analytical effort, but longed rather for relaxation from his sustained concentration of intellect and imagination on the physical order. At the same time he was so elated by the progress he was making in this order that he was inclined to assume a similar advance on the moral plane and to believe that this advance could also be achieved collectively. A collective salvation of this kind without any need of a concentration of the intellect and imagination is precisely what was opened up to him by the Rousseauistic "ideal" of brotherhood. This "ideal," as I have tried to show, was only a projection of the Arcadian imagination on the void. But in the abdication of analysis and critical judgment, which would have reduced it to a purely recreative rôle, this Arcadian dreaming was enabled to set up as a serious philosophy, and to expand into innumerable Utopias. Many who might have taken alarm at the humanitarian revolution in ethics were reassured by the very fervor with which its promoters continued to utter the old words—conscience, virtue, etc. No one puts more stress than Rousseau himself on conscience, while in the very act of transforming conscience from an inner check into an expansive emotion.

We have seen that as a result of this transformation of conscience, temperament is emancipated from both inner and outer control and that this emancipation tends in the real world to the rise of two main types—the Bohemian and the superman, both unprimitive, inasmuch as primitive man is governed not by temperament but by convention; and that what actually tends to prevail in such a temperamental world in view of the superior "hardness" of the superman, is the law of cunning and the law of force. So far as the Rousseauists set up the mere emancipation of temperament as a serious philosophy, they are to be held responsible for the results of this emancipation whether displayed in the lust of power or the lust of sensation. But the lust of power and the lust of sensation, such as they appear, for example, in the so-called realism of the later nineteenth century, are not in themselves identical with romanticism. Many of the realists, like Flaubert, as I have already pointed out, are simply bitter and disillusioned Rousseauists who are expressing their nausea at the society that has actually arisen from the emancipation of temperament in themselves and others. The essence of Rousseauistic as of other romance, I may repeat, is to be found not in any mere fact, not even in the fact of sensation, but in a certain quality of the imagination. Rousseauism is, it is true, an emancipation of impulse, especially of the impulse of sex. Practically all the examples I have chosen of the tense and beautiful moment are erotic. But what one has even here, as the imagination grows increasingly romantic, is less the reality than the dream of the beautiful moment, an intensity that is achieved only in the tower of ivory. This point can be made clear only by a fuller study of the romantic conception of love.

THOMAS ERNEST HULME   (1883-1917)

ULME has extensively influenced modern criticism because he stated, in brief and vigorous fashion, a variety of views that were to prove congenial to the modern temper but had not yet been theoretically expressed (at least in this particular combination) and critically applied to art. His critical writing, in fact, is more in the nature of a brief manifesto or declaration of principles than it is an analysis or development of a position. Hence he is not, perhaps, read so frequently now as in the late 1920's and early 1930's, even by critics and readers who repeat the same views in terms originally popularized by Hulme.

To begin with, Hulme offered to English and American critics a general credo for modern abstract *formalism*. The reaction already beginning against nineteenth-century art—against romantic vagueness and the romantic exploiting of emotion for its own sake—was carried further by Hulme, and expressed in more drastic and thoroughgoing terms. In his provocative essay, "Modern Art," he divided art, rather abruptly, into two varieties, "geometrical" and "vital," each of which expresses a basic way of regarding life. Because it leads so directly to the premises of an important modern movement, Hulme's notes on this subject deserve a fuller discussion than does his superior essay, "Romanticism and Classicism." "Vital" art tries to disclose the living and organic process of nature, though Hulme would say that it does not "disclose" but rather that it invents the quality it prizes and then projects it upon nature. This sort of art, which tends toward a "naturalistic" or "realistic" rendering of its subject, arises when man feels that he has a satisfactory and indeed organic connection with the external world. It is found in classical antiquity, and it returns in the Renaissance as the dominant form of art. Romanticism is its last stage, and, at the close of the nineteenth century, it culminated in a loose and meaningless sentimentality—"in the state of slush in which we have the misfortune to live." On the other hand, "geometrical" or abstract art—such as we find in primitive, Egyptian,

THOMAS ERNEST HULME. After attending the University of Cambridge, Hulme traveled on the Continent, returned to London, and became known in literary and social circles as a brilliant and rigorous thinker. He translated Bergson's *Introduction to Metaphysics* (1912) and wrote a few poems, but his important work was left in notebook and manuscript form when he was killed in World War I (1917).

Hulme's critical writing is found in *Speculations: Essays on Humanism and the Philosophy of Art* (ed. Herbert Read, 1924) and *Notes on Language and Style* (ed. H. Read, Seattle, 1929). For commentary, see, besides Herbert Read's Introduction to *Speculations*, A. R. Jones, *The Life and Opinions of T. E. Hulme* (1960); Wyndham Lewis, *Men Without Art* (1934); and Michael Roberts, *T. E. Hulme* (1938).

Byzantine, and some kinds of Oriental art—arises when man feels his separateness from the external world and from other men. Here, with a feeling of "space-shyness," he *imposes* form—rigid, lifeless, abstract form—thus trying to order his experience in such a way as to control it. It is into such a state of mind that the twentieth century, Hulme believed, has been moving. And he buttressed his argument by connecting it with a religious outlook which stresses man's separateness, and in which the central dogma is that of "original sin."

Hulme's division of art into these two types may be accepted as a suggestive hypothesis. But it is hardly an argument, in the form that he left it, and it leaves unanswered some of the most central concerns of critical theory. The foremost is that involved in the classical belief that form of any sort is nothing except as it is objectively *real*—except as it is found working through nature itself—and that art is of value to the degree that it reveals this form, conveying or recasting it through its own medium. Hulme's implication that the form in "vital" art is a happy delusion and a subjective creation of one's own mind is, of course, a possible interpretation. But the "geometrical" art he opposed to it is openly admitted to be subjective. It is imposed directly on nature: indeed, its principal merit, as Hulme urged it, is that it is antinatural. Nor is the attitude of "space-shyness" that underlies it developed by Hulme: he simply assumed it is inevitable, and half advocated it on romantic grounds as being "of greater intensity." If both forms of art are subjective, the difference for Hulme seemed to be that abstract art openly admits it. Like that of Irving Babbitt, if only in this one respect, Hulme's central position was thus arrived at negatively, through reacting strongly against the nineteenth century. The difference is that, for Hulme, the classic and the romantic were both of a piece in contrast to the abstract art which he urged. For Babbitt, on the other hand, the abstract formalism of Hulme would simply be one side of the same coin of which romanticism comprises the other side. Both, that is, would show a concern with the medium of art at the expense of its subject; both would illustrate the disintegration of the classical tradition by retreating from actual life, the romantic showing a subjective withdrawal from reality into an art of sentimental stock responses, while abstractionism continues this withdrawal but protests against the sentimentality of the romantic and seeks to substitute instead a more ingenious and demanding method of arousing response.

A less extreme treatment of Hulme's theory of art is that offered in his influential "Romanticism and Classicism." Here he repeated his protest against the romantic without handicapping his argument by connecting what he disliked in it with the entire Western tradition. In fact, what he here theoretically opposed to romantic art is a conception of classicism broad enough to include not only classical antiquity, but also Shakespeare, most of the Elizabethans, and the neoclassic tradition of the seventeenth and earlier eighteenth centuries. Still, the tone of his discussion suggests an ideal that may more aptly be described as neoclassic—an ideal achieved by "fancy" rather than "imagination," and characterized by a "dryness" and "hardness" of style. Both directly, and also indirectly through T. S. Eliot, this conception of poetic style was taken over and adapted in the revival of "metaphysical" poetry in the 1920's and 1930's. But its more general influence was to encourage the search, by both critics and poets, for a sophisticated urbanity of style that had not been common in English poetry since the death of Pope.

Modern Art

(1) There are two kinds of art, geometrical and vital, absolutely distinct in kind from one another. These two arts are not modifications of one and the same art but pursue different aims and are created for the satisfaction of different necessities of the mind.

(2) Each of these arts springs from and corresponds to a certain general attitude towards the world. You get long periods of time in which only one of these arts with its corresponding mental attitudes prevails. The vital art of Greece and the Renaissance corresponded to a certain attitude of mind and the geometrical has always gone with a different general attitude, of greater intensity than this.

And (3)—this is really the point I am making for—that the re-emergence of geometrical art may be the precursor of the re-emergence of the corresponding attitude towards the world, and so, of the break up of the Renaissance humanistic attitude. The fact that this change comes first in art, before it comes in thought, is easily understandable for this reason. So thoroughly are we soaked in the spirit of the period we live in, so strong is its influence over us, that we can only escape from it in an unexpected way, as it were, a side direction like art.

I am emphasising then, the absolute character of the difference between these two arts, not only because it is important for the understanding of the new art itself, but because it enables me to maintain much wider theses.

Modern Art. Delivered as a lecture in 1914; first published in *Speculations: Essays on Humanism and the Philosophy of Art* (ed. Herbert Read, 1924), and reprinted by permission of Humanities Press, Inc. and Routledge and Kegan Paul Ltd.

That is the logical order in which I present my convictions. I did not naturally arrive at them in that order. I came to believe first of all, for reasons quite unconnected with art, that the Renaissance attitude was coming to an end, and was then confirmed in that by the emergence of this art. I commenced by a change in philosophy and illustrated this by a change in art rather than vice versa. A thesis like my last one is so sweeping that it sounds a little empty. It would be quite ludicrous for me to attempt to state such a position in the space of the half page I intend to devote to it, but perhaps I can make it sound more plausible by saying how I came personally to believe it. You will have to excuse my putting it in autobiographical shape, for, after all, the break-up of a general attitude if it ever occurs will be a collection of autobiographies. First of all comes the conviction that in spite of its apparent extraordinary variety, European philosophy since the Renaissance does form a unity. You can separate philosophy into two parts, the technical and scientific part, that which more properly would be called metaphysics, and another part in which the machinery elaborated in the first is used to express the philosopher's attitude towards the world, what may be called his conclusions. These emerge in the last chapter of the book. In the first chapters the philosopher may be compared to a man in armour; he intimidates you, as a kind of impersonal machine. In the last chapter you perceive him naked, as perfectly human. Every philosopher says the world is other than it seems to be; in the last chapter he tells you what he thinks it is. As he has taken the trouble to prove it, you may assume that he regards the final picture of the world he gives as satisfactory.

Now here is my point. In a certain sense, all philosophy since the Renaissance is satisfied with a certain conception of the relation of man to the world. Now what is this conception? You get the first hint of it in the beginnings of the Renaissance itself, in a person like Pico Della Mirandola,[1] for example. You get the hint of an idea there of something, which finally culminates in a doctrine which is the opposite of the doctrine of original sin: the belief that man as a part of nature was after all something satisfactory. The change which Copernicus is supposed to have brought about is the exact contrary of the fact. Before Copernicus, man was not the centre of the world; after Copernicus he was. You get a change from a certain profundity and intensity to that flat and insipid optimism which, passing through its first stage of decay in Rousseau, has finally culminated in the state of slush in which we have the misfortune to live. If you want a proof of the radical difference between these two attitudes, you have only to look at the books which are written now on Indian religion and philosophy. There is a sheer anaemic inability to understand the stark uncompromising bleakness of this religious attitude. . . .

Consider the difference between these two kinds, then, from this point of view.

Take first the art which is most natural to us. What tendency is behind this, what need is it designed to satisfy?

This art as contrasted with geometrical art can be broadly described as naturalism or realism—using these words in their widest sense and entirely excluding the mere imitation of nature. The source of the pleasure felt by the spectator before the products of art of this kind is a feeling of increased vitality, a process which German writers on aesthetics call empathy (Einfühlung).[2] This process is perhaps a little

too complicated for me to describe it shortly here, but putting the matter in general terms, we can say that any work of art we find beautiful is an objectification of our own pleasure in activity, and our own vitality. The worth of a line or form consists in the value of the life which it contains for us. Putting the matter more simply we may say that in this art there is always a feeling of liking for, and pleasure in, the forms and movements to be found in nature. It is obvious therefore that this art can only occur in a people whose relation to outside nature is such that it admits of this feeling of pleasure and its contemplation.

Turn now to geometrical life. It most obviously exhibits no delight in nature and no striving after vitality. Its forms are always what can be described as stiff and lifeless. The dead form of a pyramid and the suppression of life in a Byzantine mosaic show that behind these arts there must have been an impulse, the direct opposite of that which finds satisfaction in the naturalism of Greek and Renaissance art.

This is what Worringer[3] calls the *tendency to abstraction.*

What is the nature of this tendency? What is the condition of mind of the people whose art is governed by it?

It can be described most generally as a feeling of separation in the face of outside nature.

While a naturalistic art is the result of a happy pantheistic relation between man and the outside world, the tendency to abstraction, on the contrary, occurs in races whose attitude to the outside world is the exact contrary of this. This feeling of separation naturally takes different forms at different levels of culture.

Take first, the case of more primitive people. They live in a world whose lack of order and seeming arbitrariness must inspire them with a certain fear. One may perhaps get a better

[1] The Italian Neoplatonist (1463-1494).

[2] "In-feeling"—an imaginative and emotional identification with the object. The doctrine of *Einfühlung* was discussed by German writers on esthetics in the late nineteenth century and later expounded in detail by Theodor Lipps, *Ästhetik* (1903-06). The word "empathy" was coined as an English equivalent by E. B. Titchener (1909). It implies a more *subjective* act of mind than does the English romantic theory of the

sympathetic imagination that is found especially in the writings of Hazlitt—more of a projection of one's own feelings upon the object than a truthful *feeling with* the object, but is otherwise much the same. It is thus a characteristic example of the way in which English psychological criticism anticipates later developments in Continental writing. (See above, pp. 273-74.)

[3] Wilhelm Worringer, whose *Abstraktion und Einfühlung* (1908) has strongly if indirectly influenced modern formalistic criticism.

description of what must be their state of mind by comparing it to the fear which makes certain people unable to cross open spaces. The fear I mean here is mental, however, not physical. They are dominated by what Worringer calls a kind of spiritual "space-shyness" in face of the varied confusion and arbitrariness of existence. In art this state of mind results in a desire to ·create a certain abstract geometrical shape, which, being durable and permanent shall be a refuge from the flux and impermanence of outside nature. The need which art satisfies here, is not the delight in the forms of nature, which is a characteristic of all vital arts, but the exact contrary. In the reproduction of natural objects there is an attempt to purify them of their characteristically living qualities in order to make them necessary and immovable. The changing is translated into something fixed and necessary. This leads to rigid lines and dead crystalline forms, for pure geometrical regularity gives a certain pleasure to men troubled by the obscurity of outside appearance. The geometrical line is something absolutely distinct from the messiness, the confusion, and the accidental details of existing things.

It must be pointed out that this condition of fear is in no sense a necessary presupposition of the tendency to abstraction. The necessary presupposition is the idea of disharmony or separation between man and nature. In peoples like the Indian or the Byzantine this feeling of separation takes quite another form.

To sum up this view of art then: it cannot be understood by itself, but must be taken as one element in a general process of adjustment between man and the outside world. The character of that relation determines the character of the art. If there is a difference of "potential" between man and the outside world, if they are at different levels, so that the relation between them is, as it were, a steep inclined plane, then the adjustment between them in art takes the form of a tendency to abstraction. If on the contrary there is no disharmony between man and the outside world, if they are both on the same level, on which man feels himself one with nature and not separate from it, then you get a naturalistic art.

Romanticism and Classicism

I WANT to maintain that after a hundred years of romanticism, we are in for a classical revival, and that the particular weapon of this new classical spirit, when it works in verse, will be fancy. And in this I imply the superiority of fancy—not superior generally or absolutely, for that would be obvious nonsense, but superior in the sense that we use the word good in empirical ethics—good for something, superior for something. I shall have to prove then two things, first that a classical revival is coming, and, secondly, for its particular purposes, fancy will be superior to imagination.

So banal have the terms Imagination and Fancy become that we imagine they must have always been in the language. Their history as two differing terms in the vocabulary of criticism is comparatively short. Originally, of course, they both mean the same thing; they first began to be differentiated by the German writers on aesthetics in the eighteenth century.[1]

I know that in using the words "classic" and "romantic" I am doing a dangerous thing. They represent five or six different kinds of antithesis, and while I may be using them in one sense you may be interpreting them in another. In this present connection I am using them in a perfectly precise and limited sense. I ought really to have coined a couple of new words, but I prefer to use the ones I have used, as I then conform to the practice of the group of polemical writers who make most use of them

Romanticism and Classicism. Posthumously published in *Speculations: Essays on Humanism and the Philosophy of Art* (ed. Herbert Read, 1924); reprinted by permission of Humanities Press, Inc. and Routledge and Kegan Paul Ltd.

[1] This was a popular superstition in English writing of the late nineteenth and early twentieth centuries, and was probably first given currency by Walter Pater. Actually this particular distinction is of English origin, and had become relatively common in England by the time of Coleridge. See above, p. 387, n. 2.

at the present day, and have almost succeeded in making them political catchwords. I mean Maurras, Lasserre and all the group connected with *L'Action Française*.

At the present time this is the particular group with which the distinction is most vital. Because it has become a party symbol. If you asked a man of a certain set whether he preferred the classics or the romantics, you could deduce from that what his politics were.

The best way of gliding into a proper definition of my terms would be to start with a set of people who are prepared to fight about it—for in them you will have no vagueness. (Other people take the infamous attitude of the person with catholic tastes who says he likes both.)

About a year ago, a man whose name I think was Fauchois gave a lecture at the Odéon on Racine, in the course of which he made some disparaging remarks about his dullness, lack of invention and the rest of it. This caused an immediate riot: fights took place all over the house; several people were arrested and imprisoned, and the rest of the series of lectures took place with hundreds of gendarmes and detectives scattered all over the place. These people interrupted because the classical ideal is a living thing to them and Racine is the great classic. That is what I call a real vital interest in literature. They regard romanticism as an awful disease from which France had just recovered.

The thing is complicated in their case by the fact that it was romanticism that made the revolution. They hate the revolution, so they hate romanticism.

I make no apology for dragging in politics here; romanticism both in England and France is associated with certain political views, and it is in taking a concrete example of the working out of a principle in action that you can get its best definition.

What was the positive principle behind all the other principles of '89? I am talking here of the revolution in as far as it was an idea; I leave out material causes—they only produce the forces. The barriers which could easily have resisted or guided these forces had been previously rotted away by ideas. This always seems to be the case in successful changes; the privileged class is beaten only when it has lost faith in itself, when it has itself been penetrated with the ideas which are working against it.

It was not the rights of man—that was a good solid practical war-cry. The thing which created enthusiasm, which made the revolution practically a new religion, was something more positive than that. People of all classes, people who stood to lose by it, were in a positive ferment about the idea of liberty. There must have been some idea which enabled them to think that something positive could come out of so essentially negative a thing. There was, and here I get my definition of romanticism. They had been taught by Rousseau that man was by nature good, that it was only bad laws and customs that had suppressed him. Remove all these and the infinite possibilities of man would have a chance. This is what made them think that something positive could come out of disorder, this is what created the religious enthusiasm. Here is the root of all romanticism: that man, the individual, is an infinite reservoir of possibilities; and if you can so rearrange society by the destruction of oppressive order then these possibilities will have a chance and you will get Progress.

One can define the classical quite clearly as the exact opposite to this. Man is an extraordinarily fixed and limited animal whose nature is absolutely constant. It is only by tradition and organisation that anything decent can be got out of him.

This view was a little shaken at the time of Darwin. You remember his particular hypothesis, that new species came into existence by the cumulative effect of small variations—this seems to admit the possibility of future progress. But at the present day the contrary hypothesis makes headway in the shape of De Vries's [2] mutation theory, that each new species comes into existence, not gradually by the accumulation of small steps, but suddenly in a jump, a kind of sport, and that once in existence it remains absolutely fixed. This enables me to keep the classical view with an appearance of scientific backing.

Put shortly, these are the two views, then. One, that man is intrinsically good, spoilt by circumstance; and the other that he is in-

[2] Hugo de Vries, a Dutch botanist and geneticist.

trinsically limited, but disciplined by order and tradition to something fairly decent. To the one party man's nature is like a well, to the other like a bucket. The view which regards man as a well, a reservoir full of possibilities, I call the romantic; the one which regards him as a very finite and fixed creature, I call the classical.

One may note here that the Church has always taken the classical view since the defeat of the Pelagian heresy and the adoption of the sane classical dogma of original sin.

It would be a mistake to identify the classical view with that of materialism. On the contrary it is absolutely identical with the normal religious attitude. I should put it in this way: That part of the fixed nature of man is the belief in the Deity. This should be as fixed and true for every man as belief in the existence of matter and in the objective world. It is parallel to appetite, the instinct of sex, and all the other fixed qualities. Now at certain times, by the use of either force or rhetoric, these instincts have been suppressed—in Florence under Savonarola, in Geneva under Calvin, and here under the Roundheads. The inevitable result of such a process is that the repressed instinct bursts out in some abnormal direction. So with religion. By the perverted rhetoric of Rationalism, your natural instincts are suppressed and you are converted into an agnostic. Just as in the case of the other instincts, Nature has her revenge. The instincts that find their right and proper outlet in religion must come out in some other way. You don't believe in a God, so you begin to believe that man is a god. You don't believe in Heaven, so you begin to believe in a heaven on earth. In other words, you get romanticism. The concepts that are right and proper in their own sphere are spread over, and so mess up, falsify and blur the clear outlines of human experience. It is like pouring a pot of treacle over the dinner table. Romanticism then, and this is the best definition I can give of it, is spilt religion.

I must now shirk the difficulty of saying exactly what I mean by romantic and classical in verse. I can only say that it means the result of these two attitudes towards the cosmos, towards man, in so far as it gets reflected in verse. The romantic, because he thinks man infinite, must always be talking about the infinite; and as there is always the bitter contrast between what you think you ought to be able to do and what man actually can, it always tends, in its later stages at any rate, to be gloomy. I really can't go any further than to say it is the reflection of these two temperaments, and point out examples of the different spirits. On the one hand I would take such diverse people as Horace, most of the Elizabethans and the writers of the Augustan age, and on the other side Lamartine, Hugo, parts of Keats, Coleridge, Byron, Shelley and Swinburne.

I know quite well that when people think of classical and romantic in verse, the contrast at once comes into their mind between, say, Racine and Shakespeare. I don't mean this; the dividing line that I intend is here misplaced a little from the true middle. That Racine is on the extreme classical side I agree, but if you call Shakespeare romantic, you are using a different definition to the one I give. You are thinking of the difference between classic and romantic as being merely one between restraint and exuberance. I should say with Nietzsche that there are two kinds of classicism, the static and the dynamic. Shakespeare is the classic of motion.

What I mean by classical in verse, then, is this. That even in the most imaginative flights there is always a holding back, a reservation. The classical poet never forgets this finiteness, this limit of man. He remembers always that he is mixed up with earth. He may jump, but he always returns back; he never flies away into the circumambient gas.

You might say if you wished that the whole of the romantic attitude seems to crystallise in verse round metaphors of flight. Hugo is always flying, flying over abysses, flying up into the eternal gases. The word infinite in every other line.

In the classical attitude you never seem to swing right along to the infinite nothing. If you say an extravagant thing which does exceed the limits inside which you know man to be fastened, yet there is always conveyed in some way at the end an impression of yourself standing outside it, and not quite believing it, or consciously putting it forward as a flourish. You never go blindly into an atmosphere more than the truth, an atmosphere too rarefied for man to breathe for long. You are always faithful to the conception of a limit. It is a question of pitch; in romantic verse you move at a certain pitch of rhetoric which you know, man being what he is, to be a little high-falutin. The kind of thing you get in Hugo or Swinburne. In the coming classical reaction that will feel just wrong. For an example of the opposite thing, a verse written in the proper classical spirit, I can take the song from Cymbeline beginning with "Fear no more the heat of the sun." I am just using this as a parable. I don't quite mean what I say here. Take the last two lines:

> Golden lads and lasses must,
> Like chimney sweepers come to dust.

Now, no romantic would have ever written that. Indeed, so ingrained is romanticism, so objectionable is this to it, that people have asserted that these were not part of the original song.

Apart from the pun, the thing that I think quite classical is the word lad. Your modern romantic could never write that. He would have to write golden youth, and take up the thing at least a couple of notes in pitch.

I want now to give the reasons which make me think that we are nearing the end of the romantic movement.

The first lies in the nature of any convention or tradition in art. A particular convention or attitude in art has a strict analogy to the phenomena of organic life. It grows old and decays. It has a definite period of life and must die. All the possible tunes get played on it and then it is exhausted; moreover its best period is its youngest. Take the case of the extraordinary efflorescence of verse in the Elizabethan period. All kinds of reasons have been given for this— the discovery of the new world and all the rest of it. There is a much simpler one. A new medium had been given them to play with—namely, blank verse. It was new and so it was easy to play new tunes on it.

The same law holds in other arts. All the masters of painting are born into the world at a time when the particular tradition from which they start is imperfect. The Florentine tradition was just short of full ripeness when Raphael came to Florence, the Bellinesque was still young when Titian was born in Venice. Landscape was still a toy or an appanage of figure-painting

when Turner and Constable [3] arose to reveal its independent power. When Turner and Constable had done with landscape they left little or nothing for their successors to do on the same lines. Each field of artistic activity is exhausted by the first great artist who gathers a full harvest from it.

This period of exhaustion seems to me to have been reached in romanticism. We shall not get any new efflorescence of verse until we get a new technique, a new convention, to turn ourselves loose in.

Objection might be taken to this. It might be said that a century as an organic unity doesn't exist, that I am being deluded by a wrong metaphor, that I am treating a collection of literary people as if they were an organism or state department. Whatever we may be in other things, an objector might urge, in literature in as far as we are anything at all—in as far as we are worth considering—we are individuals, we are persons, and as distinct persons we cannot be subordinated to any general treatment. At any period at any time, an individual poet may be a classic or a romantic just as he feels like it. You at any particular moment may think that you can stand outside a movement. You may think that as an individual you observe both the classic and the romantic spirit and decide from a purely detached point of view that one is superior to the other.

The answer to this is that no one, in a matter of judgment of beauty, can take a detached standpoint in this way. Just as physically you are not born that abstract entity, man, but the child of particular parents, so you are in matters of literary judgment. Your opinion is almost entirely of the literary history that came just before you, and you are governed by that whatever you may think. Take Spinoza's example of a stone falling to the ground. If it had a conscious mind it would, he said, think it was going to the ground because it wanted to. So you with your pretended free judgment about what is and what is not beautiful. The amount of freedom in man is much exaggerated. That we are free on cer-

---

[3] "Bellinesque"—the style developed in painting by the Bellini family, Jacopo (1400-1471), Gentile (1429-1501), and Giovanni Bellini (1430-1516). Joseph M. W. Turner (1775-1851) and John Constable (1776-1837) were noted English landscape painters.

tain rare occasions, both my religion and the views I get from metaphysics convince me. But many acts which we habitually label free are in reality automatic. It is quite possible for a man to write a book almost automatically. I have read several such products. Some observations were recorded more than twenty years ago by Robertson on reflex speech, and he found that in certain cases of dementia, where the people were quite unconscious so far as the exercise of reasoning went, that very intelligent answers were given to a succession of questions on politics and such matters. The meaning of these questions could not possibly have been understood. Language here acted after the manner of a reflex. So that certain extremely complex mechanisms, subtle enough to imitate beauty, can work by themselves—I certainly think that this is the case with judgments about beauty.

I can put the same thing in slightly different form. Here is a question of a conflict of two attitudes, as it might be of two techniques. The critic, while he has to admit that changes from one to the other occur, persists in regarding them as mere variations to a certain fixed normal, just as a pendulum might swing. I admit the analogy of the pendulum as far as movement, but I deny the further consequence of the analogy, the existence of the point of rest, the normal point.

When I say that I dislike the romantics, I dissociate two things: the part of them in which they resemble all the great poets, and the part in which they differ and which gives them their character as romantics. It is this minor element which constitutes the particular note of a century, and which, while it excites contemporaries, annoys the next generation. It was precisely that quality in Pope which pleased his friends, which we detest. Now, anyone just before the romantics who felt that, could have predicted that a change was coming. It seems to me that we stand just in the same position now. I think that there is an increasing proportion of people who simply can't stand Swinburne.

When I say that there will be another classical revival I don't necessarily anticipate a return to Pope. I say merely that now is the time for such a revival. Given people of the necessary capacity, it may be a vital thing; without them we may get a formalism something like Pope. When

it does come we may not even recognise it as classical. Although it will be classical it will be different because it has passed through a romantic period. To take a parallel example: I remember being very surprised, after seeing the Post Impressionists, to find in Maurice Denis's account of the matter that they consider themselves classical in the sense that they were trying to impose the same order on the mere flux of new material provided by the impressionist movement, that existed in the more limited materials of the painting before.

There is something now to be cleared away before I get on with my argument, which is that while romanticism is dead in reality, yet the critical attitude appropriate to it still continues to exist. To make this a little clearer: For every kind of verse, there is a corresponding receptive attitude. In a romantic period we demand from verse certain qualities. In a classical period we demand others. At the present time I should say that this receptive attitude has outlasted the thing from which it was formed. But while the romantic tradition has run dry, yet the critical attitude of mind, which demands romantic qualities from verse, still survives. So that if good classical verse were to be written to-morrow very few people would be able to stand it.

I object even to the best of the romantics. I object still more to the receptive attitude. I object to the sloppiness which doesn't consider that a poem is a poem unless it is moaning or whining about something or other. I always think in this connection of the last line of a poem of John Webster's which ends with a request I cordially endorse:

> End your moan and come away.

The thing has got so bad now that a poem which is all dry and hard, a properly classical poem, would not be considered poetry at all. How many people now can lay their hands on their hearts and say they like either Horace or Pope? They feel a kind of chill when they read them.

The dry hardness which you get in the classics is absolutely repugnant to them. Poetry that isn't damp isn't poetry at all. They cannot see that accurate description is a legitimate object of verse. Verse to them always means a bringing in of some of the emotions that are grouped round the word infinite.

The essence of poetry to most people is that it must lead them to a beyond of some kind. Verse strictly confined to the earthly and the definite (Keats is full of it) might seem to them to be excellent writing, excellent craftsmanship, but not poetry. So much has romanticism debauched us, that, without some form of vagueness, we deny the highest.

In the classic it is always the light of ordinary day, never the light that never was on land or sea. It is always perfectly human and never exaggerated: man is always man and never a god.

But the awful result of romanticism is that, accustomed to this strange light, you can never live without it. Its effect on you is that of a drug.

There is a general tendency to think that verse means little else than the expression of unsatisfied emotion. People say: "But how can you have verse without sentiment?" You see what it is: the prospect alarms them. A classical revival to them would mean the prospect of an arid desert and the death of poetry as they understand it, and could only come to fill the gap caused by that death. Exactly why this dry classical spirit should have a positive and legitimate necessity to express itself in poetry is utterly inconceivable to them. What this positive need is, I shall show later. It follows from the fact that there is another quality, not the emotion produced, which is at the root of excellence in verse. Before I get to this I am concerned with a negative thing, a theoretical point, a prejudice that stands in the way and is really at the bottom of this reluctance to understand classical verse.

It is an objection which ultimately I believe comes from a bad metaphysic of art. You are unable to admit the existence of beauty without the infinite being in some way or another dragged in.

I may quote for purposes of argument, as a typical example of this kind of attitude made vocal, the famous chapters in Ruskin's *Modern Painters*, Vol. II, on the imagination. I must say here, parenthetically, that I use this word without prejudice to the other discussion with which I shall end the paper. I only use the word here because it is Ruskin's word. All that I am concerned with just now is the attitude behind it, which I take to be the romantic.

"Imagination cannot but be serious; she sees too far, too darkly, too solemnly, too earnestly, ever to smile. There is something in the heart of everything, if we can reach it, that we shall not be inclined to laugh at. . . . Those who have so pierced and seen the melancholy deeps of things, are filled with intense passion and gentleness of sympathy." (Part III, Chap. III, § 9.)

"There is in every word set down by the imaginative mind an awful undercurrent of meaning, and evidence and shadow upon it of the deep places out of which it has come. It is often obscure, often half-told; for he who wrote it, in his clear seeing of the things beneath, may have been impatient of detailed interpretation; for if we choose to dwell upon it and trace it, it will lead us always securely back to that metropolis of the soul's dominion from which we may follow out all the ways and tracks to its farthest coasts." (Part III, Chap. III, § 5.)

Really in all these matters the act of judgment is an instinct, an absolutely unstateable thing akin to the art of the tea taster. But you must talk, and the only language you can use in this matter is that of analogy. I have no material clay to mould to the given shape; the only thing which one has for the purpose, and which acts as a substitute for it, a kind of mental clay, are certain metaphors modified into theories of aesthetic and rhetoric. A combination of these, while it cannot state the essentially unstateable intuition, can yet give you a sufficient analogy to enable you to see what it was and to recognise it on condition that you yourself have been in a similar state. Now these phrases of Ruskin's convey quite clearly to me his taste in the matter.

I see quite clearly that he thinks the best verse must be serious. That is a natural attitude for a man in the romantic period. But he is not content with saying that he prefers this kind of verse. He wants to deduce his opinion like his master, Coleridge, from some fixed principle which can be found by metaphysic.

Here is the last refuge of this romantic attitude. It proves itself to be not an attitude but a deduction from a fixed principle of the cosmos.

One of the main reasons for the existence of philosophy is not that it enables you to find truth (it can never do that) but that it does provide you a refuge for definitions. The usual idea of the thing is that it provides you with a fixed basis from which you can deduce the things you want in aesthetics. The process is the exact contrary. You start in the confusion of the fighting line, you retire from that just a little to the rear to recover, to get your weapons right. Quite plainly, without metaphor this—it provides you with an elaborate and precise language in which you really can explain definitely what you mean, but what you want to say is decided by other things. The ultimate reality is the hurly-burly, the struggle; the metaphysic is an adjunct to clear-headedness in it.

To get back to Ruskin and his objection to all that is not serious. It seems to me that involved in this is a bad metaphysical aesthetic. You have the metaphysic which in defining beauty or the nature of art always drags in the infinite. Particularly in Germany, the land where theories of aesthetics were first created, the romantic aesthetes collated all beauty to an impression of the infinite involved in the identification of our being in absolute spirit. In the least element of beauty we have a total intuition of the whole world. Every artist is a kind of pantheist.

Now it is quite obvious to anyone who holds this kind of theory that any poetry which confines itself to the finite can never be of the highest kind. It seems a contradiction in terms .to them. And as in metaphysics you get the last refuge of a prejudice, so it is now necessary for me to refute this.

Here follows a tedious piece of dialectic, but it is necessary for my purpose. I must avoid two pitfalls in discussing the idea of beauty. On the one hand there is the old classical view which is supposed to define it as lying in conformity to certain standard fixed forms; and on the other hand there is the romantic view which drags in the infinite. I have got to find a metaphysic between these two which will enable me to hold consistently that a neo-classic verse of the type I have indicated involves no contradiction in terms. It is essential to prove that beauty may be in small, dry things.

The great aim is accurate, precise and definite description. The first thing is to recognise how extraordinarily difficult this is. It is no mere matter of carefulness; you have to use language, and language is by its very nature a communal thing; that is, it expresses never the exact thing but a compromise—that which is common to you, me and everybody. But each man sees a little differently, and to get out clearly and exactly what he does see, he must have a terrific struggle with language, whether it be with words or the technique of other arts. Language has its own special nature, its own conventions and communal ideas. It is only by a concentrated effort of the mind that you can hold it fixed to your own purpose. I always think that the fundamental process at the back of all the arts might be represented by the following metaphor.[4] You know what I call architect's curves—flat pieces of wood with all different kinds of curvature. By a suitable selection from these you can draw approximately any curve you like. The artist I take to be the man who simply can't bear the idea of that "approximately." He will get the exact curve of what he sees whether it be an object or an idea in the mind. I shall here have to change my metaphor a little to get the process in his mind. Suppose that instead of your curved pieces of wood you have a springy piece of steel of the same types of curvature as the wood. Now the state of tension or concentration of mind, if he is doing anything really good in this struggle against the ingrained habit of the technique, may be represented by a man employing all his fingers to bend the steel out of its own curve and into the exact curve which you want. Something different to what it would assume naturally.

There are then two things to distinguish, first the particular faculty of mind to see things as they really are, and apart from the conventional ways in which you have been trained to see them. This is itself rare enough in all consciousness. Second, the concentrated state of mind, the grip over oneself which is necessary in the actual expression of what one sees. To prevent one falling into the conventional curves of ingrained technique, to hold on through infinite detail and trouble to the exact curve you want. Wherever you get this sincerity, you get the fundamental quality of good art without dragging in infinite or serious.

[4] This metaphor is used elsewhere by Hulme—in dealing with Bergson's Theory of Art . . . —but I have refrained from deleting it here because of its particular relevancy. [Herbert Read.]

I can now get at that positive fundamental quality of verse which constitutes excellence, which has nothing to do with infinity, with mystery or with emotions.

This is the point I aim at, then, in my argument. I prophesy that a period of dry, hard, classical verse is coming. I have met the preliminary objection founded on the bad romantic aesthetic that in such verse, from which the infinite is excluded, you cannot have the essence of poetry at all.

After attempting to sketch out what this positive quality is, I can get on to the end of my paper in this way: That where you get this quality exhibited in the realm of the emotions you get imagination, and that where you get this quality exhibited in the contemplation of finite things you get fancy.

In prose as in algebra concrete things are embodied in signs or counters which are moved about according to rules, without being visualised at all in the process. There are in prose certain type situations and arrangements of words, which move as automatically into certain other arrangements as do functions in algebra. One only changes the X's and the Y's back into physical things at the end of the process. Poetry, in one aspect at any rate, may be considered as an effort to avoid this characteristic of prose. It is not a counter language, but a visual concrete one. It is a compromise for a language of intuition which would hand over sensations bodily. It always endeavours to arrest you, and to make you continuously see a physical thing, to prevent you gliding through an abstract process. It chooses fresh epithets and fresh metaphors, not so much because they are new, and we are tired of the old, but because the old cease to convey a physical thing and become abstract counters. A poet says a ship "coursed the seas" to get a physical image, instead of the counter word "sailed." Visual meanings can only be transferred by the new bowl of metaphor; prose is an old pot that lets them leak out. Images in verse are not mere decoration, but the very essence of an intuitive language. Verse is a pedestrian taking you over the ground, prose—a train which delivers you at a destination.

I can now get on to a discussion of two words often used in this connection, "fresh" and "unexpected." You praise a thing for being "fresh." I understand what you mean, but the word besides conveying the truth conveys a secondary something which is certainly false. When you say a poem or drawing is fresh, and so good, the impression is somehow conveyed that the essential element of goodness is freshness, that it is good because it is fresh. Now this is certainly wrong, there is nothing particularly desirable about freshness *per se*. Works of art aren't eggs. Rather the contrary. It is simply an unfortunate necessity due to the nature of language and technique that the only way the element which does constitute goodness, the only way in which its presence can be detected externally, is by freshness. Freshness convinces you, you feel at once that the artist was in an actual physical state. You feel that for a minute. Real communication is so very rare, for plain speech is unconvincing. It is in this rare fact of communication that you get the root of aesthetic pleasure.

I shall maintain that wherever you get an extraordinary interest in a thing, a great zest in its contemplation which carries on the contemplator to accurate description in the sense of the word accurate I have just analysed, there you have sufficient justification for poetry. It must be an intense zest which heightens a thing out of the level of prose. I am using contemplation here just in the same way that Plato used it, only applied to a different subject: it is a detached interest. "The object of aesthetic contemplation is something framed apart by itself and regarded without memory or expectation, simply as being itself, as end not means, as individual not universal."

To take a concrete example. I am taking an extreme case. If you are walking behind a woman in the street, you notice the curious way in which the skirt rebounds from her heels. If that peculiar kind of motion becomes of such interest to you that you will search about until you can get the exact epithet which hits it off, there you have a properly aesthetic emotion. But it is the zest with which you look at the thing which decides you to make the effort. In this sense the feeling that was in Herrick's mind when he wrote "the tempestuous petticoat" was exactly the same as that which in bigger and vaguer matters makes the best romantic verse. It doesn't matter an atom that the emotion produced is not of dignified vagueness, but on the contrary amusing; the point is that exactly the same activity is at work as in the highest verse. That is the avoidance of conventional language in order to get the exact curve of the thing.

I have still to show that in the verse which is to come, fancy will be the necessary weapon of the classical school. The positive quality I have talked about can be manifested in ballad verse by extreme directness and simplicity, such as you get in "On Fair Kirkconnel Lea." But the particular verse we are going to get will be cheerful, dry and sophisticated, and here the necessary weapon of the positive quality must be fancy.

Subject doesn't matter; the quality in it is the same as you get in the more romantic people.

It isn't the scale or kind of emotion produced that decides, but this one fact: Is there any real zest in it? Did the poet have an actually realised visual object before him in which he delighted? It doesn't matter if it were a lady's shoe or the starry heavens.

Fancy is not mere decoration added on to plain speech. Plain speech is essentially inaccurate. It is only by new metaphors, that is, by fancy, that it can be made precise.

When the analogy has not enough connection with the thing described to be quite parallel with it, where it overlays the thing it described and there is a certain excess, there you have the play of fancy—that I grant is inferior to imagination.

But where the analogy is every bit of it necessary for accurate description in the sense of the word accurate I have previously described, and your only objection to this kind of fancy is that it is not serious in the effect it produces, then I think the objection to be entirely invalid. If it is sincere in the accurate sense, when the whole of the analogy is necessary to get out the exact curve of the feeling or thing you want to express—there you seem to me to have the highest verse, even though the subject be trivial and the emotions of the infinite far away.

It is very difficult to use any terminology at all for this kind of thing. For whatever word you use is at once sentimentalised. Take Coleridge's word "vital." [5] It is used loosely by all kinds of people who talk about art, to mean something vaguely and mysteriously significant. In fact, vital and mechanical is to them exactly the same antithesis as between good and bad.

Nothing of the kind; Coleridge uses it in a perfectly definite and what I call dry sense. It is just this: A mechanical complexity is the sum of its parts. Put them side by side and you get the whole. Now vital or organic is merely a convenient metaphor for a complexity of a different kind, that in which the parts cannot be said to be elements as each one is modified by the other's presence, and each one to a certain extent is the whole. The leg of a chair by itself is still a leg. My leg by itself wouldn't be.

Now the characteristic of the intellect is that it can only represent complexities of the mechanical kind. It can only make diagrams, and diagrams are essentially things whose parts are separate one from another. The intellect always analyses—when there is a synthesis it is baffled. That is why the artist's work seems mysterious. The intellect can't represent it. This is a necessary consequence of the particular nature of the intellect and the purposes for which it is formed. It doesn't mean that your synthesis is ineffable, simply that it can't be definitely stated.

Now this is all worked out in Bergson, the central feature of his whole philosophy. It is all based on the clear conception of these vital complexities which he calls "intensive" as opposed to the other kind which he calls "extensive," and the recognition of the fact that the intellect can only deal with the extensive multiplicity. To deal with the intensive you must use intuition.

Now, as I said before, Ruskin was perfectly aware of all this, but he had no such metaphysical background which would enable him to state definitely what he meant. The result is that he has to flounder about in a series of metaphors. A powerfully imaginative mind seizes and combines at the same instant all the important ideas of its poem or picture, and while it works with one of them, it is at the same instant working with and modifying all in their relation to it and never losing sight of their bearings on each other—as the motion of

[5] See above, p. 395.

a snake's body goes through all parts at once and its volition acts at the same instant in coils which go contrary ways.

A romantic movement must have an end of the very nature of the thing. It may be deplored, but it can't be helped—wonder must cease to be wonder.

I guard myself here from all the consequences of the analogy, but it expresses at any rate the inevitableness of the process. A literature of wonder must have an end as inevitably as a strange land loses its strangeness when one lives in it. Think of the lost ecstasy of the Elizabethans. "Oh my America, my new found land," think of what it meant to them and of what it means to us. Wonder can only be the attitude of a man passing from one stage to another, it can never be a permanently fixed thing.

IVOR ARMSTRONG RICHARDS   (1893-   )

RICHARDS rivals T. S. Eliot as the most important contemporary influence on recent English and especially American criticism of poetry. While the influence of Eliot has been concerned with general aims, and a reconsidering of poetic tradition in the light of his own ideals of poetic style, and has therefore shown itself largely in its effect on contemporary *taste*, the influence of Richards has been on critical *method* and *approach*. His principal effect as a critic has been twofold: to popularize among critics a renewed interest in psychology, and to redirect the interest of the critic to the text of the particular poem and to the problem of analyzing it in terms of language, imagery, and metaphor. But the two aspects are not distinct. The use of psychology advocated by Richards is not, as in the case of Sainte-Beuve, for the purpose of analyzing the writer as a whole, and for determining the relation of the given work to the writer's life and total achievement. It is rather in the great tradition of English romantic criticism:

IVOR ARMSTRONG RICHARDS. After attending Magdalene College, Cambridge (A.B. 1914), Richards became a Fellow there, taught at Peking (1929-30) and later at Harvard University (1931), to which he has since returned, first as Lecturer (1939-44), and later (1944-63) as University Professor.

Recent critical works include his *Speculative Instruments* (1955); *So Much Nearer* (1968); *Design for Escape* (1968); and a revised edition of *Science and Poetry* (1926), published under the title *Poetries and Sciences* (1970). Commentary, from diverse points of view, includes: G. R. Hamilton, *Poetry and Contemplation: a New Preface to Poetics* (Cambridge, 1937); D. W. Harding, "I. A. Richards," *Scrutiny*, I (1933), 327-38; D. G. James, *Skepticism and Poetry* (1937); John Crowe Ransom, "I. A. Richards: the Psychological Critic," in *The New Critics* (Norfolk, Conn., 1941); T. C. Pollock, "A Critique of I. A. Richards' Theory of Language and Literature," *Theory of Meaning Analyzed* (Chicago, 1942), pp. 1-25. More helpful are M. H. Abrams, "Belief and the Suspension of Disbelief," *Literature and Belief* (1958); W. H. N. Hotoph, *Language, Thought, and Comprehension* (Bloomington, Ind., 1965); and J. P. Schiller, *I. A. Richards' Theory of Literature* (New Haven, 1969).

the primary interest is the nature and working of the imagination, both as it produces or responds to art. For Richards, and especially for the Anglo-American critics of poetry who have followed him, including the "New Critics" of the past decade, the insights gained from such a psychological analysis—partly clinical but largely through introspection—are in turn applied back to the study of poetic style, and are on the whole subservient to that interest.

Richards's interest in psychology, already apparent in the *Foundations of Aesthetics* (1922) that he wrote with C. K. Ogden, is most fully expressed in the *Principles of Literary Criticism* (1924). The immediate impact of this book cannot be appreciated unless it is recalled that, since the middle of the nineteenth century, psychological criticism in England had subsided to such an extent that, to critics unfamiliar with the history of British philosophy and criticism, the approach seemed wholly novel. However, it was mainly Richards's use of recent psychological terminology and his more systematized *theoretical* discussion of the subject that marked the difference from earlier English psychological criticism. The psychological theory of criticism expounded in the *Principles of Literary Criticism* is further ramified by Richards in his *Coleridge on the Imagination* (1934).

In reviving the use of psychology as a fulcrum for the criticism of poetry, Richards, in the *Principles of Literary Criticism*, drew special attention to the imaginative and emotional impact of words. This interest in language had already taken Richards to the study of semantics in *The Meaning of Meaning* (1923), and was later to lead to his work in Basic English. But it is especially in his *Practical Criticism* (1929) that Richards's psychological study of language is closely and profitably brought to bear on the criticism of poetry. Here the recorded reactions of several readers to different poems are analyzed. Following these analyses are chapters, including the two printed below, which discuss with acumen and sensitivity the more general problems involved in responding to poetry. The influence of the book on recent textual-minded criticism has been healthful as well as extensive. But not all of Richards's followers have perhaps attained so capacious and open-minded a general outlook as that which continually appears throughout *Practical Criticism*. Earlier, in the *Principles of Literary Criticism* and also in his *Science and Poetry* (1926), Richards had reasserted—largely under the influence of Matthew Arnold—the ancient classical belief that art acts formatively in enlarging one's sensibility, deepening one's sympathies, and inducing a more organized and harmonious ability to experience life. This concept also serves as a basic premise throughout *Practical Criticism*, preventing his concentration on poetic style from being purely esthetic, formalistic, or narrowly sectarian and exclusive.

Irrelevant Associations and Stock Responses

THE PERSONAL situation of the reader inevitably (and within limits rightly) affects his reading, and many more are drawn to poetry in quest of some reflection of their latest emotional crisis than would admit in if faced with such a frank declaration as that in 11·2. Though it has been fashionable—in deference to sundry confused doctrines of "pure art" and "impersonal aesthetic emotions"—to deplore such a state of affairs, there is really no occasion. For a comparison of the feelings active in a poem with some personal feeling still present in the reader's lively recollection does give a standard, a test for reality. The dangers are that the recollected feelings may overwhelm and distort the poem and that the reader may forget that the evocation of somewhat similar feelings is probably only a part of the poem's endeavour. It exists perhaps to *control and order* such feelings and to bring them into relation with other things, not merely to arouse them. But a touchstone for reality is so valuable, and factitious or conventional feelings so common, that these dangers are worth risking.

Thus memories, whether of emotional crises or of scenes visited or incidents observed, are not to be hastily excluded as mere personal intrusions. That they are personal is nothing against them—all experience is personal—the only conditions are that they must be genuine and relevant, and must respect the liberty and autonomy of the poem. Genuine memories, for example, of "the most moving manifestations of nature" and "its loveliest and grandest aspects" (9·9 and 9·91), if they were compared with what the poem contained, would have influenced the opinions there expressed of *Poem IX.* It is the absence of such memories that allows a word like "glittering" to pass unchallenged in the last

Irrelevant Associations and Stock Responses. From *Practical Criticism* by I. A. Richards, Pt. III, Ch. 5. Reprinted by permission of Harcourt Brace Jovanovich, Inc. and Routledge and Kegan Paul Ltd. First published in 1929. The chapter is given in its entirety except for opening remarks that refer, by number, to poems and the reactions of different readers to these poems printed in Part II of the book.

line but one of the poem. At a moment when accuracy and verisimilitude in description are important, appears a word completely false to the appearances that are being described. Mountains that are "surging away into *the sunset glow*" do not glitter; they cannot, unless the sun (or moon) is fairly high in the heavens. But "glittering" is a stock epithet for icy mountains. With this we are brought to the important, neglected and curious topic of Stock Responses.

So much that passes for poetry is written, and so much reading of even the most original poetry is governed, by these fixed conventionalised reactions that their natural history will repay investigation. Their intervention, moreover, in all forms of human activity—in business, in personal relationships, in public affairs, in Courts of Justice—will be recognised, and any light which the study of poetry may throw upon their causes, their services, their disadvantages, and on the ways in which they may be overcome, should be generally welcome.

A stock response, like a stock line in shoes or hats, may be a convenience. Being readymade, it is available with less trouble than if it had to be specially made out of raw or partially prepared materials. And unless an awkward misfit is going to occur, we may agree that stock responses are much better than no responses at all. Indeed, an extensive repertory of stock responses is a necessity. Few minds could prosper if they had to work out an original, "made to measure" response to meet every situation that arose—their supplies of mental energy would be too soon exhausted and the wear and tear on their nervous systems would be too great. Clearly there is an enormous field of conventional activity over which acquired, stereotyped, habitual responses properly rule, and the only question that needs to be examined as to *these* responses is whether they are the best that practical exigencies—the range of probable situations that may arise, the necessity of quick availability and so forth—will allow. But equally clearly there are in most lives fields of activity in which stock responses, if they intervene, are disadvantageous and even danger-ous, because they may get in the way of, and prevent, a response more appropriate to the sit-uation. These unnecessary misfits may be re-marked at almost every stage of the reading of poetry, but they are especially noticeable when emotional responses are in question. . . .

But a much more subtle situation involving stock responses remains to be discussed. Here—instead of distorting the poem or of setting up an irrelevant external standard—the stock re-sponse actually is in the poem. *Poems I, IV, VII* and *IX*, with some differences in level and degree, I believe illustrate this condition of affairs. The most correct reading of them, the reading which most accords with the impulses that gave them being, is in each case, unless I am mistaken, such that every item and every strand of meaning, every cadence and every least movement of the form is fatally and irrev-ocably familiar to anyone with any acquaint-ance with English poetry. Furthermore this familiarity is *not* of the kind which passages of great poetry ever acquire, however often we may read them or however much we have them by heart. We may be weary to death of "To be or not to be . . . ," but we still know that if we were to attend to it again it could surprise us once more. The familiarity of these poems belongs to them as we first read them, it is not an acquired familiarity but native. And it im-plies, I think, that the mental movements out of which they are composed have long been parts of our intellectual and emotional repertory and that these movements are few and simple and arranged in an obvious order. In other words the familiarity is a sign of their facility as stock responses. . . .

Such stock poems are frequently very popular. They come home to a majority of readers with a minimum of trouble, for no new outlook, no new direction of feeling, is required. On the other hand, as we have seen, readers who have become more exigent often grow very indignant, the degree of their indignation being sometimes a measure, it may appear, of the distance they have themselves moved from the stock response and the recency of the development. But such cynical reflections are not always in place here, for these responses must evidently be judged by two partially independent sets of considerations

—their appropriateness to the situations to which they reply, and the degree in which they hinder more appropriate responses from developing. There are clearly stock responses which are in both ways admirable—they are right as far as they go, reasonably adequate to their situations, and they assist rather than prevent further, more refined, developments. On the other hand, no one with the necessary experience will doubt that inappropriate stock responses are common and that they are powerful enemies to poetry. Some of the *differences in origin* between good and bad responses are therefore worth tracing.

If we consider how responses in general are formed, we shall see that the chief cause of ill-appropriate, stereotyped reactions is *withdrawal from experience*. This can come about in many ways. Physically, as when a London child grows up without ever seeing the country or the sea; morally, as when a particularly heavy parent deprives a child of all the adventurous expansive side of life; through convention and inculca-tion, as when a child, being too easily persuaded what to think and to feel, develops parasitically; intellectually, as when insufficient experience is theoretically elaborated into a system that hides the real world from us.

These last two cases are the more interesting for our purpose here, though the effects of sheer ignorance and of such moral disasters as pro-duce timidity are not to be overlooked. But more often, perhaps, it is a too loose and easy growth in our responses that leads to premature fixation. Ideas, handed to us by others or produced from within, are a beguiling substitute for actual ex-perience in evoking and developing our responses. An idea—of soldiers for example—can stay the same through innumerable repetitions; our ex-perience of actual soldiers may distressingly vary. The idea, as a rule, presents one aspect; the actual things may present many. We can call up our idea by the mere use of a word. And even in the presence of the Army it is by no means certain that what we perceive will not be as much our idea as the soldiers themselves. Since a response becomes firmer through exer-cise, it is clear that those among our responses that are early hitched to an idea, rather than to the actual particularities of the object, gain a great advantage in their struggle for survival. It behoves us, therefore, to consider very carefully what kinds of things these ideas are, how we come by them and to what extent they can be trusted. . . .

We come by our ideas in three main fashions: by direct interaction with the things they represent, that is, by experience; by suggestion from other people; and by our own intellectual elaboration. Suggestion and elaboration have their evident dangers, but are indispensable means of increasing our range of ideas. It is necessary in practice to acquire ideas a great deal faster than we can possibly gain the corresponding experience, and suggestibility and elaboration though we must make them responsible for our stock responses, are after all the capacities that divide us from the brutes. Suggestion, working primarily through language, hands down to us both a good and an evil heritage. Nine-tenths, at the least, of the ideas and the annexed emotional responses that are passed on—by the cinema, the press, friends and relatives, teachers, the clergy . . .—to an average child of this century are—judged by the standards of poetry —crude and vague rather than subtle or appropriate. But the very processes by which they are transmitted explain the result. Those who hand them on received them from their fellows. And there is always a loss in transmission which becomes more serious in proportion as what is transmitted is new, delicate and subtle, or departs in any way from what is expected. Ideas and responses which cost too much labour both at the distributing end and at the reception end —both for writer and reader—are not practicable, as every journalist knows. The economics of the profession do not permit their transmission; and in any case it would be absurd to ask a million tired readers to sit down and work. It is hard enough to get thirty tired children to sit up, behave and look bright.

A very simple application of the theory of communication shows, then, that any very widespread diffusion of ideas and responses tends towards standardisation, towards a levelling down, But, as we have already agreed, any responses that work, even badly, are better than none. Once the basic level has been reached, a slow climb back may be possible. That at least is a hope that may be reasonably entertained. Meanwhile the threat to poetry in this state of affairs must be recognised. As our chief means

by which subtle ideas and responses may be communicated, poetry may have a part to play in the climb back. It is, at least, the most important repository of our standards.

We have still to consider the other influence which encourages in the individual the fixation of inappropriate responses—*speculative elaboration divorced from experience.* Thinking—in the sense of a thorough attempt to compare all the aspects of an object or situation, to analyse its parts, to reconcile one with another all its various implications, to order it in one coherent intellectual fabric with everything else we know about everything connected with it—is an arduous and not immediately profitable occupation. Accordingly, outside the scientific professions and endowed institutions and even within them, it is much less practised than we conventionally suppose.

What we usually describe as thinking is a much more attractive mental exercise; it consists in following out a train of ideas, a process which affords us most of the pleasures of thinking, in the stricter sense, without its pains and bewilderments. Such trains of associations may, and in the minds of men of genius often do, lead to new and valuable ideas. But—accidents apart— the condition for this happy result is a wide available background of relevant experience. The valuable idea is, in fact, the meeting-point, the link between separate parts of this field of experience. It unites aspects of existence that ordinarily remain unconnected, and in this lies its value. The secret of genius is perhaps nothing else than this greater availability of all experience coupled with larger stores of experience to draw upon. The man of genius seems to take in more every minute than his duller companion, and what he has received seems to be more readily at his disposal when he needs it. This obvious description of Shakespeare seems to apply in lesser degree to other good poets.

The man of less endowment (I am incidentally describing many bad poets) attempting a similar achievement with less experience and with what experience he has less available,[1] is likely to arrive at merely arbitrary results. Lacking the

[1] If we ask why one man's past experience should be less available to him than another man's, and so less useful to him in guiding his desires and thoughts, the answer must be given in terms of inhibitions. [Richards.]

control of a many-sided, still active, past experience, his *momentary* tendencies, desires, and impulses shape and settle his conclusions for him, and it is more likely to be the *attractiveness* of the idea (in the light of some particular desire) than its *relevance* that causes it to be adopted. It might be thought that the test of subsequent experience would lead such a man to abandon or correct the inappropriate ideas and responses he arrives at in this arbitrary fashion. So it does in many practical matters. We all know enthusiasts who constantly have their unreal hopes and projects dashed to the ground. But attitudes and responses of the kinds with which poetry is likely to be concerned unfortunately escape this corrective test. The erratic individual cannot himself see that his responses are inappropriate, though others might tell him. When he misreads a poem, no practical consequences arise to teach him his folly; and, similarly, if he mismanages his emotional relations with his fellow-beings he can readily persuade himself that *they* are at fault. . . .

Enough perhaps as to some of the causes of stock inappropriate responses, whether of the standardised, or the personal-whimsy, type. The only corrective in all cases must be a closer contact with reality, either directly, through experience of actual things, or mediately through other minds which are in closer contact. If good poetry owes its value in a large measure to the closeness of its contact with reality, it may thereby become a powerful weapon for breaking up unreal ideas and responses. Bad poetry certainly can be their very helpful guardian and ally. But even the best poetry, if we read into it just what we happen to have already in our minds, and do not use it as a means for reorganising ourselves, does less good than harm. . . .

The shock of discovering how alive with new aspects everything whatever is when contact with reality is restored is anaesthetising to minds that have lost their capacity to reorganise themselves; it stupefies and bewilders. Nearly all good poetry is disconcerting, for a moment at least, when we first see it for what it is. Some dear habit has to be abandoned if we are to follow it. Going forwards we are likely to find that other habitual responses, not directly concerned, seem less satisfactory. In the turmoil of disturbed routines that may ensue, the mind's hold on actuality is tested. Great poetry, indeed, is not so safe a toy as the conventional view supposes. But these indirect effects of the overthrow of even a few stock attitudes and ideas is the hope of those who think humanity may venture to improve itself. And the belief that—on the whole and accidents apart—finer, subtler, more appropriate responses are more efficient, economical, and advantageous than crude ones, is the best ground for a moderate optimism that the world-picture presents.

Doctrine in Poetry

Logic is the ethics of thinking, in the sense in which ethics is the bringing to bear of self-control, for the purpose of realising our desires.

CHARLES SAUNDERS PIERCE.

WITH most of our critical difficulties what we have had to explain is how mistakes come to be so frequent. But here we are in the opposite case, we have to explain how they come to be so rare. For it would seem evident that poetry which has been built upon firm and definite beliefs about the world, *The Divine*

Doctrine in Poetry. From *Practical Criticism* by I. A. Richards, Pt. III, Ch. 7. Reprinted by permission of Harcourt Brace Jovanovich, Inc. and Routledge and Kegan Paul Ltd. The chapter is printed entire.

Comedy or *Paradise Lost*, or Donne's *Divine Poems*, or Shelley's *Prometheus Unbound*, or Hardy's *The Dynasts*, must appear differently to readers who do and readers who do not hold similar beliefs. Yet in fact most readers, and nearly all good readers, are very little disturbed by even a direct opposition between their own beliefs and the beliefs of the poet. Lucretius and Virgil, Euripides and Aeschylus, we currently assume, are equally accessible, given the necessary scholarship, to a Roman Catholic, to a Buddhist and to a confirmed sceptic. Equally accessible in the sense that these different readers, after due study, may respond in the same way to the poetry and arrive at similar judg ments about it. And when they differ, their divergencies will commonly not be a result of their different positions with regard to the doctrines [1] of the authors, but are more likely to derive from other causes—in their temperaments and personal experience.

I have instanced religious poetry because the beliefs there concerned have the widest implications, and are the most seriously entertained of any. But the same problem arises with nearly all poetry; with mythology very evidently; with such supernatural machinery as appears in *The Rime of the Ancient Mariner:*

> The horned Moon, with one bright star
> Within the nether tip

with Blake's manifestoes; but equally, though less obtrusively, with every passage which seems to make a statement, or depend upon an assumption, that a reader may dissent from, without thereby giving proof of mental derangement.

It is essential to recognise that the problem [2] is the same whether the possible stumbling-block, the point of dissent, be trivial or important. When the point is trivial, we easily satisfy ourselves with an explanation in terms of "poetic fictions." When it is a matter of no consequence whether we assent or dissent, the theory that these disputable statements, so constantly presented to us in poetry, are merely *assumptions* introduced for poetic purposes, seems an adequate explanation. And when the statements, for example, Homer's account of "the monkey-shines of the Olympian troupe," are frankly incredible, if paraded solemnly before the bar of reasoned judgment, the same explanation applies. But as the assumptions grow more plausible, and as the consequences for our view of the world grow important, the matter seems less simple. Until, in the end, with Donne's Sonnet (*Poem III*),[3] for example, it becomes very difficult not to think that *actual belief* in the

doctrine that appears in the poem is required for its full and perfect imaginative realisation. The mere assumption of Donne's theology, as a poetic fiction, may seem insufficient in view of the intensity of the feeling which is supported and conveyed to us by its means. It is at least certain, as the protocols show (3·15, 5·42, 5·37, 5·38, 7·21), that many who try to read religious poetry find themselves strongly invited to the beliefs presented, and that doctrinal dissent is a very serious obstacle to their reading. Conversely, many successful but dissenting readers find themselves in a mental attitude towards the doctrine which, if it is not belief, closely resembles belief.

Yet if we suppose that, beyond this mere "poetic" assumption, a definite state of belief in this particular doctrine of the Resurrection of the Body is required for a full reading of Donne's poem, great difficulties at once arise. We shall have to suppose that readers who hold different beliefs incompatible with this particular doctrine must either not be able to read the poem, or must temporarily while reading it abandon their own beliefs and adopt Donne's. Both suppositions *seem* contrary to the facts, though these are matters upon which certainty is hazardous. We shall do better, however, to examine the "poetic fiction," or assumption, theory more closely and see whether when fully stated it is capable of meeting the complaint of inadequacy noticed above.

In the first place the very word "assumption" is unsuitable here. Ordinarily an assumption is a proposition, an object of thought, entertained intellectually in order to trace its logical consequences as a hypothesis. But here we are concerned very little with logical consequences and almost exclusively with emotional consequences. In the effect of the thought upon our feelings and attitudes, all its importance, for poetry, lies. But there are clearly two ways in which we may entertain an assumption: intellectually, that is in a context of other thoughts ready to support, contradict, or establish other logical relations with it; and emotionally, in a context of sentiments, feelings, desires and attitudes ready to group themselves around it. Behind the intellectual assumption stands the desire for logical consistency and order in the receptive side of the mind. But behind the emotional assumption

[1] I am not accusing these authors of doctrinal poetry in the narrow sense of verse whose sole object is to teach. But that a body of doctrine is presented by each of these poets, even by Virgil, can hardly escape any reader's notice. [Richards.]

[2] A supplementary and fuller discussion of this whole matter will be found in *Principles of Literary Criticism*, Ch. XXXII-XXXV, where difficulties, which here must be passed by, are treated in detail. [Richards.]

[3] "At the round earth's imagined corners."

stands the desire or need for order of the whole outgoing emotional side of the personality, the side that is turned towards action.

Corresponding to this distinction there are two forms of belief and similarly two forms of disbelief. Intellectual belief more resembles a weighting of an idea than anything else, a loading [4] which makes other, less heavily weighted, ideas, adjust themselves to it rather than *vice versa*. The loading may be legitimate; the quantity of evidence, its immediacy, the extent and complexity of the supporting systems of ideas are obvious forms of legitimate loading: or it may be illegitimate; our liking for the idea, its brilliance, the trouble that changing it may involve, emotional satisfactions from it, are illegitimate—*from the standpoint of intellectual belief* be it understood. The whole use of intellectual belief is to bring *all* our ideas into as perfect an ordered system as possible. We disbelieve only because we believe something else that is incompatible, as Spinoza long ago pointed out. Similarly, we perhaps only believe because it is necessary to disbelieve whatever is logically contradictory to our belief. *Neither belief nor disbelief arises*, in this intellectual sense, *unless the logical context of our ideas is in question.* Apart from these logical connections the idea is neither believed nor disbelieved, nor doubted nor questioned; it is just present. Most of the ideas of the child, of primitive man, of the peasant, of the non-intellectual world and of most poetry are in this happy condition of real intellectual disconnection.

Emotional belief is a very different matter. In primitive man, as innumerable observers have remarked, any idea which opens a ready outlet to emotion or points to a line of action in conformity with custom is quickly believed. We remain much more primitive in this phase of our behaviour than in intellectual matters. Given a need [5] (whether conscious *as a desire* or not),

any idea which can be taken as a step on the way to its fulfilment is accepted, unless some other need equally active at the moment bars it out. This acceptance, this use of the idea—by our interests, desires, feelings, attitudes, tendencies to action and what not—is emotional belief. So far as the idea is useful to them it is believed, and the sense of attachment, of adhesion, of conviction, which we feel, and to which we give the name of belief, is the result of this implication of the idea in our activities.

Most beliefs, of course, that have any strength or persistence are mixtures of intellectual and emotional belief. A purely intellectual belief need have little strength, no quality of conviction about it, for unless the idea is very original and contrary to received ideas, it needs little loading to hold its own. When we find a modern physicist, for example, passionately attached to a particular theory, we may suspect illegitimate loading, his reputation is perhaps involved in its acceptance. Conversely, a very strong emotional belief may have little persistence. Last night's revelation grows dim amid this morning's affairs, for the need which gave it such glamorous reality was only a need of the moment. Of this kind are most of the revelations received from poetry and music. But though the sense of revelation has faded, we should not suppose that the shaping influence of such experiences must be lost. The mind has found through them a pattern of response which may remain, and it is this pattern rather than the revelation which is important.

The great difference between these two kinds of belief, as I have defined them, appears most plainly if we consider what *justification* amounts to for each. Whether an intellectual belief is justified is entirely a matter of its logical place in the largest, most completely ordered, system of ideas we can attain to. Now the central, most stable, mass of our ideas has already an order and arrangement fixed for it by the facts of Nature. We must bring our ideas of these facts into correspondence with them or we promptly perish. And this order among the everyday facts of our surroundings determines the arrangement of yet another system of our

[4] To introspection this loading seems like a feeling of trust—or trustworthiness. We "side" with the belief intellectually, and though traditionally belief has been discussed along with judgment it is, as William James pointed out, more allied to choice. [Richards.]

[5] I use "need" here to stand for an imbalance mental or physical, a tendency, given suitable conditions, for a movement towards an end-state of equilibrium. A swinging pendulum might thus be said to be actuated by a need to come to rest, and to constantly overdo its

movements towards that end. We are much more like pendulums than we think, though, of course, our imbalances are infinitely more intricate. [Richards.]

ideas: namely, physical theory. These ideas are thereby weighted beyond the power of irreconcilable ideas to disturb them. Anyone who understands them cannot help believing in them, and disbelieving *intellectually* in irreconcilable ideas, provided that he brings them close enough together to perceive their irreconcilability. There are obviously countless ideas in poetry which, if put into this logical context, must be disbelieved at once.

But this intellectual disbelief does not imply that emotional belief in the same idea is either impossible or even difficult—much less that it is undesirable. For an emotional belief is not justified through any logical relations between its idea and other ideas. Its only justification is its success in meeting our needs—due regard being paid to the relative claims of our many needs one against another. It is a matter, to put it simply, of the *prudence* (in view of *all* the needs of our being) of the kind of emotional activities the belief subserves. The desirability or undesirability of an emotional belief has nothing to do with its intellectual status, provided it is kept from interfering with the intellectual system. And poetry is an extraordinarily successful device for preventing these interferences from arising.

Coleridge, when he remarked that "a willing suspension of disbelief" accompanied much poetry, was noting an important fact, but not quite in the happiest terms, for we are neither aware of a disbelief nor voluntarily suspending it in these cases. It is better to say that the question of belief or disbelief, in the intellectual sense, never arises when we are reading well. If unfortunately it does arise, either through the poet's fault or our own, we have for the moment ceased to be reading poetry and have become astronomers, or theologians, or moralists, persons engaged in quite a different type of activity.

But a possible misconception must be noted here. The intellectual exploration of the *internal* coherence of the poem, and the intellectual examination of the relations of its ideas to other ideas of ordinary experience which are *emotionally* relevant to it, are not only permissible but necessary in the reading of much poetry, as we saw in connection with the sea-harp in *Poem IX*, and in connection with the sentimentality

and stock-response problems of *Poems IV, VIII* and *XIII*. But this restricted intellectual inquiry is a different thing from the all-embracing attempt to systematise our ideas which alone brings up the problem of intellectual belief.

We can now turn back to *Poem III*, to the point from which this long analysis started. There are many readers who feel a difficulty in giving to Donne's theology just that kind of acceptance, *and no more*, that they give to Coleridge's "star within the nether tip." They feel an invitation to accord to the poem that belief in its ideas which we can hardly help supposing to have been, in Donne's mind, a powerful influence over its shaping. These readers may, perhaps, be content if we insist that the fullest possible *emotional* belief is fitting and desirable. At the same time there are many who are unable to accord *intellectual* belief to these particular theological tenets. Such readers may feel that a threatened liberty is not thereby denied them. The fact that Donne probably gave both forms of belief to these ideas need not, I think, prevent a good reader from giving the fullest emotional belief while withholding intellectual belief, or rather while not allowing the question of intellectual belief to arise. The evidence is fragmentary upon the point, largely because it has been so strangely little discussed. But the very fact that the need to discuss it has not insistently arisen—seeing how many people from how many different intellectual positions have been able to agree about the value of such doctrinal poems —points strongly in this direction. The absence of intellectual belief need not cripple emotional belief, though evidently enough in some persons it may. But the habit of attaching emotional belief only to intellectually certified ideas is strong in some people; it is encouraged by some forms of education; it is perhaps becoming, through the increased prestige of science, more common.[6]

---

[6] I have discussed this danger at length in *Science and Poetry*. There is reason to think that poetry has often arisen through fusion (or confusion) between the two forms of belief, the boundary between what is intellectually certified and what is not being much less sharply defined in former centuries and *defined in another manner*. The standard of *verification* used in science to-day is comparatively a new thing. As the scientific view of the world (including our own nature) develops, we shall probably be forced into making a division between fact and fiction that, unless we can

For those whom it conquers it means "Good-bye to poetry."

For the difficulty crops up, as I have insisted, over all poetry that departs, for its own purposes, from the most ordinary universal facts of common experience or from the most necessary deductions of scientific theory. It waylays the strict rationalist with Blake's "Sunflower," Wordsworth's "River Duddon," and Shelley's "Cloud," no less than with their more transcendental utterances. Shakespeare's Lark is as shocking as his Phoenix. Even so honest a man as Gray attributes very disputable motives to his Owl. As for Dryden's "new-kindled star," the last verse of Keats' *Ode to Melancholy,* or Landor's *Rose Aylmer*—it is very clear where we should be with them if we could not give emotional assent apart from intellectual conviction. The slightest poetry may present the problem as clearly (though not so acutely) as the greatest. And the fact that we solve it, in practice, without the least difficulty in minor cases shows, I think, that even in the major instances of philosophic and religious issues the same solution is applicable. But the temptation to confuse the two forms of belief is there greater.

For in these cases an appearance of incompleteness or insincerity may attach to emotional acceptance divorced from intellectual assent.[7] That this is simply a mistake due to a double-meaning of "belief" has been my contention. To "pretend to believe" what we "don't really believe" would certainly be insincerity, if the two kinds of believing were one and the same; but

meet it with a twofold theory of belief on the lines suggested above, would be fatal not only to poetry but to all our finer, more spiritual, responses. That is the problem. [Richards.]

[7] The most important example of this divorce that history provides is in the attitude of Confucius towards ancestor-worship. Here are the remarks of his chief English translator, James Legge, upon the matter. "It will not be supposed that I wish to advocate or defend the practice of sacrificing to the dead. My object has been to point out how Confucius recognised it, without acknowledging the faith from which it must have originated, and how he enforced it as a matter of form or ceremony. It thus connects itself with the most serious charge that can be brought against him—the charge of insincerity," *The Chinese Classics,* Vol. I, Prolegomena, Ch. V, p. 100. How far Legge was qualified to expound the Confucian doctrine of sincerity may perhaps be divined from this passage. [Richards.]

if they are not, the confusion is merely another example of the prodigious power of words over our lives. And this will be the best place to take up the uncomfortable problem of "sincerity," a word much used in criticism, but not often with any precise definition of its meaning.

The ideas, vague and precise, for which "sincere" stands must have been constantly in the reader's mind during our discussion both of Stock Responses and of Sentimentality. We can set aside at once the ordinary "business" sense in which a man is insincere when he deliberately attempts to deceive, and sincere when his statements and acts are governed by "the best of his knowledge and belief." And we can deal briefly with another sense, already touched upon in connection with *Poem VII* (see p. 95), in which a man is insincere when "he kids *himself,*" when he mistakes his own motives and so professes feelings which are different from those that are in fact actuating him. Two subtle points, however, must be noted before we set this sense aside. The feelings need not be stated or even openly expressed; it is enough if they are hinted to us. And they need not be actual personal "real, live feelings"; they may be imagined feelings. All that is required for this kind of insincerity is a discrepancy between the poem's claim upon our response and its *shaping* impulses in the poet's mind. But only the shaping impulses are relevant. A good poem can perfectly well be written for money or from pique or ambition, provided these initial external motives do not interfere with its growth. Interferences of all kinds—notably the desire to make the poem "original," "striking," or "poetic"—are, of course, the usual cause of insincerity in this sense. A sense which ought not, it may be remarked, to impute blame to the author, unless we are willing to agree that all men who are not good poets are therefore blameworthy in a high degree.

These subtleties were necessary to escape the conclusion that irony, for example—where the feeling really present is often the exact contrary to that overtly professed—is as insincere as simple readers often suppose it must be.

A more troublesome problem is raised if we ask whether an emotion, by itself and apart from its expression, can be sincere or insincere. We often speak as if this were so (witness 4·2, 4·23 and 8·51), and though sometimes no doubt this is only an effective way of saying that we approve (or disapprove) of the emotion, there are senses in which a fact about the emotion, not about our feelings about it, is meant. Sincere emotions, we say, are genuine or authentic, as opposed to spurious emotions, and the several senses which we may imply thereby are worth examining. We may mean that the emotion is genuine in the sense that every product of a perfect mind would be genuine. It would result only from the prompting situation *plus* all the relevant experience of that mind, and be free from impurities and from all interferences, from impulses that had in any way got out of place and become disordered. Since such minds are nowhere obtainable in this obstructive world, such a sense is useful only as an ideal standard by which to measure degrees of relative insincerity. "There is not a just man on earth that doeth good and sinneth not." Some great poetry, we might say, represents the closest approach to sincerity that can be found. And for extreme degrees of insincerity we should look in asylums. Possibly however, the perfect mind, if it ever appeared among us, might be put there too.

But this is plainly not a sense of sincerity which we often use, it is not what people ordinarily mean. For we would agree that stupid people can be very sincere, though their minds may be very much in a muddle, and we might even suggest that they are more likely to be sincere than the clever. Simplicity, we may think, has something to do with sincerity, for there is a sense in which "genuine" is opposed to "sophisticated." The sincere feeling, it may be suggested, is one which has been left in its natural state, not worked over and complicated by reflection. Thus strong spontaneous feelings would be more likely to be sincere than feelings that have run the gauntlet of self-criticism, and a dog, for example, might be regarded as a more sincere animal than any man.

This is certainly a sense which is frequent, though whether we should praise emotions that are sincere in this sense as much as most people do, is extremely doubtful. It is partly an echo of Rousseau's romantic fiction, the "Natural Man." Admiration for the "spontaneous" and "natural" tends to select favourable examples and turns a very blind eye to the less attractive phenomena. Moreover, many emotions which look simple and natural are nothing of the kind, they result from cultivated self-control, so consummate as to seem instantaneous. These cases, and an attractive but limited virtue in some children's behaviour, explain, I believe, the popularity of sincerity in this sense. So used, the word is of little service in criticism, for this kind of sincerity in poetry must necessarily be rare.

It will be worth while hunting a little longer for a satisfactory sense of "sincerity." Whatever it is, it is the quality we most insistently require in poetry. It is also the quality we most need as critics. And, perhaps, in the proportion that we possess it we shall acknowledge that it is not a quality that we can take for granted in ourselves as our inalienable birthright. It fluctuates with our state of health, with the quality of our recent companions, with our responsibilty and our nearness to the object, with a score of conditions that are not easy to take account of. We can *feel* very sincere when, in fact, as others can see clearly, there is no sincerity in us. Bogus forms of the virtue waylay us—confident inner assurances and invasive rootless convictions. And when we doubt our own sincerity and ask ourselves, "Do I *really* think so; do I really feel so?" an honest answer is not easily come by. A direct effort to be sincere, like other efforts to will ourselves into action, more often than not frustrates its intention. For all these reasons any light that can be gained upon the nature of sincerity, upon possible tests for it and means for inducing and promoting it, is extremely serviceable to the critic.

The most stimulating discussion of this topic is to be found in the *Chung Yung* [8] (The Doctrine of the Mean, or Equilibrium and Harmony), the treatise that embodies the most interesting and the most puzzling part of the teachings of Confucius. A more distinct (and distinguished)

[8] As might be expected, no translation that entirely commends itself is available. Those to whom Legge's edition of *The Chinese Classics*, Vol. I, is not available, may consult the tranlsation by L. A. Lyall and King Chien-Kün, *The Chung Yung or The Centre, the Common* (Longmans), very literal, but perhaps slightly too much tinctured with a Y.M.C.A. flavour. Here what is translated by others "sincerity" or "singleness" is rendered by "to be true" and "being true." [Richards.]

word than "stimulating" would be in place to describe this treatise, were the invigorating effect of a careful reading easier to define. Sincerity—the object of some idea that seems to lie in the territory that "sincerity" covers—appears there as the beginning and end of personal character, the secret of the good life, the only means to good government, the means to give full development to our own natures, to give full development to the nature of others, and very much more. This virtue is as mysterious as it is powerful; and, where so many great sinologues and Chinese scholars have confessed themselves baffled, it would be absurd for one who knows no Chinese to suggest interpretations. But some speculations generated by a reading of translations may round off this chapter.

The following extracts from the *Chung Yung* seem the most relevant to our discussion.

"Sincerity is the way of Heaven. The attainment of sincerity is the way of men. He who possesses sincerity, is he who, without an effort, hits what is right, and apprehends, without the exercise of thought; he is the sage who naturally and easily embodies the right way. He who attains to sincerity, is he who chooses what is good, and firmly holds it fast" (Legge, XX, 18). "Sincerity is that whereby self-completion is effected, and its way is that by which man must direct himself" (Legge, XXV, 1).

"In self-completion the superior man completes other men and things also . . . and this is the way by which a union is effected of the external and the internal" (XXV, 3). "In the Book of Poetry, it is said, 'In hewing an axe-handle, in hewing an axe-handle, the pattern is not far off.' We grasp one axe-handle to hew the other, and yet, if we look askance from the one to the other, we may consider them as apart" (XIII, 2). "There is a way to the attainment of sincerity in one's self; if a man does not understand what is good, he will not attain sincerity in himself" (XX, 17). "When we have intelligence resulting from sincerity, this condition is to be ascribed to nature; when we have sincerity resulting from intelligence, this condition is to be ascribed to instruction. But given the sincerity, there shall be the intelligence, given the intelligence there shall be the sincerity" (XXI). How far apart any detailed precise ex-

position in English, or in any modern Western language, must be from the form of thought of the original, is shown if we compare a more literal version of this last passage: "Being true begets light, we call that nature. Light leads to being true, we call that teaching. What is true grows light; what is light grows true" (Lyall and King Chien-Kün, p. 16).

Meditating upon this chain of pronouncements we can perhaps construct (or discover) another sense of sincerity. One important enough to justify the stress so often laid upon this quality by critics, yet not compelling us to require an impossible perfection or inviting us to sentimental (Sense 3) indiscriminate over-admiration of the ebullitions of infants. And it may be possible, by apprehending this sense more clearly, to see what general conditions will encourage sincerity and what steps may be suggested to promote this mysterious but necessary virtue in the critic.

We may take self-completion as our starting-point. The completed mind would be that perfect mind we envisaged above, in which no disorder, no mutual frustration of impulses remained. Let us suppose that in the irremediable default of this perfection, default due to man's innate constitution and to the accidents to which he is exposed, there exists *a tendency towards increased order*,[9] a tendency which takes effect unless baffled by physical interferences (disease)

---

[9] I have in several other places made prolonged and determined efforts to indicate the types of mental order I have in mind (*The Foundations of Aesthetics*, § XIV; *Principles of Literary Criticism*, Ch. XXII; *Science and Poetry*, § II), but without escaping certain large misunderstandings that I had hoped to have guarded myself against. Thus Mr. Eliot, reviewing *Science and Poetry* in *The Dial*, describes my ideal order as "Efficiency, a perfectly-working mental Roneo Steel Cabinet System," and Mr. Read performing a similar service for *Principles* in *The Criterion*, seemed to understand that where I spoke of "the organisation of impulses" I meant that kind of deliberate planning and arrangement which the controllers of a good railway or large shop must carry out. But "organisation" for me stood for that kind of interdependence of parts which we allude to when we speak of living things as "organisms"; and the "order" which I make out to be so important is not tidiness. The distinguished names cited in this foot-note will protect the reader from a sense that these explanations are insulting to his intelligence. A good idea of some of the possibilities of order and disorder in the mind may be gained from Pavlov's *Conditioned Reflexes*. [Richards.]

or by fixations of habit that prevent us from continuing to learn by experience, or by ideas too invested with emotion for other ideas that disturb them to be formed, or by too lax and volatile a bond between our interests (a frivolousness that is perhaps due to the draining off of energy elsewhere) so that no formations firm enough to build upon result.

There is much to be said in favour of such a supposition. This tendency would be a need, in the sense defined above in this chapter—deriving in fact from *the* fundamental imbalance [10] to which biological development may be supposed to be due. This development with man (and his animal neighbours) seems to be predominantly in the direction of greater complexity and finer differentiation of responses. And it is easy to conceive the organism as relieving, through this differentiation, the strain put upon it by life in a partly uncongenial environment. It is but a step further to conceive it as also tending to relieve internal strains due to these developments imposed from without. And a re-ordering of its impulses so as to reduce their interferences with one another to a minimum would be the most successful—and the "natural" —direction which this tendency would take.

Such a re-ordering would be a partial self-completion, temporary and provisional upon the external world remaining for the individual much what it had been in the past. And by such self-completion the superior man *would* "effect a union of the external and the internal." Being more at one within itself the mind thereby becomes more appropriately responsive to the outer world. I am not suggesting that this is what Confucius meant. For him "to complete other men and things too," is possibly the prerogative of the force of example, other men merely imitating the conduct of the sage. But he *may* have meant that freedom calls out freedom; that those who are "most themselves"

cause others about them to become also "more themselves"; which would, perhaps, be a more sagacious observation. Perhaps, too, "the union of the external and the internal" meant for him something different from the accordance of our thoughts and feelings with reality. But certainly, for us, this accordance is one of the fruits of sincerity.

This tendency towards a more perfect order, as it takes effect, "enables us, without effort, to hit what is right, and, without the exercise of thought, to apprehend." The "exercise of thought" here must be understood as that process of deliberately setting aside inappropriate ideas and feelings, which, in default of a sufficient inner order—a sufficient sincerity—is still very necessary. Confucius has enough to say elsewhere in the *Chung Yung* (Ch. XX, 20) of the need for unremitting research and reflection *before* sincerity is attained to clear himself from any charge of recommending "intuition" as an *alternative* to investigation. "Intuition" is the prerogative only of those who have attained to sincerity. It is only the superior man who "naturally and easily embodies the right way." And the superior man will know when his sincerity is insufficient and take ceaseless steps to remedy it. "If another man (more sincere) succeeded by one effort, *he* will use a hundred efforts. If another man succeed by ten efforts, he will use a thousand" (*Chung Yung*, XX, 20). It is the sincerity to which the superior man has already attained which enables him to know when it is insufficient; if it does not yet enable him to embody the right way, it at least enables him to refrain from embodying the wrong, as those who trust intuition too soon are likely to do. Indeed, looking back over the history of thought, we might say, "are certain to do," so heavy are the probabilities against the success of guess-work.

Sincerity, then, in this sense, is obedience to that tendency which "seeks" a more perfect order within the mind. When the tendency is frustrated (*e.g.*, by fatigue or by an idea or feeling that has lost its link with experience, or has become fixed beyond the possibility of change) we have insincerity. When confusion reigns and we are unable to decide what we think or feel (to be distinguished sharply from

[10] Whether we can profitably posit a primal imbalance in certain forms of matter for which the appearance of living substances and their development in increasingly complex forms right up to Shakespeare would be, as it were, the swings of the pendulum "attempting" to come to rest again, is a speculation that has perhaps only an amusement value. The great difficulty would be to get round the separation of the reproductive functions, but that is a difficulty for any cosmologist. [Richards.]

the case when *decided* thoughts or feelings are present, but we are unable to define or express them) we need be neither sincere nor insincere. We are in a transitional stage which may result in either. Most good critics will confess to themselves that this is the state in which a first reading of any poem of an unfamiliar type leaves them. They know that more study is needed if they are to achieve a genuine response, and they know this in virtue of the sincerity they have already attained. It follows that people with clear definite ideas and feelings, with a high degree of practical efficiency, may be insincere in this sense. Other kinds of sincerity, fidelity to convictions for example, will not save them, and indeed it may well be this fidelity which is thwarting the life of the spirit (*Chung Yung,* XXIV) in them.

Any response (however mistaken from other points of view) which embodies the present activity of this tendency to inner adjustment will be sincere, and any response that conflicts with it or inhibits it will be insincere. Thus to be sincere is to act, feel and think in accordance with "one's true nature," and to be insincere is to act, feel or think in a contrary manner. But the sense to be given to "one's true nature" is, as we have seen, a matter largely conjectural. To define it more exactly would perhaps be tedious and, for our purposes here, needless. In practice we often seem to grasp it very clearly; and all that I have attempted here is to sketch the state of affairs which we then seem to grasp. "What heaven has conferred is man's Nature; an accordance with this is the Path" (*Chung Yung,* I). Sometimes we can be certain that we have left it.[11]

On the ways in which sincerity may be increased and extended Confucius is very definite. If we seek a standard for a new response whose sincerity may be in doubt, we shall find it, he says, in the very responses which make the new

one possible. The pattern for the new axe-handle is already in our hand, though its very nearness, our firm possession of it, may hide it from us. We need, of course, a founded assurance of the sincerity of these instrumental responses themselves, and this we can gain by comparison. What is meant by "making the thoughts sincere" is the allowing no self-deception, *"as when we hate a bad smell,* and as when we love what is beautiful" (*The Great Learning,* VI, i). When we hate a bad smell we can have no doubt that our response is sincere. We can all, at least, find *some* responses beyond suspicion. These are our standard. By studying our sincerity in the fields in which we are fully competent we can extend it into the fields in which our ability is still feeling its way. This seems to be the meaning of "choosing what is good and firmly holding fast to it," where "good" stands not for our Western ethical notion so much as for the fit and proper, sane and healthy. The man who does not "hate a bad smell" "does not understand what is good"; having no basis or standards, "he will not attain to sincerity."

Together with these, the simplest most definite responses, there may be suggested also, as standards for sincerity, the responses we make to the most baffling objects that can be presented to our consciousness. Something like a technique or ritual for heightening sincerity might well be worked out. When our response to a poem after our best efforts remains uncertain, when we are unsure whether the feelings it excites come from a deep source in our experience, whether our liking or disliking is genuine, is *ours,* or an accident of fashion, a response to surface detail or to essentials, we may perhaps help ourselves by considering it in a frame of feelings whose sincerity is beyond our questioning. Such are the feelings that may be aroused by contemplation of the following:

   i. Man's loneliness (the isolation of the human situation).
   ii. The facts of birth, and of death, in their inexplicable oddity.
   iii. The inconceivable immensity of the Universe.
   iv. Man's place in the perspective of time.
   v. The enormity of his ignorance.

[11] But see *Chung Yung,* I, 2. "The path may not be left for an instant. If it could be left, it would not be the path." Possibly we can escape this difficulty by admitting that all mental activities are, to some degree, the operation of the tendency we have been speaking of. Thus all are the Path. But the Path can be obstructed, and may have loops. "The regulation of (what keeps trim) the path is instruction" (*Chung Yung,* I, 1). [Richards.]

Taking these not as targets for doctrine,[12] but as the most incomprehensible and inexhaustible objects for meditation, while their reverberation lasts pass the poem through the mind, silently reciting it as slowly as it allows. Whether what it can stir in us is important or not to us will, perhaps, show itself then. Many religious exercises and some of the practices of divination and magic may be thought to be directed in part towards a similar quest for sanction, to be rituals designed to provide standards of sincerity.

[12] The perhaps not unintentional obliquity of Mr. Eliot's interpretations of my phrases in *The Use of Poetry*, pp. 131-5, prompts me to add these references:—

i. Thinking of the key, each confirms a prison
(*The Waste Land*, l. 414).
"My external sensations are no less private to myself than are my thoughts or my feelings. In either case my experience falls within my own circle, a circle closed on the outside; and, with all its elements alike, every sphere is opaque to the others which surround it."
(F. H. Bradley, *Appearance and Reality*, p. 346.)

ii. But Love has pitched his mansion in
The place of excrement.
(*Crazy Jane talks with the Bishop*.)

iii. More distant and more solemn
Than a fading star.
(*The Hollow Men*, II.)

iii. iv, v. "Je ne sais qui m'a mis au monde, ni ce que c'est que le monde, ni que moi-même; je suis dans une ignorance terrible de toutes choses . . .
"Je vois ces effroyables espaces de l'univers qui m'enfirment, et je me trouve attaché à un coin de cette vaste étendue, sans que je sache pourquoi je suis plutôt placé en ce lieu qu'en un autre, ni pourquoi ce peu de temps qui m'est donné à vivre m'est assigné à ce point plutôt qu'à un autre de toute l'éternité qui m'a précédé et de toute celle qui me suit."

To Pascal such contemplations, when they did not lead to religious belief, seemed monstrous and insupportable, Mr. Eliot seems to think they must be trivial.

v. Enormity not enormousness. The knowledge which is the opposite of ignorance here is *knowledge how*. It is by man's fault that he is so ignorant, he has not made his thoughts sincere. Cf. p. 288. [Richards.]

EDMUND WILSON (1895-   )

A MONG contemporary critics, Edmund Wilson is distinguished by a marked independence of mind that has prevented him, at least for any length of time, from allying himself with the more sectarian movements in English and American criticism of the past thirty years. His affinities are rather with the historical and sociological criticism developed in nineteenth-century France and Germany. His interest in viewing literature in the light of social pressures has led him to experiment both with a quasi-Marxist and also, in *The Wound and the Bow* (1941), with a Freudian interpretation

EDMUND WILSON. After graduating from Princeton (1916), Wilson worked for the New York *Sun* (1916-17), served in World War I, was managing editor of *Vanity Fair* (1920-21), and was later associated with the *New Republic* and the *New Yorker*. Besides his critical writing, he has published verse, prose fiction, plays, and works on travel and social conditions.
His critical work includes especially: *Axel's Castle* (1931); *The Triple Thinkers* (1938, rev. 1948); *The Wound and the Bow* (1941, rev. 1947); *Patriotic Gore: Studies in the Literature of the American Civil War* (1962); and *The Bit Between My Teeth: a Literary Chronicle of 1950-65* (1965). For commentary, see R. M. Adams, "Masks and Delays: Edmund Wilson as Critic,"

of literature. To this extent he may be regarded as attempting to develop a systematic approach as Taine did. But unlike Taine, Wilson has always been ready to revise his position in the light of further evidence.

Indeed, Wilson's closest progenitor among French critics is Sainte-Beuve rather than Taine or Renan. Especially in his *Triple Thinkers* (1938) he revives, more sucessfully than any other contemporary writer, the vivid "psychographic" portrait that Sainte-Beuve had perfected. Again as with Sainte-Beuve, his theoretical criteria are modified by his other qualities as a critic—by an awareness, for example, of the possibilities of historical genrecriticism like that developed by Brunetière, and shown in the present provocative essay, "Is Verse a Dying Technique?"—and also by a close imaginative grasp of the text before him and a vivid sympathetic interest in the character of particular writers. Again, Wilson's interests have not been restricted to English and American literature only, or, like those of so many recent critics, to poetry alone. His work is therefore characterized by a cosmopolitan perspective rare in modern criticism—a cosmopolitanism that is further sustained by his knowledge and use of the history of criticism itself. His elastic use of various approaches is particularly apparent in his treatment of a large literary movement in *Axel's Castle* (1931), which, more than any other critical work, first connected and interpreted for the present generation the development of modern symbolism. Here especially—like Hazlitt, who is Wilson's greatest predecessor among Anglo-American journalistic critics—he has been able to approach the literature of his own day in an objective and judicial fashion. While noting sympathetically its novel and distinctive merits, he has also been able to see, in large outline and without provinciality, its possible weaknesses by viewing it in the light not only of its own day but of the history of literature as a whole.

Sewanee Review, LVI (1948), 272-86; Warner B. Bertoff, *Edmund Wilson* (Minneapolis, 1968); Edward Fiess, "Edmund Wilson: Art and Idea," *Antioch Review*, I (1941), 356-67; C. I. Glicksberg, "Edmund Wilson: Radicalism at the Crossroads," *South Atlantic Quarterly*, XXXVI (1937), 466-77; and Paul Sherman, *Edmund Wilson: a Study of Literary Vocation in Our Time* (Urbana, 1965).

Is Verse a Dying Technique?

THE MORE one reads the current criticism of poetry by poets and their reviewers, the more one becomes convinced that the discussion is proceeding on false assumptions. The writers may belong to different schools, but they all seem to share a basic confusion.

This confusion is the result of a failure to

Is Verse a Dying Technique? From *The Triple Thinkers* (1928; rev. ed., 1948); reprinted by permission of Edmund Wilson.

think clearly about what is meant by the words "prose," "verse," and "poetry"—a question which is sometimes debated but which never gets straightened out. Yet are not the obvious facts as follows?

What we mean by the words "prose" and "verse" are simply two different techniques of literary expression. Verse is written in lines with a certain number of metrical feet each; prose is written in paragraphs and has what we call rhythm. But what is "poetry," then? What I want to suggest is that "poetry" formerly meant one kind of thing but that it now means something different, and that one ought not to generalize about "poetry" by taking all the writers of verse, ancient, medieval and modern, away from their various periods and throwing them together in one's mind, but to consider both verse and prose in relation to their functions at different times.

The important thing to recognize, it seems to me, is that the literary technique of verse was once made to serve many purposes for which we now, as a rule, use prose. Solon, the Athenian statesman, expounded his political ideas in verse; the *Works and Days* of Hesiod are a shepherd's calendar in verse; his *Theogony* is versified mythology; and almost everything that in contemporary writing would be put into prose plays and novels was versified by the Greeks in epics or plays.

It is true that Aristotle tried to discriminate. "We have no common name," he wrote, "for a mime of Sophron or Xenarchus and a Socratic conversation; and we should still be without one even if the imitation in the two instances were in trimeters or elegiacs or some other kind of verse —though it is the way with people to tack on 'poet' to the name of a meter, and talk of elegiac-poets and epic-poets, thinking that they call them poets not by reason of the imitative nature of their work, but indiscriminately by reason of the meter they write in. Even if a theory of medicine or physical philosophy be put forth in a metrical form, it is usual to describe the writer in this way; Homer and Empedocles, however, have really nothing in common apart from their meter; so that, if the one is to be called a poet, the other should be termed a physicist rather than a poet." [1]

But he admitted that there was no accepted name for the creative—what he calls the "imitative"—art which had for its mediums both prose and verse; and his posterity followed the custom of which he had pointed out the impropriety by calling anything in meter a "poem." The Romans wrote treatises in verse on philosophy and astronomy and farming. The "poetic" of Horace's *Ars Poetica* applies to the whole range of ancient verse—though Horace did think it

[1] *Poetics*, I, 7.

just as well to mingle the "agreeable" with the "useful"—and this essay in literary criticism is itself written in meter. "Poetry" remained identified with verse; and since for centuries both dramas and narratives continued largely to be written in verse, the term of which Aristotle had noticed the need—a term for imaginative literature itself, irrespective of literary techniques—never came into common use.

But when we arrive at the nineteenth century, a new conception of "poetry" appears. The change is seen very clearly in the doubts which began to be felt as to whether Pope were really a poet. Now, it is true that a critic like Johnson would hardly have assigned to Pope the position of pre-eminence he does at any other period than Johnson's own; but it is *not* true that only a critic of the latter part of the eighteenth century, a critic of an "age of prose," would have considered Pope a poet. Would not Pope have been considered a poet in any age before the age of Coleridge?

But the romantics were to redefine "poetry." Coleridge, in the *Biographia Literaria,* denies that any excellent work in meter may be properly called a "poem." "The final definition . . ." he says, "may be thus worded. A poem is that species of composition which is opposed to works of science by proposing for its *immediate* object pleasure, not truth; and from all other species— (having *this* object in common with it)—it is discriminated by proposing to itself such delight from the *whole* as is compatible with a distinct gratification from each component part." This would evidently exclude the *Ars Poetica* and the *De Rerum Natura,* whose immediate objects are as much truth as pleasure. What is really happening here is that for Coleridge the function of "poetry" is becoming more specialized. Why? Coleridge answers this question in formulating an objection which may be brought against the first part of his definition: "But the communication of pleasure may be the immediate object of a work not metrically composed; and that object may have been in a high degree attained, as in novels and romances." Precisely; and the novels and romances were formerly written in verse, whereas they are now usually written in prose. In Coleridge's time, tales in verse were more and more giving place to prose novels. Before long, novels in verse such as

Aurora Leigh and *The Ring and the Book* were to seem more or less literary oddities. "Poetry," then, for Coleridge, has become something which, unless he amends his definition, may equally well be written in prose: Isaiah and Plato and Jeremy Taylor will, as he admits, be describable as "poetry." Thereafter, he seems to become somewhat muddled; but he finally arrives at the conclusion that the "peculiar property of poetry" is "the property of exciting a more continuous and equal attention than the language of prose aims at, whether colloquial or written."

The truth is that Coleridge is having difficulties in attempting to derive his new conception of poetry from the literature of the past, which has been based on the old conception. Poe, writing thirty years later, was able to get a good deal further.[2] Coleridge had said—and it seems to have been really what he was principally trying to say—that "a poem of any length neither can be, nor ought to be, all poetry." (Yet are not the *Divine Comedy* and Shakespeare's tragedies "all poetry"? Or rather, in the case of these masterpieces, is not the work as a whole really a "poem," maintained, as it is, at a consistently high level of intensity and style and with the effects of the different parts dependent on one another?) Poe predicted that "no very long poem would ever be popular again," and made "poetry" mean something even more special by insisting that it should approach the indefiniteness of music. The reason why no very long poem was ever to be popular again was simply that verse as a technique was then passing out of fashion in every department of literature except those of lyric poetry and the short idyl. The long poems of the past—Shakespeare's plays, the *Divine Comedy*, the Greek dramatists and Homer—were going to continue to be popular; but writers of that caliber in the immediate future were not going to write in verse.

Matthew Arnold was to keep on in Coleridge's direction, though by a route somewhat different from Poe's. He said, as we have heard so repeatedly, that poetry was at bottom a criticism of life; but, though one of the characteristics which true poetry might possess was "moral profundity," another was "natural magic," and "eminent manifestations of this magical power of poetry"

2 See *The Poetic Principle*, above, p. 352.

were "very rare and very precious." "Poetry" is thus, it will be seen, steadily becoming rarer. Arnold loved quoting passages of natural magic and he suggested that the lover of literature should carry around in his mind as touchstones a handful of such topnotch passages to test any new verse he encountered. His method of presenting the poets makes poetry seem fleeting and quintessential. Arnold was not happy till he had edited Byron and Wordsworth in such a way as to make it appear that their "poetry" was a kind of elixir which had to be distilled from the mass of their work—rather difficult in Byron's case: a production like *Don Juan* does not really give up its essence in the sequences excerpted by Arnold.

There was, to be sure, some point in what Arnold was trying to do for these writers: Wordsworth and Byron both often wrote badly and flatly. But they would not have lent themselves at all to this high-handed kind of anthologizing if it had not been that, by this time, it had finally become almost impossible to handle large subjects successfully in verse. Matthew Arnold could have done nothing for Dante by reducing him to a little book of extracts—nor, with all Shakespeare's carelessness, for Shakespeare. The new specialized idea of poetry appears very plainly and oddly when Arnold writes about Homer: the *Iliad* and the *Odyssey*, which had been for the Greeks fiction and scripture, have come to appear to this critic long stretches of ancient legend from which we may pick out little crystals of moral profundity and natural magic.

And in the meantime the ideas of Poe, developed by the Symbolists in France, had given rise to the *Art poétique* of Verlaine, so different from that of Horace: "Music first of all . . . no Color, only the *nuance!* . . . Shun Point, the murderer, cruel Wit and Laughter the impure. . . . Take eloquence and wring its neck! . . . Let your verse be the luck of adventure flung to the crisp morning wing that brings us a fragrance of thyme and mint—and all the rest is literature."

Eliot and Valéry followed. Paul Valéry, still in the tradition of Poe, regarded a poem as a specialized machine for producing a certain kind of "state." Eliot called poetry a "superior amusement," and he anthologized, in both his poems and his essays, even more fastidiously than Arnold. He, too, has his favorite collection of magical and quintessential passages; and he possesses an uncanny gift for transmitting to them a personal accent and imbuing them with a personal significance. And as even those passages of Eliot's poems which have not been imitated or quoted often seemed to have been pieced together out of separate lines and fragments, so his imitators came to works in broken mosaics and "pinches of glory"—to use E. M. Forster's phrase about Eliot—rather than with conventional stanzas.

The result has been an optical illusion. The critic, when he read the classic, epic, eclogue, tale or play, may have grasped it and enjoyed it as a whole; yet when the reader reads the comment of the critic, he gets the impression, looking back on the poem, that the *Divine Comedy*, say, so extraordinarily sustained and so beautifully integrated, is remarkable mainly for Eliot-like fragments. Once we know Matthew Arnold's essay, we find that the ἀνήριθμον γέλασμα of Aeschylus and the "daffodils that come before the swallow dares" of Shakespeare tend to stick out from their contexts in a way that they hardly deserve to. Matthew Arnold, unintentionally and unconsciously, has had the effect of making the poet's "poetry" seem to be concentrated in the phrase or the line.

Finally, Mr. A. E. Housman, in his lecture on *The Name and Nature of Poetry*, has declared that he cannot define poetry. He can only become aware of its presence by the symptoms he finds it producing: "Experience has taught me, when I am shaving of a morning, to keep watch over my thought, because if a line of poetry strays into my memory, my skin bristles so that the razor ceases to act. This particular symptom is accompanied by a shiver down the spine; there is another which consists in a constriction of the throat and a precipitation of water to the eyes; and there is a third which I can only describe by borrowing a phrase from one of Keats's last letters, where he says, speaking of Fanny Brawne, 'everything that reminds me of her goes through me like a spear.' The seat of this sensation is the pit of the stomach."

One recognizes these symptoms; but there are other things, too, which produce these peculiar sensations: scenes from prose plays, for example (the final curtain of *The Playboy of the Western World* could make one's hair stand on end when it was first done by the Abbey Theater), passages from prose novels (Stephen Daedalus' broodings over his mother's death in the opening episode of *Ulysses* and the end of Mrs. Bloom's soliloquy), even scenes from certain historians, such as Mirabeau's arrival in Aix at the end of Michelet's *Louis XVI*, even passages in a philosophical dialogue: the conclusion of Plato's *Symposium*. Though Housman does praise a few long English poems, he has the effect, like these other critics, of creating the impression that "poetry" means primarily lyric verse, and this only at its most poignant or most musical moments.

Now all that has been said here is, of course, not intended to belittle the value of what such people as Coleridge and Poe, Arnold and Eliot have written on the subject of poetry. These men are all themselves first-class poets; and their criticism is very important because it constitutes an attempt to explain what they have aimed at in their own verse, of what they have conceived, in their age, to be possible or impossible for their medium.

Yet one feels that in the minds of all of them a certain confusion persists between the new idea of poetry and the old—between Coleridge's conception, on the one hand, and Horace's, on the other; that the technique of prose is inevitably tending more and more to take over the material which had formerly provided the subjects for compositions in verse, and that, as the two techniques of writing are beginning to appear, side by side or combined, in a single work, it is becoming more and more impossible to conduct any comparative discussion of literature on a basis of this misleading division of it into the departments of "poetry" and of "prose."

One result of discussion on this basis, especially if carried on by verse-writers, is the creation of an illusion that contemporary "poets" of relatively small stature (though of however authentic gifts) are the true inheritors of the genius and carriers-on of the tradition of Aeschylus, Sophocles and Virgil, Dante, Shakespeare and Milton. Is it not time to discard the word "poetry" or to define it in such a way as to take account of the fact that the most intense, the most profound, the most beautifully composed and the most comprehensive of the great works of literary art (which for these reasons are also the most thrilling and give us most prickly sensations while shaving) have been written some-times in verse technique, sometimes in prose tech-nique, depending partly on the taste of the au-thor, partly on the mere current fashion. It is only when we argue these matters that we be-come involved in absurdities. When we are read-ing, we appraise correctly. Matthew Arnold cites examples of that "natural magic" which he re-gards as one of the properties of "poetry" from Chateaubriand and Maurice de Guérin, who did not write verse but prose, as well as from Shake-speare and Keats; and he rashly includes Mo-lière among the "larger and more splendid lumi-naries in the poetical heaven," though Molière was scarcely more "poetic" in any sense except perhaps that of "moral profundity" when he wrote verse than when he wrote prose and would certainly not have versified at all if the conven-tions of his time had not demanded it. One who has first come to Flaubert at a sensitive age when he is also reading Dante may have the experi-ence of finding that the paragraphs of the former remain in his mind and continue to sing just as the lines of the latter do. He has got the prose by heart unconsciously just as he has done with favorite passages of verse; he repeats them, ad-miring the form, studying the choice of words, seeing more and more significance in them. He realizes that, though Dante may be greater than Flaubert, Flaubert belongs in Dante's class. It is simply that by Flaubert's time the Dantes pre-sent their visions in terms of prose drama or fiction rather than of epics in verse. At any other period, certainly, *La Tentation de Saint Antoine* would have been written in verse instead of prose.

And if one happens to read Virgil's *Georgics* not long after having read Flaubert, the shift from verse to prose technique gets the plainest demonstration possible. If you think of Virgil with Tennyson, you have the illusion that the Virgilian poets are shrinking; but if you think of Virgil with Flaubert, you can see how a great modern prose-writer has grown out of the great classical poets. Flaubert somewhere—I think, in the Goncourt journal—expresses his admiration for Virgil; and, in method as well as in mood, the two writers are often akin. Flaubert is no less accomplished in his use of words and rhythms than Virgil; and the poet is as success-ful as the novelist in conveying emotion through objective statement. The *Georgics* were seven

years in the writing, as *Madame Bovary* was six. And the fact that—in *Madame Bovary* especially —Flaubert's elegiac feeling as well as his rural settings run so close to the characteristic vein of Virgil makes the comparison particularly in-teresting. Put the bees of the *Georgics*, for ex-ample, whose swarming Virgil thus describes:

> *aethere in alto*
> *Fit sonitus, magnum mixtae glomerantur in orbem*
> *Praecipitesque cadunt* [3]

beside the bees seen and heard by Emma Bovary on an April afternoon: "quelquefois les abeilles, tournoyant dans la lumière, frappaient contre les carreaux comme des balles d'or rebondissantes." [4]

Put

> *Et iam summa procul villarum culmina fumant,*
> *Maioresque cadunt altis de montibus umbrae* [5]

beside: "La tendresse des anciens jours leur revenait au cœur, abondante et silencieuse comme la rivière qui coulait, avec autant de mollesse qu'en apportait le parfum des seringas, et proje-tait dans leurs souvenirs des ombres plus démesurées et plus mélancoliques que celles des saules immobiles qui s'allongeaient sur l'herbe." [6] And compare Virgil's sadness and wistfulness with the sadness and nostalgia of Flaubert: the melancholy of the mountainous pastures laid waste by the cattle plague:

> *desertaque regna*
> *Pastorum, et longe saltus lateque vacantes* [7]

with the modern desolations of Paris in *L'Edu-cation sentimentale:* "Les rues étaient désertes. Quelquefois une charrette lourde passait, en

---

[3] "High in the air a sound is made; they roll up together in one large ball and plunge downwards." (*Georgics*, IV, 78-80.)

[4] "Occasionally the bees, turning in the light, strike against the panes, like rebounding balls of gold."

[5] "And now, far away, smoke rises from the highest roofs of the houses, and widening shadows fall from the high mountains." (*Eclogues*, I, 82-83.)

[6] "The tenderness of days past returned to their hearts, abundant and silent, like a running river with the swift-ness borne by the perfume of the seringa, and project-ing into their memories shades more excessive and melancholy than those of the immobile willows that stretch themselves out over the grass."

[7] "The deserted kingdoms of shepherds; and, far and wide, the ravines lie empty." (*Georgics*, III, 476-77.)

ébranlant les pavés," etc.; [8] or Palinurus, fallen into the sea, swimming with effort to the coast of Italy, but only to be murdered and left there "naked on the unknown sand," while his soul, since his corpse lies unburied, must forever be excluded from Hades, or Orpheus still calling Eurydice when his head has been torn from his body, till his tongue has grown cold and the echo of his love has been lost among the river banks—compare these with Charles Bovary, a schoolboy, looking out on fine summer evenings at the sordid streets of Rouen and sniffing for the good country odors "qui ne venaient pas jusqu'à lui" [9]—("tendebantque manus ripae ulterioris amore") [10]—or with the scene in which Emma Bovary receives her father's letter and remembers the summers of her girlhood, with the galloping colts and the bumping bees, and knows that she has spent all her illusions in maidenhood, in marriage, in adultery, as a traveler leaves something of his money at each of the inns of the road.

We find, in this connection, in Flaubert's letters the most explicit statements. "To desire to give verse-rhythm to prose, yet to leave it prose and very much prose," he wrote to Louise Colet (March 27, 1853), "and to write about ordinary life as histories and epics are written, yet without falsifying the subject, is perhaps an absurd idea. Sometimes I almost think it is. But it may also be a great experiment and very original." The truth is that Flaubert is a crucial figure. He is the first great writer in prose deliberately to try to take over for the treatment of ambitious subjects the delicacy, the precision and the intensity that have hitherto been identified with verse. Henrik Ibsen, for the poetic drama, played a role hardly less important. Ibsen began as a writer of verse and composed many short and non-dramatic poems as well as *Peer Gynt* and *Brand* and his other plays in verse, but eventually changed over to prose for the concentrated Sophoclean tragedies that affected the whole dramatic tradition. Thereafter the dramatic "poets"—the Chekhovs, the Synges and the Shaws (Hauptmann had occasional relapses)

—wrote almost invariably in prose. It was by such that the soul of the time was given its dramatic expression: there was nothing left for Rostand's alexandrines but fireworks and declamation.

In the later generation, James Joyce, who had studied Flaubert and Ibsen as well as the great classical verse-masters, set out to merge the two techniques. Dickens and Herman Melville had occasionally resorted to blank verse for passages which they meant to be elevated, but these flights had not matched their context, and the effect had not been happy. Joyce, however, now, in *Ulysses,* has worked out a new medium of his own which enables him to exploit verse metrics in a texture which is basically prose; and he has created in *Finnegans Wake* a work of which we cannot say whether it ought, in the old-fashioned phraseology, to be described as prose or verse. A good deal of *Finnegans Wake* is written in regular meter and might perfectly well be printed as verse, but, except for the interpolated songs, the whole thing is printed as prose. As one reads it, one wonders, in any case, how anything could be demanded of "poetry" by Coleridge with his "sense of novelty and freshness with old and familiar objects," by Poe with his indefiniteness of music, by Arnold with his natural magic, by Verlaine with his nuance, by Eliot with his unearthliness, or by Housman with his bristling of the beard, which the *Anna Livia Plurabelle* chapter (or canto) does not fully supply.

If, then, we take literature as a whole for our field, we put an end to many futile controversies —the controversies, for example, as to whether or not Pope is a poet, as to whether or not Whitman is a poet. If you are prepared to admit that Pope is one of the great English writers, it is less interesting to compare him with Shakespeare —which will tell you something about the development of English verse but not bring out Pope's peculiar excellence—than to compare him with Thackeray, say, with whom he has his principal theme—the vanity of the world—in common and who throws into relief the more passionate pulse and the solider art of Pope. And so the effort to apply to Whitman the ordinary standards of verse has hindered the appreciation of his careful and exquisite art.

If, in writing about "poetry," one limits one-

[8] "The streets were deserted. Occasionally a heavy wagon passed, rattling the pavements."

[9] "Which did not reach that far to him."

[10] "They reach out loving hands to the farther shore." (*Aeneid,* VI, 314.)

self to "poets" who compose in verse, one excludes too much of modern literature, and with it too much of life. The best modern work in verse has been mostly in the shorter forms, and it may be that our lyric poets are comparable to any who have ever lived, but we have had no imaginations of the stature of Shakespeare or Dante who have done their major work in verse. The horizon and even the ambition of the contemporary writer of verse has narrowed with the specialization of the function of verse itself. (Though the novelists Proust and Joyce are both masters of what used to be called "numbers," the verses of the first are negligible and those of the second minor.)

Would not D. H. Lawrence, for example, if he had lived a century earlier, probably have told his tales, as Byron and Crabbe did: in verse? Is it not just as correct to consider him the last of the great English romantic poets as one of the most original of modern English novelists? Must we not, to appreciate Virginia Woolf, be aware that she is trying to do the kind of thing that the writers of verse have done even more than she is trying to do what Jane Austen or George Eliot were doing?

Recently the techniques of prose and verse have been getting mixed up at a bewildering rate —with the prose technique steadily gaining. You have had the verse technique of Ezra Pound gradually changing into prose technique. You have had William Faulkner, who began by writing verse, doing his major work in prose fiction without ever quite mastering prose, so that he may at any moment upset us by interpolating a patch of verse. You have had Robinson Jeffers, in narrative "poems" which are as much novels as some of Lawrence's, reeling out yards of what are really prose dithyrambs with a loose hexametric base; and you have had Carl Sandburg, of *The People, Yes,* producing a queer kind of literature which oscillates between something like verse and something like the paragraphs of a newspaper "column."

Sandburg and Pound have, of course, come out of the old *vers libre,* which, though prose-like, was either epigrammatic or had the rhythms of the Whitmanesque chant. But since the Sandburg-Pound generation, a new development in verse has taken place. The sharpness and the energy disappear; the beat gives way to a de-

moralized weariness. Here the "sprung-rhythm" of Gerard Manley Hopkins has sometimes set the example. But the difference is that Hopkins' rhythms convey agitation and tension, whereas the rhythms of MacNeice and Auden let down the taut traditions of lyric verse with an effect that is often comic and probably intended to be so—these poets are not far at moments from the humorous rhymed prose of Ogden Nash. And finally—what is very strange to see—Miss Edna St. Vincent Millay in *Conversation at Midnight,* slackening her old urgent pace, dimming the ring of her numbers, has given us a curious example of metrics in full dissolution, with the stress almost entirely neglected, the lines running on for paragraphs and even the rhymes sometimes fading out. In some specimens of this recent work, the beat of verse has been so slurred and muted that it might almost as well have been abandoned. We have at last lived to see the day when the ballads of Gilbert and Hood, written without meter for comic effect in long lines that look and sound like paragraphs, have actually become the type of a certain amount of serious poetry.

You have also the paradox of Eliot attempting to revive the verse-drama with rhythms which, adapting themselves to the rhythms of colloquial speech, run sometimes closer to prose. And you have Mr. Maxwell Anderson trying to renovate the modern theater by bringing back blank verse again—with the result that, once a writer of prose dialogue distinguished by some color and wit, he has become, as a dramatic poet, banal and insipid beyond belief. The trouble is that no verse technique is more obsolete today than blank verse. The old iambic pentameters have no longer any relation whatever to the tempo and language of our lives. Yeats was the last who could write them, and he only because he inhabited, in Ireland and in imagination, a grandiose anachronistic world. You cannot deal with contemporary events in an idiom which was already growing trite in Tennyson's and Arnold's day; and if you try to combine the rhythm of blank verse with the idiom of ordinary talk, you get something—as in Anderson's *Winterset*— which lacks the merits of either. Nor can you try to exploit the worked-out rhythm without also finding yourself let in for the antiquated point of view. The comments on the action in *Winterset* are never the expression of sentiments which we ourselves could conceivably feel in connection with the events depicted: they are the echoes of Greek choruses and Elizabethan soliloquies reflecting upon happenings of a different kind.

Thus if the poets of the Auden-MacNeice school find verse turning to prose in their hands, like the neck of the flamingo in Lewis Carroll with which Alice tried to play croquet, Mr. Anderson, returning to blank verse, finds himself in the more awkward predicament of the girl in the fairy tale who could never open her mouth without having a toad jump out.

But what has happened? What, then, is the cause of this disuse into which verse technique has been falling for at least the last two hundred years? And what are we to expect in the future? Is verse to be limited now to increasingly specialized functions and finally to go out altogether? Or will it recover the domains it has lost?

To find out, if it is possible to do so, we should be forced to approach this change from the anthropological and sociological points of view. Is verse a more primitive technique than prose? Are its fixed rules like the syntax of languages, which are found to have been stiffer and more complicated the further back one goes? Aside from the question of the requirements of taste and the self-imposed difficulties of form which have always, in any period, been involved in the production of great works of art, does the easy flexibility, say, of modern English prose bear to the versification of Horace the same relation that English syntax bears to Horace's syntax, or that Horace's bears to that of the Eskimos?

It seems obvious that one of the important factors in the history of the development of verse must have been its relations with music. Greek verse grew up in fusion with music: verse and music were learned together. It was not till after Alexander the Great that prosody was detached from harmony. The Greek name for "prose" was "bare words"—that is, words divorced from music. But what the Romans took over and developed was a prosody that was purely literary. This, I believe, accounts for the fact that we seem to find in Greek poetry, if we compare it with Latin poetry, so little exact visual observation. Greek poetry is mainly for the ear. Compare a

landscape in one of the choruses of Sophocles or Aristophanes with a landscape of Virgil or Horace: the Greeks are *singing* about the landscape, the Romans are fixing it for the eye of the mind; and it is Virgil and Horace who lead the way to all the later picture poetry down to our own Imagists. Again, in the Elizabethan age, the English were extremely musical: the lyrics of Campion could hardly have been composed apart from their musical settings; and Shakespeare is permeated with music. When Shakespeare wants to make us see something, he is always compelling and brilliant; but the effect has been liquefied by music so that it sometimes gives a little the impression of objects seen under water. The main stream of English poetry continues to keep fairly close to music through Milton, the musician's son, and even through the less organ-voiced Dryden. What has really happened with Pope is that the musical background is no longer there and that the ocular sense has grown sharp again. After this, the real music of verse is largely confined to lyrics—songs—and it becomes more and more of a trick to write them so that they seem authentic—that is, so that they sound like something sung. It was the aim of the late-nineteenth-century Symbolists, who derived their theory from Poe, to bring verse closer to music again, in opposition to the school of the Parnassians, who cultivated an opaque objectivity. And the excellence of Miss Millay's lyrics is obviously connected with her musical training, as the metrical parts of Joyce—such as the Sirens episode in *Ulysses*, which attempts to render music, the response to a song of its hearer—are obviously associated with his vocal gifts. (There is of course a kind of poetry which produces plastic effects not merely by picture-making through explicit descriptions or images, but by giving the language itself—as Allen Tate is able to do—a plastic quality rather than a musical one.)

We might perhaps see a revival of verse in a period and in a society in which music played a leading role. It has long played a great role in Russia; and in the Soviet Union at the present time you find people declaiming poetry at drinking parties or while traveling on boats and trains almost as readily as they burst into song to the accordion or the balalaika, and flocking to poetry-readings just as they do to concerts. It is possible that the Russians at the present time show more of an appetite for "poetry," if not always for the best grade of literature, than any of the Western peoples. Their language, half-chanted and strongly stressed, in many ways extremely primitive, provides by itself, as Italian does, a constant stimulus to the writing of verse.

Here in the United States, we have produced some of our truest poetry in the folk-songs that are inseparable from their tunes. One is surprised, in going through the collections of American popular songs (of Abbé Niles and W. C. Handy, of Carl Sandburg, of the various students trained by Professor Kittredge), which have appeared during the last ten or fifteen years, to discover that the peopling of the continent has had as a by-product a body of folk-verse not unworthy of comparison with the similar material that went to make Percy's *Reliques*. The air of the popular song will no doubt be carrying the words that go with it into the "poetry" anthologies of the future when many of the set-pieces of "poetry," which strain to catch a music gone with Shakespeare, will have come to seem words on the page, incapable of reverberation or of flight from between the covers.

Another pressure that has helped to discourage verse has undoubtedly been the increased demand for reading matter which has been stimulated by the invention of the printing press and which, because ordinary prose is easier to write than verse, has been largely supplied by prose. Modern journalism has brought forth new art-forms; and you have had not only the masterpieces of fiction of such novelists as Flaubert and Joyce, who are also consummate artists in the sense that the great classical poets were, but also the work of men like Balzac and Dickens which lacks the tight organization and the careful attention to detail of the classical epic or drama, and which has to be read rapidly in bulk. The novels of such writers are the epics of societies: they have neither the concision of the folk-song nor the elegance of the forms of the court; they sprawl and swarm over enormous areas like the city populations they deal with. Their authors, no longer schooled in the literary tradition of the Renaissance, speak the practical everyday language of the dominant middle class, which has destroyed the Renaissance world. Even a writer like Dostoevsky rises out of this weltering literature. You cannot say that his insight is less deep, that his vision is less noble or narrower, or that his mastery of his art is less complete than that of the great poets of the past. You can say only that what he achieves he achieves by somewhat different methods.

The technique of prose today seems thus to be absorbing the technique of verse; but it is showing itself quite equal to that work of the imagination which caused men to call Homer "divine": that re-creation, in the harmony and logic of words, of the cruel confusion of life. Not, of course, that we shall have Dante and Shakespeare redone in some prose form any more than we shall have Homer in prose. In art, the same things are not done again or not done again except as copies. The point is that literary techniques are tools, which the masters of the craft have to alter in adapting them to fresh uses. To be too much attached to the traditional tools may be sometimes to ignore the new masters.

1948. The recent work of W. H. Auden has not shown a running-to-seed of the tendencies mentioned above, but has on the contrary taken the direction of returning to the older tradition of serviceable and vigorous English verse. His *New Year Letter* must be the best specimen of purely didactic verse since the end of the eighteenth century, and the alliterative Anglo-Saxon meter exploited in *The Age of Anxiety* has nothing in common with prose. It may, however, be pointed out, for the sake of my argument above, that in the speech of the girl over the sleeping boy in the fifth section of the latter poem, the poet has found it easy to slip into the rhythms and accents of Mrs. Earwicker's half-prose soliloquy at the end of *Finnegans Wake*.

NORTHROP FRYE (1912-   )

ALONE AMONG twentieth-century critics, Northrop Frye offers a comprehensive, closely argued, and systematic theory of literature. This has made him the most controversial, and probably the most influential, critic writing in English since the 1950's. In the humanities, as contrasted with sciences based on demonstrative and step-by-step argument, system is always controversial (though this is true only if it is ably presented; otherwise it is simply disregarded). For the very thing that makes system so appealing to some people also creates resistance in others: the fact that it *simplifies*. The question is whether the gains outweigh in importance what the system inevitably has to exclude or disregard for the sake of system. The controversy intensifies to the degree that what is gained and what is left out are both felt to be significant.

In the remarkable theory of literature Frye presents, the gains are enormous. The past half century has hungered for a new essentialism that will clear the ground of clutter; that will help us overcome what we feel to be the needless modern division between "popular" and "sophisticated" (or elitistic) art; that will rescue the past (primitive, classical, mediaeval, Renaissance, and so on up to yesterday) while it also appreciates and makes sense of the present and the foreseeable future; that will subsume those studies (for example, psychoanalysis or anthropology) which seem to threaten established "classical values" while, at the same time, it recognizes those classical values. All of this Frye attempts brilliantly to do. The price paid (but largely in theory rather than in Frye's own practice) is the apparent surrender of those two parts of humanistic criticism that are always most open to contention: (1) the relation of art (the frankly imaginative world man constructs) to life itself; and (2) the whole problem

NORTHROP FRYE. Born in Sherbrooke, Quebec, Frye was educated at the University of Toronto (B.A. 1933), studied theology at Emmanuel College, Toronto, and was ordained in the ministry of the United Church of Canada in 1936. Returning to literary studies, he attended Merton College, Oxford (M.A. 1941), where he became Assistant Professor of English in 1942, and then Professor in 1948 at Victoria College, Toronto. In 1959 he became Principal of the College and in 1967 University Professor at the University of Toronto.

Frye's critical works include: *Fearful Symmetry: a Study of William Blake* (1947); *Anatomy of Criticism* (1957); *The Well-Tempered Critic* (1963); *The Educated Imagination* (1963); *T. S. Eliot* (1963); *The Fables of Identity* (1963); *A Natural Perspective: the Development of Shakespearean Comedy and Romance* (1965); *The Return of Eden: Five Essays on Milton's Epics* (1965); *Fools of Time: Studies in Shakespearean Tragedy* (1967); *The Modern Century* (1967); and *A Study of English Romanticism* (1968). Commentary includes: Frank Kermode, "Northrop Frye," *Puzzles and Epiphanies* (1962); and Murray Krieger (ed.), *Northrop Frye in Modern Criticism: Selected Papers from the English Institute* (1966), containing essays by M. Krieger, Angus Fletcher, W. K. Wimsatt, G. H. Hartmann, Northrop Frye, and a bibliography of evaluation. We should state at once that Frye himself does not deny the human urgency of these two issues. He could justly say that he takes them for granted but that our need now is simply to agree on a basic alphabet for the criticism of the arts. Similarly, physicists and biologists, for example, needed at the start to set aside broader considerations of nature and to play more closely to the ground, accepting self-imposed limitations.

With this as his premise, Frye postulates the whole realm of literature (and, for that matter, art in general) as an almost self-contained universe in itself: a unique and massive product of the imagination of humankind. In Shakespeare's phrase, we "are of imagination all compact." From the beginning, and step by step as he has developed, man has encountered the world—other people, and the nonhuman world outside—through his own imagination, where he sometimes suffuses all he has encountered with his own desires and fears and sometimes objectively recognizes and assimilates. Expressing this whole experience—soliloquy, projection, imaginary dialogue, attempts to square dreams, hopes, and fears, with actuality—is the province of literature that, following the Romantics, we call "creative"— that is, "fictional" or "imaginative." * And this "second nature" that man has created is self-perpetuating, for literature develops from literature, and once it begins it is autonomous, like music or mathematics. Primitive man starts with ritual and myth, which is an "effort of the imagination to identify the human with the nonhuman world, and its most typical result is a story about a god. Later on, mythology begins to merge into literature, and myth then becomes a structural principle of story-telling" (*The Educated Imagination*, Ch. V). The word "myth," as used by Frye, does not suggest falsity. One can, for example, be devoutly religious and yet say, as does Frye, that the supreme example of myth for the literatures of the Western world is the Bible, which ideally "should be taught so early and so thoroughly that it sinks straight to the bottom of the mind, where everything that comes along later can settle on it." (The next step in literary educa-

---

by J. E. Grant. Discussions of Frye are found in A. Fletcher, *Allegory* (1964); L. T. Lemon, *The Partial Critics* (1965); F. E. Sparshott, *Structure of Aesthetics* (1963); and W. Sutton, *Modern American Criticism* (1963).

* Frye does not pretend to offer—nor has criticism generally since the start of the Romantic period (around 1770-1800) been able to offer—a means of discussing the literary value of writing that is not fictional (including oratory, history, moral philosophy, and even criticism itself). This has been one of the limitations of the Romantic legacy (as contrasted with the classical interest in "Rhetoric" from ancient Greece to the later eighteenth century); and the twentieth century, even when it has liked to consider itself "anti-Romantic," has not only inherited this limitation but has magnified it. Yet we all agree theoretically that literature, in its broadest sense, includes the entire written record of man's experience; and that some of this, which is not fictional, is of the highest literary quality. Thus the orations of Edmund Burke have been justly praised by every major prose writer of the last two centuries as one of the supreme examples of English style. And most of us would agree that Lincoln's "Gettysburg Address," Bacon's *Essays*, Johnson's *Lives of the Poets*, and Gibbon's *Decline and Fall of the Roman Empire* are, as literature, superior to most of the novels, poems, and plays that have been written. To rediscover the means of considering the literary values of such works is one of the most challenging opportunities criticism faces.

tion would be a direct acquaintance with the massive and fertile imaginative construct we call classical or Greek mythology.) In every period, the greatest writers have constantly reverted to the essential, the archetypal. The word "archetype" means literally the first, major, or ruling example or pattern. Even the lesser writer flirts with the archetypal, and we find the trashiest novel going back to the same ideas (for example, the idea of the quest). The original patterns of myths are changed through what psychoanalysis calls "displacement." This means that basic instinctual drives and goals are disguised or changed so that what is being said or wanted will seem more plausible or more aesthetically and morally acceptable.

Criticism can cut through the nonessential and help us to get our bearings, if it pushes aside all extra-literary considerations (psychological, sociological, biographical, political, historical), establishes itself on the fundamental criterion of the archetypically essential; and leaves aside the whole problem of evaluation (that is, the matter of taste). This is not to deny the importance of taste or evaluation, but, as indeed everyone knows, they are not subjects susceptible to science. We are concerned with what will permit criticism to attain some of the characteristics of a science, for criticism would then be something we could teach. We cannot "teach" literature any more than we can teach nature, though we can teach physics or biology, because literature is an object, not a subject, of study. What we can do is teach a science that will then help us *explore* literature or nature. At the same time, we are taking it for granted that man's encounter with literature, his experience of it, need not be confined to criticism—any more than his experience of nature is confined to the science of physics or biology.

Frye's first book was *Fearful Symmetry: a Study of William Blake* (1947). The process of writing this valuable critique opened up, to a scholar already well grounded in biblical and classical studies, the whole world of the "subjective imagination." Frye began immediately to reconsider the human literary effort from a synoptic view that would make room for the traditional (biblical and classical) as well as for the subjective. The result was the *Anatomy of Criticism: Four Essays* (1957), from which we reprint a part of the "Polemical Introduction" and the "Tentative Conclusion." The four parts of the book itself discuss: (1) a theory of the essential modes of narrative literature, from early myth to the present day, in relation to the kind of hero or principal character; (2) various kinds of symbolizing as they express or are appropriate to these modes; (3) Frye's general theory of literary myth—that is, the fundamental kinds of story; and (4) the theory of literary kinds, or genres. In the limited space available, it is impossible to give a fair impression of the book through just a few excerpts from these four sections, for the argument is closely reasoned, and each section depends on the other. Accordingly, in the selections from Frye that are reprinted below, a brief summary of the book has been in-

IMPLICIT IN W BLAKE IS AN UNIFIED FIELD OF LITERATURE

serted between the Introduction and Conclusion. Also reprinted as an alternative to the much longer discussions in the *Anatomy of Criticism* are two important essays: "The Archetypes of Literature" (1951), in which Frye provides, in his own words, an abbreviated statement of the critical program worked out in the *Anatomy;* and "Myth, Fiction, and Displacement" (1961), which also discusses central ideas that had been treated at length in the *Anatomy.* Both essays appear in his book *The Fables of Identity* (1963). Later books by Frye include *The Well-Tempered Critic* (1963), *The Educated Imagination* (1963), *The Modern Century* (1967), two books on Shakespeare—*A Natural Perspective* (1965), on comedy and romance, and *Fools of Time* (1967), on Shakespeare's tragedies—and *The Return of Eden: Five Essays on Milton's Epics* (1968).

The later works do not depart from or essentially qualify Frye's position in the *Anatomy,* but they extend and ramify it. They also illustrate, especially in their concern with education, something that was rather lost sight of when the *Anatomy* first appeared, and attention, whether favorably or unfavorably disposed, was focused almost entirely on his system of criticism *as* system. The reference here is to his general hope and effort as a humanist; for, like I. A. Richards, though in another way, Frye is essentially in the Arnoldian tradition as an "apologist" for literature. The tradition, of course, goes back through the Renaissance, and writers like Sir Philip Sidney, to ancient Greece. But we think of Arnold especially because he was at the threshold of the central problem that the humanist in our own century faces: How to preserve the precarious legacy of the humanities in the face of the twentieth-century rush of technology, population crowding, and paralysis or breakdown before the task of mass education. To put it more specifically: How do we save the great classics of Western literature—and save them not only for the elite but even, once again, for popular use? As with Arnold, there is a desire in Frye to recur to what we may call the "grand simplicities" of literature. We could even take as a motto for Frye's general effort as a critic Arnold's remark of more than a century ago (p. 446, above), about literature's appeal "to the great primary affections: to those elementary feelings which subsist permanently in the race, and which are independent of time. These feelings are permanent and the same; that which interests them is permanent and the same also." There are, of course, differences between the two men about the means (not to mention differences in what Frye would call "taste" as distinct from "criticism"). Secondly, Frye is more aware of history; for example, though he seeks to free us from the clutch of historical determinism, he is fascinated by the great twentieth-century cyclical theories of history (as in Spengler's *Decline of the West* or Toynbee's *Study of History*) that conceive us to be in an "autumnal" or "late" phase of our culture. Yet he is less sad than Arnold (though Arnold had a courageously gallant and even jaunty side) and, like Samuel Johnson, sees no reason for folding our hands and accepting the excuses of historical determinism. In any case, it is this essentialism, this desire to recur to the fundamental, that is Frye's greatest strength. It provides motive and creative resource in his thinking; and his concern arouses immediate response in our own generation as we seek, before the end of the twentieth century, to regain our bearings.

The Archetypes of Literature

EVERY organized body of knowledge can be learned progressively; and experience shows that there is also something progressive about the learning of literature. Our opening sentence has already got us into a semantic difficulty. Physics is an organized body of knowledge about nature, and a student of it says that he is learning physics, not that he is learning nature. Art, like nature, is the subject of a systematic study, and has to be distinguished from the study itself, which is criticism. It is therefore impossible to "learn literature": one learns about it in a certain way, but what one learns, transitively, is the criticism of literature. Similarly, the difficulty often felt in "teaching literature" arises from the fact that it cannot be done: the criticism of literature is all that can be directly taught. So while no one expects literature itself to behave like a science, there is surely no reason why criticism, as a systematic and organized study, should not be, at least partly, a science. Not a "pure" or "exact" science, perhaps, but these phrases form part of a 19th century cosmology which is no longer with us. Criticism deals with the arts and may well be something of an art itself, but it does not follow that it must be unsystematic. If it is to be related to the sciences too, it does not follow that it must be deprived of the graces of culture.

Certainly criticism as we find it in learned journals and scholarly monographs has every characteristic of a science. Evidence is examined

scientifically; previous authorities are used scientifically; fields are investigated scientifically; texts are edited scientifically. Prosody is scientific in structure; so is phonetics; so is philology. And yet in studying this kind of critical science the student becomes aware of a centrifugal movement carrying him away from literature. He finds that literature is the central division of the "humanities," flanked on one side by history and on the other by philosophy. Criticism so far ranks only as a subdivision of literature; and hence, for the systematic mental organization of the subject, the student has to turn to the conceptual framework of the historian for events, and to that of the philosopher for ideas. Even the more centrally placed critical sciences, such as textual editing, seem to be part of a "background" that recedes into history or some other non-literary field. The thought suggests itself that the ancillary critical disciplines may be related to a central expanding pattern of systematic comprehension which has not yet been established, but which, if it were established, would prevent them from being centrifugal. If such a pattern exists, then criticism would be to art what philosophy is to wisdom and history to action.

Most of the central area of criticism is at present, and doubtless always will be, the area of commentary. But the commentators have little sense, unlike the researchers, of being contained within some sort of scientific discipline: they are chiefly engaged, in the words of the gospel hymn, in brightening the corner where they are. If we attempt to get a more comprehensive idea of what criticism is about, we find ourselves wandering over quaking bogs of generalities, judicious pronouncements of value, reflective comments, perorations to works of research, and

The Archetypes of Literature. First published in *The Kenyon Review*, XIII (1951). Reprinted in Frye's *The Fables of Identity: Studies in Poetic Mythology*, copyright, 1963, by Harcourt Brace Jovanovich, Inc. The article, said Frye, is "to some extent a summarized statement of the critical program" later worked out in his *Anatomy of Criticism* (1957).

other consequences of taking the large view. But this part of the critical field is so full of pseudo-propositions, sonorous nonsense that contains no truth and no falsehood, that it obviously exists only because criticism, like nature, prefers a waste space to an empty one.

The term "pseudo-proposition" may imply some sort of logical positivist attitude on my own part. But I would not confuse the significant proposition with the factual one; nor should I consider it advisable to muddle the study of literature with a schizophrenic dichotomy between subjective-emotional and objective-descriptive aspects of meaning, considering that in order to produce any literary meaning at all one has to ignore this dichotomy. I say only that the principles by which one can distinguish a significant from a meaningless statement in criticism are not clearly defined. Our first step, therefore, is to recognize and get rid of meaningless criticism: that is, talking about literature in a way that cannot help to build up a systematic structure of knowledge. Casual value-judgments belong not to criticism but to the history of taste, and reflect, at best, only the social and psychological compulsions which prompted their utterance. All judgments in which the values are not based on literary experience but are sentimental or derived from religious or political prejudice may be regarded as casual. Sentimental judgments are usually based either on non-existent categories or antitheses ("Shakespeare studied life, Milton books") or on a visceral reaction to the writer's personality. The literary chit-chat which makes the reputations of poets boom and crash in an imaginary stock exchange is pseudo-criticism. That wealthy investor Mr. Eliot, after dumping Milton on the market, is now buying him again; Donne has probably reached his peak and will begin to taper off; Tennyson may be in for a slight flutter but the Shelley stocks are still bearish. This sort of thing cannot be part of any systematic study, for a systematic study can only progress: whatever dithers or vacillates or reacts is merely leisure-class conversation.

We next meet a more serious group of critics who say: the foreground of criticism is the impact of literature on the reader. Let us, then, keep the study of literature centripetal, and base the learning process on a structural analysis of the literary work itself. The texture of any great work of art is complex and ambiguous, and in unravelling the complexities we may take in as much history and philosophy as we please, if the subject of our study remains at the center. If it does not, we may find that in our anxiety to write about literature we have forgotten how to read it.

The only weakness in this approach is that it is conceived primarily as the antithesis of centrifugal or "background" criticism, and so lands us in a somewhat unreal dilemma, like the conflict of internal and external relations in philosophy. Antitheses are usually resolved, not by picking one side and refuting the other, or by making eclectic choices between them, but by trying to get past the antithetical way of stating the problem. It is right that the first effort of critical apprehension should take the form of a rhetorical or structural analysis of a work of art. But a purely structural approach has the same limitation in criticism that it has in biology. In itself it is simply a discrete series of analyses based on the mere existence of the literary structure, without developing any explanation of how the structure came to be what it was and what its nearest relatives are. Structural analysis brings rhetoric back to criticism, but we need a new poetics as well, and the attempt to construct a new poetics out of rhetoric alone can hardly avoid a mere complication of rhetorical terms into a sterile jargon. I suggest that what is at present missing from literary criticism is a coordinating principle, a central hypothesis which, like the theory of evolution in biology, will see the phenomena it deals with as parts of a whole. Such a principle, though it would retain the centripetal perspective of structural analysis, would try to give the same perspective to other kinds of criticism too.

The first postulate of this hypothesis is the same as that of any science: the assumption of total coherence. The assumption refers to the science, not to what it deals with. A belief in an order of nature is an inference from the intelligibility of the natural sciences; and if the natural sciences ever completely demonstrated the order of nature they would presumably exhaust their subject. Criticism, as a science, is totally intelligible; literature, as the subject of a science, is, so far as we know, an inexhaustible source of new critical discoveries, and would be even if new works of literature ceased to be written. If so, then the search for a limiting principle in literature in order to discourage the development of criticism is mistaken. The assertion that the critic should not look for more in a poem than the poet may safely be assumed to have been conscious of putting there is a common form of what may be called the fallacy of premature teleology. It corresponds to the assertion that a natural phenomenon is as it is because Providence in its inscrutable wisdom made it so.

Simple as the assumption appears, it takes a long time for a science to discover that it is in fact a totally intelligible body of knowledge. Until it makes this discovery it has not been born as an individual science, but remains an embryo within the body of some other subject. The birth of physics from "natural philosophy" and of sociology from "moral philosophy" will illustrate the process. It is also very approximately true that the modern sciences have developed in the order of their closeness to mathematics. Thus physics and astronomy assumed their modern form in the Renaissance, chemistry in the 18th century, biology in the 19th and the social sciences in the 20th. If systematic criticism, then, is developing only in our day, the fact is at least not an anachronism.

We are now looking for classifying principles lying in an area between two points that we have fixed. The first of these is the preliminary effort of criticism, the structural analysis of the work of art. The second is the assumption that there is such a subject as criticism, and that it makes, or could make, complete sense. We may next proceed inductively from structural analysis, associating the data we collect and trying to see larger patterns in them. Or we may proceed deductively, with the consequences that follow from postulating the unity of criticism. It is clear, of course, that neither procedure will work indefinitely without correction from the other. Pure induction will get us lost in haphazard guessing; pure deduction will lead to inflexible and oversimplified pigeonholing. Let us now attempt a few tentative steps in each direction, beginning with the inductive one.

II

The unity of a work of art, the basis of structural analysis, has not been produced solely by the unconditioned will of the artist, for the artist is only its efficient cause: it has form, and consequently a formal cause. The fact that revision is possible, that the poet makes changes not because he likes them better but because they are better, means that poems, like poets, are born and not made. The poet's task is to deliver the poem in as uninjured a state as possible, and if the poem is alive, it is equally anxious to be rid of him, and screams to be cut loose from his private memories and associations, his desire for self-expression, and all the other navel-strings and feeding tubes of his ego. The critic takes over where the poet leaves off, and criticism can hardly do without a kind of literary psychology connecting the poet with the poem. Part of this may be a psychological study of the poet, though this is useful chiefly in analysing the failures in his expression, the things in him which are still attached to his work. More important is the fact that every poet has his private mythology, his own spectroscopic band or peculiar formation of symbols, of much of which he is quite unconscious. In works with characters of their own, such as dramas and novels, the same psychological analysis may be extended to the interplay of characters, though of course literary psychology would analyse the behavior of such characters only in relation to literary convention.

There is still before us the problem of the formal cause of the poem, a problem deeply involved with the question of genres. We cannot say much about genres, for criticism does not know much about them. A good many critical efforts to grapple with such words as "novel" or "epic" are chiefly interesting as examples of the psychology of rumor. Two conceptions of the genre, however, are obviously fallacious, and as they are opposite extremes, the truth must lie somewhere between them. One is the pseudo-Platonic conception of genres as existing prior to and independently of creation, which confuses them with mere conventions of form like the sonnet. The other is that pseudo-biological conception of them as evolving species which turns up in so many surveys of the "development" of this or that form.

We next inquire for the origin of the genre, and turn first of all to the social conditions and cultural demands which produced it—in other words to the material cause of the work of art. This leads us into literary history, which differs from ordinary history in that its containing categories, "Gothic," "Baroque," "Romantic," and the like are cultural categories, of little use to the ordinary historian. Most literary history does not get as far as these categories, but even so we know more about it than about most kinds of critical scholarship. The historian treats literature and philosophy historically; the philosopher treats history and literature philosophically; and the so-called history of ideas approach marks the beginning of an attempt to treat history and philosophy from the point of view of an autonomous criticism.

But still we feel that there is something missing. We say that every poet has his own peculiar formation of images. But when so many poets use so many of the same images, surely there are much bigger critical problems involved than biographical ones. As Mr. Auden's brilliant essay *The Enchafèd Flood* shows, an important symbol like the sea cannot remain within the poetry of Shelley or Keats or Coleridge: it is bound to expand over many poets into an archetypal symbol of literature. And if the genre has a historical origin, why does the genre of drama emerge from medieval religion in a way so strikingly similar to the way it emerged from Greek religion centuries before? This is a problem of structure rather than origin, and suggests that there may be archetypes of genres as well as of images.

It is clear that criticism cannot be systematic unless there is a quality in literature which enables it to be so, an order of words corresponding to the order of nature in the natural sciences. An archetype should be not only a unifying category of criticism, but itself a part of a total form, and it leads us at once to the question of what sort of total form criticism can see in literature. Our survey of critical techniques has taken us as far as literary history. Total literary history moves from the primitive to the sophisticated, and here we glimpse the possibility of seeing literature as a complication of a relatively re-

stricted and simple group of formulas that can be studied in primitive culture. If so, then the search for archetypes is a kind of literary anthropology, concerned with the way that literature is informed by pre-literary categories such as ritual, myth and folk tale. We next realize that the relation between these categories and literature is by no means purely one of descent, as we find them reappearing in the greatest classics—in fact there seems to be a general tendency on the part of great classics to revert to them. This coincides with a feeling that we have all had: that the study of mediocre works of art, however energetic, obstinately remains a random and peripheral form of critical experience, whereas the profound masterpiece seems to draw us to a point at which we can see an enormous number of converging patterns of significance. Here we begin to wonder if we cannot see literature, not only as complicating itself in time, but as spread out in conceptual space from some unseen center.

This inductive movement towards the archetype is a process of backing up, as it were, from structural analysis, as we back up from a painting if we want to see composition instead of brushwork. In the foreground of the grave-digger scene in *Hamlet*, for instance, is an intricate verbal texture, ranging from the puns of the first clown to the *danse macabre* of the Yorick soliloquy, which we study in the printed text. One step back, and we are in the Wilson Knight and Spurgeon group of critics,[1] listening to the steady rain of images of corruption and decay. Here too, as the sense of the place of this scene in the whole play begins to dawn on us, we are in the network of psychological relationships which were the main interest of Bradley.[2] But after all, we say, we are forgetting the genre: *Hamlet* is a play, and an Elizabethan play. So we take another step back into the Stoll and Shaw group[3] and see the scene conventionally as part of its dramatic context. One step more, and we can

[1] Frye refers to G. Wilson Knight and Caroline Spurgeon, authors of fundamental works on Shakespeare's imagery.

[2] A. C. Bradley, whose *Shakespearean Tragedy* (1904) represents a summation of the Romantic and nineteenth-century emphasis on Shakespeare's portrayal of character.

[3] Elmer Stoll and G. B. Shaw, both of whom stressed the technical interests of Shakespeare in plot and theatrical conventions.

B1

TRACE PATTERNS IN A POEM
LITERATURE FORMS AN IDEAL ORDER

begin to glimpse the archetype of the scene, as the hero's *Liebestod* [4] and first unequivocal declaration of his love, his struggle with Laertes and the sealing of his own fate, and the sudden sobering of his mood that marks the transition to the final scene, all take shape around a leap into and return from the grave that has so weirdly yawned open on the stage.

At each stage of understanding this scene we are dependent on a certain kind of scholarly organization. We need first an editor to clean up the text for us, then the rhetorician and philologist, then the literary psychologist. We cannot study the genre without the help of the literary social historian, the literary philosopher and the student of the "history of ideas," and for the archetype we need a literary anthropologist. But now that we have got our central pattern of criticism established, all these interests are seen as converging on literary criticism instead of receding from it into psychology and history and the rest. In particular, the literary anthropologist who chases the source of the Hamlet legend from the pre-Shakespeare play to Saxo,[5] and from Saxo to nature-myths, is not running away from Shakespeare: he is drawing closer to the archetypal form which Shakespeare recreated. A minor result of our new perspective is that contradictions among critics, and assertions that this and not that critical approach is the right one, show a remarkable tendency to dissolve into unreality. Let us now see what we can get from the deductive end.

III

Some arts move in time, like music; others are presented in space, like painting. In both cases the organizing principle is recurrence, which is called rhythm when it is temporal and pattern when it is spatial. Thus we speak of the rhythm of music and the pattern of painting; but later, to show off our sophistication, we may begin to speak of the rhythm of painting and the pattern of music. In other words, all arts may be conceived both temporally and spatially. The score of a musical composition may be studied all at once; a picture may be seen as the track of an intricate dance of the eye. Literature seems to be intermediate between music and painting: its words form rhythms which approach a musical sequence of sounds at one of its boundaries, and form patterns which approach the hieroglyphic or pictorial image at the other. The attempts to get as near to these boundaries as possible form the main body of what is called experimental writing. We may call the rhythm of literature the narrative, and the pattern, the simultaneous mental grasp of the verbal structure, the meaning or significance. We hear or listen to a narrative, but when we grasp a writer's total pattern we "see" what he means.

The criticism of literature is much more hampered by the representational fallacy than even the criticism of painting. That is why we are apt to think of narrative as a sequential representation of events in an outside "life," and of meaning as a reflection of some external "idea." Properly used as critical terms, an author's narrative is his linear movement; his meaning is the integrity of his completed form. Similarly an image is not merely a verbal replica of an external object, but any unit of a verbal structure seen as part of a total pattern or rhythm. Even the letters an author spells his words with form part of his imagery, though only in special cases (such as alliteration) would they call for critical notice. Narrative and meaning thus become respectively, to borrow musical terms, the melodic and harmonic contexts of the imagery.

Rhythm, or recurrent movement, is deeply founded on the natural cycle, and everything in nature that we think of as having some analogy with works of art, like the flower or the bird's song, grows out of a profound synchronization between an organism and the rhythms of its environment, especially that of the solar year. With animals some expressions of synchronization, like the mating dances of birds, could almost be called rituals. But in human life a ritual seems to be something of a voluntary effort (hence the magical element in it) to recapture a lost rapport with the natural cycle. A farmer must harvest his crop at a certain time of year, but because this is involuntary, harvesting itself is not precisely a ritual. It is the deliberate expression of a will to synchronize human and natural energies at that time which produces the harvest songs, harvest sacrifices and harvest folk cus-

---

[4] German for "Love-Death" (as in the *Liebestod* in Wagner's *Tristan and Isolde*).

[5] Saxo Grammaticus (c. 1150-c. 1220), author of a history of Denmark, *Gesta Danorum*.

toms that we call rituals. In ritual, then, we may find the origin of narrative, a ritual being a temporal sequence of acts in which the conscious meaning or significance is latent: it can be seen by an observer, but is largely concealed from the participators themselves. The pull of ritual is toward pure narrative, which, if there could be such a thing, would be automatic and unconscious repetition. We should notice too the regular tendency of ritual to become encyclopedic. All the important recurrences in nature, the day, the phases of the moon, the seasons and solstices of the year, the crises of existence from birth to death, get rituals attached to them, and most of the higher religions are equipped with a definitive total body of rituals suggestive, if we may put it so, of the entire range of potentially significant actions in human life.

Patterns of imagery, on the other hand, or fragments of significance, are oracular in origin, and derive from the epiphanic moment, the flash of instantaneous comprehension with no direct reference to time, the importance of which is indicated by Cassirer in *Myth and Language*. By the time we get them, in the form of proverbs, riddles, commandments and etiological folk tales, there is already a considerable element of narrative in them. They too are encyclopedic in tendency, building up a total structure of significance, or doctrine, from random and empiric fragments. And just as pure narrative would be unconscious act, so pure significance would be an incommunicable state of consciousness, for communication begins by constructing narrative. The myth is the central informing power that gives archetypal significance to the ritual and archetypal narrative to the oracle. Hence the myth *is* the archetype, though it might be convenient to say myth only when referring to narrative, and archetype when speaking of significance. In the solar cycle of the day, the seasonal cycle of the year, and the organic cycle of human life, there is a single pattern of significance, out of which myth constructs a central narrative around a figure who is partly the sun, partly vegetative fertility and partly a god or archetypal human being. The crucial importance of this myth has been forced on literary critics by Jung and Frazer in particular,[6] but the several books

---

[6] Carl Jung (1875-1961), Swiss psychologist, who, by

now available on it are not always systematic in their approach, for which reason I supply the following table of its phases:

1. The dawn, spring and birth phase. Myths of the birth of the hero, of revival and resurrection, of creation and (because the four phases are a cycle) of the defeat of the powers of darkness, winter and death. Subordinate characters: the father and the mother. The archetype of romance and of most dithyrambic and rhapsodic poetry.

2. The zenith, summer, and marriage or triumph phase. Myths of apotheosis, of the sacred marriage, and of entering into Paradise. Subordinate characters: the companion and the bride. The archetype of comedy, pastoral and idyll.

3. The sunset, autumn and death phase. Myths of fall, of the dying god, of violent death and sacrifice and of the isolation of the hero. Subordinate characters: the traitor and the siren. The archetype of tragedy and elegy.

4. The darkness, winter and dissolution phase. Myths of the triumph of these powers; myths of floods and the return of chaos, of the defeat of the hero, and Götterdämmerung[7] myths. Subordinate characters: the ogre and the witch. The archetype of satire (see, for instance, the conclusion of *The Dunciad*).

The quest of the hero also tends to assimilate the oracular and random verbal structures, as we can see when we watch the chaos of local legends that results from prophetic epiphanies consolidating into a narrative mythology of departmental gods. In most of the higher religions this in turn has become the same central quest-myth that emerges from ritual, as the Messiah myth became the narrative structure of the oracles of Judaism. A local flood may beget a folk tale by accident, but a comparison of flood stories will show how quickly such tales become examples of the myth of dissolution. Finally, the tendency of both ritual and epiphany to become encyclopedic is realized in the definitive body of

studying mythology as well as drama, concluded that man possesses a "collective unconscious" apart from his experience as an individual; and Sir James Frazer (1854-1941), British anthropologist, whose book, *The Golden Bough*, in twelve volumes (1890-1915), is a monumental discussion of primitive myths and customs.

[7] "Twilight of the gods" in Norse mythology.

myth which constitutes the sacred scriptures of religions. These sacred scriptures are consequently the first documents that the literary critic has to study to gain a comprehensive view of his subject. After he has understood their structure, then he can descend from archetypes to genres, and see how the drama emerges from the ritual side of myth and lyric from the epiphanic or fragmented side, while the epic carries on the central encyclopedic structure.

Some words of caution and encouragement are necessary before literary criticism has clearly staked out its boundaries in these fields. It is part of the critic's business to show how all literary genres are derived from the quest-myth, but the derivation is a logical one within the science of criticism: the quest-myth will constitute the first chapter of whatever future handbooks of criticism may be written that will be based on enough organized critical knowledge to call themselves "introductions" or "outlines" and still be able to live up to their titles. It is only when we try to expound the derivation chronologically that we find ourselves writing pseudo-prehistorical fictions and theories of mythological contract. Again, because psychology and anthropology are more highly developed sciences, the critic who deals with this kind of material is bound to appear, for some time, a dilettante of those subjects. These two phases of criticism are largely undeveloped in comparison with literary history and rhetoric, the reason being the later development of the sciences they are related to. But the fascination which *The Golden Bough* and Jung's book on libido symbols have for literary critics is not based on dilettantism, but on the fact that these books are primarily studies in literary criticism, and very important ones.

In any case the critic who is studying the principles of literary form has a quite different interest from the psychologist's concern with states of mind or the anthropologist's with social institutions. For instance: the mental response to narrative is mainly passive; to significance mainly active. From this fact Ruth Benedict's *Patterns of Culture* develops a distinction between "Apollonian" cultures based on obedience to ritual and "Dionysiac" ones based on a tense exposure of the prophetic mind to epiphany. The critic would tend rather to note how popular literature which appeals to the inertia of the untrained mind puts a heavy emphasis on narrative values, whereas a sophisticated attempt to disrupt the connection between the poet and his environment produces the Rimbaud type of *illumination,* Joyce's solitary epiphanies, and Baudelaire's conception of nature as a source of oracles. Also how literature, as it develops from the primitive to the self-conscious, shows a gradual shift of the poet's attention from narrative to significant values, this shift of attention being the basis of Schiller's distinction between naive and sentimental poetry.

The relation of criticism to religion, when they deal with the same documents, is more complicated. In criticism, as in history, the divine is always treated as a human artifact. God for the critic, whether he finds him in *Paradise Lost* or the Bible, is a character in a human story; and for the critic all epiphanies are explained, not in terms of the riddle of a possessing god or devil, but as mental phenomena closely associated in their origin with dreams. This once established, it is then necessary to say that nothing in criticism or art compels the critic to take the attitude of ordinary waking consciousness towards the dream or the god. Art deals not with the real but with the conceivable; and criticism, though it will eventually have to have some theory of conceivability, can never be justified in trying to develop, much less assume, any theory of actuality. It is necessary to understand this before our next and final point can be made.

We have identified the central myth of literature, in its narrative aspect, with the quest-myth. Now if we wish to see this central myth as a pattern of meaning also, we have to start with the workings of the subconscious where the epiphany originates, in other words in the dream. The human cycle of waking and dreaming corresponds closely to the natural cycle of light and darkness, and it is perhaps in this correspondence that all imaginative life begins. The correspondence is largely an antithesis: it is in daylight that man is really in the power of darkness, a prey to frustration and weakness; it is in the darkness of nature that the "libido" or conquering heroic self awakes. Hence art, which Plato called a dream for awakened minds, seems to have as its final cause the resolution of the antithesis, the mingling of the sun and the hero, the realizing of a world in which the inner desire and the outward circumstance coincide. This is the same goal, of course, that the attempt to combine human and natural power in ritual has. The social function of the arts, therefore, seems to be closely connected with visualizing the goal of work in human life. So in terms of significance, the central myth of art must be the vision of the end of social effort, the innocent world of fulfilled desires, the free human society. Once this is understood, the integral place of criticism among the other social sciences, in interpreting and systematizing the vision of the artist, will be easier to see. It is at this point that we can see how religious conceptions of the final cause of human effort are as relevant as any others to criticism.

④ The importance of the god or hero in the myth lies in the fact that such characters, who are conceived in human likeness and yet have more power over nature, gradually build up the vision of an omnipotent personal community beyond an indifferent nature. It is this community which the hero regularly enters in his apotheosis. The world of this apotheosis thus begins to pull away from the rotary cycle of the quest in which all triumph is temporary. Hence if we look at the quest-myth as a pattern of imagery, we see the hero's quest first of all in terms of its fulfillment. This gives us our central pattern of archetypal images, the vision of innocence which sees the world in terms of total human intelligibility. It corresponds to, and is usually found in the form of, the vision of the unfallen world or heaven in religion. We may call it the comic vision of life, in contrast to the tragic vision, which sees the quest only in the form of its ordained cycle.

We conclude with a second table of contents, in which we shall attempt to set forth the central pattern of the comic and tragic visions. One essential principle of archetypal criticism is that the individual and the universal forms of an image are identical, the reasons being too complicated for us just now. We proceed according to the general plan of the game of Twenty Questions, or, if we prefer, of the Great Chain of Being:

1. In the comic vision the *human* world is a community, or a hero who represents the wish-fulfillment of the reader. The archetype of images of symposium, communion, order, friendship and love. In the tragic vision the human world is a tyranny or anarchy, or an individual or isolated man, the leader with his back to his followers, the bullying giant of romance, the deserted or betrayed hero. Marriage or some equivalent consummation belongs to the comic vision; the harlot, witch and other varieties of Jung's "terrible mother" belongs to the tragic one. All divine, heroic, angelic or other super-human communities follow the human pattern.

2. In the comic vision the *animal* world is a community of domesticated animals, usually a flock of sheep, or a lamb, or one of the gentler birds, usually a dove. The archetype of pastoral images. In the tragic vision the animal world is seen in terms of beasts and birds of prey, wolves, vultures, serpents, dragons and the like.

3. In the comic vision the *vegetable* world is a garden, grove or park, or a tree of life, or a rose or lotus. The archetype of Arcadian images, such as that of Marvell's green world or of Shakespeare's forest comedies. In the tragic vision it is a sinister forest like the one in *Comus* or at the opening of the *Inferno*, or a heath or wilderness, or a tree of death.

4. In the comic vision the *mineral* world is a city, or one building or temple, or one stone, normally a glowing precious stone—in fact the whole comic series, especially the tree, can be conceived as luminous or fiery. The archetype of geometrical images: the "starlit dome" belongs here. In the tragic vision the mineral world is seen in terms of deserts, rocks and ruins, or of sinister geometrical images like the cross.

5. In the comic vision the *unformed* world is a river, traditionally fourfold, which influenced the Renaissance image of the temperate body with its four humors. In the tragic vision this world usually becomes the sea, as the narrative myth of dissolution is so often a flood myth. The combination of the sea and beast images gives us the leviathan and similar water-monsters.

Obvious as this table looks, a great variety of poetic images and forms will be found to fit it. Yeats's "Sailing to Byzantium," to take a famous example of the comic vision at random, has the city, the tree, the bird, the community of sages, the geometrical gyre and the detachment from the cyclic world. It is, of course, only the gen-

[handwritten at bottom] ⊗ BLAKE'S FOUR-FOLD VISION DIFFERENT ASPECTS OF BLAKE'S LUVAH

eral comic or tragic context that determines the interpretation of any symbol: this is obvious with relatively neutral archetypes like the island, which may be Prospero's island or Circe's.

Our tables are, of course, not only elementary but grossly oversimplified, just as our inductive approach to the archetype was a mere hunch.

The important point is not the deficiencies of either procedure, taken by itself, but the fact that, somewhere and somehow, the two are clearly going to meet in the middle. And if they do meet, the ground plan of a systematic and comprehensive development of criticism has been established.

From Anatomy of Criticism

POLEMICAL INTRODUCTION

In the first part of his Introduction, Frye repeats and somewhat enlarges upon what he has already stated in the first section of the essay printed above, "The Archetypes of Literature." He then proceeds as follows:

IT IS clear that criticism cannot be a systematic study unless there is a quality in literature which enables it to be so. We have to adopt the hypothesis, then, that just as there is an order of nature behind the natural sciences, so literature is not a piled aggregate of "works," but an order of words. A belief in an order of nature, however, is an inference from the intelligibility of the natural sciences; and if the natural sciences ever completely demonstrated the order of nature they would presumably exhaust their subject. Similarly, criticism, if a science, must be totally intelligible, but literature, as the order of words which makes the science possible, is, so far as we know, an inexhaustible source of new critical discoveries, and would be even if new works of literature ceased to be written. If so, then the search for a limiting principle in literature in order to discourage the development of criticism is mistaken. The absurd quantum formula of criticism, the assertion that the critic should confine himself to "getting out" of a poem exactly what the poet may vaguely be assumed to have been aware of "putting in," is one of the many slovenly illiteracies that the absence of systematic criticism has allowed to grow up. This quantum theory is the literary form of what may be called the fallacy of premature teleology. It corresponds, in the natural

sciences, to the assertion that a phenomenon is as it is because Providence in its inscrutable wisdom made it so. That is, the critic is assumed to have no conceptual framework: it is simply his job to take a poem into which a poet has diligently stuffed a specific number of beauties or effects, and complacently extract them one by one, like his prototype Little Jack Horner.

The first step in developing a genuine poetics is to recognize and get rid of meaningless criticism, or talking about literature in a way that cannot help to build up a systematic structure of knowledge. This includes all the sonorous nonsense that we so often find in critical generalities, reflective comments, ideological perorations, and other consequences of taking a large view of an unorganized subject. It includes all lists of the "best" novels or poems or writers, whether their particular virtue is exclusiveness or inclusiveness. It includes all casual, sentimental, and prejudiced value-judgements, and all the literary chit-chat which makes the reputations of poets boom and crash in an imaginary stock exchange. That wealthy investor Mr. Eliot, after dumping Milton on the market, is now buying him again; Donne has probably reached his peak and will begin to taper off; Tennyson may be in for a slight flutter but the Shelley stocks are still bearish. This sort of thing cannot be part of any systematic study, for a systematic study can only progress: whatever dithers or vacillates or reacts is merely leisure-class gossip. The history of taste is no more a part of the

From *Anatomy of Criticism: Four Essays* (copyright © 1957, by the Princeton University Press), pp. 17-29, 341-48. Reprinted by permission of Princeton University Press.

structure of criticism than the Huxley-Wilberforce debate [1] is a part of the structure of biological science.

I believe that if this distinction is maintained and applied to the critics of the past, what they have said about real criticism will show an astonishing amount of agreement, in which the outlines of a coherent and systematic study will begin to emerge. In the history of taste, where there are no facts, and where all truths have been, in Hegelian fashion, split into half-truths in order to sharpen their cutting edges, we perhaps do feel that the study of literature is too relative and subjective ever to make any consistent sense. But as the history of taste has no organic connection with criticism, it can easily be separated. Mr. Eliot's essay *The Function of Criticism* begins by laying down the principle that the existing monuments of literature form an ideal order among themselves, and are not simply collections of the writings of individuals.[2] This is criticism, and very fundamental criticism. Much of this book attempts to annotate it. Its solidity is indicated by its consistency with a hundred other statements that could be collected from the better critics of all ages. There follows a rhetorical debate which makes tradition and its opposite into personified and contending forces, the former dignified with the titles of Catholic and Classical, the latter ridiculed by the epithet "Whiggery." This is the sort of thing that makes for confusion until we realize how easy it is to snip it off and throw it away. The debate is maintained against Mr. Middleton Murry, who is spoken of approvingly because "he is aware that there are definite positions to be taken, and that now and then one must actually reject something and select something else." There are no definite positions to be taken in chemistry or philology, and if there are any to be taken in criticism, criticism is not a field of genuine learning. For in any field of genuine learning, the only sensible response to the challenge "stand" is Falstaff's "so

I do, against my will." [3] One's "definite position" is one's weakness, the source of one's liability to error and prejudice, and to gain adherents to a definite position is only to multiply one's weakness like an infection.

The next step is to realize that criticism has a great variety of neighbors, and that the critic must enter into relations with them in any way that guarantees his own independence. He may want to know something of the natural sciences, but he need waste no time in emulating their methods. I understand that there is a Ph.D. thesis somewhere which displays a list of Hardy's novels in the order of the percentages of gloom they contain, but one does not feel that that sort of procedure should be encouraged. The critic may want to know something of the social sciences, but there can be no such thing as, for instance, a sociological "approach" to literature. There is no reason why a sociologist should not work exclusively on literary material, but if he does he should pay no attention to literary values. In his field Horatio Alger and the writer of the Elsie books [4] may well be more important than Hawthorne or Melville, and a single issue of the *Ladies' Home Journal* worth all of Henry James. The critic is similarly under no obligation to sociological values, as the social conditions favorable to the production of great art are not necessarily those at which the social sciences aim. The critic may need to know something of religion, but by theological standards an orthodox religious poem will give a more satisfactory expression of its content than a heretical one: this makes nonsense in criticism, and there is nothing to be gained by confusing the standards of the two subjects.

Literature has been always recognized to be a marketable product, its producers being the creative writers and its consumers the cultivated readers, with the critics at their head. From this point of view the critic is, in the metaphor of our opening page, the middleman. He has some wholesaler's privileges, such as free review copies, but his function, as distinct from the bookseller's, is essentially a form of consumer's re-

---

[1] A spirited debate at a meeting of the British Association at Oxford, in 1860, between the British scientist, Thomas Huxley (1825-1895), who defended Darwin's newly published *Origin of Species* (1859), and Bishop Samuel Wilberforce (1805-1873), who attacked it.

[2] See above, p. 526.

[3] I *Henry IV*, II, 2, 52.

[4] Horatio Alger (1823-1899), famous for stories of poor boys who made their fortunes; and Martha Finley (1828-1908), who wrote a series of books for young readers about the life and adventures of Elsie Dinsmore.

search. I recognize a second division of labor in literature, which, like other forms of mental construction, has a theory and a practice. The practitioner of literature and the producer of literature are not quite the same, though they overlap a good deal; the theorist of literature and the consumer of literature are not the same at all, even when they co-exist in the same man. The present book assumes that the theory of literature is as primary a humanistic and liberal pursuit as its practice. Hence, although it takes certain literary values for granted, as fully established by critical experience, it is not directly concerned with value-judgements. This fact needs explanation, as the value-judgement is often, and perhaps rightly for all I know, regarded as the distinguishing feature of the humanistic and liberal pursuit.

Value-judgements are subjective in the sense that they can be indirectly but not directly communicated. When they are fashionable or generally accepted, they look objective, but that is all. The demonstrable value-judgement is the donkey's carrot of literary criticism, and every new critical fashion, such as the current fashion for elaborate rhetorical analysis, has been accompanied by a belief that criticism has finally devised a definitive technique for separating the excellent from the less excellent. But this always turns out to be an illusion of the history of taste. Value-judgements are founded on the study of literature; the study of literature can never be founded on value-judgements. Shakespeare, we say, was one of a group of English dramatists working around 1600, and also one of the great poets of the world. The first part of this is a statement of fact, the second a value-judgement so generally accepted as to pass for a statement of fact. But it is not a statement of fact. It remains a value-judgement, and not a shred of systematic criticism can ever be attached to it.

There are two types of value-judgements, comparative and positive. Criticism founded on comparative values falls into two main divisions, according to whether the work of art is regarded as a product or as a possession. The former develops biographical criticism, which relates the work of art primarily to the man who wrote it. The latter we may call tropical criticism, and it is primarily concerned with the contemporary reader. Biographical criticism concerns itself largely with comparative questions of greatness and personal authority. It regards the poem as the oratory of its creator, and it feels most secure when it knows of a definite, and preferably heroic, personality behind the poetry. If it cannot find such a personality, it may try to project one out of rhetorical ectoplasm, as Carlyle does in his essay on Shakespeare as a "heroic" poet. Tropical criticism [5] deals comparatively with style and craftsmanship, with complexity of meaning and figurative assimilation. It tends to dislike and belittle the oratorical poets, and it can hardly deal at all with heroic personality. Both are essentially rhetorical forms of criticism, as one deals with the rhetoric of persuasive speech and the other with the rhetoric of verbal ornament, but each distrusts the other's kind of rhetoric.

Rhetorical value-judgements are closely related to social values, and are usually cleared through a customs-house of moral metaphors: sincerity, economy, subtlety, simplicity, and the like. But because poetics is undeveloped, a fallacy arises from the illegitimate extension of rhetoric into the theory of literature. The invariable mark of this fallacy is the selected tradition, illustrated with great clarity in Arnold's "touchstone" theory,[6] where we proceed from the intuition of value represented by the touchstone to a system of ranking poets in classes. The practice of comparing poets by weighing their lines (no new invention, as it was ridiculed by Aristophanes in *The Frogs*) is used by both biographical and tropical critics, mainly in order to deny first-class rating to those in favor with the opposite group.

When we examine the touchstone technique in Arnold, however, certain doubts arise about his motivation. The line from *The Tempest*, "In the dark backward and abysm of time," would do very well as a touchstone line. One feels that the line "Yet a tailor might scratch her where'er she did itch" somehow would not do,[7] though it is equally Shakespearean and equally essential to the same play. (An extreme form of the same

---

[5] Criticism concerned with "tropes" (metaphor and figurative expression).

[6] In his essay, "The Study of Poetry," prefixed to Ward's *English Poets* (1880). See above, p. 438.

[7] *The Tempest*, I, 2, 50, and II, 2, 55.

kind of criticism would, of course, deny this and insist that the line had been interpolated by a vulgar hack.) Some principle is clearly at work here which is much more highly selective than a purely critical experience of the play would be.

Arnold's "high seriousness" evidently is closely connected with the view that epic and tragedy, because they deal with ruling-class figures and require the high style of decorum, are the aristocrats of literary forms. All his Class One touchstones are from, or judged by the standards of, epic and tragedy. Hence his demotion of Chaucer and Burns to Class Two seems to be affected by a feeling that comedy and satire should be kept in their proper place, like the moral standards and the social classes which they symbolize. We begin to suspect that the literary value-judgements are projections of social ones. Why does Arnold *want* to rank poets? He says that we increase our admiration for those who manage to stay in Class One after we have made it very hard for them to do so. This being clearly nonsense, we must look further. When we read "in poetry the distinction between excellent and inferior . . . is of paramount importance . . . because of the high destinies of poetry," we begin to get a clue. We see that Arnold is trying to create a new scriptural canon out of poetry to serve as a guide for those social principles which he wants culture to take over from religion.

The treatment of criticism as the application of a social attitude is a natural enough result of what we have called the power vacuum in criticism. A systematic study alternates between inductive experience and deductive principles. In criticism rhetorical analysis provides some of the induction, and poetics, the theory of criticism, should be the deductive counterpart. There being no poetics, the critic is thrown back on prejudice derived from his existence as a social being. For prejudice is simply inadequate deduction, as a prejudice in the mind can never be anything but a major premise which is mostly submerged, like an iceberg.

It is not hard to see prejudice in Arnold, because his views have dated: it is a little harder when "high seriousness" becomes "maturity," or some other powerful persuader of more recent critical rhetoric. It is harder when the old

question of what books one would take to a desert island emerges from parlor games, where it belongs, into an expensive library alleged to constitute the scriptural canon of democratic values. Rhetorical value-judgements usually turn on questions of decorum, and the central conception of decorum is the difference between high, middle, and low styles. These styles are suggested by the class structure of society, and criticism, if it is not to reject half the facts of literary experience, obviously has to look at art from the standpoint of an ideally classless society. Arnold himself points this out when he says that "culture seeks to do away with classes." Every deliberately constructed hierarchy of values in literature known to me is based on a concealed social, moral, or intellectual analogy. This applies whether the analogy is conservative and Romantic, as it is in Arnold, or radical, giving the top place to comedy, satire, and the values of prose and reason, as it is in Bernard Shaw. The various pretexts for minimizing the communicative power of certain writers, that they are obscure or obscene or nihilistic or reactionary or what not, generally turn out to be disguises for a feeling that the views of decorum held by the ascendant social or intellectual class ought to be either maintained or challenged. These social fixations keep changing, like a fan turning in front of a light, and the changing inspires the belief that posterity eventually discovers the whole truth about art.

A selective approach to tradition, then, invariably has some ultra-critical joker concealed in it. There is no question of accepting the whole of literature as the basis of study, but a tradition (or, of course, "the" tradition) is abstracted from it and attached to contemporary social values, being then used to document those values. The hesitant reader is invited to try the following exercise. Pick three big names at random, work out the eight possible combinations of promotion and demotion (on a simplified, or two-class basis) and defend each in turn. Thus if the three names picked were Shakespeare, Milton, and Shelley, the agenda would run:

1. Demoting Shelley, on the ground that he is immature in technique and profundity of thought compared to the others.

2. Demoting Milton, on the ground that his

religious obscurantism and heavy doctrinal content impair the spontaneity of his utterance.

3. Demoting Shakespeare, on the ground that his detachment from ideas makes his dramas a reflection of life rather than a creative attempt to improve it.

4. Promoting Shakespeare, on the ground that he preserves an integrity of poetic vision which in the others is obfuscated by didacticism.

5. Promoting Milton, on the ground that his penetration of the highest mysteries of faith raises him above Shakespeare's unvarying worldliness and Shelley's callowness.

6. Promoting Shelley, on the ground that his love of freedom speaks to the heart of modern man more immediately than poets who accepted outworn social or religious values.

7. Promoting all three (for this a special style, which we may call the peroration style, should be used).

8. Demoting all three, on the ground of the untidiness of English genius when examined by French or Classical or Chinese standards.

The reader may sympathize with some of these "positions," as they are called, more than with others, and so be seduced into thinking that one of them must be right, and that it is important to decide which one it is. But long before he has finished his assignment he will realize that the whole procedure involved is an anxiety neurosis prompted by a moral censor, and is totally devoid of content. Of course, in addition to the moralists, there are poets who regard only those other poets as authentic who sound like themselves; there are critics who enjoy making religious, anti-religious, or political campaigns with toy soldiers labelled "Milton" or "Shelley" more than they enjoy studying poetry; there are students who have urgent reasons for making as much edifying reading as possible superfluous. But a conspiracy even of all these still does not make criticism.

The social dialectics applied externally to criticism, then, are, *within criticism*, pseudo-dialectics, or false rhetoric. It remains to try to define the true dialectic of criticism. On this level the biographical critic becomes the historical critic. He develops from hero-worship towards total and indiscriminate acceptance: there is nothing "in his field" that he is not prepared to read with interest. From a purely historical point of view, however, cultural phenomena are to be read in their own context without contemporary application. We study them as we do the stars, seeing their interrelationships but not approaching them. Hence historical criticism needs to be complemented by a corresponding activity growing out of tropical criticism.

We may call this ethical criticism, interpreting ethics not as a rhetorical comparison of social facts to predetermined values, but as the consciousness of the presence of society. As a critical category this would be the sense of the real presence of culture in the community. Ethical criticism, then, deals with art as a communication from the past to the present, and is based on the conception of the total and simultaneous possession of past culture. An exclusive devotion to it, ignoring historical criticism, would lead to a naive translation of all cultural phenomena into our own terms without regard to their original character. As a counterweight to historical criticism, it is designed to express the contemporary impact of all art, without selecting a tradition. Every new critical fashion has increased the appreciation of some poets and depreciated others, as the increase of interest in the metaphysical poets tended to depreciate the Romantics about twenty-five years ago. On the ethical level we can see that every increase of appreciation has been right, and every decrease wrong: that criticism has no business to react against things, but should show a steady advance toward undiscriminating catholicity. Oscar Wilde said that only an auctioneer could be equally appreciative of all kinds of art:[8] he had of course the public critic in mind, but even the public critic's job of getting the treasures of culture into the hands of the people who want them is largely an auctioneer's job. And if this is true of him, it is *a fortiori*[9] true of the scholarly critic.

The dialectic axis of criticism, then, has as one pole the total acceptance of the data of literature, and as the other the total acceptance of the potential values of those data. This is the real level of culture and of liberal education,

[8] Paraphrased from Wilde on "English Models," *English Illustrated Magazine*, VI (1889), 313-14.

[9] "For even stronger reasons."

the fertilizing of life by learning, in which the systematic progress of scholarship flows into a systematic progress of taste and understanding. On this level there is no itch to make weighty judgements, and none of the ill effects which follow the debauchery of judiciousness, and have made the word critic a synonym for an educated shrew. Comparative estimates of value are really inferences, most valid when silent ones, from critical practice, not expressed principles guiding its practice. The critic will find soon, and constantly, that Milton is a more rewarding and suggestive poet to work with than Blackmore.[10] But the more obvious this becomes, the less time he will want to waste in belaboring the point. For belaboring the point is all he can do: any criticism motivated by a desire to establish or prove it will be merely one more document in the history of taste. There is doubtless much in the culture of the past which will always be of comparatively slight value to the present. But the difference between redeemable and irredeemable art, being based on the *total* experience of criticism, can never be theoretically formulated. There are too many Cinderellas among the poets, too many stones rejected from one fashionable building that have become heads of the next corner. . . .

Criticism, in short, and aesthetics generally, must learn to do what ethics has already done. There was a time when ethics could take the simple form of comparing what man does with what he ought to do, known as the good. The "good" invariably turned out to be whatever the author of the book was accustomed to and found sanctioned by his community. Ethical writers now, though they still have values, tend to look at their problems rather differently. But a procedure which is hopelessly outmoded in ethics is still in vogue among writers on aesthetic problems. It is still possible for a critic to define as authentic art whatever he happens to like, and to go on to assert that what he happens not to like is, in terms of that definition, not authentic art. The argument has the great advantage of being irrefutable, as all circular arguments are, but it is shadow and not substance.

The odious comparisons of greatness, then, may be left to take care of themselves, for even when we feel obliged to assent to them they are still only unproductive platitudes. The real concern of the evaluating critic is with positive value, with the goodness, or perhaps the genuineness, of the poem rather than with the greatness of its author. Such criticism produces the direct value-judgement of informed good taste, the proving of art on the pulses, the disciplined response of a highly organized nervous system to the impact of poetry. No critic in his senses would try to belittle the importance of this; nevertheless there are some caveats even here. In the first place, it is superstition to believe that the swift intuitive certainty of good taste is infallible. Good taste follows and is developed by the study of literature; its precision results from knowledge, but does not produce knowledge. Hence the accuracy of any critic's good taste is no guarantee that its inductive basis in literary experience is adequate. This may still be true even after the critic has learned to base his judgements on his experience of literature and not on his social, moral, religious, or personal anxieties. Honest critics are continually finding blind spots in their taste: they discover the possibility of recognizing a valid form of poetic experience without being able to realize it for themselves.

In the second place, the positive value-judgement is founded on a direct experience which is central to criticism yet forever excluded from it. Criticism can account for it only in critical terminology, and that terminology can never recapture or include the original experience. The original experience is like the direct vision of color, or the direct sensation of heat or cold, that physics "explains" in what, from the point of view of the experience itself, is a quite irrelevant way. However disciplined by taste and skill, the experience of literature is, like literature itself, unable to speak. "If I feel physically as if the top of my head were taken off," said Emily Dickinson, "I know this is poetry."[11] This remark is perfectly sound, but it relates only to criticism as experience. The reading of literature should, like prayer in the Gospels, step

[10] Sir Richard Blackmore (d. 1729), author of forgotten epics in Miltonic blank verse.

[11] A remark made to T. W. Higginson when he visited her in August, 1870 (*Selected Poems and Letters* [ed. R. N. Linscott, 1959], p. 19).

out of the talking world of criticism into the private and secret presence of literature. Otherwise the reading will not be a genuine literary experience, but a mere reflection of critical conventions, memories, and prejudices. The presence of incommunicable experience in the center of criticism will always keep criticism an art, as long as the critic recognizes that criticism comes out of it but cannot be built on it.

Thus, though the normal development of a critic's taste is toward greater tolerance and catholicity, still criticism as knowledge is one thing, and value-judgements informed by taste are another. The attempt to bring the direct experience of literature into the structure of criticism produces the aberrations of the history of taste already dealt with. The attempt to reverse the procedure and bring criticism into direct experience will destroy the integrity of both. Direct experience, even if it is concerned with something already read hundreds of times, still tries to be a new and fresh experience each time, which is clearly impossible if the poem itself has been replaced by a critical view of the poem. To bring my own view that criticism as knowledge should constantly progress and reject nothing into direct experience would mean that the latter should progress toward a general stupor of satisfaction with everything written, which is not quite what I have in mind.

Finally, the skill developed from constant practice in the direct experience of literature is a special skill, like playing the piano, not the expression of a general attitude to life, like singing in the shower. The critic has a subjective background of experience formed by his temperament and by every contact with words he has made, including newspapers, advertisements, conversations, movies, and whatever he read at the age of nine. He has a specific skill in responding to literature which is no more like this subjective background, with all its private memories, associations, and arbitrary prejudices, than reading a thermometer is like shivering. Again, there is no one of critical ability who has not experienced intense and profound pleasure from something simultaneously with a low critical valuation of what produced it. There must be several dozen critical and aesthetic theories based on the assumption that subjective pleasure and the specific response to art are, or develop from, or ultimately become, the same thing. Yet every cultivated person who is not suffering from advanced paranoia knows that they are constantly distinct. Or, again, the ideal value may be quite different from the actual one. A critic may spend a thesis, a book, or even a life work on something that he candidly admits to be third-rate, simply because it is connected with something else that he thinks sufficiently important for his pains. No critical theory known to me takes any real account of the different systems of valuation implied by one of the most common practices of criticism. . . .

Following the Introduction, the *Anatomy of Criticism* presents four essays. *Essay I* ("Historical Criticism: Theory of Modes") focuses on the hero or principal character in literary narrative, and finds that Western literature, since the start of the Middle Ages, has run through a cycle of five periods distinguished by five different modes (in a foreshortened way, something of the same cycle had also occurred in classical antiquity). (1) *Myth.* Here the hero is altogether superior to and different from most men (that is, a god or an approximation to one). This appears in the pre-mediaeval and early mediaeval periods (late classical, Celtic, or Teutonic myths). (2) *Romance,* where the hero is superior in degree, rather than kind, to other men and his environment. If his actions are marvelous, he is still a human being (for example, mediaeval folk tales, legends of saints, romances of knight-errantry). (3) The *high mimetic* mode, in which the hero, though he is superior to other men and is a leader, is not superior to his environment (including the order of nature). This is the sort of hero of which Aristotle is thinking. This conception flowers in the European Renaissance and is associated with the tragic drama and national epic. (4) With the growth of middle-class culture there comes the *low mimetic* (as in comedy or in realistic fiction), which we associate with the rise of the novel in England after Defoe during the early and middle eighteenth century, and which parallels the development of Romanticism and continues to almost the end of the nineteenth century. The hero is superior neither to others nor to his environment. Common humanity is stressed, and with it the familiar, the homely, the natural. (5) If the hero is seen as inferior in intelligence or in freedom to act, we then have the *ironic* mode, and attention is focused on "bondage, frustration, or absurdity."

Essay II ("Ethical Criticism: Theory of Symbols") discusses various modes of using symbols that parallel what we have just summarized. (1) *Anagogy* is the symbolic expression typical of the primitive when "bare myth" is the characteristic mode. The word originally meant, in Greek, "a leading upward" and is frequently applied to mystical experience. For Frye it probably has two further overtones: in biblical criticism, it has traditionally meant a "reading of spiritual import into words"; and in psychoanalysis it applies to the transformation of unconscious drives into constructive ideals. In this early anagogic phase literature is entirely the expression of "the total dream of man," is pervaded by the subjectively human, and the mind is not just the center of reality but also the circumference, the outside limit, of reality. Nature, in other words, is "inside" the mind of man. (2) *Archetype* emerges as man's mind no longer completely swallows up his notion of the external world, and as he begins to see the world as partly "other" to himself. Fundamental patterns of image and response in man are human and subjective counterparts to an external reality that is being genuinely experienced. Man's mind is not merely projecting; it is responding to and cooperating with nature. The "archetypal," in other words, has a real objective as well as subjective applicability. "Archetype" becomes fulfilled in "Romance," the fertile transition between "bare myth" and the "high mimetic" mode. (3) Then, with the classical and "high mimetic" (in Western Europe, the period that begins with the Renaissance and continues into eighteenth-century "neoclassicism") comes *formal symbolism,* in which the symbolism is confidently expressive of contact with a reality often rationally as well as imaginatively conceived, and this symbolism observes proportion (that is, "decorum") as it fits in with larger aspects of form. (4) With the "low mimetic" mode (concerned with the familiar, the "realistic") comes *descriptive symbolism.* The tension between the "natural" and the "symbolic" increases (thus the great age of "documentary realism, the nineteenth century, was also the age of Romantic poetry"). What amounts to a growing separation takes place, in which—as in the *symboliste* movement in late nineteenth- and twentieth-century poetry (or its by-product, the concept of "pure poetry")—we cease to press the question, What does this mean as representation? The unity of the poem is in "mood," and poetic images point to each other rather than to something else. (5) Finally, in a spirit of general distrust of symbol, comes the "literal"; and in the ironic mode a "conventionalized literalism" prevails.

Essay III ("Archetypal Criticism: Theory of Myths") then turns to the historical transformation of myths and archetypal conventions through these five modes. "Apocalyptic" imagery—conceiving the world as human desire would have it—is appropriate to "the ironic mode in the late phase in which it returns to myth." In between is "analogical" imagery ("analogical"— having to do with what "corresponds"—because it is no longer confident that it is dealing with the actual identification of things but is frankly concerned with just their similarity or correspondence): an analogy of "innocence" (pastoral, etc.) typical of "romance," providing, in its imagery of an idealized world, a "human counterpart of the apocalyptic world"; an "analogy of nature and reason" typical of the "high mimetic" mode; and an "analogy of experience" in the "low mimetic" mode. Frye then discusses four basic kinds of myth, expressed in and through four basic kinds of literature: the mythos of spring (comedy), summer (romance), autumn (tragedy), and winter (irony and satire). (In Frye's earlier essay, "The Archetypes of Literature," reprinted above, "spring" was associated with "romance" and "summer" with "comedy.") Each has six phases, the last three of which parallel the first three of the next. A key concept, throughout the discussion, is expressed by the Freudian term "displacement," which in psychoanalysis refers to the changes (or distortions) that an instinctual drive or even an idea undergoes because of external circumstances or one's own inner censorship. By "displacement" Frye means the changes in original, archetypal myth as it is adapted to a particular audience to make it either rationally credible or morally acceptable.

Essay IV ("Rhetorical Criticism: Theory of Genres") turns to the various literary genres (epic, drama, lyric, and so on), using as a common denominator the concept of "rhythm" in flow. We need not summarize this essay in detail, since it is essentially a concrete application of the premises and criteria we have mentioned.

The conclusion then follows:

TENTATIVE CONCLUSION

The present book has dealt with a variety of critical techniques and approaches, most of them already used in contemporary scholarship. We have tried to show where the archetypal or mythical critic, the aesthetic form critic, the historical critic, the medieval four-level critic, the text-and-texture critic, belong in a comprehensive view of criticism. Whether the comprehensive view is right or not, I hope some sense has been communicated of what folly it would be to try to exclude any of these groups from criticism. As was said at the beginning, the present book is not designed to suggest a new program for critics, but a new perspective on their existing programs, which in themselves are valid enough. The book attacks no methods of criticism, once that subject has been defined: what it attacks are the barriers between the methods. These barriers tend to make a critic confine himself to a single method of criticism, which is unnecessary, and they tend to make him establish his primary contacts, not with other critics, but with subjects outside criticism. Hence the number of essays, not large but too large, in mythical criticism that read like bad comparative religion, in rhetorical criticism that read like bad semantics, in aesthetic criticism that read like bad metaphysics, and so on.

In this process of breaking down barriers I think archetypal criticism has a central role, and I have given it a prominent place. One element in our cultural tradition which is usually regarded as fantastic nonsense is the allegorical explanations of myths which bulk so large in medieval and Renaissance criticism and continue sporadically (e.g., Ruskin's *Queen of the Air*) to our own time. The allegorization of myth is hampered by the assumption that the explanation "is" what the myth "means." A myth being a centripetal structure of meaning, it can be made to mean an indefinite number of things, and it is more fruitful to study what in fact myths have been made to mean.

The term myth may have, and obviously does have, different meanings in different subjects. These meanings are doubtless reconcilable in the long run, but the task of reconciling them lies in the future. In literary criticism myth means ultimately *mythos,* a structural organizing principle of literary form. Commentary, we remember, is allegorization, and any great work of literature may carry an infinite amount of commentary. This fact often depresses the critic and makes him feel that everything to be said about *Hamlet,* for instance, must already have been said many times. To what has occurred to the learned and astute minds of A and B in reading *Hamlet* is added what occurs to the learned and astute minds of C, D, E, and so on, until out of sheer self-preservation most of it is left unread, or (much the same thing culturally) is assigned to specialists. Commentary which has no sense of the archetypal shape of literature as a whole, then, continues the tradition of allegorized myth, and inherits its characteristics of brilliance, ingenuity, and futility.

The only cure for this situation is the supplementing of allegorical with archetypal criticism. Things become more hopeful as soon as there is a feeling, however dim, that criticism has an end in the structure of literature as a total form, as well as a beginning in the text studied. It is not sufficient to use the text as a check on commentary, like a string tied to a kite, for one may develop a primary body of commentary around the obvious meaning, then a secondary body about the unconscious meaning, then a third body around the conventions and external relations of the poem, and so on indefinitely. This practice is not confined to modern critics, for the interpretation of Virgil's Fourth Eclogue as Messianic also assumed that Virgil was "unconsciously" prophesying the Messiah. But the poet unconsciously meant the whole corpus of his possible commentary, and it is simpler merely to say that Virgil and Isaiah use the same type of imagery dealing with the myth of the hero's birth, and that because of this similarity the Nativity Ode, for instance, is able to use both. This procedure helps to distribute the commentary, and prevents each poem from becoming a separate center of isolated scholarship.

The theory of criticism embraces the "humanities," in their educational aspect, according to our principle that it is criticism and not literature which is directly taught and learned. Hence a sense of bewilderment about the theory of criticism is readily projected as a concern over the "fate" or "plight" of the humanities. The breaking down of barriers within criticism would therefore have the long-run effect of making critics more aware of the external relations of criticism as a whole with other disciplines. This last subject is one on which I make a few final comments only because it seems to me that it would be an excess of prudence, in fact hardly honest, to shrink altogether from the larger issues of the questions here discussed.

The production of art is usually described in the "creative" metaphors of organic life. There is a curious tendency in human life to imitate some of the aspects of "lower" forms of existence, like the rituals which imitate the subtle synchronizations with the rhythms of the turning year that vegetable life makes. It is not in itself unreasonable that human culture would unconsciously assume the rhythms of an organism. Artists tend to imitate their predecessors in a slightly more sophisticated way, thus producing a tradition of cultural *aging* which goes on until some large change interrupts the process and starts it over again. Hence the containing form of historical criticism may well be some quasi-organic rhythm of cultural aging, such as is postulated in one form or another by most of the philosophical historians of our time, most explicitly by Spengler.[1] The conception of our own time as a "late" phase of a "Western" culture of which the Middle Ages was the youth, and as a phase resembling the Roman phase of an earlier Classical culture, is in practice taken for granted by everyone today, and seems to be one of the inevitable categories of the contemporary outlook. The progression of modes traced in the first essay seems to have some analogy to this view of cultural history.

Any such view, if adopted, could be decorated metaphysically to suit the tenant: but there is no reason why it should be "fatalistic," unless it is fatalism to say that one gets older every year, nor why it should include any theory of inevitable cycles in history or a pre-ordained future. Certainly it should not be perverted into a basis for rhetorical value-judgements. We get these, for instance, in the sentimental view of medieval culture which sees it as a gigantic synthesis followed by a progressive disintegration which has subdivided and specialized until it has finally landed us all in the Pretty Pass which we are in today. A movement which will restore something of the unity of medieval culture to the modern world, or some other qualities of it, has been hailed in one form or other in nearly every generation since the middle of the eighteenth century. Subsidiary forms of the same view are present in the people who cannot listen with pleasure to any music later than Mozart, or whatever terminal they choose; in the Marxists who speak of the decadence of capitalist culture; in

the alarmists who speak of a return to a new Dark Ages, and so on. All these have a more or less muddled version of some quasi-organic theory of history as their basis.

It is a commonplace of criticism that art does not evolve or improve: it produces the classic or model. One can still buy books narrating the "development" of painting from the Stone Age to Picasso, but they show no development, only a series of mutations in skill, Picasso being on much the same level as his Magdalenian[2] ancestors. Every once in a while we experience in the arts a feeling of definitive revelation. This, we may feel after a Palestrina motet or a Mozart divertimento, is the voice of music itself: this is the kind of thing that music was invented to say. Here is a simplicity which makes us realize that the simple is the opposite of the commonplace, a feeling that the boundaries of possible expression in the art have been reached for all time. This feeling belongs to direct experience, not to criticism, but it suggests the critical principle that the profoundest experiences possible to obtain in the arts are available in the art already produced.

What does improve in the arts is the comprehension of them, and the refining of society which results from it. It is the consumer, not the producer, who benefits by culture, the consumer who becomes humanized and liberally educated. There is no reason why a great poet should be a wise and good man, or even a tolerable human being, but there is every reason why his reader should be improved in his humanity as a result of reading him. Hence while the production of culture may be, like ritual, a half-involuntary imitation of organic rhythms or processes, the response to culture is, like myth, a revolutionary act of consciousness. The contemporary development of the technical ability to study the arts, represented by reproductions of painting, the recording of music, and modern libraries, forms part of a cultural revolution which makes the humanities quite as pregnant with new developments as the sciences. For the revolution is not simply in technology, but in spiritual productive power. The humanistic tradition itself rose, in its modern form, with the invention of the printing

---

[1] Frye refers to Oswald Spengler's *Decline of the West* (1918-22). The thesis is that each culture behaves like a biological organism: it grows, reaches a height, declines, and dies. Each has a "spring" (agrarian, feudal); a "summer" of great art and basic intellectual achievements (for example, the "Golden Age" of Athens or, in our own culture, the Renaissance); an "autumn" ("late-urban," sophisticated, disillusioned); and a "winter."

[2] A stone-age culture (named after the cave of La Madeleine in France) characterized by tools made skillfully from horn and bone.

press, the immediate effect of which was not to stimulate new culture so much as to codify the heritage of the past.

Nearly every work of art in the past had a social function in its own time, a function which was often not primarily an aesthetic function at all. The whole conception of "works of art" as a classification for all pictures, statues, poems, and musical compositions is a relatively modern one. We can see an aesthetic impulse at work in Peruvian textiles, palaeolithic drawings, Scythian horse ornaments, or Kwakiutl [3] masks, but in doing so we make a sophisticated abstraction which may well have been outside the mental habits of the people who produced them. Thus the question of whether a thing "is" a work of art or not is one which cannot be settled by appealing to something in the nature of the thing itself. It is convention, social acceptance, and the work of criticism in the broadest sense that determines where it belongs. It may have been originally made for use rather than pleasure, and so fall outside the general Aristotelian conception of art, but if it now exists for our pleasure it is what *we* call art.

When anything is reclassified in this way, it loses much of its original function. Even the most fanatical historical critic is bound to see Shakespeare and Homer as writers whom we admire for reasons that would have been largely unintelligible to them, to say nothing of their societies. But we can hardly be satisfied with an approach to works of art which simply strips from them their original function. One of the tasks of criticism is that of the recovery of function, not of course the restoration of an original function, which is out of the question, but the recreation of function in a new context.

Kierkegaard has written a fascinating little book called *Repetition,* in which he proposes to use this term to replace the more traditional Platonic term anamnesis or recollection. By it he apparently means, not the simple repeating of an experience, but the recreating of it which redeems or awakens it to life, the end of the process, he says, being the apocalyptic promise: "Behold, I make all things new." The preoccupation of the humanities with the past is sometimes made a reproach against them by those who forget that we face the past: it may be shadowy, but it is all that is there. Plato draws a gloomy picture of man staring at the flickering shapes made on the wall of the objective world by a fire behind us like the sun.[4] But the analogy breaks down when the shadows are those of the past, for the only light we can see them by is the Promethean fire within us. The substance of these shadows can only be in ourselves, and the goal of historical criticism, as our metaphors about it often indicate, is a kind of self-resurrection, the vision of a valley of dry bones that takes on the flesh and blood of our own vision. The culture of the past is not only the memory of mankind, but our own buried life, and study of it leads to a recognition scene, a discovery in which we see, not our past lives, but the total cultural form of our present life. It is not only the poet but his reader who is subject to the obligation to "make it new."

Without this sense of "repetition," historical criticism tends to remove the products of culture from our own sphere of interest. It must be counterpoised, as it is in all genuine historical critics, by a sense of the contemporary relevance of past art. But it is natural that this sense of contemporary relevance should often be confined to a specific issue in the present; that it should be thought of, not as expanding the perspective of present life, but as supporting a cause or thesis in the present.

If we cut through history at any point, including our own, and study a cross-section of it, we get a class structure. Culture may be employed by a social or intellectual class to increase its prestige; and in general, moral censors, selectors of great traditions, apologists of religious or political causes, aesthetes, radicals, codifiers of great books, and the like, are expressions of such class tensions. We soon realize, in studying their pronouncements, that the only really consistent moral criticism of this type would be the kind which is harnessed to an all-round revolutionary philosophy of society, such as we find not only in Marxism but in Nietzsche and in some of the rationalizations of oligarchic values in nineteenth-century Britain and twentieth-century America. In all these culture is treated as a

[3] A division of the Wakashan tribe of Indians in British Columbia, Canada.

[4] *Republic,* Bk. VII.

human productive power which in the past has been, like other productive powers, exploited by other ruling classes and is now to be revalued in terms of a better society. But as this ideal society exists only in the future, the present valuation of culture is in terms of its interim revolutionary effectiveness.

This revolutionary way of looking at culture is also as old as Plato, the selected tradition being always some version of the argument about poets in the *Republic*. As soon as we make culture a definite image of a future and perhaps attainable society, we start selecting and purging a tradition, and all the artists who don't fit (an increasing number as the process goes on) have to be thrown out. So, just as historical criticism uncorrected relates culture only to the past, ethical criticism uncorrected relates culture only to the future, to the ideal society which may eventually come if we take sufficient pains to guard the educating of our youth. For all such lines of thought end in indoctrinating the next generation, just as the moral version of Victorian progressivism led to Podsnap [5] and the blushing cheeks of the young person.

The body of work done in society, or civilization, both maintains and undermines the class structure of that society. The social energy which maintains the class structure produces perverted culture in its three chief forms: mere upper-class culture, or ostentation, mere middle-class culture, or vulgarity, and mere lower-class culture, or squalor. These three classes are called by Matthew Arnold respectively, in so far as they are classes, the barbarians, the philistines, and the populace. Revolutionary action, of whatever kind, leads to the dictatorship of one class, and the record of history seems clear that there is no quicker way of destroying the benefits of culture. If we attach our vision of culture to the conception of ruler-morality, we get the culture of barbarians; if we attach it to the conception of a proletariat, we get the culture of the populace; if we attach it to any kind of bourgeois Utopia, we get the culture of philistinism.

Whatever one thinks of dialectic materialism as a philosophy, it is certainly true that when men behave or pretend to behave like material

bodies they do behave dialectically. If England goes to war with France, all the weaknesses in the English case and all the virtues in the French case are ignored in England; not only is the traitor the lowest of criminals, but it is indignantly denied that any traitor can be honestly motivated. In war, the physical or idolatrous substitute for the real dialectic of the spirit, one lives by half-truths. The same principle applies to the verbal or mimic wars made out of "points of view," which are usually the ghosts of some kind of social conflict.

It seems better to try to get clear of all such conflicts, attaching ourselves to Arnold's other axiom that "culture seeks to do away with classes." The ethical purpose of a liberal education is to liberate, which can only mean to make one capable of conceiving society as free, classless, and urbane. No such society exists, which is one reason why a liberal education must be deeply concerned with works of imagination. The imaginative element in works of art, again, lifts them clear of the bondage of history. Anything that emerges from the total experience of criticism to form part of a liberal education becomes, by virtue of that fact, part of the emancipated and humane community of culture, whatever its original reference. Thus liberal education liberates the works of culture themselves as well as the mind they educate. The corruption out of which human art has been constructed will always remain in the art, but the imaginative quality of the art preserves it in its corruption, like the corpse of a saint. No discussion of beauty can confine itself to the formal relations of the isolated work of art; it must consider, too, the participation of the work of art in the vision of the goal of social effort, the idea of complete and classless civilization. This idea of complete civilization is also the implicit moral standard to which ethical criticism always refers, something very different from any system of morals.

The idea of the free society implied in culture can never be formulated, much less established as a society. Culture is a present social ideal which we educate and free ourselves by trying to attain, and never do attain. It teaches, with the endless patience of the book which always presents the same words whenever we open it, but it is not possessed, for the experiences and meanings attached to the words are always new. No

---

[5] A character in Dickens' *Our Mutual Friend* (1864-65), remarkable for his extreme self-satisfaction.

society can plan for its own culture unless it restricts the output of culture to socially predictable standards. The goal of ethical criticism is transvaluation, the ability to look at contemporary social values with the detachment of one who is able to compare them in some degree with the infinite vision of possibilities presented by culture. One who possesses such a standard of transvaluation is in a state of intellectual freedom. One who does not possess it is a creature of whatever social values get to him first: he has only the compulsions of habit, indoctrination, and prejudice. The current tendency to insist that man cannot be a spectator of his own life seems to me to be one of those lethal half-truths that arise in response to some kind of social malaise. Most ethical action is a mechanical reflex of habit: to get any principle of freedom in it we need some kind of theory of action, theory in the sense of *theoria,* a withdrawn or detached vision of the means and end of action which does not paralyze action, but makes it purposeful by enlightening its aims.

The two great classics of the theory of liberty in the modern world, *Areopagitica* and Mill's *Essay on Liberty,* deal of course with liberty in different contexts. For Milton culture is potential prophecy, set in judgement over against the kind of social acceptance of sanctioned error represented by the censor, whereas for Mill culture is a social critique. But allowing for this, both essays insist that liberty can begin only with an immediate and present guarantee of the autonomy of culture. In Mill unlimited liberty of thought and discussion is not only the best way of developing liberty of action, but the best way of controlling it, because it is the only means of preventing impulsive or stampeded action. In Milton liberty of conscience is not the freedom to listen to the compulsions acquired in childhood which make up the greater part of what we ordinarily call conscience, but the freedom to listen to the Word of God, which, as it is a message from an infinite mind to a finite one, can never be definitively understood by the latter.

At this point the theory of criticism seems ready to settle quietly into the larger humanistic principle that the freedom of man is inseparably bound up with his acceptance of his cultural heritage. The writer believes this, of course, and so probably do most of those who will read his book; but there may still be a residue from the parasite fallacy of criticism, which all our arguments may not yet have dispelled. This is the feeling that as criticism is based on cultural products, the more important the critic claims his work to be, the more he tends to magnify the normal pleasure that a cultivated person finds in the arts into something awful and portentous, replacing culture with aesthetic superstition, literature with bardolatry, of however sophisticated a kind.

This would be true if in fact the aesthetic or contemplative aspect of art were the final resting place for either art or criticism. Here again it is archetypal criticism that comes to our aid. We tried to show in the second essay that the moment we go from the individual work of art to the sense of the total form of the art, the art becomes no longer an object of aesthetic contemplation but an ethical instrument, participating in the work of civilization. In this shift to the ethical, criticism as well as poetry is involved, though some of the ways in which it is involved are not commonly recognized as aspects of criticism. It is obvious, for instance, that one major source of order in society is an established pattern of words. In religion this may be a scripture, a liturgy, or a creed; in politics it may be a written constitution or a set of ideological directives like the pamphlets of Lenin in present-day Russia. Such verbal patterns may remain fixed for centuries: the meanings attached to them will change out of all recognition in that time, but the feeling that the verbal structure must remain unchanged, and the consequent necessity of reinterpreting it to suit the changes of history, bring the operations of criticism into the center of society.

But we then had to complete our argument by removing all external goals from literature, thus postulating a self-contained literary universe. Perhaps in doing so we merely restored the aesthetic view on a gigantic scale, substituting Poetry for a mass of poems, aesthetic mysticism for aesthetic empiricism. The argument of our last essay, however, led to the principle that all structures in words are partly rhetorical, and hence literary, and that the notion of a scientific or philosophical verbal structure free of rhetorical elements is an illusion. If so, then our literary universe has expanded into a verbal universe, and no aesthetic principle of self-containment will work.

I am not wholly unaware that at every step of this argument there are extremely complicated philosophical problems which I am incompetent to solve as such. I am aware also, however, of something else. That something else is the confused swirl of new intellectual activities today associated with such words as communication, symbolism, semantics, linguistics, metalinguistics, pragmatics, cybernetics, and the ideas generated by and around Cassirer, Korzybsky,[6] and dozens of others in fields as remote (as they seemed until recently) as prehistory and mathematics, logic and engineering, sociology and physics. Many of these movements were instigated by a desire to free the modern mind from the tyranny of emotional rhetoric, from the advertising and propaganda that try to pervert thought by a misuse of irony into conditioned reflex. Many of them have also moved in the direction of conceptual rhetoric, reducing the content of many arguments to their ambiguous or diagrammatic structures. My knowledge of most of the books dealing with this new material is largely confined, like Moses' knowledge of God in the mount, to gazing at their spines, but it is clear to me that literary criticism has a central place in all this activity, and from the point of view of literary criticism I offer an admittedly very speculative suggestion.

We have several times hinted at an analogy between literature and mathematics. Mathematics appears to begin in the counting and measuring of objects, as a numerical commentary on the outside world. But the mathematician does not think of his subject so: for him it is an autonomous language, and there is a point at which it becomes in a measure independent of that common field of experience which we call the objective world, or nature, or existence, or reality, according to our mood. Many of its terms, such as irrational numbers, have no direct connection with the common field of experience, but depend for their meaning solely on the interrelations of the subject itself. Irrational numbers in mathematics may be compared to prepositions in verbal languages, the centripetal character of which we have noted. When we distinguish pure from applied mathematics, we are thinking of the former as a disinterested conception of numerical relationships, concerned more and more with its inner integrity, and less and less with its reference to external criteria.

We think also of literature at first as a commentary on an external "life" or "reality." But just as in mathematics we have to go from three apples to three, and from a square field to a square, so in reading a novel we have to go from literature as reflection of life to literature as autonomous language. Literature also proceeds by hypothetical possibilities, and though literature, like mathematics, is constantly useful—a word which means having a continuing relationship to the common field of experience—pure literature, like pure mathematics, contains its own meaning.

Both literature and mathematics proceed from postulates, not facts; both can be applied to external reality and yet exist also in a "pure" or self-contained form. Both, furthermore, drive a wedge between the antithesis of being and nonbeing that is so important for discursive thought. The symbol neither is nor is not the reality which it manifests. The child beginning geometry is presented with a dot and is told, first, that that is a point, and second, that it is not a point. He cannot advance until he accepts both statements at once. It is absurd that that which is no number can also be a number, but the result of accepting the absurdity was the discovery of zero. The same kind of hypothesis exists in literature, where Hamlet and Falstaff neither exist nor do not exist, and where an airy nothing is confidently located and named. We notice that rhetoric differs sharply from logic in that it invariably gives some positive quality to a negative statement. Logic counts the negatives in a statement and calls it affirmative if there is an even number, but no one in the history of communication ever took "I hain't got no money" to mean that the speaker *did* have money. Similarly in literature: Iago's urging Othello to beware of jealousy is designed to plant jealousy in Othello's mind; the negatives at the beginning of *Gerontion* [7] mean logically that Gerontion is not

[6] Ernst Cassirer (1874-1945), German philosopher and historian of ideas, a pioneer in the philosophic study of myth and symbolic forms; and Alfred Korzybsky (1879-1940), a Polish-American writer on semantics.

[7] A poem by T. S. Eliot.

a hero, but rhetorically they build up a contrasting picture of sacrifice and endurance. If the poet never affirmeth, he never denies either; [8] and in this respect Aristotle's opening statement about rhetoric, that it is the *antistrophos* or answering chorus of dialectic, breaks down.

In the final chapter of Sir James Jeans' *The Mysterious Universe,* the author speaks of the failure of physical cosmology in the nineteenth century to conceive of the universe as ultimately mechanical, and suggests that a mathematical approach to it may have better luck. The universe cannot be a machine, but it may be an interlocking set of mathematical formulas. What this means is surely that pure mathematics exists in a mathematical universe which is no longer a commentary on an outside world, but contains that world within itself. Mathematics is at first a form of understanding an objective world regarded as its content, but in the end it conceives of the content as being itself mathematical in form, and when a conception of a mathematical universe is reached, form and content become the same thing. Mathematics relates itself indirectly to the common field of experience, then, not to avoid it, but with the ultimate design of swallowing it. It appears to be a kind of informing or constructive principle in the natural sciences: it continually gives shape and coherence to them without being itself dependent on external proof or evidence, and yet finally the physical or quantitative universe appears to be contained by mathematics. The occult or mystical sound of Jeans' chapter, which nevertheless expresses a dream that has haunted mathematicians at least since Pythagoras, may be compared with the religious terminology we found ourselves compelled to use as soon as we reached the corresponding conception of a literary or verbal universe.

Other points in this analogy strike one: the curious similarity in form, for instance, between the units of literature and of mathematics, the metaphor and the equation. Both of these are, in the expanded sense of the term employed by many logicians, tautologies. But if the analogy is to hold, the question of course arises: is literature like mathematics in being substantially useful, and not just incidentally so? That is, is it true that the verbal structures of psychology,

anthropology, theology, history, law, and everything else built out of words have been informed or constructed by the same kind of myths and metaphors that we find, in their original hypothetical form, in literature?

The possibility that seems to me suggested by the present discussion is as follows. Discursive verbal structures have two aspects, one descriptive, the other constructive, a content and a form. What is descriptive is sigmatic: that is, it establishes a verbal replica of external phenomena, and its verbal symbolism is to be understood as a set of representative signs. But whatever is constructive in any verbal structure seems to me to be invariably some kind of metaphor or hypothetical identification, whether it is established among different meanings of the same word or by the use of a diagram. The assumed metaphors in their turn become the units of the myth or constructive principle of the argument. While we read, we are aware of a sequence of metaphorical identifications; when we have finished, we are aware of an organizing structural pattern or conceptualized myth.

It looks now as though Freud's view of the Oedipus complex were a psychological conception that throws some light on literary criticism. Perhaps we shall eventually decide that we have got it the wrong way round: that what happened was that the myth of Oedipus informed and gave structure to some psychological investigations at this point. Freud would in that case be exceptional only in having been well read enough to spot the source of the myth. It looks now as though the psychological discovery of an oracular mind "underneath" the conscious one forms an appropriate allegorical explanation of a poetic archetype that has run through literature from the cave of Trophonius to our own day.[9] Perhaps it was the archetype that informed the discovery: it is after all considerably older, and to explain it in this way would involve us in less anachronism. The informing of metaphysical and theological constructs by poetic myths, or by associations and diagrams analogous to poetic myths, is even more obvious.

---

[8] Cf. Sidney's "Apology for Poetry," above, p. 97.

[9] In Greek mythology Trophonius, after his death, became an oracle in a cave. Whoever consulted the oracle emerged from the cave in despair. Hence someone deeply melancholy was often said to have visited the Cave of Trophonius.

Such an approach need not be distorted into a poetic determinism, for, as has been said, it would be silly to use a reductive rhetoric to try to prove that theology, metaphysics, law, the social sciences, or whichever one or group of these we happen to dislike, are based on "nothing but" metaphors or myths. Any such proof, if we are right, would have the same kind of basis itself. Criticisms of truth or adequacy, then, are mainly criticism of content, not form. Rousseau says that the original society of nature and reason has been overlaid by the corruptions of civilization, and that a sufficiently courageous revolutionary act could reestablish it. It is nothing either for or against this argument to say that it is informed by the myth of the sleeping beauty. But we cannot agree or disagree with Rousseau until we fully understand what he does say, and while of course we can understand him well enough without extracting the myth, there is much to be gained by extracting the myth if the myth is in fact, as we are suggesting here, the source of the coherence of his argument. Such a view of the relation of myth to argument would take us very close to Plato, for whom the ultimate acts of apprehension were either mathematical or mythical.

Literature, like mathematics, is a language, and a language in itself represents no truth, though it may provide the means for expressing any number of them. But poets and critics alike have always believed in some kind of imaginative truth, and perhaps the justification for the belief is in the containment by the language of what it can express. The mathematical and the verbal universes are doubtless different ways of conceiving the same universe. The objective world affords a provisional means of unifying experience, and it is natural to infer a higher unity, a sort of beatification of common sense. But it is not easy to find any language capable of expressing the unity of this higher intellectual universe. Metaphysics, theology, history, law, have all been used, but all are verbal constructs, and the further we take them, the more clearly their metaphorical and mythical outlines show through. Whenever we construct a system of thought to unite earth with heaven, the story of the Tower of Babel recurs: [10] we discover that after all we can't quite make it, and that what we have in the meantime is a plurality of languages.

If I have read the last chapter of *Finnegans Wake* correctly, what happens there is that the dreamer, after spending the night in communion with a vast body of metaphorical identifications, wakens and goes about his business forgetting his dream, like Nebuchadnezzar, failing to use, or even to realize that he can use, the "keys to dreamland." [11] What he fails to do is therefore left for the reader to do, the "ideal reader suffering from an ideal insomnia," as Joyce calls him, in other words the critic. Some such activity as this of reforging the broken links between creation and knowledge, art and science, myth and concept, is what I envisage for criticism. Once more, I am not speaking of a change of direction or activity in criticism: I mean only that if critics go on with their own business, this will appear to be, with increasing obviousness, the social and practical result of their labors.

[10] Genesis, XI, 3-9.
[11] Daniel, IV.

Myth, Fiction, and Displacement

"MYTH" is a conception which runs through many areas of contemporary thought: anthropology, psychology, comparative religion, sociology, and several others. What follows is an attempt to explain what the term

Myth, Fiction, and Displacement. First printed in *Daedalus, Journal of the American Academy of Arts and Sciences,* Summer, 1961. Reprinted in *The Fables of Identity: Studies in Poetic Mythology,* copyright, 1963, by Harcourt Brace Jovanovich, Inc.

means in literary criticism today. Such an explanation must begin with the question: Why did the term ever get into literary criticism? There can be only one legitimate answer to such a question: because myth is and has always been an integral element of literature, the interest of poets in myth and mythology having been remarkable and constant since Homer's time.

There are two broad divisions of literary

works, which may be called the fictional and the thematic. The former comprises works of literature with internal characters, and includes novels, plays, narrative poetry, folk tales, and everything that tells a story. In thematic literature the author and the reader are the only characters involved: this division includes most lyrics, essays, didactic poetry and oratory. Each division has its own type of myth, but we shall be concerned here only with the fictional part of literature, and with myth in its more common and easily recognized form as a certain kind of narrative.

When a critic deals with a work of literature, the most natural thing for him to do is to freeze it, to ignore its movement in time and look at it as a completed pattern of words, with all its parts existing simultaneously. This approach is common to nearly all types of critical techniques: here new and old-fashioned critics are at one. But in the direct experience of literature, which is something distinct from criticism, we are aware of what we may call the persuasion of continuity, the power that keeps us turning the pages of a novel and that holds us in our seats at the theatre. The continuity may be logical, or pseudo-logical, or psychological, or rhetorical: it may reside in the surge and thunder of epic verse or in some donkey's carrot like the identity of the murderer in a detective story or the first sexual act of the heroine in a romance. Or we may feel afterwards that the sense of continuity was pure illusion, as though we had been laid under a spell.

The continuity of a work of literature exists on different rhythmical levels. In the foreground, every word, every image, even every sound made audibly or inaudibly by the words, is making its tiny contribution to the total movement. But it would take a portentous concentration to attend to such details in direct experience: they belong to the kind of critical study that is dealing with a simultaneous unity. What we are conscious of in direct experience is rather a series of larger groupings, events and scenes that make up what we call the story. In ordinary English the word "plot" means this latter sequence of gross events. For a term that would include the total movement of sounds and images, the word "narrative" seems more natural than "plot," though the choice is a matter of usage and not of in-

herent correctness. Both words translate Aristotle's *mythos,* but Aristotle meant mainly by *mythos* what we are calling plot: narrative, in the above sense, is closer to his *lexis.* The plot, then, is like the trees and houses that we focus our eyes on through a train window: the narrative is more like the weeds and stones that rush by in the foreground.

We now run into a curious difficulty. Plot, Aristotle says, is the life and soul of tragedy (and by implication of fiction generally) : [1] the essence of fiction, then, is plot or imitation of action, and characters exist primarily as functions of the plot. In our direct experience of fiction we feel how central is the importance of the steady progression of events that holds and guides our attention. Yet afterwards, when we try to remember or think about what we have seen, this sense of continuity is one of the most difficult things to recapture. What stands out in our minds is a vivid characterization, a great speech or striking image, a detached scene, bits and pieces of unusually convincing realization. A summary of a plot, say of a Scott novel, has much the same numbing effect on a hearer as a summary of last night's dream. That is not how we remember the book; or at least not why we remember it. And even with a work of fiction that we know thoroughly, such as *Hamlet,* while we keep in mind a sequence of scenes, and know that the ghost comes at the beginning and the duel with Laertes at the end, still there is something oddly discontinuous about our possession of it. With the histories this disappearance of continuity is even more striking. *The Oxford Companion to English Literature* is an invaluable reference work largely because it is so good at summarizing all the fictional plots that one has forgotten, but here is its summary of *King John:*

The play, with some departures from historical accuracy, deals with various events in King John's reign, and principally with the tragedy of young Arthur. It ends with the death of John at Swinstead Abbey. It is significant that no mention of Magna Carta appears in it. The tragic quality of the play, the poignant grief of Constance, Arthur's mother, and the political complications depicted, are relieved by the wit, humour, and gallantry of the Bastard of Faulconbridge.

[1] See above, p. 23.

This is, more or less, how we remember the play. We remember Faulconbridge and his great speech at the end; we remember the death scene of Prince Arthur; we remember Constance; we remember nothing about Magna Carta; we remember in the background the vacillating, obstinate, defiant king. But what *happened* in the play? What were the incidents that made it an imitation of an action? Does it matter? If it doesn't matter, what becomes of the principle that the characters exist for the sake of the action, the truth of which we felt so vividly while watching the play? If it does matter, are we going to invent some silly pedantic theory of unity that would rule out *King John* as legitimate drama?

Whatever the final answer, we may tentatively accept the principle that, in the direct experience of fiction, continuity is the center of our attention; our later memory, or what I call the possession of it, tends to become discontinuous. Our attention shifts from the sequence of incidents to another focus: a sense of what the work of fiction was all *about*, or what criticism usually calls its theme. And we notice that as we go on to study and reread the work of fiction, we tend, not to reconstruct the plot, but to become more conscious of the theme, and to see all incidents as manifestations of it. Thus the incidents themselves tend to remain, in our critical study of the work, discontinuous, detached from one another and regrouped in a new way. Even if we know it by heart this is still true, and if we are writing or lecturing on it, we usually start with something other than its linear action.

Now in the conception "theme," as in the conception "narrative," there are a number of distinguishable elements. One of them is "subject," which criticism can usually express by some kind of summarized statement. If we are asked what Arthur Miller's *The Crucible* is about, we say that it is about—that is, its subject is—the Salem witch trials. Similarly, the subject of *Hamlet* is Hamlet's attempt at revenge on an uncle who has murdered his father and married his mother. But the Olivier movie of *Hamlet* began with the statement (quoted from an unreliable memory): "This is the story of a man who could not make up his mind." Here is a quite different conception of theme: it expresses the theme in terms of what we may call its allegorical value. To the

extent that it is an adequate statement of the theme of *Hamlet*, it makes the play into an allegory and the chief character into a personification of Indecision. In his illuminating study of *The Ancient Mariner*, Robert Penn Warren says that the poem is written out of, and about, the general belief that the truth is implicit "in the poetic act as such, that the moral concern and the aesthetic concern are aspects of the same activity, the creative activity, and that this activity is expressive of the whole mind" (italicized in the original).[2] Here again is allegorization, of a kind that takes the theme to be what Aristotle appears to have meant primarily by *dianoia*, the "thought" or sententious reflexion that the poem suggests to a meditative reader.[3]

It seems to me that a third conception of "theme" is possible, less abstract than the subject and more direct than an allegorical translation. It is also, however, a conception for which the primitive vocabulary of contemporary criticism is ill adapted. Theme in this third sense is the *mythos* or plot examined as a simultaneous unity, when the entire shape of it is clear in our minds. In *Anatomy of Criticism* I use *dianoia* in this sense: an extension of Aristotle's meaning, no doubt, but in my opinion a justifiable one. The theme, so considered, differs appreciably from the moving plot: it is the same in substance, but we are now concerned with the details in relation to a unity, not in relation to suspense and linear progression. The unifying factors assume a new and increased importance, and the smaller details of imagery, which may escape conscious notice in direct experience, take on their proper significance. It is because of this difference that we find our memory of the progression of events dissolving as the events regroup themselves around another center of attention. Each event or incident, we now see, is a manifestation of some underlying unity, a unity that it both conceals and reveals, as clothes do the body in *Sartor Resartus*.

Further, the plot or progress of events as a whole is also a manifestation of the theme, for the same story (i.e., theme in our sense) could be told in many different ways. It is, of course, impossible to say how extensive the changes of

2 (1946), p. 103.
3 See above, p. 23.

detail would have to be before we had a differ-ent theme, but they can be surprisingly exten-sive. Chaucer's *Pardoner's Tale* is a folk tale that started in India and must have reached Chaucer from some West-European source. It also stayed in India, where Kipling picked it up and put it into the *Second Jungle Book.* Every-thing is different—setting, details, method of treatment—yet I think any reader, on whatever level of sophistication, would say that it was recognizably the same "story"—story as theme, that is, for the linear progression is what is dif-ferent. More often we have only smaller units in common, of a kind that students of folklore call motifs. Thus in Hawthorne's *The Marble Faun* we have the motif of the two heroines, one dark and one light, that we have in *Ivanhoe* and else-where; in *Lycidas* we have the motif of the "sanguine flower inscrib'd with woe," the red or purple flower that turns up everywhere in pastoral elegy, and so on. These smaller units I have elsewhere called archetypes, a word which has been connected since Plato's time with the sense of a pattern or model used in creation.

In most works of fiction we are at once aware that the *mythos* or sequence of events which holds our attention is being shaped into a unity. We are continually, if often unconsciously, at-tempting to construct a larger pattern of simul-taneous significance out of what we have so far read or seen. We feel confident that the begin-ning implies an end, and that the story is not like the soul in natural theology, starting off at an arbitrary moment in time and going on for-ever. Hence we often keep on reading even a tiresome novel "to see how it turns out." That is, we expect a certain point near the end at which linear suspense is resolved and the unifying shape of the whole design becomes conceptually visible. This point was called *anagnorisis* by Aristotle, a term for which "recognition" is a better rendering than "discovery." [4] A tragic or comic plot is not a straight line: it is a parabola following the shapes of the mouths on the con-ventional masks. Comedy has a U-shaped plot, with the action sinking into deep and often potentially tragic complications, and then sud-denly turning upward into a happy ending. Tragedy has an inverted U, with the action ris-

ing in crisis to a peripety and then plunging downward to catastrophe through a series of recognitions, usually of the inevitable conse-quences of previous acts. But in both cases what is recognized is seldom anything new; it is some-thing which has been there all along, and which, by its reappearance or manifestation, brings the end into line with the beginning.

Recognition, and the unity of theme which it manifests, is often symbolized by some kind of emblematic object. A simple example is in the sixteenth-century play, *Gammer Gurton's Needle,* the action of which is largely a great to-do over the loss of the needle, and which ends when a clown named Hodge gets it stuck in his posterior, bringing about what *Finnegans Wake* would call a culious epiphany. Fans, rings, chains and other standard props of comedy are emblematic talis-mans of the same kind. Nearly always, however, such an emblem has to do with the identification of a chief character. Birthmarks and their sym-bolic relatives have run through fiction from Odysseus' scar to the scarlet letter, and from the brand of Cain to the rose tattoo. In Greek romance and its descendants we have infants of noble birth exposed on a hillside with birth-tokens beside them; they are found by a shep-herd or farmer and brought up in a lower sta-tion of life, and the birth-tokens are produced when the story has gone on long enough. In more complex fiction the emblem may be an oblique comment on a character, as with Henry James's golden bowl; or, if it is only a motif, it may serve as what T. S. Eliot calls an objec-tive correlative. [5]

In any case, the point of recognition seems to be also a point of identification, where a hid-den truth about something or somebody emerges into view. Besides the emblem, the hero may discover who his parents or children are, or he may go through some kind of ordeal (*basanos*) that manifests his true character, or the villain may be unmasked as a hypocrite, or, as in a detective story, identified as a murderer. In the Chinese play *The Chalk Circle* we have almost every possible form of recognition in the crucial scene. A concubine bears her master a son and is then accused of having murdered him by the

[4] See above, pp. 26 and 29.

[5] In his essay on *Hamlet,* in *Selected Essays* (1932), p. 124.

wife, who has murdered him herself, and who also claims the son as her own. The concubine is tried before a foolish judge and condemned to death, then tried again before a wise one, who performs an experiment in a chalk circle resembling that of the judgment of Solomon in the Bible, and which proves that the concubine is the mother. Here we have: (a) the specific emblematic device which gives the play its name; (b) an ordeal or test which reveals character; (c) the reunion of the mother with her rightful child; and (d) the recognition of the true moral natures of concubine and wife. There are several other elements of structural importance, but these will do to go on with.

So far, however, we have been speaking of strictly controlled forms, like comedy, where the end of the linear action also manifests the unity of the theme. What shall we find if we turn to other works where the author has just let his imagination go? I put the question in the form of this very common phrase because of the way that it illustrates a curious critical muddle. Usually, when we think of "imagination" psychologically, we think of it in its Renaissance sense as a faculty that works mainly by association and outside the province of judgment. But the associative faculty is not the creative one, though the two are frequently confused by neurotics. When we think of imagination as the power that produces art, we often think of it as the designing or structural principle in creation, Coleridge's "esemplastic" power.[6] But imagination in this sense, left to itself, can only design. Random fantasy is exceedingly rare in the arts, and most of what we do have is a clever simulation of it. From primitive cultures to the *tachiste*[7] and action paintings of today, it has been a regular rule that the uninhibited imagination, in the structural sense, produces highly conventionalized art.

This rule implies, of course, that the main source of inhibitions is the need to produce a credible or plausible story, to come to terms with things as they are and not as the storyteller would like them to be for his convenience. Removing the necessity for telling a credible

story enables the teller to concentrate on its structure, and when this happens, characters turn into imaginative projections, heroes becoming purely heroic and villains purely villainous. That is, they become assimilated to their functions in the plot. We see this conventionalizing of structure very clearly in the folk tale. Folk tales tell us nothing credible about the life or manners of any society; so far from giving us dialogue, imagery or complex behavior, they do not even care whether their characters are men or ghosts or animals. Folk tales are simply abstract story-patterns, uncomplicated and easy to remember, no more hampered by barriers of language and culture than migrating birds are by customs officers, and made up of interchangeable motifs that can be counted and indexed.

Nevertheless, folk tales form a continuum with other literary fictions. We know, vaguely, that the story of Cinderella has been retold hundreds of thousands of times in middle-class fiction, and that nearly every thriller we see is a variant of Bluebeard. But it is seldom explained why even the greatest writers are interested in such tales: why Shakespeare put a folk-tale motif into nearly every comedy he wrote; why some of the most intellectualized fiction of our day, such as the later works of Thomas Mann, are based on them. Writers are interested in folk tales for the same reason that painters are interested in still-life arrangements: because they illustrate essential principles of storytelling. The writer who uses them then has the technical problem of making them sufficiently plausible or credible to a sophisticated audience. When he succeeds, he produces, not realism, but a distortion of realism in the interests of structure. Such distortion is the literary equivalent of the tendency in painting to assimilate subject-matter to geometrical form, which we see both in primitive painting and in the sophisticated primitivism of, say, Léger or Modigliani.[8]

What we see clearly in the folk tale we see less clearly in popular fiction. If we want incident for its own sake, we turn from the standard novelists to adventure stories, like those of Rider Haggard or John Buchan, where the action is close to if not actually across the boundary of

[6] See above, p. 366, n. 1.

[7] A variety of abstract expressionism (from the French word for "spot" or "blot").

[8] Fernand Léger (1881-1955), the French cubist; and Amadeo Modigliani (1884-1920), the Italian painter.

the credible. Such stories are not looser or more flexible than the classical novels, but far tighter. Gone is all sense of the leisurely acquiring of incidental experience, of exploring all facets of a character, of learning something about a specific society. A hazardous enterprise is announced at the beginning and everything is rigorously subordinated to that. In such works, while characters exist for the sake of the action, the two aspects of the action which we have defined as plot and theme are very close together. The story could hardly have been told in any other narrative shape, and our attention has so little expanding to do when it reaches the recognition that we often feel that there would be no point in reading it a second time. The subordination of character to linear action is also a feature of the detective story, for the fact that one of the characters is capable of murder is the concealed clue on which every detective story turns. Even more striking is the subordinating of moral attitude to the conventions of the story. Thus in Robert Louis Stevenson's tale, *The Body-Snatcher*, which is about the smuggling of corpses from cemeteries into medical classrooms, we read of bodies being "exposed to uttermost indignities before a class of gaping boys," and much more to the same effect. It is irrelevant to inquire whether this is really Stevenson's attitude to the use of cadavers in medical study or whether he expects it to be ours. The more sinister the crime can be felt to be, the more thrilling the thriller, and the moral attitude is being deliberately talked up to thicken the atmosphere.

The opposite extreme from such conventionalized fiction is represented by Trollope's *Last Chronicle of Barset*. Here the main story line is a kind of parody of a detective novel—such parodies of suspense are frequent in Trollope. Some money has been stolen, and suspicion falls on the Reverend Josiah Crawley, curate of Hogglestock. The point of the parody is that Crawley's character is clearly and fully set forth, and if you imagine him capable of stealing money you are simply not attending to the story. The action, therefore, appears to exist for the sake of the characters, reversing Aristotle's axiom. But this is not really true. Characters still exist only as functions of the action, but in Trollope the "action" resides in the huge social panorama that the linear events build up. Recognition is

continuous: it is in the texture of characterization, the dialogue and the comment itself, and needs no twist in the plot to dramatize a contrast between appearance and reality. And what is true of Trollope is roughly true of most mimetic fiction between Defoe and Arnold Bennett. When we read Smollett or Jane Austen or Dickens, we read them for the sake of the texture of characterization, and tend to think of the plot, when we think of it at all, as a conventional, mechanical, or even (as occasionally in Dickens) absurd contrivance included only to satisfy the demands of the literary market.

The requirement of plausibility, then, has the apparently paradoxical effect of limiting the imagination by making its design more flexible. Thus in a Dutch realistic interior the painter's ability to render the sheen of satin or the varnish of a lute both limits his power of design (for a realistic painter cannot, like Braque or Juan Gris,[9] distort his object in the interest of pictorial composition) and yet makes that design less easy to take in at a glance. In fact we often "read" Dutch pictures instead of looking at them, absorbed by their technical virtuosity but unaffected by much conscious sense of their total structure.

By this time the ambiguity in our word "imagination" is catching up with us. So far we have been using it in the sense of a structural power which, left to itself, produces rigorously predictable fictions. In this sense Bernard Shaw spoke of the romances of Marie Corelli as illustrating the triumph of imagination over mind. What is implied by "mind" here is less a structural than a reproductive power, which expresses itself in the texture of characterization and imagery. There seems no reason why this should not be called imagination too: in any case, in reading fiction there are two kinds of recognition. One is the continuous recognition of credibility, fidelity to experience, and of what is not so much lifelikeness as life-liveliness. The other is the recognition of the identity of the total design, into which we are initiated by the technical recognition in the plot.

The influence of mimetic fiction has thrown the main emphasis in criticism on the former

[9] Georges Braque (1882-1963) and Juan Gris (1887-1927), the former a French and the latter a Spanish cubist painter.

kind of recognition. Coleridge, as is well known, intended the climax of the *Biographia Literaria* to be a demonstration of the "esemplastic" or structural nature of the imagination, only to discover when the great chapter arrived that he was unable to write it. There were doubtless many reasons for this, but one was that he does not really think of imagination as a constructive power at all. He means by imagination what we have called the reproductive power, the ability to bring to life the texture of characterization and imagery. It is to this power that he applies his favorite metaphor of an organism, where the unity is some mysterious and elusive "vitality." His practical criticism of work he admires is concerned with texture: he never discusses the total design, or what we call the theme, of a Shakespeare play. It is really fancy which is his "esemplastic" power, and which he tends to think of as mechanical. His conception of fancy as a mode of memory, emancipated from time and space and playing with fixities and definites, admirably characterizes the folk tale, with its remoteness from society and its stock of interchangeable motifs. Thus Coleridge is in the tradition of critical naturalism, which bases its values on the immediacy of contact between art and nature that we continuously feel in the texture of mimetic fiction.

There is nothing wrong with critical naturalism, as far as it goes, but it does not do full justice to our feelings about the total design of a work of fiction. We shall not improve on Coleridge, however, by merely reversing his perspective, as T. E. Hulme did, and giving our favorable value-judgments to fancy, wit, and highly conventionalized forms.[10] This can start a new critical trend, but not develop the study of criticism. In the direct experience of a new work of fiction we have a sense of its unity which we derive from its persuasive continuity. As the work becomes more familiar, this sense of continuity fades out, and we tend to think of it as a discontinuous series of episodes, held together by something which eludes critical analysis. But that this unity is available for critical study as well seems clear when it emerges as a unity of "theme," as we call it, which we can study all at once, and to which we are normally initiated by

some crucial recognition in the plot. Hence we need a supplementary form of criticism which can examine the total design of fiction as something which is neither mechanical nor of secondary importance.

By a myth, as I said at the beginning, I mean primarily a certain type of story. It is a story in which some of the chief characters are gods or other beings larger in power than humanity. Very seldom is it located in history: its action takes place in a world above or prior to ordinary time, *in illo tempore*, in Mircea Eliade's phrase.[11] Hence, like the folk tale, it is an abstract story-pattern. The characters can do what they like, which means what the story-teller likes: there is no need to be plausible or logical in motivation. The things that happen in myth are things that happen only in stories; they are in a self-contained literary world. Hence myth would naturally have the same kind of appeal for the fiction writer that folk tales have. It presents him with a ready-made framework, hoary with antiquity, and allows him to devote all his energies to elaborating its design. Thus the use of myth in Joyce or Cocteau, like the use of folk tale in Mann, is parallel to the use of abstraction and other means of emphasizing design in contemporary painting; and a modern writer's interest in primitive fertility rites is parallel to a modern sculptor's interest in primitive woodcarving.

The differences between myth and folk tale, however, also have their importance. Myths, as compared with folk tales, are usually in a special category of seriousness: they are believed to have "really happened," or to have some exceptional significance in explaining certain features of life, such as ritual. Again, whereas folk tales simply interchange motifs and develop variants, myths show an odd tendency to stick together and build up bigger structures. We have creation myths, fall and flood myths, metamorphosis and dying-god myths, divine-marriage and hero-ancestry myths, etiological myths, apocalyptic myths; and writers of sacred scriptures or collectors of myth like Ovid tend to arrange these in a series. And while myths themselves

---

[10] See above, p. 564.

[11] "In that time." Eliade (1907-   ) is a Roumanian-American scholar of the history of religion.

are seldom historical, they seem to provide a kind of containing form of tradition, one result of which is the obliterating of boundaries separating legend, historical reminiscence, and actual history that we find in Homer and the Old Testament.

As a type of story, myth is a form of verbal art, and belongs to the world of art. Like art, and unlike science, it deals, not with the world that man contemplates, but with the world that man creates. The total form of art, so to speak, is a world whose content is nature but whose form is human; hence when it "imitates" nature it assimilates nature to human forms. The world of art is human in perspective, a world in which the sun continues to rise and set long after science has explained that its rising and setting are illusions. And myth, too, makes a systematic attempt to see nature in human shape: it does not simply roam at large in nature like the folk tale.

The obvious conception which brings together the human form and the natural content in myth is the god. It is not the connexion of the stories of Phaethon and Endymion with the sun and moon that makes them myths, for we could have folk tales of the same kind: it is rather their attachment to the body of stories told about Apollo and Artemis which gives them a canonical place in the growing system of tales that we call a mythology. And every developed mythology tends to complete itself, to outline an entire universe in which the "gods" represent the whole of nature in humanized form, and at the same time show in perspective man's origin, his destiny, the limits of his power, and the extension of his hopes and desires. A mythology may develop by accretion, as in Greece, or by rigorous codifying and the excluding of unwanted material, as in Israel; but the drive toward a verbal circumference of human experience is clear in both cultures.

The two great conceptual principles which myth uses in assimilating nature to human form are analogy and identity. Analogy establishes the parallels between human life and natural phenomena, and identity conceives of a "sun-god" or a "tree-god." Myth seizes on the fundamental element of design offered by nature—the cycle, as we have it daily in the sun and yearly in the seasons—and assimilates it to the human

cycle of life, death, and (analogy again) rebirth. At the same time the discrepancy between the world man lives in and the world he would like to live in develops a dialectic in myth which, as in the New Testament and Plato's *Phaedo*, separates reality into two contrasting states, a heaven and a hell.

Again, myths are often used as allegories of science or religion or morality: they may arise in the first place to account for a ritual or a law, or they may be *exempla* or parables which illustrate a particular situation or argument, like the myths in Plato or Achilles' myth of the two jars of Zeus at the end of the Iliad. Once established in their own right, they may then be interpreted dogmatically or allegorically, as all the standard myths have been for centuries, in innumerable ways. But because myths are stories, what they "mean" is inside them, in the implications of their incidents. No rendering of any myth into conceptual language can serve as a full equivalent of its meaning. A myth may be told and retold: it may be modified or elaborated, or different patterns may be discovered in it; and its life is always the poetic life of a story, not the homiletic life of some illustrated truism. When a system of myths loses all connexion with belief, it becomes purely literary, as Classical myth did in Christian Europe. Such a development would be impossible unless myths were inherently literary in structure. As it makes no difference to that structure whether an interpretation of the myth is believed in or not, there is no difficulty in speaking of a Christian mythology.

Myth thus provides the main outlines and the circumference of a verbal universe which is later occupied by literature as well. Literature is more flexible than myth, and fills up this universe more completely: a poet or novelist may work in areas of human life apparently remote from the shadowy gods and gigantic story-outlines of mythology. But in all cultures mythology merges insensibly into, and with, literature. The Odyssey is to us a work of literature, but its early place in the literary tradition, the importance of gods in its action, and its influence on the later religious thought of Greece, are all features common to literature proper and to mythology, and indicate that the difference between them is more chronological than structural. Educators are now aware that any effective teaching of literature has to recapitulate its history and begin, in early childhood, with myths, folk tales and legends.

We should expect, therefore, that there would be a great many literary works derived directly from specific myths, like the poems by Drayton and Keats about Endymion which are derived from the myth of Endymion. But the study of the relations between mythology and literature is not confined to such one-to-one relationships. In the first place, mythology as a total structure, defining as it does a society's religious beliefs, historical traditions, cosmological speculations— in short, the whole range of its verbal expressiveness—is the matrix of literature, and major poetry keeps returning to it. In every age poets who are thinkers (remembering that poets think in metaphors and images, not in propositions) and are deeply concerned with the origin or destiny or desires of mankind—with anything that belongs to the larger outlines of what literature can express—can hardly find a literary theme that does not coincide with a myth. Hence the imposing body of explicitly mythopoeic poetry in the epic and encyclopaedic forms which so many of the greatest poets use. A poet who accepts a mythology as valid for belief, as Dante and Milton accepted Christianity, will naturally use it; poets outside such a tradition turn to other mythologies as suggestive or symbolic of what might be believed, as in the adaptations of Classical or occult mythological systems made by Goethe, Victor Hugo, Shelley, or Yeats.

Similarly, the structural principles of a mythology, built up from analogy and identity, become in due course the structural principles of literature. The absorption of the natural cycle into mythology provides myth with two of these structures; the rising movement that we find in myths of spring or the dawn, of birth, marriage and resurrection, and the falling movement in myths of death, metamorphosis, or sacrifice. These movements reappear as the structural principles of comedy and tragedy in literature. Again, the dialectic in myth that projects a paradise or heaven above our world and a hell or place of shades below it reappears in literature as the idealized world of pastoral and ro-

mance and the absurd, suffering, or frustrated world of irony and satire.

The relation between myth and literature, therefore, is established by studying the genres and conventions of literature. Thus the convention of the pastoral elegy in *Lycidas* links it to Virgil and Theocritus, and thence with the myth of Adonis. Thus the convention of the foundling plot, which is the basis of *Tom Jones* and *Oliver Twist*, goes back to Menandrine comedy formulas,[12] thence to Euripides, and so back to such myths as the finding of Moses and Perseus.[13] In myth criticism, when we examine the theme or total design of a fiction, we must isolate that aspect of the fiction which is conventional, and held in common with all other works of the same category. When we begin, say, *Pride and Prejudice*, we can see at once that a story which sustains that particular mood or tone is most unlikely to end in tragedy or melodrama or mordant irony or romance. It clearly belongs to the category represented by the word "comedy," and we are not surprised to find in it the conventional features of comedy, including a foolish lover, with some economic advantages, encouraged by one of the parents, a hypocrite unmasked, misunderstandings between the chief characters eventually cleared up and happy marriages for those who deserve them. This conventional comic form is in *Pride and Prejudice* somewhat as the sonata form is in a Mozart symphony. Its presence there does not account for any of the merits of the novel, but it does account for its conventional, as distinct from its individual, structure. A serious interest in structure, then, ought naturally to lead us from *Pride and Prejudice* to a study of the comic form which it exemplifies, the conventions of which have presented much the same features from Plautus to our own day. These conventions in turn take us back into myth. When we compare the conventional plot of a play of Plautus with the Christian myth of a son appeasing the wrath of a father and redeeming his

---

[12] From Menander (342-292 B.C.), whose new form of realistic comedy influenced later Roman writers such as Plautus.

[13] For the story of the finding of Moses, see Exodus 2:3-10. Perseus, the son of Zeus by Danae, was cast adrift with his mother by Danae's husband, Acrisius, and found by a fisherman named Dictys.

bride, we can see that the latter is quite accurately described, from a literary point of view, as a divine comedy.

Whenever we find explicit mythologizing in literature, or a writer trying to indicate what myths he is particularly interested in, we should treat this as confirmatory or supporting evidence for our study of the genres and conventions he is using. Meredith's *The Egoist* is a story about a girl who narrowly escapes marrying a selfish man, which makes many references, both explicitly and indirectly in its imagery, to the two best-known myths of female sacrifice, the stories of Andromeda and Iphigeneia.[14] Such allusions would be pointless or unintelligible except as indications by Meredith of an awareness of the conventional shape of the story he is telling. Again, it is as true of poetry as it is of myth that its main conceptual elements are analogy and identity, which reappear in the two commonest figures of speech, the simile and the metaphor. Literature, like mythology, is largely an art of misleading analogies and mistaken identities. Hence we often find poets, especially young poets, turning to myth because of the scope it affords them for uninhibited poetic imagery. If Shakespeare's *Venus and Adonis* had been simply a story about a willing girl and an unwilling boy, all the resources of analogy and identity would have been left unexplored: the fanciful imagery appropriate to the mythical subject would have been merely tasteless exaggeration. Especially is this true with what may be called sympathetic imagery, the association of human and natural life:

No flower was nigh, no grass, herb, leaf, or weed,
But stole his blood and seem'd with him to bleed.[15]

The opposite extreme from such deliberate exploiting of myth is to be found in the general tendency of realism or naturalism to give imaginative life and coherence to something closely resembling our own ordinary experience. Such realism often begins by simplifying its language,

and dropping the explicit connexions with myth which are a sign of an awareness of literary tradition. Wordsworth, for example, felt that in his day Phoebus and Philomela were getting to be mere trade slang for the sun and the nightingale, and that poetry would do better to discard this kind of inorganic allusion. But, as Wordsworth himself clearly recognized, the result of turning one's back on explicit myth can only be the reconstructing of the same mythical patterns in more ordinary words:

> Paradise, and groves
> Elysian, Fortunate Fields—like those of old
> Sought in the Atlantic Main—why should they be
> A history only of departed things,
> Or a mere fiction of what never was?
> For the discerning intellect of Man,
> When wedded to this goodly universe
> In love and holy passion, shall find these
> A simple produce of the common day.[16]

To this indirect mythologizing I have elsewhere given the name of displacement. By displacement I mean the techniques a writer uses to make his story credible, logically motivated or morally acceptable—lifelike, in short. I call it displacement for many reasons, but one is that fidelity to the credible is a feature of literature that can affect only content. Life presents a continuum, and a selection from it can only be what is called a *tranche de vie*:[17] plausibility is easy to sustain, but except for death life has little to suggest in the way of plausible conclusions. And even a plausible conclusion does not necessarily round out a shape. The realistic writer soon finds that the requirements of literary form and plausible content always fight against each other. Just as the poetic metaphor is always a logical absurdity, so every inherited convention of plot in literature is more or less mad. The king's rash promise, the cuckold's jealousy, the "lived happily ever after" tag to a concluding marriage, the manipulated happy endings of comedy in general, the equally manipulated ironic endings of modern realism—none of these was suggested by any observation of human life or behavior: all exist solely as story-telling devices. Literary shape cannot come from life; it comes only from literary tradition, and so ultimately

---

[14] Andromeda, offered as sacrifice to abate the wrath of a sea-monster, was rescued by Perseus, who turned the monster to rock by showing him the Medusa's head. Iphigeneia, offered as sacrifice to Diana but saved by the goddess, is the subject of plays by Euripides, Racine, and Goethe.

[15] *Venus and Adonis*, ll. 1055-56.

[16] *The Recluse*, I, 1, 800-08.

[17] "Slice of life."

from myth. In sober realism, like the novels of Trollope, the plot, as we have noted, is often a parody plot. It is instructive to notice, too, how strong the popular demand is for such forms as detective stories, science fiction, comic strips, comic formulas like the P. G. Wodehouse stories, all of which are as rigorously conventional and stylized as the folk tale itself, works of pure "esemplastic" imagination, with the recognition turning up as predictably as the caesura in minor Augustan poetry.

One difficulty in proceeding from this point comes from the lack of any literary term which corresponds to the word "mythology." We find it hard to conceive of literature as an order of words, as a unified imaginative system that can be studied as a whole by criticism. If we had such a conception, we could readily see that literature as a whole provides a framework or context for every work of literature, just as a fully developed mythology provides a framework or context for each of its myths. Further, because mythology and literature occupy the same verbal space, so to speak, the framework or context of every work of literature can be found in mythology as well, when its literary tradition is understood. It is relatively easy to see the place of a myth in a mythology, and one of the main uses of myth criticism is to enable us to understand the corresponding place that a work of literature has in the context of literature as a whole.

Putting works of literature in such a context gives them an immense reverberating dimension of significance. (If anyone is worrying about value-judgments, I should add that establishing such a context tends to make the genuine work of literature sublime and the pinchbeck one ridiculous.) This reverberating significance, in which every literary work catches the echoes of all other works of its type in literature, and so ripples out into the rest of literature and thence into life, is often, and wrongly, called allegory. We have allegory when one literary work is joined to another, or to a myth, by a certain interpretation of meaning rather than by structure. Thus *The Pilgrim's Progress* is related allegorically to the Christian myth of redemption, and Hawthorne's story, *The Bosom Serpent*, is related allegorically to various moral serpents going back to the Book of Genesis.

Arthur Miller's *The Crucible*, already mentioned, deals with the Salem witch trials in a way that suggested McCarthyism [18] to most of its original audience. This relation in itself is allegorical. But if *The Crucible* is good enough to hold the stage after McCarthyism has become as dead an issue as the Salem trials, it would be clear that the theme of *The Crucible* is one which can always be used in literature, and that any social hysteria can form its subject matter. Social hysteria, however, is the content and not the form of the theme itself, which belongs in the category of the purgatorial or triumphant tragedy. As so often happens in literature, the only explicit clue to its mythical shape is provided by the title.

To sum up. In the direct experience of a new work of literature, we are aware of its continuity or moving power in time. As we become both more familiar with and more detached from it, the work tends to break up into a discontinuous series of felicities, bits of vivid imagery, convincing characterization, witty dialogue, and the like. The study of this belongs to what we have called critical naturalism or continuous recognition, the sense of the sharply focused reproduction of life in the fiction. But there was a feeling of unity in the original experience which such criticism does not recapture. We need to move from a criticism of "effects" to what we may call a criticism of causes, specifically the formal cause which holds the work together. The fact that such unity is available for critical study as well as for direct experience is normally symbolized by a crucial recognition, a point marking a real and not merely apparent unity in the design. Fictions like those of Trollope which appeal particularly to critical naturalism often play down or even parody such a device, and such works show the highest degree of displacement and the least conscious or explicit relationship to myth.

If, however, we go on to study the theme or total shape of the fiction, we find that it also belongs to a convention or category, like those of comedy and tragedy. With the literary cate-

[18] Frye refers to Senator Joseph McCarthy (1909-1957), who held widely publicized committee hearings in the 1950's in order to discover Communist sympathizers.

gory we reach a dead end, until we realize that literature is a reconstructed mythology, with its structural principles derived from those of myth. Then we can see that literature is in a complex setting what a mythology is in a simpler one: a total body of verbal creation. In literature, whatever has a shape has a mythical shape, and leads us toward the center of the order of words. For just as critical naturalism studies the counterpoint of literature and life, words and things, so myth criticism pulls us away from "life" toward a self-contained and autonomous literary universe. But myth, as we said at the beginning, means many things besides literary structure, and the world of words is not so self-contained and autonomous after all.

5. *Further Modern Developments*

OSCAR WILDE   (1854-1900)

OSCAR WILDE was born in Dublin, and was educated at Trinity College, Dublin, and Magdalen College, Oxford. Under the influence of the Oxford teacher and critic Walter Pater (see above, pp. 508-12) and the artist J. M. Whistler, Wilde became an apostle of the cult of "art for art's sake." He published *Poems* in 1881 and went on an extended American tour in 1882-83. His brilliant wit and good nature made him one of the most celebrated personalities of his time. Aside from his poems, he wrote moving stories for children, a novel, *The Picture of Dorian Gray* (1891), and he is still admired for his comedies of manners—*Lady Windermere's Fan* (1892), *A Woman of No Importance* (1893), and *The Importance of Being Earnest* (1895).

"The Decay of Lying" has only recently begun to be taken seriously. There are two reasons for this lag: (1) Wilde's light manner and delight in paradox; and (2) the fact that the idiom of sophisticated modern art and literature, especially after 1920, became radically different from that of the aestheticism of the 1890's. Perceptive critics argued that modern abstract or involved formalism shared much the same premises as the aestheticism of the late Victorian period, and that the real difference is that a "hard-boiled" aestheticism had replaced a "soft-boiled" one. But the argument fell on deaf ears. As we now look back on the modernist movement, we see the connection. "The Decay of Lying" overturns the whole concept of art as "imitation of nature," maintaining rather that life imitates art—that is, what man's imagination constructs in art releases the spirit for creativity, freedom, and enthusiasm; and our own lives, insofar as they amount to anything, follow that lead. Add to this the psychological fact that the more we idealize, the less satisfied we are with the bare reality—that is, "the more we study Art, the less we care for Nature"—and it seems that Nature can never compete with Art. Yet in his own time, says Wilde, artists have given up creative freedom in telling their "beautiful lies," and realism prevails. Even Henry James "writes fiction as if it were a painful duty." In many ways Wilde predicts the whole modern tendency, which now may be waning, to divorce art from nature and to advocate unlimited imaginative freedom, sometimes even to the extent of esoteric cultism. Yet if art no longer imitates life, as Wilde says, but life imitates art, then the responsibility of the artist is not less but greater.

From The Decay of Lying

PERSONS: *Cyril and Vivian.* SCENE: *the library of a country house in Nottinghamshire.*

CYRIL (*coming in through the open window from the terrace*): My dear Vivian, don't coop yourself up all day in the library. . . . Let us . . . enjoy Nature.

VIVIAN: Enjoy Nature! I am glad to say that I have entirely lost that faculty. People tell us that Art makes us love Nature more than we loved her before; that it reveals her secrets to us; and that after a careful study of Corot and Constable we see things in her that had escaped our observation. My own experience is that the more we study Art, the less we care for Nature. What Art really reveals to us is Nature's lack of design, her curious crudities, her extraordinary monotony, her absolutely unfinished condition. Nature has good intentions, of course, but, as Aristotle once said, she cannot carry them out. When I look at a landscape I cannot help seeing all its defects. It is fortunate for us, however, that Nature is so imperfect, as otherwise we should have no art at all. Art is our spirited protest, our gallant attempt to teach Nature her proper place. As for the infinite variety of Nature, that is a pure myth. It is not to be found in Nature herself. It resides in the imagination, or fancy, or cultivated blindness of the man who looks at her. . . . Now, if you promise not to interrupt too often, I will read you my article.

CYRIL: You will find me all attention.

VIVIAN (*reading . . .*): "THE DECAY OF LYING: A PROTEST.—One of the chief causes that can be assigned for the curiously commonplace character of most of the literature of our age is undoubtedly the decay of Lying as an art, a science, and a social pleasure. The ancient historians gave us delightful fiction in the form of fact; the modern novelist presents us with dull facts under the guise of fiction. The Blue-Book is rapidly becoming his ideal both for method and manner. He has his tedious *document humain,* his miserable little *coin de la création,* into which he peers with his microscope. He is to be found at the Librairie Nationale, or at the British Museum, shamelessly reading up his subject. He has not even the courage of other people's ideas, but insists on going directly to life for everything, and ultimately, between encyclopaedias and personal experience, he comes to the ground, having drawn his types from the family circle or from the weekly washerwoman, and having acquired an amount of useful information from which never, even in his most meditative moments, can he thoroughly free himself.

"The loss that results to literature in general from this false ideal of our time can hardly be overestimated. People have a careless way of talking about a 'born liar,' just as they talk about a born poet. But in both cases they are wrong. Lying and poetry are arts—arts, as Plato saw, not unconnected with each other—and they require the most careful study, the most disinterested devotion. Indeed, they have their technique, just as the more material arts of painting and sculpture have their subtle secrets of form and colour, their craft-mysteries, their deliberate artistic methods. As one knows the poet by his fine music, so one can recognize the liar by his rich rhythmic utterance, and in neither case will the casual inspiration of the moment suffice. Here, as elsewhere, practice must precede perfection. But in modern days while the fashion of writing poetry has become far too common, and should, if possible, be discouraged, the fashion of lying has almost fallen into disrepute. Many a young man starts in life with a natural gift for exaggeration which, if nurtured in congenial and sympathetic surroundings, or by the imitation of the best models, might grow into something really great and wonderful. But, as a rule, he comes to nothing. He either falls into careless habits of accuracy—"

CYRIL: My dear fellow!

VIVIAN: Please don't interrupt in the middle of a sentence. "He either falls into careless habits of accuracy, or takes to frequenting the society of the aged and the well-informed. Both things are equally fatal to his imagination, as indeed they would be fatal to the imagination of anybody, and in a short time he develops a morbid

The Decay of Lying. First published in *Nineteenth Century,* XXV (Jan., 1889). Revised and reprinted in *Intentions* (1891).

and unhealthy faculty of truth-telling, begins to verify all statements made in his presence, has no hesitation in contradicting people who are much younger than himself, and often ends by writing novels which are so life-like that no one can possibly believe in their probability. This is no isolated instance that we are giving. It is simply one example out of many; and if something cannot be done to check, or at least to modify, our monstrous worship of facts, Art will become sterile and beauty will pass away from the land. . . ."

CYRIL: There is something in what you say, and there is no doubt that whatever amusement we may find in reading a purely modern novel, we have rarely any artistic pleasure in re-reading it. And this is perhaps the best rough test of what is literature and what is not. If one cannot enjoy reading a book over and over again, there is no use reading it at all. But what do you say about the return to Life and Nature? This is the panacea that is always being recommended to us.

VIVIAN: I will read you what I say on that subject. The passage comes later on in the article, but I may as well give it to you now:—

"The popular cry of our time is 'Let us return to Life and Nature; they will recreate **Art for** us, and send the red blood coursing **through** her veins; they will shoe her feet with **swiftness** and make her hand strong.' But, alas! we are mistaken in our amiable and well-meaning efforts. Nature is always behind the age. And as for Life, she is the solvent that breaks up Art, the enemy that lays waste her house."

CYRIL: What do you mean by saying that Nature is always behind the age?

VIVIAN: Well, perhaps **that** is rather cryptic. What I mean is this. If we take Nature to mean natural simple instinct as opposed to self-conscious culture, the work produced under this influence is always old-fashioned, antiquated, and out of date. One touch of Nature may make the whole world kin, but two touches of Nature will destroy any work of Art. If, on the other hand, we regard Nature as the collection of phenomena external to man, people only discover in her what they bring to her. She has no suggestions of her own. Wordsworth went to the lakes, but he was never a lake poet. He found in stones the sermons he had already hidden there. He went moralising about the district, but his good work was produced when he returned, not to Nature but to poetry. Poetry gave him "Laodamia," and the fine sonnets, and the great Ode such as it is. Nature gave him "Martha Ray" and "Peter Bell," and the address to Mr. Wilkinson's spade.

CYRIL: I think that view might be questioned. I am rather inclined to believe in "the impulse from a vernal wood," though of course the artistic value of such an impulse depends entirely on the kind of temperament that receives it, so that the return to Nature would come to mean simply the advance to a great personality. You would agree with that, I fancy. However, proceed with your article.

VIVIAN (*reading*): "Art begins with abstract decoration, with purely imaginative and pleasurable work dealing with what is unreal and nonexistent. This is the first stage. Then Life becomes fascinated with this new wonder, and asks to be admitted into the charmed circle. Art takes life as part of her rough material, recreates it, and refashions it in fresh forms, is absolutely indifferent to fact, invents, imagines, dreams, and keeps **between** herself and reality the impenetrable barrier of beautiful style, of decorative or ideal treatment. The third stage is when Life gets the upper hand, and drives Art out into the wilderness. This is the true decadence, and it is from this that we are now suffering. . . . The whole history of these arts in Europe is the record of the struggle between Orientalism, with its frank rejection of imitation, its love of artistic convention, its dislike **to the** actual representation of any object in Nature, and our own imitative spirit. Wherever the former has been paramount, as in Byzantium, Sicily and Spain, by actual contact or in the rest of Europe by the influence of the Crusades, we have had beautiful and imaginative work in which the visible things of life are transmuted into artistic conventions, and the things that Life has not are invented and fashioned for her delight. But wherever we have returned to Life and Nature, our work has always become vulgar, common and uninteresting. . . .

"Art finds her own perfection within, and not outside of, herself. She is not to be judged by any external standard of resemblance. She is a veil, rather than a mirror. She has flowers that no forests know of, birds that no woodland possesses. She makes and unmakes many worlds, and can draw the moon from heaven with a scarlet thread. Hers are the 'forms more real than living man,' and hers the great archetypes of which things that have existence are but unfinished copies. . . .

CYRIL: . . . What do you mean by saying that life, "poor, probable, uninteresting human life," will try to reproduce the marvels of art? I can quite understand your objection to art being treated as a mirror. You think it would reduce genius to the position of a cracked looking-glass. But you don't mean to say that you seriously believe that Life imitates Art, that Life in fact is the mirror, and Art the reality?

VIVIAN: Certainly I do. Paradox though it may seem—and paradoxes are always dangerous things—it is none the less true that Life imitates art far more than Art imitates life. We have all seen in our own day in England how a certain curious and fascinating type of beauty, invented and emphasised by two imaginative painters, has so influenced Life that whenever one goes to a private view or to an artistic salon one sees, here the mystic eyes of Rossetti's dream, the long ivory throat, the strange square-cut jaw, the loosened shadowy hair that he so ardently loved, there the sweet maidenhood of "The Golden Stair," the blossom-like mouth and weary loveliness of the "Laus Amoris," the passion-pale face of Andromeda, the thin hands and lithe beauty of the Vivian in "Merlin's Dream." And it has always been so. A great artist invents a type, and Life tries to copy it, to reproduce it in a popular form, like an enterprising publisher. Neither Holbein nor Vandyck found in England what they have given us. They brought their types with them, and Life with her keen imitative faculty set herself to supply the master with models. The Greeks, with their quick artistic instinct, understood this, and set in the bride's chamber the statue of Hermes or of Apollo, that she might bear children as lovely as the works of art that she looked at in her rapture or her pain. They knew that Life gains from art not merely spirituality, depth of thought and feeling, soul-turmoil or soul-peace, but that she can form herself on the very lines and colours of art, and can reproduce the dignity of Pheidias as well as the grace of Praxiteles. Hence came their objection to realism. They disliked it on purely social grounds. They felt that it inevitably makes people ugly, and they were perfectly right. We try to improve the conditions of the race by means of good air, free sunlight, wholesome water, and hideous bare buildings for the better housing of the lower orders. But these things merely produce health, they do not produce beauty. For this, Art is required, and the true disciples of the great artist are not his studio-imitators, but those who become like his works of art, be they plastic as in Greek days, or pictorial as in modern times; in a word, Life is Art's best, Art's only pupil.

As it is with the visible arts, so it is with literature. The most obvious and the vulgarest form in which this is shown is in the case of the silly boys who, after reading the adventures of Jack Sheppard or Dick Turpin, pillage the stalls of unfortunate apple-women, break into sweet-shops at night, and alarm old gentlemen who are returning home from the city by leaping out on them in suburban lanes, with black masks and unloaded revolvers. This interesting phenomenon, which always occurs after the appearance of a new edition of either of the books I have alluded to, is usually attributed to the influence of literature on the imagination. But this is a mistake. The imagination is essentially creative, and always seeks for a new form. The boy burglar is simply the inevitable result of life's imitative instinct. He is Fact, occupied as Fact usually is, with trying to reproduce Fiction, and what we see in him is repeated on an extended scale throughout the whole of life. Schopenhauer has analysed the pessimism that characterises modern thought, but Hamlet invented it. The world has become sad because a puppet was once melancholy. . . .

CYRIL: The theory is certainly a very curious one, but to make it complete you must show that Nature, no less than Life, is an imitation of Art. Are you prepared to prove that?

VIVIAN: My dear fellow, I am prepared to prove anything.

CYRIL: Nature follows the landscape painter, then, and takes her effects from him?

VIVIAN: Certainly. Where, if not from the Impressionists, do we get those wonderful brown fogs that come creeping down our streets, blurring the gas-lamps and changing the houses into monstrous shadows? To whom, if not to them and their master, do we owe the lovely silver mists that brood over our river, and turn to faint forms of fading grace curved bridge and swaying barge? The extraordinary change that has taken place in the climate of London during the last ten years is entirely due to a particular school of Art. You smile. Consider the matter from a scientific or a metaphysical point of view, and you will find that I am right. For what is Nature? Nature is no great mother who has borne us. She is our creation. It is in our brain that she quickens to life. Things are because we see them, and what we see, and how we see it, depends on the Arts that have influenced us. To look at a thing is very different from seeing a thing. One does not see anything until one sees its beauty. Then, and then only, does it come into existence. At present, people see fogs, not because there are fogs, but because poets and painters have taught them the mysterious love-liness of such effects. There may have been fogs for centuries in London. I dare say there were. But no one saw them, and so we do not know anything about them. They did not exist till Art had invented them. Now, it must be admitted, fogs are carried to excess. They have become the mere mannerism of a clique, and the exaggerated realism of their method gives dull people bron-chitis. Where the cultured catch an effect, the uncultured catch cold. And so, let us be humane, and invite Art to turn her wonderful eyes else-where. She has done so already, indeed. That white quivering sunlight that one sees now in France, with its strange blotches of mauve, and its restless violet shadows, is her latest fancy, and, on the whole, Nature reproduces it quite admirably. Where she used to give us Corots and Daubignys, she gives us now exquisite Monets and entrancing Pissaros. Indeed there are moments, rare, it is true, but still to be ob-served from time to time, when Nature becomes absolutely modern. Of course she is not always to be relied upon. The fact is that she is in this unfortunate position. Art creates an incompa-rable and unique effect, and, having done so, passes on to other things. Nature, upon the other hand, forgetting that imitation can be made the sincerest form of insult, keeps on re-peating this effect until we all become absolutely wearied of it. Nobody of any real culture, for instance, ever talks nowadays about the beauty of a sunset. Sunsets are quite old-fashioned.

They belong to the time when Turner was the last note in art. To admire them is a distinct sign of provincialism of temperament. Upon the other hand they go on. Yesterday evening Mrs. Arundel insisted on my going to the win-dow and looking at the glorious sky, as she called it. Of course I had to look at it. She is one of those absurdly pretty Philistines to whom one can deny nothing. And what was it? It was simply a very second-rate Turner, a Turner of a bad period, with all the painter's worst faults exaggerated and over-emphasized. Of course I am quite ready to admit that Life very often commits the same error. . . . But then, when Art is more varied, Nature will, no doubt, be more varied also. That she imitates Art, I don't think even her worst enemy would deny now. It is the one thing that keeps her in touch with civilised man. But have I proved my theory to your satisfaction?

CYRIL: You have proved it to my dissatisfac-tion, which is better. But even admitting this strange imitative instinct in Life and Nature, surely you would acknowledge that Art expresses the temper of its age, the spirit of its time, the moral and social conditions that surround it, and under whose influence it is produced.

VIVIAN: Certainly not! Art never expresses anything but itself. This is the principle of my new aesthetics; and it is this, more than that vital connection between form and substance, on which Mr. Pater dwells, that makes basic the type of all the arts. Of course, nations and indi-viduals, with that healthy natural vanity which is the secret of existence, are always under the impression that it is of them that the Muses are talking, always trying to find in the calm dignity of imaginative art some mirror of their own turbid passions, always forgetting that the singer of life is not Apollo but Marsyas. Remote from reality and with her eyes turned away from the shadows of the cave, Art reveals her own per-fection, and the wondering crowd that watches the opening of the marvellous many-petalled rose fancies that it is its own history that is being told to it, its own spirit that is finding expres-sion in a new form. But it is not so. The highest art rejects the burden of the human spirit, and gains more from a new medium or a fresh ma-terial than she does from any enthusiasm for art, or from any lofty passion, or from any great awakening of the human consciousness. She develops purely on her own lines. She is not symbolic of any age. It is the ages that are her symbols. . . .

CYRIL: . . . I want you to tell me briefly the doctrines of the new aesthetics.

VIVIAN: Briefly, then, they are these. Art never expresses anything but itself. It has an independent life, just as Thought has, and develops purely on its own lines. It is not necessarily realistic in an age of realism, nor spiritual in an age of faith. So far from being the creation of its time, it is usually in direct opposition to it, and the only history that it preserves for us is the history of its own progress. Sometimes it returns upon its footsteps, and revives some antique form, as happened in the archaistic movement of late Greek Art, and in the pre-Raphaelite movement of our own day. At other times it entirely anticipates its age, and produces in one century work that it takes another century to understand, to appreciate, and to enjoy. In no case does it reproduce its age. To pass from the art of a time to the time itself is the great mistake that all historians commit.

The second doctrine is this. All bad art comes from returning to Life and Nature, and elevating them into ideals. Life and Nature may sometimes be used as part of Art's rough material, but before they are of any real service to Art they must be translated into artistic conventions. The moment Art surrenders its imaginative medium it surrenders everything. As a method Realism is a complete failure, and the two things

that every artist should avoid are modernity of form and modernity of subject-matter. To us, who live in the nineteenth century, any century is a suitable subject for art except our own. The only beautiful things are the things that do not concern us. It is, to have the pleasure of quoting myself, exactly because Hecuba is nothing to us that her sorrows are so suitable a motive for a tragedy. Besides, it is only the modern that ever becomes old-fashioned. M. Zola sits down to give us a picture of the Second Empire. Who cares for the Second Empire now? It is out of date. Life goes faster than Realism, but Romanticism is always in front of Life.

The third doctrine is that Life imitates Art far more than Art imitates Life. This results not merely from Life's imitative instinct, but from the fact that the self-conscious aim of Life is to find expression, and that Art offers it certain beautiful forms through which it may realize that energy. It is a theory that has never been put forward before, but it is extremely fruitful, and throws an entirely new light upon the history of Art.

It follows, as a corollary from this, that external Nature also imitates Art. The only effects that she can show us are effects that we have already seen through poetry, or in paintings. This is the secret of Nature's charm, as well as the explanation of Nature's weakness.

The final revelation is that Lying, the telling of beautiful untrue things, is the proper aim of Art. But of this I think I have spoken at sufficient length. . . .

WILLIAM BUTLER YEATS   (1865-1939)

WILLIAM BUTLER YEATS was born in Dublin but spent much of his youth between London and Sligo, a county on the northwest coast of Ireland that was to serve as the symbolic landscape for many of his poems. His father was associated with the Pre-Raphaelite school of painters, and Yeats himself studied painting for a time, absorbing themes, images, and symbols that form dominant motifs in his earlier poems, plays, and essays, including the one reprinted below. His interest in Celtic literature and his involvement in Irish politics and in the founding of the Irish Literary Theatre made him a commanding figure in the Irish Renaissance. World War I and the Irish Rebellion renewed his call to poetry, and the changes they wrought in him and the subsequent turmoil and reconciliation are recorded in *Michael Robartes and the Dancer* (1921), *The Tower* (1928), *The Winding Stair and Other Poems* (1933), and *Last Poems* (1936-39).

In an earlier study of Blake's engravings, Yeats had defined a symbol as "the only possible expression of some invisible essence, a transparent lamp about a spiritual flame." Here again, in this suggestive, often cryptic essay, Yeats uses symbols for defining symbolism. Sounds, colors, and forms are symbolic and, drawing on emotional powers, they awaken us to a numinous existence. Even objective reality, so often seen as all-powerful and mechanically determined, devolves from the consequences, sometimes over great spans of time, of symbols working in the imagination (cf. Shelley, above, pp. 430, 434-35). There are emotional symbols, of which Shakespeare is a great exemplar, but only a shadowy line divides them from intellectual symbols, for which Dante may serve as a model. All symbolism, however, eschews the ordinary and the popular and "only wishes to gaze on some reality, some beauty." It seeks those "wavering, meditative, organic rhythms, which are the embodiment of the imagination, that neither desires nor hates" in an extramundane realm.

The Symbolism of Poetry

I

SYMBOLISM, as seen in the writers of our day, would have no value if it were not seen also, under one "disguise or another," in every great imaginative writer," writes Mr. Arthur Symons in *The Symbolist Movement in Literature*, a subtle book which I cannot praise as I would, because it has been dedicated to me; and he goes on to show how many profound writers have in the last few years sought for a philosophy of poetry in the doctrine of symbolism, and how even in countries where it is almost scandalous to seek for any philosophy of poetry, new writers are following them in their search. We do not know what the writers of ancient times talked of among themselves, and one bull is all that remains of Shakespeare's talk, who was on the edge of modern times; and the journalist is convinced, it seems, that they talked of wine and women and politics, but never about their art, or never quite seriously about their art. He is certain that no one who had a philosophy of his art, or a theory of how he should write, has ever made a work of art, that people have no imagination who do not write without forethought and afterthought as he writes his own articles. He says this with enthusiasm, because he has heard it at so many comfortable dinner-tables, where some one had mentioned through carelessness, or foolish zeal, a book whose difficulty had offended indolence,

The Symbolism of Poetry (1900). From *Essays and Introductions* (1961). Reprinted with permission of The Macmillan Company and A. P. Watt and Son Ltd. © Mrs. William Butler Yeats, 1961.

or a man who had not forgotten that beauty is an accusation. Those formulas and generalisations, in which a hidden sergeant has drilled the ideas of journalists and through them the ideas of all but all the modern world, have created in their turn a forgetfulness like that of soldiers in battle, so that journalists and their readers have forgotten, among many like events, that Wagner spent seven years arranging and explaining his ideas before he began his most characteristic music; that opera, and with it modern music, arose from certain talks at the house of one Giovanni Bardi of Florence; and that the Pléiade laid the foundations of modern French literature with a pamphlet. Goethe has said, "a poet needs all philosophy, but he must keep it out of his work," though that is not always necessary; and almost certainly no great art, outside England, where journalists are more powerful and ideas less plentiful than elsewhere, has arisen without a great criticism, for its herald or its interpreter and protector, and it may be for this reason that great art, now that vulgarity has armed itself and multiplied itself, is perhaps dead in England.

All writers, all artists of any kind, in so far as they have had any philosophical or critical power, perhaps just in so far as they have been deliberate artists at all, have had some philosophy, some criticism of their art; and it has often been this philosophy, or this criticism, that has evoked their most startling inspiration, calling into outer life some portion of the divine life, or of the buried reality, which could alone extinguish in the emotions what their philosophy or their criticism would extinguish in the intellect. They have sought for no new thing, it may be, but only to understand and to copy the pure inspiration of early times, but because the divine life wars upon our outer life, and must needs change its weapons and its movements as we change ours, inspiration has come to them in beautiful startling shapes. The scientific movement brought with it a literature which was always tending to lose itself in externalities of all kinds, in opinion, in declamation, in picturesque writing, in word-painting, or in what Mr. Symons has called an attempt "to build in brick and mortar inside the covers of a book"; and now writers have begun to dwell upon the ele-

ment of evocation, of suggestion, upon what we call the symbolism in great writers.

I I

In "Symbolism in Painting," I tried to describe the element of symbolism that is in pictures and sculpture, and described a little the symbolism in poetry, but did not describe at all the continuous indefinable symbolism which is the substance of all style.

There are no lines with more melancholy beauty than these by Burns:—

The white moon is setting behind the white wave,
And Time is setting with me, O! [1]

and these lines are perfectly symbolical. Take from them the whiteness of the moon and of the wave, whose relation to the setting of Time is too subtle for the intellect, and you take from them their beauty. But, when all are together, moon and wave and whiteness and setting Time and the last melancholy cry, they evoke an emotion which cannot be evoked by any other arrangement of colours and sounds and forms. We may call this metaphorical writing, but it is better to call it symbolical writing, because metaphors are not profound enough to be moving, when they are not symbols, and when they are symbols they are the most perfect of all, because the most subtle, outside of pure sound, and through them one can best find out what symbols are. If one begins the reverie with any beautiful lines that one can remember, one finds they are like those by Burns. Begin with this line by Blake:—

The gay fishes on the wave when the moon sucks up the dew;

or these lines by Nash:—

Brightness falls from the air,
Queens have died young and fair,
Dust hath closed Helen's eye;

or these lines by Shakespeare:—

Timon hath made his everlasting mansion
Upon the beached verge of the salt flood;
Who once a day with his embossed froth
The turbulent surge shall cover; [2]

[1] "Oh, open the door," ll. 9-10.
[2] From, respectively, Blake's *Europa*, Plate 14, l. 3;

or take some line that is quite simple, that gets its beauty from its place in a story, and see how it flickers with the light of the many symbols that have given the story its beauty, as a sword-blade may flicker with the light of burning towers.

All sounds, all colours, all forms, either because of their preordained energies or because of long association, evoke indefinable and yet precise emotions, or, as I prefer to think, call down among us certain disembodied powers, whose footsteps over our hearts we call emotions; and when sound, and colour, and form are in a musical relation, a beautiful relation to one another, they become, as it were, one sound, one colour, one form, and evoke an emotion that is made out of their distinct evocations and yet is one emotion. The same relation exists between all portions of every work of art, whether it be an epic or a song, and the more perfect it is, and the more various and numerous the elements that have flowed into its perfection, the more powerful will be the emotion, the power, the god it calls among us. Because an emotion does not exist, or does not become perceptible and active among us, till it has found its expression, in colour or in sound or in form, or in all of these, and because no two modulations or arrangements of these evoke the same emotion, poets and painters and musicians, and in a less degree because their effects are momentary, day and night and cloud and shadow, are continually making and unmaking mankind. It is indeed only those things which seem useless or very feeble that have any power, and all those things that seem useful or strong, armies, moving wheels, modes of architecture, modes of government, speculations of the reason, would have been a little different if some mind long ago had not given itself to some emotion, as a woman gives herself to her lover, and shaped sounds or colours or forms, or all of these, into a musical relation, that their emotion might live in other minds. A little lyric evokes an emotion, and this emotion gathers others about it and melts into their being in the making of some great epic; and at last, needing an always less delicate body, or symbol, as it grows more powerful, it flows

out, with all it has gathered, among the blind instincts of daily life, where it moves a power within powers, as one sees ring within ring in the stem of an old tree. This is maybe what Arthur O'Shaughnessy meant when he made his poets say they had built Nineveh with their sighing; and I am certainly never sure, when I hear of some war, or of some religious excitement, or of some new manufacture, or of anything else that fills the ear of the world, that it has not all happened because of something that a boy piped in Thessaly. I remember once telling a seeress to ask one among the gods who, as she believed, were standing about her in their symbolic bodies, what would come of a charming but seeming trivial labour of a friend, and the form answering, "the devastation of peoples and the overwhelming of cities." I doubt indeed if the crude circumstance of the world, which seems to create all our emotions, does more than reflect, as in multiplying mirrors, the emotions that have come to solitary men in moments of poetical contemplation; or that love itself would be more than an animal hunger but for the poet and his shadow the priest, for unless we believe that outer things are the reality, we must believe that the gross is the shadow of the subtle, that things are wise before they become foolish, and secret before they cry out in the market-place. . . .

III

The purpose of rhythm, it has always seemed to me, is to prolong the moment of contemplation, the moment when we are both asleep and awake, which is the one moment of creation, by hushing us with an alluring monotony, while it holds us waking by variety, to keep us in that state of perhaps real trance, in which the mind liberated from the pressure of the will is unfolded in symbols. If certain sensitive persons listen persistently to the ticking of a watch, or gaze persistently on the monotonous flashing of a light, they fall into the hypnotic trance; and rhythm is but the ticking of a watch made softer, that one must needs listen, and various, that one may not be swept beyond memory or grow weary of listening; while the patterns of the artist are but the monotonous flash woven to take the eyes in a subtler enchantment. I have heard in meditation voices that were forgotten the moment

Thomas Nash's "In Time of Pestilence," ll. 17-19; and Shakespeare's *Timon of Athens*, V, 1, 218-21.

they had spoken; and I have been swept, when in more profound meditation, beyond all memory but of those things that came from beyond the threshold of waking life. I was writing once at a very symbolical and abstract poem, when my pen fell on the ground; and as I stooped to pick it up, I remembered some fantastic adventure that yet did not seem fantastic, and then another like adventure, and when I asked myself when these things had happened, I found that I was remembering my dreams for many nights. I tried to remember what I had done the day before, and then what I had done that morning; but all my waking life had perished from me, and it was only after a struggle that I came to remember it again, and as I did so that more powerful and startling life perished in its turn. Had my pen not fallen on the ground and so made me turn from the images that I was weaving into verse, I would never have known that meditation had become trance, for I would have been like one who does not know that he is passing through a wood because his eyes are on the pathway. So I think that in the making and in the understanding of a work of art, and the more easily if it is full of patterns and symbols and music, we are lured to the threshold of sleep, and it may be far beyond it, without knowing that we have ever set our feet upon the steps or horn or of ivory.

IV

Besides emotional symbols, symbols that evoke emotions alone,—and in this sense all alluring or hateful things are symbols, although their relations with one another are too subtle to delight us fully, away from rhythm and pattern,—there are intellectual symbols, symbols that evoke ideas alone, or ideas mingled with emotions; and outside the very definite traditions of mysticism and the less definite criticism of certain modern poets, these alone are called symbols. Most things belong to one or another kind, according to the way we speak of them and the companions we give them, for symbols, associated with ideas that are more than fragments of the shadows thrown upon the intellect by the emotions they evoke, are the playthings of the allegorist or the pedant, and soon pass away. If I say "white" or "purple" in an or-

dinary line of poetry, they evoke emotions so exclusively that I cannot say why they move me; but if I bring them into the same sentence with such obvious intellectual symbols as a cross or a crown of thorns, I think of purity and sovereignty. Furthermore, innumerable meanings, which are held to "white" or to "purple" by bonds of subtle suggestion, and alike in the emotions and in the intellect, move visibly through my mind, and move invisibly beyond the threshold of sleep, casting lights and shadows of an indefinable wisdom on what had seemed before, it may be, but sterility and noisy violence. It is the intellect that decides where the reader shall ponder over the procession of the symbols, and if the symbols are merely emotional, he gazes from amid the accidents and destinies of the world; but if the symbols are intellectual too, he becomes himself a part of pure intellect, and he is himself mingled with the procession. If I watch a rushy pool in the moonlight, my emotion at its beauty is mixed with memories of the man that I have seen ploughing by its margin, or of the lovers I saw there a night ago; but if I look at the moon herself and remember any of her ancient names and meanings, I move among divine people, and things that have shaken off our mortality, the tower of ivory, the queen of waters, the shining stag among enchanted woods, the white hare sitting upon the hilltop, the fool of Faery with his shining cup full of dreams, and it may be "make a friend of one of these images of wonder," and "meet the Lord in the air." So, too, if one is moved by Shakespeare, who is content with emotional symbols that he may come the nearer to our sympathy, one is mixed with the whole spectacle of the world; while if one is moved by Dante, or by the myth of Demeter, one is mixed into the shadow of God or of a goddess. So, too, one is furthest from symbols when one is busy doing this or that, but the soul moves among symbols and unfolds in symbols when trance, or madness, or deep meditation has withdrawn it from every impulse but its own. . . .

V

If people were to accept the theory that poetry moves us because of its symbolism, what change should one look for in the manner of our poetry? A return to the way of our fathers, a casting out of descriptions of nature for the sake of nature, of the moral law for the sake of the moral law, a casting out of all anecdotes and of that brooding over scientific opinion that so often extinguished the central flame in Tennyson, and of that vehemence that would make us do or not do certain things; or, in other words, we should come to understand that the beryl stone was enchanted by our fathers that it might unfold the pictures in its heart, and not to mirror our own excited faces, or the boughs waving outside the window. With this change of substance, this return to imagination, this understanding that the laws of art, which are the hidden laws of the world, can alone bind the imagination, would come a change of style, and we would cast out of serious poetry those energetic rhythms, as of a man running, which are the invention of the will with its eyes always on something to be done or undone; and we would seek out those wavering, meditative, organic rhythms, which

are the embodiment of the imagination, that neither desires nor hates, because it has done with time, and only wishes to gaze upon some reality, some beauty; nor would it be any longer possible for anybody to deny the importance of form, in all its kinds, for although you can expound an opinion, or describe a thing, when your words are not quite well chosen, you cannot give a body to something that moves beyond the senses, unless your words are as subtle, as complex, as full of mysterious life, as the body of a flower or of a woman. The form of sincere poetry, unlike the form of the "popular poetry," may indeed be sometimes obscure, or ungrammatical as in some of the best of the *Songs of Innocence and Experience,* but it must have the perfections that escape analysis, the subtleties that have a new meaning every day, and it must have all this whether it be but a little song made out of a moment of dreamy indolence, or some great epic made out of the dreams of one poet and of a hundred generations whose hands were never weary of the sword.

VIRGINIA WOOLF   (1882-1941)

VIRGINIA WOOLF was educated by her father, the famous scholar and critic Sir Leslie Stephen, a member of the intellectual aristocracy of late nineteenth-century England. After his death she lived with her brother and sister in the Bloomsbury district of London, which became a center (c. 1907-30) of a group of artists and writers. Without forming a "school" of thought, they championed values of skepticism and agnosticism, awareness and sensibility. In 1912 she married the political writer Leonard Woolf. Her novels—such as *Jacob's Room* (1922), *Mrs. Dalloway* (1925), *To the Lighthouse* (1927), *The Waves* (1931), and *Between the Acts* (1941) —evoke moments of consciousness, such as she describes in the essay reprinted below, in their continuous flow and in their interpenetration with reality or impingement on other minds. Her numerous essays have been collected in four volumes (1966-67).

If by the outset of this century the novel had overcome some of its earlier problems, it has nonetheless fallen in value. However humane their intentions, Wells, Bennett, and Galsworthy are grouped together as "materialists" concerned with the body and not the spirit. Inevitable repetition betrays itself in their novels, and in the novel as a genre. Life escapes their method, and "life is not a series of gig lamps symmetrically arranged; life is a luminous halo, a semi-transparent envelope surrounding us from the beginning of consciousness to the end." Yet the "materialist," after all, dealt with social issues and moral reform, and one may question whether Woolf leaves room within her definition for moral action and choice, or whether such values are harmonious with awareness and sensibility. She concludes with praise for James Joyce, though she has misgivings about his subject matter, and a suggestive comparison of the Russian and the British mind.

Modern Fiction

IN MAKING any survey, even the freest and loosest, of modern fiction, it is difficult not to take it for granted that the modern practice of the art is somehow an improvement upon the old. With their simple tools and primitive materials, it might be said, Fielding did well and Jane Austen even better, but compare their opportunities with ours! Their masterpieces certainly have a strange air of simplicity. And yet the analogy between literature and the process, to choose an example, of making motor cars scarcely holds good beyond the first glance. It is doubtful whether in the course of the centuries, though we have learnt much about making machines, we have learnt anything about making literature. We do not come to write better; all that we can be said to do is to keep moving, now a little in this direction, now in that, but with a circular tendency should the whole course of the track be viewed from a sufficiently lofty pinnacle. It need scarcely be said that we make no claim to stand, even momentarily, upon that vantage ground. On the flat, in the crowd, half blind with dust, we look back with envy to those happier warriors, whose battle is won and whose achievements wear so serene an air of accomplishment that we can scarcely refrain from

whispering that the fight was not so fierce for them as for us. It is for the historian of literature to decide; for him to say if we are now beginning or ending or standing in the middle of a great period of prose fiction, for down in the plain little is visible. We only know that certain gratitudes and hostilities inspire us; that certain paths seem to lead to fertile land, others to the dust and the desert; and of this perhaps it may be worth while to attempt some account.

Our quarrel, then, is not with the classics, and if we speak of quarrelling with Mr. Wells, Mr. Bennett, and Mr. Galsworthy, it is partly that by the mere fact of their existence in the flesh their work has a living, breathing, everyday imperfection which bids us take what liberties with it we choose. But it is also true that, while we thank them for a thousand gifts, we reserve our unconditional gratitude for Mr. Hardy, for Mr. Conrad, and in a much lesser degree for the Mr. Hudson of *The Purple Land, Green Mansions,* and *Far Away and Long Ago.* Mr. Wells, Mr. Bennett, and Mr. Galsworthy have excited so many hopes and disappointed them so persistently that our gratitude largely takes the form of thanking them for having shown us what they might have done but have not done; what we certainly could not do, but as certainly, perhaps, do not wish to do. No single phrase will sum up the charge or grievance which we have to bring against a mass of work so large in its volume and embodying so many qualities, both admirable and the reverse. If we tried to formulate our

Modern Fiction (1919). From *The Common Reader* (No. 1) (1925). Copyright 1925 by Harcourt Brace Jovanovich, Inc. Reprinted by permission of Harcourt Brace Jovanovich, Inc., Hogarth Press, Ltd., Quentin Bell, and Angelica Garnett.

meaning in one word we should say that these three writers are materialists. It is because they are concerned not with the spirit but with the body that they have disappointed us, and left us with the feeling that the sooner English fiction turns its back upon them, as politely as may be, and marches, if only into the desert, the better for its soul. Naturally, no single word reaches the centre of three separate targets. In the case of Mr. Wells it falls notably wide of the mark. And yet even with him it indicates to our thinking the fatal alloy in his genius, the great clod of clay that has got itself mixed up with the purity of his inspiration. But Mr. Bennett is perhaps the worst culprit of the three, inasmuch as he is by far the best workman. He can make a book so well constructed and solid in its craftsmanship that it is difficult for the most exacting of critics to see through what chink or crevice decay can creep in. There is not so much as a draught between the frames of the windows, or a crack in the boards. And yet—if life should refuse to live there? That is a risk which the creator of *The Old Wives' Tale*, George Cannon, Edwin Clayhanger, and hosts of other figures, may well claim to have surmounted. His characters live abundantly, even unexpectedly, but it remains to ask how do they live, and what do they live for? More and more they seem to us, deserting even the well-built villa in the Five Towns, to spend their time in some softly padded first-class railway carriage, pressing bells and buttons innumerable; and the destiny to which they travel so luxuriously becomes more and more unquestionably an eternity of bliss spent in the very best hotel in Brighton. It can scarcely be said of Mr. Wells that he is a materialist in the sense that he takes too much delight in the solidity of his fabric. His mind is too generous in its sympathies to allow him to spend much time in making things shipshape and substantial. He is a materialist from sheer goodness of heart, taking upon his shoulders the work that ought to have been discharged by Government officials, and in the plethora of his ideas and facts scarcely having leisure to realise, or forgetting to think important, the crudity and coarseness of his human beings. Yet what more damaging criticism can there be both of his earth and of his Heaven than that they are to be inhabited here and hereafter by his Joans and his Peters? Does not the inferiority of their natures tarnish whatever institutions and ideals may be provided for them by the generosity of their creator? Nor, profoundly though we respect the integrity and humanity of Mr. Galsworthy, shall we find what we seek in his pages.

If we fasten, then, one label on all these books, on which is one word, materialists, we mean by it that they write of unimportant things; that they spend immense skill and immense industry making the trivial and the transitory appear the true and the enduring.

We have to admit that we are exacting, and, further, that we find it difficult to justify our discontent by explaining what it is that we exact. We frame our question differently at different times. But it reappears most persistently as we drop the finished novel on the crest of a sigh— Is it worth while? What is the point of it all? Can it be that, owing to one of those little deviations which the human spirit seems to make from time to time, Mr. Bennett has come down with his magnificent apparatus for catching life just an inch or two on the wrong side? Life escapes; and perhaps without life nothing else is worth while. It is a confession of vagueness to have to make use of such a figure as this, but we scarcely better the matter by speaking, as critics are prone to do, of reality. Admitting the vagueness which afflicts all criticism of novels, let us hazard the opinion that for us at this moment the form of fiction most in vogue more often misses than secures the thing we seek. Whether we call it life or spirit, truth or reality, this, the essential thing, has moved off, or on, and refuses to be contained any longer in such ill-fitting vestments as we provide. Nevertheless, we go on perseveringly, conscientiously, constructing our two and thirty chapters after a design which more and more ceases to resemble the vision in our minds. So much of the enormous labour of proving the solidity, the likeness to life, of the story is not merely labour thrown away but labour misplaced to the extent of obscuring and blotting out the light of the conception. The writer seems constrained, not by his own free will but by some powerful and unscrupulous tyrant who has him in thrall, to provide a plot, to provide comedy, tragedy, love interest, and an air of probability embalming the whole so impeccable that if all his figures were to come to life they would find themselves dressed down to the last button of their coats in the fashion of the hour. The tyrant is obeyed; the novel is done to a turn. But sometimes, more and more often as time goes by, we suspect a momentary doubt, a spasm of rebellion, as the pages fill themselves in the customary way. Is life like this? Must novels be like this?

Look within and life, it seems, is very far from being "like this." Examine for a moment an ordinary mind on an ordinary day. The mind receives a myriad impressions—trivial, fantastic, evanescent, or engraved with the sharpness of steel. From all sides they come, an incessant shower of innumerable atoms; and as they fall, as they shape themselves into the life of Monday or Tuesday, the accent falls differently from of old; the moment of importance came not here but there; so that, if a writer were a free man and not a slave, if he could write what he chose, not what he must, if he could base his work upon his own feeling and not upon convention, there would be no plot, no comedy, no tragedy, no love interest or catastrophe in the accepted style, and perhaps not a single button sewn on as the Bond Street tailors would have it. Life is not a series of gig lamps symmetrically arranged; life is a luminous halo, a semi-transparent envelope surrounding us from the beginning of consciousness to the end. Is it not the task of the novelist to convey this varying, this unknown and uncircumscribed spirit, whatever aberration or complexity it may display, with as little mixture of the alien and external as possible? We are not pleading merely for courage and sincerity; we are suggesting that the proper stuff of fiction is a little other than custom would have us believe it.

It is, at any rate, in some such fashion as this that we seek to define the quality which distinguishes the work of several young writers, among whom Mr. James Joyce is the most notable, from that of their predecessors. They attempt to come closer to life, and to preserve more sincerely and exactly what interests and moves them, even if to do so they must discard most of the conventions which are commonly observed by the novelist. Let us record the atoms as they fall upon the mind in the order in which they fall, let us trace the pattern, however disconnected and incoherent in appearance, which each sight or incident scores upon the consciousness. Let us not take it for granted that life exists more fully in what is commonly thought big than in what is commonly thought small. Any one who has read *The Portrait of the Artist as a Young Man* or, what promises to be a far more interesting work, *Ulysses*, now appearing in the *Little Review*, will have hazarded some theory of this nature as to Mr. Joyce's intention. On our part, with such a fragment before us, it is hazarded rather than affirmed; but whatever the intention of the whole, there can be no question but that it is of the utmost sincerity and that the result, difficult or unpleasant as we may judge it, is undeniably important. In contrast with those whom we have called materialists, Mr. Joyce is spiritual; he is concerned at all costs to reveal the flickerings of that innermost flame which flashes its messages through the brain, and in order to preserve it he disregards with complete courage whatever seems to him adventitious, whether it be probability, or coherence, or any other of these signposts which for generations have served to support the imagination of a reader when called upon to imagine what he can neither touch nor see. The scene in the cemetery, for instance, with its brilliancy, its sordidity, its incoherence, its sudden lightning flashes of significance, does undoubtedly come so close to the quick of the mind that, on a first reading at any rate, it is difficult not to acclaim a masterpiece. If we want life itself, here surely we have it. Indeed, we find ourselves fumbling rather awkwardly if we try to say what else we wish, and for what reason a work of such originality yet fails to compare, for we must take high examples, with *Youth* or *The Mayor of Casterbridge*. It fails because of the comparative poverty of the writer's mind, we might say simply and have done with it. But it is possible to press a little further and wonder whether we may not refer our sense of being in a bright yet narrow room, confined and shut in, rather than enlarged and set free, to some limitation imposed by the method as well as by the mind. Is it the method that inhibits the creative power? Is it due to the method that we feel neither jovial nor magnanimous, but centred in a self which, in spite of its tremor of susceptibility, never embraces or creates what is outside itself and beyond? Does the emphasis laid, perhaps didactically, upon indecency, contribute to the effect of something angular and isolated? Or is it merely that in any effort of such originality it is much easier, for contemporaries especially, to feel what it lacks than to name what it gives? In any case it is a mistake to stand outside examining "methods." Any method is right, every method is right, that expresses what we wish to express, if we are writers; that brings us closer to the novelist's intention if we are readers. This method has the merit of bringing us closer to what we were prepared to call life itself; did not the reading of *Ulysses* suggest how much of life is excluded or ignored, and did it not come with a shock to open *Tristran Shandy* or even *Pendennis* and be by them convinced that there are not only other aspects of life, but more important ones into the bargain.

However this may be, the problem before the novelist at present, as we suppose it to have been in the past, is to contrive means of being free to set down what he chooses. He has to have the courage to say that what interests him is no longer "this" but "that": out of "that" alone must he construct his work. For the moderns "that," the point of interest, lies very likely in the dark places of psychology. At once, therefore, the accent falls a little differently; the emphasis is upon something hitherto ignored; at once a different outline of form becomes necessary, difficult for us to grasp, incomprehensible to our predecessors. No one but a modern, no one perhaps but a Russian, would have felt the interest of the situation which Tchekov has made into the short story which he calls "Gusev." Some Russian soldiers lie ill on board a ship which is taking them back to Russia. We are given a few scraps of their talk and some of their thoughts; then one of them dies and is carried away; the talk goes on among the others for a time, until Gusev himself dies, and looking "like a carrot or a radish" is thrown overboard. The emphasis is laid upon such unexpected places that at first it seems as if there were no emphasis at all; and then, as the eyes accustom themselves to twilight and discern the shapes of things in a room we see how complete the story is, how profound, and how truly in obedience to his vision Tchekov has chosen this, that, and the other, and placed them together to compose something new. But it is impossible to say "this is comic," or "that is tragic," nor are we certain, since short stories, we have been taught, should

be brief and conclusive, whether this, which is vague and inconclusive, should be called a short story at all.

The most elementary remarks upon modern English fiction can hardly avoid some mention of the Russian influence, and if the Russians are mentioned one runs the risk of feeling that to write of any fiction save theirs is waste of time. If we want understanding of the soul and heart where else shall we find it of comparable profundity? If we are sick of our own materialism the least considerable of their novelists has by right of birth a natural reverence for the human spirit. "Learn to make yourself akin to people. . . . But let this sympathy be not with the mind—for it is easy with the mind—but with the heart, with love towards them." In every great Russian writer we seem to discern the features of a saint, if sympathy for the sufferings of others, love towards them, endeavour to reach some goal worthy of the most exacting demands of the spirit constitute saintliness. It is the saint in them which confounds us with a feeling of our own irreligious triviality, and turns so many of our famous novels to tinsel and trickery. The conclusions of the Russian mind, thus comprehensive and compassionate, are inevitably, perhaps, of the utmost sadness. More accurately indeed we might speak of the inconclusiveness of the Russian mind. It is the sense that there is no answer, that if honestly examined life presents question after question which must be left to sound on and on after the story is over in hopeless interrogation that fills us with a deep, and finally it may be with a resentful, despair. They are right perhaps; unquestionably they see further than we do and without our gross impediments of vision. But perhaps we see something that escapes them, or why should this voice of protest mix itself with our gloom? The voice of protest is the voice of another and an ancient civilisation which seems to have bred in us the instinct to enjoy and fight rather than to suffer and understand. English fiction from Sterne to Meredith bears witness to our natural delight in humour and comedy, in the beauty of earth, in the activities of the intellect, and in the splendour of the body. But any deductions that we may draw from the comparison of two fictions so immeasurably far apart are futile save indeed as they flood us with a view of the infinite possibilities of the art and remind us that there is no limit to the horizon, and that nothing—no "method," no experiment, even of the wildest—is forbidden, but only falsity and pretence. "The proper stuff of fiction" does not exist; everything is the proper stuff of fiction, every feeling, every thought; every quality of brain and spirit is drawn upon; no perception comes amiss. And if we can imagine the art of fiction come alive and standing in our midst, she would undoubtedly bid us break her and bully her, as well as honour and love her, for so her youth is renewed and her sovereignty assured.

GEORGE SANTAYANA   (1863-1952)

GEORGE SANTAYANA was born in Madrid, came to America when he was seven, and was educated at Harvard. There he taught philosophy until 1912, when a legacy permitted him to return to Europe, where he spent the rest of his life. In *The Sense of Beauty* (1896), a major contribution to aesthetics, he connected the problems of valuation with aesthetic ideals. In numerous philosophical studies—such as the five-volume *Life of Reason* (1905-06), *Scepticism and Animal Faith* (1923), and the four-volume *Realms of Being* (1927-40)—he explored the relations between instinct and reason, naturalism and idealism, in his lucid, engaging prose style. Critical writings include *Three Philosophical Poets: Lucretius, Dante, and Goethe* (1910), *Character and Opinion in the United States* (1920), *Platonism and the Spiritual Life* (1927), and the semi-autobiographical novel *The Last Puritan* (1936).

"Penitent Art" serves as a valuable antidote to the unwitting acceptance an age can lend to its art and its artists. Far from being unconscious of the complexity of the modern age, Santayana admits that uncertainty, anxiety, and disappointment may lead an artist to throw off realism and naturalism for what are regarded as more "primary effects." When this happens, art cuts its moorings with its ally, nature, and returns to purify itself in penitential seclusion. It detaches itself systematically from reality, "emancipating the medium" by which it conveys the sensibility. Such stripping away reveals only "a mere wraith, a mere hint, a mere symbol." It is probably necessary that art (and life itself) should go through such penitent moods and even put on sackcloth and ashes; but something is to be said for being aware of what we are doing and for not being fooled by our own heady recoils and self-intoxicating slogans. The essay, "Penitent Art," admired by most critics of the last half century, has again become timely for general readers as we look back on the twentieth-century movement as a whole.

Penitent Art

ART IS like a charming woman who once had her age of innocence in the nursery, when she was beautiful without knowing it, being wholly intent on what she was making or telling or imagining.

Then she has had a season of passion and vanity, when having discovered how beautiful she was, she decked herself out in all possible pomp and finery, invented fashion after fashion to keep admiration alive, and finally began to put on rouge and false hair and too much scent, in the hope of still being a belle at seventy.

But it sometimes happens, during her long decline, that she hears a call to repentance, and thinks of being converted. Naturally, such a fine lady cannot give up her carriage; she is obliged occasionally to entertain her old friends at dinner, and to be seen now and then at the opera. Habit and the commitments she has in the world, where no function is complete without her, are too strong for her to be converted suddenly, or altogether; but henceforth something in her, in her most sensitive and thoughtful hours, upbraids her for the hollowness of her old airs and graces. It is really a sorry business, this perpetual pretence of being important and charming and charmed and beautiful.

Art seems to be passing at present through a lenten mood of this sort. Not all art, of course: somebody must still manufacture official statues and family portraits, somebody must design apartment houses, clubs, churches, skyscrapers, and stations. Visible through the academic framework of these inevitable objects, there is often much professional learning and judgment; there is even, sometimes, a hint of poetic life, or a suggestion of exotic beauty. In Mr. Sargent's painting,[1] for instance, beneath the photographic standards of the studio, we often catch a satirical

Penitent Art (1922). From *Obiter Scripta* by George Santayana. Reprinted with the permission of Charles Scribner's Sons and Constable & Co. Ltd. Copyright 1936 Charles Scribner's Sons; renewal copyright © 1964 Old Colony Trust Company.

[1] John Singer Sargent (1856-1925), American painter, known for his realistic portraits of the wealthy and socially prominent.

intention, or a philosophic idea, or love of the sensuous qualities in the model and in the accessories; a technical echo of Velasquez and Goya, though without plastic vitality or dramatic ease; a sort of Van Dyck, as it were, for the days of Edward VII; the dreadful lapse in refinement not being greater, perhaps, than is requisite for the documentary value of a true mirror of fashion in the later age. Taste of the old honest worldly sort is far from dead; it is found still in milliners and designers of fashionable garments, of furniture and ornaments. All this luxurious traditional art is as far as possible from repentance. Yet as the Magdalene was potentially a saint—perhaps always a saint really—so the most meretricious contrivances in the arts may sometimes include and betray the very principle of redemption, which is love; in this case the love of beauty. For example, here is the Russian ballet, doubling the dose of luxurious stimulation in every direction, erotic, tragic, historical, and decorative; yet see how it glides at times into simplicity, and in spite of all the paraphernalia of expert aestheticism, issues in forms of unmistakably penitent art, like pure colour and caricature.

I call pure colour and caricature penitent art, because it is only disappointment in other directions that drives artists back to these primary effects. By an austere and deliberate abstinence from everything that naturally tempts them, they achieve in this way a certain peace; but they would far rather have found it by genuinely recovering their naïveté. Sensuous splendour and caricature would then have seemed to them not the acme of abstract art, but the obvious truth of things; they would have doted on puppets and pantomime as a child dotes on dolls, without ever noticing how remote they are from reality. In the nineteenth century some romantic artists, poets, and philosophers actually tried being rebaptised, hoping that a fresh dip in the Jordan might rejuvenate them; but it was of no use. The notion of *recovering innocence* is a contradiction in terms; conversion can only initiate a non-natural life of grace; death must intervene before corruption can put on incorruption. That age was accordingly an age of revivals, of antiquaries, nothing in art and religion but retrospective; it was progressive only in things material and in the knowledge of them. Even its philosophical idealism and psychology were meant to be historical and descriptive of facts, literary and egotistical as the view of the facts might be. Romanticism thought it was exquisitely sensitive to the spirit of remote things, but in reality it was sensitive only to material perspectives, to costume and stage-setting; it grew sentimental over legends and ruins, and being moonstruck, thought it was imbibing the spirit of the past. But the past had not been consciously romantic; what the ancients actually thought and felt was understood much better before the nineteenth century than since; for formerly they were regarded simply as men, essentially contemporary—which comes much nearer the truth. Of course, the passion that can drive people to such earnest affectations must be itself genuine. Keats or Ruskin or Oscar Wilde had abundant vitality and expressed, each in his studied archaism, the profound helplessness that beset him; but what was vital in them was some sensuous or moral or revolutionary instinct of their own, such as in Shelley had existed pure; only in them it was contorted by their terrible preoccupation with being early, or rich, or choice. They were hypnotised by dead beauty; and not having invention nor influence enough to remodel their own age, they fled from it to exotic delights, sometimes primitive, sometimes luxurious, sometimes religious, and sometimes all these things at once. Similarly the revivals in architecture and in the minor crafts expressed a genuine love of colour, ornament, and beauty; they gave the snobbish middle classes a taste of cheap luxury; they could sip culture in a teacup. Yet the particular fashions revived were unstable; each successive affectation had hardly ceased to seem exquisite when it began to look foolish. Art at best is subject to fashion, because there is a margin of arbitrary variation in its forms, even when their chief lines are determined by their function; but in revived art fashion is all; it is a fancy-dress, unsatisfying even in the glamour of the ballroom, which we are positively ashamed to be seen in in the morning.

Fortunately revivals now seem to be over. Ruins and museums are interesting to the anti-quary; they stir the historical imagination, and dazzle us here and there with some ray of living beauty, like that of a jewel; but they cannot supply inspiration. In art, in poetry, unless you become as a little child you cannot enter the kingdom of heaven. Little children are what artists and poets are now striving hard to be; little children who instead of blowing a tin trumpet blow by chance through a whole orchestra, but with the same emotion as the child; or who, instead of daubing a geometrical skeleton with a piece of chalk, can daub a cross-eyed cross-section of the entire spectrum or a compound fracture of a nightmare. Such is Cubism: by no means an inexpert or meaningless thing. Before you can compose a chaos or paint the unnameable, you must train yourself to a severe abstention from all practical habits of perception; you must heroically suppress the understanding. The result, when the penance is genuinely performed, has a very deep and recondite charm; you revert to what the spinal column might feel if it had a separate consciousness, or to what the retina might see if it could be painlessly cut off from the brain; lights, patterns, dynamic suggestions, sights and memories fused together, hypnotic harmonies such as may visit a vegetative or even mineral sensibility; you become a thousand prisms and mirrors reflecting one another. This is one kind of aesthetic repentance. Vain, vain, it says to itself, was the attempt to depict or beautify external objects; let material things be what they will; what are they to the artist? Nature has the urgency of life, which art cannot rival; it has the lure, the cruelty, of actual existence, where all is sin and confusion and vanity, a hideous strife of forms devouring one another, in which all are mutilated and doomed. What is that to the spirit? Let it confess its own impotence in that field, and abandon all attempts to observe or preserve what are called *things:* let it devote itself instead to cleansing the inside of the cup, to purifying its sensibility, which is after all what nature plays upon when she seems to us to be beautiful. Perhaps in that way spirit may abstract the gold of beauty and cast the dross away—all that alloy of preoccupation with material forms and external events and moral sentiments and vain animal adventures which has so long distracted the misguided artist, when he could paint the whole world and had lost his own soul. It is always the play of sensibility, and nothing else, that lends interest to external themes; and it was an evil obsession with alien things that dragged sensibility into a slavery to things which stifled and degraded it: *salvation lies in emancipating the medium.*

To renounce representation, or be representative only by accident, is accordingly one sort of penitent art; but there is another sort, more humble and humourous. This second sort makes no attempt to resist the impulse to observe and to express external things. It does not proudly imagine that the medium, which is the human contribution to representation, can be sufficient unto itself. On the contrary, in its sensuous orchestration it is content to be rudimentary, to work in clay or in wood, and to dress in homespun. It is all feeling, all childlike tenderness, all sense of life. Persons and animals fascinate it. At the same time, warned by the fate of explicit poets and realistic painters, it does not attempt, in its portraiture, to give more than a pregnant hint, some large graphic sign, some profound caricature. Don't be rhetorical, it says; don't try to be exhaustive; all that is worth saying can be said in words of one syllable. Look long, and be brief. It is not in their material entirety and detail that things penetrate to the soul, but in their simple large identity, as a child knows his mother, nurse, or dog. Fresh inchoate forms, voices draped in mantles, people the mind, and return to it in dreams. Monsters and dwarfs were the first gods; the half, said a Greek proverb, is better than the whole. The implicit is alone important where life is concerned: nothing is more eloquent than an abstract posture, an immovable single gesture. Let art abandon reproduction and become indication. If it threatens thereby to become caricature, know that profound art can never be anything else. If men, when seen truly, take on the aspect of animals or puppets, it is because they are animals and puppets at bottom. But all caricature need not be unkind; it may be tender, or even sublime. The distortion, the single emphasis, the extreme simplification may reveal a soul which rhetoric and self-love had hidden in a false rationality. The absurd is the naked truth, the pathetic appeal of sheer fact, attempting to come into existence, like a featherless chick peeping out of its eggshell. All this pompous drapery of convention was a disguise; strip it away. Do not make maps of your images; make companions of them, make idols. Be reticent, emphatic, moody, bold; *salvation lies in caricature.*

Accustomed as they are to revivals, some critics have called this form of aesthetic penance a revival of savage art; but the mood is reversed. Savages were never rudimentary on purpose; they were not experimenting in the distortion or simplification of forms; much less, of course, did they voluntarily eliminate all representation of objects in order to deepen sensibility for the medium. They simply painted as well as they could. We have got far beyond that. Penitent art, childish as it may seem at times, is a refinement, perhaps an over-refinement; it is not so much crude or incompetent, as ascetic or morbid. It is also sometimes a little vulgar; because one of the forms of caricature and self-revelation is to be brutal, to flaunt what is out of place, what spoils the picture. Tragedy used to be noble; there is a new refinement in seeing how often it is ignoble; there is a second tragedy in that. Perhaps what we regard at first sight as a terrible decline in art may be sometimes the awakening of this sort of self-scorn. See how ugly I am, it cries, how brutish, common, and deformed! There are remains of sculpture and paintings of the late Roman Empire in some respects like our latest experiments. The decorative splendour (which was very marked) is lost; we miss the coloured marbles, the gold, the embroideries, the barbaric armour and jewels; but the stunted pathetic human figures remain in crowds. It seems that the spirit had no joy in man any more; it hid him in hieratic garments or pityingly recorded his gregarious misery. He was a corpse laid out in pontifical vestments. We too are dying; but in nature the death of one thing is commonly the birth of another. Instead of decorating a Byzantine sanctuary, our artists do penance in a psychological desert, studying their own sensations, the mysteries of sheer light and sound; and as music was long ago divorced from poetry and instrumental music from singing, so a luxurious but strident art is detaching itself from everything but its own medium. This on the decorative side; in representation the same retrenchment stops at another level. Representation too has a psychological medium; fancy must create the images which the observer or reproducer of things conceives to be their forms. These images are not the forms of things at all; not only is their perspective created by the observer, but their character, when it is truly considered, is amazingly summary, variable, and fantastic—a mere wraith, a mere hint, a mere symbol. What we suppose we see, what we *say* things look like, is rather an inventory, collected in memory and language, of many successive observations; it is discursive study, registered perhaps in discursive painting. But as the total composition never was nor ever could be a living image, so its parts are not images any longer; in being arrested they have acquired new boundaries and lost half their primitive essence. We may paint the things we see, we cannot arrest the images by which we see them; all we can do —if the images and not the things are what interest us—is to paint something that, by some occult trick of optics, may revive the image in some particular; and then, although the picture when studied discursively may not resemble the thing at all, it may bring back to us, as it were by scent, the feeling which the thing originally gave us; and we may say that it has caught the *spirit* of the thing. It is the medium that in such a case animates the object, and seems to obscure it; and this medium which we call sense in so far as things affect us through it, we call spirit in so far as it modifies our view of the things. The more we transform things in seeing them, the more we seem to spiritualise them and turn them into forms of our own sensibility, regarding the living image in us as the dramatic essence of the object. It is the business of science to correct this illusion; but the penitent artist—who has taken refuge in the spirit and is not striving to stretch his apprehension into literal truth, since the effort to depict things discursively has proved a vain and arid ambition—the penitent artist is content with the rhythms, echoes, or rays which things awaken within him; and in proportion as these reverberations are actually renewed, the poem remains a cry, the story a dream, the building a glimpse, the portrait a caricature.

PABLO PICASSO   (1881-   )

D URING his long career, Pablo Picasso has exerted a dominant influence on twentieth-century art. Born in Malaga, Spain, he held his first public exhibition in Barcelona in 1897, and since 1904 he has lived in or near Paris. Early fame rose out of his impressive leadership of the Cubist movement, but his genius has been so fecund and various that in his art, periods and styles continually rise—sometimes alongside one another—coalesce, and divide, only to reappear in new combinations in painting or sculpture. Among his numerous masterpieces is the monumental *Guernica* (1937), painted entirely in black, white, and grey, depicting destruction in a Basque town that had been bombed by German planes during the Spanish Civil War.

The passage reprinted below was dictated in Spanish to Marius de Zayas; Picasso approved the manuscript before it was translated and published in 1923. Picasso stands opposed to such theorists as Wilhelm Worringer (see above, pp. 277 and 563-4), who early in this century established polarities of naturalistic art (which mirrors the organic world and elicits our vitalistic empathy for it) and abstract art (which revolts from such naturalism and escapes to a timeless world of life-denying inorganic and geometric forms). As the foremost creator of new forms in contemporary art, Picasso makes a more radical distinction—one that is between *all* art and reality. "There are no concrete or abstract forms, but only forms which are more or less convincing lies." Yet art is more than the artificial: "Art is a lie that makes us realize truth." In a career of so many periods and styles, it should not surprise us that Picasso rejects superficial notions of "rise and decline" in the arts. He views each work in terms of its intrinsic value in confronting reality with its lies and with its truth.

Statement on Art

I CAN hardly understand the importance given to the word *research* in connection with modern painting. In my opinion to search means nothing in painting. To find, is the thing. Nobody is interested in following a man who, with his eyes fixed on the ground, spends his life looking for the pocketbook that fortune should put in his path. The one who finds something no matter what it might be, even if his intention were not to search for it, at least arouses our curiosity, if not our admiration.

Among the several sins that I have been accused of committing, none is more false than the one that I have, as the principal objective in my work, the spirit of research. When I paint my object is to show what I have found and not what I am looking for. In art intentions are not sufficient and, as we say in Spanish: love must be proved by facts and not by reasons. What one does is what counts and not what one had the intention of doing.

We all know that art is not truth. Art is a lie that makes us realize truth, at least the truth that is given us to understand. The artist must know the manner whereby to convince others of the truthfulness of his lies. If he only shows in

his work that he has searched, and re-searched, for the way to put over his lies, he would never accomplish anything.

The idea of research has often made painting go astray, and made the artist lose himself in mental lucubrations. Perhaps this has been the principal fault of modern art. The spirit of research has poisoned those who have not fully understood all the positive and conclusive elements in modern art and has made them attempt to paint the invisible and, therefore, the unpaintable.

They speak of naturalism in opposition to modern painting. I would like to know if anyone has ever seen a natural work of art. Nature and art, being two different things, cannot be the same thing. Through art we express our conception of what nature is not.

Velasquez left us his idea of the people of his epoch. Undoubtedly they were different from what he painted them, but we cannot conceive a Philip IV in any other way than the one Velasquez painted. Rubens also made a portrait of the same king and in Rubens' portrait he seems to be quite another person. We believe in the one painted by Velasquez, for he convinces us by his right of might.

From the painters of the origins, the primitives, whose work is obviously different from nature, down to those artists who, like David, Ingres and even Bouguereau, believed in painting nature as it is, art has always been art and not nature. And from the point of view of art

Statement on Art. From *Picasso: Fifty Years of His Art* by Alfred H. Barr, Jr. Copyright 1946 The Museum of Modern Art, New York, and reprinted by permission of the publisher. The "Statement by Picasso: 1923" was made in Spanish to Marius de Zayas. Picasso approved de Zayas' manuscript before it was translated into English and published, originally, in *The Arts,* New York, May 1923, under the title "Picasso Speaks."

there are no concrete or abstract forms, but only forms which are more or less convincing lies. That those lies are necessary to our mental selves is beyond any doubt, as it is through them that we form our esthetic point of view of life.

Cubism is no different from any other school of painting. The same principles and the same elements are common to all. The fact that for a long time cubism has not been understood and that even today there are people who cannot see anything in it, means nothing. I do not read English, an English book is a blank book to me. This does not mean that the English language does not exist, and why should I blame anybody else but myself if I cannot understand what I know nothing about?

I also often hear the word evolution. Repeatedly I am asked to explain how my painting evolved. To me there is no past or future in art. If a work of art cannot live always in the present it must not be considered at all. The art of the Greeks, of the Egyptians, of the great painters who lived in other times, is not an art of the past; perhaps it is more alive today than it ever was. Art does not evolve by itself, the ideas of people change and with them their mode of expression. When I hear people speak of the evolution of an artist, it seems to me that they are considering him standing between two mirrors that face each other and reproduce his image an infinite number of times, and that they contemplate the successive images of one mirror as his past, and the images of the other mirror as his future, while his real image is taken as his present. They do not consider that they all are the same images in different planes.

Variation does not mean evolution. If an artist varies his mode of expression this only means that he has changed his manner of thinking, and in changing, it might be for the better or it might be for the worse.

The several manners I have used in my art must not be considered as an evolution, or as steps toward an unknown ideal of painting. All I have ever made was made for the present and with the hope that it will always remain in the present. I have never taken into consideration the spirit of research. When I have found something to express, I have done it without thinking of the past or of the future. I do not believe I have used radically different elements in the different manners I have used in painting. If the subjects I have wanted to express have suggested different ways of expression I have never hesitated to adopt them. I have never made trials nor experiments. Whenever I had something to say, I have said it in the manner in which I have felt it ought to be said. Different motives inevitably require different methods of expression. This does not imply either evolution or progress, but an adaptation of the idea one wants to 'express and the means to express that idea.

Arts of transition do not exist. In the chronological history of art there are periods which are more positive, more complete than others. This means that there are periods in which there are better artists than in others. If the history of art could be graphically represented, as in a chart used by a nurse to mark the changes of temperature of her patient, the same silhouettes of mountains would be shown, proving that in art there is no ascendant progress, but that it follows certain ups and downs that might occur at any time. The same occurs with the work of an individual artist.

Many think that cubism is an art of transition, an experiment which is to bring ulterior results. Those who think that way have not understood it. Cubism is not either a seed or a foetus, but an art dealing primarily with forms, and when a form is realized it is there to live its own life. A mineral substance, having geometric formation, is not made so for transitory purposes, it is to remain what it is and will always have its own form. But if we are to apply the law of evolution and transformism to art, then we have to admit that all art is transitory. On the contrary, art does not enter into these philosophic absolutisms. If cubism is an art of transition I am sure that the only thing that will come out of it is another form of cubism.

Mathematics, trigonometry, chemistry, psychoanalysis, music, and whatnot, have been related to cubism to give it an easier interpretation. All this has been pure literature, not to say nonsense, which brought bad results, blinding people with theories.

Cubism has kept itself within the limits and limitations of painting, never pretending to go beyond it. Drawing, design and color are understood and practiced in cubism in the same spirit and manner that they are understood and practiced in all other schools. Our subjects might be different, as we have introduced into painting objects and forms that were formerly ignored. We have kept our eyes open to our surroundings, and also our brains.

We give to form and color all their individual significance, as far as we can see it; in our subjects we keep the joy of discovery, the pleasure of the unexpected; our subject itself must be a source of interest. But of what use is it to say what we do when everybody can see it if he wants to?

JOSÉ ORTEGA Y GASSET   (1883-1955)

JOSÉ ORTEGA Y GASSET—easily the greatest philosophical sociologist of our century to write perceptively about the arts—was born in Madrid, studied at the University there, and received his doctorate in 1904. He was professor of metaphysics at the University from 1910 to 1936. Early in his career he began writing for newspapers and journals in South America and Spain and in 1923 founded the *Revista de occidente*. He championed numerous liberal causes and in his many-faceted Voltairean way became one of the leading figures of the European intelligentsia. In 1931 he was elected deputy in the Constituent Assembly of the Spanish Republic, but at the outbreak of the Spanish Civil War in 1936 he found he could not support either side and went into exile. Returning in 1945, he remained detached from politics and the University. Among his many works are *Meditations on Quixote* (1914), which is a brilliant work on the general character of his native land, *Invertebrate Spain* (1921), *The Modern Theme* (1923), *The Revolt of the Masses* (1931), and *On Love* (1940).

The Dehumanization of Art, which had immense influence on the Continent, has long been valued by English-speaking critics as well, for providing one of the clearest distinctions that have been made between the "Modernist" movement and the nineteenth-century conceptions of the arts. Now that we see the "Modernist" movement with more perspective, and are becoming once again interested in the relation of the arts to sociological considerations, Ortega's essay is becoming even more widely appreciated. In the selection reprinted here he develops a powerful thesis with deceptive ease. Art, he argues, is undergoing a periodic divagation from reality. Aristotle had observed that poetry springs from two causes, "each of them lying deep in our nature": the instinct for imitation and the instinct for "harmonia," or form (see above, p. 21). The nineteenth century inclined toward the former, toward what Ortega calls the "core of 'lived' reality." Art became weighed down with its human content, and artistic ideas served mainly to point up objects in the natural world. In the absence of vital direction from other institutions in our culture, art had to take on many human issues, including the salvation of man. Twentieth-century art bolted from reality in order to save itself, and, as in the eighteenth century, this led to a "will to style," to derealize and, in short, to dehumanize. The icy emotionalities of Debussy's music, the lyrical objects of Mallarmé's poetry, have shown how artistic ideas may be explored in and for themselves. Why has art given up on "poor reality" and turned inward? Other critics have reasoned that it is because reality—in this century so tense and appalling— has failed man. Ortega emphasizes that the weight of tradition had grown so heavy that, in order to soar, art had to "shoot ballast," and in order to instill youthfulness, had to reject, in its jesting and ironic manner, the past itself.

From The Dehumanization of Art

UNPOPULARITY OF THE NEW ART

ALL MODERN art is unpopular, and it is so not accidentally and by chance, but essentially and by fate.

It might be said that every newcomer among styles passes through a stage of quarantine. The battle of *Hernani* comes to mind,[1] and all the other skirmishes connected with the advent of Romanticism. However, the unpopularity of present-day art is of a different kind. A distinction must be made between what is not popular and what is unpopular. A new style takes some time in winning popularity; it is not popular, but it is not unpopular either. The break-through of Romanticism, although a frequently cited example, is, as a sociological phenomenon, exactly the opposite of the present situation of art. Romanticism was very quick in winning "the

The Dehumanization of Art. First published in 1925. From *The Dehumanization of Art and Other Essays on Art, Culture, and Literature* by José Ortega y Gasset, translated by Helene Weyl (copyright Princeton University Press; rev. ed., 1968; Princeton paperback, 1968), pp. 4-6, 8-9, 11, 14, 20-23, 42-49, 50-51, 52. Reprinted by permission of Princeton University Press.

[1] Victor Hugo's *Hernani* (performed in February, 1830) violated most of the neoclassic rules of the French drama. Its performance was strongly opposed by the Academy and by classicists generally and was just as warmly espoused, in the name of liberty, by Romantics (including Balzac, Berlioz, and Delacroix). The battle raged nightly for over three months, ending in victory for the Romantic drama.

people" to whom the old classical art had never appealed. The enemy with whom Romanticism had to fight it out was precisely a select minority irretrievably sold to the classical forms of the *"ancien régime"* in poetry. The works of the romanticists were the first, after the invention of printing, to enjoy large editions. Romanticism was the prototype of a popular style. First-born of democracy, it was coddled by the masses.

Modern art, on the other hand, will always have the masses against it. It is essentially unpopular; moreover, it is antipopular. Any of its works automatically produces a curious effect on the general public. It divides the public into two groups: one very small, formed by those who are favorably inclined towards it; another very large—the hostile majority. (Let us ignore that ambiguous fauna—the snobs.) Thus the work of art acts like a social agent which segregates from the shapeless mass of the many two different castes of men.

Which is the differentiating principle that creates these two antagonistic groups? Every work of art arouses differences of opinion. Some like it, some don't; some like it more, some like it less. Such disagreements have no organic character, they are not a matter of principles. A person's chance disposition determines on which side he will fall. But in the case of the new art the split occurs in a deeper layer than that on which differences of personal taste reside. It is not that the majority does not *like* the art of the young and the minority likes it, but that the majority, the masses, do not *understand* it. The old bigwigs who were present at the performance of *Hernani* understood Victor Hugo's play very well; precisely because they understood it they disliked it. Faithfully adhering to definite aesthetic norms, they were disgusted at the new artistic values which this piece of art proposed to them.

"From a sociological point of view" the characteristic feature of the new art is, in my judgment, that it divides the public into the two classes of those who understand it and those who do not. This implies that one group possesses an organ of comprehension denied to the other—that they are two different varieties of the human species. The new art obviously addresses itself not to everybody, as did Romanticism, but to a specially gifted minority. Hence the indignation it arouses in the masses. . . .

ARTISTIC ART

If the new art is not accessible to every man this implies that its impulses are not of a generically human kind. It is an art not for men in general but for a special class of men who may not be better but who evidently are different.

One point must be clarified before we go on. What is it the majority of people call aesthetic pleasure? What happens in their minds when they "like" a work of art; for instance, a theatrical performance? The answer is easy. A man likes a play when he has become interested in the human destinies presented to him, when the love and hatred, the joys and sorrows of the personages so move his heart that he participates in it all as though it were happening in real life. And he calls a work "good" if it succeeds in creating the illusion necessary to make the imaginary personages appear like living persons. In poetry he seeks the passion and pain of the man behind the poet. Paintings attract him if he finds on them figures of men or women whom it would be interesting to meet. A landscape is pronounced "pretty" if the country it represents deserves for its loveliness or its grandeur to be visited on a trip. . . .

During the nineteenth century artists proceeded in all too impure a fashion. They reduced the strictly aesthetic elements to a minimum and let the work consist almost entirely in a fiction of human realities. In this sense all normal art of the last century must be called realistic. Beethoven and Wagner were realistic, and so was Chateaubriand as well as Zola. Seen from the vantage-point of our day Romanticism and Naturalism draw closer together and reveal their common realistic root. . . .

When we analyze the new style we find that it contains certain closely connected tendencies. It tends (1) to dehumanize art, (2) to avoid living forms, (3) to see to it that the work of art is nothing but a work of art, (4) to consider art as play and nothing else, (5) to be essentially ironical, (6) to beware of sham and hence to aspire to scrupulous realization, (7) to regard art as a thing of no transcending consequence. . . .

DEHUMANIZATION

Let us compare a painting in the new style with one of, say, 1860. The simplest procedure will be to begin by setting against one another the objects they represent: a man perhaps, a house, or a mountain. It then appears that the artist of 1860 wanted nothing so much as to give to the objects in his picture the same looks and airs they possess outside it when they occur as parts of the "lived" or "human" reality. Apart from this he may have been animated by other more intricate aesthetic ambitions, but what interests us is that his first concern was with securing this likeness. Man, house, mountain are at once recognized, they are our good old friends; whereas on a modern painting we are at a loss to recognize them. It might be supposed that the modern painter has failed to achieve resemblance. But then some pictures of the 1860's are "poorly" painted, too, and the objects in them differ considerably from the corresponding objects outside them. And yet, whatever the differences, the very blunders of the traditional artist point toward the "human" object; they are downfalls on the way toward it and somehow equivalent to the orienting words "This is a cock" with which Cervantes lets the painter Orbanejo enlighten his public. In modern paintings the opposite happens. It is not that the painter is bungling and fails to render the natural (natural = human) thing because he deviates from it, but that these deviations point in a direction opposite to that which would lead to reality.

Far from going more or less clumsily toward reality, the artist is seen going against it. He is brazenly set on deforming reality, shattering its human aspect, dehumanizing it. With the things represented on traditional paintings we could have imaginary intercourse. Many a young Englishman has fallen in love with Gioconda.[2] With the objects of modern pictures no intercourse is possible. By divesting them of their aspect of "lived" reality the artist has blown up the bridges and burned the ships that could have taken us back to our daily world. He leaves us locked up in an abstruse universe, surrounded by objects with which human dealings are inconceivable, and thus compels us to improvise other forms of intercourse completely distinct from our ordinary ways with things. We must invent unheard-of gestures to fit those singular figures. This new way of life which presupposes the annulment of spontaneous life is precisely what we call understanding and enjoyment of art. Not that this life lacks sentiments and passions, but those sentiments and passions evidently belong to a flora other than that which covers the hills and dales of primary and human life. What those ultra-objects[3] evoke in our inner artist are secondary passions, specifically aesthetic sentiments.

It may be said that, to achieve this result, it would be simpler to dismiss human forms—man, house, mountain—altogether and to construct entirely original figures. But, in the first place, this is not feasible. Even in the most abstract ornamental line a stubborn reminiscence lurks of certain "natural" forms. Secondly—and this is the crucial point—the art of which we speak is inhuman not only because it contains no things human, but also because it is an explicit act of dehumanization. In his escape from the human world the young artist cares less for the "*terminus ad quem*," the startling fauna at which he arrives, than for the "*terminus a*

quo,"[4] the human aspect which he destroys. The question is not to paint something altogether different from a man, a house, a mountain, but to paint a man who resembles a man as little as possible; a house that preserves of a house exactly what is needed to reveal the metamorphosis; a cone miraculously emerging —as the snake from his slough—from what used to be a mountain. For the modern artist, aesthetic pleasure derives from such a triumph over human matter. That is why he has to drive home the victory by presenting in each case the strangled victim.

It may be thought a simple affair to fight shy of reality, but it is by no means easy. There is no difficulty in painting or saying things which make no sense whatever, which are unintelligible and therefore nothing. One only needs to assemble unconnected words or to draw random lines. But to construct something that is not a copy of "nature" and yet possesses substance of its own is a feat which presupposes nothing less than genius. . . .

NEGATIVE INFLUENCE OF THE PAST

Elsewhere[5] I have pointed out that it is in art and pure science, precisely because they are the freest activities and least dependent on social conditions, that the first signs of any changes of collective sensibility become noticeable. A fundamental revision of man's attitude towards life is apt to find its first expression in artistic creation and scientific theory. The fine texture of both these matters renders them susceptible to the slightest breeze of the spiritual trade-winds. As in the country, opening the window of a morning, we examine the smoke rising from the chimney-stacks in order to determine the wind that will rule the day, thus we can, with a similar meteorologic purpose, study the art and science of the young generation.

The first step has been to describe the new phenomenon. Only now that this is done can we proceed to ask of which new general style of life modern art is the symptom and the harbinger. The answer requires an analysis of the causes

---

[2] The Mona Lisa by Leonardo da Vinci.

[3] "Ultraism" is one of the most appropriate names that have been coined to denote the new sensibility. [Ortega y Gasset.]

[4] Less for the "terminus *to* which" than the "terminus *from* which."

[5] In *The Modern Theme* (1931), p. 26.

that have effected this strange about-face in art. Why this desire to dehumanize? Why this disgust at living forms? Like all historical phenomena this too will have grown from a multitude of entangled roots which only a fine flair is capable of detecting. An investigation of this kind would be too serious a task to be attacked here. However, what other causes may exist, there is one which, though perhaps not decisive, is certainly very clear.

We can hardly put too much stress on the influence which at all times the past of art exerts on the future of art. In the mind of the artist a sort of chemical reaction is set going by the clash between his individual sensibility and already existing art. He does not find himself all alone with the world before him; in his relations with the world there always intervenes, like an interpreter, the artistic tradition. What will the reaction of creative originality upon the beauty of previous works be like? It may be positive or negative. Either the artist is in conformity with the past and regards it as his heritage which he feels called upon to perfect; or he discovers that he has a spontaneous indefinable aversion against established and generally acclaimed art. And as in the first case he will be pleased to settle down in the customary forms and repeat some of their sacred patterns, thus he will, in the second, not only deviate from established tradition but be equally pleased to give to his work an explicit note of protest against the time-honored norms.

The latter is apt to be overlooked when one speaks of the influence of the past on the present. That a work of a certain period may be modeled after works of another previous period has always been easily recognized. But to notice the negative influence of the past and to realize that a new style has not infrequently grown out of a conscious and relished antagonism to traditional styles seems to require somewhat of an effort.

As it is, the development of art from Romanticism to this day cannot be understood unless this negative mood of mocking aggressiveness is taken into account as a factor of aesthetic pleasure. Baudelaire praises the black Venus precisely because the classical is white. From then on the successive styles contain an ever increasing dose of derision and disparagement until in our day the new art consists almost exclusively of protests against the old. The reason is not far to seek. When an art looks back on many centuries of continuous evolution without major hiatuses or historical catastrophes its products keep on accumulating, and the weight of tradition increasingly encumbers the inspiration of the hour. Or to put it differently, an ever growing mass of traditional styles hampers the direct and original communication between the nascent artist and the world around him. In this case one or two things may happen. Either tradition stifles all creative power—as in Egypt, Byzantium, and the Orient in general—or the effect of the past on the present changes its sign and a long epoch appears in which the new art, step by step, breaks free of the old which threatened to smother it. The latter is typical of Europe whose futuristic instinct, predominant throughout its history, stands in marked contrast to the irremediable traditionalism of the Orient.

A good deal of what I have called dehumanization and disgust for living forms is inspired by just such an aversion against the traditional interpretation of realities. The vigor of the assault stands in inverse proportion to the distance. Keenest contempt is felt for nineteenth century procedures although they contain already a noticeable dose of opposition to older styles. On the other hand, the new sensibility exhibits a somewhat suspicious enthusiasm for art that is most remote in time and space, for prehistoric or savage primitivism. In point of fact, what attracts the modern artist in those primordial works is not so much their artistic quality as their candor; that is, the absence of tradition.

If we now briefly consider the question: What type of life reveals itself in this attack on past art? we come upon a strange and stirring fact. To assail all previous art, what else can it mean than to turn against Art itself? For what is art, concretely speaking, if not such art as has been made up to now?

Should that enthusiasm for pure art be but a mask which conceals surfeit with art and hatred of it? But, how can such a thing come about? Hatred of art is unlikely to develop as an isolated phenomenon; it goes hand in hand with hatred of science, hatred of State, hatred, in sum, of civilization as a whole. Is it conceivable that modern Western man bears a rankling grudge against his own historical essence? Does he feel something akin to the *odium profes- sionis* [6] of medieval monks—that aversion, after long years of monastic discipline, against the very rules that had shaped their lives? . . .[7]

DOOMED TO IRONY

When we discovered that the new style taken in its most general aspect is characterized by a tendency to eliminate all that is human and to preserve only the purely artistic elements, this seemed to betray a great enthusiasm for art. But when we then walked around the phenom- enon and looked at it from another angle we came upon an unexpected grimace of surfeit or disdain. The contradiction is obvious and must be strongly stressed. It definitely indicates that modern art is of an ambiguous nature which, as a matter of fact, does not surprise us; for ambiguous have been all important issues of these current years. . . .

The first consequence of the retreat of art upon itself is a ban on all pathos. Art laden with "humanity" had become as weighty as life itself. It was an extremely serious affair, almost sacred. At times—in Schopenhauer and Wagner —it aspired to nothing less than to save man- kind. Whereas the modern inspiration—and this is a strange fact indeed—is invariably wag- gish. The waggery may be more or less refined, it may run the whole gamut from open clownery to a slight ironical twinkle, but it is always there. And it is not that the content of the work is comical—that would mean a relapse into a mode or species of the "human" style—but that, what- ever the content, the art itself is jesting. To look for fiction as fiction—which, we have said, mod- ern art does—is a proposition that cannot be executed except with one's tongue in one's cheek.

[6] Hatred of the profession.

[7] It would be interesting to analyze the psychological mechanisms through which yesterday's art negatively affects the art of today. One is obvious: ennui. Mere repetition of style has a blunting and tiring effect. In his *Principles of Art History: the Problem of the De- velopment of Style in Later Art* (London: Bell, 1932) Heinrich Wölfflin mentions the power of boredom which has ever again mobilized art and compelled it to invent new forms. And the same applies to literature, only more so. [Ortega y Gasset.]

Art is appreciated precisely because it is recog- nized as a farce. It is this trait more than any other that makes the works of the young so in- comprehensible to serious people of less pro- gressive taste. To them modern painting and music are sheer "farce"—in the bad sense of the word—and they will not be convinced that to be a farce may be precisely the mission and the virtue of art. A "farce" in the bad sense of the word it would be if the modern artist pre- tended to equal status with the "serious" artists of the past, and a cubist painting expected to be extolled as solemnly and all but religiously as a statue by Michelangelo. But all he does is to in- vite us to look at a piece of art that is a joke and that essentially makes fun of itself. For this is what the facetious quality of the modern in- spiration comes down to. Instead of deriding other persons or things—without a victim no comedy—the new art ridicules art itself.

And why be scandalized at this? Art has never shown more clearly its magic gift than in this flout at itself. Thanks to this suicidal gesture art continues to be art, its self-negation miraculously bringing about its preservation and triumph.

I much doubt that any young person of our time can be impressed by a poem, a painting, or a piece of music that is not flavored with a dash of irony. . . .

This inevitable dash of irony, it is true, im- parts to modern art a monotony which must exasperate patience herself. But be that as it may, the contradiction between surfeit and en- thusiasm now appears resolved. The first is aroused by art as a serious affair, the second is felt for art that triumphs as a farce, laughing off everything, itself included—much as in a system of mirrors which indefinitely reflect one another no shape is ultimate, all are eventually ridiculed and revealed as pure images.

ART A THING OF NO CONSEQUENCE

[Throughout the last century] Art was impor- tant for two reasons: on account of its subjects which dealt with the profoundest problems of humanity, and on account of its own significance as a human pursuit from which the species de- rived its justification and dignity. It was a re- markable sight, the solemn air with which the great poet or the musical genius appeared before the masses—the air of a prophet and founder of religion, the majestic pose of a statesman responsible for the state of the world.

A present-day artist would be thunderstruck, I suspect, if he were trusted with so enormous a mission and, in consequence, compelled to deal in his work with matters of such scope. To his mind, the kingdom of art commences where the air feels lighter and things, free from formal fetters, begin to cut whimsical capers. In this universal pirouetting he recognizes the best warrant for the existence of the Muses. Were art to redeem man, it could do so only by saving him from the seriousness of life and restoring him to an unexpected boyishness. The symbol of art is seen again in the magic flute of the Great God Pan which makes the young goats frisk at the edge of the grove.

All modern art begins to appear comprehensible and in a way great when it is interpreted as an attempt to instill youthfulness into an ancient world. Other styles must be interpreted in connection with dramatic social or political movements, or with profound religious and philosophical currents. The new style only asks to be linked to the triumph of sports and games. It is of the same kind and origin with them. . . .

All peculiarities of modern art can be summed up in this one feature of its renouncing its importance—a feature which, in its turn, signifies nothing less than that art has changed its position in the hierarchy of human activities and interests. These activities and interests may be represented by a series of concentric circles whose radii measure the dynamic distances from the axis of life where the supreme desires are operating. All human matters—vital and cultural—revolve in their several orbits about the throbbing heart of the system. Art which—like science and politics—used to be very near the axis of enthusiasm, that backbone of our person, has moved toward the outer rings. It has lost none of its attributes, but it has become a minor issue.

The trend toward pure art betrays not arrogance, as is often thought, but modesty. Art that has rid itself of human pathos is a thing without consequence—just art with no other pretenses. . . .

THOMAS MANN   (1875-1955)

IN HIS early fiction (*Buddenbrooks, Tonio Kroger, Death in Venice*), Thomas Mann explored the predicament of the "bourgeois artist," estranged from or unfit for his vapid culture, yet foiled by his upbringing from leading a bohemian existence. His scope widened in *The Magic Mountain* (1924), in which he dramatized the intellectual forces at odds in Western civilization. He won the Nobel Prize in 1929. For political reasons Mann left Germany and emigrated to America, where he concluded his epic tetralogy of novels, *Joseph and His Brothers* (1933-43). A later novel, *Doctor Faustus* (1947), concerns a musical genius seeking to be original under the burden of an immense artistic past.

"Freud and the Future" was first delivered at a celebration honoring Freud on his eightieth birthday in May, 1936. In it Mann examines the close, often covert liaisons between science and art. Freud's mapping of the unconscious, he points out, was adumbrated by Nietzsche, Novalis, Kierkegaard, and, in particular, by the German philosopher Schopenhauer, a powerful influence behind Mann's early work. The links are double: between intellectual and psychological truth (first forged by the British empirical school and Kant); and "disease as an instrument of knowledge"—psychological and spiritual. Mann himself would often blur distinctions between the diseased genius and the ingenious disease. In the latter part of the essay Mann relates Freud's work to his own career as a writer, showing how psychological interest in human identities passes over into interest in mythical identities. Mann was working on the *Joseph* novels at the time he wrote this essay.

From Freud and the Future

MAN HAS been called *"das kranke Tier"* [1] because of the burden of strain and explicit difficulties laid upon him by his position between nature and spirit, between angel and brute. What wonder, then, that by the approach through abnormality we have succeeded in penetrating most deeply into the darkness of human nature; that the study of disease—that is to say, neurosis—has revealed itself as a first-class technique of anthropological research?

The literary artist should be the last person to be surprised at the fact. Sooner might he be surprised that he, considering his strong general and individual tendency, should have so late become aware of the close sympathetic relations which connected his own existence with psychoanalytic research and the life-work of Sigmund Freud. I realized this connection only at a time when his achievement was no longer thought of as merely a therapeutic method, whether recognized or disputed; when it had long since outgrown his purely medical implications and become a world movement which penetrated into every field of science and every domain of the intellect: literature, the history of art, religion and prehistory; mythology, folklore, pedagogy,

and what not—thanks to the practical and constructive zeal of experts who erected a structure of more general investigation round the psychiatric and medical core. Indeed, it would be too much to say that I came to psychoanalysis. It came to me. Through the friendly interest that some younger workers in the field had shown in my work, from *Little Herr Friedemann* to *Death in Venice, The Magic Mountain,* and the *Joseph* novels, it gave me to understand that in my way I "belonged"; it made me aware, as probably behoved it, of my own latent, preconscious sympathies; and when I began to occupy myself with the literature of psychoanalysis I recognized, arrayed in the ideas and the language of scientific exactitude, much that had long been familiar to me through my youthful mental experiences.

Perhaps you will kindly permit me to continue for a while in this autobiographical strain, and not take it amiss if instead of speaking of Freud I speak of myself. And indeed I scarcely trust myself to speak *about* him. What new thing could I hope to say? But I shall also, quite explicitly, be speaking in his honour in speaking of myself, in telling you how profoundly and peculiarly certain experiences decisive for my development prepared me for the Freudian experience. More than once, and in many places, I have confessed to the profound, even shattering impression made upon me as a young man

Freud and the Future (1936). From *Essays of Three Decades,* translated by H. T. Lowe-Porter (1947). Copyright 1937 and renewed 1965 by Alfred A. Knopf, Inc. Reprinted by permission of Alfred A. Knopf, Inc., and Martin Secker & Warburg Ltd.

[1] The sick animal.

by contact with the philosophy of Arthur Schopenhauer, to which then a monument was erected
in the pages of *Buddenbrooks*. Here first, in the
pessimism of a metaphysics already very strongly
equipped on the natural-science side, I encountered the dauntless zeal for truth that stands for
the moral aspect of the psychology of the unconscious. This metaphysics, in obscure revolt
against centuries-old beliefs, preached the primacy of the instinct over mind and reason; it
recognized the will as the core and the essential
foundation of the world, in man as in all other
created beings; and the intellect as secondary
and accidental, servant of the will and its pale
illuminant. This it preached not in malice, not
in the anti-human spirit of the mind-hostile doctrines of today, but in the stern love of truth
characteristic of the century which combated
idealism out of love for the ideal. It was so sincere, that nineteenth century, that—through the
mouth of Ibsen—it pronounced the lie, the lies
of life, to be indispensable. Clearly there is a
vast difference whether one assents to a lie out
of sheer hatred of truth and the spirit or for the
sake of that spirit, in bitter irony and anguished
pessimism! Yet the distinction is not clear to
everybody today.

Now, Freud, the psychologist of the unconscious, is a true son of the century of Schopenhauer and Ibsen—he was born in the middle of
it. How closely related is his revolution to Schopenhauer's, not only in its content, but also in
its moral attitude! His discovery of the great
role played by the unconscious, the id, in the
soul-life of man challenged and challenges classical psychology, to which the consciousness and
the psyche are one and the same, as offensively
as once Schopenhauer's doctrine of the will challenged philosophical belief in reason and the intellect. Certainly the early devotee of *The World
as Will and Idea* is at home in the admirable
essay that is included in Freud's *New Introductory Essays in Psychoanalysis* under the title
"The Anatomy of the Mental Personality." It
describes the soul-world of the unconscious, the
id, in language as strong, and at the same time
in as coolly intellectual, objective, and professional a tone, as Schopenhauer might have used
to describe his sinister kingdom of the will. "The
domain of the id," he says, "is the dark, inaccessible part of our personality; the little that

we know of it we have learned through the study
of dreams and of the formation of neurotic
symptoms." He depicts it as a chaos, a melting-
pot of seething excitations. The id, he thinks, is,
so to speak, open towards the somatic, and receives thence into itself compulsions which there
find psychic expression—in what substratum is
unknown. From these impulses it receives its
energy; but it is not organized, produces no
collective will, merely the striving to achieve
satisfaction for the impulsive needs operating
under the pleasure principle. In it no laws of
thought are valid, and certainly not the law of
opposites. "Contradictory stimuli exist alongside
each other without cancelling each other out or
even detracting from each other; at most they
unite in compromise forms under the compulsion of the controlling economy for the release
of energy." You perceive that this is a situation which, in the historical experience of our
own day, can take the upper hand with the ego,
with a whole mass-ego, thanks to a moral devastation which is produced by worship of the unconscious, the glorification of its dynamic as the
only life-promoting force, the systematic glorification of the primitive and irrational. For the
unconscious, the id, is primitive and irrational,
is pure dynamic. It knows no values, no good
or evil, no morality. It even knows no time, no
temporal flow, nor any effect of time upon its
psychic process. "Wish stimuli," says Freud,
"which have never overpassed the id, and impressions which have been repressed into its
depths, are virtually indestructible, they survive decade after decade as though they had just
happened. They can only be recognized as belonging to the past, devalued and robbed of their
charge of energy, by becoming conscious through
the analytic procedure." And he adds that therein
lies pre-eminently the healing effect of analytic
treatment. We perceive accordingly how antipa-
thetic deep analysis must be to an ego that is
intoxicated by a worship of the unconscious to
the point of being in a condition of subterranean
dynamic. It is only too clear and understandable
that such an ego is deaf to analysis and that the
name of Freud must not be mentioned in its
hearing.

As for the ego itself, its situation is pathetic,
well-nigh alarming. It is an alert, prominent, and
enlightened little part of the id—much as Eu-

rope is a small and lively province of the greater Asia. The ego is that part of the id which became modified by contact with the outer world; equipped for the reception and preservation of stimuli; comparable to the integument with which any piece of living matter surrounds itself. A very perspicuous biological picture. Freud writes indeed a very perspicuous prose, he is an artist of thought, like Schopenhauer, and like him a writer of European rank. The relation with the outer world is, he says, decisive for the ego, it is the ego's task to represent the world to the id—for its good! For without regard for the superior power of the outer world the id, in its blind striving towards the satisfaction of its instincts, would not escape destruction. The ego takes cognizance of the outer world, it is mindful, it honourably tries to distinguish the objectively real from whatever is an accretion from its inward sources of stimulation. It is entrusted by the id with the lever of action; but between the impulse and the action it has interposed the delay of the thought-process, during which it summons experience to its aid and thus possesses a certain regulative superiority over the pleasure principle which rules supreme in the unconscious, correcting it by means of the principle of reality. But even so, how feeble it is! Hemmed in between the unconscious, the outer world, and what Freud calls the super-ego, it leads a pretty nervous and anguished existence. Its own dynamic is rather weak. It derives its energy from the id and in general has to carry out the latter's behests. It is fain to regard itself as the rider and the unconscious as the horse. But many a time it is ridden by the unconscious; and I take leave to add what Freud's rational morality prevents him from saying, that under some circumstances it makes more progress by this illegitimate means.

But Freud's description of the id and the ego —is it not to a hair Schopenhauer's description of the Will and the Intellect, a translation of the latter's metaphysics into psychology? So he who had been initiated into the metaphysics of Schopenhauer and in Nietzsche tasted the painful pleasure of psychology—he must needs have been filled with a sense of recognition and familiarity when first, encouraged thereto by its denizens, he entered the realms of psychoanalysis and looked about him.

He found too that his new knowledge had a strange and strong retroactive effect upon the old. After a sojourn in the world of Freud, how differently, in the light of one's new knowledge, does one reread the reflections of Schopenhauer, for instance his great essay "Transcendent Speculations on Apparent Design in the Fate of the Individual"! And here I am about to touch upon the most profound and mysterious point of contact between Freud's natural-scientific world and Schopenhauer's philosophic one. For the essay I have named, a marvel of profundity and penetration, constitutes this point of contact. The pregnant and mysterious idea there developed by Schopenhauer is briefly this: that precisely as in a dream it is our own will that unconsciously appears as inexorable objective destiny, everything in it proceeding out of ourselves and each of us being the secret theatre-manager of our own dreams, so also in reality the great dream that a single essence, the will itself, dreams with us all, our fate, may be the product of our inmost selves, of our wills, and we are actually ourselves bringing about what seems to be happening to us. I have only briefly indicated here the content of the essay, for these representations are winged with the strongest and most sweeping powers of suggestion. But not only does the dream psychology which Schopenhauer calls to his aid bear an explicitly psychoanalytic character, even to the presence of the sexual argument and paradigm; but the whole complexus of thought is a philosophical anticipation of analytical conceptions, to a quite astonishing extent. For, to repeat what I said in the beginning, I see in the mystery of the unity of the ego and the world, of being and happening, in the perception of the apparently objective and accidental as a matter of the soul's own contriving, the innermost core of psychoanalytic theory.

And here there occurs to me a phrase from the pen of C. G. Jung, an able but somewhat ungrateful scion of the Freudian school, in his significant introduction to the Tibetan *Book of the Dead*. "It is so much more direct, striking, impressive, and thus convincing," he says, "to see how it happens to me than to see how I do it." A bold, even an extravagant statement, plainly betraying the calmness with which in a certain school of psychology certain things are regarded which even Schopenhauer considered prodigiously daring speculation. Would this unmasking of the "happening" as in reality "doing" be conceivable without Freud? Never! It owes him everything. It is weighted down with assumptions, it could not be understood, it could never have been written, without all that analysis has brought to light about slips of tongue and pen, the whole field of human error, the retreat into illness, the psychology of accidents, the self-punishment compulsion—in short, all the wizardry of the unconscious. Just as little, moreover, would that close-packed sentence of Jung's, including its psychological premises, have been possible without Schopenhauer's adventurous pioneering speculation. Perhaps this is the moment, my friends, to indulge on this festive occasion in a little polemic against Freud himself. He does not esteem philosophy very highly. His scientific exactitude does not permit him to regard it as a science. He reproaches it with imagining that it can present a continuous and consistent picture of the world; with overestimating the objective value of logical operations; with believing in intuitions as a source of knowledge and with indulging in positively animistic tendencies, in that it believes in the magic of words and the influence of thought upon reality. But would philosophy really be thinking too highly of itself on these assumptions? . . .

All this by the way. But it is in line with my general intention to pause a little longer at the sentence that I quoted from Jung. In this essay and also as a general method which he uses by preference, Jung applies analytical evidence to form a bridge between Occidental thought and Oriental esoteric. Nobody has focused so sharply as he the Schopenhauer-Freud perception that "the giver of all given conditions resides in ourselves—a truth which despite all evidence in the greatest as well as in the smallest things *never* becomes conscious, though it is only too often necessary, even indispensable, that it should be." A great and costly change, he thinks, is needed before we understand how the world is "given" by the nature of the soul; for man's animal nature strives against seeing himself as the maker of his own conditions. It is true that the East has always shown itself stronger than the West in the conquest of our animal nature, and we need not be surprised to hear that in its wisdom it

conceives even the gods among the "given conditions" originating from the soul and one with her, light and reflection of the human soul. This knowledge, which, according to the *Book of the Dead*, one gives to the deceased to accompany him on his way, is a paradox to the Occidental mind, conflicting with its sense of logic, which distinguishes between subject and object and refuses to have them coincide or make one proceed from the other. . . . On the whole a psychological conception of God, an idea of the godhead which is not pure condition, absolute reality, but one with the soul and bound up with it, must be intolerable to Occidental religious sense—it would be equivalent to abandoning the idea of God.

Yet religion—perhaps even etymologically—essentially implies a bond. In Genesis we have talk of the bond (covenant) between God and man, the psychological basis of which I have attempted to give in the mythological novel *Joseph and His Brothers*. Perhaps my hearers will be indulgent if I speak a little about my own work; there may be some justification for introducing it here in this hour of formal encounter between creative literature and the psychoanalytic. It is strange—and perhaps strange not only to me—that in this work there obtains precisely that psychological theology which the scholar ascribes to Oriental esoteric. This Abram is in a sense the father of God. He perceived and brought Him forth; His mighty qualities, ascribed to Him by Abram, were probably His original possession, Abram was not their inventor, yet in a sense he was, by virtue of his recognizing them and therewith, by taking thought, making them real. God's mighty qualities—and thus God Himself—are indeed something objective, exterior to Abram; but at the same time they are in him and of him as well; the power of his own soul is at moments scarcely to be distinguished from them, it consciously interpenetrates and fuses with them—and such is the origin of the bond which then the Lord strikes with Abram, as the explicit confirmation of an inward fact. The bond, it is stated, is made in the interest of both, to the end of their common sanctification. Need human and need divine here entwine until it is hard to say whether it was the human or the divine that took the initiative. In any case the arrangement shows that the holiness of man and the holiness of God constituted a twofold process, one part being most intimately bound up with the other. Wherefore else, one asks, should there be a bond at all?

The soul as "giver of the given"—yes, my friends, I am well aware that in the novel this conception reaches an ironic pitch which is not authorized either in Oriental wisdom or in psychological perception. But there is something thrilling about the unconscious and only later discovered harmony. Shall I call it the power of suggestion? But sympathy would be a better word: a kind of intellectual affinity, of which naturally psychonanalysis was earlier aware than was I, and which proceeded out of those literary appreciations which I owed to it at an earlier stage. The latest of these was an offprint of an article that appeared in *Imago,* written by a Viennese scholar of the Freudian school, under the title "On the Psychology of the Older School of Biography." The rather dry title gives no indication of the remarkable contents. The writer shows how the older and simpler type of biography and in particular the written lives of artists, nourished and conditioned by popular legend and tradition, assimilate, as it were, the life of the subject to the conventionalized stock-in-trade of biography in general, thus imparting a sort of sanction to their own performance and establishing its genuineness; making it authentic in the sense of "as it always was" and "as it has been written." For man sets store by recognition, he likes to find the old in the new, the typical in the individual. From that recognition he draws a sense of the familiar in life, whereas if it painted itself as entirely new, singular in time and space, without any possibility of resting upon the known, it could only bewilder and alarm. The question, then, which is raised by the essay, is this: can any line be sharply and unequivocally drawn between the formal stock-in-trade of legendary biography and the characteristics of the single personality—in other words, between the typical and the individual? A question negatived by its very statement. For the truth is that life is a mingling of the individual elements and the formal stock-in-trade; a mingling in which the individual, as it were, only lifts his head above the formal and impersonal elements. Much that is extra-personal, much un-

conscious identification, much that is conventional and schematic, is none the less decisive for the experience not only of the artist but of the human being in general. "Many of us," says the writer of the article, " 'live' today a biographical type, the destiny of a class or rank or calling. The freedom in the shaping of the human being's life is obviously connected with that bond which we term "lived *vita.*' " And then, to my delight, but scarcely to my surprise, he begins to cite from *Joseph,* the fundamental motif of which he says is precisely this idea of the "lived life," life as succession, as a moving in others' steps, as identification—such as Joseph's teacher, Eliezer, practises with droll solemnity. For in him is cancelled and all the Eliezers of the past gather to shape the Eliezer of the present, so that he speaks in the first person of that Eliezer who was Abram's servant, though he was far from being the same man.

I must admit that I find the train of thought extraordinarily convincing. The essay indicates the precise point at which the psychological interest passes over into the mythical. It makes it clear that the typical is actually the mythical, and that one may as well say "lived myth" as "lived life." But the mythus as lived is the epic idea embodied in my novel; and it is plain to me that when as a novelist I took the step in my subject-matter from the bourgeois and individual to the mythical and typical my personal connection with the analytic field passed into its acute stage. The mythical interest is as native to psychoanalysis as the psychological interest is to all creative writing. Its penetration into the childhood of the individual soul is at the same time a penetration into the childhood of mankind, into the primitive and mythical. Freud has told us that for him all natural science, medicine, and psychotherapy were a lifelong journey round and back to the early passion of his youth for the history of mankind, for the origins of religion and morality —an interest which at the height of his career broke out to such magnificent effect in *Totem and Taboo.* The word *Tiefenpsychologie* ("deep" psychology) has a temporal significance; the primitive foundations of the human soul are likewise primitive time, they are those profound time-sources where the myth has its home and shapes the primeval norms and forms of life.

For the myth is the foundation of life; it is the timeless schema, the pious formula into which life flows when it reproduces its traits out of the unconscious. Certainly when a writer has acquired the habit of regarding life as mythical and typical there comes a curious heightening of his artist temper, a new refreshment to his perceiving and shaping powers, which otherwise occurs much later in life; for while in the life of the human race the mythical is an early and primitive stage, in the life of the individual it is a late and mature one. What is gained is an insight into the higher truth depicted in the actual; a smiling knowledge of the eternal, the ever-being and authentic; a knowledge of the schema in which and according to which the supposed individual lives, unaware, in his naïve belief in himself as unique in space and time, of the extent to which his life is but formula and repetition and his path marked out for him by those who trod it before him. His character is a mythical role which the actor just emerged from the depths to the light plays in the illusion that it is his own and unique, that he, as it were, has invented it all himself, with a dignity and security of which his supposed unique individuality in time and space is not the source, but rather which he creates out of his deeper consciousness in order that something which was once founded and legitimized shall again be represented and once more for good or ill, whether nobly or basely, in any case after its own kind conduct itself according to pattern. Actually, if his existence consisted merely in the unique and the present, he would not know how to conduct himself at all; he would be confused, helpless, unstable in his own self-regard, would not know which foot to put foremost or what sort of face to put on. His dignity and security lie all unconsciously in the fact that with him something timeless has once more emerged into the light and become present; it is a mythical value added to the otherwise poor and valueless single character; it is native worth, because its origin lies in the unconscious.

Such is the gaze which the mythically oriented artist bends upon the phenomena about him—an ironic and superior gaze, as you can see, for the mythical knowledge resides in the gazer and not in that at which he gazes. But let us suppose that the mythical point of view could become subjective; that it could pass over into the active ego and become conscious there, proudly and darkly yet joyously, of its recurrence and its typicality, could celebrate its role and realize its own value exclusively in the knowledge that it was a fresh incarnation of the traditional upon earth. One might say that such a phenomenon alone could be the "lived myth"; nor should we think that it is anything novel or unknown. The life in the myth, life as a sacred repetition, is a historical form of life, for the man of ancient times lived thus. . . .

The ego of antiquity and its consciousness of itself were different from our own, less exclusive, less sharply defined. It was, as it were, open behind; it received much from the past and by repeating it gave it presentness again. The Spanish scholar Ortega y Gasset puts it that the man of antiquity, before he did anything, took a step backwards, like the bull-fighter who leaps back to deliver the mortal thrust. He searched the past for a pattern into which he might slip as into a diving-bell, and being thus at once disguised and protected might rush upon his present problem. Thus his life was in a sense a reanimation, an archaizing attitude. But it is just this life as reanimation that is the life as myth. Alexander walked in the footsteps of Miltiades; the ancient biographers of Caesar were convinced, rightly or wrongly, that he took Alexander as his prototype. But such "imitation" meant far more than we mean by the word today. It was a mythical identification, peculiarly familiar to antiquity; but it is operative far into modern times, and at all times is psychically possible. How often have we not been told that the figure of Napoleon was cast in the antique mould! He regretted that the mentality of the time forbade him to give himself out for the son of Jupiter Ammon, in imitation of Alexander. But we need not doubt that— at least at the period of his Eastern exploits— he mythically confounded himself with Alexander; while after he turned his face westwards he is said to have declared: "I am Charlemagne." Note that: not "I am like Charlemagne" or "My situation is like Charlemagne's," but quite simply: "I am he." That is the formulation of the myth. Life, then—at any rate, significant life— was in ancient times the reconstitution of the myth in flesh and blood; it referred to and appealed to the myth; only through it, through reference to the past, could it approve itself as genuine and significant. The myth is the legitimization of life; only through and in it does life find self-awareness, sanction, consecration. Cleopatra fulfilled her Aphrodite character even unto death—and can one live and die more significantly or worthily than in the celebration of the myth? We have only to think of Jesus and His life, which was lived in order that that which was written might be fulfilled. It is not easy to distinguish between His own consciousness and the conventionalizations of the Evangelists. But His word on the Cross, about the ninth hour, that *"Eli, Eli, lama sabachthani?"* [2] was evidently not in the least an outburst of despair and disillusionment; but on the contrary a lofty messianic sense of self. For the phrase is not original, not a spontaneous outcry. It stands at the beginning of the Twenty-second Psalm, which from one end to the other is an announcement of the Messiah. Jesus was quoting, and the quotation meant: "Yes, it is I!" Precisely thus did Cleopatra quote when she took the asp to her breast to die; and again the quotation meant: "Yes, it is I!"

Let us consider for a moment the word "celebration" which I used in this connection. It is a pardonable, even a proper usage. For life in the myth, life, so to speak, in quotation, is a kind of celebration, in that it is a making present of the past, it becomes a religious act, the performance by a celebrant of a prescribed procedure; it becomes a feast. For a feast is an anniversary, a renewal of the past in the present. Every Christmas the world-saving Babe is born again on earth, to suffer, to die, and to arise. The feast is the abrogation of time, an event, a solemn narrative being played out conformably to an immemorial pattern; the events in it take place not for the first time, but ceremonially according to the prototype. It achieves presentness as feasts do, recurring in time with their phases and hours following on each other in time as they did in the original occurrence. In antiquity each feast was essentially a dramatic performance, a mask;

it was the scenic reproduction, with priests as actors, of stories about the gods—as for instance the life and sufferings of Osiris. The Christian Middle Ages had their mystery play, with heaven, earth, and the torments of hell—just as we have it later in Goethe's *Faust;* they had their carnival farce, their folk-mime. The artist eye has a mythical slant upon life, which makes it look like a farce, like a theatrical performance of a prescribed feast, like a Punch and Judy epic, wherein mythical character puppets reel off a plot abiding from past time and now again present in a jest. It only lacks that this mythical slant pass over and become subjective in the performers themselves, become a festival and mythical consciousness of part and play, for an epic to be produced such as that in the first volume of the *Joseph and His Brothers* series, particularly in the chapter "The Great Hoaxing." There a mythical recurrent farce is tragicomically played by personages all of whom well know in whose steps they tread: Isaac, Esau, and Jacob; and who act out the cruel and grotesque tale of how Esau the Red is led by the nose and cheated of his birthright to the huge delight of all the bystanders. Joseph too is another such celebrant of life; with charming mythological hocus-pocus he enacts in his own person the Tammuz-Osiris myth, "bringing to pass" anew the story of the mangled, buried, and arisen god, playing his festival game with that which mysteriously and secretly shapes life out of its own depths—the unconscious. The mystery of the metaphysician and psychologist, that the soul is the giver of all given conditions, becomes in Joseph easy, playful, blithe—like a consummately artistic performance by a fencer or juggler. It reveals his *infantile* nature—and the word I have used betrays how closely, though seeming to wander so far afield, we have kept to the subject of our evening's homage.

Infantilism—in other words, regression to childhood—what a role this genuinely psychoanalytic element plays in all our lives! What a large share it has in shaping the life of a human being; operating, indeed, in just the way I have described: as mythical identification, as survival, as a treading in footprints already made! The bond with the father, the imitation of the father, the game of being the father, and the transfer-

[2] "My God, my God, why hast thou forsaken me?" (Matthew, XXVII, 46).

ence to father-substitute pictures of a higher and more developed type—how these infantile traits work upon the life of the individual to mark and shape it! I use the word "shape," for to me in all seriousness the happiest, most pleasurable element of what we call education (*Bildung*), the shaping of the human being, is just this powerful influence of admiration and love, this childish identification with a father-image elected out of profound affinity. The artist in particular, a passionately childlike and play-possessed being, can tell us of the mysterious yet after all obvious effect of such infantile imitation upon his own life, his productive conduct of a career which after all is often nothing but a reanimation of the hero under very different temporal and personal conditions and with very different, shall we say childish means. The *imitatio* Goethe, with its Werther and Wilhelm Meister stages, its old-age period of *Faust* and *Diwan,* can still shape and mythically mould the life of an artist—rising out of his unconscious, yet playing over—as is the artist way—into a smiling, childlike, and profound awareness.

The Joseph of the novel is an artist, playing with his *imitatio dei* upon the unconscious string; and I know not how to express the feelings which possess me—something like a joyful sense of divination of the future—when I indulge in this encouragement of the unconscious to play, to make itself fruitful in a serious product, in a narrational meeting of psychology and myth, which is at the same time a celebration of the meeting between poetry and analysis.

And now this word "future": I have used it in the title of my address, because it is this idea, the idea of the future, that I involuntarily like best to connect with the name of Freud. But even as I have been speaking I have been asking myself whether I have not been guilty of a cause of confusion; whether—from what I have said up to now—a better title might not have been something like "Freud and the Myth." And yet I rather cling to the combination of name and word and I should like to justify and make clear its relation to what I have so far said. I make bold to believe that in that novel so kin to the Freudian world, making as it does the light of psychology play upon the myth, there lie hidden seeds and elements of a new and coming sense

of our humanity. And no less firmly do I hold that we shall one day recognize in Freud's life-work the cornerstone for the building of a new anthropology and therewith of a new structure, to which many stones are being brought up to-day, which shall be the future dwelling of a wiser and freer humanity. This physicianly psychologist will, I make no doubt at all, be honoured as the path-finder towards a humanism of the future, which we dimly divine and which will have experienced much that the earlier humanism knew not of. It will be a humanism standing in a different relation to the powers of the lower world, the unconscious, the id: a relation bolder, freer, blither, productive of a riper art than any possible in our neurotic, fear-ridden, hate-ridden world. Freud is of the opinion that the significance of psychoanalysis as a science of the unconscious will in the future far outrank its value as a therapeutic method. But even as a science of the unconscious it is a therapeutic method, in the grand style, a method overarching the individual case. Call this, if you choose, a poet's utopia; but the thought is after all not unthinkable that the resolution of our great fear and our great hate, their conversion into a different relation to the unconscious which shall be more the artist's, more ironic and yet not necessarily irreverent, may one day be due to the healing effect of this very science.

The analytic revelation is a revolutionary force. With it a blithe scepticism has come into the world, a mistrust that unmasks all the schemes and subterfuges of our own souls. Once roused and on the alert, it cannot be put to sleep again. It infiltrates life, undermines its raw naïveté, takes from it the strain of its own ignorance, de-emotionalizes it, as it were, inculcates the taste for understatement, as the English call it—for the deflated rather than for the inflated word, for the cult which exerts its influence by moderation, by modesty. Modesty—what a beautiful word! In the German (*Bescheidenheit*) it originally had to do with knowing and only later got its present meaning; while the Latin word from which the English comes means a way of doing—in short, both together give us almost the sense of the French *savoir faire*—to know how to do. May we hope that this may be the fundamental temper of that more blithely objective and peaceful world which the science of the unconscious may be called to usher in?

Its mingling of the pioneer with the physicianly spirit justifies such a hope. Freud once called his theory of dreams "a bit of scientific new-found land won from superstition and mysticism." The word "won" expresses the colonizing spirit and significance of his work. "Where id was, shall be ego," he epigrammatically says. And he calls analysis a cultural labour comparable to the draining of the Zuider Zee.

HARRY LEVIN   (1912-   )

BORN in Minneapolis, Harry Levin graduated from Harvard in 1933, where, after study abroad, he returned to teach English and comparative literature, and where he now serves as Irving Babbitt Professor. One of the principal founders of the post-war study of comparative literature, he has taught as visiting professor at universities from Paris and Cambridge to Berkeley and Tokyo. His range of learning and command of languages are illustrated by a partial list of his books: *James Joyce: a Critical Introduction* (1941), still the most valuable general work on Joyce, *The Overreacher: a Study of Christopher Marlowe* (1952), *Symbolism and Fiction* (1956), *Contexts of Criticism* (1957), *The Power of Blackness: Hawthorne, Poe, and Melville* (1958), *The Question of Hamlet* (1959), *The Gates of Horn: a Study of Five French Realists* (1962), *Refractions: Essays in Comparative Literature* (1966), and *The Myth of the Golden Age in the Renaissance* (1969).

Levin's critical position is essentially open. It is characterized by nothing so much as his unwillingness to exclude any consideration—sociological or historical; biographical or psychological; stylistic, formal, or thematic—that can help us to interpret and profit from the vast written expression of man's experience that we call literature. In the essay that follows, which has been widely reprinted and translated, he is developing premises that ally him with Taine and, indirectly, with Taine's master, Sainte-Beuve, though he is developing these premises with greater subtlety and sophistication than Taine. In a revised form the essay served later as part of the opening ("Premises") of Levin's massive work on French Realism, *The Gates of Horn* (1962). Like other major critics of our century, he has concentrated on particular writers from Marlowe and Shakespeare to James Joyce. In these critical studies, he is especially drawn to continuities and developments (stylistic, thematic, historical). Though literature, as its history shows, can fulfill almost any role, it is especially valuable as a rich prism that refracts rather than mirrors, distorts, or imposes. It follows that a primary function of the critic is to note the angle of refraction and the density of the medium. To study a work of art, one must be informed in historical terms, both backward and forward from its point of origin; in sociological terms within its particular period; and with regard to the intrinsic merits of the work itself, exploring through theme and style how the work fits into its genre and how it is unique. Literature, like the church and the law, is an institution, concerned with the morality and truth of its inheritance, propositions, and legacies, unfolding in and through time.

Literature as an Institution

I. THE CONTRIBUTION OF TAINE

LITERATURE is the expression of society, as speech is the expression of man." In this aphorism the Vicomte de Bonald [1] summed up one of the bitter lessons that the French Revolution had taught the world. With the opening year of the nineteenth century, and the return of the Emigration, coincided a two-volume study by Madame de Staël: *De la Littérature considérée dans ses rapports avec les institutions sociales.*[2] This was not the first time, of course, that some relationship had been glimpsed. Renaissance humanism, fighting out the invidious quarrel between ancient and modern literatures, had concluded that each was the unique creation of its period, and had adumbrated a historical point of view. Romantic nationalism, seeking to undermine the prestige of the neo-classic school and to revive the native traditions of various countries, was now elaborating a series of geographical comparisons. It was left for Hippolyte Taine —in the vanguard of a third intellectual movement, scientific positivism—to formulate a sociological approach.[3] To the historical and geographical factors, the occasional efforts of earlier critics to discuss literature in terms of "moment"

and "race," he added a third conception, which completed and finally eclipsed them. "Milieu," as he conceived it, is the link between literary criticism and the social sciences. Thus Taine raised a host of new problems by settling an old one.

When Taine's history of English literature appeared, it smelled—to a contemporary reader, Amiel [4]—like the exhalations from a laboratory. To that sensitive Swiss idealist, it conveyed a whiff of "the literature of the future in the American style," of "the death of poetry flayed and anatomized by science." This "intrusion of technology into literature," as Amiel was shrewd enough to observe, is a responsibility which Taine shares with Balzac and Stendhal. As Taine self-consciously remarked, "From the novel to criticism and from criticism to the novel, the distance at present is not very great." Taine's critical theory is grounded upon the practice of the realists, while their novels are nothing if not critical. His recognition of the social forces behind literature coincides with their resolution to embody those forces in their works. The first to acknowledge Stendhal as a master, he welcomed Flaubert as a colleague and lived to find Zola among his disciples. "When M. Taine studies Balzac," Zola acknowledged, "he does exactly what Balzac himself does when he studies Père Grandet." There is no better way to bridge the distance between criticism and the novel, or to scrutinize the presuppositions of modern litera-

Literature as an Institution. From *Accent,* VI (Spring, 1946). Reprinted by permission of the author and the Oxford University Press.

[1] *Législation primitive* (1817), II, 228. [Levin.]
[2] *On Literature Considered in Relation to Social Institutions* (1800), a work of primary importance by the French-Swiss writer, A. L. G. Necker, Mme. de Staël (1766-1817).
[3] See above, pp. 500-06.

[4] Henri-Frederic Amiel, *Fragments d'un journal intime* (1931), II, 17. [Levin.]

ture, than by a brief reconsideration of Taine's critical method.

A tougher-minded reader than Amiel, Flaubert, noted in 1864 that—whatever the *Histoire de la littérature anglaise* left unsettled—it got rid of the uncritical notion that books dropped like meteorites from the sky.[5] The social basis of art might thereafter be overlooked, but it could hardly be disputed. Any lingering belief in poetic inspiration could hardly withstand the higher criticism that had disposed of spontaneous generation and was disposing of divine revelation. When Renan,[6] proclaiming his disbelief in mysteries, depicted Jesus as the son of man and analyzed the origins of Christianity, then Taine could depict genius as the outgrowth of environment and analyze the origins of literature. On the whole, though critics have deplored the crudity of his analyses and scholars have challenged the accuracy of his facts, his working hypothesis has won acceptance. He has become the stock example of a rigorous determinist—especially for those who think determinism is a modern version of fatalism. Taine's determinism, however, is simply an intensive application of the intellectual curiosity of his age. It is no philosopher's attempt to encroach upon the freedom of the artist's will; it is simply a historian's consciousness of what the past has already determined.

As for Taine's rigor, a more thoroughgoing historical materialist, George Plekhanov, has gone so far as to accuse him of arrant idealism.[7] A recent artist-philosopher, Jean-Paul Sartre, describes Taine's empiricism as an unsuccessful effort to set up a realistic system of metaphysics.[8] Actually his position is that of most realists, so outrageous to their early readers and so tame to later critics. His method explained too much to satisfy his contemporaries; it has not explained enough to satisfy ours. Confronted with the provocative statement, "Vice and virtue are products like vitriol and sugar," we are not shocked by the audacity that reduces moral issues to chemical formulae; we are amused at the naiveté that undertakes to solve them both by a single equation. Taine's introduction to his history of Eng-

lish literature, which abounds in dogmas of this sort, is rather a manifesto than a methodology. If, reading on, we expect the history to practise what the introduction preaches, we are amiably disappointed. Each successive author is more freely individualized. How does Taine's all-determining scheme meets its severest test? With Shakespeare, he explains, after canvassing the material factors, "all comes from within—I mean from his soul and his genius; circumstances and externals have contributed but little to his development."

The loophole that enables Taine to avoid the strict consequences of his three determinants is a fourth—a loose system of psychology. Psychology takes over where sociology has given up, and the sociologist has shown surprisingly little interest in classes or institutions. He has viewed history as a parade of influential individuals, themselves the creatures of historical influences. To understand their achievements is "a problem in psychological mechanics." The psychologist must disclose their ruling passions; he must hit upon that magnificent obsession, that "master faculty" which conditions have created within the soul of every great man. Let us not be put off by the circular logic, the mechanical apparatus, and the scientific jargon: Taine, conscientious child of his temperament and time, was an ardent individualist. His theory of character owes quite as much to Balzac as his theory of environment owes to Stendhal. Had it been the other way around, had he combined Stendhal's psychological insight with Balzac's sociological outlook, he might have been a better critic. His portrait of Balzac, for better or worse, is as monomaniacal as Balzac's portrait of Grandet.

Psychology is a knife, Dostoevsky warns us, which cuts two ways.[9] We may look for a man in his books, or we may look to the man for the explanation of his books. Taine's is the more dangerous way: to deduce the qualities of a work from a presupposition about the author. The whole *Comédie humaine* follows from the consideration that Balzac was a business man, and Livy's history is what you might expect from a writer who was really an orator. This mode of critical characterization must perforce be limited

---

[5] *Correspondance* (1929), V, 160. [Levin.]

[6] Ernest Renan (1823-1892), French Biblical scholar.

[7] *Essays in the History of Materialism* (1934), p. 235. [Levin.]

[8] *L'Imagination* (1936), p. 27. [Levin.]

[9] *The Brothers Karamazov*, tr. C. Garnett (1916), p. 785. [Levin.]

to a few broad strokes, much too exaggerated and impressionistic to be compared with the detailed nuances of Sainte-Beuve's portraiture. Most of Taine's figures bear a strong family likeness. He is most adroit at bringing out the generic traits of English literature: the response to nature, the puritan strain, the fact—in short—that it was written by Englishmen. He himself, true to his theories, remains an intransigent Frenchman, and his history—to the point where he abandons Tennyson for Musset and recrosses the channel—remains a traveller's survey of a foreign culture. Why, in spite of all temptations to interpret other cultures, should Taine have been attracted to England?

Taine's critical faculties were conditioned not by science but by romanticism, and who was Taine to repudiate his own conditioning? Madame de Staël had been drawn to Germany, and Melchior de Vogue [10] would soon be seeking the Russian soul, but English was for most Frenchmen the typically romantic literature. France had been the Bastille of classicism, while Britain had never been enslaved to the rules; untamed nature, in Saxon garb, resisted the shackles of Norman constraint. It took very little perception of the technique of English poetry for Taine to prefer blank verse to alexandrines. Form, as he construed it, was a body of artificial restrictions which inhibited free expression, and which English men of letters had somehow succeeded in doing without. One might almost say that they had developed a literature of pure content. "Not in Greece, nor in Italy, nor in Spain, nor in France," said Taine, "has an art been seen which tried so boldly to express the soul and the most intimate depths of the soul, the reality and the whole reality." What seemed to him so unprecedented is, on closer scrutiny, a complex tradition. Elizabethan drama is so much more baroque than the succinct tragedies of Racine that Taine missed its pattern altogether, and believed he was facing a chaos of first-hand and unconstrained realities. His impressions were those of Fielding's barber Partridge at the play, wholly taken in by theatrical make-believe, naively mistaking the actors for the characters they represent, quixotically confusing literature with life.[11]

[10] French writer of a work on the Russian novel (1886).

[11] *Tom Jones* (1749), Bk. XVI, Ch. V.

II. SOCIOLOGICAL CRITICISM AND SOCIAL CRITICS

Remembering Lamb's essay on the artificiality of Restoration comedy, we cannot share Taine's facile assumption that the English stage received and retained "the exact imprint of the century and the nation." We cannot accept this free translation of Hamlet's impulse to give "the very age and body of the time his form and pressure." We can admit that Taine was less of a critic than a historian, but we cannot forgive him for being such an uncritical historian. His professed willingness to trade quantities of charters for the letters of Saint Paul or the memoirs of Cellini does not indicate a literary taste; it merely states a preference for human documents as against constitutional documents. In exploiting literature for purposes of historical documentation, Taine uncovered a new mine of priceless source material. But he never learned the difference between ore and craftsmanship. In his *Philosophie de l'art*, to be sure, he could no longer sidestep esthetic and technical discussion. He was forced to concede that art could be idealistic as well as realistic, and to place Greek sculpture at a farther remove from reality than Flemish painting. This concession allowed him to turn his back on the sculpture, and to reconstruct, with a freer hand than ever, the moment, the race, and the milieu of ancient Greece.

The serious objection to environmentalism is that it failed to distinguish, not between one personality and another, but between personality and art. It encouraged scholars to write literary histories which, as Ferdinand Brunetière pointed out, were nothing but chronological dictionaries of literary biography.[12] It discouraged the realization, which Brunetière called the evolution of *genres*, that literary technique had a history of its own. It advanced a brilliant generalization, and established—as first-rate ideas will do in second-rate minds—a rule of thumb. The incidental and qualified extent to which books epitomize their epoch may vary from one example to the next. Taine's successors made no allowances for the permutations of form; rather they industrialized his process for extracting the contents of the books. The prevailing aim of literary historiography, under the sponsorship of Gustave

[12] *L'Evolution des genres dans l'histoire de la littérature* (1891), p. xii. [Levin.]

Lanson in France and other professors elsewhere, has been a kind of illustrated supplement to history. Academic research has concentrated so heavily on the backgrounds of literature that the foreground has been almost obliterated.

Meanwhile Taine's influence has been felt in the wider areas of criticism, and here it has been subordinated to political ends. Taine himself was bitterly anti-political. He did not realize the importance of ideas until he had lost faith in his own: originally he had been a proponent of the doctrines of the *philosophes,* which he blamed in his later studies, *Les Origines de la France contemporaine,* for instigating the revolution of 1789. It was a Danish critic, closely associated with Ibsen, Nietzsche, and the controversies of the eighties, who broadened the range and narrowed the tendency of literary history. For politics, and for literature too, Georg Brandes had more feeling than Taine. A cosmopolitan liberal, deeply suspicious of the ascendancy of Prussia, he found a touchstone for the romanticists in their struggles or compromises with clerical reaction and the authority of the state. Byron and Heine were his urbane prophets, the Schlegels [13] were renegades, and the revolution of 1848 was the anticlimax toward which his *Main Currents of Nineteenth Century Literature* moved. Where a book had been an end-product to Taine, to Brandes it was continuing force, and the critic's added function was to chart its repercussions.

Both aspects have been duly stressed in the critical interpretation of American writers—their reactions to their environment and their contributions to the liberal tradition. Our foremost literary historian, V. L. Parrington, extended and modified Taine's formula to fit our problems, dramatizing New England puritanism from the standpoint of western populism, and pitting a heroic Jefferson against a sinister Hamilton. His title, *Main Currents in American Thought,*[14] conveyed a fraternal salute to Brandes, and denoted an additional qualification. Parrington got around Taine's difficulty—the difficulty of using imaginative writers as historical sources—by drawing upon the moralists and the publicists. His chapters on Roger Williams and John Marshall are ample and rewarding; his accounts of Poe and Henry James are so trivial that they might better have been omitted. The latest period is inevitably the hardest, and his last volume is posthumous and fragmentary, but it seems to mark an increasing conflict between artistic and political standards. Granville Hicks, going over the same ground, was able to resolve that conflict by the simple device of discarding artistic standards.

Mr. Hicks, if he still adheres to his somewhat elusive conception of *The Great Tradition* [1933], is a Marxist critic in the sense that Parrington was a Jeffersonian critic. The choice between them is largely a matter of political standards. Jeffersonianism, naturally the most favorable climate in which to discuss American literature, has been taken in vain so often that it has begun to resist definition. Marxism, by redefining milieu in economic terms, has presented a more rigorous theory of historical causation than Taine's and a more ruthless canon of political allegiance than Brandes'. It has introduced criticism to a sociological system which is highly illuminating and a social doctrine which is highly controversial. It has tightened the relations between literature and life by oversimplifying them beyond recognition. In this respect Karl Marx, as he occasionally confessed, was no Marxist: he repeatedly cautioned his followers against expecting the arts to show a neat conformity with his views.[15] Perhaps if he had written his projected study of Balzac, he would have bequeathed them a critical method. For lack of one, they took what was available. Marxist criticism superimposed its socialistic doctrine on the deterministic method, and judged according to Marx what it had interpreted according to Taine.

Extension and modification have added their corollary to Taine's method: the relations between literature and society are reciprocal. Literature is not only the effect of social causes; it is also the cause of social effects. The critic may investigate its causes, as Taine tried to do; or he may, like Brandes and others, be more interested in its effects. So long as he is correlating works of art with trends of history, his function is relatively clear. It becomes less clear as

---

[13] See above, pp. 413-15.

[14] Published 1927-30; left incomplete at his death.

[15] Karl Marx and Friedrich Engels, *Sur la littérature et l'art,* ed. J. Freville (1936), p. 59. [Levin.]

he encounters his contemporaries, and as the issues become more immediate. He is then concerned, no longer with a secure past, but with a problematic future. An insecure present may commit him to some special partisanship, Marxist or otherwise, and incline him to judge each new work by its possible effect—whether it will advance or hinder his party's program. Since art can be a weapon, among other things, it will be judged in the heat of the battle by its polemical possibilities. We need not deny the relevance or significance of such judgments; we need only recognize that they carry us beyond the limits of esthetic questions into the field of moral values. There are times when criticism cannot conveniently stop at the border. Whenever there are boundary disputes, questions involving propaganda or regulation, we may be called upon to go afield. We shall be safe while we are aware that virtue and beauty are as intimately related as beauty and truth, and as eternally distinct.

III. THE ROLE OF CONVENTION

It was as if Taine had discovered that the earth was round, without realizing that another continent lay between Europe and Asia. The distance was longer, the route more devious, than sociological criticism had anticipated. Not that the intervening territory was unexplored; but those who had explored it most thoroughly were isolationists. Those who were most familiar with the techniques and traditions of literature were least conscious of its social responsibilities. Most of them were writers themselves, lacking in critical method perhaps, yet possessing the very skills and insights that the methodologists lacked. A few were philosophers, striving—on the high plane of idealism—toward a historical synthesis of the arts. Their concept of expressive form, inherited by the esthetic of Croce from the literary history of Francesco de Sanctis,[16] resembles the "organic principle" that Anglo-American criticism inherits from the theory of Coleridge, the preaching of Emerson, and the practice of Thoreau. By whichever name, it is too sensitive an instrument to be used effectively,

except by acute critics on acknowledged masterpieces. With cruder material, in unskilled hands, its insistence on the uniqueness of each work of art and its acceptance of the artist at his own evaluation dissolve into esthetic impressionism and romantic hero-worship.

While this school is responsible for many admirable critiques, it has never produced that "new criticism" which the late J. E. Spingarn tried vainly to define. Conceiving art as the fullest expression of individuality, it has disregarded the more analytic approaches. Taine's school, though less discriminating, has been more influential, because it conceives art as a collective expression of society. The fallacy in this conception—we have already seen—is to equate art with society, to assume a one-to-one correspondence between a book and its subject-matter, to accept the literature of an age as a complete and exact replica of the age itself. One way or another, literature is bound to tell the truth; but it has told the whole truth very seldom, and nothing but the truth hardly ever; some things are bound to be left out, and others to be exaggerated in the telling. Sins of omission can usually be traced to some restriction in the artist's freedom of speech, his range of experience, or his control of his medium. Sins of commission are inherent in the nature of his materials. The literary historian must reckon with these changing degrees of restriction and exaggeration. Literary history, if it is to be accurate, must be always correcting its aim.

To mention one conspicuous case, the relations between the sexes have received a vast—possibly a disproportionate—amount of attention from writers. From their miscellaneous and contradictory testimony it would be rash to infer very much, without allowing for the artistic taboos of one period or the exhibitionism of another. An enterprising sociologist, by measuring the exposed portions of the human figure in various paintings, has arrived at a quantitative historical index of comparative sensuality. What inference could not be drawn, by some future sciolist, from the preponderance of detective stories on the shelves of our circulating libraries? Those volumes testify, for us, to the colorless comfort of their readers' lives. We are aware, because we are not dependent on literary evidence, that ours is no unparalleled epoch of domestic crime—

---

[16] (1817-1883). His *History of Italian Literature* (1870), one of the monuments of nineteenth-century scholarship, is a broad history of Italian culture generally.

of utterly ineffectual police, of criminals who bear all the earmarks of innocence, and of detectives whose nonchalance is only equalled by their erudition. These, we are smugly aware, have not much more significance than the counters of a complicated game. Nevertheless, it is disturbing to imagine what literal-minded critics may deduce when the rules of the game have been forgotten. It suggests that we ourselves may be misreading other books through our ignorance of the lost conventions on which they hinge.

Convention may be described as a necessary difference between art and life. Some differences, strictly speaking, may be quite unnecessary: deliberate sallies of the imagination, unconscious effects of miscalculation or misunderstanding. But art must also differ from life for technical reasons: limitations of form, difficulties of expression. The artist, powerless to overcome these obstacles by himself, must have the assistance of his audience. They must agree to take certain formalities and assumptions for granted, to take the word for the deed or the shading for the shadow. The result of their unspoken agreement is a compromise between the possibilities of life and the exigencies of art. Goethe might have been speaking of convention when he said, *"In der Beschränkung zeigt sich erst der Meister."* [17] Limitation has often been a source of new forms, and difficulty—as the defenders of rhyme have argued, from Samuel Daniel to Paul Valéry—has prompted poets to their most felicitous expressions. Without some sort of conventionalization art could hardly exist. It exists by making virtues of necessities; after the necessities disappear, we forget the conventions. After perspective is invented, we misjudge the primitives; after scenery is set up, we challenge the unities. And Taine, forgetting that feminine roles were played by boys, is appalled at finding masculine traits in Elizabethan heroines.

His former classmate, Francisque Sarcey, who became—through forty years of playgoing—the most practical of critics, might have supplied the needed correction for Taine's theories. "It is inadequate to repeat that the theater is a representation of human life," Sarcey had learned. "It would be a more precise definition to say

that dramatic art is the sum of conventions, universal or local, eternal or temporary, which help —when human life is represented on the stage— to give a public the illusion of truth." [18] This illusion may be sustained in the novel more easily than on the stage; but it is still an illusion, as Maupassant frankly admitted. Although drama may be the most conventional of literary forms, and fiction the least, even fiction is not entirely free. Even Proust, the most unconventional of novelists, must resort to the convention of eavesdropping in order to sustain the needs of first-person narrative. We need not condone such melodramatic stratagems; we can observe that the modern novel has endeavored to get along without them; upon fuller consideration we may even conclude that the whole modern movement of realism, technically considered, is an endeavor to emancipate literature from the sway of conventions.

IV. TOWARD AN INSTITUTIONAL METHOD

This provisional conclusion would explain why literary historians, under the influence of realism, have slighted literary form. In their impatience to lay bare the so-called content of a work, they have missed a more revealing characteristic: the way the artist handles the appropriate conventions. Whether it is possible, or even desirable, to eliminate artifice from art— that is one of the largest questions that criticism must face. But realistic novelists who declare their intentions of transcribing life have an obvious advantage over realistic critics who expect every book to be a literal transcript. Stendhal, when he declares that "a novel is a mirror riding along a highway," [19] is in a position to fulfil his picaresque intention. When Taine echoes this precept, defining the novel as "a kind of portable mirror which can be conveyed everywhere, and which is most convenient for reflecting all aspects of nature and life," he puts the mirror before the horse. He is then embarrassed to discover so few reflections of the *ancien régime* in French novels of the eighteenth century. His revulsion from neo-classical general-

[17] "It is under limitations that the master first shows himself" (from Goethe's "Nature and Art").

[18] "Essai d'une esthétique de théâtre," *Quarante ans du théâtre* (1900), I, 132. [Levin.]

[19] *Le Rouge et le Noir*, ed. H. Martineau (1927), I, 132. [Levin.]

ities and his preference for descriptive details carry him back across the channel, from Marmontel and Crébillon *fils* to Fielding and Smollett. Some mirrors, Taine finally discovered, are less reliable than others.

The metaphor of the mirror held up to nature, the idea that literature reflects life, was mentioned by Plato only to be rejected. By the time of Cicero it was already a commonplace of criticism. It was applied by the ancients to comedy, the original vehicle of realism; later it became a byword for artistic didacticism, for the medieval zeal to see vice exposed and virtue emulated. When Shakespeare invoked it, he had a definite purpose which those who quote him commonly ignore. Hamlet is not merely describing a play, he is exhorting the players. His advice is a critique of bad acting as well as an apology for the theater, a protest against unnatural conventions as well as a plea for realism. Like modern critics who derive their metaphors from photography, he implies a further comparison with more conventionalized modes of art—particularly with painting. To hold up a photograph or a mirror, as it were, is to compare the "abstract and brief chronicles of the time" with the distorted journeywork that "imitated humanity so abominably." [20] Art should be a reflection of life, we are advised, not a distortion—as it has all too frequently been. Criticism, in assuming that art invariably reflects and forgetting that it frequently distorts, wafts us through the looking-glass into a sphere of its own, where everything is clear and cool, logical and literal, and more surrealistic than real.

In questioning the attempts of scholars to utilize Shakespeare as the mirror of his time, Professor Stoll has reminded them that their business is to separate historical fact from literary illusion, to distinguish the object from its reflected image. [21] Literature, instead of reflecting life, refracts it. Our task, in any given case, is to determine the angle of refraction. Since the angle depends upon the density of the medium, it is always shifting, and the task is never easy. We are aided today, however, by a more flexible and accurate kind of critical apparatus than

Taine was able to employ. An acquaintance with artistic conventions, which can best be acquired through comparative studies in technique, should complement an awareness of social backgrounds. "Literature is complementary to life." [22] This formula of Lanson's is broad enough to include the important proviso that there is room in the world of art for ideals and projects, fantasies and anxieties, which do not ordinarily find a habitation in the world of reality. But, in recognizing that literature adds something to life or that it subtracts something from life, we must not overlook the most important consideration of all—that literature is at all times an intrinsic part of life. It is, if we can work out the implications of Leslie Stephen's phrase, "a particular function of the whole social organism."

The organic character of this relationship has been most explicitly formulated by a statesman and historian, Prosper de Barante. Writing of the ideas behind the French revolution while they were still fresh in men's minds, his comprehension of their political interplay was broader than Taine's. "In the absence of regular institutions," wrote Barante, "literature became one." [23] The truth, though it has long been obscured by a welter of personalities and technicalities, is that literature has always been an institution. Like other institutions, the church or the law, it cherishes a unique phase of human experience and controls a special body of precedents and devices; it tends to incorporate a self-perpetuating discipline, while responding to the main currents of each succeeding period; it is continually accessible to all the impulses of life at large, but it must translate them into its own terms and adapt them to its peculiar forms. Once we have grasped this fact, we begin to perceive how art may belong to society and yet be autonomous within its own limits, and are no longer puzzled by the apparent polarity of social and formal criticism. These, in the last analysis, are complementary frames of reference whereby we may discriminate the complexities of a work of art. In multiplying these discriminations between external impulses and internal peculiari-

---

[20] *Hamlet*, II, ii, 547 f., and III, ii, 39 f. [Levin.]

[21] E. E. Stoll, *From Shakespeare to Joyce* (1949), p. 28. [Levin.]

[22] Gustave Lanson, "L'Histoire litteraire et la sociologie," *Revue de metaphysique et de morale* (1904), XII.

[23] *De la littérature francaise pendant le dix-huitième siècle* (1854), p. 5. [Levin.]

ties—in other words, between the effects of environment and convention—our ultimate justification is to understand the vital process to which they are both indispensable.

To consider the novel as an institution, then, imposes no dogma, exacts no sacrifice, and excludes none of the critical methods that have proved illuminating in the past. If it tends to subordinate the writer's personality to his achievement, it requires no further apology, for criticism has long been unduly subordinated to biography. The tendency of the romanticists to live their writings and write their lives, and the consequent success of their critics as biographers, did much to justify this subordination; but even Sainte-Beuve's "natural history of souls," though it unified and clarified an author's works by fitting them into the pattern of his career, was too ready to dismiss their purely artistic qualities as "rhetoric." More recently the doctrines of Freud, while imposing a topheavy vocabulary upon the discussion of art, have been used to corroborate and systematize the sporadic intuitions of artists; but the psychologists, like the sociologists, have been more interested in utilizing books for documentary purposes than in exploring their intrinsic nature. Meanwhile, on the popular level, the confusion between a novelist and his novels has been consciously exploited. A series of novelized biographies, calling itself *Le Roman des grandes existences*,[24] invites the common reader to proceed from "the prodigious life of Balzac" through "the mournful life of Baudelaire" to "the wise and merry life of Montaigne."

If fiction has seldom been discussed on a plane commensurate with its achievements, it is because we are too often sidetracked by personalities. If, with Henry James, we recognize the novelist's intention as a figure in a carpet, we must recognize that he is guided by his material, his training, his commission, by the size and shape of his loom, and by his imagination to the extent that it accepts and masters those elements. Psychology—illuminating as it has been—has treated literature too often as a record of personal idiosyncrasies, too seldom as the basis of a collective consciousness. Yet it is

on that basis that the greatest writers have functioned. Their originality has been an ability to "seize on the public mind," in Bagehot's opinion; conventions have changed and styles have developed as lesser writers caught "the traditional rhythm of an age." The irreducible element of individual talent would seem to play the same role in the evolution of *genres* that natural selection plays in the origin of species. Amid the mutations of modern individualism, we may very conceivably have overstressed the private aspects of writing. One convenience of the institutional method is that it gives due credit to the never-ending collaboration between writer and public. It sees no reason to ignore what is relevant in the psychological prepossessions of the craftsman, and it knows that he is ultimately to be judged by the technical resources of his craftsmanship; but it attains its clearest and most comprehensive scope by centering on his craft—on his social status and his historical function as participant in a skilled group and a living tradition.

When Edgar Quinet announced a course at the Collège de France in *La Littérature et les institutions comparées de l'Europe méridionelle*,[25] he was requested by Guizot's ministry to omit the word "institutions" and to limit himself to purely literary discussion. When he replied that this would be impossible, his course was suspended, and his further efforts went directly into those reform agitations which culminated in the democratic revolution of the following year, 1848. Thereby proceeding from sociological to social criticism, he demonstrated anew what French critics and novelists have understood particularly well—the dynamic interaction between ideas and events. In a time which has seen that demonstration repeated on so vast a scale, the institutional forces that impinge upon literature are self-evident. The responsibilities that literature owes to itself, and the special allegiance it exacts from us, should also become apparent when we conceive it as an institution in its own right. The misleading dichotomy between substance and form, which permits literary historians, like Parrington, to dismiss "belle-

[24] "The novel (or romance) of great lives."

[25] "The Literature and Institutions of Southern Europe Compared."

tristic philandering," and esthetic impressionists, like Mr. R. P. Blackmur,[26] to dispose of "separable content," should disappear as soon as abstract categories are dropped and concrete relations are taken up. And the jurisdictional

[26] See below, p. 691.

conflict between truth and beauty should dissolve when esthetics discovers the truth about beauty; when criticism becomes—as Bacon intended, and Renan and Sainte-Beuve remembered, and all too many other critics have forgotten—the science of art.

JEAN-PAUL SARTRE (1905-   )

JEAN-PAUL SARTRE, philosopher, novelist, dramatist critic, and leading savant of existentialism, was born in Paris where he has spent much of his life. Early studies such as *Imagination* and *The Psychology of Imagination* and the novel *Nausea* received theoretical underpinning in *Being and Nothingness* (1943), partly written while Sartre, a member of the French Resistance, was a prisoner of war. After the war he turned to the novel (*The Age of Reason, The Reprieve, Iron in the Soul*), to drama (*No Exit, The Condemned of Altona*), and to criticism—in studies of Tintoretto, Genet, Baudelaire, Camus, Giacometti, and Flaubert among others. The first part of his autobiography, *The Words*, was published in 1964. In that year Sartre was awarded the Nobel Prize, which he declined.

Although the framework of the theory of *What Is Literature?* (1947) was present earlier, the experience of World War II helped form its sometimes desperate moral tone and earnestness. Writing is an *action* and hence must be concerned with moral consequences. What would happen, a writer must ask, if everyone were to read what I have written? Appealing to the imaginative generosity of his reader, a writer paradoxically uses words as "traps" to catch his reader's feelings; in exchange for the reader's surrender of freedom, the writer must prove committed (*engagé*) to the reader's freedom— that is, to mankind's continual struggle for freedom. Existential anguish or *Angst* may result from the growing consciousness of freedom; but insincerity in the quest for freedom—on the part of writer or reader—signals "bad faith," a repudiation of their mutual commitment and responsibility.

From What Is Literature?

ON THE ONE hand, the literary object has no other substance than the reader's subjectivity; Raskolnikov's [1] waiting is *my* waiting which I lend him. Without this impatience of the reader he would remain only a collection of signs. His hatred of the police magistrate who questions him is my hatred which has been solicited and wheedled out of me by signs, and the police magistrate himself would not 'exist without the hatred I have for him via Raskolnikov. That is what animates him, it is his very flesh.

But on the other hand, the words are there like traps to arouse our feelings and to reflect them toward us. Each word is a path of transcendence; it shapes our feelings, names them, and attributes them to an imaginary personage who takes it upon himself to live them for us and who has no other substance than these borrowed passions; he confers objects, perspectives, and a horizon upon them. . . .

The writer should not seek to *overwhelm*; otherwise he is in contradiction with himself; if he wishes to *make demands* he must propose only the task to be fulfilled. Hence, the character of pure presentation which appears essential to the work of art. The reader must be able to make a certain aesthetic withdrawal. This is what Gautier foolishly confused with "art for art's sake" and the Parnassians with the imperturbability of the artist. It is simply a matter of precaution, and Genet more justly calls it the author's politeness toward the reader.[2] But that does not mean that the writer makes an appeal to some sort of abstract and conceptual freedom. One certainly creates the aesthetic object with feelings; if it is touching, it appears through our tears; if it is comic, it will be recognized by laughter. However, these feelings are of a particular kind. They have their origin

in freedom; they are loaned. The belief which I accord the tale is freely assented to. It is a Passion, in the Christian sense of the word, that is, a freedom which resolutely puts itself into a state of passivity to obtain a certain transcendent effect by this sacrifice. The reader renders himself credulous; he descends into credulity which, though it ends by enclosing him like a dream, is at every moment conscious of being free. An effort is sometimes made to force the writer into this dilemma: "Either one believes in your story, and it is intolerable, or one does not believe in it, and it is ridiculous." But the argument is absurd because the characteristic of aesthetic consciousness is to be a belief by means of engagement, by oath, a belief sustained by fidelity to one's self and to the author, a perpetually renewed choice to believe. I can awaken at every moment, and I know it; but I do not want to; reading is a free dream. So that all feelings which are exacted on the basis of this imaginary belief are like particular modulations of my freedom. Far from absorbing or masking it, they are so many different ways it has chosen to reveal itself to itself. Raskolnikov, as I have said, would only be a shadow, without the mixture of repulsion and friendship which I feel for him and which makes him live. . . .

To write is thus both to disclose the world and to offer it as a task to the generosity of the reader. It is to have recourse to the consciousness of others in order to make one's self be recognized as *essential* to the totality of being; it is to wish to live this essentiality by means of interposed persons; but, on the other hand, as the real world is revealed only by action, as one can feel himself in it only by exceeding it in order to change it, the novelist's universe would lack thickness if it were not discovered in a movement to transcend it. It has often been observed that an object in a story does not derive its density of existence from the number and length of the descriptions devoted to it, but from the complexity of its connections with the different characters. The more often the characters handle it, take it up, and put it down,

What Is Literature? (1947). Translated by Bernard Frechtman, copyright 1949 Philosophical Library. Reprinted by permission of Literary Masterworks, Inc.

[1] The principal character in Dostoevsky's *Crime and Punishment* (1866).

[2] The poet and novelist, Théophile Gautier (1811-1872), and the novelist Jean Genet (1910-   ).

in short, go beyond it toward their own ends, the more real will it appear. Thus, of the world of the novel, that is, the totality of men and things, we may say that in order for it to offer its maximum density the disclosure-creation by which the reader discovers it must also be an imaginary engagement in the action; in other words, the more disposed one is to change it, the more alive it will be. The error of realism has been to believe that the real reveals itself to contemplation, and that consequently one could draw an impartial picture of it. How could that be possible, since the very perception is partial, since by itself the naming is already a modification of the object? And how could the writer, who wants himself to be essential to this universe, want to be essential to the injustice which this universe comprehends? Yet, he must be; but if he accepts being the creator of injustices, it is in a movement which goes beyond them toward their abolition. As for me who read, if I create and keep alive an unjust world, I can not help making myself responsible for it. And the author's whole art is bent on obliging me to *create* what he *discloses*, therefore to compromise myself. So both of us bear the responsibility for the universe. And precisely because this universe is supported by the joint effort of our two freedoms, and because the author, with me as medium, has attempted to integrate it into the human, it must appear truly *in itself*, in its very marrow, as being shot through and through with a freedom which has taken human freedom as its end, and if it is not really the city of ends that it ought to be, it must at least be a stage along the way; in a word, it must be a becoming and it must always be considered and presented not as a crushing mass which weighs us down, but from the point of view of its going beyond toward that city of ends. However bad and hopeless the humanity which it paints may be, the work must have an air of generosity. Not, of course, that this generosity is to be expressed by means of edifying discourses and virtuous characters; it must not even be premeditated, and it is quite true that fine sentiments do not make fine books. But it must be the very warp and woof of the book, the stuff out of which the people and things are cut; whatever the subject, a sort of essential lightness must appear everywhere and remind us that the work is never

a natural datum, but an *exigence* and a *gift*. And if I am given this world with its injustices, it is not so that I might contemplate them coldly, but that I might animate them with my indignation, that I might disclose them and create them with their nature as injustices, that is, as abuses to be suppressed. Thus, the writer's universe will only reveal itself in all its depth to the examination, the admiration, and the indignation of the reader; and the generous love is a promise to maintain, and the generous indignation is a promise to change, and the admiration a promise to imitate; although literature is one thing and morality a quite different one, at the heart of the aesthetic imperative we discern the moral imperative. For, since the one who writes recognizes, by the very fact that he takes the trouble to write, the freedom of his readers, and since the one who reads, by the mere fact of his opening the book, recognizes the freedom of the writer, the work of art, from whichever side you approach it, is an act of confidence in the freedom of men. And since readers, like the author, recognize this freedom only to demand that it manifest itself, the work can be defined as an imaginary presentation of the world insofar as it demands human freedom. The result of which is that there is no "gloomy literature," since, however dark may be the colors in which one paints the world, he paints it only so that free men may feel their freedom as they face it. Thus, there are only good and bad novels. The bad novel aims to please by flattering, whereas the good one is an exigence and an act of faith. But above all, the unique point of view from which the author can present the world to those freedoms whose concurrence he wishes to bring about is that of a world to be impregnated always with more freedom. It would be inconceivable that this unleashing of generosity provoked by the writer could be used to authorize an injustice, and that the reader could enjoy his freedom while reading a work which approves or accepts or simply abstains from condemning the subjection of man by man. One can imagine a good novel being written by an American Negro even if hatred of the whites were spread all over it, because it is the freedom of his race that he demands through this hatred. And, as he invites me to assume the attitude of generosity, the moment I feel myself a pure freedom I can not bear to identify myself with a race of oppressors. Thus, I require of all freedoms that they demand the liberation of colored people against the white race and against myself insofar as I am a part of it, but nobody can suppose for a moment that it is possible to write a good novel in praise of anti-Semitism. For, the moment I feel that my freedom is indissolubly linked with that of all other men, it can not be demanded of me that I use it to approve the enslavement of a part of these men. Thus, whether he is an essayist, a pamphleteer, a satirist, or a novelist, whether he speaks only of individual passions or whether he attacks the social order, the writer, a free man addressing free men, has only one subject—freedom.

Hence, any attempt to enslave his readers threatens him in his very art. A blacksmith can be affected by fascism in his life as a man, but not necessarily in his craft; a writer will be affected in both, and even more in his craft than in his life. I have seen writers, who before the war, called for fascism with all their hearts, smitten with sterility at the very moment when the Nazis were loading them with honors. . . .

One does not write for slaves. The art of prose is bound up with the only regime in which prose has meaning, democracy. When one is threatened, the other is too. And it is not enough to defend them with the pen. A day comes when the pen is forced to stop, and the writer must then take up arms. Thus, however you might have come to it, whatever the opinions you might have professed, literature throws you into battle. Writing is a certain way of wanting freedom; once you have begun, you are engaged, willy-nilly.

Engaged in what? Defending freedom? That's easy to say. Is it a matter of acting as guardian of ideal values like Benda's clerk before the betrayal,[3] or is it concrete, everyday freedom which must be protected by our taking sides in political and social struggles? The question is tied up with another one, one very simple in appearance but which nobody ever asks himself: "For whom does one write?"

[3] Sartre refers to *La Trahison des clercs* (1927)—translated as *The Treason of the Intellectuals*—by the French classical humanist, Julien Benda (1867-1956).

WALLACE STEVENS   (1879-1955)

WALLACE STEVENS was born in Reading, Pennsylvania, attended Harvard University and New York Law School, and settled in a business career in Hartford, Connecticut, where from 1916 until his death he was associated with a life insurance company. His first volume of poetry, *Harmonium,* was not published until he was forty-four. It was followed by *Ideas of Order* (1936), *The Man with the Blue Guitar* (1937), *Transport to Summer* (1947), *The Auroras of Autumn* (1950), the criticism contained in *The Necessary Angel* (1951), and the poetry and criticism collected in *Opus Posthumous* (1957).

"Two or Three Ideas" was first read at the New England section of the College English Association and forms what he regarded as an artist's credo in an age of disbelief. The first idea, that the style of the poem and its meaning are one, derives from general Romantic theory (cf. Coleridge's definition of a symbol as "consubstantial with the truths of which they are the conductors," above, p. 386). The second idea is that the style of "the gods" and "the gods" themselves are one, that "the gods" reflect the inmost imaginative aspirations of their creators—or as Stevens wrote in a late poem, "A mythology reflects its region." Stevens' third idea builds from these first two premises: "In a time that is largely humanistic . . . it is for the poet to supply the satisfactions of belief, in his measure and in his style." The poet does not presume upon the god, but upon the priest, and the revelation that he bodies forth is nothing less than a "revelation of reality" (cf. Hazlitt, above, p. 330). Ultimately the style of men and men themselves are one, and imagination and reality are fused in the union poetry provides.

From Two or Three Ideas

IN AN AGE of disbelief, or, what is the same thing, in a time that is largely humanistic, in one sense or another, it is for the poet to supply the satisfactions of belief, in his measure and in his style. I say in his measure to indicate that the figures of the philosopher, the artist, the teacher, the moralist and other figures, including the poet, find themselves, in such a time, to be figures of an importance greatly enhanced by the requirements both of the individual and of society; and I say in his style by way of confining the poet to his role and thereby of intensifying that role. It is this that I want to talk about today. I want to try to formulate a conception of perfection in poetry with reference to the present time and the near future and to speculate on the activities possible to it as it deploys itself throughout the lives of men and women. I think of it as a role of the utmost seriousness. It is, for one thing, a spiritual role. One might stop to draw an ideal portrait of the poet. But that would be parenthetical. In any case, we do not say that the philosopher, the artist or the teacher is to take the place of the gods. Just so, we do not say that the poet is to take the place of the gods.

To see the gods dispelled in mid-air and dissolve like clouds is one of the great human experiences. It is not as if they had gone over the

horizon to disappear for a time; nor as if they had been overcome by other gods of greater power and profounder knowledge. It is simply that they came to nothing. Since we have always shared all things with them and have always had a part of their strength and, certainly, all of their knowledge, we shared likewise this experience of annihilation. It was their annihilation, not ours, and yet it left us feeling that in a measure, we, too, had been annihilated. It left us feeling dispossessed and alone in a solitude, like children without parents, in a home that seemed deserted, in which the amical rooms and halls had taken on a look of hardness and emptiness. What was most extraordinary is that they left no mementoes behind, no thrones, no mystic rings, no texts either of the soil or of the soul. It was as if they had never inhabited the earth. There was no crying out for their return. They were not forgotten because they had been a part of the glory of the earth. At the same time, no man ever muttered a petition in his heart for the restoration of those unreal shapes. There was always in every man the increasingly human self, which instead of remaining the observer, the non-participant, the delinquent, became constantly more and more all there was or so it seemed; and whether it was so or merely seemed so still left it for him to resolve life and the world in his own terms.

Thinking about the end of the gods creates singular attitudes in the mind of the thinker. One attitude is that the gods of classical mythol-

Two or Three Ideas (1951). From *Opus Posthumous*, ed. S. F. Morse. Copyright © 1957 by Elsie Stevens and Holly Stevens. Reprinted by permission of Alfred A. Knopf, Inc., and Faber & Faber Ltd.

ogy were merely aesthetic projections. They were not the objects of belief. They were expressions of delight. Perhaps delight is too active a word. It is true that they were engaged with the future world and the immortality of the soul. It is true, also, that they were the objects of veneration and therefore of religious dignity and sanctity. But in the blue air of the Mediterranean these white and a little colossal figures had a special propriety, a special felicity. Could they have been created for that propriety, that felicity? Notwithstanding their divinity, they were close to the people among whom they moved. Is it one of the normal activities of humanity, in the solitude of reality and in the unworthy treatment of solitude, to create companions, a little colossal as I have said, who, if not superficially explicative, are, at least, assumed to be full of the secret of things and who in any event bear in themselves even, if they do not always wear it, the peculiar majesty of mankind's sense of worth, neither too much nor too little? To a people of high intelligence, whose gods have benefited by having been accepted and addressed by the superior minds of a superior world, the symbolic paraphernalia of the very great becomes unnecessary and the very great become the very natural. However all that may be, the celestial atmosphere of these deities, their ultimate remote celestial residences are not matters of chance. Their fundamental glory is the fundamental glory of men and women, who being in need of it create it, elevate it, without too much searching of its identity.

The people, not the priests, made the gods. The personages of immortality were something more than the conceptions of priests, although they may have picked up many of the conceits of priests. Who were the priests? Who have always been the high priests of any of the gods? Certainly not those officials or generations of officials who administered rites and observed rituals. The great and true priest of Apollo was he that composed the most moving of Apollo's hymns. The really illustrious archimandrite of Zeus was the one that made the being of Zeus people the whole of Olympus and the Olympian land, just as the only marvelous bishops of heaven have always been those that made it seem like heaven. I said a moment ago that we had not forgotten the gods. What is it that we remember of them? In the case of those masculine do we remember their ethics or is it their port and mien, their size, their color, not to speak of their adventures, that we remember? In the case of those feminine do we remember, as in the case of Diana, their fabulous chastity or their beauty? Do we remember those masculine in any way differently from the way in which we remember Ulysses and other men of supreme interest and excellence? In the case of those feminine do we remember Venus in any way differently from the way in which we remember Penelope and other women of much mark and feeling? In short, while the priests helped to realize the gods, it was the people that spoke of them and to them and heard their replies.

Let us stop now and restate the ideas which we are considering in relation to one another. The first is that the style of a poem and the poem itself are one; the second is that the style of the gods and the gods themselves are one; the third is that in an age of disbelief, when the gods have come to an end, when we think of them as the aesthetic projections of a time that has passed, men turn to a fundamental glory of their own and from that create a style of bearing themselves in reality. They create a new style of a new bearing in a new reality. This third idea, then, may be made to conform to the way in which the other two have been expressed by saying that the style of men and men themselves are one.

W. H. AUDEN   (1907-   )

WYSTAN HUGH AUDEN was born in York, England, was educated at Oxford, and was a schoolmaster for a time. He became associated with a group of writers, now known as the "Auden circle," which included Stephen Spender, C. Day Lewis and Christopher Isherwood. In 1939 he emigrated to the United States and in 1946 became an American citizen. Among the most versatile writers in the century, he has published many volumes of poetry—*Look Stranger!* (1936), *Another Time* (1940), *For the Time Being* (1944), *The Shield of Achilles* (1955), *Homage to Clio* (1960), *About the House* (1965), *City Without Walls* (1969)—collaborated with Isherwood on three plays (among them *The Ascent of F-6*), made libretti for several operas, translated prose and poetry from many languages, and written several volumes of critical essays, such as *The Enchafed Flood* (1949) and *The Dyer's Hand* (1962).

"Making, Knowing, Judging" was Auden's inaugural lecture as Professor of Poetry at Oxford, a post he held from 1956 to 1961. Religious metaphors proliferate, and underlying his metaphors are some of the themes that dominate his poetry: the "enjoyment of being," the "consciousness of beyondness," and man's halting striving towards virtue. A poet's art is not religion, but it points to some of the questions that religion itself asks. By its formal and ritualistic nature "a poem is a rite." Words become the means by which passive awe or awareness is transformed into active homage. Neither exclusively worldly nor otherworldly, sacred nor profane, poetry treads the enchanted ground between, adjusting in a given age the one to the other. Poetry begins with sacred encounters and may even try to express them, but more often it moves among the things of this world and praises them "for being and happening."

From Making, Knowing, Judging

THE IMPULSE to create a work of art is felt when, in certain persons, the passive awe provoked by sacred beings or events is transformed into a desire to express that awe in a rite of worship or homage, and to be fit homage this rite must be beautiful. This rite has no magical or idolatrous intention; nothing is expected in return. Nor is it, in a Christian sense, an act of devotion. If it praises the Creator, it does so indirectly by praising His creatures—

Making, Knowing, Judging (1956). From *The Dyer's Hand and Other Essays* (1962). Copyright © 1956 by

among which may be human notions of the Divine Nature. With God as redeemer, it has, so far as I can see, little if anything to do.

In poetry the rite is verbal; it pays homage by naming. I suspect that the predisposition of a mind towards the poetic medium may have its origin in an error. A nurse, let us suppose, says to a child, "Look at the moon!" The child looks and for him this is a sacred encounter. In his mind the word *moon* is not a name of a sacred object but one of its most important properties and, therefore, numinous. The notion of writing poetry cannot occur to him, of course, until he has realized that names and things are not identical and that there cannot be an intelligible sacred language, but I wonder if, when he has discovered the social nature of language, he would attach such importance to one of its uses, that of naming, if he had not previously made this false identification.

The pure poem, in the French sense of *la poésie pure* would be, I suppose, a celebration of the numinous-in-itself in abstraction from all cases and devoid of any profane reference whatsoever—a sort of *sanctus, sanctus, sanctus*. If it could be written, which is doubtful, it would not necessarily be the best poem.

A poem is a rite; hence its formal and ritualistic character. Its use of language is deliberately and ostentatiously different from talk. Even when it employs the diction and rhythms of conversation, it employs them as a deliberate informality, presupposing the norm with which they are intended to contrast.

The form of a rite must be beautiful, exhibiting, for example, balance, closure and aptness to that which it is the form of. It is over this last quality of aptness that most of our aesthetic quarrels arise, and must arise, whenever our sacred and profane worlds differ.

To the Eyes of a Miser, a Guinea is far more beautiful than the Sun & a bag worn with the use of Money has more beautiful proportions than a Vine filled with Grapes.[1]

Blake, it will be noticed, does not accuse the Miser of lacking imagination.

The value of a profane thing lies in what it

[1] Blake's letter to Rev. Trusler, August 23, 1799, *Poetry and Prose* (1965), ed. D. Erdman and H. Bloom, p. 677.

usefully does, the value of a sacred thing lies in what it *is*; a sacred thing may also have a function but it does not have to. The apt name for a profane being, therefore, is the word or words that accurately describe his function—a Mr. Smith, a Mr. Weaver. The apt name for a sacred being is the word or words which worthily express his importance—Son of Thunder, The Well-Wishing One.

Great changes in artistic style always reflect some alteration in the frontier between the sacred and profane in the imagination of a society. Thus, to take an architectural example, a seventeenth-century monarch had the same function as that of a modern State official—he had to govern. But in designing his palace, the Baroque architect did not aim, as a modern architect aims when designing a government building, at making an office in which the king could govern as easily and efficiently as possible; he was trying to make a home fit for God's earthly representative to inhabit; in so far as he thought at all about what the king would do in it as a ruler, he thought of his ceremonial not his practical actions.

Even today few people find a functionally furnished living-room beautiful because, to most of us, a sitting-room is not merely a place to sit in; it is also a shrine for father's chair.

Thanks to the social nature of language, a poet can relate any one sacred being or event to any other. The relation may be harmonious, an ironic contrast or a tragic contradiction like the great man or the beloved and death; he can relate them to every other concern of the mind, the demands of desire, reason and conscience, and he can bring them into contact and contrast with the profane. Again the consequences can be happy, ironic, tragic and, in relation to the profane, comic. How many poems have been written, for example, upon one of these three themes:

This was sacred but now it is profane. Alas, or thank goodness!

This is sacred but ought it to be?

This is sacred but is that so important?

But it is from the sacred encounters of his imagination that a poet's impulse to write a poem arises. Thanks to language, he need not name them directly unless he wishes; he can describe one in terms of another and translate those that are private or irrational or socially unacceptable into such as are acceptable to reason and society. Some poems are directly *about* the sacred beings they were written *for*; others are not, and in that case no reader can tell what was the original encounter which provided the impulse for the poem. Nor, probably, can the poet himself. Every poem he writes involves his whole past. Every love-poem, for instance, is hung with trophies of lovers gone, and among these there may be some very peculiar objects indeed. The lovely lady of the present may number among her predecessors an overshot water-wheel. But the encounter, be it novel or renewed by recollection from the past, must be suffered by a poet before he can write a genuine poem.

Whatever its actual content and overt interest, every poem is rooted in imaginative awe. Poetry can do a hundred and one things, delight, sadden, disturb, amuse, instruct—it may express every possible shade of emotion, and describe every conceivable kind of event, but there is only one thing that all poetry must do; it must praise all it can for being and for happening.

R. P. BLACKMUR (1904-1965)

BORN in Springfield, Massachusetts, Richard Palmer Blackmur received no formal education beyond high school. But even before he was appointed professor at Princeton (1948), he had become one of the leaders of the highly academic movement known as the "New Criticism," which, through close rhetorical analysis, sought to free literary studies from the then conventional academic historicism. His works include three volumes of poetry and, more important, seven of criticism, of which *Language as Gesture* (1952), *The Lion and the Honeycomb* (1955), *Form and Value in Modern Poetry* (1957), *Eleven Essays in the European Novel* (1964), and the posthumous *A Primer of Ignorance* (1967) are representative.

In "The Great Grasp of Unreason," first delivered as a lecture at the Library of Congress in 1956, taking his epigraph from Sophocles' *Antigone*, "the unjust minds of the just," Blackmur diagnoses the "unreason of behavior" in the twentieth century. Can we grasp, like King Lear on the heath, "reason in madness"? Traditionally Blackmur finds "bourgeois humanism . . . the treasure of residual reason in live relation to the madness of the senses," and out of such humanism, in the brilliant decade of the 1920's, came *Ulysses, The Waste Land, The Magic Mountain, The Tower*, and *The Counterfeiters*. This fertile bourgeois humanism may now be facing a period of fatigue or even decline, but our need to strive for its renewal has no alternative, for nothing approaches it in potential fertility. Meanwhile, in what Blackmur considers a post-Christian world, we may wrest metaphysical knowledge from literature itself—"an irregular metaphysic," to be sure, but still of value "for the control of man's irrational powers." In this essay, as in Blackmur's career generally, we have an example of the way in which the New Criticism of the 1930's to the 1950's proved, after all, to be largely a domestic quarrel with—and finally a return to—Matthew Arnold and much that Arnold represented. At the start, there were differences in poetic taste (typified by T. S. Eliot) and of approach (typified by I. A. Richards). But the premises were much the same: above all, the premise of the centrality of literary studies in what Arnold called "culture," and especially in an age without strong religious convictions. The original movement of the New Criticism, insofar as it differed from Arnold, was primarily a movement toward a stricter and more involved formalism. But when it found itself in the 1960's faced with a militant anti-elitism—sociological in its interest rather than formalistic—it began to return to the Arnoldian fold, at least in general spirit, and, despite justifiable pride in what it had done, in something of an autumnal mood.

From The Great Grasp of Unreason

[In poetry and literature generally] we have not only an enormous increase in potential or required audience but also a diminution, relatively if not absolutely, in the means of reaching, let alone controlling, that audience. So put, we see at once how the new knowledges, so managed, so esoteric, have been reflected in the habit and superficial character of poetry and the poet himself. He has found himself speaking a private language and has grown proud of it.

What else could the writer do but invent a vital dogma of self-sufficiency?—and I do not say he was not right in doing so. Faced with the dissolution of thought and the isolation of the artist, faced with the new industrialization of intellect, what else could he do but declare his independence and self-sufficient supremacy both as intellectual and as artist? Let us admit the new independence came partly out of the old claims for and defenses of poetry from Aristotle through Shelley, partly from the nineteenth-century claims made by Ruskin and Arnold, all of which allied art deeply to society, but partly—and this is the

biggest emotional part—from the blow of the First World War and what seemed the alienation of the artist from a society increasingly less aesthetically-minded—less interested in the vivid apprehension of the values of the individual. It is when you have lost, or think you are about to lose, the objective recognition of your values, that you assert them most violently and in their most extreme form—as every unrequited lover knows. You either go into the desert, kill yourself, pull your shell over your head, or set up in a new business: in any case, whether lover or artist, being as conspicuous as possible about it. To be either a dandy or dirty, and especially where out of keeping, is always a good role; and to be an anchorite or an oracle combines the advantages of both. You are in any case among enemies.

A Russian socialist, Georgi Plekhanov, thought this sort of attitude develops when artists feel a "hopeless contradiction between their aims and the aims of the society to which they belong. Artists must be very hostile to their society and they must see no hope of changing it." But let us put it one more way—as near neutral as possible. It has always been difficult to pay for art out of the running expenses of any form of society, and it has become unusually difficult under finance-

The Great Grasp of Unreason, the first of Blackmur's 1956 Library of Congress Lectures, "Anni Mirabiles, 1921-1925: Reason in the Madness of Letters," in *A Primer of Ignorance* (1967). Reprinted by permission of Harcourt Brace Jovanovich, Inc.

capitalism (or any current money-based form of democracy) to find a means to go beyond the economy or find a special privy-purse. Also, it has always been difficult to find a sure or satisfactory audience for the living artist; and this has become increasingly difficult in societies like our own where education has become both universal and largely technical—at any rate less generalizably literate—and which has at the same time enormously multiplied the number of its artists. So, too, it has always been difficult for the artist to find the means of expressing his own direct apprehension of life in conventions which were, or could be made, part of the conventions of society in general; and this, also—this problem of communication—has become excessively difficult in a society which tends to reject the kind of faithful conventions under which the artist has usually worked, and a society in which, under the urban process, and under the weight of the new knowledges, so much of thought has been given over to mechanism which had formerly operated under faith. These are the conditions under which the artist has felt, in his exaggeration of them, isolated and has asserted himself under the general state of mind that runs from art for art's sake through surrealism to *Existenz*—It is no wonder. Yet it was Coleridge who, as reported in *Table Talk*, put the matter most succinctly—there were, he said, three silent revolutions in the history of England: "When the professions fell off from the Church; when literature fell off from the professions; and when the press fell off from literature." I will not say what the fourth silent revolution is: it is ours, and now going on.

But if we cannot name the fourth revolution we can discern some of its features in a sketch of some of the materials that go to make up our immediate intellectual history. We can touch on some of the conditions and forces of our minds. We can look into our fictions to see what gave them idiom. Idiom is the twist of truth, the twist, like that of the strands of a rope, which keeps its component fictions together. History is old and twisted beyond our reach in time. But the sense of moving background which we call history began to grow with Gibbon and we began to feel it imperative in the last ninety years—or since the war of 1870. We now take into account the extremes of several forms of time as part of our history which had not got much into history before that date—time outside the chronicle and the chronometer alike. We have time in anthropology, ethnology, mythology, psychology, physics, and mathematics, and as a response to these times we have changed our heroes.

Politics began to pretend a century and a half ago that the good society had no hero but itself, and did so on the conviction that the old heroes were malevolent. As the old Chinese believed, a great man was a national calamity. About 1870 two opposed heroic shapes were thrown up by society: the artist as hero and the heroic proletariat. Mussolini, Hitler, Stalin came to represent the hero (by dictatorship) of the scum of the earth. The scum on the pond is the reimagined primeval slime, and we are nothing if we are not primeval. In psychoanalysis we regurgitate the scum, only to discover it inexhaustible. Taboos become totems. St. Francis of Assisi becomes Vicar of our scummiest behavior. Society takes on the aspect of uniform motion. The artist is the hero who struggles against uniform motion, a struggle in marmalade.

For the artist regards uniform motion as the last torpor of life. Torpor is the spread of momentum, but we prefer to believe it is the running down of things. For three generations we have heroized the second law of thermodynamics, which is the law of the dissipation or gradual unavailability of energy within any system—which is the law of entropy or the incapacity for fresh idiom, time and perception going backwards. Entropy, from the point of view of the rational imagination, is disorder and is indeed its field. Actually, we have been as busy, as violent, and as concentrated as the ant-heap. We are torpid only because we are glutted with energy and feel it only as trouble. The strains are out of phase with each other and we have techniques only for the troubles.

If we say this sort of thing as example—and we could say so much more—are we not the first age which is self-conscious of its own fictions; and hence the first age of true Pyrrhonism:[1] doubting the value as well as the fact? We believe only in the techniques of manipulating and counting. Not in choice, not in the imperative,

[1] Used generally now for scepticism (originally referring to the doctrines of Pyrrho of Elis [c. 300 B.C.], who maintained the impossibility of certainty in knowledge).

chiefly in opinion. Thus we believe in the analysis of conduct as a means of discounting behavior, in the drum-majorette of fourteen as a means of showing sex as force without having to take account of it.

Our age is full of great hymns to the puerile, what in medicine and art are called images of fundamental frustration. If you look in the Oxford dictionary, all the early meanings of frustration were positive. You frustrated villainy, which was desirable. Now we frustrate our own good, and we lend Hamlet our own frustrations. In the history of the word there is part of the history of our psyche. When we recognize frustration as a *fundamental* condition of life, it ought no longer to be frustration, but fate, tragedy, damnation, the Cross, the other side of every infatuation. But we would not think we expressed ourselves if we said so.

Here one does not exactly ask if we are to have a deliberate resurrection of the dark ages, one only looks in the closet and under the bed and remembers how Freud said that our dreams make it possible for us to sleep. If the dark ages had had a mind, it would have been both cyclical and on sale to the devil. We migrate from one to the other, from hope without longing to longing without hope, and on the whole we prefer instruments to speculation, method to madness, as if we would obliterate the *daring* part of consciousness, which looks into the glass to see. We prefer, even in our art, poetry, and religion, confused alarms on lonely shores.

It is considerations like these which make us reflect that there may actually be a new phase of culture at hand: mass culture. But it may be only that too much of our research leads us into the mass-part of man's soul: into the anonymous and communal saga in which the actions of the individual are construed as sinister and somehow less than his own. Thus the superman or hero tends to be either the mass-man or the arch-criminal or the pure heel. It is the glory of James Joyce that in the figures of Bloom and H. C. Earwicker he worked against all these in a valiant attempt to create a new kingdom of man: an independent, individual morality against the society that made it necessary. Yet he deflected the common mode of research very little. He was a proper author and redeemed the validity of experience in the theorems he called his art. Besides Joyce, there are the others, to whom we shall come if we hold out.

What holds us, what keeps us, what moves us, must be a combination of our under-momentum and our bourgeois humanism. These are the correctives as they are the aching sources, the true enliveners, of our great men. Bourgeois humanism (the treasure of residual reason in live relation to the madness of the senses) is the only conscious art of the mind designed to deal with our megalopolitan mass society: it alone knows what to *do with* momentum in its new guise; and it alone knows it must be more than itself without losing itself in order to succeed.

The decay of the prestige of bourgeois humanism was perhaps necessary, but only as an interim, a condition of interregnum, when new forces overran us. In order to restore the humanism we have to overcome the forces. We have to take stock, too, of the multiplication in the number of the artists and to remember their insistent disrelatedness. It was never to have been expected that society—especially a centralized state like our own—would be willing to pay for the cost of the artists who as a class, and often individually, raised the severest problems of that society: images of the deep anarchies out of which the order of the state must be remade if that order is to be vital. But it ought to have been expected that the incentive of the artists themselves should have remained fixed on that living relation between anarchy and order. Instead, we have the apparition of the arts asserting their authority in a combination of the spontaneous and the arbitrary, in pure poetry and pure expression and pure trouble. Instead of creation in honesty, we have assertion in desperation; we have a fanaticism of the accidental instead of a growth of will. The true anarchy of spirit should always show (or always *has* showed) a tory flavor. It is the artist above all who *realizes* that revolutions—however fresh, violent and destructive, however aspiring, or groping, or contagious—have always *already* taken place; as private murder represents a relation already at crisis or already sundered. Revolution and murder are only the gross cost, assessed too late: the usury of dead institutions.

The anarchy of our artists is in response to facts as well as in evasion of facts. The two great external facts of our time are the explosion of

populations and the explosions of the new energies. The two great internal facts of our time
are the recreation of the devil (or pure behavior) in a place of authority and the development
of techniques for finding destructive troubles in
the psyche of individuals. With neither of these
pairs of facts, without a vital order in society,
can the individual keep up except as corrosion
may be said to keep up with the salts that cause
it—to the point of incoherence in purpose and
collapse of structure. The two pairs of facts are
I think related. The devil and the techniques are
the slow form of population and energy explosions. But if we let this relation transpire in the
mind we see we have the power to cope with the
facts themselves; for we then behold the nature
of our troubles in what used to be called the
unity of apperception. To say this is to involve
bourgeois humanism once again. It may not be
the right force, or the right muse, but they are
the only ones we know, and the only ones which
we know have within themselves the capacity to
generate by absorbing disorder into order. We
can remember in the past it was the artists who
taught society this skill.

The latter end of our time—1920-1950—is an
age of critique: critique as a means of criticism
and critique as a means of creation. Critique
as criticism we see in the expanding omnivorous techniques for the examination of poetry.
Critique as creation we see in Proust, Mann,
Joyce, and Kafka. Critique is the wiggling extreme articulation of vital elements into an order
of vision: especially the elements of the new
powers and the new troubles.

With critique as creation we shall have much
to do. Here I want a passing emphasis on criticism in its widest sense. Some of the criticism
merely extends along new lines the malicious
criticism of knowledge (the attack on the validity
of perception) which is the net practical result
of the current of philosophy beginning with
Berkeley and running into the sands of the Exis-
tentialists. Epistemology was taught to prevent
knowledge or at least to gravel it with doubts;
so most criticism of poetry. All the apprehensive
powers of the mind have been put at such a dis-
count that they are felt to be irrational, when
actually they are the fountainhead and fountain
reach of reason herself. It strikes me here that
in result upon our general mind, modern physics

and mathematics make a parallel extension of
the same malicious criticism of knowledge: as
refinement of critical abstraction, good for manipulation, rotten for apprehension—that is, for
the sensual knowledge that is the immediate rock
of physics and the thing indexed by mathematics.
As compared to literary criticism, the critique
supplied by physics is both more malice and
more knowledge and is also more remote from
the apprehending reason. The effect of these
malicious critiques is profound: almost they dissolve our sense of the texture of moral experience. It is the writhing of actual knowledge
under these malicious techniques that makes
choice and purpose and taste so difficult, uncertain, and fractious. We tend to relapse from all
human creation back into almost pure momentum (in analogy to pure sensation), with all our
activity becoming mere sports on the movement
of inertia. Thus it is we seem to manipulate for
manipulation's sake and find the *acte gratuite* a
liberation when it ought to be a warning, an explosion when it ought to be a play, a gesture, a
feint. It is thus that we *become* our problem
when we ought to exemplify some effort at the
solution of it. We become, in Dante's language,
the War of the Journey without active knowledge
of the War of the Pity. It is the two Wars that
need the Muses; either, taken solely, puerilizes
man.

The malicious criticism of knowledge is reflected also in the unmoored diabolism that makes
so many mansions in the modern sensibility, and
makes them uninhabitable sink-holes of terror
and dismay, full of the uncleanly and aborted
approximations of the unseemly. Hysteria, which
ought to be the clue to reality, becomes its
creator. This we see in Freud, who began his
studies with the etiology of hysteria and proceeded with its deification: as if all the gross
responses unconformable with conduct could ordain conduct. The sequence is interesting: hyp-
notism, psychical research, hysteria, neurosis,
psychosis, psychoanalysis. The very title, *Psycho-
pathology of Everyday Life,* in itself a lie, told
that we might mistake the conditions of our
struggle for its object; in short, a malicious criticism of knowledge. It is a queer thing that we
should desire to make experience itself suicidal
to its own impulses: queer but actual. The devil
always takes the form of the actual, most con-

spicuously in an expressionistic age. But only the bourgeois humanist would know this.

But it must be the bourgeois humanist in his role as artist who knows—for it is he who is nearest the expressionism of our times, the artist thrown up as a heroic type and a heroic image. And indeed it has been that class which has known most, or expressed the most—especially in that explosion of talent that took place in the twenties, crystallizing between 1922 and 1925 in *Ulysses, The Waste Land, The Magic Mountain, The Tower, The Counterfeiters,* and a great deal more. It is a version of the general *artistic* problem which gave condition to this explosion that I have been leading up to. All these books came deeply from the bourgeois humanistic tradition and come as near masterpieces as our age provides. They were a part of the great expressionistic period between the wars, not only in literature but in all the arts. Older talents crystallized and reached pinnacles and took on new dimensions; new talents were flung off like sparks from a Catharine wheel or the blobs of light from a roman candle. Expressionism—what I say is both myself in truth and creates a new world—tends to pyrotechnics; the fireworks are within us and are all around us and are their own meaning—subject to the least possible external control or common predictable forms of understanding. In expressionistic art we see what the forces are which we have to control by other means: the actual forces of human nature, of nonrational behavior, and of the industriously rational machinations of the devil—the diabolic, the demonic, and the chthonic—the life that is in our soil. Expressionism compacts the Faustian spirit and the adventures of our conduct. This is a new claim for the arts, and perhaps the most ambitious yet in the long series since Aristotle. It is precisely the opposite from Shelley's claim that poets are the unacknowledged legislators of the world. It constitutes for itself rather the claim to undermine, to readjust, to put into fresh order the frames or forms in which we make the adventure of conduct tangible to our minds, and it therefore denies validity to pre-existent legislation on human relations.

No wonder all that we mean by the state and most of what we mean by public morals turn stony against expressionistic art. No wonder, too, that for all its talent and all its novelty, expressionistic art has never been popular with the new mass society that threw it off as a new turn—a new force—of the mind. It has been popular rather with the human fragments which the mass society also threw off—with the remainder of the old élites and with the new professional and intellectual proletariats: all those of us who, in Toynbee's phrase, are *in* but not *of* the great mass society. All art is in a sense the daydream arrested and compacted in form. Most people like their daydreams to conform to their normal expectations and their immediate ambitions and to do so in familiar forms. Most of us like either happy endings or a lonely glory in our affairs. We dream to get rid of our reality and to charm the lights of love. Here popular art helps us out. More serious art—high-brow art—is also daydream, but it insists on responding to the pressures that make our dreams so strange and so full of prophecy: nightmare or revelation. Instead of rationalizing our experience we give our experience what form we can and set reason new and almost impossible tasks to perform. We recreate reality in rivalry with our own wishes. I think of Thomas Hardy who tried to write popular melodramatic novels for money out of ordinary melodramatic daydreams but, in what we call his better novels, found himself responding to and shaping dark forces. I think also of Henry James who wanted to write the best possible popular novels, but never knew what the deep moral troubles in his psyche were that prevented him (the very troubles which as he expressed them give him stature) until, in August 1914, he saw that *this* is what we have been leading up to all along.

We have had another war since then, and the enclosure of the two wars suggests certain things about the talent that lay between them—or at least puts certain things in a violent murky light. We lived in a time of troubles, when the very torpor of our momentum let us see what monsters and what heroes we could make of ourselves in imagination—the monsters of our behavior newly seen, and the heroes of our struggle with that conduct newly construed. Newly seen and newly construed: for not only did we live in a time of troubles, we lived also in a time when we were learning a whole set of techniques for finding—even creating—trouble: new ways of undermining personality and conviction and belief and human relation. I myself can remember when the Oedipus complex was a shattering shock and a neurosis was a ravening worm. It was not till later that we had the law of uncertainty in mathematical physics, which broke the last healthy remnants of moral determinism. But we had psychology which dissolved the personality into bad behavior, we had anthropology which dissolved religion into a competition, world- and history-wide, of monsters, and we had psychiatry which cured the disease by making a monument of it and sociology which flattened us into the average of the lonely crowd. We had thus the tools with which to construct the age of anxiety out of the older debris. Almost, the tools guided the hands and predicted the work. As if that were not enough, the same monsters, and more intolerable heroes (those who accepted the monsters) began their work in the world of managers. It was in 1922 that Mussolini made his march on Rome; and by 1939 the Faustian spirit within had come very near succumbing to the dictatorship of the scum of the earth without.

It need not have happened that way, but the risk of its happening that way was very great, and is still with us; and the arts have more than ever the job of enforcing new tasks upon reason: to show poetry as the wisdom of our violent knowledge—which is what Giambattisto Vico said, in 1744, that poetry could do in his great work, *Principi di una Scienza Nuova*, the new way of looking at knowledge. It was also, I think, how he came to say that justice was an emanation of the human conscience, and therefore changed as times and forces changed.

In the darkness and hope of these remarks something else we have long known shows the more clearly: the shifting contour and widening focus, not of one or two generations, but of three or four centuries, in the burdening and the possible scope of literature as it is a development in history. It is not the atheists and agnostics but the committed men like Reinhold Niebuhr and Arnold Toynbee who habitually say that we live in a post-Christian world; and the history of literature bears them out. In Shakespeare justice is the endless jar of right and wrong as it strikes upon the conscience. We feel in Shakespeare what troubled Joyce's Stephen Dedalus so much: the agenbite of inwit, or remorse of conscience. In Shakespeare, as in Montaigne, and not again going backwards till Dante, nor going forward till Pascal, you feel the constant explosions of violently irrational forces upon the conscience. These explosions were of their talent. From the First World War onward the explosions are commonplace, though the talent may be less or at least less acceptable. Except Dante, who I think prophesied it, we are all heirs to a realignment of the usurping and abdicating institutions which manage our relations to our irrational experience. There are many ways of putting this. Here is Marcel Raymond, who is trying to explain the apparition of nonrational French poetry from 1870 onwards: "An explosion of the irrational elements in the human personality had occurred in the era of the Counter-Reformation and Baroque art, but at that time the Church had determined the course of the mystical upsurge without much difficulty. Two centuries later, after the critique of the 'philosophers,' she was no longer in the same commanding position. It was the task of art (but not of art alone) to gratify some of the human demands that religion had thus far been able to exercise.

"From then on poetry tended to become an ethic or some sort of irregular instrument of metaphysical knowledge. Poets were obsessed by the need to 'change' life, as Rimbaud puts it, to change man and to bring him into direct contact with existence. The novelty lies less in the fact that in the intention, which gradually emerges from the realm of the unconscious, of reconquering man's irrational powers and of transcending the dualism of the self and the universe." (Raymond goes on to remark that modern civilization and Romanticism crystallized at the same moment.[2])

An irregular metaphysic for the control of man's irrational powers, if I may so condense M. Raymond, these words on the sequence of these remarks seem to me to enlighten the motive-power, the *moving* power, of the extraordinary outburst of creative talent in the twenties. No wonder it is sometimes called a rival creation.

Let me list a few in literature. Pirandello wrote *Six Characters in Search of an Author* in 1921, *Henry IV* in 1922: or how it is we struggle for

[2] Marcel Raymond, *De Baudelaire au Surrealisme* (Paris, 1940), pp. 11-12.

identity. Ortega y Gasset wrote *Invertebrate Spain* in 1922, *Revolt of the Masses,* in 1930. Valéry published *Charmes* in 1922: the identity of the spirit with its senses. For that year Proust had *Sodome et Gomorrhe:* the beast which springs and is sprung of spirit. Ezra Pound had finished *Hugh Selwyn Mauberly* and some of his most characteristic *Cantos* in 1921: the artist as hero *manqué.* Wallace Stevens' *Harmonium* appeared in 1923: a dandy finding an old chaos in the sun. Mann's *Magic Mountain* came in 1924: the intellect entered literature at a new level to meet and merge with the sick and the unseemly. Two years later, 1926, Gide produced his *Counterfeiters:* the migratory black devil in Puritanism. And so on.

For our purposes, we have only to remember that Eliot's *Waste Land* and Joyce's *Ulysses* appeared in 1922, and that around that year hovers Yeats' most powerful work. Do not these works, as we lump them in one image which we cannot swallow and of which we cannot free ourselves, constitute a deep plea for the wisdom of our violent knowledge? Is not the poetry in them precisely the wisdom with which we respond to the great grasp of unreason?

DOUGLAS BUSH   (1896-   )

O NE of the two or three major classical humanists of our century to be closely concerned with modern literature as well—indeed with every period of literature from the Renaissance to the present—is Douglas Bush, who was born in Ontario, Canada, and who studied at the University of Toronto and at Harvard. He taught at the University of Minnesota (1927-36) and Harvard (1936-66), where he served as Gurney Professor of English Literature. His scholarship and criticism in the fields of the classical tradition and English literature are of unrivaled amplitude and depth. Among his many works are *Mythology and the Renaissance Tradition in English Poetry* (1932), *Mythology and the Romantic Tradition in English Poetry* (1937), *The Renaissance and English Humanism* (1939), *English Literature in the Earlier Seventeenth Century* (1943), *Paradise Lost in Our Time* (1945), *Science and English Poetry* (1952), *John Milton* (1964), *John Keats* (1966), and *Pagan Myth and Christian Tradition in English Poetry* (1968).

As with almost every principal critic of our century, the works for which Douglas Bush has been most famous have been studies of particular writers and periods: the great Oxford History of the earlier seventeenth century, the memorable studies of Milton and Renaissance humanism, of Keats and the Romantics, and by far the most authoritative and capacious historical studies of the use of myth in English poetry from the Renaissance to the present. Of no other critic concerned with English literature since 1950 can it so truthfully be said—as has been often said of Bush—that he is "an authority to authorities." Yet no one of even comparable authority has written with such wit, lucidity, grace, and imaginative balance. Essentially, Douglas Bush is in the great Arnoldian tradition. Our question is how to preserve the humanities in a rapidly changing and uncertain age, and not only to preserve, but to create with and through the best of what we inherit. Almost every major critic of our century, who survived into the 1960's, has returned to this position. The difference is that Bush, with perhaps a few others of our century, takes a longer view than Arnold. Their awareness of the problem is deeper; and they bring more to bear historically than Arnold had at his command. In the following essay, "Literary History and Literary Criticism," Bush acknowledges our debt to the wealth of humanistic studies in this century. Such literary history and criticism has been many-sided and open, like literature itself, to "the complex pressures of religious, philosophical, scientific, ethical, social, political, and aesthetic ideas." Bush points out that the sheer bulk of scholarship and criticism, which he quickly surveys, has nonetheless become a burden, and we run the risk of burying the work under the commentaries. Then Bush sets down, in order of importance, the values by which a student might best be guided.

Literary History and Literary Criticism

I CONFESS that every time I have looked through the program for this Congress I have been stricken with inarticulate paralysis. Almost every topic is a reminder of the infinite extent of literature and criticism and of one's own infinite ignorance. While there may be polymaths among us who have no reason to be so troubled, it can probably be assumed that most scholars and critics have some acquaintance with despair, unless they early reconciled themselves to picking up pebbles on the shore or cultivating their own small garden.

The scope of the program and one's individual sense of total inadequacy in some sense dramatize a general problem which nowadays confronts not merely literary humanists but workers in all areas of intellectual endeavor. There is just too much to know, not only of literature itself and

Literary History and Literary Criticism. Reprinted by permission from *Literary History and Literary Criticism: Acta of the Ninth Congress International Federation for Modern Languages and Literature Held at New York University, August 25 to 31, 1963,* ed. Leon Edel, Kenneth McKee, and W. M. Gibson, © 1964 by New York University.

the vast amount of scholarship and criticism but of cultural history in general, since the study of literature takes in everything that man has felt and thought and done, including science and the arts. Up through the nineteenth century "literature" as a matter of course meant only or chiefly European literature; now the conventional boundaries have been widely extended, and both the more and the less familiar bodies of writing have been studied in breadth and depth by relatively new armies of professional scholars and critics. The contrast between the literary scene in 1963 and that of 1863 does not need elaboration, although it is so significant in various ways that I shall be coming back to it.

These self-evident considerations—and again the list of topics and of foreign experts in our program—are good warrant for caution, and I shall stay discreetly within the limits of scholarship and criticism in the English-speaking world. Whether attitudes and movements in this restricted area are parallel to, or quite different from, those found in continental Europe and elsewhere, they are important in themselves and complex enough for a brief survey.

We might recall some tendencies and landmarks in the England and America of the last hundred years and especially the last fifty or so. In England, for a good part of that period it was assumed that one read one's native literature for oneself, without academic instruction. While academic scholarship of the modern kind was being produced, in the outer world criticism was mainly impressionistic "appreciation." The critical work of the early 1900's that proved to be of most enduring importance was A. C. Bradley's *Shakespearean Tragedy*, the culminating product of the nineteenth-century romantic tradition; in literary history a large landmark was [W. J.] Courthope's philosophic *History of English Poetry*. But if we had to name the single figure most typical of English criticism and literary history in that period, it would be George Saintsbury, the amateur *par excellence*, the quite unphilosophical embodiment of omnivorous gusto. Saintsbury's history of English literature and his larger history of criticism surveyed countless individual writers with only minimal recognition of the movement of ideas, of critical and cultural processes and patterns. While France and Italy also had their traditions of impressionism, we may think of the semi-scientific principles of Taine or of the philosophical De Sanctis.[1] During the last forty years professionalism in England has grown much stronger, though there are still a good many books written for, and sometimes apparently by, the general reader (not that that is such a bad thing, since it implies a popular audience).

In the nineteenth century the United States had its amateurs, like Poe—whose impact on France was so significant—and James Russell Lowell. There was also such a scholarly historian of American literature as Moses Coit Tyler. But we may associate the general rise of American literary scholarship with the establishment and growth of graduate schools in the major universities. In this country the professional attitude has been much more firmly fixed than the amateur; one conspicuous early achievement was Child's great edition of the popular ballads.[2] To

speak roughly, from about 1880 to about 1916 there was virtually a single movement in literary scholarship, that is, the writing of literary history according to the genetic method, a method derived from European science and the literary stress on milieu. This meant the tracing of literary sources and literary influences, and during most of this long period the material was predominantly medieval literature, which lent itself most readily to such investigations and which had such illustrious European explorers as Gaston Paris. The aim and method, however, were extended over later literature as well, and continued to flourish through the 1930's, after rival aims and methods had appeared. The total result, whether in rounded works or small fragments, was a learned, comprehensive, and solidly detailed body of literary history from which we have all learned. Its chief shortcoming was that its historical preoccupations slighted criticism and critical values, so that it remained largely an external record of purely literary relationships. One book which may be called at once a culmination and a distinguished exception was John Livingston Lowes's *The Road to Xanadu* (1927).

While this useful if limited approach to literature is still practiced to some degree (and in recent years has been rehabilitated by a more critical historicism), it gave way to a succession of movements which sought to get closer to the inner significance and artistic value of literature. The second great wave in the United States was the history of ideas. Irving Babbitt, the Harvard professor of French, had been a crusader, on his own ethical and anti-Romantic plane. More disinterested modes of inquiry seem to have begun about 1916 on several literary fronts, in the writings of a number of literary scholars and of the philosopher Arthur O. Lovejoy. This new movement, in part a revolt against the tyranny of external fact, had a strong appeal for those, especially the young, who craved more nourishment from literature than literary history had provided. For many years many notable scholars have been rewriting the history of literature— and not merely of literature—with a fresh understanding of the complex pressures of religious,

---

[1] For Taine, see above, pp. 500-01, and for De Sanctis, see above, p. 679.

[2] Bush refers to Francis James Child (1825-1896), whose *English and Scottish Popular Ballads* (first pub-

lished in 8 vols., 1857-58, expanded in later editions), remains the authoritative collection.

philosophical, scientific, ethical, social, political, and aesthetic ideas. There is no need of citing authors of the many books and articles, American and English, which are part of everyone's equipment. The study of ideas has not only re-created literary history at a new depth; it has come closer to criticism through its philosophical illumination of countless individual works and authors.

But neither the older literary history nor the history of ideas carried within itself any criteria of aesthetic values, since a poor writer might illustrate influences or ideas as well as, or even better than, a great one. Also, both methods were focused primarily on backgrounds or specific strains in literature and did not essay fully rounded accounts of particular works. To fill this partial vacuum the so-called "new criticism" came into being; the name, in America, arrived some time after the method had been in full swing. The close analysis of rhetorical structure and texture had been employed with the classics ever since antiquity, but classical education had long been declining and with it the capacity for intensive reading. To recall some familiar facts, the modern revival or adaptation of rhetorical analysis began with the general stimulus of the anti-Romantic T. E. Hulme and T. S. Eliot and the more rigorous principles and practice of I. A. Richards and his disciples, such as William Empson. Although the new criticism started in England, it spread widely and rapidly in the United States, so that before long no department of English could count itself respectable unless it included at least one new critic. The virtues and the limitations of the new criticism everyone knows. Although literary history and the history of ideas are valuable disciplines in themselves, it is individual works that stir us, and the new criticism focused directly on them. It taught slack generations to read, to analyze the functional components of works of art, form, imagery, diction, rhythm, and such qualities as irony, ambiguity, and paradox. It also tended, if not consistently, to take works out of their historical setting; and it could emphasize some elements, such as imagery, at the expense of others and thereby fall into overreading or misreading. Speaking recently of such dangers, Professor M. H. Abrams judiciously affirmed that "The necessary but not sufficient condition for a com-

petent reader of poetry remains what it has always been—a keen eye for the obvious." [3] In general the new criticism has had more success with short poems of an intellectual cast than with other things from pure lyrics to epics, plays, and novels.

Some other approaches to literature may be mentioned more briefly. They range from a mainly social view (which in the 1930's could be dogmatic Marxism) to the aims and scientific methods of technical bibliography. Apropos of the latter, it might be observed that of late years scholarly acumen and rigor have been assisted by time-saving machines for the collating of texts and the like—a new and startling version of the wedding of Mercury and Philology. Another and less scientific approach—though it can claim scientific origins and authority—has come from the psychology of Freud and others. This has often inclined to loose or extreme exploitation of over-simple formulas; it has also, as in some large works by French scholar-critics, utilized psychology in more general and flexible ways. Then there is the neo-Aristotelian school, centered in the University of Chicago, which has put critical emphasis on structure; and there are other forms of formalism. There are the structural linguists, who have quickly become a considerable army, but whose work I am not qualified to assess. Some scholars, trained in the old way as literary historians, have brought literary and other kinds of learning to the theory and practice of criticism. And a number of important scholars and critics cannot be readily classified. To add a last topic to this overcrowded paragraph, from the new critics onward there has been an inclination to deny biography a place in or near criticism, but, for one recent and distinguished interpretative work, there are the volumes on Henry James by the local chairman of this Congress, Professor Leon Edel. Among other new works that fuse biography and criticism are two by younger colleagues of mine, Herschel Baker's *William Hazlitt* and W. J. Bate's *John Keats*.

In this country perhaps the most fashionable critical mode of the past decade or more has

[3] "Five Ways of Reading *Lycidas*," *Varieties of Literary Experience*, ed. Stanley Burnshaw (New York, 1962), p. 23. [Bush.]

been the myth-and-symbol doctrine. Like the new criticism, it began in England but has flourished chiefly in America. It may be said to have started with Maud Bodkin's *Archetypal Patterns in Poetry* (1934); its authoritative bible is the fresh, acute, learned, and lively *Anatomy of Criticism* (1957) by Northrop Frye. This doctrine has grown out of psychology and anthropology, especially the writings of Jung, out of such seminal works of modern literature as *The Waste Land* and *Ulysses*, and in some sense out of the new criticism, although that father does not care to acknowledge any parenthood. In capable hands, this method has added new dimensions to many works of literature or has firmly defined dimensions and traditional patterns felt only vaguely before. In less capable hands it can yield quite erratic fancies, since the wandering eye sees myths and symbols everywhere, and some products are paralleled only by the medieval religious allegorizations of Ovid. Even at its best this method, having such a special focus, can hardly render a full account of any particular work. Its most general limitation is that, like the old literary history and the history of ideas, it does not contain in itself any criteria of aesthetic value; of course, like literary historians and historians of ideas, myth-and-symbol critics may acquire such criteria from elsewhere and use them.

To return to literary history, which includes both formal histories of periods and genres and innumerable particular contributions, we have noticed the two main kinds, the strictly literary and the ideological. Most of the formal histories of English literature, large and small, are mainly literary, although the largest, the *Cambridge History*, cast its net over wide areas. I take it that in the theme of our program "literary history" means both kinds. But there have been and are diverse opinions about the proper scope of histories of literature—and a few strongminded individualists object to their being written at all. Some people would confine history to works of conscious art and to the historical charting of these in aesthetic terms. Others would argue that the serious botanist is not content with flowers in a bouquet but wants to examine root, branches, leaves, and even soil, the whole organism in its habitat. In other words, literary history can be conceived as the record not only

of works of art but of all forms of culture expressed in the written word. Both kinds of course must be critical and in some sense philosophical. I think that there is room and need for both kinds, although I favor the broader conception. Literary history devoted wholly to aesthetic concerns is likely to be "too thin breathing," as Keats's Endymion said of his direct pursuit of an abstract ideal; it is a diet for epicures and needs some roughage. The broader kind of history does much to re-create the mental worlds of the authors it deals with; and it makes a much stronger appeal to the general reader, if he still exists or can be brought back into existence. In this connection I might say that it seems to me deplorable that the one consecutive survey of English literature in popular form should be the Pelican volumes edited by Boris Ford and written by the heirs of *Scrutiny*; there are good sections, but not enough to redeem the whole.

To sum up the accomplishment of our own century, it can be safely said that an immense amount of varied learning and infinite rays of philosophical and critical light have been brought to bear on the whole range of English and American literature, that we now have—or groups of specialists now have—vastly richer knowledge and understanding than anyone possessed or dreamed of in the later nineteenth century. The whole scale and aim and method of study have gone well beyond what was for centuries considered appropriate for the ancient classics only. In 1888 Arnold could say that "Shelley is not a classic, whose various readings are to be noted with earnest attention"; [4] now, of course, Shelley and all the other major and many minor poets are edited with meticulous textual apparatus. Most of us could not, without hesitation, recall the chief scholarly and critical books that were around 1890 available for students of English and American literature; now there are whole libraries. During this period professional journals have multiplied to a number that makes the head swim. In the annual international bibliography in *PMLA* the list of books and articles on English and American literature runs, in recent years, to more than six thousand.

[4] "Shelley," *Essays in Criticism, Second Series* (2d ed., 1898), p. 206.

This has been, I hope, a fair if meager outline of the American and English scene. Obviously the catholic impressionist orthodoxy of the age of Saintsbury has given place to a variety of protestant creeds and sects, not all in harmony with one another and some claiming an exclusive hold upon truth. Obviously also, no one person could or would be a practicing adherent of all the diverse creeds and methods. We all do what we best can and like to do. But, since the map presents a confusing number of roads, divergent, parallel, or convergent, we may well ask not merely where we go from here but where we are now. I cannot answer either question, but I shall venture to make some comments; I shall probably not escape the dangers both of seeming to pontificate and of being much too elementary for this very learned and sophisticated audience.

1. The name of Arnold recalls his broad definition of criticism, which made no specific reference to literature at all and was indeed virtually the same as his definition of culture. In our time criticism in that large sense is carried on, by philosophic publicists and others, but criticism in the narrower sense, as we have seen, has been moving along very diverse roads, most of them leading to partial rather than total views of a work or an author. Ideally, criticism seeks to define and analyze both the substantive materials and the aesthetic components of a particular work, both being considered as the means of expressing a theme; it seeks also to interpret that theme and to assess the total value of the work in itself and in relation to comparable works. The terms of this rough definition need to be enlarged though not essentially altered if the critic is dealing with more than one work or with an author's whole output. Along with the critic's own quest of light and satisfaction, his main object is to mediate between a work or author and a reader presumably less instructed and enlightened, at least on this particular topic. As Mr. Eliot succinctly put it, the function of criticism is the elucidation of works of art and the correction of taste; and, as he also said, comparison and analysis are the critic's chief instruments.[5]

[5] "The Function of Criticism," *Selected Essays* (1932), p. 21.

2. Since the great mass of great literature belongs to the past, adequate criticism must grow out of historical knowledge, cultural and linguistic, as well as out of intuitive insight. Every work must be understood on its own terms as the product of a particular mind in a particular setting, and that mind and setting must be re-created through all the resources that learning and the historical imagination can muster—not excluding the author's intention, if that is known. The very pastness of a work, as Lionel Trilling[6] has emphasized, is part of its meaning for us and must be realized to the best of our power. The doctrine that a work of art is self-sufficient and may not receive extraneous illustration is arbitrary and irrational. There are no short cuts to the past or present significance of a work of the past, though uninformed criticism has the advantage that Sir Robert Walpole[7] found in having bawdy conversation at the dinner table—that all could join in on equal terms. We can of course achieve only limited degrees of truth in trying to re-create the outward and inward conditions in which a work of art was engendered, but, unless we try, we cannot distinguish between its local and temporal and its universal and timeless elements; indeed we may not be able to understand some works at all.

One example of unhistorical distortion is the way in which, during the 1920's and later, John Donne was turned into a skeptical, rootless, alienated, twentieth-century intellectual. Or we might take such an example of wrongheadedness as the book on *Paradise Lost* by A. J. A. Waldock, who belabored the poem because its characters and narrative were not those of a realistic novel and who, in regard to religious and even ethical values, was simply tone deaf. Thomas Rymers, when they appear, suffer from lack of knowledge or lack of imagination or both.[8] One function of literary history is to correct the vagaries of unhistorical criticism. History and criticism were taken as one and indi-

[6] "The Sense of the Past," *The Liberal Imagination* (1950). [Bush.]

[7] (1676-1745), Prime Minister of England (1721-42), father of the famous eighteenth-century letter writer, Horace Walpole.

[8] Thomas Rymer (1641-1713), an extreme neoclassic rationalist, noted for his systematic rigidity as a critic. See above, p. 9.

visible by Edmund Wilson (who is probably tired of being called the dean of American critics): in dedicating *Axel's Castle* (1931) to his Princeton teacher, Christian Gauss, Mr. Wilson said that it was principally from him that he acquired his idea of what literary criticism ought to be, "a history of man's ideas and imaginings in the setting of the conditions which have shaped them."

3. While criticism cannot attain to anything like scientific objectivity, it should seek to avoid personal bias. Mr. Eliot long ago quoted the saying of Rémy de Gourmont, that every critic, if he is sincere, tries to erect his personal impressions into laws. In that sense, the great law-giver of our time is F. R. Leavis.[9] A critic cannot escape his own temperamental and intellectual limitations, and should not deny his own convictions and standards, but he should be open-mindedly receptive to works of art and the critical ideas of others. This might seem a truism if there were not critics who appear otherwise disposed. The various kinds of criticism already outlined can be the means of illumination; they can also be idols of the cave. What are we to say when a learned and often acute critic of *Paradise Lost* finds in the poem phallicism, castration complexes, and other elements of the rigmarole? Miltonic criticism yields an especially rich harvest of prejudice and aberration. While Mr. Eliot's poetry has long been classical and in no need of defense, it has long been recognized that his early criticism was in part an oblique justification of his own poetic methods, among them the use of concrete particulars. Mr. Eliot could apply this principle to *L'Allegro* without regard to Milton's purpose: the ploughman and the rest were not made individuals, as Wordsworth would have seen them. But Milton needed typical, ideal figures in a landscape, and the effect would have been ruined if he had told us that the ploughman, like Wordsworth's Simon Lee, had weak ankles that swelled. Similarly Dr. Leavis denounced Milton's description of paradise because it did not give the immediate

9 (1895-   ), noted Cambridge critic, co-founder and editor of *Scrutiny* (1932-53), author of *Determinations* (1934), *Revaluation* (1936), *The Great Tradition* (1948), and other works in which his approach combines close textual criticism with social and moral principles of evaluation.

sensation of being in a garden; here again, in a symbolic pattern of perfection in which the garden and its inhabitants must be kept at an aesthetic distance, realistic particularity would have been fatal.

4. Since criticism is not a science and cannot be made one by any amount of theorizing, it should follow the world's great critics in the belief that the most precise and subtle ideas about literature can be expressed in ordinary language. Some English exponents of "Cambridge English" and some Americans are given to horrid pseudo-scientific diction embedded in shapeless, jagged, cacophonous sentences. Jargon does not make simple ideas scientific and profound; it only inspires profound distrust of the user's aesthetic sensitivity. I might mention a sinister declaration I had from a sophomore who came in to tell me that he was a Thomist in his thinking and also to speak about his low marks. I asked "Did you ever in all your reading encounter such clotted jargon as this paper?" Said he, "I write the English of the future."

5. Of literature, especially poetry, in the modern languages a very large part is bound up with the classics, and it may be thought that modern criticism suffers from the general decline of classical education. Such education, to be sure, is no guarantee of insight, but it is likely to promote centrality and rationality of outlook and clarity of style and to be an asset worth more than methodologies.

6. A sixth generality, which belongs to the other end of the spectrum, can also be put briefly. Academic scholars and critics nowadays are as a rule much more aware of contemporary writing than they used to be, much more aware that literature is not something that stopped decades ago and was enshrined in a museum, but something that goes on, continually augmented by people who live among us. And there is much more osmosis than there was between the academy and the outer world of writers. Such awareness of the present is good in itself and it helps to vitalize our sense of the past.

7. My last comment requires some elaboration. During the twenty-five centuries from Homer to about 1800, the long stretch of time that brought forth a very high proportion of the world's great literature, there was only a

trickle of what can be termed specific criticism; and literary history, though called for by Bacon,[10] did not appear in England until the eighteenth century. It would seem that literature can thrive without either, and that perhaps we have no good reason for existing. I would not deny for a moment the splendid achievements of modern scholarship and criticism, which were briefly celebrated earlier, and to which we are all grateful debtors; but the picture has its other side and candor compels a look at that.

With all our solid grounds for satisfaction, even complacency, there are grounds also for depression, though I do not know whether this is widespread; possibly foreign scholars and critics feel it less, or less directly, than many of us in the United States, which has by far the largest army of workers in the vineyard and produces by far the largest quantity of grapes, juicy or dry. Of course there are practical and professional pressures that explain some of this activity. But whatever the writers' motives, from the desire for promotion to the sharing of a fresh insight, it is an obvious fact that no one, even if he had nothing to do but read, could assimilate more than a fraction of the material that deals with his own special interests, much less anything beyond these. No one can pick his way through a few sections of one of the annual bibliographies before another huge volume has fallen upon him. A footnote is blown up into an article, an article into a book. Again and again, reading articles and books that in large measure say what has been said many times before, we ask the question asked under wartime restrictions: "Was this trip necessary?" Some critical analyses seem designed to supersede and bury the original work. Criticism has become less of an art than a grim industry or solemn priest-craft, and in the process has lost most of the infectious gusto that used to inspire amateur impressionism in less doggedly conscientious times. In short, the great achievements of scholarship and criticism have their pathological side, and we seem to have encountered the law of diminishing returns. Then, to look outside our immediate professional concerns, when and how do we enlarge our acquaintance with the infinite body of the world's great literature and the extra-literary works that we should know? But one recoils from considering the answer to that question.

In the present state of the cultural and the political world I do not think that we can afford to continue our recent course without taking more thought about where we stand and where we are going. I can only ask forgiveness if I end with gratuitous sermonizing, though I imagine that I am expressing a general uneasiness. We students of literature assembled here, representing many countries with more or less venerable literary traditions, may have for the moment a feeling of confident strength and security. But that feeling, if we have it, is surely something of an illusion. Without repeating the clichés about possible annihilation, we must still recognize the fact that, after some two millennia of leadership, the humanities have in our time been downgraded by the dazzling discoveries of science and, to a lesser degree, by the large promises of social science. The past twenty or thirty years have witnessed the birth of a new scientific civilization. We and other tribes of humanists—and some scientists—deny the multiplying and aggressive claims of the sciences that they are the supreme or the only guides for mankind, we maintain that the humanities are still the realm of value and the central habitation of the human spirit, but we are engaged in what has the appearance of a losing battle. Possibly, if he survives, man will discover that he cannot live, literally or metaphorically, in the mechanized and dehumanized world of science and technology, and the Zeitgeist[11] will alter its present course. But we cannot put our faith in that dubious deity; perhaps we cannot do much of anything. Yet we can surely do something better than go our accustomed ways without regard to the advent of a new dark age.

In the study of literature as in the sciences modern specialization has of course added enormously and rapidly to the total sum of knowledge and enlightenment, but the individual specialists, if not reduced to the humble function of coral insects, have at any rate been impoverished. The serious humanists of the Renaissance were intellectual and cultural, ethical and political leaders of their world. A century ago the

---

[10] *Advancement of Learning*, Bk. II, Sect. 3, par. 4.

[11] Spirit of the age (literally, "time spirit").

Sainte-Beuves and Arnolds could address a large public with authority and be heard. How many literary humanists nowadays have any semblance of that general authority? Such men as Sainte-Beuve and Arnold were amateurs in a number of literatures; most of us are experts in patches of one. It is not our fault that a once consider-able and fairly homogeneous public has almost if not quite disappeared, yet we have done more to assist than to check the process. We seldom think of addressing any but an academic audi-ence, old or young; we write for other scholars and critics on relatively esoteric matters and seldom try, in Arnoldian language, to enlarge the saving remnant. There was, to be sure, in-difference or hostility toward the humanities in ancient Athens and Renaissance Europe, but now the adverse odds are immensely heavier. We ourselves, in our libraries or in the com-pany of colleagues, are so sure of our own faith in literature that we forget how minute a por-tion of the human race we are, how alien and meaningless that faith is to most of mankind, how greatly the world has changed from the relative security and traditionalism of the nine-teenth century. I do not mean that we should forsake true learning for the pulpit (as I am now doing in addressing a body of the elect), that we should go about giving inspirational hurrahs for the humanities—though even such utterances can be desirable at times. But I do believe that we should turn a much larger part of our energies to sharing our central faith, that we should not allow ourselves to be drawn away from the essential values of literature, that we should put much less effort into the indiscrimi-nate advancement of knowledge. As I said at the start, there is already far too much to know, in literature itself, without taking account of scholarship and criticism at all. We are in a perpetual rat race, neglecting original works because we must keep up with new knowledge and opinions. Perhaps, as I remarked before, these baneful pressures are worse in this coun-try than elsewhere—I do not know. But foreign scholars may still agree that the study of litera-ture, with all its visible and splendid accom-plishment, could be in a much healthier state, that it could reflect much more truly and fully our highest faith and aims. If we cannot any longer achieve or deserve the status of the early humanists, we can at least strive not to dwindle into a society of antiquaries and connoisseurs "Housed in a dream, at distance from the kind." [12]

[12] Wordsworth, "Elegiac Stanzas Suggested by a Picture of Peele Castle," l. 54.

INDEX

INDEX

In this Index, the most important page references and, under topics, the names of those critics who discuss the particular topic in detail have been italicized.

M H ABRAMS "THE MIRROR AND THE LAMP"

```
                    UNIVERSE
                 ( MIMETIC THEORIES)
                        ↑
                        |
           WORK         |
              ↖    ↗    |
   ARTIST     ↙      ↘  →  AUDIENCE
 ( EXPRESSIVE THEORIES)|  ( PRAGMATIC THEORIES)
                        |
                        ↓
                    WORK
                 ( NEW CRITICS)
```

SUBJECT - OBJECT DISTINCTION
     18C   20C   ?

    O O   OO   O

ALL LITERARY CRITICISM IS BASED ON LINGUISTICS (SEUSSERE)
① LANGUAGE IS STUDIED AS IF IT WERE A REAL OBJECT
   THE SPEAKER IS SEPARATE
② STRUCTURAL LINGUINISTICS CANNOT SEPARATE FORM
   FROM MEANING - IT TREATS LANGUAGE AS IT APPEARS
   ON THE PAGE, NOT THE WAY IT IS PROCESSED IN
   THE MIND -
   CANNOT EXPLAIN:
      Ⓐ LANGUAGE ACQUISITION IN CHILDREN
      Ⓑ LANGUAGE TRANSLATIONS
      Ⓒ AMBIGUITY (NAVY WITNESSES SMOKE)
      Ⓓ COMMUNICATION WITHOUT LANGUAGE STRUCTURE
③ ALL LITERARY CRITICISM IS A FORM OF EPISTOMOLOGY
   (THEORY OF KNOWLEDGE)
      Ⓐ KNOWER   ALL FOUND IN
      Ⓑ OBJECT   UNIVERSE - AUDIENCE - ARTIST
      Ⓒ PROCESS

④ THE STRUCTURALIST SEUSSERE SAYS THAT NOTHING CAN
  PRECEDE KNOWLEDGE (NOT SO WITH EASTERN RELIGIONS)

⑤ STRUCTURAL LINGUISTICS LEVELS OF LANGUAGE
      SOUND (SURFACE)
        THOUGHT
        PASHYANTI
        KNOWER

PLATO - WORLD IS EXPRESSION OF A REALITY OTHER
THAN ITSELF - REFLECTION OF IDEAL.

ARISTOTLE'S INFLUENCE TO 1750
LONGINUS'S INFLUENCE 1750 TO PRESENT
   ① STRESSED METAPHORE AND IMAGE
   ② METAPHORE - METAPHORIA - GREEK FOR TRANSPORT
     GETTING YOU BEYOND THE ORDINARY TO A HIGHER STATE
   ③ METAPHORE IS TRANSPORT FOR LONGINUS

               SURFACE
                 SUBLIME

   ④ LANGUAGE CAN TAKE US PAST THE LIMITS OF TIME AND
   SPACE TO THE UNLIMITLESS MIND.

ARISTOTLE
   KATHARSIS

       PITY ← TERROR (SAME EMOTION - PHYSIOLOGICAL)
               ↳ OF OWN MORTALITY
        ↳ FOR SOMEONE

       ONCE PURGED THAN COMPASSION IS POSSIBLE (CLEAR
       VISION OF HEART WITHOUT EMOTION)
   YOU MUST EXPERIENCE BEFORE WRITING ABOUT IT (YOU
   CANNOT PRETEND) - PEOPLE EXPERIENCE REALITY IN DIFFERENT
   WAYS.

IMITATION OF NATURE
   ST. THOMAS AQUINAS
   ① NATURA NATURATA - NATURE AS OBJECT (OBJECTIVE)
                FACTS, NUMBERS, PHOTO-LIKE GLANCES)
   ② NATURA NATURANS - NATURE AS SHE IS IN PROCESS, AS
                  SHE OPERATES

   INTELLECTUAL KNOWLEDGE - BOOK LEARNING
   KNOWLEDGE OF CONATURALITY - EXPERIENCE
   • BOOK LEARNING MUST BE INTEGRATED INTO EXPERIENCE
   • EXAMPLE: BOOK LEARNING   EXPERIENCE
            GRAMMAR   WRITING AN ESSAY
        TO WRITE THE ESSAY WELL THE GRAMMAR MUST
       ALREADY HAVE BEEN INTEGRATED INTO EXPERIENCE.

SIR PHILIP SIDNEY
   ① POETRY EXCEEDS ALL OTHER FORMS OF EXPRESSION
   ② POETRY BEAUTIFIES THE LANGUAGE
   ③ HUMAN QUALITIES ARE PERSONIFIED IN THE GREEK
     MYTHS (ROMAN, NORSE, ETC)
   ④ MORAL: TOO ABSTRACT
   HISTORY: TOO RELATIVE
   POET: COMBINES THE ABSTRACT AND RELATIVE FOR
     EFFECTIVE TEACHING

HUME: MAN IS MADE UP OF A BUNDLE OF
PERCEPTIONS ALWAYS IN A STATE OF FLUX.
IF TRUE THEN (REASON IS INADEQUATE)
IMPOSSIBLE TO GAIN KNOWLEDGE ABOUT
ANYTHING INCLUDING OUR SELVES — WITHOUT
KNOWLEDGE OF SELF NO OTHER KNOWLEDGE
IS POSSIBLE.

KANT: TRIES TO DISPROVE HUME BY ASKING
WHAT HOLDS THIS BUNDLE OF PERCEPTIONS
TOGETHER — HIS ANSWER IS THE "TRANSCENDENTAL
UNITY OF APPERCEPTION" — CANNOT BE GIVEN
IN EXPERIENCE — HE SHOULD HAVE REFERRED
ONLY TO HIS PERCEPTIONS, NOT EVERYONE'S.

ROMANTIC AGE: IMAGINATION REPLACES REASON
A TURN INWARD FROM THE OUTER WORLD
PRIVATE V. PUBLIC VOICE
"ANTHILL POETRY" EASTERN STORY OF POET
WHO SAT BY WHERE THE RIVER OF LIFE
(GANGES) AND THE RIVER OF DEATH (
CONVERGED AND THOUGHT ABOUT LIFE'S
MEANING.